HISTORY OF THE
CONQUEST OF MEXICO

William Hickling Prescott was born into a prosperous, old New England family in 1796. In 1811 he entered Harvard, where his academic record was good but undistinguished; he had serious difficulties with mathematics, and in later life the prospect of appraising the mathematical achievements of the aboriginal Mexicans almost prevented him from completing his work. Near the end of his junior year, a crust of bread thrown during a melee in the student commons caused virtual blindness in his left eye; the weakness of his other eye, caused by infection, sometimes prevented him from carrying on any kind of literary work. Throughout his life, Prescott's vision seems to have fluctuated from good to total blindness, and he often resorted to the use of a noctograph, a writing grid with parallel wires that guided a stylus over a chemically treated surface. Substantial portions of all his books and correspondence were composed on this device. He died in 1859.

ALSO BY W. H. PRESCOTT

History of the Conquest of Peru (Phoenix Press)
History of the Reign of Ferdinand and Isabella
History of Spanish Literature
History of Philip II

HISTORY OF
THE CONQUEST
OF MEXICO

W. H. Prescott

'Victrices aquilas alium laturus in orbem.'
LUCAN, Pharsalia, lib. v., v. 238

PHOENIX
PRESS

5 UPPER SAINT MARTIN'S LANE
LONDON
WC2H 9EA

A PHOENIX PRESS PAPERBACK

First published by Harper & Brothers in 1843
This paperback edition published in 2002
by Phoenix Press,
a division of The Orion Publishing Group Ltd,
Orion House, 5 Upper St Martin's Lane,
London WC2H 9EA

Phoenix Press
Sterling Publishing Co Inc
387 Park Avenue South
New York
NY 10016-8810
USA

A CIP catalogue record for this book
is available from the British Library.

Printed and bound in Great Britain by
Clays Ltd, St Ives plc

ISBN 1 84212 574 5

PREFACE.

—o—

As the Conquest of Mexico has occupied the pens of Solís and of Robertson, two of the ablest historians of their respective nations, it might seem that little could remain at the present day to be gleaned by the historical inquirer. But Robertson's narrative is necessarily brief, forming only part of a more extended work; and neither the British nor the Castilian author was provided with the important materials for relating this event which have been since assembled by the industry of Spanish scholars. The scholar who led the way in these researches was Don Juan Baptista Muñoz, the celebrated historiographer of the Indies, who, by a royal edict, was allowed free access to the national archives, and to all libraries, public, private, and monastic, in the kingdom and its colonies. The result of his long labours was a vast body of materials, of which unhappily he did not live to reap the benefit himself. His manuscripts were deposited, after his death, in the archives of the Royal Academy of History at Madrid; and that collection was subsequently augmented by the manuscripts of Don Vargas Ponçe, President of the Academy, obtained, like those of Muñoz, from different quarters, but especially from the archives of the Indies at Seville.

On my application to the Academy, in 1838, for permission to copy that part of this inestimable collection relating to Mexico and Peru, it was freely acceded to, and an eminent German scholar, one of their own number, was appointed to superintend the collation and transcription of the manuscripts; and this, it may be added, before I had any claim on the courtesy of that respectable body, as one of its associates. This conduct shows the advance of a liberal spirit in the Peninsula since the time of Dr. Robertson, who complains that he was denied admission to the most important public repositories. The favour with which my own application was regarded, however, must chiefly be attributed to the kind offices of the venerable President of the Academy, Don Martin Fernandez de Navarrete ; a scholar whose personal character has secured to him the same high consideration at home which his literary labours have obtained abroad. To this eminent person I am under still further obligations, for the free use which he has allowed me to make of his own manuscripts,— the fruits of a life of accumulation, and the basis of those valuable publications with which he has at different times illustrated the Spanish colonial history.

From these three magnificent collections, the result of half a century's careful researches, I have obtained a mass of unpublished documents relating to the Conquest and Settlement of Mexico and of Peru, comprising altogether about eight thousand folio pages. They consist of instructions of the Court, military and private journals, correspondence of the great actors in the scenes, legal instruments, contemporary chronicles, and the like, drawn from all the principal places in the extensive colonial empire of Spain, as well as from the public archives in the Peninsula.

I have still further fortified the collection by gleaning such materials from Mexico itself as had been overlooked by my illustrious predecessors in these researches. For these I am indebted to the courtesy of Count Cortina, and, yet more, to that of Don Lúcas Alaman, Minister of Foreign Affairs in Mexico; but, above all, to my excellent friend, Don Angel Calderon de la Barca, late Minister Plenipotentiary to that country from the Court of Madrid,—a gentleman whose high and estimable qualities, even more than his station, secured him the public confidence, and gained him free access to every place of interest and importance in Mexico.

I have also to acknowledge the very kind offices rendered to me by the Count Camaldoli at Naples; by the Duke of Serradifalco in Sicily, a nobleman whose science gives additional lustre to his rank ; and by the Duke of Monteleone, the present representative of Cortés, who has courteously opened the archives of his family to my inspection. To these names must also be added that of Sir Thomas Phillips, Bart., whose precious collection of manuscripts probably surpasses in extent that of any private gentleman in Great Britain, if not in Europe ; that of M. Ternaux-Compans, the proprietor of the valuable literary collection of Don Antonio Uguina, including the papers of Muñoz, the fruits of which he is giving to the world in his excellent translations ; and, lastly, that of my friend and countryman, Arthur Middleton, Esq., late Chargé-d'Affaires from the United States at the Court of Madrid, for the efficient aid he has afforded me in prosecuting my inquiries in that capital.

In addition to this stock of original documents obtained through these various sources, I have diligently provided myself with such printed works as have reference to the subject, including the magnificent publications, which have appeared both in France and England, on the Antiquities of Mexico, which, from their cost and colossal dimensions, would seem better suited to a public than a private library.

Having thus stated the nature of my materia.s, and the sources whence they are derived, it remains for me to add a few observations on the general plan and composition of the work. Among the remarkable achievements of the Spaniards in the sixteenth century, there is no one more striking to the imagination than the conquest of Mexico. The subversion of a great empire by a handful of adventurers, taken with all its strange and picturesque accompaniments, has the air of romance rather than of sober history; and it is not easy to treat such a theme according to the severe rules prescribed by historical criticism. But, notwithstanding the seductions of the subject, I have conscientiously endeavoured to distinguish fact from fiction, and to establish the narrative on as broad a basis as possible of contemporary evidence; and I have taken occasion to corroborate the text by ample citations from authorities, usually in the original, since few of them can be very accessible to the reader. In these extracts I have scrupulously conformed to the ancient orthography, however obsolete and even barbarous, rather than impair in any degree the integrity of the original document.

Although the subject of the work is, properly, only the Conquest of Mexico, I have prepared the way for it by such a view of the civilization of the ancient Mexicans as might acquaint the reader with the character of this extraordinary race, and enable him to understand the difficulties which the Spaniards had to encounter in their subjugation. This introductory part of the work, with the essay in the Appendix which properly belongs to the Introduction, although both together making only half a volume, has cost me as much labour, and nearly as much time, as the remainder of the history. If I shall have succeeded in giving the reader a just idea of the true nature and extent of the civilization to which the Mexicans had attained, it will not be labour lost.

The story of the Conquest terminates with the fall of the capital. Yet I have preferred to continue the narrative to the death of Cortés, relying on the interest which the development of his character in his military career may have excited in the reader. I am not insensible to the hazard I incur by such a course. The mind, previously occupied with one great idea, that of the subversion of the capital, may feel the prolongation of the story beyond that point superfluous, if not tedious, and may find it difficult, after the excitement caused by witnessing a great national catastrophe, to take an interest in the adventures of a private individual. Solís took the more politic course of concluding his narrative with the fall of Mexico, and thus leaves his readers with the full impression of that memorable event, undisturbed, on their minds. To prolong the narrative is to expose the historian to the error so much censured by the French critics in some of their most celebrated dramas, where the author, by a premature *dénouement* has impaired the interest of his piece. It is the defect that necessarily attaches, though in a greater degree, to the history of Columbus, in which petty adventures among a group of islands make up the sequel of a life that opened with the magnificent discovery of a World,—a defect, in short, which it has required all the genius of Irving and the magical charm of his style perfectly to overcome.

Notwithstanding these objections, I have been induced to continue the narrative, partly from deference to the opinion of several Spanish scholars, who considered that the biography of Cortés had not been fully exhibited, and partly from the circumstance of my having such a body of original materials for this biography at my command. And I cannot regret that I have adopted this course; since, whatever lustre the Conquest may reflect on Cortés as a military achievement, it gives but an imperfect idea of his enlightened spirit and of his comprehensive and versatile genius.

To the eye of the critic there may seem some incongruity in a plan which combines objects so dissimilar as those embraced by the present history, where the Introduction, occupied with the antiquities and origin of a nation, has somewhat the character of a *philosophic* theme, while the conclusion is strictly *biographical*, and the two may be supposed to match indifferently with the main body, or *historical* portion, of the work. But I may hope that such objections will be found to have less weight in practice than in theory ; and, if properly managed, that the general views of the Introduction will prepare the reader for the particulars of the Conquest, and that the great public events narrated in this will, without violence, open the way to the remaining personal history of the hero who is the soul of it. Whatever incongruity may exist in other respects, I may hope that the *unity of interest*, the only unity held of much importance by modern critics, will be found still to be preserved.

The distance of the present age from the period of the narrative might be presumed to secure the historian from undue prejudice or partiality. Yet by the American and the English reader, acknowledging so different a moral standard from that of the sixteenth century, I may possibly be thought too indulgent to the errors of the Conquerors ; while by a Spaniard, accustomed to the undiluted panegyric of Solís, I may be deemed to have dealt too hardly with them. To such I can only say that, while, on the one hand, I have not hesitated to expose in their strongest colours the excesses of the Conquerors, on the other, I have given them the benefit of such mitigating reflections as might be suggested by the circumstances and the period in which they lived. I have endeavoured not only to present a picture true in itself, but to place it in its proper light, and to put the spectator in a proper point of view for seeing it to the best advantage. I have endeavoured, at the expense of some repetition, to surround him with the spirit of the times, and, in a word, to make him, if I may so express myself, a contemporary of the sixteenth century. Whether, and how far, I have succeeded in this, he must determine.

For one thing, before I conclude, I may reasonably ask the reader's indulgence. Owing to the state of my eyes, I have been obliged to use a writing-case made for the blind, which does not permit the writer to see his own manuscript. Nor have I ever corrected, or even read, my own original draft. As the chirography, under these disadvantages, has been too often careless and obscure, occasional errors, even with the utmost care of my secretary, must have necessarily occurred in the transcription, somewhat increased by the barbarous phraseology imported from my Mexican authorities. I cannot expect that these errors have always been detected even by the vigilant eye of the perspicacious critic to whom the proof-sheets have been subjected.

In the Preface to the " History of Ferdinand and Isabella," I lamented that, while occupied with that subject, two of its most attractive parts had engaged the attention of the most popular of American authors, Washington Irving. By a singular chance, something like the reverse of this has taken place in the composition of the present history, and I have found myself unconsciously taking up ground which he was preparing to occupy. It was not till I had become master of my rich collection of materials that I was acquainted with this circumstance ; and, had he persevered in his design, I should unhesitatingly have abandoned my own, if not from courtesy, at least from policy; for, though armed with the weapons of Achilles, this could give me no hope of success in a competition with Achilles himself. But no sooner was that distinguished writer informed of the preparations I had made, than, with the gentlemanly spirit which will surprise no one who has the pleasure of his acquaintance, he instantly announced to me his attention of leaving the subject open to me. While I do but justice to Mr. Irving by this statement, I feel the prejudice it does to myself in the unavailing regret I am exciting in the bosom of the reader.

I must not conclude this Preface, too long protracted as it is already, without a word of acknowledgment to my friend George Ticknor, Esq.,— the friend of many years,—for his patient revision of my manuscript; a labour of love, the worth of which those only can estimate who are acquainted with his extraordinary erudition and his nice critical taste. If I have reserved his name for the last in the list of those to whose good offices I am indebted, it is most assuredly not because I value his services least.

WILLIAM H. PRESCOTT.

BOSTON, *October* 1, 1843.

NOTE.—The author's emendations of this history include many additional notes, which, being often contradictory to the text, have been printed between brackets. They were chiefly derived from the copious annotations of Don José F. Ramirez and Don Lúcas Alaman to the two Spanish translations published in Mexico. There could be no stronger guarantee of the value and general accuracy of the work than the minute labour bestowed upon it by these distinguished scholars.—ED.

MAPS.—The maps for this work are the result of a laborious investigation by a skilful and competent hand. Humboldt's are the only maps of New Spain which can lay claim to the credit of tolerable accuracy. They have been adopted as the basis of those for the present History; and an occasional deviation from them has been founded on a careful comparison with the verbal accounts of Gomara, Bernal Diaz, Clavigero, and, above all, of Cortés, illustrated by his meagre commentator Lorenzana. Of these, Cortés is generally the most full and exact in his statement of distances, though it is to be regretted that he does not more frequently afford a hint as to the bearings of the places. As it is desirable to present the reader with a complete and unembarrassed view of the route of Cortés, the names of all other places than those which occur in this work have been discarded, while a considerable number have been now introduced which are not to be found on any previous chart. The position of these must necessarily be, in some degree, hypothetical; but as it has been determined by a study of the narratives of contemporary historians and by the measurement of distances, the result, probably, cannot in any instance be much out of the way. The ancient names have been retained, so as to present a map of the country as it was at the time of the Conquest.

CONTENTS.

—o—

BOOK I.

INTRODUCTION.—VIEW OF THE AZTEC CIVILIZATION.

CHAPTER I.

ANCIENT MEXICO—CLIMATE AND PRODUCTS—PRIMITIVE RACES—AZTEC EMPIRE.

CHAPTER II.

SUCCESSION TO THE CROWN—AZTEC NOBILITY—JUDICIAL SYSTEM—LAWS AND REVENUES—MILITARY INSTITUTIONS.

CHAPTER III.

MEXICAN MYTHOLOGY—THE SACERDOTAL ORDER—THE TEMPLES—HUMAN SACRIFICES.

CHAPTER IV.

MEXICAN HIEROGLYPHICS—MANUSCRIPTS—ARITHMETIC—CHRONOLOGY—
ASTRONOMY.

CHAPTER V.

AZTEC AGRICULTURE—MECHANICAL ARTS—MERCHANTS—DOMESTIC
MANNERS.

CHAPTER VI.

TEZCUCANS—THEIR GOLDEN AGE—ACCOMPLISHED PRINCES—DECLINE
OF THEIR MONARCHY.

BOOK II.

DISCOVERY OF MEXICO.

CHAPTER I.

SPAIN UNDER CHARLES V.—PROGRESS OF DISCOVERY—COLONIAL POLICY
—CONQUEST OF CUBA—EXPEDITIONS TO YUCATAN.

CHAPTER VII.

CHAPTER VIII.

BOOK III.
MARCH TO MEXICO.

CHAPTER I.

CHAPTER II.

CHAPTER III.

DECISIVE VICTORY—INDIAN COUNCIL—NIGHT ATTACK—NEGOTIATIONS WITH THE ENEMY—TLASCALAN HERO.

CHAPTER IV.

DISCONTENTS IN THE ARMY — TLASCALAN SPIES — PEACE WITH THE REPUBLIC—EMBASSY FROM MONTEZUMA.

CHAPTER V.

SPANIARDS ENTER TLASCALA—DESCRIPTION OF THE CAPITAL—ATTEMPTED CONVERSION—AZTEC EMBASSY—INVITED TO CHOLULA.

CHAPTER VI.

CITY OF CHOLULA—GREAT TEMPLE—MARCH TO CHOLULA—RECEPTION OF THE SPANIARDS—CONSPIRACY DETECTED.

CHAPTER VII.

TERRIBLE MASSACRE—TRANQUILLITY RESTORED—REFLECTIONS ON THE MASSACRE—FURTHER PROCEEDINGS—ENVOYS FROM MONTEZUMA.

CHAPTER VIII.

CHAPTER IX.

BOOK IV.

RESIDENCE IN MEXICO.

CHAPTER I.

CHAPTER II.

CHAPTER III.

CHAPTER IV.

CHAPTER V.

CHAPTER VI.

CHAPTER VII.

CHAPTER VIII.

DISCONTENT OF THE TROOPS—INSURRECTION IN THE CAPITAL—RETURN OF CORTÉS—GENERAL SIGNS OF HOSTILITY—MASSACRE BY ALVARADO —RISING OF THE AZTECS.

BOOK V.

EXPULSION FROM MEXICO.

CHAPTER I.

DESPERATE ASSAULT ON THE QUARTERS—FURY OF THE MEXICANS—SALLY OF THE SPANIARDS—MONTEZUMA ADDRESSES THE PEOPLE—DANGEROUSLY WOUNDED.

CHAPTER II.

STORMING OF THE GREAT TEMPLE—SPIRIT OF THE AZTECS—DISTRESSES OF THE GARRISON—SHARP COMBATS IN THE CITY—DEATH OF MONTEZUMA.

CHAPTER III.

CHAPTER IV.

CHAPTER V.

CHAPTER VI.

CHAPTER VII.

BOOK VI.

SIEGE AND SURRENDER OF MEXICO.

CHAPTER I.

CHAPTER II.

CHAPTER III.

CHAPTER VII.

CHAPTER VIII.

BOOK VII.

CONCLUSION—SUBSEQUENT CAREER OF CORTÉS.

CHAPTER I.

CHAPTER II.

MODERN MEXICO—SETTLEMENT OF THE COUNTRY—CONDITION OF THE
NATIVES—CHRISTIAN MISSIONARIES—CULTIVATION OF THE SOIL—
VOYAGES AND EXPEL TIONS.

CHAPTER III.

DEFECTION OF OLID—DREADFUL MARCH TO HONDURAS—EXECUTION OF
GUATEMOZIN—DOÑA MARINA—ARRIVAL AT HONDURAS.

CHAPTER IV.

DISTURBANCES IN MEXICO—RETURN OF CORTÉS—DISTRUST OF THE COURT
—CORTÉS RETURNS TO SPAIN—DEATH OF SANDOVAL—BRILLIANT
RECEPTION OF CORTÉS—HONOURS CONFERRED ON HIM.

CHAPTER V.

APPENDIX.

PART I.

ORIGIN OF THE MEXICAN CIVILIZATION—ANALOGIES WITH THE OLD WORLD.

PART II.

ORIGINAL DOCUMENTS.

HISTORY OF THE
CONQUEST OF MEXICO

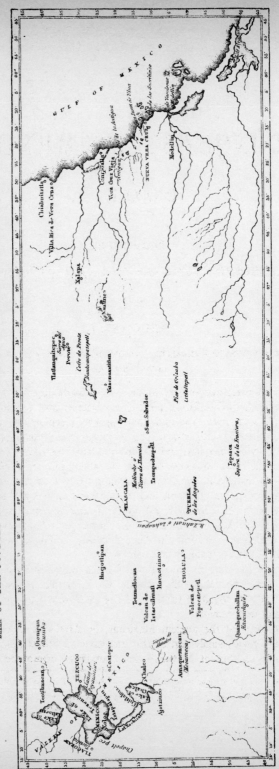

MAP OF THE COUNTRY TRAVERSED BY THE SPANIARDS ON THEIR MARCH TO MEXICO.

CONQUEST OF MEXICO.

BOOK I.

Introduction.

PRELIMINARY VIEW OF THE AZTEC CIVILIZATION.

—o—

CHAPTER I.

ANCIENT MEXICO.—CLIMATE AND PRODUCTS.—PRIMITIVE RACES.—
AZTEC EMPIRE.

OF all that extensive empire which once acknowledged the authority of
Spain in the New World, no portion, for interest and importance, can be
compared with Mexico;—and this equally, whether we consider the
variety of its soil and climate; the inexhaustible stores of its mineral
wealth; its scenery, grand and picturesque beyond example; the character
of its ancient inhabitants, not only far surpassing in intelligence that of the
other North American races, but reminding us, by their monuments, of the
primitive civilization of Egypt and Hindostan; or, lastly, the peculiar circumstances of its Conquest, adventurous and romantic as any legend
devised by Norman or Italian bard of chivalry. It is the purpose of the
present narrative to exhibit the history of this Conquest, and that of the
remarkable man by whom it was achieved.

But, in order that the reader may have a better understanding of the
subject, it will be well, before entering on it, to take a general survey of
the political and social institutions of the races who occupied the land at
the time of its discovery.

The country of the ancient Mexicans, or Aztecs as they were called,
formed but a very small part of the extensive territories comprehended in
the modern republic of Mexico.[1] Its boundaries cannot be defined with

---

[1] Extensive indeed, if we may trust Archbishop
Lorenzana, who tells us, "It is doubtful if the
country of New Spain does not border on Tartary
and Greenland;—by the way of California, on the
former, and by New Mexico, on the latter"! Historia de Nueva-España (México, 1770), p. 38, nota.

A

certainty. They were much enlarged in the latter days of the empire, when they may be considered as reaching from about the eighteenth degree north, to the twenty-first, on the Atlantic; and from the fourteenth to the nineteenth, including a very narrow strip, on the Pacific.[1] In its greatest breadth, it could not exceed five degrees and a half, dwindling, as it approached its south-eastern limits, to less than two. It covered, probably, less than sixteen thousand square leagues.[2] Yet such is the remarkable formation of this country, that, though not more than twice as large as New England, it presented every variety of climate, and was capable of yielding nearly every fruit, found between the equator and the Arctic circle.

All along the Atlantic, the country is bordered by a broad tract, called the *tierra caliente,* or hot region, which has the usual high temperature of equinoctial lands. Parched and sandy plains are intermingled with others, of exuberant fertility, almost impervious from thickets of aromatic shrubs and wild flowers, in the midst of which tower up trees of that magnificent growth which is found only within the tropics. In this wilderness of sweets lurks the fatal *malaria,* engendered, probably, by the decomposition of rank vegetable substances in a hot and humid soil. The season of the bilious fever,—*vómito,* as it is called,—which scourges these coasts, continues from the spring to the autumnal equinox, when it is checked by the cold winds that descend from Hudson's Bay. These winds in the winter season frequently freshen into tempests, and sweeping down the Atlantic coast and the winding Gulf of Mexico, burst with the fury of a hurricane on its unprotected shores, and on the neighbouring West India islands. Such are the mighty spells with which Nature has surrounded this land of enchantment, as if to guard the golden treasures locked up within its bosom. The genius and enterprise of man have proved more potent than her spells.

After passing some twenty leagues across this burning region, the traveller finds himself rising into a purer atmosphere. His limbs recover their

---

[1] I have conformed to the limits fixed by Clavigero. He has, probably, examined the subject with more thoroughness and fidelity than most of his countrymen, who differ from him, and who assign a more liberal extent to the monarchy. (See his Storia antica del Messico (Cesena, 1780), dissert. 7.) The abbé, however, has not informed his readers on what frail foundations his conclusions rest. The extent of the Aztec empire is to be gathered from the writings of historians since the arrival of the Spaniards, and from the picture-rolls of tribute paid by the conquered cities; both sources extremely vague and defective. See the MSS. of the Mendoza Collection, in Lord Kingsborough's magnificent publication (Antiquities of Mexico, comprising Facsimiles of Ancient Paintings and Hieroglyphics, together with the Monuments of New Spain. London, 1830.) The difficulty of the inquiry is much increased by the fact of the conquests having been made, as will be seen hereafter, by the united arms of three powers, so that it is not always easy to tell to which party they eventually belonged. The affair is involved in so much uncertainty that Clavigero, notwithstanding the positive assertions in his text, has not ventured, in his map, to define the precise limits of the empire, either towards the north, where it mingles with the Tezcucan empire, or towards the south, where, indeed, he has fallen into the egregious blunder of asserting that, while the Mexican territory reached to the fourteenth degree, it did not include any portion of Guatemala. (See tom. i. p. 29, and tom. iv. dissert. 7.) The Tezcucan chronicler Ixtlilxochitl puts in a sturdy claim for the paramount empire of his own nation. Historia Chichimeca, MS., cap. 39, 53, et alibi.

[2] Eighteen to twenty thousand, according to Humboldt, who considers the Mexican territory to have been the same with that occupied by the modern intendancies of Mexico, Puebla, Vera Cruz, Oaxaca, and Valladolid. (Essai politique sur le Royaume de Nouvelle-Espagne (Paris, 1825), tom. i. p. 196.) This last, however, was all, or nearly all, included in the rival kingdom of Michoacán, as he himself more correctly states in another part of his work. Comp. tom. ii. p. 164.

elasticity. He breathes more freely, for his senses are not now oppressed by the sultry heats and intoxicating perfumes of the valley. The aspect of nature, too, has changed, and his eye no longer revels among the gay variety of colours with which the landscape was painted there. The vanilla, the indigo, and the flowering cacao-groves disappear as he advances. The sugar-cane and the glossy-leaved banana still accompany him; and, when he has ascended about four thousand feet, he sees in the unchanging verdure, and the rich foliage of the liquid-amber tree, that he has reached the height where clouds and mists settle, in their passage from the Mexican Gulf. This is the region of perpetual humidity; but he welcomes it with pleasure, as announcing his escape from the influence of the deadly *vómito*.[1] He has entered the *tierra templada*, or temperate region, whose character resembles that of the temperate zone of the globe. The features of the scenery become grand, and even terrible. His road sweeps along the base of mighty mountains, once gleaming with volcanic fires, and still resplendent in their mantles of snow, which serve as beacons to the mariner, for many a league at sea. All around he beholds traces of their ancient combustion, as his road passes along vast tracts of lava, bristling in the innumerable fantastic forms into which the fiery torrent has been thrown by the obstacles in its career. Perhaps, at the same moment, as he casts his eye down some steep slope, or almost unfathomable ravine, on the margin of the road, he sees their depths glowing with the rich blooms and enamelled vegetation of the tropics. Such are the singular contrasts presented, at the same time, to the senses, in this picturesque region!

Still pressing upwards, the traveller mounts into other climates, favourable to other kinds of cultivation. The yellow maize, or Indian corn, as we usually call it, has continued to follow him up from the lowest level; but he now first sees fields of wheat, and the other European grains brought into the country by the Conquerors. Mingled with them, he views the plantations of the aloe or maguey (*Agave Americana*), applied to such various and important uses by the Aztecs. The oaks now acquire a sturdier growth, and the dark forests of pine announce that he has entered the *tierra fria*, or cold region,—the third and last of the great natural terraces into which the country is divided. When he has climbed to the height of between seven and eight thousand feet, the weary traveller sets his foot on the summit of the Cordillera of the Andes,—the colossal range that, after traversing South America and the Isthmus of Darien, spreads out, as it enters Mexico, into that vast sheet of table-land which maintains an elevation of more than six thousand feet, for the distance of nearly two hundred leagues, until it gradually declines in the higher latitudes of the north.[2]

---

[1] The traveller who enters the country across the dreary sand-hills of Vera Cruz will hardly recognize the truth of the above description. He must look for it in other parts of the *tierra caliente*. Of recent tourists, no one has given a more gorgeous picture of the impressions made on his senses by these sunny regions than Latrobe, who came on shore at Tampico (Rambler in Mexico (New York, 1836), chap. 1),—a traveller, it may be added, whose descriptions of man and nature in our own country, where we can judge, are distinguished by a sobriety and fairness that entitle him to confidence in his delineation of other countries.

[2] This long extent of country varies in elevation

Across this mountain rampart a chain of volcanic hills stretches, in a westerly direction, of still more stupendous dimensions, forming, indeed, some of the highest land on the globe. Their peaks, entering the limits of perpetual snow, diffuse a grateful coolness over the elevated plateaus below; for these last, though termed "cold," enjoy a climate the mean temperature of which is not lower than that of the central parts of Italy.[1] The air is exceedingly dry; the soil, though naturally good, is rarely clothed with the luxuriant vegetation of the lower regions. It frequently, indeed, has a parched and barren aspect, owing partly to the greater evaporation which takes place on these lofty plains, through the diminished pressure of the atmosphere, and partly, no doubt, to the want of trees to shelter the soil from the fierce influence of the summer sun. In the time of the Aztecs, the table-land was thickly covered with larch, oak, cypress, and other forest trees, the extraordinary dimensions of some of which, remaining to the present day, show that the curse of barrenness in later times is chargeable more on man than on nature. Indeed, the early Spaniards made as indiscriminate war on the forest as did our Puritan ancestors, though with much less reason. After once conquering the country, they had no lurking ambush to fear from the submissive, semi-civilized Indian, and were not, like our forefathers, obliged to keep watch and ward for a century. This spoliation of the ground, however, is said to have been pleasing to their imaginations, as it reminded them of the plains of their own Castile,—the table-land of Europe;[2] where the nakedness of the landscape forms the burden of every traveller's lament who visits that country.

Midway across the continent, somewhat nearer the Pacific than the Atlantic Ocean, at an elevation of nearly seven thousand five hundred feet, is the celebrated Valley of Mexico. It is of an oval form, about sixty-seven leagues in circumference,[3] and is encompassed by a towering rampart of porphyritic rock, which nature seems to have provided, though ineffectually, to protect it from invasion.

The soil, once carpeted with a beautiful verdure and thickly sprinkled with stately trees, is often bare, and, in many places, white with the incrustation of salts caused by the draining of the waters. Five lakes are spread

---

from 5570 to 8856 feet,—equal to the height of the passes of Mount Cenis or the Great St. Bernard. The table-land stretches still three hundred leagues farther, before it declines to a level of 2624 feet. Humboldt, Essai politique, tom. i. pp. 157, 255.

[1] About 62° Fahrenheit, or 17° Réaumur. (Humboldt, Essai politique, tom. i. p. 273.) The more elevated plateaus of the table-land, as the Valley of Toluca, about 8500 feet above the sea, have a stern climate, in which the thermometer, during a great part of the day, rarely rises beyond 45° F. Idem (loc. cit.), and Malte-Brun (Universal Geography, English translation, book 83), who is, indeed, in this part of his work, but an echo of the former writer.

[2] The elevation of the Castiles, according to the authority repeatedly cited, is about 350 toises, or 2100 feet above the ocean. (Humboldt's Dissertation, apud Laborde, Itinéraire descriptif de l'Espagne (Paris, 1827), tom. i. p. 5.) It is rare to find plains in Europe of so great a height.

[3] Archbishop Lorenzana estimates the circuit of the Valley at ninety leagues, correcting at the same time the statement of Cortés, which puts it at seventy, very near the truth, as appears from the result of M. de Humboldt's measurement, cited in the text. Its length is about eighteen leagues, by twelve and a half in breadth. (Humboldt, Essai politique, tom. ii. p. 29.—Lorenzana, Hist. de Nueva-España, p. 101.) Humboldt's map of the Valley of Mexico forms the third in his "Atlas géographique et physique," and, like all the others in the collection, will be found of inestimable value to the traveller, the geologist, and the historian.

over the Valley, occupying one-tenth of its surface.[1] On the opposite borders of the largest of these basins, much shrunk in its dimensions [2] since the days of the Aztecs, stood the cities of Mexico and Tezcuco, the capitals of the two most potent and flourishing states of Anahuac, whose history, with that of the mysterious races that preceded them in the country,[3] exhibits some of the nearest approaches to civilization to be met with anciently on the North American continent.

Of these races the most conspicuous were the Toltecs. Advancing from a northerly direction, but from what region is uncertain,[4] they entered the

---

[1] Humboldt, Essai politique, tom. ii. pp. 29, 44-49. — Malte-Brun, book 85. This latter geographer assigns only 6700 feet for the level of the Valley, contradicting himself (comp. book 83), or rather Humboldt, to whose pages he helps himself *plenis manibus*, somewhat too liberally, indeed, for the scanty references at the bottom of his page.

[2] Torquemada accounts in part for this diminution by supposing that, as God permitted the waters, which once covered the whole earth, to subside after mankind had been nearly exterminated for their iniquities, so he allowed the waters of the Mexican lake to subside, in token of goodwill and reconciliation, after the idolatrous races of the land had been destroyed by the Spaniards! (Monarchía Indiana (Madrid, 1723), tom. i. p. 309.) Quite as probable, if not as orthodox, an explanation, may be found in the active evaporation of these upper regions, and in the fact of an immense drain having been constructed, during the lifetime of the good father, to reduce the waters of the principal lake and protect the capital from inundation.

[3] [It is perhaps to be regretted that, instead of a meagre notice of the Toltecs with a passing allusion to earlier races, the author did not give a separate chapter to the history of the country during the ages preceding the Conquest. That history, it is true, resting on tradition or on questionable records mingled with legendary and mythological relations, is full of obscurity and doubt. But, whatever its uncertainty in regard to details, it presents a mass of general facts supported by analogy and by the stronger evidence of language and of the existing relics of the past. The number and diversity of the architectural and other remains found on the soil of Mexico and the adjacent regions, and the immense variety of the spoken languages, with the vestiges of others that have passed out of use,—all perhaps derived originally from a common stock, but exhibiting different stages of development or decay, and capable of being classified into several distinct families,—point to conclusions that render the subject one of the most attractive fields for critical investigation. These concurrent testimonies leave no doubt that, like portions of the Old World similarly favoured in regard to climate, soil, and situation, the central regions of America were occupied from a very remote period by nations which made distinct advances in civilization, and passed through a cycle of revolutions comparable to that of which the Valley of the Euphrates and other parts of Asia were anciently the scene. The useful arts were known and practised, wealth was accumulated, social systems exhibiting a certain refinement and a peculiar complexity were organized, states were established which flourished, decayed,—either from the effects of isolation or an inherent incapacity for continuance,—and were finally overthrown by invaders, by whom the experiment was repeated, though not always with equal success. Some of these nations passed away, leaving no trace but their names; others, whose very names are unknown, left mysterious monuments imbedded in the soil or records that are undecipherable. Of those that still remain, comprising about a dozen distinct

races speaking a hundred and twenty different dialects, we have the traditions preserved either in their own records or in those of the Spanish discoverers. The task of constructing out of these materials a history shorn of the adornments of mythology and fable has been attempted by the Abbé Brasseur de Bourbourg (Histoire des Nations civilisées du Mexique et de l'Amérique-Centrale, durant les Siècles antérieurs à Christophe Colomb, 4 vols., Paris, 1857-59), and, whatever may be thought of the method he has pursued, his research is unquestionable, and his views—very different from those which he has since put forth—merit attention. A more practical effort has been made by Don Manuel Orozco y Berra to trace the order, diffusion, and relations of the various races by the differences, the intermixtures, and the geographical limits of their languages. (Geografía de las Lenguas y Carta etnográfica de México, precedidas de un Ensayo de Clasificacion de las mismas Lenguas y de Apuntes para las Inmigraciones de las Tribus, México, 1864.)—ED.]

[4] [The uncertainty is not diminished by our being told that Tollan, Tullan, Tulan, or Tula (called also Tlapallan and Huehuetlapallan) was the original seat of this people, since we are still left in doubt whether the country so designated—like Aztlan, the supposed point of departure of the Aztecs—is to be located in New Mexico, California, the north-western extremity of America, or in Asia. M. Brasseur de Bourbourg (whose later speculations, in which the name plays a conspicuous part, will be noticed more appropriately in the Appendix) found in the Quiché manuscripts mention of four Tollans, one of them "in the east, on the other side of the sea." "But," he adds, "in what part of the world is it to be placed? *C'est là encore une question bien difficile à résoudre.*" (Hist. des Nations civilisées du Mexique, tom. i. pp. 167, 168.) Nor will the etymology much help us. According to Buschmann, *Tollan* is derived from *tolin*, reed, and signifies "place of reeds,"—"Ort der Binsen, Platz mit Binsen gewachsen, *juncetum*." (Ueber die aztekischen Ortsnamen, S. 682.) He refers, however, to a different derivation, suggested by a writer who has made it the basis of one of those extraordinary theories which are propounded from time to time, to account for the first diffusion of the human race, and more particularly for the original settlement of America. According to this theory, the cradle of mankind was the Himalayan Mountains. "But the collective name of these lofty regions was very anciently designated by appellations the roots of which were *Tal, Tol, Tul*, meaning tall, high, . . as it does yet in many languages, the English, Chinese, and Arabic for instance. Such were *Tolo, T'hala, Talaha, Tulan*, etc., in the old Sanscrit and primitive languages of Asia. Whence came the Asiatic *Atlas* and also the *Atlantes* of the Greeks, who, spreading through the world westerly, gave these names to many other places and nations. . . . The Talas or Atlantes occupied or conquered Europe and Africa, nay, went to America in very early times. . . . In Greece they became *Atalantes, Talautians* of Epirus, *Aetolians*. . . . They gave

territory of Anahuac,[1] probably before the close of the seventh century. Of course, little can be gleaned with certainty respecting a people whose written records have perished, and who are known to us only through the traditionary legends of the nations that succeeded them.[2] By the general agreement of these, however, the Toltecs were well instructed in agriculture and many of the most useful mechanic arts; were nice workers of metals; invented the complex arrangement of time adopted by the Aztecs; and, in short, were the true fountains of the civilization which distinguished this part of the continent in later times.[3] They established their capital at Tula, north of the Mexican Valley, and the remains of extensive buildings were to be discerned there at the time of the Conquest.[4] The noble ruins of religious and other edifices, still to be seen in various parts of New Spain, are referred to this people, whose name, *Toltec*, has passed into a synonym for *architect*.[5] Their shadowy history reminds us of those primitive races who preceded the ancient Egyptians in the march of civilization; fragments of whose monuments, as they are seen at this day, incorporated with

name to Italy, *Aitala* meaning land eminent, . . . to the Atlantic Ocean, and to the great Atlantis, or America, called in the Hindu books, *Atala* or *Tala-tolo*, the fourth world, where dwelt giants or powerful men. . . . America is also filled with their names and deeds from Mexico and Carolina to Peru: the *Tol-tecas*, people of Tol, and Aztlan, *Otolum* near Palenque, many towns of *Tula* and *Tolu*; the *Talas* of Michuacan, the *Matalans*, *Atalans*, *Tulukis*, etc., of North America." (C. S. Rafinesque, Atlantic Journal, Philadelphia, 1832-33.) It need hardly be added that Tula has also been identified with the equally unknown and long-sought-for *ultima Thule*, with the simplifying effect of bringing two streams of inquiry into one channel. Meanwhile, by a different kind of criticism, the whole question is dissipated into thin air, *Tollan* and *Aztlan* being resolved into names of mere mythical import, and the regions thus designated transferred from the earth to the bright domain of the sky, from which the descriptions in the legends appear to have been borrowed. See Brinton, Myths of the New World, pp. 88, 89.—ED.]

[1] Anahuac, according to Humboldt, comprehended only the country between the fourteenth and twenty-first degrees of north latitude. (Essai politique, tom. i. p. 197.) According to Clavigero, it included nearly all since known as New Spain. (Stor. del Messico, tom. i. p. 27.) Veytia uses it, also, as synonymous with New Spain. (Historia antigua de Méjico (Méjico, 1836), tom. i. cap. 12.) The first of these writers probably allows too little, as the latter do too much, for its boundaries. Ixtlilxochitl says it extended four hundred leagues south of the Otomi country. (Hist. Chichimeca, MS., cap.

73.) The word Anahuac signifies *near the water*. It was, probably, first applied to the country around the lakes in the Mexican Valley, and gradually extended to the remoter regions occupied by the Aztecs and the other semi-civilized races. Or possibly the name may have been intended, as Veytia suggests (Hist. antig., lib. 1, cap. 1), to denote the land between the waters of the Atlantic and Pacific.*

[2] Clavigero talks of Boturini's having written "on the faith of the Toltec historians." (Stor. del Messico, tom. i. p. 128.) But that scholar does not pretend to have ever met with a Toltec manuscript himself, and had heard of only one in the possession of Ixtlilxochitl. (See his Idea de una nueva Historia general de la América Septentrional (Madrid, 1746), p. 110.) The latter writer tells us that his account of the Toltec and Chichimec races was "derived from interpretation" (probably of the Tezcucan paintings), "and from the traditions of old men;" poor authority for events which had passed centuries before. Indeed, he acknowledges that their narratives were so full of absurdity and falsehood that he was obliged to reject nine-tenths of them. (See his Relaciones, MS., no. 5.) The cause of truth would not have suffered much, probably, if he had rejected nine-tenths of the remainder.†

[3] Ixtlilxochitl, Hist. Chich., MS., cap. 2.—Idem, Relaciones, MS., no. 2.—Sahagun, Historia general de las Cosas de Nueva-España (México, 1829), lib. 10, cap. 29.—Veytia, Hist. antig., lib. 1, cap. 27

[4] Sahagun, Hist. de Nueva-España, lib. 10, cap. 29.

[5] Sahagun, ubi supra.—Torquemada, Monarch. Ind., lib. 1, cap. 14.

* [This suggestion of Veytia is unworthy of attention,—refuted by the actual application and appropriateness of the name, and by the state of geographical knowledge and ideas at the period when it must have originated. A modern traveller, describing the appearance of the great plains as seen from the summit of Popocatepetl, remarks, "Even now that the lakes have shrunk to a fraction of their former size, we could see the fitness of the name given in old times to the Valley of Mexico, *Anahuac*, that is, By the water-side." Tylor, Anahuac: or Mexico and the Mexicans, Ancient and Modern (London, 1861), p. 270.—ED.]

† [Ixtlilxochitl's language does not necessarily imply that he considered any of the relations he had received as false or absurd, nor does he say that he had rejected nine-tenths of them. What he has written is, he asserts, "The true history of the Toltecs," though it does not amount to nine-tenths of the whole ("de lo que ello fué"), *i.e.*, of what had been contained in the original records; these records having perished, and he himself having abridged the accounts he had been able to obtain of their contents, as well for the sake of brevity as because of the marvellous character of the relations ("son tan estrañas las cosas y tan peregrinas y nunca oidas"). The sources of his information are also incorrectly described; but a further mention of them will be found in a note at the end of this Book.—ED.]

the buildings of the Egyptians themselves, give to these latter the appearance of almost modern constructions.[1]

After a period of four centuries, the Toltecs, who had extended their sway over the remotest borders of Anahuac,[2] having been greatly reduced, it is said, by famine, pestilence, and unsuccessful wars, disappeared from the land as silently and mysteriously as they had entered it. A few of them still lingered behind, but much the greater number, probably, spread over the region of Central America and the neighbouring isles; and the traveller now speculates on the majestic ruins of Mitla and Palenque, as possibly the work of this extraordinary people.[3]

After the lapse of another hundred years, a numerous and rude tribe, called the Chichimecs, entered the deserted country from the regions of the far North-west. They were speedily followed by other races, of higher civilization, perhaps of the same family with the Toltecs, whose language they appear to have spoken. The most noted of these were the Aztecs or Mexicans, and the Acolhuans. The latter, better known in later times by the name of Tezcucans, from their capital, Tezcuco,[4] on the eastern border of the Mexican lake, were peculiarly fitted, by their comparatively mild religion and manners, for receiving the tincture of civilization which could be derived from the few Toltecs that still remained in the country.[5] This,

---

[1] Description de l'Égypte (Paris, 1809), Antiquités, tom. i. cap. 1. Veytia has traced the migrations of the Toltecs with sufficient industry, scarcely rewarded by the necessarily doubtful credit of the results. Hist. antig., lib. 2, cap. 21–33.

[2] Ixtlilxochitl, Hist. Chich., MS., cap. 73.

[3] Veytia, Hist. antig., lib. 1, cap. 33.—Ixtlilxochitl, Hist. Chich., MS., cap. 3.—Idem, Relaciones, MS., nos. 4, 5.—Father Torquemada—perhaps misinterpreting the Tezcucan hieroglyphics—has accounted for this mysterious disappearance of the Toltecs by such *fee-faw-fum* stories of giants and demons as show his appetite for the marvellous was fully equal to that of any of his calling. See his Monarch. Ind., lib. 1, cap. 14.

[This supposition, neither adopted nor rejected in the text, was, as Mr. Tylor remarks, "quite tenable at the time that Prescott wrote," being founded on the statements of early writers and partially supported by the conclusions of Mr. Stephens, who believed that the ruined cities of Oaxaca, Chiapa, Yucatan, and Guatemala dated from a comparatively recent period, and were still flourishing at the time of the Spanish Conquest; and that their inhabitants, the ancestors, as he contends, of the degenerate race that now occupies the soil, were of the same stock and spoke the same language as the Mexicans. (Incidents of Travel in Central America, Chiapas, and Yucatan.) But these opinions have been refuted by later investigators. Orozco y Berra, in an elaborate and satisfactory examination of the question, discusses all the evidence relating to it, compares the remains in the southern provinces with those of the Valley of Mexico, points out the essential differences in the architecture, sculpture, and inscriptions, and arrives at the conclusion that there was "no point of contact or resemblance" between the two civilizations. He considers that of the southern provinces, though of a far higher grade, as long anterior in time to the Toltec domination,—the work of a

people which had passed away, under the assaults of barbarism, at a period prior to all traditions, leaving no name and no trace of their existence save those monuments which, neglected and forgotten by their successors, have become the riddle of later generations. Geografía de las Lenguas de México, pp. 122–131. See also Tylor, Anahuac, p. 189, et seq.—ED.]

[4] *Tezcuco* signifies "place of detention;" as several of the tribes who successively occupied Anahuac were said to have halted some time at the spot. Ixtlilxochitl, Hist. Chich., MS., cap. 10.*

[5] [It is difficult to reconcile the two statements that the Toltecs "were the true fountains of the civilization which distinguished this part of the continent in later times," and that they "disappeared from the land as silently and mysteriously as they had entered it," leaving an interval of more than a century before the appearance of the Aztecs and the Acolhuans. If the latter received from the former the knowledge of those arts in which they speedily rivalled them, it must have been by more direct communication and transmission than can be inferred from the mention of a small fraction of the Toltec population as remaining in the country,—a fact which has itself the appearance of having been invented to meet the difficulty. Orozco y Berra compares this transitional period with that which followed the overthrow of the Roman Empire; but if in the former case there was, in his own words, "no conquest, but only an occupation, no war because no one to contend with," the analogy altogether fails. Brasseur de Bourbourg reduces the interval between the departure of the Toltecs and the arrival of the Chichimecs to a few years, and supposes that a considerable number of the former inhabitants remained scattered through the Valley. If, however, it be allowable to substitute probabilities for doubtful relations, it is an easier solution to believe that no interval occurred and that no emigration took place.— ED.]

---

* ["Ueber die Etymologie lässt sich nichts sicheres sagen," says Buschmann, "so zuversichtlich auch Prescott, wohl nach Ixtlilxochitl den Namen durch *place of detention* übersetzt." Ueber die aztekischen Ortsnamen, S. 697.—ED.]

in their turn, they communicated to the barbarous Chichimecs, a large portion of whom became amalgamated with the new settlers as one nation.[1]

Availing themselves of the strength derived, not only from this increase of numbers, but from their own superior refinement, the Acolhuans gradually stretched their empire over the ruder tribes in the north ; while their capital was filled with a numerous population, busily employed in many of the more useful and even elegant arts of a civilized community. In this palmy state, they were suddenly assaulted by a warlike neighbour, the Tepanecs, their own kindred, and inhabitants of the same valley as themselves. Their provinces were overrun, their armies beaten, their king assassinated, and the flourishing city of Tezcuco became the prize of the victor. From this abject condition the uncommon abilities of the young prince, Nezahualcoyotl, the rightful heir to the crown, backed by the efficient aid of his Mexican allies, at length redeemed the state, and opened to it a new career of prosperity, even more brilliant than the former.[2]

The Mexicans, with whom our history is principally concerned, came also, as we have seen, from the remote regions of the North,—the populous hive of nations in the New World, as it has been in the Old.[3] They arrived on the borders of Anahuac towards the beginning of the thirteenth century, some time after the occupation of the land by the kindred races. For a long time they did not establish themselves in any permanent residence, but continued shifting their quarters to different parts of the Mexican Valley, enduring all the casualties and hardships of a migratory life. On one occasion they were enslaved by a more powerful tribe ; but their ferocity soon made them formidable to their masters.[4] After a series of wanderings and adventures which need not shrink from comparison with the most extravagant legends of the heroic ages of antiquity, they at length halted on the south-western borders of the principal lake, in the year

---

[1] The historian speaks, in one page, of the Chichimecs burrowing in caves, or, at best, in cabins of straw, and, in the next, talks gravely of their *señoras, infantas,* and *caballeros !** Ibid., cap. 9, et seq.—Veytia, Hist. antig., lib. 2, cap. 1-10.— Camargo, Historia de Tlascala, MS.

[2] Ixtlilxochitl, Hist. Chich., MS., cap. 9-20.— Veytia, Hist. antig., lib. 2, cap. 29-54.

[3] [Some recent writers have contended that Mexico must have been peopled originally by migrations from the South. Aztec names and communities, and traces of Toltec settlements long anterior to the occupation of Anahuac by the same people, are found in several parts of Central America. The most primitive traditions, as well as the remains of the earliest civilization, belong also to the same quarter. This latter fact, however, is considered by Orozco y Berra as itself an evidence of the migrations having been from the North, the first comers having been naturally attracted southward by a warmer climate, and more fertile soil, or pushed onward in this direction by successive invasions from behind. Contradictory inferences have in like manner been drawn from the existence of Aztec remains and settlements in New Mexico and Arizona. All that can be said with confidence is that neither of the opposing theories rests on a secure and sufficient basis.—ED.]

[4] These were the Colhuans, not Acolhuans, with whom Humboldt, and most writers since, have confounded them.† See his Essai politique, tom. i. p. 414 ; ii. p. 37.

* [The confusion arises from the fact that the name of Chichimecs, originally that of a single tribe, and subsequently of its many offshoots, was also used, like the term *barbarians* in mediæval Italy to designate successive hordes, of whatever race, being sometimes employed as a mark of contempt, and sometimes assumed as an honourable appellation. It is found applied to the Otomies, the Toltecs, and many other races.—ED.]

† [Humboldt, strictly speaking, has not confounded the Colhuans with the Acolhuans, but has written, in the places cited, the latter name for the former. "Letzterer Name," says Buschmann, "ist der erstere mit dem Zusatz von *atl* Wasser,—Wasser Colhuer." (Ueber die aztekischen Ortsnamen, S. 690.) Yet the two tribes, according to the same authority, were entirely distinct, one alone—though which, he is unable to determine—being of the Nahuatlac race. Orozco y Berra, however, makes them both of this stock, the Acolhuans being one of the main branches, the Colhuans merely the descendants of the Toltec remnant in Anahuac.—ED.]

1325. They there beheld, perched on the stem of a prickly pear, which shot out from the crevice of a rock that was washed by the waves, a royal eagle of extraordinary size and beauty, with a serpent in his talons, and his broad wings opened to the rising sun. They hailed the auspicious omen, announced by an oracle as indicating the site of their future city, and laid its foundations by sinking piles into the shallows; for the low marshes were half buried under water. On these they erected their light fabrics of reeds and rushes, and sought a precarious subsistence from fishing, and from the wild fowl which frequented the waters, as well as from the cultivation of such simple vegetables as they could raise on their floating gardens. The place was called Tenochtitlan, in token of its miraculous origin, though only known to Europeans by its other name of Mexico,[1] derived from their war-god, Mexitli.[2] The legend of its foundation is still further commemorated by the device of the eagle and the cactus, which form the arms of the modern Mexican republic. Such were the humble beginnings of the Venice of the Western World.[3]

The forlorn condition of the new settlers was made still worse by domestic feuds. A part of the citizens seceded from the main body, and formed a separate community on the neighbouring marshes. Thus divided, it was long before they could aspire to the acquisition of territory on the main land. They gradually increased, however, in numbers, and strengthened themselves yet more by various improvements in their polity and military discipline, while they established a reputation for courage as well as cruelty in war which made their name terrible throughout the Valley. In the early part of the fifteenth century, nearly a hundred years from the foundation of the city, an event took place which created an entire revolution in the circumstances and, to some extent, in the character of the Aztecs. This was the subversion of the Tezcucan monarchy by the Tepanecs, already noticed. When the oppressive conduct of the victors had at length aroused a spirit of resistance, its prince, Nezahualcoyotl, succeeded, after incredible perils and escapes, in mustering such a force as, with the aid of the Mexicans, placed him on a level with his enemies. In two successive battles, these were defeated with great slaughter, their chief

---

[1] [This is not quite correct, since the form used in the letters of Cortés and other early documents is *Temixtitan*, which is explained as a corruption of Tenochtitlan. The letters *x* and *ch* are convertible, and have the same sound,—that of the English *sh*. *Mexico* is *Mexitl* with the place-designation *co, tl* final being dropped before an affix.—ED.]

[2] Clavigero gives good reasons for preferring the etymology of Mexico above noticed, to various others. (See his Stor. del Messico, tom. i. p. 168, nota.) The name *Tenochtitlan* signifies *tunal* (a cactus) *on a stone.* Esplicacion de la Col. de Mendoza, apud Antiq. of Mexico, vol. iv.

[3] "Datur hæc venia antiquitati," says Livy, "ut, miscendo humana divinis, primordia urbium augustiora faciat." Hist., Præf.—See, for the above paragraph, Col. de Mendoza, plate 1, apud Antiq. of Mexico, vol. i.,—Ixtlilxochitl, Hist. Chich., MS., cap. 10,—Toribio, Historia de los Indios, MS., Parte 3, cap. 8,—Veytia, Hist. antig., lib. 2, cap. 15.

—Clavigero, after a laborious examination, assigns the following dates to some of the prominent events noticed in the text. No two authorities agree on them; and this is not strange, considering that Clavigero—the most inquisitive of all—does not always agree with himself. (Compare his dates for the coming of the Acolhuans; tom. i. p. 147, and tom. iv., dissert. 2:)—

	A.D.
The Toltecs arrived in Anahuac	648
They abandoned the country	1051
The Chichimecs arrived	1170
The Acolhuans arrived about	1200
The Mexicans reached Tula	1196
They founded Mexico	1325

See his dissert. 2, sec. 12. In the last date, the one of most importance, he is confirmed by the learned Veytia, who differs from him in all the others. Hist. antig., lib. 2, cap. 15.

slain, and their territory, by one of those sudden reverses which characterize the wars of petty states, passed into the hands of the conquerors. It was awarded to Mexico, in return for its important services.

Then was formed that remarkable league, which, indeed, has no parallel in history. It was agreed between the states of Mexico, Tezcuco, and the neighbouring little kingdom of Tlacopan, that they should mutually support each other in their wars, offensive and defensive, and that in the distribution of the spoil one-fifth should be assigned to Tlacopan, and the remainder be divided, in what proportions is uncertain, between the other powers. The Tezcucan writers claim an equal share for their nation with the Aztecs. But this does not seem to be warranted by the immense increase of territory subsequently appropriated by the latter. And we may account for any advantage conceded to them by the treaty, on the supposition that, however inferior they may have been originally, they were at the time of making it, in a more prosperous condition than their allies, broken and dispirited by long oppression. What is more extraordinary than the treaty itself, however, is the fidelity with which it was maintained. During a century of uninterrupted warfare that ensued, no instance occurred where the parties quarrelled over the division of the spoil, which so often makes shipwreck of similar confederacies among civilized states.[1]

The allies for some time found sufficient occupation for their arms in their own valley; but they soon overleaped its rocky ramparts, and by the middle of the fifteenth century, under the first Montezuma, had spread down the sides of the table-land to the borders of the Gulf of Mexico. Tenochtitlan, the Aztec capital, gave evidence of the public prosperity. Its frail tenements were supplanted by solid structures of stone and lime. Its population rapidly increased. Its old feuds were healed. The citizens who had seceded were again brought under a common government with the main body, and the quarter they occupied was permanently connected with the parent city; the dimensions of which, covering the same ground, were much larger than those of the modern capital of Mexico.[2]

Fortunately, the throne was filled by a succession of able princes, who knew how to profit by their enlarged resources and by the martial enthusiasm of the nation. Year after year saw them return, loaded with the spoils of conquered cities, and with throngs of devoted captives, to their capital. No state was able long to resist the accumulated strength of

---

[1] The loyal Tezcucan chronicler claims the supreme dignity for his own sovereign, if not the greatest share of the spoil, by this imperial compact. (Hist. Chich., cap. 32.) Torquemada, on the other hand, claims one-half of all the conquered lands for Mexico. (Monarch. Ind., lib. 2, cap. 40.) All agree in assigning only one-fifth to Tlacopan; and Veytia (Hist. antig., lib. 3, cap. 3) and Zurita (Rapport sur les différentes Classes de Chefs de la Nouvelle-Espagne, trad. de Ternaux (Paris, 1840), p. 11), both very competent critics, acquiesce in an equal division between the two principal states in the confederacy. An ode, still extant, of Nezahualcoyotl, in its Castilian version, bears testimony to the singular union of the three powers:—

"solo se acordarán en las Naciones
lo bien que gobernáron
las *tres Cabezas* que el Imperio honráron."
Cantares del Emperador
Nezahualcoyotl, MS.

[2] See the plans of the ancient and modern capital, in Bullock's "Mexico," first edition. The original of the ancient map was obtained by that traveller from the collection of the unfortunate Boturini; if, as seems probable, it is the one indicated on page 13 of his Catalogue, I find no warrant for Mr. Bullock's statement that it was the one prepared for Cortés by the order of Montezuma.

the confederates. At the beginning of the sixteenth century, just before the arrival of the Spaniards, the Aztec dominion reached across the continent, from the Atlantic to the Pacific; and, under the bold and bloody Ahuitzotl, its arms had been carried far over the limits already noticed as defining its permanent territory, into the farthest corners of Guatemala and Nicaragua. This extent of empire, however limited in comparison with that of many other states, is truly wonderful, considering it as the acquisition of a people whose whole population and resources had so recently been comprised within the walls of their own petty city, and considering, moreover, that the conquered territory was thickly settled by various races, bred to arms like the Mexicans, and little inferior to them in social organization. The history of the Aztecs suggests some strong points of resemblance to that of the ancient Romans, not only in their military successes, but in the policy which led to them.[1]

The most important contribution, of late years, to the early history of Mexico is the *Historia antigua* of the Lic. Don Mariano Veytia, published in the city of Mexico, in 1836. This scholar was born of an ancient and highly respectable family at Puebla, 1718. After finishing his academic education, he went to Spain, where he was kindly received at court. He afterwards visited several other countries of Europe, made himself acquainted with their languages, and returned home well stored with the fruits of a discriminating observation and diligent study. The rest of his life he devoted to letters; especially to the illustration of the national history and antiquities. As the executor of the unfortunate Boturini, with whom he had contracted an intimacy in Madrid, he obtained access to his valuable collection of manuscripts in Mexico, and from them, and every other source which his position in society and his eminent character opened to him, he composed various works, none of which, however, except the one before us, has been admitted to the honours of the press. The time of his death is not given by his editor, but it was probably not later than 1780.

Veytia's history covers the whole period from the first occupation of Anahuac to the middle of the fifteenth century, at which point his labours were unfortunately terminated by his death. In the early portion he has endeavoured to trace the migratory movements and historical annals of the principal races who entered the country. Every page bears testimony to the extent and fidelity of his researches; and, if we feel but moderate confidence in the results, the fault is not imputable to him, so much as to the dark and doubtful nature of the subject. As he descends to later ages, he is more occupied with the fortunes of the Tezcucan than with those of the Aztec dynasty, which have been amply discussed by others of his countrymen. The premature close of his labours prevented him, probably, from giving that attention to the domestic institutions of the people he describes, to which they are entitled as the most important subject of inquiry to the historian. The deficiency has been supplied by his judicious editor, Orteaga, from other sources. In the early part of his work, Veytia has explained the chronological system of the Aztecs, but, like most writers preceding the accurate Gama, with indifferent success. As a critic, he certainly ranks much higher than the annalists who preceded him, and, when his own religion is not involved, shows a discriminating judgment. When

---

[1] Clavigero, Stor. del Messico, tom. i. lib. 2.—Torquemada, Monarch. Ind., tom. i. lib. 2.—Boturini, Idea, p. 146.—Col. of Mendoza, Part 1, and Codex Telleriano-Remensis, apud Antiq. of Mexico, vols. i., vi.—Machiavelli has noticed it as one great cause of the military successes of the Romans, "that they associated themselves, in their wars, with other states, as the principal," and expresses his astonishment that a similar policy should not have been adopted by ambitious republics in later times. (See his Discorsi sopra T. Livio, lib. 2, cap. 4, apud Opere (Geneva, 1798).) This, as we have seen above, was the very course pursued by the Mexicans.

it is, he betrays a full measure of the credulity which still maintains its hold on too many even of the well-informed of his countrymen. The editor of the work has given a very interesting letter from the Abbé Clavigero to Veytia, written when the former was a poor and humble exile, and in the tone of one addressing a person of high standing and literary eminence. Both were employed on the same subject. The writings of the poor abbé, published again and again, and translated into various languages, have spread his fame throughout Europe; while the name of Veytia, whose works have been locked up in their primitive manuscript, is scarcely known beyond the boundaries of Mexico.

CHAPTER II.

SUCCESSION TO THE CROWN.—AZTEC NOBILITY.—JUDICIAL SYSTEM.—LAWS AND REVENUES.—MILITARY INSTITUTIONS.

THE form of government differed in the different states of Anahuac. With the Aztecs and Tezcucans it was monarchical and nearly absolute. The two nations resembled each other so much in their political institutions that one of their historians has remarked, in too unqualified a manner indeed, that what is told of one may be always understood as applying to the other.[1] I shall direct my inquiries to the Mexican polity, borrowing an illustration occasionally from that of the rival kingdom.

The government was an elective monarchy. Four of the principal nobles, who had been chosen by their own body in the preceding reign, filled the office of electors, to whom were added, with merely an honorary rank, however, the two royal allies of Tezcuco and Tlacopan. The sovereign was selected from the brothers of the deceased prince, or, in default of them, from his nephews. Thus the election was always restricted to the same family. The candidate preferred must have distinguished himself in war, though, as in the case of the last Montezuma, he were a member of the priesthood.[2] This singular mode of supplying the throne had some advantages. The candidates received an education which fitted them for the royal dignity, while the age at which they were chosen not only secured the nation against the evils of minority, but afforded ample means for estimating their qualifications for the office. The result, at all events, was favourable; since the throne, as already noticed, was filled by a succession of able princes, well qualified to rule over a warlike and ambitious people. The scheme of election, however defective, argues a more refined and calculating policy than was to have been expected from a barbarous nation.[3]

---

[1] Ixtlilxochitl, Hist. Chich., MS., cap. 36.

[2] This was an exception.—In Egypt, also, the king was frequently taken from the warrior caste, though obliged afterwards to be instructed in the mysteries of the priesthood · ὁ δὲ ἐκ μαχίμων ἀποδεδειγμένος εὐθὺς ἐγίνετο τῶν ἱέρων. Plutarch, de Isid. et Osir., sec. 9.

[3] Torquemada, Monarch. Ind., lib. 2, cap. 18; lib. 11, cap. 27.—Clavigero, Stor. del Messico, tom. ii. p. 112.—Acosta, Naturall and Morall Historie of

The new monarch was installed in his regal dignity with much parade of religious ceremony, but not until, by a victorious campaign, he had obtained a sufficient number of captives to grace his triumphal entry into the capital and to furnish victims for the dark and bloody rites which stained the Aztec superstition. Amidst this pomp of human sacrifice he was crowned. The crown, resembling a mitre in its form, and curiously ornamented with gold, gems, and feathers, was placed on his head by the lord of Tezcuco, the most powerful of his royal allies. The title of *King*, by which the earlier Aztec princes are distinguished by Spanish writers, is supplanted by that of *Emperor* in the later reigns, intimating, perhaps, his superiority over the confederated monarchies of Tlacopan and Tezcuco.[1]

The Aztec princes, especially towards the close of the dynasty, lived in a barbaric pomp, truly Oriental. Their spacious palaces were provided with halls for the different councils who aided the monarch in the transaction of business. The chief of these was a sort of privy council, composed in part, probably, of the four electors chosen by the nobles after the accession, whose places, when made vacant by death, were immediately supplied as before. It was the business of this body, so far as can be gathered from the very loose accounts given of it, to advise the king, in respect to the government of the provinces, the administration of the revenues, and, indeed, on all great matters of public interest.[2]

In the royal buildings were accommodations, also, for a numerous body-guard of the sovereign, made up of the chief nobility. It is not easy to determine with precision, in these barbarian governments, the limits of the several orders. It is certain there was a distinct class of nobles, with large landed possessions, who held the most important offices near the person of the prince, and engrossed the administration of the provinces and cities.[3] Many of these could trace their descent from the founders of the Aztec monarchy. According to some writers of authority, there were thirty great *caciques*, who had their residence, at least a part of the year, in the capital, and who could muster a hundred thousand vassals each on their estates.[4] Without relying on such wild statements, it is clear, from the testimony of the Conquerors, that the country was occupied by numerous powerful chieftains, who lived like independent princes on their domains. If it be true that the kings encouraged, or, indeed, exacted, the residence of these

---

the East and West Indies, Eng. trans. (London, 1604.)—According to Zurita, an election by the nobles took place only in default of heirs of the deceased monarch. (Rapport, p. 15.) The minute historical investigation of Clavigero may be permitted to outweigh this general assertion.

[1] Sahagun, Hist. de Nueva-España, lib. 6, cap. 9, 10, 14; lib. 8, cap. 31, 34.—See, also, Zurita, Rapport, pp. 20-23.—Ixtlilxochitl stoutly claims this supremacy for his own nation. (Hist. Chich., MS., cap. 34.) His assertions are at variance with facts stated by himself elsewhere, and are not countenanced by any other writer whom I have consulted.

[2] Sahagun, who places the elective power in a much larger body, speaks of four senators, who formed a state council. (Hist. de Nueva-España, lib. 8, cap. 30.) Acosta enlarges the council beyond the number of the electors. (Lib. 6, ch. 26.) No two writers agree.

[3] Zurita enumerates four orders of chiefs, all of whom were exempted from imposts and enjoyed very considerable privileges. He does not discriminate the several ranks with much precision. Rapport, p. 47, et seq.

[4] See, in particular, Herrera, Historia general de los Hechos de los Castellanos en las Islas y Tierra firme del Mar Océano (Madrid, 1730), dec. 2, lib. 7, cap. 12.

nobles in the capital, and required hostages in their absence, it is evident that their power must have been very formidable.[1]

Their estates appear to have been held by various tenures, and to have been subject to different restrictions. Some of them, earned by their own good swords or received as the recompense of public services, were held without any limitation, except that the possessors could not dispose of them to a plebeian.[2] Others were entailed on the eldest male issue, and, in default of such, reverted to the crown. Most of them seem to have been burdened with the obligation of military service. The principal chiefs of Tezcuco, according to its chronicler, were expressly obliged to support their prince with their armed vassals, to attend his court, and aid him in the council. Some, instead of these services, were to provide for the repairs of his buildings, and to keep the royal demesnes in order, with an annual offering, by way of homage, of fruits and flowers. It was usual, if we are to believe historians, for a new king, on his accession, to confirm the investiture of estates derived from the crown.[3]

It cannot be denied that we recognize, in all this, several features of the feudal system, which, no doubt, lose nothing of their effect under the hands of the Spanish writers, who are fond of tracing analogies to European institutions. But such analogies lead sometimes to very erroneous conclusions. The obligation of military service, for instance, the most essential principle of a fief, seems to be naturally demanded by every government from its subjects. As to minor points of resemblance, they fall far short of that harmonious system of reciprocal service and protection which embraced, in nice gradation, every order of a feudal monarchy. The kingdoms of Anahuac were in their nature despotic, attended, indeed, with many mitigating circumstances unknown to the despotisms of the East; but it is chimerical to look for much in common—beyond a few accidental forms and ceremonies—with those aristocratic institutions of the Middle Ages which made the court of every petty baron the precise image in miniature of that of his sovereign.

The legislative power, both in Mexico and Tezcuco, resided wholly with the monarch. This feature of despotism, however, was in some measure counteracted by the constitution of the judicial tribunals,—of more importance, among a rude people, than the legislative, since it is easier to make good laws for such a community than to enforce them, and the best laws, badly administered, are but a mockery. Over each of the principal

---

[1] Carta de Cortés, ap. Lorenzana, Hist. de Nueva-España, p. 110.—Torquemada, Monarch. Ind., lib. 2, cap. 80; lib. 14, cap. 6.—Clavigero, Stor. del Messico, tom. ii. p. 121.—Zurita, Rapport, pp. 48, 65.—Ixtlilxochitl (Hist. Chich., MS., cap. 34) speaks of thirty great feudal chiefs, some of them Tezcucan and Tlacopan, whom he styles "grandees of the empire"! He says nothing of the great *tail* of 100,000 vassals to each, mentioned by Torquemada and Herrera.

[2] *Macehual,*—a word equivalent to the French word *roturier.* Nor could fiefs originally be held by plebeians in France. See Hallam's Middle Ages (London, 1819), vol. ii. p. 207.

[3] Ixtlilxochitl, Hist. Chich., MS., ubi supra.—Zurita, Rapport, ubi supra.—Clavigero, Stor. del Messico, tom. ii. pp. 122-124.—Torquemada, Monarch. Ind., lib. 14, cap. 7.—Gomara, Crónica de Nueva-España, cap. 199, ap. Barcia, tom. ii.—Boturini (Idea, p. 165) carries back the origin of *fiefs* in Anahuac to the twelfth century. Carli says, "Le système politique y étoit féodal." In the next page he tells us, "Personal merit alone made the distinction of the nobility"! (Lettres Américaines, trad. Fr. (Paris, 1788), tom. i. let. 11.) Carli was a writer of a lively imagination.

cities, with its dependent territories, was placed a supreme judge, appointed by the crown, with original and final jurisdiction in both civil and criminal cases. There was no appeal from his sentence to any other tribunal, nor even to the king. He held his office during life; and any one who usurped his ensigns was punished with death.[1]

Below this magistrate was a court, established in each province, and consisting of three members. It held concurrent jurisdiction with the supreme judge in civil suits, but in criminal an appeal lay to his tribunal. Besides these courts, there was a body of inferior magistrates, distributed through the country, chosen by the people themselves in their several districts. Their authority was limited to smaller causes, while the more important were carried up to the higher courts. There was still another class of subordinate officers, appointed also by the people, each of whom was to watch over the conduct of a certain number of families and report any disorder or breach of the laws to the higher authorities.[2]

In Tezcuco the judicial arrangements were of a more refined character;[3] and a gradation of tribunals finally terminated in a general meeting or parliament, consisting of all the judges, great and petty, throughout the kingdom, held every eighty days in the capital, over which the king presided in person. This body determined all suits which, from their importance or difficulty, had been reserved for its consideration by the lower tribunals. It served, moreover, as a council of state, to assist the monarch in the transaction of public business.[4]

Such are the vague and imperfect notices that can be gleaned, respecting the Aztec tribunals, from the hieroglyphical paintings still preserved, and from the most accredited Spanish writers. These, being usually ecclesiastics, have taken much less interest in this subject than in matters connected with religion. They find some apology, certainly, in the early destruction of most of the Indian paintings, from which their information was, in part, to be gathered.

On the whole, however, it must be inferred that the Aztecs were suffi-

---

[1] This magistrate, who was called *cihuacoatl,*[*] was also to audit the accounts of the collectors of the taxes in his district. (Clavigero, Stor. del Messico, tom. ii. p. 127.—Torquemada, Monarch. Ind., lib. ii, cap. 25.) The Mendoza Collection contains a painting of the courts of justice under Montezuma, who introduced great changes in them. (Antiq. of Mexico, vol. i., Plate 70.) According to the interpreter, an appeal lay from them, in certain cases, to the king's council. Ibid., vol. vi. p. 79.

[2] Clavigero, Stor. del Messico, tom. ii. pp. 127, 128.—Torquemada, Monarch. Ind., ubi supra.—In this arrangement of the more humble magistrates we are reminded of the Anglo-Saxon hundreds and tithings, especially the latter, the members of which were to watch over the conduct of the families in their districts and bring the offenders to justice. The hard penalty of mutual responsibility was not known to the Mexicans.

[3] Zurita, so temperate, usually, in his language, remarks that, in the capital, "Tribunals were instituted which might compare in their organization with the royal audiences of Castile." (Rapport, p. 93.) His observations are chiefly drawn from the Tezcucan courts, which in their forms of procedure, he says, were like the Aztec. (Loc. cit.)

[4] Boturini, Idea, p. 87.—Torquemada, Monarch. Ind., lib. ii, cap. 26.—Zurita compares this body to the Castilian córtes. It would seem, however, according to him, to have consisted only of twelve principal judges, besides the king. His meaning is somewhat doubtful. (Rapport, pp. 94, 101, 106.) M. de Humboldt, in his account of the Aztec courts, has confounded them with the Tezcucan. Comp. Vues des Cordillères et Monumens des Peuples indigènes de l'Amérique (Paris, 1810), p. 55, and Clavigero, Stor. del Messico, tom. ii. pp. 128, 129.

[*] [This word, a compound of *cihuatl,* woman, and *coatl,* serpent, was the name of a divinity, the mythical mother of the human species. Its typical application may have had reference to justice, or law, as the source of social order.—ED.]

ciently civilized to evince a solicitude for the rights both of property and of persons. The law, authorizing an appeal to the highest judicature in criminal matters only, shows an attention to personal security, rendered the more obligatory by the extreme severity of their penal code, which would naturally have made them more cautious of a wrong conviction. The existence of a number of co-ordinate tribunals, without a central one of supreme authority to control the whole, must have given rise to very discordant interpretations of the law in different districts. But this is an evil which they shared in common with most of the nations of Europe.

The provision for making the superior judges wholly independent of the crown was worthy of an enlightened people. It presented the strongest barrier that a mere constitution could afford against tyranny. It is not, indeed, to be supposed that, in a government otherwise so despotic, means could not be found for influencing the magistrate. But it was a great step to fence round his authority with the sanction of the law; and no one of the Aztec monarchs, so far as I know, is accused of an attempt to violate it.

To receive presents or a bribe, to be guilty of collusion in any way with a suitor, was punished, in a judge, with death. Who, or what tribunal, decided as to his guilt, does not appear. In Tezcuco this was done by the rest of the court. But the king presided over that body. The Tezcucan prince Nezahualpilli, who rarely tempered justice with mercy, put one judge to death for taking a bribe, and another for determining suits in his own house,—a capital offence, also, by law.[1]

The judges of the higher tribunals were maintained from the produce of a part of the crown lands, reserved for this purpose. They, as well as the supreme judge, held their offices for life. The proceedings in the courts were conducted with decency and order. The judges wore an appropriate dress, and attended to business both parts of the day, dining always, for the sake of despatch, in an apartment of the same building where they held their session; a method of proceeding much commended by the Spanish chroniclers, to whom despatch was not very familiar in their own tribunals. Officers attended to preserve order, and others summoned the parties and produced them in court. No counsel was employed; the parties stated their own case and supported it by their witnesses. The oath of the accused was also admitted in evidence. The statement of the case, the testimony, and the proceedings of the trial were all set forth by a clerk, in hieroglyphical paintings, and handed over to the court. The paintings were executed with so much accuracy that in all suits respecting real property they were allowed to be produced as good authority in the Spanish tribunals, very long after the Conquest; and a chair for their study and interpretation was established at Mexico in 1553, which has

---

[1] "If this should be done now, what an excellent ching it would be!" exclaims Sahagun's Mexican editor. Hist. de Nueva-España. tom. ii. p. 304, nota.—Zurita, Rapport, p. 102.—Torquemada, Monarch. Ind., ubi supra.—Ixtlilxochitl, Hist. Chich., MS., cap. 67.

long since shared the fate of most other provisions for learning in that unfortunate country.[1]

A capital sentence was indicated by a line traced with an arrow across the portrait of the accused. In Tezcuco, where the king presided in the court, this, according to the national chronicler, was done with extraordinary parade. His description, which is of rather a poetical cast, I give in his own words. " In the royal palace of Tezcuco was a courtyard, on the opposite sides of which were two halls of justice. In the principal one, called the 'tribunal of God,' was a throne of pure gold, inlaid with turquoises and other precious stones. On a stool in front was placed a human skull, crowned with an immense emerald of a pyramidal form, and surmounted by an aigrette of brilliant plumes and precious stones. The skull was laid on a heap of military weapons, shields, quivers, bows, and arrows. The walls were hung with tapestry, made of the hair of different wild animals, of rich and various colours, festooned by gold rings and embroidered with figures of birds and flowers. Above the throne was a canopy of variegated plumage, from the centre of which shot forth resplendent rays of gold and jewels. The other tribunal, called 'the King's,' was also surmounted by a gorgeous canopy of feathers, on which were emblazoned the royal arms. Here the sovereign gave public audience and communicated his despatches. But when he decided important causes, or confirmed a capital sentence, he passed to the 'tribunal of God,' attended by the fourteen great lords of the realm, marshalled according to their rank. Then, putting on his mitred crown, incrusted with precious stones, and holding a golden arrow, by way of sceptre, in his left hand, he laid his right upon the skull, and pronounced judgment." [2] All this looks rather fine for a court of justice, it must be owned. But it is certain that the Tezcucans, as we shall see hereafter, possessed both the materials and the skill requisite to work them up in this manner. Had they been a little further advanced in refinement, one might well doubt their having the bad taste to do so.

The laws of the Aztecs were registered, and exhibited to the people, in their hieroglyphical paintings. Much the larger part of them, as in every nation imperfectly civilized, relates rather to the security of persons than of property. The great crimes against society were all made capital. Even the murder of a slave was punished with death. Adulterers, as among the Jews, were stoned to death. Thieving, according to the degree of the offence, was punished by slavery or death. Yet the Mexicans could have been under no great apprehension of this crime, since the entrances to their dwellings were not secured by bolts or fastenings of any kind. It was a capital offence to remove the boundaries of another's lands ; to alter the

[1] Zurita, Rapport, pp. 95, 100, 103.—Sahagun, Hist. de Nueva-España, loc. cit.—Humboldt, Vues des Cordillères, pp. 55, 56.—Torquemada, Monarch. Ind., lib. 11, cap. 25.—Clavigero says the accused might free himself by oath : " il reo poteva purgarsi col giuramento." (Stor. del Messico, tom. ii. p. 129.) What rogue, then, could ever have been convicted?

[2] Ixtlilxochitl, Hist. Chich., MS., cap. 36.— These various objects had a symbolical meaning, according to Boturini, Idea, p. 84.

established measures; and for a guardian not to be able to give a good account of his ward's property. These regulations evince a regard for equity in dealings, and for private rights, which argues a considerable progress in civilization. Prodigals, who squandered their patrimony, were punished in like manner; a severe sentence, since the crime brought its adequate punishment along with it. Intemperance, which was the burden, moreover, of their religious homilies, was visited with the severest penalties; as if they had foreseen in it the consuming canker of their own as well as of the other Indian races in later times. It was punished in the young with death, and in older persons with loss of rank and confiscation of property. Yet a decent conviviality was not meant to be proscribed at their festivals, and they possessed the means of indulging it, in a mild fermented liquor, called *pulque*, which is still popular, not only with the Indian, but the European population of the country.[1]

The rites of marriage were celebrated with as much formality as in any Christian country; and the institution was held in such reverence that a tribunal was instituted for the sole purpose of determining questions relating to it. Divorces could not be obtained until authorized by a sentence of this court, after a patient hearing of the parties.

But the most remarkable part of the Aztec code was that relating to slavery. There were several descriptions of slaves: prisoners taken in war who were almost always reserved for the dreadful doom of sacrifice; criminals, public debtors, persons who, from extreme poverty, voluntarily resigned their freedom, and children who were sold by their own parents. In the last instance, usually occasioned also by poverty, it was common for the parents, with the master's consent, to substitute others of their children successively, as they grew up; thus distributing the burden as equally as possible among the different members of the family. The willingness of freemen to incur the penalties of this condition is explained by the mild form in which it existed. The contract of sale was executed in the presence of at least four witnesses. The services to be exacted were limited with great precision. The slave was allowed to have his own family, to hold property, and even other slaves. His children were free. No one could be born to slavery in Mexico;[2] an honourable distinction, not known, I believe, in any civilized community where slavery has been sanctioned.[3] Slaves were not sold by their masters, unless when these

---

[1] Paintings of the Mendoza Collection, Pl. 72, and Interpretation, ap. Antiq. of Mexico, vol. vi. p. 87.—Torquemada, Monarch. Ind., lib. 12, cap. 7.—Clavigero, Stor. del Messico, tom. ii. pp. 130-134.—Camargo, Hist. de Tlascala, MS.—They could scarcely have been an intemperate people, with these heavy penalties hanging over them. Indeed, Zurita bears testimony that those Spaniards who thought they were greatly erred. (Rapport, p. 112.) M. Ternaux's translation of a passage of the Anonymous Conqueror, "aucun peuple n'est aussi sobre" (Recueil de Pièces relatives à la Conquête du Mexique, ap. Voyages, etc. (Paris, 1838), p. 54), may give a more favourable impression, however, than

that intended by his original, whose remark is confined to abstemiousness in eating. See the Relatione, ap. Ramusio, Raccolta delle Navigationi et Viaggi (Venetia, 1554-1565).

[2] In ancient Egypt the child of a slave was born free, if the father were free. (Diodorus, Bibl. Hist., lib. 1, sec. 80.) This, though more liberal than the code of most countries, fell short of the Mexican.

[3] In Egypt the same penalty was attached to the murder of a slave as to that of a freeman. (Ibid., lib. 1, sec. 77.) Robertson speaks of a class of slaves held so cheap in the eye of the Mexican law that one might kill them with impunity. (History of America (ed. London, 1776), vol. iii. p. 164.) This,

were driven to it by poverty. They were often liberated by them at their death, and sometimes, as there was no natural repugnance founded on difference of blood and race, were married to them. Yet a refractory or vicious slave might be led into the market, with a collar round his neck, which intimated his bad character, and there be publicly sold, and on a second sale, reserved for sacrifice.[1]

Such are some of the most striking features of the Aztec code, to which the Tezcucan bore great resemblance.[2] With some exceptions, it is stamped with the severity, the ferocity indeed, of a rude people, hardened by familiarity with scenes of blood, and relying on physical instead of moral means for the correction of evil.[3] Still, it evinces a profound respect for the great principles of morality, and as clear a perception of these principles as is to be found in the most cultivated nations.

The royal revenues were derived from various sources. The crown lands, which appear to have been extensive, made their returns in kind. The places in the neighbourhood of the capital were bound to supply workmen and materials for building the king's palaces and keeping them in repair. They were also to furnish fuel, provisions, and whatever was necessary for his ordinary domestic expenditure, which was certainly on no stinted scale.[4] The principal cities, which had numerous villages and a large territory dependent on them, were distributed into districts, with each a share of the lands allotted to it, for its support. The inhabitants paid a stipulated part of the produce to the crown. The vassals of the great chiefs, also, paid a portion of their earnings into the public treasury; an arrangement not at all in the spirit of the feudal institutions.[5]

In addition to this tax on all the agricultural produce of the kingdom, there was another on its manufactures. The nature and the variety of the tributes will be best shown by an enumeration of some of the principal articles. These were cotton dresses, and mantles of feather-work exquisitely made; ornamented armour; vases and plates of gold; gold dust, bands and bracelets; crystal, gilt, and varnished jars and goblets; bells, arms, and utensils of copper; reams of paper; grain, fruits, copal,

---

however, was not in Mexico, but in Nicaragua (see his own authority, Herrera, Hist. general, dec. 3, lib. 4, cap. 2), a distant country, not incorporated in the Mexican empire, and with laws and institutions very different from those of the latter.

[1] Torquemada, Monarch. Ind., lib. 12, cap. 15; lib. 14, cap. 16, 17.—Sahagun, Hist. de Nueva-España, lib. 8, cap. 14.—Clavigero, Stor. del Messico, tom. ii. pp. 134-136.

[2] Ixtlilxochitl, Hist. Chich., MS., cap. 38, and Relaciones, MS.—The Tezcucan code, indeed, as digested under the great Nezahualcoyotl, formed the basis of the Mexican, in the latter days of the empire. Zurita, Rapport, p. 95.

[3] In this, at least, they did not resemble the Romans; of whom their countryman could boast, "Gloriari licet, nulli gentium mitiores placuisse poenas." Livy, Hist., lib. 1, cap. 28.

[4] The Tezcucan revenues were, in like manner, paid in the produce of the country. The various branches of the royal expenditure were defrayed by specified towns and districts; and the whole arrange-

ments here, and in Mexico, bore a remarkable resemblance to the financial regulations of the Persian empire, as reported by the Greek writers (see Herodotus, Clio, sec. 192); with this difference, however, that the towns of Persia proper were not burdened with tributes, like the conquered cities. Idem, Thalia, sec. 97.

[5] Lorenzana, Hist. de Nueva-España, p. 172.—Torquemada, Monarch. Ind., lib. 2, cap. 89; lib. 14, cap. 7.—Boturini, Idea, p. 166.—Camargo, Hist. de Tlascala, MS.—Herrera, Hist. general, dec. 2, lib. 7, cap. 13.—The people of the provinces were distributed into *calpulli*, or tribes, who held the lands of the neighbourhood in common. Officers of their own appointment parcelled out these lands among the several families of the *calpulli*; and on the extinction or removal of a family its lands reverted to the common stock, to be again distributed. The individual proprietor had no power to alienate them. The laws regulating these matters were very precise, and had existed ever since the occupation of the country by the Aztecs. Zurita, Rapport, pp. 51-62.

amber, cochineal, cacao, wild animals and birds, timber, lime, mats, &c.[1] In this curious medley of the most homely commodities and the elegant superfluities of luxury, it is singular that no mention should be made of silver, the great staple of the country in later times, and the use of which was certainly known to the Aztecs.[2]

Garrisons were established in the larger cities,—probably those at a distance and recently conquered,—to keep down revolt, and to enforce the payment of the tribute.[3] Tax-gatherers were also distributed throughout the kingdom, who were recognized by their official badges, and dreaded from the merciless rigour of their exactions. By a stern law, every defaulter was liable to be taken and sold as a slave. In the capital were spacious granaries and warehouses for the reception of the tributes. A receiver-general was quartered in the palace, who rendered in an exact account of the various contributions, and watched over the conduct of the inferior agents, in whom the least malversation was summarily punished. This functionary was furnished with a map of the whole empire, with a minute specification of the imposts assessed on every part of it. These imposts, moderate under the reigns of the early princes, became so burdensome under those at the close of the dynasty, being rendered still more oppressive by the manner of collection, that they bred disaffection throughout the land, and prepared the way for its conquest by the Spaniards.[4]

Communication was maintained with the remotest parts of the country by means of couriers. Post-houses were established on the great roads, about two leagues distant from each other. The courier, bearing his despatches in the form of a hieroglyphical painting, ran with them to the first station, where they were taken by another messenger and carried forward to the next, and so on till they reached the capital. These couriers, trained from childhood, travelled with incredible swiftness,

---

[1] The following items of the tribute furnished by different cities will give a more precise idea of its nature :—20 chests of ground chocolate ; 40 pieces of armour, of a particular device ; 2400 loads of large mantles, of twisted cloth ; 800 loads of small mantles, of rich wearing apparel ; 5 pieces of armour, of rich feathers ; 60 pieces of armour, of common feathers ; a chest of beans ; a chest of *chian ;* a chest of maize ; 8000 reams of paper ; likewise 2000 loaves of very white salt, refined in the shape of a mould, for the consumption only of the lords of Mexico ; 8000 lumps of unrefined copal ; 400 small baskets of white refined copal ; 100 copper axes ; 80 loads of red chocolate ; 800 *xicaras,* out of which they drank chocolate ; a little vessel of small turquoise stones ; 4 chests of timber, full of maize ; 4000 loads of lime ; tiles of gold, of the size of an oyster, and as thick as the finger ; 40 bags of cochineal ; 20 bags of gold dust, of the finest quality ; a diadem of gold, of a specified pattern ; 20 lip-jewels of clear amber, ornamented with gold ; 200 loads of chocolate ; 100 pots or jars of liquid-amber ; 8000 *handfuls* of rich scarlet feathers ; 40 tiger-skins ; 1600 bundles of cotton, etc. etc. Col. de Mendoza, part 2, ap. Antiq. of Mexico, vols. i., vi.

[2] Mapa de Tributos, ap. Lorenzana, Hist. de Nueva-España.—Tribute-roll, ap. Antiq. of Mexico, vol. i., and Interpretation, vol. vi. pp. 17–44.—The Mendoza Collection, in the Bodleian Library at Oxford, contains a roll of the cities of the Mexican empire, with the specific tributes exacted from them. It is a copy made after the Conquest, with a pen, on European paper. (See Foreign Quarterly Review, No. XVII. Art. 4.) An original painting of the same roll was in Boturini's museum. Lorenzana has given us engravings of it, in which the outlines of the Oxford copy are filled up, though somewhat rudely. Clavigero considers the explanations in Lorenzana's edition very inaccurate (Stor. del Messico, tom. i. p. 25), a judgment confirmed by Aglio, who has transcribed the entire collection of the Mendoza papers, in the first volume of the Antiquities of Mexico. It would have much facilitated reference to his plates if they had been numbered ;—a strange omission !

[3] The caciques, who submitted to the allied arms, were usually confirmed in their authority, and the conquered places allowed to retain their laws and usages. (Zurita, Rapport, p. 67.) The conquests were not always partitioned, but sometimes, singularly enough, were held in common by the three powers. Ibid., p. 11.

[4] Col. of Mendoza, ap. Antiq. of Mexico, vol. vi. p. 17.—Carta de Cortés, ap. Lorenzana, Hist. de Nueva-España, p. 110.—Torquemada, Monarch. Ind., lib. 14, cap. 6, 8.—Herrera, Hist. general, dec. 2, lib. 7, cap. 13.—Sahagun, Hist. de Nueva-España, lib. 8, cap. 18, 19.

—not four or five leagues an hour, as an old chronicler would make us believe, but with such speed that despatches were carried from one to two hundred miles a day.[1] Fresh fish was frequently served at Montezuma's table in twenty-four hours from the time it had been taken in the Gulf of Mexico, two hundred miles from the capital. In this way intelligence of the movements of the royal armies was rapidly brought to court; and the dress of the courier, denoting by its colour the nature of his tidings, spread joy or consternation in the towns through which he passed.[2]

But the great aim of the Aztec institutions, to which private discipline and public honours were alike directed, was the profession of arms. In Mexico, as in Egypt, the soldier shared with the priest the highest consideration. The king, as we have seen, must be an experienced warrior. The tutelary deity of the Aztecs was the god of war. A great object of their military expeditions was to gather hecatombs of captives for his altars. The soldier who fell in battle was transported at once to the region of ineffable bliss in the bright mansions of the Sun.[3] Every war, therefore, became a crusade; and the warrior, animated by a religious enthusiasm like that of the early Saracen or the Christian crusader, was not only raised to a contempt of danger, but courted it, for the imperishable crown of martyrdom. Thus we find the same impulse acting in the most opposite quarters of the globe, and the Asiatic, the European, and the American, each earnestly invoking the holy name of religion in the perpetration of human butchery.

The question of war was discussed in a council of the king and his chief nobles. Ambassadors were sent, previously to its declaration, to require the hostile state to receive the Mexican gods and to pay the customary tribute. The persons of ambassadors were held sacred throughout Anahuac. They were lodged and entertained in the great towns at the public charge, and were everywhere received with courtesy, so long as they did not deviate from the highroads on their route. When they did, they forfeited their privileges. If the embassy proved unsuccessful, a defiance, or open declaration of war, was sent; quotas were drawn from the conquered provinces, which were always subjected to military

---

[1] The Hon. C. A. Murray, whose imperturbable good-humour under real troubles forms a contrast, rather striking, to the sensitiveness of some of his predecessors to imaginary ones, tells us, among other marvels, that an Indian of his party travelled a hundred miles in four-and-twenty hours. (Travels in North America (New York, 1839), vol. i. p. 193.) The Greek who, according to Plutarch, brought the news of victory to Platæa, a hundred and twenty-five miles, in a day, was a better traveller still. Some interesting facts on the pedestrian capabilities of man in the savage state are collected by Buffon, who concludes, truly enough, "L'homme civilisé ne connaît pas ses forces." (Histoire naturelle : De la Jeunesse.)

[2] Torquemada, Monarch. Ind., lib. 14, cap. 1.—The same wants led to the same expedients in ancient Rome, and still more ancient Persia.

"Nothing in the world is borne so swiftly," says Herodotus, "as messages by the Persian couriers;" which his commentator Valckenaer prudently qualifies by the exception of the carrier-pigeon. (Herodotus, Hist., Urania, sec. 98, nec non Adnot. ed. Schweighäuser.) Couriers are noticed, in the thirteenth century, in China, by Marco Polo. Their stations were only three miles apart, and they accomplished five days' journey in one. (Viaggi di Marco Polo, lib. 2, cap. 20, ap. Ramusio, tom. ii.) A similar arrangement for posts subsists there at the present day, and excites the admiration of a modern traveller. (Anderson, British Embassy to China (London, 1796), p. 282.) In all these cases, the posts were for the use of government only.

[3] Sahagun, Hist. de Nueva-España, lib ↄ Apend., cap. 3

service, as well as the payment of taxes ; and the royal army, usually with
the monarch at its head, began its march.[1]

The Aztec princes made use of the incentives employed by European
monarchs to excite the ambition of their followers. They established
various military orders, each having its privileges and peculiar insignia.
There seems, also, to have existed a sort of knighthood, of inferior degree.
It was the cheapest reward of martial prowess, and whoever had not
reached it was excluded from using ornaments on his arms or his person,
and obliged to wear a coarse white stuff, made from the threads of the
aloe, called *nequen.* Even the members of the royal family were not
excepted from this law, which reminds one of the occasional practice of
Christian knights, to wear plain armour, or shields without device, till
they had achieved some doughty feat of chivalry. Although the military
orders were thrown open to all, it is probable that they were chiefly filled
with persons of rank, who, by their previous training and connections,
were able to come into the field under peculiar advantages.[2]

The dress of the higher warriors was picturesque and often magnificent.
Their bodies were covered with a close vest of quilted cotton, so thick as
to be impenetrable to the light missiles of Indian warfare. This garment
was so light and serviceable that it was adopted by the Spaniards. The
wealthier chiefs sometimes wore, instead of this cotton mail, a cuirass
made of thin plates of gold or silver. Over it was thrown a surcoat of
the gorgeous feather-work in which they excelled.[3] Their helmets were
sometimes of wood, fashioned like the heads of wild animals, and sometimes of silver, on the top of which waved a *panache* of variegated plumes,
sprinkled with precious stones and ornaments of gold. They wore also
collars, bracelets, and earrings of the same rich materials.[4]

Their armies were divided into bodies of eight thousand men ; and these,
again, into companies of three or four hundred, each with its own commander.
The national standard, which has been compared to the ancient Roman, displayed, in its embroidery of gold and feather-work, the armorial ensigns of the
state. These were significant of its name, which, as the names of both
persons and places were borrowed from some material object, was easily
expressed by hieroglyphical symbols. The companies and the great chiefs
had also their appropriate banners and devices, and the gaudy hues of
their many-coloured plumes gave a dazzling splendour to the spectacle.

---

[1] Zurita, Rapport, pp. 68, 120.—Col. of Mendoza.
ap. Antiq. of Mexico, vol. i. Pl. 67 ; vol. vi. p. 74.
—Torquemada, Monarch. Ind., lib. 14, cap. 1.—
The reader will find a remarkable resemblance to
these military usages in those of the early Romans.
Comp. Liv., Hist., lib. 1, cap. 32 ; lib. 4, cap. 30, et
alibi.

[2] Ibid., lib. 14, cap. 4, 5.—Acosta, lib. 6, ch. 26.
—Col. of Mendoza, ap. Antiq. of Mexico, vol. i. Pl.
65 ; vol. vi. p. 72.—Camargo, Hist. de Tlascala, MS.

[3] "Their mail, if mail it may be called, was woven
Of vegetable down, like finest flax,
Bleached to the whiteness of new-fallen snow.

.   .   .   .

Others, of higher office, were arrayed

In feathery breastplates, of more gorgeous hue
Than the gay plumage of the mountain-cock,
Than the pheasant's glittering pride. But what
        were these,
Or what the thin gold hauberk, when opposed
To arms like ours in battle ? "
                              Madoc, Part 1, canto 7.

Beautiful painting ! One may doubt, however,
the propriety of the Welshman's vaunt, before the
use of firearms.

[4] Sahagun, Hist. de Nueva-España, lib. 2, cap.
27 ; lib. 8, cap. 12.—Relatione d'un gentil' huomo,
ap. Ramusio, tom. iii. p. 305.—Torquemada, Monarch. Ind., ubi supra.

Their tactics were such as belong to a nation with whom war, though a trade, is not elevated to the rank of a science. They advanced singing, and shouting their war-cries, briskly charging the enemy, as rapidly retreating, and making use of ambuscades, sudden surprises, and the light skirmish of guerilla warfare. Yet their discipline was such as to draw forth the encomiums of the Spanish conquerors. "A beautiful sight it was," says one of them, "to see them set out on their march, all moving forward so gayly, and in so admirable order!"[1] In battle they did not seek to kill their enemies, so much as to take them prisoners; and they never scalped, like other North American tribes. The valour of a warrior was estimated by the number of his prisoners; and no ransom was large enough to save the devoted captive.[2]

Their military code bore the same stern features as their other laws. Disobedience of orders was punished with death. It was death, also, for a soldier to leave his colours, to attack the enemy before the signal was given, or to plunder another's booty or prisoners. One of the last Tezcucan princes, in the spirit of an ancient Roman, put two sons to death—after having cured their wounds—for violating the last-mentioned law.[3]

I must not omit to notice here an institution the introduction of which in the Old World is ranked among the beneficent fruits of Christianity. Hospitals were established in the principal cities, for the cure of the sick and the permanent refuge of the disabled soldier; and surgeons were placed over them, "who were so far better than those in Europe," says an old chronicler, "that they did not protract the cure in order to increase the pay."[4]

Such is the brief outline of the civil and military polity of the ancient Mexicans; less perfect than could be desired in regard to the former, from the imperfection of the sources whence it is drawn. Whoever has had occasion to explore the early history of modern Europe has found how vague and unsatisfactory is the political information which can be gleaned from the gossip of monkish annalists. How much is the difficulty increased in the present instance, where this information, first recorded in the dubious language of hieroglyphics, was interpreted in another language, with which the Spanish chroniclers were imperfectly acquainted, while it related to institutions of which their past experience enabled them to form no adequate conception! Amidst such uncertain lights, it is in vain to expect nice accuracy of detail. All that can be done is to attempt an outline of the more prominent features, that a correct impression, so far as it goes, may be produced on the mind of the reader.

---

[1] Relatione d'un gentil' huomo, ubi supra.

[2] Col. of Mendoza, ap. Antiq. of Mexico, vol. i. Pl. 65, 66; vol. vi. p. 73.—Sahagun, Hist. de Nueva-España, lib. 8, cap. 12.—Toribio, Hist. de los Indios, MS., Parte I. cap. 7.—Torquemada, Monarch. Ind., lib. 14, cap. 3.—Relatione d'un gentil' huomo, ap. Ramusio, loc. cit.—Scalping may claim high authority, or, at least, antiquity. The Father of History gives an account of it among the Scythians, showing that they performed the operation, and wore the hideous trophy, in the same manner as our North American Indians. (Herodot., Hist., Melpomene, sec. 64.) Traces of the same savage custom are also found in the laws of the Visigoths, among the Franks, and even the Anglo-Saxons. See Guizot, Cours d'Histoire moderne (Paris, 1829), tom. i. p. 283.

[3] Ixtlilxochitl, Hist. Chich., MS., cap. 67.

[4] Torquemada, Monarch. Ind., lib. 12, cap. 6; lib. 14, cap. 3.—Ixtlilxochitl, Hist. Chich., MS., cap. 36.

Enough has been said, however, to show that the Aztec and Tezcucan races were advanced in civilization very far beyond the wandering tribes of North America.[1]   The degree of civilization which they had reached, as inferred by their political institutions, may be considered, perhaps, not much short of that enjoyed by our Saxon ancestors under Alfred.   In respect to the nature of it, they may be better compared with the Egyptians; and the examination of their social relations and culture may suggest still stronger points of resemblance to that ancient people.

Those familiar with the modern Mexicans will find it difficult to conceive that the nation should ever have been capable of devising the enlightened polity which we have been considering.   But they should remember that in the Mexicans of our day they see only a conquered race; as different from their ancestors as are the modern Egyptians from those who built,— I will not say, the tasteless pyramids,—but the temples and palaces whose magnificent wrecks strew the borders of the Nile, at Luxor and Karnac. The difference is not so great as between the ancient Greek, and his degenerate descendant, lounging among the masterpieces of art which he has scarcely taste enough to admire,—speaking the language of those still more imperishable monuments of literature which he has hardly capacity to comprehend.   Yet he breathes the same atmosphere, is warmed by the same sun, nourished by the same scenes, as those who fell at Marathon and won the trophies of Olympic Pisa.   The same blood flows in his veins that flowed in theirs.   But ages of tyranny have passed over him; he belongs to a conquered race.

The American Indian has something peculiarly sensitive in his nature. He shrinks instinctively from the rude touch of a foreign hand.   Even when this foreign influence comes in the form of civilization, he seems to sink and pine away beneath it.   It has been so with the Mexicans. Under the Spanish domination, their numbers have silently melted away. Their energies are broken.   They no longer tread their mountain plains with the conscious independence of their ancestors.   In their faltering step and meek and melancholy aspect we read the sad characters of the conquered race.   The cause of humanity, indeed, has gained.   They live under a better system of laws, a more assured tranquillity, a purer faith.

---

[1] Zurita is indignant at the epithet of *barbarians* bestowed on the Aztecs; an epithet, he says, "which could come from no one who had personal knowledge of the capacity of the people or their institutions, and which in some respects is quite as well merited by the European nations." (Rapport, p. 200, et seq.)   This is strong language. Yet no one had better means of knowing than this eminent jurist, who for nineteen years held a post in the royal *audiences* of New Spain.   During his long residence in the country he had ample opportunity of acquainting himself with its usages, both through his own personal observation and intercourse with the natives, and through the first missionaries who came over after the Conquest.   On his return to Spain, probably about 1560, he occupied himself with an answer to queries which had been propounded by the government, on the character of the Aztec laws and institutions, and on that of the modifications introduced by the Spaniards.   Much of his treatise is taken up with the latter subject. In what relates to the former he is more brief than could be wished, from the difficulty, perhaps, of obtaining full and satisfactory information as to the details.   As far as he goes, however, he manifests a sound and discriminating judgment.   He is very rarely betrayed into the extravagance of expression so visible in the writers of the time; and this temperance, combined with his uncommon sources of information, makes his work one of highest authority on the limited topics within its range.   The original manuscript was consulted by Clavigero, and, indeed, has been used by other writers.   The work is now accessible to all, as one of the series of translations from the pen of the indefatigable Ternaux.

But all does not avail. Their civilization was of the hardy character which belongs to the wilderness. The fierce virtues of the Aztec were all his own. They refused to submit to European culture,—to be engrafted on a foreign stock. His outward form, his complexion, his lineaments, are substantially the same; but the moral characteristics of the nation, all that constituted its individuality as a race, are effaced for ever.

Two of the principal authorities for this chapter are Torquemada and Clavigero. The former, a Provincial of the Franciscan order, came to the New World about the middle of the sixteenth century. As the generation of the Conquerors had not then passed away, he had ample opportunities of gathering the particulars of their enterprise from their own lips. Fifty years, during which he continued in the country, put him in possession of the traditions and usages of the natives, and enabled him to collect their history from the earliest missionaries, as well as from such monuments as the fanaticism of his own countrymen had not then destroyed. From these ample sources he compiled his bulky tomes, beginning, after the approved fashion of the ancient Castilian chroniclers, with the creation of the world, and embracing the whole circle of the Mexican institutions, political, religious, and social, from the earliest period to his own time. In handling these fruitful themes, the worthy father has shown a full measure of the bigotry which belonged to his order at that period. Every page, too, is loaded with illustrations from Scripture or profane history, which form a whimsical contrast to the barbaric staple of his story; and he has sometimes fallen into serious errors, from his misconception of the chronological system of the Aztecs. But, notwithstanding these glaring defects in the composition of the work, the student, aware of his author's infirmities, will find few better guides than Torquemada in tracing the stream of historic truth up to the fountain-head; such is his manifest integrity, and so great were his facilities for information on the most curious points of Mexican antiquity. No work, accordingly, has been more largely consulted and copied, even by some who, like Herrera, have affected to set little value on the sources whence its information was drawn. (Hist. general, dec. 6, lib. 6, cap. 19.) The *Monarchía Indiana* was first published at Seville, 1615 (Nic. Antonio, Bibliotheca Nova (Matriti, 1783), tom. ii. p. 787), and since, in a better style, in three volumes folio, at Madrid, in 1723.

The other authority, frequently cited in the preceding pages, is the Abbé Clavigero's *Storia antica del Messico*. It was originally printed towards the close of the last century, in the Italian language, and in Italy, whither the author, a native of Vera Cruz, and a member of the order of the Jesuits, had retired, on the expulsion of that body from Spanish America, in 1767. During a residence of thirty-five years in his own country, Clavigero had made himself intimately acquainted with its antiquities, by the careful examination of paintings, manuscripts, and such other remains as were to be found in his day. The plan of his work is nearly as comprehensive as that of his predecessor, Torquemada; but the later and more cultivated period in which he wrote is visible in the superior address with which he has managed his complicated subject. In the elaborate disquisitions in his concluding volume, he has done much to rectify the chronology and the various inaccuracies of preceding writers. Indeed, an avowed object of his work was to vindicate his countrymen from what he conceived to be the misrepresentations of Robertson, Raynal, and De Pau. In regard to the last two he was perfectly successful. Such an ostensible design might naturally suggest unfavourable ideas of his impartiality. But, on the whole, he seems to have conducted the discussion with good faith; and if he has been led by national zeal to overcharge the picture with brilliant colours, he will be found much more temperate, in this respect, than those who preceded him, while he has applied sound principles of criticism, of which they were incapable. In a word, the diligence of his researches has gathered into one focus the scattered lights of tradition and antiquarian lore, purified in a great measure from the mists of superstition which obscure the best productions of an earlier period. Fom these causes, the work, notwithstanding its occasional prolixity, and the disagreeable aspect given to it by the profusion of uncouth names in the Mexican orthography, which bristle over every page, has found merited favour with the public, and created something like a popular interest in the subject. Soon after its publication at Cesena, in 1780, it was translated into English and more lately into Spanish and German.

CHAPTER III.

MEXICAN MYTHOLOGY.—THE SACERDOTAL ORDER.—THE TEMPLES.— HUMAN SACRIFICES.

THE civil polity of the Aztecs is so closely blended with their religion that without understanding the latter it is impossible to form correct ideas of their government or their social institutions. I shall pass over, for the present, some remarkable traditions, bearing a singular resemblance to those found in the Scriptures, and endeavour to give a brief sketch of their mythology and their careful provisions for maintaining a national worship.

Mythology may be regarded as the poetry of religion, or rather as the poetic development of the religious principle in a primitive age. It is the effort of untutored man to explain the mysteries of existence, and the secret agencies by which the operations of nature are conducted. Although the growth of similar conditions of society, its character must vary with that of the rude tribes in which it originates ; and the ferocious Goth, quaffing mead from the skulls of his slaughtered enemies, must have a very different mythology from that of the effeminate native of Hispaniola, loitering away his hours in idle pastimes, under the shadow of his bananas.

At a later and more refined period, we sometimes find these primitive legends combined into a regular system under the hands of the poet, and the rude outline moulded into forms of ideal beauty, which are the objects of adoration in a credulous age, and the delight of all succeeding ones. Such were the beautiful inventions of Hesiod and Homer, "who," says the Father of History, "created the theogony of the Greeks ;" an assertion not to be taken too literally, since it is hardly possible that any man should create a religious system for his nation.[1] They only filled up the shadowy outlines of tradition with the bright touches of their own imaginations, until they had clothed them in beauty which kindled the imaginations of others. The power of the poet, indeed, may be felt in a similar way in a much riper period of society. To say nothing of the "Divina Commedia," who is there that rises from the perusal of "Paradise Lost"

---

[1] ποιήσαντες θεογονίην Ἕλλησι. Herodotus, Euterpe, sec. 53.—Heeren hazards a remark equally strong, respecting the epic poets of India, "who," says he, "have supplied the numerous gods that fill her Pantheon." Historical Researches, Eng. trans (Oxford, 1833), vol. iii. p. 139.

without feeling his own conceptions of the angelic hierarchy quickened by those of the inspired artist, and a new and sensible form, as it were, given to images which had before floated dim and undefined before him?

The last-mentioned period is succeeded by that of philosophy; which, disclaiming alike the legends of the primitive age and the poetical embellishments of the succeeding one, seeks to shelter itself from the charge of impiety by giving an allegorical interpretation to the popular mythology, and thus to reconcile the latter with the genuine deductions of science.

The Mexican religion had emerged from the first of the periods we have been considering, and, although little affected by poetical influences, had received a peculiar complexion from the priests, who had digested as thorough and burdensome a ceremonial as ever existed in any nation. They had, moreover, thrown the veil of allegory over early tradition, and invested their deities with attributes savouring much more of the grotesque conceptions of the Eastern nations in the Old World, than of the lighter fictions of Greek mythology, in which the features of humanity, however exaggerated, were never wholly abandoned.[1]

In contemplating the religious system of the Aztecs, one is struck with its apparent incongruity, as if some portion of it had emanated from a comparatively refined people, open to gentle influences, while the rest breathes a spirit of unmitigated ferocity. It naturally suggests the idea of two distinct sources, and authorizes the belief that the Aztecs had inherited from their predecessors a milder faith, on which was afterwards engrafted their own mythology. The latter soon became dominant, and gave its dark colouring to the creeds of the conquered nations,—which the Mexicans, like the ancient Romans, seem willingly to have incorporated into their own,—until the same funereal superstition settled over the farthest borders of Anahuac.

The Aztecs recognized the existence of a supreme Creator and Lord of the universe. They addressed him, in their prayers, as "the God by whom we live," "omnipresent, that knoweth all thoughts, and giveth all gifts," "without whom man is as nothing," "invisible, incorporeal, one God, of *perfect perfection* and purity," "under whose wings we find repose and a sure defence." These sublime attributes infer no inadequate conception of the true God. But the idea of unity—of a being with whom volition is action, who has no need of inferior ministers to execute his purposes— was too simple, or too vast, for their understandings; and they sought relief, as usual, in a plurality of deities, who presided over the elements, the changes of the seasons, and the various occupations of man.[2] Of these, there were thirteen principal deities, and more than two hundred

---

[1] The Hon. Mountstuart Elphinstone has fallen into a similar train of thought, in a comparison of the Hindoo and Greek Mythology, in his "History of India," published since the remarks in the text were written. (See Book I. ch. 4.) The same chapter of this truly philosophic work suggests some curious points of resemblance to the Aztec religious institutions, that may furnish pertinent illustrations to the mind bent on tracing the affinities of the Asiatic and American races.

[2] Ritter has well shown, by the example of the Hindoo system, how the idea of unity suggests, of itself, that of plurality. History of Ancient Philosophy, Eng. trans. (Oxford, 1838), book 2, ch. 1.

inferior; to each of whom some special day or appropriate festival was consecrated.[1]

At the head of all stood the terrible Huitzilopochtli, the Mexican Mars; although it is doing injustice to the heroic war-god of antiquity to identify him with this sanguinary monster. This was the patron deity of the nation. His fantastic image was loaded with costly ornaments. His temples were the most stately and august of the public edifices; and his altars reeked with the blood of human hecatombs in every city of the empire. Disastrous indeed must have been the influence of such a superstition on the character of the people.[2]

A far more interesting personage in their mythology was Quetzalcoatl, god of the air, a divinity who, during his residence on earth, instructed the natives in the use of metals, in agriculture, and in the arts of government. He was one of those benefactors of their species, doubtless, who have been deified by the gratitude of posterity. Under him, the earth teemed with fruits and flowers, without the pains of culture. An ear of Indian corn was as much as a single man could carry. The cotton, as it grew, took, of its own accord, the rich dyes of human art. The air was filled with

---

[1] Sahagun, Hist. de Nueva-España, lib. 6, passim. —Acosta, lib. 5, ch. 9.—Boturini, Idea, p. 8, et seq. —Ixtlilxochitl, Hist. Chich., MS., cap. 1.—Camargo, Hist. de Tlascala, MS.—The Mexicans, according to Clavigero, believed in an evil Spirit, the enemy of the human race, whose barbarous name signified "Rational Owl." (Stor. del Messico, tom. ii. p. 2.) The curate Bernaldez speaks of the Devil being embroidered on the dresses of Columbus's Indians, in the likeness of an owl. (Historia de los Reyes Católicos, MS., cap. 131.) This must not be confounded, however, with the evil Spirit in the mythology of the North American Indians (see Heckewelder's Account, ap. Transactions of the American Philosophical Society, Philadelphia, vol. i. p. 205), still less with the evil Principle of the Oriental nations of the Old World. It was only one among many deities, for evil was found too liberally mingled in the natures of most of the Aztec gods—in the same manner as with the Greeks—to admit of its personification by any one.

[2] Sahagun, Hist. de Nueva-España, lib. 3, cap. 1, et seq.—Acosta, lib. 5, ch. 9.—Torquemada, Monarch. Ind., lib. 6, cap. 21.—Boturini, Idea, pp. 27, 28.—Huitzilopochtli is compounded of two words, signifying "humming-bird," and "left," from his image having the feathers of this bird on its left foot (Clavigero, Stor. del Messico, tom. ii. p. 17); an amiable etymology for so ruffian a deity.*— The fantastic forms of the Mexican idols were in the highest degree symbolical. See Gama's learned exposition of the devices on the statue of the goddess found in the great square of Mexico. (Descripcion de las Dos Piedras (México, 1832), Parte 1, pp. 34-44.) The tradition respecting the origin of this god, or, at least, his appearance on earth, is curious. He was born of a woman. His mother, a devout person, one day, in her attendance on the temple, saw a ball of bright-coloured feathers floating in the air. She took it, and deposited it in her bosom. She soon after found herself pregnant, and the dread deity was born, coming into the world, like Minerva, all armed,—with a spear in the right hand, a shield in the left, and his head surmounted by a crest of green plumes. (See Clavigero, Stor. del Messico, tom. ii. p. 10, et seq.) A similar notion in respect to the incarnation of their principal deity existed among the people of India beyond the Ganges, of China, and of Thibet. "Budh," says Milman, in his learned and luminous work on the History of Christianity, "according to a tradition known in the West, was born of a virgin. So were the Fohi of China, and the Schakaof of Thibet, no doubt the same, whether a mythic or a real personage. The Jesuits in China, says Barrow, were appalled at finding in the mythology of that country the counterpart of the Virgo Deipara." (Vol. i. p. 99, note.) The existence of similar religious ideas in remote regions, inhabited by different races, is an interesting subject of study; furnishing, as it does, one of the most important links in the great chain of communication which binds together the distant families of nations.

* [The name may possibly have referred to the whispered oracles and intimations in dreams—such as "a little bird of the air" is still fabled to convey—by which, according to the legend, the deity had guided his people in their migrations and conquests. That it had a symbolical meaning will hardly be doubted, and M. Brasseur de Bourbourg, who had originally explained it as "Huitzil the Left-handed,"—the proper name of a deified hero with the addition of a descriptive epithet,—has since found one of too deep an import to be briefly expounded or easily understood. (Quatre Lettres sur le Mexique (Paris, 1868), p. 201, et al.) *Mexitl,* another name of the same deity, is translated "the hare of the aloes." In some accounts the two are distinct personages. Mythological science rejects the legend, and regards the Aztec war-god as a "nature-deity," a personification of the lightning, this being a natural type of warlike might, of which the common symbol, the serpent, was represented among the decorations of the idol. (Myths of the New World, p. 118.) More commonly he has been identified with the sun, and Mr. Tylor, while declining "to attempt a general solution of this inextricable compound parthenogenetic deity," notices the association of his principal festival with the winter's solstice, and the fact that his paste idol was then shot through with an arrow, as tending to show that the life and death of the deity were emblematic of the year's, "while his functions of war-god may have been of later addition." Primitive Culture, tom. ii. p. 279.—Ed.]

intoxicating perfumes and the sweet melody of birds. In short, these were the halcyon days, which find a place in the mythic systems of so many nations in the Old World. It was the *golden age* of Anahuac.

From some cause, not explained, Quetzalcoatl incurred the wrath of one of the principal gods, and was compelled to abandon the country. On his way he stopped at the city of Cholula, where a temple was dedicated to his worship, the massy ruins of which still form one of the most interesting relics of antiquity in Mexico. When he reached the shores of the Mexican Gulf, he took leave of his followers, promising that he and his descendants would revisit them hereafter, and then, entering his wizard skiff, made of serpents' skins, embarked on the great ocean for the fabled land of Tlapallan. He was said to have been tall in stature, with a white skin, long, dark hair, and a flowing beard. The Mexicans looked confidently to the return of the benevolent deity ; and this remarkable tradition, deeply cherished in their hearts, prepared the way, as we shall see hereafter, for the future success of the Spaniards.[1]

---

[1] Codex Vaticanus, Pl. 15, and Codex Telleriano-Remensis, Part. 2, Pl. 2, ap. Antiq. of Mexico, vols. i., vi.—Sahagun, Hist. de Nueva-España, lib. 3, cap. 3, 4, 13, 14.—Torquemada, Monarch. Ind., lib. 6, cap. 24.—Ixtlilxochitl, Hist. Chich., MS., cap. 1.—Gomara, Crónica de la Nueva-España, cap. 222, ap. Barcia, Historiadores primitivos de las Indias Occidentales (Madrid, 1749), tom. ii.—Quetzalcoatl signifies "feathered serpent." The last syllable means, likewise, a "twin ;" which furnished an argument for Dr. Siguenza, to identify this god with the apostle Thomas (Didymus signifying also a twin), who, he supposes, came over to America to preach the gospel. In this rather startling conjecture he is supported by several of his devout countrymen, who appear to have as little doubt of the fact as of the advent of St. James, for a similar purpose, in the mother-country. See the various authorities and arguments set forth with becoming gravity in Dr. Mier's dissertation in Bustamante's edition of Sahagun (lib. 3, Suplem.), and Veytia (tom. i. pp. 160–200). Our ingenious countryman McCulloh carries the Aztec god up to a still more respectable antiquity, by identifying him with the patriarch Noah. Researches, Philosophical and Antiquarian, concerning the Aboriginal History of America (Baltimore, 1829), p. 233.*

* [Under the modern system of mythical interpretation, which has been applied by Dr. Brinton with singular force and ingenuity to the traditions of the New World, Quetzalcoatl, "the central figure of Toltec mythology," with the corresponding figures found in the legends of the Mayas, Quichés, Peruvians, and other races, loses all personal existence, and becomes a creation of that primitive religious sentiment which clothed the uncomprehended powers of nature with the attributes of divinity. His name, "Bird-Serpent," unites the emblems of the wind and the lightning. " He is both lord of the eastern light and the winds. As the former, he was born of a virgin in the land of Tula or Tlapallan, in the distant Orient, and was high-priest of that happy realm. The morning star was his symbol. . . . Like all the dawn heroes, he too was represented as of white complexion, clothed in long white robes, and, as most of the Aztec gods, with a full and flowing beard. When his earthly work was done, he too returned to the east, assigning as a reason that the sun, the ruler of Tlapallan, demanded his presence. But the real motive was that he had been overcome by Tezcatlipoca, otherwise called Yoalliehecatl, the wind or spirit of the night, who had descended from heaven by a spider's web and presented his rival with a draught pretended to confer immortality, but, in fact, producing uncontrollable longing for home. For the wind and the light both depart when the gloaming draws near, or when the clouds spread their dark and shadowy webs along the mountains and pour the vivifying rain upon the fields. . . . Wherever he went, all manner of singing-birds bore him company, emblems of the whistling breezes. When he finally disappeared in the far east, he sent back four trusty youths, who had ever shared his fortunes, incomparably swift and light of foot, with directions to divide the earth between them and rule it till he should return and resume his power." (The Myths of the New World, p. 180, et seq.) So far as mere physical attributes are concerned, this analysis may be accepted as a satisfactory elucidation of the class of figures to which it relates. But the grand and distinguishing characteristic of these figures is the moral and intellectual eminence ascribed to them. They are invested with the highest qualities of humanity,—attributes neither drawn from the external phenomena of nature nor born of any rude sentiment of wonder and fear. Their lives and doctrines are in strong contrast with those of the ordinary divinities of the same or other lands, and they are objects not of a propitiatory worship, but of a pious veneration. Can we, then, assent to the conclusion that under this aspect also they were "wholly mythical," "creations of the religious fancy," "ideals summing up in themselves the best traits, the most approved virtues, of whole nations"? (Ibid., pp. 293, 294.) This would seem to imply that nations may attain to lofty conceptions of moral truth and excellence by a process of selection, without any standard or point of view furnished by living embodiments of the ideal. But this would be as impossible as to arrive at conceptions of the highest forms and ideas of art independently of the special genius and actual productions of the artist. In the one case, as in the other, the ideal is derived originally from examples shaped by finer and deeper intuitions than those of the masses. "Im Anfang war die That." The mere fact, therefore, that the Mexican people recognized an exalted ideal of purity and wisdom is a sufficient proof that men had existed among them who displayed these qualities in an eminent degree. The status of their civilization, imperfect as it was, can be accounted for only in the same way. Compara-

We have not space for further details respecting the Mexican divinities, the attributes of many of whom were carefully defined, as they descended, in regular gradation, to the *penates* or household gods, whose little images were to be found in the humblest dwelling.

The Aztecs felt the curiosity, common to man in almost every stage of civilization, to lift the veil which covers the mysterious past and the more awful future. They sought relief, like the nations of the Old Continent, from the oppressive idea of eternity, by breaking it up into distinct cycles, or periods of time, each of several thousand years' duration. There were four of these cycles, and at the end of each, by the agency of one of the elements, the human family was swept from the earth, and the sun blotted out from the heavens, to be again rekindled.[1]

They imagined three separate states of existence in the future life. The wicked, comprehending the greater part of mankind, were to expiate their sins in a place of everlasting darkness. Another class, with no other merit than that of having died of certain diseases capriciously selected, were to enjoy a negative existence of indolent contentment. The highest place was reserved, as in most warlike nations, for the heroes who fell in battle, or in sacrifice. They passed at once into the presence of the Sun, whom they accompanied with songs and choral dances in his bright progress through the heavens ; and, after some years, their spirits went to animate the clouds and singing-birds of beautiful plumage, and to revel amidst the rich blossoms and odours of the gardens of paradise.[2] Such was the heaven of the Aztecs; more refined in its character than that of the more polished pagan, whose elysium reflected only the martial sports or sensual gratifications of this life.[3] In the destiny they assigned to the wicked, we discern similar traces of refinement ; since the absence of all physical torture forms a striking

---

[1] Cod. Vat., Pl. 7-10, Antiq. of Mexico, vols. i., vi.—Ixtlilxochitl, Hist. Chich., MS., cap. 1.—M. de Humboldt has been at some pains to trace the analogy between the Aztec cosmogony and that of Eastern Asia. He has tried, though in vain, to find a multiple which might serve as the key to the calculations of the former. (Vues des Cordillères, pp. 202-212.) In truth, there seems to be a material discordance in the Mexican statements, both in regard to the number of revolutions and their duration. A manuscript before me, of Ixtlilxochitl, reduces them to three, before the present state of the world, and allows only 4394 years for them (Sumaria Relacion, MS., No. 1); Gama, on the faith of an ancient Indian MS. in Boturini's Catalogue (viii. 13), reduces the duration still lower (Descripcion de las Dos Piedras, Parte 1, p. 49, et seq.); while the cycles of the Vatican paintings take up near 18,000 years.—It is interesting to observe how the wild *conjectures* of an ignorant age have been confirmed by the more recent *discoveries* in geology, making it probable that the earth has experienced a number of convulsions, possibly thousands of years distant from each other, which have swept away the races then existing, and given a new aspect to the globe.

[2] Sahagun, Hist. de Nueva-España, lib. 3, Apend.—Cod. Vat., ap. Antiq. of Mexico, Pl. 1-5.—Torquemada, Monarch. Ind., lib. 13, cap. 48.—The last writer assures us "that, as to what the Aztecs said of their going to hell, they were right ; for, as they died in ignorance of the true faith, they have, without question, all gone there to suffer everlasting punishment"! Ubi supra.

[3] It conveys but a poor idea of these pleasures, that the shade of Achilles can say "he had rather be the slave of the meanest man on earth, than sovereign among the dead." (Odyss., A. 488-490.) The Mahometans believe that the souls of martyrs pass, after death, into the bodies of birds, that haunt the sweet waters and bowers of Paradise. (Sale's Koran (London, 1825), vol. i. p. 106.)—The Mexican heaven may remind one of Dante's, in its *material* enjoyments ; which, in both, are made up of light, music, and motion. The sun, it must also be remembered, was a spiritual conception with the Aztec :—

" He sees with other eyes than theirs ; where they
  Behold a sun, he spies a deity."

tive mythology may resolve into its original elements a personification of the forces of nature woven by the religious fancy of primitive races, but it cannot sever that chain of discoverers and civilizers by which mankind has been drawn from the abysses of savage ignorance, and by which its progress, when uninterrupted, has been always maintained.—ED.]

contrast to the schemes of suffering so ingeniously devised by the fancies of the most enlightened nations.[1] In all this, so contrary to the natural suggestions of the ferocious Aztec, we see the evidences of a higher civilization,[2] inherited from their predecessors in the land.

Our limits will allow only a brief allusion to one or two of their most interesting ceremonies. On the death of a person, his corpse was dressed in the peculiar habiliments of his tutelar deity. It was strewed with pieces of paper, which operated as charms against the dangers of the dark road he was to travel. A throng of slaves, if he were rich, was sacrificed at his obsequies. His body was burned, and the ashes, collected in a vase, were preserved in one of the apartments of his house. Here we have successively the usages of the Roman Catholic, the Mussulman, the Tartar, and the ancient Greek and Roman; curious coincidences, which may show how cautious we should be in adopting conclusions founded on analogy.[3]

A more extraordinary coincidence may be traced with Christian rites, in the ceremony of naming their children. The lips and bosom of the infant were sprinkled with water, and "the Lord was implored to permit the holy drops to wash away the sin that was given to it before the foundation of the world; so that the child might be born anew."[4] We are reminded of Christian morals, in more than one of their prayers, in which they used regular forms. "Wilt thou blot us out, O Lord, for ever? Is this punishment intended, not for our reformation, but for our destruction?" Again, "Impart to us, out of thy great mercy, thy gifts, which we are not worthy to receive through our own merits." "Keep peace with all," says another petition; "bear injuries with humility; God, who sees, will avenge you." But the most striking parallel with Scripture is in the remarkable declaration that "he who looks too curiously on a woman commits adultery with his eyes."[5] These pure and elevated maxims, it is true, are

---

[1] It is singular that the Tuscan bard, while exhausting his invention in devising modes of bodily torture, in his "Inferno," should have made so little use of the *moral* sources of misery. That he has not done so might be reckoned a strong proof of the rudeness of the time, did we not meet with examples of it in a later day; in which a serious and sublime writer, like Dr. Watts, does not disdain to employ the same coarse machinery for moving the conscience of the reader.

[2] [It should perhaps be regarded rather as evidence of a low civilization, since the absence of any strict ideas of retribution is a characteristic of the notions in regard to a future life entertained by savage races. See Tylor, Primitive Culture, vol. ii. p. 76, et seq.—ED.]

[3] Carta del Lic. Zuazo (Nov. 1521), MS.—Acosta, lib. 5. cap. 8.—Torquemada, Monarch. Ind., lib. 13, cap. 45.—Sahagun, Hist. de Nueva-España, lib. 3, Apend.—Sometimes the body was buried entire, with valuable treasures, if the deceased was rich. The "Anonymous Conqueror," as he is called, saw gold to the value of 3000 castellanos drawn from one of these tombs. Relatione d'un gentil' huomo, ap. Ramusio, tom. iii. p. 310.

[4] This interesting rite, usually solemnized with great formality, in the presence of the assembled friends and relatives, is detailed with minuteness by Sahagun (Hist. de Nueva-España, lib. 6, cap. 37), and by Zuazo (Carta, MS.), both of them eyewitnesses. For a version of part of Sahagun's account, see Appendix, Part 1, note 26.*

[5] "¿Es posible que este azote y este castigo no se nos dá para nuestra correccion y enmienda, sino para total destruccion y asolamiento?" (Sahagun, Hist. de Nueva-España, lib. 6, cap. 1.) "Y esto por sola vuestra liberalidad y magnificencia lo habeis de hacer, que ninguno es digno ni merecedor de recibir vuestra larguezas por su dignidad y merecimiento, sino que por vuestra benignidad." (Ibid., lib. 6, cap. 2.) "Sed sufridos y reportados, que Dios bien os vé y responderá por vosotros, y él os vengará (á) sed humildes con todos, y con esto os hará Dios merced y tambien honra." (Ibid., lib. 6, cap. 17.) "Tampoco mires con curiosidad el gesto y disposicion de la gente principal, mayormente de las mugeres, y sobre todo de las casadas, porque dice el refran que él que curiosamente mira á la muger adultera con la vista." (Ibid., lib. 6, cap. 22.)

* [A similar rite of baptism, founded on the natural symbolism of the purifying power of water, was practised by other races in America, and had existed in the East, as the reader need hardly be told, long anterior to Christianity.—ED.]

mixed up with others of a puerile, and even brutal chaiacter, arguing thɑt confusion of the moral perceptions which is natural in the twilight of civi- lization. One would not expect, however, to meet, in such a state of society, with doctrines as sublime as any inculcated by the enlightened codes of ancient philosophy.[1]

But, although the Aztec mythology gathered nothing from the beautiful inventions of the poet, or from the refinements of philosophy, it was much indebted, as I have noticed, to the priests, who endeavoured to dazzle the imagination of the people by the most formal and pompous ceremonial. The influence of the priesthood must be greatest in an imperfect state of civilization, where it engrosses all the scanty science of the time in its own body. This is particularly the case when the science is of that spurious kind which is less occupied with the real phenomena of nature than with the fanciful chimeras of human superstition. Such are the sciences of astrology and divination, in which the Aztec priests were well initiated ; and, while they seemed to hold the keys of the future in their own hands, they impressed the ignorant people with sentiments of superstitious awe, beyond that which has probably existed in any other country,—even in ancient Egypt.

The sacerdotal order was very numerous ; as may be inferred from the statement that five thousand priests were, in some way or other, attached to the principal temple in the capital. The various ranks and functions of this multitudinous body were discriminated with great exactness. Those best instructed in music took the management of the choirs. Others arranged the festivals conformably to the calendar. Some superintended the education of youth, and others had charge of the hieroglyphical paint- ings and oral traditions ; while the dismal rites of sacrifice were reserved for the chief dignitaries of the order. At the head of the whole establish- ment were two high-priests, elected from the order, as it would seem, by the king and principal nobles, without reference to birth, but solely for their qualifications, as shown by their previous conduct in a subordinate station. They were equal in dignity, and inferior only to the sovereign, who rarely acted without their advice in weighty matters of public concern.[2]

---

[1] [On reviewing the remarkable coincidences shown in the above pages with the sentiments and even the phraseology of Scripture, we cannot but admit there is plausible ground for Mr. Gallatin's conjecture that the Mexicans, after the Conquest, attributed to their remote ancestors ideas which more properly belonged to a generation coeval with the Conquest, and brought into contact with the Europeans. "The substance," he remaɪks, "may be true ; but several of the prayers convey elevated and correct notions of a Supreme Being, which appear to me altogether inconsistent with that which we know to have been their practical religion and worship." * Transactions of the American Ethnological Society, i. 210.]

[2] Sahagun, Hist. de Nueva-España, lib. 2, Apend. ; lib. 3, cap. 9.—Torquemada, Monarch. Ind., lib. 8, cap. 20 ; lib. 9, cap. 3, 56.—Gomara, Crón. cap. 215, ap. Barcia, tom. ii.—Toribio, Hist. de los Indios, MS., Parte 1, cap. 4.—Clavigero says.

* [It is evident that an inconsistency such as belongs to all religions, and to human nature in general, affords no sufficient ground for doubting the authenticity of the prayers reported by Sahagun. Similar specimens of prayers used by the Peruvians have been preserved, and, like those of the Aztecs, exhibit, in their recognition of spiritual as distinct from material blessings, a contrast to the forms of petition employed by the wholly uncivilized races of the north. They are in harmony with the purer conceptions of morality which those nations are admitted to have possessed, and which formed the real basis of their civiliza- tion.—Eᴅ.]

The priests were each devoted to the service of some particular deity; and had quarters provided within the spacious precincts of their temple, at least, while engaged in immediate attendance there,—for they were allowed to marry, and have families of their own. In this monastic residence they lived in all the stern severity of conventual discipline. Thrice during the day, and once at night, they were called to prayers. They were frequent in their ablutions and vigils, and mortified the flesh by fasting and cruel penance,—drawing blood from their bodies by flagellation, or by piercing them with tne thorns of the aloe ; in short, by practising all those austerities to which fanaticism (to borrow the strong language of the poet) has resorted, in every age of the world,

" In hopes to merit heaven by making earth a hell."[1]

The great cities were divided into districts placed under the charge of a sort of parochial clergy, who regulated every act of religion within their precincts. It is remarkable that they administered the rites of confession and absolution. The secrets of the confessional were held inviolable, and penances were imposed of much the same kind as those enjoined in the Roman Catholic Church. There were two remarkable peculiarities in the Aztec ceremony. The first was, that, as the repetition of an offence once atoned for was deemed inexpiable, confession was made but once in a man's life, and was usually deferred to a late period of it, when the penitent unburdened his conscience and settled at once the long arrears of iniquity. Another peculiarity was, that priestly absolution was received in place of the legal punishment of offences, and authorized an acquittal in case of arrest. Long after the Conquest, the simple natives, when they came under the arm of the law, sought to escape by producing the certificate of their confession.[2]

One of the most important duties of the priesthood was that of education, to which certain buildings were appropriated within the enclosure of the principal temple. Here the youth of both sexes, of the higher and middling orders, were placed at a very tender age. The girls were intrusted to the care of priestesses ; for women were allowed to exercise

that the high-priest was necessarily a person of rank. (Stor. del Messico, tom. ii. p. 37.) I find no authority for this, not even in his oracle, Torquemada, who expressly says, " There is no warrant for the assertion, however probable the fact may be." (Mon. Ind., lib. 9, cap. 5.) It is contradicted by Sahagun, whom I have followed as the highest authority in these matters. Clavigero had no other knowledge of Sahagun's work than what was filtered through the writings of Torquemada and later authors.

[1] Sahagun, Hist. de Nueva-España, ubi supra.—Torquemada, Monarch. Ind., lib. 9, cap. 25.—Gomara, Crón., ap. Barcia, ubi supra.—Acosta, lib. 5, cap. 14, 17.

[2] Sahagun, Hist. de Nueva-España, lib. 1, cap. 12; lib. 6, cap. 7.—The address of the confessor, on these occasions, contains some things too remarkable to be omitted. " O merciful Lord," he says, in his prayer, " thou who knowest the secrets of all hearts, let thy forgiveness and favour descend, like the pure waters of heaven, to wash away the stains from the soul. Thou knowest that this poor man *has sinned not from his own free-will*, but from the influence of the sign under which he was born." After a copious exhortation to the penitent, enjoining a variety of mortifications and minute ceremonies by way of penance, and particularly urging the necessity of instantly procuring *a slave for sacrifice* to the Deity, the priest concludes with inculcating charity to the poor. " Clothe the naked and feed the hungry, whatever privations it may cost thee ; for remember, *their flesh is like thine, and they are men like thee.*" Such is the strange medley of truly Christian benevolence and heathenish abominations which pervades the Aztec litany,—intimating sources widely different.

C

sacerdotal functions, except those of sacrifice.[1]   In these institutions the boys were drilled in the routine of monastic discipline; they decorated the shrines of the gods with flowers, fed the sacred fires, and took part in the religious chants and festivals.   Those in the higher school—the *Calmecac*, as it was called—were initiated in their traditionary lore, the mysteries of hieroglyphics, the principles of government, and such branches of astronomical and natural science as were within the compass of the priesthood.   The girls learned various feminine employments, especially to weave and embroider rich coverings for the altars of the gods. Great attention was paid to the moral discipline of both sexes.   The most perfect decorum prevailed;   and offences were punished with extreme rigour, in some instances with death itself.   Terror, not love, was the spring of education with the Aztecs.[2]

At a suitable age for marrying, or for entering into the world, the pupils were dismissed, with much ceremony, from the convent, and the recommendation of the principal often introduced those most competent to responsible situations in public life.   Such was the crafty policy of the Mexican priests, who, by reserving to themselves the business of instruction, were enabled to mould the young and plastic mind according to their own wills, and to train it early to implicit reverence for religion and its ministers; a reverence which still maintained its hold on the iron nature of the warrior, long after every other vestige of education had been effaced by the rough trade to which he was devoted.

To each of the principal temples, lands were annexed for the maintenance of the priests.   These estates were augmented by the policy or devotion of successive princes, until, under the last Montezuma, they had swollen to an enormous extent, and covered every district of the empire. The priests took the management of their property into their own hands; and they seem to have treated their tenants with the liberality and indulgence characteristic of monastic corporations.   Besides the large supplies drawn from this source, the religious order was enriched with the first-fruits, and such other offerings as piety or superstition dictated.   The surplus beyond what was required for the support of the national worship was distributed in alms among the poor; a duty strenuously prescribed by their moral code.   Thus we find the same religion inculcating lessons of pure philanthropy, on the one hand, and of merciless extermination, as we shall soon

---

[1] The Egyptian gods were also served by priestesses. (See Herodotus, Euterpe, sec. 54.) Tales of scandal similar to those which the Greeks circulated respecting them, have been told of the Aztec virgins. (See Le Noir's dissertation, ap. Antiquités Mexicaines (Paris, 1834), tom. ii. p. 7, note.) The early missionaries, credulous enough, certainly, give no countenance to such reports; and Father Acosta, on the contrary, exclaims, "In truth, it is very strange to see that this false opinion of religion hath so great force among these yoong men and maidens of Mexico, that they will serve the Divell with so great rigor and austerity, which many of us doe not in the service of the most high

God; the which is a great shame and confusion." Eng. trans., lib. 5, cap. 16.

[2] Toribio, Hist. de los Indios, MS., Parte 1, cap. 9.—Sahagun, Hist. de Nueva-España, lib. 2, Apend.; lib. 3, cap. 4–8.—Zurita, Rapport, pp. 123–126.—Acosta, lib. 5, cap. 15, 16.—Torquemada, Monarch. Ind., lib. 9, cap. 11–14. 30, 31.—"They were taught," says the good father last cited, "to eschew vice, and cleave to virtue,—*according to their notions of them*; namely, to abstain from wrath, to offer violence and do wrong to no man,—in short, to perform the duties plainly pointed out by natural religion."

see, on the other. The inconsistency will not appear incredible to those who are familiar with the history of the Roman Catholic Church, in the early ages of the Inquisition.[1]

The Mexican temples—*teocallis*, " houses of God," as they were called[2] —were very numerous. There were several hundreds in each of the principal cities, many of them, doubtless, very humble edifices. They were solid masses of earth, cased with brick or stone, and in their form somewhat resembled the pyramidal structures of ancient Egypt. The bases of many of them were more than a hundred feet square, and they towered to a still greater height. They were distributed into four or five stories, each of smaller dimensions than that below. The ascent was by a flight of steps, at an angle of the pyramid, on the outside. This led to a sort of terrace or gallery, at the base of the second story, which passed quite round the building to another flight of stairs, commencing also at the same angle as the preceding and directly over it, and leading to a similar terrace ; so that one had to make the circuit of the temple several times before reaching the summit. In some instances the stairway led directly up the centre of the western face of the building. The top was a broad area, on which were erected one or two towers, forty or fifty feet high, the sanctuaries in which stood the sacred images of the presiding deities. Before these towers stood the dreadful stone of sacrifice, and two lofty altars, on which fires were kept, as inextinguishable as those in the temple of Vesta. There were said to be six hundred of these altars, on smaller buildings within the enclosure of the great temple of Mexico, which, with those on the sacred edifices in other parts of the city, shed a brilliant illumination over its streets, through the darkest night.[3]

From the construction of their temples, all religious services were public. The long processions of priests winding round their massive sides, as they rose higher and higher towards the summit, and the dismal rites of sacrifice performed there, were all visible from the remotest corners of the capital, impressing on the spectator's mind a superstitious veneration for the mysteries of his religion, and for the dread ministers by whom they were interpreted.

This impression was kept in full force by their numerous festivals,

1 Torquemada, Monarch. Ind., lib. 8, cap. 20, 21. —Camargo, Hist. de Tlascala, MS.—It is impossible not to be struck with the great resemblance, not merely in a few empty forms, but in the whole way of life, of the Mexican and Egyptian priesthood. Compare Herodotus (Euterpe, passim) and Diodorus (lib. 1, sec. 73, 81). The English reader may consult, for the same purpose, Heeren (Hist. Res., vol. v. chap. 2), Wilkinson (Manners and Customs of the Ancient Egyptians (London, 1837), vol. i. pp. 257-279), the last writer especially,—who has contributed, more than all others, towards opening to us the interior of the social life of this interesting people.

2 [Humboldt has noticed the curious similarity of the word *teocalli* with the Greek compound—actual or possible—θεοκαλία ; and Buschmann observes, " Die Uebereinstimmung des mex. teotl und θεός,

arithmetisch sehr hoch anzuschlagen wegen des Doppelvocals, zeigt wie weit es der Zufall in Wortähnlichkeiten zwischen ganz verschiedenen Sprachen bringen kann." Ueber die aztekischen Ortsnamen, S. 627.—ED.]

3 Rel. d'un gentil' huomo, ap. Ramusio, tom. iii. fol. 307.—Camargo, Hist. de Tlascala, MS.—Acosta, lib. 5, cap. 13.—Gomara, Crón., cap. 80, ap. Barcia, tom. ii.—Toribio, Hist. de los Indios, MS., Parte 1, cap. 4.—Carta del Lic. Zuazo, MS.—This last writer, who visited Mexico immediately after the Conquest, in 1521, assures us that some of the smaller temples, or pyramids, were filled with earth impregnated with odoriferous gums and gold dust ; the latter sometimes in such quantities as probably to be worth a million of *castellanos* ! (Ubi supra.) These were the temples of Mammon, indeed ! But I find no confirmation of such golden reports.

Every month was consecrated to some protecting deity; and every week, nay, almost every day, was set down in their calendar for some appropriate celebration; so that it is difficult to understand how the ordinary business of life could have been compatible with the exactions of religion. Many of their ceremonies were of a light and cheerful complexion, consisting of the national songs and dances, in which both sexes joined. Processions were made of women and children crowned with garlands and bearing offerings of fruits, the ripened maize, or the sweet incense of copal and other odoriferous gums, while the altars of the deity were stained with no blood save that of animals.[1] These were the peaceful rites derived from their Toltec predecessors, on which the fierce Aztecs engrafted a superstition too loathsome to be exhibited in all its nakedness, and one over which I would gladly draw a veil altogether, but that it would leave the reader in ignorance of their most striking institution, and one that had the greatest influence in forming the national character.

Human sacrifices were adopted by the Aztecs early in the fourteenth century, about two hundred years before the Conquest.[2] Rare at first, they became more frequent with the wider extent of their empire; till, at length, almost every festival was closed with this cruel abomination. These religious ceremonials were generally arranged in such a manner as to afford a type of the most prominent circumstances in the character or history of the deity who was the object of them. A single example will suffice.

One of their most important festivals was that in honour of the god Tezcatlipoca, whose rank was inferior only to that of the Supreme Being. He was called "the soul of the world," and supposed to have been its creator. He was depicted as a handsome man, endowed with perpetual youth. A year before the intended sacrifice, a captive, distinguished for his personal beauty, and without a blemish on his body, was selected to represent this deity. Certain tutors took charge of him, and instructed him how to perform his new part with becoming grace and dignity. He was arrayed in a splendid dress, regaled with incense and with a profusion of sweet-scented flowers, of which the ancient Mexicans were as fond as their descendants at the present day. When he went abroad, he was attended by a train of the royal pages, and as he halted in the streets to play some favourite melody, the crowd prostrated themselves before him, and did him homage as the representative of their good deity. In this way he led an easy, luxurious life, till within a month of his sacrifice. Four beautiful girls, bearing the names of the principal goddesses, were then selected to share the honours of his bed; and with them he continued

---

1 Cod. Tel.-Rem., Pl. 1, and Cod. Vat., passim, ap. Antiq. of Mexico, vols. i., vi.—Torquemada, Monarch. Ind., lib. 10, cap. 10, et seq.—Sahagun, Hist. de Nueva-España, lib. 2, passim.—Among the offerings, quails may be particularly noticed, for the incredible quantities of them sacrificed and consumed at many of the festivals.

2 The traditions of their origin have somewhat of a fabulous tinge. But, whether true or false, they are equally indicative of unparalleled ferocity in the people who could be the subject of them. Clavigero, Stor. del Messico, tom. i. p. 167, et seq.; also Humboldt (who does not appear to doubt them), Vues des Cordillères, p. 95.

to live in idle dalliance, feasted at the banquets of the principal nobles, who paid him all the honours of a divinity.

At length the fatal day of sacrifice arrived. The term of his shortlived glories was at an end. He was stripped of his gaudy apparel, and bade adieu to the fair partners of his revelries. One of the royal barges transported him across the lake to a temple which rose on its margin, about a league from the city. Hither the inhabitants of the capital flocked, to witness the consummation of the ceremony. As the sad procession wound up the sides of the pyramid, the unhappy victim threw away his gay chaplets of flowers, and broke in pieces the musical instruments with which he had solaced the hours of captivity. On the summit he was received by six priests, whose long and matted locks flowed disorderly over their sable robes, covered with hieroglyphic scrolls of mystic import. They led him to the sacrificial stone, a huge block of jasper, with its upper surface somewhat convex. On this the prisoner was stretched. Five priests secured his head and his limbs; while the sixth, clad in a scarlet mantle, emblematic of his bloody office, dexterously opened the breast of the wretched victim with a sharp razor of *itztli*,—a volcanic substance, hard as flint,—and, inserting his hand in the wound, tore out the palpitating heart. The minister of death, first holding this up towards the sun, an object of worship throughout Anahuac, cast it at the feet of the deity to whom the temple was devoted, while the multitudes below prostrated themselves in humble adoration. The tragic story of this prisoner was expounded by the priests as the type of human destiny, which, brilliant in its commencement, too often closes in sorrow and disaster.[1]

Such was the form of human sacrifice usually practised by the Aztecs. It was the same that often met the indignant eyes of the Europeans in their progress through the country, and from the dreadful doom of which they themselves were not exempted. There were, indeed, some occasions when preliminary tortures, of the most exquisite kind,—with which it is unnecessary to shock the reader,—were inflicted, but they always terminated with the bloody ceremony above described. It should be remarked, however, that such tortures were not the spontaneous suggestions of cruelty, as with the North American Indians, but were all rigorously prescribed in the Aztec ritual, and doubtless were often inflicted with the same compunctious visitings which a devout familiar of the Holy Office might at times experience in executing its stern decrees.[2] Women, as well as the

---

[1] Sahagun, Hist. de Nueva-España, lib. 2, cap. 2, 5, 24, et alibi.—Herrera, Hist. general, dec. 3, lib. 2, cap. 16.—Torquemada, Monarch. Ind., lib. 7, cap. 19; lib. 10, cap. 14.—Rel. d'un gentil' huomo, ap. Ramusio, tom. iii. fol. 307.—Acosta, lib. 5, cap. 9-21.—Carta del Lic. Zuazo, MS.— Relacion por el Regimiento de Vera Cruz (Julio, 1519), MS.—Few readers, probably, will sympathize with the sentence of Torquemada, who concludes his tale of woe by coolly dismissing "the soul of the victim, to sleep with those of his false gods, in hell!" Lib. 10, cap. 23.

[2] Sahagun, Hist. de Nueva-España, lib. 2, cap. 10, 29.—Gomara, Crón., cap. 219, ap. Barcia, tom. ii.—Toribio, Hist. de los Indios, MS., Parte 1, cap. 6-11.—The reader will find a tolerably exact picture of the nature of these tortures in the twenty-first canto of the "Inferno." The fantastic creations of the Florentine poet were nearly realized, at the very time he was writing, by the barbarians of an unknown world. One sacrifice, of a less revolting character, deserves to be mentioned. The Spaniards called it the "gladiatorial sacrifice," and it may remind one of the bloody games of antiquity. A

other sex, were sometimes reserved for sacrifice. On some occasions, particularly in seasons of drought, at the festival of the insatiable Tlaloc, the god of rain, children, for the most part infants, were offered up. As they were borne along in open litters, dressed in their festal robes, and decked with the fresh blossoms of spring, they moved the hardest heart to pity, though their cries were drowned in the wild chant of the priests, who read in their tears a favourable augury for their petition. These innocent victims were generally bought by the priests of parents who were poor, but who stifled the voice of nature, probably less at the suggestions of poverty than of a wretched superstition.[1]

The most loathsome part of the story—the manner in which the body of the sacrificed captive was disposed of—remains yet to be told. It was delivered to the warrior who had taken him in battle, and by him, after being dressed, was served up in an entertainment to his friends. This was not the coarse repast of famished cannibals, but a banquet teeming with delicious beverages and delicate viands, prepared with art, and attended by both sexes, who, as we shall see hereafter, conducted themselves with all the decorum of civilized life. Surely, never were refinement and the extreme of barbarism brought so closely in contact with each other.[2]

Human sacrifices have been practised by many nations, not excepting the most polished nations of antiquity ;[3] but never by any, on a scale to be compared with those in Anahuac. The amount of victims immolated on its accursed altars would stagger the faith of the least scrupulous believer. Scarcely any author pretends to estimate the yearly sacrifices throughout the empire at less than twenty thousand, and some carry the number as high as fifty thousand ![4]

On great occasions, as the coronation of a king or the consecration of a temple, the number becomes still more appalling. At the dedication of the great temple of Huitzilopochtli, in 1486, the prisoners, who for some

---

captive of distinction was sometimes furnished with arms, and brought against a number of Mexicans in succession. If he defeated them all, as did occasionally happen, he was allowed to escape. If vanquished, he was dragged to the block and sacrificed in the usual manner. The combat was fought on a huge circular stone, before the assembled capital. Sahagun, Hist. de Nueva-España, lib. 2, cap. 21.—Rel. d'un gentil' huomo, ap. Ramusio, tom. iii. fol. 305.

[1] Sahagun, Hist. de Nueva-España, lib. 2, cap. 1, 4, 21, et alibi.—Torquemada, Monarch. Ind., lib. 10, cap. 10.—Clavigero, Stor. del Messico, tom. ii. pp. 76, 82.

[2] Carta del Lic. Zuazo, MS. — Torquemada, Monarch. Ind., lib. 7, cap. 19.—Herrera, Hist. general, dec. 3, lib. 2, cap. 17.—Sahagun, Hist. de Nueva-España, lib. 2. cap. 21, et alibi.—Toribio, Hist. de los Indios, MS., Parte 1, cap. 2.

[3] To say nothing of Egypt, where, notwithstanding the indications on the monuments, there is strong reason for doubting it. (Comp. Herodotus, Euterpe, sec. 45.) It was of frequent occurrence among the Greeks, as every schoolboy knows. In Rome, it was so common as to require to be interdicted by an express law, less than a hundred years before the Christian era,—a law recorded in a very honest strain of exultation by Pliny (Hist. Nat., lib. 30,

sec. 3, 4) ; notwithstanding which, traces of the existence of the practice may be discerned to a much later period. See, among others, Horace, Epod., In Canidiam.

[4] See Clavigero, Stor. del Messico, tom. ii. p. 49.—Bishop Zumárraga, in a letter written a few years after the Conquest, states that 20,000 victims were yearly slaughtered in the capital. Torquemada turns this into 20,000 *infants.* (Monarch. Ind., lib. 7, cap. 21.) Herrera, following Acosta, says 20,000 victims on a specified day of the year throughout the kingdom. (Hist. general, dec. 2, lib. 2, cap. 16.) Clavigero, more cautious, infers that this number may have been sacrificed annually throughout Anahuac. (Ubi supra.) Las Casas, however, in his reply to Sepulveda's assertion, that no one who had visited the New World put the number of yearly sacrifices at less than 20,000, declares that "this is the estimate of brigands, who wish to find an apology for their own atrocities, and that the real number was not above 50" ! (Œuvres, ed. Llorente (Paris, 1822), tom. i. pp. 365, 386.) Probably the good Bishop's arithmetic here, as in most other instances, came more from his heart than his head. With such loose and contradictory data, it is clear that any specific number is mere conjecture, undeserving the name of calculation.

years had been reserved for the purpose, were drawn from all quarters to the capital. They were ranged in files, forming a procession nearly two miles long. The ceremony consumed several days, and seventy thousand captives are said to have perished at the shrine of this terrible deity! But who can believe that so numerous a body would have suffered themselves to be led unresistingly like sheep to the slaughter? Or how could their remains, too great for consumption in the ordinary way, be disposed of, without breeding a pestilence in the capital? Yet the event was of recent date, and is unequivocally attested by the best-informed historians.[1] One fact may be considered certain. It was customary to preserve the skulls of the sacrificed in buildings appropriated to the purpose. The companions of Cortés counted one hundred and thirty-six thousand in one of these edifices![2] Without attempting a precise calculation, therefore, it is safe to conclude that thousands were yearly offered up, in the different cities of Anahuac, on the bloody altars of the Mexican divinities.[3]

Indeed, the great object of war, with the Aztecs, was quite as much to gather victims for their sacrifices as to extend their empire. Hence it was that an enemy was never slain in battle, if there were a chance of taking him alive. To this circumstance the Spaniards repeatedly owed their preservation. When Montezuma was asked " why he had suffered the republic of Tlascala to maintain her independence on his borders," he replied, " that she might furnish him with victims for his gods "! As the supply began to fail, the priests, the Dominicans of the New World, bellowed aloud for more, and urged on their superstitious sovereign by the denunciations of celestial wrath. Like the militant churchmen of Christendom in the Middle Ages, they mingled themselves in the ranks, and were conspicuous in the thickest of the fight, by their hideous aspect and frantic gestures. Strange, that, in every country, the most fiendish passions of the human heart have been those kindled in the name of religion![4]

---

[1] I am within bounds. Torquemada states the number, most precisely, at 72,344 (Monarch. Ind., lib. 2, cap. 63); Ixtlilxochitl, with equal precision, at 80,400. (Hist. Chich., MS.) *¿ Quien sabe?* The latter adds that the captives massacred in the capital, in the course of that memorable year, exceeded 100,000! (Loc. cit.) One, however, has to read but a little way, to find out that the science of numbers—at least where the party was not an eye-witness—is anything but an exact science with these ancient chroniclers. The Codex Telleriano-Remensis, written some fifty years after the Conquest, reduces the amount to 20,000. (Antiq. of Mexico, vol. i. Pl. 19; vol. vi. p. 141, Eng. note.) Even this hardly warrants the Spanish interpreter in calling king Ahuitzotl a man "of a mild and moderate disposition," *templada y benigna condicion!* Ibid., vol. v. p. 49.

[2] Gomara states the number on the authority of two soldiers, whose names he gives, who took the trouble to count the grinning horrors in one of these Golgothas, where they were so arranged as to produce the most hideous effect. The existence of these conservatories is attested by every writer of the time.

[3] The "Anonymous Conqueror" assures us, as a fact beyond dispute, that the Devil introduced himself into the bodies of the idols, and persuaded the silly priests that his only diet was human hearts! It furnishes a very satisfactory solution, to his mind, of the frequency of sacrifices in Mexico. Rel. d'un gentil' huomo, ap. Ramusio, tom. iii. fol. 307.

[4] The Tezcucan priests would fain have persuaded the good king Nezahualcoyotl, on occasion of a pestilence, to appease the gods by the sacrifice of some of his own subjects, instead of his enemies; on the ground that they would not only be obtained more easily, but would be fresher victims, and more acceptable. (Ixtlilxochitl, Hist. Chich., MS., cap. 41.) This writer mentions a cool arrangement entered into by the allied monarchs with the republic of Tlascala and her confederates. A battle-field was marked out, on which the troops of the hostile nations were to engage at stated seasons, and thus supply themselves with subjects for sacrifice. The victorious party was not to pursue his advantage by invading the other's territory, and they were to continue, in all other respects, on the most amicable footing. (Ubi supra.) The historian, who follows in the track of the Tezcucan Chronicler, may often find occasion to shelter himself, like Ariosto, with

" Mettendolo Turpin, lo metto anch' io."

The influence of these practices on the Aztec character was as disastrous as might have been expected. Familiarity with the bloody rites of sacrifice steeled the heart against human sympathy, and begat a thirst for carnage, like that excited in the Romans by the exhibitions of the circus. The perpetual recurrence of ceremonies, in which the people took part, associated religion with their most intimate concerns, and spread the gloom of superstition over the domestic hearth, until the character of the nation wore a grave and even melancholy aspect, which belongs to their descendants at the present day. The influence of the priesthood, of course, became unbounded. The sovereign thought himself honoured by being permitted to assist in the services of the temple. Far from limiting the authority of the priests to spiritual matters, he often surrendered his opinion to theirs, where they were least competent to give it. It was their opposition that prevented the final capitulation which would have saved the capital. The whole nation, from the peasant to the prince, bowed their necks to the worst kind of tyranny, that of a blind fanaticism.

In reflecting on the revolting usages recorded in the preceding pages, one finds it difficult to reconcile their existence with anything like a regular form of government, or an advance in civilization.[1] Yet the Mexicans had many claims to the character of a civilized community. One may, perhaps, better understand the anomaly, by reflecting on the condition of some of the most polished countries in Europe, in the sixteenth century, after the establishment of the modern Inquisition,—an institution which yearly destroyed its thousands, by a death more painful than the Aztec sacrifices ; which armed the hand of brother against brother, and, setting its burning seal upon the lip, did more to stay the march of improvement than any other scheme ever devised by human cunning.

Human sacrifice, however cruel, has nothing in it degrading to its victim. It may be rather said to ennoble him by devoting him to the gods. Although so terrible with the Aztecs, it was sometimes voluntarily embraced by them, as the most glorious death, and one that opened a sure passage into paradise.[2] The Inquisition, on the other hand, branded its

---

[1] [Don José F. Ramirez, the distinguished Mexican scholar, has made this sentence the text for a disquisition of fifty pages or more, one object of which is to show that the existence of human sacrifices is not irreconcilable with an advance in civilization. This leads him into an argument of much length, covering a broad range of historical inquiry, and displaying much learning as well as a careful consideration of the subject. In one respect, however, he has been led into an important error by misunderstanding the drift of my remarks, where, speaking of cannibalism, I say, " It is impossible the people who practise it should make any great progress in moral or intellectual culture" (p. 41). This observation, referring solely to cannibalism, the critic cites as if applied by me to human sacrifices. Whatever force, therefore, his reasoning may have in respect to the latter, it cannot be admitted to apply to the former. The distance is wide between human sacrifices and cannibalism ; though Señor Ramirez diminishes this distance by regarding both one and the other simply as religious exercises, springing from the devotional principle in our nature.* He enforces his views by a multitude of examples from history, which show how extensively these revolting usages of the Aztecs—on a much less gigantic scale indeed—have been practised by the primitive races of the Old World, some of whom, at a later period, made high advances in civilization. Ramirez, Notas y Esclarecimientos á la Historia del Conquista de México del Señor W. Prescott, appended to Navarro's translation.]

[2] Rel. d'un gentil' huomo, ap. Ramusio, tom. iii. fol. 307.—Among other instances is that of Chimalpopoca, third king of Mexico, who doomed himself, with a number of his lords, to this death, to wipe off

* [The practice of eating, or tasting, the victim has been generally associated with sacrifice, from the idea either of the sacredness of the offering or of the deity's accepting the soul, the immaterial part, or the blood as containing the principle of life, and leaving the flesh to his worshippers.—Ed.]

victims with infamy in this world, and consigned them to everlasting perdition in the next.

One detestable feature of the Aztec superstition, however, sunk it far below the Christian. This was its cannibalism; though, in truth, the Mexicans were not cannibals in the coarsest acceptation of the term. They did not feed on human flesh merely to gratify a brutish appetite, but in obedience to their religion. Their repasts were made of the victims whose blood had been poured out on the altar of sacrifice. This is a distinction worthy of notice.[1] Still, cannibalism, under any form or whatever sanction, cannot but have a fatal influence on the nation addicted to it. It suggests ideas so loathsome, so degrading to man, to his spiritual and immortal nature, that it is impossible the people who practise it should make any great progress in moral or intellectual culture. The Mexicans furnish no exception to this remark. The civilization which they possessed descended from the Toltecs, a race who never stained their altars, still less their banquets, with the blood of man.[2] All that deserved the name of science in Mexico came from this source; and the crumbling ruins of edifices attributed to them, still extant in various parts of New Spain, show a decided superiority in their architecture over that of the later races of Anahuac. It is true, the Mexicans made great proficiency in many of the social and mechanic arts, in that material culture,—if I may so call it,—the natural growth of increasing opulence, which ministers to the gratification of the senses. In purely intellectual progress they were behind the Tezcucans, whose wise sovereigns came into the abominable rites of their neighbours with reluctance and practised them on a much more moderate scale.[3]

In this state of things, it was beneficently ordered by Providence that the land should be delivered over to another race, who would rescue it from the brutish superstitions that daily extended wider and wider with extent of empire.[4] The debasing institutions of the Aztecs furnish the best apology for their conquest. It is true, the conquerors brought along with them the Inquisition. But they also brought Christianity, whose benign radiance would still survive when the fierce flames of fanaticism should be extinguished; dispelling those dark forms of horror which had so long brooded over the fair regions of Anahuac.

---

an indignity offered him by a brother monarch. (Torquemada, Monarch. Ind., lib. 2, cap. 28.) This was the law of honour with the Aztecs.

[1] Voltaire, doubtless, intends this, when he says, "Ils n'étaient point anthropophages, comme un très-petit nombre de peuplades Américaines." (Essai sur les Mœurs, chap. 147.)

[2] [The remark in the text admits of some qualification. According to an ancient Tezcucan chronicler, quoted by Señor Ramirez, the Toltecs celebrated occasionally the worship of the god Tlaloc with human sacrifices. The most important of these was the offering up once a year of five or six maidens, who were immolated in the usual horrid way of tearing out their hearts. It does not appear that the Toltecs consummated the sacrifice by devouring the flesh of the victim. This seems to have been the only exception to the blameless character of the Toltec rites. Tlaloc was the oldest deity in the Aztec mythology in which he found a suitable place. Yet, as the knowledge of him was originally derived from the Toltecs, it cannot be denied that this people, as Ramirez says, possessed in their peculiar civilization the germs of those sanguinary institutions which existed on so appalling a scale in Mexico. See Ramirez, Notas y Esclarecimientos, ubi supra.]

[3] Ixtlilxochitl, Hist. Chich., MS., cap. 45, et alibi.

[4] No doubt the ferocity of character engendered by their sanguinary rites greatly facilitated their conquests. Machiavelli attributes to a similar cause, in part, the military successes of the Romans. (Discorsi sopra T. Livio, lib. 2, cap. 2.) The same chapter contains some ingenious reflections—much more ingenious than candid—on the opposite tendencies of Christianity.

The most important authority in the preceding chapter, and, indeed, wherever the Aztec religion is concerned, is Bernardino de Sahagun, a Franciscan friar, contemporary with the Conquest. His great work, *Historia universal de Nueva-España*, has been recently printed for the first time. The circumstances attending its compilation and subsequent fate form one of the most remarkable passages in literary history.

Sahagun was born in a place of the same name, in old Spain. He was educated at Salamanca, and, having taken the vows of St. Francis, came over as a missionary to Mexico in the year 1529. Here he distinguished himself by his zeal, the purity of his life, and his unwearied exertions to spread the great truths of religion among the natives. He was the guardian of several conventual houses, successively, until he relinquished these cares, that he might devote himself more unreservedly to the business of preaching, and of compiling various works designed to illustrate the antiquities of the Aztecs. For these literary labours he found some facilities in the situation which he continued to occupy, of reader, or lecturer, in the College of Santa Cruz, in the capital.

The "Universal History" was concocted in a singular manner. In order to secure to it the greatest possible authority, he passed some years in a Tezcucan town, where he conferred daily with a number of respectable natives unacquainted with Castilian. He propounded to them queries, which they, after deliberation, answered in their usual method of writing, by hieroglyphical paintings. These he submitted to other natives, who had been educated under his own eye in the College of Santa Cruz ; and the latter, after a consultation among themselves, gave a written version, in the Mexican tongue, of the hieroglyphics. This process he repeated in another place, in some part of Mexico, and subjected the whole to a still further revision by a third body in another quarter. He finally arranged the combined results into a regular history, in the form it now bears ; composing it in the Mexican language, which he could both write and speak with great accuracy and elegance,—greater, indeed, than any Spaniard of the time.

The work presented a mass of curious information, that attracted much attention among his brethren. But they feared its influence in keeping alive in the natives a too vivid reminiscence of the very superstitions which it was the great object of the Christian clergy to eradicate. Sahagun had views more liberal than those of his order, whose blind zeal would willingly have annihilated every monument of art and human ingenuity which had not been produced under the influence of Christianity. They refused to allow him the necessary aid to transcribe his papers, which he had been so many years in preparing, under the pretext that the expense was too great for their order to incur. This occasioned a further delay of several years. What was worse, his provincial got possession of his manuscripts, which were soon scattered among the different religious houses in the country.

In this forlorn state of his affairs, Sahagun drew up a brief statement of the nature and contents of his work, and forwarded it to Madrid. It fell into the hands of Don Juan de Ovando, president of the Council for the Indies, who was so much interested in it that he ordered the manuscripts to be restored to their author, with the request that he would at once set about translating them into Castilian. This was accordingly done. His papers were recovered, though not without the menace of ecclesiastical censures ; and the octogenarian author began the work of translation from the Mexican, in which they had been originally written by him thirty years before. He had the satisfaction to complete the task, arranging the Spanish version in a parallel column with the original, and adding a vocabulary, explaining the difficult Aztec terms and phrases; while the text was supported by the numerous paintings on which it was founded. In this form, making two bulky volumes in folio, it was sent to Madrid. There seemed now to be no further reason for postponing its publication, the importance of which could not be doubted. But from this moment it disappears ; and we hear nothing further of it, for more than two centuries, except only as a valuable work, which had once existed, and was probably buried in some one of the numerous cemeteries of learning in which Spain abounds.

At length, towards the close of the last century, the indefatigable Muñoz succeeded in disinterring the long-lost manuscript from the place tradition had assigned to it,—the library of a convent at Tolosa, in Navarre, the northern extremity of Spain. With his usual ardour, he transcribed the whole work with his own hands, and added it to the inestimable collection, of which, alas ! he was destined not to reap the full benefit himself. From this transcript Lord Kingsborough was enabled to procure the copy which was published in 1830, in the sixth volume of his magnificent compilation. In it he expresses an honest satisfaction at being the first to give Sahagun's work to the world. But in this supposition he was mistaken. The very year preceding, an edition of it, with annotations, appeared in Mexico, in three volumes octavo. It was prepared by Busta-mante,—a scholar to whose editorial activity his country is largely indebted,—from a copy of the Muñoz manuscript which came into his possession. Thus this remarkable work, which was denied the honours of the press during the author's lifetime, after passing into oblivion, reappeared, at the distance of nearly three centuries, not in his own country, but in foreign lands widely remote from each other, and that almost simultaneously. The story is extraordinary, though unhappily not so extraordinary in Spain as it would be elsewhere.

Sahagun divided his history into twelve books. The first eleven are occupied with the social institutions of Mexico, and the last with the Conquest. On the religion of the country he is particularly full. His great object evidently was, to give a clear view of its mythology, and of the burdensome ritual which belonged to it. Religion entered so intimately into the most private concerns and usages of the Aztecs, that Sahagun's work must be a text-book for every student of their antiquities. Torquemada availed himself of a manuscript copy, which fell into his hands before it was sent to Spain, to enrich his own pages,—a circumstance more fortunate for his readers than for Sahagun's reputation, whose work, now that it is published, loses much of the originality and interest which would otherwise attach to it. In one respect it is invaluable ; as presenting a complete collection of the various forms of prayer, accommodated to every possible emergency, in use by the Mexicans. They are often clothed in dignified and beautiful language, showing that sublime speculative tenets are quite compatible with the most degrading practices of superstition. It is much to be regretted that we have not the eighteen hymns inserted by the author in his book, which would have particular interest, as the only specimen of devotional poetry preserved of the Aztecs. The hieroglyphical paintings, which accompanied the text, are also missing. If they have escaped the hands of fanaticism, both may reappear at some future day.

Sahagun produced several other works of a religious or philological character. Some of these were voluminous, but none have been printed. He lived to a very advanced age, closing a life of activity and usefulness, in 1590, in the capital of Mexico. His remains were followed to the tomb by a numerous concourse of his own countrymen, and of the natives, who lamented in him the loss of unaffected piety, benevolence, and learning.

CHAPTER IV.

MEXICAN HIEROGLYPHICS.—MANUSCRIPTS.—ARITHMETIC.—CHRONOLOGY. —ASTRONOMY.

It is a relief to turn from the gloomy pages of the preceding chapter to a brighter side of the picture, and to contemplate the same nation in its generous struggle to raise itself from a state of barbarism and to take a positive rank in the scale of civilization. It is not the less interesting, that these efforts were made on an entirely new theatre of action, apart from those influences that operate in the Old World; the inhabitants of which, forming one great brotherhood of nations, are knit together by sympathies that make the faintest spark of knowledge, struck out in one quarter, spread gradually wider and wider, until it has diffused a cheering light over the remotest. It is curious to observe the human mind, in this new position, conforming to the same laws as on the ancient continent, and taking a similar direction in its first inquiries after truth,—so similar, indeed, as, although not warranting, perhaps, the idea of imitation, to suggest at least that of a common origin.

In the Eastern hemisphere we find some nations, as the Greeks, for instance, early smitten with such a love of the beautiful as to be unwilling to dispense with it even in the graver productions of science; and other nations, again, proposing a severer end to themselves, to which even imagination and elegant art were made subservient. The productions of such a people must be criticised, not by the ordinary rules of taste, but by their adaptation to the peculiar end for which they were designed. Such were the Egyptians in the Old World,[1] and the Mexicans in the New. We have already had occasion to notice the resemblance borne by the latter nation to the former in their religious economy. We shall be more struck with it in their scientific culture, especially their hieroglyphical writing and their astronomy.

To describe actions and events by delineating visible objects seems to be a natural suggestion, and is practised, after a certain fashion, by the rudest savages. The North American Indian carves an arrow on the bark of trees to show his followers the direction of his march, and some other sign to show the success of his expeditions. But to paint intelligibly a consecutive series of these actions—forming what Warburton has happily called *picture-writing* [2]—requires a combination of ideas that amounts to a positively intellectual effort. Yet further, when the object of the painter, instead of being limited to the present, is to penetrate the past, and to gather from its dark recesses lessons of instruction for coming generations, we see the dawnings of a literary culture, and recognize the proof of a decided civilization in the attempt itself, however imperfectly it may be executed. The literal imitation of objects will not answer for this more complex and extended plan. It would occupy too much space, as well as time in the execution. It then becomes necessary to abridge the pictures, to confine the drawing to outlines, or to such prominent parts of the bodies delineated as may readily suggest the whole. This is the *representative* or *figurative* writing, which forms the lowest stage of hieroglyphics.

---

[1] "An Egyptian temple," says Denon, strikingly, "is an open volume, in which the teachings of science, morality, and the arts are recorded. Everything seems to speak one and the same language, and breathes one and the same spirit." The passage is cited by Heeren, Hist. Res., vol. v. p. 178

[2] Divine Legation, ap. Works (London, 1811), vol. iv. b. 4, sec. 4.—The Bishop of Gloucester, in his comparison of the various hieroglyphical systems of the world, shows his characteristic sagacity and boldness by announcing opinions little credited then, though since established. He affirmed the existence of an Egyptian alphabet, but was not aware of the phonetic property of hieroglyphics,—the great literary discovery of our age.

But there are things which have no type in the material world; abstract ideas, which can only be represented by visible objects supposed to have some quality analogous to the idea intended. This constitutes *symbolical* writing, the most difficult of all to the interpreter, since the analogy between the material and immaterial object is often purely fanciful, or local in its application. Who, for instance, could suspect the association which made a beetle represent the universe, as with the Egyptians, or a serpent typify time, as with the Aztecs?

The third and last division is the *phonetic*, in which signs are made to represent sounds, either entire words, or parts of them. This is the nearest approach of the hieroglyphical series to that beautiful invention, the alphabet, by which language is resolved into its elementary sounds, and an apparatus supplied for easily and accurately expressing the most delicate shades of thought.

The Egyptians were well skilled in all three kinds of hieroglyphics. But, although their public monuments display the first class, in their ordinary intercourse and written records, it is now certain that they almost wholly relied on the phonetic character. Strange that, having thus broken down the thin partition which divided them from an alphabet, their latest monuments should exhibit no nearer approach to it than their earliest.[1] The Aztecs, also, were acquainted with the several varieties of hieroglyphics. But they relied on the figurative infinitely more than on the others. The Egyptians were at the top of the scale, the Aztecs at the bottom.

In casting the eye over a Mexican manuscript, or map, as it is called, one is struck with the grotesque caricatures it exhibits of the human figure; monstrous, overgrown heads, on puny, misshapen bodies, which are themselves hard and angular in their outlines, and without the least skill in composition. On closer inspection, however, it is obvious that it is not so much a rude attempt to delineate nature, as a conventional symbol, to express the idea in the most clear and forcible manner; in the same way as the pieces of similar value on a chessboard, while they correspond with one another in form, bear little resemblance, usually, to the objects they represent. Those parts of the figure are most distinctly traced which are the most important. So, also, the colouring, instead of the delicate gradations of nature, exhibits only gaudy and violent contrasts, such as may produce the most vivid impression. " For even colours," as Gama observes, " speak in the Aztec hieroglyphics." [2]

But in the execution of all this the Mexicans were much inferior to the Egyptians. The drawings of the latter, indeed, are exceedingly defective,

---

[1] It appears that the hieroglyphics on the most recent monuments of Egypt contain no larger infusion of phonetic characters than those which existed eighteen centuries before Christ; showing no advance, in this respect, for twenty-two hundred years! (See Champollion, Précis du Système hiéroglyphique des anciens Égyptiens (Paris, 1824), pp. 242, 281.) It may seem more strange that the enchorial alphabet, so much more commodious, should not

have been substituted. But the Egyptians were familiar with their hieroglyphics from infancy, which, moreover, took the fancies of the most illiterate, probably in the same manner as our children are attracted and taught by the picture-alphabets in an ordinary spelling-book.

[2] Descripcion histórica y cronológica de las Dos Piedras (México, 1832), Parte 2, p. 39.

when criticised by the rules of art; for they were as ignorant of perspective as the Chinese, and only exhibited the head in profile, with the eye in the centre, and with total absence of expression. But they handled the pencil more gracefully than the Aztecs, were more true to the natural forms of objects, and, above all, showed great superiority in abridging the original figure by giving only the outline, or some characteristic or essential feature. This simplified the process, and facilitated the communication of thought. An Egyptian text has almost the appearance of alphabetical writing in its regular lines of minute figures. A Mexican text looks usually like a collection of pictures, each one forming the subject of a separate study. This is particularly the case with the delineations of mythology; in which the story is told by a conglomeration of symbols, that may remind one more of the mysterious anaglyphs sculptured on the temples of the Egyptians, than of their written records.

The Aztecs had various emblems for expressing such things as, from their nature, could not be directly represented by the painter; as, for example, the years, months, days, the seasons, the elements, the heavens, and the like. A "tongue" denoted speaking; a "footprint," travelling; a "man sitting on the ground," an earthquake. These symbols were often very arbitrary, varying with the caprice of the writer; and it requires a nice discrimination to interpret them, as a slight change in the form or position of the figure intimated a very different meaning.[1] An ingenious writer asserts that the priests devised secret symbolic characters for the record of their religious mysteries. It is possible. But the researches of Champollion lead to the conclusion that the similar opinion formerly entertained respecting the Egyptian hieroglyphics is without foundation.[2]

Lastly, they employed, as above stated, phonetic signs, though these were chiefly confined to the names of persons and places; which, being derived from some circumstance or characteristic quality, were accommodated to the hieroglyphical system. Thus, the town *Cimatlan* was compounded of *cimatl*, a "root," which grew near it, and *tlan*, signifying "near;" *Tlaxcallan* meant "the place of bread," from its rich fields of corn; *Huexotzinco*, "a place surrounded by willows." The names of persons were often significant of their adventures and achievements. That of the great Tezcucan prince Nezahualcoyotl signified "hungry fox," intimating his sagacity, and his distresses in early life.[3] The emblems of such names

---

[1] Gama, Descripcion, Parte 2, pp. 32, 44.—Acosta, lib. 6, cap. 7.—The continuation of Gama's work, recently edited by Bustamante, in Mexico, contains, among other things, some interesting remarks on the Aztec hieroglyphics. The editor has rendered a good service by this further publication of the writings of this estimable scholar, who has done more than any of his countrymen to explain the mysteries of Aztec science.

[2] Gama, Descripcion, Parte 2, p. 32.—Warburton, with his usual penetration, rejects the idea of mystery in the figurative hieroglyphics. (Divine Legation, s. 4, sec. 4.) If there was any mystery reserved for be initiated, Champollion thinks it may have been the

system of the anaglyphs. (Précis, p. 360.) Why may not this be true, likewise, of the monstrous symbolical combinations which represented the Mexican deities?

[3] Boturini, Idea, pp. 77–83.—Gama, Descripcion, Parte 2, pp. 34–43.—Heeren is not aware, or does not allow, that the Mexicans used phonetic characters of any kind. (Hist. Res., vol. v. p. 45.) They, indeed, reversed the usual order of proceeding, and, instead of adapting the hieroglyphic to the name of the object, accommodated the name of the object to the hieroglyphic. This, of course, could not admit of great extension. We find phonetic characters, however, applied in some instances to common as well as proper names.

were no sooner seen, than they suggested to every Mexican the person and place intended, and, when painted on their shields or embroidered on their banners, became the armorial bearings by which city and chieftain were distinguished, as in Europe in the age of chivalry.[1]

But, although the Aztecs were instructed in all the varieties of hieroglyphical painting, they chiefly resorted to the clumsy method of direct representation. Had their empire lasted, like the Egyptian, several thousand years, instead of the brief space of two hundred, they would doubtless, like them, have advanced to the more frequent use of the phonetic writing. But, before they could be made acquainted with the capabilities of their own system, the Spanish Conquest, by introducing the European alphabet, supplied their scholars with a more perfect contrivance for expressing thought, which soon supplanted the ancient pictorial character.[2]

Clumsy as it was, however, the Aztec picture-writing seems to have been adequate to the demands of the nation, in their imperfect state of civilization. By means of it were recorded all their laws, and even their regulations for domestic economy; their tribute-rolls, specifying the imposts of the various towns; their mythology, calendars, and rituals; their political annals, carried back to a period long before the foundation of the city. They digested a complete system of chronology, and could specify with accuracy the dates of the most important events in their history; the year being inscribed on the margin, against the particular circumstance recorded. It is true, history, thus executed, must necessarily be vague and fragmentary. Only a few leading incidents could be presented. But in this it did not differ much from the monkish chronicles of the dark ages, which often dispose of years in a few brief sentences,—quite long enough for the annals of barbarians.[3]

In order to estimate aright the picture-writing of the Aztecs, one must regard it in connection with oral tradition, to which it was auxiliary. In the colleges of the priests the youth were instructed in astronomy, history, mythology, etc. ; and those who were to follow the profession of hieroglyphical painting, were taught the application of the characters appropriated to each of these branches. In an historical work, one had charge of the chronology, another of the events. Every part of the labour was thus mechanically distributed.[4] The pupils, instructed in all that was before

[1] Boturini, Idea, ubi supra.

[2] Clavigero has given a catalogue of the Mexican historians of the sixteenth century,—some of whom are often cited in this history,—which bears honourable testimony to the literary ardour and intelligence of the native races. Stor. del Messico, tom. i., Pref. —Also, Gama, Descripcion, Parte 1, passim.

[3] M. de Humboldt's remark, that the Aztec annals, from the close of the eleventh century, " exhibit the greatest method and astonishing minuteness" (Vues des Cordillères, p. 137), must be received with some qualification. The reader would scarcely understand from it that there are rarely more than one or two facts recorded in any year, and sometimes not one in a dozen or more. The necessary looseness and uncertainty of these historical records are made apparent by the remarks of the Spanish interpreter of the Mendoza Codex, who tells us that the natives, to whom it was submitted, were very long in coming to an agreement about the proper signification of the paintings. Antiq. of Mexico, vol. vi. p. 87.

[4] Gama, Descripcion, Parte 2, p. 30.—Acosta, lib. 6, cap. 7.—"Tenian para cada género," says Ixtlilxochitl, "sus Escritores, unos que trataban de los Anales, poniendo por su órden las cosas que acaecian en cada un año, con dia, mes, y hora; otros tenian á su cargo las Genealogías, y descendencia de los Reyes, Señores, y Personas de linaje, asentando por cuenta y razon los que nacian, y borraban los que morian con la misma cuenta. Unos tenian cuidado de las pinturas, de los términos, límites, y mojoneras de las Ciudades, Pro-

known in their several departments, were prepared to extend still further the boundaries of their imperfect science. The hieroglyphics served as a sort of stenography, a collection of notes, suggesting to the initiated much more than could be conveyed by a literal interpretation. This combination of the written and the oral comprehended what may be called the literature of the Aztecs.[1]

Their manuscripts were made of different materials,—of cotton cloth, or skins nicely prepared; of a composition of silk and gum; but, for the most part, of a fine fabric from the leaves of the aloe, *Agave Americana*, called by the natives *maguey*, which grows luxuriantly over the table-lands of Mexico. A sort of paper was made from it, resembling somewhat the Egyptian *papyrus*,[2] which, when properly dressed and polished, is said to have been more soft and beautiful than parchment. Some of the specimens, still existing, exhibit their original freshness, and the paintings on them retain their brilliancy of colours. They were sometimes done up into rolls, but more frequently into volumes, of moderate size, in which the paper was shut up, like a folding screen, with a leaf or tablet of wood at each extremity, that gave the whole, when closed, the appearance of a book. The length of the strips was determined only by convenience. As the pages might be read and referred to separately, this form had obvious advantages over the rolls of the ancients.[3]

At the time of the arrival of the Spaniards, great quantities of these manuscripts were treasured up in the country. Numerous persons were employed in painting, and the dexterity of their operations excited the astonishment of the Conquerors. Unfortunately, this was mingled with other and unworthy feelings. The strange, unknown characters inscribed on them excited suspicion. They were looked on as magic scrolls, and were regarded in the same light with the idols and temples, as the symbols of a pestilent superstition, that must be extirpated. The first archbishop of Mexico, Don Juan de Zumárraga,—a name that should be as immortal as that of Omar,—collected these paintings from every quarter, especially

---

vincias, Pueblos, y Lugares, y de las suertes, y repartimiento de las tierras cuyas eran, y á quien pertenecian; otros de los libros de Leyes, ritos, y ceremonias que usaban." Hist. Chich., MS., Prólogo.

[1] According to Boturini, the ancient Mexicans were acquainted with the Peruvian method of recording events by means of the *quippus*,—knotted strings of various colours,—which were afterwards superseded by hieroglyphical painting. (Idea, p. 86.) He could discover, however, but a single specimen, which he met with in Tlascala, and that had nearly fallen to pieces with age. McCulloh suggests that it may have been only a wampum belt, such as is common among our North American Indians. (Researches, p. 201.) The conjecture is plausible enough. Strings of wampum, of various colours, were used by the latter people for the similar purpose of registering events. The insulated fact, recorded by Boturini, is hardly sufficient—unsupported, so far as I know, by any other testimony—to establish the existence of *quippus* among the Aztecs, who had but little in common with the Peruvians.

[2] Pliny, who gives a minute account of the *papyrus* reed of Egypt, notices the various manufactures obtained from it, as ropes, cloth, paper, etc. It also served as a thatch for the roofs of houses, and as food and drink for the natives. (Hist. Nat., lib. ii, cap. 20-22.) It is singular that the American *agave*, a plant so totally different, should also have been applied to all these various uses.

[3] Lorenzana, Hist. de Nueva-España, p. 8.—Boturini, Idea, p. 96.—Humboldt, Vues des Cordillères, p. 52.—Peter Martyr Anglerius, De Orbe Novo (Compluti, 1530), dec. 3, cap. 8; dec. 5, cap. 10.—Martyr has given a minute description of the Indian maps sent home soon after the invasion of New Spain. His inquisitive mind was struck with the evidence they afforded of a positive civilization. Ribera, the friend of Cortés, brought back a story that the paintings were designed as patterns for embroiderers and jewellers. But Martyr had been in Egypt, and he felt little hesitation in placing the Indian drawings in the same class with those he had seen on the obelisks and temples of that country.

from Tezcuco, the most cultivated capital in Anahuac, and the great depository of the national archives. He then caused them to be piled up in a " mountain-heap "—as it is called by the Spanish writers themselves— in the market-place of Tlatelolco, and reduced them all to ashes ! [1] His greater countryman, Archbishop Ximenes, had celebrated a similar *auto-da-fe* of Arabic manuscripts, in Granada, some twenty years before. Never did fanaticism achieve two more signal triumphs than by the annihilation of so many curious monuments of human ingenuity and learning ! [2]

The unlettered soldiers were not slow in imitating the example of their prelate. Every chart and volume which fell into their hands was wantonly destroyed ; so that, when the scholars of a later and more enlightened age anxiously sought to recover some of these memorials of civilization, nearly all had perished, and the few surviving were jealously hidden by the natives. [3] Through the indefatigable labours of a private individual, how-ever, a considerable collection was eventually deposited in the archives of Mexico, but was so little heeded there that some were plundered, others decayed piecemeal from the damps and mildews, and others, again, were used up as waste paper ! [4] We contemplate with indignation the cruel-ties inflicted by the early conquerors. But indignation is qualified with contempt when we see them thus ruthlessly trampling out the spark of knowledge, the common boon and property of all mankind. We may well doubt which has the stronger claim to civilization, the victor or the vanquished.

A few of the Mexican manuscripts have found their way, from time to time, to Europe, and are carefully preserved in the public libraries of its capitals. They are brought together in the magnificent work of Lord Kingsborough ; but not one is there from Spain. The most important of them, for the light it throws on the Aztec institutions, is the Mendoza Codex ; which, after its mysterious disappearance for more than a century, has at length reappeared in the Bodleian Library at Oxford. It has been several times engraved. [5] The most brilliant in colouring, probably, is the

---

[1] Ixtlilxochitl, Hist. Chich., MS., Prólogo.—Idem, Sum. Relac., MS.—[" The name of Zumár-raga," says Señor Alaman, "has other and very different titles to immortality from that mentioned by Mr. Prescott,—titles founded on his virtues and apostolic labours, especially on the fervid zeal with which he defended the natives and the manifold benefits he secured to them. The loss that history suffered by the destruction of the Indian manu-scripts by the missionaries has been in a great measure repaired by the writings of the missionaries themselves." Conquista de Méjico (trad. de Vega), tom. i. p. 60.]—Writers are not agreed whether the conflagration took place in the square of Tlatelolco or Tezcuco. Comp. Clavigero, Stor. del Messico, tom. ii. p. 188, and Bustamante's Pref. to Ixtlilxo-chitl, Cruautés des Conquérans, trad. de Ternaux, p. xvii.

[2] It has been my lot to record both these dis-plays of human infirmity, so humbling to the pride of intellect. See the History of Ferdinand and Isa-bella, Part 2, chap. 6.

[3] Sahagun, Hist. de Nueva-España, lib. 10, cap.

27.—Bustamante, Mañanas de Alameda (México, 1836), tom. ii., Prólogo.

[4] Very many of the documents thus painfully amassed in the archives of the Audience of Mexico were sold, according to Bustamante, as wrapping-paper, to apothecaries, shopkeepers, and rocket-makers ! Boturini's noble collection has not fared much better.

[5] The history of this famous collection is familiar to scholars. It was sent to the Emperor Charles the Fifth, not long after the Conquest, by the viceroy Mendoza, Marques de Mondejar. The vessel fell into the hands of a French cruiser, and the manu-script was taken to Paris. It was afterwards bought by the chaplain of the English embassy, and coming into the possession of the antiquary Purchas, was engraved, *in extenso*, by him, in the third volume of his "Pilgrimage." After its publication, in 1625, the Aztec original lost its importance, and fell into ob-livion so completely that, when at length the public curiosity was excited in regard to its fate, no trace of it could be discovered. Many were the specula-tions of scholars, at home and abroad, respecting it,

Borgian collection, in Rome.[1]　The most curious, however, is the Dresden Codex, which has excited less attention than it deserves.　Although usually classed among Mexican manuscripts, it bears little resemblance to them in its execution; the figures of objects are more delicately drawn, and the characters, unlike the Mexican, appear to be purely arbitrary, and are possibly phonetic.[2]　Their regular arrangement is quite equal to the Egyptian.　The whole infers a much higher civilization than the Aztec, and offers abundant food for curious speculation.[3]

Some few of these maps have interpretations annexed to them, which were obtained from the natives after the Conquest.[4]　The greater part are without any, and cannot now be unriddled.　Had the Mexicans made free use of a phonetic alphabet, it might have been originally easy, by mastering the comparatively few signs employed in this kind of communi-

---

and Dr. Robertson settled the question as to its existence in England, by declaring that there was no Mexican relic in that country, except a golden goblet of Montezuma. (History of America (London, 1796), vol. iii. p. 370.) Nevertheless, the identical Codex, and several other Mexican paintings, have been since discovered in the Bodleian Library. The circumstance has brought some obloquy on the historian, who, while prying into the collections of Vienna and the Escorial, could be so blind to those under his own eyes. The oversight will not appear so extraordinary to a thorough - bred collector, whether of manuscripts, or medals, or any other rarity. The Mendoza Codex is, after all, but a copy, coarsely done with a pen on European paper. Another copy, from which Archbishop Lorenzana engraved his tribute-rolls in Mexico, existed in Boturini's collection. A third is in the Escorial, according to the Marquis of Spineto. (Lectures on the Elements of Hieroglyphics (London), Lect. 7.) This may possibly be the original painting. The entire Codex, copied from the Bodleian maps, with its Spanish and English interpretations, is included in the noble compilation of Lord Kingsborough. (Vols. i., v., vi.) It is distributed into three parts, embracing the civil history of the nation, the tributes paid by the cities, and the domestic economy and discipline of the Mexicans, and, from the fulness of the interpretation, is of much importance in regard to these several topics.

[1] It formerly belonged to the Giustiniani family, but was so little cared for that it was suffered to fall into the mischievous hands of the domestics' children, who made sundry attempts to burn it. Fortunately, it was painted on deer-skin, and, though somewhat singed, was not destroyed. (Humboldt, Vues des Cordillères, p. 89, et seq.) It is impossible to cast the eye over this brilliant assemblage of forms and colours without feeling how hopeless must be the attempt to recover a key to the Aztec mythological symbols; which are here distributed with the symmetry, indeed, but in all the endless combinations, of the kaleidoscope. It is in the third volume of Lord Kingsborough's work.

[2] Humboldt, who has copied some pages of it in his "Atlas pittoresque," intimates no doubt of its Aztec origin. (Vues des Cordillères, pp. 266, 267.) M. Le Noir even reads in it an exposition of Mexican Mythology, with occasional analogies to that of

Egypt and of Hindostan. (Antiquités Mexicaines, tom. ii., Introd.) The fantastic forms of hieroglyphic symbols may afford analogies for almost anything.

[3] The history of this Codex, engraved entire in the third volume of the "Antiquities of Mexico," goes no further back than 1739, when it was purchased at Vienna for the Dresden Library. It is made of the American agave. The figures painted on it bear little resemblance, either in feature or form, to the Mexican. They are surmounted by a sort of head-gear, which looks something like a modern peruke. On the chin of one we may notice a beard, a sign often used after the Conquest to denote a European. Many of the persons are sitting cross-legged. The profiles of the faces, and the whole contour of the limbs, are sketched with a spirit and freedom very unlike the hard, angular outlines of the Aztecs. The characters, also, are delicately traced, generally in an irregular but circular form, and are very minute. They are arranged, like the Egyptian, both horizontally and perpendicularly, mostly in the former manner, and, from the prevalent direction of the profiles, would seem to have been read from right to left. Whether phonetic or ideographic, they are of that compact and purely conventional sort which belongs to a well-digested system for the communication of thought. One cannot but regret that no trace should exist of the quarter whence this MS. was obtained; perhaps some part of Central America, from the region of the mysterious races who built the monuments of Mitla and Palenque; though, in truth, there seems scarcely more resemblance in the symbols to the Palenque bas-reliefs than to the Aztec paintings.*

[4] There are three of these : the Mendoza Codex; the Telleriano-Remensis,—formerly the property of Archbishop Tellier,—in the Royal Library of Paris; and the Vatican MS., No. 3738. The interpretation of the last bears evident marks of its recent origin; probably as late as the close of the sixteenth or the beginning of the seventeenth century, when the ancient hieroglyphics were read with the eye of faith rather than of reason. Whoever was the commentator (comp. Vues des Cordillères, pp. 203, 204; and Antiq. of Mexico, vol. vi. pp. 155, 222), he has given such an exposition as shows the old Aztecs to have been as orthodox Christians as any subjects of the Pope.

* [Mr. Stephens, who, like Humboldt, considered the Dresden Codex a Mexican manuscript, compared the characters of it with those on the altar of Copan, and drew the conclusion that the inhabitants of that place and of Palenque must have spoken the same language as the Aztecs. Prescott's opinion has, however, been confirmed by later critics, who have shown that the hieroglyphics of the Dresden Codex are quite different from those at Copan and Palenque, while the Mexican writing bears not the least resemblance to either. See Orozco y Berra, Geografía de las Lenguas de México. p 101.—ED.]

cation, to have got a permanent key to the whole.[1]   A brief inscription has furnished a clue to the vast labyrinth of Egyptian hieroglyphics.   But the Aztec characters, representing individuals, or, at most, species, require to be made out separately ; a hopeless task, for which little aid is to be expected from the vague and general tenor of the few interpretations now existing.   There was, as already mentioned, until late in the last century, a professor in the University of Mexico, especially devoted to the study of the national picture-writing.   But, as this was with a view to legal proceedings, his information, probably, was limited to deciphering titles.   In less than a hundred years after the Conquest, the knowledge of the hieroglyphics had so far declined that a diligent Tezcucan writer complains he could find in the country only two persons, both very aged, at all competent to interpret them.[2]

It is not probable, therefore, that the art of reading these picture-writings will ever be recovered ; a circumstance certainly to be regretted.   Not that the records of a semi-civilized people would be likely to contain any new truth or discovery important to human comfort or progress ; but they could scarcely fail to throw some additional light on the previous history of the nation, and that of the more polished people who before occupied the country.   This would be still more probable, if any literary relics of their Toltec predecessors were preserved ; and, if report be true, an important compilation from this source was extant at the time of the invasion, and may have perhaps contributed to swell the holocaust of Zumárraga.[3]   It is no great stretch of fancy to suppose that such records might reveal the successive links in the mighty chain of migration of the primitive races, and, by carrying us back to the seat of their possessions in the Old World, have solved the mystery which has so long perplexed the learned, in regard to the settlement and civilization of the New.[4]

---

[1] The total number of Egyptian hieroglyphics discovered by Champollion amounts to 864 ; and of these 130 only are phonetic, notwithstanding that this kind of character is used far more frequently than both the others. Précis, p. 263;—also Spineto, Lectures, Lect. 3.

[2] Ixtlilxochitl, Hist. Chich., MS., Dedic.—Boturini, who travelled through every part of the country in the middle of the last century, could not meet with an individual who could afford him the least clue to the Aztec hieroglyphics. So completely had every vestige of their ancient language been swept away from the memory of the natives. (Idea, p. 116.) If we are to believe Bustamante, however, a complete key to the whole system is, at this moment, *somewhere* in Spain. It was carried home, at the time of the process against Father Mier, in 1795. The name of the Mexican Champollion who discovered it is Borunda. Gama, Descripcion, tom. ii. p. 33, nota.

[3] *Teoamoxtli*, "the divine book," as it was called.

According to Ixtlilxochitl, it was composed by a Tezcucan doctor, named Huematzin, towards the close of the seventeenth century. (Relaciones, MS.) It gave an account of the migrations of his nation from Asia, of the various stations on their journey, of their social and religious institutions, their science, arts, etc., etc., a good deal too much for one book. *Ignotum pro mirifico.*   It has never been seen by a European.*   A copy is said to have been in possession of the Tezcucan chroniclers on the taking of their capital.   (Bustamante, Crónica Mexicana (México, 1822), carta 3.) Lord Kingsborough, who can scent out a Hebrew root be it buried never so deep, has discovered that the *Teoamoxtli* was the Pentateuch.   Thus, *teo* means "divine," *amotl*, "paper" or "book," and *moxtli* "*appears* to be Moses ;"—"Divine Book of Moses"!   Antiq. of Mexico, vol. vi. p. 204, nota.

[4] [Such a supposition would require a "stretch of fancy" greater than any which the mind of the mere

---

* [It must have been seen by many Europeans, if we accept either the statement of the Baron de Waldeck, in 1838 (Voyage pittoresque et archéologique dans la Province d'Yucatan), that it was then in his possession, or the theories of Brasseur de Bourbourg, who identifies it with the Dresden Codex and certain other hieroglyphical manuscripts, and who believes himself to have found the key to it, and consequently to the origin of the Mexican history and civilization, in one of the documents in Boturini's collection, to which he has given the name of the Codex Chimalpopoca. Quatre Lettres sur le Mexique (Paris, 1868).—Ed.]

Besides the hieroglyphical maps, the traditions of the country were embodied in the songs and hymns, which, as already mentioned, were carefully taught in the public schools.   These were various, embracing the mythic legends of a heroic age, the warlike achievements of their own, or the softer tales of love and pleasure.[1]   Many of them were composed by scholars and persons of rank, and are cited as affording the most authentic record of events.[2]   The Mexican dialect was rich and expressive, though inferior to the Tezcucan, the most polished of the idioms of Anahuac. None of the Aztec compositions have survived, but we can form some estimate of the general state of poetic culture from the odes which have come down to us from the royal house of Tezcuco.[3]   Sahagun has furnished us with translations of their more elaborate prose, consisting of prayers and public discourses, which give a favourable idea of their eloquence, and show that they paid much attention to rhetorical effect.   They are said to have had, also, something like theatrical exhibitions, of a pantomimic sort, in which the faces of the performers were covered with masks, and the figures of birds or animals were frequently represented ; an imitation to which they may have been led by the familiar delineation of such objects in their hieroglyphics.[4]   In all this we see the dawning of a literary culture, surpassed, however, by their attainments in the severer walks of mathematical science.

They devised a system of notation in their arithmetic sufficiently simple. The first twenty numbers were expressed by a corresponding number of dots.   The first five had specific names ; after which they were represented by combining the fifth with one of the four preceding ; as five and one for six, five and two for seven, and so on.   Ten and fifteen had each a separate name, which was also combined with the first four, to express a higher quantity.   These four, therefore, were the radical characters of their oral arithmetic, in the same manner as they were of the written with the ancient Romans ; a more simple arrangement, probably, than any existing among Europeans.[5]   Twenty was expressed by a separate hieroglyphic,—a flag. Larger sums were reckoned by twenties, and, in writing, by repeating the number of flags.   The square of twenty, four hundred, had a separate sign,

---

historical inquirer is capable of taking. To admit the probability of the Asiatic origin of the American races, and of the indefinite antiquity of the Mexican civilization, is something very different from believing that this civilization, already developed in the degree required for the existence and preservation of its own records during so long a period and so great a migration, can have been transplanted from the one continent to the other. It would be easier to accept the theory, now generally abandoned, that the original settlers owed their civilization to a body of colonists from Phœnicia. In view of so hazardous a conjecture, it is difficult to understand why Buschmann has taken exception to the "sharp criticism" to which Prescott has subjected the sources of Mexican history, and his "low estimate of their value and credibility."—ED.]

[1] Boturini, Idea, pp. 90–97.—Clavigero, Stor. del Messico, tom. ii. pp. 174–178.

[2] "Los cantos con que las observaban Autores muy graves en su modo de ciencia y facultad, pues fuéron los mismos Reyes, y de la gei te mas ilustre y entendida, que siempre observáron y adquiriéron la verdad, y esta con tanta razon, quánta pudiéron tener los mas graves y fidedignos Autores." Ixtlilxochitl, Hist. Chich., MS., Prólogo.

[3] See chap. 6 of this Introduction.

[4] See some account of these mummeries in Acosta (lib. 5, cap. 30),—also Clavigero (Stor. del Messico, ubi supra).   Stone models of masks are sometimes found among the Indian ruins, and engravings of them are both in Lord Kingsborough's work and in the Antiquités Mexicaines.

[5] Gama, Descripcion, Parte 2, Apend. 2.—Gama, in comparing the language of Mexican notation with the decimal system of the Europeans and the ingenious binary system of Leibnitz, confounds oral with written arithmetic.

that of a plume, and so had the cube of twenty, or eight thousand, which was denoted by a purse, or sack. This was the whole arithmetical apparatus of the Mexicans, by the combination of which they were enabled to indicate any quantity. For greater expedition, they used to denote fractions of the larger sums by drawing only a part of the object. Thus, half or three-fourths of a plume, or of a purse, represented that proportion of their respective sums, and so on.[1] With all this, the machinery will appear very awkward to us, who perform our operations with so much ease by means of the Arabic or, rather, Indian ciphers. It is not much more awkward, however, than the system pursued by the great mathematicians of antiquity, unacquainted with the brilliant invention, which has given a new aspect to mathematical science, of determining the value, in a great measure, by the relative position of the figures.

In the measurement of time, the Aztecs adjusted their civil year by the solar. They divided it into eighteen months of twenty days each. Both months and days were expressed by peculiar hieroglyphics,—those of the former often intimating the season of the year, like the French months at the period of the Revolution. Five complementary days, as in Egypt,[2] were added, to make up the full number of three hundred and sixty-five. They belonged to no month, and were regarded as peculiarly unlucky. A month was divided into four weeks, of five days each, on the last of which was the public fair, or market-day.[3] This arrangement, differing from that of the nations of the Old Continent, whether of Europe or Asia,[4] has the advantage of giving an equal number of days to each month, and of comprehending entire weeks, without a fraction, both in the months and in the year.[5]

As the year is composed of nearly six hours more than three hundred and sixty-five days, there still remained an excess, which, like other nations who have framed a calendar, they provided for by intercalation ; not, indeed, every fourth year, as the Europeans,[6] but at longer intervals, like some of the Asiatics.[7] They waited till the expiration of fifty-two vague years, when they interposed thirteen days, or rather twelve and a half, this

---

1 Gama, ubi supra.—This learned Mexican has given a very satisfactory treatise on the arithmetic of the Aztecs, in his second part.

2 Herodotus, Euterpe, sec. 4.

3 Sahagun, Hist. de Nueva-España, lib. 4, Apend. —According to Clavigero, the fairs were held on the days bearing the sign of the year. Stor. del Messico, tom. ii. p. 62.

4 The people of Java, according to Sir Stamford Raffles, regulated their markets, also, by a week of five days. They had, besides, our week of seven. (History of Java (London, 1830), vol. i. pp. 531, 532.) The latter notion of time, of general use throughout the East, is the oldest monument existing of astronomical science. See La Place, Exposition du Système du Monde (Paris, 1808), lib. 5, chap. 1.

5 Veytia, Hist. antigua de Méjico (Méjico, 1806), tom. i. cap. 6, 7.—Gama, Descripcion, Parte 1, pp. 33, 34, et alibi.—Boturini, Idea, pp. 4, 44, et seq.— Cod. Tel.-Rem., ap. Antiq. of Mexico, vol. vi. p. 104.—Camargo, Hist. de Tlascala, MS.—Toribio, Hist. de los Indios, MS., Parte 1, cap. 5.

6 Sahagun intimates doubts of this. "They celebrated another feast every four years in honour of the elements of fire, and it is probable and has been conjectured that it was on these occasions that they made their intercalation, counting six days of *nemontemi*," as the unlucky complementary days were called. (Hist. de Nueva-España, lib. 4, Apend.) But this author, however good an authority for the superstitions, is an indifferent one for the science of the Mexicans.

7 The Persians had a cycle of one hundred and twenty years, of three hundred and sixty-five days each, at the end of which they intercalated thirty days. (Humboldt, Vues des Cordillères, p. 177.) This was the same as thirteen after the cycle of fifty-two years of the Mexicans, but was less accurate than their probable intercalation of twelve days and a half. It is obviously indifferent, as far as accuracy is concerned, which multiple of four is selected to form the cycle ; though, the shorter the interval of intercalation, the less, of course, will be the temporary departure from the true time.

being the number which had fallen in arrear. Had they inserted thirteen, it would have been too much, since the annual excess over three hundred and sixty-five is about eleven minutes less than six hours. But, as their calendar at the time of the Conquest was found to correspond with the European (making allowance for the subsequent Gregorian reform), they would seem to have adopted the shorter period of twelve days and a half,[1] which brought them, within an almost inappreciable fraction, to the exact length of the tropical year, as established by the most accurate observations.[2] Indeed, the intercalation of twenty-five days in every hundred and four years shows a nicer adjustment of civil to solar time than is presented by any European calendar; since more than five centuries must elapse before the loss of an entire day.[3] Such was the astonishing precision displayed by the Aztecs, or, perhaps, by their more polished Toltec predecessors, in these computations, so difficult as to have baffled, till a comparatively recent period, the most enlightened nations of Christendom.[4]

The chronological system of the Mexicans, by which they determined the date of any particular event, was also very remarkable. The epoch from which they reckoned corresponded with the year 1091 of the Christian era. It was the period of the reform of their calendar, soon after their migration from Aztlan. They threw the years, as already noticed, into great cycles, of fifty-two each, which they called "sheafs," or "bundles," and represented by a quantity of reeds bound together by a string. As often as this hieroglyphic occurs in their maps, it shows the number of half-centuries. To enable them to specify any particular year, they divided the

---

[1] This is the conclusion to which Gama arrives, after a very careful investigation of the subject. He supposes that the "bundles," or cycles, of fifty-two years—by which, as we shall see, the Mexicans computed time—ended alternately at midnight and midday. (Descripcion, Parte 1, p. 52, et seq.) He finds some warrant for this in Acosta's account (lib. 6, cap. 2), though contradicted by Torquemada (Monarch. Ind., lib. 5, cap. 33), and, as it appears, by Sahagun,—whose work, however, Gama never saw (Hist. de Nueva-España, lib. 7, cap. 9),—both of whom place the close of the year at midnight. Gama's hypothesis derives confirmation from a circumstance I have not seen noticed. Besides the "bundle" of fifty-two years, the Mexicans had a larger cycle of one hundred and four years, called "an old age." As this was not used in their reckonings, which were carried on by their "bundles," it seems highly probable that it was designed to express the period which would bring round the commencement of the smaller cycles to the same hour, and in which the intercalary days, amounting to twenty-five, might be comprehended without a fraction.

[2] This length, as computed by Zach, at 365d. 5h. 48m. 48sec., is only 2m. 9sec. longer than the Mexican; which corresponds with the celebrated calculation of the astronomers of the Caliph Almamon, that fell short about two minutes of the true time. See La Place, Exposition, p. 350.

[3] "El corto exceso de 4hor. 38min. 40seg., que hay de mas de los 25 dias en el período de 104 años, no puede componer un dia entero, hasta que pasen mas de cinco de estos periodos máximos ó 538 años." (Gama, Descripcion, Parte 1, p. 23.) Gama estimates the solar year at 365d. 5h. 48m. 50sec.

[4] The ancient Etruscans arranged their calendar in cycles of 110 solar years, and reckoned the year at 365d. 5h. 40m.; at least this seems probable, says Niebuhr. (History of Rome, Eng. trans. (Cambridge, 1828), vol. i. pp. 113, 238.) The early Romans had not wit enough to avail themselves of this accurate measurement, which came within nine minutes of the true time. The Julian reform, which assumed 365d. 5¼h. as the length of the year, erred as much, or rather more, on the other side. And when the Europeans, who adopted this calendar, landed in Mexico, their reckoning was nearly eleven days in advance of the exact time,—or, in other words, of the reckoning of the barbarous Aztecs; a remarkable fact.—Gama's researches led to the conclusion that the year of the new cycle began with the Aztecs on the ninth of January; a date considerably earlier than that usually assigned by the Mexican writers. (Descripcion, Parte 2, pp. 49-52.) By postponing the intercalation to the end of fifty-two years, the annual loss of six hours made every fourth year begin a day earlier. Thus, the cycle commencing on the ninth of January, the fifth year of it began on the eighth, the ninth year on the seventh, and so on; so that the last day of the series of fifty-two years fell on the twenty-sixth of December, when the intercalation of thirteen days rectified the chronology and carried the commencement of the new year to the ninth of January again. Torquemada, puzzled by the irregularity of the new-year's day, asserts that the Mexicans were unacquainted with the annual excess of six hours, and therefore never intercalated! (Monarch. Ind., lib. 10, cap. 36.) The interpreter of the Vatican Codex has fallen into a series of blunders on the same subject, still more ludicrous. (Antiq. of Mexico, vol. vi. Pl. 16.) So soon had the Aztec science fallen into oblivion after the Conquest!

great cycle into four smaller cycles, or indictions, of thirteen years each. They then adopted two periodical series of signs, one consisting of their numerical dots, up to thirteen, the other, of four hieroglyphics of the years.[1] These latter they repeated in regular succession, setting against each one a number of the corresponding series of dots, continued also in regular succession up to thirteen. The same system was pursued through the four

FIRST INDICTION.			SECOND INDICTION.		
Year of the Cycle.			Year of the Cycle.		
1.	•		14.	•	
2.	• •		15.	• •	
3.	• • •		16.	• • •	
4.	• • • •		17.	• • • •	
5.	• • • • •		18.	• • • • •	
6.	• • • • • •		19.	• • • • • •	
7.	• • • • • • •		20.	• • • • • • •	
8.	• • • • • • • •		21.	• • • • • • • •	
9.	• • • • • • • • •		22.	• • • • • • • • •	
10.	• • • • • • • • • •		23.	• • • • • • • • • •	
11.	• • • • • • • • • • •		24.	• • • • • • • • • • •	
12.	• • • • • • • • • • • •		25.	• • • • • • • • • • • •	
13.	• • • • • • • • • • • • •		26.	• • • • • • • • • • • • •	

indictions, which thus, it will be observed, began always with a different hieroglyphic of the year from the preceding; and in this way each of the hieroglyphics was made to combine successively with each of the numerical signs, but never twice with the same; since four, and thirteen, the factors of fifty-two,—the number of years in the cycle,—must admit of just as

---

[1] These hieroglyphics were a "rabbit," a "reed," a "flint," a "house." They were taken as symbolical of the four elements, air, water, fire, earth, according to Veytia. (Hist. antig., tom. i. cap. 5.) It is not easy to see the connection between the terms "rabbit" and "air," which lead the respective series.*

* [The fleet and noiseless motions of the animal seem to offer an obvious explanation of the symbol.— ED.]

many combinations as are equal to their product. Thus every year had its appropriate symbol, by which it was at once recognized. And this symbol, preceded by the proper number of "bundles" indicating the half-centuries, showed the precise time which had elapsed since the national epoch of 1091.[1] The ingenious contrivance of a periodical series, in place of the cumbrous system of hieroglyphical notation, is not peculiar to the Aztecs, and is to be found among various nations on the Asiatic continent,—the same in principle, though varying materially in arrangement.[2]

The solar calendar above described might have answered all the purposes of the people ; but the priests chose to construct another for themselves. This was called a "lunar reckoning," though nowise accommodated to the revolutions of the moon.[3] It was formed, also, of two periodical series, one of them consisting of thirteen numerical signs, or dots, the other, of the twenty hieroglyphics of the days. But, as the product of these combinations would be only 260, and as some confusion might arise from the repetition of the same terms for the remaining 105 days of the year, they invented a third series, consisting of nine additional hieroglyphics, which, alternating with the two preceding series, rendered it impossible that the three should coincide twice in the same year, or indeed in less than 2340 days ; since $20 \times 13 \times 9 = 2340$.[4] Thirteen was a mystic number, of frequent use in their tables.[5] Why they resorted to that of nine, on this occasion, is not so clear.[6]

---

[1] The foregoing table of two of the four indictions of thirteen years each will make the text more clear. The first column shows the actual year of the great cycle, or "bundle." The second, the numerical dots used in their arithmetic. The third is composed of their hieroglyphics for rabbit, reed, flint, house, in their regular order.

By pursuing the combinations through the two remaining indictions, it will be found that the same number of dots will never coincide with the same hieroglyphic. These tables are generally thrown into the form of wheels, as are those also of their months and days, having a very pretty effect. Several have been published, at different times, from the collections of Siguenza and Boturini. The wheel of the great cycle of fifty-two years is encompassed by a serpent, which was also the symbol of "an age," both with the Persians and Egyptians. Father Toribio seems to misapprehend the nature of these chronological wheels : "Tenian rodelas y escudos, y en ellas pintadas las figuras y armas de sus Demonios con su blason." Hist. de los Indios, MS., Parte 1, cap. 4.

[2] Among the Chinese, Japanese, Moghols, Mantchous, and other families of the Tartar race. Their series are composed of symbols of their five elements, and the twelve zodiacal signs, making a cycle of sixty years' duration. Their several systems are exhibited, in connection with the Mexican, in the luminous pages of Humboldt (Vues des Cordillères, p. 149), who draws important consequences from the comparison, to which we shall have occasion to return hereafter.

[3] In this calendar, the months of the tropical year were distributed into cycles of thirteen days, which, being repeated twenty times,—the number of days in a solar month,—completed the lunar, or astrological, year of 260 days ; when the reckoning began again. "By the contrivance of these *trecenas* (terms of thirteen days) and the cycle of fifty-two years," says Gama, "they formed a luni-solar period,

most exact for astronomical purposes." (Descripcion, Parte 1, p. 27.) He adds that these *trecenas* were suggested by the periods in which the moon is visible before and after conjunction. (Loc. cit.) It seems hardly possible that a people capable of constructing a calendar so accurately on the true principles of solar time should so grossly err as to suppose that in this reckoning they really "represented the daily revolutions of the moon." "The whole Eastern world," says the learned Niebuhr, "has followed the moon in its calendar ; the free scientific division of a vast portion of time is peculiar to the West. Connected with the West is that primeval extinct world which we call the New." History of Rome, vol. i. p. 239.

[4] They were named "companions," and "lords of the night," and were supposed to preside over the night, as the other signs did over the day. Boturini, Idea, p. 57.

[5] Thus, their astrological year was divided into months of thirteen days ; there were thirteen years in their indictions, which contained each three hundred and sixty-five periods of thirteen days, etc. It is a curious fact that the number of lunar months of thirteen days contained in a cycle of fifty-two years, with the intercalation, should correspond precisely with the number of years in the great Sothic period of the Egyptians, namely, 1491 ; a period in which the seasons and festivals came round to the same place in the year again. The coincidence may be accidental. But a people employing periodical series and astrological calculations have generally some meaning in the numbers they select and the combinations to which they lead.

[6] According to Gama (Descripcion, Parte 1, pp. 75, 76), because 360 can be divided by nine without a fraction ; the nine "companions" not being attached to the five complementary days. But 4, a mystic number much used in their arithmetical combinations, would have answered the same purpose

This second calendar rouses a holy indignation in the early Spanish missionaries, and Father Sahagun loudly condemns it, as "most unhallowed, since it is founded neither on natural reason, nor on the influence of the planets, nor on the true course of the year ; but is plainly the work of necromancy, and the fruit of a compact with the Devil ! "[1] One may doubt whether the superstition of those who invented the scheme was greater than that of those who thus impugned it. At all events, we may, without having recourse to supernatural agency, find in the human heart a sufficient explanation of its origin; in that love of power, that has led the priesthood of many a faith to affect a mystery the key to which was in their own keeping.

By means of this calendar, the Aztec priests kept their own records, regulated the festivals and seasons of sacrifice, and made all their astrological calculations.[2] The false science of astrology is natural to a state of society partially civilized, where the mind, impatient of the slow and cautious examination by which alone it can arrive at truth, launches at once into the regions of speculation, and rashly attempts to lift the veil— the impenetrable veil—which is drawn around the mysteries of nature. It is the characteristic of true science to discern the impassable, but not very obvious, limits which divide the province of reason from that of speculation. Such knowledge comes tardily. How many ages have rolled away, in which powers that, rightly directed, might have revealed the great laws of nature, have been wasted in brilliant but barren reveries on alchemy and astrology !

The latter is more particularly the study of a primitive age ; when the mind, incapable of arriving at the stupendous fact that the myriads of minute lights glowing in the firmament are the centres of systems as glorious as our own, is naturally led to speculate on their probable uses, and to connect them in some way or other with man, for whose convenience every other object in the universe seems to have been created. As the eye of the simple child of nature watches, through the long nights, the stately march of the heavenly bodies, and sees the bright hosts coming up, one after another, and changing with the changing seasons of the year, he

---

equally well. In regard to this, McCulloh observes, with much shrewdness, " It seems impossible that the Mexicans, so careful in constructing their cycle, should abruptly terminate it with 360 revolutions, whose natural period of termination is 2340." And he supposes the nine "companions" were used in connection with the cycles of 260 days, in order to throw them into the larger ones, of 2340 ; eight of which, with a ninth of 260 days, he ascertains to be equal to the great solar period of 52 years. (Researches, pp. 207, 208.) This is very plausible. But in fact the combinations of the two first series, forming the cycle of 260 days, were always interrupted at the end of the year, since each new year began with the same hieroglyphic of the days. The third series of the "companions" was intermitted, as above stated, on the five unlucky days which closed the year, in order, if we may believe Boturini, that the first day of the solar year might have annexed to

it the first of the nine "companions," which signified "Lord of the year " (Idea, p. 57) ; a result which might have been equally well secured, without any intermission at all, by taking 5, another favourite number, instead of 9, as the divisor. As it was, however, the cycle, as far as the third series was concerned, did terminate with 360 revolutions. The subject is a perplexing one, and I can hardly hope to have presented it in such a manner as to make it perfectly clear to the reader.

[1] Hist. de Nueva-España, lib. 4, Introd.

[2] " Dans les pays les plus différents," says Benjamin Constant, concluding some sensible reflections on the sources of the sacerdotal power, " chez les peuples de mœurs les plus opposées, le sacerdoce a dû au culte des éléments et des astres un pouvoir dont aujourd'hui nous concevons à peine l'idée." De la Religion (Paris, 1825), lib. 3, ch. 5.

naturally associates them with those seasons, as the periods over which they hold a mysterious influence. In the same manner, he connects their appearance with any interesting event of the time, and explores, in their flaming characters, the destinies of the new-born infant.[1] Such is the origin of astrology, the false lights of which have continued from the earliest ages to dazzle and bewilder mankind, till they have faded away in the superior illumination of a comparatively recent period.

The astrological scheme of the Aztecs was founded less on the planetary influences than on those of the arbitrary signs they had adopted for the months and days. The character of the leading sign in each lunar cycle of thirteen days gave a complexion to the whole ; though this was qualified in some degree by the signs of the succeeding days, as well as by those of the hours. It was in adjusting these conflicting forces that the great art of the diviner was shown. In no country, not even in ancient Egypt, were the dreams of the astrologer more implicitly deferred to. On the birth of a child, he was instantly summoned. The time of the event was accurately ascertained ; and the family hung in trembling suspense, as the minister of Heaven cast the horoscope of the infant and unrolled the dark volume of destiny. The influence of the priest was confessed by the Mexican in the very first breath which he inhaled.[2]

We know little further of the astronomical attainments of the Aztecs. That they were acquainted with the cause of eclipses is evident from the representation, on their maps, of the disk of the moon projected on that of the sun.[3] Whether they had arranged a system of constellations is uncertain ; though that they recognized some of the most obvious, as the Pleiades, for example, is evident from the fact that they regulated their festivals by them. We know of no astronomical instruments used by them, except the dial.[4] An immense circular block of carved stone, disinterred in 1790, in the great square of Mexico, has supplied an acute and learned scholar with the means of establishing some interesting facts in regard to Mexican science.[5] This colossal fragment, on which the calendar is engraved,

---

[1] "It is a gentle and affectionate thought,
    That, in immeasurable heights above us,
  At our first birth the wreath of love was woven
  With sparkling stars for flowers."
          COLERIDGE : Translation of
                Wallenstein, act 2, sc. 4.
Schiller is more true to poetry than history, when he tells us, in the beautiful passage of which this is part, that the worship of the stars took the place of classic mythology. It existed long before it.
[2] Gama has given us a complete almanac of the astrological year, with the appropriate signs and divisions, showing with what scientific skill it was adapted to its various uses. (Descripcion, Parte 1, pp. 25-31, 62-76.) Sahagun has devoted a whole book to explaining the mystic import and value of these signs, with a minuteness that may enable one to cast up a scheme of nativity for himself. (Hist. de Nueva-España, lib. 4.) It is evident he fully believed the magic wonders which he told. "It was a deceitful art," he says, "pernicious and idolatrous, and was never contrived by human reason." The good father was certainly no philosopher.

[3] See, among others, the Cod. Tel.-Rem., Part 4, Pl. 22, ap. Antiq. of Mexico, vol. i.
[4] "It can hardly be doubted," says Lord Kingsborough, "that the Mexicans were acquainted with many scientifical instruments of strange invention, as compared with our own ; whether the *telescope* may not have been of the number is uncertain ; but the thirteenth plate of M. Dupaix's *Monuments*, Part Second, which represents a man holding something of a similar nature to his eye, affords reason to suppose that they knew how to improve the powers of vision." (Antiq. of Mexico, vol. vi. p. 15, note.) The instrument alluded to is rudely carved on a conical rock. It is raised no higher than the neck of the person who holds it, and looks—to my thinking—as much like a musket as a telescope ; though I shall not infer the use of firearms among the Aztecs from this circumstance. (See vol. iv. Pl. 15.) Captain Dupaix, however, in his commentary on the drawing, sees quite as much in it as his lordship. Ibid., vol. v. p. 241.
[5] Gama, Descripcion, Parte 1, sec. 4 : Parte 2, Apend.—Besides this colossal fragment, Gama met

shows that they had the means of settling the hours of the day with precision, the periods of the solstices and of the equinoxes, and that of the transit of the sun across the zenith of Mexico.[1]

We cannot contemplate the astronomical science of the Mexicans, so disproportioned to their progress in other walks of civilization, without astonishment. An acquaintance with some of the more obvious principles of astronomy is within the reach of the rudest people. With a little care, they may learn to connect the regular changes of the seasons with those of the place of the sun at his rising and setting. They may follow the march of the great luminary through the heavens, by watching the stars that first brighten on his evening track or fade in his morning beams. They may measure a revolution of the moon, by marking her phases, and may even form a general idea of the number of such revolutions in a solar year. But that they should be capable of accurately adjusting their festivals by the movements of the heavenly bodies, and should fix the true length of the tropical year, with a precision unknown to the great philosophers of antiquity, could be the result only of a long series of nice and patient observations, evincing no slight progress in civilization.[2] But whence could the rude inhabitants of these mountain-regions have derived this curious erudition? Not from the barbarous hordes who roamed over the higher latitudes of the North; nor from the more polished races on the Southern continent, with whom, it is apparent, they had no intercourse. If we are driven, in our embarrassment, like the greatest astronomer of our age, to seek the solution among the civilized communities of Asia, we shall still be perplexed by finding, amidst general resemblance of outline, sufficient discrepancy in the details to vindicate, in the judgments of many, the Aztec claim to originality.[3]

I shall conclude the account of Mexican science with that of a remarkable festival, celebrated by the natives at the termination of the great cycle of fifty-two years. We have seen, in the preceding chapter, their tradition of the destruction of the world at four successive epochs. They looked forward confidently to another such catastrophe, to take place, like the preceding, at the close of a cycle, when the sun was to be effaced from the heavens, the human race from the earth, and when the darkness of chaos was to settle on the habitable globe. The cycle would end in the latter

---

with some others, designed, probably, for similar scientific uses, at Chapoltepec. Before he had leisure to examine them, however, they were broken up for materials to build a furnace,—a fate not unlike that which has too often befallen the monuments of ancient art in the Old World.

[1] In his second treatise on the cylindrical stone, Gama dwells more at large on its scientific construction, as a vertical sundial, in order to dispel the doubts of some sturdy sceptics on this point. (Descripcion, Parte 2, Apend. 1.) The civil day was distributed by the Mexicans into sixteen parts, and began, like that of most of the Asiatic nations, with sunrise. M. de Humboldt, who probably never saw Gama's second treatise, allows only eight intervals. Vues des Cordillères. p. 128.

[2] "Un calendrier," exclaims the enthusiastic Carli, "qui est réglé sur la révolution annuelle du soleil, non-seulement par l'addition de cinq jours tous les ans, mais encore par la correction du bissextile, doit sans doute être regardé comme une opération déduite d'une étude réfléchie, et d'une grande combinaison. Il faut donc supposer chez ces peuples une suite d'observations astronomiques, une idée distincte de la sphère, de la déclinaison de l'écliptique, et l'usage d'un calcul concernant les jours et les heures des apparitions solaires." Lettres Américaines, tom. i. let. 23.

[3] La Place, who suggests the analogy, frankly admits the difficulty. Système du Monde, lib. 5, ch. 3.

part of December, and as the dreary season of the winter solstice approached, and the diminished light of day gave melancholy presage of its speedy extinction, their apprehensions increased; and on the arrival of the five "unlucky" days which closed the year they abandoned themselves to despair.[1]   They broke in pieces the little images of their household gods, in whom they no longer trusted.   The holy fires were suffered to go out in the temples, and none were lighted in their own dwellings.   Their furniture and domestic utensils were destroyed; their garments torn in pieces; and everything was thrown into disorder, for the coming of the evil genii who were to descend on the desolate earth.

On the evening of the last day, a procession of priests, assuming the dress and ornaments of their gods, moved from the capital towards a lofty mountain, about two leagues distant.   They carried with them a noble victim, the flower of their captives, and an apparatus for kindling the *new fire*, the success of which was an augury of the renewal of the cycle.   On reaching the summit of the mountain, the procession paused till midnight; when, as the constellation of the Pleiades approached the zenith,[2] the *new fire* was kindled by the friction of the sticks placed on the wounded breast of the victim.[3]   The flame was soon communicated to a funeral pile, on which the body of the slaughtered captive was thrown.   As the light streamed up towards heaven, shouts of joy and triumph burst forth from the countless multitudes who covered the hills, the terraces of the temples, and the house-tops, with eyes anxiously bent on the mount of sacrifice. Couriers, with torches lighted at the blazing beacon, rapidly bore them over every part of the country; and the cheering element was seen brightening on altar and hearthstone, for the circuit of many a league, long before the sun, rising on his accustomed track, gave assurance that a new cycle had commenced its march, and that the laws of nature were not to be reversed for the Aztecs.

The following thirteen days were given up to festivity.   The houses were cleansed and whitened.   The broken vessels were replaced by new ones.   The people, dressed in their gayest apparel, and crowned with garlands and chaplets of flowers, thronged in joyous procession to offer up their oblations and thanksgivings in the temples.   Dances and games were instituted, emblematical of the regeneration of the world.   It was the carnival of the Aztecs; or rather the national jubilee, the great secular

---

[1] M. Jomard errs in placing the *new fire*, with which ceremony the old cycle properly concluded, at the winter solstice.   It was not till the 26th of December, if Gama is right.   The cause of M. Jomard's error is his fixing it before, instead of after, the complementary days.   See his sensible letter on the Aztec calendar, in the Vues des Cordillères, p. 309.

[2] At the actual moment of their culmination, according to both Sahagun (Hist. de Nueva-España, lib. 4, Apend.) and Torquemada (Monarch. Ind., lib. 10, cap. 33, 36).   But this could not be, as that took place at midnight, in November, so late as the

last secular festival, which was early in Montezuma's reign, in 1507.   (Gama, Descripcion, Parte 1, p. 50, nota.—Humboldt, Vues des Cordillères, pp. 181, 182.)   The longer we postpone the beginning of the new cycle, the greater must be the discrepancy.

[3] "On his bare breast the cedar boughs are
        laid ;
    On his bare breast, dry sedge and odor-
        ous gums,
    Laid ready to receive the sacred spark,
    And blaze, to herald the ascending Sun,
    Upon his living altar."
            SOUTHEY's Madoc, part 2, canto 26.

festival, like that of the Romans, or ancient Etruscans, which few alive had witnessed before, or could expect to see again.[1]

M. de Humboldt remarked, many years ago, " It were to be wished that some government would publish at its own expense the remains of the ancient American civilization ; for it is only by the comparison of several monuments that we can succeed in discovering the meaning of these allegories, which are partly astronomical and partly mystic." This enlightened wish has now been realized, not by any government, but by a private individual, Lord Kingsborough. The great work published under his auspices, and so often cited in this Introduction, appeared in London in 1830. When completed it will reach to nine volumes, seven of which are now before the public. Some idea of its magnificence may be formed by those who have not seen it, from the fact that copies of it, with coloured plates, sold originally at £175, and, with uncoloured, at £120. The price has been since much reduced. It is designed to exhibit a complete view of the ancient Aztec MSS., with such few interpretations as exist ; the beautiful drawings of Castañeda relating to Central America, with the commentary of Dupaix; the unpublished history of Father Sahagun ; and, last, not least, the copious annotations of his lordship.

Too much cannot be said of the mechanical execution of the book,—its splendid typography, the apparent accuracy and the delicacy of the drawings, and the sumptuous quality of the materials. Yet the purchaser would have been saved some superfluous expense, and the reader much inconvenience, if the letterpress had been in volumes of an ordinary size. But it is not uncommon, in works on this magnificent plan, to find utility in some measure sacrificed to show.

The collection of Aztec MSS., if not perfectly complete, is very extensive, and reflects great credit on the diligence and research of the compiler. It strikes one as strange, however, that not a single document should have been drawn from Spain. Peter Martyr speaks of a number having been brought thither in his time. (De Insulis nuper Inventis, p. 368.) The Marquis Spineto examined one in the Escorial, being the same with the Mendoza Codex, and perhaps the original, since that at Oxford is but a copy. (Lectures, Lect. 7.) Mr. Waddilove, chaplain of the British embassy to Spain, gave a particular account of one to Dr. Robertson, which he saw in the same library and considered an Aztec calendar. Indeed, it is scarcely possible that the frequent voyagers to the New World should not have furnished the mother-country with abundant specimens of this most interesting feature of Aztec civilization. Nor should we fear that the present liberal government would seclude these treasures from the inspection of the scholar.

Much cannot be said in favour of the arrangement of these codices. In some of them, as the Mendoza Codex, for example, the plates are not even numbered ; and one who would study them by the corresponding interpretation must often bewilder himself in the maze of hieroglyphics, without a clue to guide him. Neither is there any attempt to enlighten us as to the positive value and authenticity of the respective documents, or even their previous history, beyond a barren reference to the particular library from which they have been borrowed. Little light, indeed, can be expected on these matters ; but we have not that little. The defect of arrangement is chargeable on other parts of the work. Thus, for instance, the sixth book of Sahagun is transferred from the body of the history to which it belongs, to a preceding volume ; while the grand hypothesis of his lordship, for which the work was concocted, is huddled into notes, hitched on random

---

[1] I borrow the words of the summons by which the people were called to the *ludi seculares*, the secular games of ancient Rome, " *quos nec spectâsset quisquam, nec spectaturus esset.*" (Suetonius, Vita Tib. Claudii, lib. 5.) The old Mexican chroniclers warm into something like eloquence in their descriptions of the Aztec festival. (Torquemada, Monarch. Ind., lib. 10, cap. 33.—Toribio Hist. de los Indios, MS., Parte 1, cap. 5.—Sahagun, Hist. de Nueva-España, lib. 7, cap. 9-12. See, also, Gama, Descripcion, Parte 1, pp. 52-54,—Clavigero, Stor. del Messico, tom. ii. pp. 84-86.) The English reader will find a more brilliant colouring of the same scene in the canto of Madoc above cited —" On the Close of the Century."

passages of the text, with a good deal less connection than the stories of Queen Scheherezade, in the " Arabian Nights," and not quite so entertaining.

The drift of Lord Kingsborough's speculations is, to establish the colonization of Mexico by the Israelites. To this the whole battery of his logic and learning is directed. For this, hieroglyphics are unriddled, manuscripts compared, monuments delineated. His theory, however, whatever be its merits, will scarcely become popular ; since, instead of being exhibited in a clear and comprehensive form, readily embraced by the mind, it is spread over an infinite number of notes, thickly sprinkled with quotations from languages ancient and modern, till the weary reader, floundering about in the ocean of fragments, with no light to guide him, feels like Milton's Devil, working his way through chaos,—

> " Neither sea.
> Nor good dry land ; nigh foundered, on he fares."

It would be unjust, however, not to admit that the noble author, if his logic is not always convincing, shows much acuteness in detecting analogies ; that he displays familiarity with his subject, and a fund of erudition, though it often runs to waste ; that, whatever be the defects of arrangement, he has brought together a most rich collection of unpublished materials to illustrate the Aztec and, in a wider sense, American antiquities ; and that by this munificent undertaking, which no government, probably, would have, and few individuals could have, executed, he has entitled himself to the lasting gratitude of every friend of science.

Another writer whose works must be diligently consulted by every student of Mexican antiquities is Antonio Gama. His life contains as few incidents as those of most scholars. He was born at Mexico, in 1735, of a respectable family, and was bred to the law. He early showed a preference for mathematical studies, conscious that in this career lay his strength. In 1771 he communicated his observations on the eclipse of that year to the French astronomer M. de Lalande, who published them in Paris, with high commendations of the author. Gama's increasing reputation attracted the attention of government ; and he was employed by it in various scientific labours of importance. His great passion, however, was the study of Indian antiquities. He made himself acquainted with the history of the native races, their traditions, their languages, and, as far as possible, their hieroglyphics. He had an opportunity of showing the fruits of this preparatory training, and his skill as an antiquary, on the discovery of the great calendar-stone, in 1790. He produced a masterly treatise on this, and another Aztec monument, explaining the objects to which they were devoted, and pouring a flood of light on the astronomical science of the aborigines, their mythology, and their astrological system. He afterwards continued his investigations in the same path, and wrote treatises on the dial, hieroglyphics, and arithmetic of the Indians. These, however, were not given to the world till a few years since, when they were published, together with a reprint of the former work, under the auspices of the industrious Bustamante. Gama died in 1802, leaving behind him a reputation for great worth in private life,—one in which the bigotry that seems to enter too frequently into the character of the Spanish-Mexican was tempered by the liberal feelings of a man of science. His reputation as a writer stands high for patient acquisition, accuracy, and acuteness. His conclusions are neither warped by the love of theory so common in the philosopher, nor by the easy credulity so natural to the antiquary. He feels his way with the caution of a mathematician, whose steps are demonstrations. M. de Humboldt was largely indebted to his first work, as he has emphatically acknowledged. But, notwithstanding the eulogiums of this popular writer, and his own merits, Gama's treatises are rarely met with out of New Spain, and his name can hardly be said to have a transatlantic reputation.

CHAPTER V.

IT is hardly possible that a nation so far advanced as the Aztecs in mathematical science should not have made considerable progress in the mechanical arts, which are so nearly connected with it. Indeed, intellectual progress of any kind implies a degree of refinement that requires a certain cultivation of both useful and elegant art. The savage wandering through the wide forest, without shelter for his head or raiment for his back, knows no other wants than those of animal appetites, and, when they are satisfied, seems to himself to have answered the only ends of existence. But man, in society, feels numerous desires, and artificial tastes spring up, accommodated to the various relations in which he is placed, and perpetually stimulating his invention to devise new expedients to gratify them.

There is a wide difference in the mechanical skill of different nations ; but the difference is still greater in the inventive power which directs this skill and makes it available. Some nations seem to have no power beyond that of imitation, or, if they possess invention, have it in so low a degree that they are constantly repeating the same idea, without a shadow of alteration or improvement ; as the bird builds precisely the same kind of nest which those of its own species built at the beginning of the world. Such, for example, are the Chinese, who have probably been familiar for ages with the germs of some discoveries, of little practical benefit to themselves, but which, under the influence of European genius, have reached a degree of excellence that has wrought an important change in the constitution of society.

Far from looking back and forming itself slavishly on the past, it is characteristic of the European intellect to be ever on the advance. Old discoveries become the basis of new ones. It passes onward from truth to truth, connecting the whole by a succession of links, as it were, into the great chain of science which is to encircle and bind together the universe. The light of learning is shed over the labours of art. New avenues are opened for the communication both of person and of thought. New facilities are devised for subsistence. Personal comforts, of every kind, are inconceivably multiplied, and brought within the reach of the poorest. Secure of these, the thoughts travel into a nobler region than that of the senses ; and the appliances of art are made to minister to the demands of an elegant taste and a higher moral culture.

The same enlightened spirit, applied to agriculture, raises it from a mere mechanical drudgery, or the barren formula of traditional precepts, to the dignity of a science. As the composition of the earth is analyzed, man learns the capacity of the soil that he cultivates ; and, as his empire is gradually extended over the elements of nature, he gains the power to stimulate her to her most bountiful and various production. It is with satisfaction that we can turn to the land of our fathers, as the one in which the experiment has been conducted on the broadest scale and attended with results that the world has never before witnessed. With equal truth, we may point to the Anglo-Saxon race in both hemispheres, as that whose enterprising genius has contributed most essentially to the great interests of humanity, by the application of science to the useful arts.

Husbandry, to a very limited extent, indeed, was practised by most of the rude tribes of North America. Wherever a natural opening in the forest, or a rich strip of *interval*, met their eyes, or a green slope was found along the rivers, they planted it with beans and Indian corn.[1] The cultivation was slovenly in the extreme, and could not secure the improvident natives from the frequent recurrence of desolating famines. Still, that they tilled the soil at all was a peculiarity which honourably distinguished them from other tribes of hunters, and raised them one degree higher in the scale of civilization.

Agriculture in Mexico was in the same advanced state as the other arts of social life. In few countries, indeed, has it been more respected. It was closely interwoven with the civil and religious institutions of the nation. There were peculiar deities to preside over it ; the names of the months and of the religious festivals had more or less reference to it. The public taxes, as we have seen, were often paid in agricultural produce. All except the soldiers and great nobles, even the inhabitants of the cities, cultivated the soil. The work was chiefly done by the men ; the women scattering the seed, husking the corn, and taking part only in the lighter labours of the field.[2] In this they presented an honourable contrast to the other tribes of the continent, who imposed the burden of agriculture, severe as it is in the North, on their women.[3] Indeed, the sex was as tenderly regarded by the Aztecs in this matter, as it is, in most parts of Europe, at the present day.

There was no want of judgment in the management of their ground.

---

[1] This latter grain, according to Humboldt, was found by the Europeans in the New World, from the South of Chili to Pennsylvania (Essai politique, tom. ii. p. 408); he might have added, to the St. Lawrence. Our Puritan fathers found it in abundance on the New England coast, wherever they landed. See Morton, New England's Memorial (Boston, 1826), p. 68.—Gookin, Massachusetts, Historical Collections, chap. 3.

[2] Torquemada, Monarch. Ind., lib. 13, cap. 31.— "Admirable example for our times," exclaims the good father, "when women are not only unfit for the labours of the field, but have too much levity to attend to their own household !"

[3] A striking contrast also to the Egyptians, with whom some antiquaries are disposed to identify the ancient Mexicans. Sophocles notices the effeminacy of the men in Egypt, who stayed at home tending the loom, while their wives were employed in severe labours out of doors :—

Ὦ πάντ᾽ ἐκείνω τοῖς ἐν Αἰγύπτῳ νόμοις
Φύσιν κατεικασθέντε καὶ βίου τροφάς,
Ἐκεῖ γὰρ οἱ μὲν ἄρσενες κατὰ στέγας
Θακοῦσιν ἱστουργοῦντες· αἱ δὲ σύννομοι
Τἄξω βίου τροφεῖα πορσύνουσ᾽ ἀεί.

Sophocl., Œdip. Col., v. 337-341.

When somewhat exhausted, it was permitted to recover by lying fallow. Its extreme dryness was relieved by canals, with which the land was partially irrigated; and the same end was promoted by severe penalties against the destruction of the woods, with which the country, as already noticed, was well covered before the Conquest. Lastly, they provided for their harvests ample granaries, which were admitted by the Conquerors to be of admirable construction. In this provision we see the forecast of civilized man.[1]

Among the most important articles of husbandry, we may notice the banana, whose facility of cultivation and exuberant returns are so fatal to habits of systematic and hardy industry.[2] Another celebrated plant was the cacao, the fruit of which furnished the chocolate,—from the Mexican *chocolatl*,—now so common a beverage throughout Europe.[3] The vanilla, confined to a small district of the sea-coast, was used for the same purposes, of flavouring their food and drink, as with us.[4] The great staple of the country, as, indeed, of the American continent, was maize, or Indian corn, which grew freely along the valleys, and up the steep sides of the Cordilleras to the high level of the table-land. The Aztecs were as curious in its preparation, and as well instructed in its manifold uses, as the most expert New England housewife. Its gigantic stalks, in these equinoctial regions, afford a saccharine matter, not found to the same extent in northern latitudes, and supplied the natives with sugar little inferior to that of the cane itself, which was not introduced among them till after the Conquest.[5] But the miracle of nature was the great Mexican aloe, or *maguey*, whose clustering pyramids of flowers, towering above their dark coronals of leaves, were seen sprinkled over many a broad acre of the table-land. As we have already noticed, its bruised leaves afforded a paste from which paper was manufactured;[6] its juice was fermented into an intoxicating beverage, *pulque*, of which the natives, to this day, are excessively fond;[7] its leaves further supplied an impenetrable thatch for the more humble dwellings; thread, of which coarse stuffs were made, and strong cords, were drawn from its tough and twisted fibres; pins and

[1] Torquemada, Monarch. Ind., lib. 13, cap. 32.— Clavigero, Stor. del Messico, tom. ii. pp. 153-155. —"Jamas padeciéron hambre," says the former writer, "sino en pocas ocasiones." If these famines were rare, they were very distressing, however, and lasted very long. Comp. Ixtlilxochitl, Hist. Chich., MS., cap. 41, 71, et alibi.

[2] Oviedo considers the *musa* an imported plant; and Hernandez, in his copious catalogue, makes no mention of it at all. But Humboldt, who has given much attention to it, concludes that, if some species were brought into the country, others were indigenous. (Essai politique, tom. ii. pp. 382-388.) If we may credit Clavigero, the banana was the forbidden fruit that tempted our poor mother Eve! Stor. del Messico, tom. i. p. 49, nota.

[3] Rel. d'un gentil' huomo, ap. Ramusio, tom. iii. fol. 306.—Hernandez, De Historiâ Plantarum Novæ Hispaniæ (Matriti, 1790), lib. 6, cap. 87.

[4] Sahagun, Hist. de Nueva-España, lib. 8, cap. 13, et alibi.

[5] Carta del Lic. Zuazo, MS.—He extols the honey of the maize, as equal to that of bees. (Also Oviedo, Hist. natural de las Indias, cap. 4, ap. Barcia, tom. i.) Hernandez, who celebrates the manifold ways in which the maize was prepared, derives it from the Haytian word *mahiz*. Hist. Plantarum, lib. 6, cap. 44, 45.

[6] And is still, in one spot at least, San Angel,— three leagues from the capital. Another mill was to have been established, a few years since, in Puebla. Whether this has actually been done, I am ignorant. See the Report of the Committee on Agriculture to the Senate of the United States, March 12, 1838.

[7] Before the Revolution, the duties on the *pulque* formed so important a branch of revenue that the cities of Mexico, Puebla, and Toluca alone paid $817,739 to government. (Humboldt, Essai politique, tom. ii. p. 47.) It requires time to reconcile Europeans to the peculiar flavour of this liquor, on the merits of which they are consequently much divided. There is but one opinion among the natives. The English reader will find a good account of its manufacture in Ward's Mexico, vol. ii. pp. 55-60.

E

needles were made of the thorns at the extremity of its leaves ; and the root, when properly cooked, was converted into a palatable and nutritious food. The *agave*, in short, was meat, drink, clothing, and writing-materials for the Aztec ! Surely, never did Nature enclose in so compact a form so many of the elements of human comfort and civilization ![1]

It would be obviously out of place to enumerate in these pages all the varieties of plants, many of them of medicinal virtue, which have been introduced from Mexico into Europe. Still less can I attempt a catalogue of its flowers, which, with their variegated and gaudy colours, form the greatest attraction of our greenhouses. The opposite climates embraced within the narrow latitudes of New Spain have given to it, probably, the richest and most diversified flora to be found in any country on the globe. These different products were systematically arranged by the Aztecs, who understood their properties, and collected them into nurseries, more extensive than any then existing in the Old World. It is not improbable that they suggested the idea of those "gardens of plants" which were introduced into Europe not many years after the Conquest.[2]

The Mexicans were as well acquainted with the mineral as with the vegetable treasures of their kingdom. Silver, lead, and tin they drew from the mines of Tasco ; copper from the mountains of Zacotollan. These were taken not only from the crude masses on the surface, but from veins wrought in the solid rock, into which they opened extensive galleries. In fact, the traces of their labours furnished the best indications for the early Spanish miners.[3] Gold, found on the surface, or gleaned from the beds of rivers, was cast into bars, or, in the form of dust, made part of the regular tribute of the southern provinces of the empire. The use of iron, with which the soil was impregnated, was unknown to them. Notwithstanding its abundance, it demands so many processes to prepare it for use that it has commonly been one of the last metals pressed into the service of man. The age of iron has followed that of brass, in fact as well as in fiction.[4]

---

[1] Hernandez enumerates the several species of the maguey, which are turned to these manifold uses, in his learned work, De Hist. Plantarum. (Lib. 7, cap. 71, et seq.) M. de Humboldt considers them all varieties of the *Agave Americana*, familiar in the southern parts both of the United States and Europe. (Essai politique, tom. ii. p. 487, et seq.) This opinion has brought on him a rather sour rebuke from our countryman the late Dr. Perrine, who pronounces them a distinct species from the American *agave*, and regards one of the kinds, the *pita*, from which the fine thread is obtained, as a totally distinct genus. (See the Report of the Committee on Agriculture.) Yet the Baron may find authority for all the properties ascribed by him to the maguey, in the most accredited writers who have resided more or less time in Mexico. See, among others, Hernandez, ubi supra.—Sahagun, Hist. de Nueva-España, lib. 9, cap. 2 ; lib. 11, cap. 7.—Toribio, Hist. de los Indios, MS., Parte 3, cap. 19.—Carta del Lic. Zuazo, MS. The last, speaking of the maguey, which produces the fermented drink, says expressly, "With what remain of these leaves they manufacture excellent and very fine cloth, resembling

holland, or the finest linen." It cannot be denied, however, that Dr. Perrine shows himself intimately acquainted with the structure and habits of the tropical plants, which, with such patriotic spirit, he proposed to introduce into Florida.

[2] The first regular establishment of this kind, according to Carli, was at Padua, in 1545. Lettres Américaines, tom. i. chap. 21.

[3] [Though I have conformed to the views of Humboldt in regard to the knowledge of mining possessed by the ancient Mexicans, Señor Ramirez thinks the conclusions to which I have been led are not warranted by the ancient writers. From the language of Bernal Diaz and of Sahagun, in particular, he infers that their only means of obtaining the precious metals was by gathering such detached masses as were found on the surface of the ground or in the beds of the rivers. The small amount of silver in their possession he regards as an additional proof of their ignorance of the proper method and their want of the requisite tools for extracting it from the earth. See Ramirez, Notas y Esclarecimientos, p. 73.]

[4] P. Martyr, De Orbe Novo, Decades (Compluti,

They found a substitute in an alloy of tin and copper, and, with tools made of this bronze, could cut not only metals, but, with the aid of a silicious dust, the hardest substances, as basalt, porphyry, amethysts, and emeralds.[1]   They fashioned these last, which were found very large, into many curious and fantastic forms.   They cast, also, vessels of gold and silver, carving them with their metallic chisels in a very delicate manner. Some of the silver vases were so large that a man could not encircle them with his arms.   They imitated very nicely the figures of animals, and, what was extraordinary, could mix the metals in such a manner that the feathers of a bird, or the scales of a fish, should be alternately of gold and silver. The Spanish goldsmiths admitted their superiority over themselves in these ingenious works.[2]

They employed another tool, made of *itztli,* or obsidian, a dark transparent mineral, exceedingly hard, found in abundance in their hills.   They made it into knives, razors, and their serrated swords.   It took a keen edge, though soon blunted.   With this they wrought the various stones and alabasters employed in the construction of their public works and principal dwellings.   I shall defer a more particular account of these to the body of the narrative, and will only add here that the entrances and angles of the buildings were profusely ornamented with images, sometimes of their fantastic deities, and frequently of animals.[3]   The latter were executed with great accuracy.   "The former," according to Torquemada, "were the hideous reflection of their own souls.   And it was not till after they had been converted to Christianity that they could model the true figure of a man."[4]   The old chronicler's facts are well founded, whatever we may think of his reasons.   The allegorical phantasms of his religion, no doubt, gave a direction to the Aztec artist, in his delineation of the human figure; supplying him with an imaginary beauty in the personification of divinity itself.   As these superstitions lost their hold on his mind, it opened to the influences of a purer taste; and, after the Conquest, the Mexicans furnished many examples of correct, and some of beautiful, portraiture.

1530), dec. 5, p. 191.—Acosta, lib. 4, cap. 3.—Humboldt, Essai politique, tom. iii. pp. 114-125.—Torquemada, Monarch. Ind., lib. 13, cap. 34.
"Men wrought in brass," says Hesiod, "when iron did not exist."

Χαλκῷ δ' ἐργάζοντο· μέλας δ' οὐκ ἔσκε
σίδηρος.

Hesiod,
Ἔργα καὶ Ἡμεραι.

The Abbé Raynal contends that the ignorance of iron must necessarily have kept the Mexicans in a low state of civilization, since without it "they could have produced no work in metal, worth looking at, no masonry nor architecture, engraving nor sculpture." (History of the Indies, Eng. trans., vol. iii. b. 6.) Iron, however, if known, was little used by the ancient Egyptians, whose mighty monuments were hewn with bronze tools; while their weapons and domestic utensils were of the same material, as appears from the green colour given to them in their paintings.

[1] Gama, Descripcion, Parte 2, pp. 25-29.—Torquemada, Monarch. Ind., ubi supra.
[2] Sahagun, Hist. de Nueva-España, lib. 9, cap. 15-17.—Boturini, Idea, p. 77.—Torquemada, Monarch. Ind., loc. cit.—Herrera, who says they could also enamel, commends the skill of the Mexican goldsmiths in making birds and animals with movable wings and limbs, in a most curious fashion. (Hist. general, dec. 2, lib. 7, cap. 15.) Sir John Maundeville, as usual,

"With his hair on end
At his own wonders,"

notices the "gret marvayle" of similar pieces of mechanism at the court of the grand Chane of Cathay. See his Voiage and Travaile, chap. 20.
[3] Herrera, Hist. general, dec. 2, lib. 7, cap. 11.—Torquemada, Monarch. Ind., lib. 13, cap. 34.—Gama, Descripcion, Parte 2, pp. 27, 28.
[4] "Parece, que permitia Dios, que la figura de sus cuerpos se asimilase á la que tenian sus almas por el pecado, en que siempre permanecian." Monarch. Ind., lib. 13, cap. 34.

Sculptured images were so numerous that the foundations of the cathedral in the *plaza mayor*, the great square of Mexico, are said to be entirely composed of them.[1] This spot may, indeed, be regarded as the Aztec forum,—the great depository of the treasures of ancient sculpture, which now lie hid in its bosom. Such monuments are spread all over the capital, however, and a new cellar can hardly be dug, or foundation laid, without turning up some of the mouldering relics of barbaric art. But they are little heeded, and, if not wantonly broken in pieces at once, are usually worked into the rising wall or supports of the new edifice.[2] Two celebrated bas-reliefs of the last Montezuma and his father, cut in the solid rock, in the beautiful groves of Chapoltepec, were deliberately destroyed, as late as the last century, by order of the government![3] The monuments of the barbarian meet with as little respect from civilized man as those of the civilized man from the barbarian.[4]

The most remarkable piece of sculpture yet disinterred is the great calendar-stone, noticed in the preceding chapter. It consists of dark porphyry, and in its original dimensions, as taken from the quarry, is computed to have weighed nearly fifty tons. It was transported from the mountains beyond Lake Chalco, a distance of many leagues, over a broken country intersected by watercourses and canals. In crossing a bridge which traversed one of these latter, in the capital, the supports gave way, and the huge mass was precipitated into the water, whence it was with difficulty recovered. The fact that so enormous a fragment of porphyry could be thus safely carried for leagues, in the face of such obstacles, and without the aid of cattle,—for the Aztecs, as already mentioned, had no animals of draught,—suggests to us no mean ideas of their mechanical skill and of their machinery, and implies a degree of cultivation little inferior to that demanded for the geometrical and astronomical science displayed in the inscriptions on this very stone.[5]

The ancient Mexicans made utensils of earthenware for the ordinary purposes of domestic life, numerous specimens of which still exist.[6] They made cups and vases of a lackered or painted wood, impervious to wet, and gaudily coloured. Their dyes were obtained from both mineral and

---

[1] Clavigero, Stor. del Messico, tom. ii. p. 195.

[2] Gama, Descripcion, Parte 1, p. 1. Besides the *plaza mayor*, Gama points out the Square of Tlatelolco, as a great cemetery of ancient relics. It was the quarter to which the Mexicans retreated, on the siege of the capital.

[3] Torquemada, Monarch. Ind., lib. 13, cap. 34.—Gama, Descripcion, Parte 2, pp. 81–83.—These statues are repeatedly noticed by the old writers. The last was destroyed in 1754, when it was seen by Gama, who highly commends the execution of it. Ibid.

[4] This wantonness of destruction provokes the bitter animadversion of Martyr, whose enlightened mind respected the vestiges of civilization wherever found. "The conquerors," he says, "seldom repaired the buildings that were defaced. They would rather sack twenty stately cities than erect one good edifice." De Orbe Novo, dec. 5, cap. 10.

[5] Gama, Descripcion Parte 1, pp. 110–114.—

Humboldt, Essai politique, tom. ii. p. 40.—Ten thousand men were employed in the transportation of this enormous mass, according to Tezozomoc, whose narrative, with all the accompanying prodigies, is minutely transcribed by Bustamante. The Licentiate shows an appetite for the marvellous which might excite the envy of a monk of the Middle Ages. (See Descripcion, nota, loc. cit.) The English traveller Latrobe accommodates the wonders of nature and art very well to each other, by suggesting that these great masses of stone were transported by means of the mastodon, whose remains are occasionally disinterred in the Mexican Valley. Rambler in Mexico, p. 145.

[6] A great collection of ancient pottery, with various other specimens of Aztec art, the gift of Messrs. Poinsett and Keating, is deposited in the Cabinet of the American Philosophical Society, at Philadelphia. See the Catalogue, ap. Transactions, vol. iii. p. 510.

vegetable substances. Among them was the rich crimson of the cochineal, the modern rival of the famed Tyrian purple. It was introduced into Europe from Mexico, where the curious little insect was nourished with great care on plantations of cactus, since fallen into neglect.[1] The natives were thus enabled to give a brilliant colouring to the webs which were manufactured, of every degree of fineness, from the cotton raised in abundance throughout the warmer regions of the country. They had the art, also, of interweaving with these the delicate hair of rabbits and other animals, which made a cloth of great warmth as well as beauty, of a kind altogether original; and on this they often laid a rich embroidery, of birds, flowers, or some other fanciful device.[2]

But the art in which they most delighted was their *plumaje*, or feather-work. With this they could produce all the effect of a beautiful mosaic. The gorgeous plumage of the tropical birds, especially of the parrot tribe, afforded every variety of colour; and the fine down of the humming-bird, which revelled in swarms among the honeysuckle bowers of Mexico, supplied them with soft aerial tints that gave an exquisite finish to the picture. The feathers, pasted on a fine cotton web, were wrought into dresses for the wealthy, hangings for apartments, and ornaments for the temples. No one of the American fabrics excited such admiration in Europe, whither numerous specimens were sent by the Conquerors. It is to be regretted that so graceful an art should have been suffered to fall into decay.[3]

There were no shops in Mexico, but the various manufactures and agricultural products were brought together for sale in the great market-places of the principal cities. Fairs were held there every fifth day, and were thronged by a numerous concourse of persons, who came to buy or sell from all the neighbouring country. A particular quarter was allotted to each kind of article. The numerous transactions were conducted without confusion, and with entire regard to justice, under the inspection of magistrates appointed for the purpose. The traffic was carried on partly by barter, and partly by means of a regulated currency, of different values. This consisted of transparent quills of gold dust; of bits of tin, cut in the form of a ⊤; and of bags of cacao, containing a specified number of grains. "Blessed money," exclaims Peter Martyr, "which exempts its possessors from avarice, since it cannot be long hoarded, nor hidden under ground!"[4]

---

[1] Hernandez, Hist. Plantarum, lib. 6, cap. 116.

[2] Carta del Lic. Zuazo, MS.—Herrera, Hist. general, dec. 2, lib. 7, cap. 15.—Boturini, Idea, p. 77.—It is doubtful how far they were acquainted with the manufacture of silk. Carli supposes that what Cortés calls silk was only the fine texture of hair, or down, mentioned in the text. (Lettres Américaines, tom. i. let. 21.) But it is certain they had a species of caterpillar, unlike our silkworm, indeed, which spun a thread that was sold in the markets of ancient Mexico. See the Essai politique (tom. iii. pp. 66-69), where M. de Humboldt has collected some interesting facts in regard to the culture of silk by the Aztecs. Still, that the fabric should be a matter of uncertainty at all shows that it could not have reached any great excellence or extent.

[3] Carta del Lic. Zuazo, MS.—Acosta, lib. 4, cap. 37.—Sahagun, Hist. de Nueva-España, lib. 9, cap. 18-21.—Toribio, Hist. de los Indios, MS., Parte 1, cap. 15.—Rel. d'un gentil' huomo, ap. Ramusio, tom. iii. fol. 306.—Count Carli is in raptures with a specimen of feather-painting which he saw in Strasbourg. "Never did I behold anything so exquisite," he says, "for brilliancy and nice gradation of colour, and for beauty of design. No European artist could have made such a thing." (Lettres Américaines, let. 21, note.) There is still one place, Patzquaro, where, according to Bustamante, they preserve some knowledge of this interesting art, though it is practised on a very limited scale and at great cost. Sahagun, ubi supra, nota.

[4] "O felicem monetam, quæ suavem utilemque

There did not exist in Mexico that distinction of castes found among the Egyptian and Asiatic nations. It was usual, however, for the son to follow the occupation of his father. The different trades were arranged into something like guilds; each having a particular district of the city appropriated to it, with its own chief, its own tutelar deity, its peculiar festivals, and the like. Trade was held in avowed estimation by the Aztecs. "Apply thyself, my son," was the advice of an aged chief, "to agriculture, or to feather-work, or some other honourable calling. Thus did your ancestors before you. Else how would they have provided for themselves and their families? Never was it heard that nobility alone was able to maintain its possessor."[1] Shrewd maxims, that must have sounded somewhat strange in the ear of a Spanish *hidalgo !* [2]

But the occupation peculiarly respected was that of the merchant. It formed so important and singular a feature of their social economy as to merit a much more particular notice than it has received from historians. The Aztec merchant was a sort of itinerant trader, who made his journeys to the remotest borders of Anahuac, and to the countries beyond, carrying with him merchandise of rich stuffs, jewellery, slaves, and other valuable commodities. The slaves were obtained at the great market of Azcapozalco, not many leagues from the capital, where fairs were regularly held for the sale of these unfortunate beings. They were brought thither by their masters, dressed in their gayest apparel, and instructed to sing, dance, and display their little stock of personal accomplishments, so as to recommend themselves to the purchaser. Slave-dealing was an honourable calling among the Aztecs.[3]

With this rich freight the merchant visited the different provinces, always bearing some present of value from his own sovereign to their chiefs, and usually receiving others in return, with a permission to trade. Should this be denied him, or should he meet with indignity or violence, he had the means of resistance in his power. He performed his journeys with a number of companions of his own rank, and a large body of inferior attendants who were employed to transport the goods. Fifty or sixty pounds were the usual load for a man. The whole caravan went armed, and so well provided against sudden hostilities that they could make good their defence, if necessary, till reinforced from home. In one instance, a body of these militant traders stood a siege of four years in the town of Ayotlan, which they finally took from the enemy.[4] Their own government, however, was

præbet humano generi potum, et a tartareâ peste avaritiæ suos immunes servat possessores, quod suffodi aut diu servari nequeat!" De Orbe Novo, dec. 5, cap. 4.—(See, also, Carta de Cortés, ap. Lorenzana, p. 100, et seq.—Sahagun, Hist. de Nueva-España, lib. 8, cap. 36.—Toribio, Hist. de los Indios, MS., Parte 3, cap. 8.—Carta del Lic. Zuazo, MS.) The substitute for money throughout the Chinese empire was equally simple in Marco Polo's time, consisting of bits of stamped paper, made from the inner bark of the mulberry-tree. See Viaggi di Messer Marco Polo, gentil' huomo Veneziano, lib. 2, cap. 18, ap. Ramusio, tom. ii.

1 "Procurad de saber algun *oficio honroso,* como es el hacer obras de pluma y otros oficios mecánicos. . . . Mirad que tengais cuidado de lo tocante á la agricultura. . . . En ninguna parte he visto que alguno se mantenga por su nobleza." Sahagun, Hist. de Nueva-España, lib. 6, cap. 17.
2 Col. de Mendoza, ap. Antiq. of Mexico, vol. i. Pl. 71; vol. vi. p. 86.—Torquemada, Monarch. Ind., lib. 2, cap. 41.
3 Sahagun, Hist. de Nueva-España, lib. 9, cap. 4, 10-14.
4 Ibid., lib. 9, cap. 2.

always prompt to embark in a war on this ground, finding it a very convenient pretext for extending the Mexican empire. It was not unusual to allow the merchants to raise levies themselves, which were placed under their command. It was, moreover, very common for the prince to employ the merchants as a sort of spies, to furnish him information of the state of the countries through which they passed, and the dispositions of the inhabitants towards himself.[1]

Thus their sphere of action was much enlarged beyond that of a humble trader, and they acquired a high consideration in the body politic. They were allowed to assume insignia and devices of their own. Some of their number composed what is called by the Spanish writers a council of finance; at least, this was the case in Tezcuco.[2] They were much consulted by the monarch, who had some of them constantly near his person, addressing them by the title of " uncle," which may remind one of that of *primo*, or " cousin," by which a grandee of Spain is saluted by his sovereign. They were allowed to have their own courts, in which civil and criminal cases, not excepting capital, were determined ; so that they formed an independent community, as it were, of themselves. And, as their various traffic supplied them with abundant stores of wealth, they enjoyed many of the most essential advantages of an hereditary aristocracy.[3]

That trade should prove the path to eminent political preferment in a nation but partially civilized, where the names of soldier and priest are usually the only titles to respect, is certainly an anomaly in history. It forms some contrast to the standard of the more polished monarchies of the Old World, in which rank is supposed to be less dishonoured by a life of idle ease or frivolous pleasure than by those active pursuits which promote equally the prosperity of the state and of the individual. If civilization corrects many prejudices, it must be allowed that it creates others.

We shall be able to form a better idea of the actual refinement of the natives by penetrating into their domestic life and observing the intercourse between the sexes. We have, fortunately, the means of doing this. We shall there find the ferocious Aztec frequently displaying all the sensibility of a cultivated nature ; consoling his friends under affliction, or congratulating them on their good fortune, as on occasion of a marriage, or of the birth or the baptism of a child, when he was punctilious in his visits, bringing presents of costly dresses and ornaments, or the more simple offering of flowers, equally indicative of his sympathy. The visits at these times,

---

1 Sahagun, Hist. de Nueva-España, lib. 9, cap. 2, 4.—In the Mendoza Codex is a painting representing the execution of a cacique and his family, with the destruction of his city, for maltreating the persons of some Aztec merchants. Antiq. of Mexico, vol. i. Pl. 67.

2 Torquemada, Monarch. Ind., lib. 2, cap. 41.— Ixtlilxochitl gives a curious story of one of the royal family of Tezcuco, who offered, with two *other* merchants, *otros mercaderes*, to visit the court of a hostile cacique and bring him dead or alive to the capital. They availed themselves of a drunken revel,

at which they were to have been sacrificed, to effect their object. Hist. Chich., MS., cap. 62.

3 Sahagun, Hist. de Nueva-España, lib. 9, cap. 2, 5.—The ninth book is taken up with an account of the merchants, their pilgrimages, the religious rites on their departure, and the sumptuous way of living on their return. The whole presents a very remarkable picture, showing they enjoyed a consideration, among the half-civilized nations of Anahuac, to which there is no parallel, unless it be that possessed by the merchant-princes of an Italian republic, or the princely merchants of our own.

though regulated with all the precision of Oriental courtesy, were accompanied by expressions of the most cordial and affectionate regard.[1]

The discipline of children, especially at the public schools, as stated in a previous chapter, was exceedingly severe.[2]   But after she had come to a mature age the Aztec maiden was treated by her parents with a tenderness from which all reserve seemed banished.   In the counsels to a daughter about to enter into life, they conjured her to preserve simplicity in her manners and conversation, uniform neatness in her attire, with strict attention to personal cleanliness.   They inculcated modesty, as the great ornament of a woman, and implicit reverence for her husband; softening their admonitions by such endearing epithets as showed the fulness of a parent's love.[3]

Polygamy was permitted among the Mexicans, though chiefly confined, probably, to the wealthiest classes.[4]   And the obligations of the married vow, which was made with all the formality of a religious ceremony, were fully recognized, and impressed on both parties.   The women are described by the Spaniards as pretty, unlike their unfortunate descendants of the present day, though with the same serious and rather melancholy cast of countenance.   Their long black hair, covered, in some parts of the country, by a veil made of the fine web of the *pita*, might generally be seen wreathed with flowers, or, among the richer people, with strings of precious stones, and pearls from the Gulf of California.   They appear to have been treated with much consideration by their husbands, and passed their time in indolent tranquillity, or in such feminine occupations as spinning, embroidery, and the like, while their maidens beguiled the hours by the rehearsal of traditionary tales and ballads.[5]

The women partook equally with the men of social festivities and entertainments.   These were often conducted on a large scale, both as regards the number of guests and the costliness of the preparations. Numerous attendants, of both sexes, waited at the banquet.   The halls were scented with perfumes, and the courts strewed with odoriferous herbs and flowers, which were distributed in profusion among the guests, as they

---

[1] Sahagun, Hist. de Nueva-España, lib. 6, cap. 23-37.—Camargo, Hist. de Tlascala, MS.—These complimentary attentions were paid at stated seasons, even during pregnancy.   The details are given with abundant gravity and minuteness by Sahagun, who descends to particulars which his Mexican editor, Bustamante, has excluded, as somewhat too unreserved for the public eye.   If they were more so than some of the editor's own notes, they must have been very communicative indeed.

[2] Zurita, Rapport, pp. 112-134.—The Third Part of the Col. de Mendoza (Antiq. of Mexico, vol. i.) exhibits the various ingenious punishments devised for the refractory child.   The flowery path of knowledge was well strewed with thorns for the Mexican tyro.

[3] Zurita, Rapport, pp. 151-160.—Sahagun has given us the admonitions of both father and mother to the Aztec maiden on her coming to years of discretion.   What can be more tender than the beginning of the mother's exhortation?   "Hija mia muy amada, muy querida palomita : ya has oido y notado las palabras que tu señor padre te ha dicho ; ellas son palabras preciosas, y que raramente se dicen ni

se oyen, las quales han procedido de las entrañas y corazon en que estaban atesoradas ; y tu muy amado padre bien sabe que eres su hija, engendrada de él, eres su sangre y su carne, y sabe Dios nuestro señor que es asi ; aunque eres muger, é imágen de tu padre ¿ que mas te puedo decir, hija mia, de lo que ya esta dicho?" (Hist. de Nueva-España, lib. 6, cap. 19.)   The reader will find this interesting document, which enjoins so much of what is deemed most essential among civilized nations, translated entire in the Appendix, Part 2, No. 1.

[4] Yet we find the remarkable declaration, in the counsels of a father to his son, that, for the multiplication of the species, God ordained one man only for one woman.   "Nota, hijo mio, lo que te digo, mira que el mundo ya tiene este estilo de engendrar y multiplicar, y para esta generacion y multiplicacion, ordenó Dios que una muger usase de un varon, y un varon de una muger."   Sahagun, Hist. de Nueva-España, lib. 6, cap. 21.

[5] Ibid., lib. 6, cap. 21-23 ; lib. 8, cap. 23.—Rel. d'un gentil' huomo, ap. Ramusio, tom. iii. fol. 305.— Carta del Lic Zuazo, MS.

arrived. Cotton napkins and ewers of water were placed before them, as they took their seats at the board ; for the venerable ceremony of ablution [1] before and after eating was punctiliously observed by the Aztecs.[2] Tobacco was then offered to the company, in pipes, mixed up with aromatic substances, or in the form of cigars, inserted in tubes of tortoise-shell or silver. They compressed the nostrils with the fingers, while they inhaled the smoke, which they frequently swallowed. Whether the women, who sat apart from the men at table, were allowed the indulgence of the fragrant weed, as in the most polished circles of modern Mexico, is not told us. It is a curious fact that the Aztecs also took the dried leaf in the pulverized form of snuff.[3]

The table was well provided with substantial meats, especially game ; among which the most conspicuous was the turkey, erroneously supposed, as its name imports, to have come originally from the East.[4] These more solid dishes were flanked by others of vegetables and fruits, of every delicious variety found on the North American continent. The different viands were prepared in various ways, with delicate sauces and seasoning, of which the Mexicans were very fond. Their palate was still further regaled by confections and pastry, for which their maize-flour and sugar supplied ample materials. One other dish, of a disgusting nature, was sometimes added to the feast, especially when the celebration partook of a

---

[1] As old as the heroic age of Greece, at least. We may fancy ourselves at the table of Penelope, where water in golden ewers was poured into silver basins for the accommodation of her guests, before beginning the repast :—

Χέρνιβα δ' ἀμφίπολος προχόῳ ἐπέχευε
φέρουσα
Καλῇ, χρυσείῃ, ὑπὲρ ἀργυρέοιο λέβητος,
Νίψασθαι· παρὰ δὲ ξεστὴν ἐτάνυσσε
τράπεζαν.   ΟΔΥΣΣ. Α.

The feast affords many other points of analogy to the Aztec, inferring a similar stage of civilization in the two nations. One may be surprised, however, to find a greater profusion of the precious metals in the barren isle of Ithaca than in Mexico. But the poet's fancy was a richer mine than either.

[2] Sahagun, Hist. de Nueva-España, lib. 6, cap. 22.—Amidst some excellent advice of a parent to his son, on his general deportment, we find the latter punctiliously enjoined not to take his seat at the board till he has washed his face and hands, and not to leave it till he has repeated the same thing, and *cleansed his teeth.* The directions are given with a precision worthy of an Asiatic. "Al principio de la comida labarte has las manos y la boca, y donde te juntares con otros á comer, no te sientes luego ; mas antes tomarás el agua y la jícara para que se laben los otros, y echarles has agua á los manos, y despues de esto, cojerás lo que se ha caido por el suelo y barrerás el lugar de la comida, y tambien despues de comer lavarás te las manos y la boca, y limpiarás los dientes." Ibid., loc. cit.

[3] Rel. d'un gentil' huomo, ap. Ramusio, tom. iii. fol. 306.—Sahagun, Hist. de Nueva-España, lib. 4, cap. 37.—Torquemada, Monarch. Ind., lib. 13, cap. 23.—Clavigero, Stor. del Messico, tom. ii. p. 227.—The Aztecs used to smoke after dinner, to prepare for the *siesta,* in which they indulged themselves as regularly as an old Castilian.—Tobacco, in Mexican

yetl, is derived from a Haytian word, *tabaco.* The natives of Hispaniola, being the first with whom the Spaniards had much intercourse, have supplied Europe with the names of several important plants. —Tobacco, in some form or other, was used by almost all the tribes of the American continent, from the North-west Coast to Patagonia. (See McCulloh, Researches, pp. 91–94.) Its manifold virtues, both social and medicinal, are profusely panegyrized by Hernandez, in his Hist. Plantarum, lib. 2, cap. 109.

[4] This noble bird was introduced into Europe from Mexico. The Spaniards called it *gallopavo,* from its resemblance to the peacock. See Rel. d'un gentil' huomo, ap. Ramusio (tom. iii. fol. 306) ; also Oviedo (Rel. Sumaria, cap. 38), the earliest naturalist who gives an account of the bird, which he saw soon after the Conquest, in the West Indies, whither it had been brought, as he says, from New Spain. The Europeans, however, soon lost sight of its origin, and the name "turkey" intimated the popular belief of its Eastern origin. Several eminent writers have maintained its Asiatic or African descent ; but they could not impose on the sagacious and better-instructed Buffon. (See Histoire naturelle, art. *Dindon.*) The Spaniards saw immense numbers of turkeys in the domesticated state, on their arrival in Mexico, where they were more common than any other poultry. They were found wild, not only in New Spain, but all along the continent, in the less frequented places, from the North-western territory of the United States to Panamá. The wild turkey is larger, more beautiful, and every way an incomparably finer bird than the tame. Franklin, with some point, as well as pleasantry, insists on its preference to the bald eagle as the national emblem. (See his Works, vol. x. p. 63, in Spark's excellent edition.) Interesting notices of the history and habits of the wild turkey may be found in the Ornithology both of Buonaparte and of that enthusiastic lover of nature, Audubon, *vox Meleagris, Gallopavo.*

religious character.   On such occasions a slave was sacrificed, and his flesh, elaborately dressed, formed one of the chief ornaments of the banquet. Cannibalism, in the guise of an Epicurean science, becomes even the more revolting.[1]

The meats were kept warm by chafing-dishes.   The table was ornamented with vases of silver, and sometimes gold, of delicate workmanship.   The drinking-cups and spoons were of the same costly materials, and likewise of tortoise-shell.   The favourite beverage was the *chocolatl*, flavoured with vanilla and different spices.   They had a way of preparing the froth of it, so as to make it almost solid enough to be eaten, and took it cold.[2] The fermented juice of the maguey, with a mixture of sweets and acids, supplied, also, various agreeable drinks, of different degrees of strength, and formed the chief beverage of the elder part of the company.[3]

As soon as they had finished their repast, the young people rose from the table, to close the festivities of the day with dancing.   They danced gracefully, to the sound of various instruments, accompanying their movements with chants of a pleasing though somewhat plaintive character.[4] The older guests continued at table, sipping *pulque*, and gossiping about other times, till the virtues of the exhilarating beverage put them in good humour with their own.   Intoxication was not rare in this part of the company, and, what is singular, was excused in them, though severely punished in the younger.   The entertainment was concluded by a liberal distribution of rich dresses and ornaments among the guests, when they withdrew, after midnight, "some commending the feast, and others condemning the bad taste or extravagance of their host; in the same manner," says an old Spanish writer, "as with us."[5]   Human nature is, indeed, much the same all the world over.

In this remarkable picture of manners, which I have copied faithfully from the records of earliest date after the Conquest, we find no resemblance

---

[1] Sahagun, Hist. de Nueva-España, lib. 4, cap. 37 ; lib. 8, cap. 13 ; lib. 9, cap. 10–14.—Torquemada, Monarch. Ind., lib. 13, cap. 23.—Rel. d'un gentil' huomo, ap. Ramusio, tom. ii. fol. 306.—Father Sahagun has gone into many particulars of the Aztec *cuisine*, and the mode of preparing sundry savoury messes, making, all together, no despicable contribution to the noble science of gastronomy.

[2] The froth, delicately flavoured with spices and some other ingredients, was taken cold by itself. It had the consistency almost of a solid ; and the "Anonymous Conqueror" is very careful to inculcate the importance of " opening the mouth wide, in order to facilitate deglutition, that the foam may dissolve gradually, and descend imperceptibly, as it were, into the stomach." It was so nutritious that a single cup of it was enough to sustain a man through the longest day's march. (Fol. 300.) The old soldier discusses the beverage *con amore*.

[3] Sahagun, Hist. de Nueva-España, lib. 4, cap. 37 ; lib. 8, cap. 13.—Torquemada, Monarch. Ind., lib. 13, cap. 23.—Rel. d'un gentil' huomo, ap. Ramusio, tom. iii. fol. 306.

[4] Herrera, Hist. general, dec. 2, lib. 7, cap. 8.— Torquemada, Monarch. Ind., lib. 14, cap. 11.—The Mexican nobles entertained minstrels in their houses,

who composed ballads suited to the times, or the achievements of their lord, which they chanted, to the accompaniment of instruments, at the festivals and dances. Indeed, there was more or less dancing at most of the festivals, and it was performed in the courtyards of the houses, or in the open squares of the city. (Ibid., ubi supra.) The principal men had, also, buffoons and jugglers in their service, who amused them and astonished the Spaniards by their feats of dexterity and strength (Acosta, lib. 6, cap. 23 ; also Clavigero (Stor. del Messico, tom. ii. pp. 179–186), who has designed several representations of these exploits, truly surprising.) It is natural that a people of limited refinement should find their enjoyment in material rather than intellectual pleasures, and, consequently, should excel in them. The Asiatic nations, as the Hindoos and Chinese, for example, surpass the more polished Europeans in displays of agility and legerdemain.

[5] " Y de esta manera pasaban gran rato de la noche, y se despedian, é iban á sus casas, unos alabando la fiesta, y otros murmurando de las demasías y excesos, cosa mui ordinaria en los que á semejantes actos se juntan." Torquemada, Monarch. Ind., lib. 13, cap. 23.—Sahagun, Hist. de Nueva-España, lib. 9, cap. 10–14

to the other races of North American Indians. Some resemblance we may trace to the general style of Asiatic pomp and luxury. But in Asia, woman, far from being admitted to unreserved intercourse with the other sex, is too often jealously immured within the walls of the harem. European civilization, which accords to this loveliest portion of creation her proper rank in the social scale, is still more removed from some of the brutish usages of the Aztecs. That such usages should have existed with the degree of refinement they showed in other things is almost inconceivable. It can only be explained as the result of religious superstition ; superstition which clouds the moral perception, and perverts even the natural senses, till man, civilized man, is reconciled to the very things which are most revolting to humanity. Habits and opinions founded on religion must not be taken as conclusive evidence of the actual refinement of a people.

The Aztec character was perfectly original and unique. It was made up of incongruities apparently irreconcilable. It blended into one the marked peculiarities of different nations, not only of the same phase of civilization, but as far removed from each other as the extremes of barbarism and refinement. It may find a fitting parallel in their own wonderful climate, capable of producing, on a few square leagues of surface, the boundless variety of vegetable forms which belong to the frozen regions of the North, the temperate zone of Europe, and the burning skies of Arabia and Hindostan.

One of the works repeatedly consulted and referred to in this Introduction is Boturini's *Idea de una nueva Historia general de la América Septentrional.* The singular persecutions sustained by its author, even more than the merits of his book, have associated his name inseparably with the literary history of Mexico. The Chevalier Lorenzo Boturini Benaduci was a Milanese by birth, of an ancient family, and possessed of much learning. From Madrid, where he was residing, he passed over to New Spain, in 1735, on some business of the Countess of Santibañez, a lineal descendant of Montezuma. While employed on this, he visited the celebrated shrine of Our Lady of Guadaloupe, and, being a person of devout and enthusiastic temper, was filled with the desire of collecting testimony to establish the marvellous fact of her apparition. In the course of his excursions, made with this view, he fell in with many relics of Aztec antiquity, and conceived —what to a Protestant, at least, would seem much more rational—the idea of gathering together all the memorials he could meet with of the primitive civilization of the land.

In pursuit of this double object, he penetrated into the remotest parts of the country, living much with the natives, passing his nights sometimes in their huts, sometimes in caves and the depths of the lonely forests. Frequently months would elapse without his being able to add anything to his collection ; for the Indians had suffered too much not to be very shy of Europeans. His long intercourse with them, however, gave him ample opportunity to learn their language and popular traditions, and, in the end, to amass a large stock of materials, consisting of hieroglyphical charts on cotton, skins, and the fibre of the maguey ; besides a considerable body of Indian manuscripts, written after the Conquest. To all these must be added the precious documents for placing beyond controversy the miraculous apparition of the Virgin. With this treasure he returned, after a pilgrimage of eight years, to the capital.

His zeal, in the meanwhile, had induced him to procure from Rome a bull authorizing the coronation of the sacred image at Guadaloupe. The bull, however, though sanctioned by the Audience of New Spain, had never been approved by the Council of the Indies. In consequence of this informality, Boturini was arrested in the midst of his proceedings, his papers were taken from him, and, as he declined to give an inventory of them, he was thrown into prison, and confined in the same apartment with two criminals ! Not long afterward he was sent to Spain. He there presented a memorial to the Council of the Indies, setting forth his manifold grievances, and soliciting redress. At the same time, he drew up his "Idea," above noticed, in which he displayed the catalogue of his *museum* in New Spain, declaring, with affecting earnestness, that "he would not exchange these treasures for all the gold and silver, diamonds and pearls, in the New World."

After some delay, the Council gave an award in his favour ; acquitting him of any intentional violation of the law, and pronouncing a high encomium on his deserts. His papers, however, were not restored. But his Majesty was graciously pleased to appoint him Historiographer-General of the Indies, with a salary of one thousand dollars per annum. The stipend was too small to allow him to return to Mexico. He remained in Madrid, and completed there the first volume of a "General History of North America," in 1749. Not long after this event, and before the publication of the work, he died. The same injustice was continued to his heirs ; and, notwithstanding repeated applications in their behalf, they were neither put in possession of their unfortunate kinsman's collection, nor received a remuneration for it. What was worse,—as far as the public was concerned,—the collection itself was deposited in apartments of the vice-regal palace at Mexico, so damp that they gradually fell to pieces, and the few remaining were still further diminished by the pilfering of *the curious*. When Baron Humboldt visited Mexico, not one-eighth of this inestimable treasure was in existence !

I have been thus particular in the account of the unfortunate Boturini, as affording, on the whole, the most remarkable example of the serious obstacles and persecutions which literary enterprise, directed in the path of the national antiquities, has, from some cause or other, been exposed to in New Spain.

Boturini's manuscript volume was never printed, and probably never will be, if indeed it is in existence. This will scarcely prove a great detriment to science or to his own reputation. He was a man of a zealous temper, strongly inclined to the marvellous, with little of that acuteness requisite for penetrating the tangled mazes of antiquity, or of the philosophic spirit fitted for calmly weighing its doubts and difficulties. His "Idea" affords a sample of his peculiar mind. With abundant learning, ill assorted and ill digested, it is a jumble of fact and puerile fiction, interesting details, crazy dreams, and fantastic theories. But it is hardly fair to judge by the strict rules of criticism a work which, put together hastily, as a catalogue of literary treasures, was designed by the author rather to show what might be done, than that he could do it himself. It is rare that talents for action and contemplation are united in the same individual, Boturini was eminently qualified, by his enthusiasm and perseverance, for collecting the materials necessary to illustrate the antiquities of the country. It requires a more highly gifted mind to avail itself of them.

CHAPTER VI.

THE TEZCUCANS.—THEIR GOLDEN AGE.—ACCOMPLISHED PRINCES.—
DECLINE OF THEIR MONARCHY.

THE reader would gather but an imperfect notion of the civilization of Anahuac, without some account of the Acolhuans, or Tezcucans, as they are usually called; a nation of the same great family with the Aztecs, whom they rivalled in power and surpassed in intellectual culture and the arts of social refinement. Fortunately, we have ample materials for this in the records left by Ixtlilxochitl, a lineal descendant of the royal line of Tezcuco, who flourished in the century of the Conquest. With every opportunity for information he combined much industry and talent, and, if his narrative bears the high colouring of one who would revive the faded glories of an ancient but dilapidated house, he has been uniformly commended for his fairness and integrity, and has been followed without misgiving by such Spanish writers as could have access to his manuscripts.[1] I shall confine myself to the prominent features of the two reigns which may be said to embrace the golden age of Tezcuco, without attempting to weigh the probability of the details, which I will leave to be settled by the reader, according to the measure of his faith.

The Acolhuans came into the Valley, as we have seen, about the close of the twelfth century, and built their capital of Tezcuco on the eastern borders of the lake, opposite to Mexico. From this point they gradually spread themselves over the northern portion of Anahuac, when their career was checked by an invasion of a kindred race, the Tepanecs, who, after a desperate struggle, succeeded in taking their city, slaying their monarch, and entirely subjugating his kingdom.[2] This event took place about 1418; and the young prince, Nezahualcoyotl, the heir to the crown, then fifteen years old, saw his father butchered before his eyes, while he himself lay concealed among the friendly branches of a tree which overshadowed the spot.[3] His subsequent history is as full of romantic daring and perilous escapes as that of the renowned Scanderbeg or of the "young Chevalier."[4]

Not long after his flight from the field of his father's blood, the Tezcucan prince fell into the hands of his enemy, was borne off in triumph to his city, and was thrown into a dungeon. He effected his escape, however, through the connivance of the governor of the fortress, an old servant of

---

1 For a criticism on this writer, see the Postscript to this chapter.
2 See Chapter I. of this Introduction, p. 8.
3 Ixtlilxochitl, Relaciones, MS., No. 9.—Idem, Hist. Chich., MS., cap. 19.
4 The adventures of the former hero are told with

his usual spirit by Sismondi (Républiques Italiennes, chap. 79). It is hardly necessary, for the latter, to refer the English reader to Chambers's " History of the Rebellion of 1745;" a work which proves how thin is the partition in human life which divides romance from reality.

his family, who took the place of the royal fugitive, and paid for his loyalty with his life. He was at length permitted, through the intercession of the reigning family in Mexico, which was allied to him, to retire to that capital, and subsequently to his own, where he found a shelter in his ancestral palace. Here he remained unmolested for eight years, pursuing his studies under an old preceptor, who had had the care of his early youth, and who instructed him in the various duties befitting his princely station.[1]

At the end of this period the Tepanec usurper died, bequeathing his empire to his son, Maxtla, a man of fierce and suspicious temper. Nezahualcoyotl hastened to pay his obeisance to him, on his accession. But the tyrant refused to receive the little present of flowers which he laid at his feet, and turned his back on him in presence of his chieftains. One of his attendants, friendly to the young prince, admonished him to provide for his own safety, by withdrawing, as speedily as possible, from the palace, where his life was in danger. He lost no time, consequently, in retreating from the inhospitable court, and returned to Tezcuco. Maxtla, however, was bent on his destruction. He saw with jealous eye the opening talents and popular manners of his rival, and the favour he was daily winning from his ancient subjects.[2]

He accordingly laid a plan for making away with him at an evening entertainment. It was defeated by the vigilance of the prince's tutor, who contrived to mislead the assassins and to substitute another victim in the place of his pupil.[3] The baffled tyrant now threw off all disguise, and sent a strong party of soldiers to Tezcuco, with orders to enter the palace, seize the person of Nezahualcoyotl, and slay him on the spot. The prince, who became acquainted with the plot through the watchfulness of his preceptor, instead of flying, as he was counselled, resolved to await his enemies. They found him playing at ball, when they arrived, in the court of his palace. He received them courteously, and invited them in, to take some refreshments after their journey. While they were occupied in this way, he passed into an adjoining saloon, which excited no suspicion, as he was still visible through the open doors by which the apartments communicated with each other. A burning censer stood in the passage, and, as it was fed by the attendants, threw up such clouds of incense as obscured his movements from the soldiers. Under this friendly veil he succeeded in making his escape by a secret passage, which communicated with a large earthen pipe formerly used to bring water to the palace.[4] Here he remained till nightfall, when, taking advantage of the obscurity, he found his way into the suburbs, and sought a shelter in the cottage of one of his father's vassals.

---

[1] Ixtlilxochitl, Relaciones, MS., No. 10.
[2] Idem, Relaciones, MS., No. 10.—Hist. Chich., MS., cap. 20-24.
[3] Idem, Hist. Chich., MS., cap. 25. The contrivance was effected by means of an extraordinary personal resemblance of the parties; a fruitful source of comic—as every reader of the drama knows—though rarely of tragic interest.

[4] It was customary, on entering the presence of a great lord, to throw aromatics into the censer. "Hecho en el brasero incienso y copal, que era uso y costumbre donde estaban los Reyes y Señores, cada vez que los criados entraban con mucha reverencia y acatamiento echaban sahumerio en el brasero; y así con este perfume se obscurecia algo la sala." Ixtlilxochitl, Relaciones, MS., No. 11.

The Tepanec monarch, enraged at this repeated disappointment, ordered instant pursuit. A price was set on the head of the royal fugitive. Whoever should take him, dead or alive, was promised, however humble his degree, the hand of a noble lady, and an ample domain along with it. Troops of armed men were ordered to scour the country in every direction. In the course of the search, the cottage in which the prince had taken refuge was entered. But he fortunately escaped detection by being hid under a heap of maguey fibres used for manufacturing cloth. As this was no longer a proper place of concealment, he sought a retreat in the mountainous and woody district lying between the borders of his own state and Tlascala.[1]

Here he led a wretched, wandering life, exposed to all the inclemencies of the weather, hiding himself in deep thickets and caverns, and stealing out, at night, to satisfy the cravings of appetite; while he was kept in constant alarm by the activity of his pursuers, always hovering on his track. On one occasion he sought refuge from them among a small party of soldiers, who proved friendly to him, and concealed him in a large drum around which they were dancing. At another time he was just able to turn the crest of a hill as his enemies were climbing it on the other side, when he fell in with a girl who was reaping *chia*,—a Mexican plant, the seed of which was much used in the drinks of the country. He persuaded her to cover him up with the stalks she had been cutting. When his pursuers came up, and inquired if she had seen the fugitive, the girl coolly answered that she had, and pointed out a path as the one he had taken. Notwithstanding the high rewards offered, Nezahualcoyotl seems to have incurred no danger from treachery, such was the general attachment felt to himself and his house. "Would you not deliver up the prince, if he came in your way?" he inquired of a young peasant who was unacquainted with his person. "Not I," replied the other. "What, not for a fair lady's hand, and a rich dowry beside?" rejoined the prince. At which the other only shook his head and laughed.[2] On more than one occasion his faithful people submitted to torture, and even to lose their lives, rather than disclose the place of his retreat.[3]

However gratifying such proofs of loyalty might be to his feelings, the situation of the prince in these mountain solitudes became every day more distressing. It gave a still keener edge to his own sufferings to witness those of the faithful followers who chose to accompany him in his wanderings. "Leave me," he would say to them, "to my fate! Why should you throw away your own lives for one whom fortune is never weary of persecuting?" Most of the great Tezcucan chiefs had consulted

[1] Ixtlilxochitl, Hist. Chich., MS., cap. 26.—Relaciones, MS., No. 11.—Veytia, Hist. antig., lib. 2, cap. 47.

[2] "Nezahualcoiotzin le dixo, que si viese á quien buscaban, si lo iría á denunciar? respondió, que no; tornándole á replicar diciéndole, que haria mui mal en perder una muger hermosa y lo demas que el rey Maxtla prometia, el mancebo se rió de todo, no haciendo caso ni de lo uno ni de lo otro." Ixtlilxochitl, Hist. Chich., MS., cap. 27.

[3] Ibid., MS., cap. 26, 27.—Relaciones, MS., No. 11.—Veytia, Hist. antig., lib. 2, cap. 47, 48.

their interest by a timely adhesion to the usurper. But some still clung to their prince, preferring proscription, and death itself, rather than desert him in his extremity.[1]

In the meantime, his friends at a distance were active in measures for his relief. The oppressions of Maxtla, and his growing empire, had caused general alarm in the surrounding states, who recalled the mild rule of the Tezcucan princes. A coalition was formed, a plan of operations concerted, and, on the day appointed for a general rising, Nezahualcoyotl found himself at the head of a force sufficiently strong to face his Tepanec adversaries. An engagement came on, in which the latter were totally discomfited; and the victorious prince, receiving everywhere on his route the homage of his joyful subjects, entered his capital, not like a proscribed outcast, but as the rightful heir, and saw himself once more enthroned in the halls of his fathers.

Soon after, he united his forces with the Mexicans, long disgusted with the arbitrary conduct of Maxtla. The allied powers, after a series of bloody engagements with the usurper, routed him under the walls of his own capital. He fled to the baths, whence he was dragged out, and sacrificed with the usual cruel ceremonies of the Aztecs; the royal city of Azcapozalco was razed to the ground, and the wasted territory was henceforth reserved as the great slave-market for the nations of Anahuac.[2]

These events were succeeded by the remarkable league among the three powers of Tezcuco, Mexico, and Tlacopan, of which some account has been given in a previous chapter.[3] Historians are not agreed as to the precise terms of it; the writers of the two former nations each insisting on the paramount authority of his own in the coalition. All agree in the subordinate position of Tlacopan, a state, like the others, bordering on the lake. It is certain that in their subsequent operations, whether of peace or war, the three states shared in each other's councils, embarked in each other's enterprises, and moved in perfect concert together, till just before the coming of the Spaniards.

The first measure of Nezahualcoyotl, on returning to his dominions, was a general amnesty. It was his maxim "that a monarch might punish, but revenge was unworthy of him."[4] In the present instance he was averse even to punish, and not only freely pardoned his rebel nobles, but conferred on some, who had most deeply offended, posts of honour and confidence. Such conduct was doubtless politic, especially as their alienation was owing, probably, much more to fear of the usurper than to any disaffection towards himself. But there are some acts of policy which a magnanimous spirit only can execute.

The restored monarch next set about repairing the damages sustained

---

[1] Ixtlilxochitl, MSS., ubi supra.—Veytia, ubi supra.

[2] Ixtlilxochitl, Hist. Chich., MS., cap. 28—31.—Relaciones, MS., No. 11.—Veytia, Hist. antig., lib. 2, cap. 51—54.

[3] See page 10 of this volume.

[4] "Que venganza no es justo la procuren los Reyes, sino castigar al que lo mereciere." MS. de Ixtlilxochitl.

under the late misrule, and reviving, or rather remodelling, the various departments of government. He framed a concise, but comprehensive, code of laws, so well suited, it was thought, to the exigencies of the times, that it was adopted as their own by the two other members of the triple alliance. It was written in blood, and entitled the author to be called the Draco rather than "the Solon of Anahuac," as he is fondly styled by his admirers.[1] Humanity is one of the best fruits of refinement. It is only with increasing civilization that the legislator studies to economize human suffering, even for the guilty ; to devise penalties not so much by way of punishment for the past as of reformation for the future.[2]

He divided the burden of government among a number of departments, as the council of war, the council of finance, the council of justice. This last was a court of supreme authority, both in civil and criminal matters, receiving appeals from the lower tribunals of the provinces, which were obliged to make a full report, every four months, or eighty days, of their own proceedings to this higher judicature. In all these bodies, a certain number of citizens were allowed to have seats with the nobles and professional dignitaries. There was, however, another body, a council of state, for aiding the king in the despatch of business, and advising him in matters of importance, which was drawn altogether from the highest order of chiefs. It consisted of fourteen members ; and they had seats provided for them at the royal table.[3]

Lastly, there was an extraordinary tribunal, called the council of music, but which, differing from the import of its name, was devoted to the encouragement of science and art. Works on astronomy, chronology, history, or any other science, were required to be submitted to its judgment, before they could be made public. This censorial power was of some moment, at least with regard to the historical department, where the wilful perversion of truth was made a capital offence by the bloody code of Nezahualcoyotl. Yet a Tezcucan author must have been a bungler, who could not elude a conviction under the cloudy veil of hieroglyphics. This body, which was drawn from the best instructed persons in the kingdom, with little regard to rank, had supervision of all the productions of art, and of the nicer fabrics. It decided on the qualifications of the professors in the various branches of science, on the fidelity of their instructions to their pupils, the deficiency of which was severely punished, and it instituted examinations of these latter. In short, it was a general board of education for the country. On stated days, historical compositions, and poems treating of moral or traditional topics, were recited before

---

[1] See Clavigero, Stor. dèl Messico, tom. i. p. 247.—Nezahualcoyotl's code consisted of eighty laws, of which thirty-four only have come down to us, according to Veytia. (Hist. antig., tom. iii. p. 224, nota.) Ixtlilxochitl enumerates several of them. Hist. Chich., MS., cap. 38, and Relaciones, MS., Ordenanzas.

[2] Nowhere are these principles kept more steadily in view than in the various writings of our adopted countryman Dr. Lieber, having more or less to do with the theory of legislation. Such works could not have been produced before the nineteenth century.

[3] Ixtlilxochitl, Hist. Chich.,MS., cap. 36.—Veytia, Hist. antig., lib. 3, cap. 7.—According to Zurita, the principal judges, at their general meetings every four months, constituted also a sort of parliament or córtes, for advising the king on matters of state. See his Rapport, p. 106 ; also *ante*, p. 15.

F

it by their authors. Seats were provided for the three crowned heads of the empire, who deliberated with the other members on the respective merits of the pieces, and distributed prizes of value to the successful competitors.[1]

Such are the marvellous accounts transmitted to us of this institution; an institution certainly not to have been expected among the aborigines of America. It is calculated to give us a higher idea of the refinement of the people than even the noble architectural remains which still cover some parts of the continent. Architecture is, to a certain extent, a sensual gratification. It addresses itself to the eye, and affords the best scope for the parade of barbaric pomp and splendour. It is the form in which the revenues of a semi-civilized people are most likely to be lavished. The most gaudy and ostentatious specimens of it, and sometimes the most stupendous, have been reared by such hands. It is one of the first steps in the great march of civilization. But the institution in question was evidence of still higher refinement. It was a literary luxury, and argued the existence of a taste in the nation which relied for its gratification on pleasures of a purely intellectual character.

The influence of this academy must have been most propitious to the capital, which became the nursery not only of such sciences as could be compassed by the scholarship of the period, but of various useful and ornamental arts. Its historians, orators, and poets were celebrated throughout the country.[2] Its archives, for which accommodations were provided in the royal palace, were stored with the records of primitive ages.[3] Its idiom, more polished than the Mexican, was, indeed, the purest of all the Nahuatlac dialects, and continued, long after the Conquest, to be that in which the best productions of the native races were composed. Tezcuco claimed the glory of being the Athens of the Western world.[4]

Among the most illustrious of her bards was the emperor himself,—for the Tezcucan writers claim this title for their chief, as head of the imperial alliance. He doubtless appeared as a competitor before that very academy where he so often sat as a critic. Many of his odes descended to a late generation, and are still preserved, perhaps, in some of the dusty repositories

1 Ixtlilxochitl, Hist. Chich., MS., cap. 36.—Clavigero, Stor. del Messico, tom. ii. p. 137.—Veytia, Hist. antig., lib. 3, cap. 7.—"Concurrian á este consejo las tres cabezas del imperio, en ciertos dias, á oir cantar las poesías históricas antiguas y modernas, para instruirse de toda su historia, y tambien cuando habia algun nuevo invento en cualquiera facultad, para examinarlo, aprobarlo, ó reprobarlo. Delante de las sillas de los reyes habia una gran mesa cargada de joyas de oro y plata, pedrería, plumas, y otras cosas estimables, y en los rincones de la sala muchas de mantas de todas calidades, para premios de las habilidades y estímulo de los profesores, las cuales alhajas repartian los reyes, en los dias que concurrian, á los que se aventajaban en el ejercicio de sus facultades." Ibid.

2 Veytia, Hist. antig., lib. 3, cap. 7.—Clavigero, Stor. del Messico, tom. i. p. 247.—The latter author enumerates four historians, some of much repute, of the royal house of Tezcuco, descendants of the great Nezahualcoyotl. See his Account of Writers, tom. i. pp. 6-21.

3 "En la ciudad de Tezcuco estaban los Archivos Reales de todas las cosas referidas, por haver sido la Metrópoli de todas las ciencias, usos, y buenas costumbres, porque los Reyes que fuéron de ella se preciáron de esto." (Ixtlilxochitl, Hist. Chich., MS., Prólogo.) It was from the poor wreck of these documents, once so carefully preserved by his ancestors, that the historian gleaned the materials, as he informs us, for his own works.

4 "Aunque es tenida la lengua Mejicana por materna, y la Tezcucana por mas cortesana y pulida." (Camargo, Hist. de Tlascala, MS.) "Tezcuco," says Boturini, "where the noblemen sent their sons to acquire the most polished dialect of the Nahuatlac language, and to study poetry, moral philosophy, the heathen theology, astronomy, medicine, and history." Idea, p. 142.

of Mexico or Spain.[1] The historian Ixtlilxochitl has left a translation, in Castilian, of one of the poems of his royal ancestor. It is not easy to render his version into corresponding English rhyme, without the perfume of the original escaping in this double filtration.[2] They remind one of the rich breathings of Spanish-Arab poetry, in which an ardent imagination is tempered by a not unpleasing and moral melancholy.[3] But, though sufficiently florid in diction, they are generally free from the meretricious ornaments and hyperbole with which the minstrelsy of the East is usually tainted. They turn on the vanities and mutability of human life,—a topic very natural for a monarch who had himself experienced the strangest mutations of fortune. There is mingled in the lament of the Tezcucan bard, however, an Epicurean philosophy, which seeks relief from the fears of the future in the joys of the present. "Banish care," he says : "if there are bounds to pleasure, the saddest life must also have an end. Then weave the chaplet of flowers, and sing thy songs in praise of the all-powerful God ; for the glory of this world soon fadeth away. Rejoice in the green freshness of thy spring ; for the day will come when thou shalt sigh for these joys in vain ; when the sceptre shall pass from thy hands, thy servants shall wander desolate in thy courts, thy sons, and the sons of thy nobles, shall drink the dregs of distress, and all the pomp of thy victories and triumphs shall live only in their recollection. Yet the remembrance of the just shall not pass away from the nations, and the good thou hast done shall ever be held in honour. The goods of this life, its glories and its riches, are but lent to us, its substance is but an illusory shadow, and the things of to-day shall change on the coming of the morrow. Then gather the fairest flowers from thy gardens, to bind round thy brow, and seize the joys of the present ere they perish."[4]

But the hours of the Tezcucan monarch were not all passed in idle dalliance with the Muse, nor in the sober contemplations of philosophy, as at a later period. In the freshness of youth and early manhood he led

---

[1] "He composed sixty songs," says the author last quoted, "which have probably perished by the incendiary hands of the ignorant." (Idea, p. 79.) Boturini had translations of two of these in his museum (Catálogo, p. 8), and another has since come to light.

[2] Difficult as the task may be, it has been executed by the hand of a fair friend, who, while she has adhered to the Castilian with singular fidelity, has shown a grace and flexibility in her poetical movements which the Castilian version, and probably the Mexican original, cannot boast. See both translations in Appendix, Part 2, No. 2.

[3] Numerous specimens of this may be found in Condé's "Dominacion de los Arabes en España." None of them are superior to the plaintive strains of the royal Abderahman on the solitary palm-tree which reminded him of the pleasant land of his birth. See Parte 2, cap. 9.

[4] " Io tocaré cantando
El músico instrumento sonoroso,
Tú de flores gozando
Danza, y festeja á Dios que es poderoso ;
O gozemos de esta gloria,
Porque la humana vida es transitoria."
MS. DE IXTLILXOCHITL.

The sentiment, which is common enough, is expressed with uncommon beauty by the English poet Herrick :—

" Gather the rosebuds while you may ;
   Old Time is still a flying ;
The fairest flower that blooms to-day
   To-morrow may be dying."

And with still greater beauty, perhaps, by Racine :—

" Rions, chantons, dit cette troupe impie,
De fleurs en fleurs, de plaisirs en plaisirs,
       Promenons nos désirs.
Sur l'avenir insensé qui se fie.
De nos ans passagers le nombre est incertain.
Hâtons-nous aujourd'hui de jouir de la vie ;
Qui sait si nous serons demain ? "
       ATHALIE, Acte 2.

It is interesting to see under what different forms the same sentiment is developed by different races and in different languages. It is an Epicurean sentiment, indeed, but its universality proves its truth to nature.

the allied armies in their annual expeditions, which were certain to result in a wider extent of territory to the empire.[1]   In the intervals of peace he fostered those productive arts which are the surest sources of public prosperity.   He encouraged agriculture above all; and there was scarcely a spot so rude, or a steep so inaccessible, as not to confess the power of cultivation.   The land was covered with a busy population, and towns and cities sprang up in places since deserted or dwindled into miserable villages.[2]

From resources thus enlarged by conquest and domestic industry, the monarch drew the means for the large consumption of his own numerous household,[3] and for the costly works which he executed for the convenience and embellishment of the capital.   He filled it with stately edifices for his nobles, whose constant attendance he was anxious to secure at his court.[4]   He erected a magnificent pile of buildings which might serve both for a royal residence and for the public offices.   It extended, from east to west, twelve hundred and thirty-four yards, and from north to south, nine hundred and seventy-eight.   It was encompassed by a wall of unburnt bricks and cement, six feet wide and nine high for one half of the circumference, and fifteen feet high for the other half.   Within this enclosure were two courts.   The outer one was used as the great market-place of the city, and continued to be so until long after the Conquest, —if, indeed, it is not now.   The interior court was surrounded by the council-chambers and halls of justice.   There were also accommodations there for the foreign ambassadors; and a spacious saloon, with apartments opening into it, for men of science and poets, who pursued their studies in this retreat or met together to hold converse under its marble porticoes. In this quarter, also, were kept the public archives, which fared better under the Indian dynasty than they have since under their European successors.[5]

Adjoining this court were the apartments of the king, including those

---

1 Some of the provinces and places thus conquered were held by the allied powers in common ; Tlacopan, however, only receiving one-fifth of the tribute.   It was more usual to annex the vanquished territory to that one of the two great states to which it lay nearest. See Ixtlilxochitl, Hist. Chich., MS., cap. 38.—Zurita, Rapport, p. 11.

2 Ixtlilxochitl, Hist. Chich., MS., cap. 41. The same writer, in another work, calls the population of Tezcuco, at this period, double of what it was at the Conquest ; founding his estimate on the royal registers, and on the numerous remains of edifices still visible in his day, in places now depopulated. "Parece en las historias que en este tiempo, antes que se destruyesen, havia doblado mas gente de la que halló al tiempo que vino Cortés, y los demas Españoles : porque yo hallo en los padrones reales, que el menor pueblo tenía 1100 vecinos, y de allí para arriba, y ahora no tienen 200 vecinos, y aun en algunas partes de todo punto se han acabado. . . . Como se hecha de ver en las ruinas, hasta los mas altos montes y sierras tenian sus sementeras, y casas principales para vivir y morar." Relaciones, MS., No 9.

3 Torquemada has extracted the particulars of

the yearly expenditure of the palace from the royal account-book, which came into the historian's possession. The following are some of the items, namely : 4,900,300 fanegas of maize (the *fanega* is equal to about one hundred pounds; 2,744,000 fanegas of cacao ; 8000 turkeys ; 1300 baskets of salt ; besides an incredible quantity of game of every kind, vegetables, condiments, etc. (Monarch. Ind., lib. 2, cap. 53.) See, also, Ixtlilxochitl, Hist. Chich., MS., cap. 35.

4 There were more than four hundred of these lordly residences : "Asi mismo hizo edificar muchas casas y palacios para los señores y cavalleros, que asistian en su corte, cada uno conforme á la calidad y méritos de su persona, las quales llegáron á ser mas de quatrocientas casas de señores y cavalleros de solar conocido." Ibid., cap. 38.

5 Ixtlilxochitl, Hist. Chich., MS., cap. 36. "Esta plaza cercada de portales, y tenia asi mismo por la parte del poniente otra sala grande, y muchos quartos á la redonda, que era la universidad, en donde asistian todos los poetas, históricos, y philósophos del reyno, divididos en sus claves, y academias, conforme era la facultad de cada uno, y así mismo estaban aquí los archivos reales."

for the royal harem, as liberally supplied with beauties as that of an Eastern sultan. Their walls were incrusted with alabasters and richly-tinted stucco, or hung with gorgeous tapestries of variegated feather-work. They led through long arcades, and through intricate labyrinths of shrubbery, into gardens where baths and sparkling fountains were overshadowed by tall groves of cedar and cypress. The basins of water were well stocked with fish of various kinds, and the aviaries with birds glowing in all the gaudy plumage of the tropics. Many birds and animals which could not be obtained alive were represented in gold and silver so skilfully as to have furnished the great naturalist Hernandez with models for his work.[1]

Accommodations on a princely scale were provided for the sovereigns of Mexico and Tlacopan when they visited the court. The whole of this lordly pile contained three hundred apartments, some of them fifty yards square.[2] The height of the building is not mentioned. It was probably not great, but supplied the requisite room by the immense extent of ground which it covered. The interior was doubtless constructed of light materials, especially of the rich woods which, in that country, are remarkable, when polished, for the brilliancy and variety of their colours. That the more solid materials of stone and stucco were also liberally employed is proved by the remains at the present day; remains which have furnished an inexhaustible quarry for the churches and other edifices since erected by the Spaniards on the site of the ancient city.[3]

We are not informed of the time occupied in building this palace. But two hundred thousand workmen, it is said, were employed on it.[4] However this may be, it is certain that the Tezcucan monarchs, like those of Asia and ancient Egypt, had the control of immense masses of men, and would sometimes turn the whole population of a conquered city, including the women, into the public works.[5] The most gigantic monuments of architecture which the world has witnessed would never have been reared by the hands of freemen.

---

[1] This celebrated naturalist was sent by Philip II. to New Spain, and he employed several years in compiling a voluminous work on its various natural productions, with drawings illustrating them. Although the government is said to have expended sixty thousand ducats in effecting this great object, the volumes were not published till long after the author's death. In 1651 a mutilated edition of the part of the work relating to medical botany appeared at Rome.—The original MSS. were supposed to have been destroyed by the great fire in the Escorial, not many years after. Fortunately, another copy, in the author's own hand, was detected by the indefatigable Muñoz, in the library of the Jesuits' College at Madrid, in the latter part of the last century; and a beautiful edition, from the famous press of Ibarra, was published in that capital, under the patronage of government, in 1790. (Hist. Plantarum, Præfatio. —Nic. Antonio, Bibliotheca Hispana Nova (Matriti, 1790), tom. ii. p. 432.) The work of Hernandez is a monument of industry and erudition, the more remarkable as being the first on this difficult subject. And, after all the additional light from the labours of later naturalists, it still holds its place as a book of the highest authority, for the perspicuity, fidelity,

and thoroughness with which the multifarious topics in it are discussed.

[2] Ixtlilxochitl, Hist. Chich., MS., cap. 36.

[3] " Some of the terraces on which it stood," says Mr. Bullock, speaking of this palace, "are still entire, and covered with cement, very hard, and equal in beauty to that found in ancient Roman buildings. . . . The great church, which stands close by, is almost entirely built of the materials taken from the palace, many of the sculptured stones from which may be seen in the walls, though most of the ornaments are turned inwards. Indeed, our guide informed us that whoever built a house at Tezcuco made the ruins of the palace serve as his quarry." (Six Months in Mexico, chap. 26.) Torquemada notices the appropriation of the materials to the same purpose. Monarch. Ind., lib. 2, cap. 45.

[4] Ixtlilxochitl, MS., ubi supra.

[5] Thus, to punish the Chalcas for their rebellion, the whole population were compelled, women as well as men, says the chronicler so often quoted, to labour on the royal edifices for four years together ; and large granaries were provided with stores for their maintenance in the meantime. Idem, Hist Chich., MS., cap. 46.

Adjoining the palace were buildings for the king's children, who, by his various wives, amounted to no less than sixty sons and fifty daughters.[1] Here they were instructed in all the exercises and accomplishments suited to their station ; comprehending, what would scarcely find a place in a royal education on the other side of the Atlantic, the arts of working in metals, jewellery, and feather-mosaic. Once in every four months, the whole household, not excepting the youngest, and including all the officers and attendants on the king's person, assembled in a grand saloon of the palace, to listen to a discourse from an orator, probably one of the priesthood. The princes, on this occasion, were all dressed in *nequen*, the coarsest manufacture of the country. The preacher began by enlarging on the obligations of morality and of respect for the gods, especially important in persons whose rank gave such additional weight to example. He occasionally seasoned his homily with a pertinent application to his audience, if any member of it had been guilty of a notorious delinquency. From this wholesome admonition the monarch himself was not exempted, and the orator boldly reminded him of his paramount duty to show respect for his own laws. The king, so far from taking umbrage, received the lesson with humility ; and the audience, we are assured, were often melted into tears by the eloquence of the preacher.[2] This curious scene may remind one of similar usages in the Asiatic and Egyptian despotisms, where the sovereign occasionally condescended to stoop from his pride of place and allow his memory to be refreshed with the conviction of his own mortality.[3] It soothed the feelings of the subject to find himself thus placed, though but for a moment, on a level with his king ; while it cost little to the latter, who was removed too far from his people to suffer anything by this short-lived familiarity. It is probable that such an act of public humiliation would have found less favour with a prince less absolute.

Nezahualcoyotl's fondness for magnificence was shown in his numerous villas, which were embellished with all that could make a rural retreat delightful. His favourite residence was at Tezcotzinco, a conical hill about two leagues from the capital.[4] It was laid out in terraces, or hanging gardens, having a flight of steps five hundred and twenty in number, many of them hewn in the natural porphyry.[5] In the garden on the summit was a reservoir of water, fed by an aqueduct that was carried over hill and valley, for several miles, on huge buttresses of masonry. A large rock stood in the midst of this basin, sculptured with the hieroglyphics representing the

---

[1] If the people in general were not much addicted to polygamy, the sovereign, it must be confessed,— and it was the same, we shall see, in Mexico,— made ample amends for any self-denial on the part of his subjects.

[2] Ixtlilxochitl, Hist. Chich., MS., cap. 37.

[3] The Egyptian priests managed the affair in a more courtly style, and, while they prayed that all sorts of kingly virtues might descend on the prince, they threw the blame of actual delinquencies on his ministers ; thus, "not by the bitterness of reproof," says Diodorus, "but by the allurements of praise,

enticing him to an honest way of life." Lib. 1, cap. 70.

[4] Ixtlilxochitl, Hist. Chich., MS., cap. 42.—See Appendix, Part 2, No. 3, for the original description of this royal residence.

[5] "Quinientos y veynte escalones." Davilla Padilla, Historia de la Provincia de Santiago (Madrid, 1596), lib. 2, cap. 81.—This writer, who lived in the sixteenth century, counted the steps himself. Those which were not cut in the rock were crumbling into ruins, as, indeed, every part of the establishment was even then far gone to decay.

years of Nezahualcoyotl's reign and his principal achievements in each.[1] On a lower level were three other reservoirs, in each of which stood a marble statue of a woman, emblematic of the three states of the empire. Another tank contained a winged lion, (?) cut out of the solid rock, bearing in its mouth the portrait of the emperor.[2] His likeness had been executed in gold, wood, feather-work, and stone; but this was the only one which pleased him.

From these copious basins the water was distributed in numerous channels through the gardens, or was made to tumble over the rocks in cascades, shedding refreshing dews on the flowers and odoriferous shrubs below. In the depths of this fragrant wilderness, marble porticoes and pavilions were erected, and baths excavated in the solid porphyry, which are still shown by the ignorant natives as the "baths of Montezuma"![3] The visitor descended by steps cut in the living stone and polished so bright as to reflect like mirrors.[4] Towards the base of the hill, in the midst of cedar groves, whose gigantic branches threw a refreshing coolness over the verdure in the sultriest seasons of the year,[5] rose the royal villa, with its light arcades and airy halls, drinking in the sweet perfumes of the gardens. Here the monarch often retired, to throw off the burden of state and refresh his wearied spirits in the society of his favourite wives, reposing during the noontide heats in the embowering shades of his paradise, or mingling, in the cool of the evening, in their festive sports and dances. Here he entertained his imperial brothers of Mexico and Tlacopan, and followed the hardier pleasures of the chase in the noble woods that stretched for miles around his villa, flourishing in all their primeval majesty. Here, too, he often repaired in the latter days of his life, when age had tempered ambition and cooled the ardour of his blood, to pursue in solitude the studies of philosophy and gather wisdom from meditation.

The extraordinary accounts of the Tezcucan architecture are confirmed, in the main, by the relics which still cover the hill of Tezcotzinco or are half buried beneath its surface. They attract little attention, indeed, in the country, where their true history has long since passed into oblivion;[6]

---

[1] On the summit of the mount, according to Padilla, stood an image of a *coyotl*,—an animal resembling a fox,—which, according to tradition, represented an Indian famous for his fasts. It was destroyed by that stanch iconoclast, Bishop Zumárraga, as a relic of idolatry. (Hist. de Santiago, lib. 2, cap. 81.) This figure was, no doubt, the emblem of Nezahualcoyotl himself, whose name, as elsewhere noticed, signified "hungry fox."

[2] "Hecho de una peña un leon de mas de dos brazas de largo con sus alas y plumas: estaba hechado y mirando á la parte del oriente, en cuia boca asomaba un rostro, que era el mismo retrato del Rey." Ixtlilxochitl, Hist. Chich., MS., cap. 42.

[3] Bullock speaks of a "beautiful basin, twelve feet long by eight wide, having a well five feet by four, deep in the centre," etc., etc. Whether truth lies in the bottom of this well is not so clear. Latrobe describes the baths as "two singular basins, perhaps two feet and a half in diameter, not large enough for any monarch bigger than Oberon to take a duck in." (Comp. Six Months in Mexico, chap.

26; and Rambler in Mexico, Let. 7.) Ward speaks much to the same purpose (Mexico in 1827 (London, 1828), vol. ii. p. 296), which agrees with verbal accounts I have received of the same spot.

[4] "Gradas hechas de la misma peña tan bien gravadas y lizas que parecian espejos." (Ixtlilxochitl, MS., ubi supra.) The travellers just cited notice the beautiful polish still visible in the porphyry.

[5] Padilla saw entire pieces of cedar among the ruins, ninety feet long and four in diameter. Some of the massive portals, he observed, were made of a single stone. (Hist. de Santiago, lib. 11, cap. 81.) Peter Martyr notices an enormous wooden beam, used in the construction of the palaces of Tezcuco, which was one hundred and twenty feet long by eight feet in diameter! The accounts of this and similar huge pieces of timber were so astonishing, he adds, that he could not have received them except on the most unexceptionable testimony. De Orbe Novo, dec. 5, cap. 10.

[6] It is much to be regretted that the Mexican government should not take a deeper interest in the

while the traveller whose curiosity leads him to the spot speculates on their probable origin, and, as he stumbles over the huge fragments of sculptured porphyry and granite, refers them to the primitive races who spread their colossal architecture over the country long before the coming of the Acolhuans and the Aztecs.[1]

The Tezcucan princes were used to entertain a great number of concubines. They had but one lawful wife, to whose issue the crown descended.[2] Nezahualcoyotl remained unmarried to a late period. He was disappointed in an early attachment, as the princess who had been educated in privacy to be the partner of his throne gave her hand to another. The injured monarch submitted the affair to the proper tribunal. The parties, however, were proved to have been ignorant of the destination of the lady, and the court, with an independence which reflects equal honour on the judges who could give and the monarch who could receive the sentence, acquitted the young couple. This story is sadly contrasted by the following.[3]

The king devoured his chagrin in the solitude of his beautiful villa of Tezcotzinco, or sought to divert it by travelling. On one of his journeys he was hospitably entertained by a potent vassal, the old lord of Tepechpan, who, to do his sovereign more honour, caused him to be attended at the banquet by a noble maiden, betrothed to himself, and who, after the fashion of the country, had been educated under his own roof. She was of the blood royal of Mexico, and nearly related, moreover, to the Tezcucan monarch. The latter, who had all the amorous temperament of the South, was captivated by the grace and personal charms of the youthful Hebe, and conceived a violent passion for her. He did not disclose it to any one, however, but, on his return home, resolved to gratify it, though at the expense of his own honour, by sweeping away the only obstacle which stood in his path.

He accordingly sent an order to the chief of Tepechpan to take command of an expedition set on foot against the Tlascalans. At the same time he instructed two Tezcucan chiefs to keep near the person of the old lord, and bring him into the thickest of the fight, where he might lose his life. He assured them this had been forfeited by a great crime, but that, from regard for his vassal's past services, he was willing to cover up his disgrace by an honourable death.

The veteran, who had long lived in retirement on his estates, saw

---

Indian antiquities. What might not be effected by a few hands drawn from the idle garrisons of some of the neighbouring towns and employed in excavating this ground, " the Mount Palatine " of Mexico ! But, unhappily, the age of violence has been succeeded by one of apathy.

[1] " They are doubtless," says Mr. Latrobe, speaking of what he calls " these inexplicable ruins," " rather of Toltec than Aztec origin, and, perhaps, with still more probability, attributable to a people of an age yet more remote." (Rambler in Mexico, Let. 7.) " I am of opinion," says Mr. Bullock, " that these were antiquities prior to the discovery of America, and erected by a people whose history was lost even before the building of the city of Mexico.—Who can solve this difficulty ? " (Six Months in Mexico, ubi supra.) The reader who takes Ixtlilxochitl for his guide will have no great trouble in solving it. He will find here, as he might, probably, in some other instances, that one need go little higher than the Conquest for the origin of antiquities which claim to be coeval with Phœnicia and ancient Egypt.

[2] Zurita, Rapport, p. 12
[3] Ixtlilxochitl, Hist. Chich., MS., cap. 43.

himself with astonishment called so suddenly and needlessly into action, for which so many younger men were better fitted. He suspected the cause, and, in the farewell entertainment to his friends, uttered a presentiment of his sad destiny. His predictions were too soon verified ; and a few weeks placed the hand of his virgin bride at her own disposal.

Nezahualcoyotl did not think it prudent to break his passion publicly to the princess so soon after the death of his victim. He opened a correspondence with her through a female relative, and expressed his deep sympathy for her loss. At the same time, he tendered the best consolation in his power, by an offer of his heart and hand. Her former lover had been too well stricken in years for the maiden to remain long inconsolable. She was not aware of the perfidious plot against his life ; and, after a decent time, she was ready to comply with her duty, by placing herself at the disposal of her royal kinsman.

It was arranged by the king, in order to give a more natural aspect to the affair and prevent all suspicion of the unworthy part he had acted, that the princess should present herself in his grounds at Tezcotzinco, to witness some public ceremony there. Nezahualcoyotl was standing in a balcony of the palace when she appeared, and inquired, as if struck with her beauty for the first time, " who the lovely young creature was, in his gardens." When his courtiers had acquainted him with her name and rank, he ordered her to be conducted to the palace, that she might receive the attentions due to her station. The interview was soon followed by a public declaration of his passion ; and the marriage was celebrated not long after, with great pomp, in the presence of his court, and of his brother monarchs of Mexico and Tlacopan.[1]

This story, which furnishes so obvious a counterpart to that of David and Uriah, is told with great circumstantiality, both by the king's son and grandson, from whose narratives Ixtlilxochitl derived it.[2] They stigmatize the action as the basest in their great ancestor's life. It is indeed too base not to leave an indelible stain on any character, however pure in other respects, and exalted.

The king was strict in the execution of his laws, though his natural disposition led him to temper justice with mercy. Many anecdotes are told of the benevolent interest he took in the concerns of his subjects, and of his anxiety to detect and reward merit, even in the most humble. It was common for him to ramble among them in disguise, like the celebrated caliph in the " Arabian Nights," mingling freely in conversation, and ascertaining their actual condition with his own eyes.[3]

On one such occasion, when attended only by a single lord, he met with a boy who was gathering sticks in a field for fuel. He inquired of him

---

[1] Ixtlilxochitl, Hist. Chich., MS., cap. 43.
[2] Idem, ubi supra.
[3] " En traje de cazador (que lo acostumbraba á hacer muy de ordinario), saliendo á solas, y disfrazado para que no fuese conocido, á reconocer las faltas y necesidad que havia en la república para remediarlas." Ixtlilxochitl, Historia Chichimeca, MS., cap. 46.

" why he did not go into the neighbouring forest, where he would find plenty of them." To which the lad answered, " It was the king's wood, and he would punish him with death if he trespassed there." The royal forests were very extensive in Tezcuco, and were guarded by laws full as severe as those of the Norman tyrants in England. " What kind of man is your king ? " asked the monarch, willing to learn the effect of these pro- hibitions on his own popularity. " A very hard man," answered the boy, " who denies his people what God has given them." [1] Nezahualcoyotl urged him not to mind such arbitrary laws, but to glean his sticks in the forest, as there was no one present who would betray him. But the boy sturdily refused, bluntly accusing the disguised king, at the same time, of being a traitor, and of wishing to bring him into trouble.

Nezahualcoyotl, on returning to the palace, ordered the child and his parents to be summoned before him. They received the orders with astonishment, but, on entering the presence, the boy at once recognized the person with whom he had discoursed so unceremoniously, and he was filled with consternation. The good-natured monarch, however, relieved his apprehensions, by thanking him for the lesson he had given him, and, at the same time, commended his respect for the laws, and praised his parents for the manner in which they had trained their son. He then dismissed the parties with a liberal largess, and afterwards mitigated the severity of the forest laws, so as to allow persons to gather any wood they might find on the ground, if they did not meddle with the standing timber. [2]

Another adventure is told of him, with a poor woodman and his wife, who had brought their little load of billets for sale to the market-place of Tezcuco. The man was bitterly lamenting his hard lot, and the difficulty with which he earned a wretched subsistence, while the master of the palace before which they were standing lived an idle life, without toil, and with all the luxuries in the world at his command.

He was going on in his complaints, when the good woman stopped him, by reminding him he might be overheard. He was so, by Nezahualcoyotl himself, who, standing screened from observation at a latticed window which overlooked the market, was amusing himself, as he was wont, with observing the common people chaffering in the square. He immediately ordered the querulous couple into his presence. They appeared trembling and conscience-struck before him. The king gravely inquired what they had said. As they answered him truly, he told them they should reflect that, if he had great treasures at his command, he had still greater calls for them ; that, far from leading an easy life, he was oppressed with the whole burden of government ; and concluded by admonishing them " to be more cautious in future, as walls had ears." [3] He then ordered his

---

[1] " Un hombresillo miserable, pues quita á los hombres lo que Dios á manos llenas les da." Ixtlilxo- chitl, loc. cit.

[2] Ibid., cap. 46.

[3] " Porque las paredes oian." (Ixtlilxochitl, loc. cit.) A European proverb among the American aborigines looks too strange not to make one suspect the hand of the chronicler.

officers to bring a quantity of cloth and a generous supply of cacao (the coin of the country), and dismissed them. "Go," said he; "with the little you now have, you will be rich; while, with all my riches, I shall still be poor."[1]

It was not his passion to hoard. He dispensed his revenues munifi cently, seeking out poor but meritorious objects on whom to bestow them. He was particularly mindful of disabled soldiers, and those who had in any way sustained loss in the public service, and, in case of their death, extended assistance to their surviving families. Open mendicity was a thing he would never tolerate, but chastised it with exemplary rigour.[2]

It would be incredible that a man of the enlarged mind and endowments of Nezahualcoyotl should acquiesce in the sordid superstitions of his countrymen, and still more in the sanguinary rites borrowed by them from the Aztecs. In truth, his humane temper shrunk from these cruel cere- monies, and he strenuously endeavoured to recall his people to the more pure and simple worship of the ancient Toltecs. A circumstance produced a temporary change in his conduct.

He had been married some years to the wife he had so unrighteously obtained, but was not blessed with issue. The priests represented that it was owing to his neglect of the gods of his country, and that his only remedy was to propitiate them by human sacrifice. The king reluc tantly consented, and the altars once more smoked with the blood of slaughtered captives. But it was all in vain; and he indignantly exclaimed, "These idols of wood and stone can neither hear nor feel; much less could they make the heavens, and the earth, and man, the lord of it. These must be the work of the all-powerful, unknown God, Creator of the universe, on whom alone I must rely for consolation and support."[3]

He then withdrew to his rural palace of Tezcotzinco, where he remained forty days, fasting and praying at stated hours, and offering up no other sacrifice than the sweet incense of copal, and aromatic herbs and gums. At the expiration of this time, he is said to have been comforted by a vision assuring him of the success of his petition. At all events, such proved to be the fact; and this was followed by the cheering intelligence of the triumph of his arms in a quarter where he had lately experienced some humiliating reverses.[4]

Greatly strengthened in his former religious convictions, he now openly professed his faith, and was more earnest to wean his subjects from their degrading superstitions and to substitute nobler and more spiritual

---

1 "Le dijo, que con aquello poco le bastaba, y viviria bien aventurado; y él, con toda la máquina que le parecia que tenia arto, no tenia nada; y así lo despidió." Ixtlilxochitl, loc. cit.

2 Ibid.

3 "Verdaderamente los Dioses que io adoro, que son idolos de piedra que no hablan, ni sienten, no pudiéron hacer ni formar la hermosura del cielo, el sol, luna, y estrellas que lo hermosean, y dan luz á la tierra, rios, aguas y fuentes, árboles, y plantas que la hermosean, las gentes que la poseen, y todo lo criado; algun Dios muy poderoso, oculto, y no conocido es el Criador de todo el universo. El solo es él que puede consolarme en mi afliccion, y socor- rerme en tan grande angustia como mi corazon siente." MS. de Ixtlilxochitl.

4 MS. de Ixtlilxochitl.—The manuscript here quoted is one of the many left by the author on the antiquities of his country, and forms part of a volu- minous compilation made in Mexico by Father Vega, in 1702, by order of the Spanish government. See Appendix, Part 2, No. 2.

conceptions of the Deity. He built a temple in the usual pyramidal form, and on the summit a tower nine stories high, to represent the nine heavens; a tenth was surmounted by a roof painted black, and profusely gilded with stars, on the outside, and incrusted with metals and precious stones within. He dedicated this to "*the unknown God, the Cause of causes.*"[1] It seems probable, from the emblem on the tower, as well as from the complexion of his verses, as we shall see, that he mingled with his reverence for the Supreme the astral worship which existed among the Toltecs.[2] Various musical instruments were placed on the top of the tower, and the sound of them, accompanied by the ringing of a sonorous metal struck by a mallet, summoned the worshippers to prayers, at regular seasons.[3] No image was allowed in the edifice, as unsuited to the "invisible God;" and the people were expressly prohibited from profaning the altars with blood, or any other sacrifices than that of the perfume of flowers and sweet-scented gums.

The remainder of his days was chiefly spent in his delicious solitudes of Tezcotzinco, where he devoted himself to astronomical and, probably, astrological studies, and to meditation on his immortal destiny,—giving utterance to his feelings in songs, or rather hymns, of much solemnity and pathos. An extract from one of these will convey some idea of his religious speculations. The pensive tenderness of the verses quoted in a preceding page is deepened here into a mournful, and even gloomy, colouring; while the wounded spirit, instead of seeking relief in the convivial sallies of a young and buoyant temperament, turns for consolation to the world beyond the grave :—

"All things on earth have their term, and, in the most joyous career of their vanity and splendour, their strength fails, and they sink into the dust. All the round world is but a sepulchre; and there is nothing which lives on its surface that shall not be hidden and entombed beneath it. Rivers, torrents, and streams move onward to their destination. Not one flows back to its pleasant source. They rush onward, hastening to bury themselves in the deep bosom of the ocean. The things of yesterday are no more to-day; and the things of to-day shall cease perhaps, on the morrow.[4] The cemetery is full of the loathsome dust of bodies once quickened by living souls, who occupied thrones, presided over assemblies, marshalled armies, subdued provinces, arrogated to themselves worship, were puffed up with vainglorious pomp, and power, and empire.

---

[1] "Al Dios no conocido, causa de las causas." MS. de Ixtlilxochitl.

[2] Their earliest temples were dedicated to the sun. The moon they worshipped as his wife, and the stars as his sisters. (Veytia, Hist. antig., tom. i. cap. 25.) The ruins still existing at Teotihuacan, about seven leagues from Mexico, are supposed to have been temples raised by this ancient people in honour of the two great deities. Boturini, Idea, p. 42.

[3] MS. de Ixtlilxochitl.—"This was evidently a *gong*," says Mr. Ranking, who treads with enviable confidence over the "suppositos cineres," in the path of the antiquary. See his Historical Researches on the Conquest of Peru, Mexico, etc., by the Mongols (London, 1827), p. 310.

[4] "Toda la redondez de la tierra es un sepulcro : no hay cosa que sustente que con titulo de piedad no la esconda y entierre. Corren los rios, los arroyos, las fuentes, y las aguas, y ningunas retroceden para sus alegres nacimientos : aceléranse con ansia para los vastos dominios de Tlulóca [Neptuno], y cuanto mas se arriman á sus dilatadas márgenes, tanto mas van labrando las melancólicas urnas para sepultarse. Lo que fué ayer no es hoy, ni lo de hoy se afianza que será mañana."

" But these glories have all passed away, like the fearful smoke that issues from the throat of Popocatepetl, with no other memorial of their existence than the record on the page of the chronicler.

" The great, the wise, the valiant, the beautiful,—alas! where are they now? They are all mingled with the clod; and that which has befallen them shall happen to us, and to those that come after us. Yet let us take courage, illustrious nobles and chieftains, true friends and loyal subjects, —*let us aspire to that heaven where all is eternal and corruption cannot come.*[1] The horrors of the tomb are but the cradle of the Sun, and the dark shadows of death are brilliant lights for the stars."[2] The mystic import of the last sentence seems to point to that superstition respecting the mansions of the Sun, which forms so beautiful a contrast to the dark features of the Aztec mythology.

At length, about the year 1470,[3] Nezahualcoyotl, full of years and honours, felt himself drawing near his end. Almost half a century had elapsed since he mounted the throne of Tezcuco. He had found his kingdom dismembered by faction and bowed to the dust beneath the yoke of a foreign tyrant. He had broken that yoke; had breathed new life into the nation, renewed its ancient institutions, extended wide its domain; had seen it flourishing in all the activity of trade and agriculture, gathering strength from its enlarged resources, and daily advancing higher and higher in the great march of civilization. All this he had seen, and might fairly attribute no small portion of it to his own wise and beneficent rule. His long and glorious day was now drawing to its close; and he contemplated the event with the same serenity which he had shown under the clouds of its morning and in its meridian splendour.

A short time before his death, he gathered around him those of his children in whom he most confided, his chief counsellors, the ambassadors of Mexico and Tlacopan, and his little son, the heir to the crown, his only offspring by the queen. He was then not eight years old, but had already given, as far as so tender a blossom might, the rich promise of future excellence.[4]

After tenderly embracing the child, the dying monarch threw over him the robes of sovereignty. He then gave audience to the ambassadors,

---

[1] "Aspiremos al cielo, que allí todo es eterno y nada se corrompe."

[2] " El horror del sepulcro es lisongera cuna para él, y las funestas sombras, brillantes luces para los astros."—The original text and a Spanish translation of this poem first appeared, I believe, in a work of Granados y Galvez. (Tardes Americanas (México, 1778), p. 90, et seq.) The original is in the Otomi tongue, and both, together with a French version, have been inserted by M. Ternaux-Compans in the Appendix to his translation of Ixtlilxochitl's Hist. des Chichimèques (tom. i. pp. 359-367). Bustamante, who has, also, published the Spanish version in his Galería de antiguos Príncipes Mejicanos (Puebla, 1821 (pp. 16, 17),), calls it the " Ode of the Flower," which was recited at a banquet of the great Tezcucan nobles. If this last, however, be the same mentioned

by Torquemada (Monarch. Ind., lib. 2, cap. 45), it must have been written in the Tezcucan tongue; and, indeed, it is not probable that the Otomi, an Indian dialect, so distinct from the languages of Anahuac, however well understood by the royal poet, could have been comprehended by a miscellaneous audience of his countrymen.

[3] An approximation to a date is the most one can hope to arrive at with Ixtlilxochitl, who has entangled his chronology in a manner beyond my skill to unravel. Thus, after telling us that Nezahualcoyotl was fifteen years old when his father was slain in 1418, he says he died at the age of seventy-one, in 1462. *Instar omnium.* Comp. Hist. Chich., MS., cap. 18, 19, 49.

[4] MS. de Ixtlilxochitl,—also Hist. Chich., MS., cap. 49.

and, when they had retired, made the boy repeat the substance of the
conversation. He followed this by such counsels as were suited to his
comprehension, and which, when remembered through the long vista of
after-years, would serve as lights to guide him in his government of the
kingdom. He besought him not to neglect the worship of " the unknown
God," regretting that he himself had been unworthy to know him, and
intimating his conviction that the time would come when he should be
known and worshipped throughout the land.[1]

He next addressed himself to that one of his sons in whom he placed
the greatest trust, and whom he had selected as the guardian of the realm.
" From this hour," said he to him, " you will fill the place that I have
filled, of father to this child ; you will teach him to live as he ought ; and
by your counsels he will rule over the empire. Stand in his place, and be
his guide, till he shall be of age to govern for himself." Then, turning to
his other children, he admonished them to live united with one another,
and to show all loyalty to their prince, who, though a child, already manifested a discretion far above his years. " Be true to him," he added, " and
he will maintain you in your rights and dignities."[2]

Feeling his end approaching, he exclaimed, " Do not bewail me with
idle lamentations. But sing the song of gladness, and show a courageous
spirit, that the nations I have subdued may not believe you disheartened,
but may feel that each one of you is strong enough to keep them in obedience !" The undaunted spirit of the monarch shone forth even in the
agonies of death. That stout heart, however, melted, as he took leave of
his children and friends, weeping tenderly over them, while he bade each
a last adieu. When they had withdrawn, he ordered the officers of the
palace to allow no one to enter it again. Soon after, he expired, in the
seventy-second year of his age, and the forty-third of his reign.[3]

Thus died the greatest monarch, and, if one foul blot could be effaced,
perhaps the best, who ever sat upon an Indian throne. His character is
delineated with tolerable impartiality by his kinsman, the Tezcucan chronicler : " He was wise, valiant, liberal ; and, when we consider the magna
nimity of his soul, the grandeur and success of his enterprises, his deep
policy, as well as daring, we must admit him to have far surpassed every
other prince and captain of this New World. He had few failings himself
and rigorously punished those of others. He preferred the public to his
private interest ; was most charitable in his nature, often buying articles,
at double their worth, of poor and honest persons, and giving them away
again to the sick and infirm. In seasons of scarcity he was particularly
bountiful, remitting the taxes of his vassals, and supplying their wants from
the royal granaries. He put no faith in the idolatrous worship of the

---

[1] "No consentiendo que haya sacrificios de gente
humana, que Dios se enoja de ello, castigando con
rigor á los que lo hicieren ; que el dolor que llevo
es no tener luz, ni conocimiento, ni ser merecedor
de conocer tan gran Dios, el qual tengo por cierto

que ya que los presentes no lo conozcan, *ha de venir
tiempo en que sea conocido y adorado en esta tierra.*"
MS de Ixtlilxochitl.

[2] Idem, ubi supra ; also Hist. Chich., MS., cap. 49.

[3] Idem, Hist. Chich., MS., cap. 49.

country. He was well instructed in moral science, and sought, above all things, to obtain light for knowing the true God. He believed in one God only, the Creator of heaven and earth, by whom we have our being, who never revealed himself to us in human form, nor in any other ; with whom the souls of the virtuous are to dwell after death, while the wicked will suffer pains unspeakable. He invoked the Most High, as ' He by whom we live,' and 'Who has all things in himself.' He recognized the Sun for his father, and the Earth for his mother. He taught his children not to confide in idols, and only to conform to the outward worship of them from deference to public opinion.[1] If he could not entirely abolish human sacrifices, derived from the Aztecs, he at least restricted them to slaves and captives." [2]

I have occupied so much space with this illustrious prince that but little remains for his son and successor, Nezahualpilli. I have thought it better, in our narrow limits, to present a complete view of a single epoch, the most interesting in the Tezcucan annals, than to spread the inquiries over a broader but comparatively barren field. Yet Nezahualpilli, the heir to the crown, was a remarkable person, and his reign contains many incidents which I regret to be obliged to pass over in silence.[3]

He had, in many respects, a taste similar to his father's, and, like him, displayed a profuse magnificence in his way of living and in his public edifices. He was more severe in his morals, and, in the execution of justice, stern even to the sacrifice of natural affection. Several remarkable instances of this are told ; one, among others, in relation to his eldest son, the heir to the crown, a prince of great promise. The young man entered into a poetical correspondence with one of his father's concubines, the lady of Tula, as she was called, a woman of humble origin, but of uncommon endowments. She wrote verses with ease, and could discuss graver matters with the king and his ministers. She maintained a separate establishment, where she lived in state, and acquired, by her beauty and accomplishments, great ascendency over her royal lover.[4] With this favourite the prince carried on a correspondence in verse,—whether of an amorous nature does not appear. At all events, the offence was capital. It was submitted to the regular tribunal, who pronounced sentence of death on the unfortunate youth ; and the king, steeling his heart against all

---

[1] " Solia amonestar á sus hijos en secreto que no adorasen á aquellas figuras de ídolos, y que aquello que hiciesen en público fuese *solo por cumplimiento.*" Ixtlilxochitl.

[2] Idem, ubi supra.

[3] The name *Nezahualpilli* signifies " the prince for whom one has fasted,"—in allusion, no doubt, to the long fast of his father previous to his birth. (See Ixtlilxochitl, Hist. Chich., MS., cap. 45.) I have explained the meaning of the equally euphonious name of his parent, Nezahualcoyotl. (*Ante*, ch. 4.) If it be true that

" Cæsar or Epaminondas
Could ne'er without names have been known to us,"

it is no less certain that such names as those of the two Tezcucan princes, so difficult to be pronounced or remembered by a European, are most unfavourable to immortality.

[4] " De las concubinas la que mas privó con el rey fué la que llamaban la Señora de Tula, no por linage, sino porque era hija de un mercader, y era tan sabia que competia con el rey y con los mas sabios de su reyno, y era en la poesía muy aventajada, que con estas gracias y dones naturales tenia al rey muy sugeto á su voluntad de tal manera que lo que queria alcanzaba de él, y así vivia sola por sí con grande aparato y magestad en unos palacios que el rey le mandó edificar." Ixtlilxochitl, Hist. Chich., MS., cap. 57.

entreaties and the voice of nature, suffered the cruel judgment to be carried into execution. We might, in this case, suspect the influence of baser passions on his mind, but it was not a solitary instance of his inexorable justice towards those most near to him. He had the stern virtue of an ancient Roman, destitute of the softer graces which make virtue attractive. When the sentence was carried into effect, he shut himself up in his palace for many weeks, and commanded the doors and windows of his son's residence to be walled up, that it might never again be occupied.[1]

Nezahualpilli resembled his father in his passion for astronomical studies, and is said to have had an observatory on one of his palaces.[2] He was devoted to war in his youth, but, as he advanced in years, resigned himself to a more indolent way of life, and sought his chief amusement in the pursuit of his favourite science, or in the soft pleasures of the sequestered gardens of Tezcotzinco. This quiet life was ill suited to the turbulent temper of the times, and of his Mexican rival Montezuma. The distant provinces fell off from their allegiance; the army relaxed its discipline; disaffection crept into its ranks; and the wily Montezuma, partly by violence, and partly by stratagems unworthy of a king, succeeded in plundering his brother monarch of some of his most valuable domains. Then it was that he arrogated to himself the title and supremacy of emperor, hitherto borne by the Texcucan princes as head of the alliance. Such is the account given by the historians of that nation, who in this way explain the acknowledged superiority of the Aztec sovereign, both in territory and consideration, on the landing of the Spaniards.[3]

These misfortunes pressed heavily on the spirits of Nezahualpilli. Their effect was increased by certain gloomy prognostics of a near calamity which was to overwhelm the country.[4] He withdrew to his retreat, to brood in secret over his sorrows. His health rapidly declined; and in the year 1515, at the age of fifty-two, he sank into the grave;[5] happy, at least, that by this timely death he escaped witnessing the fulfilment of his own predictions, in the ruin of his country, and the extinction of the Indian dynasties for ever.[6]

---

[1] Ixtlilxochitl, Hist. Chich., MS., cap. 67.—The Tezcucan historian records several appalling examples of this severity,—one in particular, in relation to his guilty wife. The story, reminding one of the tales of an Oriental harem, has been translated for the Appendix, Part 2, No. 4. See also Torquemada (Monarch. Ind., lib. 2, cap. 66), and Zurita (Rapport, pp. 108, 109). He was the terror, in particular, of all unjust magistrates. They had little favour to expect from the man who could stifle the voice of nature in his own bosom in obedience to the laws. As Suetonius said of a prince who had not his virtue, "Vehemens et in coercendis quidem delictis immodicus." Vita Galbæ, sec. 9.

[2] Torquemada saw the remains of this, *or what passed for such*, in his day. Monarch. Ind., lib. 2, cap. 64.

[3] Ixtlilxochitl, Hist. Chich., MS., cap. 73, 74.— This sudden transfer of empire from the Tezcucans, at the close of the reigns of two of their ablest monarchs, is so improbable that one cannot but doubt if they ever possessed it,—at least, to the extent claimed by the patriotic historian. See *ante*, chap. 1, p. 10, note 1, and the corresponding text.

[4] Ibid., cap. 72.—The reader will find a particular account of these prodigies, better authenticated than most miracles, in a future page of this History.

[5] Ibid., cap. 75.—Or, rather, at the age of fifty, if the historian is right in placing his birth, as he does in a preceding chapter, in 1465. (See cap. 46.) It is not easy to decide what is true, when the writer does not take the trouble to be true to himself.

[6] His obsequies were celebrated with sanguinary pomp. Two hundred male and one hundred female slaves were sacrificed at his tomb. His body was consumed, amidst a heap of jewels, precious stuffs, and incense, on a funeral pile; and the ashes, deposited in a golden urn, were placed in the great temple of Huitzilopochtli, for whose worship the king, notwithstanding the lessons of his father, had some partiality. Ixtlilxochitl.

In reviewing the brief sketch here presented of the Tezcucan monarchy, we are strongly impressed with the conviction of its superiority, in all the great features of civilization, over the rest of Anahuac. The Mexicans showed a similar proficiency, no doubt, in the mechanic arts, and even in mathematical science. But in the science of government, in legislation, in speculative doctrines of a religious nature, in the more elegant pursuits of poetry, eloquence, and whatever depended on refinement of taste and a polished idiom, they confessed themselves inferior, by resorting to their rivals for instruction and citing their works as the masterpieces of their tongue. The best histories, the best poems, the best code of laws, the purest dialect, were all allowed to be Tezcucan. The Aztecs rivalled their neighbours in splendour of living, and even in the magnificence of their structures. They displayed a pomp and ostentatious pageantry truly Asiatic. But this was the development of the material rather than the intellectual principle. They wanted the refinement of manners essential to a continued advance in civilization. An insurmountable limit was put to theirs by that bloody mythology which threw its withering taint over the very air that they breathed.

The superiority of the Tezcucans was owing, doubtless, in a great measure to that of the two sovereigns whose reigns we have been depicting. There is no position which affords such scope for ameliorating the condition of man as that occupied by an absolute ruler over a nation imperfectly civilized. From his elevated place, commanding all the resources of his age, it is in his power to diffuse them far and wide among his people. He may be the copious reservoir on the mountain-top, drinking in the dews of heaven, to send them in fertilizing streams along the lower slopes and valleys, clothing even the wilderness in beauty. Such were Nezahualcoyotl and his illustrious successor, whose enlightened policy, extending through nearly a century, wrought a most salutary revolution in the condition of their country. It is remarkable that we, the inhabitants of the same continent, should be more familiar with the history of many a barbarian chief, both in the Old and New World, than with that of these truly great men, whose names are identified with the most glorious period in the annals of the Indian races.

What was the actual amount of the Tezcucan civilization it is not easy to determine, with the imperfect light afforded us. It was certainly far below anything which the word conveys, measured by a European standard. In some of the arts, and in any walk of science, they could only have made, as it were, a beginning. But they had begun in the right way, and already showed a refinement in sentiment and manners, a capacity for receiving instruction, which, under good auspices, might have led them on to indefinite improvement. Unhappily, they were fast falling under the dominion of the warlike Aztecs. And that people repaid the benefits received from their more polished neighbours by imparting to them their own ferocious superstition, which, falling like a mildew on the land, would soon have blighted its rich blossoms of promise and turned even its fruits to dust and ashes.

G

Fernando de Alva Ixtlilxochitl, who flourished in the beginning of the sixteenth century,[1] was a native of Tezcuco, and descended in a direct line from the sovereigns of that kingdom. The royal posterity became so numerous in a few generations that it was common to see them reduced to great poverty and earning a painful subsistence by the most humble occupations. Ixtlilxochitl, who was descended from the principal wife or queen of Nezahualpilli, maintained a very respectable position. He filled the office of interpreter to the viceroy, to which he was recommended by his acquaintance with the ancient hieroglyphics and his knowledge of the Mexican and Spanish languages. His birth gave him access to persons of the highest rank in his own nation, some of whom occupied important civil posts under the new government, and were thus enabled to make large collections of Indian manuscripts, which were liberally opened to him. He had an extensive library of his own, also, and with these means diligently pursued the study of the Tezcucan antiquities. He deciphered the hieroglyphics, made himself master of the songs and traditions, and fortified his narrative by the oral testimony of some very aged persons, who had themselves been acquainted with the Conquerors. From such authentic sources he composed various works in the Castilian, on the primitive history of the Toltec and the Tezcucan races, continuing it down to the subversion of the empire by Cortés. These various accounts, compiled under the title of *Relaciones,* are, more or less, repetitions and abridgments of each other ; nor is it easy to understand why they were thus composed. The *Historia Chichimeca* is the best digested and most complete of the whole series, and as such has been the most frequently consulted for the preceding pages.

Ixtlilxochitl's writings have many of the defects belonging to his age. He often crowds the page with incidents of a trivial, and sometimes improbable, character. The improbability increases with the distance of the period ; for distance, which diminishes objects to the natural eye, exaggerates them to the mental. His chronology, as I have more than once noticed. is inextricably entangled. He has often lent a too willing ear to traditions and reports which would startle the more sceptical criticism of the present time. Yet there is an appearance of good faith and simplicity in his writings, which may convince the reader that when he errs it is from no worse cause than national partiality. And surely such partiality is excusable in the descendant of a proud line, shorn of its ancient splendours, which it was soothing to his own feelings to revive again —though with something more than their legitimate lustre—on the canvas of history. It should also be considered that, if his narrative is sometimes startling, his researches penetrate into the mysterious depths of antiquity, where light and darkness meet and melt into each other, and where everything is still further liable to distortion, as seen through the misty medium of hieroglyphics.[2]

With these allowances, it will be found that the Tezcucan historian has just claims to our admiration for the compass of his inquiries and the sagacity with which they have been conducted. He has introduced us to the knowledge of the most polished people of Anahuac, whose records, if preserved, could not, at a much later period, have been comprehended ; and he has thus afforded a standard of comparison which much raises our ideas of American civilization. His language is simple, and, occasionally, eloquent and touching. His descriptions are highly picturesque. He abounds in familiar anecdote ; and the natural graces of his manner, in detailing the more striking events of history and the personal adventures of his heroes, entitle him to the name of the Livy of Anahuac.

I shall be obliged to enter hereafter into his literary merits, in connection with the

---

[1] [Ixtlilxochitl wrote in the early part of the seventeenth century. A certificate which he presented to the viceroy bears the date of November 18, 1608. The error is apparently a clerical one ; though a previous passage in the text seems to indicate some confusion on the author's part.—ED.]

[2] [Señor Ramirez objects to this remark, on the ground that, however obscure the hieroglyphics may now seem, at the time of Ixtlilxochitl, they were, in his language, "as plain as our letters to those who were acquainted with them." Notas y Esclarecimientos, p. 10.—ED.]

narrative of the Conquest; for which he is a prominent authority. His earlier annals—
though no one of his manuscripts has been printed—have been diligently studied by the
Spanish writers in Mexico, and liberally transferred to their pages; and his reputation,
like Sahagun's, has doubtless suffered by the process. His *Historia Chichimeca* is now
turned into French by M. Ternaux-Compans, forming part of that inestimable series of
translations from unpublished documents which have so much enlarged our acquaintance
with the early American history. I have had ample opportunity of proving the merits
of his version of Ixtlilxochitl, and am happy to bear my testimony to the fidelity and
elegance with which it is executed.

NOTE.—It was my intention to conclude this Introductory portion of the work with
an inquiry into the *Origin of the Mexican Civilization.* "But the general question of
the origin of the inhabitants of a continent," says Humboldt, "is beyond the limits prescribed to history; perhaps it is not even a philosophic question." "For the majority
of readers," says Livy, "the origin and remote antiquities of a nation can have comparatively little interest." The criticism of these great writers is just and pertinent;
and, on further consideration, I have thrown the observations on this topic, prepared
with some care, into the Appendix (Part I); to which those who feel sufficient curiosity
in the discussion can turn before entering on the narrative of the Conquest.

BOOK II.

DISCOVERY OF MEXICO.

———

CHAPTER I.

SPAIN UNDER CHARLES V.—PROGRESS OF DISCOVERY.—COLONIAL POLICY.
—CONQUEST OF CUBA.—EXPEDITIONS TO YUCATAN.

(1516–1518.)

IN the beginning of the sixteenth century, Spain occupied perhaps the
most prominent position on the theatre of Europe. The numerous states
into which she had been so long divided were consolidated into one
monarchy. The Moslem crescent, after reigning there for eight centuries,
was no longer seen on her borders. The authority of the crown did not,
as in later times, overshadow the inferior orders of the state. The people
enjoyed the inestimable privilege of political representation, and exercised
it with manly independence. The nation at large could boast as great a
degree of constitutional freedom as any other, at that time, in Christendom.
Under a system of salutary laws and an equitable administration, domestic
tranquillity was secured, public credit established, trade, manufactures, and
even the more elegant arts, began to flourish; while a higher education
called forth the first blossoms of that literature which was to ripen into
so rich a harvest before the close of the century. Arms abroad kept pace
with arts at home. Spain found her empire suddenly enlarged by important acquisitions both in Europe and Africa, while a New World beyond
the waters poured into her lap treasures of countless wealth and opened
an unbounded field for honourable enterprise.

Such was the condition of the kingdom at the close of the long and
glorious reign of Ferdinand and Isabella, when on the 23d of January
1516, the sceptre passed into the hands of their daughter Joanna, or rather
their grandson, Charles the Fifth, who alone ruled the monarchy during
the long and imbecile existence of his unfortunate mother. During the
two years following Ferdinand's death, the regency, in the absence of
Charles, was held by Cardinal Ximenes, a man whose intrepidity, extra-

ordinary talents, and capacity for great enterprises were accompanied by a haughty spirit, which made him too indifferent as to the means of their execution. His administration, therefore, notwithstanding the uprightness of his intentions, was, from his total disregard of forms, unfavourable to constitutional liberty; for respect for forms is an essential element of freedom. With all his faults, however, Ximenes was a Spaniard; and the object he had at heart was the good of his country.

It was otherwise on the arrival of Charles, who, after a long absence, came as a foreigner into the land of his fathers. (November 1517.) His manners, sympathies, even his language, were foreign, for he spoke the Castilian with difficulty. He knew little of his native country, of the character of the people or their institutions. He seemed to care still less for them; while his natural reserve precluded that freedom of communication which might have counteracted, to some extent, at least, the errors of education. In everything, in short, he was a foreigner, and resigned himself to the direction of his Flemish counsellors with a docility that gave little augury of his future greatness.

On his entrance into Castile, the young monarch was accompanied by a swarm of courtly sycophants, who settled, like locusts, on every place of profit and honour throughout the kingdom. A Fleming was made grand chancellor of Castile; another Fleming was placed in the archiepiscopal see of Toledo. They even ventured to profane the sanctity of the córtes, by intruding themselves on its deliberations. Yet that body did not tamely submit to these usurpations, but gave vent to its indignation in tones becoming the representatives of a free people.[1]

The deportment of Charles, so different from that to which the Spaniards had been accustomed under the benign administration of Ferdinand and Isabella, closed all hearts against him; and, as his character came to be understood, instead of the spontaneous outpourings of loyalty which usually greet the accession of a new and youthful sovereign, he was everywhere encountered by opposition and disgust. In Castile, and afterwards in Aragon, Catalonia, and Valencia, the commons hesitated to confer on him the title of *King* during the lifetime of his mother; and, though they eventually yielded this point, and associated his name with hers in the sovereignty, yet they reluctantly granted the supplies he demanded, and, when they did so, watched over their appropriation with a vigilance which left little to gratify the cupidity of the Flemings. The language of the legislature on these occasions, though temperate and respectful, breathes a spirit of resolute independence not to be found, probably, on the parlia-

---

[1] The following passage — one among many— from that faithful mirror of the times, Peter Martyr's correspondence, does ample justice to the intemperance, avarice, and intolerable arrogance of the Flemings. The testimony is worth the more, as coming from one who, though resident in Spain, was not a Spaniard. "Crumenas auro fulcire inhiant; huic uni studio invigilant. Nec detrectat juvenis Rex. Farcit quacunque posse datur; non satiat tamen. Quæ qualisve sit gens hæc, depingere adhuc nescio. Insufflat vulgus hic in omne genus hominum non arctoum. Minores faciunt Hispanos, quam si nati essent inter eorum cloacas. Rugiunt jam Hispani, labra mordent, submurmurant taciti, fatorum vices tales esse conqueruntur, quod ipsi domitores regnorum ita floccifiant ab his, quorum Deus unicus (sub rege temperato) Bacchus est cum Citherea." Opus Epistolarum (Amstelodami, 1610), ep. 608.

mentary records of any other nation at that period.   No wonder that
Charles should have early imbibed a disgust for these popular assemblies,
—the only bodies whence truths so unpalatable could find their way to
the ears of the sovereign ! [1]   Unfortunately, they had no influence on his
conduct ; till the discontent, long allowed to fester in secret, broke out in
that sad war of the *comunidades*, which shook the state to its foundations
and ended in the subversion of its liberties. [2]

The same pestilent foreign influence was felt, though much less sensibly,
in the colonial administration.   This had been placed, in the preceding
reign, under the immediate charge of the two great tribunals, the Council
of the Indies, and the *Casa de Contratacion*, or India House, at Seville.
It was their business to further the progress of discovery, watch over the
infant settlements, and adjust the disputes which grew up in them.   But
the licenses granted to private adventurers did more for the cause of discovery than the patronage of the crown or its officers.   The long peace,
enjoyed with slight interruption by Spain in the early part of the sixteenth
century, was most auspicious for this ; and the restless cavalier, who could
no longer win laurels on the fields of Africa or Europe, turned with eagerness to the brilliant career opened to him beyond the ocean.

It is difficult for those of our time, as familiar from childhood with the
most remote places on the globe as with those in their own neighbourhood,
to picture to themselves the feelings of the men who lived in the sixteenth
century.   The dread mystery which had so long hung over the great deep
had, indeed, been removed.   It was no longer beset with the same undefined
horrors as when Columbus launched his bold bark on its dark and unknown
waters.   A new and glorious world had been thrown open.   But as to the
precise spot where that world lay, its extent, its history, whether it were
island or continent,—of all this they had very vague and confused conceptions.   Many, in their ignorance, blindly adopted the erroneous conclusion
into which the great Admiral had been led by his superior science,—that
the new countries were a part of Asia ; and, as the mariner wandered among

[1] Yet the nobles were not all backward in manifesting their disgust.   When Charles would have
conferred the famous Burgundian order of the Golden
Fleece on the Count of Benavente, that lord refused
it, proudly telling him, "I am a Castilian.   I desire
no honours but those of my own country, in my
opinion quite as good as—indeed, better than—those
of any other."   Sandoval, Historia de la Vida y
Hechos del Emperador Cárlos V. (Ambéres, 1681),
tom. i. p. 103.

[2] [The tone of the preceding paragraphs is that of
the Spanish chroniclers of the seventeenth century,
and shows how the author, despite his natural candour and impartiality of mind, had acquired insensibly the habit of considering questions that affected
Spain from the national point of view of the class of
writers with whom his studies had made him most
familiar.   Spain is called the "native country" of
Charles V., and the "land of his fathers," although,
as hardly any reader will need to be reminded, he
was born in the Netherlands and was of Spanish
descent only on the maternal side.   The term
"foreigner" is applied to him as if it indicated
some vicious trait in his nature ; and the training

which he had received as the heir to the Austro-
Burgundian dominions is spoken of as erroneous,
merely because it had not fitted him for a different
position.   His manners are contrasted with those of
native Spanish sovereigns, as if wanting in gracious-
ness and affability ; yet the Spaniards, who alone
ever made this complaint, recognized their own
ideal of royal demeanour in that of the taciturn and
phlegmatic Philip II.   In like manner, Charles is
supposed to have made his first acquaintance with
free institutions on his arrival in Spain ; whereas he
had been brought up in a country where the power
of the sovereign was perhaps more closely restricted
by the chartered rights and immunities of the subject than was the case in any other part of Europe.
That the union of Spain and the Netherlands was a
most incongruous one, disastrous to the freedom, the
independence, and the development of both countries, is undeniable ; but it was not Charles's early
partiality for the one, but his successor's far stronger
partiality for the other, which rendered the incom-
patibility apparent and led to a rupture of the connection.—ED.]

the Bahamas, or steered his caravel across the Caribbean Seas, he fancied he was inhaling the rich odours of the spice-islands in the Indian Ocean. Thus every fresh discovery, interpreted by this previous delusion, served to confirm him in his error, or, at least, to fill his mind with new perplexities.

The career thus thrown open had all the fascinations of a desperate hazard, on which the adventurer staked all his hopes of fortune, fame, and life itself. It was not often, indeed, that he won the rich prize which he most coveted; but then he was sure to win the meed of glory scarcely less dear to his chivalrous spirit; and, if he survived to return to his home, he had wonderful stories to recount, of perilous chances among the strange people he had visited, and the burning climes whose rank fertility and magnificence of vegetation so far surpassed anything he had witnessed in his own. These reports added fresh fuel to imaginations already warmed by the study of those tales of chivalry which formed the favourite reading of the Spaniards at that period. Thus romance and reality acted on each other, and the soul of the Spaniard was exalted to that pitch of enthusiasm which enabled him to encounter the terrible trials that lay in the path of the discoverer. Indeed, the life of the cavalier of that day was romance put into action. The story of his adventures in the New World forms one of the most remarkable pages in the history of man.

Under this chivalrous spirit of enterprise, the progress of discovery had extended, by the beginning of Charles the Fifth's reign, from the Bay of Honduras, along the winding shores of Darien, and the South American continent, to the Rio de la Plata. The mighty barrier of the Isthmus had been climbed, and the Pacific descried, by Nuñez de Balboa, second only to Columbus in his valiant band of "ocean chivalry." The Bahamas and Caribbee Islands had been explored, as well as the Peninsula of Florida on the northern continent. This latter point had been reached by Sebastian Cabot in his descent along the coast from Labrador, in 1497. So that before 1518, the period when our narrative begins, the eastern borders of both the great continents had been surveyed through nearly their whole extent. The shores of the great Mexican Gulf, however, sweeping with a wide circuit far into the interior, remained still concealed, with the rich realms that lay beyond, from the eye of the navigator. The time had now come for their discovery.

The business of colonization had kept pace with that of discovery. In several of the islands, and in various parts of Terra Firma, and in Darien, settlements had been established, under the control of governors who affected the state and authority of viceroys. Grants of land were assigned to the colonists, on which they raised the natural products of the soil, but gave still more attention to the sugar-cane, imported from the Canaries. Sugar, indeed, together with the beautiful dye-woods of the country and the precious metals, formed almost the only articles of export in the infancy of the colonies, which had not yet introduced those other staples of the West Indian commerce which in our day constitute its principal wealth.

Yet the precious metals, painfully gleaned from a few scanty sources, would have made poor returns, but for the gratuitous labour of the Indians.

The cruel system of *repartimientos*, or distribution of the Indians as slaves among the conquerors, had been suppressed by Isabella. Although subsequently countenanced by the government, it was under the most careful limitations. But it is impossible to license crime by halves,—to authorize injustice at all, and hope to regulate the measure of it. The eloquent remonstrances of the Dominicans,—who devoted themselves to the good work of conversion in the New World with the same zeal that they showed for persecution in the Old,—but, above all, those of Las Casas, induced the regent, Ximenes, to send out a commission with full powers to inquire into the alleged grievances and to redress them. It had authority, moreover, to investigate the conduct of the civil officers, and to reform any abuses in their administration. This extraordinary commission consisted of three Hieronymite friars and an eminent jurist, all men of learning and unblemished piety.

They conducted the inquiry in a very dispassionate manner, but, after long deliberation, came to a conclusion most unfavourable to the demands of Las Casas, who insisted on the entire freedom of the natives. This conclusion they justified on the grounds that the Indians would not labour without compulsion, and that, unless they laboured, they could not be brought into communication with the whites, nor be converted to Christianity. Whatever we may think of this argument, it was doubtless urged with sincerity by its advocates, whose conduct through their whole administration places their motives above suspicion. They accompanied it with many careful provisions for the protection of the natives. But in vain. The simple people, accustomed all their days to a life of indolence and ease, sank under the oppressions of their masters, and the population wasted away with even more frightful rapidity than did the aborigines in our own country under the operation of other causes. It is not necessary to pursue these details further, into which I have been led by the desire to put the reader in possession of the general policy and state of affairs in the New World at the period when the present narrative begins.[1]

Of the islands, Cuba was the second discovered ; but no attempt had been made to plant a colony there during the lifetime of Columbus, who, indeed, after skirting the whole extent of its southern coast, died in the conviction that it was part of the continent.[2] At length, in 1511, Diego, the son and successor of the "Admiral," who still maintained the seat of

---

[1] I will take the liberty to refer the reader who is desirous of being more minutely acquainted with the Spanish colonial administration and the state of discovery previous to Charles V., to the "History of the Reign of Ferdinand and Isabella" (Part 2, ch. 9, 26), where the subject is treated *in extenso.**

[2] See the curious document attesting this, and drawn up by order of Columbus, ap. Navarrete, Coleccion de los Viages y de Descubrimientos (Madrid, 1825), tom. ii. Col. Dip., No. 76.

* [All the documents relative to the commission sent out by Ximenes, including many reports from the commissioners, have been printed in the Col. de Doc. inéd. relativos al Descubrimiento, Conquista y Colonizacion de las Posesiones españolas en América y Oceanía, tom. i.—ED.]

government in Hispaniola, finding the mines much exhausted there, proposed to occupy the neighbouring island of Cuba, or Fernandina, as it was called in compliment to the Spanish monarch.[1] He prepared a small force for the conquest, which he placed under the command of Don Diego Velasquez; a man described by a contemporary as "possessed of considerable experience in military affairs, having served seventeen years in the European wars; as honest, illustrious by his lineage and reputation, covetous of glory, and somewhat more covetous of wealth."[2] The portrait was sketched by no unfriendly hand.

Velasquez, or rather his lieutenant, Narvaez, who took the office on himself of scouring the country, met with no serious opposition from the inhabitants, who were of the same family with the effeminate natives of Hispaniola. The conquest, through the merciful interposition of Las Casas, "the protector of the Indians," who accompanied the army in its march, was effected without much bloodshed. One chief, indeed, named Hatuey, having fled originally from St. Domingo to escape the oppression of its invaders, made a desperate resistance, for which he was condemned by Velasquez to be burned alive. It was he who made that memorable reply, more eloquent than a volume of invective. When urged at the stake to embrace Christianity, that his soul might find admission into heaven, he inquired if the white men would go there. On being answered in the affirmative, he exclaimed, "Then I will not be a Christian; for I would not go again to a place where I must find men so cruel!"[3]

After the conquest, Velasquez, now appointed governor, diligently occupied himself with measures for promoting the prosperity of the island. He formed a number of settlements, bearing the same names with the modern towns, and made St. Jago, on the south-east corner, the seat of government.[4] He invited settlers by liberal grants of land and slaves. He encouraged them to cultivate the soil, and gave particular attention to the sugar-cane, so profitable an article of commerce in later times. He was, above all, intent on working the gold-mines, which promised better returns than those in Hispaniola. The affairs of his government did not prevent him, meanwhile, from casting many a wistful glance at the discoveries going forward on the continent, and he longed for an opportunity to embark in these golden adventures himself. Fortune gave him the occasion he desired.

An *hidalgo* of Cuba, named Hernandez de Cordova, sailed with three

---

[1] The island was originally called by Columbus Juana, in honour of Prince John, heir to the Castilian crown. After his death it received the name of Fernandina, at the king's desire. The Indian name has survived both. Herrera, Hist. general, Descrip., cap. 6.

[2] "Erat Didacus, ut hoc in loco de eo semel tantum dicamus, veteranus miles, rei militaris gnarus, quippe qui septem et decem annos in Hispania militiam exercitus fuerat, homo probus, opibus, genere et fama clarus, honoris cupidus, pecuniæ aliquanto cupidior." De Rebus gestis Ferdinandi Cortesii, MS.

[3] The story is told by Las Casas in his appalling record of the cruelties of his countrymen in the New World, which charity — and common sense — may excuse us for believing the good father has greatly overcharged. Brevissima Relacion de la Destruycion de las Indias (Venetia, 1643), p. 28.

[4] Among the most ancient of these establishments we find the Havana, Puerto del Príncipe, Trinidad, St. Salvador, and Matanzas, or *the Slaughter*, so called from a massacre of the Spaniards there by the Indians. Bernal Diaz, Hist. de la Conquista, cap. 8.

vessels on an expedition to one of the neighbouring Bahama Islands, in quest of Indian slaves. (February 8, 1517.)   He encountered a succession of heavy gales which drove him far out of his course, and at the end of three weeks he found himself on a strange and unknown coast.   On landing and asking the name of the country, he was answered by the natives, " *Tectetan,*" meaning, " I do not understand you," — but which the Spaniards, misinterpreting into the name of the place, easily corrupted into Yucatan.   Some writers give a different etymology.[1]   Such mistakes, however, were not uncommon with the early discoverers, and have been the origin of many a name on the American continent.[2]

Cordova had landed on the north-eastern end of the peninsula, at Cape Catoche.   He was astonished at the size and solid materials of the buildings, constructed of stone and lime, so different from the frail tenements of reeds and rushes which formed the habitations of the islanders.   He was struck, also, with the higher cultivation of the soil, and with the delicate texture of the cotton garments and gold ornaments of the natives.   Everything indicated a civilization far superior to anything he had before witnessed in the New World.   He saw the evidence of a different race, moreover, in the warlike spirit of the people.   Rumours of the Spaniards had perhaps, preceded them, as they were repeatedly asked if they came from the east ; and, wherever they landed, they were met with the most deadly hostility.   Cordova himself, in one of his skirmishes with the Indians, received more than a dozen wounds, and one only of his party escaped unhurt.   At length, when he had coasted the peninsula as far as Campeachy, he returned to Cuba, which he reached after an absence of several months, having suffered all the extremities of ill which these pioneers of the ocean were sometimes called to endure, and which none but the most courageous spirit could have survived.   As it was, half the original number, consisting of one hundred and ten men, perished, including their brave commander, who died soon after his return.   The reports he had brought back of the country, and, still more, the specimens of curiously wrought gold, convinced Velasquez of the importance of this discovery, and he prepared with all despatch to avail himself of it.[3]

He accordingly fitted out a little squadron of four vessels for the newly-discovered lands, and placed it under the command of his nephew, Juan de Grijalva, a man on whose probity, prudence, and attachment to himself he knew he could rely.   The fleet left the port of St. Jago de Cuba, May 1,

---

[1] Gomara, Historia de las Indias, cap. 52, ap. Barcia, tom. ii.—Bernal Diaz says the word came from the vegetable *yuca,* and *tale* the name for a hillock in which it is planted. (Hist. de la Conquista, cap. 6.)   M. Waldeck finds a much more plausible derivation in the Indian word *Ouyouckatan,* "listen to what they say."   Voyage pittoresque, p. 25.

[2] Two navigators, Solis and Pinzon, had descried the coast as far back as 1506, according to Herrera, though they had not taken possession of it. (Hist. general, dec. 1, lib. 6, cap. 17.)   It is, indeed, remarkable it should so long have eluded discovery, considering that it is but two degrees distant from Cuba.

[3] Oviedo, General y natural Historia de las Indias, MS., lib. 33, cap. 1.—De Rebus gestis, MS.—Carta del Cabildo de Vera Cruz (July 10, 1519), MS.—Bernal Diaz denies that the original object of the expedition, in which he took part, was to procure slaves, though Velasquez had proposed it. (Hist. de la Conquista, cap. 2.)   But he is contradicted in this by the other contemporary records above cited.

1518.[1] It took the course pursued by Cordova, but was driven some-what to the south, the first land that it made being the island of Cozumel. From this quarter Grijalva soon passed over to the continent, and coasted the peninsula, touching at the same places as his predecessor. Every-where he was struck, like him, with the evidences of a higher civilization, especially in the architecture ; as he well might be, since this was the region of those extraordinary remains which have become recently the subject of so much speculation. He was astonished, also, at the sight of large stone crosses, evidently objects of worship, which he met with in various places. Reminded by these circumstances of his own country, he gave the peninsula the name of " New Spain," a name since appropriated to a much wider extent of territory.[2]

Wherever Grijalva landed, he experienced the same unfriendly recep-tion as Cordova ; though he suffered less, being better prepared to meet it. In the *Rio de Tabasco,* or *Grijalva,* as it is often called, after him, he held an amicable conference with a chief who gave him a number of gold plates fashioned into a sort of armour. As he wound round the Mexican coast, one of his captains, Pedro de Alvarado, afterwards famous in the Conquest, entered a river, to which he, also, left his own name. In a neighbouring stream, called the *Rio de Vanderas,* or " River of Banners," from the ensigns displayed by the natives on its borders, Grijalva had the first com-munication with the Mexicans themselves.

The cacique who ruled over this province had received notice of the approach of the Europeans, and of their extraordinary appearance. He was anxious to collect all the information he could respecting them and the motives of their visit, that he might transmit them to his master, the Aztec emperor.[3] A friendly conference took place between the parties on shore, where Grijalva landed with all his force, so as to make a suitable impression on the mind of the barbaric chief. The interview lasted some hours, though, as there was no one on either side to interpret the language of the other, they could communicate only by signs. They, however, interchanged presents, and the Spaniards had the satisfaction of receiving, for a few worthless toys and trinkets, a rich treasure of jewels, gold orna-ments and vessels, of the most fantastic forms and workmanship.[4]

Grijalva now thought that in this successful traffic—successful beyond his most sanguine expectations—he had accomplished the chief object of his mission. He steadily refused the solicitations of his followers to plant a colony on the spot,—a work of no little difficulty in so populous and powerful a country as this appeared to be. To this, indeed, he was

[1] Itinerario de la Isola de Iuchathan, novamente ritrovata per il Signor Joan de Grijalva, per il suo Capellano, MS.—The chaplain's word may be taken for the date, which is usually put at the 8th of April.
[2] De Rebus gestis, MS.—Itinerario del Capel-lano, MS.
[3] According to the Spanish authorities, the cacique was sent with these presents from the Mexican sovereign, who had received previous tidings of the approach of the Spaniards. I have followed Sahagun, who obtained his intelligence directly from the natives. Historia de la Conquista, MS., cap. 2.
[4] Gomara has given the *per* and *contra* of this negotiation, in which gold and jewels of the value of fifteen or twenty thousand *pesos de oro* were ex-changed for glass beads, pins, scissors, and other trinkets common in an assorted cargo for savages. Crónica, cap. 6.

inclined, but deemed it contrary to his instructions, which limited him to barter with the natives. He therefore despatched Alvarado in one of the caravels back to Cuba, with the treasure and such intelligence as he had gleaned of the great empire in the interior, and then pursued his voyage along the coast.

He touched at San Juan de Ulua, and at the *Isla de los Sacrificios*, so called by him from the bloody remains of human victims found in one of the temples. He then held on his course as far as the province of Panuco, where, finding some difficulty in doubling a boisterous headland, he returned on his track, and, after an absence of nearly six months, reached Cuba in safety. Grijalva has the glory of being the first navigator who set foot on the Mexican soil and opened an intercourse with the Aztecs.[1]

On reaching the island, he was surprised to learn that another and more formidable armament had been fitted out to follow up his own discoveries, and to find orders, at the same time, from the governor, couched in no very courteous language, to repair at once to St. Jago. He was received by that personage not merely with coldness, but with reproaches for having neglected so fair an opportunity of establishing a colony in the country he had visited. Velasquez was one of those captious spirits who, when things do not go exactly to their minds, are sure to shift the responsibility of the failure from their own shoulders, where it should lie, to those of others. He had an ungenerous nature, says an old writer, credulous, and easily moved to suspicion.[2] In the present instance it was most unmerited. Grijalva, naturally a modest, unassuming person, had acted in obedience to the instructions of his commander, given before sailing, and had done this in opposition to his own judgment and the importunities of his followers. His conduct merited anything but censure from his employer.[3]

When Alvarado had returned to Cuba with his golden freight, and the accounts of the rich empire of Mexico which he had gathered from the natives, the heart of the governor swelled with rapture as he saw his dreams of avarice and ambition so likely to be realized. Impatient of the long absence of Grijalva, he despatched a vessel in search of him under the command of Olid, a cavalier who took an important part afterwards in the Conquest. Finally he resolved to fit out another armament on a sufficient scale to insure the subjugation of the country.

He previously solicited authority for this from the Hieronymite commission in St. Domingo. He then despatched his chaplain to Spain with the royal share of the gold brought from Mexico, and a full account of the intelligence gleaned there. He set forth his own manifold services, and

[1] Itinerario del Capellano, MS.—Carta de Vera Cruz, MS.

[2] "Hombre de terrible condicion," says Herrera, citing the good Bishop of Chiapa, " para los que le servian, i aiudaban, i que facilmente se indignaba contra aquellos." Hist. general, dec. 2, lib. 3, cap. 10.

[3] At least, such is the testimony of Las Casas, who knew both the parties well, and had often conversed with Grijalva upon his voyage. Historia general de las Indias, MS., lib. 3, cap. 113.

solicited from the court full powers to go on with the conquest and colonization of the newly-discovered regions.[1] Before receiving an answer, he began his preparations for the armament, and, first of all, endeavoured to find a suitable person to share the expense of it and to take the command. Such a person he found, after some difficulty and delay, in Hernando Cortés; the man of all others best calculated to achieve this great enterprise,—the last man to whom Velasquez, could he have foreseen the results, would have confided it.

CHAPTER II.

HERNANDO CORTÉS. — HIS EARLY LIFE. — VISITS THE NEW WORLD. — HIS RESIDENCE IN CUBA.—DIFFICULTIES WITH VELASQUEZ.—ARMADA INTRUSTED TO CORTÉS.

(1518.)

HERNANDO CORTÉS was born at Medellin, a town in the south-east corner of Estremadura,[2] in 1485.[3] He came of an ancient and respectable family; and historians have gratified the national vanity by tracing it up to the Lombard kings, whose descendants crossed the Pyrenees and established themselves in Aragon under the Gothic monarchy.[4] This royal genealogy was not found out till Cortés had acquired a name which would confer distinction on any descent, however noble. His father, Martin Cortés de Monroy, was a captain of infantry, in moderate circumstances, but a man of unblemished honour ; and both he and his wife, Doña Catalina Pizarro Altamirano, appear to have been much regarded for their excellent qualities.[5]

In his infancy Cortés is said to have had a feeble constitution, which strengthened as he grew older.[6] At fourteen, he was sent to Salamanca,

[1] Itinerario del Capellano, MS.—Las Casas, Hist. de las Indias, MS., lib. 3, cap. 113.—The most circumstantial account of Grijalva's expedition is to be found in the *Itinerary* of his chaplain above quoted. The original is lost, but an indifferent Italian version was published at Venice in 1522. A copy, which belonged to Ferdinand Columbus, is still extant in the library of the great church of Seville. The book had become so exceedingly rare, however, that the historiographer Muñoz made a transcript of it with his own hand ; and from his manuscript that in my possession was taken.

[2] [The house in which he was born, in the Calle de la Feria, was preserved until the present century, and many a traveller has lodged there, desirous, says Alaman, of sleeping in the mansion where the hero was born. In the year 1809 the building was destroyed by the French, and only a few fragments of wall now remain to commemorate the birthplace of the Conqueror. Alaman, Disertaciones históricas, tom. ii. p. 2.]

[3] Gomara, Crónica, cap. 1.—Bernal Diaz, Hist. de la Conquista, cap. 203. I find no more precise notice of the date of his birth, except, indeed, by Pizarro y Orellana, who tells us "that Cortés came

into the world the same day that that *infernal beast, the false heretic Luther*, entered it,—by way of compensation, no doubt, since the labours of the one to pull down the true faith were counterbalanced by those of the other to maintain and extend it"! (Varones ilustres del Nuevo-Mundo (Madrid, 1639), p. 66.) But this statement of the good cavalier, which places the birth of our hero in 1483, looks rather more like a zeal for "the true faith" than for historic.

[4] Argensola, in particular, has bestowed great pains on the *prosapia* of the house of Cortés ; which he traces up, nothing doubting, to Narnes Cortés, king of Lombardy and Tuscany. Anales de Aragon (Zaragoza, 1630), pp. 621-625.—Also, Caro de Torres, Historia de las Ordenes militares (Madrid, 1629), fol. 103.

[5] De Rebus gestis, MS.—Las Casas, who knew the father, bears stronger testimony to his poverty than to his noble birth. "Un escudero," he says of him, "que yo conocí harto pobre y humilde, aunque cristiano, viejo *y dizen que hidalgo.*" Hist. de las Indias, MS., lib. 3, cap. 27.

[6] [His parents had cast lots to decide which of the apostles should be chosen as his patron saint. The

as his father, who conceived great hopes from his quick and showy parts, proposed to educate him for the law, a profession which held out better inducements to the young aspirant than any other.   The son, however, did not conform to these views.   He showed little fondness for books, and, after loitering away two years at college, returned home, to the great chagrin of his parents.   Yet his time had not been wholly misspent, since he had laid up a little store of Latin, and learned to write good prose, and even verses " of some estimation, considering "—as an old writer quaintly remarks—" Cortés as the author." [1]   He now passed his days in the idle, unprofitable manner of one who, too wilful to be guided by others, proposes no object to himself.   His buoyant spirits were continually breaking out in troublesome frolics and capricious humours, quite at variance with the orderly habits of his father's household.   He showed a particular inclination for the military profession, or rather for the life of adventure to which in those days it was sure to lead.   And when, at the age of seventeen, he proposed to enroll himself under the banners of the Great Captain, his parents, probably thinking a life of hardship and hazard abroad preferable to one of idleness at home, made no objection.

The youthful cavalier, however, hesitated whether to seek his fortunes under that victorious chief, or in the New World, where gold as well as glory was to be won, and where the very dangers had a mystery and romance in them inexpressibly fascinating to a youthful fancy.   It was in this direction, accordingly, that the hot spirits of that day found a vent, especially from that part of the country where Cortés lived, the neighbourhood of Seville and Cadiz, the focus of nautical enterprise.   He decided on this latter course, and an opportunity offered in the splendid armament fitted out under Don Nicolas de Ovando, successor to Columbus.   An unlucky accident defeated the purpose of Cortés. [2]

As he was scaling a high wall, one night, which gave him access to the apartment of a lady with whom he was engaged in an intrigue, the stones gave way, and he was thrown down with much violence and buried under the ruins.   A severe contusion, though attended with no other serious consequences, confined him to his bed till after the departure of the fleet. [3]

Two years longer he remained at home, profiting little, as it would seem, from the lesson he had received.   At length he availed himself of another opportunity presented by the departure of a small squadron of vessels bound to the Indian islands.   He was nineteen years of age when he bade adieu to his native shores in 1504,—the same year in which Spain lost the best and greatest in her long line of princes, Isabella the Catholic.

---

[1] Argensola, Anales, p. 220.—Las Casas and Bernal Diaz both state that he was Bachelor of Laws at Salamanca. (Hist. de las Indias, MS., ubi supra.—Hist. de la Conquista, cap. 203.) The lot fell upon Peter, which explains the especial devotion which Cortés professed, through his whole life, to that saint, to whose watchful care he attributed the improvement in his health.   Alaman, Disertaciones históricas, tom. ii. p. 4.]

degree was given probably in later life, when the University might feel a pride in claiming him among her sons.

[2] De Rebus gestis, MS. — Gomara, Crónica, cap. 1.

[3] De Rebus gestis, MS.—Gomara, Ibid.—Argensola states the cause of his detention concisely enough : "Suspendió el viaje, *por enamorado y por quartanario.*"   Anales, p. 621.

The vessel in which Cortés sailed was commanded by one Alonso Quintero. The fleet touched at the Canaries, as was common in the outward passage. While the other vessels were detained there taking in supplies, Quintero secretly stole out by night from the island, with the design of reaching Hispaniola and securing the market before the arrival of his companions. A furious storm which he encountered, however, dismasted his ship, and he was obliged to return to port and refit. The convoy consented to wait for their unworthy partner, and after a short detention they all sailed in company again. But the faithless Quintero, as they drew near the Islands, availed himself once more of the darkness of the night, to leave the squadron with the same purpose as before. Unluckily for him, he met with a succession of heavy gales and head-winds, which drove him from his course, and he wholly lost his reckoning. For many days the vessel was tossed about, and all on board were filled with apprehensions, and no little indignation against the author of their calamities. At length they were cheered one morning with the sight of a white dove, which, wearied by its flight, lighted on the topmast. The biographers of Cortés speak of it as a miracle.[1] Fortunately it was no miracle, but a very natural occurrence, showing incontestably that they were near land. In a short time, by taking the direction of the bird's flight, they reached the island of Hispaniola; and, on coming into port, the worthy master had the satisfaction to find his companions arrived before him, and their cargoes already sold.[2]

Immediately on landing, Cortés repaired to the house of the governor, to whom he had been personally known in Spain. Ovando was absent on an expedition into the interior, but the young man was kindly received by the secretary, who assured him there would be no doubt of his obtaining a liberal grant of land to settle on. "But I came to get gold," replied Cortés, "not to till the soil, like a peasant."

On the governor's return, Cortés consented to give up his roving thoughts, at least for a time, as the other laboured to convince him that he would be more likely to realize his wishes from the slow, indeed, but sure, returns of husbandry, where the soil and the labourers were a free gift to the planter, than by taking his chance in the lottery of adventure, in which there were so many blanks to a prize. He accordingly received a grant of land with a *repartimiento* of Indians, and was appointed notary of the town or settlement of Acua. His graver pursuits, however, did not prevent his indulgence of the amorous propensities which belong to the sunny clime where he was born; and this frequently involved him in affairs of honour, from which, though an expert swordsman, he carried away scars that accompanied him to his grave.[3] He occasionally, moreover, found the means of

---

[1] Some thought it was the Holy Ghost in the form of this dove: "Sanctum esse Spiritum, qui, in illius alitis specie, ut mœstos et afflictos solaretur, venire erat dignatus" (De Rebus gestis, MS.); a conjecture which seems very reasonable to Pizarro y Orellana, since the expedition was to "redound so much to the spread of the Catholic faith, and the Castilian monarchy"! Varones ilustres, p. 70.

[2] Gomara, Crónica, cap. 2.

[3] Bernal Diaz, Hist. de la Conquista, cap. 203.

breaking up the monotony of his way of life by engaging in the military expeditions which, under the command of Ovando's lieutenant, Diego Velasquez, were employed to suppress the insurrections of the natives. In this school the young adventurer first studied the wild tactics of Indian warfare ; he became familiar with toil and danger, and with those deeds of cruelty which have too often, alas ! stained the bright scutcheons of the Castilian chivalry in the New World.   He was only prevented by illness —a most fortunate one, on this occasion—from embarking in Nicuessa's expedition, which furnished a tale of woe not often matched in the annals of Spanish discovery.   Providence reserved him for higher ends.

At length, in 1511, when Velasquez undertook the conquest of Cuba, Cortés willingly abandoned his quiet life for the stirring scenes there opened, and took part in the expedition.   He displayed, throughout the invasion, an activity and courage that won him the approbation of the commander; while his free and cordial manners, his good humour and lively sallies of wit, made him the favourite of the soldiers.   " He gave little evidence," says a contemporary, " of the great qualities which he afterwards showed."   It is probable these qualities were not known to himself; while to a common observer his careless manners and jocund repartees might well seem incompatible with anything serious or profound ; as the real depth of the current is not suspected under the light play and sunny sparkling of the surface.[1]

After the reduction of the island, Cortés seems to have been held in great favour by Velasquez, now appointed its governor.   According to Las Casas, he was made one of his secretaries.[2]   He still retained the same fondness for gallantry, for which his handsome person afforded obvious advantages, but which had more than once brought him into trouble in earlier life.   Among the families who had taken up their residence in Cuba was one of the name of Xuarez, from Granada in Old Spain.   It consisted of a brother, and four sisters remarkable for their beauty.   With one of them, named Catalina, the susceptible heart of the young soldier became enamoured.[3]   How far the intimacy was carried is not quite certain.   But it appears he gave his promise to marry her,—a promise which, when the time came, and reason, it may be, had got the better of passion, he showed no alacrity in keeping.   He resisted, indeed, all remonstrances to this effect, from the lady's family, backed by the governor, and somewhat sharpened, no doubt, in the latter by the particular interest he took in one of the fair sisters, who is said not to have repaid it with ingratitude.

Whether the rebuke of Velasquez or some other cause of disgust rankled

---

[1] De Rebus gestis, MS.—Gomara, Crónica, cap. 3, 4.—Las Casas, Hist. de las Indias, MS., lib. 3, cap. 27.

[2] Hist. de las Indias, MS., loc. cit.—" Res omnes arduas difficilosque per Cortesium, quem in dies magis magisque amplectebatur, Velasquius agit. Ex eo ducis favore et gratia magna Cortesio invidia est orta."   De Rebus gestis, MS.

[3] Solís has found a patent of nobility for this lady also,—" doncella noble y recatada." (Historia de la Conquista de Méjico (Paris, 1838), lib. 1, cap. 9.) Las Casas treats her with less ceremony : "Una hermana de *un* Juan Xuarez, *gente pobre.*" Hist. de las Indias, MS., lib. 3, cap. 17.

in the breast of Cortés, he now became cold towards his patron, and connected himself with a disaffected party tolerably numerous in the island. They were in the habit of meeting at his house and brooding over their causes of discontent, chiefly founded, it would appear, on what they conceived an ill requital of their services in the distribution of lands and offices. It may well be imagined that it could have been no easy task for the ruler of one of these colonies, however discreet and well intentioned, to satisfy the indefinite cravings of speculators and adventurers, who swarmed, like so many famished harpies, in the track of discovery in the New World.[1]

The malcontents determined to lay their grievances before the higher authorities in Hispaniola, from whom Velasquez had received his commission. The voyage was one of some hazard, as it was to be made in an open boat, across an arm of the sea eighteen leagues wide; and they fixed on Cortés, with whose fearless spirit they were well acquainted, as the fittest man to undertake it. The conspiracy got wind, and came to the governor's ears before the departure of the envoy, whom he instantly caused to be seized, loaded with fetters, and placed in strict confinement. It is even said he would have hung him, but for the interposition of his friends.[2] The fact is not incredible. The governors of these little territories, having entire control over the fortunes of their subjects, enjoyed an authority far more despotic than that of the sovereign himself. They were generally men of rank and personal consideration; their distance from the mother-country withdrew their conduct from searching scrutiny, and, when that did occur, they usually had interest and means of corruption at command sufficient to shield them from punishment. The Spanish colonial history, in its earlier stages, affords striking instances of the extraordinary assumption and abuse of powers by these petty potentates; and the sad fate of Vasquez Nuñez de Balboa, the illustrious discoverer of the Pacific, though the most signal, is by no means a solitary example, that the greatest services could be requited by persecution and an ignominious death.

The governor of Cuba, however, although irascible and suspicious in his nature, does not seem to have been vindictive, nor particularly cruel. In the present instance, indeed, it may well be doubted whether the blame would not be more reasonably charged on the unfounded expectations of his followers than on himself.

Cortés did not long remain in durance. He contrived to throw back one of the bolts of his fetters, and, after extricating his limbs, succeeded in forcing open a window with the irons so as to admit of his escape. He was lodged on the second floor of the building, and was able to let himself

---

[1] Gomara, Crónica, cap. 4.—Las Casas, Hist. de las Indias, MS., ubi supra.—De Rebus gestis, MS. –Memorial de Benito Martinez, Capellan de D. Velasquez, contra H. Cortés, MS.

[2] Las Casas, Hist. de las Indias, MS. ubi supra.

down to the pavement without injury, and unobserved.   He then made the best of his way to a neighbouring church, where he claimed the privilege of sanctuary.

Velasquez, though incensed at his escape, was afraid to violate the sanctity of the place by employing force.   But he stationed a guard in the neighbourhood, with orders to seize the fugitive if he should forget himself so far as to leave the sanctuary.   In a few days this happened.   As Cortés was carelessly standing without the walls in front of the building, an *alguacil* suddenly sprang on him from behind and pinioned his arms, while others rushed in and secured him.   This man, whose name was Juan Escudero, was afterwards hung by Cortés for some offence in New Spain.[1]

The unlucky prisoner was again put in irons, and carried on board a vessel to sail the next morning for Hispaniola, there to undergo his trial. Fortune favoured him once more.   He succeeded, after much difficulty and no little pain, in passing his feet through the rings which shackled them. He then came cautiously on deck, and, covered by the darkness of the night, stole quietly down the side of the ship into a boat that lay floating below. He pushed off from the vessel with as little noise as possible.   As he drew near the shore, the stream became rapid and turbulent.   He hesitated to trust his boat to it, and, as he was an excellent swimmer, prepared to breast it himself, and boldly plunged into the water.   The current was strong, but the arm of a man struggling for life was stronger ; and, after buffeting the waves till he was nearly exhausted, he succeeded in gaining a landing; when he sought refuge in the same sanctuary which had protected him before.   The facility with which Cortés a second time effected his escape may lead one to doubt the fidelity of his guards; who perhaps looked on him as the victim of persecution, and felt the influence of those popular manners which seem to have gained him friends in every society into which he was thrown.[2]

For some reason not explained,—perhaps from policy,—he now relinquished his objections to the marriage with Catalina Xuarez.   He thus secured the good offices of her family.   Soon afterwards the governor himself relented, and became reconciled to his unfortunate enemy.   A strange story is told in connection with this event.   It is said his proud spirit refused to accept the proffers of reconciliation made him by Velasquez ; and that one evening, leaving the sanctuary, he presented himself unexpectedly before the latter in his own quarters, when on a military excursion at some distance from the capital.   The governor, startled by the sudden apparition of his enemy completely armed before him, with some dismay inquired the meaning of it.   Cortés answered by insisting on a full explanation of his previous conduct.   After some hot discussion the

---

[1] Las Casas, Hist. de las Indias, MS., loc. cit.— Memorial de Martinez, MS.
[2] Gomara, Crónica, cap. 4.—Herrera tells a silly story of his being unable to swim, and throwing himself on a plank, which, after being carried out to sea, was washed ashore with him at flood tide. Hist. general, dec. 1, lib. 9, cap. 8.

interview terminated amicably; the parties embraced, and, when a messenger arrived to announce the escape of Cortés, he found him in the apartments of his Excellency, where, having retired to rest, both were actually sleeping in the same bed! The anecdote is repeated without distrust by more than one biographer of Cortés.[1] It is not very probable, however, that a haughty, irascible man like Velasquez should have given such uncommon proofs of condescension and familiarity to one, so far beneath him in station, with whom he had been so recently in deadly feud; nor, on the other hand, that Cortés should have had the silly temerity to brave the lion in his den, where a single nod would have sent him to the gibbet,—and that, too, with as little compunction or fear of consequences as would have attended the execution of an Indian slave.[2]

The reconciliation with the governor, however brought about, was permanent. Cortés, though not re-established in the office of secretary, received a liberal *repartimiento* of Indians, and an ample territory in the neighbourhood of St. Jago, of which he was soon after made *alcalde.* He now lived almost wholly on his estate, devoting himself to agriculture with more zeal than formerly. He stocked his plantation with different kinds of cattle, some of which were first introduced by him into Cuba.[3] He wrought, also, the gold-mines which fell to his share, and which in this island promised better returns than those in Hispaniola. By this course of industry he found himself, in a few years, master of some two or three thousand *castellanos*, a large sum for one in his situation. "God, who alone knows at what cost of Indian lives it was obtained," exclaims Las Casas, "will take account of it!"[4] His days glided smoothly away in these tranquil pursuits, and in the society of his beautiful wife, who, however ineligible as a connection, from the inferiority of her condition, appears to have fulfilled all the relations of a faithful and affectionate partner. Indeed, he was often heard to say at this time, as the good bishop above quoted remarks, "that he lived as happily with her as if she had been the daughter of a duchess." Fortune gave him the means in after-life of verifying the truth of his assertion.[5]

Such was the state of things, when Alvarado returned with the tidings of Grijalva's discoveries and the rich fruits of his traffic with the natives. The news spread like wildfire throughout the island; for all saw in it the promise of more important results than any hitherto obtained. The governor, as already noticed, resolved to follow up the track of discovery

[1] Gomara, Crónica, cap. 4.—"Cœnat cubatque Cortesius cum Velasquio eodem in lecto. Qui postero die fugæ Cortesii nuntius venerat, Velasquium et Cortesium juxta accubantes intuitus, miratur." De Rebus gestis, MS.

[2] Las Casas, who remembered Cortés at this time "so poor and lowly that he would have gladly received any favour from the least of Velasquez' attendants," treats the story of the bravado with contempt. "Por lo qual si él [Velasquez] sintiera de Cortés una puncta de alfiler de cerviguillo ó presuncion, ó lo ahorcara ó á lo menos lo echara de la

tierra y lo sumiera en ella sin que alzara cabeza en su vida." Hist. de las Indias, MS., lib. 3, cap. 27.

[3] "Pecuariam primus quoque habuit, in insulamque induxit, omni pecorum genere ex Hispania petito." De Rebus gestis, MS.

[4] "Los que por sacarle el oro muriéron Dios abrá tenido mejor cuenta que yo." Hist. de las Indias, MS., lib. 3, cap. 27. The text is a free translatior

[5] "Estando conmigo, me lo dixo que estava tan contento con ella como si fuera hija de una Duquessa." Hist. de las Indias, MS., ubi supra.—Gomara, Crónica, cap. 4.

with a more considerable armament; and he looked around for a proper person to share the expense of it and to take the command.

Several hidalgos presented themselves, whom, from want of proper qualifications, or from his distrust of their assuming an independence of their employer, he, one after another, rejected. There were two persons in St. Jago in whom he placed great confidence,—Amador de Lares, the *contador*, or royal treasurer,[1] and his own secretary, Andres de Duero. Cortés was also in close intimacy with both these persons; and he availed himself of it to prevail on them to recommend him as a suitable person to be intrusted with the expedition. It is said he reinforced the proposal by promising a liberal share of the proceeds of it. However this may be, the parties urged his selection by the governor with all the eloquence of which they were capable. That officer had had ample experience of the capacity and courage of the candidate. He knew, too, that he had acquired a fortune which would enable him to co-operate materially in fitting out the armament. His popularity in the island would speedily attract followers to his standard.[2] All past animosities had long since been buried in oblivion, and the confidence he was now to repose in him would insure his fidelity and gratitude. He lent a willing ear, therefore, to the recommendation of his counsellors, and, sending for Cortés, announced his purpose of making him Captain-General of the Armada.[3]

Cortés had now attained the object of his wishes,—the object for which his soul had panted ever since he had set foot in the New World. He was no longer to be condemned to a life of mercenary drudgery, nor to be cooped up within the precincts of a petty island; but he was to be placed on a new and independent theatre of action, and a boundless prospective was opened to his view, which might satisfy not merely the wildest cravings of avarice, but, to a bold, aspiring spirit like his, the far more importunate cravings of ambition. He fully appreciated the importance of the late discoveries, and read in them the existence of the great empire in the far West, dark hints of which had floated, from time to time, to the Islands, and of which more certain glimpses had been caught by those who had reached the continent. This was the country intimated to the "Great Admiral" in his visit to Honduras in 1502, and which he might have reached had he held on a northern course, instead of striking to the south in quest of an imaginary strait. As it was, " he had but opened the gate," to use his own bitter expression, "for others to enter." The time had at length come when they were to enter it; and the young adventurer, whose magic lance was to dissolve the spell which had so long hung over these mysterious regions, now stood ready to assume the enterprise.

---

[1] The treasurer used to boast he had passed some two-and-twenty years in the wars of Italy. He was a shrewd personage, and Las Casas, thinking that country a slippery school for morals, warned the governor, he says, more than once "to beware of the twenty-two years in Italy." Hist. de las Indias, MS., lib. 3, cap. 113.

[2] "Si él no fuera por Capitan, que no fuera la tercera parte de la gente que con él fué." Declaracion de Puertocarrero, MS. (Coruña, 30 de Abril 1520.)
[3] Bernal Diaz, Hist. de la Conquista, cap. 19.— De Rebus gestis, MS.—Gomara, Crónica, cap. 7.— Las Casas, Hist. general de las Indias, MS., lib. 3, cap. 113.

From this hour the deportment of Cortés seemed to undergo a change. His thoughts, instead of evaporating in empty levities or idle flashes of merriment, were wholly concentrated on the great object to which he was devoted. His elastic spirits were shown in cheering and stimulating the companions of his toilsome duties, and he was roused to a generous enthusiasm, of which even those who knew him best had not conceived him capable. He applied at once all the money in his possession to fitting out the armament. He raised more by the mortgage of his estates, and by giving his obligations to some wealthy merchants of the place, who relied for their reimbursement on the success of the expedition; and, when his own credit was exhausted, he availed himself of that of his friends.

The funds thus acquired he expended in the purchase of vessels, provisions, and military stores, while he invited recruits by offers of assistance to such as were too poor to provide for themselves, and by the additional promise of a liberal share of the anticipated profits.[1]

All was now bustle and excitement in the little town of St. Jago. Some were busy in refitting the vessels and getting them ready for the voyage; some in providing naval stores; others in converting their own estates into money in order to equip themselves; every one seemed anxious to contribute in some way or other to the success of the expedition. Six ships, some of them of a large size, had already been procured; and three hundred recruits enrolled themselves in the course of a few days, eager to seek their fortunes under the banner of this daring and popular chieftain.

How far the governor contributed towards the expenses of the outfit is not very clear. If the friends of Cortés are to be believed, nearly the whole burden fell on him; since, while he supplied the squadron without remuneration, the governor sold many of his own stores at an exorbitant profit.[2] Yet it does not seem probable that Velasquez, with such ample means at his command, should have thrown on his deputy the burden of the expedition, nor that the latter—had he done so—could have been in a condition to meet these expenses, amounting, as we are told, to more than twenty thousand gold ducats. Still it cannot be denied that an ambitious man like Cortés, who was to reap all the glory of the enterprise, would very naturally be less solicitous to count the gains of it, than his employer, who, inactive at home, and having no laurels to win, must look on the pecuniary profits as his only recompense. The question gave rise, some years later,

---

[1] Declaracion de Puertocarrero, MS.—Carta de Vera Cruz, MS.—Probanza en la Villa Segura, MS. (4 de Oct. 1520.)

[2] The letter from the Municipality of Vera Cruz, after stating that Velasquez bore only one-third of the original expense, adds, "Y sepan Vras. Magestades que la mayor parte de la dicha tercia parte que el dicho Diego Velasquez gastó en hacer la dicha armada fué emplear sus dineros en vinos y en ropas, y en otras cosas de poco valor para nos lo vender acá en mucha mas cantidad de lo que á él le costó, por manera que podemos decir que entre nosotros los Españoles vasallos de Vras. Reales Altezas ha hecho Diego Velasquez su rescate y granosea de sus dineros cobrandolos muy bien." (Carta de Vera Cruz, MS.) Puertocarrero and Montejo, also, in their depositions taken in Spain, both speak of Cortés' having furnished two-thirds of the cost of the flotilla. (Declaracion de Puertocarrero, MS.—Declaracion de Montejo, MS. (29 de Abril 1520).) The letter from Vera Cruz, however, was prepared under the eye of Cortés; and the last two were his confidential officers.

to a furious litigation between the parties, with which it is not necessary at present to embarrass the reader.

It is due to Velasquez to state that the instructions delivered by him for the conduct of the expedition cannot be charged with a narrow or mercenary spirit.   The first object of the voyage was to find Grijalva, after which the two commanders were to proceed in company together.   Reports had been brought back by Cordova, on his return from the first visit to Yucatan, that six Christians were said to be lingering in captivity in the interior of the country.   It was supposed they might belong to the party of the unfortunate Nicuessa, and orders were given to find them out, if possible, and restore them to liberty.   But the great object of the expedition was barter with the natives.   In pursuing this, special care was to be taken that they should receive no wrong, but be treated with kindness and humanity.   Cortés was to bear in mind, above all things, that the object which the Spanish monarch had most at heart was the conversion of the Indians. He was to impress on them the grandeur and goodness of his royal master, to invite them " to give in their allegiance to him, and to manifest it by regaling him with such comfortable presents of gold, pearls, and precious stones as, by showing their own goodwill, would secure his favour and protection."   He was to make an accurate survey of the coast, sounding its bays and inlets for the benefit of future navigators.   He was to acquaint himself with the natural products of the country, with the character of its different races, their institutions and progress in civilization ; and he was to send home minute accounts of all these, together with such articles as he should obtain in his intercourse with them.   Finally, he was to take *the most careful care* to omit nothing that might redound to the service of God or his sovereign.[1]

Such was the general tenor of the instructions given to Cortés ; and they must be admitted to provide for the interests of science and humanity, as well as for those which had reference only to a commercial speculation. It may seem strange, considering the discontent shown by Velasquez with his former captain, Grijalva, for not colonizing, that no directions should have been given to that effect here.   But he had not yet received from Spain the warrant for investing his agents with such powers ; and that which had been obtained from the Hieronymite fathers in Hispaniola conceded only the right to traffic with the natives.   The commission at the same time recognized the authority of Cortés as Captain-General of the expedition.[2]

---

[1] The instrument, in the original Castilian, will be found in Appendix, Part 2, No. 5. It is often referred to by writers who never saw it, as the Agreement between Cortés and Velasquez. It is, in fact, only the instructions given by this latter to his officer, who was no party to it.

[2] Declaracion de Puertocarrero, MS.—Gomara, Crónica, cap. 7.—Velasquez soon after obtained from the crown authority to colonize the new countries, with the title of *adelantado* over them The instrument was dated at Barcelona, Nov. 13th, 1518. (Herrera, Hist. general, dec. 2, lib. 3, cap. 8.) Empty privileges ! Las Casas gives a caustic etymology of the title of *adelantado,* so often granted to the Spanish discoverers. "Adelantados porque se adelantaran en hazer males y daños tan gravisimos á gentes pacificas." Hist. de las Indias, MS., lib. 3, cap. 117.

CHAPTER III.

JEALOUSY OF VELASQUEZ.—CORTÉS EMBARKS.—EQUIPMENT OF HIS FLEET.—
HIS PERSON AND CHARACTER.—RENDEZVOUS AT HAVANA.—STRENGTH
OF HIS ARMAMENT.

(1519.)

THE importance given to Cortés by his new position, and, perhaps, a somewhat more lofty bearing, gradually gave uneasiness to the naturally suspicious temper of Velasquez, who became apprehensive that his officer, when away where he would have the power, might also have the inclination, to throw off his dependence on him altogether. An accidental circumstance at this time heightened these suspicions. A mad fellow, his jester, one of those crack-brained wits—half wit, half fool—who formed in those days a common appendage to every great man's establishment, called out to the governor, as he was taking his usual walk one morning with Cortés towards the port, "Have a care, master Velasquez, or we shall have to go a hunting, some day or other, after this same captain of ours!" "Do you hear what the rogue says?" exclaimed the governor to his companion. "Do not heed him," said Cortés: "he is a saucy knave, and deserves a good whipping." The words sank deep, however, in the mind of Velasquez,—as, indeed, true jests are apt to stick.

There were not wanting persons about his Excellency who fanned the latent embers of jealousy into a blaze. These worthy gentlemen, some of them kinsmen of Velasquez, who probably felt their own deserts somewhat thrown into the shade by the rising fortunes of Cortés, reminded the governor of his ancient quarrel with that officer, and of the little probability that affronts so keenly felt at the time could ever be forgotten. By these and similar suggestions, and by misconstructions of the present conduct of Cortés, they wrought on the passions of Velasquez to such a degree that he resolved to intrust the expedition to other hands.[1]

He communicated his design to his confidential advisers, Lares and Duero, and these trusty personages reported it without delay to Cortés, although, "to a man of half his penetration," says Las Casas, "the thing would have been readily divined from the governor's altered demeanour."[2] The two functionaries advised their friend to expedite matters as much as possible, and to lose no time in getting his fleet ready for sea, if he would

[1] "Deterrebat," says the anonymous biographer, eum Cortesii natura imperii avida, fiducia sui ingens, et nimius sumptus in classe parandâ. Timere itaque Velasquius cœpit, si Cortesius cum eâ classe iret, nihil ad se vel honoris vel lucri rediturum." De Rebus gestis, MS.—Bernal Diaz, Hist. de la Conquista, cap. 19.—Las Casas, Hist. de las Indias, MS., cap. 114.

[2] "Cortés no avia menester mas para entendello de mirar el gesto á Diego Velasquez segun su astuta viveza y mundana sabiduría." Hist. de las Indias, MS., cap. 114.

retain the command of it.   Cortés showed the same prompt decision on this occasion which more than once afterwards in a similar crisis gave the direction to his destiny.

He had not yet got his complement of men, nor of vessels, and was very inadequately provided with supplies of any kind.   But he resolved to weigh anchor that very night.   He waited on his officers, informed them of his purpose, and probably of the cause of it; and at midnight, when the town was hushed in sleep, they all went quietly on board, and the little squadron dropped down the bay.   First, however, Cortés had visited the person whose business it was to supply the place with meat, and relieved him of all his stock on hand, notwithstanding his complaint that the city must suffer for it on the morrow, leaving him, at the same time, in payment, a massive gold chain of much value, which he wore round his neck.[1]

Great was the amazement of the good citizens of St. Jago when, at dawn, they saw that the fleet, which they knew was so ill prepared for the voyage, had left its moorings and was busily getting under way.   The tidings soon came to the ears of his Excellency, who, springing from his bed, hastily dressed himself, mounted his horse, and, followed by his retinue, galloped down to the quay.   Cortés, as soon as he descried their approach, entered an armed boat, and came within speaking-distance of the shore.   "And is it thus you part from me?" exclaimed Velasquez: "a courteous way of taking leave, truly!"   "Pardon me," answered Cortés; "time presses, and there are some things that should be done before they are even thought of.   Has your Excellency any commands?" But the mortified governor had no commands to give; and Cortés, politely waving his hand, returned to his vessel, and the little fleet instantly made sale for the port of Macaca, about fifteen leagues distant. (November 18, 1518.)   Velasquez rode back to his house to digest his chagrin as he best might; satisfied, probably, that he had made at least two blunders,—one in appointing Cortés to the command, the other in attempting to deprive him of it.   For, if it be true that by giving our confidence by halves we can scarcely hope to make a friend, it is equally true that by withdrawing it when given we shall make an enemy.[2]

This clandestine departure of Cortés has been severely criticised by some writers, especially by Las Casas.[3]   Yet much may be urged in vindication of his conduct.   He had been appointed to the command by the voluntary act of the governor, and this had been fully ratified by the

---

[1] Las Casas had the story from Cortés' own mouth. Hist. de las Indias, MS., cap. 114.—Gomara, Crónica, cap. 7.—De Rebus gestis, MS.

[2] Las Casas, Hist. de las Indias, MS., cap. 114.—Herrera, Hist. general, dec. 2, lib. 3, cap. 12.—Solis, who follows Bernal Diaz in saying that Cortés parted openly and amicably from Velasquez, seems to consider it a great slander on the character of the former to suppose that he wanted to break with the governor so soon, when he had received so little provocation. (Conquista, lib. 1, cap. 10.) But it is not necessary to suppose that Cortés intended a rupture with his employer by this clandestine movement, but only to secure himself in the command.   At all events, the text conforms in every particular to the statement of Las Casas, who, as he knew both the parties well, and resided on the island at the time, had ample means of information.

[3] Hist. de las Indias, MS., cap. 114.

authorities of Hispaniola. He had at once devoted all his resources to the undertaking, incurring, indeed, a heavy debt in addition. He was now to be deprived of his commission, without any misconduct having been alleged or at least proved against him. Such an event must overwhelm him in irretrievable ruin, to say nothing of the friends from whom he had so largely borrowed, and the followers who had embarked their fortunes in the expedition on the faith of his commanding it. There are few persons, probably, who, under these circumstances, would have felt called tamely to acquiesce in the sacrifice of their hopes to a groundless and arbitrary whim. The most to have been expected from Cortés was that he should feel obliged to provide faithfully for the interests of his employer in the conduct of the enterprise. How far he felt the force of this obligation will appear in the sequel.

From Macaca, where Cortés laid in such stores as he could obtain from the royal farms, and which, he said, he considered as "a loan from the king," he proceeded to Trinidad; a more considerable town, on the southern coast of Cuba. Here he landed, and, erecting his standard in front of his quarters, made proclamation, with liberal offers to all who would join the expedition. Volunteers came in daily, and among them more than a hundred of Grijalva's men, just returned from their voyage and willing to follow up the discovery under an enterprising leader. The fame of Cortés attracted, also, a number of cavaliers of family and distinction, some of whom, having accompanied Grijalva, brought much information valuable for the present expedition. Among these hidalgos may be mentioned Pedro de Alvarado and his brothers, Cristóval de Olid, Alonso de Avila, Juan Velasquez de Leon, a near relation of the governor, Alonso Hernandez de Puertocarrero, and Gonzalo de Sandoval,—all of them men who took a most important part in the Conquest. Their presence was of great moment, as giving consideration to the enterprise; and, when they entered the little camp of the adventurers, the latter turned out to welcome them amidst lively strains of music and joyous salvos of artillery.

Cortés meanwhile was active in purchasing military stores and provisions. Learning that a trading-vessel laden with grain and other commodities for the mines was off the coast, he ordered out one of his caravels to seize her and bring her into port. He paid the master in bills for both cargo and ship, and even persuaded this man, named Sedeño, who was wealthy, to join his fortunes to the expedition. He also despatched one of his officers, Diego de Ordaz, in quest of another ship, of which he had tidings, with instructions to seize it in like manner, and to meet him with it off Cape St. Antonio, the westerly point of the island.[1] By this he effected another object, that of getting rid of Ordaz, who was one of the governor's household, and an inconvenient spy on his own actions.

---

[1] Las Casas had this, also, from the lips of Cortés in later life. "Todo esto me dixo el mismo Cortés, con otras cosas cerca dello despues de Mar- | ques; . . . reindo y mofando é con estas formales palabras, *Á la mi fée andube por allí como un gentil cosario.*" Hist. de las Indias, MS., cap. 115.

While thus occupied, letters from Velasquez were received by the commander of Trinidad, requiring him to seize the person of Cortés and to detain him, as he had been deposed from the command of the fleet, which was given to another. This functionary communicated his instructions to the principal officers in the expedition, who counselled him not to make the attempt, as it would undoubtedly lead to a commotion among the soldiers, that might end in laying the town in ashes. Verdugo thought it prudent to conform to this advice.[1]

As Cortés was willing to strengthen himself by still further reinforcements, he ordered Alvarado with a small body of men to march across the country to the Havana, while he himself would sail round the westerly point of the island and meet him there with a squadron. In this port he again displayed his standard, making the usual proclamation. He caused all the large guns to be brought on shore, and, with the small-arms and crossbows, to be put in order. As there was abundance of cotton raised in this neighbourhood, he had the jackets of the soldiers thickly quilted with it, for a defence against the Indian arrows, from which the troops in the former expeditions had grievously suffered. He distributed his men into eleven companies, each under the command of an experienced officer; and it was observed that, although several of the cavaliers in the service were the personal friends and even kinsmen of Velasquez, he appeared to treat them all with perfect confidence.

His principal standard was of black velvet, embroidered with gold, and emblazoned with a red cross amidst flames of blue and white, with this motto in Latin beneath: "Friends, let us follow the Cross; and under this sign, if we have faith, we shall conquer." He now assumed more state in his own person and way of living, introducing a greater number of domestics and officers into his household, and placing it on a footing becoming a man of high station. This state he maintained through the rest of his life.[2]

Cortés at this time was thirty-three, or perhaps thirty-four, years of age. In stature he was rather above the middle size. His complexion was pale; and his large dark eye gave an expression of gravity to his countenance, not to have been expected in one of his cheerful temperament. His figure was slender, at least until later life; but his chest was deep, his shoulders broad, his frame muscular and well proportioned. It presented the union of agility and vigour which qualified him to excel in fencing, horsemanship, and the other generous exercises of chivalry. In his diet he was temperate, careless of what he ate, and drinking little; while to toil and privation he seemed perfectly indifferent. His dress, for he did not disdain the impression produced by such adventitious aids, was such as to set off his

[1] De Rebus gestis, MS.—Gomara, Crónica, cap. 8.
—Las Casas, Hist. de las Indias, MS., cap. 114, 115.
[2] Bernal Diaz, Hist. de la Conquista, cap. 24.—
De Rebus gestis, MS.—Gomara, Crónica, cap. 8.

—Las Casas, Hist. de las Indias, MS., cap. 115.—
The legend on the standard was, doubtless, suggested by that on the *labarum*,—the sacred banner of Constantine.

handsome person to advantage; neither gaudy nor striking, but rich. He wore few ornaments, and usually the same; but those were of great price. His manners, frank and soldier-like, concealed a most cool and calculating spirit. With his gayest humour there mingled a settled air of resolution, which made those who approached him feel they must obey, and which infused something like awe into the attachment of his most devoted followers. Such a combination, in which love was tempered by authority, was the one probably best calculated to inspire devotion in the rough and turbulent spirits among whom his lot was to be cast.

The character of Cortés seems to have undergone some change with change of circumstances; or, to speak more correctly, the new scenes in which he was placed called forth qualities which before lay dormant in his bosom. There are some hardy natures that require the heats of excited action to unfold their energies; like the plants which, closed to the mild influence of a temperate latitude, come to their full growth, and give forth their fruits, only in the burning atmosphere of the tropics. Such is the portrait left to us by his contemporaries of this remarkable man; the instrument selected by Providence to scatter terror among the barbarian monarchs of the Western World, and lay their empires in the dust.[1]

Before the preparations were fully completed at the Havana, the commander of the place, Don Pedro Barba, received despatches from Velasquez ordering him to apprehend Cortés and to prevent the departure of his vessels; while another epistle from the same source was delivered to Cortés himself, requesting him to postpone his voyage till the governor could communicate with him, as he proposed, in person. "Never," exclaims Las Casas, "did I see so little knowledge of affairs shown, as in this letter of Diego Velasquez,—that he should have imagined that a man who had so recently put such an affront on him would defer his departure at his bidding!"[2] It was, indeed, hoping to stay the flight of the arrow by a word, after it had left the bow.

The Captain-General, however, during his short stay, had entirely conciliated the goodwill of Barba. And, if that officer had had the inclination, he knew he had not the power, to enforce his principal's orders, in the face of a resolute soldiery, incensed at this ungenerous persecution of their commander, and "all of whom," in the words of the honest chronicler who bore part in the expedition, "officers and privates would have cheerfully laid down their lives for him."[3] Barba contented himself, therefore, with explaining to Velasquez the impracticability of the attempt, and at the same time endeavoured to tranquillize his apprehensions by asserting his own confidence in the fidelity of Cortés. To this the latter added a communication of his own, couched "in the soft terms he knew

---

[1] The most minute notices of the person and habits of Cortés are to be gathered from the narrative of the old cavalier Bernal Diaz, who served so long under him, and from Gomara, the general's chaplain. See in particular the last chapter of Gomara's Crónica, and cap. 203 of the Hist. de la Conquista.

[2] Las Casas, Hist. de las Indias, MS., cap. 115.

[3] Bernal Diaz, Hist. de la Conquista, cap. 24.

so well how to use," [1] in which he implored his Excellency to rely on his devotion to his interests, and concluded with the comfortable assurance that he and the whole fleet, God willing, would sail on the following morning.

Accordingly, on the 10th of February 1519, the little squadron got under way, and directed its course towards Cape St. Antonio, the appointed place of rendezvous. When all were brought together, the vessels were found to be eleven in number; one of them, in which Cortés himself went, was of a hundred tons' burden, three others were from seventy to eighty tons; the remainder were caravels and open brigantines. The whole was put under the direction of Antonio de Alaminos, as chief pilot; a veteran navigator, who had acted as pilot to Columbus in his last voyage, and to Cordova and Grijalva in the former expeditions to Yucatan.

Landing on the Cape and mustering his forces, Cortés found they amounted to one hundred and ten mariners, five hundred and fifty-three soldiers, including thirty-two crossbowmen, and thirteen arquebusiers, besides two hundred Indians of the island, and a few Indian women for menial offices. He was provided with ten heavy guns, four lighter pieces called falconets, and with a good supply of ammunition. [2] He had besides sixteen horses. They were not easily procured; for the difficulty of transporting them across the ocean in the flimsy craft of that day made them rare and incredibly dear in the Islands. [3] But Cortés rightfully estimated the importance of cavalry, however small in number, both for their actual service in the field, and for striking terror into the savages. With so paltry a force did he enter on a conquest which even his stout heart must have shrunk from attempting with such means, had he but foreseen half its real difficulties!

Before embarking, Cortés addressed his soldiers in a short but animated harangue. He told them they were about to enter on a noble enterprise, one that would make their name famous to after-ages. He was leading them to countries more vast and opulent than any yet visited by Europeans. "I hold out to you a glorious prize," continued the orator, "but it is to be won by incessant toil. Great things are achieved only by great exertions, and glory was never the reward of sloth. [4] If I have

---

[1] Bernal Diaz, Hist. de la Conquista, cap. 24.

[2] Bernal Diaz, Hist. de la Conquista, cap. 26.— There is some discrepancy among authorities in regard to the numbers of the army. The Letter from Vera Cruz, which should have been exact, speaks in round terms of only four hundred soldiers. (Carta de Vera Cruz, MS.) Velasquez himself, in a communication to the Chief Judge of Hispaniola, states the number at six hundred. (Carta de Diego Velasquez al Lic. Figueroa, MS.) I have adopted the estimates of Bernal Diaz, who, in his long service, seems to have become intimately acquainted with every one of his comrades, their persons, and private history.

[3] Incredibly dear indeed, since, from the statements contained in the depositions at Villa Segura, it appears that the cost of the horses for the expedition was from four to five hundred *pesos de oro* each!

"Si saben que de caballos que el dicho Señor Capitan General Hernando Cortés ha comprado para servir en la dicha Conquista, que son diez é ocho, que le han costado á quatrocientos cinquenta é á quinientos pesos ha pagado, é que deve mas de ocho mil pesos de oro dellos." (Probanza en Villa Segura, MS.) The estimation of these horses is sufficiently shown by the minute information. Bernal Diaz has thought proper to give of every one of them; minute enough for the pages of a sporting calendar. See Hist. de la Conquista, cap. 23.

[4] "Io vos propongo grandes premios, mas embueltos en grandes trabajos; pero la virtud no quiere ociosidad." (Gomara, Crónica, cap. 9.) It is the thought so finely expressed by Thomson:—

"For sluggard's brow the laurel never grows;
Renown is not the child of indolent repose."

laboured hard and staked my all on this undertaking, it is for the love of that renown which is the noblest recompense of man. But, if any among you covet riches more, be but true to me, as I will be true to you and to the occasion, and I will make you masters of such as our countrymen have never dreamed of! You are few in number, but strong in resolution; and, if this does not falter, doubt not but that the Almighty, who has never deserted the Spaniard in his contest with the infidel, will shield you, though encompassed by a cloud of enemies; for your cause is a *just cause*, and you are to fight under the banner of the Cross. Go forward, then," he concluded, "with alacrity and confidence, and carry to a glorious issue the work so auspiciously begun."[1]

The rough eloquence of the general, touching the various chords of ambition, avarice, and religious zeal, sent a thrill through the bosoms of his martial audience; and, receiving it with acclamations, they seemed eager to press forward under a chief who was to lead them not so much to battle, as to triumph.

Cortés was well satisfied to find his own enthusiasm so largely shared by his followers. Mass was then celebrated with the solemnities usual with the Spanish navigators when entering on their voyages of discovery. The fleet was placed under the immediate protection of St. Peter, the patron saint of Cortés, and, weighing anchor, took its departure on the eighteenth day of February 1519 for the coast of Yucatan.[2]

---

[1] The text is a very condensed abridgment of the original speech of Cortés,—or of his chaplain, as the case may be. See it, in Gomara, Crónica, cap. 9.

[2] Las Casas, Hist. de las Indias, MS., cap. 115. —Gomara, Crónica, cap. 10.—De Rebus gestis, MS.—"Tantus fuit armorum apparatus," exclaims the author of the last work, "quo alterum terrarum orbem bellis Cortesius concutit; ex tam parvis opibus tantum imperium Carolo facit; aperitque omnium primus Hispanæ genti Hispaniam novam!" The author of this work is unknown. It seems to have been part of a great compilation "De Orbe Novo," written, probably, on the plan of a series of biographical sketches, as the introduction speaks of a life of Columbus preceding this of Cortés. It was composed, as it states, while many of the old Con-querors were still surviving, and is addressed to the son of Cortés. The historian, therefore, had ample means of verifying the truth of his own statements, although they too often betray, in his partiality for his hero, the influence of the patronage under which the work was produced. It runs into a prolixity of detail which, however tedious, has its uses in a contemporary document. Unluckily, only the first book was finished, or, at least, has survived; terminating with the events of this chapter. It is written in Latin, in a pure and perspicuous style, and is conjectured with some plausibility to be the work of Calvet de Estrella, Chronicler of the Indies. The original exists in the Archives of Simancas, where it was discovered and transcribed by Muñoz, from whose copy that in my library was taken.

CHAPTER IV.

(1519.)

ORDERS were given for the vessels to keep as near together as possible,
and to take the direction of the *capitania*, or admiral's ship, which carried
a beacon-light in the stern during the night. But the weather, which had
been favourable, changed soon after their departure, and one of those
tempests set in which at this season are often found in the latitudes of the
West Indies. It fell with terrible force on the little navy, scattering it far
asunder, dismantling some of the ships, and driving them all considerably
south of their proposed destination.

Cortés, who had lingered behind to convoy a disabled vessel, reached
the island of Cozumel last. On landing, he learned that one of his
captains, Pedro de Alvarado, had availed himself of the short time he had
been there, to enter the temples, rifle them of their few ornaments, and, by
his violent conduct, so far to terrify the simple natives that they had fled
for refuge into the interior of the island. Cortés, highly incensed at these
rash proceedings, so contrary to the policy he had proposed, could not
refrain from severely reprimanding his officer in the presence of the army.
He commanded two Indian captives, taken by Alvarado, to be brought
before him, and explained to them the pacific purpose of his visit. This
he did through the assistance of his interpreter, Melchorejo, a native of
Yucatan, who had been brought back by Grijalva, and who during his
residence in Cuba had picked up some acquaintance with the Castilian.
He then dismissed them loaded with presents, and with an invitation
to their countrymen to return to their homes without fear of further
annoyance. This humane policy succeeded. The fugitives, reassured,
were not slow in coming back ; and an amicable intercourse was
established, in which Spanish cutlery and trinkets were exchanged for the
gold ornaments of the natives ; a traffic in which each party congratulated
itself—a philosopher might think with equal reason—on outwitting the
other.

The first object of Cortés was to gather tidings of the unfortunate
Christians who were reported to be still lingering in captivity on the
neighbouring continent. From some traders in the island he obtained
such a confirmation of the report that he sent Diego de Ordaz with two
brigantines to the opposite coast of Yucatan, with instructions to remain

there eight days. Some Indians went as messengers in the vessels, who consented to bear a letter to the captives informing them of the arrival of their countrymen in Cozumel, with a liberal ransom for their release. Meanwhile the general proposed to make an excursion to the different parts of the island, that he might give employment to the restless spirits of the soldiers, and ascertain the resources of the country.

It was poor and thinly peopled. But everywhere he recognized the vestiges of a higher civilization than what he had before witnessed in the Indian islands. The houses were some of them large, and often built of stone and lime. He was particularly struck with the temples, in which were towers constructed of the same solid materials, and rising several stories in height. In the court of one of these he was amazed by the sight of a cross, of stone and lime, about ten palms high. It was the emblem of the god of rain. Its appearance suggested the wildest conjectures, not merely to the unlettered soldiers, but subsequently to the European scholar, who speculated on the character of the races that had introduced there the sacred symbol of Christianity. But no such inference, as we shall see hereafter, could be warranted.[1] Yet it must be regarded as a curious fact that the Cross should have been venerated as the object of religious worship both in the New World and in regions of the Old where the light of Christianity had never risen.[2]

The next object of Cortés was to reclaim the natives from their gross idolatry and to substitute a purer form of worship. In accomplishing this he was prepared to use force, if milder measures should be ineffectual. There was nothing which the Spanish government had more earnestly at heart than the conversion of the Indians. It forms the constant burden of their instructions, and gave to the military expeditions in this western hemisphere somewhat of the air of a crusade. The cavalier who embarked in them entered fully into these chivalrous and devotional feelings. No doubt was entertained of the efficacy of conversion, however sudden might be the change or however violent the means. The sword was a good argument, when the tongue failed; and the spread of Mahometanism had shown that seeds sown by the hand of violence, far from perishing in the ground,

---

[1] See Appendix, Part I, Note 27.
[2] Carta de Vera Cruz, MS.—Bernal Diaz, Hist. de la Conquista, cap. 25, et seq.—Gomara, Crónica, cap. 10, 15.—Las Casas, Hist. de las Indias, MS., lib. 3, cap. 115.—Herrera, Hist. general, dec. 2, lib. 4, cap. 6.—Martyr, de Insulis nuper inventis (Coloniæ, 1574), p. 344.—While these pages were passing through the press, but not till two years after they were written, Mr. Stephens's important and interesting volumes appeared, containing the account of his second expedition to Yucatan. In the latter part of the work he describes his visit to Cozumel, now an uninhabited island covered with impenetrable forests. Near the shore he saw the remains of ancient Indian structures, which he conceives may possibly have been the same that met the eyes of Grijalva and Cortés, and which suggest to him some important inferences. He is led into further reflections on the existence of the cross as a symbol of worship among the islanders. (Incidents of Travel in Yucatan (New York, 1843), vol. ii. chap. 20.) As the discussion of these matters would lead me too far from the track of our narrative, I shall take occasion to return to them hereafter, when I treat of the architectural remains of the country.*

* [In the passages here referred to, the author has noticed various proofs of the existence of the cross as a symbol of worship among pagan nations both in the Old World and the New. The fact has been deemed a very puzzling one; yet the explanation, as traced by Dr. Brinton, is sufficiently simple: "The arms of the cross were designed to point to the cardinal points and represent the four winds,—the rain-bringers." Hence the name given to it in the Mexican language, signifying "Tree of our Life,"—a term well calculated to increase the wonderment of the Spanish discoverers. Myths of the New World, p. 96, et al.—ED.]

would spring up and bear fruit to after-time. If this were so in a bad cause, how much more would it be true in a good one! The Spanish cavalier felt he had a high mission to accomplish as a soldier of the Cross. However unauthorized or unrighteous the war into which he had entered may seem to us, to him it was a holy war. He was in arms against the infidel. Not to care for the soul of his benighted enemy was to put his own in jeopardy. The conversion of a single soul might cover a multitude of sins. It was not for morals that he was concerned, but for *the faith*. This, though understood in its most literal and limited sense, comprehended the whole scheme of Christian morality. Whoever died in the faith, however immoral had been his life, might be said to die in the Lord. Such was the creed of the Castilian knight of that day, as imbibed from the preachings of the pulpit, from cloisters and colleges at home, from monks and missionaries abroad,—from all save one, whose devotion, kindled at a purer source, was not, alas! permitted to send forth its radiance far into the thick gloom by which he was encompassed.[1]

No one partook more fully of the feelings above described than Hernan Cortés. He was, in truth, the very mirror of the time in which he lived, reflecting its motley characteristics, its speculative devotion and practical license, but with an intensity all his own. He was greatly scandalized at the exhibition of the idolatrous practices of the people of Cozumel, though untainted, as it would seem, with human sacrifices. He endeavoured to persuade them to embrace a better faith, through the agency of two ecclesiastics who attended the expedition,—the licentiate Juan Diaz and Father Bartolomé de Olmedo. The latter of these godly men afforded the rare example—rare in any age—of the union of fervent zeal with charity, while he beautifully illustrated in his own conduct the precepts which he taught. He remained with the army through the whole expedition, and by his wise and benevolent counsels was often enabled to mitigate the cruelties of the Conquerors, and to turn aside the edge of the sword from the unfortunate natives.

These two missionaries vainly laboured to persuade the people of Cozumel to renounce their abominations, and to allow the Indian idols, in which the Christians recognized the true lineaments of Satan,[2] to be thrown down and demolished. The simple natives, filled with horror at the proposed profanation, exclaimed that these were the gods who sent them the sunshine and the storm, and, should any violence be offered, they would be sure to avenge it by sending their lightnings on the heads of its perpetrators.

Cortés was probably not much of a polemic. At all events, he preferred on the present occasion action to argument, and thought that the best way

---

[1] See the biographical sketch of the good bishop Las Casas, the "Protector of the Indians," in the Postscript at the close of the present Book.

[2] "It may have been that the devil appeared to them as he is, and left these forms stamped on their imagination, so that the imitative power of the artist reveals itself in the ugliness of the image." Solís, Conquista, p. 39.

to convince the Indians of their error was to prove the falsehood of the prediction. He accordingly, without further ceremony, caused the venerated images to be rolled down the stairs of the great temple, amidst the groans and lamentations of the natives. An altar was hastily constructed, an image of the Virgin and Child placed over it, and mass was performed by Father Olmedo and his reverend companion for the first time within the walls of a temple in New Spain. The patient ministers tried once more to pour the light of the gospel into the benighted understandings of the islanders, and to expound the mysteries of the Catholic faith. The Indian interpreter must have afforded rather a dubious channel for the transmission of such abstruse doctrines. But they at length found favour with their auditors, who, whether overawed by the bold bearing of the invaders, or convinced of the impotence of deities that could not shield their own shrines from violation, now consented to embrace Christianity.[1]

While Cortés was thus occupied with the triumphs of the Cross, he received intelligence that Ordaz had returned from Yucatan without tidings of the Spanish captives. Though much chagrined, the general did not choose to postpone longer his departure from Cozumel. The fleet had been well stored with provisions by the friendly inhabitants, and, embarking his troops, Cortés, in the beginning of March, took leave of its hospitable shores. The squadron had not proceeded far, however, before a leak in one of the vessels compelled them to return to the same port. The detention was attended with important consequences ; so much so, indeed, that a writer of the time discerns in it "a great mystery and - miracle."[2]

Soon after landing, a canoe with several Indians was seen making its way from the neighbouring shores of Yucatan. On reaching the island, one of the men inquired, in broken Castilian, "if he were among Christians," and, being answered in the affirmative, threw himself on his knees and returned thanks to Heaven for his delivery. He was one of the unfortunate captives for whose fate so much interest had been felt. His name was Gerónimo de Aguilar, a native of Ecija, in Old Spain, where he had been regularly educated for the Church. He had been established with the colony at Darien, and on a voyage from that place to Hispaniola, eight years previous, was wrecked near the coast of Yucatan. He escaped with several of his companions in the ship's boat, where some perished from hunger and exposure, while others were sacrificed, on their reaching land, by the cannibal natives of the peninsula. Aguilar was preserved

---

[1] Carta de Vera Cruz, MS.—Gomara, Crónica, cap. 13.—Herrera, Hist. general, dec. 2, lib. 4, cap. 7.—Ixtlilxochitl, Hist. Chich., MS., cap. 78.— Las Casas, whose enlightened views in religion would have done honour to the present age, insists on the futility of these forced conversions, by which it was proposed in a few days to wean men from the idolatry which they had been taught to reverence from the cradle. "The only way of doing this," he says, "is by long, assiduous, and faithful preaching, until the heathen shall gather some ideas of the true nature of the Deity and of the doctrines they are to embrace. Above all, the lives of the Christians should be such as to exemplify the truth of these doctrines, that, seeing this, the poor Indian may glorify the Father, and acknowledge him, who has such worshippers, for the true and only God." See the original remarks, which I quote *in extenso*, as a good specimen of the bishop's style when kindled by his subject into eloquence, in Appendix, Part 2, No. 6.

[2] " Muy gran misterio y milagro de Dios." Carta de Vera Cruz, MS.

I

from the same dismal fate by escaping into the interior, where he fell into the hands of a powerful cacique, who, though he spared his life, treated him at first with great rigour. The patience of the captive, however, and his singular humility, touched the better feelings of the chieftain, who would have persuaded Aguilar to take a wife among his people, but the ecclesiastic steadily refused, in obedience to his vows. This admirable constancy excited the distrust of the cacique, who put his virtue to a severe test by various temptations, and much of the same sort as those with which the Devil is said to have assailed St. Anthony.[1] From all these fiery trials, however, like his ghostly predecessor, he came out unscorched. Continence is too rare and difficult a virtue with barbarians, not to challenge their veneration, and the practice of it has made the reputation of more than one saint in the Old as well as the New World. Aguilar was now intrusted with the care of his master's household and his numerous wives. He was a man of discretion, as well as virtue ; and his counsels were found so salutary that he was consulted on all important matters. In short, Aguilar became a great man among the Indians.

It was with much regret, therefore, that his master received the proposals for his return to his countrymen, to which nothing but the rich treasure of glass beads, hawk-bells, and other jewels of like value, sent for his ransom, would have induced him to consent. When Aguilar reached the coast, there had been so much delay that the brigantines had sailed ; and it was owing to the fortunate return of the fleet to Cozumel that he was enabled to join it.

On appearing before Cortés, the poor man saluted him in the Indian style, by touching the earth with his hand and carrying it to his head. The commander, raising him up, affectionately embraced him, covering him at the same time with his own cloak, as Aguilar was simply clad in the habiliments of the country, somewhat too scanty for a European eye. It was long, indeed, before the tastes which he had acquired in the freedom of the forest could be reconciled to the constraints either of dress or manners imposed by the artificial forms of civilization. Aguilar's long residence in the country had familiarized him with the Mayan dialects of Yucatan, and, as he gradually revived his Castilian, he became of essential importance as an interpreter. Cortés saw the advantage of this from the first, but he could not fully estimate all the consequences that were to flow from it.[2]

The repairs of the vessels being at length completed, the Spanish commander once more took leave of the friendly natives of Cozumel, and set

---

[1] They are enumerated by Herrera with a minuteness which may claim at least the merit of giving a much higher notion of Aguilar's virtue than the barren generalities of the text. (Hist. general, dec. 2, lib. 4, cap. 6–8.) The story is prettily told by Washington Irving. Voyages and Discoveries of the Companions of Columbus (London, 1833), p. 263, et seq.

[2] Camargo, Historia de Tlascala, MS.—Oviedo, Hist. de las Indias, MS., lib. 33, cap. 1.—Martyr, De Insulis, p. 347.—Bernal Diaz, Hist. de la Conquista, cap. 29.—Carta de Vera Cruz, MS.—Las Casas, Hist. de las Indias, MS.. lib. 3, cap. 115, 116.

sail on the 4th of March. Keeping as near as possible to the coast of Yucatan, he doubled Cape Catoche, and with flowing sheets swept down the broad bay of Campeachy, fringed with the rich dye-woods which have since furnished so important an article of commerce to Europe. He passed Potonchan, where Cordova had experienced a rough reception from the natives; and soon after reached the mouth of the *Rio de Tabasco*, or *Grijalva*, in which that navigator had carried on so lucrative a traffic. Though mindful of the great object of his voyage,—the visit to the Aztec territories,—he was desirous of acquainting himself with the resources of this country, and determined to ascend the river and visit the great town on its borders.

The water was so shallow, from the accumulation of sand at the mouth of the stream, that the general was obliged to leave the ships at anchor and to embark in the boats with a part only of his forces. The banks were thickly studded with mangrove-trees, that, with their roots shooting up and interlacing one another, formed a kind of impervious screen or network, behind which the dark forms of the natives were seen glancing to and fro with the most menacing looks and gestures. Cortés, much surprised at these unfriendly demonstrations, so unlike what he had had reason to expect, moved cautiously up the stream. When he had reached an open place, where a large number of Indians were assembled, he asked, through his interpreter, leave to land, explaining at the same time his amicable intentions. But the Indians, brandishing their weapons, answered only with gestures of angry defiance. Though much chagrined, Cortés thought it best not to urge the matter further that evening, but withdrew to a neighbouring island, where he disembarked his troops, resolved to effect a landing on the following morning.

When day broke, the Spaniards saw the opposite banks lined with a much more numerous array than on the preceding evening, while the canoes along the shore were filled with bands of armed warriors. Cortés now made his preparations for the attack. He first landed a detachment of a hundred men under Alonso de Avila, at a point somewhat lower down the stream, sheltered by a thick grove of palms, from which a road, as he knew, led to the town of Tabasco, giving orders to his officer to march at once on the place, while he himself advanced to assault it in front.[1]

Then, embarking the remainder of his troops, Cortés crossed the river in face of the enemy; but, before commencing hostilities, that he might "act with entire regard to justice, and in obedience to the instructions of the Royal Council,"[2] he first caused proclamation to be made, through the interpreter, that he desired only a free passage for his men, and that

---

[1] Bernal Diaz, Hist. de la Conquista, cap. 31.—Carta de Vera Cruz, MS.—Gomara, Crónica, cap. 18.—Las Casas, Hist. de las Indias, MS., lib. 3, cap. 118.—Martyr, De Insulis, p. 348.—There are some discrepancies between the statements of Bernal Diaz and the Letter from Vera Cruz; both by parties who were present.

[2] Carta de Vera Cruz, MS —Bernal Diaz, Hist. de la Conquista, cap. 31.

he proposed to revive the friendly relations which had formerly subsisted between his countrymen and the natives. He assured them that if blood were spilt the sin would lie on their heads, and that resistance would be useless, since he was resolved at all hazards to take up his quarters that night in the town of Tabasco. This proclamation, delivered in lofty tone, and duly recorded by the notary, was answered by the Indians—who might possibly have comprehended one word in ten of it—with shouts of defiance and a shower of arrows.[1]

Cortés, having now complied with all the requisitions of a loyal cavalier, and shifted the responsibility from his own shoulders to those of the Royal Council, brought his boats alongside of the Indian canoes. They grappled fiercely together, and both parties were soon in the water, which rose above the girdle. The struggle was not long, though desperate. The superior strength of the Europeans prevailed, and they forced the enemy back to land. Here, however, they were supported by their countrymen, who showered down darts, arrows, and blazing billets of wood on the heads of the invaders. The banks were soft and slippery, and it was with difficulty the soldiers made good their footing. Cortés lost a sandal in the mud, but continued to fight barefoot, with great exposure of his person, as the Indians, who soon singled out the leader, called to one another, "Strike at the chief!"

At length the Spaniards gained the bank, and were able to come into something like order, when they opened a brisk fire from their arquebuses and crossbows. The enemy, astounded by the roar and flash of the firearms, of which they had had no experience, fell back, and retreated behind a breastwork of timber thrown across the way. The Spaniards, hot in the pursuit, soon carried these rude defences, and drove the Tabascans before them towards the town, where they again took shelter behind their palisades.

Meanwhile Avila had arrived from the opposite quarter, and the natives, taken by surprise, made no further attempt at resistance, but abandoned the place to the Christians. They had previously removed their families and effects. Some provisions fell into the hands of the victors, but little gold, "a circumstance," says Las Casas, "which gave them no particular satisfaction."[2] It was a very populous place. The houses were mostly of mud ; the better sort of stone and lime ; affording proofs in the inhabitants

---

[1] "See," exclaims the Bishop of Chiapa, in his caustic vein, "the reasonableness of this 'requisition,' or, to speak more correctly, the folly and insensibility of the Royal Council, who could find, in the refusal of the Indians to receive it, a good pretext for war." (Hist. de las Indias, MS., lib. 3, cap. 118.) In another place he pronounces an animated invective against the iniquity of those who covered up hostilities under this empty form of words, the import of which was utterly incomprehensible to the barbarians. (Ibid., lib. 3, cap. 57.) The famous formula, used by the Spanish con-querors on this occasion, was drawn up by Dr. Palacios Reubios, a man of letters, and a member of the King's council. "But I laugh at him and his letters," exclaims Oviedo, "if he thought a word of it could be comprehended by the untutored Indians!" (Hist. de las Ind., MS., lib. 29, cap. 7.) The regular Manifesto, *requirimiento*, may be found translated in the concluding pages of Irving's "Voyages of the Companions of Columbus."

[2] "Halláronlas llenas de maiz é gallinas y otros vastimentos, oro ninguno, de lo que ellos no resciviéron mucho plazer." Hist de las Ind , MS., ubi supra.

of a superior refinement to that found in the Islands, as their stout resistance had given evidence of superior valour.[1]

Cortés, having thus made himself master of the town, took formal possession of it for the crown of Castile. He gave three cuts with his sword on a large *ceiba*-tree which grew in the place, and proclaimed aloud that he took possession of the city in the name and behalf of the Catholic sovereigns, and would maintain and defend the same with sword and buckler against all who should gainsay it. The same vaunting declaration was also made by the soldiers, and the whole was duly recorded and attested by the notary. This was the usual simple but chivalric form with which the Spanish cavaliers asserted the royal title to the conquered territories in the New World. It was a good title, doubtless, against the claims of any other European potentate.

The general took up his quarters that night in the courtyard of the principal temple. He posted his sentinels, and took all the precautions practised in wars with a civilized foe. Indeed, there was reason for them. A suspicious silence seemed to reign through the place and its neighbourhood; and tidings were brought that the interpreter, Melchorejo, had fled, leaving his Spanish dress hanging on a tree. Cortés was disquieted by the desertion of this man, who would not only inform his countrymen of the small number of the Spaniards, but dissipate any illusions that might be entertained of their superior natures.

On the following morning, as no traces of the enemy were visible, Cortés ordered out a detachment under Alvarado, and another under Francisco de Lujo, to reconnoitre. The latter officer had not advanced a league, before he learned the position of the Indians, by their attacking him in such force that he was fain to take shelter in a large stone building, where he was closely besieged. Fortunately, the loud yells of the assailants, like most barbarous nations seeking to strike terror by their ferocious cries, reached the ears of Alvarado and his men, who, speedily advancing to the relief of their comrades, enabled them to force a passage through the enemy. Both parties retreated, closely pursued, on the town, when Cortés, marching out to their support, compelled the Tabascans to retire.

A few prisoners were taken in this skirmish. By them Cortés found his worst apprehensions verified. The country was everywhere in arms. A force consisting of many thousands had assembled from the neighbouring provinces, and a general assault was resolved on for the next day. To the general's inquiries why he had been received in so different a

---

[1] Peter Martyr gives a glowing picture of this Indian capital. "Ad fluminis ripam protentum dicunt esse oppidum, quantum non ausim dicere: mille quingentorum passuum, ait Alaminus nauclerus, et domorum quinque ac viginti millium: stringunt alij, ingens tamen fatentur et celebre. Hortis intersecantur domus, quæ sunt *egregiè lapidibus et calce fabrefactæ, maximâ industriâ et architectorum arte.*" (De Insulis, p. 349.) With his usual inquisitive spirit, he gleaned all the particulars from the old pilot Alaminos, and from two of the officers of Cortés who revisited Spain in the course of that year. Tabasco was in the neighbourhood of those ruined cities of Yucatan which have lately been the theme of so much speculation. The encomiums of Martyr are not so remarkable as the apathy of other contemporary chroniclers.

manner from his predecessor, Grijalva, they answered that "the conduct of the Tabascans then had given great offence to the other Indian tribes, who taxed them with treachery and cowardice ; so that they had promised, on any return of the white men, to resist them in the same manner as their neighbours had done." [1]

Cortés might now well regret that he had allowed himself to deviate from the direct object of his enterprise, and to become entangled in a doubtful war which could lead to no profitable result. But it was too late to repent. He had taken the step, and had no alternative but to go forward. To retreat would dishearten his own men at the outset, impair their confidence in him as their leader, and confirm the arrogance of his foes, the tidings of whose success might precede him on his voyage and prepare the way for greater mortifications and defeats. He did not hesitate as to the course he was to pursue, but, calling his officers together, announced his intention to give battle the following morning. [2]

He sent back to the vessels such as were disabled by their wounds, and ordered the remainder of the forces to join the camp. Six of the heavy guns were also taken from the ships, together with all the horses. The animals were stiff and torpid from long confinement on board ; but a few hours' exercise restored them to their strength and usual spirit. He gave the command of the artillery—if it may be dignified with the name— to a soldier named Mesa, who had acquired some experience as an engineer in the Italian wars. The infantry he put under the orders of Diego de Ordaz, and took charge of the cavalry himself. It consisted of some of the most valiant gentlemen of his little band, among whom may be mentioned Alvarado, Velasquez de Leon, Avila, Puertocarrero, Olid, Montejo. Having thus made all the necessary arrangements, and settled his plan of battle, he retired to rest,—but not to slumber. His feverish mind, as may well be imagined, was filled with anxiety for the morrow, which might decide the fate of his expedition ; and, as was his wont on such occasions, he was frequently observed, during the night, going the rounds, and visiting the sentinels, to see that no one slept upon his post.

At the first glimmering of light he mustered his army, and declared his purpose not to abide, cooped up in the town, the assault of the enemy, but to march at once against him. For he well knew that the spirits rise with action, and that the attacking party gathers a confidence from the very movement, which is not felt by the one who is passively, perhaps anxiously, awaiting the assault. The Indians were understood to be encamped on a level ground a few miles distant from the city, called the plain of Ceutla. The general commanded that Ordaz should march with the foot, including the artillery, directly across the country, and attack

---

[1] Bernal Diaz, Hist. de la Conquista, cap. 31, 32.—Gomara, Crónica, cap. 18.—Las Casas, Hist. de las Indias, MS., lib. 3, cap. 118, 119.—Ixtlilxochitl, Hist. Chich., MS., cap. 78, 79.

[2] According to Solis, who quotes the address of Cortés on the occasion, he summoned a council of his captains to advise him as to the course he should pursue. (Conquista, cap. 19.) It is possible ; but I find no warrant for it anywhere.

them in front, while he himself would fetch a circuit with the horse, and turn their flank when thus engaged, or fall upon their rear.

These dispositions being completed, the little army heard mass and then sallied forth from the wooden walls of Tabasco. It was Lady-day, the twenty-fifth of March,—long memorable in the annals of New Spain. The district around the town was checkered with patches of maize, and, on the lower level, with plantations of cacao,—supplying the beverage, and perhaps the coin, of the country, as in Mexico. These plantations, requiring constant irrigation, were fed by numerous canals and reservoirs of water, so that the country could not be traversed without great toil and difficulty. It was, however, intersected by a narrow path or causeway over which the cannon could be dragged.

The troops advanced more than a league on their laborious march, without descrying the enemy. The weather was sultry, but few of them were embarrassed by the heavy mail worn by the European cavaliers at that period. Their cotton jackets, thickly quilted, afforded a tolerable protection against the arrows of the Indians, and allowed room for the freedom and activity of movement essential to a life of rambling adventure in the wilderness.

At length they came in sight of the broad plains of Ceutla, and beheld the dusky lines of the enemy stretching, as far as the eye could reach, along the edge of the horizon. The Indians had shown some sagacity in the choice of their position; and, as the weary Spaniards came slowly on, floundering through the morass, the Tabascans set up their hideous battle-cries, and discharged volleys of arrows, stones, and other missiles, which rattled like hail on the shields and helmets of the assailants. Many were severely wounded before they could gain the firm ground, where they soon cleared a space for themselves, and opened a heavy fire of artillery and musketry on the dense columns of the enemy, which presented a fatal mark for the balls. Numbers were swept down at every discharge; but the bold barbarians, far from being dismayed, threw up dust and leaves to hide their losses, and, sounding their war-instruments, shot off fresh flights of arrows in return.

They even pressed closer on the Spaniards, and, when driven off by a vigorous charge, soon turned again, and, rolling back like the waves of the ocean, seemed ready to overwhelm the little band by weight of numbers. Thus cramped, the latter had scarcely room to perform their necessary evolutions, or even to work their guns with effect.[1]

The engagement had now lasted more than an hour, and the Spaniards, sorely pressed, looked with great anxiety for the arrival of the horse—which some unaccountable impediments must have detained—to relieve them from their perilous position. At this crisis, the farthest columns of

[1] Las Casas, Hist. de las Indias, MS., lib. 3, cap. 119.—Gomara, Crónica, cap. 19, 20 —Herrera, Hist. general, dec. 2, lib. 4, cap. 11.—Martyr, De Insulis, p. 350.—Ixtlilxochitl, Hist. Chich., MS., cap. 79.— Bernal Diaz, Hist. de la Conquista, cap. 33, 36.— Carta de Vera Cruz, MS.

the Indian army were seen to be agitated and thrown into a disorder that rapidly spread through the whole mass. It was not long before the ears of the Christians were saluted with the cheering war-cry of "San Jago and San Pedro!" and they beheld the bright helmets and swords of the Castilian chivalry flashing back the rays of the morning sun, as they dashed through the ranks of the enemy, striking to the right and left, and scattering dismay around them. The eye of faith, indeed, could discern the patron Saint of Spain, himself, mounted on his grey war-horse, heading the rescue and trampling over the bodies of the fallen infidels![1]

The approach of Cortés had been greatly retarded by the broken nature of the ground. When he came up, the Indians were so hotly engaged that he was upon them before they observed his approach. He ordered his men to direct their lances at the faces of their opponents,[2] who, terrified at the monstrous apparition,—for they supposed the rider and the horse, which they had never before seen, to be one and the same,[3]—were seized with a panic. Ordaz availed himself of it to command a general charge along the line, and the Indians, many of them throwing away their arms, fled without attempting further resistance.

Cortés was too content with the victory to care to follow it up by dipping his sword in the blood of the fugitives. He drew off his men to a copse of palms which skirted the place, and under their broad canopy the soldiers offered up thanksgivings to the Almighty for the victory vouchsafed them. The field of battle was made the site of a town, called, in honour of the day on which the action took place, *Santa María de la Victoria,* long afterwards the capital of the province.[4] The number of those who fought or fell in the engagement is altogether doubtful. Nothing, indeed, is more uncertain than numerical estimates of barbarians. And they gain nothing in probability when they come, as in the present instance, from the reports of their enemies. Most accounts, however, agree that the Indian force consisted of five squadrons of eight thousand men each. There is more discrepancy as to the number of slain, varying

---

[1] Ixtlilxochitl, Hist. Chich., MS., cap. 79.— "Cortés supposed it was his own tutelar saint, St. Peter," says Pizarro y Orellana; "but the common and indubitable opinion is that it was our glorious apostle St. James, the bulwark and safeguard of our nation." (Varones ilustres, p. 73.) "Sinner that I am," exclaims honest Bernal Diaz, in a more sceptical vein, "it was not permitted to me to see either the one or the other of the Apostles on this occasion." Hist. de la Conquista, cap. 34.*

[2] It was the order—as the reader may remember

—given by Cæsar to his followers in his battle with Pompey :—

"Adversosque jubet ferro confundere vultus."
LUCAN, Pharsalia, lib. 7, v. 575.

[3] "Equites," says Paolo Giovio, "unum integrum Centaurorum specie animal esse existimarent." Elogia Virorum Illustrium (Basil, 1696), lib. 6, p. 229.
[4] Clavigero, Stor. del Messico, tom. iii. p. 11.

* [The remark of Bernal Diaz is not to be taken as ironical. His faith in the same vision on subsequent occasions is expressed without demur. In the present case he recognized the rider of the grey horse as a Spanish cavalier, Francisco de Morla. It appears from the account of Andrés de Tápia, another companion of Cortés, whose narrative has been recently published, that, owing to canals and other impediments, the cavalry was unable to effect the intended détour, and it therefore returned and joined the infantry. The latter, meanwhile, having seen a cavalier on a grey horse charging the Indians in their rear, supposed that the cavalry had penetrated to that quarter. Cortés, on hearing this, exclaimed, "Adelante, compañeros, que Dios es con nosotros." (Icazbalceta, Col. de Doc. para la Hist. de México, tom. i.) Tápia says nothing about St. James or St. Peter, and perhaps suspected that the incident was a ruse contrived by Cortés. Generally, however, such legends seem to be sufficiently explained by the religious belief and excited imagination of the narrators. See the remarks, on this point, of Macaulay, who notices the account of Diaz, in the introduction to his lay of the Battle of the Lake Regillus.—ED.]

from one to thirty thousand! In this monstrous discordance, the common disposition to exaggerate may lead us to look for truth in the neighbour-hood of the smallest number. The loss of the Christians was inconsider-able; not exceeding—if we receive their own reports, probably, from the same causes, much diminishing the truth—two killed and less than a hundred wounded! We may readily comprehend the feelings of the Con-querors, when they declared that "Heaven must have fought on their side, since their own strength could never have prevailed against such a multitude of enemies!"[1]

Several prisoners were taken in the battle, among them two chiefs. Cortés gave them their liberty, and sent a message by them to their countrymen "that he would overlook the past, if they would come in at once and tender their submission. Otherwise he would ride over the land, and put every living thing in it, man, woman, and child, to the sword!" With this formidable menace ringing in their ears, the envoys departed.

But the Tabascans had no relish for further hostilities. A body of inferior chiefs appeared the next day, clad in dark dresses of cotton, intimating their abject condition, and implored leave to bury their dead. It was granted by the general, with many assurances of his friendly dis-position; but at the same time he told them he expected their principal caciques, as he would treat with none other. These soon presented themselves, attended by a numerous train of vassals, who followed with timid curiosity to the Christian camp. Among their propitiatory gifts were twenty female slaves, which, from the character of one of them, proved of infinitely more consequence than was anticipated by either Spaniards or Tabascans. Confidence was soon restored, and was suc-ceeded by a friendly intercourse, and the interchange of Spanish toys for the rude commodities of the country, articles of food, cotton, and a few gold ornaments of little value. When asked where the precious metal was procured, they pointed to the west, and answered, "Culhua," "Mexico." The Spaniards saw this was no place for them to traffic, or to tarry in. Yet here, they were not many leagues distant from a potent and opulent city, or what once had been so, the ancient Palenque. But its glory may have even then passed away, and its name have been forgotten by the surrounding nations.

Before his departure the Spanish commander did not omit to provide for one great object of his expedition, the conversion of the Indians. He first represented to the caciques that he had been sent thither by a powerful monarch on the other side of the water, for whom he had now

---

[1] "Crean Vras. Reales Altezas por cierto, que esta batalla fué vencida mas por voluntad de Dios que por nras, fuerzas, porque para con quarenta mil hombres de guerra, poca defensa fuera quatrozientos que nosotros eramos." (Carta de Vera Cruz, MS.—Gomara, Crónica, cap. 20.—Bernal Diaz, Hist. de la Conquista, cap. 35.) It is Las Casas, who, regu-lating his mathematics, as usual, by his feelings, rates the Indian loss at the exorbitant amount cited in the text. "This," he concludes, dryly, "was the first preaching of the gospel by Cortés in New Spain!" Hist. de las Indias, MS., lib. 3, cap. 119.

a right to claim their allegiance. He then caused the reverend fathers Olmedo and Diaz to enlighten their minds, as far as possible, in regard to the great truths of revelation, urging them to receive these in place of their own heathenish abominations. The Tabascans, whose perceptions were no doubt materially quickened by the discipline they had undergone, made but a faint resistance to either proposal. The next day was Palm Sunday, and the general resolved to celebrate their conversion by one of those pompous ceremonials of the Church, which should make a lasting impression on their minds.

A solemn procession was formed of the whole army, with the ecclesiastics at their head, each soldier bearing a palm branch in his hand. The concourse was swelled by thousands of Indians of both sexes, who followed in curious astonishment at the spectacle. The long files bent their way through the flowery savannas that bordered the settlement, to the principal temple, where an altar was raised, and the image of the presiding deity was deposed to make room for that of the Virgin with the infant Saviour. Mass was celebrated by Father Olmedo, and the soldiers who were capable joined in the solemn chant. The natives listened in profound silence, and, if we may believe the chronicler of the event who witnessed it, were melted into tears; while their hearts were penetrated with reverential awe for the God of those terrible beings who seemed to wield in their own hands the thunder and the lightning.[1]

The Roman Catholic communion has, it must be admitted, some decided advantages over the Protestant, for the purposes of proselytism. The dazzling pomp of its service and its touching appeal to the sensibilities affect the imagination of the rude child of nature much more powerfully than the cold abstractions of Protestantism, which, addressed to the reason, demand a degree of refinement and mental culture in the audience to comprehend them. The respect, moreover, shown by the Catholic for the material representations of Divinity, greatly facilitates the same object. It is true, such representations are used by him only as incentives, not as the objects of worship. But this distinction is lost on the savage, who finds such forms of adoration too analogous to his own to impose any great violence on his feelings. It is only required of him to transfer his homage from the image of Quetzalcoatl, the benevolent deity who walked among men, to that of the Virgin or the Redeemer; from the Cross, which he has worshipped as the emblem of the god of rain, to the same Cross, the symbol of salvation.

These solemnities concluded, Cortés prepared to return to his ships, well satisfied with the impression made on the new converts, and with the conquests he had thus achieved for Castile and Christianity. The soldiers, taking leave of their Indian friends, entered the boats with the palm branches

---

[1] Gomara, Crónica, cap. 21, 22.—Carta de Vera Cruz, MS.—Martyr, De Insulis, p. 351.—Las Casas, Hist. de las Indias, MS., ubi supra.

in their hands, and, descending the river, re-embarked on board their vessels, which rode at anchor at its mouth. A favourable breeze was blowing, and the little navy, opening its sails to receive it, was soon on its way again to the golden shores of Mexico.

CHAPTER V.

VOYAGE ALONG THE COAST.—DOÑA MARINA.—SPANIARDS LAND IN MEXICO. —INTERVIEW WITH THE AZTECS.

(1519.)

THE fleet held its course so near the shore that the inhabitants could be seen on it; and, as it swept along the winding borders of the Gulf, the soldiers, who had been on the former expedition with Grijalva, pointed out to their companions the memorable places on the coast. Here was the *Rio de Alvarado,* named after the gallant adventurer, who was present also in this expedition; there the *Rio de Vanderas,* in which Grijalva had carried on so lucrative a commerce with the Mexicans; and there the *Isla de los Sacrificios,* where the Spaniards first saw the vestiges of human sacrifice on the coast. Puertocarrero, as he listened to these reminiscences of the sailors, repeated the words of the old ballad of Montesinos, " Here is France, there is Paris, and there the waters of the Duero,"[1] etc. " But I advise you," he added, turning to Cortés, " to look out only for the rich lands, and the best way to govern them." " Fear not," replied his commander : " if Fortune but favours me as she did Orlando, and I have such gallant gentlemen as you for my companions, I shall understand myself very well."[2]

The fleet had now arrived off San Juan de Ulua, the island so named by Grijalva. The weather was temperate and serene, and crowds of natives were gathered on the shore of the mainland, gazing at the strange phenomenon, as the vessels glided along under easy sail on the smooth bosom of the waters. It was the evening of Thursday in Passion Week. The air came pleasantly off the shore, and Cortés, liking the spot, thought he might safely anchor under the lee of the island, which would shelter him from the *nortes* that sweep over these seas with fatal violence in the winter, sometimes even late in the spring.

The ships had not been long at anchor, when a light pirogue, filled with

---

[1] " Cata Francia, Montesinos,
Cata Paris la ciudad,
Cata las aguas de Duero
Do van á dar en la mar."

They are the words of the popular old ballad, first published, I believe, in the Romancero de Ambéres, and lately by Duran, Romances caballerescos é históricos, Parte 1, p. 82.

[2] Bernal Diaz, Hist. de la Conquista, cap. 37.

natives, shot off from the neighbouring continent, and steered for the general's vessel, distinguished by the royal ensign of Castile floating from the mast.   The Indians came on board with a frank confidence, inspired by the accounts of the Spaniards spread by their countrymen who had traded with Grijalva.   They brought presents of fruits and flowers and little ornaments of gold, which they gladly exchanged for the usual trinkets. Cortés was baffled in his attempts to hold a conversation with his visitors by means of the interpreter, Aguilar, who was ignorant of the language ; the Mayan dialects, with which he was conversant, bearing too little resemblance to the Aztec.   The natives supplied the deficiency, as far as possible, by the uncommon vivacity and significance of their gestures,— the hieroglyphics of speech ; but the Spanish commander saw with chagrin the embarrassments he must encounter in future for want of a more perfect medium of communication.[1]   In this dilemma, he was informed that one of the female slaves given to him by the Tabascan chiefs was a native Mexican, and understood the language.   Her name—that given to her by the Spaniards—was Marina ; and, as she was to exercise a most important influence on their fortunes, it is necessary to acquaint the reader with something of her character and history.

She was born at Painalla, in the province of Coatzacualco, on the south-eastern borders of the Mexican empire.   Her father, a rich and powerful cacique, died when she was very young.   Her mother married again, and, having a son, she conceived the infamous idea of securing to this offspring of her second union Marina's rightful inheritance.   She accordingly feigned that the latter was dead, but secretly delivered her into the hands of some itinerant traders of Xicallanco.   She availed herself, at the same time, of the death of a child of one of her slaves, to substitute the corpse for that of her own daughter, and celebrated the obsequies with mock solemnity. These particulars are related by the honest old soldier Bernal Diaz, who knew the mother, and witnessed the generous treatment of her afterwards by Marina.   By the merchants the Indian maiden was again sold to the cacique of Tabasco, who delivered her, as we have seen, to the Spaniards.

From the place of her birth, she was well acquainted with the Mexican tongue, which, indeed, she is said to have spoken with great elegance. Her residence in Tabasco familiarized her with the dialects of that country, so that she could carry on a conversation with Aguilar, which he in turn rendered into the Castilian.   Thus a certain though somewhat circuitous channel was opened to Cortés for communicating with the Aztecs ; a circumstance of the last importance to the success of his enterprise.   It was not very long, however, before Marina, who had a lively genius, made

---

1 Las Casas notices the significance of the Indian gestures as implying a most active imagination : "Señas é meneos con que los Yndios mucho mas que otras generaciones entienden y se dan á entender, por   tener muy bivos los sentidos exteriores y tambien los interiores, mayormente que es admirable su imaginacion." Hist. de las Indias, MS., lib. 3, cap. 120.

herself so far mistress of the Castilian as to supersede the necessity of any other linguist. She learned it the more readily, as it was to her the language of love.

Cortés, who appreciated the value of her services from the first, made her his interpreter, then his secretary, and, won by her charms, his mistress, she had a son by him, Don Martin Cortés, *comendador* of the Military Order of St. James, less distinguished by his birth than his unmerited persecutions.

Marina was at this time in the morning of life. She is said to have possessed uncommon personal attractions,[1] and her open, expressive features indicated her generous temper. She always remained faithful to the countrymen of her adoption; and her knowledge of the language and customs of the Mexicans, and often of their designs, enabled her to extricate the Spaniards, more than once, from the most embarrassing and perilous situations. She had her errors, as we have seen. But they should be rather charged to the defects of early education, and to the evil influence of him to whom in the darkness of her spirit she looked with simple confidence for the light to guide her. All agree that she was full of excellent qualities, and the important services which she rendered the Spaniards have made her memory deservedly dear to them; while the name of Malinche[2]—the name by which she is still known in Mexico—was pronounced with kindness by the conquered races, with whose misfortunes she showed an invariable sympathy.[3]

With the aid of his two intelligent interpreters, Cortés entered into conversation with his Indian visitors. He learned that they were Mexicans, or rather subjects of the great Mexican empire, of which their own province formed one of the comparatively recent conquests. The country was ruled by a powerful monarch, called Moctheuzoma, or by Europeans more commonly Montezuma,[4] who dwelt on the mountain plains of the interior, nearly seventy leagues from the coast; their own province

---

[1] "Hermosa como Diosa," *beautiful as a goddess,* says Camargo of her. (Hist. de Tlascala, MS.) A modern poet pays her charms the following not inelegant tribute :—

"Admira tan lúcida cabalgada
Y espectáculo tal Doña Marina,
India noble al caudillo presentada,
De fortuna y belleza peregrina.
. . . .
Con despejado espíritu y viveza
Gira la vista en el concurso mudo ;
Rico manto de extrema sutileza
Con chapas de oro autorizarla pudo,
Prendido con bizarra gentileza
Sobre los pechos en ayroso nudo ;
Reyna parece de la Indiana Zona,
Varonil y hermosísima Amazona."

MORATIN, Las Naves de Cortés destruidas.

[2] ["Malinche" is a corruption of the Aztec word "Malintzin," which is itself a corruption of the Spanish name "Marina." The Aztecs, having no *r* in their alphabet, substituted *l* for it, while the termination *tzin* was added in token of respect, so

that the name was equivalent to Doña or Lady Marina. Conquista de Méjico (trad. de Vega, anotada por D. Lúcas Alaman), tom. ii. pp. 17, 269.]

[3] Las Casas, Hist. de las Indias, MS., lib. 3, cap. 120.—Gomara, Crónica, cap. 25, 26.—Clavigero, Stor. del Messico, tom. iii. pp. 12-14.—Oviedo, Hist. de las Indias, MS., lib. 33, cap. 1.—Ixtlilxochitl, Hist. Chich., MS., cap. 79.—Camargo, Hist. de Tlascala, MS.—Bernal Diaz, Hist. de la Conquista, cap. 37, 38.—There is some discordance in the notices of the early life of Marina. I have followed Bernal Diaz—from his means of observation, the best authority. There is happily no difference in the estimate of her singular merits and services.

[4] The name of the Aztec monarch, like those of most persons and places in New Spain, has been twisted into all possible varieties of orthography. Cortés, in his letters, calls him "Muteczuma." Modern Spanish historians usually spell his name "Motezuma." I have preferred to conform to the name by which he is usually known to English readers. It is the one adopted by Bernal Diaz, and by most writers near the time of the Conquest. Alaman, Disertaciones históricas, tom. i., apénd. 2.

was governed by one of his nobles, named Teuhtlile, whose residence was eight leagues distant. Cortés acquainted them in turn with his own friendly views in visiting their country, and with his desire of an interview with the Aztec governor. He then dismissed them loaded with presents, having first ascertained that there was abundance of gold in the interior, like the specimens they had brought.

Cortés, pleased with the manners of the people and the goodly reports of the land, resolved to take up his quarters here for the present. The next morning, April 21, being Good Friday, he landed, with all his force, on the very spot where now stands the modern city of Vera Cruz. Little did the Conqueror imagine that the desolate beach on which he first planted his foot was one day to be covered by a flourishing city, the great mart of European and Oriental trade, the commercial capital of New Spain.[1]

It was a wide and level plain, except where the sand had been drifted into hillocks by the perpetual blowing of the *norte*. On these sandhills he mounted his little battery of guns, so as to give him the command of the country. He then employed the troops in cutting down small trees and bushes which grew near, in order to provide a shelter from the weather. In this he was aided by the people of the country, sent, as it appeared, by the governor of the district to assist the Spaniards. With their help stakes were firmly set in the earth, and covered with boughs, and with mats and cotton carpets, which the friendly natives brought with them. In this way they secured, in a couple of days, a good defence against the scorching rays of the sun, which beat with intolerable fierceness on the sands. The place was surrounded by stagnant marshes, the exhalations from which, quickened by the heat into the pestilent malaria, have occasioned in later times wider mortality to Europeans than all the hurricanes on the coast. The bilious disorders, now the terrible scourge of the *tierra caliente*, were little known before the Conquest. The seeds of the poison seem to have been scattered by the hand of civilization ; for it is only necessary to settle a town, and draw together a busy European population, in order to call out the malignity of the venom which had before lurked innoxious in the atmosphere.[2]

While these arrangements were in progress, the natives flocked in from the adjacent district, which was tolerably populous in the interior, drawn by a natural curiosity to see the wonderful strangers. They brought with them fruits, vegetables, flowers in abundance, game, and many dishes

[1] Ixtlilxochitl, Hist. Chich., MS., cap. 79.—Clavigero, Stor. del Messico, tom. iii. p. 16.—New Vera Cruz, as the present town is called, is distinct, as we shall see hereafter, from that established by Cortés, and was not founded till the close of the sixteenth century, by the Conde de Monterey, Viceroy of Mexico. It received its privileges as a city from Philip III. in 1615. Ibid., tom. iii. p. 30, nota.

[2] The epidemic of the *matlazahuatl*, so fatal to the Aztecs, is shown by M. de Humboldt to have been essentially different from the *vómito*, or bilious fever of our day. Indeed, this disease is not noticed

by the early conquerors and colonists, and, Clavigero asserts, was not known in Mexico till 1725. (Stor. del Messico, tom. i. p. 117, nota.) Humboldt, however, arguing that the same physical causes must have produced similar results, carries the disease back to a much higher antiquity, of which he discerns some traditional and historic vestiges. "Il ne faut pas confondre l'époque," he remarks, with his usual penetration, "à laquelle une maladie a été décrite pour la première fois, parce qu'elle a fait de grands ravages dans un court espace de temps, avec l'époque de sa première apparition." Essai politique, tom. iv. p. 161 et seq., and 179.

cooked after the fashion of the country, with little articles of gold and other ornaments. They gave away some as presents, and bartered others for the wares of the Spaniards; so that the camp, crowded with a motley throng of every age and sex, wore the appearance of a fair. From some of the visitors Cortés learned the intention of the governor to wait on him the following day.

This was Easter. Teuhtlile arrived, as he had announced, before noon. He was attended by a numerous train, and was met by Cortés, who conducted him with much ceremony to his tent, where his principal officers were assembled. The Aztec chief returned their salutations with polite though formal courtesy. Mass was first said by Father Olmedo, and the service was listened to by Teuhtlile and his attendants with decent reverence. A collation was afterwards served, at which the general entertained his guest with Spanish wines and confections. The interpreters were then introduced, and a conversation commenced between the parties.

The first inquiries of Teuhtlile were respecting the country of the strangers and the purport of their visit. Cortés told him that " he was the subject of a potent monarch beyond the seas, who ruled over an immense empire, and had kings and princes for his vassals; that, acquainted with the greatness of the Mexican emperor, his master had desired to enter into a communication with him, and had sent him as his envoy to wait on Montezuma with a present in token of his goodwill, and a message which he must deliver in person." He concluded by inquiring of Teuhtlile when he could be admitted to his sovereign's presence.

To this the Aztec noble somewhat haughtily replied, " How is it that you have been here only two days, and demand to see the emperor?" He then added, with more courtesy, that " he was surprised to learn there was another monarch as powerful as Montezuma, but that, if it were so, he had no doubt his master would be happy to communicate with him. He would send his couriers with the royal gift brought by the Spanish commander, and, so soon as he had learned Montezuma's will, would communicate it."

Teuhtlile then commanded his slaves to bring forward the present intended for the Spanish general. It consisted of ten loads of fine cottons, several mantles of that curious feather-work whose rich and delicate dyes might vie with the most beautiful painting, and a wicker basket filled with ornaments of wrought gold, all calculated to inspire the Spaniards with high ideas of the wealth and mechanical ingenuity of the Mexicans.

Cortés received these presents with suitable acknowledgments, and ordered his own attendants to lay before the chief the articles designed for Montezuma. These were an armchair richly carved and painted, a crimson cap of cloth, having a gold medal emblazoned with St. George and the dragon, and a quantity of collars, bracelets, and other ornaments of cut glass, which, in a country where glass was not to be had, might claim to have the value of real gems, and no doubt passed for such with the inexperienced Mexican. Teuhtlile observed a soldier in the camp with a shining gilt helmet on his head, which he said reminded him of one worn by the god Quetzalcoatl in Mexico; and he showed a desire that Montezuma should see it. The coming of the Spaniards, as the reader will soon see, was associated with some traditions of this same deity. Cortés expressed his willingness that the casque should be sent to the emperor, intimating a hope that it would be returned filled with the gold dust of the country, that he might be able to compare its quality with that of his own! He further told the governor, as we are informed by his chaplain, "that the Spaniards were troubled with a disease of the heart, for which gold was a specific remedy"![1] "In short," says Las Casas, "he contrived to make his want of gold very clear to the governor."[2]

While these things were passing, Cortés observed one of Teuhtlile's attendants busy with a pencil, apparently delineating some object. On looking at his work, he found that it was a sketch on canvas of the Spaniards, their costumes, arms, and in short different objects of interest, giving to each its appropriate form and colour. This was the celebrated picture-writing of the Aztecs, and as Teuhtlile informed him, this man was employed in portraying the various objects for the eye of Montezuma, who would thus gather a more vivid notion of their appearance than from any description by words. Cortés was pleased with the idea; and, as he knew how much the effect would be heightened by converting still life into action, he ordered out the cavalry on the beach, the wet sands of which afforded a firm footing for the horses. The bold and rapid movements of the troops, as they went through their military exercises; the apparent ease with which they managed the fiery animals on which they were mounted; the glancing of their weapons, and the shrill cry of the trumpet, all filled the spectators with astonishment; but when they heard the thunders of the cannon, which Cortés ordered to be fired at the same time, and witnessed the volumes of smoke and flame issuing from these terrible engines, and the rushing sound of the balls, as they dashed through the trees of the neighbouring forest, shivering their branches into fragments, they were filled with consternation, from which the Aztec chief himself was not wholly free.

Nothing of all this was lost on the painters, who faithfully recorded, after their fashion, every particular; not omitting the ships,—"the water-houses," as they called them, of the strangers,—which, with their dark hulls and snow-white sails reflected from the water, were swinging lazily at anchor on the calm bosom of the bay. All was depicted with a fidelity that excited in their turn the admiration of the Spaniards, who, doubtless, unprepared for this exhibition of skill, greatly overestimated the merits of the execution.[3]

---

[1] Gom ra, Crónica, cap. 26.
[2] Las Casas, Hist. de las Indias, MS., lib. 3, cap. 119.

[3] [According to a curious document published by Icazbalceta (Col. de Doc. para la Hist. de México, tom. ii.), two of the principal caciques present on

These various matters completed, Teuhtlile with his attendants withdrew from the Spanish quarters, with the same ceremony with which he had entered them; leaving orders that his people should supply the troops with provisions and other articles requisite for their accommodation, till further instructions from the capital.[1]

CHAPTER VI.

ACCOUNT OF MONTEZUMA.—STATE OF HIS EMPIRE.—STRANGE PROGNOSTICS. —EMBASSY AND PRESENTS.—SPANISH ENCAMPMENT.

(1519.)

WE must now take leave of the Spanish camp in the *tierra caliente*, and transport ourselves to the distant capital of Mexico, where no little sensation was excited by the arrival of the wonderful strangers on the coast. The Aztec throne was filled at that time by Montezuma the Second, nephew of the last, and grandson of a preceding monarch. He had been elected to the regal dignity in 1502, in preference to his brothers, for his superior qualifications both as a soldier and a priest,—a combination of offices sometimes found in the Mexican candidates, as it was more frequently in the Egyptian. In early youth he had taken an active part in the wars of the empire, though of late he had devoted himself more exclusively to the services of the temple; and he was scrupulous in his attentions to all the burdensome ceremonial of the Aztec worship. He maintained a grave and reserved demeanour, speaking little and with prudent deliberation. His deportment was well calculated to inspire ideas of superior sanctity.[2]

When his election was announced to him, he was found sweeping down the stairs in the great temple of the national war-god. He received the messengers with a becoming humility, professing his unfitness for so responsible a station. The address delivered as usual on the occasion was made by his relative Nezahualpilli, the wise king of Tezcuco.[3] It has, fortunately, been preserved, and presents a favourable specimen of Indian eloquence. Towards the conclusion, the orator exclaims, "Who can

---

this occasion communicated secretly with Cortés, and, declaring themselves disaffected subjects of Montezuma, offered to facilitate the advance of the Spaniards by furnishing the general with paintings in which the various features of the country would be correctly delineated. The offer was accepted, and on the next visit the paintings were produced, and proved subsequently of great service to Cortés, who rewarded the donors with certain grants. But the genuineness of this paper, though supported by so distinguished a scholar as Señor Ramirez, is more than questionable.—ED.]

1 Ixtlilxochitl, Relaciones, MS., No. 13.—Idem, Hist. Chich., MS., cap. 79.—Gomara, Crónica, cap.

25, 26.—Bernal Diaz, Hist. de la Conquista, cap. 38.—Herrera, Hist. general, dec. 2, lib. 5, cap. 4.— Carta de Vera Cruz, MS.—Torquemada, Monarch. Ind., lib. 4, cap. 13-15.—Tezozomoc, Crón. Mexicana, MS., cap. 107.

2 His name suited his nature; Montezuma, according to Las Casas, signifying, in the Mexican, "sad or severe man." Hist. de las Indias, MS., lib. 3, cap. 120.—Ixtlilxochitl, Hist. Chich., MS., cap. 70. —Acosta, lib. 7, cap. 20.—Col. de Mendoza, pp. 13-16; Codex Tel.-Rem., p. 143, ap. Antiq. of Mexico, vol. vi.

3 For a full account of this prince, see Book I., chap. 6.

K

doubt that the Aztec empire has reached the zenith of its greatness, since the Almighty has placed over it one whose very presence fills every beholder with reverence? Rejoice, happy people, that you have now a sovereign who will be to you a steady column of support; a father in distress, a more than brother in tenderness and sympathy; one whose aspiring soul will disdain all the profligate pleasures of the senses and the wasting indulgence of sloth. And thou, illustrious youth, doubt not that the Creator, who has laid on thee so weighty a charge, will also give strength to sustain it; that He, who has been so liberal in times past, will shower yet more abundant blessings on thy head, and keep thee firm in thy royal seat through many long and glorious years." These golden prognostics, which melted the royal auditor into tears, were not destined to be realized.[1]

Montezuma displayed all the energy and enterprise in the commencement of his reign which had been anticipated from him. His first expedition against a rebel province in the neighbourhood was crowned with success, and he led back in triumph a throng of captives for the bloody sacrifice that was to grace his coronation. This was celebrated with uncommon pomp. Games and religious ceremonies continued for several days, and among the spectators who flocked from distant quarters were some noble Tlascalans, the hereditary enemies of Mexico. They were in disguise, hoping thus to elude detection. They were recognized, however, and reported to the monarch. But he only availed himself of the information to provide them with honourable entertainment and a good place for witnessing the games. This was a magnanimous act, considering the long-cherished hostility between the nations.

In his first years, Montezuma was constantly engaged in war, and frequently led his armies in person. The Aztec banners were seen in the farthest provinces on the Gulf of Mexico, and the distant regions of Nicaragua and Honduras. The expeditions were generally successful; and the limits of the empire were more widely extended than at any preceding period.

Meanwhile the monarch was not inattentive to the interior concerns of the kingdom. He made some important changes in the courts of justice, and carefully watched over the execution of the laws, which he enforced with stern severity. He was in the habit of patrolling the streets of his capital in disguise, to make himself personally acquainted with the abuses in it. And with more questionable policy, it is said, he would sometimes try the integrity of his judges by tempting them with large bribes to swerve from their duty, and then called the delinquent to strict account for yielding to the temptation.

He liberally recompensed all who served him. He showed a similar

[1] The address is fully reported by Torquemada (Monarch. Ind., lib. 3, cap. 68), who came into the country little more than half a century after its delivery. It has been recently republished by Bustamante. Tezcuco en los últimos Tiempos (México, 1826), pp. 256–258.

munificent spirit in his public works, constructing and embellishing the temples, bringing water into the capital by a new channel, and establishing a hospital, or retreat for invalid soldiers, in the city of Colhuacan.[1]

These acts, so worthy of a great prince, were counterbalanced by others of an opposite complexion. The humility, displayed so ostentatiously before his elevation, gave way to an intolerable arrogance. In his pleasure-houses, domestic establishment, and way of living, he assumed a pomp unknown to his predecessors. He secluded himself from public observation, or, when he went abroad, exacted the most slavish homage; while in the palace he would be served only, even in the most menial offices, by persons of rank. He, further, dismissed several plebeians, chiefly poor soldiers of merit, from the places they had occupied near the person of his predecessor, considering their attendance a dishonour to royalty. It was in vain that his oldest and sagest counsellors remonstrated on a conduct so impolitic.

While he thus disgusted his subjects by his haughty deportment, he alienated their affections by the imposition of grievous taxes. These were demanded by the lavish expenditure of his court. They fell with peculiar heaviness on the conquered cities. This oppression led to frequent insurrection and resistance; and the latter years of his reign present a scene of unintermitting hostility, in which the forces of one half of the empire were employed in suppressing the commotions of the other. Unfortunately, there was no principle of amalgamation by which the new acquisitions could be incorporated into the ancient monarchy as parts of one whole. Their interests, as well as sympathies, were different. Thus the more widely the Aztec empire was extended, the weaker it became; resembling some vast and ill-proportioned edifice, whose disjointed materials, having no principle of cohesion, and tottering under their own weight, seem ready to fall before the first blast of the tempest.

In 1516 died the Tezcucan king, Nezahualpilli; in whom Montezuma lost his most sagacious counsellor. The succession was contested by his two sons, Cacama and Ixtlilxochitl. The former was supported by Montezuma. The latter, the younger of the princes, a bold, aspiring youth, appealing to the patriotic sentiment of his nation, would have persuaded them that his brother was too much in the Mexican interests to be true to his own country. A civil war ensued, and ended by a compromise, by which one half of the kingdom, with the capital, remained to Cacama, and the northern portion to his ambitious rival. Ixtlilxochitl became from that time the mortal foe of Montezuma.[2]

A more formidable enemy still was the little republic of Tlascala, lying midway between the Mexican Valley and the coast. It had maintained its

---

[1] Acosta, lib. 7, cap. 22.—Sahagun, Hist. de Nueva-España, lib. 8, Prólogo, et cap. 1.—Torque-mada, Monarch. Ind., lib. 3, cap. 73, 74, 81.—Col. de Mendoza, pp. 14, 85, ap. Antiq. of Mexico, vol. vi.

[2] Clavigero, Stor. del Messico, tom. i. pp. 267, 274, 275.—Ixtlilxochitl, Hist. Chich., MS., cap. 70-76.—Acosta, lib. 7, cap. 21.

independence for more than two centuries against the allied forces of the empire. Its resources were unimpaired, its civilization scarcely below that of its great rival states, and for courage and military prowess it had established a name inferior to none other of the nations of Anahuac.

Such was the condition of the Aztec monarchy on the arrival of Cortés; —the people disgusted with the arrogance of the sovereign; the provinces and distant cities outraged by fiscal exactions; while potent enemies in the neighbourhood lay watching the hour when they might assail their formidable rival with advantage. Still the kingdom was strong in its internal resources, in the will of its monarch, in the long habitual deference to his authority,—in short, in the terror of his name, and in the valour and discipline of his armies, grown grey in active service, and well drilled in all the tactics of Indian warfare. The time had now come when these imperfect tactics and rude weapons of the barbarian were to be brought into collision with the science and enginery of the most civilized nations of the globe.

During the latter years of his reign, Montezuma had rarely taken part in his military expeditions, which he left to his captains, occupying himself chiefly with his sacerdotal functions. Under no prince had the priesthood enjoyed greater consideration and immunities. The religious festivals and rites were celebrated with unprecedented pomp. The oracles were consulted on the most trivial occasions; and the sanguinary deities were propitiated by hecatombs of victims dragged in triumph to the capital from the conquered or rebellious provinces. The religion, or, to speak correctly, the superstition of Montezuma proved a principal cause of his calamities.

In a preceding chapter I have noticed the popular traditions respecting Quetzalcoatl, that deity with a fair complexion and flowing beard, so unlike the Indian physiognomy, who, after fulfilling his mission of benevolence among the Aztecs, embarked on the Atlantic Sea for the mysterious shores of Tlapallan.[1] He promised, on his departure, to return at some future day with his posterity, and resume the possession of his empire. That day was looked forward to with hope or with apprehension, according to the interest of the believer, but with general confidence, throughout the wide borders of Anahuac. Even after the Conquest it still lingered among the Indian races, by whom it was as fondly cherished as the advent of their king Sebastian continued to be by the Portuguese, or that of the Messiah by the Jews.[2]

A general feeling seems to have prevailed in the time of Montezuma that the period for the return of the deity and the full accomplishment of his promise was near at hand. This conviction is said to have gained ground from various preternatural occurrences, reported with more or less detail by

1 *Ante*, Book I., chap. 3, pp. 28, 29, and note 1.
2 Tezozomoc, Crón. Mexicana, MS., cap. 107.— Ixtlilxochitl, Hist. Chich., MS., cap. 1.—Torquemada, Monarch. Ind., lib. 4, cap. 14; lib. 6, cap.

24.—Codex Vaticanus, ap. Antiq. of Mexico, vol. vi.—Sahagun, Hist. de Nueva-España, lib. 8, cap. 7.—Ibid., MS., lib. 12, cap. 3, 4.

all the most ancient historians.[1] In 1510 the great lake of Tezcuco, without the occurrence of a tempest, or earthquake, or any other visible cause,
became violently agitated, overflowed its banks, and, pouring into the
streets of Mexico, swept off many of the buildings by the fury of the waters.
In 1511 one of the turrets of the great temple took fire, equally without
any apparent cause, and continued to burn in defiance of all attempts to
extinguish it. In the following years, three comets were seen; and not
long before the coming of the Spaniards a strange light broke forth in the
east. It spread broad at its base on the horizon, and rising in a pyramidal
form tapered off as it approached the zenith. It resembled a vast sheet or
flood of fire, emitting sparkles, or, as an old writer expresses it, " seemed
thickly powdered with stars." [2] At the same time, low voices were heard in
the air, and doleful wailings, as if to announce some strange, mysterious
calamity ! The Aztec monarch, terrified at the apparitions in the heavens,
took counsel of Nezahualpilli, who was a great proficient in the subtle
science of astrology. But the royal sage cast a deeper cloud over his spirit
by reading in these prodigies the speedy downfall of the empire.[3]

Such are the strange stories reported by the chroniclers, in which it is
not impossible to detect the glimmerings of truth.[4] Nearly thirty years
had elapsed since the discovery of the Islands by Columbus, and more
than twenty since his visit to the American continent. Rumours, more or
less distinct, of this wonderful appearance of the white men, bearing in
their hands the thunder and the lightning, so like in many respects to the
traditions of Quetzalcoatl, would naturally spread far and wide among the
Indian nations. Such rumours, doubtless, long before the landing of the
Spaniards in Mexico, found their way up the grand plateau, filling the
minds of men with anticipations of the near coming of the period when the
great deity was to return and receive his own again.

In the excited state of their imaginations, prodigies became a familiar
occurrence. Or rather, events not very uncommon in themselves, seen
through the discoloured medium of fear, were easily magnified into prodigies ; and the accidental swell of the lake, the appearance of a comet, and
the conflagration of a building were all interpreted as the special annuncia-
tions of Heaven.[5] Thus it happens in those great political convulsions

---

1 " Tenia por cierto," says Las Casas of Montezuma, " segun sus prophetas ó agoreros le avian
certificado, que su estado é rriquezas y prosperidad
avia de perezer dentro de pocos años por çiertas
gentes que avian de venir en sus dias, que de su
felicidad lo derrocase, y por esto vivia siempre con
temor y en tristeça y sobresaltado." Hist. de las
Indias, MS., lib. 3, cap. 120.
2 Camargo, Hist. de Tlascala, MS.—The Interpreter of the Codex Tel.-Rem. intimates that this
scintillating phenomenon was probably nothing
more than an eruption of one of the great volcanoes
of Mexico. Antiq. of Mexico, vol. vi. p. 144.
3 Sahagun, Hist. de Nueva-España, MS., lib. 12,
cap. 1.—Camargo, Hist. de Tlascala, MS.—Acosta,
lib. 7, cap. 23.—Herrera, Hist. general, dec. 2, lib.
5, cap. 5.—Ixtlilxochitl, Hist. Chich., MS., cap. 74.
4 I omit the most extraordinary miracle of all,—
though legal attestations of its truth were furnished

the court of Rome (see Clavigero, Stor. del Messico, tom. i. p. 289),—namely, the resurrection of
Montezuma's sister, Papantzin, four days after her
burial, to warn the monarch of the approaching ruin
of his empire. It finds credit with one writer, at
least, in the nineteenth century ! See the note of
Sahagun's Mexican editor, Bustamante, Hist. de
Nueva-España, tom. ii. p. 270.
5 Lucan gives a fine enumeration of such prodigies witnessed in the Roman capital in a similar
excitement. (Pharsalia, lib. 1, v. 523, et seq.)
Poor human nature is much the same everywhere.
Machiavelli has thought the subject worthy of a
separate chapter in his Discourses. The philosopher even intimates a belief in the existence of
beneficent intelligences who send these portents as
a sort of *premonitories*, to warn mankind of the
coming tempest. Discorsi sopra Tito Livio, lib. 1,
cap. 56.

which shake the foundations of society,—the mighty events that cast their
shadows before them in their coming.   Then it is that the atmosphere is
agitated with the low, prophetic murmurs with which Nature, in the moral
as in the physical world, announces the march of the hurricane :—

> " When from the shores
> And forest-rustling mountains comes a voice,
> That, solemn sounding, bids the world prepare ! "

When tidings were brought to the capital of the landing of Grijalva on
the coast, in the preceding year, the heart of Montezuma was filled with
dismay.   He felt as if the destinies which had so long brooded over the
royal line of Mexico were to be accomplished, and the sceptre was to pass
away from his house for ever.   Though somewhat relieved by the departure
of the Spaniards, he caused sentinels to be stationed on the heights ; and,
when the Europeans returned under Cortés, he doubtless received the
earliest notice of the unwelcome event.   It was by his orders, however,
that the provincial governor had prepared so hospitable a reception for
them.   The hieroglyphical report of these strange visitors, now forwarded
to the capital, revived all his apprehensions.   He called, without delay, a
meeting of his principal counsellors, including the kings of Tezcuco and
Tlacopan, and laid the matter before them.[1]

There seems to have been much division of opinion in that body.
Some were for resisting the strangers at once, whether by fraud or by
open force.   Others contended that, if they were supernatural beings,
fraud and force would be alike useless.   If they were, as they pretended,
ambassadors from a foreign prince, such a policy would be cowardly
and unjust.   That they were not of the family of Quetzalcoatl was argued
from the fact that they had shown themselves hostile to his religion ;
for tidings of the proceedings of the Spaniards in Tabasco, it seems,
had already reached the capital.   Among those in favour of giving
them a friendly and honourable reception was the Tezcucan king,
Cacama.

But Montezuma, taking counsel of his own ill-defined apprehensions,
preferred a half-way course,—as usual, the most impolitic.   He resolved
to send an embassy, with such a magnificent present to the strangers
as should impress them with high ideas of his grandeur and resources ;
while at the same time he would forbid their approach to the capital.
This was to reveal at once both his wealth and his weakness.[2]

While the Aztec court was thus agitated by the arrival of the Spaniards,
they were passing their time in the *tierra caliente*, not a little annoyed by
the excessive heats and suffocating atmosphere of the sandy waste on

---

[1] Las Casas, Hist. de las Indias, MS., lib. 3,
cap. 120.—Ixtlilxochitl, Hist. Chich., MS., cap.
80.—Idem, Relaciones, MS.—Sahagun, Hist. de
Nueva-España, MS., lib. 12, cap. 3, 4.—Tezozomoc,
Crón. Mexicana, MS., cap. 108.

[2] Tezozomoc, Crón. Mexicana, MS., loc. cit.—
Camargo, Hist. de Tlascala, MS.—Ixtlilxochitl,
Hist. Chich., MS., cap. 80.

which they were encamped. They experienced every alleviation that could be derived from the attentions of the friendly natives. These, by the governor's command, had constructed more than a thousand huts or booths of branches and matting, which they occupied in the neighbourhood of the camp. Here they prepared various articles of food for the tables of Cortés and his officers, without any recompense; while the common soldiers easily obtained a supply for themselves, in exchange for such trifles as they brought with them for barter. Thus the camp was liberally provided with meat and fish dressed in many savoury ways, with cakes of corn, bananas, pine-apples, and divers luscious vegetables of the tropics, hitherto unknown to the Spaniards. The soldiers contrived, moreover, to obtain many little bits of gold, of no great value, indeed, from the natives; a traffic very displeasing to the partisans of Velasquez, who considered it an invasion of his rights. Cortés, however, did not think it prudent, in this matter, to balk the inclinations of his followers.[1]

At the expiration of seven, or eight days at most. the Mexican embassy presented itself before the camp. It may seem an incredibly short space of time, considering the distance of the capital was near seventy leagues. But it may be remembered that tidings were carried there by means of posts, as already noticed, in the brief space of four-and-twenty hours;[2] and four or five days would suffice for the descent of the envoys to the coast, accustomed as the Mexicans were to long and rapid travelling. At all events, no writer states the period occupied by the Indian emissaries on this occasion as longer than that mentioned.

The embassy, consisting of two Aztec nobles, was accompanied by the governor, Teuhtlile, and by a hundred slaves, bearing the princely gifts of Montezuma. One of the envoys had been selected on account of the great resemblance which, as appeared from the painting representing the camp, he bore to the Spanish commander. And it is a proof of the fidelity of the painting, that the soldiers recognized the resemblance, and always distinguished the chief by the name of the "Mexican Cortés."

On entering the general's pavilion, the ambassadors saluted him and his officers with the usual signs of reverence to persons of great consideration, touching the ground with their hands and then carrying them to their heads, while the air was filled with clouds of incense, which rose up from the censers borne by their attendants. Some delicately wrought mats of the country (*petates*) were then unrolled, and on them the slaves displayed the various articles they had brought. They were of the most miscellaneous kind : shields, helmets, cuirasses, embossed with plates and ornaments of pure gold; collars and bracelets of the same metal, sandals, fans. *panaches* and crests of variegated feathers, intermingled with gold and

---

[1] Bernal Diaz, Hist. de la Conquista, cap. 39.— | [2] *Ante*, Book 1, chapter 2, page 21
Gomara, Crónica, cap. 27, ap. Barcia, tom. ii.

silver thread, and sprinkled with pearls and precious stones ; imitations of birds and animals in wrought and cast gold and silver, of exquisite work-manship ; curtains, coverlets, and robes of cotton, fine as silk, of rich and various dyes, interwoven with feather-work that rivalled the delicacy of painting.[1]   There were more than thirty loads of cotton cloth in addition. Among the articles was the Spanish helmet sent to the capital, and now returned filled to the brim with grains of gold.   But the things which excited the most admiration were two circular plates of gold and silver, "as large as carriage-wheels."   One, representing the sun, was richly carved with plants and animals,—no doubt, denoting the Aztec century. It was thirty palms in circumference, and was valued at twenty thousand *pesos de oro.*   The silver wheel, of the same size, weighed fifty marks.[2]

The Spaniards could not conceal their rapture at the exhibition of treas-ures which so far surpassed all the dreams in which they had indulged. For, rich as were the materials, they were exceeded—according to the testimony of those who saw these articles afterwards in Seville, where they could coolly examine them—by the beauty and richness of the work-manship.[3]

When Cortés and his officers had completed their survey, the ambas-sadors courteously delivered the message of Montezuma.   "It gave their master great pleasure," they said, "to hold this communication with so powerful a monarch as the King of Spain, for whom he felt the most profound respect.   He regretted much that he could not enjoy a personal

---

[1] From the checkered figure of some of these coloured cottons, Peter Martyr infers, the Indians were acquainted with chess ! He notices a curious fabric made of the hair of animals, feathers, and cotton thread, interwoven together. "Plumas illas et concinnant inter cuniculorum villos interque gosampij stamina ordiuntur, et intexunt operose adeo, ut quo pacto id faciant non bene intellexeri-mus." De Orbe Novo (Parisiis, 1587), dec. 5, cap. 10.

[2] Bernal Diaz, Hist. de la Conquista, cap. 39.—Oviedo, Hist. de las Ind., MS., lib. 33, cap. 1.—Las Casas, Hist. de las Indias, MS., lib. 3, cap. 120.—Gomara, Crónica, cap. 27, ap. Barcia, tom. ii.—Carta de Vera Cruz, MS.—Herrera, Hist. general, dec. 2, lib. 5, cap. 5.—Robertson cites Bernal Diaz as reckoning the value of the silver plate at 20,000 *pesos*, or about £5000. (History of America, vol. ii. note 75.) But Bernal Diaz speaks only of the value of the gold plate, which he esti-mates at 20,000 *pesos de oro*, different from the *pesos*, dollars, or ounces of silver, with which the historian confounds them. As the mention of the *peso de oro* will often recur in these pages, it will be well to make the reader acquainted with its probable value. Nothing is more difficult than to ascertain the actual value of the currency of a distant age ; so many circumstances occur to embarrass the calcu-lation, besides the general depreciation of the pre-cious metals, such as the adulteration of specific coins, and the like. Señor Clemencin, the Secretary of the Royal Academy of History, in the sixth volume of its *Memorias*, has computed with great accuracy the value of the different denominations of the Spanish currency at the close of the fifteenth century, the period just preceding that of the con-quest of Mexico. He makes no mention of the *peso de oro* in his tables But he ascertains the precise

value of the gold ducat, which will answer our pur-pose as well. (Memorias de la Real Academia de Historia (Madrid, 1821), tom. vi. Ilust. 20.) Oviedo, a contemporary of the Conquerors, informs us that the *peso de oro* and the *castellano* were of the same value, and that was precisely one-third greater than the value of the ducat. (Hist. del Ind., lib. vi., cap. 8, ap. Ramusio, Navigationi et Viaggi (Venetia, 1565), tom. iii.) Now, the ducat, as appears from Clemencin, reduced to our own currency, would be equal to eight dollars and seventy-five cents. *The peso de oro, therefore, was equal to eleven dollars and sixty-seven cents, or two pounds twelve shil-lings and sixpence sterling.* Keeping this in mind, it will be easy for the reader to determine the actual value, in *pesos de oro*, of any sum that may be here-after mentioned.

[3] ¡ Cierto cosas de ver !" exclaims Las Casas, who saw them with the Emperor Charles V. in Seville, in 1520. "Quedáron todos los que viéron aquestas cosas tan ricas y tan bien artifíciadas y ermosísimas como de cosas nunca vistas," etc. (Hist. de las Indias, MS., lib. 3, cap. 120.) "Muy hermosas," says Oviedo, who saw them in Valla-dolid, and describes the great wheels more minutely ; "todo era mucho de ver !" (Hist. de las Indias, MS., loc. cit.) The inquisitive Martyr, who ex-amined them carefully, remarks, yet more emphati-cally, "Si quid unquam honoris humana ingenia in huiuscemodi artibus sunt adepta, principatum iure merito ista consequentur. Aurum, gemmasque non admiror quidem, quâ industriâ, quóve studio superet opus materiam, stupeo. Mille figuras et facies mille prospexi quæ scribere nequeo. Quid oculos hominum suâ pulchritudine æque possit allicere meo iudicio vidi nunquam." De Orbe Novo, dec. 4, cap. 9.

interview with the Spaniards, but the distance of his capital was too great; since the journey was beset with difficulties, and with too many dangers from formidable enemies, to make it possible. All that could be done, therefore, was for the strangers to return to their own land, with the proofs thus afforded them of his friendly disposition."

Cortés, though much chagrined at this decided refusal of Montezuma to admit his visit, concealed his mortification as he best might, and politely expressed his sense of the emperor's munificence. "It made him only the more desirous," he said, "to have a personal interview with him. He should feel it, indeed, impossible to present himself again before his own sovereign, without having accomplished this great object of his voyage; and one who had sailed over two thousand leagues of ocean held lightly the perils and fatigues of so short a journey by land." He once more requested them to become the bearers of his message to their master, together with a slight additional token of his respect.

This consisted of a few fine Holland shirts, a Florentine goblet, gilt and somewhat curiously enamelled, with some toys of little value,—a sorry return for the solid magnificence of the royal present. The ambassadors may have thought as much. At least, they showed no alacrity in charging themselves either with the present or the message, and, on quitting the Castilian quarters, repeated their assurance that the general's application would be unavailing.[1]

The splendid treasure, which now lay dazzling the eyes of the Spaniards, raised in their bosoms very different emotions, according to the difference of their characters. Some it stimulated with the ardent desire to strike at once into the interior and possess themselves of a country which teemed with such boundless stores of wealth. Others looked on it as the evidence of a power altogether too formidable to be encountered with their present insignificant force. They thought, therefore, it would be most prudent to return and report their proceedings to the governor of Cuba, where preparations could be made commensurate with so vast an undertaking. There can be little doubt as to the impression made on the bold spirit of Cortés, on which difficulties ever operated as incentives, rather than discouragements, to enterprise. But he prudently said nothing,— at least in public, — preferring that so important a movement should flow from the determination of his whole army, rather than from his own individual impulse.

Meanwhile the soldiers suffered greatly from the inconveniences of their position amidst burning sands and the pestilent effluvia of the neighbouring marshes, while the venomous insects of these hot regions left them no repose, day or night. Thirty of their number had already sickened and died; a loss that could ill be afforded by the little band. To add to their troubles, the coldness of the Mexican chiefs had extended to their

[1] Las Casas, Hist. de las Indias, MS., lib. 3, cap. 121.—Bernal Diaz, Hist. de la Conquista, cap. 39.— Ixtlilxochitl, Hist. Chich., MS., cap. 80.—Gomara, Crónica, cap. 27, ap. Barcia, tom. ii.

followers; and the supplies for the camp were not only much diminished, but the prices set on them were exorbitant. The position was equally unfavourable for the shipping, which lay in an open roadstead, exposed to the fury of the first *norte* which should sweep the Mexican Gulf.

The general was induced by these circumstances to despatch two vessels, under Francisco de Montejo, with the experienced Alaminos for his pilot, to explore the coast in a northerly direction, and see if a safer port and more commodious quarters for the army could not be found there.

After the lapse of ten days the Mexican envoys returned. They entered the Spanish quarters with the same formality as on the former visit, bearing with them an additional present of rich stuffs and metallic ornaments, which, though inferior in value to those before brought, were estimated at three thousand ounces of gold. Besides these, there were four precious stones, of a considerable size, resembling emeralds, called by the natives *chalchuites*, each of which, as they assured the Spaniards, was worth more than a load of gold, and was designed as a mark of particular respect for the Spanish monarch.[1] Unfortunately, they were not worth as many loads of earth in Europe.

Montezuma's answer was in substance the same as before. It contained a positive prohibition for the strangers to advance nearer to the capital, and expressed his confidence that, now they had obtained what they had most desired, they would return to their own country without unnecessary delay. Cortés received this unpalatable response courteously, though somewhat coldly, and, turning to his officers, exclaimed, "This is a rich and powerful prince indeed; yet it shall go hard but we will one day pay him a visit in his capital!"

While they were conversing the bell struck for vespers. At the sound, the soldiers, throwing themselves on their knees, offered up their orisons before the large wooden cross planted in the sands. As the Aztec chiefs gazed with curious surprise, Cortés thought it a favourable occasion to impress them with what he conceived to be a principal object of his visit to the country. Father Olmedo accordingly expounded, as briefly and clearly as he could, the great doctrines of Christianity, touching on the atonement, the passion, and the resurrection, and concluding with assuring his astonished audience that it was their intention to extirpate the idolatrous practices of the nation and to substitute the pure worship of the true God. He then put into their hands a little image of the Virgin with the infant Redeemer, requesting them to place it in their temples instead of their sanguinary deities. How far the Aztec lords comprehended the mysteries of the faith, as conveyed through the double version of Aguilar and Marina, or how well they perceived the subtle distinctions between

---

[1] Bernal Diaz, Hist. de la Conquista, cap. 40.— Father Sahagun thus describes these stones, so precious in Mexico that the use of them was interdicted to any but the nobles: "The *chalchuites* are of a green colour mixed with white, and are not trans- parent. They are much worn by persons of rank, and, attached to the wrist by a thread, are a token of the nobility of the wearer." Hist. de Nueva-España, lib. 11, cap. 8.

their own images and those of the Roman Church, we are not informed. There is reason to fear, however, that the seed fell on barren ground ; for, when the homily of the good father ended, they withdrew with an air of dubious reserve very different from their friendly manners at the first interview. The same night every hut was deserted by the natives, and the Spaniards saw themselves suddenly cut off from supplies in the midst of a desolate wilderness. The movement had so suspicious an appearance that Cortés apprehended an attack would be made on his quarters, and took precautions accordingly. But none was meditated.

The army was at length cheered by the return of Montejo from his exploring expedition, after an absence of twelve days. He had run down the Gulf as far as Panuco, where he experienced such heavy gales, in attempting to double that headland, that he was driven back, and had nearly foundered. In the whole course of the voyage he had found only one place tolerably sheltered from the north winds. Fortunately, the adjacent country, well watered by fresh, running streams, afforded a favourable position for the camp ; and thither, after some deliberation, it was determined to repair.[1]

CHAPTER VII.

TROUBLES IN THE CAMP.—PLAN OF A COLONY.—MANAGEMENT OF CORTÉS.— MARCH TO CEMPOALLA.—PROCEEDINGS WITH THE NATIVES.—FOUNDATION OF VERA CRUZ.

(1519.)

THERE is no situation which tries so severely the patience and discipline of the soldier as a life of idleness in camp, where his thoughts, instead of being bent on enterprise and action, are fastened on himself and the inevitable privations and dangers of his condition. This was particularly the case in the present instance, where, in addition to the evils of a scanty subsistence, the troops suffered from excessive heat, swarms of venomous insects, and the other annoyances of a sultry climate. They were, moreover, far from possessing the character of regular forces, trained to subordination under a commander whom they had long been taught to reverence and obey. They were soldiers of fortune, embarked with him in an adventure in which all seemed to have an equal stake, and they regarded their captain—the captain of a day—as little more than an equal.

There was a growing discontent among the men at their longer residence in this strange land. They were still more dissatisfied on learning the

---

[1] Camargo, Hist. de Tlascala, MS.—Las Casas, Hist. de ias Indias, MS., lib. 3, cap. 121.—Bernal Diaz, Hist. de la Conquista, cap. 40, 41.—Herrera, Hist. general, dec. 2, lib. 5, cap. 6.—Gomara, Crónica, cap. 29, ap. Barcia, tom. ii.

general's intention to remove to the neighbourhood of the port discovered by Montejo. "It was time to return," they said, "and report
what had been done to the governor of Cuba, and not linger on these
barren shores until they had brought the whole Mexican empire on their
heads!" Cortés evaded their importunities as well as he could, assuring
them there was no cause for despondency. "Everything so far had gone
on prosperously, and, when they had taken up a more favourable position,
there was no reason to doubt they might still continue the same profitable
intercourse with the natives."

While this was passing, five Indians made their appearance in the camp
one morning, and were brought to the general's tent. Their dress and
whole appearance were different from those of the Mexicans. They wore
rings of gold, and gems of bright blue stone in their ears and nostrils, while
a gold leaf delicately wrought was attached to the under lip. Marina was
unable to comprehend their language, but, on her addressing them in
Aztec, two of them, it was found, could converse in that tongue. They
said they were natives of Cempoalla, the chief town of the Totonacs, a
powerful nation who had come upon the great plateau many centuries
back, and, descending its eastern slope, settled along the sierras and broad
plains which skirt the Mexican Gulf towards the north. Their country was
one of the recent conquests of the Aztecs, and they experienced such
vexatious oppressions from their conquerors as made them very impatient
of the yoke. They informed Cortés of these and other particulars. The
fame of the Spaniards had reached their master, who sent these messengers
to request the presence of the wonderful strangers in his capital.

This communication was eagerly listened to by the general, who, it will
be remembered, was possessed of none of those facts, laid before the
reader, respecting the internal condition of the kingdom, which he had no
reason to suppose other than strong and united. An important truth now
flashed on his mind, as his quick eye descried in this spirit of discontent
a potent lever, by the aid of which he might hope to overturn this barbaric
empire. He received the mission of the Totonacs most graciously, and
after informing himself, as far as possible, of their dispositions and resources, dismissed them with presents, promising soon to pay a visit to
their lord.[1]

Meanwhile, his personal friends, among whom may be particularly mentioned Alonso Hernandez Puertocarrero, Cristóbal de Olid, Alonso de
Avila, Pedro de Alvarado and his brothers, were very busy in persuading
the troops to take such measures as should enable Cortés to go forward
in those ambitious plans for which he had no warrant from the powers of
Velasquez. "To return now," they said, "was to abandon the enterprise
on the threshold, which, under such a leader, must conduct to glory and
incalculable riches. To return to Cuba would be to surrender to the

greedy governor the little gains they had already got. The only way was to persuade the general to establish a permanent colony in the country, the government of which would take the conduct of matters into its own hands and provide for the interests of its members. It was true, Cortés had no such authority from Velasquez. But the interests of the sovereigns, which were paramount to every other, imperatively demanded it."

These conferences could not be conducted so secretly, though held by night, as not to reach the ears of the friends of Velasquez.[1] They remonstrated against the proceedings, as insidious and disloyal. They accused the general of instigating them, and, calling on him to take measures without delay for the return of the troops to Cuba, announced their own intention to depart, with such followers as still remained true to the governor.

Cortés, instead of taking umbrage at this high-handed proceeding, or even answering in the same haughty tone, mildly replied "that nothing was further from his desire than to exceed his instructions. He, indeed, preferred to remain in the country, and continue his profitable intercourse with the natives. But, since the army thought otherwise, he should defer to their opinion, and give orders to return, as they desired." On the following morning, proclamation was made for the troops to hold themselves in readiness to embark at once on board the fleet, which was to sail for Cuba.[2]

Great was the sensation caused by their general's order. Even many of those before clamorous for it, with the usual caprice of men whose wishes are too easily gratified, now regretted it. The partisans of Cortés were loud in their remonstrances. "They were betrayed by the general," they cried, and, thronging round his tent, called on him to countermand his orders. "We came here," said they, "expecting to form a settlement, if the state of the country authorized it. Now it seems you have no warrant from the governor to make one. But there are interests, higher than those of Velasquez, which demand it. These territories are not his property, but were discovered for the sovereigns;[3] and it is necessary to plant a colony to watch over their interests, instead of wasting time in idle barter, or, still worse, of returning, in the present state of affairs, to Cuba. If you refuse," they concluded, "we shall protest against your conduct as disloyal to their Highnesses."

---

[1] The letter from the *cabildo* of Vera Cruz says nothing of these midnight conferences. Bernal Diaz, who was privy to them, is a sufficient authority. See Hist. de la Conquista, cap. 42.

[2] Gomara, Crónica, cap. 30.—Las Casas, Hist. de las Indias, MS., lib. 3, cap. 121.—Ixtlilxochitl, Hist. Chich., MS., cap. 80.—Bernal Diaz, Ibid., loc. cit.—Declaracion de Puertocarrero, MS.—The deposition of a respectable person like Puertocarrero, taken in the spring of the following year, after his return to Spain, is a document of such authority that I have transferred it entire, in the original, to the Appendix, Part 2, No. 7.

[3] Sometimes we find the Spanish writers referring to "the sovereigns," sometimes to "the emperor:" in the former case intending Queen Joanna, the crazy mother of Charles V., as well as himself. Indeed, all public acts and ordinances ran in the name of both. The title of "Highness," which until the reign of Charles V. had usually—not uniformly, as Robertson imagines (History of Charles V., vol. ii. p. 59)—been applied to the sovereign, now gradually gave way to that of "Majesty," which Charles affected after his election to the imperial throne. The same title is occasionally found in the correspondence of the Great Captain, and other courtiers of the reign of Ferdinand and Isabella.

Cortés received this remonstrance with the embarrassed air of one by whom it was altogether unexpected. He modestly requested time for deliberation, and promised to give his answer on the following day. At the time appointed, he called the troops together, and made them a brief address. "There was no one," he said, "if he knew his own heart, more deeply devoted than himself to the welfare of his sovereigns and the glory of the Spanish name. He had not only expended his all, but incurred heavy debts, to meet the charges of this expedition, and had hoped to reimburse himself by continuing his traffic with the Mexicans. But, if the soldiers thought a different course advisable, he was ready to postpone his own advantage to the good of the state."[1] He concluded by declaring his willingness to take measures for settling a colony *in the name of the Spanish sovereigns*, and to nominate a magistracy to preside over it.[2]

For the *alcaldes* he selected Puertocarrero and Montejo, the former cavalier his fast friend, and the latter the friend of Velasquez, and chosen for that very reason; a stroke of policy which perfectly succeeded. The *regidores*, *alguacil*, treasurer, and other functionaries were then appointed, all of them his personal friends and adherents. They were regularly sworn into office, and the new city received the title of *Villa Rica de Vera Cruz*, "The Rich Town of the True Cross;" a name which was considered as happily intimating that union of spiritual and temporal interests to which the arms of the Spanish adventurers in the New World were to be devoted.[3] Thus, by a single stroke of the pen, as it were, the camp was transformed into a civil community, and the whole framework and even title of the city were arranged, before the site of it had been settled.

The new municipality were not slow in coming together; when Cortés presented himself, cap in hand, before that august body, and, laying the powers of Velasquez on the table, respectfully tendered the resignation of his office of Captain-General, "which, indeed," he said, "had necessarily expired, since the authority of the governor was now superseded by that of the magistracy of Villa Rica de Vera Cruz." He then, with a profound obeisance, left the apartment.[4]

The council, after a decent time spent in deliberation, again requested his presence. "There was no one," they said, "who, on mature reflection,

---

[1] According to Robertson, Cortés told his men that he had proposed to establish a colony on the coast, before marching into the country; but he abandoned his design, at their entreaties to set out at once on the expedition. In the very next page we find him organizing this same colony. (History of America, vol. ii. pp. 241, 242.) The historian would have been saved this inconsistency, if he had followed either of the authorities whom he cites, Bernal Diaz and Herrera, or the letter from Vera Cruz, of which he had a copy. They all concur in the statement in the text.

[2] Las Casas, Hist. de las Indias, MS., lib. 3, cap. 122.—Carta de Vera Cruz, MS.—Declaracion de Montejo, MS.—Declaracion de Puertocarrero, MS. —"Our general, after some urging, acquiesced," says the blunt old soldier Bernal Diaz; "for, as the proverb says, 'You ask me to do what I have already made up my mind to.'" *Tu me lo ruegas, é yo me lo quiero*. Hist. de la Conquista, cap. 42.

[3] According to Bernal Diaz, the title of "Vera Cruz" was intended to commemorate their landing on Good Friday. Hist. de la Conquista, cap. 42.

[4] Solis, whose taste for speech-making might have satisfied even the Abbé Mably (see his Treatise, "De la Manière d'écrire l'Histoire"), has put a very flourishing harangue on this occasion into the mouth of his hero, of which there is not a vestige in any contemporary account. (Conquista, lib. 2, cap. 7.) Dr. Robertson has transferred it to his own eloquent pages, without citing his author, indeed, who, considering he came a century and a half after the Conquest, must be allowed to be not the best, especially when the only voucher for a fact.

appeared to them so well qualified to take charge of the interests of the community, both in peace and in war, as himself; and they unanimously named him, in behalf of their Catholic Highnesses, Captain-General and Chief Justice of the colony." He was further empowered to draw, on his own account, one-fifth of the gold and silver which might hereafter be obtained by commerce or conquest from the natives.[1] Thus clothed with supreme civil and military jurisdiction, Cortés was not backward in asserting his authority. He found speedy occasion for it.

The transactions above described had succeeded each other so rapidly that the governor's party seemed to be taken by surprise, and had formed no plan of opposition. When the last measure was carried, however, they broke forth into the most indignant and opprobrious invectives, denouncing the whole as a systematic conspiracy against Velasquez. These accusations led to recrimination from the soldiers of the other side, until from words they nearly proceeded to blows. Some of the principal cavaliers, among them Velasquez de Leon, a kinsman of the governor, Escobar, his page, and Diego de Ordaz, were so active in instigating these turbulent movements that Cortés took the bold measure of putting them all in irons and sending them on board the vessels. He then dispersed the common file by detaching many of them with a strong party under Alvarado to forage the neighbouring country and bring home provisions for the destitute camp.

During their absence, every argument that cupidity or ambition could suggest was used to win the refractory to his views. Promises, and even gold, it is said, were liberally lavished; till, by degrees, their understandings were opened to a clearer view of the merits of the case. And when the foraging party reappeared with abundance of poultry and vegetables, and the cravings of the stomach—that great laboratory of disaffection, whether in camp or capital—were appeased, good humour returned with good cheer, and the rival factions embraced one another as companions in arms, pledged to a common cause. Even the high-mettled hidalgos on board the vessels did not long withstand the general tide of reconciliation, but one by one gave in their adhesion to the new government. What is more remarkable is that this forced conversion was not a hollow one, but from this time forward several of these very cavaliers became the most steady and devoted partisans of Cortés.[2]

---

[1] "Lo peor de todo que le otorgámos," says Bernal Diaz, somewhat peevishly, was, "que le dariamos el quinto del oro de lo que se huuiesse, despues de sacado el Real quinto." (Hist. de la Conquista, cap. 42.) The letter from Vera Cruz says nothing of this fifth. The reader who would see the whole account of this remarkable transaction in the original may find it in the Appendix, Part 2, No. 8.

[2] Carta de Vera Cruz, MS.—Gomara, Crónica, cap. 30, 31.—Las Casas, Hist. de las Indias, MS., lib. 3, cap. 122.—Ixtlilxochitl, Hist. Chich., MS., cap. 80.—Bernal Diaz, Hist. de la Conquista, cap. 42.—Declaraciones de Montejo y Puertocarrero, MSS.—In the process of Narvaez against Cortes.

the latter is accused of being possessed with the Devil, as only Lucifer could have thus gained him the affections of the soldiery. (Demanda de Narvaez, MS.) Solís, on the other hand, sees nothing but good faith and loyalty in the conduct of the general, who acted from a sense of duty! (Conquista, lib. 2, cap. 6, 7.) Solís is even a more steady apologist for his hero than his own chaplain, Gomara, or the worthy magistrates of Vera Cruz. A more impartial testimony than either, probably, may be gathered from honest Bernal Diaz, so often quoted. A hearty champion of the cause, he was by no means blind to the defects or the merits of his leader.

Such was the address of this extraordinary man, and such the ascendency which in a few months he had acquired over these wild and turbulent spirits! By this ingenious transformation of a military into a civil community, he had secured a new and effectual basis for future operations. He might now go forward without fear of check or control from a superior, —at least from any other superior than the crown, under which alone he held his commission. In accomplishing this, instead of incurring the charge of usurpation or of transcending his legitimate powers, he had transferred the responsibility, in a great measure, to those who had imposed on him the necessity of action. By this step, moreover, he had linked the fortunes of his followers indissolubly with his own. They had taken their chance with him, and, whether for weal or for woe, must abide the consequences. He was no longer limited to the narrow concerns of a sordid traffic, but, sure of their co-operation, might now boldly meditate, and gradually disclose, those lofty schemes which he had formed in his own bosom for the conquest of an empire.[1]

Harmony being thus restored, Cortés sent his heavy guns on board the fleet, and ordered it to coast along the shore to the north as far as Chiahuitztla, the town near which the destined port of the new city was situated; proposing, himself, at the head of his troops, to visit Cempoalla, on the march. The road lay for some miles across the dreary plains in the neighbourhood of the modern Vera Cruz. In this sandy waste no signs of vegetation met their eyes, which, however, were occasionally refreshed by glimpses of the blue Atlantic, and by the distant view of the magnificent Orizaba, towering, with his spotless diadem of snow, far above his colossal brethren of the Andes.[2] As they advanced, the country gradually assumed a greener and richer aspect. They crossed a river, probably a tributary of the *Rio de la Antigua*, with difficulty, on rafts, and on some broken canoes that were lying on the banks. They now came in view of very different scenery,—wide-rolling plains covered with a rich carpet of verdure and overshadowed by groves of cocoas and feathery palms, among whose tall, slender stems were seen deer, and various wild animals with which the Spaniards were unacquainted. Some of the horsemen gave chase to the deer, and wounded, but did not succeed in killing them. They saw, also, pheasants and other birds; among them

---

[1] This may appear rather indifferent logic to those who consider that Cortés appointed the very body who, in turn, appointed him to the command. But the affectation of legal forms afforded him a thin varnish for his proceedings, which served his purpose, for the present at least, with the troops. For the future, he trusted to his good star—in other words, to the success of his enterprise—to vindicate his conduct to the Emperor. He did not miscalculate.

[2] The name of the mountain is not given, and probably was not known, but the minute description in the MS. of Vera Cruz leaves no doubt that it was the one mentioned in the text. "Entre las quales así una que excede en mucha altura á todas las otras y de ella se vee y descubre gran parte de la mar y de la tierra, y es tan alta, que si el dia no es bien claro, no se puede divisar ni ver lo alto de ella, porque de la mitad arriba está toda cubierta de nubes : y algunos veces, cuando hace muy claro dia, se vee por cima de las dichas nubes lo alto de ella, y está tan blanco, que lo jusgamos por nieve." (Carta de Vera Cruz, MS.) This huge volcano was called *Citlaltepetl*, or "Star-Mountain," by the Mexicans, —perhaps from the fire which once issued from its conical summit, far above the clouds. It stands in the intendancy of Vera Cruz, and rises, according to Humboldt's measurement, to the enormous height of 17,368 feet above the ocean. (Essai politique, tom. i. p. 265.) It is the highest peak but one in the whole range of the Mexican Cordilleras.

the wild turkey, the pride of the American forest, which the Spaniards described as a species of peacock.[1]

On their route they passed through some deserted villages, in which were Indian temples, where they found censers, and other sacred utensils, and manuscripts of the *agave* fibre, containing the picture-writing, in which, probably, their religious ceremonies were recorded. They now beheld, also, the hideous spectacle, with which they became afterwards familiar, of the mutilated corpses of victims who had been sacrificed to the accursed deities of the land. The Spaniards turned with loathing and indignation from a display of butchery which formed so dismal a contrast to the fair scenes of nature by which they were surrounded.

They held their course along the banks of the river, towards its source, when they were met by twelve Indians, sent by the cacique of Cempoalla to show them the way to his residence. At night they bivouacked in an open meadow, where they were well supplied with provisions by their new friends. They left the stream on the following morning, and, striking northerly across the country, came upon a wide expanse of luxuriant plains and woodland, glowing in all the splendour of tropical vegetation. The branches of the stately trees were gaily festooned with clustering vines of the dark-purple grape, variegated convolvuli, and other flowering parasites of the most brilliant dyes. The undergrowth of prickly aloe, matted with wild rose and honeysuckle, made in many places an almost impervious thicket. Amid this wilderness of sweet-swelling buds and blossoms fluttered numerous birds of the parrot tribe, and clouds of butterflies, whose gaudy colours, nowhere so gorgeous as in the *tierra caliente*, rivalled those of the vegetable creation ; while birds of exquisite song, the scarlet cardinal, and the marvellous mocking-bird, that comprehends in his own notes the whole music of a forest, filled the air with delicious melody. The hearts of the stern Conquerors were not very sensible to the beauties of nature. But the magical charms of the scenery drew forth unbounded expressions of delight, and as they wandered through this " terrestrial paradise," as they called it, they fondly compared it to the fairest regions of their own sunny land.[2]

As they approached the Indian city, they saw abundant signs of cultivation, in the trim gardens and orchards that lined both sides of the road.

---

[1] Carta de Vera Cruz, MS.—Bernal Diaz, Hist. de la Conquista, cap. 44.

[2] Gomara, Crónica, cap. 32, ap. Barcia, tom. ii.— Herrera, Hist. general, dec. 2, lib. 5, cap. 1.— Oviedo, Hist. de las Ind., MS., lib. 33, cap. 1.— " Mui hermosas vegas y riberas tales y tan hermosas que en toda España no pueden ser mejores ansí de apacibles á la vista como de fructíferas." (Carta de Vera Cruz, MS.) The following poetical apostrophe, by Lord Morpeth, to the scenery of Cuba, equally applicable to that of the *tierra caliente*, will give the reader a more animated picture of the glories of these sunny climes than my own prose can. The verses, which have never been published, breathe the generous sentiment characteristic of their noble author :—

" Ye tropic forests of unfading green,
  Where the palm tapers and the orange glows,
Where the light bamboo waves her feathery screen,
  And her far shade the matchless *ceiba* throws !

" Ye cloudless ethers of unchanging blue,
  Save where the rosy streaks of eve give way
To the clear sapphire of your midnight hue,
  The burnished azure of your perfect day !

" Yet tell me not my native skies are bleak,
  That flushed with liquid wealth no cane-fields
    wave ;
For Virtue pines, and Manhood dares not speak,
  And Nature's glories brighten round the Slave."

L

They were now met by parties of the natives, of either sex, who increased in numbers with every step of their progress. The women, as well as men, mingled fearlessly among the soldiers, bearing bunches and wreaths of flowers, with which they decorated the neck of the general's charger, and hung a chaplet of roses about his helmet. Flowers were the delight of this people. They bestowed much care in their cultivation, in which they were well seconded by a climate of alternate heat and moisture, stimulating the soil to the spontaneous production of every form of vegetable life. The same refined taste, as we shall see, prevailed among the warlike Aztecs, and has survived the degradation of the nation in their descendants of the present day.[1]

Many of the women appeared, from their richer dress and numerous attendants, to be persons of rank. They were clad in robes of fine cotton, curiously coloured, which reached from the neck—in the inferior orders, from the waist—to the ankles. The men wore a sort of mantle of the same material, *á la Morisca*, in the Moorish fashion, over their shoulders, and belts or sashes about the loins. Both sexes had jewels and ornaments of gold round their necks, while their ears and nostrils were perforated with rings of the same metal.

Just before reaching the town, some horsemen who had ridden in advance returned with the amazing intelligence "that they had been near enough to look within the gates, and found the houses all plated with burnished silver!" On entering the place, the silver was found to be nothing more than a brilliant coating of stucco, with which the principal buildings were covered; a circumstance which produced much merriment among the soldiers at the expense of their credulous comrades. Such ready credulity is a proof of the exalted state of their imaginations, which were prepared to see gold and silver in every object around them.[2] The edifices of the better kind were of stone and lime, or bricks dried in the sun; the poorer were of clay and earth. All were thatched with palm leaves, which, though a flimsy roof, apparently, for such structures, were so nicely interwoven as to form a very effectual protection against the weather.

The city was said to contain from twenty to thirty thousand inhabitants. This is the most moderate computation, and not improbable.[3] Slowly and silently the little army paced the narrow and now crowded streets of Cempoalla, inspiring the natives with no greater wonder than they them-

1 "The same love of flowers," observes one of the most delightful of modern travellers, "distinguishes the natives now, as in the times of Cortés. And it presents a strange anomaly," she adds, with her usual acuteness; "this love of flowers having existed along with their sanguinary worship and barbarous sacrifices." Madame Calderon de la Barca, Life in Mexico, vol. i. let. 12.

2 "Con la imaginacion que llevaban, i buenos deseos, todo se les antojaba plata i oro lo que relucia." Gomara, Crónica, cap. 32, ap. Barcia, tom. ii.

3 This is Las Casas' estimate. (Hist. de las Ind., MS., lib. 3, cap. 121.) Torquemada hesitates between twenty, fifty, and one hundred and fifty thousand, each of which he names at different times! (Clavigero, Stor. del Messico, tom. iii. p. 26, nota.) The place was gradually abandoned, after the Conquest, for others, in a more favourable position, probably, for trade. Its ruins were visible at the close of the last century. See Lorenzana, Hist. de Nueva-España, p. 39, nota.

selves experienced at the display of a policy and refinement so far superior to anything they had witnessed in the New World.[1] The cacique came out in front of his residence to receive them. He was a tall and very corpulent man, and advanced leaning on two of his attendants. He received Cortés and his followers with great courtesy, and, after a brief interchange of civilities, assigned the army its quarters in a neighbouring temple, into the spacious courtyard of which a number of apartments opened, affording excellent accommodations for the soldiery.

Here the Spaniards were well supplied with provisions, meat cooked after the fashion of the country, and maize made into bread-cakes. The general received, also, a present of considerable value from the cacique, consisting of ornaments of gold and fine cottons. Notwithstanding these friendly demonstrations, Cortés did not relax his habitual vigilance, nor neglect any of the precautions of a good soldier. On his route, indeed, he had always marched in order of battle, well prepared against surprise. In his present quarters, he stationed his sentinels with like care, posted his small artillery so as to command the entrance, and forbade any soldier to leave the camp without orders, under pain of death.[2]

The following morning, Cortés, accompanied by fifty of his men, paid a visit to the lord of Cempoalla in his own residence. It was a building of stone and lime, standing on a steep terrace of earth, and was reached by a flight of stone steps. It may have borne resemblance in its structure to some of the ancient buildings found in Central America. Cortés, leaving his soldiers in the courtyard, entered the mansion with one of his officers, and his fair interpreter, Doña Marina.[3] A long conference ensued, from which the Spanish general gathered much light respecting the state of the country. He first announced to the chief that he was the subject of a great monarch who dwelt beyond the waters; that he had come to the Aztec shores to abolish the inhuman worship which prevailed there, and to introduce the knowledge of the true God. The cacique replied that their gods, who sent them the sunshine and the rain, were good enough for them; that he was the tributary of a powerful monarch also, whose capital stood on a lake far off among the mountains, —a stern prince, merciless in his exactions, and, in case of resistance, or any offence, sure to wreak his vengeance by carrying off their young men and maidens to be sacrificed to his deities. Cortés assured him that he would never consent to such enormities; he had been sent by his sovereign to redress abuses and to punish the oppressor;[4] and, if the Totonacs would be true to him, he would enable them to throw off the detested yoke of the Aztecs.

---

[1] "Porque viven mas política y rasonablemente que ninguna de las gentes que hasta oy en estas partes se ha visto." Carta de Vera Cruz, MS.
[2] Las Casas, Hist. de las Indias, MS., lib. 3, cap. 121.—Carta de Vera Cruz, MS.—Gomara, Crónica, cap. 33, ap. Barcia, tom. ii.—Oviedo, Hist. de las Indias, MS., lib. 33, cap. 1.

[3] The courteous title of *doña* is usually given by the Spanish chroniclers to this accomplished Indian.
[4] "He had come only to redress injuries, to protect the captive, to succour the weak, and to overthrow tyranny." (Gomara, Crónica, cap. 33, ap. Barcia, tom. ii.) Are we reading the adventures—it is the language—of Don Quixote or Amadis de Gaula?

The cacique added that the Totonac territory contained about thirty towns and villages, which could muster a hundred thousand warriors,—a number much exaggerated.[1] There were other provinces of the empire, he said, where the Aztec rule was equally odious; and between him and the capital lay the warlike republic of Tlascala, which had always maintained its independence of Mexico. The fame of the Spaniards had gone before them, and he was well acquainted with their terrible victory at Tabasco. But still he looked with doubt and alarm to a rupture with "the great Montezuma," as he always styled him; whose armies, on the least provocation, would pour down from the mountain regions of the West, and, rushing over the plains like a whirlwind, sweep off the wretched people to slavery and sacrifice !

Cortés endeavoured to reassure him, by declaring that a single Spaniard was stronger than a host of Aztecs. At the same time, it was desirable to know what nations would co-operate with him, not so much on his account as theirs, that he might distinguish friend from foe and know whom he was to spare in this war of extermination. Having raised the confidence of the admiring chief by this comfortable and politic vaunt, he took an affectionate leave, with the assurance that he would shortly return and concert measures for their future operations, when he had visited his ships in the adjoining port and secured a permanent settlement there.[2]

The intelligence gained by Cortés gave great satisfaction to his mind. It confirmed his former views, and showed, indeed, the interior of the monarchy to be in a state far more distracted than he had supposed. If he had before scarcely shrunk from attacking the Aztec empire, in the true spirit of a knight-errant, with his single arm, as it were, what had he now to fear, when one half of the nation could be thus marshalled against the other ? In the excitement of the moment, his sanguine spirit kindled with an enthusiasm which overleaped every obstacle. He communicated his own feelings to the officers about him, and, before a blow was struck, they already felt as if the banners of Spain were waving in triumph from the towers of Montezuma ! But many a bloody field was to be fought, many a peril and privation to be encountered, before that consummation could be attained.

Taking leave of the hospitable Indian, on the following day the Spaniards took the road to Chiahuitztla,[3] about four leagues distant, near which was the port discovered by Montejo, where their ships were now riding at anchor. They were provided by the cacique with four hundred Indian porters, *tamanes*, as they were called, to transport the baggage. These men easily carried fifty pounds' weight five or six leagues in a day. They were in use all over the Mexican empire, and the Spaniards found

---

[1] Gomara, Crónica, cap. 36.—Cortés, in his Second Letter to the Emperor Charles V., estimates the number of fighting-men at 50,000. Relacion segunda, ap. Lorenzana, p. 40.

[2] Las Casas, Hist. de las Indias, MS., lib. 3, cap. 121.—Ixtlilxochitl, Hist. Chich., MS., cap. 81.—Oviedo, Hist. de las Indias, MS., lib. 33, cap. 1.

[3] The historian, with the aid of Clavigero, himself a Mexican, may rectify frequent blunders of former writers, in the orthography of Aztec names. Both Robertson and Solís spell the name of this place *Quiabislan.* Blunders in such a barbarous nomenclature must be admitted to be very pardonable.

them of great service, henceforth, in relieving the troops from this part of their duty. They passed through a country of the same rich, voluptuous character as that which they had lately traversed, and arrived early next morning at the Indian town, perched like a fortress on a bold, rocky eminence that commanded the Gulf. Most of the inhabitants had fled, but fifteen of the principal men remained, who received them in a friendly manner, offering the usual compliments of flowers and incense. The people of the place, losing their fears, gradually returned. While conversing with the chiefs, the Spaniards were joined by the worthy cacique of Cempoalla, borne by his men on a litter. He eagerly took part in their deliberations. The intelligence gained here by Cortés confirmed the accounts already gathered of the feelings and resources of the Totonac nation.

In the midst of their conference, they were interrupted by a movement among the people, and soon afterwards five men entered the great square or market-place, where they were standing. By their lofty port, their peculiar and much richer dress, they seemed not to be of the same race as these Indians. Their dark, glossy hair was tied in a knot on the top of the head. They had bunches of flowers in their hands, and were followed by several attendants, some bearing wands with cords, others fans, with which they brushed away the flies and insects from their lordly masters. As these persons passed through the place, they cast a haughty look on the Spaniards, scarcely deigning to return their salutations. They were immediately joined, in great confusion, by the Totonac chiefs, who seemed anxious to conciliate them by every kind of attention.

The general, much astonished, inquired of Marina what it meant. She informed him they were Aztec nobles, empowered to receive the tribute for Montezuma. Soon after, the chiefs returned with dismay painted on their faces. They confirmed Marina's statement, adding that the Aztecs greatly resented the entertainment afforded the Spaniards without the Emperor's permission, and demanded in expiation twenty young men and women for sacrifice to the gods. Cortés showed the strongest indignation at this insolence. He required the Totonacs not only to refuse the demand, but to arrest the persons of the collectors and throw them into prison. The chiefs hesitated, but he insisted on it so peremptorily that they at length complied, and the Aztecs were seized, bound hand and foot, and placed under a guard.

In the night, the Spanish general procured the escape of two of them, and had them brought secretly before him. He expressed his regret at the indignity they had experienced from the Totonacs ; told them he would provide means for their flight, and to-morrow would endeavour to obtain the release of their companions. He desired them to report this to their master, with assurances of the great regard the Spaniards entertained for him, notwithstanding his ungenerous behaviour in leaving them to perish from want on his barren shores. He then sent the Mexican nobles down to the port, whence they were carried to another part of the coast by water, for fear of the violence of the Totonacs. These were greatly incensed at the escape of the prisoners, and would have sacrificed the remainder at once, but for the Spanish commander, who evinced the utmost horror at the proposal, and ordered them to be sent for safe custody on board the fleet. Soon after, they were permitted to join their companions. This artful proceeding, so characteristic of the policy of Cortés, had, as we shall see hereafter, all the effect intended on Montezuma. It cannot be commended, certainly, as in the true spirit of chivalry. Yet it has not wanted its panegyrist among the national historians ! [1]

By order of Cortés, messengers were despatched to the Totonac towns to report what had been done, calling on them to refuse the payment of further tribute to Montezuma. But there was no need of messengers. The affrighted attendants of the Aztec lords had fled in every direction, bearing the tidings, which spread like wildfire through the country, of the daring insult offered to the majesty of Mexico. The astonished Indians, cheered with the sweet hope of regaining their ancient liberty, came in numbers to Chiahuitztla, to see and confer with the formidable strangers. The more timid, dismayed at the thought of encountering the power of Montezuma, recommended an embassy to avert his displeasure by timely concessions. But the dexterous management of Cortés had committed them too far to allow any reasonable expectation of indulgence from this quarter. After some hesitation, therefore, it was determined to embrace the protection of the Spaniards, and to make one bold effort for the recovery of freedom. Oaths of allegiance were taken by the chiefs to the Spanish sovereigns, and duly recorded by Godoy, the royal notary. Cortés, satisfied with the important acquisition of so many vassals to the crown, set out soon after for the destined port, having first promised to revisit Cempoalla, where his business was but partially accomplished. [2]

The spot selected for the new city was only half a league distant, in a wide and fruitful plain, affording a tolerable haven for the shipping. Cortés was not long in determining the circuit of the walls, and the sites of the fort, granary, town-house, temple, and other public buildings. The friendly Indians eagerly assisted, by bringing materials, stone, lime, wood, and bricks dried in the sun. Every man put his hand to the work. The general laboured with the meanest of the soldiers, stimulating their exertions by his example as well as voice. In a few weeks the task was accomplished, and a town rose up, which, if not quite worthy of the aspiring name it bore, answered most of the purposes for which it was intended. It served as a good *point d'appui* for future operations ; a place of retreat for the disabled, as well as for the army in case of reverses ; a magazine

[1] "Grande artífice," exclaims Solís, "de medir lo que disponia con lo que recelaba ; y prudente capitan él que sabe caminar en alcance de las contingencias"! Conquista, lib. 2, cap. 9.
[2] Ixtlilxochitl, Hist. Chich., MS., cap. 81.—Rel.

Seg. de Cortés, ap. Lorenzana, p. 40.—Gomara, Crónica, cap. 34-36, ap. Barcia, tom. ii.—Bernal Diaz, Conquista, cap. 46, 47.—Herrera, Hist. general, dec. 2, lib. 5, cap. 10, 11.

for stores, and for such articles as might be received from or sent to the mother-country; a port for the shipping; a position of sufficient strength to overawe the adjacent country.[1]

It was the first colony—the fruitful parent of so many others—in New Spain. It was hailed with satisfaction by the simple natives, who hoped to repose in safety under its protecting shadow. Alas! they could not read the future, or they would have found no cause to rejoice in this harbinger of a revolution more tremendous than any predicted by their bards and prophets. It was not the good Quetzalcoatl who had returned to claim his own again, bringing peace, freedom, and civilization in his train. Their fetters, indeed, would be broken, and their wrongs be amply avenged on the proud head of the Aztec. But it was to be by that strong arm which should bow down equally the oppressor and the oppressed. The light of civilization would be poured on their land. But it would be the light of a consuming fire, before which their barbaric glory, their institutions, their very existence and name as a nation, would wither and become extinct! Their doom was sealed when the white man had set his foot on their soil.

CHAPTER VIII.

ANOTHER AZTEC EMBASSY.—DESTRUCTION OF THE IDOLS.—DESPATCHES SENT TO SPAIN.—CONSPIRACY IN THE CAMP.—THE FLEET SUNK.

(1519.)

WHILE the Spaniards were occupied with their new settlement, they were surprised by the presence of an embassy from Mexico. The account of the imprisonment of the royal collectors had spread rapidly through the country. When it reached the capital, all were filled with amazement at the unprecedented daring of the strangers. In Montezuma every other feeling, even that of fear, was swallowed up in indignation; and he showed his wonted energy in the vigorous preparations which he instantly made to punish his rebellious vassals and to avenge the insult offered to the majesty of the empire. But when the Aztec officers liberated by Cortés reached the capital and reported the courteous treatment they had

---

[1] Carta de Vera Cruz, MS.—Bernal Diaz, Conquista, cap. 48.—Oviedo, Hist. de las Ind., MS., lib. 33, cap. 1.—Declaracion de Montejo, MS.—Notwithstanding the advantages of its situation, La Villa Rica was abandoned in a few years for a neighbouring position to the south, not far from the mouth of the Antigua. This second settlement was known by the name of *Vera Cruz Vieja*, "Old Vera Cruz." Early in the seventeenth century this place, also, was abandoned for the present city, *Nueva Vera Cruz*, or New Vera Cruz, as it is called. (See *ante*, p. 142, note 1.) Of the true cause of these successive migrations we are ignorant. If, as is pretended, it was on account of the *vómito*, the inhabitants, one would suppose, can have gained little by the exchange. (See Humboldt, Essai politique, tom. ii. p. 210.) A want of attention to these changes has led to much confusion and inaccuracy in the ancient maps. Lorenzana has not escaped them in his chart and topographical account of the route of Cortés.

received from the Spanish commander, Montezuma's anger was mitigated, and his superstitious fears, getting the ascendency again, induced him to resume his former timid and conciliatory policy.   He accordingly sent an embassy, consisting of two youths, his nephews, and four of the ancient nobles of his court, to the Spanish quarters.   He provided them, in his usual munificent spirit, with a princely donation of gold, rich cotton stuffs, and beautiful mantles of the *plumaje*, or feather embroidery.   The envoys, on coming before Cortés, presented him with the articles, at the same time offering the acknowledgments of their master for the courtesy he had shown in liberating his captive nobles.   He was surprised and afflicted, however, that the Spaniards should have countenanced his faithless vassals in their rebellion.   He had no doubt they were the strangers whose arrival had been so long announced by the oracles, and of the same lineage with himself.[1]   From deference to them he would spare the Totonacs, while they were present.   But the time for vengeance would come.

Cortés entertained the Indian chieftains with frank hospitality.   At the same time, he took care to make such a display of his resources as, while it amused their minds, should leave a deep impression of his power.   He then, after a few trifling gifts, dismissed them with a conciliatory message to their master, and the assurance that he should soon pay his respects to him in his capital, where all misunderstanding between them would be readily adjusted.

The Totonac allies could scarcely credit their senses, when they gathered the nature of this interview.   Notwithstanding the presence of the Spaniards, they had looked with apprehension to the consequences of their rash act ; and their feelings of admiration were heightened into awe for the strangers who, at this distance, could exercise so mysterious an influence over the terrible Montezuma.[2]

Not long after, the Spaniards received an application from the cacique of Cempoalla to aid him in a dispute in which he was engaged with a neighbouring city.   Cortés marched with a part of his forces to his support. On the route, one Morla, a common soldier, robbed a native of a couple of fowls.   Cortés, indignant at this violation of his orders before his face, and aware of the importance of maintaining a reputation for good faith with his allies, commanded the man to be hung up, at once, by the roadside, in face of the whole army.   Fortunately for the poor wretch, Pedro de Alvarado, the future conqueror of Quiché, was present, and ventured to cut down the body, while there was yet life in it.   He, probably, thought enough had been done for example, and the loss of a single life, unnecessarily, was more than the little band could afford.   The anecdote is characteristic, as showing the strict discipline maintained by Cortés over

---

1 "Teniendo respeto á que tiene por cierto, que somos los que sus antepassados les auian dicho, que auian de venir á sus tierras, é que deuemos de ser de sus linajes." Bernal Diaz, Hist. de la Conquista, cap. 48.

2 Gomara, Crónica, cap. 37.—Ixtlilxochitl, Hist. Chich., MS., cap. 82.

his men, and the freedom assumed by his captains, who regarded him on terms nearly of equality,—as a fellow-adventurer with themselves. This feeling of companionship led to a spirit of insubordination among them, which made his own post as commander the more delicate and difficult.

On reaching the hostile city, but a few leagues from the coast, they were received in an amicable manner; and Cortés, who was accompanied by his allies, had the satisfaction of reconciling these different branches of the Totonac family with each other, without bloodshed. He then returned to Cempoalla, where he was welcomed with joy by the people, who were now impressed with as favourable an opinion of his moderation and justice as they had before been of his valour. In token of his gratitude, the Indian cacique delivered to the general eight Indian maidens, richly dressed, wearing collars and ornaments of gold, with a number of female slaves to wait on them. They were daughters of the principal chiefs, and the cacique requested that the Spanish captains might take them as their wives. Cortés received the damsels courteously, but told the cacique they must first be baptized, as the sons of the Church could have no commerce with idolaters.[1] He then declared that it was a great object of his mission to wean the natives from their heathenish abominations, and besought the Totonac lord to allow his idols to be cast down, and the symbols of the true faith to be erected in their place.

To this the other answered, as before, that his gods were good enough for him; nor could all the persuasion of the general, nor the preaching of Father Olmedo, induce him to acquiesce. Mingled with his polytheism, he had conceptions of a Supreme and Infinite Being, Creator of the Universe, and his darkened understanding could not comprehend how such a Being could condescend to take the form of humanity, with its infirmities and ills, and wander about on earth, the voluntary victim of persecution from the hands of those whom his breath had called into existence.[2] He plainly told the Spaniards that he would resist any violence offered to his gods, who would, indeed, avenge the act themselves, by the instant destruction of their enemies.

But the zeal of the Christians had mounted too high to be cooled by remonstrance or menace. During their residence in the land, they had witnessed more than once the barbarous rites of the natives, their cruel sacrifices of human victims, and their disgusting cannibal repasts.[3] Their souls sickened at these abominations, and they agreed with one voice to

---

[1] "De buena gana recibirian las Doncellas como fuesen Christianas; porque de otra manera, no era permitido á hombres, hijos de la Iglesia de Dios, tener comercio con idólatras." Herrera, Hist. general, dec. 2, lib. 5, cap. 13.

[2] Herrera, Hist. general, dec. 2, lib. 5, cap. 13.— Las Casas, Hist. de las Indias, MS., lib. 3, cap. 122.—Herrera has put a very edifying harangue, on this occasion, into the mouth of Cortés, which savours much more of the priest than the soldier. Does he not confound him with Father Olmedo?

[3] "Esto habemos visto," says the Letter of Vera Cruz, "algunos de nosotros, y los que lo han visto dizen que es la mas terrible y la mas espantosa cosa de ver que jamas han visto." Still more strongly speaks Bernal Diaz. (Hist. de la Conquista, cap. 51.) The Letter computes that there were fifty or sixty persons thus butchered in each of the *teocallis* every year; giving an annual consumption, in the countries which the Spaniards had then visited, of three or four thousand victims! (Carta de Vera Cruz, MS.) However loose this arithmetic may be, the general fact is appalling.

stand by their general, when he told them that "Heaven would never smile on their enterprise if they countenanced such atrocities, and that, for his own part, he was resolved the Indian idols should be demolished that very hour, if it cost him his life." To postpone the work of conversion was a sin. In the enthusiasm of the moment, the dictates of policy and ordinary prudence were alike unheeded.

Scarcely waiting for his commands, the Spaniards moved towards one of the principal *teocallis*, or temples, which rose high on a pyramidal foundation, with a steep ascent of stone steps in the middle. The cacique, divining their purpose, instantly called his men to arms. The Indian warriors gathered from all quarters, with shrill cries and clashing of weapons; while the priests, in their dark cotton robes, with dishevelled tresses matted with blood, flowing wildly over their shoulders, rushed frantic among the natives, calling on them to protect their gods from violation ! All was now confusion, tumult, and warlike menace, where so lately had been peace and the sweet brotherhood of nations.

Cortés took his usual prompt and decided measures. He caused the cacique and some of the principal inhabitants and priests to be arrested by his soldiers. He then commanded them to quiet the people, for, if an arrow was shot against a Spaniard, it should cost every one of them his life. Marina, at the same time, represented the madness of resistance, and reminded the cacique that if he now alienated the affections of the Spaniards he would be left without a protector against the terrible vengeance of Montezuma. These temporal considerations seem to have had more weight with the Totonac chieftain than those of a more spiritual nature. He covered his face with his hands, exclaiming that the gods would avenge their own wrongs.

The Christians were not slow in availing themselves of his tacit acquiescence. Fifty soldiers, at a signal from their general, sprang up the great stairway of the temple, entered the building on the summit, the walls of which were black with human gore, tore the huge wooden idols from their foundations, and dragged them to the edge of the terrace. Their fantastic forms and features, conveying a symbolic meaning, which was lost on the Spaniards, seemed in their eyes only the hideous lineaments of Satan. With great alacrity they rolled the colossal monsters down the steps of the pyramid, amidst the triumphant shouts of their own companions, and the groans and lamentations of the natives. They then consummated the whole by burning them in the presence of the assembled multitude.

The same effect followed as in Cozumel. The Totonacs, finding their deities incapable of preventing or even punishing this profanation of their shrines, conceived a mean opinion of their power, compared with that of the mysterious and formidable strangers. The floor and walls of the *teocalli* were then cleansed, by command of Cortés, from their foul impurities : a fresh coating of stucco was laid on them by the Indian masons ; and an altar was raised, surmounted by a lofty cross, and hung with garlands of roses. A procession was next formed, in which some of the principal Totonac priests, exchanging their dark mantles for robes of white, carried lighted candles in their hands ; while an image of the Virgin, half smothered under the weight of flowers, was borne aloft, and, as the procession climbed the steps of the temple, was deposited above the altar. Mass was performed by Father Olmedo, and the impressive character of the ceremony and the passionate eloquence of the good priest touched the feelings of the motley audience, until Indians as well as Spaniards, if we may trust the chronicler, were melted into tears and audible sobs. The Protestant missionary seeks to enlighten the understanding of his convert by the pale light of reason. But the bolder Catholic, kindling the spirit by the splendour of the spectacle and by the glowing portrait of an agonized Redeemer, sweeps along his hearers in a tempest of passion, that drowns everything like reflection. He has secured his convert, however, by the hold on his affections,—an easier and more powerful hold, with the untutored savage, than reason.

An old soldier named Juan de Torres, disabled by bodily infirmity, consented to remain and watch over the sanctuary and instruct the natives in its services. Cortés then, embracing his Totonac allies, now brothers in religion as in arms, set out once more for the Villa Rica, where he had some arrangements to complete previous to his departure for the capital.[1]

He was surprised to find that a Spanish vessel had arrived there in his absence, having on board twelve soldiers and two horses. It was under the command of a captain named Saucedo, a cavalier of the ocean, who had followed in the track of Cortés in quest of adventure. Though a small, they afforded a very seasonable body of recruits for the little army. By these men, the Spaniards were informed that Velasquez, the governor of Cuba, had lately received a warrant from the Spanish government to establish a colony in the newly-discovered countries.

Cortés now resolved to put a plan in execution which he had been some time meditating. He knew that all the late acts of the colony, as well as his own authority, would fall to the ground without the royal sanction. He knew, too, that the interest of Velasquez, which was great at court, would, so soon as he was acquainted with his secession, be wholly employed to circumvent and crush him. He resolved to anticipate his movements, and to send a vessel to Spain with despatches addressed to the emperor himself, announcing the nature and extent of his discoveries, and to obtain, if possible, the confirmation of his proceedings. In order to conciliate his master's goodwill, he further proposed to send him such a present as should suggest lofty ideas of the importance of his own services to the crown. To effect this, the royal fifth he considered

---

[1] Las Casas, Hist. de las Indias, MS., lib. 3, cap. 122.—Bernal Diaz, Hist. de la Conquista, cap. 51, 52.—Gomara, Crónica, cap. 43.—Herrera, Hist. general, dec. 2, lib. 5, cap. 13, 14.—Ixtlilxochitl, Hist. Chich., MS., cap. 83.

inadequate. He conferred with his officers, and persuaded them to relinquish their share of the treasure. At his instance, they made a similar
application to the soldiers; representing that it was the earnest wish of the
general, who set the example by resigning his own fifth, equal to the share
of the crown. It was but little that each man was asked to surrender, but
the whole would make a present worthy of the monarch for whom it was
intended. By this sacrifice they might hope to secure his indulgence for
the past and his favour for the future; a temporary sacrifice, that would
be well repaid by the security of the rich possessions which awaited them
in Mexico. A paper was then circulated among the soldiers, which all
who were disposed to relinquish their shares were requested to sign.
Those who declined should have their claims respected, and receive the
amount due to them. No one refused to sign; thus furnishing another
example of the extraordinary power obtained by Cortés over these rapacious spirits, who, at his call, surrendered up the very treasures which had
been the great object of their hazardous enterprise![1]

He accompanied this present with a letter to the emperor, in which he
gave a full account of all that had befallen him since his departure from
Cuba; of his various discoveries, battles, and traffic with the natives;
their conversion to Christianity; his strange perils and sufferings; many
particulars respecting the lands he had visited, and such as he could collect
in regard to the great Mexican monarchy and its sovereign. He stated
his difficulties with the governor of Cuba, the proceedings of the army in
reference to colonization, and besought the emperor to confirm their acts,
as well as his own authority, expressing his entire confidence that he should
be able, with the aid of his brave followers, to place the Castilian crown in
possession of this great Indian empire.[2]

This was the celebrated *First Letter*, as it is called, of Cortés, which has
hitherto eluded every search that has been made for it in the libraries of

---

[1] Bernal Diaz, Hist. de la Conquista, cap. 53.—
Ixtlilxochitl, Hist. Chich., MS., cap. 82.—Carta de
Vera Cruz, MS.
A complete inventory of the articles received from
Montezuma is contained in the *Carta de Vera
Cruz.*—The following are a few of the items :—
Two collars made of gold and precious stones.
A hundred ounces of gold ore, that their High-
nesses might see in what state the gold came from
the mines.
Two birds made of green feathers, with feet,
beaks, and eyes of gold,—and, in the same piece
with them, animals of gold, resembling snails.
A large alligator's head of gold.
A bird of green feathers, with feet, beak, and eyes
of gold.
Two birds made of thread and feather-work,
having the quills of their wings and tails, their feet,
eyes, and the ends of their beaks, of gold,—standing
upon two reeds covered with gold, which are raised
on balls of feather-work and gold embroidery, one
white and the other yellow, with seven tassels of
feather-work hanging from each of them.
A large silver wheel weighing forty-eight marks,
several bracelets and leaves of the same metal,

together with five smaller shields, the whole weighing sixty-two marks of silver.
A box of feather-work embroidered on leather,
with a large plate of gold, weighing seventy ounces,
in the midst.
Two pieces of cloth woven with feathers; another
with variegated colours; and another worked with
black and white figures.
A large wheel of gold, with figures of strange
animals on it, and worked with tufts of leaves;
weighing three thousand eight hundred ounces.
A fan of variegated feather-work, with thirty-
seven rods plated with gold.
Five fans of variegated feathers,—four of which
have ten, and the other thirteen, rods embossed
with gold.
Sixteen shields of precious stones, with feathers
of various colours hanging from their rims.
Two pieces of cotton very richly wrought with
black and white embroidery.
Six shields, each covered with a plate of gold,
with something resembling a golden mitre in the
centre.
[2] "Una muy larga Carta," says Gomara, in his
loose analysis of it. Crónica, cap. 40.

Europe.[1] Its existence is fully established by references to it, both in his own subsequent letters, and in the writings of contemporaries.[2] Its general purport is given by his chaplain, Gomara. The importance of the document has doubtless been much overrated; and, should it ever come to light, it will probably be found to add little of interest to the matter contained in the letter from Vera Cruz, which has formed the basis of the preceding portion of our narrative. Cortés had no sources of information beyond those open to the authors of the latter document. He was even less full and frank in his communications, if it be true that he suppressed all notice of the discoveries of his two immediate predecessors.[3]

The magistrates of the Villa Rica, in their epistle, went over the same ground with Cortés; concluding with an emphatic representation of the misconduct of Velasquez, whose venality, extortion, and selfish devotion to his personal interests, to the exclusion of those of his sovereigns as well as of his own followers, they placed in a most clear and unenviable light.[4] They implored the government not to sanction his interference with the new colony, which would be fatal to its welfare, but to commit the undertaking to Hernando Cortés, as the man most capable, by his experience and conduct, of bringing it to a glorious termination.[5]

---

[1] Dr. Robertson states that the Imperial Library at Vienna was examined for this document, at his instance, but without success. (History of America, vol. ii. note 70.) I have not been more fortunate in the researches made for me in the British Museum, the Royal Library of Paris, and that of the Academy of History at Madrid. The last is a great depository for the colonial historical documents; but a very thorough inspection of its papers makes it certain that this is wanting to the collection. As the emperor received it on the eve of his embarkation for Germany, and the Letter of Vera Cruz, forwarded at the same time, is in the library of Vienna, this would seem, after all, to be the most probable place of its retreat.

[2] "By a ship," says Cortés, in the very first sentence of his Second Letter to the emperor, "which I despatched from this your sacred majesty's province of New Spain on the 16th of July of the year 1519, I sent your highness a very long and particular relation of what had happened from my coming hither up to that time." (Rel. Seg. de Cortés, ap. Lorenzana, p. 38.) "Cortés wrote," says Bernal Diaz, "as he informed us, an accurate report, but we did not see his letter." (Hist. de la Conquista, cap. 53.) (Also, Oviedo, Hist. de las Ind., MS., lib. 33, cap. 1, and Gomara, ut supra.) Were it not for these positive testimonies, one

might suppose that the Carta de Vera Cruz had suggested an *imaginary* letter of Cortés. Indeed, the copy of the former document belonging to the Spanish Academy of History—and perhaps the original at Vienna—bears the erroneous title of "Primera Relacion de Cortés." *

[3] This is the imputation of Bernal Diaz, reported on hearsay, as he admits he never saw the letter himself. Hist. de la Conquista, cap. 54.

[4] "Fingiendo mill cautelas," says Las Casas, politely, of this part of the letter, "y afirmando otras muchas falsedades é mentiras"! Hist. de las Indias, MS., lib. 3, cap. 122.

[5] This document is of the greatest value and interest, coming as it does from the best instructed persons in the camp. It presents an elaborate record of all then known of the countries they had visited, and of the principal movements of the army, to the time of the foundation of the Villa Rica. The writers conciliate our confidence by the circumspect tone of their narration. "Querer dar," they say, "á Vuestra Magestad todas las particularidades de esta tierra y gente de ella, podria ser que en algo se errase la relacion, porque muchas de ellas no se han visto mas de por informaciones de los naturales de ella, y por esto no nos entremetemos á dar mas de aquello que por muy cierto y verdadero Vras. Reales Altezas podrán mandar tener." The account given of

* [There can be little doubt that the "Letter of Vera Cruz" is the document referred to by Cortés, writing in October 1520, as the "muy larga y particular Relacion" which he had "despatched" to the emperor in the summer of the preceding year. This language would not necessarily imply that the letter so described bore his own signature, while it was a natural mode of designating one of which he was the real author. It is easy to understand why, holding as yet no direct commission from the crown, he should have been less solicitous to appear as the narrator of his own exploits than to give them an appearance of official sanction and cover up his irregularity in not addressing his report to Velasquez, the official superior from whose control he was seeking to emancipate himself. Nor is it necessary, in accepting this hypothesis, to reject the statement of Bernal Diaz that Cortés sent to the emperor a relation under his own hand which he did not show to his companions. It seems to have been his habit on subsequent occasions, when sending a detailed report, to accompany it with a briefer and more private letter, giving a summary of what was contained in the longer document, sometimes with the addition of other matter, to be read by the emperor himself. One such letter, cited hereafter (book vii., chap. iii., note), mentions "una relacion bien larga y particular," which he was sending under the same date. That letters of this kind should not always have been preserved can excite no surprise; but it is highly improbable that the same fate should have befallen a full official report, the first of a series otherwise complete and disseminated by means of copies.—ED.]

With this letter went also another in the name of the citizen-soldiers of Villa Rica, tendering their dutiful submission to the sovereigns, and requesting the confirmation of their proceedings, above all, that of Cortés as their general.

The selection of the agents for the mission was a delicate matter, as on the result might depend the future fortunes of the colony and its commander. Cortés intrusted the affair to two cavaliers on whom he could rely; Francisco de Montejo, the ancient partisan of Velasquez, and Alonso Hernandez de Puertocarrero. The latter officer was a near kinsman of the Count of Medellin, and it was hoped his high connections might secure a favourable influence at court.

Together with the treasure, which seemed to verify the assertion that "the land teemed with gold as abundantly as that whence Solomon drew the same precious metal for his temple," [1] several Indian manuscripts were sent. Some were of cotton, others of the Mexican *agave*. Their unintelligible characters, says a chronicler, excited little interest in the Conquerors. As evidence of intellectual culture, however, they formed higher objects of interest to a philosophic mind than those costly fabrics which attested only the mechanical ingenuity of the nation. [2] Four Indian slaves were added as specimens of the natives. They had been rescued from the cages in which they were confined for sacrifice. One of the best vessels of the fleet was selected for the voyage, manned by fifteen seamen, and placed under the direction of the pilot Alaminos. He was directed to hold his course through the Bahama channel, north of Cuba, or Fernandina, as it was then called, and on no account to touch at that island, or any other in the Indian Ocean. With these instructions the good ship took its departure on the 26th of July, freighted with the treasures and the good wishes of the community of the Villa Rica de Vera Cruz.

After a quick run the emissaries made the island of Cuba, and, in direct disregard of orders, anchored before Marien, on the northern side of the island. This was done to accommodate Montejo, who wished to visit a plantation owned by him in the neighbourhood. While off the port, a sailor got on shore, and crossing the island to St. Jago, the capital, spread everywhere tidings of the expedition, until they reached the ears of Velasquez. It was the first intelligence which had been received of the armament since its departure; and, as the governor listened to the recital,

---

Velasquez, however, must be considered as an *ex parte* testimony, and, as such, admitted with great reserve. It was essential to their own vindication, to vindicate Cortés. The letter has never been printed. The original exists, as above stated, in the Imperial Library at Vienna. The copy in my possession, covering more than sixty pages folio, is taken from that of the Academy of History at Madrid. *

[1] "A nuestra parecer se debe creer, que ai en esta tierra tanto quanto en aquella de donde se dize aver llevado Salomon el oro para el templo." Carta de Vera Cruz, MS.

[2] Peter Martyr, pre-eminent above his contemporaries for the enlightened views he took of the new discoveries, devotes half a chapter to the Indian manuscripts, in which he recognized the evidence of a civilization analogous to the Egyptian. De Orbe Novo, dec. 4, cap. 8.

* [The letter has since been printed, from the original at Vienna, in the Col. de Doc. inéd. para la Hist. de España, tom. i.—Ed.]

it would not be easy to paint the mingled emotions of curiosity, astonishment, and wrath which agitated his bosom. In the first sally of passion, he poured a storm of invective on the heads of his secretary and treasurer, the friends of Cortés, who had recommended him as the leader of the expedition. After somewhat relieving himself in this way, he despatched two fast-sailing vessels to Marien with orders to seize the rebel ship, and, in case of her departure, to follow and overtake her.

But before the ships could reach that port the bird had flown, and was far on her way across the broad Atlantic. Stung with mortification at this fresh disappointment, Velasquez wrote letters of indignant complaint to the government at home, and to the Hieronymite fathers in Hispaniola, demanding redress. He obtained little satisfaction from the latter. He resolved, however, to take the matter into his own hands, and set about making formidable preparations for another squadron, which should be more than a match for that under his rebellious officer. He was indefatigable in his exertions, visiting every part of the island, and straining all his resources to effect his purpose. The preparations were on a scale that necessarily consumed many months.

Meanwhile the little vessel was speeding her prosperous way across the waters, and, after touching at one of the Azores, came safely into the harbour of St. Lucar, in the month of October. However long it may appear in the more perfect nautical science of our day, it was reckoned a fair voyage for that. Of what befell the commissioners on their arrival, their reception at court, and the sensation caused by their intelligence, I defer the account to a future chapter.[1]

Shortly after the departure of the commissioners, an affair occurred of a most unpleasant nature. A number of persons with the priest Juan Diaz at their head, ill-affected, from some cause or other, towards the administration of Cortés, or not relishing the hazardous expedition before them, laid a plan to seize one of the vessels, make the best of their way to Cuba, and report to the governor the fate of the armament. It was conducted with so much secrecy that the party had got their provisions, water, and everything necessary for the voyage, on board, without detection; when the conspiracy was betrayed, on the very night they were to sail, by one of their own number, who repented the part he had taken in it. The general caused the persons implicated to be instantly apprehended. An examination was instituted. The guilt of the parties was placed beyond a doubt. Sentence of death was passed on two of the ringleaders; another, the pilot, was condemned to lose his feet, and several others to be whipped. The priest, probably the most guilty of the whole, claiming the usual benefit of clergy, was permitted to escape.

---

[1] Bernal Diaz, Hist. de la Conquista, cap. 54-57.—Gomara, Crónica, cap. 40.—Herrera, Hist. general, dec. 2, lib. 5, cap. 14.—Carta de Vera Cruz, MS.—Martyr's copious information was chiefly derived from his conversations with Alaminos and the two envoys, on their arrival at court. De Orbe Novo, dec. 4, cap. 6, et alibi; also Idem, Opus Epistolarum (Amstelodami, 1670), ep. 650.

One of those condemned to the gallows was named Escudero, the very alguacil who, the reader may remember, so stealthily apprehended Cortés before the sanctuary in Cuba.[1] The general, on signing the death-warrants, was heard to exclaim, "Would that I had never learned to write!" It was not the first time, it was remarked, that the exclamation had been uttered in similar circumstances.[2]

The arrangements being now finally settled at the Villa Rica, Cortés sent forward Alvarado, with a large part of the army, to Cempoalla, where he soon after joined them with the remainder. The late affair of the conspiracy seems to have made a deep impression on his mind. It showed him that there were timid spirits in the camp on whom he could not rely, and who he feared might spread the seeds of disaffection among their companions. Even the more resolute, on any occasion of disgust or disappointment hereafter, might falter in purpose, and, getting possession of the vessels, abandon the enterprise. This was already too vast, and the odds were too formidable, to authorize expectation of success with diminution of numbers. Experience showed that this was always to be apprehended while means of escape were at hand.[3] The best chance for success was to cut off these means. He came to the daring resolution to destroy the fleet, without the knowledge of his army.

When arrived at Cempoalla, he communicated his design to a few of his devoted adherents, who entered warmly into his views. Through them he readily persuaded the pilots, by means of those golden arguments which weigh more than any other with ordinary minds, to make such a report of the condition of the fleet as suited his purpose. The ships, they said, were grievously racked by the heavy gales they had encountered, and, what was worse, the worms had eaten into their sides and bottoms until most of them were not seaworthy, and some, indeed, could scarcely now be kept afloat.

Cortés received the communication with surprise; "for he could well dissemble," observes Las Casas, with his usual friendly comment, "when it suited his interests." "If it be so," he exclaimed, "we must make the best of it! Heaven's will be done!"[4] He then ordered five of the worst conditioned to be dismantled, their cordage, sails, iron, and whatever was movable, to be brought on shore, and the ships to be sunk. A survey was made of the others, and, on a similar report, four more were condemned in the same manner. Only one small vessel remained!

---

[1] See *ante,* p. 114.

[2] Bernal Diaz, Hist. de la Conquista, cap. 57.—Oviedo, Hist. de las Ind., MS., lib. 33, cap. 2.—Las Casas, Hist. de las Indias, MS., lib. 3, cap. 122.—Demanda de Narvaez, MS.—Rel. Seg. de Cortés, ap. Lorenzana, p. 41.—It was the exclamation of Nero, as reported by Suetonius. "Et cum de supplicio cujusdam capite damnati ut ex more subscriberet, admoneretur, 'Quam vellem,' inquit, 'nescire literas!'" Lib. 6, cap. 10.

[3] "Y porque," says Cortés, "demas de los que por ser criados y amigos de Diego Velasquez tenian voluntad de salir de la Tierra, habia otros, que por verla tan grande, y de tanta gente, y tal, y ver los pocos Españoles que eramos, estaban del mismo propósito; creyendo, que si allí los navíos dejasse, se me alzarian con ellos, y yéndose todos los que de esta voluntad estavan, yo quedaria casi solo."

[4] "Mostró quando se lo dixéron mucho sentimiento Cortés, porque savia bien haçer fingimientos quando le era provechoso, y rrespondióles que mirasen vien en ello, é que si no estavan para navegar que diesen gracias á Dios por ello, pues no se podia hacer mas." Las Casas, Hist. de las Indias, MS., lib. 3, cap. 122.

When the intelligence reached the troops in Cempoalla, it caused the deepest consternation. They saw themselves cut off by a single blow from friends, family, country! The stoutest hearts quailed before the prospect of being thus abandoned on a hostile shore, a handful of men arrayed against a formidable empire. When the news arrived of the destruction of the five vessels first condemned, they had acquiesced in it as a necessary measure, knowing the mischievous activity of the insects in these tropical seas. But, when this was followed by the loss of the remaining four, suspicions of the truth flashed on their minds. They felt they were betrayed. Murmurs, at first deep, swelled louder and louder, menacing open mutiny. "Their general," they said, "had led them like cattle to be butchered in the shambles!"[1] The affair wore a most alarming aspect. In no situation was Cortés ever exposed to greater danger from his soldiers.[2]

His presence of mind did not desert him at this crisis. He called his men together, and, employing the tones of persuasion rather than authority, assured them that a survey of the ships showed they were not fit for service. If he had ordered them to be destroyed, they should consider, also, that his was the greatest sacrifice, for they were his property,—all, indeed, he possessed in the world. The troops, on the other hand, would derive one great advantage from it, by the addition of a hundred able-bodied recruits, before required to man the vessels. But, even if the fleet had been saved, it could have been of little service in their present expedition; since they would not need it if they succeeded, while they would be too far in the interior to profit by it if they failed. He besought them to turn their thoughts in another direction. To be thus calculating chances and means of escape was unworthy of brave souls. They had set their hands to the work; to look back, as they advanced, would be their ruin. They had only to resume their former confidence in themselves and their general, and success was certain. "As for me," he concluded, "I have chosen my part. I will remain here while there is one to bear me company. If there be any so craven as to shrink from sharing the dangers of our glorious enterprise, let them go home, in God's name. There is still one vessel left. Let them take that and return to Cuba. They can tell there how they deserted their commander and their comrades, and patiently wait till we return loaded with the spoils of the Aztecs."[3]

The politic orator had touched the right chord in the bosoms of the soldiers. As he spoke, their resentment gradually died away. The faded visions of future riches and glory, rekindled by his eloquence, again floated before their imaginations. The first shock over, they felt ashamed of their

---

[1] "Decian, que los queria meter en el matadero." Gomara, Crónica, cap. 42.

[2] "Al cavo lo ovieron de sentir la gente y ayna se le amotinaran muchos, y esta fué uno de los peligros que pasaron por Cortés de muchos que para matallo de los mismos Españoles estuvo." Las Casas, Hist. de las Indias, MS., lib. 3, cap. 122.

[3] "Que ninguno seria tan cobarde y tan pusilánime que queria estimar su vida mas que la suya, ni de tan debil corazon que dudase de ir con él á México, donde tanto bien le estaba aparejado, y que si acaso se determinaba alguno de dejar de hacer este se podia ir bendito de Dios á Cuba en el navío que habia dexado, de que antes de mucho se arrepentiria, y pelaria las barbas, viendo la buena ventura que esperaba le sucederia." Ixtlilxochitl, Hist. Chich., MS., cap. 82.

temporary distrust. The enthusiasm for their leader revived, for they felt that under his banner only they could hope for victory ; and, as he concluded, they testified the revulsion of their feelings by making the air ring with their shouts, " To Mexico ! to Mexico ! "

The destruction of his fleet by Cortés is, perhaps, the most remarkable passage in the life of this remarkable man. History, indeed, affords examples of a similar expedient in emergencies somewhat similar ; but none where the chances of success were so precarious and defeat would be so disastrous.[1] Had he failed, it might well seem an act of madness. Yet it was the fruit of deliberate calculation. He had set fortune, fame, life itself, all upon the cast, and must abide the issue. There was no alternative in his mind but to succeed or perish. The measure he adopted greatly increased the chance of success. But to carry it into execution, in the face of an incensed and desperate soldiery, was an act of resolution that has few parallels in history.[2]

Fray Bartolomé de las Casas, Bishop of Chiapa, whose " History of the Indies " forms an important authority for the preceding pages, was one of the most remarkable men of

---

[1] Perhaps the most remarkable of these examples is that of Julian, who, in his unfortunate Assyrian invasion, burnt the fleet which had carried him up the Tigris. The story is told by Gibbon, who shows very satisfactorily that the fleet would have proved a hindrance rather than a help to the emperor in his further progress. See History of the Decline and Fall, vol. ix. p. 177, of Milman's excellent edition.

[2] The account given in the text of the destruction of the fleet is not that of Bernal Diaz, who states it to have been accomplished not only with the knowledge, but entire approbation of the army, though at the suggestion of Cortés. (Hist. de la Conquista, cap. 58.) This version is sanctioned by Dr. Robertson (History of America, vol. ii. pp. 253, 254). One should be very slow to depart from the honest record of the old soldier, especially when confirmed by the discriminating judgment of the Historian of America. But Cortés expressly declares in his letter to the emperor that he ordered the vessels to be sunk, without the knowledge of his men, from the apprehension that, if the means of escape were open, the timid and disaffected might at some future time avail themselves of them. (Rel. Seg. de Cortés, ap. Lorenzana, p. 41.) The cavaliers Montejo and Puertocarrero, on their visit to Spain, stated, in their depositions, that the general destroyed the fleet on information received from the pilots. (Declaraciones,

MSS.) Narvaez in his accusation of Cortés, and Las Casas, speak of the act in terms of unqualified reprobation, charging him, moreover, with bribing the pilots to bore holes in the bottoms of the ships in order to disable them. (Demanda de Narvaez, MS.—Hist. de las Indias, MS., lib. 3, cap. 122.) The same account of the transaction, though with a very different commentary as to its merits, is repeated by Oviedo (Hist. de las Ind., MS., lib. 33, cap. 2), Gomara (Crónica, cap. 42), and Peter Martyr (De Orbe Novo, dec. 5, cap. 1), all of whom had access to the best sources of information. The affair, so remarkable as the act of one individual, becomes absolutely incredible when considered as the result of so many independent wills. It is not improbable that Bernal Diaz, from his known devotion to the cause, may have been one of the few to whom Cortés confided his purpose. The veteran, in writing his narrative, many years after, may have mistaken a part for the whole, and in his zeal to secure to the army a full share of the glory of the expedition, too exclusively appropriated by the general (a great object, as he tells us, of his history), may have distributed among his comrades the credit of an exploit which, in this instance, at least, properly belonged to their commander. Whatever be the cause of the discrepancy, his solitary testimony can hardly be sustained against the weight of contemporary evidence from such competent sources.*

---

* [Prescott's account of the circumstances attending the destruction of the fleet has been contested at great length by Señor Ramirez, who insists on accepting the statements of Bernal Diaz without qualification, and ascribing to the army an equal share with the general in the merit of the act. He remarks with truth that the language of Cortés—" Tuve manera, como so color que los dichos navíos no estaban para navegar, los eché á la costa"—contains no *express declaration*, as stated by Prescott, that the order for the fleet to be sunk was given without the knowledge of the army, but would, at the most, lead to an inference to that effect. " Nor can even this," he adds, " be admitted, since, in order to persuade the soldiers that the ships were unfit for sailing, he must have had an understanding with the mariners who were to make the statement, and with his friends who were to confirm it." This is, however, very inefficient reasoning. It is not pretended that Cortés had no confidants and agents in the transaction. The question of real importance is, was the resolution taken, as Bernal Diaz asserts, *openly and by the advice* of the whole army,—" claramente, por consejo de todos los demas soldados"? or was it formed by Cortés, and were measures taken for giving effect to it, without any communication with the mass of his followers? The newly-discovered relation of Tápia is cited by Señor Ramirez as " in perfect accordance with the testimony of Diaz, and destructive of every supposition of mystery and secrecy." Yet Tápia says, with Herrera, that Cortés caused holes to be bored in the ships, and their unserviceable condition to be reported to him, and thereupon gave orders for their destruction ; no mention being made of the concurrence of the soldiers at any stage of the proceedings.—ED.]

the sixteenth century. He was born at Seville in 1474. His father accompanied Columbus, as a common soldier, in his first voyage to the New World ; and he acquired wealth enough by his vocation to place his son at the University of Salamanca. During his residence there, he was attended by an Indian page, whom his father had brought with him from Hispaniola. Thus the uncompromising advocate for freedom began his career as the owner of a slave himself. But he did not long remain so, for his slave was one of those subsequently liberated by the generous commands of Isabella.

In 1498 he completed his studies in law and divinity, took his degree of licentiate, and in 1502 accompanied Oviedo, in the most brilliant armada which had been equipped for the Western World. Eight years after, he was admitted to priest's orders in St. Domingo, an event somewhat memorable, since he was the first person consecrated in that holy office in the colonies. On the occupation of Cuba by the Spaniards, Las Casas passed over to that island, where he obtained a curacy in a small settlement. He soon, however, made himself known to the governor, Velasquez, by the fidelity with which he discharged his duties, and especially by the influence which his mild and benevolent teaching obtained for him over the Indians. Through his intimacy with the governor, Las Casas had the means of ameliorating the condition of the conquered race, and from this time he may be said to have consecrated all his energies to this one great object. At this period, the scheme of *repartimientos,* introduced soon after the discoveries of Columbus, was in full operation, and the aboriginal population of the islands was rapidly melting away under a system of oppression which has been seldom paralleled in the annals of mankind. Las Casas, outraged at the daily exhibition of crime and misery, returned to Spain to obtain some redress from government. Ferdinand died soon after his arrival. Charles was absent, but the reins were held by Cardinal Ximenes, who listened to the complaints of the benevolent missionary, and, with his characteristic vigour, instituted a commission of three Hieronymite friars, with full authority, as already noticed in the text, to reform abuses. Las Casas was honoured, for his exertions, with the title of " Protector General of the Indians."

The new commissioners behaved with great discretion. But their office was one of consummate difficulty, as it required time to introduce important changes in established institutions. The ardent and impetuous temper of Las Casas, disdaining every consideration of prudence, overleaped all these obstacles, and chafed under what he considered the lukewarm and temporizing policy of the commissioners. As he was at no pains to conceal his disgust, the parties soon came to a misunderstanding with each other ; and Las Casas again returned to the mother-country, to stimulate the government, if possible, to more effectual measures for the protection of the natives.

He found the country under the administration of the Flemings, who discovered from the first a wholesome abhorrence of the abuses practised in the colonies, and who, in short, seemed inclined to tolerate no peculation or extortion but their own. They acquiesced, without much difficulty, in the recommendations of Las Casas, who proposed to relieve the natives by sending out Castilian labourers and by importing negro slaves into the islands. This last proposition has brought heavy obloquy on the head of its author, who has been freely accused of having thus introduced negro slavery into the New World. Others, with equal groundlessness, have attempted to vindicate his memory from the reproach of having recommended the measure at all. Unfortunately for the latter assertion, Las Casas, in his History of the Indies, confesses, with deep regret and humiliation, his advice on this occasion, founded on the most erroneous views, as he frankly states ; since, to use his own words, " the same law applies equally to the negro as to the Indian." But, so far from having introduced slavery by this measure into the islands, the importation of blacks there dates from the beginning of the century. It was recommended by some of the wisest and most benevolent persons in the colony, as the means of diminishing the amount of human suffering; since the African was more fitted by his constitution to endure the climate and the severe toil imposed on the slave, than the feeble and effeminate islander. It was a suggestion of humanity, however mistaken and, considering the circumstances under which it occurred, and the age, it may well be forgiven in Las Casas, especially taking into view that, as he became more enlightened himself, he was so ready to testify his regret at having unadvisedly countenanced the measure.

The experiment recommended by Las Casas was made, but, through the apathy of Fonseca, president of the Indian Council, not heartily,—and it failed. The good missionary now proposed another and much bolder scheme. He requested that a large tract of country in Tierra Firme, in the neighbourhood of the famous pearl-fisheries, might be ceded to him for the purpose of planting a colony there, and of converting the natives to Christianity. He required that none of the authorities of the islands, and no military force, especially, should be allowed to interfere with his movements. He pledged himself by peaceful means alone to accomplish all that had been done by violence in other quarters. He asked only that a certain number of labourers should attend him, invited by a bounty from government, and that he might further be accompanied by fifty Dominicans, who were to be distinguished like himself by a peculiar dress, that should lead the natives to suppose them a different race of men from the Spaniards. This proposition was denounced as chimerical and fantastic by some, whose own opportunities of observation entitled their judgment to respect. These men declared the Indian, from his nature, incapable of civilization. The question was one of such moment that Charles the Fifth ordered the discussion to be conducted before him. The opponent of Las Casas was first heard, when the good missionary, in answer, warmed by the noble cause he was to maintain, and nothing daunted by the august presence in which he stood, delivered himself with a fervent eloquence that went directly to the hearts of his auditors. "The Christian religion," he concluded, "is equal in its operation, and is accommodated to every nation on the globe. It robs no one of his freedom, violates none of his inherent rights, on the ground that he is a slave by nature, as pretended ; and it well becomes your Majesty to banish so monstrous an oppression from your kingdoms in the beginning of your reign, that the Almighty may make it long and glorious."

In the end Las Casas prevailed. He was furnished with the men and means for establishing his colony, and in 1520 embarked for America. But the result was a lamentable failure. The country assigned to him lay in the neighbourhood of a Spanish settlement, which had already committed some acts of violence on the natives. To quell the latter, now thrown into commotion, an armed force was sent by the young "Admiral" from Hispaniola. The very people, among whom Las Casas was to appear as the messenger of peace, were thus involved in deadly strife with his countrymen. The enemy had been before him in his own harvest. While waiting for the close of these turbulent scenes, the labourers, whom he had taken out with him, dispersed, in despair of effecting their object. And after an attempt to pursue, with his faithful Dominican brethren, the work of colonization further, other untoward circumstances compelled them to abandon the project altogether. Its unfortunate author, overwhelmed with chagrin, took refuge in the Dominican monastery in the island of Hispaniola. The failure of the enterprise should, no doubt, be partly ascribed to circumstances beyond the control of its projector. Yet it is impossible not to recognize in the whole scheme, and in the conduct of it, the hand of one much more familiar with books than men, who, in the seclusion of the cloister, had meditated and matured his benevolent plans, without fully estimating the obstacles that lay in their way, and who counted too confidently on meeting the same generous enthusiasm in others which glowed in his own bosom.

He found, in his disgrace, the greatest consolation and sympathy from the brethren of St. Dominic, who stood forth as the avowed champions of the Indians on all occasions, and showed themselves as devoted to the cause of freedom in the New World as they had been hostile to it in the Old. Las Casas soon became a member of their order, and, in his monastic retirement, applied himself for many years to the performance of his spiritual duties, and the composition of various works, all directed, more or less, to vindicate the rights of the Indians. Here, too, he commenced his great work, the "Historia general de las Indias," which he pursued, at intervals of leisure, from 1527 till a few years before his death. His time, however, was not wholly absorbed by these labours ; and he found means to engage in several laborious missions. He preached the gospel among the natives of Nicaragua and Guatemala, and succeeded in converting and reducing to obedience some wild tribes in the latter province, who had defied the arms of his countrymen. In all these pious labours he was sustained by his Dominican brethren. At length, in 1539, he crossed the waters again, to seek further assistance and recruits among the members of his order.

A great change had taken place in the board that now presided over the colonial department. The cold and narrow-minded Fonseca, who, during his long administration, had, it may be truly said, shown himself the enemy of every great name and good measure connected with the Indians, had died. His place, as president of the Indian Council, was filled by Loaysa, Charles's confessor. This functionary, general of the Dominicans, gave ready audience to Las Casas, and showed a goodwill to his proposed plans of reform. Charles, too, now grown older, seemed to feel more deeply the responsibility of his station, and the necessity of redressing the wrongs, too long tolerated, of his American subjects. The state of the colonies became a common topic of discussion, not only in the council, but in the court ; and the representations of Las Casas made an impression that manifested itself in the change of sentiment more clearly every day. He promoted this by the publication of some of his writings at this time, and especially of his "Brevísima Relacion," or Short Account of the Destruction of the Indies, in which he sets before the reader the manifold atrocities committed by his countrymen in different parts of the New World in the prosecution of their conquests. It is a tale of woe. Every line of the work may be said to be written in blood. However good the motives of its author, we may regret that the book was ever written. He would have been certainly right not to spare his countrymen ; to exhibit their misdeeds in their true colours, and by this appalling picture—for such it would have been—to have recalled the nation, and those who governed it, to a proper sense of the iniquitous career it was pursuing on the other side of the water. But, to produce a more striking effect, he has lent a willing ear to every tale of violence and rapine, and magnified the amount to a degree which borders on the ridiculous. The wild extravagance of his numerical estimates is of itself sufficient to shake confidence in the accuracy of his statements generally. Yet the naked truth was too startling in itself to demand the aid of exaggeration. The book found great favour with foreigners ; was rapidly translated into various languages, and ornamented with characteristic designs, which seemed to put into action all the recorded atrocities of the text. It excited somewhat different feelings in his own countrymen, particularly the people of the colonies, who considered themselves the subjects of a gross, however undesigned, misrepresentation ; and in his future intercourse with them it contributed, no doubt, to diminish his influence and consequent usefulness, by the spirit of alienation, and even resentment, which it engendered.

Las Casas' honest intentions, his enlightened views and long experience, gained him deserved credit at home. This was visible in the important regulations made at this time for the better government of the colonies, and particularly in respect to the aborigines. A code of laws, *Las Nuevas Leyes,* was passed, having for their avowed object the enfranchisement of this unfortunate race ; and in the wisdom and humanity of its provisions it is easy to recognize the hand of the Protector of the Indians. The history of Spanish colonial legislation is the history of the impotent struggles of the government in behalf of the natives, against the avarice and cruelty of its subjects. It proves that an empire powerful at home—and Spain then was so—may be so widely extended that its authority shall scarcely be felt in its extremities.

The government testified their sense of the signal services of Las Casas by promoting him to the bishopric of Cuzco, one of the richest sees in the colonies. But the disinterested soul of the missionary did not covet riches or preferment. He rejected the proffered dignity without hesitation. Yet he could not refuse the bishopric of Chiapa.

a country which, from the poverty and ignorance of its inhabitants, offered a good field for his spiritual labours. In 1544, though at the advanced age of seventy, he took upon himself these new duties, and embarked, for the fifth and last time, for the shores of America. His fame had preceded him. The colonists looked on his coming with apprehension, regarding him as the real author of the new code, which struck at their ancient immunities, and which he would be likely to enforce to the letter. Everywhere he was received with coldness. In some places his person was menaced with violence. But the venerable presence of the prelate, his earnest expostulations, which flowed so obviously from conviction, and his generous self-devotion, so regardless of personal considerations, preserved him from this outrage. Yet he showed no disposition to conciliate his opponents by what he deemed an unworthy concession ; and he even stretched the arm of authority so far as to refuse the sacraments to any who still held an Indian in bondage. This high-handed measure not only outraged the planters, but incurred the disapprobation of his own brethren in the Church. Three years were spent in disagreeable altercation without coming to any decision. The Spaniards, to borrow their accustomed phraseology on these occasions, "obeying the law, but not fulfilling it," applied to the court for further instructions ; and the bishop, no longer supported by his own brethren, thwarted by the colonial magistrates, and outraged by the people, relinquished a post where his presence could be no longer useful, and returned to spend the remainder of his days in tranquillity at home.

Yet, though withdrawn to his Dominican convent, he did not pass his hours in slothful seclusion. He again appeared as the champion of Indian freedom in the famous controversy with Sepulveda, one of the most acute scholars of the time, and far surpassing Las Casas in elegance and correctness of composition. But the Bishop of Chiapa was his superior in argument, at least in this discussion, where he had right and reason on his side. In his "Thirty Propositions," as they are called, in which he sums up the several points of his case, he maintains that the circumstance of infidelity in religion cannot deprive a nation of its political rights ; that the Holy See, in its grant of the New World to the Catholic sovereigns, designed only to confer the right of converting its inhabitants to Christianity, and of thus winning a peaceful authority over them ; and that no authority could be valid which rested on other foundations. This was striking at the root of the colonial empire as assumed by Castile. But the disinterested views of Las Casas, the respect entertained for his principles, and the general conviction, it may be, of the force of his arguments, prevented the court from taking umbrage at their import, or from pressing them to their legitimate conclusion. While the writings of his adversary were interdicted from publication, he had the satisfaction to see his own printed and circulated in every quarter.

From this period his time was distributed among his religious duties, his studies, and the composition of his works, especially his History. His constitution, naturally excellent, had been strengthened by a life of temperance and toil ; and he retained his faculties unimpaired to the last. He died after a short illness, July 1566, at the great age of ninety-two, in his monastery of Atocha, at Madrid.

The character of Las Casas may be inferred from his career. He was one of those to whose gifted minds are revealed those glorious moral truths which, like the lights of heaven, are fixed and the same for ever, but which, though now familiar, were hidden from all but a few penetrating intellects by the general darkness of the time in which he lived. He was a reformer, and had the virtues and errors of a reformer. He was inspired by one great and glorious idea. This was the key to all his thoughts, to all that he said and wrote, to every act of his long life. It was this which urged him to lift the voice of rebuke in the presence of princes, to brave the menaces of an infuriated populace, to cross seas, to traverse mountains and deserts, to incur the alienation of friends, the hostility of enemies, to endure obloquy, insult, and persecution. It was this, too, which made him reckless of obstacles, led him to count too confidently on the co-operation of others, animated his discussion, sharpened his invective, too often steeped his pen in the gall of personal vituperation, led him into gross exaggeration and over-colouring in his statements, and a blind credulity of evil that rendered him unsafe as a counsellor and unsuccessful in the practical concerns of life. His views were pure and elevated. But his manner of enforcing them was not always so commendable. This may be gathered not only from the testimony of the colonists generally, who, as parties interested, may be supposed to have been prejudiced, but from that of the members of his own profession, persons high in office, and of integrity beyond suspicion, not to add that of missionaries engaged in the same good work with himself. These, in their letters and reported conversations, charged the Bishop of Chiapa with an arrogant, uncharitable temper, which deluded his judgment, and vented itself in unwarrantable crimination against such as resisted his projects or differed from him in opinion. Las Casas, in short, was a man. But, if he had the errors of humanity, he had virtues that rarely belong to it. The best commentary on his character is the estimation which he obtained in the court of his sovereign. A liberal pension was settled on him after his last return from America, which he chiefly expended on charitable objects. No measure of importance relating to the Indians was taken without his advice. He lived to see the fruits of his efforts in the positive amelioration of their condition, and in the popular admission of those great truths which it had been the object of his life to unfold. And who shall say how much of the successful efforts and arguments since made in behalf of persecuted humanity may be traced to the example and the writings of this illustrious philanthropist?

His compositions were numerous, most of them of no great length. Some were printed in his time ; others have since appeared, especially in the French translation of Llorente. His great work, which occupied him at intervals for more than thirty years, the *Historia general de las Indias*, still remains in manuscript. It is in three volumes, divided into as many parts, and embraces the colonial history from the discovery of the country by Columbus to the year 1520. The style of the work, like that of all his writings, is awkward, disjointed, and excessively diffuse, abounding in repetitions, irrelevant digressions, and pedantic citations. But it is sprinkled over with passages of a different kind ; and, when he is roused by the desire to exhibit some gross wrong to the natives, his simple language kindles into eloquence, and he expounds those great and immutable principles of natural justice which in his own day were so little understood. His defect as a historian is that he wrote history, like everything else, under the influence of one dominant idea. He is always pleading the cause of the persecuted native. This gives a colouring to events which passed under his own eyes, and filled him with a too easy confidence in those which he gathered from the reports of others. Much of the preceding portion of our narrative which relates to affairs in Cuba must have come under his personal observation. But he seems incapable of shaking off his early deference to Velasquez, who, as we have noticed, treated him, while a poor curate in the island, with peculiar confidence. For Cortés, on the other hand, he appears to have felt a profound contempt. He witnessed the commencement of his career, when he was standing, cap in hand, as it were, at the proud governor's door, thankful even for a smile of recognition. Las Casas remembered all this, and, when he saw the Conqueror of Mexico rise into a glory and renown that threw his former patron into the shade,—and most unfairly, as Las Casas deemed, at the expense of that patron,—the good bishop could not withhold his indignation, nor speak of him otherwise than with a sneer, as a mere upstart adventurer.

It is the existence of defects like these, and the fear of the misconception likely to be produced by them, that have so long prevented the publication of his history At his death, he left it to the convent of San Gregorio, at Valladolid, with directions that it should not be printed for forty years, nor be seen during that time by any layman or member of the fraternity. Herrera, however, was permitted to consult it, and he liberally transferred its contents to his own volumes, which appeared in 1601. The Royal Academy of History revised the first volume of Las Casas some years since, with a view to the publication of the whole work. But the indiscreet and imaginative style of the composition, according to Navarrete, and the consideration that its most important facts were already known through other channels, induced that body to abandon the design. With deference to their judgment, this seems to me a mistake. Las Casas, with every deduction, is one of the great writers of the nation ; great from the important truths which he discerned when none else could see them, and from the courage with which he proclaimed them to the world. They are scattered over his History as well as his other writings. They are not, however, the passages transcribed by Herrera. In the statement of fact, too, however partial and prejudiced, no one will impeach his integrity ; and, as an enlightened contemporary, his evidence is of undeniable value. It is due to the memory of Las Casas that, if his work be given to the public at all, it should not be through the garbled extracts of one who was no fair interpreter of his opinions. Las Casas does not speak for himself in the courtly pages of Herrera. Yet the History should not be published without a suitable commentary to enlighten the student and guard him against any undue prejudices in the writer. We may hope that the entire manuscript will one day be given to the world under the auspices of that distinguished body which has already done so much in this way for the illustration of the national annals.

The life of Las Casas has been several times written. The two memoirs most worthy of notice are that by Llorente, late Secretary of the Inquisition, prefixed to his French translation of the bishop's controversial writings, and that by Quintana, in the third volume of his " Españoles célebres," where it presents a truly noble specimen of biographical composition, enriched by a literary criticism as acute as it is candid. I have gone to the greater length in this notice, from the interesting character of the man, and the little that is known of him to the English reader. I have also transferred a passage from his work in the original to the Appendix, that the Spanish scholar may form an idea of his style of composition. He ceases to be an authority for us henceforth, as his account of the expedition of Cortés terminates with the destruction of the navy.

BOOK III.

MARCH TO MEXICO.

—o—

CHAPTER I.

PROCEEDINGS AT CEMPOALLA.—THE SPANIARDS CLIMB THE TABLE-LAND.
—PICTURESQUE SCENERY. — TRANSACTIONS WITH THE NATIVES.—
EMBASSY TO TLASCALA.

(1519.)

WHILE at Cempoalla, Cortés received a message from Escalante, his commander at Villa Rica, informing him that there were four strange ships hovering off the coast, and that they took no notice of his repeated signals. This intelligence greatly alarmed the general, who feared they might be a squadron sent by the governor of Cuba to interfere with his movements. In much haste, he set out at the head of a few horsemen, and, ordering a party of light infantry to follow, posted back to Villa Rica. The rest of the army he left in charge of Alvarado and of Gonzalo de Sandoval, a young officer who had begun to give evidence o. the uncommon qualities which have secured to him so distinguished a rank among the conquerors of Mexico.

Escalante would have persuaded the general, on his reaching the town, to take some rest, and allow him to go in search of the strangers. But Cortés replied with the homely proverb, " A wounded hare takes no nap,"[1] and, without stopping to refresh himself or his men, pushed on three or four leagues to the north, where he understood the ships were at anchor. On the way, he fell in with three Spaniards, just landed from them. To his eager inquiries whence they came, they replied that they belonged to a squadron fitted out by Francisco de Garay, governor of Jamaica. This person, the year previous, had visited the Florida coast, and obtained from Spain—where he had some interest at court—authority over the countries he might discover in that vicinity. The three men, consisting of a notary and two witnesses, had been sent on shore to warn their countrymen under Cortés to desist from what was considered an encroach-

---

[1] " Cabra coja no tenga siesta."

ment on the territories of Garay. Probably neither the governor of Jamaica nor his officers had any very precise notion of the geography and limits of these territories.

Cortés saw at once there was nothing to apprehend from this quarter. He would have been glad, however, if he could by any means have induced the crews of the ships to join his expedition. He found no difficulty in persuading the notary and his companions. But when he came in sight of the vessels, the people on board distrusting the good terms on which their comrades appeared to be with the Spaniards, refused to send their boat ashore. In this dilemma Cortés had recourse to a stratagem.

He ordered three of his own men to exchange dresses with the new-comers. He then drew off his little band in sight of the vessels, affecting to return to the city. In the night, however, he came back to the same place, and lay in ambush, directing the disguised Spaniards, when the morning broke, and they could be discerned, to make signals to those on board. The artifice succeeded. A boat put off, filled with armed men, and three or four leaped on shore. But they soon detected the deceit, and Cortés springing from his ambush, made them prisoners. Their comrades in the boat, alarmed, pushed off, at once, for the vessels, which soon got under way, leaving those on shore to their fate. Thus ended the affair. Cortés returned to Cempoalla, with the addition of half-a-dozen able-bodied recruits, and, what was of more importance, relieved in his own mind from the apprehension of interference with his operations.[1]

He now made arrangements for his speedy departure from the Totonac capital. The forces reserved for the expedition amounted to about four hundred foot and fifteen horse, with seven pieces of artillery. He obtained, also, from the cacique of Cempoalla, thirteen hundred warriors, and a thousand *tamanes*, or porters, to drag the guns and transport the baggage. He took forty more of their principal men as hostages, as well as to guide him on the way and serve him by their counsels among the strange tribes he was to visit. They were, in fact, of essential service to him throughout the march.[2]

The remainder of his Spanish force he left in garrison at Villa Rica de Vera Cruz, the command of which he had intrusted to the alguacil, Juan de Escalante, an officer devoted to his interests. The selection was judicious. It was important to place there a man who would resist any hostile interference from his European rivals, on the one hand, and maintain the present friendly relations with the natives, on the other. Cortés

---

[1] Oviedo, Hist. de las Ind., MS., lib. 33, cap. 1.—Rel. Seg. de Cortés, ap. Lorenzana, pp. 42-45.—Bernal Diaz, Hist. de la Conquista, cap. 59, 60.

[2] Gomara, Crónica, cap. 44.—Ixtlilxochitl, Hist. Chich., MS., cap. 83.—Bernal Diaz, Hist. de la Conquista, cap. 61.—The number of the Indian auxiliaries stated in the text is much larger than that allowed by either Cortés or Diaz. But both these actors in the drama show too obvious a desire to magnify their own prowess, by exaggerating the numbers of their foes and diminishing their own, to be entitled to much confidence in their estimates.

recommended the Totonac chiefs to apply to this officer in case of any difficulty, assuring them that so long as they remained faithful to their new
sovereign and religion they should find a sure protection in the Spaniards.

Before marching, the general spoke a few words of encouragement to
his own men. He told them they were now to embark in earnest on an
enterprise which had been the great object of their desires, and that the
blessed Saviour would carry them victorious through every battle with
their enemies. "Indeed," he added, "this assurance must be our stay,
for every other refuge is now cut off but that afforded by the providence
of God and your own stout hearts." [1] He ended by comparing their
achievements to those of the ancient Romans, "in phrases of honeyed
eloquence far beyond anything I can repeat," says the brave and simple-
hearted chronicler who heard them. Cortés was, indeed, master of that
eloquence which went to the soldiers' hearts. For their sympathies were
his, and he shared in that romantic spirit of adventure which belonged
to them. "We are ready to obey you," they cried as with one voice.
"Our fortunes, for better or worse, are cast with yours." [2] Taking leave,
therefore, of their hospitable Indian friends, the little army, buoyant
with high hopes and lofty plans of conquest, set forward on the march
to Mexico.

It was the sixteenth of August 1519. During the first day, their road
lay through the *tierra caliente*, the beautiful land where they had been so
long lingering; the land of the vanilla, cochineal, cacao (not till later days
of the orange and the sugar-cane), products which, indigenous to Mexico,
have now become the luxuries of Europe; the land where the fruits and
the flowers chase one another in unbroken circle through the year; where
the gales are loaded with perfumes till the sense aches at their sweetness,
and the groves are filled with many-coloured birds, and insects whose
enamelled wings glisten like diamonds in the bright sun of the tropics.
Such are the magical splendours of this paradise of the senses. Yet
Nature, who generally works in a spirit of compensation, has provided
one here; since the same burning sun which quickens into life these
glories of the vegetable and animal kingdoms calls forth the pestilent
malaria, with its train of bilious disorders, unknown to the cold skies
of the North. The season in which the Spaniards were there, the rainy
months of summer, was precisely that in which the *vómito* rages with
greatest fury; when the European stranger hardly ventures to set his
foot on shore, still less to linger there a day. We find no mention made
of it in the records of the Conquerors, nor any notice, indeed, of an
uncommon mortality. The fact doubtless corroborates the theory of
those who postpone the appearance of the yellow fever till long after the

---

[1] No teniamos otro socorro, ni ayuda sino el de
Dios; porque ya no teniamos nauíos para ir á Cuba,
salvo nuestro buen pelear y coraçones fuertes."
Bernal Diaz, Hist. de la Conquista, cap. 59.

[2] "Y todos á vna le respondímos, que hariamos
lo que ordenasse, que echada estaua la suerte de la
buena ó mala ventura." Loc. cit.

occupation of the country by the whites. It proves, at least, that, if existing before, it must have been in a very much mitigated form.

After some leagues of travel over roads made nearly impassable by the summer rains, the troops began the gradual ascent—more gradual on the eastern than the western declivities of the Cordilleras—which leads up to the table-land of Mexico. At the close of the second day they reached Xalapa, a place still retaining the same Aztec name that it has communicated to the drug raised in its environs, the medicinal virtues of which are now known throughout the world.[1] This town stands midway up the long ascent, at an elevation where the vapours from the ocean, touching in their westerly progress, maintain a rich verdure throughout the year. Though somewhat infected with these marine fogs, the air is usually bland and salubrious. The wealthy resident of the lower regions retires here for safety in the heats of summer, and the traveller hails its groves of oak with delight, as announcing that he is above the deadly influence of the *vómito*.[2] From this delicious spot, the Spaniards enjoyed one of the grandest prospects in nature. Before them was the steep ascent—much steeper after this point—which they were to climb. On the right rose the Sierra Madre, girt with its dark belt of pines, and its long lines of shadowy hills stretching away in the distance. To the south, in brilliant contrast, stood the mighty Orizaba, with his white robe of snow descending far down his sides, towering in solitary grandeur, the giant spectre of the Andes. Behind them, they beheld, unrolled at their feet, the magnificent *tierra caliente*, with its gay confusion of meadows, streams, and flowering forests, sprinkled over with shining Indian villages, while a faint line of light on the edge of the horizon told them that there was the ocean, beyond which were the kindred and country they were many of them never more to see.

Still winding their way upward, amidst scenery as different as was the temperature from that of the regions below, the army passed through settlements containing some hundreds of inhabitants each, and on the fourth day reached a "strong town," as Cortés terms it, standing on a rocky eminence, supposed to be that now known by the Mexican name of Naulinco. Here they were hospitably entertained by the inhabitants, who were friends of the Totonacs. Cortés endeavoured, through Father Olmedo, to impart to them some knowledge of Christian truths, which were kindly received, and the Spaniards were allowed to erect a cross in the place, for the future adoration of the natives. Indeed, the route of the army might be tracked by these emblems of man's salvation, raised wherever a willing population of Indians invited it, suggesting a very

---

[1] Jalap, *Convolvulus jalapæ*. The *x* and *j* are convertible consonants in the Castilian.

[2] The heights of Xalapa are crowned with a convent dedicated to St. Francis, erected in later days by Cortés, showing, in its solidity, like others of the period built under the same auspices, says an agreeable traveller, a military as well as religious design. Tudor's Travels in North America (London, 1834), vol. ii. p. 186.

different idea from what the same memorials intimate to the traveller in these mountain solitudes in our day.[1]

The troops now entered a rugged defile, the Bishop's Pass,[2] as it is called, capable of easy defence against an army. Very soon they experienced a most unwelcome change of climate. Cold winds from the mountains, mingled with rain, and, as they rose still higher, with driving sleet and hail, drenched their garments, and seemed to penetrate to their very bones. The Spaniards, indeed, partially covered by their armour and thick jackets of quilted cotton, were better able to resist the weather, though their long residence in the sultry regions of the valley made them still keenly sensible to the annoyance. But the poor Indians, natives of the *tierra caliente*, with little protection in the way of covering, sank under the rude assault of the elements, and several of them perished on the road.

The aspect of the country was as wild and dreary as the climate. Their route wound along the spur of the huge Cofre de Perote, which borrows its name, both in Mexican and Castilian, from the coffer-like rock on its summit.[3] It is one of the great volcanoes of New Spain. It exhibits now, indeed, no vestige of a crater on its top, but abundant traces of volcanic action at its base, where acres of lava, blackened scoriæ, and cinders proclaim the convulsions of nature, while numerous shrubs and mouldering trunks of enormous trees, among the crevices, attest the antiquity of these events. Working their toilsome way across this scene of desolation, the path often led them along the borders of precipices, down whose sheer depths of two or three thousand feet the shrinking eye might behold another climate, and see all the glowing vegetation of the tropics choking up the bottom of the ravines.

After three days of this fatiguing travel, the wayworn army emerged through another defile, the *Sierra del Agua*.[4] They soon came upon an open reach of country, with a genial climate, such as belongs to the temperate latitudes of southern Europe. They had reached the level of

---

[1] Oviedo, Hist. de las Ind., MS., lib. 33, cap. 1.—Rel. Seg. de Cortés, ap. Lorenzana, p. 40.—Gomara, Crónica, cap. 44.—Ixtlilxochitl, Hist. Chich., MS., cap. 83.—"Every hundred yards of our route," says the traveller last quoted, speaking of this very region, "was marked by the melancholy erection of a wooden cross, denoting, according to the custom of the country, the commission of some horrible murder on the spot where it was planted." (Travels in North America, vol. ii. p. 188.)—[Señor Alaman stoutly defends his countrymen from this gross exaggeration, as he pronounces it, of Mr. Tudor. For although it is unhappily true, he says, that travellers were formerly liable to be attacked in going from the city of Mexico to Vera Cruz, and that the *diligence* which passes over this road is still frequently stopped, yet it is very seldom that personal violence is offered. "Foreign tourists are prone to believe all the stories of atrocities that are related to them, and generally, at inns, fall into the society of persons who take delight in furnishing a large supply of such materials. The crosses that are to be met with in the country are not so numerous as is pretended ; nor are all of them memorials of assassinations committed in the places where they

have been erected. Many are merely objects of devotion, and others indicate the spot where two roads diverge from each other. We must, nevertheless, confess that this matter is one that demands all the attention of the government ; while the candid foreigner will doubtless admit that it is not easy to exercise police supervision over roads on which the central points of population lie far apart, as in countries like ours, instead of being so near that a watch can be maintained from them over the intermediate spaces, as is the case in most countries of Europe, and in a great part of the United States." Conquista de Méjico (trad. de Vega), tom. i. p. 251.]

[2] *El Paso del Obispo.* Cortés named it *Puerto del Nombre de Dios.* Viaje, ap. Lorenzana, p. ii.

[3] The Aztec name is Nauhcampatepetl, from *nauhcampa*, "anything square," and *tepetl*, "a mountain."—Humboldt, who waded through forests and snows to its summit, ascertained its height to be 4089 metres, = 13,414 feet above the sea. See his Vues des Cordillères, p. 234, and Essai politique, vol. i. p. 266.

[4] The same mentioned in Cortés' Letter as the *Puerto de la Leña.* Viaje, ap. Lorenzana, p. iii.

more than seven thousand feet above the ocean, where the great sheet of table-land spreads out for hundreds of miles along the crests of the Cordilleras. The country showed signs of careful cultivation, but the products were, for the most part, not familiar to the eyes of the Spaniards. Fields and hedges of the various tribes of the cactus, the towering organum, and plantations of aloes with rich yellow clusters of flowers on their tall stems, affording drink and clothing to the Aztec, were everywhere seen. The plants of the torrid and temperate zones had disappeared, one after another, with the ascent into these elevated regions. The glossy and dark-leaved banana, the chief, as it is the cheapest, aliment of the countries below, had long since faded from the landscape. The hardy maize, however, still shone with its golden harvests in all the pride of cultivation, the great staple of the higher equally with the lower terraces of the plateau.

Suddenly the troops came upon what seemed the environs of a populous city, which, as they entered it, appeared to surpass even that of Cempoalla in the size and solidity of its structures.[1] These were of stone and lime, many of them spacious and tolerably high. There were thirteen *teocallis* in the place; and in the suburbs they had seen a receptacle, in which, according to Bernal Diaz, were stored a hundred thousand skulls of human victims, all piled and ranged in order! He reports the number as one he had ascertained by counting them himself.[2] Whatever faith we may attach to the precise accuracy of his figures, the result is almost equally startling. The Spaniards were destined to become familiar with this appalling spectacle as they approached nearer to the Aztec capital.

The lord of the town ruled over twenty thousand vassals. He was tributary to Montezuma, and a strong Mexican garrison was quartered in the place. He had probably been advised of the approach of the Spaniards, and doubted how far it would be welcome to his sovereign. At all events, he gave them a cold reception, the more unpalatable after the extraordinary sufferings of the last few days. To the inquiry of Cortés, whether he were subject to Montezuma, he answered, with real or affected surprise, "Who is there that is not a vassal of Montezuma?"[3] The general told him, with some emphasis, that *he* was not. He then explained whence and why he came, assuring him that he served a monarch who had princes for his vassals as powerful as the Aztec monarch himself.

The cacique, in turn, fell nothing short of the Spaniard in the pompous display of the grandeur and resources of the Indian emperor. He told his guest that Montezuma could muster thirty great vassals, each master

1 Now known by the euphonious Indian name of Tlatlauqnitepec. (Viaje, ap. Lorenzana, p. iv.) It is the *Cocotlan* of Bernal Diaz. (Hist. de la Conquista, cap. 61.) The old Conquerors made sorry work with the Aztec names, both of places and persons, for which they must be allowed to have had ample excuse.

2 "Puestos tantos rimeros de calaueras de muertos, que se podian bien contar, segun el concierto con que estauan puestas, que me parece que eran mas de cien mil, y digo otra vez sobre cien mil." Ibid., ubi supra.

3 "El qual casi admirado de lo que le preguntaba, me respondió, diciendo; ¿ que quién no era vasallo de Muctezuma? queriendo decir, que allí era Señor del Mundo." Rel. Seg. de Cortés, ap. Lorenzana, p. 47.

of a hundred thousand men![1] His revenues were immense, as every subject, however poor, paid something. They were all expended on his magnificent state and in support of his armies. These were continually in the field, while garrisons were maintained in most of the large cities of the empire. More than twenty thousand victims, the fruit of his wars, were annually sacrificed on the altars of his gods! His capital, the cacique said, stood in a lake, in the centre of a spacious valley. The lake was commanded by the emperor's vessels, and the approach to the city was by means of causeways, several miles long, connected in parts by wooden bridges, which, when raised, cut off all communication with the country. Some other things he added, in answer to queries of his guest, in which, as the reader may imagine, the crafty or credulous cacique varnished over the truth with a lively colouring of romance. Whether romance, or reality, the Spaniards could not determine. The particulars they gleaned were not of a kind to tranquillize their minds, and might well have made bolder hearts than theirs pause, ere they advanced. But far from it. "The words which we heard," says the stout old cavalier so often quoted, "however they may have filled us with wonder, made us— such is the temper of the Spaniard—only the more earnest to prove the adventure, desperate as it might appear."[2]

In a further conversation Cortés inquired of the chief whether his country abounded in gold, and intimated a desire to take home some, as specimens, to his sovereign. But the Indian lord declined to give him any, saying it might displease Montezuma. "Should he command it," he added, "my gold, my person, and all I possess, shall be at your disposal." The general did not press the matter further.

The curiosity of the natives was naturally excited by the strange dresses, weapons, horses, and dogs of the Spaniards. Marina, in satisfying their inquiries, took occasion to magnify the prowess of her adopted countrymen, expatiating on their exploits and victories, and stating the extraordinary marks of respect they had received from Montezuma. This intelligence seems to have had its effect ; for soon after the cacique gave the general some curious trinkets of gold, of no great value, indeed, but as a testimony of his goodwill. He sent him, also, some female slaves to prepare bread for the troops, and supplied the means of refreshment and repose, more important to them, in the present juncture, than all the gold of Mexico.[3]

The Spanish general, as usual, did not neglect the occasion to inculcate

---

[1] "Tiene mas de 30 Príncipes á sí subjectos, que cada uno dellos tiene cient mill hombres é mas de pelea." (Oviedo, Hist. de las Ind., MS., lib. 33, cap. 1.) This marvellous tale is gravely repeated by more than one Spanish writer, in their accounts of the Aztec monarchy, not as the assertion of this chief, but as a veritable piece of statistics. See, among others, Herrera, Hist. general, dec. 2, lib. 7, cap. 12.—Solis, Conquista, lib. 3, cap. 16.

[2] Bernal Diaz, Hist. de la Conquista, cap. 61.—

There is a slight ground-swell of glorification in the Captain's narrative, which may provoke a smile,— not a sneer, for it is mingled with too much real courage and simplicity of character.

[3] For the preceding pages, besides authorities cited in course, see Peter Martyr, De Orbe Novo, dec. 5, cap. 1,—Ixtlilxochitl, Hist. Chich., MS., cap. 83,—Gomara, Crónica, cap. 44,—Torquemada, Monarch. Ind., lib. 4, cap. 26.

the great truths of revelation on his host, and to display the atrocity of the Indian superstitions. The cacique listened with civil but cold indifference. Cortés, finding him unmoved, turned briskly round to his soldiers, exclaiming that now was the time to plant the Cross! They eagerly seconded his pious purpose, and the same scenes might have been enacted as at Cempoalla, with perhaps very different results, had not Father Olmedo, with better judgment, interposed. He represented that to introduce the Cross among the natives, in their present state of ignorance and incredulity, would be to expose the sacred symbol to desecration so soon as the backs of the Spaniards were turned. The only way was to wait patiently the season when more leisure should be afforded to instil into their minds a knowledge of the truth. The sober reasoning of the good father prevailed over the passions of the martial enthusiasts.

It was fortunate for Cortés that Olmedo was not one of those frantic friars who would have fanned his fiery temper on such occasions into a blaze. It might have had a most disastrous influence on his fortunes; for he held all temporal consequences light in comparison with the great work of conversion, to effect which the unscrupulous mind of the soldier, trained to the stern discipline of the camp, would have employed force whenever fair means were ineffectual.[1] But Olmedo belonged to that class of benevolent missionaries—of whom the Roman Catholic Church, to its credit, has furnished many examples—who rely on spiritual weapons for the great work, inculcating those doctrines of love and mercy which can best touch the sensibilities and win the affections of their rude audience. These, indeed, are the true weapons of the Church, the weapons employed in the primitive ages, by which it has spread its peaceful banners over the farthest regions of the globe. Such were not the means used by the conquerors of America, who, rather adopting the policy of the victorious Moslems in their early career, carried with them the sword in one hand and the Bible in the other. They imposed obedience in matters of faith, no less than of government, on the vanquished, little heeding whether the conversion were genuine, so that it conformed to the outward observances of the Church. Yet the seeds thus recklessly scattered must have perished but for the missionaries of their own nation, who, in later times, worked over the same ground, living among the Indians as brethren, and, by long and patient culture, enabling the germs of truth to take root and fructify in their hearts.

The Spanish commander remained in the city four or five days, to recruit his fatigued and famished forces; and the modern Indians still point out, or did, at the close of the last century, a venerable cypress,

---

[1] The general clearly belonged to the church militant, mentioned by Butler:—

" Such as do build their faith upon
The holy text of pike and gun,
And prove their doctrines orthodox
By apostolic blows and knocks."

under the branches of which was tied the horse of the *Conquistador*,—the Conqueror, as Cortés was styled, *par excellence.*[1] Their route now opened on a broad and verdant valley, watered by a noble stream,—a circumstance of not too frequent occurrence on the parched table-land of New Spain. The soil was well protected by woods,—a thing still rarer at the present day; since the invaders, soon after the Conquest, swept away the magnificent growth of timber, rivalling that of our Southern and Western States in variety and beauty, which covered the plateau under the Aztecs.[2]

All along the river, on both sides of it, an unbroken line of Indian dwellings, " so near as almost to touch one another," extended for three or four leagues ; arguing a population much denser than at present.[3] On a rough and rising ground stood a town that might contain five or six thousand inhabitants, commanded by a fortress, which, with its walls and trenches, seemed to the Spaniards quite "on a level with similar works in Europe." Here the troops again halted, and met with friendly treatment.[4]

Cortés now determined his future line of march. At the last place he had been counselled by the natives to take the route of the ancient city of Cholula, the inhabitants of which, subjects of Montezuma, were a mild race, devoted to mechanical and other peaceful arts, and would be likely to entertain him kindly. Their Cempoallan allies, however, advised the Spaniards not to trust the Cholulans, " a false and perfidious people," but to take the road to Tlascala, that valiant little republic which had so long maintained its independence against the arms of Mexico. The people were frank as they were fearless, and fair in their dealings. They had always been on terms of amity with the Totonacs, which afforded a strong guarantee for their amicable disposition on the present occasion.

The arguments of his Indian allies prevailed with the Spanish commander, who resolved to propitiate the goodwill of the Tlascalans by an embassy. He selected four of the principal Cempoallans for this, and sent by them a martial gift,—a cap of crimson cloth, together with a sword and a crossbow, weapons which, it was observed, excited general admiration among the natives. He added a letter, in which he asked permission to pass through their country. He expressed his admiration of the valour of the Tlascalans, and of their long resistance to the Aztecs,

---

[1] " Arbol grande, dicho *ahuehuete.*" (Viaje, ap. Lorenzana, p. iii.) The *Cupressus disticha* of Linnæus. See Humboldt, Essai politique, tom. ii. p. 54, note.

[2] It is the same taste which has made the Castiles, the table-land of the Peninsula, so naked of wood. Prudential reasons, as well as taste, however, seem to have operated in New Spain. A friend of mine on a visit to a noble *hacienda*, but uncommonly barren of trees, was informed by the proprietor that they were cut down to prevent the lazy Indians on the plantation from wasting their time by loitering in their shade !

[3] It confirms the observations of M. de Humboldt. " Sans doute lors de la première arrivée des Espagnols, toute cette côte, depuis la rivière de Papaloa-

pan (Alvarado) jusqu'à Huaxtecapan, était plus habitée et mieux cultivée qu'elle ne l'est aujourd'hui. Cependant à mesure que les conquérans montèrent au plateau, ils trouvèrent les villages plus rapprochés les uns des autres, les champs divisés en portions plus petites, le peuple plus policé." Humboldt, Essai politique, tom. ii. p. 202.

[4] The correct Indian name of the town, *Yxtaca maxtitlan, Yztacmastitan* of Cortés, will hardly be recognized in the *Xalacingo* of Diaz. The town was removed, in 1601, from the top of the hill to the plain. On the original site are still visible remains of carved stones of large dimensions, attesting the elegance of the ancient fortress or palace of the cacique. Viaje, ap. Lorenzana, p. v.

whose proud empire he designed to humble.[1] It was not to be expected that this epistle, indited in good Castilian, would be very intelligible to the Tlascalans. But Cortés communicated its import to the ambassadors. Its mysterious characters might impress the natives with an idea of superior intelligence, and the letters serve instead of those hieroglyphical missives which formed the usual credentials of an Indian ambassador.[2]

The Spaniards remained three days in this hospitable place, after the departure of the envoys, when they resumed their progress. Although in a friendly country, they marched always as if in a land of enemies, the horse and light troops in the van, with the heavy-armed and baggage in the rear, all in battle-array. They were never without their armour, waking or sleeping, lying down with their weapons by their sides. This unintermitting and restless vigilance was, perhaps, more oppressive to the spirits than even bodily fatigue. But they were confident in their superiority in a fair field, and felt that the most serious danger they had to fear from Indian warfare was surprise. "We are few against many, brave companions," Cortés would say to them; "be prepared, then, not as if you were going to battle, but as if actually in the midst of it!"[3]

The road taken by the Spaniards was the same which at present leads to Tlascala; not that, however, usually followed in passing from Vera Cruz to the capital, which makes a circuit considerably to the south, towards Puebla, in the neighbourhood of the ancient Cholula. They more than once forded the stream that rolls through this beautiful plain, lingering several days on the way, in hopes of receiving an answer from the Indian republic. The unexpected delay of the messengers could not be explained, and occasioned some uneasiness.

As they advanced into a country of rougher and bolder features, their progress was suddenly arrested by a remarkable fortification. It was a stone wall nine feet in height, and twenty in thickness, with a parapet, a foot and a half broad, raised on the summit for the protection of those who defended it. It had only one opening, in the centre, made by two semicircular lines of wall overlapping each other for the space of forty paces, and affording a passage-way between, ten paces wide, so contrived, therefore, as to be perfectly commanded by the inner wall. This fortification, which extended more than two leagues, rested at either end on the bold natural buttresses formed by the sierra. The work was built of immense blocks of stones nicely laid together without cement;[4] and

---

[1] "Estas cosas y otras de gran persuasion contenia la carta, pero como no sabian leer no pudiéron entender lo que contenia." Camargo, Hist. de Tlascala, MS.

[2] For an account of the diplomatic usages of the people of Anahuac, see *ante*, p. 21.

[3] "Mira, señores compañeros, ya veis que somos pocos, hemos de estar siempre tan apercebidos, y aparejados, como si aora viessemos venir los contra-

rios á pelear, y no solamente vellos venir, sino hazer cuenta que estamos ya en la batalla con ellos." Bernal Diaz, Hist. de la Conquista, cap. 62.

[4] According to the writer last cited, the stones were held by a cement so hard that the men could scarcely break it with their pikes. (Hist. de la Conquista, cap. 62.) But the contrary statement, in the general's letter, is confirmed by the present appearance of the wall. Viaje, ap. Lorenzana, p. vii.

the remains still existing, among which are rocks of the whole breadth of the rampart, fully attest its solidity and size.[1]

This singular structure marked the limits of Tlascala, and was intended, as the natives told the Spaniards, as a barrier against the Mexican invasions. The army paused, filled with amazement at the contemplation of this Cyclopean monument, which naturally suggested reflections on the strength and resources of the people who had raised it. It caused them, too, some painful solicitude as to the probable result of their mission to Tlascala, and their own consequent reception there. But they were too sanguine to allow such uncomfortable surmises long to dwell in their minds. Cortés put himself at the head of his cavalry, and, calling out, "Forward, soldiers, the Holy Cross is our banner, and under that we shall conquer," led his little army through the undefended passage, and in a few moments they trod the soil of the free republic of Tlascala.[2]

CHAPTER II.

REPUBLIC OF TLASCALA.—ITS INSTITUTIONS.—EARLY HISTORY.—DISCUSSIONS IN THE SENATE.—DESPERATE BATTLES.

(1519.)

BEFORE advancing further with the Spaniards into the territory of Tlascala, it will be well to notice some traits in the character and institutions of the nation, in many respects the most remarkable in Anahuac. The Tlascalans belonged to the same great family with the Aztecs.[3] They came on the grand plateau about the same time with the kindred races, at the close of the twelfth century, and planted themselves on the western borders of the lake of Tezcuco. Here they remained many years, engaged in the usual pursuits of a bold and partially civilized people. From some cause or other, perhaps their turbulent temper, they incurred the enmity of surrounding tribes. A coalition was formed against them ; and a bloody battle was fought on the plains of Poyauhtlan, in which the Tlascalans were completely victorious.

Disgusted, however, with their residence among nations with whom they found so little favour, the conquering people resolved to migrate.

---

[1] Viaje, ap. Lorenzana, p. vii.—The attempts of the Archbishop to identify the route of Cortés have been very successful. It is a pity that his map illustrating the itinerary should be so worthless.

[2] Camargo, Hist. de Tlascala, MS.—Gomara, Crónica, cap. 44, 45.—Ixtlilxochitl, Hist. Chich., MS., cap. 83.—Herrera, Hist. general, dec. 2, lib. 6, cap. 3.—Oviedo, Hist. de las Ind., MS., lib. 33, cap. 2.—Peter Martyr, De Orbe Novo, dec. 5, cap. 1.

[3] The Indian chronicler, Camargo, considers his nation a branch of the Chichimec. (Hist. de Tlascala, MS.) So, also, Torquemada. (Monarch. Ind., lib. 3, cap. 9.) Clavigero, who has carefully investigated the antiquities of Anahuac, calls it one of the seven Nahuatlac tribes. (Stor. del Messico, tom. i. p. 153, nota.) The fact is not of great moment, since they were all cognate races, speaking the same tongue, and, probably, migrated from their country in the far North at nearly the same time.

They separated into three divisions, the largest of which, taking a southern course by the great *volcan* of Mexico, wound round the ancient city of Cholula, and finally settled in the district of country overshadowed by the sierra of Tlascala. The warm and fruitful valleys, locked up in the embraces of this rugged brotherhood of mountains, afforded means of subsistence for an agricultural people, while the bold eminences of the sierra presented secure positions for their towns.

After the lapse of years, the institutions of the nation underwent an important change. The monarchy was divided first into two, afterwards into four separate states, bound together by a sort of federal compact, probably not very nicely defined. Each state, however, had its lord or supreme chief, independent in his own territories, and possessed of co-ordinate authority with the others in all matters concerning the whole republic. The affairs of government, especially all those relating to peace and war, were settled in a senate or council, consisting of the four lords with their inferior nobles.

The lower dignitaries held of the superior, each in his own district, by a kind of feudal tenure, being bound to supply his table and enable him to maintain his state in peace, as well as to serve him in war.[1] In return, he experienced the aid and protection of his suzerain. The same mutual obligations existed between him and the followers among whom his own territories were distributed.[2] Thus a chain of feudal dependencies was established, which, if not contrived with all the art and legal refinements of analogous institutions in the Old World, displayed their most prominent characteristics in its personal relations, the obligations of military service on the one hand, and protection on the other. This form of government, so different from that of the surrounding nations, subsisted till the arrival of the Spaniards. And it is certainly evidence of considerable civilization that so complex a polity should have so long continued, undisturbed by violence or faction in the confederate states, and should have been found competent to protect the people in their rights, and the country from foreign invasion.

The lowest order of the people, however, do not seem to have enjoyed higher immunities than under the monarchical governments; and their rank was carefully defined by an appropriate dress, and by their exclusion from the insignia of the aristocratic orders.[3]

---

[1] The descendants of these petty nobles attached as great value to their pedigrees as any Biscayan or Asturian in Old Spain. Long after the Conquest, they refused, however needy, to dishonour their birth by resorting to mechanical or other plebeian occupations, *oficios viles y bajos*. "Los descendientes de estos son estimados por hombres calificados, que aunque sean pobrísimos no usan oficios mecánicos ni tratos bajos ni viles, ni jamas se permiten cargar ni cabar con coas y azadones, diciendo que son hijos Idalgos en que no han de aplicarse á estas cosas soeces y bajas, sino servir en guerras y fronteras, como Idalgos, y morir como hombres peleando." Camargo, Hist. de Tlascala, MS.

[2] "Cualquier Tecuhtli que formaba un Tecalli,

que es casa de Mayorazgo, todas aquellas tierras que le caian en suerte de repartimiento, con montes, fuentes, rios, ó lagunas tomase para la casa principal la mayor y mejor suerte ó pagos de tierra, y luego las demas que quedaban se partian por sus soldados amigos y parientes, igualmente, y todos estos están obligados á reconocer la casa mayor y acudir á ella, á alzarla y repararla, y á ser continuos en reconocer á ella de aves, caza, flores, y ramos para el sustento de la casa del Mayorazgo, y el que lo es está obligado á sustentarlos y á regalarlos, como amigos de aquella casa y parientes de ella." Ibid., MS.

[3] Camargo, Hist. de Tlascala, MS.

The nation, agricultural in its habits, reserved its highest honours, like most other rude—unhappily, also, civilized—nations, for military prowess. Public games were instituted, and prizes decreed to those who excelled in such manly and athletic exercises as might train them for the fatigues of war. Triumphs were granted to the victorious general, who entered the city, leading his spoils and captives in long procession, while his achievements were commemorated in national songs, and his effigy, whether in wood or stone, was erected in the temples. It was truly in the martial spirit of republican Rome.[1]

An institution not unlike knighthood was introduced, very similar to one existing also among the Aztecs. The aspirant to the honours of this barbaric chivalry watched his arms and fasted fifty or sixty days in the temple, then listened to a grave discourse on the duties of his new profession. Various whimsical ceremonies followed, when his arms were restored to him; he was led in solemn procession through the public streets, and the inauguration was concluded by banquets and public rejoicings. The new knight was distinguished henceforth by certain peculiar privileges, as well as by a badge intimating his rank. It is worthy of remark that this honour was not reserved exclusively for military merit, but was the recompense, also, of public services of other kinds, as wisdom in council, or sagacity and success in trade. For trade was held in as high estimation by the Tlascalans as by the other people of Anahuac.[2]

The temperate climate of the table-land furnished the ready means for distant traffic. The fruitfulness of the soil was indicated by the name of the country,—*Tlascala* signifying the "land of bread." Its wide plains, to the slopes of its rocky hills, waved with yellow harvests of maize, and with the bountiful maguey, a plant which, as we have seen, supplied the materials for some important fabrics. With these, as well as the products of agricultural industry, the merchant found his way down the sides of the Cordilleras, wandered over the sunny regions at their base, and brought back the luxuries which nature had denied to his own.[3]

The various arts of civilization kept pace with increasing wealth and public prosperity; at least, these arts were cultivated to the same limited extent, apparently, as among the other people of Anahuac. The Tlascalan tongue, says the national historian, simple as beseemed that of a mountain region, was rough compared with the polished Tezcucan or the popular Aztec dialect, and, therefore, not so well fitted for composition. But the Tlascalans made like proficiency with the kindred nations in the rudiments of science. Their calendar was formed on the same plan. Their religion,

1 "Los grandes recibimientos que hacian á los capitanes que venian y alcanzaban victoria en las guerras, las fiestas y solenidades con que se solenizaban á manera de triunfo, que los metian en andas en su puebla, trayendo consigo á los vencidos; y por eternizar sus hazañas se las cantaban publicamente, y ansi quedaban memoradas y con estatuas que les ponian en los templos." Camargo, Hist. de Tlascala. MS.

2 For the whole ceremony of inauguration,—though, as it seems, having especial reference to the merchant-knights,—see Appendix, Part 2, No. 9, where the original is given from Camargo.
3 "Ha bel paese," says the Anonymous Conqueror, speaking of Tlascala at the time of the invasion, "di pianure et mõtagne, et è provincia popolosa et vi si raccoglie molto pane." Rel d'un gentil' huomo, ap. Ramusio, tom. iii. p. 308.

their architecture, many of their laws and social usages, were the same, arguing a common origin for all. Their tutelary deity was the same ferocious war-god as that of the Aztecs, though with a different name; their temples, in like manner, were drenched with the blood of human victims, and their boards groaned with the same cannibal repasts.[1]

Though not ambitious of foreign conquest, the prosperity of the Tlascalans, in time, excited the jealousy of their neighbours, and especially of the opulent state of Cholula. Frequent hostilities arose between them, in which the advantage was almost always on the side of the former. A still more formidable foe appeared in later days in the Aztecs, who could ill brook the independence of Tlascala when the surrounding nations had acknowledged, one after another, their influence or their empire. Under the ambitious Axayacatl, they demanded of the Tlascalans the same tribute and obedience rendered by other people of the country. If it were refused, the Aztecs would raze their cities to their foundations, and deliver the land to their enemies.

To this imperious summons, the little republic proudly replied, "Neither they nor their ancestors had ever paid tribute or homage to a foreign power, and never would pay it. If their country was invaded, they knew how to defend it, and would pour out their blood as freely in defence of their freedom now as their fathers did of yore, when they routed the Aztecs on the plains of Poyauhtlan!"[2]

This resolute answer brought on them the forces of the monarchy. A pitched battle followed, and the sturdy republicans were victorious. From this period, hostilities between the two nations continued with more or less activity, but with unsparing ferocity. Every captive was mercilessly sacrificed. The children were trained from the cradle to deadly hatred against the Mexicans; and, even in the brief intervals of war, none of those intermarriages took place between the people of the respective countries, which knit together in social bonds most of the other kindred races of Anahuac.

In this struggle the Tlascalans received an important support in the accession of the Othomis, or Otomies,—as usually spelt by Castilian writers,—a wild and warlike race originally spread over the table-land north of the Mexican Valley. A portion of them obtained a settlement in the republic, and were speedily incorporated in its armies. Their courage and fidelity to the nation of their adoption showed them worthy of trust, and the frontier places were consigned to their keeping. The mountain barriers by which Tlascala is encompassed afforded many strong natural positions for defence against invasion. The country was open towards the east, where a valley, of some six miles in breadth, invited the

---

[1] A full account of the manners, customs, and domestic policy of Tlascala is given by the national historian, throwing much light on the other states of Anahuac, whose social institutions seem to have been all cast in the same mould.

[2] Camargo, Hist. de Tlascala, MS.—Torquemada, Monarch. Ind., lib. 2, cap. 70.

approach of an enemy. But here it was that the jealous Tlascalans erected the formidable rampart which had excited the admiration of the Spaniards, and which they manned with a garrison of Otomies.

Efforts for their subjugation were renewed on a greater scale after the accession of Montezuma. His victorious arms had spread down the declivities of the Andes to the distant provinces of Vera Paz and Nicaragua.[1] And his haughty spirit was chafed by the opposition of a petty state whose territorial extent did not exceed ten leagues in breadth by fifteen in length.[2] He sent an army against them under the command of a favourite son. His troops were beaten, and his son was slain. The enraged and mortified monarch was roused to still greater preparations. He enlisted the forces of the cities bordering on his enemy, together with those of the empire, and with this formidable army swept over the devoted valleys of Tlascala. But the bold mountaineers withdrew into the recesses of their hills, and, coolly awaiting their opportunity, rushed like a torrent on the invaders, and drove them back, with dreadful slaughter, from their territories.

Still, notwithstanding the advantages gained over the enemy in the field, the Tlascalans were sorely pressed by their long hostilities with a foe so far superior to themselves in numbers and resources. The Aztec armies lay between them and the coast, cutting off all communication with that prolific region, and thus limited their supplies to the products of their own soil and manufacture. For more than half a century they had neither cotton, nor cacao, nor salt. Indeed, their taste had been so far affected by long abstinence from these articles that it required the lapse of several generations after the Conquest to reconcile them to the use of salt at their meals.[3] During the short intervals of war, it is said, the Aztec nobles, in the true spirit of chivalry, sent supplies of these commodities as presents, with many courteous expressions of respect, to the Tlascalan chiefs. This intercourse, we are assured by the Indian chronicler, was unsuspected by the people. Nor did it lead to any further correspondence, he adds, between the parties, prejudicial to the liberties of the republic, " which maintained its customs and good government inviolate, and the worship of its gods." [4]

Such was the condition of Tlascala at the coming of the Spaniards ; holding, it might seem, a precarious existence under the shadow of the formidable power which seemed suspended like an avalanche over her head, but still strong in her own resources, stronger in the indomitable

---

[1] Camargo (Hist. de Tlascala, MS.) notices the extent of Montezuma's conquests, — a debatable ground for the historian.

[2] Torquemada, Monarch. Ind., lib. 3, cap. 16.— Solis says, "The Tlascalan territory was fifty leagues in circumference, ten long, from east to west, and four broad, from north to south." (Conquista de Méjico, lib. 3, cap. 3.) It must have made a curious figure in geometry !

[3] Camargo, Hist. de Tlascala, MS.

[4] "Los Señores Mejicanos v Tezcucanos en tiempo que ponian treguas por algunas temporadas embiaban á los Señores de Tlaxcalla grandes presentes y dádivas de oro, ropa, y cacao, y sal, y de todas las cosas de que carecian, sin que la gente plebeya lo entendiese, y se saludaban secretamente, guardándose el decoro que se debian : mas con todos estos trabajos la órden de su república jamas se dejaba de gobernar con la rectitud de sus costumbres guardando inviolablemente el culto de sus Dioses." Ibid., MS.

temper of her people ; with a reputation established throughout the land for good faith and moderation in peace, for valour in war, while her uncompromising spirit of independence secured the respect even of her enemies. With such qualities of character, and with an animosity sharpened by long, deadly hostility with Mexico, her alliance was obviously of the last importance to the Spaniards, in their present enterprise. It was not easy to secure it.[1]

The Tlascalans had been made acquainted with the advance and victorious career of the Christians, the intelligence of which had spread far and wide over the plateau. But they do not seem to have anticipated the approach of the strangers to their own borders. They were now much embarrassed by the embassy demanding a passage through their territories. The great council was convened, and a considerable difference of opinion prevailed in its members. Some, adopting the popular superstition, supposed the Spaniards might be the white and bearded men foretold by the oracles.[2] At all events, they were the enemies of Mexico, and as such might co-operate with them in their struggle with the empire. Others argued that the strangers could have nothing in common with them. Their march throughout the land might be tracked by the broken images of the Indian gods and desecrated temples. How did the Tlascalans even know that they were foes to Montezuma ? They had received his embassies, accepted his presents, and were now in the company of his vassals on the way to his capital.

These last were the reflections of an aged chief, one of the four who presided over the republic. His name was Xicotencatl. He was nearly blind, having lived, as is said, far beyond the limits of a century.[3] His son, an impetuous young man of the same name with himself, commanded a powerful army of Tlascalan and Otomi warriors, near the eastern frontier. It would be best, the old man said, to fall with this force at once on the Spaniards. If victorious, the latter would then be in their power. If defeated, the senate could disown the act as that of the general, not of the republic.[4] The cunning counsel of the chief found favour with his hearers, though assuredly not in the spirit of chivalry, nor of the good faith for which his countrymen were celebrated. But with an Indian, force and stratagem, courage and deceit, were equally admissible in war, as they were among the barbarians of ancient Rome.[5] The Cempoallan envoys were to be detained under pretence of assisting at a religious sacrifice.

---

[1] The Tlascalan chronicler discerns in this deep-rooted hatred of Mexico the hand of Providence, who wrought out of it an important means for subverting the Aztec empire. Hist. de Tlascala, MS.

[2] " Si bien os acordais, como tenemos de nuestra antiguedad como han de venir gentes á la parte donde sale el sol, y que han de emparentar con nosotros, y que hemos de ser todos unos ; y que han de ser blancos y barbudos." Ibid., MS.

[3] To the ripe age of one hundred and forty ! if we may credit Camargo. Solís, who confounds this

veteran with his son, has put a flourishing harangue in the mouth of the latter, which would be a rare gem of Indian eloquence,—were it not Castilian. Conquista, lib. 2, cap. 16.

[4] Camargo, Hist. de Tlascala, MS.—Herrera, Hist. general, dec. 2, lib. 6, cap. 3.—Torquemada, Monarch. Ind., lib. 4, cap. 27.—There is sufficient contradiction, as well as obscurity, in the proceedings reported of the council, which it is not easy to reconcile altogether with subsequent events.

[5] " Dolus an virtus, quis in hoste requirat ? "

Meanwhile, Cortés and his gallant band, as stated in the preceding chapter, had arrived before the rocky rampart on the eastern confines of Tlascala. From some cause or other, it was not manned by its Otomi garrison, and the Spaniards passed in, as we have seen, without resistance. Cortés rode at the head of his body of horse, and ordering the infantry to come on at a quick pace, went forward to reconnoitre. After advancing three or four leagues, he descried a small party of Indians, armed with sword and buckler, in the fashion of the country. They fled at his approach. He made signs for them to halt, but, seeing that they only fled the faster, he and his companions put spurs to their horses, and soon came up with them. The Indians, finding escape impossible, faced round, and, instead of showing the accustomed terror of the natives at the strange and appalling aspect of a mounted trooper, they commenced a furious assault on the cavaliers. The latter, however, were too strong for them, and would have cut their enemy to pieces without much difficulty, when a body of several thousand Indians appeared in sight, coming briskly on to the support of their countrymen.

Cortés, seeing them, despatched one of his party in all haste, to accelerate the march of his infantry. The Indians, after discharging their missiles, fell furiously on the little band of Spaniards. They strove to tear the lances from their grasp, and to drag the riders from the horses. They brought one cavalier to the ground, who afterwards died of his wounds, and they killed two of the horses, cutting through their necks with their stout broadswords—if we may believe the chronicler—at a blow![1] In the narrative of these campaigns there is sometimes but one step—and that a short one—from history to romance. The loss of the horses, so important and so few in number, was seriously felt by Cortés, who could have better spared the life of the best rider in the troop.

The struggle was a hard one. But the odds were as overwhelming as any recorded by the Spaniards in their own romances, where a handful of knights is arrayed against legions of enemies. The lances of the Christians did terrible execution here also; but they had need of the magic lance of Astolpho, that overturned myriads with a touch, to carry them safe through so unequal a contest. It was with no little satisfaction, therefore, that they beheld their comrades rapidly advancing to their support.

No sooner had the main body reached the field of battle, than, hastily forming, they poured such a volley from their muskets and crossbows as staggered the enemy. Astounded, rather than intimidated, by the terrible report of the firearms, now heard for the first time in these regions, the Indians made no further effort to continue the fight, but drew off in good order, leaving the road open to the Spaniards. The latter, too well satisfied to be rid of the annoyance to care to follow the retreating foe, again held on their way.

---

[1] "I les matáron dos Caballos, de dos cuchilladas, i segun algunos, que lo viércn cortáron á cercen de in golpe cada pescueço, con riendas, i todas' Gomara, Crónica, cap. 45.

Their route took them through a country sprinkled over with Indian cottages, amidst flourishing fields of maize and maguey, indicating an industrious and thriving peasantry. They were met here by two Tlascalan envoys, accompanied by two of the Cempoallans. The former, presenting themselves before the general, disavowed the assault on his troops, as an unauthorized act, and assured him of a friendly reception at their capital. Cortés received the communication in a courteous manner, affecting to place more confidence in its good faith than he probably felt.

It was now growing late, and the Spaniards quickened their march, anxious to reach a favourable ground for encampment before nightfall. They found such a spot on the borders of a stream that rolled sluggishly across the plain. A few deserted cottages stood along the banks, and the fatigued and famished soldiers ransacked them in quest of food. All they could find was some tame animals resembling dogs. These they killed and dressed without ceremony, and, garnishing their unsavoury repast with the fruit of the *tuna*, the Indian fig, which grew wild in the neighbourhood, they contrived to satisfy the cravings of appetite. A careful watch was maintained by Cortés, and companies of a hundred men each relieved each other in mounting guard through the night. But no attack was made. Hostilities by night were contrary to the system of Indian tactics.[1]

By break of day on the following morning, it being the second of September, the troops were under arms. Besides the Spaniards, the whole number of Indian auxiliaries might now amount to three thousand; for Cortés had gathered recruits from the friendly places on his route,—three hundred from the last. After hearing mass, they resumed their march. They moved in close array; the general had previously admonished the men not to lag behind, or wander from the ranks a moment, as stragglers would be sure to be cut off by their stealthy and vigilant enemy. The horsemen rode three abreast, the better to give one another support; and Cortés instructed them in the heat of fight to keep together, and never to charge singly. He taught them how to carry their lances that they might not be wrested from their hands by the Indians, who constantly attempted it. For the same reason, they should avoid giving thrusts, but aim their weapons steadily at the faces of their foes.[2]

They had not proceeded far, when they were met by the two remaining Cempoallan envoys, who with looks of terror informed the general that they had been treacherously seized and confined, in order to be sacrificed at an approaching festival of the Tlascalans, but in the night had succeeded in making their escape. They gave the unwelcome tidings, also, that a large force of the natives was already assembled to oppose the progress of the Spaniards.

[1] Rel. Seg. de Cortés, ap. Lorenzana, p. 50.—Camargo, Hist. de Tlascala, MS.—Bernal Díaz, Hist. de la Conquista, cap. 62.—Gomara, Crónica, cap. 45.—Oviedo, Hist. de las Ind., MS., lib. 33, cap. 3, 41.—Sahagun, Hist. de Nueva-España, MS., lib. 12, cap. 10.

[2] "Que quando rompiessemos por los esquadrones, que lleuassen las lanças por las caras, y no parassen á dar lançadas, porque no les echassen mano dellas." Bernal Díaz, Hist. de la Conquista, cap. 62.

Soon after, they came in sight of a body of Indians, about a thousand, apparently, all armed, and brandishing their weapons, as the Christians approached, in token of defiance. Cortés, when he had come within hearing, ordered the interpreters to proclaim that he had no hostile intentions, but wished only to be allowed a passage through their country, which he had entered as a friend. This declaration he commanded the royal notary, Godoy, to record on the spot, that, if blood were shed, it might not be charged on the Spaniards. This pacific proclamation was met, as usual on such occasions, by a shower of darts, stones, and arrows, which fell like rain on the Spaniards, rattling on their stout harness, and in some instances penetrating to the skin. Galled by the smart of their wounds, they called on the general to lead them on, till he sounded the well-known battle-cry, "St. Jago, and at them!"[1]

The Indians maintained their ground for a while with spirit, when they retreated with precipitation, but not in disorder.[2] The Spaniards, whose blood was heated by the encounter, followed up their advantage with more zeal than prudence, suffering the wily enemy to draw them into a narrow glen or defile intersected by a little stream of water, where the broken ground was impracticable for artillery, as well as for the movements of cavalry. Pressing forward with eagerness, to extricate themselves from their perilous position, to their great dismay, on turning an abrupt angle of the pass, they came in presence of a numerous army, choking up the gorge of the valley, and stretching far over the plains beyond. To the astonished eyes of Cortés, they appeared a hundred thousand men, while no account estimates them at less than thirty thousand.[3]

They presented a confused assemblage of helmets, weapons, and many-coloured plumes, glancing bright in the morning sun, and mingled with banners, above which proudly floated one that bore as a device the heron on a rock. It was the well-known ensign of the house of Titcala, and, as well as the white and yellow stripes on the bodies, and the like colours on the feather-mail of the Indians, showed that they were the warriors of Xicotencatl.[4]

As the Spaniards came in sight, the Tlascalans set up a hideous war-cry, or rather whistle, piercing the ear with its shrillness, and which, with the beat of their melancholy drums, that could be heard for half a league or more,[5]

---

[1] "Entonces dixo Cortés, 'Santiago, y á ellos.'" Bernal Diaz, Hist. de la Conquista, cap. 63.

[2] "Una gentil contienda," says Gomara of this skirmish. Crónica, cap. 46.

[3] Rel. Seg. de Cortés, ap. Lorenzana, p. 51. According to Gomara (Crónica, cap. 46), the enemy mustered 80,000. So, also, Ixtlilxochitl. (Hist. Chich., MS., cap. 83.) Bernal Diaz says, more than 40,000. (Hist. de la Conquista, cap. 63.) But Herrera (Hist. general, dec. 2, lib. 6, cap. 5) and Torquemada (Monarch. Ind., lib. 4, cap. 20) reduce them to 30,000. One might as easily reckon the leaves in a forest, as the numbers of a confused throng of barbarians. As this was only one of several armies kept on foot by the Tlascalans, the smallest amount is, probably, too large. The whole population of the state, according to Clavigero, who would not be likely to underrate it, did not exceed half a million at the time of the invasion. Stor. del Messico, tom. i. p. 156.

[4] "La divisa y armas de la casa y cabecera de Titcala es una garga blanca sobre un peñasco." (Camargo, Hist. de Tlascala, MS.) "El capitan general," says Bernal Diaz, "que se dezia Xicotenga, y con sus diuisas de blanco y colorado, porque aquella diuisa y librea era de aquel Xicotenga." Hist. de la Conquista, cap. 63.

[5] "Llaman Teponaztle ques de un trozo de madero concavado y de una pieza rollizo y, como decimos, hueco por de dentro, que suena algunas veces mas de media legua y con el atambor hace estraña y suave consonancia." (Camargo, Hist. de Tlascala

might well have filled the stoutest heart with dismay. This formidable host came rolling on towards the Christians, as if to overwhelm them by their very numbers. But the courageous band of warriors, closely serried together and sheltered under their strong panoplies, received the shock unshaken, while the broken masses of the enemy, chafing and heaving tumultuously around them, seemed to recede only to return with new and accumulated force.

Cortés, as usual, in the front of danger, in vain endeavoured, at the head of the horse, to open a passage for the infantry. Still his men, both cavalry and foot, kept their array unbroken, offering no assailable point to their foe. A body of the Tlascalans, however, acting in concert, assaulted a soldier named Moran, one of the best riders in the troop. They succeeded in dragging him from his horse, which they despatched with a thousand blows. The Spaniards, on foot, made a desperate effort to rescue their comrade from the hands of the enemy,—and from the horrible doom of the captive. A fierce struggle now began over the body of the prostrate horse. Ten of the Spaniards were wounded, when they succeeded in retrieving the unfortunate cavalier from his assailants, but in so disastrous a plight that he died on the following day. The horse was borne off in triumph by the Indians, and his mangled remains were sent, a strange trophy, to the different towns of Tlascala. The circumstance troubled the Spanish commander, as it divested the animal of the super-natural terrors with which the superstition of the natives had usually surrounded it. To prevent such a consequence, he had caused the two horses, killed on the preceding day, to be secretly buried on the spot.

The enemy now began to give ground gradually, borne down by the riders, and trampled under the hoofs of their horses. Through the whole of this sharp encounter the Indian allies were of great service to the Spaniards. They rushed into the water, and grappled their enemies, with the desperation of men who felt that "their only safety was in the despair of safety."[1] "I see nothing but death for us," exclaimed a Cempoallan chief to Marina; "we shall never get through the pass alive." "The God of the Christians is with us," answered the intrepid woman; "and He will carry us safely through."[2]

Amidst the din of battle, the voice of Cortés was heard, cheering on his soldiers. "If we fail now," he cried, "the Cross of Christ can never be planted in the land. Forward, comrades! When was it ever known that a Castilian turned his back on a foe?"[3] Animated by the words and heroic bearing of their general, the soldiers, with desperate efforts, at

---

MS.) Clavigero, who gives a drawing of this same drum, says it is still used by the Indians, and may be heard two or three miles. Stor. del Messico, tom. ii. p. 179.

[1] "Una illis fuit spes salutis, desperâsse de salute." (P. Martyr, De Orbe Novo, dec. 1, cap. 1.) It is said with the classic energy of Tacitus.

[2] "Respondióle Marina, que no tuviese miedo, porque el Dios de los Christianos, que es muy poderoso, i los queria mucho, los sacaria de peligro." Herrera, Hist. general, dec. 2, lib. 6, cap. 5.

[3] Ibid., ubi supra.

length succeeded in forcing a passage through the dark columns of the enemy, and emerged from the defile on the open plain beyond.

Here they quickly recovered their confidence with their superiority. The horse soon opened a space for the manœuvres of the artillery. The close files of their antagonists presented a sure mark; and the thunders of the ordnance vomiting forth torrents of fire and sulphurous smoke, the wide desolation caused in their ranks and the strangely mangled carcasses of the slain, filled the barbarians with consternation and horror. They had no weapons to cope with these terrible engines, and their clumsy missiles, discharged from uncertain hands, seemed to fall ineffectual on the charmed heads of the Christians. What added to their embarrassment was, the desire to carry off the dead and wounded from the field, a general practice among the people of Anahuac, but one which necessarily exposed them, while thus employed, to still greater loss.

Eight of their principal chiefs had now fallen, and Xicotencatl, finding himself wholly unable to make head against the Spaniards in the open field, ordered a retreat. Far from the confusion of a panic-struck mob, so common among barbarians, the Tlascalan force moved off the ground with all the order of a well-disciplined army. Cortés, as on the preceding day, was too well satisfied with his present advantage to desire to follow it up. It was within an hour of sunset, and he was anxious before nightfall to secure a good position, where he might refresh his wounded troops and bivouac for the night.[1]

Gathering up his wounded, he held on his way, without loss of time, and before dusk reached a rocky eminence, called *Tzompachtepetl*, or "the hill of Tzompach." It was crowned by a sort of tower or temple, the remains of which are still visible.[2] His first care was given to the wounded, both men and horses. Fortunately, an abundance of provisions was found in some neighbouring cottages; and the soldiers, at least all who were not disabled by their injuries, celebrated the victory of the day with feasting and rejoicing.

As to the number of killed or wounded on either side, it is matter of loosest conjecture. The Indians must have suffered severely, but the practice of carrying off the dead from the field made it impossible to know to what extent. The injury sustained by the Spaniards appears to have been principally in the number of their wounded. The great object of the natives of Anahuac in their battles was to make prisoners, who might grace their triumphs and supply victims for sacrifice. To this brutal superstition the Christians were indebted, in no slight degree, for their personal preservation. To take the reports of the Conquerors, their own losses in action were always inconsiderable. But whoever has had occasion to consult the ancient chroniclers of Spain in relation to its wars

[1] Oviedo, Hist. de las Ind., MS., lib. 33, cap. 3, 45.—Ixtlilxochitl, Hist. Chich., MS., cap. 83.— Rel. Seg. de Cortés, ap. Lorenzana, p. 51.—Bernal

Diaz, Hist. de la Conquista, cap. 63.—Gomara, Crónica, cap. 40.
[2] Viaje de Cortés, ap. Lorenzana, p. ix.

with the infidel, whether Arab or American, will place little confidence in numbers.[1]

The events of the day had suggested many topics for painful reflection to Cortés. He had nowhere met with so determined a resistance within the borders of Anahuac; nowhere had he encountered native troops so formidable for their weapons, their discipline, and their valour. Far from manifesting the superstitious terrors felt by the other Indians at the strange arms and aspect of the Spaniards, the Tlascalans had boldly grappled with their enemy, and only yielded to the inevitable superiority of his military science. How important would the alliance of such a nation be in a struggle with those of their own race,—for example, with the Aztecs! But how was he to secure this alliance? Hitherto, all overtures had been rejected with disdain; and it seemed probable that every step of his progress in this populous land was to be fiercely contested. His army, especially the Indians, celebrated the events of the day with feasting and dancing, songs of merriment, and shouts of triumph. Cortés encouraged it, well knowing how important it was to keep up the spirits of his soldiers. But the sounds of revelry at length died away; and, in the still watches of the night, many an anxious thought must have crowded on the mind of the general, while his little army lay buried in slumber in its encampment around the Indian hill.

CHAPTER III.

DECISIVE VICTORY.—INDIAN COUNCIL.—NIGHT-ATTACK.——NEGOTIATIONS WITH THE ENEMY.—TLASCALAN HERO.

(1519.)

THE Spaniards were allowed to repose undisturbed the following day, and to recruit their strength after the fatigue and hard fighting of the preceding They found sufficient employment, however, in repairing and cleaning their weapons, replenishing their diminished stock of arrows, and getting everything in order for further hostilities, should the severe lesson they had inflicted on the enemy prove insufficient to discourage him. On the second day, as Cortés received no overtures from the Tlascalans, he determined to send an embassy to their camp, proposing a cessation of hostilities, and expressing his intention to visit their capital as a friend.

---

[1] According to Cortés, not a Spaniard fell—though many were wounded—in this action so fatal to the infidel! Diaz allows one. In the famous battle of Navas de Tolosa, between the Spaniards and Arabs, in 1212, equally matched in military science at that time, there were left 200,000 of the latter on the field; and, to balance this bloody roll, only five- and-twenty Christians! See the estimate in Alfonso IX.'s veracious letter, ap. Mariana (Hist. de España, lib. 2, cap. 24). The official returns of the old Castilian crusaders, whether in the Old World or the New, are scarcely more trustworthy than a French *imperial* bulletin in our day.

He selected two of the principal chiefs taken in the late engagement, as the bearers of the message.

Meanwhile, averse to leaving his men longer in a dangerous state of inaction, which the enemy might interpret as the result of timidity or exhaustion, he put himself at the head of the cavalry and such light troops as were most fit for service, and made a foray into the neighbouring country. It was a mountainous region, formed by a ramification of the great sierra of Tlascala, with verdant slopes and valleys teeming with maize and plantations of maguey, while the eminences were crowned with populous towns and villages. In one of these, he tells us, he found three thousand dwellings.[1] In some places he met with a resolute resistance, and on these occasions took ample vengeance by laying the country waste with fire and sword. After a successful inroad he returned laden with forage and provisions and driving before him several hundred Indian captives. He treated them kindly, however, when arrived in camp, endeavouring to make them understand that these acts of violence were not dictated by his own wishes, but by the unfriendly policy of their countrymen. In this way he hoped to impress the nation with the conviction of his power on the one hand, and of his amicable intentions, if met by them in the like spirit, on the other.

On reaching his quarters, he found the two envoys returned from the Tlascalan camp. They had fallen in with Xicotencatl at about two leagues' distance, where he lay encamped with a powerful force. The cacique gave them audience at the head of his troops. He told them to return with the answer, " that the Spaniards might pass on as soon as they chose to Tlascala ; and, when they reached it, their flesh would be hewn from their bodies, for sacrifice to the gods ! If they preferred to remain in their own quarters, he would pay them a visit there the next day."[2] The ambassadors added that the chief had an immense force with him, consisting of five battalions of ten thousand men each. They were the flower of the Tlascalan and Otomi warriors, assembled under the banners of their respective leaders, by command of the senate, who were resolved to try the fortunes of the state in a pitched battle and strike one decisive blow for the extermination of the invaders.[3]

This bold defiance fell heavily on the ears of the Spaniards, not prepared for so pertinacious a spirit in their enemy. They had had ample proof of

---

[1] Rel. Seg. de Cortés, ap. Lorenzana, p. 52.— Oviedo, who made free use of the manuscripts of Cortés, writes thirty-nine houses. (Hist. de las Ind., MS., lib. 33, cap. 3.) This may perhaps be explained by the sign for a thousand, in Spanish notation bearing great resemblance to the figure 9. Martyr, who had access also to the Conqueror's manuscript, confirms the larger and, *a priori*, less probable number.

[2] " Que fuessemos á su pueblo adonde está su padre, q̃ allá harian las pazes cõ hartarse de nuestras carnes, y honrar sus dioses con nuestros coraçones, y sangre, é que para otro dia de mañana

veriamos su respuesta." Bernal Diaz, Hist. de la Conquista, cap. 64.

[3] More than one writer repeats a story of the Tlascalan general sending a good supply of provisions, at this time, to the famished army of the Spaniards ; to put them in stomach, it may be, for the fight. (Gomara, Crónica, cap. 46.—Ixtlilxochitl, Hist. Chich., MS., cap. 83.) This ultra-chivalrous display from the barbarian is not very probable, and Cortés' own account of his successful foray may much better explain the abundance which reigned in his camp.

his courage and formidable prowess. They were now, in their crippled condition, to encounter him with a still more terrible array of numbers. The war, too, from the horrible fate with which it menaced the vanquished, wore a peculiarly gloomy aspect, that pressed heavily on their spirits. "We feared death," says the lion-hearted Diaz, with his usual simplicity, "for we were men." There was scarcely one in the army that did not confess himself that night to the reverend Father Olmedo, who was occupied nearly the whole of it with administering absolution, and with the other solemn offices of the Church. Armed with the blessed sacraments, the Catholic soldier lay tranquilly down to rest, prepared for any fate that might betide him under the banner of the Cross.[1]

As the battle was now inevitable, Cortés resolved to march out and meet the enemy in the field. This would have a show of confidence that might serve the double purpose of intimidating the Tlascalans and inspiriting his own men, whose enthusiasm might lose somewhat of its heat if compelled to await the assault of their antagonists, inactive in their own intrenchments. The sun rose bright on the following morning, the fifth of September 1519, an eventful day in the history of the Spanish Conquest. The general reviewed his army, and gave them, preparatory to marching, a few words of encouragement and advice. The infantry he instructed to rely on the point rather than the edge of their swords, and to endeavour to thrust their opponents through the body. The horsemen were to charge at half speed, with their lances aimed at the eyes of the Indians. The artillery, the arquebusiers, and crossbowmen were to support one another, some loading while others discharged their pieces, that there should be an unintermitted firing kept up through the action. Above all, they were to maintain their ranks close and unbroken, as on this depended their preservation.

They had not advanced a quarter of a league, when they came in sight of the Tlascalan army. Its dense array stretched far and wide over a vast plain or meadow-ground about six miles square. Its appearance justified the report which had been given of its numbers.[2] Nothing could be more picturesque than the aspect of these Indian battalions, with the naked bodies of the common soldiers gaudily painted, the fantastic helmets of the chiefs glittering with gold and precious stones, and the glowing panoplies of feather-work which decorated their persons.[3] Innumerable spears and darts, tipped with points of transparent *itztli* or fiery copper, sparkled

---

[1] Rel. Seg. de Cortés, ap. Lorenzana, p. 52.—Ixtlilxochitl, Hist. Chich., MS., cap. 83.—Gomara, Crónica, cap. 46, 47.—Oviedo, Hist. de las Ind., MS., lib. 33, cap. 3.—Bernal Diaz, Hist. de la Conquista, cap. 64.

[2] Through the magnifying lens of Cortés, there appeared to be 150,000 men (Rel. Seg., ap. Lorenzana, p. 52); a number usually preferred by succeeding writers.

[3] " Not half so gorgeous, for their May-day mirth
   All wreathed and ribanded, our youths and maids,
As these stern *Tlascalans* in war attire !

The golden glitterance, and the feather-mail
More gay than glittering gold ; and round the helm
A coronal of high upstanding plumes,
Green as the spring grass in a sunny shower ;
Or scarlet bright, as in the wintry wood
The clustered holly ; or of purple tint ;
Whereto shall that be likened ? to what gem
Indiademed, what flower, what insect's wing ?
With war-songs and wild music they came on ;
We, the while kneeling, raised with one accord
The hymn of supplication."
      Southey's Madoc, Part 1, canto 7.

bright in the morning sun, like the phosphoric gleams playing on the surface of a troubled sea, while the rear of the mighty host was dark with the shadows of banners, on which were emblazoned the armorial bearings of the great Tlascalan and Otomi chieftains.[1] Among these, the white heron on the rock, the cognizance of the house of Xicotencatl, was conspicuous, and, still more, the golden eagle with outspread wings, in the fashion of a Roman *signum*, richly ornamented with emeralds and silver-work, the great standard of the republic of Tlascala.[2]

The common file wore no covering except a girdle round the loins. Their bodies were painted with the appropriate colours of the chieftain whose banner they followed. The feather-mail of the higher class of warriors exhibited, also, a similar selection of colours for the like object, in the same manner as the colour of the tartan indicates the peculiar clan of the Highlander.[3] The caciques and principal warriors were clothed in quilted cotton tunics, two inches thick, which, fitting close to the body, protected also the thighs and the shoulders. Over these the wealthier Indians wore cuirasses of thin gold plate, or silver. Their legs were defended by leathern boots or sandals, trimmed with gold. But the most brilliant part of their costume was a rich mantle of the *plumaje* or feather-work, embroidered with curious art, and furnishing some resemblance to the gorgeous surcoat worn by the European knight over his armour in the Middle Ages. This graceful and picturesque dress was surmounted by a fantastic headpiece made of wood or leather, representing the head of some wild animal, and frequently displaying a formidable array of teeth. With this covering the warrior's head was enveloped, producing a most grotesque and hideous effect.[4] From the crown floated a splendid panache of the richly variegated plumage of the tropics, indicating, by its form and colours, the rank and family of the wearer. To complete their defensive armour, they carried shields or targets, made sometimes of wood covered with leather, but more usually of a light frame of reeds quilted with cotton, which were preferred, as tougher and less liable to fracture than the former. They had other bucklers, in which the cotton was

---

[1] The standards of the Mexicans were carried in the centre, those of the Tlascalans in the rear of the army. (Clavigero, Stor. del Messico, vol. ii. p. 145.) According to the Anonymous Conqueror, the banner-staff was attached to the back of the ensign, so that it was impossible to be torn away "Ha ogni cōpagnia il suo Alfiere con la sua insegna inhastata, et in tal modo ligata sopra le spalle, che non gli da alcun disturbo di poter combattere ne far ció che vuole, et la porta cosi ligata bene al corpo, che se nō fanno del suo corpo pezzi, non se gli puo sligare, ne torgliela mai." Rel. d'un gentil' huomo, ap. Ramusio, tom. iii. fol. 305.

[2] Camargo, Hist. de Tlascala, MS.—Herrera, Hist. general, dec. 2, lib. 6, cap. 6.—Gomara, Crónica, cap. 46.—Bernal Diaz, Hist. de la Conquista, cap. 64.—Oviedo, Hist. de las Ind., MS., lib. 33, cap. 45.—The last two authors speak of the device of "a white bird like an ostrich," as that of the republic. They have evidently confounded it with that of the Indian general. Camargo, who has given the heraldic emblems of the four great families of Tlascala, notices the white heron as that of Xicotencatl.

[3] The accounts of the Tlascalan chronicler are confirmed by the Anonymous Conqueror and by Bernal Diaz, both eyewitnesses; though the latter frankly declares that had he not seen them with his own eyes he should never have credited the existence of orders and badges among the barbarians, like those found among the civilized nations of Europe. Hist. de la Conquista, cap. 64, et alibi.—Camargo, Hist. de Tlascala, MS.—Rel. d'un gentil' huomo, ap. Ramusio, tom. iii. fol. 305.

[4] "Portano in testa," says the Anonymous Conqueror. "per difesa una cosa come teste di serpēti, ò di tigri, ò di leoni, ò di lupi, che ha le mascelle, et è la testa dell' huomo messa nella testa di q̄sto animale come se lo volesse diuorare: sono di legno, et sopra vi é la pēna, et di piastra d'oro et di pietre preciose corte, che è cosa marauigliosa da vedere." Rel. d'un gentil' huomo, ap. Ramusio, tom. iii. fol. 305.

covered with an elastic substance, enabling them to be shut up in a more compact form, like a fan or umbrella. These shields were decorated with showy ornaments, according to the taste or wealth of the wearer, and fringed with a beautiful pendant of feather-work.

Their weapons were slings, bows and arrows, javelins, and darts. They were accomplished archers, and would discharge two or even three arrows at a time. But they most excelled in throwing the javelin. One species of this, with a thong attached to it, which remained in the slinger's hand, that he might recall the weapon, was especially dreaded by the Spaniards. These various weapons were pointed with bone, or the mineral *itztli* (obsidian), the hard vitreous substance already noticed as capable of taking an edge like a razor, though easily blunted. Their spears and arrows were also frequently headed with copper. Instead of a sword, they bore a two-handed staff, about three feet and a half long, in which, at regular distances, were inserted, transversely, sharp blades of *itztli*,—a formidable weapon, which, an eyewitness assures us, he had seen fell a horse at a blow.[1]

Such was the costume of the Tlascalan warrior, and, indeed, of that great family of nations generally who occupied the plateau of Anahuac. Some parts of it, as the targets and the cotton mail or *escaupil*, as it was called in Castilian, were so excellent that they were subsequently adopted by the Spaniards, as equally effectual in the way of protection, and superior on the score of lightness and convenience to their own. They were of sufficient strength to turn an arrow or the stroke of a javelin, although impotent as a defence against firearms. But what armour is not? Yet it is probably no exaggeration to say that, in convenience, gracefulness, and strength, the arms of the Indian warrior were not very inferior to those of the polished nations of antiquity.[2]

As soon as the Castilians came in sight, the Tlascalans set up their yell of defiance, rising high above the wild barbaric minstrelsy of shell, atabal, and trumpet, with which they proclaimed their triumphant anticipations of victory over the paltry forces of the invaders. When the latter had come within bowshot, the Indians hurled a tempest of missiles, that darkened the sun for a moment as with a passing cloud, strewing the earth around with heaps of stones and arrows.[3] Slowly and steadily the little band of Spaniards held on its way amidst this arrowy shower, until it had reached what appeared the proper distance for delivering its fire with full effect. Cortés then halted, and, hastily forming his troops, opened a general well-directed fire along the whole line. Every shot bore its errand of

---

[1] "I saw one day an Indian make a thrust at the horse of a cavalier with whom he was fighting, which pierced its breast, and penetrated so deep that it immediately fell dead; and the same day I saw another Indian cut the neck of a horse, which fell dead at his feet." Rel. d'un gentil' huomo, ap. Ramusio, tom. iii. fol. 305.

[2] Particular notices of the military dress and appointments of the American tribes on the plateau may be found in Camargo, Hist. de Tlascala, MS., —Clavigero, Stor. del Messico, tom. ii. p. 101, et seq.,—Acosta, lib. 6, cap. 26,—Rel. d'un gentil' huomo, ap. Ramusio, tom. iii. fol. 305, et auct. al.

[3] "Que granizo de piedra de los honderos! Pues flechas todo el suelo hecho parva de varas todas de á dos gajos, que passan qualquiera arma, y las entrañas adonde no ay defensa." Bernal Diaz, Hist de la Conquista, cap. 65.

death; and the ranks of the Indians were mowed down faster than their comrades in the rear could carry off their bodies, according to custom, from the field. The balls in their passage through the crowded files, bearing splinters of the broken harness and mangled limbs of the warriors, scattered havoc and desolation in their path. The mob of barbarians stood petrified with dismay, till at length, galled to desperation by their intolerable suffering, they poured forth simultaneously their hideous war-shriek and rushed impetuously on the Christians.

On they came like an avalanche, or mountain torrent, shaking the solid earth and sweeping away every obstacle in its path. The little army of Spaniards opposed a bold front to the overwhelming mass. But no strength could withstand it. They faltered, gave way, were borne along before it, and their ranks were broken and thrown into disorder. It was in vain the general called on them to close again and rally. His voice was drowned by the din of fight and the fierce cries of the assailants. For a moment, it seemed that all was lost. The tide of battle had turned against them, and the fate of the Christians was sealed.

But every man had that within his bosom which spoke louder than the voice of the general. Despair gave unnatural energy to his arm. The naked body of the Indian afforded no resistance to the sharp Toledo steel; and with their good swords the Spanish infantry at length succeeded in staying the human torrent. The heavy guns from a distance thundered on the flank of the assailants, which, shaken by the iron tempest, was thrown into disorder. Their very numbers increased the confusion, as they were precipitated on the masses in front. The horse at the same moment, charging gallantly under Cortés, followed up the advantage, and at length compelled the tumultuous throng to fall back with greater precipitation and disorder than that with which they had advanced.

More than once in the course of the action a similar assault was attempted by the Tlascalans, but each time with less spirit and greater loss. They were too deficient in military science to profit by their vast superiority in numbers. They were distributed into companies, it is true, each serving under its own chieftain and banner. But they were not arranged by rank and file, and moved in a confused mass, promiscuously heaped together. They knew not how to concentrate numbers on a given point, or even how to sustain an assault, by employing successive detachments to support and relieve one another. A very small part only of their array could be brought into contact with an enemy inferior to them in amount of forces. The remainder of the army, inactive and worse than useless, in the rear, served only to press tumultuously on the advance and embarrass its movements by mere weight of numbers, while on the least alarm they were seized with a panic and threw the whole body into inextricable confusion. It was, in short, the combat of the ancient Greeks and Persians over again. Still, the great numerical superiority of the Indians might have enabled them, at a severe cost of their own lives, indeed, to wear out, in time, the constancy of the Spaniards, disabled by wounds and incessant fatigue. But, fortunately for the latter, dissensions arose among their enemies. A Tlascalan chieftain, commanding one of the great divisions, had taken umbrage at the haughty demeanour of Xicotencatl, who had charged him with misconduct or cowardice in the late action. The injured cacique challenged his rival to single combat. This did not take place. But, burning with resentment, he chose the present occasion to indulge it, by drawing off his forces, amounting to ten thousand men, from the field. He also persuaded another of the commanders to follow his example.

Thus reduced to about half his original strength, and that greatly crippled by the losses of the day, Xicotencatl could no longer maintain his ground against the Spaniards. After disputing the field with admirable courage for four hours, he retreated and resigned it to the enemy. The Spaniards were too much jaded, and too many were disabled by wounds, to allow them to pursue; and Cortés, satisfied with the decisive victory he had gained, returned in triumph to his position on the hill of Tzompach.

The number of killed in his own ranks had been very small, notwith-standing the severe loss inflicted on the enemy. These few he was careful to bury where they could not be discovered, anxious to conceal not only the amount of the slain, but the fact that the whites were mortal.[1] But very many of the men were wounded, and all the horses. The trouble of the Spaniards was much enhanced by the want of many articles important to them in their present exigency. They had neither oil nor salt, which, as before noticed, was not to be obtained in Tlascala. Their clothing, accommodated to a softer climate, was ill adapted to the rude air of the mountains; and bows and arrows, as Bernal Diaz sarcastically remarks, formed an indifferent protection against the inclemency of the weather.[2]

Still, they had much to cheer them in the events of the day; and they might draw from them a reasonable ground for confidence in their own resources, such as no other experience could have supplied. Not that the results could authorize anything like contempt for their Indian foe. Singly and with the same weapons, he might have stood his ground against the Spaniard.[3] But the success of the day established the

[1] So says Bernal Diaz; who at the same time, by the epithets *los muertos, los cuerpos,* plainly contradicts his previous boast that only one Christian fell in the fight. (Hist. de la Conquista, cap. 65.) Cortés has not the grace to acknowledge that one.

[2] Oviedo, Hist. de las Ind., MS., lib. 33, cap. 3.—Rel. Seg. de Cortés, ap. Lorenzana, p. 52.—Herrera, Hist. general, dec. 2, lib. 6, cap. 6.—Ixtlilxochitl, Hist. Chich., MS., cap. 83.—Gomara, Crónica, cap. 46.—Torquemada, Monarch. Ind., lib. 4, cap. 32.—Bernal Diaz, Hist. de la Conquista, cap. 65, 66.—The warm, chivalrous glow of feeling which colours the rude composition of the last chronicler makes him a better painter than his more correct and

classical rivals. And, if there is somewhat too much of the self-complacent tone of the *quorum pars magna fui* in his writing, it may be pardoned in the hero of more than a hundred battles and almost as many wounds.

[3] The Anonymous Conqueror bears emphatic testimony to the valour of the Indians, specifying instances in which he had seen a single warrior defend himself for a long time against two, three, and even four Spaniards! "Sono fra loro di valētissimi huomini et che ossano morir ostinatissimamēte. Et io ho veduto un d' essi difendersi valētemente da duoi cavalli leggieri, et un altro da tre, et quattro." Rel. d' un gentil' huomo, ap. Ramusio, tom. iii. fol. 305.

superiority of science and discipline over mere physical courage and numbers. It was fighting over again, as we have said, the old battle of the European and the Asiatic. But the handful of Greeks who routed the hosts of Xerxes and Darius, it must be remembered, had not so obvious an advantage on the score of weapons as was enjoyed by the Spaniards in these wars. The use of firearms gave an ascendency which cannot easily be estimated; one so great, that a contest between nations equally civilized, which should be similar in all other respects to that between the Spaniards and the Tlascalans, would probably be attended with a similar issue. To all this must be added the effect produced by the cavalry. The nations of Anahuac had no large domesticated animals, and were unacquainted with any beast of burden. Their imaginations were bewildered when they beheld the strange apparition of the horse and his rider moving in unison and obedient to one impulse, as if possessed of a common nature; and as they saw the terrible animal, with his " neck clothed in thunder," bearing down their squadrons and trampling them in the dust, no wonder they should have regarded him with the mysterious terror felt for a supernatural being. A very little reflection on the manifold grounds of superiority, both moral and physical, possessed by the Spaniards in this contest, will surely explain the issue, without any disparagement to the courage or capacity of their opponents.[1]

Cortés, thinking the occasion favourable, followed up the important blow he had struck by a new mission to the capital, bearing a message of similar import with that recently sent to the camp. But the senate was not yet sufficiently humbled. The late defeat caused, indeed, general consternation. Maxixcatzin, one of the four great lords who presided over the republic, reiterated with greater force the arguments before urged by him for embracing the proffered alliance of the strangers. The armies of the state had been beaten too often to allow any reasonable hope of successful resistance; and he enlarged on the generosity shown by the politic Conqueror to his prisoners—so unusual in Anahuac—as an additional motive for an alliance with men who knew how to be friends as well as foes.

But in these views he was overruled by the war-party, whose animosity was sharpened, rather than subdued, by the late discomfiture. Their hostile feelings were further exasperated by the younger Xicotencatl, who burned for an opportunity to retrieve his disgrace, and to wipe away the stain which had fallen for the first time on the arms of the republic.

In their perplexity they called in the assistance of the priests, whose authority was frequently invoked in the deliberations of the American chiefs. The latter inquired, with some simplicity, of these interpreters of fate, whether the strangers were supernatural beings, or men of flesh and blood like themselves. The priests, after some consultation, are said to

---

[1] The appalling effect of the cavalry on the natives reminds one of the confusion into which the Roman legions were thrown by the strange appearance of the elephants in their first engagements with Pyrrhus, as told by Plutarch in his life of that prince.

have made the strange answer that the Spaniards, though not gods, were
children of the Sun, that they derived their strength from that luminary,
and when his beams were withdrawn their powers would also fail. They
recommended a night-attack, therefore, as one which afforded the best
chance of success. This apparently childish response may have had in
it more of cunning than credulity. It was not improbably suggested by
Xicotencatl himself, or by the caciques in his interest, to reconcile the
people to a measure which was contrary to the military usages—indeed, it
may be said, to the public law—of Anahuac. Whether the fruit of artifice
or superstition, it prevailed ; and the Tlascalan general was empowered,
at the head of a detachment of ten thousand warriors, to try the effect
of an assault by night on the Christian camp.

The affair was conducted with such secrecy that it did not reach the
ears of the Spaniards. But their general was not one who allowed himself,
sleeping or waking, to be surprised on his post. Fortunately, the night
appointed was illumined by the full beams of an autumnal moon ; and
one of the vedettes perceived by its light, at a considerable distance, a
large body of Indians moving towards the Christian lines. He was not
slow in giving the alarm to the garrison.

The Spaniards slept, as has been said, with their arms by their side ;
while their horses, picketed near them, stood ready saddled, with the
bridle hanging at the bow. In five minutes the whole camp was under
arms ; when they beheld the dusky columns of the Indians cautiously
advancing over the plain, their heads just peering above the tall maize
with which the land was partially covered. Cortés determined not to
abide the assault in his intrenchments, but to sally out and pounce on
the enemy when he had reached the bottom of the hill.

Slowly and stealthily the Indians advanced, while the Christian camp,
hushed in profound silence, seemed to them buried in slumber. But no
sooner had they reached the slope of the rising ground than they were
astounded by the deep battle-cry of the Spaniards, followed by the
instantaneous apparition of the whole army, as they sallied forth from the
works and poured down the sides of the hill. Brandishing aloft their
weapons, they seemed to the troubled fancies of the Tlascalans like so
many spectres or demons hurrying to and fro in mid-air, while the uncertain
light magnified their numbers and expanded the horse and his rider into
gigantic and unearthly dimensions.

Scarcely awaiting the shock of their enemy, the panic-struck barbarians
let off a feeble volley of arrows, and, offering no other resistance, fled
rapidly and tumultuously across the plain. The horse easily overtook the
fugitives, riding them down and cutting them to pieces without mercy,
until Cortés, weary with slaughter, called off his men, leaving the field
loaded with the bloody trophies of victory.[1]

[1] Rel. Seg. de Cortés, ap. Lorenzana, pp. 53, 54. | P. Martyr, De Orbe Novo, dec. 2, cap. 2.—Torque-
—Oviedo, Hist. de las Ind., MS., lib. 33, cap. 3.— | mada, Monarch. Ind., lib. 4, cap. 32.—Herrera,

The next day, the Spanish commander, with his usual policy after a decisive blow had been struck, sent a new embassy to the Tlascalan capital. The envoys received their instructions through the interpreter, Marina. That remarkable woman had attracted general admiration by the constancy and cheerfulness with which she endured all the privations of the camp. Far from betraying the natural weakness and timidity of her sex, she had shrunk from no hardship herself, and had done much to fortify the drooping spirits of the soldiers ; while her sympathies, whenever occasion offered, had been actively exerted in mitigating the calamities of her Indian countrymen.[1]

Through his faithful interpreter, Cortés communicated the terms of his message to the Tlascalan envoys. He made the same professions of amity as before, promising oblivion of all past injuries ; but if this proffer were rejected, he would visit their capital as a conqueror, raze every house in it to the ground, and put every inhabitant to the sword ! He then dismissed the ambassadors with the symbolical presents of a letter in one hand and an arrow in the other.

The envoys obtained respectful audience from the council of Tlascala, whom they found plunged in deep dejection by their recent reverses. The failure of the night-attack had extinguished every spark of hope in their bosoms. Their armies had been beaten again and again, in the open field and in secret ambush. Stratagem and courage, all their resources, had alike proved ineffectual against a foe whose hand was never weary and whose eye was never closed. Nothing remained but to submit. They selected four principal caciques, whom they intrusted with a mission to the Christian camp. They were to assure the strangers of a free passage through the country, and a friendly reception in the capital. The proffered friendship of the Spaniards was cordially embraced, with many awkward excuses for the past. The envoys were to touch at the Tlascalan camp on their way, and inform Xicotencatl of their proceedings. They were to require him, at the same time, to abstain from all further hostilities and to furnish the white men with an ample supply of provisions.

But the Tlascalan deputies, on arriving at the quarters of that chief, did not find him in the humour to comply with these instructions. His repeated collisions with the Spaniards, or, it may be, his constitutional courage, left him inaccessible to the vulgar terrors of his countrymen. He regarded the strangers not as supernatural beings, but as men like himself. The animosity of a warrior had rankled into a deadly hatred from the mortifications he had endured at their hands, and his head teemed with plans for recovering his fallen honours and for taking vengeance on the invaders of his country. He refused to disband any of the force, still

Hist. general, dec. 2, lib. 6, cap. 8.—Bernal Diaz, Hist. de la Conquista, cap. 66.

[1] "Though she heard them every day talk of killing us and eating our flesh, though she had seen us surrounded in past battles, and knew that we were now all of us wounded and suffering, yet we never saw any weakness in her, but a courage far beyond that of woman." Bernal Diaz, Hist. de la Conquista, cap. 66.

formidable, under his command, or to send supplies to the enemy's camp. He further induced the ambassadors to remain in his quarters and relinquish their visit to the Spaniards. The latter, in consequence, were kept in ignorance of the movements in their favour which had taken place in the Tlascalan capital.[1]

The conduct of Xicotencatl is condemned by Castilian writers as that of a ferocious and sanguinary barbarian. It is natural they should so regard it. But those who have no national prejudice to warp their judgments may come to a different conclusion. They may find much to admire in that high, unconquerable spirit, like some proud column standing alone in its majesty amidst the fragments and ruins around it. They may see evidences of a clear-sighted sagacity, which, piercing the thin veil of insidious friendship proffered by the Spaniards, and penetrating the future, discerned the coming miseries of his country ; the noble patriotism of one who would rescue that country at any cost, and, amidst the gathering darkness, would infuse his own intrepid spirit into the hearts of his nation, to animate them to a last struggle for independence.

CHAPTER IV.

DISCONTENTS IN THE ARMY.— TLASCALAN SPIES.— PEACE WITH THE REPUBLIC.—EMBASSY FROM MONTEZUMA.

(1519.)

DESIROUS to keep up the terror of the Castilian name by leaving the enemy no respite, Cortés, on the same day that he despatched the embassy to Tlascala, put himself at the head of a small corps of cavalry and light troops to scour the neighbouring country. He was at that time so ill from fever, aided by medical treatment,[2] that he could hardly keep his seat in the saddle. It was a rough country, and the sharp winds from the frosty summits of the mountains pierced the scanty covering of the troops and chilled both men and horses. Four or five of the animals gave out, and the general, alarmed for their safety, sent them back to the camp. The soldiers, discouraged by this ill omen, would have persuaded him to return. But he made answer,. "We fight under the banner of the Cross ; God is stronger than nature," [3] and continued his march.

It led through the same kind of checkered scenery of rugged hill and

---

[1] Bernal Diaz, Hist. de la Conquista, cap. 67.— Camargo, Hist. de Tlascala, MS.—Ixtlilxochitl, Hist. Chich., MS., cap. 83.

[2] The effect of the medicine—though rather a severe dose, according to the precise Diaz—was suspended during the general's active exertions. Gomara, however, does not consider this a miracle.

(Crónica, cap. 49.) Father Sandoval does. (Hist. de Cárlos Quinto, tom. i. p. 127.) Solís, after a conscientious inquiry into this perplexing matter, decides—strange as it may seem—against the father! Conquista, lib. 2, cap. 20.

[3] "Dios es sobre natura." Rel. Seg. de Cortés, ap. Lorenzana, p. 54.

cultivated plain as that already described, well covered with towns and villages, some of them the frontier posts occupied by the Otomies. Practising the Roman maxim of lenity to the submissive foe, he took full vengeance on those who resisted, and, as resistance too often occurred, marked his path with fire and desolation. After a short absence, he returned in safety, laden with the plunder of a successful foray. It would have been more honourable to him had it been conducted with less rigour. The excesses are imputed by Bernal Diaz to the Indian allies, whom in the heat of victory it was found impossible to restrain.[1] On whose head soever they fall, they seem to have given little uneasiness to the general, who declares in his letter to the emperor Charles the Fifth, " As we fought under the standard of the Cross,[2] for the true Faith, and the service of your Highness, Heaven crowned our arms with such success that, while multitudes of the infidel were slain, little loss was suffered by the Castilians."[3] The Spanish Conquerors, to judge from their writings, unconscious of any worldly motive lurking in the bottom of their hearts, regarded themselves as soldiers of the Church, fighting the great battle of Christianity, and in the same edifying and comfortable light are regarded by most of the national historians of a later day.[4]

On his return to the camp, Cortés found a new cause of disquietude, in discontents which had broken out among the soldiery. Their patience was exhausted by a life of fatigue and peril to which there seemed to be no end. The battles they had won against such tremendous odds had not advanced them a jot. The idea of their reaching Mexico, says the old soldier so often quoted, " was treated as a jest by the whole army ; "[5] and the indefinite prospect of hostilities with the ferocious people among whom they were now cast threw a deep gloom over their spirits.

Among the malcontents were a number of noisy, vapouring persons, such as are found in every camp, who, like empty bubbles, are sure to rise to the surface and make themselves seen in seasons of agitation. They were, for the most part, of the old faction of Velasquez, and had estates in Cuba, to which they turned many a wistful glance as they receded more and more from the coast. They now waited on the general, not in

[1] Hist. de la Conquista, cap. 64.—Not so Cortés, who says, boldly, "I burned more than ten towns." (Ibid., p. 52.) His reverend commentator specifies the localities of the Indian towns destroyed by him in his forays. Viaje, ap. Lorenzana, pp. ix.–xi.

[2] [Lorenzana speaks of two standards as borne by Cortés in the Conquest, one having the image of the Virgin emblazoned on it, the other that of the Cross. It may be the latter which is still preserved in the Museum of Artillery at Madrid. (Rel. Seg. de Cortés, ap. Lorenzana, p. 52, nota.) In a letter written to me from that capital, a few years since, by my friend Mr. George Summer, he remarks, "In Madrid, in the Museum of Artillery, is a small mahogany box, about a foot square, locked and sealed, which contains, as the inscription shows it states, the *pendon* which Hernan Cortés carried to the conquest of Mexico. On applying to the Brigadier Leon de Palacio, the director of the museum, he was so kind as not only to order this to be opened, but to come himself with me to examine it. The standard is probably the same which Lorenzana, in 1770, speaks of as being then in the Secretario de Gobierno. It is of red Damascus silk, and has marks of the painting once upon it, but is now completely in rags."]

[3] "É como trayamos la Bandera de la Cruz, y puñabamos por nuestra Fe, y por servicio de Vuestra Sacra Magestad, en su muy Real ventura nos dió Dios tanta victoria, que les matámos mucha gente, sin que los nuestros recibiessen daño." Rel. Seg. de Cortés, ap. Lorenzana, p. 52.

[4] "It was a notable thing," exclaims Herrera, "to see with what humility and devotion all returned praising God, who gave them victories so miraculously, by which it was clearly apparent that they were favoured with the divine assistance."

[5] "Porque entrar en México, teníamoslo por cosa de risa, á causa de sus grandes fuerças." Bernal Diaz, Hist. de la Conquista, cap. 66.

a mutinous spirit of resistance (for they remembered the lesson in Villa Rica), but with the design of frank expostulation, as with a brother adventurer in a common cause.[1] The tone of familiarity thus assumed was eminently characteristic of the footing of equality on which the parties in the expedition stood with one another.

Their sufferings, they told him, were too great to be endured. All the men had received one, most of them two or three wounds. More than fifty had perished, in one way or another, since leaving Vera Cruz. There was no beast of burden but led a life preferable to theirs. For, when the night came, the former could rest from his labours; but they, fighting or watching, had no rest, day nor night. As to conquering Mexico, the very thought of it was madness. If they had encountered such opposition from the petty republic of Tlascala, what might they not expect from the great Mexican empire? There was now a temporary suspension of hostilities. They should avail themselves of it to retrace their steps to Vera Cruz. It is true, the fleet there was destroyed; and by this act, unparalleled for rashness even in Roman annals, the general had become responsible for the fate of the whole army. Still there was one vessel left. That might be despatched to Cuba for reinforcements and supplies; and, when these arrived, they would be enabled to resume operations with some prospect of success.

Cortés listened to this singular expostulation with perfect composure. He knew his men, and, instead of rebuke or harsher measures, replied in the same frank and soldier-like vein which they had affected.

There was much truth, he allowed, in what they said. The sufferings of the Spaniards had been great; greater than those recorded of any heroes in Greek or Roman story. So much the greater would be their glory. He had often been filled with admiration as he had seen his little host encircled by myriads of barbarians, and felt that no people but Spaniards could have triumphed over such formidable odds. Nor could they, unless the arm of the Almighty had been over them. And they might reasonably look for his protection hereafter; for was it not in his cause they were fighting? They had encountered dangers and difficulties, it was true. But they had not come here expecting a life of idle dalliance and pleasure. Glory, as he had told them at the outset, was to be won only by toil and danger. They would do him the justice to acknowledge that he had never shrunk from his share of both. This was a truth, adds the honest chronicler who heard and reports the dialogue, which no one could deny. But, if they had met with hardships, he continued, they had been everywhere victorious. Even now they were enjoying the fruits of this, in the plenty which reigned in the camp. And they would soon see the

---

[1] Diaz indignantly disclaims the idea of mutiny, which Gomara attached to this proceeding. "What they said to him was by way of counsel, and because they believed it were well said, and not with any other intent, since they followed him ever, bravely and loyally; nor is it strange that in an army some good soldiers should offer counsel to their captain, especially when such hardships have been endured as were by us." Hist. de la Conquista, cap. 71.

Tlascalans, humbled by their late reverses, suing for peace on any terms. To go back now was impossible. The very stones would rise up against them. The Tlascalans would hunt them in triumph down to the water's edge. And how would the Mexicans exult at this miserable issue of their vainglorious vaunts! Their former friends would become their enemies; and the Totonacs, to avert the vengeance of the Aztecs, from which the Spaniards could no longer shield them, would join in the general cry. There was no alternative, then, but to go forward in their career. And he besought them to silence their pusillanimous scruples, and, instead of turning their eyes towards Cuba, to fix them on Mexico, the great object of their enterprise.

While this singular conference was going on, many other soldiers had gathered round the spot; and the discontented party, emboldened by the presence of their comrades, as well as by the general's forbearance, replied that they were far from being convinced. Another such victory as the last would be their ruin. They were going to Mexico only to be slaughtered. Until, at length, the general's patience being exhausted, he cut the argument short, by quoting a verse from an old song, implying that it was better to die with honour than to live disgraced,—a sentiment which was loudly echoed by the greater part of his audience, who, notwithstanding their occasional murmurs, had no design to abandon the expedition, still less the commander to whom they were passionately devoted. The malcontents, disconcerted by this rebuke, slunk back to their own quarters, muttering half-smothered execrations on the leader who had projected the enterprise, the Indians who had guided him, and their own countrymen who supported him in it.[1]

Such were the difficulties that lay in the path of Cortés: a wily and ferocious enemy; a climate uncertain, often unhealthy; illness in his own person, much aggravated by anxiety as to the manner in which his conduct would be received by his sovereign; last, not least, disaffection among his soldiers, on whose constancy and union he rested for the success of his operations,—the great lever by which he was to overturn the empire of Montezuma.

On the morning following this event, the camp was surprised by the appearance of a small body of Tlascalans, decorated with badges, the white colour of which intimated peace. They brought a quantity of provisions, and some trifling ornaments, which, they said, were sent by the Tlascalan general, who was weary of the war and desired an accommodation with the Spaniards. He would soon present himself to arrange this in person. The intelligence diffused general joy, and the emissaries received a friendly welcome.

---

[1] This conference is reported, with some variety, indeed, by nearly every historian. (Rel. Seg. de Cortés, ap. Lorenzana, p. 55.—Oviedo, Hist. de las Ind., MS., lib. 33, cap. 3.—Gomara, Crónica, cap. 51 52.—Ixtlilxochitl, Hist. Chich., MS., cap. 80.— Herrera, Hist. general, dec. 2, lib. 6, cap. 9.—P. Martyr, De Orbe Novo, dec. 5, cap. 2.) I have abridged the account given by Bernal Diaz, one of the audience, though not one of the parties to the dialogue,—for that reason the better authority.

A day or two elapsed, and, while a few of the party left the Spanish quarters, the others, about fifty in number, who remained, excited some distrust in the bosom of Marina. She communicated her suspicions to Cortés that they were spies. He caused several of them, in consequence, to be arrested, examined them separately, and ascertained that they were employed by Xicotencatl to inform him of the state of the Christian camp, preparatory to a meditated assault, for which he was mustering his forces. Cortés, satisfied of the truth of this, determined to make such an example of the delinquents as should intimidate his enemy from repeating the attempt. He ordered their hands to be cut off, and in that condition sent them back to their countrymen, with the message "that the Tlascalans might come by day or night; they would find the Spaniards ready for them." [1]

The doleful spectacle of their comrades returning in this mutilated state filled the Indian camp with horror and consternation. The haughty crest of their chief was humbled. From that moment he lost his wonted buoyancy and confidence. His soldiers, filled with superstitious fear, refused to serve longer against a foe who could read their very thoughts and divine their plans before they were ripe for execution. [2]

The punishment inflicted by Cortés may well shock the reader by its brutality. But it should be considered, in mitigation, that the victims of it were spies, and, as such, by the laws of war, whether among civilized or savage nations, had incurred the penalty of death. The amputation of the limbs was a milder punishment, and reserved for inferior offences. If we revolt at the barbarous nature of the sentence, we should reflect that it was no uncommon one at that day; not more uncommon, indeed, than whipping and branding with a hot iron were in our own country at the beginning of the present century, or than cropping the ears was in the preceding one. A higher civilization, indeed, rejects such punishments, as pernicious in themselves, and degrading to humanity. But in the sixteenth century they were openly recognized by the laws of the most polished nations in Europe. And it is too much to ask of any man, still less one bred to the iron trade of war, to be in advance of the refinement of his age. We may be content if, in circumstances so unfavourable to humanity, he does not fall below it.

All thoughts of further resistance being abandoned, the four delegates of the Tlascalan republic were now allowed to proceed on their mission. They were speedily followed by Xicotencatl himself, attended by a numerous train of military retainers. As they drew near the Spanish lines, they were easily recognized by the white and yellow colours of their

---

[1] Diaz says only seventeen lost their hands, the rest their thumbs. (Hist. de la Conquista, cap. 70.) Cortés does not flinch from confessing, the hands of the whole fifty : "I ordered that all the fifty should have their hands cut off ; and I sent them to tell their lord that let him come when he would, by night or day, they should see who we were." Rel. Seg. de Cortés, ap. Lorenzana, p. 53.

[2] "De que los Tlascaltecas se admiráron, entendiendo que Cortés les entendia sus pensamientos." Ixtlilxochitl, Hist. Chich., MS., cap. 83.

uniforms, the livery of the house of Titcala. The joy of the army was great at this sure intimation of the close of hostilities; and it was with difficulty that Cortes was enabled to restore the men to tranquillity and the assumed indifference which it was proper to maintain in presence of an enemy.

The Spaniards gazed with curious eye on the valiant chief who had so long kept his enemies at bay, and who now advanced with the firm and fearless step of one who was coming rather to bid defiance than to sue for peace. He was rather above the middle size, with broad shoulders, and a muscular frame intimating great activity and strength. His head was large, and his countenance marked with the lines of hard service rather than of age, for he was but thirty-five. When he entered the presence of Cortés, he made the usual salutation by touching the ground with his hand and carrying it to his head; while the sweet incense of aromatic gums rolled up in clouds from the censers carried by his slaves.

Far from a pusillanimous attempt to throw the blame on the senate, he assumed the whole responsibility of the war. He had considered the white men, he said, as enemies, for they came with the allies and vassals of Montezuma. He loved his country, and wished to preserve the independence which she had maintained through her long wars with the Aztecs. He had been beaten. They might be the strangers who, it had been so long predicted, would come from the east, to take possession of the country. He hoped they would use their victory with moderation, and not trample on the liberties of the republic. He came now in the name of his nation, to tender their obedience to the Spaniards, assuring them they would find his countrymen as faithful in peace as they had been firm in war.

Cortés, far from taking umbrage, was filled with admiration at the lofty spirit which thus disdained to stoop beneath misfortunes. The brave man knows how to respect bravery in another. He assumed, however, a severe aspect, as he rebuked the chief for having so long persisted in hostilities. Had Xicotencatl believed the word of the Spaniards, and accepted their proffered friendship sooner, he would have spared his people much suffering, which they well merited by their obstinacy. But it was impossible, continued the general, to retrieve the past. He was willing to bury it in oblivion, and to receive the Tlascalans as vassals to the emperor, his master. If they proved true, they should find him a sure column of support; if false, he would take such vengeance on them as he had intended to take on their capital had they not speedily given in their submission. It proved an ominous menace for the chief to whom it was addressed.

The cacique then ordered his slaves to bring forward some trifling ornaments of gold and feather-embroidery, designed as presents. They were of little value, he said, with a smile, for the Tlascalans were poor. They had little gold, not even cotton, nor salt. The Aztec emperor had left them nothing but their freedom and their arms. He offered this gift only as a token of his goodwill. "As such I receive it," answered Cortés, "and, coming from the Tlascalans, set more value on it than I should from any other source, though it were a house full of gold ; " — a politic as well as magnanimous reply, for it was by the aid of this goodwill that he was to win the gold of Mexico.[1]

Thus ended the bloody war with the fierce republic of Tlascala, during the course of which the fortunes of the Spaniards more than once had trembled in the balance. Had it been persevered in but a little longer, it must have ended in their confusion and ruin, exhausted as they were by wounds, watching, and fatigues, with the seeds of disaffection rankling among themselves. As it was, they came out of the fearful contest with untarnished glory. To the enemy they seemed invulnerable, bearing charmed lives, proof alike against the accidents of fortune and the assaults of man. No wonder that they indulged a similar conceit in their own bosoms, and that the humblest Spaniard should have fancied himself the subject of a special interposition of Providence, which shielded him in the hour of battle and reserved him for a higher destiny.

While the Tlascalans were still in the camp, an embassy was announced from Montezuma. Tidings of the exploits of the Spaniards had spread far and wide over the plateau. The emperor, in particular, had watched every step of their progress, as they climbed the steeps of the Cordilleras and advanced over the broad table-land on their summit. He had seen them, with great satisfaction, take the road to Tlascala, trusting that, if they were mortal men, they would find their graves there. Great was his dismay when courier after courier brought him intelligence of their successes, and that the most redoubtable warriors on the plateau had been scattered like chaff by the swords of this handful of strangers.

His superstitious fears returned in full force. He saw in the Spaniards "the men of destiny," who were to take possession of his sceptre. In his alarm and uncertainty, he sent a new embassy to the Christian camp. It consisted of five great nobles of his court, attended by a train of two hundred slaves. They brought with them a present, as usual, dictated partly by fear and in part by the natural munificence of his disposition. It consisted of three thousand ounces of gold, in grains, or in various manufactured articles, with several hundred mantles and dresses of embroidered cotton and the picturesque feather-work. As they laid these at the feet of Cortés, they told him they had come to offer the congratulations of their master on the late victories of the white men. The emperor only regretted that it would not be in his power to receive them in his capital, where the numerous population was so unruly that their safety would be placed in jeopardy. The mere intimation of the Aztec emperor's wishes, in the

---

[1] Rel. Seg. de Cortés, ap. Lorenzana, pp. 56, 57. —Oviedo, Hist. de las Ind., MS., lib. 33, cap. 3.— Gomara, Crónica, cap. 53.—Bernal Diaz, Hist. de la Conquista, cap. 71, et seq.—Sahagun, Hist. de Nueva-España, MS., lib. 12, cap. 11.

most distant way, would have sufficed with the Indian nations. It had very little weight with the Spaniards; and the envoys, finding this puerile expression of them ineffectual, resorted to another argument, offering a tribute in their master's name to the Castilian sovereign, provided the Spaniards would relinquish their visit to his capital. This was a greater error: it was displaying the rich casket with one hand which he was unable to defend with the other. Yet the author of this pusillanimous policy, the unhappy victim of superstition, was a monarch renowned among the Indian nations for his intrepidity and enterprise,—the terror of Anahuac!

Cortés, while he urged his own sovereign's commands as a reason for disregarding the wishes of Montezuma, uttered expressions of the most profound respect for the Aztec prince, and declared that if he had not the means of requiting his munificence, as he could wish, at present, he trusted *to repay him, at some future day, with good works!* [1]

The Mexican ambassadors were not much gratified with finding the war at an end, and a reconciliation established between their mortal enemies and the Spaniards. The mutual disgust of the two parties with each other was too strong to be repressed even in the presence of the general, who saw with satisfaction the evidences of a jealousy which, undermining the strength of the Indian emperor, was to prove the surest source of his own success. [2]

Two of the Aztec envoys returned to Mexico, to acquaint their sovereign with the state of affairs in the Spanish camp. The others remained with the army, Cortés being willing that they should be personal spectators of the deference shown him by the Tlascalans. Still he did not hasten his departure for their capital. Not that he placed reliance on the injurious intimations of the Mexicans respecting their good faith. Yet he was willing to put this to some longer trial, and at the same time to re-establish his own health more thoroughly before his visit. Meanwhile, messengers daily arrived from the city, pressing his journey, and were finally followed by some of the aged rulers of the republic, attended by a numerous retinue, impatient of his long delay. They brought with them a body of five hundred *tamanes*, or *men of burden*, to drag his cannon and relieve his own forces from this fatiguing part of their duty. It was impossible to defer his departure longer; and after mass, and a solemn thanksgiving to the great Being who had crowned their arms with triumph, the Spaniards bade adieu to the quarters which they had occupied for nearly three weeks on the hill of Tzompach. The strong tower, or *teocalli*, which commanded it,

---

[1] "Cortés recibió con alegría aquel presente, y dixo que se lo tenia en merced, y que él lo pagaria al señor Monteçuma en buenas obras." Bernal Diaz, Hist. de la Conquista, cap. 73.

[2] He dwells on it in his letter to the emperor. "Seeing the discord and division between them, I felt not a little pleasure, for it appeared to me to suit well with my design, and that through this means I might the more easily subjugate them. Moreover I remembered a text of the Evangelist, which says, 'Every kingdom divided against itself is brought to desolation.' I treated therefore with both parties, and thanked each in secret for the intelligence it had given me, professing to regard it with greater friendship than the other." Rel. Seg. de Cortés, ap. Lorenzana, p. 61.

was called, in commemoration of their residence, "the tower of victory;" and the few stones which still survive of its ruins point out to the eye of the traveller a spot ever memorable in history for the courage and constancy of the early Conquerors.[1]

CHAPTER V.

SPANIARDS ENTER TLASCALA.—DESCRIPTION OF THE CAPITAL.—ATTEMPTED CONVERSION.—AZTEC EMBASSY.—INVITED TO CHOLULA.

(1519.)

THE city of Tlascala, the capital of the republic of the same name, lay at the distance of about six leagues from the Spanish camp. The road led into a hilly region, exhibiting in every arable patch of ground the evidence of laborious cultivation. Over a deep *barranca*, or ravine, they crossed on a bridge of stone, which, according to tradition,—a slippery authority,—is the same still standing, and was constructed originally for the passage of the army.[2] They passed some considerable towns on their route, where they experienced a full measure of Indian hospitality. As they advanced, the approach to a populous city was intimated by the crowds who flocked out to see and welcome the strangers; men and women in their picturesque dresses, with bunches and wreaths of roses, which they gave to the Spaniards, or fastened to the necks and caparisons of their horses, in the same manner as at Cempoalla. Priests, with their white robes, and long matted tresses floating over them, mingled in the crowd, scattering volumes of incense from their burning censers. In this way the multitudinous and motley procession defiled through the gates of the ancient capital of Tlascala. It was the twenty-third of September 1519, the anniversary of which is still celebrated by the inhabitants as a day of jubilee.[3]

The press was now so great that it was with difficulty the police of the city could clear a passage for the army; while the *azoteas*, or flat terraced roofs of the buildings, were covered with spectators, eager to catch a glimpse of the wonderful strangers. The houses were hung with festoons

---

[1] Herrera, Hist. general, dec. 2, lib. 6, cap. 10.—Oviedo, Hist. de las Ind., MS., lib. 33, cap. 4.—Gomara, Crónica, cap. 54.—Martyr, De Orbe Novo, dec. 5, cap. 2.—Bernal Diaz, Hist. de la Conquista, cap. 72-74.—Ixtlilxochitl, Hist. Chich., MS., cap. 83.

[2] "Á distancia de un quarto de legua caminando á esta dicha ciudad se encuentra una barranca honda, que tiene para pasar *un Puente de cal y canto de bóveda*, y es tradicion en el pueblo de San Salvador, que se hizo en aquellos dias, que estubo allí Cortés para que pase." (Viaje, ap. Lorenzana, p. xi.) If the antiquity of this *arched* stone bridge could be established, it would settle a point much mooted in respect to Indian architecture. But the construction of so solid a work in so short a time is a fact requiring a better voucher than the villagers of San Salvador.

[3] Clavigero, Stor. del Messico, tom. iii. p. 53.—"Recibimiento el mas solene y famoso que en el mundo se ha visto," exclaims the enthusiastic historian of the republic. He adds that "more than a hundred thousand men flocked out to receive the Spaniards; a thing that appears impossible," *que parece cosa imposible!* It does indeed. Camargo Hist. de Tlascala, MS.

of flowers, and arches of verdant boughs, intertwined with roses and honey-suckle, were thrown across the streets. The whole population abandoned itself to rejoicing; and the air was rent with songs and shouts of triumph, mingled with the wild music of the national instruments, that might have excited apprehensions in the breasts of the soldiery had they not gathered their peaceful import from the assurance of Marina and the joyous counte-nances of the natives.

With these accompaniments, the procession moved along the principal streets to the mansion of Xicotencatl, the aged father of the Tlascalan general, and one of the four rulers of the republic. Cortés dismounted from his horse to receive the old chieftain's embrace. He was nearly blind, and satisfied, as far as he could, a natural curiosity respecting the person of the Spanish general, by passing his hand over his features. He then led the way to a spacious hall in his palace, where a banquet was served to the army. In the evening they were shown to their quarters, in the buildings and open ground surrounding one of the principal *teocallis;* while the Mexican ambassadors, at the desire of Cortés, had apartments assigned them next to his own, that he might the better watch over their safety in this city of their enemies.[1]

Tlascala was one of the most important and populous towns on the table-land. Cortés, in his letter to the emperor, compares it to Granada, affirming that it was larger, stronger, and more populous than the Moorish capital at the time of the conquest, and quite as well built.[2] But, notwith-standing we are assured by a most respectable writer at the close of the last century that its remains justify the assertion,[3] we shall be slow to believe that its edifices could have rivalled those monuments of Oriental magnificence, whose light aerial forms still survive after the lapse of ages, the admiration of every traveller of sensibility and taste. The truth is, that Cortés, like Columbus, saw objects through the warm medium of his own fond imagination, giving them a higher tone of colouring and larger dimensions than were strictly warranted by the fact. It was natural that the man who had made such rare discoveries should unconsciously magnify their merits to his own eyes and to those of others.

The houses were built, for the most part, of mud or earth; the better sort of stone and lime, or bricks dried in the sun. They were unprovided with doors or windows, but in the apertures for the former hung mats fringed with pieces of copper or something which, by its tinkling sound, would give notice of any one's entrance. The streets were narrow and dark. The population must have been considerable, if, as Cortés asserts,

---

1 Sahagun, Hist. de Nueva-España, MS., lib. 12, cap. 11.—Rel. Seg. de Cortés, ap. Lorenzana, p. 59.—Camargo, Hist. de Tlascala, MS.—Gomara, Crónica, cap. 54.—Herrera, Hist. general, dec. 2, lib. 6, cap. 11.

2 "La qual ciudad es tan grande, y de tanta admiracion, que aunque mucho de lo, que de ella podria decir, dexe, lo poco que diré creo es casi increible, porque es muy mayor que Granada, y muy mas fuerte, y de tan buenos Edificios, y de muy mucha mas gente, que Granada tenia al tiempo que se ganó." Rel. Seg. de Cortés, ap. Lorenzana, p. 58.

3 "En las Ruinas, que aun hoy se vén en Tlax-cala, se conoce, que no es ponderacion." Rel. Seg. de Cortés, p. 58. Nota del editor, Lorenzana.

thirty thousand souls were often gathered in the market on a public day. These meetings were a sort of fairs, held, as usual, in all the great towns, every fifth day, and attended by the inhabitants of the adjacent country, who brought there for sale every description of domestic produce and manufacture with which they were acquainted. They peculiarly excelled in pottery, which was considered as equal to the best in Europe.[1] It is a further proof of civilized habits that the Spaniards found barbers' shops, and baths both of vapour and hot water, familiarly used by the inhabitants. A still higher proof of refinement may be discerned in a vigilant police which repressed everything like disorder among the people.[2]

The city was divided into four quarters, which might rather be called so many separate towns, since they were built at different times, and separated from each other by high stone walls, defining their respective limits. Over each of these districts ruled one of the four great chiefs of the republic, occupying his own spacious mansion and surrounded by his own immediate vassals. Strange arrangement,—and more strange that it should have been compatible with social order and tranquillity! The ancient capital, through one quarter of which flowed the rapid current of the Zahuatl, stretched along the summits and sides of hills, at whose base are now gathered the miserable remains of its once flourishing population.[3] Far beyond, to the south-east, extended the bold sierra of Tlascala, and the huge Malinche, crowned with the usual silver diadem of the highest Andes, having its shaggy sides clothed with dark-green forests of firs, gigantic sycamores, and oaks whose towering stems rose to the height of forty or fifty feet, unencumbered by a branch. The clouds, which sailed over from the distant Atlantic, gathered round the lofty peaks of the sierra, and, settling into torrents, poured over the plains in the neighbourhood of the city, converting them, at such seasons, into swamps. Thunder-storms, more frequent and terrible here than in other parts of the table-land, swept down the sides of the mountains and shook the frail tenements of the capital to their foundations. But, although the bleak winds of the sierra gave an austerity to the climate, unlike the sunny skies and genial temperature of the lower regions, it was far more favourable to the development of both the physical and moral energies. A bold and hardy peasantry was nurtured among the recesses of the hills, fit equally to cultivate the land in peace and to defend it in war. Unlike the spoiled child of Nature, who derives such facilities of subsistence from her too prodigal hand as supersede the necessity of exertion on his own part, the Tlascalan earned his bread—from a soil not ungrateful, it is true—by

---

[1] "Nullum est fictile vas apud nos, quod arte superet ab illis vasa formata." Martyr, De Orbe Novo, dec. 5, cap. 2.

[2] Camargo, Hist. de Tlascala, MS.—Rel. Seg. de Cortés, ap. Lorenzana, p. 59.—Oviedo, Hist. de las Ind., MS., lib. 33, cap. 4.—Ixtlilxochitl, Hist. Chich., MS., cap. 83.—The last historian enumerates such a number of contemporary Indian author-

ities for his narrative as of itself argues no inconsiderable degree of civilization in the people.

[3] Herrera, Hist. general, dec. 2, lib. 6, cap. 12.—The population of a place which Cortés could compare with Granada had dwindled by the beginning of the present century to 3400 inhabitants, of whom less than a thousand were of the Indian stock. See Humboldt, Essai politique, tom. ii. p. 158.

the sweat of his brow. He led a life of temperance and toil. Cut off by his long wars with the Aztecs from commercial intercourse, he was driven chiefly to agricultural labour, the occupation most propitious to purity of morals and sinewy strength of constitution. His honest breast glowed with the patriotism, or local attachment to the soil, which is the fruit of its diligent culture ; while he was elevated by a proud consciousness of independence, the natural birthright of the child of the mountains. Such was the race with whom Cortés was now associated for the achievement of his great work.

Some days were given by the Spaniards to festivity, in which they were successively entertained at the hospitable boards of the four great nobles, in their several quarters of the city. Amidst these friendly demonstrations, however, the general never relaxed for a moment his habitual vigilance, or the strict discipline of the camp ; and he was careful to provide for the security of the citizens by prohibiting, under severe penalties, any soldier from leaving his quarters without express permission. Indeed, the severity of his discipline provoked the remonstrance of more than one of his officers, as a superfluous caution ; and the Tlascalan chiefs took some exception at it, as inferring an unreasonable distrust of them. But, when Cortés explained it, as in obedience to an established military system, they testified their admiration, and the ambitious young general of the republic proposed to introduce it, if possible, into his own ranks.[1]

The Spanish commander, having assured himself of the loyalty of his new allies, next proposed to accomplish one of the great objects of his mission, their conversion to Christianity. By the advice of Father Olmedo, always opposed to precipitate measures, he had deferred this till a suitable opportunity presented itself for opening the subject. Such a one occurred when the chiefs of the state proposed to strengthen the alliance with the Spaniards by the intermarriage of their daughters with Cortés and his officers. He told them this could not be while they continued in the darkness of infidelity. Then, with the aid of the good friar, he expounded as well as he could the doctrines of the Faith, and, exhibiting the image of the Virgin with the infant Redeemer, told them that there was the God in whose worship alone they would find salvation, while that of their own false idols would sink them in eternal perdition.

It is unnecessary to burden the reader with a recapitulation of his homily, which contained, probably, dogmas quite as incomprehensible to the untutored Indian as any to be found in his own rude mythology. But, though it failed to convince his audience, they listened with a deferential awe. When he had finished, they replied they had no doubt that the God of the Christians must be a good and a great God, and as such they were willing to give him a place among the divinities of Tlascala. The

---

[1] Sahagun, Hist. de Nueva-España, MS., lib. 12, cap. 11.—Camargo, Hist. de Tlascala, MS.—Gomara, Crónica, cap. 54, 55.—Herrera, Hist. general, dec. 2, lib. 6, cap. 13.—Bernal Diaz, Hist. de la Conquista, cap. 75.

polytheistic system of the Indians, like that of the ancient Greeks, was of that accommodating kind which could admit within its elastic folds the deities of any other religion, without violence to itself.[1]   But every nation, they continued, must have its own appropriate and tutelary deities.   Nor could they, in their old age, abjure the service of those who had watched over them from youth.   It would bring down the vengeance of their gods, and of their own nation, who were as warmly attached to their religion as their liberties, and would defend both with the last drop of their blood !

It was clearly inexpedient to press the matter further at present.   But the zeal of Cortés, as usual, waxing warm by opposition, had now mounted too high for him to calculate obstacles; nor would he have shrunk, probably, from the crown of martyrdom in so good a cause.   But, fortunately, at least for the success of his temporal cause, this crown was not reserved for him.

The good monk, his ghostly adviser, seeing the course things were likely to take, with better judgment interposed to prevent it.   He had no desire, he said, to see the same scenes acted over again as at Cempoalla.   He had no relish for forced conversions.   They could hardly be lasting.   The growth of an hour might well die with the hour.   Of what use was it to overturn the altar, if the idol remained enthroned in the heart ? or to destroy the idol itself, if it were only to make room for another ?   Better to wait patiently the effect of time and teaching to soften the heart and open the understanding, without which there could be no assurance of a sound and permanent conviction.   These rational views were enforced by the remonstrances of Alvarado, Velasquez de Leon, and those in whom Cortés placed most confidence; till, driven from his original purpose, the military polemic consented to relinquish the attempt at conversion for the present, and to refrain from a repetition of scenes which, considering the different mettle of the population, might have been attended with very different results from those at Cozumel and Cempoalla.[2]

In the course of our narrative we have had occasion to witness more than once the good effects of the interposition of Father Olmedo.   Indeed, it is scarcely too much to say that his discretion in spiritual matters contributed as essentially to the success of the expedition as did the sagacity and courage of Cortés in temporal.   He was a true disciple in the school of Las Casas.   His heart was unscathed by that fiery fanaticism which sears and hardens whatever it touches.   It melted with the warm glow of Christian charity.   He had come out to the New World as a missionary

---

[1] Camargo notices this elastic property in the religions of Anahuac: "Este modo de hablar y decir que les querrá dar otro Dios, es saber que cuando estas gentes tenian noticia de algun Dios de buenas propiedades y costumbres, que le rescibiesen admitiéndole por tal, porque otras gentes advenedizas trujéron muchos ídolos que tubiéron por Dioses, y á este fin y propósito decian, que Cortés les traia otro Dios." Hist. de Tlascala, MS.

[2] Ixtlilxochitl, Hist. Chich., MS., cap. 84.—Gomara, Crónica, cap. 56.—Bernal Diaz, Hist. de la

Conquista, cap. 76, 77.—This is not the account of Camargo.   According to him, Cortés gained his point : the nobles led the way by embracing Christianity, and the idols were broken. (Hist. de Tlascala, MS.)   But Camargo was himself a Christianized Indian, who lived in the next generation after the Conquest, and may very likely have felt as much desire to relieve his nation from the reproach of infidelity as a modern Spaniard would to scour out the stain—*mala raza y mancha*—of Jewish or Moorish lineage from his escutcheon.

among the heathen, and he shrunk from no sacrifice but that of the welfare of the poor benighted flock to whom he had consecrated his days. If he followed the banners of the warrior, it was to mitigate the ferocity of war, and to turn the triumphs of the Cross to a good account for the natives themselves, by the spiritual labours of conversion. He afforded the uncommon example—not to have been looked for, certainly, in a Spanish monk of the sixteenth century—of enthusiasm controlled by reason, a quickening zeal tempered by the mild spirit of toleration.

But, though Cortés abandoned the ground of conversion for the present, he compelled the Tlascalans to break the fetters of the unfortunate victims reserved for sacrifice; an act of humanity unhappily only transient in its effects, since the prisons were filled with fresh victims on his departure.

He also obtained permission for the Spaniards to perform the services of their own religion unmolested. A large cross was erected in one of the great courts or squares. Mass was celebrated every day in the presence of the army and of crowds of natives, who, if they did not comprehend its full import, were so far edified that they learned to reverence the religion of their conquerors. The direct interposition of Heaven, however, wrought more for their conversion than the best homily of priest or soldier. Scarcely had the Spaniards left the city—the tale is told on very respectable authority—when a thin, transparent cloud descended and settled like a column on the cross, and, wrapping it round in its luminous folds, continued to emit a soft, celestial radiance through the night, thus proclaiming the sacred character of the symbol, on which was shed the halo of divinity![1]

The principle of toleration in religious matters being established, the Spanish general consented to receive the daughters of the caciques. Five or six of the most beautiful of the Indian maidens were assigned to as many of his principal officers, after they had been cleansed from the stains of infidelity by the waters of baptism. They received, as usual, on this occasion, good Castilian names, in exchange for the barbarous nomenclature of their own vernacular.[2] Among them, Xicotencatl's daughter, Doña Luisa, as she was called after her baptism, was a princess of the highest estimation and authority in Tlascala. She was given by her father to Alvarado, and their posterity intermarried with the noblest families of Castile. The frank and joyous manners of this cavalier made him a great favourite with the Tlascalans; and his bright, open countenance, fair complexion, and golden locks gave him the name of *Tonatiuh* the "Sun." The Indians often pleased their fancies by fastening a *sobriquet*, or some characteristic epithet, on the Spaniards. As Cortés was always attended, on public occasions, by Doña Marina, or Malinche, as she was called by

---

[1] The miracle is reported by Herrera (Hist. general, dec. 2, lib. 6, cap. 15), and *believed* by Solis. Conquista de Méjico, lib. 3, cap. 5.
[2] To avoid the perplexity of selection, it was common for the missionary to give the same names to all the Indians baptized on the same day. Thus, one day was set apart for the Johns, another for the Peters, and so on; an ingenious arrangement, much more for the convenience of the clergy than of the converts. See Camargo, Hist. de Tlascala, MS.

the natives, they distinguished him by the same name. By these epithets, originally bestowed in Tlascala, the two Spanish captains were popularly designated among the Indian nations.[1]

While these events were passing, another embassy arrived from the court of Mexico. It was charged, as usual, with a costly donative of embossed gold plate, and rich embroidered stuffs of cotton and feather-work. The terms of the message might well argue a vacillating and timid temper in the monarch, did they not mask a deeper policy. He now invited the Spaniards to his capital, with the assurance of a cordial welcome. He besought them to enter into no alliance with the base and barbarous Tlascalans; and he invited them to take the route of the friendly city of Cholula, where arrangements, according to his orders, were made for their reception.[2]

The Tlascalans viewed with deep regret the general's proposed visit to Mexico. Their reports fully confirmed all he had before heard of the power and ambition of Montezuma. His armies, they said, were spread over every part of the continent. His capital was a place of great strength, and as, from its insular position, all communication could be easily cut off with the adjacent country, the Spaniards, once entrapped there, would be at his mercy. His policy, they represented, was as insidious as his ambition was boundless. "Trust not his fair words," they said, "his courtesies, and his gifts. His professions are hollow, and his friendships are false." When Cortés remarked that he hoped to bring about a better understanding between the emperor and them, they replied it would be impossible; however smooth his words, he would hate them at heart.

They warmly protested, also, against the general's taking the route of Cholula. The inhabitants, not brave in the open field, were more dangerous from their perfidy and craft. They were Montezuma's tools, and would do his bidding. The Tlascalans seemed to combine with this distrust a superstitious dread of the ancient city, the headquarters of the religion of Anahuac. It was here that the god Quetzalcoatl held the pristine seat of his empire. His temple was celebrated throughout the land, and the priests were confidently believed to have the power, as they themselves boasted, of opening an inundation from the foundations of his shrine, which should bury their enemies in the deluge. The Tlascalans further reminded Cortés that, while so many other and distant places had sent to him at Tlascala to testify their goodwill and offer their allegiance to his sovereigns, Cholula, only six leagues distant, had done neither.

---

[1] Camargo, Hist. de Tlascala, MS.—Bernal Diaz, Hist. de la Conquista, cap. 74; 77.—According to Camargo, the Tlascalans gave the Spanish commander 300 damsels to wait on Marina; and the kind treatment and instruction they received led some of the chiefs to surrender their own daughters, " con propósito de que *si acaso* algunas se empreñasen quedase entre ellos generacion de hombres tan valientes y temidos."

[2] Bernal Diaz, Hist. de la Conquista, cap. 80.— Rel. Seg. de Cortés, ap. Lorenzana, p. 60.—Martyr, De Orbe Novo, dec. 5, cap. 2.—Cortés notices only one Aztec mission, while Diaz speaks of three. The former, from brevity, falls so much short of the whole truth, and the latter, from forgetfulness perhaps, goes so much beyond it, that it is not always easy to decide between them. Diaz did not compile his narrative till some fifty years after the Conquest; a lapse of time which may excuse many errors, but must considerably impair our confidence in the minute accuracy of his details. A more intimate acquaintance with his chronicle does not strengthen this confidence.

The last suggestion struck the general more forcibly than any of the preceding. He instantly despatched a summons to the city, requiring a formal tender of its submission.

Among the embassies from different quarters which had waited on the Spanish commander, while at Tlascala, was one from Ixtlilxochitl, son of the great Nezahualpilli, and an unsuccessful competitor with his elder brother—as noticed in a former part of our narrative—for the crown of Tezcuco.[1] Though defeated in his pretensions, he had obtained a part of the kingdom, over which he ruled with a deadly feeling of animosity towards his rival, and to Montezuma, who had sustained him. He now offered his services to Cortés, asking his aid, in return, to place him on the throne of his ancestors. The politic general returned such an answer to the aspiring young prince as might encourage his expectations and attach him to his interests. It was his aim to strengthen his cause by attracting to himself every particle of disaffection that was floating through the land.

It was not long before deputies arrived from Cholula, profuse in their expressions of goodwill, and inviting the presence of the Spaniards in their capital. The messengers were of low degree, far beneath the usual rank of ambassadors. This was pointed out by the Tlascalans; and Cortés regarded it as a fresh indignity. He sent in consequence a new summons, declaring if they did not instantly send him a deputation of their principal men he would deal with them as *rebels* to his own sovereign, the rightful lord of these realms![2] The menace had the desired effect. The Cholulans were not inclined to contest, at least for the present, his magnificent pretensions. Another embassy appeared in the camp, consisting of some of the highest nobles; who repeated the invitation for the Spaniards to visit their city, and excused their own tardy appearance by apprehensions for their personal safety in the capital of their enemies. The explanation was plausible, and was admitted by Cortés.

The Tlascalans were now more than ever opposed to his projected visit. A strong Aztec force, they had ascertained, lay in the neighbourhood of Cholula, and the people were actively placing their city in a posture of defence. They suspected some insidious scheme concerted by Montezuma to destroy the Spaniards.

These suggestions disturbed the mind of Cortés, but did not turn him from his purpose. He felt a natural curiosity to see the venerable city so celebrated in the history of the Indian nations. He had, besides, gone too far to recede,—too far, at least, to do so without a show of apprehension implying a distrust in his own resources which could not fail to have

1 *Ante*, p. 147.

2 " Si no viniessen, iria sobre ellos, y los destruiria, y procederia contra ellos como contra personas rebeldes; diciéndoles, como todas estas Partes, y otras muy mayores Tierras, y Señorios eran de Vuestra Alteza." (Rel. Seg. de Cortés, ap. Lorenzana, p. 63.) "Rebellion" was a very convenient term, fastened in like manner by the countrymen of Cortés on the Moors for defending the possessions which they had held for eight centuries in the Peninsula. It justified very rigorous reprisals. (See the History of Ferdinand and Isabella, Part I. chap. 13, et alibi.)

a bad effect on his enemies, his allies, and his own men. After a brief consultation with his officers, he decided on the route to Cholula.[1]

It was now three weeks since the Spaniards had taken up their residence within the hospitable walls of Tlascala, and nearly six since they entered her territory. They had been met on the threshold as enemies, with the most determined hostility. They were now to part with the same people as friends and allies; fast friends, who were to stand by them, side by side, through the whole of their arduous struggle. The result of their visit, therefore, was of the last importance; since on the co-operation of these brave and warlike republicans greatly depended the ultimate success of the expedition.

CHAPTER VI.

CITY OF CHOLULA.—GREAT TEMPLE.—MARCH TO CHOLULA.—RECEPTION
OF THE SPANIARDS.—CONSPIRACY DETECTED.

(1519.)

THE ancient city of Cholula, capital of the republic of that name, lay nearly six leagues south of Tlascala, and about twenty east, or rather south-east, of Mexico. It was said by Cortés to contain twenty thousand houses within the walls, and as many more in the environs;[2] though now dwindled to a population of less than sixteen thousand souls.[3] Whatever was its real number of inhabitants, it was unquestionably, at the time of the Conquest, one of the most populous and flourishing cities in New Spain.

It was of great antiquity, and was founded by the primitive races who overspread the land before the Aztecs.[4] We have few particulars of its form of government, which seems to have been cast on a republican model similar to that of Tlascala. This answered so well that the state maintained its independence down to a very late period, when, if not reduced to vassalage by the Aztecs, it was so far under their control as to enjoy few of the benefits of a separate political existence. Their connection with Mexico brought the Cholulans into frequent collision with their neighbours and

---

[1] Rel. Seg. de Cortés, ap. Lorenzana, pp. 62, 63. —Oviedo, Hist. de las Ind., MS., lib. 33, cap. 4.— Ixtlilxochitl, Hist. Chich., MS., cap. 84.—Gomara, Crónica, cap. 58.—Martyr, de Orbe Novo, dec. 5, cap. 2.—Herrera, Hist. general, dec. 2, lib. 6, cap. 18.—Sahagun, Hist. de Nueva-España, MS., lib. 12, cap. 11.

[2] Rel. Seg., ap. Lorenzana, p. 67.—According to Las Casas, the place contained 30,000 *vecinos*, or about 150,000 inhabitants. (Brevissima Relatione della Distruttione dell' Indie Occidentale (Venetia, •643).) This latter, being the smaller estimate, is

a priori the more credible; especially—a rare occurrence—when in the pages of the good Bishop of Chiapa.

[3] Humboldt, Essai politique, tom. iii. p. 159.

[4] Veytia carries back the foundation of the city to the Ulmecs, a people who preceded the Toltecs. (Hist. antig., tom. i. cap. 13, 20.) As the latter, after occupying the land several centuries, have left not a single written record, probably, of their existence, it will be hard to disprove the licentiate's assertion,—still harder to prove it.

kindred the Tlascalans. But, although far superior to them in refinement and the various arts of civilization, they were no match in war for the bold mountaineers, the Swiss of Anahuac. The Cholulan capital was the great commercial emporium of the plateau. The inhabitants excelled in various mechanical arts, especially that of working in metals, the manufacture of cotton and agave cloths, and of a delicate kind of pottery, rivalling, it was said, that of Florence in beauty.[1] But such attention to the arts of a polished and peaceful community naturally indisposed them to war, and disqualified them for coping with those who made war the great business of life. The Cholulans were accused of effeminacy, and were less distinguished—it is the charge of their rivals—by their courage than their cunning.[2]

But the capital, so conspicuous for its refinement and its great antiquity, was even more venerable for the religious traditions which invested it. It was here that the god Quetzalcoatl paused in his passage to the coast, and passed twenty years in teaching the Toltec inhabitants the arts of civilization. He made them acquainted with better forms of government, and a more spiritualized religion, in which the only sacrifices were the fruits and flowers of the season.[3] It is not easy to determine what he taught, since his lessons have been so mingled with the licentious dogmas of his own priests and the mystic commentaries of the Christian missionary.[4] It is probable that he was one of those rare and gifted beings who, dissipating the darkness of the age by the illumination of their own genius, are deified by a grateful posterity and placed among the lights of heaven.

It was in honour of this benevolent deity that the stupendous mound was erected on which the traveller still gazes with admiration as the most colossal fabric in New Spain, rivalling in dimensions, and somewhat resembling in form, the pyramidal structures of ancient Egypt. The date of its erection is unknown; for it was found there when the Aztecs entered on the plateau. It had the form common to the Mexican *teocallis*, that of a truncated pyramid, facing with its four sides the cardinal points, and divided into the same number of terraces. Its original outlines, however, have been effaced by the action of time and of the elements, while the exuberant growth of shrubs and wild flowers, which have mantled over its surface, give it the appearance of one of those symmetrical elevations thrown up by the caprice of nature rather than by the industry of man. It is doubtful, indeed, whether the interior be not a natural hill; though it seems not improbable that it is an artificial composition of stone and

[1] Herrera, Hist. general, dec. 2, lib. 7, cap. 2.
[2] Camargo, Hist. de Tlascala, MS.—Gomara, Crónica, cap. 58.—Torquemada, Monarch. Ind., lib. 3, cap. 19.
[3] Veytia, Hist. antig., tom. i. cap. 15, et seq.—Sahagun, Hist. de Nueva-España, lib. 1, cap. 5; lib. 3.
[4] Later divines have found in these teachings of the Toltec god, or high-priest, the germs of some of the great mysteries of the Christian faith, as those of the Incarnation, and the Trinity, for example. In the teacher himself they recognize no less a person than St. Thomas the Apostle! See the Dissertation of the irrefragable Dr. Mier, with an edifying commentary by Señor Bustamante, ap. Sahagun. (Hist. de Nueva-España, tom. i., Suplemento.) The reader will find further particulars of this matter in Appendix, Part 1, of this History

earth, deeply incrusted, as is certain, in every part, with alternate strata of brick and clay.[1]

The perpendicular height of the pyramid is one hundred and seventy-seven feet. Its base is one thousand four hundred and twenty-three feet long, twice as long as that of the great pyramid of Cheops. It may give some idea of its dimensions to state that its base, which is square, covers about forty-four acres, and the platform on its truncated summit embraces more than one. It reminds us of those colossal monuments of brickwork which are still seen in ruins on the banks of the Euphrates, and, in much higher preservation, on those of the Nile.[2]

On the summit stood a sumptuous temple, in which was the image of the mystic deity, "god of the air," with ebon features, unlike the fair complexion which he bore upon earth, wearing a mitre on his head waving with *plumes of fire*, with a resplendent collar of gold round his neck, pendants of mosaic turquoise in his ears, a jewelled sceptre in one hand, and a shield curiously painted, the emblem of his rule over the winds, in the other.[3] The sanctity of the place, hallowed by hoary tradition, and the magnificence of the temple and its services, made it an object of veneration throughout the land, and pilgrims from the farthest corners of Anahuac came to offer up their devotions at the shrine of Quetzalcoatl.[4] The number of these was so great as to give an air of mendicity to the motley population of the city ; and Cortés, struck with the novelty, tells us that he saw multitudes of beggars, such as are to be found in the enlightened capitals of Europe ;[5]—a whimsical criterion of civilization, which must place our own prosperous land somewhat low in the scale.

Cholula was not the resort only of the indigent devotee. Many of the kindred races had temples of their own in the city, in the same manner as some Christian nations have in Rome, and each temple was provided with its own peculiar ministers for the service of the deity to whom it was consecrated. In no city was there seen such a concourse of priests, so many processions, such pomp of ceremonial, sacrifice, and religious festivals. Cholula was, in short, what Mecca is among Mahometans, or Jerusalem among Christians ; it was the Holy City of Anahuac.[6]

---

[1] Such, on the whole, seems to be the judgment of M. de Humboldt, who has examined this interesting monument with his usual care. (Vues des Cordillères, p. 27, et seq.—Essai politique, tom. ii. p. 150, et seq.) The opinion derives strong confirmation from the fact that a road, cut some years since across the tumulus, laid open a large section of it, in which the alternate layers of brick and clay are distinctly visible. (Ibid., loc. cit.) The present appearance of this monument, covered over with the verdure and vegetable mould of centuries, excuses the scepticism of the more superficial traveller.

[2] Several of the pyramids of Egypt, and the ruins of Babylon, are, as is well known, of brick. An inscription on one of the former, indeed, celebrates this material as superior to stone. (Herodotus, Euterpe, sec. 136.)—Humboldt furnishes an apt illustration of the size of the Mexican *teocalli*, by comparing it to a mass of bricks covering a square

four times as large as the Place Vendôme, and of twice the height of the Louvre. Essai politique, tom. ii. p. 152.

[3] A minute account of the costume and insignia of Quetzalcoatl is given by Father Sahagun, who saw the Aztec gods before the arm of the Christian convert had tumbled them from "their pride of place." See Historia de Nueva-España, lib. 1, cap. 3.

[4] They came from the distance of two hundred leagues, says Torquemada. Monarch. Ind., lib. 3, cap. 19.

[5] "Hay mucha gente pobre, y que piden entre los Ricos por las Calles, y por las Casas, y Mercados, como hacen los Pobres en España, y en otras partes que hay *Gente de razon*." Rel. Seg., ap. Lorenzana, pp. 67, 68.

[6] Torquemada, Monarch. Ind., lib. 3, cap. 19.— Gomara, Crónica, cap. 61.—Camargo, Hist. de Tlascala, MS.

The religious rites were not performed, however, in the pure spirit originally prescribed by its tutelary deity. His altars, as well as those of the numerous Aztec gods, were stained with human blood; and six thousand victims *are said* to have been annually offered up at their sanguinary shrines![1] The great number of these may be estimated from the declaration of Cortés that he counted four hundred towers in the city;[2] yet no temple had more than two, many only one. High above the rest rose the great "pyramid of Cholula," with its undying fires flinging their radiance far and wide over the capital, and proclaiming to the nations that there was the mystic worship—alas! how corrupted by cruelty and superstition!—of the good deity who was one day to return and resume his empire over the land.

Nothing could be more grand than the view which met the eye from the area on the truncated summit of the pyramid. Towards the west stretched that bold barrier of porphyritic rock which nature has reared around the Valley of Mexico, with the huge Popocatepetl and Iztaccihuatl standing like two colossal sentinels to guard the entrance to the enchanted region. Far away to the east was seen the conical head of Orizaba soaring high into the clouds, and nearer, the barren though beautifully-shaped Sierra de la Malinche, throwing its broad shadows over the plains of Tlascala. Three of these are volcanoes higher than the highest mountain-peak in Europe, and shrouded in snows which never melt under the fierce sun of the tropics. At the foot of the spectator lay the sacred city of Cholula, with its bright towers and pinnacles sparkling in the sun, reposing amidst gardens and verdant groves, which then thickly studded the cultivated environs of the capital. Such was the magnificent prospect which met the gaze of the Conquerors, and may still, with slight change, meet that of the modern traveller, as from the platform of the great pyramid his eye wanders over the fairest portion of the beautiful plateau of Puebla.[3]

But it is time to return to Tlascala. On the appointed morning the Spanish army took up its march to Mexico by the way of Cholula. It was followed by crowds of the citizens, filled with admiration at the intrepidity of men who, so few in number, would venture to brave the great Montezuma in his capital. Yet an immense body of warriors offered to share the dangers of the expedition; but Cortés, while he showed his gratitude for their goodwill, selected only six thousand of the volunteers

---

[1] Herrera, Hist. general, dec. 2, lib. 7, cap. 2.—Torquemada, Monarch. Ind., ubi supra.

[2] "É certifico á Vuestra Alteza, que yo conté desde una Mezquita quatrocientas, y tantas Torres en la dicha Ciudad, y todas son de Mezquitas." Rel. Seg., ap. Lorenzana, p. 67.

[3] The city of Puebla de los Ángeles was founded by the Spaniards soon after the Conquest, on the site of an insignificant village in the territory of Cholula, a few miles to the east of that capital. It is, perhaps, the most considerable city in New Spain, after Mexico itself, which it rivals in beauty. It seems to have inherited the religious pre-eminence of the ancient Cholula, being distinguished, like her, for the number and splendour of its churches, the multitude of its clergy, and the magnificence of its ceremonies and festivals. These are fully displayed in the pages of travellers who have passed through the place on the usual route from Vera Cruz to the capital. (See, in particular, Bullock's Mexico, vol. i. chap. 6.) The environs of Cholula, still irrigated as in the days of the Aztecs, are equally remarkable for the fruitfulness of the soil. The best wheatlands, according to a very respectable authority, yield in the proportion of eighty for one. Ward's Mexico, vol. ii. p. 270.—See, also, Humboldt, Essai politique, tom. ii. p. 158; tom. iv. p. 330.

to bear him company.[1] He was unwilling to encumber himself with an unwieldy force that might impede his movements, and probably did not care to put himself so far in the power of allies whose attachment was too recent to afford sufficient guarantee for their fidelity.

After crossing some rough and hilly ground, the army entered on the wide plain which spreads out for miles around Cholula. At the elevation of more than six thousand feet above the sea, they beheld the rich products of various climes growing side by side, fields of towering maize, the juicy aloe, the *chilli* or Aztec pepper, and large plantations of the cactus on which the brilliant cochineal is nourished. Not a rood of land but was under cultivation;[2] and the soil—an uncommon thing on the table-land—was irrigated by numerous streams and canals, and well shaded by woods, that have disappeared before the rude axe of the Spaniards. Towards evening they reached a small stream, on the banks of which Cortés determined to take up his quarters for the night, being unwilling to disturb the tranquillity of the city by introducing so large a force into it at an unseasonable hour.

Here he was soon joined by a number of Cholulan caciques and their attendants, who came to view and welcome the strangers. When they saw their Tlascalan enemies in the camp, however, they exhibited signs of displeasure, and intimated an apprehension that their presence in the town might occasion disorder. The remonstrance seemed reasonable to Cortés, and he accordingly commanded his allies to remain in their present quarters, and to join him as he left the city on the way to Mexico.

On the following morning he made his entrance at the head of his army into Cholula, attended by no other Indians than those from Cempoalla, and a handful of Tlascalans, to take charge of the baggage. His allies, at parting, gave him many cautions respecting the people he was to visit, who, while they affected to despise them as a nation of traders, employed the dangerous arms of perfidy and cunning. As the troops drew near the city, the road was lined with swarms of people of both sexes and every age, old men tottering with infirmity, women with children in their arms, all eager to catch a glimpse of the strangers, whose persons, weapons, and horses were objects of intense curiosity to eyes which had not hitherto ever encountered them in battle. The Spaniards, in turn, were filled with admiration at the aspect of the Cholulans, much superior in dress and general appearance to the nations they had hitherto seen. They were particularly struck with the costume of the higher classes, who wore fine embroidered mantles, resembling the graceful *albornoz*, or Moorish cloak,

---

[1] According to Cortés, a hundred thousand men offered their services on this occasion! "And although I forbade it, and requested that they would not go, since there was no necessity for it, yet I was followed by as many as a hundred thousand men well fitted for war, who came with me to the distance of nearly two leagues from the city, and then through my pressing importunities were induced to return, with the exception of five or six thousand, who continued in my company." (Rel. Seg., ap. Lorenzana, p. 64.) This, which must have been nearly the whole fighting force of the republic, does not startle Oviedo (Historia de las Indias, MS., cap. 4) nor Gomara, Crónica, cap. 58.
[2] The words of the *Conquistador* are yet stronger. "There is not a *hand's-breadth* of land that is not cultivated." Rel. Seg., ap. Lorenzana, p. 67.

in their texture and fashion.[1] They showed the same delicate taste for flowers as the other tribes of the plateau, decorating their persons with them, and tossing garlands and bunches among the soldiers. An immense number of priests mingled with the crowd, swinging their aromatic censers, while music from various kinds of instruments gave a lively welcome to the visitors, and made the whole scene one of gay, bewildering enchantment. If it did not have the air of a triumphal procession so much as at Tlascala, where the melody of instruments was drowned by the shouts of the multitude, it gave a quiet assurance of hospitality and friendly feeling not less grateful.

The Spaniards were also struck with the cleanliness of the city, the width and great regularity of the streets, which seemed to have been laid out on a settled plan, with the solidity of the houses, and the number and size of the pyramidal temples. In the court of one of these, and its surrounding buildings, they were quartered.[2]

They were soon visited by the principal lords of the place, who seemed solicitous to provide them with accommodations. Their table was plentifully supplied, and, in short, they experienced such attentions as were calculated to dissipate their suspicions, and made them impute those of their Tlascalan friends to prejudice and old national hostility.

In a few days the scene changed. Messengers arrived from Montezuma, who, after a short and unpleasant intimation to Cortés that his approach occasioned much disquietude to their master, conferred separately with the Mexican ambassadors still in the Castilian camp, and then departed, taking one of the latter along with them. From this time the deportment of their Cholulan hosts underwent a visible alteration. They did not visit the quarters as before, and, when invited to do so, excused themselves on pretence of illness. The supply of provisions was stinted, on the ground that they were short of maize. These symptoms of alienation, independently of temporary embarrassment, caused serious alarm in the breast of Cortés, for the future. His apprehensions were not allayed by the reports of the Cempoallans, who told him that in wandering round the city they had seen several streets barricadoed, the *azoteas*, or flat roofs of the houses, loaded with huge stones and other missiles, as if preparatory to an assault, and in some places they had found holes covered over with

[1] "All the inhabitants of rank wear, besides their other clothing, *albornoces*, differing from those of Africa inasmuch as they have pockets, but very similar in form, in material, and in the bordering." Rel. Seg. de Cortés, ap. Lorenzana, p. 67.

[2] Rel. Seg. de Cortés, ap. Lorenzana, p. 67.— Ixtlilxochitl, Hist. Chich., MS., cap. 84.—Oviedo, Hist. de las Ind., MS., lib. 33, cap. 4.—Bernal Diaz, Hist. de la Conquista, cap. 82.—The Spaniards compared Cholula to the beautiful Valladolid, according to Herrera, whose description of the entry is very animated: "Saliéronle otro dia á recibir mas de diez mil ciudadanos en diversas tropas, con rosas, flores, pan, aves, i frutas, i mucha música. Llegaba vn esquadron á dar la bien llegada á Hernando Cortés, i con buena órden se iba apartando, dando lugar á que otro llegase. . . . En llegando á la ciudad, que pareció mucho á los Castellanos, en el asiento, i perspectiva, á Valladolid, salió la demas gente, quedando mui espantada de ver las figuras, talles, i armas de los Castellanos. Saliéron los sacerdotes con vestiduras blancas, como sobrepellices, i algunas cerradas por delante, los braços defuera, con fluecos de algodon en las orillas. Unos llevaban figuras de ídolos en las manos, otros sahumerios; otros tocaban cornetas, atabalejos, i diversas músicas, i todos iban cantando, i llegaban á encensar á los Castellanos. Con esta pompa entráron en Chulula." Hist. general, dec. 2, lib. 7, cap. 1.

branches, and upright stakes planted within, as if to embarrass the movements of the cavalry.[1]   Some Tlascalans coming in, also, from their camp,
informed the general that a great sacrifice, mostly of children, had been
offered up in a distant quarter of the town, to propitiate the favour of the
gods, apparently for some intended enterprise.   They added that they
had seen numbers of the citizens leaving the city with their women and
children, as if to remove them to a place of safety.   These tidings confirmed the worst suspicions of Cortés, who had no doubt that some hostile
scheme was in agitation.   If he had felt any, a discovery by Marina, the
good angel of the expedition, would have turned these doubts into certainty.

The amiable manners of the Indian girl had won her the regard of
the wife of one of the caciques, who repeatedly urged Marina to visit
her house, darkly intimating that in this way she would escape the fate
that awaited the Spaniards.   The interpreter, seeing the importance of
obtaining further intelligence at once, pretended to be pleased with the
proposal, and affected, at the same time, great discontent with the white
men, by whom she was detained in captivity.   Thus throwing the credulous Cholulan off her guard, Marina gradually insinuated herself into her
confidence, so far as to draw from her a full account of the conspiracy.

It originated, she said, with the Aztec emperor, who had sent rich
bribes to the great caciques, and to her husband among others, to secure
them in his views.   The Spaniards were to be assaulted as they marched
out of the capital, when entangled in its streets, in which numerous
impediments had been placed to throw the cavalry into disorder.   A force
of twenty thousand Mexicans was already quartered at no great distance
from the city, to support the Cholulans in the assault.   It was confidently
expected that the Spaniards, thus embarrassed in their movements, would
fall an easy prey to the superior strength of their enemy.   A sufficient
number of prisoners was to be reserved to grace the sacrifices of Cholula,
the rest were to be led in fetters to the capital of Montezuma.

While this conversation was going on, Marina occupied herself with
putting up such articles of value and wearing apparel as she proposed to
take with her in the evening, when she could escape unnoticed from the
Spanish quarters to the house of her Cholulan friend, who assisted her
in the operation.   Leaving her visitor thus employed, Marina found an
opportunity to steal away for a few moments, and, going to the general's
apartment, disclosed to him her discoveries.   He immediately caused the
cacique's wife to be seized, and, on examination, she fully confirmed the
statement of his Indian mistress.

The intelligence thus gathered by Cortés filled him with the deepest

---

[1] Cortés, indeed, noticed these same alarming
appearances on his entering the city, thus suggesting
the idea of a premeditated treachery.   "On the
road we noticed many indications such as the natives
of this province had told us of; for we found the
royal road barred up and another opened, and some
holes dug,—though not many,—and some of the
streets of the city barricadoed, and many stones
upon the roofs ; which put us more upon our guard
and caused us to exercise great caution." Rel. Seg.,
ap. Lorenzana, p. 64.

alarm. He was fairly taken in the snare. To fight or to fly seemed equally difficult. He was in a city of enemies, where every house might be converted into a fortress, and where such embarrassments were thrown in the way as might render the manœuvres of his artillery and horse nearly impracticable. In addition to the wily Cholulans, he must cope, under all these disadvantages, with the redoubtable warriors of Mexico. He was like a traveller who has lost his way in the darkness among precipices, where any step may dash him to pieces, and where to retreat or to advance is equally perilous.

He was desirous to obtain still further confirmation and particulars of the conspiracy. He accordingly induced two of the priests in the neighbourhood, one of them a person of much influence in the place, to visit his quarters. By courteous treatment, and liberal largesses of the rich presents he had received from Montezuma,—thus turning his own gifts against the giver,—he drew from them a full confirmation of the previous report. The emperor had been in a state of pitiable vacillation since the arrival of the Spaniards. His first orders to the Cholulans were to receive the strangers kindly. He had recently consulted his oracles anew, and obtained for answer that Cholula would be the grave of his enemies; for the gods would be sure to support him in avenging the sacrilege offered to the Holy City. So confident were the Aztecs of success, that numerous manacles, or poles with thongs which served as such, were already in the place to secure the prisoners.

Cortés, now feeling himself fully possessed of the facts, dismissed the priests, with injunctions of secrecy, scarcely necessary. He told them it was his purpose to leave the city on the following morning, and requested that they would induce some of the principal caciques to grant him an interview in his quarters. He then summoned a council of his officers, though, as it seems, already determined as to the course he was to take.

The members of the council were differently affected by the startling intelligence, according to their different characters. The more timid, disheartened by the prospect of obstacles which seemed to multiply as they drew nearer the Mexican capital, were for retracing their steps and seeking shelter in the friendly city of Tlascala. Others, more persevering, but prudent, were for taking the more northerly route, originally recommended by their allies. The greater part supported the general, who was ever of opinion that they had no alternative but to advance. Retreat would be ruin. Half-way measures were scarcely better, and would infer a timidity which must discredit them with both friend and foe. Their true policy was to rely on themselves,—to strike such a blow as should intimidate their enemies and show them that the Spaniards were as incapable of being circumvented by artifice as of being crushed by weight of numbers and courage in the open field.

When the caciques, persuaded by the priests, appeared before Cortés, he contented himself with gently rebuking their want of hospitality, and assured them the Spaniards would be no longer a burden to their city, as he proposed to leave it early on the following morning. He requested, moreover, that they would furnish a reinforcement of two thousand men to transport his artillery and baggage. The chiefs, after some consultation, acquiesced in a demand which might in some measure favour their own designs.

On their departure, the general summoned the Aztec ambassadors before him. He briefly acquainted them with his detection of the treacherous plot to destroy his army, the contrivance of which, he said, was imputed to their master, Montezuma. It grieved him much, he added, to find the emperor implicated in so nefarious a scheme, and that the Spaniards must now march as enemies against the prince whom they had hoped to visit as a friend.

The ambassadors, with earnest protestations, asserted their entire ignorance of the conspiracy, and their belief that Montezuma was equally innocent of a crime which they charged wholly on the Cholulans. It was clearly the policy of Cortés to keep on good terms with the Indian monarch, to profit as long as possible by his good offices, and to avail himself of his fancied security—such feelings of security as the general could inspire him with—to cover his own future operations. He affected to give credit, therefore, to the assertion of the envoys, and declared his unwillingness to believe that a monarch who had rendered the Spaniards so many friendly offices would now consummate the whole by a deed of such unparalleled baseness. The discovery of their twofold duplicity, he added, sharpened his resentment against the Cholulans, on whom he would take such vengeance as should amply requite the injuries done both to Montezuma and the Spaniards. He then dismissed the ambassadors, taking care, notwithstanding this show of confidence, to place a strong guard over them, to prevent communication with the citizens.[1]

That night was one of deep anxiety to the army. The ground they stood on seemed loosening beneath their feet, and any moment might be the one marked for their destruction. Their vigilant general took all possible precautions for their safety, increasing the number of the sentinels, and posting his guns in such a manner as to protect the approaches to the camp. His eyes, it may well be believed, did not close during the night. Indeed, every Spaniard lay down in his arms, and every horse stood saddled and bridled, ready for instant service. But no assault was meditated by the Indians, and the stillness of the hour was undisturbed except by the occasional sounds heard in a populous city, even when buried in slumber, and by the hoarse cries of the priests from the turrets of the *teocallis*, proclaiming through their trumpets the watches of the night.[2]

[1] Bernal Diaz, Hist. de la Conquista, cap. 83.—Gomara, Crónica, cap. 59.—Rel. Seg. de Cortés, ap. Lorenzana, p. 65.—Torquemada, Monarch, Ind., lib. 4, cap. 39.—Oviedo, Hist. de las Ind., MS., lib. 83, cap. 4.—Martyr, De Orbe Novo, dec. 5, cap. 2.—Herrera, Hist. general, dec. 2, lib. 7, cap. 1.—Argensola, Anales, lib. 1, cap. 85.

[2] "Las horas de la noche las regulaban por las estrellas, y tocaban los ministros del templo que estaban destinados para este fin, ciertos instrumentos como vocinas, con que hacian conocer al pueblo el tiempo." Gama, Descripcion, Parte 1, p. 14.

CHAPTER VII.

TERRIBLE MASSACRE.—TRANQUILLITY RESTORED.—REFLECTIONS ON THE
MASSACRE.—FURTHER PROCEEDINGS.—ENVOYS FROM MONTEZUMA.

(1519.)

WITH the first streak of morning light, Cortés was seen on horseback,
directing the movements of his little band. The strength of his forces he
drew up in the great square or court, surrounded partly by buildings, as
before noticed, and in part by a high wall. There were three gates of
entrance, at each of which he placed a strong guard. The rest of his
troops, with his great guns, he posted without the enclosure, in such a
manner as to command the avenues and secure those within from interruption in their bloody work. Orders had been sent the night before to the
Tlascalan chiefs to hold themselves ready, at a concerted signal, to march
into the city and join the Spaniards.

The arrangements were hardly completed, before the Cholulan caciques
appeared, leading a body of levies, *tamanes*, even more numerous than had
been demanded. They were marched at once into the square, commanded, as we have seen, by the Spanish infantry, which was drawn up
under the walls. Cortés then took some of the caciques aside. With a
stern air, he bluntly charged them with the conspiracy, showing that he
was well acquainted with all the particulars. He had visited their city, he
said, at the invitation of their emperor; had come as a friend; had respected
the inhabitants and their property; and, to avoid all cause of umbrage,
had left a great part of his forces without the walls. They had received
him with a show of kindness and hospitality, and, reposing on this, he had
been decoyed into the snare, and found this kindness only a mask to cover
the blackest perfidy.

The Cholulans were thunderstruck at the accusation. An undefined awe
crept over them as they gazed on the mysterious strangers and felt themselves in the presence of beings who seemed to have the power of reading
the thoughts scarcely formed in their bosoms. There was no use in pre-
varication or denial before such judges. They confessed the whole, and
endeavoured to excuse themselves by throwing the blame on Montezuma.
Cortés, assuming an air of higher indignation at this, assured them that the
pretence should not serve, since, even if well founded, it would be no
justification; and he would now make such an example of them for their
treachery that the report of it should ring throughout the wide borders of
Anahuac!

The fatal signal, the discharge of an arquebuse, was then given. In
an instant every musket and crossbow was levelled at the unfortunate

Q

Cholulans in the courtyard, and a frightful volley poured into them as they stood crowded together like a herd of deer in the centre. They were taken by surprise, for they had not heard the preceding dialogue with the chiefs. They made scarcely any resistance to the Spaniards, who followed up the discharge of their pieces by rushing on them with their swords; and, as the half-naked bodies of the natives afforded no protection, they hewed them down with as much ease as the reaper mows down the ripe corn in harvest-time. Some endeavoured to scale the walls, but only afforded a surer mark to the arquebusiers and archers. Others threw themselves into the gateways, but were received on the long pikes of the soldiers who guarded them. Some few had better luck in hiding themselves under the heaps of slain with which the ground was soon loaded.

While this work of death was going on, the countrymen of the slaughtered Indians, drawn together by the noise of the massacre, had commenced a furious assault on the Spaniards from without. But Cortés had placed his battery of heavy guns in a position that commanded the avenues, and swept off the files of the assailants as they rushed on. In the intervals between the discharges, which, in the imperfect state of the science in that day, were much longer than in ours, he forced back the press by charging with the horse into the midst. The steeds, the guns, the weapons of the Spaniards were all new to the Cholulans. Notwithstanding the novelty of the terrific spectacle, the flash of firearms mingling with the deafening roar of the artillery as its thunders reverberated among the buildings, the despairing Indians pushed on to take the places of their fallen comrades.

While this fierce struggle was going forward, the Tlascalans, hearing the concerted signal, had advanced with quick pace into the city. They had bound, by order of Cortés, wreaths of sedge round their heads, that they might the more surely be distinguished from the Cholulans.[1] Coming up in the very heat of the engagement, they fell on the defenceless rear of the townsmen, who, trampled down under the heels of the Castilian cavalry on one side, and galled by their vindictive enemies on the other, could no longer maintain their ground. They gave way, some taking refuge in the nearest buildings, which, being partly of wood, were speedily set on fire. Others fled to the temples. One strong party, with a number of priests at its head, got possession of the great *teocalli*. There was a vulgar tradition, already alluded to, that on removal of part of the walls the god would send forth an inundation to overwhelm his enemies. The superstitious Cholulans with great difficulty succeeded in wrenching away some of the stones in the walls of the edifice. But dust, not water, followed. Their false god deserted them in the hour of need. In despair they flung them-

---

[1] "Usáron los de Tlaxcalla de un aviso muy bueno y les dió Hernando Cortés porque fueran conocidos y no morir entre los enemigos por yerro, porque sus armas y divisas eran casi de una manera; . . . y ansí se pusiéron en las cabezas unas guirnaldas de esparto á manera de torzales, y con esto eran conocidos los de nuestra parcialidad que no fué pequeño aviso." Camargo, Hist. de Tlascala, MS.

selves into the wooden turrets that crowned the temple, and poured down stones, javelins, and burning arrows on the Spaniards, as they climbed the great staircase which, by a flight of one hundred and twenty steps, scaled the face of the pyramid. But the fiery shower fell harmless on the steel bonnets of the Christians, while they availed themselves of the burning shafts to set fire to the wooden citadel, which was speedily wrapt in flames. Still the garrison held out, and though quarter, *it is said*, was offered, only one Cholulan availed himself of it. The rest threw themselves headlong from the parapet, or perished miserably in the flames.[1]

All was now confusion and uproar in the fair city which had so lately reposed in security and peace. The groans of the dying, the frantic supplications of the vanquished for mercy, were mingled with the loud battle-cries of the Spaniards as they rode down their enemy, and with the shrill whistle of the Tlascalans, who gave full scope to the long-cherished rancour of ancient rivalry. The tumult was still further swelled by the incessant rattle of musketry, and the crash of falling timbers, which sent up a volume of flame that outshone the ruddy light of morning, making altogether a hideous confusion of sights and sounds that converted the Holy City into a Pandemonium. As resistance slackened, the victors broke into the houses and sacred places, plundering them of whatever valuables they contained, plate, jewels, which were found in some quantity, wearing apparel and provisions, the two last coveted even more than the former by the simple Tlascalans, thus facilitating a division of the spoil much to the satisfaction of their Christian confederates. Amidst this universal license, it is worthy of remark, the commands of Cortés were so far respected that no violence was offered to women or children, though these, as well as numbers of the men, were made prisoners to be swept into slavery by the Tlascalans.[2] These scenes of violence had lasted some hours, when Cortés, moved by the entreaties of some Cholulan chiefs who had been reserved from the massacre, backed by the prayers of the Mexican envoys, consented, out of regard, as he said, to the latter, the representatives of Montezuma, to call off the soldiers, and put a stop, as well as he could, to further outrage.[3] Two of the caciques were, also, permitted to go to their countrymen with assurances of pardon and protection to all who would return to their obedience.

These measures had their effect. By the joint efforts of Cortés and the caciques, the tumult was with much difficulty appeased. The assailants, Spaniards and Indians, gathered under their respective banners, and the

---

1 Camargo, Hist. de Tlascala, MS.—Oviedo, Hist. de las Ind., MS., lib. 33, cap. 4, 45.—Torquemada, Monarch. Ind., lib. 4, cap. 40.—Ixtlilxochitl, Hist. Chich., MS., cap. 84.—Gomara, Crónica, cap. 60.

2 "They killed nearly six thousand persons, but touched neither women nor children, for so it had been ordered." Herrera, Hist. general, dec. 2, lib. 7, cap. 2.

3 [Andrés de Tápia, who participated in the massacre, says that the work of destroying the city ("el trabajar por destruir la cibdad") went on for two days, before Cortés gave orders for it to cease, and that it was not till two or three days later that the inhabitants, many of whom had fled to the mountains and neighbouring territory, obtained pardon and leave to return. Col. de Doc. para la Hist. de México, publicada por Joaquin García Icazbalceta, tom. ii.—ED.]

Cholulans, relying on the assurance of their chiefs, gradually returned to their homes.

The first act of Cortés was to prevail on the Tlascalan chiefs to liberate their captives.[1] Such was their deference to the Spanish commander that they acquiesced, though not without murmurs, contenting themselves, as they best could, with the rich spoil rifled from the Cholulans, consisting of various luxuries long since unknown in Tlascala. His next care was to cleanse the city from its loathsome impurities, particularly from the dead bodies which lay festering in heaps in the streets and great square. The general, in his letter to Charles the Fifth, admits three thousand slain, most accounts say six, and some swell the amount yet higher. As the eldest and principal cacique was among the number, Cortés assisted the Cholulans in installing a successor in his place.[2] By these pacific measures confidence was gradually restored. The people in the environs, reassured, flocked into the capital to supply the place of the diminished population. The markets were again opened ; and the usual avocations of an orderly, industrious community were resumed. Still, the long piles of black and smouldering ruins proclaimed the hurricane which had so lately swept over the city, and the walls surrounding the scene of slaughter in the great square, which were standing more than fifty years after the event, told the sad tale of the Massacre of Cholula.[3]

This passage in their history is one of those that have left a dark stain on the memory of the Conquerors. Nor can we contemplate at this day, without a shudder, the condition of this fair and flourishing capital thus invaded in its privacy and delivered over to the excesses of a rude and ruthless soldiery. But, to judge the action fairly, we must transport ourselves to the age when it happened. The difficulty that meets us in the outset is, to find a justification of the right of conquest, at all. But it should be remembered that religious infidelity, at this period, and till a

---

[1] Bernal Diaz, Hist. de la Conquista, cap. 83.—Ixtlilxochitl, Hist. Chich. MS., ubi supra.

[2] Bernal Diaz, Hist. de la Conquista, cap. 83.—The descendants of the principal Cholulan cacique are living at this day in Puebla, according to Bustamante. See Gomara, Crónica, trad. de Chimalpain (México, 1826), tom. i. p. 98, nota.

[3] Rel. Seg. de Cortés, ap. Lorenzana, p. 66.—Camargo, Hist. de Tlascala, MS.—Ixtlilxochitl, Hist. Chich., MS., cap. 84.—Oviedo, Hist. de las Ind., MS., lib. 33, cap. 4, 45.—Bernal Diaz, Hist. de la Conquista, cap. 83.—Gomara, Crónica, cap. 60.—Sahagun, Hist. de Nueva-España, MS., lib. 12, cap. 11.—Las Casas, in his printed treatise on the Destruction of the Indies, garnishes his account of these transactions with some additional and rather startling particulars. According to him, Cortés caused a hundred or more of the caciques to be impaled or roasted at the stake ! He adds the report that, while the massacre in the courtyard was going on, the Spanish general repeated a scrap of an old *romance*, describing Nero as rejoicing over the burning ruins of Rome :—

" Mira Nero de Tarpeya,
 A Roma como se ardia.

Gritos dan niños y viejos,
 Y él de nada se dolia."
 (Brevísima Relacion, p. 46.)

This is the first instance, I suspect, on record of any person being ambitious of finding a parallel for himself in that emperor ! Bernal Diaz, who had seen " the interminable narrative," as he calls it, of Las Casas, treats it with great contempt. His own version—one of those chiefly followed in the text—was corroborated by the report of the missionaries, who, after the Conquest, visited Cholula, and investigated the affair with the aid of the priests and several old survivors who had witnessed it. It is confirmed in its substantial details by the other contemporary accounts. The excellent Bishop of Chiapa wrote with the avowed object of moving the sympathies of his countrymen in behalf of the oppressed natives ; a generous object, certainly, but one that has too often warped his judgment from the strict line of historic impartiality. He was not an eyewitness of the transactions in New Spain, and was much too willing to receive whatever would make for his case, and to " over-red," if I may so say, his argument with such details of blood and slaughter as, from their very extravagance, carry their own refutation with them.

much later, was regarded—no matter whether founded on ignorance or education, whether hereditary or acquired, heretical or pagan—as a sin to be punished with fire and fagot in this world, and eternal suffering in the next. This doctrine, monstrous as it is, was the creed of the Romish, in other words, of the Christian Church,—the basis of the Inquisition, and of those other species of religious persecutions which have stained the annals, at some time or other, of nearly every nation in Christendom.[1] Under this code, the territory of the heathen, wherever found, was regarded as a sort of religious waif, which, in default of a legal proprietor, was claimed and taken possession of by the Holy See, and as such was freely given away by the head of the Church, to any temporal potentate whom he pleased, that would assume the burden of conquest.[2] Thus, Alexander the Sixth generously granted a large portion of the Western hemisphere to the Spaniards, and of the Eastern to the Portuguese. These lofty pretensions of the successors of the humble fisherman of Galilee, far from being nominal, were acknowledged and appealed to as conclusive in controversies between nations.[3]

With the right of conquest, thus conferred, came also the obligation, on which it may be said to have been founded, to retrieve the nations sitting in darkness from eternal perdition. This obligation was acknowledged by the best and the bravest, the gownsman in his closet, the missionary, and the warrior in the crusade. However much it may have been debased by temporal motives and mixed up with worldly considerations of ambition and avarice, it was still active in the mind of the Christian conqueror. We have seen how far paramount it was to every calculation of personal interest in the breast of Cortés. The concession of the Pope, then, founded on, and enforcing, the imperative duty of conversion,[4]

---

[1] For an illustration of the above remark the reader is referred to the closing pages of chap. 7, Part II., of the "History of Ferdinand and Isabella," where I have taken some pains to show how deep settled were these convictions in Spain at the period with which we are now occupied. The world had gained little in liberality since the age of Dante, who could coolly dispose of the great and good of antiquity in one of the circles of Hell because—no fault of theirs, certainly—they had come into the world too soon. The memorable verses, like many others of the immortal bard, are a proof at once of the strength and weakness of the human understanding. They may be cited as a fair exponent of the popular feeling at the beginning of the sixteenth century :—

" Ch' ei non peccaro, e, s'egli hanno mercedi,
Non basta, *perch' e' non ebber battesmo,*
Ch' è porta della fede che tu credi.
E, se furon dinanzi al Cristianesmo,
Non adorar debitamente Dio ;
E di questi cotai son io medesmo
Per tai difetti, e non per altro rio.
Semo perduti, e sol di tanto offesi
Che sanza speme vivemo in disio."
                INFERNO, canto 4.

[2] It is in the same spirit that the laws of Oleron, the máritime code of so high authority in the Middle Ages, abandon the property of the infidel, in common with that of pirates, as fair spoil to the true believer ! " S'ilz sont pyrates, pilleurs, ou escumeurs de mer, ou Turcs, *et autres contraires et ennemis de nostredicte foy catholicque,* chascun peut prendre sur telles manieres de gens, *comme sur chiens, si peut l'on les desrobber et spolier de leurs biens sans pugnition.* C'est le jugement." Jugemens d'Oleron, Art. 45, ap. Collection de Lois maritimes, par J. M. Pardessus (ed. Paris, 1828), tom. i. p. 351.

[3] The famous bull of partition became the basis of the treaty of Tordesillas, by which the Castilian and Portuguese governments determined the boundary-line of their respective discoveries ; a line that secured the vast empire of Brazil to the latter, which from priority of occupation should have belonged to their rivals. See the History of Ferdinand and Isabella, Part I., chap. 18 ; Part II., chap. 9,—the closing pages of each.

[4] It is the condition, unequivocally expressed and reiterated, on which Alexander VI., in his famous bulls of May 3d and 4th, 1493, conveys to Ferdinand and Isabella full and absolute right over all such territories in the Western World as may not have been previously occupied by Christian princes. See these precious documents, *in extenso,* apud Navarrete, Coleccion de los Viages y Descubrimientos (Madrid, 1825), tom. ii. Nos. 17. 18.

was the assumed basis—and, in the apprehension of that age, a sound one —of the right of conquest.[1]

This right could not, indeed, be construed to authorize any unnecessary act of violence to the natives. The present expedition, up to the period of its history at which we are now arrived, had probably been stained with fewer of such acts than almost any similar enterprise of the Spanish discoverers in the New World. Throughout the campaign, Cortés had prohibited all wanton injuries to the natives in person or property, and had punished the perpetrators of them with exemplary severity. He had been faithful to his friends, and, with perhaps a single exception, not unmerciful to his foes. Whether from policy or principle, it should be recorded to his credit; though, like every sagacious mind, he may have felt that principle and policy go together.

He had entered Cholula as a friend, at the invitation of the Indian emperor, who had a real, if not avowed, control over the state. He had been received as a friend, with every demonstration of goodwill; when, without any offence of his own or his followers, he found they were to be the victims of an insidious plot,—that they were standing on a mine which might be sprung at any moment and bury them all in its ruins. His safety, as he truly considered, left no alternative but to anticipate the blow of his enemies. Yet who can doubt that the punishment thus inflicted was excessive,—that the same end might have been attained by directing the blow against the guilty chiefs, instead of letting it fall on the ignorant rabble who but obeyed the commands of their masters? But when was it ever seen that fear, armed with power, was scrupulous in the exercise of it? or that the passions of a fierce soldiery, inflamed by conscious injuries, could be regulated in the moment of explosion?

We shall, perhaps, pronounce more impartially on the conduct of the Conquerors if we compare it with that of our own contemporaries under somewhat similar circumstances. The atrocities at Cholula were not so bad as those inflicted on the descendants of these very Spaniards, in the

---

[1] The ground on which Protestant nations assert a natural right to the fruits of their discoveries in the New World is very different. They consider that the earth was intended for cultivation, and that Providence never designed that hordes of wandering savages should hold a territory far more than necessary for their own maintenance, to the exclusion of civilized man. Yet it may be thought, as far as 'improvement of the soil is concerned, that this argument would afford us but an indifferent tenure for much of our own unoccupied and uncultivated territory, far exceeding what is demanded for our present or prospective support. As to a right founded on difference of civilization, this is obviously a still more uncertain criterion. It is to the credit of our Puritan ancestors that they did not avail themselves of any such interpretation of the law of nature, and still less rely on the powers conceded by King James's patent, asserting rights as absolute, nearly, as those claimed by the Roman See. On the contrary, they established their title to the soil by fair purchase of the aborigines; thus forming an honourable contrast to the policy pursued by too many of the settlers on the American continents. It should be remarked that, whatever difference of opinion may have subsisted between the Roman Catholic— or rather the Spanish and Portuguese—nations and the rest of Europe, in regard to the true foundation of their titles in a moral view, they have always been content, in their controversies with one another, to rest them exclusively on priority of discovery. For a brief view of the discussion, see Vattel (Droit des Gens, sec. 209), and especially Kent (Commentaries on American Law, vol. iii. lec. 51), where it is handled with much perspicuity and eloquence. The argument, as founded on the law of nations, may be found in the celebrated case of Johnson v. McIntosh. (Wheaton, Reports of Cases in the Supreme Court of the United States, vol. viii. p. 543, et seq.) If it were not treating a grave discussion too lightly, I should crave leave to refer the reader to the renowned Diedrich Knickerbocker's History of New York (book 1, chap. 5) for a luminous disquisition on this knotty question. At all events, he will find there the popular arguments subjected to the test of ridicule; a test showing, more than any reasoning can, how much, or rather how little, they are really worth.

late war of the Peninsula, by the most polished nations of our time ; by the British at Badajoz, for example,—at Tarragona, and a hundred other places, by the French. The wanton butchery, the ruin of property, and, above all, those outrages worse than death, from which the female part of the population were protected at Cholula, show a catalogue of enormities quite as black as those imputed to the Spaniards, and without the same apology for resentment,—with no apology, indeed, but that afforded by a brave and patriotic resistance. The consideration of these events, which, from their familiarity, make little impression on our senses, should render us more lenient in our judgments of the past, showing, as they do, that man in a state of excitement, savage or civilized, is much the same in every age. It may teach us—it is one of the best lessons of history—that, since such are the *inevitable* evils of war, even among the most polished people, those who hold the destinies of nations in their hands, whether rulers or legislators, should submit to every sacrifice, save that of honour, before authorizing an appeal to arms. The extreme solicitude to avoid these calamities, by the aid of peaceful congresses and impartial mediation, is, on the whole, the strongest evidence, stronger than that afforded by the progress of science and art, of our boasted advance in civilization.

It is far from my intention to vindicate the cruel deeds of the old Conquerors. Let them lie heavy on their heads. They were an iron race, who perilled life and fortune in the cause ; and, as they made little account of danger and suffering for themselves, they had little sympathy to spare for their unfortunate enemies. But, to judge them fairly, we must not do it by the lights of our own age. We must carry ourselves back to theirs, and take the point of view afforded by the civilization of their time. Thus only can we arrive at impartial criticism in reviewing the generations that are past. We must extend to them the same justice which we shall have occasion to ask from posterity, when, by the light of a higher civilization, it surveys the dark or doubtful passages in our own history, which hardly arrest the eye of the contemporary.

But, whatever be thought of this transaction in a moral view, as a stroke of policy it was unquestionable. The nations of Anahuac had beheld, with admiration mingled with awe, the little band of Christian warriors steadily advancing along the plateau in face of every obstacle, overturning army after army with as much ease, apparently, as the good ship throws off the angry billows from her bows, or rather like the lava, which, rolling from their own volcanoes, holds on its course unchecked by obstacles, rock, tree, or building, bearing them along, or crushing and consuming them in its fiery path. The prowess of the Spaniards—"the white gods," as they were often called [1]—made them to be thought invincible. But it was not till their arrival at Cholula that the natives learned how terrible was their vengeance ; and they trembled !

---

[1] *Los Dioses blancos.*—Camargo, Hist. de Tlascala, MS.—Torquemada, Monarch. Ind., lib. 4, cap. 40.

None trembled more than the Aztec emperor on his throne among the mountains. He read in these events the dark characters traced by the finger of Destiny.[1]   He felt his empire melting away like a morning mist. He might well feel so.   Some of the most important cities in the neighbourhood of Cholula, intimidated by the fate of that capital, now sent their envoys to the Castilian camp, tendering their allegiance, and propitiating the favour of the strangers by rich presents of gold and slaves.[2]   Montezuma, alarmed at these signs of defection, took counsel again of his impotent deities; but, although the altars smoked with fresh hecatombs of human victims, he obtained no cheering response.   He determined, therefore, to send another embassy to the Spaniards, disavowing any participation in the conspiracy of Cholula.

Meanwhile Cortés was passing his time in that capital.   He thought that the impression produced by the late scenes, and by the present restoration of tranquillity, offered a fair opportunity for the good work of conversion.   He accordingly urged the citizens to embrace the Cross and abandon the false guardians who had abandoned them in their extremity. But the traditions of centuries rested on the Holy City, shedding a halo of glory around it as "the sanctuary of the gods," the religious capital of Anahuac.   It was too much to expect that the people would willingly resign this pre-eminence and descend to the level of an ordinary community.   Still Cortés might have pressed the matter, however unpalatable, but for the renewed interposition of the wise Olmedo, who persuaded him to postpone it till after the reduction of the whole country.[3]

The Spanish general, however, had the satisfaction to break open the cages in which the victims for sacrifice were confined, and to dismiss the trembling inmates to liberty and life.   He also seized upon the great *teocalli*, and devoted that portion of the building which, being of stone, had escaped the fury of the flames, to the purposes of a Christian church; while a crucifix of stone and lime, of gigantic dimensions, spreading out its arms above the city, proclaimed that the population below was under the protection of the Cross.   On the same spot now stands a temple overshadowed by dark cypresses of unknown antiquity, and dedicated to Our Lady *de los Remedios*.   An image of the Virgin presides over it, *said* to have been left by the Conqueror himself;[4] and an Indian ecclesiastic, a descendant of the ancient Cholulans, performs the peaceful services of the Roman Catholic communion on the spot where his ancestors celebrated the sanguinary rites of the mystic Quetzalcoatl.[5]

---

[1] Sahagun, Hist. de Nueva-España, MS., lib. 12, cap. 11.—In an old Aztec harangue, made as a matter of form on the accession of a prince, we find the following remarkable prediction: "Perhaps ye are dismayed at the prospect of the terrible calamities that are one day to overwhelm us, calamities foreseen and foretold, though not felt, by our fathers! . . . when the destruction and desolation of the empire shall come, when all shall be plunged in darkness. when the hour shall arrive in which they shall make us slaves throughout the land, and we shall be condemned to the lowest and most degrading offices!" (Ibid., lib. 6, cap. 16.)   This random shot of prophecy, which I have rendered literally, shows how strong and settled was the apprehension of some impending revolution.

[2] Herrara, Hist. general, dec. 2, lib. 7, cap. 3.
[3] Bernal Diaz, Hist. de la Conquista, cap. 83.
[4] Veytia, Hist. antig., tom. i. cap. 13.
[5] Humboldt, Vues des Cordillères, p. 32.

During the occurrence of these events, envoys arrived from Mexico. They were charged, as usual, with a rich present of plate and ornaments of gold, among others, artificial birds in imitation of turkeys, with plumes of the same precious metal. To these were added fifteen hundred cotton dresses of delicate fabric. The emperor even expressed his regret at the catastrophe of Cholula, vindicated himself from any share in the conspiracy, which he said had brought deserved retribution on the heads of its authors, and explained the existence of an Aztec force in the neighbourhood by the necessity of repressing some disorders there.[1]

One cannot contemplate this pusillanimous conduct of Montezuma without mingled feelings of pity and contempt. It is not easy to reconcile his assumed innocence of the plot with many circumstances connected with it. But it must be remembered here, and always, that his history is to be collected solely from Spanish writers and such of the natives as flourished after the Conquest, when the country had become a colony of Spain. Not an Aztec record of the primitive age survives, in a form capable of interpretation.[2] It is the hard fate of this unfortunate monarch to be wholly indebted for his portraiture to the pencil of his enemies.

More than a fortnight had elapsed since the entrance of the Spaniards into Cholula, and Cortés now resolved without loss of time to resume his march towards the capital. His rigorous reprisals had so far intimidated the Cholulans that he felt assured he should no longer leave an active enemy in his rear, to annoy him in case of retreat. He had the satisfaction, before his departure, to heal the feud—in outward appearance, at least—that had so long subsisted between the Holy City and Tlascala, and which, under the revolution which so soon changed the destinies of the country, never revived.

It was with some disquietude that he now received an application from his Cempoallan allies to be allowed to withdraw from the expedition and return to their own homes. They had incurred too deeply the resentment of the Aztec emperor, by their insults to his collectors, and by their co-operation with the Spaniards, to care to trust themselves in his capital. It was in vain Cortés endeavoured to reassure them by promises of his protection. Their habitual distrust and dread of "the great Montezuma" were not to be overcome. The general learned their determination with regret, for they had been of infinite service to the cause by their stanch fidelity and courage. All this made it the more difficult for him to resist

---

[1] Rel. Seg. de Cortés, ap. Lorenzana, p. 69.—Gomara, Crónica, cap. 63.—Oviedo, Hist. de las Indias, MS., lib. 33, cap. 5.—Ixtlilxochitl, Hist. Chich., MS., cap. 84.

[2] The language of the text may appear somewhat too unqualified, considering that three Aztec codices exist with interpretations. (See *ante*, pp. 49-51.) But they contain very few and general allusions to Montezuma, and these strained through commentaries of Spanish monks, oftentimes manifestly irreconcilable with the genuine Aztec notions. Even such writers as Ixtlilxochitl and Camargo, from whom, considering their Indian descent, we might expect more independence, seem less solicitous to show this, than their loyalty to the new faith and country of their adoption. Perhaps the most honest Aztec record of the period is to be obtained from the volumes, the twelfth book particularly, of Father Sahagun, embodying the traditions of the natives soon after the Conquest. This portion of his great work was rewritten by its author, and considerable changes were made in it, at a later period of his life. Yet it may be doubted if the reformed version reflects the traditions of the country as faithfully as the original, which is still in manuscript, and which I have chiefly followed.

their reasonable demand. Liberally recompensing their services, therefore, from the rich wardrobe and treasures of the emperor, he took leave of his faithful followers, before his own departure from Cholula. He availed himself of their return to send letters to Juan de Escalante, his lieutenant at Vera Cruz, acquainting him with the successful progress of the expedition. He enjoined on that officer to strengthen the fortifications of the place, so as the better to resist any hostile interference from Cuba,—an event for which Cortés was ever on the watch,—and to keep down revolt among the natives. He especially commended the Totonacs to his protection, as allies whose fidelity to the Spaniards exposed them, in no slight degree, to the vengeance of the Aztecs.[1]

CHAPTER VIII.

MARCH RESUMED.—ASCENT OF THE GREAT VOLCANO.—VALLEY OF MEXICO —IMPRESSION ON THE SPANIARDS.—CONDUCT OF MONTEZUMA.— THEY DESCEND INTO THE VALLEY.

(1519.)

EVERYTHING being now restored to quiet in Cholula, the allied army of Spaniards and Tlascalans set forward in high spirits, and resumed the march on Mexico. The road lay through the beautiful savannas and luxuriant plantations that spread out for several leagues in every direction. On the march, they were met occasionally by embassies from the neighbouring places, anxious to claim the protection of the white men, and to propitiate them by gifts, especially of gold, their appetite for which was generally known throughout the country.

Some of these places were allies of the Tlascalans, and all showed much discontent with the oppressive rule of Montezuma. The natives cautioned the Spaniards against putting themselves in his power by entering his capital; and they stated, as evidence of his hostile disposition, that he had caused the direct road to it to be blocked up, that the strangers might be compelled to choose another, which, from its narrow passes and strong positions, would enable him to take them at great disadvantage.

The information was not lost on Cortés, who kept a strict eye on the movements of the Mexican envoys, and redoubled his own precautions against surprise.[2] Cheerful and active, he was ever where his presence was needed, sometimes in the van, at others in the rear, encouraging the

---

[1] Bernal Diaz, Hist. de la Conquista, cap. 84, 85. —Rel. Seg. de Cortés, ap. Lorenzana, p. 67.— Gomara, Crónica, cap. 60.—Oviedo, Hist. de las Ind., MS., lib. 33, cap. 5.

[2] "We walked," says Diaz, in the homely but expressive Spanish proverb, "with our beards over our shoulders"—*la barba sobre el ombro*. Hist. de la Conquista, cap. 86.

weak, stimulating the sluggish, and striving to kindle in the breasts or others the same courageous spirit which glowed in his own. At night he never omitted to go the rounds, to see that every man was at his post. On one occasion his vigilance had wellnigh proved fatal to him. He approached so near a sentinel that the man, unable to distinguish his person in the dark, levelled his crossbow at him, when fortunately an exclamation of the general, who gave the watchword of the night, arrested a movement which might else have brought the campaign to a close and given a respite for some time longer to the empire of Montezuma.

The army came at length to the place mentioned by the friendly Indians, where the road forked, and one arm of it was found, as they had foretold, obstructed with large trunks of trees, and huge stones which had been strewn across it. Cortés inquired the meaning of this from the Mexican ambassadors. They said it was done by the emperor's orders, to prevent their taking a route which, after some distance, they would find nearly impracticable for the cavalry. They acknowledged, however, that it was the most direct road; and Cortés, declaring that this was enough to decide him in favour of it, as the Spaniards made no account of obstacles, commanded the rubbish to be cleared away. Some of the timber might still be seen by the roadside, as Bernal Diaz tells us, many years after. The event left little doubt in the general's mind of the meditated treachery of the Mexicans. But he was too politic to betray his suspicions.[1]

They were now leaving the pleasant champaign country, as the road wound up the bold sierra which separates the great plateaus of Mexico and Puebla. The air, as they ascended, became keen and piercing; and the blasts, sweeping down the frozen sides of the mountains, made the soldiers shiver in their thick harness of cotton, and benumbed the limbs of both men and horses.

They were passing between two of the highest mountains on the North American continent; Popocatepetl, "the hill that smokes," and Iztaccihuatl, or "white woman,"[2]—a name suggested, doubtless, by the bright robe of snow spread over its broad and broken surface. A puerile superstition of the Indians regarded these celebrated mountains as gods, and Iztaccihuatl as the wife of her more formidable neighbour.[3] A tradition of a higher character described the northern volcano as the abode of the departed spirits of wicked rulers, whose fiery agonies in their prison-house caused the fearful bellowings and convulsions in times of eruption. It was the classic fable of antiquity.[4] These superstitious legends had invested the

[1] Bernal Diaz, Hist. de la Conquista, cap. 86.— Rel. Seg. de Cortés, ap. Lorenzana, p. 70.—Torquemada, Monarch. Ind., lib. 4, cap. 41.

[2] "Llamaban al volcan Popocatépetl, y á la sierra nevada Iztaccihuatl, que quiere decir la sierra que humea, y la blanca muger." Camargo, Hist. de Tlascala, MS.

[3] "La Sierra nevada y el volcan los tenian por Dioses; y que el volcan y la Sierra nevada eran marido y muger." Ibid., MS.

[4] Gomara, Crónica, cap. 62.

"Ætna Giganteos nunquam tacitura triumphos,
Enceladi bustum, qui saucia terga revinctus
Spirat inexhaustum flagranti pectore sulphur."

Claudian, De Rapt. Pros., lib. 1, v. 152.

mountain with a mysterious horror, that made the natives shrink from attempting its ascent, which, indeed, was from natural causes a work of incredible difficulty.

The great *volcan*,[1] as Popocatepetl was called, rose to the enormous height of 17,852 feet above the level of the sea ; more than 2000 feet above the "monarch of mountains,"—the highest elevation in Europe.[2] During the present century it has rarely given evidence of its volcanic origin, and "the hill that smokes" has almost forfeited its claim to the appellation. But at the time of the Conquest it was frequently in a state of activity, and raged with uncommon fury while the Spaniards were at Tlascala ; an evil omen, it was thought, for the natives of Anahuac. Its head, gathered into a regular cone by the deposit of successive eruptions, wore the usual form of volcanic mountains when not disturbed by the falling in of the crater. Soaring towards the skies, with its silver sheet of everlasting snow, it was seen far and wide over the broad plains of Mexico and Puebla, the first object which the morning sun greeted in his rising, the last where his evening rays were seen to linger, shedding a glorious effulgence over its head, that contrasted strikingly with the ruinous waste of sand and lava immediately below, and the deep fringe of funereal pines that shrouded its base.

The mysterious terrors which hung over the spot, and the wild love of adventure, made some of the Spanish cavaliers desirous to attempt the ascent, which the natives declared no man could accomplish and live. Cortés encouraged them in the enterprise, willing to show the Indians that no achievement was above the dauntless daring of his followers. One of his captains, accordingly, Diego Ordaz, with nine Spaniards, and several Tlascalans, encouraged by their example, undertook the ascent. It was attended with more difficulty than had been anticipated.

The lower region was clothed with a dense forest, so thickly matted that in some places it was scarcely possible to penetrate it. It grew thinner, however, as they advanced, dwindling by degrees into a straggling, stunted vegetation, till, at the height of somewhat more than thirteen thousand feet, it faded away altogether. The Indians who had held on thus far, intimidated by the strange subterraneous sounds of the volcano, even then in a state of combustion, now left them. The track opened on a black surface of glazed volcanic sand and of lava, the broken fragments of which, arrested in its boiling progress in a thousand fantastic forms, opposed continual impediments to their advance. Amidst these, one huge rock, the *Pico del Fraile*, a conspicuous object from below, rose to the perpendicular height of a hundred and fifty feet, compelling them

---

[1] The old Spaniards called any lofty mountain by that name, though never having given signs of combustion. Thus, Chimborazo was called a *volcan de nieve*, or "snow volcano" (Humboldt, Essai politique, tom. i. p. 162); and that enterprising traveller, Stephens, notices the *volcan de agua*, "water volcano," in the neighbourhood of Antigua Guate-mala. Incidents of Travel in Chiapas, Central America, and Yucatan (New York, 1841), vol. i. chap. 13.

[2] Mont Blanc, according to M. de Saussure, is 15,670 feet high. For the estimate of Popocatepetl, see an elaborate communication in the "Revista Mexicana," tom. ii. No. 4.

to take a wide circuit. They soon came to the limits of perpetual snow, where new difficulties presented themselves, as the treacherous ice gave an imperfect footing, and a false step might precipitate them into the frozen chasms that yawned around. To increase their distress, respiration in these aerial regions became so difficult that every effort was attended with sharp pains in the head and limbs. Still they pressed on, till, drawing nearer the crater, such volumes of smoke, sparks, and cinders were belched forth from its burning entrails, and driven down the sides of the mountain, as nearly suffocated and blinded them. It was too much even for their hardy frames to endure, and, however reluctantly, they were compelled to abandon the attempt on the eve of its completion. They brought back some huge icicles,—a curious sight in these tropical regions, —as a trophy of their achievement, which, however imperfect, was sufficient to strike the minds of the natives with wonder, by showing that with the Spaniards the most appalling and mysterious perils were only as pastimes. The undertaking was eminently characteristic of the bold spirit of the cavalier of that day, who, not content with the dangers that lay in his path, seemed to court them from the mere Quixotic love of adventure. A report of the affair was transmitted to the emperor Charles the Fifth, and the family of Ordaz was allowed to commemorate the exploit by assuming a burning mountain on their escutcheon.[1]

The general was not satisfied with the result. Two years after, he sent up another party, under Francisco Montaño, a cavalier of determined resolution. The object was to obtain sulphur to assist in making gunpowder for the army. The mountain was quiet at this time, and the expedition was attended with better success. The Spaniards, five in number, climbed to the very edge of the crater, which presented an irregular ellipse at its mouth, more than a league in circumference. Its depth might be from eight hundred to a thousand feet. A lurid flame burned gloomily at the bottom, sending up a sulphureous steam, which, cooling as it rose, was precipitated on the sides of the cavity. The party cast lots, and it fell on Montaño himself, to descend in a basket into this hideous abyss, into which he was lowered by his companions to the depth of four hundred feet! This was repeated several times, till the adventurous cavalier had collected a sufficient quantity of sulphur for the wants of the army.[2] This doughty enterprise excited general admiration at the time. Cortés concludes his report of it to the emperor with the judicious reflection that it would be less inconvenient, on the whole, to import their powder from Spain.[3]

[1] Rel. Seg. de Cortés, ap. Lorenzana, p. 70.—Oviedo, Hist. de las Ind., MS., lib. 33, cap. 5.—Bernal Diaz, Hist. de la Conquista, cap. 78.—The latter writer speaks of the ascent as made when the army lay at Tlascala, and of the attempt as perfectly successful. The general's letter, written soon after the event, with no motive for misstatement, is the better authority. See, also, Herrera, Hist. general, dec. 2, lib. 6, cap. 18.—Rel. d'un gentil' huomo, ap. Ramusio, tom. iii. p. 308.—Gomara, Crónica, cap. 62.

[2] [Montaño's family remained in Mexico after the Conquest, and his daughter received a pension from the government. Alaman, Disertaciones históricas, tom. i. apénd. 2.]

[3] Rel. Ter. y Quarta de Cortés, ap. Lorenzana, pp. 318, 380.—Herrera, Hist. general, dec. 3, lib. 3, cap. 1.—Oviedo, Hist. de las Ind., MS., lib. 33,

But it is time to return from our digression, which may perhaps be excused, as illustrating, in a remarkable manner, the chimerical spirit of enterprise—not inferior to that in his own romances of chivalry—which glowed in the breast of the Spanish cavalier in the sixteenth century.

The army held on its march through the intricate gorges of the sierra. The route was nearly the same as that pursued at the present day by the courier from the capital to Puebla, by the way of Mecameca.[1] It was not that usually taken by travellers from Vera Cruz, who follow the more circuitous road round the northern base of Iztaccihuatl, as less fatiguing than the other, though inferior in picturesque scenery and romantic points of view. The icy winds, that now swept down the sides of the mountains, brought with them a tempest of arrowy sleet and snow, from which the Christians suffered even more than the Tlascalans, reared from infancy among the wild solitudes of their own native hills. As night came on, their sufferings would have been intolerable, but they luckily found a shelter in the commodious stone buildings which the Mexican government had placed at stated intervals along the roads for the accommodation of the traveller and their own couriers. It little dreamed it was providing a protection for its enemies.

The troops, refreshed by a night's rest, succeeded, early on the following day, in gaining the crest of the sierra of Ahualco, which stretches like a curtain between the two great mountains on the north and south. Their progress was now comparatively easy, and they marched forward with a buoyant step, as they felt they were treading the soil of Montezuma.

They had not advanced far, when, turning an angle of the sierra, they suddenly came on a view which more than compensated the toils of the preceding day. It was that of the Valley of Mexico, or Tenochtitlan, as more commonly called by the natives; which, with its picturesque assemblage of water, woodland, and cultivated plains, its shining cities and shadowy hills, was spread out like some gay and gorgeous panorama before them. In the highly rarefied atmosphere of these upper regions, even remote objects have a brilliancy of colouring and a distinctness of outline which seem to annihilate distance.[2] Stretching far away at their feet, were seen noble forests of oak, sycamore, and cedar, and beyond, yellow fields of maize and the towering maguey, intermingled with orchards and blooming gardens; for flowers, in such demand for their

---

cap. 41.—M. de Humboldt doubts the fact of Montaño's descent into the crater, thinking it more probable that he obtained the sulphur through some lateral crevice in the mountain. (Essai politique, tom. i. p. 164.)* No attempt—at least, no successful one—was made to gain the summit of Popocatepetl, since this of Montaño, till the present century. In 1827 it was reached in two expeditions, and again in 1833 and 1834. A very full account of the last, containing many interesting details and scientific observations, was written by Federico de Gerolt,

one of the party, and published in the periodical already referred to. (Revista Mexicana, tom. i. pp. 461-482.) The party from the topmost peak, which commanded a full view of the less elevated Iztaccihuatl, saw no vestige of a crater in that mountain, contrary to the opinion usually received.

[1] Humboldt, Essai politique, tom. iv. p. 17.

[2] The lake of Tezcuco, on which stood the capital of Mexico, is 2277 metres—nearly 7500 feet—above the sea. Humboldt, Essai politique, tom. ii. p. 45.

* [There would seem to have been no grounds for the doubt expressed by Humboldt, as the sulphur is now nearly exhausted, having been regularly collected by Indian labourers, lowered into the crater by means of a rope of hide attached to a windlass. Tylor, Anahuac, p. 269.—ED.]

religious festivals, were even more abundant in this populous valley than in other parts of Anahuac. In the centre of the great basin were beheld the lakes, occupying then a much larger portion of its surface than at present; their borders thickly studded with towns and hamlets, and, in the midst,—like some Indian empress with her coronal of pearls,—the fair city of Mexico, with her white towers and pyramidal temples, reposing, as it were, on the bosom of the waters,—the far-famed "Venice of the Aztecs." High over all rose the royal hill of Chapoltepec, the residence of the Mexican monarchs, crowned with the same grove of gigantic cypresses which at this day fling their broad shadows over the land. In the distance beyond the blue waters of the lake, and nearly screened by intervening foliage, was seen a shining speck, the rival capital of Tezcuco, and, still farther on, the dark belt of porphyry, girdling the Valley around, like a rich setting which Nature had devised for the fairest of her jewels.

Such was the beautiful vision which broke on the eyes of the Conquerors. And even now, when so sad a change has come over the scene; when the stately forests have been laid low, and the soil, unsheltered from the fierce radiance of a tropical sun, is in many places abandoned to sterility; when the waters have retired, leaving a broad and ghastly margin white with the incrustation of salts, while the cities and hamlets on their borders have mouldered into ruins;—even now that desolation broods over the land-scape, so indestructible are the lines of beauty which Nature has traced on its features, that no traveller, however cold, can gaze on them with any other emotions than those of astonishment and rapture.[1]

What, then, must have been the emotions of the Spaniards, when, after working their toilsome way into the upper air, the cloudy tabernacle parted before their eyes, and they beheld these fair scenes in all their pristine magnificence and beauty! It was like the spectacle which greeted the eyes of Moses from the summit of Pisgah, and, in the warm glow of their feelings, they cried out, "It is the promised land!"[2]

But these feelings of admiration were soon followed by others of a very different complexion, as they saw in all this the evidences of a civilization and power far superior to anything they had yet encountered. The more timid, disheartened by the prospect, shrunk from a contest so unequal, and demanded, as they had done on some former occasions, to be led back again to Vera Cruz. Such was not the effect produced on the sanguine spirit of the general. His avarice was sharpened by the display of the dazzling spoil at his feet; and, if he felt a natural anxiety at the formidable odds, his confidence was renewed, as he gazed on the lines of his veterans, whose weather-beaten visages and battered armour told of battles won

---

[1] It is unnecessary to refer to the pages of modern travellers, who, however they may differ in taste, talent, or feeling, all concur in the impressions produced on them by the sight of this beautiful valley.

[2] Torquemada, Monarch. Ind., lib. 4, cap. 41.—

It may call to the reader's mind the memorable view of the fair plains of Italy which Hannibal displayed to his hungry barbarians after a similar march through the wild passes of the Alps, as reported by the prince of historic painters. Livy, Hist., lib. 21, cap. 35.

and difficulties surmounted, while his bold barbarians, with appetites whetted by the view of their enemies' country, seemed like eagles on the mountains, ready to pounce upon their prey. By argument, entreaty, and menace, he endeavoured to restore the faltering courage of the soldiers, urging them not to think of retreat, now that they had reached the goal for which they had panted, and the golden gates were opened to receive them. In these efforts he was well seconded by the brave cavaliers, who held honour as dear to them as fortune ; until the dullest spirits caught somewhat of the enthusiasm of their leaders, and the general had the satisfaction to see his hesitating columns, with their usual buoyant step, once more on their march down the slopes of the sierra.[1]

With every step of their progress, the woods became thinner; patches of cultivated land more frequent ; and hamlets were seen in the green and sheltered nooks, the inhabitants of which, coming out to meet them, gave the troops a kind reception. Everywhere they heard complaints of Montezuma, especially of the unfeeling manner in which he carried off their young men to recruit his armies, and their maidens for his harem. These symptoms of discontent were noticed with satisfaction by Cortés, who saw that Montezuma's "mountain-throne," as it was called, was indeed seated on a volcano, with the elements of combustion so active within that it seemed as if any hour might witness an explosion. He encouraged the disaffected natives to rely on his protection, as he had come to redress their wrongs. He took advantage, moreover, of their favourable dispositions, to scatter among them such gleams of spiritual light as time and the preaching of Father Olmedo could afford.

He advanced by easy stages, somewhat retarded by the crowd of curious inhabitants gathered on the highways to see the strangers, and halting at every spot of interest or importance. On the road, he was met by another embassy from the capital. It consisted of several Aztec lords, freighted, as usual, with a rich largess of gold, and robes of delicate furs and feathers. The message of the emperor was couched in the same deprecatory terms as before. He even condescended to bribe the return of the Spaniards, by promising, in that event, four loads of gold to the general, and one to each of the captains,[2] with a yearly tribute to their sovereign. So effectually had the lofty and naturally courageous spirit of the barbarian monarch been subdued by the influence of superstition !

But the man whom the hostile array of armies could not daunt was not to be turned from his purpose by a woman's prayers. He received the embassy with his usual courtesy, declaring, as before, that he could not answer it to his own sovereign if he were now to return without visiting the emperor in his capital. It would be much easier to arrange matters

---

1 Torquemada, Monarch. Ind., ubi supra.—Herrera, Hist. general, dec. 2, lib. 7, cap. 3.—Gomara, Crónica, cap. 64.—Oviedo, Hist. de las Ind., MS., lib. 33, cap. 5.

2 A load for a Mexican *tamane* was about fifty pounds, or eight hundred ounces. Clavigero, Stor. del Messico, tom. iii. p. 69, nota.

by a personal interview than by distant negotiation. The Spaniards came in the spirit of peace. Montezuma would so find it; but, should their presence prove burdensome to him, it would be easy for them to relieve him of it.[1]

The Aztec monarch, meanwhile, was a prey to the most dismal apprehensions. It was intended that the embassy above noticed should reach the Spaniards before they crossed the mountains. When he learned that this was accomplished, and that the dread strangers were on their march across the Valley, the very threshold of his capital, the last spark of hope died away in his bosom. Like one who suddenly finds himself on the brink of some dark and yawning gulf, he was too much bewildered to be able to rally his thoughts, or even to comprehend his situation. He was the victim of an absolute destiny, against which no foresight or precautions could have availed. It was as if the strange beings who had thus invaded his shores had dropped from some distant planet, so different were they from all he had ever seen, in appearance and manners; so superior—though a mere handful in numbers—to the banded nations of Anahuac in strength and science and all the fearful accompaniments of war! They were now in the Valley. The huge mountain screen, which nature had so kindly drawn around it for its defence, had been overleaped. The golden visions of security and repose in which he had so long indulged, the lordly sway descended from his ancestors, his broad imperial domain, were all to pass away. It seemed like some terrible dream,—from which he was now, alas! to awake to a still more terrible reality.

In a paroxysm of despair, he shut himself up in his palace, refused food, and sought relief in prayer and in sacrifice. But the oracles were dumb. He then adopted the more sensible expedient of calling a council of his principal and oldest nobles. Here was the same division of opinion which had before prevailed. Cacama, the young king of Tezcuco, his nephew, counselled him to receive the Spaniards courteously, as ambassadors, so styled by themselves, of a foreign prince. Cuitlahua, Montezuma's more warlike brother, urged him to muster his forces on the instant, and drive back the invaders from his capital or die in its defence. But the monarch found it difficult to rally his spirits for this final struggle. With downcast eye and dejected mien, he exclaimed, "Of what avail is resistance, when the gods have declared themselves against us?[2] Yet I mourn most for the old and infirm, the women and children, too feeble to fight or to fly. For myself and the brave men around me, we must bare our breasts to the storm, and meet it as we may!" Such are the sorrowful and sympathetic tones in which the Aztec emperor is said to have uttered the

[1] Sahagun, Hist. de Nueva-España, MS., lib. 12, cap. 12.—Rel. Seg. de Cortés, ap. Lorenzana, p. 73.—Herrera, Hist. general, dec. 2, lib. 7, cap. 3.—Gomara, Crónica, cap. 64.—Oviedo, Hist. de las Ind., MS., lib. 33, cap. 5.—Bernal Diaz, Hist. de la Conquista, cap. 87.

[2] This was not the sentiment of the Roman hero:—

"Victrix causa Diis placuit, sed victa Catoni!"

LUCAN, lib. 1, v. 128.

bitterness of his grief. He would have acted a more glorious part had he put his capital in a posture of defence, and prepared, like the last of the Palæologi, to bury himself under its ruins.[1]

He straightway prepared to send a last embassy to the Spaniards, with his nephew, the lord of Tezcuco, at its head, to welcome them to Mexico.

The Christian army, meanwhile, had advanced as far as Amaquemecan, a well-built town of several thousand inhabitants. They were kindly received by the cacique, lodged in large, commodious, stone buildings, and at their departure presented, among other things, with gold to the amount of three thousand *castellanos*.[2] Having halted there a couple of days, they descended among flourishing plantations of maize and of maguey, the latter of which might be called the Aztec vineyards, towards the lake of Chalco. Their first resting-place was Ajotzinco, a town of considerable size, with a great part of it then stand ng on piles in the water. It was the first specimen which the Spaniards had seen of this maritime architecture. The canals which intersected the city, instead of streets, presented an animated scene, from the number of barks which glided up and down freighted with provisions and other articles for the inhabitants. The Spaniards were particularly struck with the style and commodious structure of the houses, built chiefly of stone, and with the general aspect of wealth and even elegance which prevailed there.

Though received with the greatest show of hospitality, Cortés found some occasion for distrust in the eagerness manifested by the people to see and approach the Spaniards.[3] Not content with gazing at them in the roads, some even made their way stealthily into their quarters, and fifteen or twenty unhappy Indians were shot down by the sentinels as spies. Yet there appears, as well as we can judge at this distance of time, to have been no real ground for such suspicion. The undisguised jealousy of the court, and the cautions he had received from his allies, whiie they very properly put the general on his guard, seem to have given an unnatural acuteness, at least in the present instance, to his perceptions of danger.[4]

---

[1] Sahagun, Hist. de Nueva-España, MS., lib. 12, cap. 13.—Torquemada, Monarch. Ind., lib. 4, cap. 44.—Gomara, Crónica, cap. 63.

[2] "El señor de esta provincia y pueblo me dió hasta quarenta esclavas, y tres mil castellanos ; y dos dias que allí estuve nos proveyó muy cumplidamente de todo lo necesario para nuestra comida." Rel. Seg. de Cortés, ap. Lorenzana, p. 74.

[3] " De todas partes era infinita la gente que de un cabo é de otro concurrian á mirar á los Españoles, é maravillábanse mucho de los ver. Tenian grande espacio é atencion en mirar los caballos ; derian,

'Estos son Teules,' que quiere decir Demonios." Oviedo, Hist. de las Ind., MS., lib. 33, cap. 45.

[4] Cortés tells the affair coolly enough to the emperor. "And that night I kept such guard that of the spies—as well those who came across the water in canoes as those who descended from the sierra to watch for an opportunity of accomplishing their design—fifteen or twenty were discovered in the morning that had been killed by our men ; so that few returned with the information they had come to get." Rel. Seg. de Cortés, ap. Lorenzana, p. 74.*

* [Cortés cannot be blamed for adopting such precautions as any good general would have thought it culpable to neglect ; while his repeated warnings to the natives not to approach the camp after sunset show his anxiety to impress them with a sense of the danger. "Sabed," he said to the chiefs, "que estos que conmigo vienen no duermen de noche, é si duermen es un poco cuando es de dia ; é de noche están con sus armas, é cualquiera que ven que anda en pié ó entra do ellos están, luego lo matan ; é yo no basto á lo resistir ; por tanto, hacedlo así saber á toda vuestra gente, é decildes que despues de puesto el sol ninguna venga do estamos, porque morirá, é á mí me pesará de los que murieren." Relacion hecha por el Señor Andrés de Tápia sobre la Conquista de México.—Ed.]

Early on the following morning, as the army was preparing to leave the place, a courier came, requesting the general to postpone his departure till after the arrival of the king of Tezcuco, who was advancing to meet him. It was not long before he appeared, borne in a palanquin or litter, richly decorated with plates of gold and precious stones, having pillars curiously wrought, supporting a canopy of green plumes, a favourite colour with the Aztec princes. He was accompanied by a numerous suite of nobles and inferior attendants. As he came into the presence of Cortés, the lord of Tezcuco descended from his palanquin, and the obsequious officers swept the ground before him as he advanced. He appeared to be a young man of about twenty-five years of age, with a comely presence, erect and stately in his deportment. He made the Mexican salutation usually addressed to persons of high rank, touching the earth with his right hand, and raising it to his head. Cortés embraced him as he rose, when the young prince informed him that he came as the representative of Montezuma, to bid the Spaniards welcome to his capital. He then presented the general with three pearls of uncommon size and lustre. Cortés, in return, threw over Cacama's neck a chain of cut glass, which, where glass was as rare as diamonds, might be admitted to have a value as real as the latter. After this interchange of courtesies, and the most friendly and respectful assurances on the part of Cortés, the Indian prince withdrew, leaving the Spaniards strongly impressed with the superiority of his state and bearing over anything they had hitherto seen in the country.[1]

Resuming its march, the army kept along the southern borders of the lake of Chalco, overshadowed, at that time, by noble woods, and by orchards glowing with autumnal fruits, of unknown names, but rich and tempting hues. More frequently it passed through cultivated fields waving with the yellow harvest, and irrigated by canals introduced from the neighbouring lake; the whole showing a careful and economical husbandry, essential to the maintenance of a crowded population.

Leaving the mainland, the Spaniards came on the great dike or causeway, which stretches some four or five miles in length and divides lake Chalco from Xochicalco on the west. It was a lance in breadth in the narrowest part, and in some places wide enough for eight horsemen to ride abreast. It was a solid structure of stone and lime, running directly through the lake, and struck the Spaniards as one of the most remarkable works which they had seen in the country.

As they passed along, they beheld the gay spectacle of multitudes of Indians darting up and down in their light pirogues, eager to catch a glimpse of the strangers, or bearing the products of the country to the neighbouring cities. They were amazed, also, by the sight of the *chinampas,*

[1] Rel. Seg. de Cortés, ap. Lorenzana, p. 75.—Gomara, Crónica, cap. 64.—Ixtlilxochitl, Hist. Chich., MS., cap. 85.—Oviedo, Hist. de las Ind., MS., lib. 33, cap. 5.—"We esteemed it a great matter, and said amongst ourselves, If this cacique appeared in such state, what must be that displayed by the great Montezuma?" Bernal Diaz, Hist. de la Conquista, cap. 87.

or floating gardens,—those wandering islands of verdure, to which we shall
have occasion to return hereafter,—teeming with flowers and vegetables, and
moving like rafts over the waters. All round the margin, and occasionally
far in the lake, they beheld little towns and villages, which, half concealed
by the foliage, and gathered in white clusters round the shore, looked in
the distance like companies of wild swans riding quietly on the waves. A
scene so new and wonderful filled their rude hearts with amazement. It
seemed like enchantment; and they could find nothing to compare it with
but the magical pictures in the " Amadis de Gaula."[1] Few pictures,
indeed, in that or any other legend of chivalry, could surpass the realities
of their own experience. The life of the adventurer in the New World
was romance put into action. What wonder, then, if the Spaniard of that
day, feeding his imagination with dreams of enchantment at home and
with its realities abroad, should have displayed a Quixotic enthusiasm,—
a romantic exaltation of character, not to be comprehended by the colder
spirits of other lands !

Midway across the lake the army halted at the town of Cuitlahuac, a
place of moderate size, but distinguished by the beauty of the buildings,
—the most beautiful, according to Cortés, that he had yet seen in the
country.[2] After taking some refreshment at this place, they continued
their march along the dike. Though broader in this northern section,
the troops found themselves much embarrassed by the throng of Indians,
who, not content with gazing on them from the boats, climbed up the
causeway and lined the sides of the road. The general, afraid that his
ranks might be disordered, and that too great familiarity might diminish
a salutary awe in the natives, was obliged to resort not merely to command, but menace, to clear a passage. He now found, as he advanced,
a considerable change in the feelings shown towards the government.
He heard only of the pomp and magnificence, nothing of the oppressions,
of Montezuma. Contrary to the usual fact, it seemed that the respect for
the court was greatest in its immediate neighbourhood.

From the causeway, the army descended on that narrow point of land
which divides the waters of the Chalco from the Tezcucan lake, but which
in those days was overflowed for many a mile now laid bare.[3] Traversing
this peninsula, they entered the royal residence of Iztapalapan, a place

---

[1] "Nos quedámos admirados," exclaims Diaz,
with simple wonder, "y deziamos que parecia á las
casas de encantamento, que cuentan en el libro de
Amadis !" Hist. de la Conquista, cap. 87. An
edition of this celebrated romance in its Castilian
dress had appeared before this time, as the prologue
to the second edition of 1521 speaks of a former one
in the reign of the " Catholic Sovereigns." See
Cervantes, Don Quixote, ed. Pellicer (Madrid, 1797),
tom. i., Discurso prelim.

[2] "Una ciudad, la mas hermosa, aunque pequeña,
que hasta entonces habiamos visto, assi de muy bien
obradas Casas, y Torres, como de la buena órden,
que en el fundamento de ella habia por ser armada
toda sobre Agua." (Rel. Seg. de Cortés, ap. Lorenzana, p. 76.) The Spaniards gave this aquatic city
the name of Venezuela, or Little Venice. Toribio,
Hist. de los Indios, MS., Parte 2, cap. 4.

[3] M. de Humboldt has dotted the *conjectural*
limits of the ancient lake in his admirable chart of
the Mexican Valley. (Atlas géographique et physique de la Nouvelle-Espagne (Paris, 1811), carte
3.) Notwithstanding his great care, it is not easy
always to reconcile his topography with the itineraries of the Conquerors, so much has the face of
the country been changed by natural and artificial
causes. It is still less possible to reconcile their
narratives with the maps of Clavigero, Lopez,
Robertson, and others, defying equally topography
and history.

containing twelve or fifteen thousand houses, according to Cortés.[1] It was governed by Cuitlahua, the emperor's brother, who, to do greater honour to the general, had invited the lords of some neighbouring cities, of the royal house of Mexico, like himself, to be present at the interview. This was conducted with much ceremony, and, after the usual present of gold and delicate stuffs,[2] a collation was served to the Spaniards in one of the great halls of the palace. The excellence of the architecture here, also, excited the admiration of the general, who does not hesitate, in the glow of his enthusiasm, to pronounce some of the buildings equal to the best in Spain.[3] They were of stone, and the spacious apartments had roofs of odorous cedar-wood, while the walls were tapestried with fine cotton stained with brilliant colours.

But the pride of Iztapalapan, on which its lord had freely lavished his care and his revenues, was its celebrated gardens. They covered an immense tract of land ; were laid out in regular squares, and the paths intersecting them were bordered with trellises, supporting creepers and aromatic shrubs that loaded the air with their perfumes. The gardens were stocked with fruit-trees, imported from distant places, and with the gaudy family of flowers which belonged to the Mexican flora, scientifically arranged, and growing luxuriant in the equable temperature of the table-land. The natural dryness of the atmosphere was counteracted by means of aqueducts and canals that carried water into all parts of the grounds.

In one quarter was an aviary, filled with numerous kinds of birds, remarkable in this region both for brilliancy of plumage and of song. The gardens were intersected by a canal communicating with the lake of Tezcuco, and of sufficient size for barges to enter from the latter. But the most elaborate piece of work was a huge reservoir of stone, filled to a considerable height with water well supplied with different sorts of fish. This basin was sixteen hundred paces in circumference, and was surrounded by a walk, made also of stone, wide enough for four persons to go abreast. The sides were curiously sculptured, and a flight of steps led to the water below, which fed the aqueducts above noticed, or, collected into fountains, diffused a perpetual moisture.

Such are the accounts transmitted of these celebrated gardens, at a period when similar horticultural establishments were unknown in Europe ;[4] and we might well doubt their existence in this semi-civilized land, were it not a matter of such notoriety at the time and so explicitly attested by the invaders. But a generation had scarcely passed after the Conquest,

---

[1] Several writers notice a visit of the Spaniards to Tezcuco on the way to the capital. (Torquemada, Monarch. Ind., lib. 4, cap. 42.—Solis, Conquista, lib. 3, cap. 9.—Herrera, Hist. general, dec. 2, lib. 7, cap. 4.—Clavigero, Stor. del Messico, tom. iii. p. 74.) This improbable episode—which, it may be remarked, has led these authors into some geographical perplexities, not to say blunders—is altogether too remarkable to have been passed over in silence in the minute relation of Bernal Diaz, and that of Cortés, neither of whom alludes to it.

[2] "É me diéron," says Cortés, "hasta tres, ó quatro mil Castellanos, y algunas Esclavas, y Ropa, é me hiciéron muy buen acogimiento." Rel. Seg., ap. Lorenzana, p. 76.

[3] "Tiene el Señor de ella unas Casas nuevas, que aun no están acabadas, que son tan buenas como las mejores de España, digo de grandes y bien labradas." Ibid., p. 77.

[4] The earliest instance of a Garden of Plants in Europe is said to have been at Padua, in 1545. Carli, Lettres Américaines, tom. i. let. 21.

before a sad change came over these scenes so beautiful. The town itself was deserted, and the shore of the lake was strewed with the wreck of buildings which once were its ornament and its glory. The gardens shared the fate of the city. The retreating waters withdrew the means of nourishment, converting the flourishing plains into a foul and unsightly morass, the haunt of loathsome reptiles; and the water-fowl built her nest in what had once been the palaces of princes ! [1]

In the city of Iztapalapan, Cortés took up his quarters for the night. We may imagine what a crowd of ideas must have pressed on the mind of the Conqueror, as, surrounded by these evidences of civilization, he prepared with his handful of followers to enter the capital of a monarch who, as he had abundant reason to know, regarded him with distrust and aversion. This capital was now but a few miles distant, distinctly visible from Iztapalapan. And as its long lines of glittering edifices, struck by the rays of the evening sun, trembled on the dark-blue waters of the lake, it looked like a thing of fairy creation, rather than the work of mortal hands. Into this city of enchantment Cortés prepared to make his entry on the following morning.[2]

CHAPTER IX.

ENVIRONS OF MEXICO.—INTERVIEW WITH MONTEZUMA.—ENTRANCE INTO
THE CAPITAL.—HOSPITABLE RECEPTION.—VISIT TO THE EMPEROR.

(1519.)

WITH the first faint streak of dawn, the Spanish general was up, mustering his followers. They gathered, with beating hearts, under their respective banners, as the trumpet sent forth its spirit-stirring sounds across water and woodland, till they died away in distant echoes among the mountains. The sacred flames on the altars of numberless *teocallis*, dimly seen through the grey mists of morning,[3] indicated the site of the capital, till temple, tower, and palace were fully revealed in the glorious illumination which the sun, as he rose above the eastern barrier, poured over the beautiful Valley. It was the eighth of November 1519; a

---

[1] Rel. Seg. de Cortés, ubi supra.— Herrera, Hist. general, dec. 2, lib. 7, cap. 44.—Sahagun, Hist. de Nueva-España, MS., lib. 12, cap. 13.—Oviedo, Hist. de las Ind., MS., lib. 33, cap. 5.—Bernal Diaz, Hist. de la Conquista, cap. 87.

[2] " There Aztlan stood upon the farther shore ;
Amid the shade of trees its dwellings rose,
Their level roofs with turrets set around,
And battlements all burnished white, which shone
Like silver in the sunshine. I beheld
The imperial city, her far-circling walls,
Her garden groves and stately palaces,
Her temples mountain size, her thousand roots ;

And when I saw her might and majesty,
My mind misgave me then."
    SOUTHEY'S Madoc, Part 1, canto 6.

[3] [Alaman objects to my speaking of the "grey mists of morning" in connection with the Aztec capital. 'In the beginning of November," he says, "there is no such thing as a mist to be seen in the morning, or indeed in any part of the day, in the Valley of Mexico, where the weather is uncommonly bright and beautiful. The historian," he adds, "has confounded the climate of Mexico with that of England or the United States." Conquista de Méjico (trad. de Vega), tom. i. p. 337.]

conspicuous day in history, as that on which the Europeans first set foot in the capital of the Western World.

Cortés with his little body of horse formed a sort of advanced guard to the army. Then came the Spanish infantry, who in a summer's campaign had acquired the discipline and the weather-beaten aspect of veterans. The baggage occupied the centre ; and the rear was closed by the dark files [1] of Tlascalan warriors. The whole number must have fallen short of seven thousand ; of which less than four hundred were Spaniards. [2]

For a short distance, the army kept along the narrow tongue of land that divides the Tezcucan from the Chalcan waters, when it entered on the great dike, which, with the exception of an angle near the commencement, stretches in a perfectly straight line across the salt floods of Tezcuco to the gates of the capital. It was the same causeway, or rather the basis of that, which still forms the great southern avenue of Mexico. [3] The Spaniards had occasion more than ever to admire the mechanical science of the Aztecs, in the geometrical precision with which the work was executed, as well as the solidity of its construction. It was composed of huge stones well laid in cement, and wide enough, throughout its whole extent, for ten horsemen to ride abreast.

They saw, as they passed along, several large towns, resting on piles, and reaching far into the water,—a kind of architecture which found great favour with the Aztecs, being in imitation of that of their metropolis. [4] The busy population obtained a good subsistence from the manufacture of salt, which they extracted from the waters of the great lake. The duties on the traffic in this article were a considerable source of revenue to the crown.

Everywhere the Conquerors beheld the evidence of a crowded and thriving population, exceeding all they had yet seen. The temples and principal buildings of the cities were covered with a hard white stucco, which glistened like enamel in the level beams of the morning. The margin of the great basin was more thickly gemmed than that of Chalco with towns and hamlets. [5] The water was darkened by swarms of canoes

---

[1] [A Spanish translator incorrectly renders the words "dark files" by *indisciplinadas filas*, "undisciplined files." Señor Alaman, correcting, in this instance at least, the translation instead of the original, objects to this language. We may talk, says the critic, of the different kind of discipline peculiar to the Tlascalans, but not of their want of discipline, a defect which can hardly be charged on the most warlike nation of Anahuac. Conquista de Méjico (trad. de Vega), tom. i. p. 337.]

[2] He took about 6000 warriors from Tlascala ; and some few of the Cempoallan and other Indian allies continued with him. The Spanish force on leaving Vera Cruz amounted to about 400 foot and 15 horse. In the remonstrance of the disaffected soldiers, after the murderous Tlascalan combats, they speak of having lost fifty of their number since the beginning of the campaign. *Ante*, p. 218.

[3] "La calzada d'Iztapalapan est fondée sur cette même digue ancienne, sur laquelle Cortéz fit des prodiges de valeur dans ses rencontres avec les assiégés." (Humboldt, Essai politique, tom. ii. p. 57.) [At present the road of Tlalplan, or St. Augustine of the Caves (San Augustin de las Cuevas). Conquista de Méjico (trad. de Vega), tom. i. p. 338.]

[4] Among these towns were several containing from three to five or six thousand dwellings, according to Cortés, whose barbarous orthography in proper names will not easily be recognized by Mexican or Spaniard. Rel. Seg., ap. Lorenzana, p. 78.

[5] Father Toribio Benavente does not stint his panegyric in speaking of the neighbourhood of the capital, which he saw in its glory. "Creo, que en toda nuestra Europa hay pocas ciudades que tengan tal asiento y tal comarca, con tantos pueblos á la redonda de sí y tan bien asentados." Hist. de los Indios, MS., Parte 3, cap. 7.

filled with Indians,[1] who clambered up the sides of the causeway and gazed with curious astonishment on the strangers. And here, also, they beheld those fairy islands of flowers, overshadowed occasionally by trees of considerable size, rising and falling with the gentle undulation of the billows. At the distance of half a league from the capital, they encountered a solid work or curtain of stone, which traversed the dike. It was twelve feet high, was strengthened by towers at the extremities, and in the centre was a battlemented gateway, which opened a passage to the troops. It was called the Fort of Xoloc, and became memorable in after-times as the position occupied by Cortés in the famous siege of Mexico.

Here they were met by several hundred Aztec chiefs, who came out to announce the approach of Montezuma and to welcome the Spaniards to his capital. They were dressed in the fanciful gala costume of the country, with the *maxtlatl*, or cotton sash, around their loins, and a broad mantle of the same material, or of the brilliant feather-embroidery, flowing gracefully down their shoulders. On their necks and arms they displayed collars and bracelets of turquoise mosaic, with which delicate plumage was curiously mingled,[2] while their ears, under-lips, and occasionally their noses, were garnished with pendants formed of precious stones, or crescents of fine gold. As each cacique made the usual formal salutation of the country separately to the general, the tedious ceremony delayed the march more than an hour. After this, the army experienced no further interruption till it reached a bridge near the gates of the city. It was built of wood, since replaced by one of stone, and was thrown across an opening of the dike, which furnished an outlet to the waters when agitated by the winds or swollen by a sudden influx in the rainy season. It was a draw-bridge ; and the Spaniards, as they crossed it, felt how truly they were committing themselves to the mercy of Montezuma, who, by thus cutting off their communications with the country, might hold them prisoners in his capital.[3]

In the midst of these unpleasant reflections, they beheld the glittering retinue of the emperor emerging from the great street which led then, as it still does, through the heart of the city.[4] Amidst a crowd of Indian

---

[1] It is not necessary, however, to adopt Herrera's account of 50,000 canoes, which, he says, were constantly employed in supplying the capital with provisions ! (Hist. general, dec. 2, lib. 7, cap. 14.) The poet-chronicler Saavedra is more modest in his estimate :—

　　" Dos mil y mas canoas cada dia
　　Bastecen el gran pueblo Mexicano
　　De la mas y la menos niñeria
　　Que es necesario al alimento humano."
　　　　　　　El Peregrino Indiano, canto ii.

[2] " Usaban unos brazaletes de musaico, hechos de turquezas con unas plumas ricas que salian de ellos, que eran mas altas que la cabeza, y bordadas con plumas ricas y con oro, y unas bandas de oro, que subian con las plumas." Sahagun, Hist. de Nueva-España, lib. 8, cap. 9.

[3] Gonzalo de las Casas, Defensa, MS., Parte i, cap. 24.—Gomara, Crónica, cap. 65.—Bernal Diaz, Hist. de la Conquista, cap. 88.—Oviedo, Hist. de

las Ind., MS., lib. 33, cap. 5.—Rel. Seg. de Cortés, ap. Lorenzana, pp. 78, 79. — Ixtlilxochitl, Hist. Chich., MS., cap. 85.

[4] Cardinal Lorenzana says, the street intended was, probably, that crossing the city from the Hospital of San Antonio. (Rel. Seg. de Cortés, p. 79, nota.) This is confirmed by Sahagun. " Y así en aquel trecho que está desde la Iglesia de San Antonio (que ellos llaman Xuluco) que va por cave las casas de Alvarado, hácia el Hospital de la Concepcion, salió Moctezuma á recibir de paz á D. Hernando Cortés." Hist. de Nueva-España, MS., lib. 12, cap. 16. [The present Calle del Rastro, which continues, under different names, from the guard-house of San Antonio Abad to the Plaza. According to an early tradition, Montezuma and Cortés met in front of the spot where the Hospital of Jesus now stands, and the site for the building was chosen on that account. Conquista de Méjico (trad. de Vega), tom. i. p. 339.]

nobles, preceded by three officers of state bearing golden wands,[1] they saw the royal palanquin blazing with burnished gold. It was borne on the shoulders of nobles, and over it a canopy of gaudy feather-work, powdered with jewels and fringed with silver, was supported by four attendants of the same rank. They were barefooted, and walked with a slow, measured pace, and with eyes bent on the ground. When the train had come within a convenient distance, it halted, and Montezuma, descending from his litter, came forward, leaning on the arms of the lords of Tezcuco and Iztapalapan, his nephew and brother, both of whom, as we have seen, had already been made known to the Spaniards. As the monarch advanced under the canopy, the obsequious attendants strewed the ground with cotton tapestry, that his imperial feet might not be contaminated by the rude soil. His subjects of high and low degree, who lined the sides of the causeway, bent forward with their eyes fastened on the ground as he passed, and some of the humbler class prostrated themselves before him.[2] Such was the homage paid to the Indian despot, showing that the slavish forms of Oriental adulation were to be found among the rude inhabitants of the Western World.

Montezuma wore the girdle and ample square cloak, *tilmatli*, of his nation. It was made of the finest cotton, with the embroidered ends gathered in a knot round his neck. His feet were defended by sandals having soles of gold, and the leathern thongs which bound them to his ankles were embossed with the same metal. Both the cloak and sandals were sprinkled with pearls and precious stones, among which the emerald and the *chalchivitl*—a green stone of higher estimation than any other among the Aztecs—were conspicuous. On his head he wore no other ornament than a *panache* of plumes of the royal green, which floated down his back, the badge of military, rather than of regal, rank.

He was at this time about forty years of age. His person was tall and thin, but not ill made. His hair, which was black and straight, was not very long; to wear it short was considered unbecoming persons of rank. His beard was thin; his complexion somewhat paler than is often found in his dusky, or rather copper-coloured, race. His features, though serious in their expression, did not wear the look of melancholy, indeed, of dejection, which characterizes his portrait, and which may well have settled on them at a later period. He moved with dignity, and his whole demeanour, tempered by an expression of benignity not to have been anticipated from the reports circulated of his character, was worthy of a great prince. Such is the portrait left to us of the celebrated Indian emperor in this his first interview with the white men.[3]

The army halted as he drew near. Cortés, dismounting, threw his reins

---

[1] Carta del Lic. Zuazo, MS.

[2] "Toda la gente que estaba en las calles se le humiliaban y hacian profunda reverencia y grande acatamiento sin levantar los ojos á le mirar, sino que todos estaban hasta que él era pasado, *tan inclinados como frayles en Gloria Patri.*" Toribio, Hist. de los Indios, MS., Parte 3, cap. 7.

[3] For the preceding account of the equipage and appearance of Montezuma, see Bernal Diaz, Hist. de la Conquista, cap. 88,—Carta de Zuazo, MS.,—

to a page, and, supported by a few of the principal cavaliers, advanced to meet him. The interview must have been one of uncommon interest to both. In Montezuma, Cortés beheld the lord of the broad realms he had traversed, whose magnificence and power had been the burden of every tongue. In the Spaniard, on the other hand, the Aztec prince saw the strange being whose history seemed to be so mysteriously connected with his own; the predicted one of his oracles; whose achievements proclaimed him something more than human. But, whatever may have been the monarch's feelings, he so far suppressed them as to receive his guest with princely courtesy, and to express his satisfaction at personally seeing him in his capital.[1] Cortés responded by the most profound expressions of respect, while he made ample acknowledgments for the substantial proofs which the emperor had given the Spaniards of his munificence. He then hung round Montezuma's neck a sparkling chain of coloured crystal, accompanying this with a movement as if to embrace him, when he was restrained by the two Aztec lords, shocked at the menaced profanation of the sacred person of their master.[2] After the interchange of these civilities, Montezuma appointed his brother to conduct the Spaniards to their residence in the capital, and, again entering his litter, was borne off amidst prostrate crowds in the same state in which he had come. The Spaniards quickly followed, and, with colours flying and music playing, soon made their entrance into the southern quarter of Tenochtitlan.[3]

Here, again, they found fresh cause for admiration in the grandeur of the city and the superior style of its architecture. The dwellings of the poorer class were, indeed, chiefly of reeds and mud. But the great avenue through which they were now marching was lined with the houses of the nobles, who were encouraged by the emperor to make the capital their residence. They were built of a red porous stone drawn from quarries in the neighbourhood, and, though they rarely rose to a second story, often covered a large space of ground. The flat roofs, *azoteas*, were protected by stone parapets, so that every house was a fortress. Sometimes these roofs resembled parterres of flowers, so thickly were they covered with them, but more frequently these were cultivated in broad terraced gardens, laid out between the edifices.[4] Occasionally a great square or market-

---

Ixtlilxochitl, Hist. Chich., MS., cap. 85,—Gomara, Crónica, 65,—Oviedo, Hist. de las Ind., MS., ubi supra, et cap. 45,—Acosta, lib. 7, cap. 22,—Sahagun, Hist. de Nueva-España, MS., lib. 12, cap. 16,—Toribio, Hist. de los Indios, MS., Parte 3, cap. 7.—The noble Castilian or rather Mexican bard, Saavedra, who belonged to the generation after the Conquest, has introduced most of the particulars in his rhyming chronicle. The following specimen will probably suffice for the reader :—

" Yva el gran Moteçuma atauiado
De manta açul y blanca con gran falda,
De algodon muy sutil y delicado,
Y al remate vna concha de esmeralda :
En la parte que el nudo tiene dado,
Y una tiara á modo de guirnalda,

Zapatos que de oro son las suelas
Asidos con muy ricas correhuelas."
EL PEREGRINO INDIANO, canto II.

[1] "Satis vultu læto," says Martyr, "an stomacho sedatus, et an hospites per vim quis unquam libens susceperit, experti loquantur." De Orbe Novo, dec. 5, cap. 3.

[2] Rel. Seg. de Cortés, ap. Lorenzana, p. 79.

[3] "Entráron en la ciudad de Méjico á punto de guerra, tocando los atambores, y con banderas desplegadas," etc. Sahagun, Hist. de Nueva-España, MS., lib. 12, cap. 15.

[4] "Et giardini alti e bassi, che era cosa maravigliosa da vedere." Rel. d'un gentil' huomo, ap. Ramusio, tom. iii. fol. 309.

place intervened, surrounded by its porticoes of stone and stucco; or a pyramidal temple reared its colossal bulk, crowned with its tapering sanctuaries, and altars blazing with inextinguishable fires. The great street facing the southern causeway, unlike most others in the place, was wide, and extended some miles in nearly a straight line, as before noticed, through the centre of the city. A spectator standing at one end of it, as his eye ranged along the deep vista of temples, terraces, and gardens, might clearly discern the other, with the blue mountains in the distance, which, in the transparent atmosphere of the table-land, seemed almost in contact with the buildings.

But what most impressed the Spaniards was the throngs of people who swarmed through the streets and on the canals, filling every doorway and window and clustering on the roofs of the buildings. "I well remember the spectacle," exclaims Bernal Diaz: "it seems now, after so many years, as present to my mind as if it were but yesterday."[1] But what must have been the sensations of the Aztecs themselves as they looked on the portentous pageant! as they heard, now for the first time, the well-cemented pavement ring under the iron tramp of the horses,—the strange animals which fear had clothed in such supernatural terrors; as they gazed on the children of the East, revealing their celestial origin in their fair complexions; saw the bright falchions and bonnets of steel, a metal to them unknown, glancing like meteors in the sun, while sounds of unearthly music—at least such as their rude instruments had never wakened—floated in the air! But every other emotion was lost in that of deadly hatred, when they beheld their detested enemy the Tlascalan stalking, in defiance, as it were, through their streets, and staring around with looks of ferocity and wonder, like some wild animal of the forest who had strayed by chance from his native fastnesses into the haunts of civilization.[2]

As they passed down the spacious street, the troops repeatedly traversed bridges suspended above canals, along which they saw the Indian barks gliding swiftly with their little cargoes of fruits and vegetables for the markets of Tenochtitlan.[3] At length they halted before a broad area near the centre of the city, where rose the huge pyramidal pile dedicated to the patron war-god of the Aztecs, second only, in size as well as sanctity, to the temple of Cholula, and covering the same ground now in part occupied by the great cathedral of Mexico.[4]

---

[1] "¿Quien podrá," exclaims the old soldier, "dezir la multitud de hombres, y mugeres, y muchachos, que estauan en las calles, é açuteas, y en Canoas en aquellas acequias, que nos salian á mirar? Era cosa de notar, que agora que lo estoy escriuiendo, se me representa todo delante de mis ojos, como si ayer fuera quando esto passó." Hist. de la Conquista, cap. 88.

[2] "Ad spectaculum," says the penetrating Martyr, "tandem Hispanis placidum, quia diu optatum, Tenustiatanis prudentibus forte aliter, quia verentur fore, vt hi hospites quietem suam Elysiam veniant perturbaturi; de populo secus, qui nil sentit æque delectabile, quàm res novas ante oculos in presenti-

arum habere, de futuro nihil anxius." De Orbe Novo, dec. 5, cap. 3.

[3] The euphonious name of *Tenochtitlan* is commonly derived from Aztec words signifying "the *tuna*, or cactus, on a rock," the appearance of which, as the reader may remember, was to determine the site of the future capital. (Toribio, Hist. de los Indios, Parte 3, cap. 7.—Esplic. de la Coleccion de Mendoza, ap. Antiq. of Mexico, vol. iv.) Another etymology derives the word from *Tenoch*, the name of one of the founders of the monarchy.

[4] ["Por algunos manuscritos que he consultado é investigaciones que he hecho, me inclino á creer, que el templo se estendia desde la esquina de la

Facing the western gate of the enclosure of the temple, stood a low range of stone buildings, spreading over a wide extent of ground, the palace of Axayacatl, Montezuma's father, built by that monarch about fifty years before.[1] It was appropriated as the barracks of the Spaniards. The emperor himself was in the courtyard, waiting to receive them. Approaching Cortés, he took from a vase of flowers, borne by one of his slaves, a massy collar, in which the shell of a species of crawfish, much prized by the Indians, was set in gold and connected by heavy links of the same metal. From this chain depended -eight ornaments, also of gold, made in resemblance of the same shellfish, a span in length each, and of delicate workmanship;[2] for the Aztec goldsmiths were confessed to have shown skill in their craft not inferior to their brethren of Europe.[3] Montezuma, as he hung the gorgeous collar round the general's neck, said, " This palace belongs to you, Malinche "[4] (the epithet by which he always addressed him), " and your brethren. Rest after your fatigues, for you have much need to do so, and in a little while I will visit you again." So saying, he withdrew with his attendants, evincing in this act a delicate consideration not to have been expected in a barbarian.

Cortés' first care was to inspect his new quarters. The building, though spacious, was low, consisting of one floor, except, indeed, in the centre, where it rose to an additional story. The apartments were of great size, and afforded accommodations, according to the testimony of the Conquerors themselves, for the whole army![5] The hardy mountaineers of Tlascala were, probably, not very fastidious, and might easily find a shelter in the outbuildings, or under temporary awnings in the ample courtyards. The best apartments were hung with gay cotton draperies, the floors covered with mats or rushes. There were, also, low stools made of single pieces of wood elaborately carved, and in most of the apartments beds made of the palm leaf, woven into a thick mat, with coverlets, and sometimes canopies, of cotton. These mats were the only beds used by the natives, whether of high or low degree.[6]

After a rapid survey of this gigantic pile, the general assigned his troops their respective quarters, and took as vigilant precautions for security as

---

calle de *Plateros* y *Empedradillo* hasta la de *Cordobanes;* y de P. á O., desde el tercio ó cuarto de la placeta del *Empedradillo*, hasta penetrar unas cuantas varas hácia el O., dentro de las aceras que miran al P., y forman las calles del *Seminario* y del *Relox.* Ramirez, Notas y Esclarecimientos, p. 103.]

[1] Clavigero, Stor. del Messico, tom. iii. p. 78.—It occupied what is now the corner of the streets "Del Indio Triste" and "Tacuba."* Humboldt, Vues des Cordillères, p. 7, et seq.

[2] Rel. Seg. de Cortés, ap. Lorenzana, p. 88.—Gonzalo de las Casas, Defensa, MS., Parte 1, cap. 24.

[3] Boturini says, greater, by the acknowledgment of the goldsmiths themselves. "Los plateros de Madrid, viendo algunas Piezas, y Brazaletes de oro,

con que se armaban en guerra los Reyes, y Capitanes Indianos, confessáron, que eran inimitables en Europa." (Idea, p. 78.) And Oviedo, speaking of their work in jewellery, remarks, " Io vi algunas piedras jaspes, calcidonias, jacintos, corniolas, é plasmas de esmeraldas, é otras de otras especies labradas é fechas, cabezas de Aves, é otras hechas animales é otras figuras, que dudo haber en España ni en Italia quien las supiera hacer con tanta perficion." Hist. de las Ind., MS., lib. 33, cap. 11.

[4] *Ante*, p. 229.

[5] Bernal Diaz, Hist. de la Conquista, cap. 88.—Rel. Seg. de Cortés, ap. Lorenzana, p. 80.

[6] Bernal Diaz, Ibid., loc. cit.—Oviedo, Hist. de las Ind., MS., lib. 33, cap. 5.—Sahagun, Hist. de Nueva-España, MS., lib. 12, cap. 16.

* [Consequently, says Alaman, it must have faced the east, not the west gate of the Temple. Conquista de Méjico, tom. i. p. 343.—ED.]

if he had anticipated a siege instead of a friendly entertainment. The place was encompassed by a stone wall of considerable thickness, with towers or heavy buttresses at intervals, affording a good means of defence. He planted his cannon so as to command the approaches, stationed his sentinels along the works, and, in short, enforced in every respect as strict military discipline as had been observed in any part of the march. He well knew the importance to his little band, at least for the present, of conciliating the goodwill of the citizens; and, to avoid all possibility of collision, he prohibited any soldier from leaving his quarters without orders, under pain of death. Having taken these precautions, he allowed his men to partake of the bountiful collation which had been prepared for them.

They had been long enough in the country to become reconciled to, if not to relish, the peculiar cooking of the Aztecs. The appetite of the soldier is not often dainty, and on the present occasion it cannot be doubted that the Spaniards did full justice to the savoury productions of the royal kitchen. During the meal they were served by numerous Mexican slaves, who were, indeed, distributed through the palace, anxious to do the bidding of the strangers. After the repast was concluded, and they had taken their *siesta*, not less important to a Spaniard than food itself, the presence of the emperor was again announced.

Montezuma was attended by a few of his principal nobles. He was received with much deference by Cortés; and, after the parties had taken their seats, a conversation commenced between them, through the aid of Doña Marina, while the cavaliers and Aztec chieftains stood around in respectful silence.

Montezuma made many inquiries concerning the country of the Spaniards, their sovereign, the nature of his government, and especially their own motives in visiting Anahuac. Cortés explained these motives by the desire to see so distinguished a monarch and to declare to him the true Faith professed by the Christians. With rare discretion, he contented himself with dropping this hint, for the present, allowing it to ripen in the mind of the emperor, till a future conference. The latter asked whether those white men who in the preceding year had landed on the eastern shores of his empire were their countrymen. He showed himself well informed of the proceedings of the Spaniards from their arrival in Tabasco to the present time, information of which had been regularly transmitted in the hieroglyphical paintings. He was curious, also, in regard to the rank of his visitors in their own country; inquiring if they were the kinsmen of the sovereign. Cortés replied, they were kinsmen of one another, and subjects of their great monarch, who held them all in peculiar estimation. Before his departure, Montezuma made himself acquainted with the names of the principal cavaliers, and the position they occupied in the army.

At the conclusion of the interview, the Aztec prince commanded his attendants to bring forward the presents prepared for his guests. They consisted of cotton dresses, enough to supply every man, it is said, including the allies, with a suit !¹ And he did not fail to add the usual accompaniment of gold chains and other ornaments, which he distributed in profusion among the Spaniards. He then withdrew with the same ceremony with which he had entered, leaving every one deeply impressed with his munificence and his affability, so unlike what they had been taught to expect by what they now considered an invention of the enemy.²

That evening the Spaniards celebrated their arrival in the Mexican capital by a general discharge of artillery. The thunders of the ordnance, reverberating among the buildings and shaking them to their foundations, the stench of the sulphureous vapour that rolled in volumes above the walls of the encampment, reminding the inhabitants of the explosions of the great *volcan*, filled the hearts of the superstitious Aztecs with dismay. It proclaimed to them that their city held in its bosom those dread beings whose path had been marked with desolation, and who could call down the thunderbolts to consume their enemies ! It was doubtless the policy of Cortés to strengthen this superstitious feeling as far as possible, and to impress the natives, at the outset, with a salutary awe of the supernatural powers of the Spaniards.³

On the following morning, the general requested permission to return the emperor's visit, by waiting on him in his palace. This was readily granted, and Montezuma sent his officers to conduct the Spaniards to his presence. Cortés dressed himself in his richest habit, and left the quarters attended by Alvarado, Sandoval, Velasquez, and Ordaz, together with five or six of the common file.

The royal habitation was at no great distance. It stood on the ground, to the south-west of the cathedral, since covered in part by the *Casa del Estado*, the palace of the dukes of Monteleone, the descendants of Cortés.⁴ It was a vast, irregular pile of low stone buildings, like that garrisoned by the Spaniards.⁵ So spacious was it, indeed, that, as one of the Conquerors assures us, although he had visited it more than once, for the express

---

1 "Muchas y diversas Joyas de Oro, y Plata, y Plumajes, y con fasta cinco ó seis mil Piezas de Ropa de Algodon muy ricas, y de diversas maneras texida, y labrada." (Rel. Seg. de Cortés, ap. Lorenzana, p. 80.) Even this falls short of truth, according to Diaz. "Tenia apercebido el gran Moteçuma muy ricas joyas de oro, y de muchas hechuras, que dió á nuestro Capitan, é assí mismo á cada vno de nuestros Capitanes dió cositas de oro, y tres cargas de mantas de labores ricas de pluma, y entre todos los soldados tambien nos dió á cada vno á dos cargas de mantas, con alegria, y en todo parecia gran señor." (Hist. de la Conquista, cap. 89.) "Sex millia vestium, aiunt qui eas vidêre." Martyr, De Orbe Novo, dec. 5, cap. 3.

2 Ixtlilxochitl, Hist. Chich., MS., cap. 85.— Gomara, Crónica, cap. 66.—Herrera, Hist. general, dec. 2, lib. 7, cap. 6.—Bernal Diaz, Hist. de la Conquista, cap. 88.—Oviedo, Hist. de las Ind., MS., lib. 33, cap. 5.

3 "La noche siguiente jugáron la artillería por la solemnidad de haber llegado sin daño á donde deseaban; pero los Indios como no usados á los truenos de la artillería, mal edor de la pólvora, recibiéron grande alteracion y miedo toda aquella noche." Sahagun, Hist. de Nueva-España, MS., lib. 12, cap. 17.

4 "C'est là que la famille construisit le bel édifice dans lequel se trouvent les archives del Estado, et qui est passé avec tout l'héritage au duc Napolitain de Monteleone." (Humboldt, Essai politique, tom. ii. p. 72.) The inhabitants of modern Mexico have large obligations to this inquisitive traveller for the care he has taken to identify the memorable localities of their capital. It is not often that a philosophical treatise is also a good *manuel du voyageur*.

5 [The palace of Montezuma, according to Ramirez, "occupied the site where the national palace now stands, including that of the university and the adjacent houses, and extending to the Plaza del Volador, or new market-place. This was the ordinary residence of the last Montezuma, and the place where he was actually made prisoner." Notas y Esclarecimientos, p. 103.]

purpose, he had been too much fatigued each time by wandering through the apartments ever to see the whole of it.[1] It was built of the red porous stone of the country, *tetzontli*, was ornamented with marble, and on the façade over the principal entrance were sculptured the arms or device of Montezuma, an eagle bearing an ocelot in his talons.[2]

In the courts through which the Spaniards passed, fountains of crystal water were playing, fed from the copious reservoir on the distant hill of Chapoltepec, and supplying in their turn more than a hundred baths in the interior of the palace. Crowds of Aztec nobles were sauntering up and down in these squares, and in the outer halls, loitering away their hours in attendance on the court. The apartments were of immense size, though not lofty. The ceilings were of various sorts of odoriferous wood ingeniously carved; the floors covered with mats of the palm leaf. The walls were hung with cotton richly stained, with the skins of wild animals, or gorgeous draperies of feather-work wrought in imitation of birds, insects, and flowers, with the nice art and glowing radiance of colours that might compare with the tapestries of Flanders. Clouds of incense rolled up from censers and diffused intoxicating odours through the apartments. The Spaniards might well have fancied themselves in the voluptuous precincts of an Eastern harem, instead of treading the halls of a wild barbaric chief in the Western World.[3]

On reaching the hall of audience, the Mexican officers took off their sandals, and covered their gay attire with a mantle of *nequen*, a coarse stuff made of the fibres of the maguey, worn only by the poorest classes. This act of humiliation was imposed on all, except the members of his own family, who approached the sovereign.[4] Thus barefooted, with downcast eyes and formal obeisance, they ushered the Spaniards into the royal presence.

They found Montezuma seated at the further end of a spacious saloon and surrounded by a few of his favourite chiefs. He received them kindly, and very soon Cortés, without much ceremony, entered on the subject which was uppermost in his thoughts. He was fully aware of the importance of gaining the royal convert, whose example would have such an influence on the conversion of his people. The general, therefore, prepared to display the whole store of his theological science, with the

---

[1] "Et io entrai più di quattro volte in una casa del gran Signor non per altro effetto che per vederla, et ogni volta vi camminauo tanto che mi stancauo, et mai la fini di vedere tutta." Rel. d'un gentil' huomo ap. Ramusio, tom. iii. fol. 309.

[2] Gomara, Crónica, cap. 71. — Herrera, Hist. general, dec. 2, lib. 7, cap. 9.—The authorities call it "tiger," an animal not known in America. I have ventured to substitute the "ocelot," *tlalocelotl* of Mexico, a native animal, which, being of the same family, might easily be confounded by the Spaniards with the tiger of the Old Continent.

[3] Toribio, Hist. de los Indios, MS., Parte 3, cap. 7.—Herrera, Hist. general, dec. 2, lib. 7, cap. 9.—Gomara, Crónica, cap. 71.—Bernal Diaz, Hist. de

la Conquista, cap. 91.—Oviedo, Hist. de las Ind., MS., lib. 33, cap. 5, 46.—Rel. Seg. de Cortés, ap. Lorenzana, pp. 111-114.

[4] "Para entrar en su palacio, á que ellos llaman Tecpa, todos se descalzaban, y los que entraban á negociar con él habian de llevar mantas groseras encima de si, y si eran grandes señores ó en tiempo de frio, sobre las mantas buenas que llevaban vestidas, ponian una manta grosera y pobre ; y para hablarle, estaban muy humiliados y sin levantar los ojos." (Toribio, Hist. de los Indios, MS., Parte 3, cap. 7.) There is no better authority than this worthy missionary for the usages of the ancient Aztecs, of which he had such large personal knowledge.

most winning arts of rhetoric he could command, while the interpretation was conveyed through the silver tones of Marina, as inseparable from him, on these occasions, as his shadow.

He set forth, as clearly as he could, the ideas entertained by the Church in regard to the holy mysteries of the Trinity, the Incarnation, and the Atonement. From this he ascended to the origin of things, the creation of the world, the first pair, paradise, and the fall of man. He assured Montezuma that the idols he worshipped were Satan under different forms. A sufficient proof of it was the bloody sacrifices they imposed, which he contrasted with the pure and simple rite of the mass. Their worship would sink him in perdition. It was to snatch his soul, and the souls of his people, from the flames of eternal fire by opening to them a purer faith, that the Christians had come to his land. And he earnestly besought him not to neglect the occasion, but to secure his salvation by embracing the Cross, the great sign of human redemption.

The eloquence of the preacher was wasted on the insensible heart of his royal auditor. It doubtless lost somewhat of its efficacy, strained through the imperfect interpretation of so recent a neophyte as the Indian damsel. But the doctrines were too abstruse in themselves to be comprehended at a glance by the rude intellect of a barbarian. And Montezuma may have, perhaps, thought it was not more monstrous to feed on the flesh of a fellow-creature than on that of the Creator himself.[1] He was, besides, steeped in the superstitions of his country from his cradle. He had been educated in the straitest sect of her religion, had been himself a priest before his election to the throne, and was now the head both of the religion and the state. Little probability was there that such a man would be open to argument or persuasion, even from the lips of a more practised polemic than the Spanish commander. How could he abjure the faith that was intertwined with the dearest affections of his heart and the very elements of his being? How could he be false to the gods who had raised him to such prosperity and honours, and whose shrines were intrusted to his especial keeping?

He listened, however, with silent attention, until the general had concluded his homily. He then replied that he knew the Spaniards had held this discourse wherever they had been. He doubted not their God was, as they said, a good being. His gods, also, were good to him. Yet what his visitor said of the creation of the world was like what he had been taught to believe.[2] It was not worth while to discourse further of the matter. His ancestors, he said, were not the original proprietors of the land. They had occupied it but a few ages, and had been led there

---

[1] The ludicrous effect—if the subject be not too grave to justify the expression—of a literal belief in the doctrine of transubstantiation in the mother-country, even at this day, is well illustrated by Blanco White, **Letters** from Spain (London, 1822), let. 1.

[2] "Y en esso de la creacion del mundo assí lo tenemos nosotros creido muchos tiempos passados." (Bernal Diaz, Hist. de la Conquista, cap. 90.) For some points of resemblance between the Aztec and Hebrew traditions, see Book 1, chap. 3, and Appendix, Part 1, of this History.

by a great Being, who, after giving them laws and ruling over the nation for a time, had withdrawn to the regions where the sun rises. He had declared, on his departure, that he or his descendants would again visit them and resume his empire.[1] The wonderful deeds of the Spaniards, their fair complexions, and the quarter whence they came, all showed they were his descendants. If Montezuma had resisted their visit to his capital, it was because he had heard such accounts of their cruelties,— that they sent the lightning to consume his people, or crushed them to pieces under the hard feet of the ferocious animals on which they rode. He was now convinced that these were idle tales; that the Spaniards were kind and generous in their natures; they were mortals, of a different race, indeed, from the Aztecs, wiser, and more valiant,—and for this he honoured them.

"You, too," he added, with a smile, "have been told, perhaps, that I am a god, and dwell in palaces of gold and silver.[2] But you see it is false. My houses, though large, are of stone and wood like those of others; and as to my body," he said, baring his tawny arm, "you see it is flesh and bone like yours. It is true, I have a great empire inherited from my ancestors; lands, and gold, and silver. But your sovereign beyond the waters is, I know, the rightful lord of all. I rule in his name. You, Malinche, are his ambassador; you and your brethren shall share these things with me. Rest now from your labours. You are here in your own dwellings, and everything shall be provided for your subsistence. I will see that your wishes shall be obeyed in the same way as my own."[3] As the monarch concluded these words, a few natural tears suffused his eyes, while the image of ancient independence, perhaps, flitted across his mind.[4]

Cortés, while he encouraged the idea that his own sovereign was the great Being indicated by Montezuma, endeavoured to comfort the monarch by the assurance that his master had no desire to interfere with his authority, otherwise than, out of pure concern for his welfare, to effect his conversion and that of his people to Christianity. Before the emperor dismissed his visitors he consulted his munificent spirit, as usual, by distributing rich stuffs and trinkets of gold among them, so that the poorest soldier, says Bernal Diaz, one of the party, received at least two heavy collars of the precious metal for his share. The iron hearts of the

---

[1] "É siempre hemos tenido, que los que de él descendiessen habian de venir á sojuzgar esta tierra, y á nosotros como á sus Vasallos." Rel. Seg. de Cortés, ap. Lorenzana, p. 81.

[2] "Y luego el Monteçuma dixo riendo, porque en todo era muy regozijado en su hablar de gran señor: Malinche, bien sé que te han dicho essos de Tlascala, con quien tanta amistad aueis tomado, que yo que soy como Dios, ó Teule, que quanto ay en mis casas es todo oro, é plata, y piedras ricas." Bernal Diaz, Hist. de la Conquista, cap. 90.

[3] "É por tanto Vos sed cierto, que os obedecerémos, y ternémos por señor en lugar de esse gran señor, que decis, y que en ello no habia falta, ni engaño alguno; é bien podeis en toda la tierra, digo,

que en la que yo en mi Señorío poseo, mandar á vuestra voluntad, porque será obedecido y fecho, y todo lo que nosotros tenemos es para lo que Vos de ello quisieredes disponer." Rel. Seg. de Cortés, ubi supra.

[4] Martyr, De Orbe Novo, dec. 5, cap. 3.—Gomara, Crónica, cap. 66.—Oviedo, Hist. de las Ind., MS., lib. 33, cap. 5.—Gonzalo de las Casas, MS., Parte 1, cap. 24.—Cortés, in his brief notes of this proceeding, speaks only of the interview with Montezuma in the Spanish quarters, which he makes the scene of the preceding dialogue. Bernal Diaz transfers this to the subsequent meeting in the palace. In the only fact of importance, the dialogue itself, both substantially agree.

Spaniards were touched with the emotion displayed by Montezuma, as well as by his princely spirit of liberality. As they passed him, the cavaliers, with bonnet in hand, made him the most profound obeisance, and "on the way home," continues the same chronicler, "we could discourse of nothing but the gentle breeding and courtesy of the Indian monarch, and of the respect we entertained for him."[1]

Speculations of a graver complexion must have pressed on the mind of the general, as he saw around him the evidences of a civilization, and consequently power, for which even the exaggerated reports of the natives —discredited from their apparent exaggeration—had not prepared him. In the pomp and burdensome ceremonial of the court he saw that nice system of subordination and profound reverence for the monarch which characterize the semi-civilized empires of Asia. In the appearance of the capital, its massy yet elegant architecture, its luxurious social accommodations, its activity in trade, he recognized the proofs of the intellectual progress, mechanical skill, and enlarged resources of an old and opulent community; while the swarms in the streets attested the existence of a population capable of turning these resources to the best account.

In the Aztec he beheld a being unlike either the rude republican Tlascalan or the effeminate Cholulan, but combining the courage of the one with the cultivation of the other. He was in the heart of a great capital, which seemed like an extensive fortification, with its dikes and its drawbridges, where every house might be easily converted into a castle. Its insular position removed it from the continent, from which, at the mere nod of the sovereign, all communication might be cut off, and the whole warlike population be at once precipitated on him and his handful of followers. What could superior science avail against such odds?[2]

As to the subversion of Montezuma's empire, now that he had seen him in his capital, it must have seemed a more doubtful enterprise than ever. The recognition which the Aztec prince had made of the feudal supremacy, if I may so say, of the Spanish sovereign, was not to be taken too literally. Whatever show of deference he might be disposed to pay the latter under the influence of his present—perhaps temporary—delusion, it was not to be supposed that he would so easily relinquish his actual power and possessions, or that his people would consent to it. Indeed, his sensitive apprehensions in regard to this very subject, on the coming of the Spaniards, were sufficient proof of the tenacity with which he clung to his authority. It is true that Cortés had a strong lever for future operations in the superstitious reverence felt for himself both by prince and people.

[1] "Assí nos despedímos con grandes cortesías del, y nos fuýmos á nuestros aposentos, é ibamos platicando de la buena manera é criança que en todo tenia, é que nosotros en todo le tuuiessemos mucho acato, é con las gorras de armas colchadas quitadas, quando delante dél passassemos." Bernal Diaz, Hist. de la Conquista, cap. 90.

[2] "Y assi," says Toribio de Benavente, "estaba tan fuerte esta ciudad, que parecia no bastar poder humano para ganarla; porque ademas de su fuerza y municion que tenia, era cabeza y Señoría de toda la tierra, y el Señor de ella (Moteczuma) gloriábase en su silla y en la fortaleza de su ciudad, y en la muchedumbre de sus vassallos." Hist. de los Indios, MS., Parte 3, cap. 8.

It was undoubtedly his policy to maintain this sentiment unimpaired in both, as far as possible.[1]   But, before settling any plan of operations, it was necessary to make himself personally acquainted with the topography and local advantages of the capital, the character of its population, and the real nature and amount of its resources.   With this view, he asked the emperor's permission to visit the principal public edifices.

Antonio de Herrera, the celebrated chronicler of the Indies, was born of a respectable family at Cuella, in Old Spain, in 1549.   After passing through the usual course of academic discipline in his own country, he went to Italy, to which land of art and letters the Spanish youth of that time frequently resorted to complete their education.   He there became acquainted with Vespasian Gonzaga, brother of the duke of Mantua, and entered into his service.   He continued with this prince after he was made Viceroy of Navarre, and was so highly regarded by him, that, on his deathbed, Gonzaga earnestly commended him to the protection of Philip the Second.   This penetrating monarch soon discerned the excellent qualities of Herrera, and raised him to the post of Historiographer of the Indies,—an office for which Spain is indebted to Philip.   Thus provided with a liberal salary, and with every facility for pursuing the historical researches to which his inclination led him, Herrera's days glided peacefully away in the steady, but silent, occupations of a man of letters.   He continued to hold the office of historian of the colonies through Philip the Second's reign, and under his successors, Philip the Third and the Fourth ; till in 1625 he died at the advanced age of seventy-six, leaving behind him a high character for intellectual and moral worth.

Herrera wrote several works, chiefly historical.   The most important, that on which his reputation rests, is his *Historia general de las Indias occidentales.*   It extends from the year 1492, the time of the discovery of America, to 1554, and is divided into eight decades.   Four of them were published in 1601, and the remaining four in 1615, making in all five volumes in folio.   The work was subsequently republished in 1730, and has been translated into most of the languages of Europe.   The English translator, Stevens, has taken great liberties with his original, in the way of abridgment and omission, but the execution of his work is, on the whole, superior to that of most of the old English versions of the Castilian chroniclers.

Herrera's vast subject embraces the whole colonial empire of Spain in the New World. The work is thrown into the form of annals, and the multifarious occurrences in the distant regions of which he treats are all marshalled with exclusive reference to their chronology, and made to move together *pari passu.*   By means of this tasteless arrange-ment the thread of interest is perpetually snapped, the reader is hurried from one scene to another, without the opportunity of completing his survey of any.   His patience is exhausted and his mind perplexed with partial and scattered glimpses, instead of gather-ing new light as he advances from the skilful development of a continuous and well-digested narrative.   This is the great defect of a plan founded on a slavish adherence to chronology.   The defect becomes more serious when the work, as in the present instance, is of vast compass and embraces a great variety of details having little relation to each other.   In such a work we feel the superiority of a plan like that which Robertson has pursued in his " History of America," where every subject is allowed to occupy its own independent place, proportioned to its importance, and thus to make a distinct and individual impression on the reader.

Herrera's position gave him access to the official returns from the colonies, state

---

[1] " Many are of opinion," says Father Acosta, "that, if the Spaniards had continued the course they began, they might easily have disposed of Montezuma and his kingdom, and introduced the law of Christ, without much bloodshed." Lib. 7, cap. 25.

papers, and whatever documents existed in the public offices for the illustration of the colonial history. Among these sources of information were some manuscripts, with which it is not now easy to meet ; as, for example, the memorial of Alonso de Ojeda, one of the followers of Cortés, which has eluded my researches both in Spain and Mexico. Other writings, as those of Father Sahagun, of much importance in the history of Indian civilization, were unknown to the historian. Of such manuscripts as fell into his hands, Herrera made the freest use. From the writings of Las Casas, in particular, he borrowed without ceremony. The bishop had left orders that his " History of the Indies " should not be published till at least forty years after his death. Before that period had elapsed, Herrera had entered on his labours, and, as he had access to the papers of Las Casas, he availed himself of it to transfer whole pages, nay, chapters, of his narrative in the most unscrupulous manner to his own work. In doing this, he made a decided improvement on the manner of his original, reduced his cumbrous and entangled sentences to pure Castilian, omitted his turgid declamation and his unreasonable invectives. But, at the same time, he also excluded the passages that bore hardest on the conduct of his country-men, and those bursts of indignant eloquence which showed a moral sensibility in the Bishop of Chiapa that raised him so far above his age. By this sort of metempsychosis, if one may so speak, by which the letter and not the spirit of the good missionary was transferred to Herrera's pages, he rendered the publication of Las Casas' history, in some measure, superfluous ; and this circumstance has, no doubt, been one reason for its having been so long detained in manuscript.

Yet, with every allowance for the errors incident to rapid composition, and to the pedantic chronological system pursued by Herrera, his work must be admitted to have extraordinary merit. It displays to the reader the whole progress of Spanish conquest and colonization in the New World for the first sixty years after the discovery. The individual actions of his complicated story, though unskilfully grouped together, are unfolded in a pure and simple style, well suited to the gravity of his subject. If at first sight he may seem rather too willing to magnify the merits of the early discoverers and to throw a veil over their excesses, it may be pardoned, as flowing, not from moral insensi-bility, but from the patriotic sentiment which made him desirous, as far as might be, to wipe away every stain from the escutcheon of his nation, in the proud period of her renown. It is natural that the Spaniard who dwells on this period should be too much dazzled by the display of her gigantic efforts, scrupulously to weigh their moral character, or the merits of the cause in which they were made. Yet Herrera's national partiality never makes him the apologist of crime ; and, with the allowances fairly to be conceded, he may be entitled to the praise so often given him of integrity and candour.

It must not be forgotten that, in addition to the narrative of the early discoveries of the Spaniards, Herrera has brought together a vast quantity of information in respect to the institutions and usages of the Indian nations, collected from the most authentic sources. This gives his work a completeness beyond what is to be found in any other on the same subject. It is, indeed, a noble monument of sagacity and erudition ; and the student of history, and still more the historical compiler, will find himself unable to advance a single step among the early colonial settlements of the New World without reference to the pages of Herrera.

Another writer on Mexico, frequently consulted in the course of the present narrative, is Toribio de Benavente, or *Motolinia*, as he is still more frequently called, from his Indian cognomen. He was one of the twelve Franciscan missionaries who, at the request of Cortés, were sent out to New Spain immediately after the Conquest, in 1523. Toribio's humble attire, naked feet, and, in short, the poverty-stricken aspect which belongs to his order, frequently drew from the natives the exclamation of *Motolinia*, or " poor man." It was the first Aztec word the signification of which the missionary learned, and he was so much pleased with it, as intimating his own condition, that he henceforth assumed it as his name. Toribio employed himself zealously with his brethren in the great object of their mission. He travelled on foot over various parts of Mexico.

Guatemala, and Nicaragua. Wherever he went, he spared no pains to wean the natives from their dark idolatry, and to pour into their minds the light of revelation. He showed even a tender regard for their temporal as well as spiritual wants, and Bernal Diaz testifies that he has known him to give away his own robe to clothe a destitute and suffering Indian. Yet this charitable friar, so meek and conscientious in the discharge of his Christian duties, was one of the fiercest opponents of Las Casas, and sent home a remonstrance against the Bishop of Chiapa, couched in terms the most opprobrious and sarcastic. It has led the bishop's biographer, Quintana, to suggest that the friar's thread-bare robe may have covered somewhat of worldly pride and envy. It may be so. Yet it may also lead us to distrust the discretion of Las Casas himself, who could carry measures with so rude a hand as to provoke such unsparing animadversions from his fellow-labourers in the vineyard.

Toribio was made guardian of a Franciscan convent at Tezcuco. In this situation he continued active in good works, and at this place, and in his different pilgrimages, is stated to have baptized more than four hundred thousand natives. His efficacious piety was attested by various miracles. One of the most remarkable was when the Indians were suffering from great drought, which threatened to annihilate the approaching harvests. The good father recommended a solemn procession of the natives to the church of Santa Cruz, with prayers and a vigorous flagellation. The effect was soon visible in such copious rains as entirely relieved the people from their apprehensions, and in the end made the season uncommonly fruitful. The counterpart to this prodigy was afforded a few years later, while the country was labouring under excessive rains; when, by a similar remedy, the evil was checked, and a like propitious influence exerted on the season as before. The exhibition of such miracles greatly edified the people, says his biographer, and established them firmly in the Faith. Probably Toribio's exemplary life and conversation, so beautifully illustrating the principles which he taught, did quite as much for the good cause as his miracles.

Thus passing his days in the peaceful and pious avocations of the Christian missionary, the worthy ecclesiastic was at length called from the scene of his earthly pilgrimage, in what year is uncertain, but at an advanced age, for he survived all the little band of missionaries who had accompanied him to New Spain. He died in the convent of San Francisco at Mexico, and his panegyric is thus emphatically pronounced by Torquemada, a brother of his own order : "He was a truly apostolic man, a great teacher of Christianity, beautiful in the ornament of every virtue, jealous of the glory of God, a friend of evangelical poverty, most true to the observance of his monastic rule, and zealous in the conversion of the heathen."

Father Toribio's long personal intercourse with the Mexicans, and the knowledge of their language, which he was at much pains to acquire, opened to him all the sources of information respecting them and their institutions, which existed at the time of the Conquest. The results he carefully digested in the work so often cited in these pages, the *Historia de los Indios de Nueva-España*, making a volume of manuscript in folio. It is divided into three parts. 1. The religion, rites, and sacrifices of the Aztecs. 2. Their conversion to Christianity, and their manner of celebrating the festivals of the Church. 3. The genius and character of the nation, their chronology and astrology, together with notices of the principal cities and the staple productions of the country. Notwithstanding the methodical arrangement of the work, it is written in the rambling, unconnected manner of a commonplace-book, into which the author has thrown at random his notices of such matters as most interested him in his survey of the country. His own mission is ever before his eyes, and the immediate topic of discussion, of whatever nature it may be, is at once abandoned to exhibit an event or an anecdote that can illustrate his ecclesiastical labours. The most startling occurrences are recorded with all the credulous gravity which is so likely to win credit from the vulgar ; and a stock of miracles is duly attested by the historian, of more than sufficient magnitude to supply the wants of the infant religious communities of New Spain.

Yet amidst this mass of pious *incredibilia* the inquirer into the Aztec antiquities will find much curious and substantial information. Toribio's long and intimate relations with the natives put him in possession of their whole stock of theology and science ; and as his manner, though somewhat discursive, is plain and unaffected, there is no obscurity in the communication of his ideas. His inferences, coloured by the superstitions of the age and the peculiar nature of his profession, may be often received with distrust. But, as his integrity and his means of information were unquestionable, his work becomes of the first authority in relation to the antiquities of the country, and its condition at tne period of the Conquest. As an educated man, he was enabled to penetrate deeper than the illiterate soldiers of Cortés, men given to action rather than to speculation. Yet Toribio's manuscript, valuable as it is to the historian, has never been printed, and has too little in it of popular interest, probably, ever to be printed. Much that it contains has found its way, in various forms, into subsequent compilations. The work itself is very rarely to be found. Dr. Robertson had a copy, as it seems from the catalogue of MSS. published with his "History of America;" though the author's name is not prefixed to it. There is no copy, I believe, in the library of the Academy of History at Madrid ; and for that in my possession I am indebted to the kindness of that curious bibliographer, Mr. O. Rich, now consul for the United States at Minorca.

Pietro Martire de Angleria, or Peter Martyr, as he is called by English writers, belonged to an ancient and highly respectable family of Arona in the north of Italy. In 1487 he was induced by the count of Tendilla, the Spanish ambassador at Rome, to return with him to Castile. He was graciously received by Queen Isabella, always desirous to draw around her enlightened foreigners, who might exercise a salutary influence on the rough and warlike nobility of Castile. Martyr, who had been educated for the Church, was persuaded by the queen to undertake the instruction of the young nobles at the court. In this way he formed an intimacy with some of the most illustrious men of the nation, who seem to have cherished a warm personal regard for him through the remainder of his life. He was employed by the Catholic sovereigns in various concerns of public interest, was sent on a mission to Egypt, and was subsequently raised to a distinguished post in the cathedral of Granada. But he continued to pass much of his time at court, where he enjoyed the confidence of Ferdinand and Isabella, and of their successor, Charles the Fifth, till in 1525 he died, at the age of seventy.

Martyr's character combined qualities not often found in the same individual,—an ardent love of letters, with a practical sagacity that can only result from familiarity with men and affairs. Though passing his days in the gay and dazzling society of the capital, he preserved the simple tastes and dignified temper of a philosopher. His correspondence, as well as his more elaborate writings, if the term elaborate can be applied to any of his writings, manifests an enlightened and oftentimes independent spirit ; though one would have been better pleased had he been sufficiently independent to condemn the religious intolerance of the government. But Martyr, though a philosopher, was enough of a courtier to look with a lenient eye on the errors of princes. Though deeply imbued with the learning of antiquity, and a scholar at heart, he had none of the feelings of the recluse, but took the most lively interest in the events that were passing around him. His various writings, including his copious correspondence, are for this reason the very best mirror of the age in which he lived.

His inquisitive mind was particularly interested by the discoveries that were going on in the New World. He was allowed to be present at the sittings of the Council of the Indies when any communication of importance was made to it ; and he was subsequently appointed a member of that body. All that related to the colonies passed through his hands. The correspondence of Columbus, Cortés, and the other discoverers with the court of Castile was submitted to his perusal. He became personally acquainted with these illustrious persons on their return home, and frequently, as we find from his letters, entertained them at his own table. With these advantages, his testimony becomes but one degree removed from that of the actors themselves in the great drama. In one respect it is of a higher kind, since it is free from the prejudice and passion which a personal interest in events is apt to beget. The testimony of Martyr is that of a philosopher, taking a clear and comprehensive survey of the ground, with such lights of previous knowledge to guide him as none of the actual discoverers and conquerors could pretend to. It is true, this does not prevent his occasionally falling into errors ; the errors of credulity,—not, however, of the credulity founded on superstition, but that which arises from the uncertain nature of the subject, where phenomena so unlike anything with which he had been familiar were now first disclosed by the revelation of an unknown world.

He may be more fairly charged with inaccuracies of another description, growing out of haste and inadvertence of composition. But even here we should be charitable. For he confesses his sins with a candour that disarms criticism. In truth, he wrote rapidly, and on the spur of the moment, as occasion served. He shrunk from the publication of his writings, when it was urged on him, and his Decades *De Orbe Novo*, in which he embodied the results of his researches in respect to the American discoveries, were not published entire till after his death. The most valuable and complete edition of this work—the one referred to in the present pages—is the edition of Hakluyt, published at Paris in 1587.

Martyr's works are all in Latin, and that not the purest ; a circumstance rather singular, considering his familiarity with the classic models of antiquity. Yet he evidently handled the dead languages with the same facility as the living. Whatever defects may be charged on his manner, in the selection and management of his topics he shows the superiority of his genius. He passes over the trivial details which so often encumber the literal narratives of the Spanish voyagers, and fixes his attention on the great results of their discoveries,—the products of the country, the history and institutions of the races, their character and advance in civilization. In one respect his writings are of peculiar value. They show the state of feeling which existed at the Castilian court during the progress of discovery. They furnish, in short, the reverse side of the picture ; and, when we have followed the Spanish conquerors in their wonderful career of adventure in the New World, we have only to turn to the pages of Martyr to find the impression produced by them on the enlightened minds of the Old. Such a view is necessary to the completeness of the historical picture.

If the reader is curious to learn more of this estimable scholar, he will find the particulars given in "The History of Ferdinand and Isabella" (Part I. chap. 14, Postscript, and chap. 19), for the illustration of whose reign his voluminous correspondence furnishes the most authentic materials.

BOOK IV.

RESIDENCE IN MEXICO.

—o—

CHAPTER I.

TEZCUCAN LAKE.—DESCRIPTION OF THE CAPITAL.—PALACES AND MUSEUMS.
—ROYAL HOUSEHOLD.—MONTEZUMA'S WAY OF LIFE.

(1519.)

THE ancient city of Mexico covered the same spot occupied by the
modern capital. The great causeways touched it in the same points; the
streets ran in much the same direction, nearly from north to south and
from east to west; the cathedral in the *plaza mayor* stands on the same
ground that was covered by the temple of the Aztec war-god; and the four
principal quarters of the town are still known among the Indians by their
ancient names. Yet an Aztec of the days of Montezuma, could he behold
the modern metropolis, which has risen with such phœnix-like splendour
from the ashes of the old, would not recognize its site as that of his own
Tenochtitlan. For the latter was encompassed by the salt floods of
Tezcuco, which flowed in ample canals through every part of the city;
while the Mexico of our day stands high and dry on the mainland, nearly
a league distant, at its centre, from the water. The cause of this apparent
change in its position is the diminution of the lake, which, from the
rapidity of evaporation in these elevated regions, had become perceptible
before the Conquest, but which has since been greatly accelerated by
artificial causes.[1]

The average level of the Tezcucan lake, at the present day, is but four
feet lower than the great square of Mexico.[2] It is considerably lower than
the other great basins of water which are found in the Valley. In the
heavy swell sometimes caused by long and excessive rains, these latter

---

[1] The lake, it seems, had perceptibly shrunk before the Conquest, from the testimony of Motolinia,
who entered the country soon after. Toribio, Hist.
de los Indios, MS., Parte 3, cap. 6.

[2] Humboldt, Essai politique, tom. ii. p. 95.—
Cortés supposed there were regular tides in this
lake. (Rel. Seg., ap. Lorenzana, p. 101.) This

sorely puzzles the learned Martyr (De Orbe Novo,
dec. 5, cap. 3); as it has more than one philosopher
since, whom it has led to speculate on a subterraneous communication with the ocean! What the
general called "tides" was probably the periodical
swells caused by the prevalence of certain regular
winds.

reservoirs anciently overflowed into the Tezcuco, which, rising with the accumulated volume of, waters, burst through the dikes, and, pouring into the streets of the capital, buried the lower part of the buildings under a deluge. This was comparatively a light evil when the houses stood on piles so elevated that boats might pass under them ; when the streets were canals, and the ordinary mode of communication was by water. But it became more disastrous as these canals, filled up with the rubbish of the ruined Indian city, were supplanted by streets of solid earth, and the foundations of the capital were gradually reclaimed from the watery element. To obviate this alarming evil, the famous drain of Huehuetoca was opened, at an enormous cost, in the beginning of the seventeenth century, and Mexico, after repeated inundations, has been at length placed above the reach of the flood.[1] But what was gain to the useful, in this case, as in some others, has been purchased at the expense of the beautiful. By this shrinking of the waters, the bright towns and hamlets once washed by them have been removed some miles into the interior, while a barren strip of land, ghastly from the incrustation of salts formed on the surface, has taken the place of the glowing vegetation which once enamelled the borders of the lake, and of the dark groves of oak, cedar, and sycamore which threw their broad shadows over its bosom.

The *chinampas*, that archipelago of wandering islands, to which our attention was drawn in the last chapter, have, also, nearly disappeared. These had their origin in the detached masses of earth, which, loosening from the shores, were still held together by the fibrous roots with which they were penetrated. The primitive Aztecs, in their poverty of land, availed themselves of the hint thus afforded by nature. They constructed rafts of reeds, rushes, and other fibrous materials, which, tightly knit together, formed a sufficient basis for the sediment that they drew up from the bottom of the lake. Gradually islands were formed, two or three hundred feet in length, and three or four feet in depth, with a rich stimulated soil, on which the economical Indian raised his vegetables and flowers for the markets of Tenochtitlan. Some of these *chinampas* were even firm enough to allow the growth of small trees, and to sustain a hut for the residence of the person that had charge of it, who with a long pole, resting on the sides or the bottom of the shallow basin, could change the position of his little territory at pleasure, which with its rich freight of vegetable stores was seen moving like some enchanted island over the water.[2]

The ancient dikes were three in number. That of Iztapalapan, by which the Spaniards entered, approaching the city from the south. That of Tepejacac, on the north, which, continuing the principal street, might

[1] Humboldt has given a minute account of this tunnel, which he pronounces one of the most stupendous hydraulic works in existence, and the completion of which, in its present form, does not date earlier than the latter part of the last century. See his Essai politique, tom. ii. p. 105, et seq.

[2] Humboldt, Essai politique, tom. ii. p. 87, et seq.— Clavigero, Stor. del Messico, tom. ii. p. 153.

be regarded, also, as a continuation of the first causeway. Lastly, the
dike of Tlacopan, connecting the island-city with the continent on the
west. This last causeway, memorable for the disastrous retreat of the
Spaniards, was about two miles in length. They were all built in the same
substantial manner, of lime and stone, were defended by drawbridges, and
were wide enough for ten or twelve horsemen to ride abreast.[1]

The rude founders of Tenochtitlan built their frail tenements of reeds
and rushes on the group of small islands in the western part of the lake.
In process of time, these were supplanted by more substantial buildings.
A quarry in the neighbourhood, of a red porous amygdaloid, *tetzontli*, was
opened, and a light, brittle stone drawn from it and wrought with little
difficulty. Of this their edifices were constructed, with some reference to
architectural solidity, if not elegance. Mexico, as already noticed, was
the residence of the great chiefs, whom the sovereign encouraged, or
rather compelled, from obvious motives of policy, to spend part of the
year in the capital. It was also the temporary abode of the great lords
of Tezcuco and Tlacopan, who shared, nominally at least, the sovereignty
of the empire.[2] The mansions of these dignitaries, and of the principal
nobles, were on a scale of rude magnificence corresponding with their state.
They were low, indeed,—seldom of more than one floor, never exceeding
two. But they spread over a wide extent of ground, were arranged in a
quadrangular form, with a court in the centre, and were surrounded by
porticoes embellished with porphyry and jasper, easily found in the
neighbourhood, while not unfrequently a fountain of crystal water in the
centre shed a grateful coolness through the air. The dwellings of the
common people were also placed on foundations of stone, which rose to
the height of a few feet and were then succeeded by courses of unbaked
bricks, crossed occasionally by wooden rafters.[3] Most of the streets were
mean and narrow. Some few, however, were wide and of great length.
The principal street, conducting from the great southern causeway,
penetrated in a straight line the whole length of the city, and afforded
a noble vista, in which the long lines of low stone edifices were broken
occasionally by intervening gardens, rising on terraces and displaying all
the pomp of Aztec horticulture.

The great streets, which were coated with a hard cement, were intersected by numerous canals. Some of these were flanked by a solid way,
which served as a footwalk for passengers, and as a landing-place where
boats might discharge their cargoes. Small buildings were erected at

<hr/>

[1] Toribio, Hist. de los Indios, MS., Parte 3, cap. 8.—Cortés, indeed, speaks of four causeways. (Rel. Seg., ap. Lorenzana, p. 102.) He may have reckoned an arm of the southern one leading to Cojohuacan, or possibly the great aqueduct of Chapoltepec.

[2] *Ante*, p. 10.

[3] Martyr gives a particular account of these dwellings, which shows that even the poorer classes were comfortably lodged. "Populares vero domus cingulo virili tenus lapideæ sunt et ipsæ, ob lacunæ incrementum per fluxum aut fluviorum in ea labentium alluvies. Super fundamentis illis magnis, lateribus tum coctis, tum æstivo sole siccatis, immixtis trabibus reliquam molem construunt; uno sunt communes domus contentæ tabulato. In solo parum hospitantur propter humiditatem, tecta non tegulis sed bitumine quodam terreo vestiunt; ad solem captandum commodior est ille modus, breviore tempore consumi debere credendum est." De Orbe Novo, dec. 5, cap. 10.

intervals, as stations for the revenue officers who collected the duties on different articles of merchandise. The canals were traversed by numerous bridges, many of which could be raised, affording the means of cutting off communication between different parts of the city.[1]

From the accounts of the ancient capital, one is reminded of those aquatic cities in the Old World, the positions of which have been selected from similar motives of economy and defence; above all, of Venice,[2]—if it be not rash to compare the rude architecture of the American Indian with the marble palaces and temples—alas, how shorn of their splendour! —which crowned the once proud mistress of the Adriatic.[3] The example of the metropolis was soon followed by the other towns in the vicinity. Instead of resting their foundations on *terra firma*, they were seen advancing far into the lake, the shallow waters of which in some parts do not exceed four feet in depth.[4] Thus an easy means of intercommunication was opened, and the surface of this inland "sea," as Cortés styles it, was darkened by thousands of canoes[5]—an Indian term—industriously engaged in the traffic between these little communities. How gay and picturesque must have been the aspect of the lake in those days, with its shining cities, and flowering islets rocking, as it were, at anchor on the fair bosom of its waters!

The population of Tenochtitlan at the time of the Conquest is variously stated. No contemporary writer estimates it at less than sixty thousand houses, which, by the ordinary rules of reckoning, would give three hundred thousand souls.[6] If a dwelling often contained, as is asserted, several families, it would swell the amount considerably higher.[7] Nothing is more uncertain than estimates of numbers among barbarous communities,

[1] Toribio, Hist. de los Indios, MS., Parte 3, cap. 8.—Rel. Seg. de Cortés, ap. Lorenzana, p. 108.—Oviedo, Hist. de las Ind., MS., lib. 33, cap. 10, 11.—Rel. d'un gentil' huomo, ap. Ramusio, tom. iii. fol. 309.

[2] Martyr was struck with the resemblance. "Uti de illustrissima civitate Venetiarum legitur, ad tumulum in ea sinus Adriatici parte visum, fuisse constructam." Martyr, De Orbe Novo, dec. 5, cap. 10.

[3] May we not apply, without much violence, to the Aztec capital, Giovanni della Casa's spirited sonnet, contrasting the origin of Venice with its meridian glory?

"Questi Palazzi e queste logge or colte
    D'ostro, di marmo e di figure elette,
    Fur poche e basse case insieme accolte
    Deserti lidi e povere Isolette.
Ma genti ardite d'ogni vizio sciolte
    Premeano il mar con picciole barchette,
    Che qui non per domar provincie molte,
    Ma fuggir servitù s' eran ristrette
Non era ambizion ne' petti loro;
    Ma 'l mentire abborrian più che la morte,
    Nè vi regnava ingorda fame d' oro.
Se 'l Ciel v' ha dato più beata sorte,
    Non sien quelle virtù che tanto onoro,
    Dalle nuove ricchezze oppresse emorte."

[4] "Le lac de Tezcuco n'a généralement que trois à cinq mètres de profondeur. Dans quelques endroits le fond se trouve même déjà à moins d'un mètre." Humboldt, Essai politique, tom. ii. p. 49.

[5] "Y cada dia entran gran multitud de Indios cargados de bastimentos y tributos, así por tierra como por agua, en acales ó barcas, que *en lengua de las Islas llaman Canoas*." Toribio, Hist. de los Indios, MS., Parte 3, cap. 6.

[6] "Esta la cibdad de Méjico ó *Teneztutan*, que será de sesenta mil vecinos." (Carta del Lic. Zuazo, MS.) "Tenustitanam ipsam inquiunt sexaginta circiter esse millium domorum." (Martyr, De Orbe Novo, dec. 5, cap. 3.) "Era Méjico, quando Cortés entró, pueblo de sesenta mil casas." (Gomara, Crónica, cap. 78.) Toribio says, vaguely, "Los moradores y gente era innumerable." (Hist. de los Indios, MS., Parte 3, cap. 8.) The Italian translation of the "Anonymous Conqueror," who survives only in translation, says, indeed, "meglio di sessanta mila *habitatori*" (Rel. d'un gentil' huomo, ap. Ramusio, tom. iii. fol. 309); owing, probably, to a blunder in rendering the word *vecinos*, the ordinary term in Spanish statistics, which, signifying *householders*, corresponds with the Italian *fuochi*. See, also, Clavigero. (Stor. del Messico, tom. iii. p. 86, nota.) Robertson rests *exclusively* on this Italian translation for his estimate. (History of America, vol. ii. p. 281.) He cites, indeed, two other authorities in the same connection; Cortés, who says nothing of the population, and Herrera, who confirms the popular statement of "sesenta mil casas." (Hist. general, dec. 2, lib. 7, cap. 13.) The fact is of some importance.

[7] "In the smallest houses, with few exceptions, two, four, and even six families resided together." Herrera, Hist. general, dec. 2, lib. 7, cap. 13.

who necessarily live in a more confused and promiscuous manner than civilized, and among whom no regular system is adopted for ascertaining the population. The concurrent testimony of the Conquerors; the extent of the city, which was said to be nearly three leagues in circumference;[1] the immense size of its great market-place; the long lines of edifices, vestiges of whose ruins may still be found in the suburbs, miles from the modern city;[2] the fame of the metropolis throughout Anahuac, which, however, could boast many large and populous places; lastly, the economical husbandry and the ingenious contrivances to extract aliment from the most unpromising sources,[3]—all attest a numerous population, far beyond that of the present capital.[4]

A careful police provided for the health and cleanliness of the city. A thousand persons are said to have been daily employed in watering and sweeping the streets,[5] so that a man—to borrow the language of an old Spaniard—"could walk through them with as little danger of soiling his feet as his hands."[6] The water, in a city washed on all sides by the salt floods, was extremely brackish. A liberal supply of the pure element,

---

[1] Rel. d'un gentil' huomo, ap. Ramusio, tom. iii. fol. 309.

[2] "C'est sur le chemin qui mène à Tanepantla et aux Ahuahuetes que l'on peut marcher plus d'une heure entre les ruines de l'ancienne ville. On y reconnaît, ainsi que sur la route de Tacuba et d'Iztapalapan, combien Mexico, rebâti par Cortéz, est plus petit que l'était Tenochtitlan sous le dernier des Montezuma. L'énorme grandeur du marché de Tlatelolco, dont on reconnaît encore les limites, prouve combien la population de l'ancienne ville doit avoir été considérable." (Humboldt, Essai politique, tom. ii. p. 43.

[3] A common food with the lower classes was a glutinous scum found in the lakes, which they made into a sort of cake, having a savour not unlike cheese. (Bernal Diaz, Hist. de la Conquista, cap. 92.)—[This "scum" consists in fact of the eggs of aquatic insects, with which cakes are made, in the same manner as with the spawn of fishes. Conquista de Méjico (trad. de Vega), tom. i. p. 366.]*

[4] One is confirmed in this inference by comparing the two maps at the end of the first edition of Bullock's "Mexico;" one of the modern city, the other of the ancient, taken from Boturini's museum, and showing its regular arrangement of streets and canals; as regular, indeed, as the squares on a chessboard.†

[5] Clavigero, Stor. del Messico, tom. i. p. 274.

[6] "Era tan barrido y el suelo tan asentado y liso, que aunque la planta del pie fuera tan delicada como la de la mano no recibiera el pie detrimento ninguno en andar descalzo." Toribio, Hist. de los Indios, MS., Parte 3, cap. 7.

* [Little can be inferred, in regard to the difference of population, from the use of the *ahuahutle*, as these cakes are called, since it is still a favourite article of food at Tezcuco, where the eggs are found in great abundance, and sold in the market both in the prepared state and in lumps as collected at the edge of the lake. "The flies which produce these eggs are called by the Mexicans *axayacatl*, or *water-face*,—*Corixa femorata*, and *Notonecta unifasciata*, according to MM. Meneville and Virlet d'Aoust." Tylor, Anahuac, p. 156.—ED.]

† [The doubts so often excited by the descriptions of ancient Mexico in the accounts of the Spanish discoverers, like the similar incredulity formerly entertained in regard to the narrations of Herodotus, are dispelled by a critical investigation in conjunction with the results of modern explorations. Among recent travellers, Mr. Edward B. Tylor, whose learning and acumen have been displayed in various ethnological studies, is entitled to especial confidence. In company with Mr. Christy, the well-known collector, he examined the ploughed fields in the neighbourhood of Mexico, making repeated trials whether it was possible to stand in any spot where no relic of the former population was within reach. "But this," he says, "we could not do. Everywhere the ground was full of unglazed pottery and obsidian." "We noticed by the sides of the road, and where ditches had been cut, numbers of old Mexican stone floors covered with stucco. The earth has accumulated above them to the depth of two or three feet, so that their position is like that of the Roman pavements so often found in Europe; and we may guess, from what we saw exposed, how great must be the number of such remains still hidden, and how vast a population must once have inhabited this plain, now almost deserted." "When we left England," he adds, "we both doubted the accounts of the historians of the Conquest, believing that they had exaggerated the numbers of the population, and the size of the cities, from a natural desire to make the most of their victories, and to write as wonderful a history as they could, as historians are prone to do. But our examination of Mexican remains soon induced us to withdraw this accusation, and even made us inclined to blame the chroniclers for having had no eyes for the wonderful things that surrounded them. I do not mean by this that we felt inclined to swallow the monstrous exaggerations of Solis and Gomara and other Spanish chroniclers, who seemed to think that it was as easy to say a thousand as a hundred, and that it sounded much better. But when this class of writers are set aside, and the more valuable authorities severely criticised, it does not seem to us that the history thus extracted from these sources is much less reliable than European history of the same period. There is, perhaps, no better way of expressing this opinion than to say that what we saw of Mexico tended generally to confirm Prescott's History of the Conquest, and but seldom to make his statements appear to us improbable." Anahuac, p. 147.—ED.]

however, was brought from Chapoltepec, "the grasshopper's hill," less than a league distant. It was brought through an earthen pipe, along a dike constructed for the purpose. That there might be no failure in so essential an article when repairs were going on, a double course of pipes was laid. In this way a column of water of the size of a man's body was conducted into the heart of the capital, where it fed the fountains and reservoirs of the principal mansions. Openings were made in the aqueduct as it crossed the bridges, and thus a supply was furnished to the canoes below, by means of which it was transported to all parts of the city.[1]

While Montezuma encouraged a taste for architectural magnificence in his nobles, he contributed his own share towards the embellishment of the city. It was in his reign that the famous calendar stone, weighing, probably, in its primitive state, nearly fifty tons, was transported from its native quarry, many leagues distant, to the capital, where it still forms one of the most curious monuments of Aztec science. Indeed, when we reflect on the difficulty of hewing such a stupendous mass from its hard basaltic bed without the aid of iron tools, and that of transporting it such a distance across land and water without the help of animals, we may well feel admiration at the mechanical ingenuity and enterprise of the people who accomplished it.[2]

Not content with the spacious residence of his father, Montezuma erected another on a yet more magnificent scale. It occupied, as before mentioned, the ground partly covered by the private dwellings on one side of the *plaza mayor* of the modern city. This building, or, as it might more correctly be styled, pile of buildings, spread over an extent of ground so vast that, as one of the Conquerors assures us, its terraced roof might have afforded ample room for thirty knights to run their courses in a regular tourney.[3] I have already noticed its interior decorations, its fanciful draperies, its roofs inlaid with cedar and other odoriferous woods, held together without a nail, and, probably, without a knowledge of the arch,[4] its numerous and spacious apartments, which Cortés, with enthusiastic hyperbole, does not hesitate to declare superior to anything of the kind in Spain.[5]

Adjoining the principal edifice were others, devoted to various objects. One was an armoury, filled with the weapons and military dresses worn by the Aztecs, all kept in the most perfect order, ready for instant use. The emperor was himself very expert in the management of the *maquahuitl*,

[1] Rel. Seg. de. Cortés, ap. Lorenzana, p. 108.—Carta del Lic. Zuazo, MS.—Rel. d'un gentil' huomo, ap. Ramusio, tom. iii. fol. 309.

[2] These immense masses, according to Martyr, who gathered his information from eyewitnesses, were transported by means of long files of men, who dragged them with ropes over huge wooden rollers. (De Orbe Novo, dec. 5, cap. 10.) It was the manner in which the Egyptians removed their enormous blocks of granite, as appears from numerous reliefs sculptured on their buildings.

[3] Rel. d'un gentil' huomo, ap. Ramusio, tom. iii. fol. 309.

[4] "Ricos edificios," says the Licentiate Zuazo, speaking of the buildings in Anahuac generally, "ecepto que no se halla alguno con *boveda*." (Carta, MS.) The writer made large and careful observation, the year after the Conquest. His assertion, if it be received, will settle a question much mooted among antiquaries.

[5] "His residence within the city was so marvellous for its beauty and vastness that it seems to me almost impossible to describe it. I shall therefore say no more of it than that there is nothing like it in Spain." Rel. Seg., ap. Lorenzana, p. 111.

or Indian sword, and took great delight in witnessing athletic exercises and the mimic representation of war by his young nobility. Another building was used as a granary, and others as warehouses for the different articles of food and apparel contributed by the districts charged with the maintenance of the royal household.

There were, also, edifices appropriated to objects of quite another kind. One of these was an immense aviary, in which birds of splendid plumage were assembled from all parts of the empire. Here was the scarlet cardinal, the golden pheasant, the endless parrot tribe with their rainbow hues (the royal green predominant), and that miniature miracle of nature, the humming-bird, which delights to revel among the honeysuckle bowers of Mexico.[1] Three hundred attendants had charge of this aviary, who made themselves acquainted with the appropriate food of its inmates, oftentimes procured at great cost, and in the moulting season were careful to collect the beautiful plumage, which, with its many-coloured tints, furnished the materials for the Aztec painter.

A separate building was reserved for the fierce birds of prey; the voracious vulture tribes and eagles of enormous size, whose home was in the snowy solitudes of the Andes. No less than five hundred turkeys, the cheapest meat in Mexico, were allowed for the daily consumption of these tyrants of the feathered race.

Adjoining this aviary was a menagerie of wild animals, gathered from the mountain forests, and even from the remote swamps of the *tierra caliente*. The resemblance of the different species to those in the Old World, with which no one of them, however, was identical, led to a perpetual confusion in the nomenclature of the Spaniards, as it has since done in that of better-instructed naturalists. The collection was still further swelled by a great number of reptiles and serpents remarkable for their size and venomous qualities, among which the Spaniards beheld the fiery little animal "with the castanets in his tail," the terror of the American wilderness.[2] The serpents were confined in long cages lined with down or feathers, or in troughs of mud and water. The beasts and birds of prey were provided with apartments large enough to allow of their moving about, and secured by a strong lattice-work, through which light and air were freely admitted. The whole was placed under the charge of numerous keepers, who acquainted themselves with the habits of their prisoners and provided for their comfort and cleanliness. With what deep interest would the enlightened naturalist of that day — an

---

[1] Herrera's account of these feathered insects, if one may so style them, shows the fanciful errors into which even men of science were led in regard to the new tribes of animals discovered in America: "There are some birds in the country of the size of butterflies, with long beaks, brilliant plumage, much esteemed for the curious works made of them. Like the bees, they live on flowers, and the dew which settles on them; and when the rainy season is over, and the dry weather sets in, they fasten themselves to the trees by their beaks and soon die. But in the following year, when the new rains come, they come to life again"! Hist. general, dec. 2, lib. 10, cap. 21.

[2] "Pues mas tenian," says the honest Captain Diaz, "en aquella maldita casa muchas Víboras, y Culebras emponçoñadas, que traen en las colas vnos que suenan como cascabeles; estas son las peores Víboras de todas." Hist. de la Conquista, cap. 91.

Oviedo, or a Martyr, for example — have surveyed this magnificent collection, in which the various tribes which roamed over the Western wilderness, the unknown races of an unknown world, were brought into one view! How would they have delighted to study the peculiarities of these new species, compared with those of their own hemisphere, and thus have risen to some comprehension of the general laws by which Nature acts in all her works! The rude followers of Cortés did not trouble themselves with such refined speculations. They gazed on the spectacle with a vague curiosity not unmixed with awe; and, as they listened to the wild cries of the ferocious animals and the hissings of the serpents, they almost fancied themselves in the infernal regions.[1]

I must not omit to notice a strange collection of human monsters, dwarfs, and other unfortunate persons in whose organization Nature had capriciously deviated from her regular laws. Such hideous anomalies were regarded by the Aztecs as a suitable appendage of state. It is even said they were in some cases the result of artificial means, employed by unnatural parents desirous to secure a provision for their offspring by thus qualifying them for a place in the royal museum![2]

Extensive gardens were spread out around these buildings, filled with fragrant shrubs and flowers, and especially with medicinal plants.[3] No country has afforded more numerous species of these last than New Spain; and their virtues were perfectly understood by the Aztecs, with whom medical botany may be said to have been studied as a science. Amidst this labyrinth of sweet-scented groves and shrubberies, fountains of pure water might be seen throwing up their sparkling jets and scattering refreshing dews over the blossoms. Ten large tanks, well stocked with fish, afforded a retreat on their margins to various tribes of water-fowl, whose habits were so carefully consulted that some of these ponds were of salt water, as that which they most loved to frequent. A tessellated pavement of marble enclosed the ample basins, which were overhung by light and fanciful pavilions, that admitted the perfumed breezes of the gardens, and offered a grateful shelter to the monarch and his mistresses in the sultry heats of summer.[4]

But the most luxurious residence of the Aztec monarch, at that season, was the royal hill of Chapoltepec,—a spot consecrated, moreover, by the ashes of his ancestors. It stood in a westerly direction from the capital, and its base was, in his day, washed by the waters of the Tezcuco. On

---

[1] "Digamos aora," exclaims Captain Diaz, "las cosas infernales que hazian, quando bramauan los Tigres y Leones, y aullauan los Adiues y Zorros, y silbauan las Sierpes, era grima oirlo, y parecia infierno." Hist. de la Conquista, cap. 91.

[2] Ibid., ubi supra.—Rel. Seg. de Cortés, ap. Lorenzana, pp. 111-113.—Carta del Lic. Zuazo, MS.—Toribio, Hist. de los Indios, MS., Parte 3, cap. 7.—Oviedo, Hist. de las Ind., MS., lib. 33, tap. 11, 46.

[3] Montezuma, according to Gomara, would allow no fruit-trees, considering them as unsuitable to

pleasure-grounds. (Crónica, cap. 75.) Toribio says, to the same effect, "Los Indios Señores no procuran árboles de fruta, porque se la traen sus vasallos, sino árboles de floresta, de donde cojan rosas, y adonde se crian aves, así para gozar del canto, como para las tirar con Cerbatana, de la cual son grandes tiradores." Hist. de los Indios, MS., Parte 3, cap. 6.

[4] Toribio, Hist. de los Indios, MS., Parte 3, cap. 6.—Rel. Seg. de Cortés, ubi supra.—Oviedo, Hist. de las Ind., MS., lib. 33, cap. 11.

its lofty crest of porphyritic rock there now stands the magnificent, though desolate, castle erected by the young viceroy Galvez at the close of the seventeenth century.[1] The view from its windows is one of the finest in the environs of Mexico. The landscape is not disfigured here, as in many other quarters, by the white and barren patches, so offensive to the sight; but the eye wanders over an unbroken expanse of meadows and cultivated fields, waving with rich harvests of European grain. Montezuma's gardens stretched for miles around the base of the hill. Two statues of that monarch and his father, cut in bas-relief in the porphyry, were spared till the middle of the last century;[2] and the grounds are still shaded by gigantic cypresses, more than fifty feet in circumference, which were centuries old at the time of the Conquest.[3] The place is now a tangled wilderness of wild shrubs, where the myrtle mingles its dark, glossy leaves with the red berries and delicate foliage of the pepper-tree. Surely there is no spot better suited to awaken meditation on the past; none where the traveller, as he sits under those stately cypresses grey with the moss of ages, can so fitly ponder on the sad destinies of the Indian races and the monarch who once held his courtly revels under the shadow of their branches.

The domestic establishment of Montezuma was on the same scale of barbaric splendour as everything else about him. He could boast as many wives as are found in the harem of an Eastern sultan.[4] They were lodged in their own apartments, and provided with every accommodation, according to their ideas, for personal comfort and cleanliness. They passed their hours in the usual feminine employments of weaving and embroidery, especially in the graceful feather-work, for which such rich materials were furnished by the royal aviaries. They conducted themselves with strict decorum, under the supervision of certain aged females, who acted in the respectable capacity of duennas, in the same manner as in the religious houses attached to the *teocallis*. The palace was supplied with numerous baths, and Montezuma set the example, in his own person, of frequent ablutions. He bathed at least once, and changed his dress four times, it is said, every day.[5] He never put on the same apparel a second time, but gave it away to his attendants. Queen Elizabeth, with a similar taste for costume, showed a less princely spirit in hoarding her discarded suits. Her wardrobe was, probably, somewhat more costly than that of the Indian emperor.

Besides his numerous female retinue, the halls and antechambers were

[1] [It is used at the present day for a military school. Conquista de Méjico (trad. de Vega), tom. i. p. 370.]

[2] Gomara, a competent critic, who saw them just before their destruction, praises their execution. Gama, Descripcion, Parte 2, pp. 81–83. Also, *ante*, p. 68.

[3] [Yet the whole of this beautiful grove was not spared. The axes of the Conquerors levelled such of the trees as grew round the fountain of Chapoltepec and dropped their decayed leaves into its

waters. The order of the municipality, dated February 28, 1527, is quoted by Alaman, Disertaciones históricas, tom. ii. p. 290.]

[4] No less than one thousand, if we believe Gomara; who adds the edifying intelligence, "que huvo vez, que tuvo ciento i cincuenta preñadas á un tiempo!"

[5] "Vestíase todos los dias quatro maneras de vestiduras todas nuevas, y nunca mas se las vestia otra vez." Rel. Seg. de Cortés, ap. Lorenzana, p. 114.

filled with nobles in constant attendance on his person, who served also as a sort of body-guard. It had been usual for plebeians of merit to fill certain offices in the palace. But the haughty Montezuma refused to be waited upon by any but men of noble birth. They were not unfrequently the sons of the great chiefs, and remained as hostages in the absence of their fathers; thus serving the double purpose of security and state.[1]

His meals the emperor took alone. The well-matted floor of a large saloon was covered with hundreds of dishes.[2] Sometimes Montezuma himself, but more frequently his steward, indicated those which he preferred, and which were kept hot by means of chafing-dishes.[3] The royal bill of fare comprehended, besides domestic animals, game from the distant forests, and fish which, the day before, was swimming in the Gulf of Mexico! They were dressed in manifold ways, for the Aztec *artistes*, as we have already had occasion to notice, had penetrated deep into the mysteries of culinary science.[4]

The meats were served by the attendant nobles, who then resigned the office of waiting on the monarch to maidens selected for their personal grace and beauty. A screen of richly gilt and carved wood was drawn around him, so as to conceal him from vulgar eyes during the repast. He was seated on a cushion, and the dinner was served on a low table covered with a delicate cotton cloth. The dishes were of the finest ware of Cholula. He had a service of gold, which was reserved for religious celebrations. Indeed, it would scarcely have comported with even his princely revenues to have used it on ordinary occasions, when his table-equipage was not allowed to appear a second time, but was given away to his attendants. The saloon was lighted by torches made of a resinous wood, which sent forth a sweet odour and, probably, not a little smoke, as they burned. At his meal, he was attended by five or six of his ancient counsellors, who stood at a respectful distance, answering his questions, and occasionally rejoiced by some of the viands with which he complimented them from his table.

This course of solid dishes was succeeded by another of sweetmeats and pastry, for which the Aztec cooks, provided with the important requisites of maize-flour, eggs, and the rich sugar of the aloe, were famous. Two

---

[1] Bernal Diaz, Hist. de la Conquista, cap. 91.—Gomara, Crónica, cap. 67, 71, 76.—Rel. Seg. de Cortés, ap. Lorenzana, pp. 113, 114.—Toribio, Hist. de los Indios, MS., Parte 3, cap. 7.—"Á la puerta de la sala estaba vn patio mui grande en que habia cien aposentos de 25 ó 30 pies de largo cada vno sobre sí en torno de dicho patio, é allí estaban los Señores principales aposentados como guardas del palacio ordinarias, y estos tales aposentos se llaman galpones, los quales á la contina ocupan mas de 600 hombres, que jamas se quitaban de allí, é cada vno de aquellos tenian mas de 30 servidores de manera que á lo menos nunca faltaban 3000 hombres de guerra en esta guarda cotediana del palacio." (Oviedo, Hist. de las Ind., MS., lib. 33, cap. 46.) A very curious and full account of Montezuma's household is given by this author, as he gathered it

from the Spaniards who saw it in its splendour. As Oviedo's history still remains in manuscript, I have transferred the chapter in the original Castilian to Appendix, Part 2, No. 10.

[2] Bernal Diaz, Hist. de la Conquista, cap. 91.—Rel. Seg. de Cortés, ubi supra.

[3] "Y porque la Tierra es fria trahian debaxo de cada plato y escudilla de manjar un braserico con brasa, porque no se enfriasse." Rel. Seg. de Cortés, ap. Lorenzana, p. 113.

[4] Bernal Diaz has given us a few items of the royal *carte*. The first cover is rather a startling one, being a fricassee or stew of little children! "*carnes de muchachos de poca edad.*" He admits, however, that this is somewhat apocryphal. Ibid., ubi supra.

girls were occupied at the farther end of the apartment, during dinner, in preparing fine rolls and wafers, with which they garnished the board from time to time. The emperor took no other beverage than the *chocolatl*, a potation of chocolate, flavoured with vanilla and other spices, and so prepared as to be reduced to a froth of the consistency of honey, which gradually dissolved in the mouth. This beverage, if so it could be called, was served in golden goblets, with spoons of the same metal or of tortoise-shell finely wrought. The emperor was exceedingly fond of it, to judge from the quantity—no less than fifty jars or pitchers—prepared for his own daily consumption.[1] Two thousand more were allowed for that of his household.[2]

The general arrangement of the meal seems to have been not very unlike that of Europeans. But no prince in Europe could boast a dessert which could compare with that of the Aztec emperor. For it was gathered fresh from the most opposite climes; and his board displayed the products of his own temperate region, and the luscious fruits of the tropics, plucked the day previous, from the green groves of the *tierra caliente*, and transmitted with the speed of steam, by means of couriers, to the capital. It was as if some kind fairy should crown our banquets with the spicy products that but yesterday were growing in a sunny isle of the far-off Indian seas![3]

After the emperor's appetite was appeased, water was handed to him by the female attendants in a silver basin, in the same manner as had been done before commencing his meal; for the Aztecs were as constant in their ablutions, at these times, as any nation of the East. Pipes were then brought, made of a varnished and richly-gilt wood, from which he inhaled, sometimes through the nose, at others through the mouth, the fumes of an intoxicating weed, "called *tobacco*,"[4] mingled with liquid amber. While this soothing process of fumigation was going on, the emperor enjoyed the exhibitions of his mountebanks and jugglers, of whom a regular corps was attached to the palace. No people, not even those of China or Hindostan, surpassed the Aztecs in feats of agility and legerdemain.[5]

Sometimes he amused himself with his jester; for the Indian monarch had his jesters, as well as his more refined brethren of Europe, at that day. Indeed, he used to say that more instruction was to be gathered from them than from wiser men, for they dared to tell the truth. At other times he witnessed the graceful dances of his women, or took delight in

---

1 "*Lo que yo ví,*" says Diaz, speaking from his own observation, "que traian sobre cincuenta jarros grandes hechos de buen cacao con su espuma, y de lo que bebia." Hist. de la Conquista, cap. 91.

2 Ibid., ubi supra.—Rel. Seg. de Cortés, ap. Lorenzana, pp. 113, 114.—Oviedo, Hist. de las Ind., MS., lib. 33, cap. 11, 46.—Gomara, Crónica, cap. 67.

3 [This description, as Señor Alaman observes, seems to have a tincture of romance, since many of the fruits now produced in such abundance in Mexico were unknown there previous to the Con-

quest. Conquista de Méjico (trad. de Vega), tom. i. p. 373.—ED.]

4 "Tambien le ponian en la mesa tres cañutos muy pintados, y dorados, y dentro traian liquid-ámbar, rebuelto con vnas yervas *que se dize tabaco.*" Bernal Diaz, Hist. de la Conquista, cap. 91.

5 The feats of jugglers and tumblers were a favourite diversion with the Grand Khan of China, as Sir John Maundeville informs us. (Voiage and Travaille, chap. 22.) The Aztec mountebanks had such repute, that Cortes sent two of them to Rome to amuse his Holiness Clement VII. Clavigero, Stor. del Messico, tom. ii. p. 186.

listening to music,—if the rude minstrelsy of the Mexicans deserve that name,—accompanied by a chant, in slow and solemn cadence, celebrating the heroic deeds of great Aztec warriors, or of his own princely line.

When he had sufficiently refreshed his spirits with these diversions, he composed himself to sleep, for in his *siesta* he was as regular as a Spaniard. On awaking, he gave audience to ambassadors from foreign states or his own tributary cities, or to such caciques as had suits to prefer to him. They were introduced by the young nobles in attendance, and, whatever might be their rank, unless of the blood royal, they were obliged to submit to the humiliation of shrouding their rich dresses under the coarse mantle of *nequen*, and entering barefooted, with downcast eyes, into the presence. The emperor addressed few and brief remarks to the suitors, answering them generally by his secretaries; and the parties retired with the same reverential obeisance, taking care to keep their faces turned towards the monarch. Well might Cortés exclaim that no court, whether of the Grand Seignior or any other infidel, ever displayed so pompous and elaborate a ceremonial![1]

Besides the crowd of retainers already noticed, the royal household was not complete without a host of artisans constantly employed in the erection or repair of buildings, besides a great number of jewellers and persons skilled in working metals, who found abundant demand for their trinkets among the dark-eyed beauties of the harem. The imperial mummers and jugglers were also very numerous, and the dancers belonging to the palace occupied a particular district of the city, appropriated exclusively to them.

The maintenance of this little host, amounting to some thousands of individuals, involved a heavy expenditure, requiring accounts of a complicated and, to a simple people, it might well be, embarrassing nature. Everything, however, was conducted with perfect order; and all the various receipts and disbursements were set down in the picture-writing of the country. The arithmetical characters were of a more refined and conventional sort than those for narrative purposes; and a separate apartment was filled with hieroglyphical ledgers, exhibiting a complete view of the economy of the palace. The care of all this was intrusted to a treasurer, who acted as a sort of major-domo in the household, having a general superintendence over all its concerns. This responsible office, on the arrival of the Spaniards, was in the hands of a trusty cacique named Tápia.[2]

Such is the picture of Montezuma's domestic establishment and way of living, as delineated by the Conquerors and their immediate followers,

---

[1] "Ninguno de los Soldanes, ni otro ningun señor infiel, de los que hasta agora se tiene noticia, no creo, que tantas, ni tales ceremonias en servicio tengan." Rel. Seg. de Cortés, ap. Lorenzana, p. 115.
[2] Bernal Diaz, Hist. de la Conquista, cap. 91.— Carta del Lic. Zuazo, MS.—Oviedo, Hist. de las Ind., MS., ubi supra.—Toribio, Hist. de los Indios,

MS., Parte 3, cap. 7.—Rel. Seg. de Cortés, ap. Lorenzana, pp. 110-115.—Rel. d'un gentil' huomo, ap. Ramusio, tom. iii. fol. 306.
[The name, which is Spanish, not Aztec, was that given to him by the Conquerors, perhaps with some reference to one of their own number, Andrés de Tápia.—Er]

who had the best means of information ;[1] too highly coloured, it may be, by the proneness to exaggerate, which was natural to those who first witnessed a spectacle so striking to the imagination, so new and unexpected. I have thought it best to present the full details, trivial though they may seem to the reader, as affording a curious picture of manners so superior in point of refinement to those of the other aboriginal tribes on the North American continent.   Nor are they, in fact, so trivial, when we reflect that in these details of private life we possess a surer measure of civilization than in those of a public nature.

In surveying them we are strongly reminded of the civilization of the East; not of that higher, intellectual kind which belonged to the more polished Arabs and the Persians, but that semi-civilization which has distinguished, for example, the Tartar races, among whom art, and even science, have made, indeed, some progress in their adaptation to material wants and sensual gratification, but little in reference to the higher and more ennobling interests of humanity.   It is characteristic of such a people to find a puerile pleasure in a dazzling and ostentatious pageantry; to mistake show for substance, vain pomp for power; to hedge round the throne itself with a barren and burdensome ceremonial, the counterfeit of real majesty.

Even this, however, was an advance in refinement, compared with the rude manners of the earlier Aztecs.   The change may, doubtless, be referred in some degree to the personal influence of Montezuma.   In his younger days he had tempered the fierce habits of the soldier with the milder profession of religion.   In later life he had withdrawn himself still more from the brutalizing occupations of war, and his manners acquired a refinement, tinctured, it may be added, with an effeminacy, unknown to his martial predecessors.

The condition of the empire, too, under his reign, was favourable to this change.   The dismemberment of the Tezcucan kingdom on the death of the great Nezahualpilli had left the Aztec monarchy without a rival; and it soon spread its colossal arms over the farthest limits of Anahuac.   The aspiring mind of Montezuma rose with the acquisition of wealth and power; and he displayed the consciousness of new importance by the assumption of unprecedented state.   He affected a reserve unknown to his predecessors, withdrew his person from the vulgar eye, and fenced himself round with an elaborate and courtly etiquette.   When he went abroad, it was in state, on some public occasion, usually to the great temple, to take part in the religious services; and as he passed along he exacted from his people, as we have seen, the homage of an adulation worthy of an Oriental despot.[2]   His haughty demeanour touched the pride

---

[1] If the historian will descend but a generation later for his authorities, he may find materials for as good a chapter as any in Sir John Maundeville or the Arabian Nights.

[2] "Referre in tanto rege piget superbam mutationem vestis, et desideratas humi jacentium adulationes." (Livy, Hist., lib. 9, cap. 18.) The remarks of the Roman historian in reference to Alexander, after he was infected by the manners of Persia, fit equally well the Aztec emperor.

of his more potent vassals, particularly those who, at a distance, felt them-selves nearly independent of his authority. His exactions, demanded by the profuse expenditure of his palace, scattered broadcast the seeds of discontent; and, while the empire seemed towering in its most palmy and prosperous state, the canker had eaten deepest into its heart.

CHAPTER II.

MARKET OF MEXICO.—GREAT TEMPLE.—INTERIOR SANCTUARIES.
—SPANISH QUARTERS.

(1519.)

FOUR days had elapsed since the Spaniards made their entry into Mexico. Whatever schemes their commander may have revolved in his mind, he felt that he could determine on no plan of operations till he had seen more of the capital and ascertained by his own inspection the nature of its resources. He accordingly, as was observed at the close of the last Book, sent to Montezuma, asking permission to visit the great *teocalli*, and some other places in the city.

The friendly monarch consented without difficulty. He even prepared to go in person to the great temple to receive his guests there,—it may be, to shield the shrine of his tutelar deity from any attempted profanation. He was acquainted, as we have already seen, with the proceedings of the Spaniards on similar occasions in the course of their march. Cortés put himself at the head of his little corps of cavalry, and nearly all the Spanish foot, as usual, and followed the caciques sent by Montezuma to guide him. They proposed first to conduct him to the great market of Tlatelolco, in the western part of the city.

On the way, the Spaniards were struck, in the same manner as they had been on entering the capital, with the appearance of the inhabitants, and their great superiority in the style and quality of their dress over the people of the lower countries.[1] The *tilmatli*, or cloak thrown over the shoulders and tied round the neck, made of cotton of different degrees of fineness, according to the condition of the wearer, and the ample sash around the loins, were often wrought in rich and elegant figures and edged with a deep fringe or tassel. As the weather was now growing cool, mantles of fur or of the gorgeous feather-work were sometimes substituted. The latter

---

[1] "La Gente de esta Ciudad es de mas manera y primor en su vestido, y servicio, que no la otra de estas otras Provincias, y Ciudades: porque como allí estaba siempre este Señor Muteczuma, y todos los Señores sus Vasallos ocurrian siempre á la Ciudad, habia en ella mas manera, y policía en todas las cosas." Rel. Seg. de Cortés, ap Lorenzana, p. 109.

combined the advantage of great warmth with beauty.[1]   The Mexicans had also the art of spinning a fine thread of the hair of the rabbit and other animals, which they wove into a delicate web that took a permanent dye.

The women, as in other parts of the country, seemed to go about as freely as the men.   They wore several skirts or petticoats of different lengths, with highly-ornamented borders, and sometimes over them loose flowing robes, which reached to the ankles.   These, also, were made of cotton, for the wealthier classes, of a fine texture, prettily embroidered.[2] No veils were worn here, as in some other parts of Anahuac, where they were made of the aloe thread, or of the light web of hair, above noticed. The Aztec women had their faces exposed ; and their dark, raven tresses floated luxuriantly over their shoulders, revealing features which, although of a dusky or rather cinnamon hue, were not unfrequently pleasing, while touched with the serious, even sad expression characteristic of the national physiognomy.[3]

On drawing near to the *tianguez,* or great market, the Spaniards were astonished at the throng of people pressing towards it, and on entering the place their surprise was still further heightened by the sight of the multitudes assembled there, and the dimensions of the enclosure, thrice as large as the celebrated square of Salamanca.[4]   Here were met together traders from all parts, with the products and manufactures peculiar to their countries ; the goldsmiths of Azcapozalco ; the potters and jewellers of Cholula, the painters of Tezcuco, the stonecutters of Tenajocan, the hunters of Xilotepec, the fishermen of Cuitlahuac, the fruiterers of the warm countries, the mat and chair makers of Quauhtitlan, and the florists of Xochimilco,—all busily engaged in recommending their respective wares and in chaffering with purchasers.[5]

The market-place was surrounded by deep porticoes, and the several articles had each its own quarter allotted to it.   Here might be seen cotton piled up in bales, or manufactured into dresses and articles of domestic use, as tapestry, curtains, coverlets, and the like.   The richly stained and nice fabrics reminded Cortés of the *alcaycería,* or silk-market, of Granada. There was the quarter assigned to the goldsmiths, where the purchaser might find various articles of ornament or use formed of the precious metals, or curious toys, such as we have already had occasion to notice, made in imitation of birds and fishes, with scales and feathers alternately

---

[1] Zuazo, speaking of the beauty and warmth of this national fabric, says, "Ví muchas mantas de á dos haces labradas de plumas de papos de aves tan suaves, que trayendo la mano por encima á pelo y á pospelo, no era mas que vna manta zebellina mui bien adobada : hice pesar vna dellas ; no pesó mas de seis onzas. Dicen que en el tiempo del Ynbierno una abasta para encima de la camisa sin otro cobertor ni mas ropa encima de la cama."   Carta, MS.

[2] " Sono lunghe & large, lauorate di bellisimi, & molto gentili lauori sparsi per esse, cō le loro frangie,

ò orletti ben lauorati che compariscono benissimo." Rel. d'un gentil' huomo, ap. Ramusio, tom. iii. fol. 305.

[3] Ibid., fol. 305.   [4] Ibid., fol. 309.

[5] " Quivi concorrevano i Pentolai, ed i Giojellieri di Cholulla, gli Orefici d' Azcapozalco, i Pittori di Tezcuco, gli Scarpellini di Tenajocan, i Cacciatori di Xilotepec, i Pescatori di Cuitlahuac, i fruttajuoli de' paesi caldi, gli artefici di stuoje, e di scranne di Quauhtitlan ed i coltivatori de' fiori di Xochimilco." Clavigero, Stor. del Messico, tom. ii. p. 165.

of gold and silver, and with movable heads and bodies.   These fantastic little trinkets were often garnished with precious stones, and showed a patient, puerile ingenuity in the manufacture, like that of the Chinese.[1]

In an adjoining quarter were collected specimens of pottery coarse and fine, vases of wood elaborately carved, varnished or gilt, of curious and sometimes graceful forms.   There were also hatchets made of copper alloyed with tin, the substitute, and, as it proved, not a bad one, for iron. The soldier found here all the implements of his trade : the casque fashioned into the head of some wild animal, with its grinning defences of teeth, and bristling crest dyed with the rich tint of the cochineal ; [2] the *escaupil*, or quilted doublet of cotton, the rich surcoat of feather-mail, and weapons of all sorts, copper-headed lances and arrows, and the broad *maquahuitl*, the Mexican sword, with its sharp blades of *itztli*.   Here were razors and mirrors of this same hard and polished mineral, which served so many of the purposes of steel with the Aztecs.[3]   In the square were also to be found booths occupied by barbers, who used these same razors in their vocation.   For the Mexicans, contrary to the popular and erroneous notions respecting the aborigines of the New World, had beards, though scanty ones.   Other shops or booths were tenanted by apothecaries, well provided with drugs, roots, and different medicinal preparations.   In other places, again, blank books or maps for the hieroglyphical picture-writing were to be seen folded together like fans, and made of cotton, skins, or more commonly the fibres of the agave, the Aztec papyrus.

Under some of the porticoes they saw hides raw and dressed, and various articles for domestic or personal use made of the leather.   Animals, both wild and tame, were offered for sale, and near them, perhaps, a gang of slaves, with collars round their necks, intimating they were likewise on sale,—a spectacle unhappily not confined to the barbarian markets of Mexico, though the evils of their condition were aggravated there by the consciousness that a life of degradation might be consummated at any moment by the dreadful doom of sacrifice.

The heavier materials for building, as stone, lime, timber, were considered too bulky to be allowed a place in the square, and were deposited in the adjacent streets on the borders of the canals.   It would be tedious

---

[1] "Oro y plata, piedras de valor, con otros plumajes é argenterias maravillosas, y con tanto primor fabricadas que excede todo ingenio humano para comprenderlas y alcanzarlas." (Carta del Lic. Zuazo, MS.) The licentiate then enumerates several of these elegant pieces of mechanism. Cortés is not less emphatic in his admiration : "Contrahechas de oro, y plata, y piedras y plumas, tan al natural lo de Oro, y Plata, que no ha Platero en el Mundo que mejor lo hiciesse, y lo de las Piedras, que no baste juicio comprehender con que Instrumentos se hiciesse tan perfecto, y lo de Pluma, que ni de Cera, ni en ningun broslado se podria hacer tan maravillosamente." (Rel. Seg., ap. Lorenzana, p. 110.) Peter Martyr, a less prejudiced critic than Cortés, who saw and examined many of these golden trinkets afterwards in Castile, bears the same testimony to the exquisite character of the workmanship, which, he says, far surpassed the value of the material. De Orbe Novo, dec. 5, cap. 10.

[2] Herrera makes the unauthorized assertion, repeated by Solís, that the Mexicans were unacquainted with the value of the cochineal till it was taught them by the Spaniards. (Herrera, Hist. general, dec. 4, lib. 8, cap. 11.) The natives, on the contrary, took infinite pains to rear the insect on plantations of the cactus, and it formed one of the staple tributes to the crown from certain districts. See the tribute-rolls, ap. Lorenzana, Nos. 23, 24.—Hernandez, Hist. Plantarum, lib. 6, cap. 116.—Also, Clavigero, Stor. del Messico, tom. i. p. 114, nota.

[3] *Ante*, p. 67.

to enumerate all the various articles, whether for luxury or daily use, which were collected from all quarters in this vast bazaar. I must not omit to mention, however, the display of provisions, one of the most attractive features of the *tianguez ;* meats of all kinds, domestic poultry, game from the neighbouring mountains, fish from the lakes and streams, fruits in all the delicious abundance of these temperate regions, green vegetables, and the unfailing maize. There was many a viand, too, ready dressed, which sent up its savoury steams provoking the appetite of the idle passenger; pastry, bread of the Indian corn, cakes, and confectionery.[1] Along with these were to be seen cooling or stimulating beverages, the spicy foaming *chocolatl* with its delicate aroma of vanilla, and the inebriating *pulque*, the fermented juice of the aloe. All these commodities, and every stall and portico, were set out, or rather smothered, with flowers, showing—on a much greater scale, indeed—a taste similar to that displayed in the markets of modern Mexico. Flowers seem to be the spontaneous growth of this luxuriant soil; which, instead of noxious weeds, as in other regions, is ever ready, without the aid of man, to cover up its nakedness with this rich and variegated livery of Nature.[2]

I will spare the reader the repetition of all the particulars enumerated by the bewildered Spaniards, which are of some interest as evincing the various mechanical skill and the polished wants, resembling those of a refined community rather than of a nation of savages. It was the *material* civilization, which belongs neither to the one nor the other. The Aztec had plainly reached that middle station, as far above the rude races of the New World as it was below the cultivated communities of the Old.

As to the numbers assembled in the market, the estimates differ, as usual. The Spaniards often visited the place, and no one states the amount at less than forty thousand! Some carry it much higher.[3] Without relying too much on the arithmetic of the Conquerors, it is certain that on this occasion, which occurred every fifth day, the city swarmed with a motley crowd of strangers, not only from the vicinity, but from many leagues around; the causeways were thronged, and the lake was darkened by canoes filled with traders flocking to the great *tianguez*. It resembled, indeed, the periodical fairs in Europe, not as they exist now,

---

[1] Zuazo, who seems to have been nice in these matters, concludes a paragraph of dainties with the following tribute to the Aztec *cuisine :* "Vendense huebos asados, crudos, en tortilla, é diversidad de guisados que se suelen guisar, con otras cazuelas y pasteles, que en el mal cocinado de Medina, ni en otros lugares de Tlamencos dicen que hai ni se pueden hallar tales trujamanes." Carta, MS.

[2] Ample details—many more than I have thought it necessary to give—of the Aztec market of Tlatelolco may be found in the writings of all the old Spaniards who visited the capital. Among otheis, see Rel. Seg. de Cortés, ap. Lorenzana, pp. 103–105. Toribio, Hist. de los Indios, MS., Parte 3, cap. 7.—Carta del Lic. Zuazo, MS.—Rel. d'un

gentil' huomo, ap. Ramusio, tom. iii. fol. 309.—Bernal Diaz, Hist. de la Conquista, cap. 92.

[3] Zuazo raises it to 80,000 ! (Carta, MS.) Cortés to 60,000. (Rel. Seg., ubi supra.) The most modest computation is that of the "Anonymous Conqueror," who says from 40,000 to 50,000. "Et il giorno del mercato, che si fa di cinque in cinque giorni, vi sono da quaranta ò cinquanta mila persone" (Rel. d'un gentil' huomo, ap. Ramusio, tom. iii. fol. 309); a confirmation, by-the-by, of the supposition that the estimated population of the capital, found in the Italian version of this author, is a misprint. (See *ante*, p. 283, note 6.) He would hardly have crowded an amount equal to the whole of it into the market.

but as they existed in the Middle Ages, when, from the difficulties of intercommunication, they served as the great central marts for commercial intercourse, exercising a most important and salutary influence on the community.

The exchanges were conducted partly by barter, but more usually in the currency of the country. This consisted of bits of tin stamped with a character like a T, bags of cacao, the value of which was regulated by their size, and, lastly, quills filled with gold dust.[1] Gold was part of the regular currency, it seems, in both hemispheres. In their dealings it is singular that they should have had no knowledge of scales and weights. The quantity was determined by measure and number.[2]

The most perfect order reigned throughout this vast assembly. Officers patrolled the square, whose business it was to keep the peace, to collect the duties imposed on the different articles of merchandise, to see that no false measures or fraud of any kind were used, and to bring offenders at once to justice. A court of twelve judges sat in one part of the *tianguez*, clothed with those ample and summary powers which in despotic countries are often delegated even to petty tribunals. The extreme severity with which they exercised these powers, in more than one instance, proves that they were not a dead letter.[3]

The *tianguez* of Mexico was naturally an object of great interest, as well as wonder, to the Spaniards. For in it they saw converged into one focus, as it were, all the rays of civilization scattered throughout the land. Here they beheld the various evidences of mechanical skill, of domestic industry, the multiplied resources, of whatever kind, within the compass of the natives. It could not fail to impress them with high ideas of the magnitude of these resources, as well as of the commercial activity and social subordination by which the whole community was knit together; and their admiration is fully evinced by the minuteness and energy of their descriptions.[4]

From this bustling scene the Spaniards took their way to the great *teocalli*, in the neighbourhood of their own quarters. It covered, with the subordinate edifices, as the reader has already seen, the large tract of ground now occupied by the cathedral, part of the market-place, and some of the adjoining streets.[5] It was the spot which had been consecrated to the same object, probably, ever since the foundation of the city. The present building, however, was of no great antiquity, having been constructed by Ahuitzotl, who celebrated its dedication, in 1486, by that

---

1 [From the description of the coin, Ramirez infers that it was not stamped, but cut, in the form mentioned in the text. This is confirmed by one or two specimens of the kind still preserved in the National Museum at Mexico. Ramirez, Notas y Esclarecimientos, p. 102.]

2 *Ante*, p. 60.

3 Toribio, Hist. de los Indios, MS., Parte 3, cap. 7 —Rel. Seg., ap. Lorenzana, p. 104.—Oviedo, Hist. de las Ind., MS., lib. 33, cap. 10.—Bernal Diaz, Hist. de la Conquista, loc. cit.

4 "There were amongst us," says Diaz, "soldiers who had been in many parts of the world,—in Constantinople and in Rome and through all Italy,—and who said that a market-place so large, so well ordered and regulated, and so filled with people, they had never seen." Hist. de la Conquista, loc. cit.

5 Clavigero, Stor. del Messico, tom. ii. p. 27.

hecatomb of victims of which such incredible reports are to be found in the chronicles.[1]

It stood in the midst of a vast area, encompassed by a wall of stone and lime, about eight feet high, ornamented on the outer side by figures of serpents, raised in relief, which gave it the name of the *coatepantli,* or "wall of serpents." This emblem was a common one in the sacred sculpture of Anahuac, as well as of Egypt. The wall, which was quadrangular, was pierced by huge battlemented gateways, opening on the four principal streets of the capital. Over each of the gates was a kind of arsenal, filled with arms and warlike gear; and, if we may credit the report of the Conquerors, there were barracks adjoining, garrisoned by ten thousand soldiers, who served as a sort of military police for the capital, supplying the emperor with a strong arm in case of tumult or sedition.[2]

The *teocalli* itself was a solid pyramidal structure of earth and pebbles, coated on the outside with hewn stones, probably of the light, porous kind employed in the buildings of the city.[3] It was probably square, with its sides facing the cardinal points.[4] It was divided into five bodies or stories, each one receding so as to be of smaller dimensions than that immediately below it,—the usual form of the Aztec *teocallis,* as already described, and bearing obvious resemblance to some of the primitive pyramidal structures in the Old World.[5] The ascent was by a flight of steps on the outside, which reached to the narrow terrace or platform at the base of the second story, passing quite round the building, when a second stairway conducted to a similar landing at the base of the third. The breadth of this walk was just so much space as was left by the retreating story next above it. From this construction the visitor was obliged to pass round the whole edifice four times in order to reach the top. This had a most imposing effect in the religious ceremonials, when the pompous procession of priests with their wild minstrelsy came sweeping round the huge sides of the pyramid, as they rose higher and higher, in the presence of gazing multitudes, towards the summit.

The dimensions of the temple cannot be given with any certainty. The Conquerors judged by the eye, rarely troubling themselves with anything like an accurate measurement. It was, probably, not much

---

[1] *Ante,* p. 38.—[A minute account of the site and extent of the ground covered by the great temple is given by Alaman (Disertaciones históricas, tom. ii. pp. 246-248.) The Mexicans are largely indebted to this eminent scholar for his elaborate researches into the topography and antiquities of the Aztec capital.]

[2] "Et di più v' hauea vna guarnigione di dieci mila huomini di guerra, tutti eletti per huomini valenti, & questi accompagnauano & guardauano la sua persona, & quando si facea qualche rumore ò ribellione nella città ò nel paese circumuicino, andauano questi, ò parte d' essi per Capitani." Rel. d'un gentil' huomo, ap. Ramusio, tom. iii. fol. 309.

[3] Humboldt, Essai politique, tom. ii. p. 40.—On paving the square, not long ago, round the modern

cathedral, there were found large blocks of sculptured stone buried between thirty and forty feet deep in the ground. Ibid., loc. cit.

[4] Clavigero calls it oblong, on the alleged authority of the "Anonymous Conqueror." (Stor. del Messico, tom. ii. p. 27, nota.) But the latter says not a word of the shape, and his contemptible woodcut is too plainly destitute of all proportion to furnish an inference of any kind. (Comp. Rel. d'un gentil' huomo, ap. Ramusio, tom. iii. fol. 307.) Torquemada and Gomara both say it was square (Monarch. Ind., lib. 8, cap. 11;—Crónica, cap. 80); and Toribio de Benavente, speaking generally of the Mexican temples, says they had that form, Hist. de los Ind., MS., Parte 1, cap. 12.

[5] See Appendix, Part 1.

less than three hundred feet square at the base;[1] and, as the Spaniards counted a hundred and fourteen steps, was, probably, less than one hundred feet in height.[2]

When Cortés arrived before the *teocalli*, he found two priests and several caciques commissioned by Montezuma to save him the fatigue of the ascent by bearing him on their shoulders, in the same manner as had been done to the emperor. But the general declined the compliment, preferring to march up at the head of his men. On reaching the summit, they found it a vast area, paved with broad flat stones. The first object that met their view was a large block of jasper, the peculiar shape of which showed it was the stone on which the bodies of the unhappy victims were stretched for sacrifice. Its convex surface, by raising the breast, enabled the priest to perform his diabolical task more easily, of removing the heart. At the other end of the area were two towers or sanctuaries, consisting of three stories, the lower one of stone and stucco, the two upper of wood elaborately carved. In the lower division stood the images of their gods; the apartments above were filled with utensils for their religious services, and with the ashes of some of their Aztec princes, who had fancied this airy sepulchre. Before each sanctuary stood an altar, with that undying fire upon it, the extinction of which boded as much evil to the empire as that of the Vestal flame would have done in ancient Rome. Here, also, was the huge cylindrical drum made of serpents' skins, and struck only on extraordinary occasions, when it sent forth a melancholy sound that might be heard for miles,—a sound of woe in after-times to the Spaniards.

Montezuma, attended by the high-priest, came forward to receive Cortés as he mounted the area. "You are weary, Malinche," said he to him, "with climbing up our great temple." But Cortés, with a politic vaunt, assured him "the Spaniards were never weary"! Then, taking him by the hand, the emperor pointed out the localities of the neighbourhood. The temple on which they stood, rising high above all other edifices in the capital, afforded the most elevated as well as central point of view. Below them, the city lay spread out like a map, with its streets and canals intersecting each other at right angles, its terraced roofs blooming like so many parterres of flowers. Every place seemed alive with business and

---

[1] Clavigero, calling it oblong, adopts Torquemada's estimate—not Sahagun's, as he pretends, which he never saw, and who gives no measurement of the building—for the length, and Gomara's estimate, which is somewhat less, for the breadth. (Stor. del Messico, tom. ii. p. 28, nota.) As both his authorities make the building square, this spirit of accommodation is whimsical enough. Toribio, who did measure a *teocalli* of the usual construction in the town of Tenayuca, found it to be forty *brazas*, or two hundred and forty feet, square. (Hist. de los Ind., MS., Parte 1, cap. 12.) The great temple of Mexico was undoubtedly larger, and, in the want of better authorities, one may accept Torquemada, who makes it a little more than three hundred and sixty Toledan, equal to three hundred and eight French feet, square. (Monarch. Ind., lib. 8, cap. 11.) How can M. de Humboldt speak of the "great concurrence of testimony" in regard to the dimensions of the temple? (Essai politique, tom. ii. p. 41.) No two authorities agree.

[2] Bernal Diaz says he counted one hundred and fourteen steps. (Hist. de la Conquista, cap. 92.) Toribio says that more than one person who had numbered them told him they exceeded a hundred. (Hist. de los Indios, MS., Parte 1, cap. 12.) The steps could hardly have been less than eight or ten inches high, each; Clavigero assumes that they were a foot, and that the building, therefore, was a hundred and fourteen feet high, precisely. (Stor. del Messico, tom. ii. pp. 28, 29.) It is seldom safe to use anything stronger than *probably* in history.

bustle; canoes were glancing up and down the canals, the streets were crowded with people in their gay, picturesque costume, while from the market-place they had so lately left a confused hum of many sounds and voices rose upon the air.[1] They could distinctly trace the symmetrical plan of the city, with its principal avenues issuing, as it were, from the four gates of the *coatepantli* and connecting themselves with the causeways, which formed the grand entrances to the capital. This regular and beautiful arrangement was imitated in many of the inferior towns, where the great roads converged towards the chief *teocalli*, or cathedral, as to a common focus.[2] They could discern the insular position of the metropolis, bathed on all sides by the salt floods of the Tezcuco, and in the distance the clear fresh waters of the Chalco; far beyond stretched a wide prospect of fields and waving woods, with the burnished walls of many a lofty temple rising high above the trees and crowning the distant hill-tops.[3] The view reached in an unbroken line to the very base of the circular range of mountains, whose frosty peaks glittered as if touched with fire in the morning ray; while long, dark wreaths of vapour, rolling up from the hoary head of Popocatepetl, told that the destroying element was, indeed, at work in the bosom of the beautiful Valley.

Cortés was filled with admiration at this grand and glorious spectacle, and gave utterance to his feelings in animated language to the emperor, the lord of these flourishing domains. His thoughts, however, soon took another direction; and, turning to Father Olmedo, who stood by his side, he suggested that the area would afford a most conspicuous position for the Christian Cross, if Montezuma would but allow it to be planted there. But the discreet ecclesiastic, with the good sense which on these occasions seems to have been so lamentably deficient in his commander, reminded him that such a request, at present, would be exceedingly ill timed, as the Indian monarch had shown no dispositions as yet favourable to Christianity.[4]

Cortés then requested Montezuma to allow him to enter the sanctuaries and behold the shrines of his gods. To this the latter, after a short conference with the priests, assented, and conducted the Spaniards into the building. They found themselves in a spacious apartment incrusted on the sides with stucco, on which various figures were sculptured, representing the Mexican calendar, perhaps, or the priestly ritual. At one end of the saloon was a recess with a roof of timber richly carved and gilt.

1 "Tornámos á ver la gran plaça, y la multitud de gente que en ella auia, vnos comprado, y otros vendiendo, que solamente el rumor, y zumbido de las vozes, y palabras que allí auia, sonaua mas que de vna legua!" Bernal Diaz, Hist. de la Conquista, cap. 92.

2 "Y por honrar mas sus templos sacaban los caminos muy derechos por cordel de una y de dos leguas que era cosa harto de ver, desde lo Alto del principal templo, como venian de todos los pueblos menores y barrios; salian los caminos muy derechos y iban á dar al patio de los teocallis." Toribio, Hist. de los Indios, MS., Parte 1, cap. 12.

3 "No se contentaba el Demonio con los [Teucales] ya dichos, sino que en cada pueblo, en cada barrio, y á cuarto de legua, tenian otros patios pequeños adonde habia tres ó cuatro teocallis, y en algunos mas, en otras partes solo uno, y en cada Mogote ó Cerrejon uno ó dos, y por los caminos y entre los Maizales, habia otros muchos pequeños, y todos estaban blancos y encalados, que parecian y abultaban mucho, que en la tierra bien poblada parecia que todo estaba lleno de casas, en especial de los patios del Demonio, que eran muy de ver." Toribio, Hist. de los Indios, MS., ubi supra.

4 Bernal Diaz, Hist. de la Conquista, ubi supra.

Before the altar in this sanctuary stood the colossal image of Huitzilo-pochtli, the tutelary deity and war-god of the Aztecs. His countenance was distorted into hideous lineaments of symbolical import. In his right hand he wielded a bow, and in his left a bunch of golden arrows, which a mystic legend had connected with the victories of his people. The huge folds of a serpent, consisting of pearls and precious stones, were coiled round his waist, and the same rich materials were profusely sprinkled over his person. On his left foot were the delicate feathers of the humming-bird, which, singularly enough, gave its name to the dread deity.[1] The most conspicuous ornament was a chain of gold and silver hearts alternate, suspended round his neck, emblematical of the sacrifice in which he most delighted. A more unequivocal evidence of this was afforded by three human hearts smoking and almost palpitating, as if recently torn from the victims, and now lying on the altar before him !

The adjoining sanctuary was dedicated to a milder deity. This was Tezcatlipoca, next in honour to that invisible Being, the Supreme God, who was represented by no image and confined by no temple. It was Tezcatlipoca who created the world and watched over it with a provi-dential care. He was represented as a young man, and his image, of polished black stone, was richly garnished with gold plates and ornaments, among which a shield burnished like a mirror was the most characteristic emblem, as in it he saw reflected all the doings of the world. But the homage to this god was not always of a more refined or merciful character than that paid to his carnivorous brother ; for five bleeding hearts were also seen in a golden platter on his altar.

The walls of both these chapels were stained with human gore. "The stench was more intolerable," exclaims Diaz, "than that of the slaughter-houses in Castile !" And the frantic forms of the priests, with their dark robes clotted with blood, as they flitted to and fro, seemed to the Spaniards to be those of the very ministers of Satan ![2]

From this foul abode they gladly escaped into the open air; when Cortés, turning to Montezuma, said, with a smile, "I do not comprehend how a great and wise prince, like you, can put faith in such evil spirits as these idols, the representatives of the Devil! If you will but permit us to erect here the true Cross, and place the images of the blessed Virgin and her Son in your sanctuaries, you will soon see how your false gods will shrink before them !"

Montezuma was greatly shocked at this sacrilegious address. "These are the gods," he answered, "who have led the Aztecs on to victory since they were a nation, and who send the seed-time and harvest in their

---

[1] *Ante*, p. 28.
[2] "Y tenia en las paredes tantas costras de sangre, y el suelo todo bañado dello, que en los mataderos de Castilla no auia tanto hedor." Bernal Diaz, Hist. de la Conquista, ubi supra.—Rel. Seg. de

Cortés, ap. Lorenzana, pp. 105, 106.—Carta del Lic. Zuazo, MS.—See, also, for notices of these deities, Sahagun, lib. 3, cap. 1, et seq.—Torquemada, Monarch. Ind., lib. 6, cap. 20, 21.—Acosta, lib. 5, cap. 9.

seasons. Had I thought you would have offered them this outrage, I would not have admitted you into their presence."

Cortés, after some expressions of concern at having wounded the feelings of the emperor, took his leave. Montezuma remained, saying that he must expiate, if possible, the crime of exposing the shrines of the divinities to such profanation by the strangers.[1]

On descending to the court, the Spaniards took a leisurely survey of the other edifices in the enclosure. The area was protected by a smooth stone pavement, so polished, indeed, that it was with difficulty the horses could keep their legs. There were several other *teocallis*, built generally on the model of the great one, though of much inferior size, dedicated to the different Aztec deities.[2] On their summits were the altars crowned with perpetual flames, which, with those on the numerous temples in other quarters of the capital, shed a brilliant illumination over its streets through the long nights.[3]

Among the *teocallis* in the enclosure was one consecrated to Quetzal-coatl, circular in its form, and having an entrance in imitation of a dragon's mouth, bristling with sharp fangs and dropping with blood. As the Spaniards cast a furtive glance into the throat of this horrible monster, they saw collected there implements of sacrifice and other abominations of fearful import. Their bold hearts shuddered at the spectacle, and they designated the place not inaptly as the "Hell."[4]

One other structure may be noticed as characteristic of the brutish nature of their religion. This was a pyramidal mound or tumulus, having a complicated framework of timber on its broad summit. On this was strung an immense number of human skulls, which belonged to the victims, mostly prisoners of war, who had perished on the accursed stone of sacrifice. Two of the soldiers had the patience to count the number of these ghastly trophies, and reported it to be one hundred and thirty-six thousand![5]

---

[1] Bernal Diaz, Hist. de la Conquista, ubi supra.—Whoever examines Cortés' great letter to Charles V. will be surprised to find it stated that, instead of any acknowledgment to Montezuma, he threw down his idols and erected the Christian emblems in their stead. (Rel. Seg., ap. Lorenzana, p. 106.) This was an event of much later date. The *Conquistador* wrote his despatches too rapidly and concisely to give heed always to exact time and circumstance. We are quite as likely to find them attended to in the long-winded, gossiping,—inestimable chronicle of Diaz.

[2] "Quarenta torres muy altas y bien obradas." Rel. Seg. de Cortés, ap. Lorenzana, p. 105.

[3] "Delante de todos estos altares habia braçeros que toda la noche hardian, y en las salas tambien tenian sus fuegos." Toribio, Hist. de los Indios, MS., Parte 1, cap. 12.

[4] Bernal Diaz, Ibid., ubi supra.—Toribio, also, notices this temple with the same complimentary epithet. "La boca hecha como de infierno y en ella pintada la boca de una temerosa Sierpe con terribles colmillos y dientes, y en algunas de estas los colmillos eran de bulto, que verlo y entrar dentro ponia gran temor y grima, en especial el infierno que estaba en México, que parecia traslado del verdadero infierno." Hist. de los Indios, MS., Parte 1, cap. 4.

[5] Bernal Diaz, ubi supra.—"Andrés de Tápia, *que me lo dijo*, i Gonçalo de Umbria, las contáron vn Dia, i halláron ciento i treinta i seis mil Calaberas, en las Vigas, i Gradas." Gomara, Crónica, cap. 82.*

* [Gomara is so often accused of exaggeration and falsehood that it is satisfactory to find his exactness, in the present instance, established by the evidence of Tápia himself, who thus describes the manner in which the estimate was made: "É quien esto escribe, y un Gonzalo de Umbréa, contaron los palos que habie, é multiplicando á cinco cabezas cada palo de los que entre viga y viga estaban, . . . hallamos haber ciento treinta y seis mill cabezas, *sin las de las torres.*" (Icazbalceta, Col. de Doc. para la Hist. de México, tom. iii.) The original of this "Relacion," recently discovered, is in the library of the Academy of History at Madrid. It is an unfinished narrative, valuable as the production of one of the chief companions of Cortés, and for the confirmation it affords of other contemporaneous accounts of the Conquest. —Ed.]

Belief might well be staggered, did not the Old World present a worthy counterpart in the pyramidal Golgothas which commemorated the triumphs of Tamerlane.[1]

There were long ranges of buildings in the enclosure, appropriated as the residence of the priests and others engaged in the offices of religion. The whole number of them was said to amount to several thousand. Here were, also, the principal seminaries for the instruction of youth of both sexes, drawn chiefly from the higher and wealthier classes. The girls were taught by elderly women who officiated as priestesses in the temples, a custom familiar, also, to Egypt. The Spaniards admit that the greatest care for morals, and the most blameless deportment, were maintained in these institutions. The time of the pupils was chiefly occupied, as in most monastic establishments, with the minute and burdensome ceremonial of their religion. The boys were likewise taught such elements of science as were known to their teachers, and the girls initiated in the mysteries of embroidery and weaving, which they employed in decorating the temples. At a suitable age they generally went forth into the world to assume the occupations fitted to their condition, though some remained permanently devoted to the services of religion.[2]

The spot was also covered by edifices of a still different character. There were granaries filled with the rich produce of the church-lands and with the first-fruits and other offerings of the faithful. One large mansion was reserved for strangers of eminence who were on a pilgrimage to the great *teocalli*. The enclosure was ornamented with gardens, shaded by ancient trees and watered by fountains and reservoirs from the copious streams of Chapoltepec. The little community was thus provided with almost everything requisite for its own maintenance and the services of the temple.[3]

It was a microcosm of itself, a city within a city, and, according to the assertion of Cortés, embraced a tract of ground large enough for five hundred houses.[4] It presented in this brief compass the extremes of barbarism, blended with a certain civilization, altogether characteristic of the Aztecs. The rude Conquerors saw only the evidence of the former. In the fantastic and symbolical features of the deities they beheld the literal lineaments of Satan; in the rites and frivolous ceremonial, his own especial code of damnation; and in the modest deportment and careful nurture of the inmates of the seminaries, the snares by which he was to beguile his deluded victims![5] Before a century had elapsed, the descen-

---

[1] Three collections, thus fancifully disposed, of these grinning horrors—in all 230,000—are noticed by Gibbon! (Decline and Fall, ed. Milman, vol. i. p. 52; vol. xii. p. 45.) A *European* scholar commends " the conqueror's piety, his moderation, and his justice"! Rowe's Dedication of "Tamerlane."

[2] *Ante*, pp. 33, 34.—The desire of presenting the reader with a complete view of the actual state of the capital at the time of its occupation by the Spaniards has led me in this and the preceding chapter into a few repetitions of remarks on the Aztec institutions in the Introductory Book of this History.

[3] Toribio, Hist. de los Indios, MS., Parte 1, cap. 12.—Gomara, Crónica, cap. 80.—Rel. d'un gentil' huomo, ap. Ramusio, tom. iii. fol. 309.

[4] "Es tan grande que dentro del circuito de ella, que es todo cercado de Muro muy alto, se podia muy bien facer una Villa de quinientos Vecinos." Rel. Seg., ap. Lorenzana, p. 105.

[5] "Todas estas mugeres," says Father Toribio, "estaban aquí sirviendo al demonio por sus propios intereses; las unas porque el Demonio las hiciese modestas," etc. Hist. de los Indios, MS., Parte 1, cap. 9.

dants of these same Spaniards discerned in the mysteries of the Aztec religion the features, obscured and defaced, indeed, of the Jewish and Christian revelations![1] Such were the opposite conclusions of the unlettered soldier and of the scholar. A philosopher, untouched by superstition, might well doubt which of the two was the more extraordinary.

The sight of the Indian abominations seems to have kindled in the Spaniards a livelier feeling for their own religion; since on the following day they asked leave of Montezuma to convert one of the halls in their residence into a chapel, that they might celebrate the services of the Church there. The monarch, in whose bosom the feelings of resentment seem to have soon subsided, easily granted their request, and sent some of his own artisans to aid them in the work.

While it was in progress, some of the Spaniards observed what appeared to be a door recently plastered over. It was a common rumour that Montezuma still kept the treasures of his father, King Axayacatl, in this ancient palace. The Spaniards, acquainted with this fact, felt no scruple in gratifying their curiosity by removing the plaster. As was anticipated, it concealed a door. On forcing this, they found the rumour was no exaggeration. They beheld a large hall filled with rich and beautiful stuffs, articles of curious workmanship of various kinds, gold and silver in bars and in the ore, and many jewels of value. It was the private hoard of Montezuma, the contributions, it may be, of tributary cities, and once the property of his father. " I was a young man," says Diaz, who was one of those that obtained a sight of it, " and it seemed to me as if all the riches of the world were in that room!"[2] The Spaniards, notwithstanding their elation at the discovery of this precious deposit, seem to have felt some commendable scruples as to appropriating it to their own use, —at least for the present. And Cortés, after closing up the wall as it was before, gave strict injunctions that nothing should be said of the matter, unwilling that the knowledge of its existence by his guests should reach the ears of Montezuma.

Three days sufficed to complete the chapel; and the Christians had the satisfaction to see themselves in possession of a temple where they might worship God in their own way, under the protection of the Cross and the blessed Virgin. Mass was regularly performed by the fathers Olmedo and Diaz, in the presence of the assembled army, who were most earnest and exemplary in their devotions, partly, says the chronicler above quoted, from the propriety of the thing, and partly for its edifying influence on the benighted heathen.[3]

---

1 See Appendix, Part i.

2 "Y luego lo supímos entre todos los demas Capitanes, y soldados, y lo entrámos á ver muy secretamente, y como yo lo ví, digo que me admiré, é como en aquel tiempo era mancebo, y no auía visto en mi vida riquezas como aquellas, tuue por cierto, que en el mundo no deuiera auer otras tantas!" Hist. de la Conquista, cap. 93.

3 Ibid., loc. cit.

CHAPTER III.

ANXIETY OF CORTÉS.—SEIZURE OF MONTEZUMA.—HIS TREATMENT BY THE
SPANIARDS.—EXECUTION OF HIS OFFICERS.—MONTEZUMA IN IRONS.—
REFLECTIONS.

(1519.)

THE Spaniards had been now a week in Mexico. During this time they
had experienced the most friendly treatment from the emperor. But the
mind of Cortés was far from easy. He felt that it was quite uncertain
how long this amiable temper would last. A hundred circumstances
might occur to change it. Montezuma might very naturally feel the
maintenance of so large a body too burdensome on his treasury. The
people of the capital might become dissatisfied at the presence of so
numerous an armed force within their walls. Many causes of disgust
might arise betwixt the soldiers and the citizens. Indeed, it was scarcely
possible that a rude, licentious soldiery, like the Spaniards, could be
long kept in subjection without active employment.[1] The danger was
even greater with the Tlascalans, a fierce race now brought into daily
contact with the nation who held them in loathing and detestation.
Rumours were already rife among the allies, whether well founded or not,
of murmurs among the Mexicans, accompanied by menaces of raising
the bridges.[2]

Even should the Spaniards be allowed to occupy their present quarters
unmolested, it was not advancing the great object of the expedition.
Cortés was not a whit nearer gaining the capital, so essential to his
meditated subjugation of the country; and any day he might receive
tidings that the crown, or, what he most feared, the governor of Cuba,
had sent a force of superior strength to wrest from him a conquest but
half achieved. Disturbed by these anxious reflections, he resolved to
extricate himself from his embarrassment by one bold stroke. But he
first submitted the affair to a council of the officers in whom he most
confided, desirous to divide with them the responsibility of the act, and,
no doubt, to interest them more heartily in its execution by making it in
some measure the result of their combined judgments.

When the general had briefly stated the embarrassments of their position,
the council was divided in opinion. All admitted the necessity of some

---

[1] "We Spaniards," says Cortés, frankly, "are
apt to be somewhat unmanageable and troublesome."
Rel. Seg., ap. Lorenzana, p. 84.
[2] Gomara, Crónica, cap. 83.—There is reason to
doubt the truth of these stories. "Segun una carta
original que tengo en mi poder firmada de las tres
cabezas de la Nueva-España en donde escriben á la
Magestad del Emperador Nuestro Señor (que Dios

tenga en su Santo Reyno) disculpan en ella á
Motecuhzoma y á los Mexicanos de esto, y de lo
demas que se les argulló, que lo cierto era que fué
invencion de los Tlascaltecas, y de algunos de los
Españoles que veian la hora de salirse de miedo de
la Ciudad, y poner en cobro innumerables riquezas
que habian venido á sus manos." Ixtlilxochitl,
Hist. Chich., MS., cap. 85.

U

instant action. One party were for retiring secretly from the city, and getting beyond the causeways before their march could be intercepted. Another advised that it should be done openly, with the knowledge of the emperor, of whose goodwill they had had so many proofs. But both these measures seemed alike impolitic. A retreat under these circumstances, and so abruptly made, would have the air of a flight. It would be construed into distrust of themselves; and anything like timidity on their part would be sure not only to bring on them the Mexicans, but the contempt of their allies, who would, doubtless, join in the general cry.

As to Montezuma, what reliance could they place on the protection of a prince so recently their enemy, and who, in his altered bearing, must have taken counsel of his fears rather than his inclinations?

Even should they succeed in reaching the coast, their situation would be little better. It would be proclaiming to the world that, after all their lofty vaunts, they were unequal to the enterprise. Their only hopes of their sovereign's favour, and of pardon for their irregular proceedings, were founded on success. Hitherto, they had only made the discovery of Mexico; to retreat would be to leave conquest and the fruits of it to another. In short, to stay and to retreat seemed equally disastrous.

In this perplexity, Cortés proposed an expedient which none but the most daring spirit, in the most desperate extremity, would have conceived. This was to march to the royal palace and bring Montezuma to the Spanish quarters, by fair means if they could persuade him, by force if necessary,—at all events, to get possession of his person. With such a pledge, the Spaniards would be secure from the assault of the Mexicans, afraid by acts of violence to compromise the safety of their prince. If he came by his own consent, they would be deprived of all apology for doing so. As long as the emperor remained among the Spaniards, it would be easy, by allowing him a show of sovereignty, to rule in his name, until they had taken measures for securing their safety and the success of their enterprise. The idea of employing a sovereign as a tool for the government of his own kingdom, if a new one in the age of Cortés, is certainly not so in ours.[1]

A plausible pretext for the seizure of the hospitable monarch—for the most barefaced action seeks to veil itself under some show of decency—

---

[1] Rel. Seg. de Cortés, ap. Lorenzana, p. 84.— Ixtlilxochitl, Hist. Chich., MS., cap. 85.—Peter Martyr, De Orbe Novo, dec. 5, cap. 3.—Oviedo, Hist. de las Ind., MS., lib 33, cap. 6.—Bernal Diaz gives a very different report of this matter. According to him, a number of officers and soldiers, of whom he was one, suggested the capture of Montezuma to the general, who came into the plan with hesitation. (Hist. de la Conquista, cap. 93.) This is contrary to the character of Cortés, who was a man to lead, not to be led, on such occasions. It is contrary to the general report of historians, though these, it must be confessed, are mainly built on the general's narrative. It is contrary to anterior probability; since, if the conception seems almost too desperate to have seriously entered into the head of any one man, how much more improbable is it that it should have originated with a number! Lastly, it is contrary to the positive written statement of Cortés to the emperor, publicly known and circulated, confirmed in print by his chaplain, Gomara, and all this when the thing was fresh and when the parties interested were alive to contradict it. We cannot but think that the captain here, as in the case of the burning of the ships, assumes rather more for himself and his comrades than the facts will strictly warrant; an oversight for which the lapse of half a century—to say nothing of his avowed anxiety to show up the claims of the latter—may furnish some apology

was afforded by a circumstance of which Cortés had received intelligence at Cholula.[1] He had left, as we have seen, a faithful officer, Juan de Escalante, with a hundred and fifty men, in garrison at Vera Cruz, on his departure for the capital. He had not been long absent when his lieutenant received a message from an Aztec chief named Quauhpopoca, governor of a district to the north of the Spanish settlement, declaring his desire to come in person and tender his allegiance to the Spanish authorities at Vera Cruz. He requested that four of the white men might be sent to protect him against certain unfriendly tribes through which his road lay. This was not an uncommon request, and excited no suspicion in Escalante. The four soldiers were sent ; and on their arrival two of them were murdered by the false Aztec. The other two made their way back to the garrison.[2]

The commander marched at once, with fifty of his men, and several thousand Indian allies, to take vengeance on the cacique. A pitched battle followed. The allies fled from the redoubted Mexicans. The few Spaniards stood firm, and with the aid of their firearms and the blessed Virgin, who was distinctly seen hovering over their ranks in the van, they made good the field against the enemy. It cost them dear, however; since seven or eight Christians were slain, and among them the gallant Escalante himself, who died of his injuries soon after his return to the fort. The Indian prisoners captured in the battle spoke of the whole proceeding as having taken place at the instigation of Montezuma.[3]

One of the Spaniards fell into the hands of the natives, but soon after perished of his wounds. His head was cut off and sent to the Aztec emperor. It was uncommonly large and covered with hair ; and, as Montezuma gazed on the ferocious features, rendered more horrible by death, he seemed to read in them the dark lineaments of the destined destroyers of his house. He turned from it with a shudder, and commanded that it should be taken from the city, and not offered at the shrine of any of his gods.

Although Cortés had received intelligence of this disaster at Cholula, he had concealed it within his own breast, or communicated it to very few only of his most trusty officers, from apprehension of the ill effect it might have on the spirits of the common soldiers.

The cavaliers whom Cortés now summoned to the council were men of the same mettle with their leader. Their bold, chivalrous spirits seemed

---

[1] Even Gomara has the candour to style it a "pretext,"—*achaque.* Crónica, cap. 83.

[2] Bernal Diaz states the affair, also, differently. According to him, the Aztec governor was enforcing the payment of the customary tribute from the Totonacs, when Escalante, interfering to protect his allies, now subjects of Spain, was slain in an action with the enemy. (Hist. de la Conquista, cap. 93.) Cortés had the best means of knowing the facts, and wrote at the time. He does not usually shrink from avowing his policy, however severe, towards the natives ; and I have thought it fair to give him the benefit of his own version of the story.

[3] Oviedo, Hist. de las Ind., MS., lib. 33, cap. 5. —Rel. Seg. de Cortés, ap. Lorenzana, pp. 83, 84.— The apparition of the Virgin was seen only by the Aztecs, who, it is true, had to make out the best case for their defeat they could to Montezuma; a suspicious circumstance, which, however, did not stagger the Spaniards. "Assuredly all of us soldiers who accompanied Cortés held the belief that the divine mercy and Our Lady the Virgin Mary were always with us. and this was the truth." Bernal Diaz, Hist. de la Conquista, cap. 94.

to court danger for its own sake. If one or two, less adventurous, were startled by the proposal he made, they were soon overruled by the others, who, no doubt, considered that a desperate disease required as desperate a remedy.

That night Cortés was heard pacing his apartment to and fro, like a man oppressed by thought or agitated by strong emotion. He may have been ripening in his mind the daring scheme for the morrow.[1] In the morning the soldiers heard mass as usual, and Father Olmedo invoked the blessing of Heaven on their hazardous enterprise. Whatever might be the cause in which he was embarked, the heart of the Spaniard was cheered with the conviction that the saints were on his side![2]

Having asked an audience from Montezuma, which was readily granted, the general made the necessary arrangements for his enterprise. The principal part of his force was drawn up in the courtyard, and he stationed a considerable detachment in the avenues leading to the palace, to check any attempt at rescue by the populace. He ordered twenty-five or thirty of the soldiers to drop in at the palace, as if by accident, in groups of three or four at a time, while the conference was going on with Montezuma. He selected five cavaliers, in whose courage and coolness he placed most trust, to bear him company; Pedro de Alvarado, Gonzalo de Sandoval, Francisco de Lujo, Velasquez de Leon, and Alonso de Avila,—brilliant names in the annals of the Conquest. All were clad, as well as the common soldiers, in complete armour, a circumstance of too familiar occurrence to excite suspicion.

The little party were graciously received by the emperor, who soon, with the aid of the interpreters, became interested in a sportive conversation with the Spaniards, while he indulged his natural munificence by giving them presents of gold and jewels. He paid the Spanish general the particular compliment of offering him one of his daughters as his wife; an honour which the latter respectfully declined, on the ground that he was already accommodated with one in Cuba, and that his religion forbade a plurality.

When Cortés perceived that a sufficient number of his soldiers were assembled, he changed his playful manner, and in a serious tone briefly acquainted Montezuma with the treacherous proceedings in the *tierra caliente*, and the accusation of him as their author. The emperor listened to the charge with surprise, and disavowed the act, which he said could only have been imputed to him by his enemies. Cortés expressed his belief in his declaration, but added that, to prove it true, it would be necessary to send for Quauhpopoca and his accomplices, that they might be examined and dealt with according to their deserts. To this Monte-

---

[1] "Paseóse vn gran rato solo, i cuidadoso de aquel gran hecho, que emprendia, i que aun á él mesmo le parecia temerario, pero necesario para su intento, andando." Gomara, Crónica, cap. 83.

[2] Diaz says, "All that night we spent in prayer, beseeching the Father of Mercies that he would so direct the matter that it should contribute to his holy service." Hist. de la Conquista, cap. 95.

zuma made no objection. Taking from his wrist, to which it was attached, a precious stone, the royal signet, on which was cut the figure of the War-god,[1] he gave it to one of his nobles, with orders to show it to the Aztec governor, and require his instant presence in the capital, together with all those who had been accessory to the murder of the Spaniards. If he resisted, the officer was empowered to call in the aid of the neighbouring towns to enforce the mandate.

When the messenger had gone, Cortés assured the monarch that this prompt compliance with his request convinced him of his innocence. But it was important that his own sovereign should be equally convinced of it. Nothing would promote this so much as for Montezuma to transfer his residence to the palace occupied by the Spaniards, till on the arrival of Quauhpopoca the affair could be fully investigated. Such an act of condescension would, of itself, show a personal regard for the Spaniards, incompatible with the base conduct alleged against him, and would fully absolve him from all suspicion![2]

Montezuma listened to this proposal, and the flimsy reasoning with which it was covered, with looks of profound amazement. He became pale as death; but in a moment his face flushed with resentment, as, with the pride of offended dignity, he exclaimed, "When was it ever heard that a great prince, like myself, voluntarily left his own palace to become a prisoner in the hands of strangers!"

Cortés assured him he would not go as a prisoner. He would experience nothing but respectful treatment from the Spaniards, would be surrounded by his own household, and hold intercourse with his people as usual. In short, it would be but a change of residence, from one of his palaces to another, a circumstance of frequent occurrence with him. It was in vain. "If I should consent to such a degradation," he answered, "my subjects never would!"[3] When further pressed, he offered to give up one of his sons and two of his daughters to remain as hostages with the Spaniards, so that he might be spared this disgrace.

Two hours passed in this fruitless discussion, till a high-mettled cavalier, Velasquez de Leon, impatient of the long delay, and seeing that the attempt, if not the deed, must ruin them cried out, "Why do we waste words on this barbarian? We have gone too far to recede now. Let us seize him, and, if he resists, plunge our swords into his body!"[4] The fierce tone and menacing gestures with which this was uttered alarmed the monarch, who inquired of Marina what the angry Spaniard said. The interpreter explained it in as gentle a manner as she could, beseeching him "to accompany the white men to their quarters, where he would be

[1] According to Ixtlilxochitl, it was his own portrait. "Se quitó del brazo una rica piedra, donde está esculpido su rostro (que era lo mismo que un sello Real)." Hist. Chich., MS., cap. 85.

[2] Rel. Seg. de Cortés, ap. Lorenzana, p. 86.

[3] "Quando Io lo consintiera, los mios no pasarian por ello." Ixtlilxochitl, Hist. Chich., MS., cap. 85.

[4] "¿ Que haze v. m. ya con tantas palabras? O le lleuemos preso, ó le darémos de estocadas, por esso tornadle á dezir, que si da vozes, ó haze alboroto, que le mataréis, porque mas vale que desta vez asseguremos nuestras vidas, ó las perdamos." Bernal Diaz, Hist. de la Conquista, cap. 95.

treated with all respect and kindness, while to refuse them would but expose himself to violence, perhaps to death." Marina, doubtless, spoke to her sovereign as she thought, and no one had better opportunity of knowing the truth than herself.

This last appeal shook the resolution of Montezuma. It was in vain that the unhappy prince looked around for sympathy or support. As his eyes wandered over the stern visages and iron forms of the Spaniards, he felt that his hour was indeed come; and, with a voice scarcely audible from emotion, he consented to accompany the strangers,—to quit the palace, whither he was never more to return. Had he possessed the spirit of the first Montezuma, he would have called his guards around him, and left his life-blood on the threshold, sooner than have been dragged a dishonoured captive across it. But his courage sank under circumstances. He felt he was the instrument of an irresistible Fate![1]

No sooner had the Spaniards got his consent, than orders were given for the royal litter. The nobles who bore and attended it could scarcely believe their senses when they learned their master's purpose. But pride now came to Montezuma's aid, and, since he must go, he preferred that it should appear to be with his own free-will. As the royal retinue, escorted by the Spaniards, marched through the street with downcast eyes and dejected mien, the people assembled in crowds, and a rumour ran among them that the emperor was carried off by force to the quarters of the white men. A tumult would have soon arisen but for the intervention of Montezuma himself, who called out to the people to disperse, as he was visiting his friends of his own accord; thus sealing his ignominy by a declaration which deprived his subjects of the only excuse for resistance. On reaching the quarters, he sent out his nobles with similar assurances to the mob, and renewed orders to return to their homes.[2]

He was received with ostentatious respect by the Spaniards, and selected the suite of apartments which best pleased him. They were soon furnished with fine cotton tapestries, feather-work, and all the elegancies of Indian upholstery. He was attended by such of his household as he chose, his wives and his pages, and was served with his usual pomp and luxury at his meals.[3] He gave audience, as in his own palace, to his subjects, who

---

[1] Oviedo has some doubts whether Montezuma's conduct is to be viewed as pusillanimous or as prudent. "Al coronista le parece, segun lo que se puede colegir de esta materia, que Montezuma era, ó mui falto de ánimo, ó pusilánimo, ó mui prudente, aunque en muchas cosas, los que lé viéron lo loan de mui señor y mui liberal; y en sus razonamientos mostraba ser de buen juicio." He strikes the balance, however, in favour of pusillanimity. "Un Príncipe tan grande como Montezuma no se habia de dexar incurrir en tales términos, ni consentir ser detenido de tan poco número de Españoles, ni de otra generacion alguna; mas como Dios tiene ordenado lo que ha de ser, ninguno puede huir de su juicio." Historia de las Indias, MS., lib. 33, cap. 6.
[2] The story of the seizure of Montezuma may be found, with the usual discrepancies in the details, in

Rel. Seg. de Cortés, ap. Lorenzana, pp. 84–86,—Bernal Diaz, Hist. de la Conquista, cap. 95,—Ixtlilxochitl, Hist. Chich., MS., cap. 85,—Oviedo, Hist. de las Ind., MS., lib. 33, cap. 6,—Gomara, Crónica, cap. 83,—Herrera, Hist. general, dec. 2, lib. 8, cap. 2, 3,—Martyr, De Orbe Novo, dec. 5, cap. 3.
[3] [According to Tápia, his servants brought him at each meal more than four hundred dishes of meat, game, and fish, intermingled with vegetables and fruits: "é debajo de cada plato de los que á sus servidores les parecie que él comerie, venia un braserico con lumbre; . . . siempre le traian platos nuevos en que comie, é jamas comie en cada plato mas de una vez, ni se vistie ropa mas de una vez; é lavábase el cuerpo cada dia dos veces." Icazbalceta, Col. de Doc. para la Hist. de México, tom. ii.—ED.]

were admitted to his presence, few, indeed, at a time, under the pretext of greater order and decorum. From the Spaniards themselves he met with a formal deference. No one, not even the general himself approached him without doffing his casque and rendering the obeisance due to his rank. Nor did they ever sit in his presence, without being invited by him to do so.[1]

With all this studied ceremony and show of homage, there was one circumstance which too clearly proclaimed to his people that their sovereign was a prisoner. In the front of the palace a patrol of sixty men was established, and the same number in the rear. Twenty of each corps mounted guard at once, maintaining a careful watch, day and night.[2] Another body, under command of Velasquez de Leon, was stationed in the royal antechamber. Cortés punished any departure from duty, or relaxation of vigilance, in these sentinels, with the utmost severity.[3] He felt, as indeed every Spaniard must have felt, that the escape of the emperor now would be their ruin. Yet the task of this unintermitting watch sorely added to their fatigues. " Better this dog of a king should die," cried a soldier one day, " than that we should wear out our lives in this manner." The words were uttered in the hearing of Montezuma, who gathered something of their import, and the offender was severely chastised by order of the general.[4] Such instances of disrespect, however, were very rare. Indeed, the amiable deportment of the monarch, who seemed to take pleasure in the society of his jailers, and who never allowed a favour or attention from the meanest soldier to go unrequited, inspired the Spaniards with as much attachment as they were capable of feeling—for a barbarian.[5]

Things were in this posture, when the arrival of Quauhpopoca from the coast was announced. He was accompanied by his son and fifteen Aztec chiefs. He had travelled all the way, borne, as became his high rank, in a litter. On entering Montezuma's presence, he threw over his dress the coarse robe of *nequen*, and made the usual humiliating acts of obei-

---

[1] " Siempre que ante él passauamos, y aunque fuesse Cortés, le quitauamos los bonetes de armas ó cascos, que siempre estauamos armados, y él nos hazia gran mesura, y honra á todos. . . . Digo que no se sentauan Cortés ni ningun Capitan, hasta que el Monteçuma les mandaua dar sus assentaderos ricos, y les mandaua assentar." Bernal Diaz, Hist. de la Conquista, cap. 95, 100.

[2] Herrera, Hist. general, dec. 2, lib. 8, cap. 3.

[3] On one occasion, three soldiers, who left their posts without orders, were sentenced to run the gantlet,—a punishment little short of death. Ibid., ubi supra.

[4] Bernal Diaz, Hist. de la Conquista, cap. 97.

[5] [The patriotic sensibilities of Señor Ramirez are somewhat disturbed by my application of the term *barbarians* to his Aztec countrymen.* This word, with the corresponding epithet of *savages*, forms the key, he seems to think, to my descriptions of the ancient Mexicans. " Regarded from this point of view," he says, " the astounding examples of heroism and self-devotion so rarely met with in the history of the world are interpreted not as a voluntary sacrifice inspired by the holy love of country and of freedom, but as the effect of a brutish hatred and stupid ferocity." There may be some foundation for these strictures, though somewhat too highly coloured. And one cannot deny that, as he reflects on the progress made by the Aztecs in the knowledge of the useful arts, and, indeed, to a certain extent, of science, he must admit their claim to a higher place in the scale of civilization than that occupied by barbarians,—to one, in truth, occupied by the semi-civilized races of China and Hindostan. But there is another side of the picture, not presented by the Eastern nations, in those loathsome abominations which degraded the Aztec character to a level with the lowest stages of humanity, and makes even the term *barbarian* inadequate to express the ferocity of his nature.]

* [This sensibility is the more natural that Señor Ramirez claims descent not from the conquering but from the conquered race,—a fact which may also account for his rigorous judgments on the acts and character of Cortés.—ED.]

sance. The poor parade of courtly ceremony was the more striking when placed in contrast with the actual condition of the parties.

The Aztec governor was coldly received by his master, who referred the affair (had he the power to do otherwise?) to the examination of Cortés. It was, doubtless, conducted in a sufficiently summary manner. To the general's query, whether the cacique was the subject of Montezuma, he replied, "And what other sovereign could I serve?" implying that his sway was universal.[1] He did not deny his share in the transaction, nor did he seek to shelter himself under the royal authority till sentence of death was passed on him and his followers, when they all laid the blame of their proceedings on Montezuma.[2] They were condemned to be burnt alive in the area before the palace. The funeral piles were made of heaps of arrows, javelins, and other weapons, drawn by the emperor's permission from the arsenals round the great *teocalli*, where they had been stored to supply means of defence in times of civic tumult or insurrection. By this politic precaution Cortés proposed to remove a ready means of annoyance in case of hostilities with the citizens.

To crown the whole of these extraordinary proceedings, Cortés, while preparations for the execution were going on, entered the emperor's apartment, attended by a soldier bearing fetters in his hands. With a severe aspect, he charged the monarch with being the original contriver of the violence offered to the Spaniards, as was now proved by the declaration of his own instruments. Such a crime, which merited death in a subject, could not be atoned for, even by a sovereign, without some punishment. So saying, he ordered the soldier to fasten the fetters on Montezuma's ankles. He coolly waited till it was done, then, turning his back on the monarch, quitted the room.

Montezuma was speechless under the infliction of this last insult. He was like one struck down by a heavy blow, that deprives him of all his faculties. He offered no resistance. But, though he spoke not a word, low, ill-suppressed moans, from time to time, intimated the anguish of his spirit. His attendants, bathed in tears, offered him their consolations. They tenderly held his feet in their arms, and endeavoured, by inserting their shawls and mantles, to relieve them from the pressure of the iron. But they could not reach the iron which had penetrated into his soul. He felt that he was no more a king.

Meanwhile, the execution of the dreadful doom was going forward in the courtyard. The whole Spanish force was under arms, to check any interruption that might be offered by the Mexicans. But none was attempted. The populace gazed in silent wonder, regarding it as the

[1] "Y despues que confesáron haber muerto los Españoles, les hice interrogar si ellos eran Vasallos de Muteczuma? Y el dicho Qualpopoca respondió, que si habia otro Señor, de quien pudiesse serlo? casi diciendo, que no habia otro, y que si eran." Rel. Seg. de Cortés, ap. Lorenzana, p. 87.

[2] "É assimismo les pregunte, si lo que allí se habia hecho si habia sido por su mandado? y dijéron que no, aunque despues, al tiempo que en ellos se executó la sentencia, que fuessen quemados, todos á una voz dijéron, que era verdad que el dicho Muteczuma se lo habia embiado á mandar, y que por su mandado lo habian hecho." Rel. Seg. de Cortés, ap. Lorenzana, loc. cit.

sentence of the emperor. The manner of the execution, too, excited less surprise, from their familiarity with similar spectacles, aggravated, indeed, by additional horrors, in their own diabolical sacrifices. The Aztec lord and his companions, bound hand and foot to the blazing piles, submitted without a cry or a complaint to their terrible fate. Passive fortitude is the virtue of the Indian warrior; and it was the glory of the Aztec, as of the other races on the North American continent, to show how the spirit of the brave man may triumph over torture and the agonies of death.

When the dismal tragedy was ended, Cortés re-entered Montezuma's apartment. Kneeling down, he unclasped his shackles with his own hand, expressing at the same time his regret that so disagreeable a duty as that of subjecting him to such a punishment had been imposed on him. This last indignity had entirely crushed the spirit of Montezuma; and the monarch whose frown, but a week since, would have made the nations of Anahuac tremble to their remotest borders, was now craven enough to thank his deliverer for his freedom, as for a great and unmerited boon![1]

Not long after, the Spanish general, conceiving that his royal captive was sufficiently humbled, expressed his willingness that he should return, if he inclined, to his own palace. Montezuma declined it; alleging, it is said, that his nobles had more than once importuned him to resent his injuries by taking arms against the Spaniards, and that, were he in the midst of them, it would be difficult to avoid it, or to save his capital from bloodshed and anarchy.[2] The reason did honour to his heart, if it was the one which influenced him. It is probable that he did not care to trust his safety to those haughty and ferocious chieftains, who had witnessed the degradation of their master, and must despise his pusillanimity, as a thing unprecedented in an Aztec monarch. It is also said that, when Marina conveyed to him the permission of Cortés, the other interpreter, Aguilar, gave him to understand the Spanish officers never would consent that he should avail himself of it.[3]

Whatever were his reasons, it is certain that he declined the offer; and the general, in a well-feigned or real ecstasy, embraced him, declaring "that he loved him as a brother, and that every Spaniard would be zealously devoted to his interests, since he had shown himself so mindful of theirs!" Honeyed words, "which," says the shrewd old chronicler who was present, "Montezuma was wise enough to know the worth of."

The events recorded in this chapter are certainly some of the most extraordinary on the page of history. That a small body of men, like the Spaniards, should have entered the palace of a mighty prince, have seized

---

[1] Gomara, Crónica, cap. 89.—Oviedo, Hist. de las Ind., MS., lib. 33, cap. 6.—Bernal Diaz, Hist. de la Conquista, cap. 95.—One may doubt whether pity or contempt predominates in Martyr's notice of this event. "Infelix tunc Muteczuma re adeo noua perculsus, formidine repletur, decidit animo, neque iam erigere caput audet, aut suorum auxilia implo-

rare. Ille vero pœnam se meruisse fassus est, vti agnus mitis. Æquo animo pati videtur has regulas grammaticalibus duriores, imberbibus pueris dictatas, omnia placide fert, ne seditio ciuium et procerum oriatur." De Orbe Novo, dec. 5, cap. 3.

[2] Rel. Seg. de Cortés, ap. Lorenzana, p. 18.

[3] Bernal Diaz, Hist. de la Conquista, ubi supra.

his person in the midst of his vassals, have borne him off a captive to their quarters,—that they should have put to an ignominious death before his face his nigh officers, for executing, probably, his own commands, and have crowned the whole by putting the monarch in irons like a common malefactor,—that this should have been done, not to a drivelling dotard in the decay of his fortunes, but to a proud monarch in the plenitude of his power, in the very heart of his capital, surrounded by thousands and tens of thousands, who trembled at his nod and would have poured out their blood like water in his defence,—that all this should have been done by a mere handful of adventurers, is a thing too extravagant, altogether too improbable, for the pages of romance ! It is, nevertheless, literally true. Yet we shall not be prepared to acquiesce in the judgments of contemporaries who regarded these acts with admiration. We may well distrust any grounds on which it is attempted to justify the kidnapping of a friendly sovereign,—by those very persons, too, who were reaping the full benefit of his favours.

To view the matter differently, we must take the position of the Conquerors and assume with them the original right of conquest. Regarded from this point of view, many difficulties vanish. If conquest were a duty, whatever was necessary to effect it was right also. Right and expedient become convertible terms. And it can hardly be denied that the capture of the monarch was expedient, if the Spaniards would maintain their hold on the empire.[1]

The execution of the Aztec governor suggests other considerations. If he were really guilty of the perfidious act imputed to him by Cortés, and if Montezuma disavowed it, the governor deserved death, and the general was justified by the law of nations in inflicting it.[2] It is by no means so clear, however, why he should have involved so many in this sentence ; most, perhaps all, of whom must have acted under his authority. The cruel manner of the death will less startle those who are familiar with the established penal codes in most civilized nations in the sixteenth century.

But, if the governor deserved death, what pretence was there for the outrage on the person of Montezuma ? If the former was guilty, the latter surely was not. But, if the cacique only acted in obedience to orders, the responsibility was transferred to the sovereign who gave the orders. They could not both stand in the same category.

It is vain, however, to reason on the matter on any abstract principles of right and wrong, or to suppose that the Conquerors troubled themselves with the refinements of casuistry. Their standard of right and

---

[1] Archbishop Lorenzana, as late as the close of the last century, finds good Scripture warrant for the proceeding of the Spaniards. "Fué grande prudencia, y Arte militar haber asegurado á el Emperador, porque sino quedaban expuestos Hernan Cortés, y sus soldados á perecer á traycion, y teniendo seguro á el Emperador se aseguraba á sí mismo, pues los Españoles no se confian ligeramente : Jonathas fué muerto, y sorprendido por haberse confiado de Triphon." Rel. Seg. de Cortés, p. 84, nota.

[2] See Puffendorf, De Jure Naturæ et Gentium, lib. 8, cap. 6, sec. 10.—Vattel, Law of Nations, book 3, chap. 8, sec. 141.

wrong, in reference to the natives, was a very simple one. Despising them as an outlawed race, without God in the world, they, in common with their age, held it to be their "mission" (to borrow the cant phrase of our own day) to conquer and to convert. The measures they adopted certainly facilitated the first great work of conquest. By the execution of the caciques they struck terror not only into the capital, but throughout the country. It proclaimed that not a hair of a Spaniard was to be touched with impunity! By rendering Montezuma contemptible in his own eyes and those of his subjects, Cortés deprived him of the support of his people and forced him to lean on the arm of the stranger. It was a politic proceeding,—to which few men could have been equal who had a touch of humanity in their natures.

A good criterion of the moral sense of the actors in these events is afforded by the reflections of Bernal Diaz, made some fifty years, it will be remembered, after the events themselves, when the fire of youth had become extinct, and the eye, glancing back through the vista of half a century, might be supposed to be unclouded by the passions and prejudices which throw their mist over the present. "Now that I am an old man," says the veteran, "I often entertain myself with calling to mind the heroical deeds of early days, till they are as fresh as the events of yesterday. I think of the seizure of the Indian monarch, his confinement in irons, and the execution of his officers, till all these things seem actually passing before me. And, as I ponder on our exploits, I feel that it was not of ourselves that we performed them, but that it was the providence of God which guided us. Much food is there here for meditation!"[1] There is so, indeed, and for a meditation not unpleasing, as we reflect on the advance, in speculative morality at least, which the nineteenth century has made over the sixteenth. But should not the consciousness of this teach us charity? Should it not make us the more distrustful of applying the standard of the present to measure the actions of the past?

---

[1] "Osar quemar sus Capitanes delante de sus Palacios, y echalle grillos entre tanto que se hazia la Justicia, que muchas vezes aora que soy viejo me paro á considerar las cosas heroicas que en aquel tiempo passámos, que me parece las veo presentes: Y digo que nuestros hechos, que no los haziamos nosotros, sino que venian todos encaminados por Dios. . . . Porque ay mucho que ponderar en ello." Hist. de la Conquista, cap. 95.

CHAPTER IV.

MONTEZUMA'S DEPORTMENT.—HIS LIFE IN THE SPANISH QUARTERS.—
MEDITATED INSURRECTION.—LORD OF TEZCUCO SEIZED.—FURTHER
MEASURES OF CORTÉS.

(1520.)

THE settlement of La Villa Rica de Vera Cruz was of the last importance
to the Spaniards. It was the port by which they were to communicate
with Spain; the strong post on which they were to retreat in case of
disaster, and which was to bridle their enemies and give security to their
allies; the *point d'appui* for all their operations in the country. It was
of great moment, therefore, that the care of it should be intrusted to
proper hands.

A cavalier, named Alonso de Grado, had been sent by Cortés to take
the place made vacant by the death of Escalante. He was a person
of greater repute in civil than military matters, and would be more likely,
it was thought, to maintain peaceful relations with the natives than a
person of more belligerent spirit. Cortés made—what was rare with him
—a bad choice. He soon received such accounts of troubles in the
settlement from the exactions and negligence of the new governor, that
he resolved to supersede him.

He now gave the command to Gonzalo de Sandoval, a young cavalier,
who had displayed, through the whole campaign, singular intrepidity
united with sagacity and discretion; while the good-humour with which
he bore every privation, and his affable manners, made him a favourite
with all, privates as well as officers. Sandoval accordingly left the camp
for the coast. Cortés did not mistake his man a second time.

Notwithstanding the actual control exercised by the Spaniards through
their royal captive, Cortés felt some uneasiness when he reflected that it
was in the power of the Indians at any time to cut off his communications with the surrounding country and hold him a prisoner in the capital
He proposed, therefore, to build two vessels of sufficient size to transport
his forces across the lake, and thus to render himself independent of the
causeways. Montezuma was pleased with the idea of seeing those
wonderful " water-houses," of which he had heard so much, and readily
gave permission to have the timber in the royal forests felled for the
purpose. The work was placed under the direction of Martin Lopez, an
experienced shipbuilder. Orders were also given to Sandoval to send
up from the coast a supply of cordage, sails, iron, and other necessary
materials, which had been judiciously saved on the destruction of the fleet.[1]

---

[1] Bernal Diaz, Hist. de la Conquista, cap. 96.

The Aztec emperor, meanwhile, was passing his days in the Spanish quarters in no very different manner from what he had been accustomed to in his own palace. His keepers were too well aware of the value of their prize, not to do everything which could make his captivity comfortable and disguise it from himself. But the chain will gall, though wreathed with roses. After Montezuma's breakfast, which was a light meal of fruits or vegetables, Cortés or some of his officers usually waited on him, to learn if he had any commands for them. He then devoted some time to business. He gave audience to those of his subjects who had petitions to prefer or suits to settle. The statement of the party was drawn up on the hieroglyphic scrolls, which were submitted to a number of counsellors or judges, who assisted him with their advice on these occasions. Envoys from foreign states or his own remote provinces and cities were also admitted, and the Spaniards were careful that the same precise and punctilious etiquette should be maintained towards the royal puppet as when in the plenitude of his authority.

After business was despatched, Montezuma often amused himself with seeing the Castilian troops go through their military exercises. He, too, had been a soldier, and in his prouder days had led armies in the field. It was very natural he should take an interest in the novel display of European tactics and discipline. At other times he would challenge Cortés or his officers to play at some of the national games. A favourite one was called *totoloque*, played with golden balls aimed at a target or mark of the same metal. Montezuma usually staked something of value,—precious stones or ingots of gold. He lost with good-humour ; indeed, it was of little consequence whether he won or lost, since he generally gave away his winnings to his attendants.[1] He had, in truth, a most munificent spirit. His enemies accused him of avarice. But, if he were avaricious, it could have been only that he might have the more to give away.

Each of the Spaniards had several Mexicans, male and female, who attended to his cooking and various other personal offices. Cortés, considering that the maintenance of this host of menials was a heavy tax on the royal exchequer, ordered them to be dismissed, excepting one to be retained for each soldier. Montezuma, on learning this, pleasantly remonstrated with the general on his careful economy, as unbecoming a royal establishment, and, countermanding the order, caused additional accommodations to be provided for the attendants, and their pay to be doubled.

On another occasion, a soldier purloined some trinkets of gold from the treasure kept in the chamber, which, since Montezuma's arrival in the Spanish quarters, had been reopened. Cortés would have punished the man for the theft, but the emperor, interfering, said to him, " Your countrymen are welcome to the gold and other articles, if you will but

---

[1] Bernal Diaz, Hist. de la Conquista, cap. 97.

spare those belonging to the gods." Some of the soldiers, making the most of his permission, carried off several hundred loads of fine cotton to their quarters. When this was represented to Montezuma, he only replied, " What I have once given I never take back again." [1]

While thus indifferent to his treasures, he was keenly sensitive to personal slight or insult. When a common soldier once spoke to him angrily, the tears came into the monarch's eyes, as it made him feel the true character of his impotent condition. Cortés, on becoming acquainted with it, was so much incensed that he ordered the soldier to be hanged, but, on Montezuma's intercession, commuted this severe sentence for a flogging. The general was not willing that any one but himself should treat his royal captive with indignity. Montezuma was desired to procure a further mitigation of the punishment. But he refused, saying "that, if a similar insult had been offered by any one of his subjects to Malinche, he would have resented it in like manner." [2]

Such instances of disrespect were very rare. Montezuma's amiable and inoffensive manners, together with his liberality, the most popular of virtues with the vulgar, made him generally beloved by the Spaniards. [3] The arrogance for which he had been so distinguished in his prosperous days deserted him in his fallen fortunes. His character in captivity seems to have undergone something of that change which takes place in the wild animals of the forest when caged within the walls of the menagerie.

The Indian monarch knew the name of every man in the army, and was careful to discriminate his proper rank. [4] For some he showed a strong partiality. He obtained from the general a favourite page, named Orteguilla, who, being in constant attendance on his person, soon learned enough of the Mexican language to be of use to his countrymen. Montezuma took great pleasure, also, in the society of Velasquez de Leon, the captain of his guard, and Pedro de Alvarado, *Tonatiuh*, or " the Sun," as he was called by the Aztecs, from his yellow hair and sunny countenance. The sunshine, as events afterwards showed, could sometimes be the prelude to a terrible tempest.

Notwithstanding the care taken to cheat him of the tedium of captivity, the royal prisoner cast a wistful glance, now and then, beyond the walls of his residence to the ancient haunts of business or pleasure. He intimated a desire to offer up his devotions at the great temple, where he was once so constant in his worship. The suggestion startled Cortés. It was too reasonable, however, for him to object to it without wholly discarding the appearances which he was desirous to maintain. But he secured Montezuma's return by sending an escort with him of a hundred and fifty

---

[1] Gomara, Crónica, cap. 84. — Herrera, Hist. general, dec. 2, lib. 8, cap. 4.
[2] Herrera, Hist. general, dec. 2, lib. 8, cap. 5.
[3] " En esto era tan bien mirado, que todos le queriamos con gran amor, porque verdaderamente era gran señor en todas las cosas que le viamos

hazer." Bernal Diaz, Hist. de la Conquista, cap 100.
[4] " Y él bien conocia á todos, y sabia nuestros nombres, y aun calidades, y era tan bueno que á todos nos daua joyas, á otros mantas é Indias hermosas." Ibid., cap. 97.

soldiers under the same resolute cavaliers who had aided in his seizure. He told him, also, that in case of any attempt to escape his life would instantly pay the forfeit. Thus guarded, the Indian prince visited the *teocalli*, where he was received with the usual state, and, after performing his devotions, he returned again to his quarters.[1]

It may well be believed that the Spaniards did not neglect the opportunity afforded by his residence with them, of instilling into him some notions of the Christian doctrine. Fathers Diaz and Olmedo exhausted all their battery of logic and persuasion to shake his faith in his idols, but in vain. He, indeed, paid a most edifying attention, which gave promise of better things. But the conferences always closed with the declaration that "the God of the Christians was good, but the gods of his own country were the true gods for him."[2] It is said, however, they extorted a promise from him that he would take part in no more human sacrifices. Yet such sacrifices were of daily occurrence in the great temples of the capital; and the people were too blindly attached to their bloody abominations for the Spaniards to deem it safe, for the present at least, openly to interfere.

Montezuma showed, also, an inclination to engage in the pleasures of the chase, of which he once was immoderately fond. He had large forests reserved for the purpose on the other side of the lake. As the Spanish brigantines were now completed, Cortés proposed to transport him and his suite across the water in them. They were of a good size, strongly built. The largest was mounted with four falconets, or small guns. It was protected by a gaily-coloured awning stretched over the deck, and the royal ensign of Castile floated proudly from the mast. On board of this vessel, Montezuma, delighted with the opportunity of witnessing the nautical skill of the white men, embarked with a train of Aztec nobles and a numerous guard of Spaniards. A fresh breeze played on the waters, and the vessel soon left behind it the swarms of light pirogues which darkened their surface. She seemed like a thing of life in the eyes of the astonished natives, who saw her, as if disdaining human agency, sweeping by with snowy pinions as if on the wings of the wind, while the thunders from her sides, now for the first time breaking on the silence of this " island sea," showed that the beautiful phantom was clothed in terror.[3]

The royal chase was well stocked with game; some of which the emperor shot with arrows, and others were driven by the numerous attendants into nets.[4] In these woodland exercises, while he ranged over his wild domain, Montezuma seemed to enjoy again the sweets of

[1] Bernal Diaz, Hist. de la Conquista, cap. 98.

[2] According to Solís, the Devil closed his heart against these good men; though, in the historian's opinion, there is no evidence that this evil counsellor actually appeared and conversed with Montezuma after the Spaniards had displayed the Cross in Mexico. Conquista, lib. 3, cap. 20

[3] Bernal Diaz, Hist. de la Conquista, cap. 99.— Rel. Seg. de Cortés, ap. Lorenzana, p. 88.

[4] He sometimes killed his game with a tube, a sort of air-gun, through which he blew little balls at birds and rabbits. "La Caça á que Moteçuma iba por la Laguna, era á tirar á Pájaros, á Conejos, con Cerbatana, de la qual era diestro." Herrera, Hist. general, dec. 2, lib. 8, cap. 4.

liberty. It was but the shadow of liberty, however; as in his quarters, at home, he enjoyed but the shadow of royalty. At home or abroad, the eye of the Spaniard was always upon him.

But, while he resigned himself without a struggle to his inglorious fate, there were others who looked on it with very different emotions. Among them was his nephew Cacama, lord of Tezcuco, a young man not more than twenty-five years of age, but who enjoyed great consideration from his high personal qualities, especially his intrepidity of character. He was the same prince who had been sent by Montezuma to welcome the Spaniards on their entrance into the Valley; and, when the question of their reception was first debated in the council, he had advised to admit them honourably as ambassadors of a foreign prince, and, if they should prove different from what they pretended, it would be time enough then to take up arms against them. That time, he thought, had now come.

In a former part of this work, the reader has been made acquainted with the ancient history of the Acolhuan or Tezcucan monarchy, once the proud rival of the Aztec in power, and greatly its superior in civilization.[1] Under its last sovereign, Nezahuilpilli, its territory is said to have been grievously clipped by the insidious practices of Montezuma, who fomented dissensions and insubordination among his subjects. On the death of the Tezcucan prince, the succession was contested, and a bloody war ensued between his eldest son, Cacama, and an ambitious younger brother, Ixtlilxochitl. This was followed by a partition of the kingdom, in which the latter chieftain held the mountain districts north of the capital, leaving the residue to Cacama. Though shorn of a large part of his hereditary domain, the city was itself so important that the lord of Tezcuco still held a high rank among the petty princes of the Valley. His capital, at the time of the Conquest, contained, according to Cortés, a hundred and fifty thousand inhabitants.[2] It was embellished with noble buildings, rivalling those of Mexico itself, and the ruins still to be met with on its ancient site attest that it was once the abode of princes.[3]

The young Tezcucan chief beheld with indignation and no slight contempt the abject condition of his uncle. He endeavoured to rouse him to manly exertion, but in vain. He then set about forming a league

---

[1] *Ante*, Book I. chap. 6.

[2] "É llámase esta Ciudad Tezcuco, y será de hasta treinta mil Vecinos." (Rel. Seg., ap. Lorenzana, p. 94.) According to the licentiate Zuazo, double that number,—*sesenta mil Vecinos*. (Carta, MS.) Scarcely probable, as Mexico had no more. Toribio speaks of it as covering a league one way by six another! (Hist. de los Indios, MS., Parte 3, cap. 7.) This must include the environs to a considerable extent. The language of the old chroniclers is not the most precise.

[3] A description of the capital in its glory is thus given by an eyewitness. "Esta Ciudad era la segunda cosa principal de la tierra, y así habia en Tezcuco muy grandes edificios de templos del Demonio, y muy gentiles casas y aposentos de Señores, entre los cuales, fué muy cosa de ver la casa del Señor principal, así la vieja con su huerta cercada de mas de mil cedros muy grandes y muy hermosos, de los cuales hoy dia están los mas en pie, aunque la casa está asolada, otra casa tenia que se podia aposentar en ella un egército, con muchos jardines, y un muy grande estanque, que por debajo de tierra solian entrar á él con barcas." (Toribio, Hist. de los Indios, MS., Parte 3, cap. 7.) The last relics of this palace were employed in the fortifications of the city in the revolutionary war of 1810. (Ixtlilxochitl, Venida de los Esp., p. 78, nota.) Tezcuco is now an insignificant little place, with a population of a few thousand inhabitants. Its architectural remains, as still to be discerned, seem to have made a stronger impression on Mr. Bullock than on most travellers. Six Months in Mexico, chap. 27.

with several of the neighbouring caciques to rescue his kinsman and to break the detested yoke of the strangers. He called on the lord of Iztapalapan, Montezuma's brother, the lord of Tlacopan, and some others of most authority, all of whom entered heartily into his views. He then urged the Aztec nobles to join them; but they expressed an unwillingness to take any step not first sanctioned by the emperor.[1] They entertained, undoubtedly, a profound reverence for their master; but it seems probable that jealousy of the personal views of Cacama had its influence on their determination. Whatever were their motives, it is certain that by this refusal they relinquished the best opportunity ever presented for retrieving their sovereign's independence and their own.

These intrigues could not be conducted so secretly as not to reach the ears of Cortés, who, with his characteristic promptness, would have marched at once on Tezcuco and trodden out the spark of "rebellion"[2] before it had time to burst into a flame. But from this he was dissuaded by Montezuma, who represented that Cacama was a man of resolution, backed by a powerful force, and not to be put down without a desperate struggle. He consented, therefore, to negotiate, and sent a message of amicable expostulation to the cacique. He received a haughty answer in return. Cortés rejoined in a more menacing tone, asserting the supremacy of his own sovereign, the emperor of Castile. To this Cacama replied, "He acknowledged no such authority; he knew nothing of the Spanish sovereign or his people, nor did he wish to know anything of them."[3] Montezuma was not more successful in his application to Cacama to come to Mexico and allow him to mediate his differences with the Spaniards, with whom he assured the prince he was residing as a friend. But the young lord of Tezcuco was not to be so duped. He understood the position of his uncle, and replied "that when he did visit his capital it would be to rescue it, as well as the emperor himself, and their common gods, from bondage. He should come, not with his hand in his bosom, but on his sword,—to drive out the detested strangers who had brought such dishonour on their country!"[4]

Cortés, incensed at this tone of defiance, would again have put himself in motion to punish it, but Montezuma interposed with his more politic

[1] "Cacama reprehendió asperamente á la Nobleza Mexicana porque consentia hacer semejantes desacatos á quatro Estrangeros y que no les mataban; se escusaban con decirles les iban á la mano y no les consentian tomar las Armas para libertarlo, y tomar sí una tan gran deshonra como era la que los Estrangeros les habian hecho en prender á su señor, y quemar á Quauhpopocatzin, los demas sus Hijos y Deudos sin culpa, con las Armas y Municion que tenian para la defenza y guarda de la ciudad, y de su autoridad tomar para sí los tesoros del Rey, y de los Dioses, y otras libertades y desvergüenzas que cada dia pasaban, y aunque todo esto vehian lo disimulaban por no enojar á Motecuhzoma que tan amigo y casado estaba con ellos." Ixtlilxochitl, Hist. Chich., MS., cap. 86.

[2] It is the language of Cortés. "Y este señor *se rebeló*, assí contra el servicio de Vuestra Alteza, á

quien se habia ofrecido, como contra el dicho Muteczuma." Rel. Seg., ap. Lorenzana, p. 95.—Voltaire, with his quick eye for the ridiculous, notices this arrogance in his tragedy of Alzire:—

"Tu vois de ces tyrans la fureur despotique:
Ils pensent que pour eux le Ciel fit l'Amérique,
Qu'ils en sont nés les Rois; et Zamore à leurs yeux
Tout souverain qu'il fut, n'est qu'un séditieux."

ALZIRE, act 4, sc. 3.

[3] Gomara, Crónica, cap 91.
[4] "I que para reparar la Religion, i restituir los Dioses, guardar el Reino, cobrar la fama, i libertad á él, i á México, iria de mui buena gana, mas no las manos en el seno, sino en la Espada, para matar los Españoles, que tanta mengua, i afrenta havian hecho á la Nacion de Culhúa." Ibid., cap. 91.

X

arts. He had several of the Tezcucan nobles, he said, in his pay ;[1] and it would be easy, through their means, to secure Cacama's person, and thus break up the confederacy, at once, without bloodshed. The maintaining of a corps of stipendiaries in the courts of neighbouring princes was a refinement which showed that the Western barbarian understood the science of political intrigue as well as some of his royal brethren on the other side of the water.

By the contrivance of these faithless nobles, Cacama was induced to hold a conference, relative to the proposed invasion, in a villa which overhung the Tezcucan lake, not far from his capital. Like most of the principal edifices, it was raised so as to admit the entrance of boats beneath it. In the midst of the conference, Cacama was seized by the conspirators, hurried on board a bark in readiness for the purpose, and transported to Mexico. When brought into Montezuma's presence, the high-spirited chief abated nothing of his proud and lofty bearing. He taxed his uncle with his perfidy, and a pusillanimity so unworthy of his former character and of the royal house from which he was descended. By the emperor he was referred to Cortés, who, holding royalty but cheap in an Indian prince, put him in fetters.[2]

There was at this time in Mexico a brother of Cacama, a stripling much younger than himself. At the instigation of Cortés, Montezuma, pretending that his nephew had forfeited the sovereignty by his late *rebellion*, declared him to be deposed, and appointed Cuicuitzca in his place. The Aztec sovereigns had always been allowed a paramount authority in questions relating to the succession. But this was a most unwarrantable exercise of it. The Tezcucans acquiesced, however, with a ready ductility, which showed their allegiance hung but lightly on them, or, what is more probable, that they were greatly in awe of the Spaniards ; and the new prince was welcomed with acclamations to his capital.[3]

Cortés still wanted to get into his hands the other chiefs who had entered into the confederacy with Cacama. This was no difficult matter. Montezuma's authority was absolute, everywhere but in his own palace. By his command, the caciques were seized each in his own city, and brought in chains to Mexico, where Cortés placed them in strict confinement with their leader.[4]

---

[1] "Pero que él tenia en su Tierra de el dicho Cacamazin muchas Personas Principales, que vivian con él, y les daba su salario." Rel. Seg. de Cortés, ap. Lorenzana, p. 95.

[2] Rel. Seg. de Cortés, ap. Lorenzana, pp. 95, 96. —Oviedo, Hist. de las Ind., MS., lib. 33, cap. 8.— Ixtlilxochitl, Hist.Chich., MS., cap. 86.—The latter author dismisses the capture of Cacama with the comfortable reflection " that it saved the Spaniards much embarrassment, and greatly facilitated the introduction of the Catholic faith."

[3] Cortés calls the name of this prince Cucuzca. (Rel. Seg., ap. Lorenzana, p. 96.) In the orthography of Aztec words, the general was governed by his ear, and was wrong nine times out of ten.—

Bustamante, in his catalogue of Tezcucan monarchs, omits him altogether. He probably regards him as an intruder, who had no claim to be ranked among the rightful sovereigns of the land. (Galería de antiguos Príncipes (Puebla, 1821), p. 21.) Sahagun has, in like manner, struck his name from the royal roll of Tezcuco. Hist. de Nueva-España, lib. 8, cap. 3.

[4] The exceeding lenity of the Spanish commander, on this occasion, excited general admiration, if we are to credit Solís, throughout the Aztec empire ! "Tuvo notable aplauso en todo el imperio este género de castigo sin sangre, que se atribuyó al superior juicio de los Españoles, porque no esperaban de Motezuma semejante moderacion." Conquista, lib. 4, cap. 2.

He had now triumphed over all his enemies. He had set his foot on the necks of princes; and the great chief of the Aztec empire was but a convenient tool in his hands for accomplishing his purposes. His first use of this power was to ascertain the actual resources of the monarchy. He sent several parties of Spaniards, guided by the natives, to explore the regions where gold was obtained. It was gleaned mostly from the beds of rivers, several hundred miles from the capital.

His next object was to learn if there existed any good natural harbour for shipping on the Atlantic coast, as the road of Vera Cruz left no protection against the tempests that at certain seasons swept over these seas. Montezuma showed him a chart on which the shores of the Mexican Gulf were laid down with tolerable accuracy.[1] Cortés, after carefully inspecting it, sent a commission, consisting of ten Spaniards, several of them pilots, and some Aztecs, who descended to Vera Cruz and made a careful survey of the coast for nearly sixty leagues south of that settlement, as far as the great river Coatzacualco, which seemed to offer the best—indeed, the only—accommodations for a safe and suitable harbour. A spot was selected as the site of a fortified post, and the general sent a detachment of a hundred and fifty men under Velasquez de Leon to plant a colony there.

He also obtained a grant of an extensive tract of land in the fruitful province of Oaxaca, where he proposed to lay out a plantation for the crown. He stocked it with the different kinds of domesticated animals peculiar to the country, and with such indigenous grains and plants as would afford the best articles for export. He soon had the estate under such cultivation that he assured his master, the emperor Charles the Fifth, it was worth twenty thousand ounces of gold.[2]

---

[1] Rel. Seg. de Cortés, ap. Lorenzana, p. 91.

[2] "Damus quæ dant," says Martyr, briefly, in reference to this valuation. (De Orbe Novo, dec. 5, cap. 3.) Cortés notices the reports made by his people, of large and beautiful edifices in the province of Oaxaca. (Rel. Seg., ap. Lorenzana, p. 89.) It is here, also, that some of the most elaborate specimens of Indian architecture are still to be seen, in the ruins of Mitla.

CHAPTER V.

MONTEZUMA SWEARS ALLEGIANCE TO SPAIN.—ROYAL TREASURES.—THEIR DIVISION.—CHRISTIAN WORSHIP IN THE TEOCALLI.—DISCONTENTS OF THE AZTECS.

(1520.)

CORTÉS now felt his authority sufficiently assured to demand from Montezuma a formal recognition of the supremacy of the Spanish emperor. The Indian monarch had intimated his willingness to acquiesce in this, on their very first interview. He did not object, therefore, to call together his principal caciques for the purpose. When they were assembled, he made them an address, briefly stating the object of the meeting. They were all acquainted, he said, with the ancient tradition that the great Being who had once ruled over the land had declared, on his departure, that he should return at some future time and resume his sway. That time had now arrived. The white men had come from the quarter where the sun rises, beyond the ocean, to which the good deity had withdrawn. They were sent by their master to reclaim the obedience of his ancient subjects. For himself, he was ready to acknowledge his authority. "You have been faithful vassals of mine," continued Montezuma, "during the many years that I have sat on the throne of my fathers. I now expect that you will show me this last act of obedience by acknowledging the great king beyond the waters to be your lord, also, and that you will pay him tribute in the same manner as you have hitherto done to me."[1] As he concluded, his voice was nearly stifled by his emotion, and the tears fell fast down his cheeks.

His nobles, many of whom, coming from a distance, had not kept pace with the changes which had been going on in the capital, were filled with astonishment as they listened to his words and beheld the voluntary abasement of their master, whom they had hitherto reverenced as the omnipotent lord of Anahuac. They were the more affected, therefore, by the sight of his distress.[2] His will, they told him, had always been their law. It should be so now; and, if he thought the sovereign of the strangers was the ancient lord of their country, they were willing to acknowledge him as such still. The oaths of allegiance were then administered with all due solemnity, attested by the Spaniards present, and a

---

[1] "Y mucho os ruego, pues á todos os es notorio todo esto, que assí como hasta aquí á mí me habeis tenido, y obedecido por Señor vuestro, de aquí adelante tengais, y obedescais á este Gran Rey, pues él es vuestro natural Señor, y en su lugar tengais á este su Capitan : y todos los Tributos, y Servicios. que fasta aquí á mí me haciades, los haced, y dad á él, porque yo assimismo tengo de contribuir, y servir con todo lo que me mandaré." Rel. Seg. de Cortés, ap. Lorenzana, p. 97.

[2] "Lo qual todo les dijo llorando, con las mayores lágrimas, y suspiros, que un hombre podia manifestar ; é assimismo todos aquellos Señores, que le estaban oiendo, lloraban tanto, que en gran rato no le pudiéron responder." Ibid., loc. cit.

full record of the proceedings was drawn up by the royal notary, to be sent to Spain.[1] There was something deeply touching in the ceremony by which an independent and absolute monarch, in obedience less to the dictates of fear than of conscience, thus relinquished his hereditary rights in favour of an unknown and mysterious power. It even moved those hard men who were thus unscrupulously availing themselves of the confiding ignorance of the natives; and, though "it was in the regular way of their own business," says an old chronicler, "there was not a Spaniard who could look on the spectacle with a dry eye"![2]

The rumour of these strange proceedings was soon circulated through the capital and the country. Men read in them the finger of Providence. The ancient tradition of Quetzalcoatl was familiar to all; and where it had slept scarcely noticed in the memory, it was now revived with many exaggerated circumstances. It was said to be part of the tradition that the royal line of the Aztecs was to end with Montezuma; and his name, the literal signification of which is "sad" or "angry lord," was construed into an omen of his evil destiny.[3]

Having thus secured this great feudatory to the crown of Castile, Cortés suggested that it would be well for the Aztec chiefs to send his sovereign such a gratuity as would conciliate his goodwill by convincing him of the loyalty of his new vassals.[4] Montezuma consented that his collectors should visit the principal cities and provinces, attended by a number of Spaniards, to receive the customary tributes, in the name of the Castilian sovereign. In a few weeks most of them returned, bringing back large quantities of gold and silver plate, rich stuffs, and the various commodities in which the taxes were usually paid.

To this store Montezuma added, on his own account, the treasure of Axayacatl, previously noticed, some part of which had been already given to the Spaniards. It was the fruit of long and careful hoarding,—of extortion, it may be,—by a prince who little dreamed of its final destination. When brought into the quarters, the gold alone was sufficient to

[1] Solis regards this ceremony as supplying what was before defective in the title of the Spaniards to the country. The remarks are curious, even from a professed casuist: "Y siendo una como insinuacion misteriosa del titulo que se debió despues al derecho de las armas, sobre justa provocacion, como lo verémos en su lugar: circunstancia particular, que concurrió en la conquista de Méjico para mayor justificacion de aquel dominio, sobre las demas consideraciones generales que no solo hiciéron lícita la guerra en otras partes, sino legítima y razonable siempre que se puso en términos de medio necesario para la introduccion del Evangelio." Conquista, lib. 4, cap. 3.

[2] Bernal Diaz, Hist. de la Conquista, cap. 101.—Solis, Conquista, loc. cit.—Herrera, Hist. general, dec. 2, lib. 9, cap. 4.—Ixtlilxochitl, Hist. Chich., MS., cap. 87.—Oviedo considers the grief of Montezuma as sufficient proof that his homage, far from being voluntary, was extorted by necessity. The historian appears to have seen the drift of events more clearly than some of the actors in them. "Y en la verdad si como Cortés lo dice, ó escrivió, passó en efecto, mui gran cosa me parece la con-

ciencia y liberalidad de Montezuma en esta su restitucion é obediencia al Rey de Castilla, por la simple ó cautelosa informacion de Cortés, que le podia hacer para ello; Mas aquellas lágrimas con que dice, que Montezuma hizo su oracion, é amonestamiento, despojándose de su señorío, é las de aquellos con que les respondiéron aceptando lo que les mandaba, y exortaba, y á mi parecer su llanto queria decir, ó enseñar otra cosa de lo que él, y ellos dixéron; porque las obediencias que se suelen dar á los Príncipes con riza, é con cámaras; é diversidad de Música, é leticia, enseñales de placer, se suele hacer; é no con lucto ni lágrimas, é sollozos, ni estando preso quien obedece; porque como dice Marco Varron: Lo que por fuerza se da no es servicio sino robo." Hist. de las Ind., MS., lib. 33, cap. 9.

[3] Gomara, Crónica, cap. 92.—Clavigero, Stor. del Messico, tom. ii. p. 256.

[4] "Pareceria que ellos comenzaban á servir, y Vuestra Alteza tendria mas concepto de las voluntades, que á su servicio mostraban." Rel. Seg. de Cortés, ap. Lorenzana, p. 98.

make three great heaps. It consisted partly of native grains; part had been melted into bars; but the greatest portion was in utensils, and various kinds of ornaments and curious toys, together with imitations of birds, insects, or flowers, executed with uncommon truth and delicacy. There were, also, quantities of collars, bracelets, wands, fans, and other trinkets, in which the gold and feather-work were richly powdered with pearls and precious stones. Many of the articles were even more admirable for the workmanship than for the value of the materials;[1] such, indeed,—if we may take the report of Cortés to one who would himself have soon an opportunity to judge of its veracity, and whom it would not be safe to trifle with,—as no monarch in Europe could boast in his dominions![2]

Magnificent as it was, Montezuma expressed his regret that the treasure was no larger. But he had diminished it, he said, by his former gifts to the white men. "Take it," he added, "Malinche, and let it be recorded in your annals that Montezuma sent this present to your master."[3]

The Spaniards gazed with greedy eyes on the display of riches,[4] now their own, which far exceeded all hitherto seen in the New World, and fell nothing short of the *El Dorado* which their glowing imaginations had depicted. It may be that they felt somewhat rebuked by the contrast which their own avarice presented to the princely munificence of the barbarian chief. At least, they seemed to testify their sense of his superiority by the respectful homage which they rendered him, as they poured forth the fulness of their gratitude.[5] They were not so scrupulous, however, as to manifest any delicacy in appropriating to themselves the donative, a small part of which was to find its way into the royal coffers. They clamoured loudly for an immediate division of the spoil, which the general would have postponed till the tributes from the remoter provinces had been gathered in. The goldsmiths of Azcapozalco were sent for to take in pieces the larger and coarser ornaments, leaving untouched those of more delicate workmanship. Three days were consumed in this labour, when the heaps of gold were cast into ingots and stamped with the royal arms.

Some difficulty occurred in the division of the treasure, from the want of weights, which, strange as it appears, considering their advancement

---

[1] Peter Martyr, distrusting some extravagance in this statement of Cortés, found it fully confirmed by the testimony of others. "Referunt non credenda. Credenda tamen, quando vir talis ad Cæsarem et nostri collegii Indici senatores audeat exscribere. Addes insuper se multa prætermittere, ne tanta recensendo sit molestus. *Idem affirmant qui ad nos inae regrediuntur.*" De Orbe Novo, dec. 5, cap. 3.

[2] "Las quales, demas de su valor, eran tales, y tan maravillosas, que consideradas por su novedad, y estrañeza, no tenian precio, ni es de creer, que alguno de todos los Príncipes del Mundo de quien se tiene noticia, las pudiesse tener tales, y de tal calidad." Rel. Seg. de Cortés, ap. Lorenzana, p.

99.—See, also, Oviedo, Hist. de las Ind., MS., lib. 33, cap. 9,—Bernal Diaz, Hist. de la Conquista, cap. 104.

[3] "Dezilde en vuestros anales y cartas: Esto os embia vuestro buen vassallo Monteçuma." Bernal Diaz, ubi supra.

[4]   "Fluctibus auri
      Expleri calor ille nequit."
            CLAUDIAN, In Ruf., lib. 1.

[5] "Y quãdo aquello le oyó Cortés, y todos nosotros, estuvímos espantados de la gran bondad, y liberalidad del gran Monteçuma, y con mucho acato le quitámos todos las gorras de armas, y le diximos, que se lo teniamos en merced, y con palabras de mucho amor," etc. Bernal Diaz, ubi supra.

in the arts, were, as already observed, unknown to the Aztecs. The deficiency was soon supplied by the Spaniards, however, with scales and weights of their own manufacture, probably not the most exact. With the aid of these they ascertained the value of the royal fifth to be thirty-two thousand and four hundred *pesos de oro*.[1] Diaz swells it to nearly four times that amount.[2] But their desire of securing the emperor's favour makes it improbable that the Spaniards should have defrauded the exchequer of any part of its due; while, as Cortés was responsible for the sum admitted in his letter, he would be still less likely to overstate it. His estimate may be received as the true one.

The whole amounted, therefore, to one hundred and sixty-two thousand *pesos de oro*, independently of the fine ornaments and jewellery, the value of which Cortés computes at five hundred thousand ducats more. There were, besides, five hundred marks of silver, chiefly in plate, drinking-cups, and other articles of luxury. The inconsiderable quantity of the silver, as compared with the gold, forms a singular contrast to the relative proportions of the two metals since the occupation of the country by the Europeans.[3] The whole amount of the treasure, reduced to our own currency, and making allowance for the change in the value of gold since the beginning of the sixteenth century, was about six million three hundred thousand dollars, or one million four hundred and seventeen thousand pounds sterling; a sum large enough to show the incorrectness of the popular notion that little or no wealth was found in Mexico.[4] It was, indeed, small in comparison with that obtained by the conquerors of Peru. But few European monarchs of that day could boast a larger treasure in their coffers.[5]

The division of the spoil was a work of some difficulty. A perfectly equal division of it among the Conquerors would have given them more

---

[1] Rel. Seg. de Cortés, ap. Lorenzana, p. 99.— This estimate of the royal fifth is confirmed (with the exception of the four hundred ounces) by the affidavits of a number of witnesses cited on behalf of Cortés to show the amount of the treasure. Among these witnesses we find some of the most respectable names in the army, as Olid, Ordaz, Avila, the priests Olmedo and Diaz,—the last, it may be added, not too friendly to the general. The instrument, which is without date, is in the collection of Vargas Ponçe. Probanza fecha á pedimento de Juan de Lexalde, MS.

[2] " Eran tres montones *de oro*, y pesado huvo en ellos sobre *seis cientos mil pesos*, como adelante diré, sin la plata, é otras muchas riquezas." Hist. de la Conquista, cap. 104.

[3] The quantity of silver taken from the American mines has exceeded that of gold in the ratio of forty-six to one. (Humboldt, Essai politique, tom. iii. p. 401.) The value of the latter metal, says Clemencin, which on the discovery of the New World was only eleven times greater than that of the former, has now come to be sixteen times. (Memorias de la Real Acad. de Hist., tom. vi. Ilust. 20.) This does not vary materially from Smith's estimate made after the middle of the last century. (Wealth of Nations, book i, chap. 11.) The difference would have been much more considerable, but for the greater demand for silver for objects of ornament and use.

[4] Dr. Robertson, preferring the authority, it seems, of Diaz, speaks of the value of the treasure as 600,000 *pesos*. (History of America, vol. ii. pp. 296, 298.) The value of the *peso* is an ounce of silver, or dollar, which, making allowance for the depreciation of silver, represented, in the time of Cortés, nearly four times its value at the present day. But that of the *peso de oro* was nearly three times that sum, or eleven dollars sixty-seven cents. (See *ante*, p. 152, note 2.) Robertson makes his own estimate, so much reduced below that of his original, an argument for doubting the existence, in any great quantity, of either gold or silver in the country. In accounting for the scarcity of the former metal in this argument, he falls into an error in stating that gold was not one of the standards by which the value of other commodities in Mexico was estimated. Comp. *ante*, p. 69.

[5] Many of them, indeed, could boast little or nothing in their coffers. Maximilian of Germany, and the more prudent Ferdinand of Spain, left scarcely enough to defray their funeral expenses. Even as late as the beginning of the next century we find Henry IV. of France embracing his minister, Sully, with rapture when he informed him that, by dint of great economy, he had 36,000,000 livres— about 1,500,000 pounds sterling—in his treasury. See Mémoires, du Duc de Sully, tom. iii. liv. 27.

than three thousand pounds sterling apiece; a magnificent booty! But one-fifth was to be deducted for the crown. An equal portion was reserved for the general, pursuant to the tenor of his commission. A large sum was then allowed to indemnify him and the governor of Cuba for the charges of the expedition and the loss of the fleet. The garrison of Vera Cruz was also to be provided for. Ample compensation was made to the principal cavaliers. The cavalry, arquebusiers, and cross-bowmen each received double pay. So that when the turn of the common soldiers came there remained not more than a hundred *pesos de oro* for each; a sum so insignificant, in comparison with their expectations, that several refused to accept it.[1]

Loud murmurs now rose among the men. "Was it for this," they said, "that we left our homes and families, perilled our lives, submitted to fatigue and famine, and all for so contemptible a pittance? Better to have stayed in Cuba and contented ourselves with the gains of a safe and easy traffic. When we gave up our share of the gold at Vera Cruz, it was on the assurance that we should be amply requited in Mexico. We have, indeed, found the riches we expected; but no sooner seen, than they are snatched from us by the very men who pledged us their faith!" The malcontents even went so far as to accuse their leaders of appropriating to themselves several of the richest ornaments before the partition had been made; an accusation that receives some countenance from a dispute which arose between Mexia, the treasurer for the crown, and Velasquez de Leon, a relation of the governor, and a favourite of Cortés. The treasurer accused this cavalier of purloining certain pieces of plate before they were submitted to the royal stamp. From words the parties came to blows. They were good swordsmen; several wounds were given on both sides, and the affair might have ended fatally, but for the interference of Cortés, who placed both under arrest.

He then used all his authority and insinuating eloquence to calm the passions of his men. It was a delicate crisis. He was sorry, he said, to see them so unmindful of the duty of loyal soldiers and cavaliers of the Cross, as to brawl like common banditti over their booty. The division, he assured them, had been made on perfectly fair and equitable principles. As to his own share, it was no more than was warranted by his commission. Yet, if they thought it too much, he was willing to forego his just claims and divide with the poorest soldier. Gold, however welcome, was not the chief object of his ambition. If it were theirs, they should still reflect that the present treasure was little in comparison with what awaited them hereafter; for had they not the whole country and its mines at their disposal? It was only necessary that they should not give an opening to the enemy, by their discord, to circumvent and to crush them. With these honeyed words, of which he had good store for all fitting occasions, says

---

[1] "Por ser tan poco, muchos soldados huuo que no lo quisiéron recebir." Bernal Diaz, Hist. de la Conquista, cap. 105.

an old soldier,[1] for whose benefit, in part, they were intended, he succeeded in calming the storm for the present; while in private he took
more effectual means, by presents judiciously administered, to mitigate
the discontents of the importunate and refractory. And, although there
were a few of more tenacious temper, who treasured this in their memories
against a future day, the troops soon returned to their usual subordination.
This was one of those critical conjunctures which taxed all the address
and personal authority of Cortés. He never shrunk from them, but on
such occasions was true to himself. At Vera Cruz he had persuaded his
followers to give up what was but the earnest of future gains. Here he
persuaded them to relinquish these gains themselves. It was snatching
the prey from the very jaws of the lion. Why did he not turn and rend
him?

To many of the soldiers, indeed, it mattered little whether their share
of the booty were more or less. Gaming is a deep-rooted passion in the
Spaniard, and the sudden acquisition of riches furnished both the means
and the motive for its indulgence. Cards were easily made out of old
parchment drum-heads, and in a few days most of the prize-money,
obtained with so much toil and suffering, had changed hands, and many
of the improvident soldiers closed the campaign as poor as they had commenced it. Others, it is true, more prudent, followed the example of
their officers, who, with the aid of the royal jewellers, converted their gold
into chains, services of plate, and other portable articles of ornament or
use.[2]

Cortés seemed now to have accomplished the great objects of the expedition. The Indian monarch had declared himself the feudatory of the
Spanish. His authority, his revenues, were at the disposal of the general.
The conquest of Mexico seemed to be achieved, and that without a blow.
But it was far from being achieved. One important step yet remained to
be taken, towards which the Spaniards had hitherto made little progress,—
the conversion of the natives. With all the exertions of Father Olmedo,
backed by the polemic talents of the general,[3] neither Montezuma nor his
subjects showed any disposition to abjure the faith of their fathers.[4] The
bloody exercises of their religion, on the contrary, were celebrated with
all the usual circumstance and pomp of sacrifice before the eyes of the
Spaniards.

---

[1] "Palabras muy melifluas; . . . razones mui
bien dichas, que las sabia bien proponer." Bernal
Diaz, ubi supra.

[2] Bernal Diaz, Hist. de la Conquista, cap. 105,
106.—Gomara, Crónica, cap. 93.—Herrera, Hist.
general, dec. 2, lib. 8, cap. 5.

[3] "Ex jureconsulto Cortesius theologus effectus,"
says Martyr, in his pithy manner. De Orbe Novo,
dec. 5, cap. 4.

[4] According to Ixtlilxochitl, Montezuma got as
far on the road to conversion as the *Credo* and the
Ave Maria, both of which he could repeat; but
his baptism was postponed, and he died before receiving it. That he ever consented to receive it is
highly improbable. I quote the historian's words,

in which he further notices the general's unsuccessful labours among the Indians: " Cortés comenzó
á dar órden de la conversion de los Naturales, diciéndoles, que pues eran vasallos del Rey de España
que se tornasen Cristianos como él lo era, y así se
comenzáron á Bautizar algunos aunque fuéron muy
pocos, y Motecuhzoma aunque pidió el Bautismo, y
sabia algunas de las oraciones como eran el Ave
María, y el Credo, se dilató por la Pasqua siguiente,
que era la de Resurreccion, y fué tan desdichado
que nunca alcanzó tanto bien, y los Nuestros con la
dilacion y aprieto en que se viéron, se descuidáron,
de que pesó á todos mucho muriese sin Bautismo."
Hist. Chich., MS., cap. 87.

Unable further to endure these abominations, Cortés, attended by several of his cavaliers, waited on Montezuma. He told the emperor that the Christians could no longer consent to have the services of their religion shut up within the narrow walls of the garrison. They wished to spread its light far abroad, and to open to the people a full participation in the blessings of Christianity. For this purpose they requested that the great *teocalli* should be delivered up, as a fit place where their worship might be conducted in the presence of the whole city.

Montezuma listened to the proposal with visible consternation. Amidst all his troubles he had leaned for support on his own faith, and, indeed, it was in obedience to it that he had shown such deference to the Spaniards as the mysterious messengers predicted by the oracles. "Why," said he, "Malinche, why will you urge matters to an extremity, that must surely bring down the vengeance of our gods, and stir up an insurrection among my people, who will never endure this profanation of their temples?"[1]

Cortés, seeing how greatly he was moved, made a sign to his officers to withdraw. When left alone with the interpreters, he told the emperor that he would use his influence to moderate the zeal of his followers, and persuade them to be contented with one of the sanctuaries of the *teocalli*. If that were not granted, they should be obliged to take it by force, and to roll down the images of his false deities in the face of the city. "We fear not for our lives," he added, "for, though our numbers are few, the arm of the true God is over us." Montezuma, much agitated, told him that he would confer with the priests.

The result of the conference was favourable to the Spaniards, who were allowed to occupy one of the sanctuaries as a place of worship. The tidings spread great joy throughout the camp. They might now go forth in open day and publish their religion to the assembled capital. No time was lost in availing themselves of the permission. The sanctuary was cleansed of its disgusting impurities. An altar was raised, surmounted by a crucifix and the image of the Virgin. Instead of the gold and jewels which blazed on the neighbouring pagan shrine, its walls were decorated with fresh garlands of flowers; and an old soldier was stationed to watch over the chapel and guard it from intrusion.

When these arrangements were completed, the whole army moved in solemn procession up the winding ascent of the pyramid. Entering the sanctuary, and clustering round its portals, they listened reverentially to the service of the mass, as it was performed by the fathers Olmedo and Diaz. And, as the beautiful *Te Deum* rose towards heaven, Cortés and his soldiers, kneeling on the ground, with tears streaming from their eyes,

---

[1] "O Malinche, y como nos quereis echar á perder á toda esta ciudad, porque estarán mui enojados nuestros Dioses contra nosotros, y aun vuestras vidas no sé en que pararán." Bernal Diaz, Hist. de la Conquista, cap. 107.

poured forth their gratitude to the Almighty for this glorious triumph of the Cross.[1]

It was a striking spectacle,—that of these rude warriors lifting up their orisons on the summit of this mountain temple, in the very capital of heathendom, on the spot especially dedicated to its unhallowed mysteries. Side by side the Spaniard and the Aztec knelt down in prayer; and the Christian hymn mingled its sweet tones of love and mercy with the wild chant raised by the Indian priest in honour of the war-god of Anahuac! It was an unnatural union, and could not long abide.

A nation will endure any outrage sooner than that on its religion. This is an outrage both on its principles and its prejudices; on the ideas instilled into it from childhood, which have strengthened with its growth, until they become a part of its nature,—which have to do with its highest interests here and with the dread hereafter. Any violence to the religious sentiment touches all alike, the old and the young, the rich and the poor, the noble and the plebeian. Above all, it touches the priests, whose personal consideration rests on that of their religion, and who, in a semi civilized state of society, usually hold an unbounded authority. Thus it was with the Brahmins of India, the Magi of Persia, the Roman Catholic clergy in the Dark Ages, the priests of Ancient Egypt and Mexico.

The people had borne with patience all the injuries and affronts hitherto put on them by the Spaniards. They had seen their sovereign dragged as a captive from his own palace, his ministers butchered before his eyes, his treasure seized and appropriated, himself in a manner deposed from his royal supremacy. All this they had seen, without a struggle to prevent it. But the profanation of their temples touched a deeper feeling, of which the priesthood were not slow to take advantage.[2]

The first intimation of this change of feeling was gathered from Montezuma himself. Instead of his usual cheerfulness, he appeared grave and abstracted, and instead of seeking, as he was wont, the society of the Spaniards, seemed rather to shun it. It was noticed, too, that conferences were more frequent between him and the nobles, and especially the priests. His little page, Orteguilla, who had now picked up a tolerable acquaintance with the Aztec, contrary to Montezuma's usual practice, was not allowed to attend him at these meetings. These circumstances could not fail to awaken most uncomfortable apprehensions in the Spaniards.

---

[1] This transaction is told with more discrepancy than usual by the different writers. Cortés assures the emperor that he occupied the temple, and turned out the false gods by force, in spite of the menaces of the Mexicans. (Rel. Seg., ap. Lorenzana, p. 106.) The improbability of this Quixotic feat startles Oviedo, who nevertheless reports it. (Hist. de las Ind., MS., lib. 33, cap. 10.) It looks, indeed, very much as if the general was somewhat too eager to set off his militant zeal to advantage in the eyes of his master. The statements of Diaz, and of other chroniclers, conformably to that in the text, seem far the most probable. Comp. Diaz, Hist. de la Conquista, ubi supra.—Herrera, Hist. general, dec. 2, lib. 8, cap. 6.—Argensola, Anales, lib. 1, cap. 88.

[2] "Para mí yo tengo por marabilla, é grande, la mucha paciencia de Montezuma, y de los Indios principales, que assí viéron tratar sus Templos, é Idolos: Mas su disimulacion adelante se mostró ser otra cosa viendo, que vna Gente Extrangera, é de tan poco número, les prendió su Señor é porque formas los hacia tributarios, é se castigaban é quemaban los principales, é se aniquilaban y disipaban sus templos, é hasta en aquellos y sus antecesores estaban. Recia cosa me parece soportarla con tanta quietud; pero adelante, como lo dirá la Historia, mostró el tiempo lo que en el pecho estaba oculto en todos los Indios generalmente." Oviedo, Hist. de las Ind., MS., lib. 33, cap. 10.

Not many days elapsed, however, before Cortés received an invitation, or rather a summons, from the emperor to attend him in his apartment. The general went with some feelings of anxiety and distrust, taking with him Olid, captain of the guard, and two or three other trusty cavaliers. Montezuma received them with cold civility, and, turning to the general, told him that all his predictions had come to pass. The gods of his country had been offended by the violation of their temples. They had threatened the priests that they would forsake the city if the sacrilegious strangers were not driven from it, or rather sacrificed on the altars in expiation of their crimes.[1] The monarch assured the Christians it was from regard for their safety that he communicated this ; and, " if you have any regard for it yourselves," he concluded, " you will leave the country without delay. I have only to raise my finger, and every Aztec in the land will rise in arms against you." There was no reason to doubt his sincerity. For Montezuma, whatever evils had been brought on him by the white men, held them in reverence as a race more highly gifted than his own, while for several, as we have seen, he had conceived an attachment, flowing, no doubt, from their personal attentions and deference to himself.

Cortés was too much master of his feelings to show how far he was startled by this intelligence. He replied, with admirable coolness, that he should regret much to leave the capital so precipitately, when he had no vessels to take him from the country. If it were not for this, there could be no obstacle to his leaving it at once. He should also regret another step to which he should be driven, if he quitted it under these circumstances,—that of taking the emperor along with him.

Montezuma was evidently troubled by this last suggestion. He inquired how long it would take to build the vessels, and finally consented to send a sufficient number of workmen to the coast, to act under the orders of the Spaniards ; meanwhile, he would use his authority to restrain the impatience of the people, under the assurance that the white men would leave the land when the means for it were provided. He kept his word. A large body of Aztec artisans left the capital with the most experienced Castilian shipbuilders, and, descending to Vera Cruz, began at once to fell the timber and build a sufficient number of ships to transport the Spaniards back to their own country. The work went forward with apparent alacrity. But those who had the direction of it, it is said, received private instructions from the general to interpose as many delays

---

1 According to Herrera, it was the Devil himself who communicated this to Montezuma, and he reports the substance of the dialogue between the parties. (Hist. general, dec. 2, lib. 9, cap. 6.) Indeed, the apparition of Satan in his own bodily presence, on this occasion, is stoutly maintained by most historians of the time. Oviedo, a man of enlarged ideas on most subjects, speaks with a little more qualification on this : " Porque la Misa y Evangelio, que predicaban y decian los christianos, le [al Diablo] daban gran tormento ; y débese pensar, si verdad es, que esas gentes tienen tanta conversacion y comunicacion con nuestro adversario, *como se tiene por cierto en estas Indias*, que no le podia á nuestro enemigo placer con los misterios y sacramentos de la sagrada religion christiana." Hist. de las Ind., MS., lib. 33, cap. 47.

as possible, in hopes of receiving in the meantime such reinforcements from Europe as would enable him to maintain his ground.[1]

The whole aspect of things was now changed in the Castilian quarters. Instead of the security and repose in which the troops had of late indulged, they felt a gloomy apprehension of danger, not the less oppressive to the spirits that it was scarcely visible to the eye;—like the faint speck just descried above the horizon by the voyager in the tropics, to the common gaze seeming only a summer cloud, but which to the experienced mariner bodes the coming of the hurricane.   Every precaution that prudence could devise was taken to meet it.   The soldier, as he threw himself on his mats for repose, kept on his armour.   He ate, drank, slept, with his weapons by his side.   His horse stood ready caparisoned, day and night, with the bridle hanging at the saddle-bow.   The guns were carefully planted so as to command the great avenues.   The sentinels were doubled, and every man, of whatever rank, took his turn in mounting guard.   The garrison was in a state of siege.[2]   Such was the uncomfortable position of the army when, in the beginning of May 1520, six months after their arrival in the capital, tidings came from the coast which gave greater alarm to Cortés than even the menaced insurrection of the Aztecs.

---

[1] " É Cortés proveió de maestros é personas que entendiesen en la labor de los Navíos, é dixo despues á los Españoles desta manera : Señores y hermanos, este Señor Montezuma quiere que nos vamos de la tierra, y conviene que se hagan Navíos. Id con estos Indios é córtese la madera ; é entretanto Dios nos proveherá de gente é socorro ; por tanto, poned tal dilacion que parezca que haceis algo y se haga con ella lo que nos conviene ; é siempre me escrivid é avisad que tales estáis en la Montaña, é que no sientan los Indios nuestra disimulacion. É así se puso por obra." (Oviedo, Hist. de las Ind., MS., lib. 33, cap. 47.) So, also, Gomara. (Crónica, cap. 95.) Diaz denies any such secret orders, alleging that Martin Lopez, the principal builder, assured him they made all the expedition possible in getting three ships on the stocks. Hist. de la Conquista, cap. 108.

[2] " I may say without vaunting," observes our stout-hearted old chronicler, Bernal Diaz, "that I was so accustomed to this way of life, that since the conquest of the country I have never been able to lie down undressed, or in a bed ; yet I sleep as sound as if I were on the softest down. Even when I make the rounds of my *encomienda*, I never take a bed with me, unless, indeed, I go in the company of other cavaliers, who might impute this to parsimony. But even then I throw myself on it with my clothes on. Another thing I must add, that I cannot sleep long in the night without getting up to look at the heavens and the stars, and stay a while in the open air, and this without a bonnet or covering of any sort on my head. And, thanks to God, I have received no harm from it. I mention these things, that the world may understand of what stuff we, the true Conquerors, were made, and how well drilled we were to arms and watching." Hist. de la Conquista, cap. 108.

CHAPTER VI.

FATE OF CORTÉS' EMISSARIES.—PROCEEDINGS IN THE CASTILIAN COURT.—
PREPARATIONS OF VELASQUEZ.—NARVAEZ LANDS IN MEXICO.—POLITIC
CONDUCT OF CORTÉS.—HE LEAVES THE CAPITAL.

(1520.)

BEFORE explaining the nature of the tidings alluded to in the preceding
chapter, it will be necessary to cast a glance over some of the transactions
of an earlier period.   The vessel, which, as the reader may remember, bore
the envoys Puertocarrero and Montejo with the despatches from Vera
Cruz, after touching, contrary to orders, at the northern coast of Cuba,
and spreading the news of the late discoveries, held on its way uninterrupted towards Spain, and early in October 1519 reached the little port
of San Lucar.   Great was the sensation caused by her arrival and the
tidings which she brought ; a sensation scarcely inferior to that created by
the original discovery of Columbus.   For now, for the first time, all the
magnificent anticipations formed of the New World seemed destined to be
realized.

Unfortunately, there was a person in Seville at this time, named Benito
Martin, chaplain of Velasquez, the governor of Cuba.   No sooner did this
man learn the arrival of the envoys, and the particulars of their story,
than he lodged a complaint with the *Casa de Contratacion*,—the Royal
Indian House,—charging those on board the vessel with mutiny and
rebellion against the authorities of Cuba, as well as with treason to the
crown.[1]   In consequence of his representations, the ship was taken possession of by the public officers, and those on board were prohibited from
removing their own effects, or anything else, from her.   The envoys were
not even allowed the funds necessary for the expenses of the voyage, nor a
considerable sum remitted by Cortés to his father, Don Martin.   In this
embarrassment they had no alternative but to present themselves, as
speedy as possible, before the emperor, deliver the letters with which they
had been charged by the colony, and seek redress for their own grievances.
They first sought out Martin Cortés, residing at Medellin, and with him
made the best of their way to court.

Charles the Fifth was then on his first visit to Spain after his accession.
It was not a long one ; long enough, however, to disgust his subjects, and,
in a great degree, to alienate their affections.   He had lately received

---

[1] In the collection of MSS. made by Don Vargas
Ponçe, former President of the Academy of History,
is a Memorial of this same Benito Martin to the
emperor, setting forth the services of Velasquez and
the ingratitude and revolt of Cortés and his followers.   The paper is without date ; written after
the arrival of the envoys, probably at the close of
1519 or the beginning of the following year.

intelligence of his election to the imperial crown of Germany. From that hour his eyes were turned to that quarter. His stay in the Peninsula was prolonged only that he might raise supplies for appearing with splendour on the great theatre of Europe. Every act showed too plainly that the diadem of his ancestors was held lightly in comparison with the imperial bauble in which neither his countrymen nor his own posterity could have the slightest interest. The interest was wholly personal.

Contrary to established usage, he had summoned the Castilian córtes to meet at Compostella, a remote town in the north, which presented no other advantage than that of being near his place of embarkation.[1] On his way thither he stopped some time at Tordesillas, the residence of his unhappy mother, Joanna "the Mad." It was here that the envoys from Vera Cruz presented themselves before him, in March 1520. At nearly the same time, the treasures brought over by them reached the court, where they excited unbounded admiration.[2] Hitherto, the returns from the New World had been chiefly in vegetable products, which, if the surest, are also the slowest sources of wealth. Of gold they had as yet seen but little, and that in its natural state or wrought into the rudest trinkets. The courtiers gazed with astonishment on the large masses of the precious metal, and the delicate manufacture of the various articles, especially of the richly tinted feather-work. And, as they listened to the accounts, written and oral, of the great Aztec empire, they felt assured that the Castilian ships had at length reached the golden Indies, which hitherto had seemed to recede before them.

In this favourable mood there is little doubt the monarch would have granted the petition of the envoys, and confirmed the irregular proceedings of the Conquerors, but for the opposition of a person who held the highest office in the Indian department. This was Juan Rodriguez de Fonseca, formerly dean of Seville, now bishop of Burgos. He was a man of noble family, and had been intrusted with the direction of the colonial concerns on the discovery of the New World. On the establishment of the Royal Council of the Indies by Ferdinand the Catholic, he had been made its president, and had occupied that post ever since. His long continuance in a position of great importance and difficulty is evidence of capacity for business. It was no uncommon thing in that age to find ecclesiastics in high civil, and even military, employments. Fonseca appears to have been an active, efficient person, better suited to a secular than to a religious vocation. He had, indeed, little that was religious in his temper ; quick to take offence and slow to forgive. His resentments seem to have been nourished and perpetuated like a part of his own nature. Unfortunately,

---

[1] Sandoval, indeed, gives a singular reason,— that of being near the coast, so as to enable Chièvres and the other Flemish bloodsuckers to escape suddenly, if need were, with their ill-gotten treasures, from the country. Hist. de Cárlos Quinto, tom. i. p. 203, ed. Pamplona, 1634.

[2] See the letter of Peter Martyr to his noble friend and pupil, the Marquis de Mondejar, written two months after the arrival of the vessel from Vera Cruz. Opus Epist., ep. 650.

his peculiar position enabled him to display them towards some of the most illustrious men of his time. From pique at some real or fancied slight from Columbus, he had constantly thwarted the plans of the great navigator. He had shown the same unfriendly feeling towards the Admiral's son, Diego, the heir of his honours ; and he now, and from this time forward, showed a similar spirit towards the Conqueror of Mexico. The immediate cause of this was his own personal relations with Velasquez, to whom a near relative was betrothed.[1]

Through this prelate's representations, Charles, instead of a favourable answer to the envoys, postponed his decision till he should arrive at Coruña, the place of embarkation.[2] But here he was much pressed by the troubles which his impolitic conduct had raised, as well as by preparations for his voyage. The transaction of the colonial business, which, long postponed, had greatly accumulated on his hands, was reserved for the last week in Spain. But the affairs of the " young admiral " consumed so large a portion of this, that he had no time to give to those of Cortés, except, indeed, to instruct the board at Seville to remit to the envoys so much of their funds as was required to defray the charges of the voyage. On the 16th of May 1520 the impatient monarch bade adieu to his distracted kingdom, without one attempt to settle the dispute between his belligerent vassals in the New World, and without an effort to promote the magnificent enterprise which was to secure to him the possession of an empire. What a contrast to the policy of his illustrious predecessors, Ferdinand and Isabella ![3]

The governor of Cuba, meanwhile, without waiting for support from home, took measures for redress into his own hands. We have seen in a preceding chapter how deeply he was moved by the reports of the proceedings of Cortés, and of the treasures which his vessel was bearing to Spain. Rage, mortification, disappointed avarice, distracted his mind. He could not forgive himself for trusting the affair to such hands. On the very week in which Cortés had parted from him to take charge of the fleet, a *capitulation* had been signed by Chárles the Fifth, conferring on Velasquez the title of *adelantado*, with great augmentation of his original powers.[4] The governor resolved, without loss of time, to send such a force to the Mexican coast as should enable him to assert his new authority to its full extent and to take vengeance on his rebellious officer. He began his preparations as early as October.[5] At first he proposed to

---

1 Zuñiga, Anales eclesiásticos y seculares de Sevilla (Madrid, 1677), fol. 414.—Herrera, Hist. general, dec. 2, lib. 5, cap. 14 ; lib. 9, cap. 17, et alibi.

2 Velasquez, it appears, had sent home an account of the doings of Cortés and of the vessel which touched with the treasures at Cuba, as early as October 1519. Carta de Velasquez al Lic. Figueroa, MS., Nov. 17, 1519.

3 "With loud music from clarions and flutes, and with great demonstrations of joy, they weighed anchor and unfurled their sails to the wind, leaving unhappy Spain oppressed with sorrows and misfor-

tunes." Sandoval, Hist. de Cárlos Quinto, tom. i. p. 219.

4 The instrument was dated at Barcelona, Nov. 13, 1518. Cortés left St. Jago the 18th of the same month. Herrera, Hist. general, dec. 2, lib. 3, cap. 11.

5 Gomara (Crónica, cap. 96) and Robertson (History of America, vol. ii. pp. 304, 466) consider that the new dignity of *adelantado* stimulated the governor to this enterprise. By a letter of his own writing in the Muñoz collection, it appears he had begun operations some months previous to his receiving

assume the command in person. But his unwieldy size, which disqualified him for the fatigues incident to such an expedition, or, according to his own account, tenderness for his Indian subjects, then wasted by an epidemic, induced him to devolve the command on another.[1]

The person whom he selected was a Castilian hidalgo, named Pánfilo de Narvaez. He had assisted Velasquez in the reduction of Cuba, where his conduct cannot be wholly vindicated from the charge of inhumanity which too often attaches to the early Spanish adventurers. From that time he continued to hold important posts under the government, and was a decided favourite with Velasquez. He was a man of some military capacity, though negligent and lax in his discipline. He possessed undoubted courage, but it was mingled with an arrogance, or rather overweening confidence in his own powers, which made him deaf to the suggestions of others more sagacious than himself. He was altogether deficient in that prudence and calculating foresight demanded in a leader who was to cope with an antagonist like Cortés.[2]

The governor and his lieutenant were unwearied in their efforts to assemble an army. They visited every considerable town in the island, fitting out vessels, laying in stores and ammunition, and encouraging volunteers to enlist by liberal promises. But the most effectual bounty was the assurance of the rich treasures that awaited them in the golden regions of Mexico. So confident were they in this expectation, that all classes and ages vied with one another in eagerness to embark in the expedition, until it seemed as if the whole white population would desert the island and leave it to its primitive occupants.[3]

The report of these proceedings soon spread through the Islands, and drew the attention of the Royal Audience of St. Domingo. This body was intrusted, at that time, not only with the highest judicial authority in the colonies, but with a civil jurisdiction, which, as "the Admiral" complained, encroached on his own rights. The tribunal saw with alarm the proposed expedition of Velasquez, which, whatever might be its issue in regard to the parties, could not fail to compromise the interests of the crown. They chose accordingly one of their number, the licentiate Ayllon, a man of prudence and resolution, and despatched him to Cuba, with instructions to interpose his authority, and stay, if possible, the proceedings of Velasquez.[4]

On his arrival he found the governor in the western part of the island, busily occupied in getting the fleet ready for sea. The licentiate explained to him the purport of his mission, and the views entertained of the

---

notice of his appointment. Carta de Velasquez al Señor de Xêvres, Isla Fernandina, MS., Octubre 12, 1519.

[1] Carta de Velasquez al Lic. Figueroa, MS., Nov. 17, 1519.

[2] The person of Narvaez is thus whimsically described by Diaz: "He was tall, stout-limbed, with a large head and red beard, an agreeable presence, a voice deep and sonorous, as if it rose from a cavern. He was a good horseman and valiant." Hist. de la Conquista, cap. 205.

[3] The danger of such a result is particularly urged in a memorandum of the licentiate Ayllon. Carta al Emperador Guaniguanico, Marzo 4, 1520, MS.

[4] Processo y Pesquiza hecha por la Real Audiencia de la Española, Santo Domingo, Diciembre 24, 1519, MS.

proposed enterprise by the Royal Audience. The conquest of a powerful country like Mexico required the whole force of the Spaniards, and, if one half were employed against the other, nothing but ruin could come of it. It was the governor's duty, as a good subject, to forego all private animosities, and to sustain those now engaged in the great work by sending them the necessary supplies. He might, indeed, proclaim his own powers and demand obedience to them. But, if this were refused, he should leave the determination of his dispute to the authorized tribunals, and employ his resources in prosecuting discovery in another direction, instead of hazarding all by hostilities with his rival.

This admonition, however sensible and salutary, was not at all to the taste of the governor. He professed, indeed, to have no intention of coming to hostilities with Cortés. He designed only to assert his lawful jurisdiction over territories discovered under his own auspices. At the same time, he denied the right of Ayllon or of the Royal Audience to interfere in the matter. Narvaez was still more refractory, and, as the fleet was now ready, proclaimed his intention to sail in a few hours. In this state of things, the licentiate, baffled in his first purpose of staying the expedition, determined to accompany it in person, that he might prevent, if possible, by his presence, an open rupture between the parties.[1]

The squadron consisted of eighteen vessels, large and small. It carried nine hundred men, eighty of whom were cavalry, eighty more arquebusiers, one hundred and fifty crossbowmen, with a number of heavy guns, and a large supply of ammunition and military stores. There were, besides, a thousand Indians, natives of the island, who went, probably, in a menial capacity.[2] So gallant an armada—with one exception[3]—never before rode in the Indian seas. None to compare with it had ever been fitted out in the Western World.

Leaving Cuba early in March 1520, Narvaez held nearly the same course as Cortés, and running down what was then called the "island of Yucatan,"[4] after a heavy tempest, in which some of his smaller vessels foundered, anchored, April 23, off San Juan de Ulua. It was the place where Cortés, also, had first landed; the sandy waste covered by the present city of Vera Cruz.

Here the commander met with a Spaniard, one of those sent by the general from Mexico to ascertain the resources of the country, especially its mineral products. This man came on board the fleet, and from him the Spaniards gathered the particulars of all that had occurred since the departure of the envoys from Vera Cruz,—the march into the interior, the bloody battles with the Tlascalans, the occupation of Mexico, the rich

[1] Parecer del Lic. Ayllon al Adelantado Diego Velasquez, Isla Fernandina, 1520, MS.

[2] Relacion del Lic. Ayllon, Santo Domingo, 30 de Agosto, 1520, MS.—Processo y Pesquiza por la Real Audiencia, MS.—According to Diaz, the ordnance amounted to twenty cannon. Hist. de la Conquista, cap. 109.

[3] The great fleet under Ovando, 1501, in which Cortés had intended to embark for the New World. Herrera, Hist. general, dec. 1, lib. 4, cap. 11.

[4] "De allí seguimos el viage por toda la costa de la Isla de Yucatan." Relacion del Lic. Ayllon, MS.

treasures found in it, and the seizure of the monarch, by means of which, concluded the soldier, " Cortés rules over the land like its own sovereign, so that a Spaniard may travel unarmed from one end of the country to the other, without insult or injury."[1] His audience listened to this marvellous report with speechless amazement, and the loyal indignation of Narvaez waxed stronger and stronger, as he learned the value of the prize which had been snatched from his employer.

He now openly proclaimed his intention to march against Cortés and punish him for his rebellion. He made this vaunt so loudly, that the natives, who had flocked in numbers to the camp, which was soon formed on shore, clearly comprehended that the new-comers were not friends, but enemies, of the preceding. Narvaez determined, also,—though in opposition to the counsel of the Spaniard, who quoted the example of Cortés, —to establish a settlement on this unpromising spot ; and he made the necessary arrangements to organize a municipality. He was informed by the soldier of the existence of the neighbouring colony at Villa Rica, commanded by Sandoval, and consisting of a few invalids, who, he was assured, would surrender on the first summons. Instead of marching against the place, however, he determined to send a peaceful embassy to display his powers and demand the submission of the garrison.[2]

These successive steps gave serious displeasure to Ayllon, who saw they must lead to inevitable collision with Cortés. But it was in vain he remonstrated and threatened to lay the proceedings of Narvaez before the government. The latter, chafed by his continued opposition and sour rebuke, determined to rid himself of a companion who acted as a spy on his movements. He caused him to be seized and sent back to Cuba. The licentiate had the address to persuade the captain of the vessel to change her destination for St. Domingo ; and, when he arrived there, a formal report of his proceedings, exhibiting in strong colours the disloyal conduct of the governor and his lieutenant, was prepared, and despatched by the Royal Audience to Spain.[3]

Sandoval meanwhile had not been inattentive to the movements of Narvaez. From the time of his first appearance on the coast, that vigilant officer, distrusting the object of the armament, had kept his eye on him. No sooner was he apprised of the landing of the Spaniards, than the commander of Villa Rica sent off his few disabled soldiers to a place of safety in the neighbourhood. He then put his works in the best posture of defence that he could, and prepared to maintain the place to the last

---

[1] " La cual tierra sabe é ha visto este testigo, que el dicho Hernando Cortés tiene pacífica, é le sirven é obedecen todos los Indios ; é que cree este testigo que lo hacen por cabsa que el dicho Hernando Cortés tiene preso á un Cacique que dicen Montesuma, que es Señor de lo mas de la tierra, á lo que este testigo alcanza, al cual los Indios obedecen, é facen lo que les manda, é los Cristianos andan por toda esta tierra seguros, é un solo Cristiano la ha atravesado toda sin temor." Processo y Pesquiza hecha por la Real Audiencia de la Española, MS.

[2] Relacion del Lic. Ayllon, MS.—Demanda de Zavallos en nombre de Narvaez, MS.

[3] This report is to be found among the MSS. of Vargas Ponçe, in the archives of the Royal Academy of History. It embraces a hundred and ten folio pages, and is entitled " El Processo y Pesquiza hecha por la Real Audiencia de la Española é tierra nuevamente descubierta. Para el Consejo de su Majestad."

extremity. His men promised to stand by him, and, the more effectually to fortify the resolution of any who might falter, he ordered a gallows to be set up in a conspicuous part of the town! The constancy of his men was not put to the trial.

The only invaders of the place were a priest, a notary, and four other Spaniards, selected for the mission, already noticed, by Narvaez. The ecclesiastic's name was Guevara. On coming before Sandoval, he made him a formal address, in which he pompously enumerated the services and claims of Velasquez, taxed Cortés and his adherents with rebellion, and demanded of Sandoval to tender his submission, as a loyal subject, to the newly constituted authority of Narvaez.

The commander of La Villa Rica was so much incensed at this uncere-monious mention of his companions in arms that he assured the reverend envoy that nothing but respect for his cloth saved him from the chastise-ment he merited. Guevara now waxed wroth in his turn, and called on the notary to read the proclamation. But Sandoval interposed, promising that functionary that if he attempted to do so, without first producing a warrant of his authority from the crown, he should be soundly flogged. Guevara lost all command of himself at this, and, stamping on the ground, repeated his orders in a more peremptory tone than before. Sandoval was not a man of many words. He simply remarked that the instrument should be read to the general himself in Mexico. At the same time, he ordered his men to procure a number of sturdy *tamanes*, or Indian porters, on whose backs the unfortunate priest and his companions were bound like so many bales of goods. They were then placed under a guard of twenty Spaniards, and the whole caravan took its march for the capital. Day and night they travelled, stopping only to obtain fresh relays of carriers; and as they passed through populous towns, forests, and culti-vated fields, vanishing as soon as seen, the Spaniards, bewildered by the strangeness of the scene, as well as of their novel mode of conveyance, hardly knew whether they were awake or in a dream. In this way, at the end of the fourth day, they reached the Tezcucan lake in view of the Aztec capital.[1]

Its inhabitants had already been made acquainted with the fresh arrival of white men on the coast. Indeed, directly on their landing, intelligence had been communicated to Montezuma, who is said (it does not seem probable) to have concealed it some days from Cortés.[2] At length, inviting him to an interview, he told him there was no longer any obstacle to his leaving the country, as a fleet was ready for him. To the inquiries of the astonished general, Montezuma replied by pointing to a hieroglyphical map sent him from the coast, on which the ships, the Spaniards themselves,

1 "É iban espantados de que veian tātas ciudades y pueblos grandes, que les traian de comer, y vnos los dexavan, y otros los tomavan, y andar por su camino. Dizé que iban pensando si era en can-tamiento, ó sueño." Bernal Diaz, Hist. de la Conquista, cap. 111. — Demanda de Zavallos, MS.

2 "Ya auia tres dias que lo sabia el Moteçuma, y Cortés no sabia cosa ninguna." Bernal Diaz, Hist. de la Conquista, cap. 110.

and their whole equipment were minutely delineated. Cortés, suppressing all emotions but those of pleasure, exclaimed, " Blessed be the Redeemer for his mercies ! " On returning to his quarters, the tidings were received by the troops with loud shouts, the firing of cannon, and other demonstrations of joy. They hailed the new-comers as a reinforcement from Spain. Not so their commander. From the first, he suspected them to be sent by his enemy, the governor of Cuba. He communicated his suspicions to his officers, through whom they gradually found their way among the men. The tide of joy was instantly checked. Alarming apprehensions succeeded, as they dwelt on the probability of this suggestion and on the strength of the invaders. Yet their constancy did not desert them ; and they pledged themselves to remain true to their cause, and, come what might, to stand by their leader. It was one of those occasions that proved the entire influence which Cortés held over these wild adventurers. All doubts were soon dispelled by the arrival of the prisoners from Villa Rica.

One of the convoy, leaving the party in the suburbs, entered the city, and delivered a letter to the general from Sandoval, acquainting him with all the particulars. Cortés instantly sent to the prisoners, ordered them to be released, and furnished them with horses to make their entrance into the capital,—a more creditable conveyance than the backs of *tamanes.* On their arrival, he received them with marked courtesy, apologized for the rude conduct of his officers, and seemed desirous by the most assiduous attentions to soothe the irritation of their minds. He showed his good-will still further by lavishing presents on Guevara and his associates, until he gradually wrought such a change in their dispositions that from enemies he converted them into friends, and drew forth many important particulars respecting not merely the designs of their leader, but the feelings of his army. The soldiers, in general, they said, far from desiring a rupture with those of Cortés, would willingly co-operate with them, were it not for their commander. They had no feelings of resentment to gratify. Their object was gold. The personal influence of Narvaez was not great, and his arrogance and penurious temper had already gone far to alienate from him the affections of his followers. These hints were not lost on the general.

He addressed a letter to his rival in the most conciliatory terms. He besought him not to proclaim their animosity to the world, and, by kindling a spirit of insubordination in the natives, unsettle all that had been so far secured. A violent collision must be prejudicial even to the victor, and might be fatal to both. It was only in union that they could look for success. He was ready to greet Narvaez as a brother in arms, to share with him the fruits of conquest, and, if he could produce a royal commission, to submit to his authority. Cortés well knew he had no such commission to show.[1]

---

[1] Oviedo, Hist. de las Ind., MS., lib. 33, cap. 47.—Rel. Seg. de Cortés. ap. Lorenzana, pp. 117-120

Soon after the departure of Guevara and his comrades,[1] the general determined to send a special envoy of his own. The person selected for this delicate office was Father Olmedo, who, through the campaign, had shown a practical good sense, and a talent for affairs, not always to be found in persons of his spiritual calling. He was intrusted with another epistle to Narvaez, of similar import with the preceding. Cortés wrote, also, to the licentiate Ayllon, with whose departure he was not acquainted, and to Andres de Duero, former secretary of Velasquez, and his own friend, who had come over in the present fleet. Olmedo was instructed to converse with these persons in private, as well as with the principal officers and soldiers, and, as far as possible, to infuse into them a spirit of accommodation. To give greater weight to his arguments, he was furnished with a liberal supply of gold.

During this time, Narvaez had abandoned his original design of planting a colony on the sea-coast, and had crossed the country to Cempoalla, where he had taken up his quarters. He was here when Guevara returned and presented the letter of Cortés.

Narvaez glanced over it with a look of contempt, which was changed into one of stern displeasure as his envoy enlarged on the resources and formidable character of his rival, counselling him by all means to accept his proffers of amity. A different effect was produced on the troops, who listened with greedy ears to the accounts given of Cortés, his frank and liberal manners, which they involuntarily contrasted with those of their own commander, the wealth in his camp, where the humblest private could stake his ingot and chain of gold at play, where all revelled in plenty, and the life of the soldier seemed to be one long holiday. Guevara had been admitted only to the sunny side of the picture.

The impression made by these accounts was confirmed by the presents of Olmedo. The ecclesiastic delivered his missives, in like manner, to Narvaez, who ran through their contents with feelings of anger which found vent in the most opprobrious invectives against his rival; while one of his captains, named Salvatierra, openly avowed his attention to cut off the rebel's ears and broil them for his breakfast![2] Such impotent sallies did not alarm the stout-hearted friar, who soon entered into communication with many of the officers and soldiers, whom he found better inclined to an accommodation. His insinuating eloquence, backed by his liberal largesses, gradually opened a way into their hearts, and a party was formed, under the very eye of their chief, better affected to his rival's interests than to his own. The intrigue could not be conducted so secretly as wholly to elude the suspicions of Narvaez, who would have arrested Olmedo and placed him under confinement, but for the interposition of

---

[1] "Our commander said so many kind things to them," says Diaz, "and *anointed their fingers* so plentifully with gold, that, though they came like roaring lions, they went home perfectly tame!" Hist. de la Conquista, cap. 111.

[2] Bernal Diaz, Hist. de la Conquista, cap. 112.

Duero. He put a stop to his further machinations by sending him back again to his master. But the poison was left to do its work.

Narvaez made the same vaunt as at his landing, of his design to march against Cortés and apprehend him as a traitor. The Cempoallans learned with astonishment that their new guests, though the countrymen, were enemies of their former. Narvaez, also, proclaimed his intention to release Montezuma from captivity and restore him to his throne. It is said he received a rich present from the Aztec emperor, who entered into a correspondence with him.[1] That Montezuma should have treated him with his usual munificence, supposing him to be the friend of Cortés, is very probable. But that he should have entered into a secret communication, hostile to the general's interests, is too repugnant to the whole tenor of his conduct to be lightly admitted.

These proceedings did not escape the watchful eye of Sandoval. He gathered the particulars partly from deserters who fled to Villa Rica, and partly from his own agents, who in the disguise of natives mingled in the enemy's camp. He sent a full account of them to Cortés, acquainted him with the growing defection of the Indians, and urged him to take speedy measures for the defence of Villa Rica if he would not see it fall into the enemy's hands. The general felt that it was time to act.

Yet the selection of the course to be pursued was embarrassing in the extreme. If he remained in Mexico and awaited there the attack of his rival, it would give the latter time to gather round him the whole forces of the empire, including those of the capital itself, all willing, no doubt, to serve under the banners of a chief who proposed the liberation of their master. The odds were too great to be hazarded.

If he marched against Narvaez, he must either abandon the city and the emperor, the fruit of all his toils and triumphs, or, by leaving a garrison to hold them in awe, must cripple his strength, already far too weak to cope with that of his adversary. Yet on this latter course he decided. He trusted less, perhaps, to an open encounter of arms than to the influence of his personal address and previous intrigues, to bring about an amicable arrangement. But he prepared himself for either result.

In the preceding chapter it was mentioned that Velasquez de Leon was sent with a hundred and fifty men to plant a colony on one of the great rivers emptying into the Mexican Gulf. Cortés, on learning the arrival of Narvaez, had despatched a messenger to his officer, to acquaint him with the fact and to arrest his further progress. But Velasquez had already received notice of it from Narvaez himself, who, in a letter written

---

[1] Bernal Diaz, Hist. de la Conquista, cap. 111.— Oviedo says that Montezuma called a council of his nobles, in which it was decided to let the troops of Narvaez into the capital, and then to crush them at one blow, with those of Cortés! (Hist. de las Ind., MS., lib. 33, cap. 47.) Considering the awe in which the latter alone were held by the Mexicans, a more improbable tale could not be devised. But nothing is too improbable for history,—though, according to Boileau's maxim, it may be for fiction.

soon after his landing, had adjured him in the name of his kinsman, the governor of Cuba, to quit the banners of Cortés and come over to him. That officer, however, had long since buried the feelings of resentment which he had once nourished against his general, to whom he was now devotedly attached, and who had honoured him throughout the campaign with particular regard. Cortés had early seen the importance of securing this cavalier to his interests. Without waiting for orders, Velasquez abandoned his expedition, and commenced a countermarch on the capital, when he received the general's commands to await him in Cholula.

Cortés had also sent to the distant province of Chinantla, situated far to the south-east of Cholula, for a reinforcement of two thousand natives. They were a bold race, hostile to the Mexicans, and had offered their services to him since his residence in the metropolis. They used a long spear in battle, longer, indeed, than that borne by the Spanish or German infantry. Cortés ordered three hundred of their double-headed lances to be made for him, and to be tipped with copper instead of *itztli.* With this formidable weapon he proposed to foil the cavalry of his enemy.

The command of the garrison in his absence he intrusted to Pedro de Alvarado,—the *Tonatiuh* of the Mexicans,—a man possessed of many commanding qualities, of an intrepid though somewhat arrogant spirit, and his warm personal friend. He inculcated on him moderation and forbearance. He was to keep a close watch on Montezuma, for on the possession of the royal person rested all their authority in the land. He was to show him the deference alike due to his high station and demanded by policy. He was to pay uniform respect to the usages and the prejudices of the people; remembering that though his small force would be large enough to overawe them in times of quiet, yet should they be once roused it would be swept away like chaff before the whirlwind.

From Montezuma he exacted a promise to maintain the same friendly relations with his lieutenant which he had preserved towards himself. This, said Cortés, would be most grateful to his own master, the Spanish sovereign. Should the Aztec prince do otherwise, and lend himself to any hostile movement, he must be convinced that he would fall the first victim of it.

The emperor assured him of his continued goodwill. He was much perplexed, however, by the recent events. Were the Spaniards at his court, or those just landed, the true representatives of their sovereign? Cortés, who had hitherto maintained a reserve on the subject, now told him that the latter were indeed his countrymen, but traitors to his master. As such, it was his painful duty to march against them, and, when he had chastised their rebellion, he should return, before his departure from the land, in triumph to the capital. Montezuma offered to support him with five thousand Aztec warriors; but the general declined it, not choosing to encumber himself with a body of doubtful, perhaps disaffected, auxiliaries.

He left in garrison, under Alvarado, one hundred and forty men, two-thirds of his whole force.[1] With these remained all the artillery, the greater part of the little body of horse, and most of the arquebusiers. He took with him only seventy soldiers, but they were men of the most mettle in the army and his stanch adherents. They were lightly armed, and encumbered with as little baggage as possible. Everything depended on celerity of movement.

Montezuma, in his royal litter, borne on the shoulders of his nobles, and escorted by the whole Spanish infantry, accompanied the general to the causeway. There, embracing him in the most cordial manner, they parted, with all the external marks of mutual regard. It was about the middle of May 1520, more than six months since the entrance of the Spaniards into Mexico. During this time they had lorded it over the land with absolute sway. They were now leaving the city in hostile array, not against an Indian foe, but their own countrymen. It was the beginning of a long career of calamity,—checkered, indeed, by occasional triumphs,—which was yet to be run before the Conquest could be completed.[2]

CHAPTER VII.

CORTÉS DESCENDS FROM THE TABLE-LAND.—NEGOTIATES WITH NARVAEZ. —PREPARES TO ASSAULT HIM.—QUARTERS OF NARVAEZ.—ATTACK BY NIGHT.—NARVAEZ DEFEATED.

(1520.)

TRAVERSING the southern causeway, by which they had entered the capital, the little party were soon on their march across the beautiful Valley. They climbed the mountain screen which Nature had so ineffectually drawn around it, passed between the huge volcanoes that, like faithless watch-dogs on their posts, have long since been buried in slumber, threaded the intricate defiles where they had before experienced such bleak and tempestuous weather, and, emerging on the other side, descended the western slope which opens on the wide expanse of the fruitful plateau of Cholula. They heeded little of what they saw on their rapid march, nor whether

---

[1] In the Mexican edition of the letters of Cortés, it is called five hundred men. (Rel. Seg., ap. Lorenzana, p. 122.) But this was more than his whole Spanish force. In Ramusio's version of the same letter, printed as early as 1565, the number is stated as in the text. (Navigationi et Viaggi, fol. 244.) In an instrument without date, containing the affidavits of certain witnesses as to the management of the royal fifth by Cortés, it is said there were one hundred and fifty soldiers left in the capital under Alvarado. (Probanza fecha en la nueva España del mar océano á pedimento de Juan Ochoa

de Lexalde, en nombre de Hernando Cortés, MS.) The account in the Mexican edition is unquestionably an error.

[2] Carta de la Villa de Vera Cruz á el Emperador, MS. This letter without date was probably written in 1520.—See, also, for the preceding pages, Probanza fecha á pedimento de Juan Ochoa, MS.,—Herrera, Hist. general, dec. 2, lib. 9, cap. 1, 21; lib. 10, cap. 1,—Rel. Seg. de Cortés, ap. Lorenzana, pp. 119, 120,—Bernal Diaz, Hist. de la Conquista, cap. 112-115,—Oviedo, Hist. de las Ind., MS., lib. 33, cap. 47.

it was cold or hot. The anxiety of their minds made them indifferent to outward annoyances; and they had fortunately none to encounter from the natives, for the name of Spaniard was in itself a charm,—a better guard than helm or buckler to the bearer.

In Cholula, Cortés had the inexpressible satisfaction of meeting Velasquez de Leon, with the hundred and twenty soldiers intrusted to his command for the formation of a colony. That faithful officer had been some time at Cholula, waiting for the general's approach. Had he failed, the enterprise of Cortés must have failed also.[1] The idea of resistance, with his own handful of followers, would have been chimerical. As it was, his little band was now trebled, and acquired a confidence in proportion.

Cordially embracing their companions in arms, now knit together more closely than ever by the sense of a great and common danger, the combined troops traversed with quick step the streets of the sacred city, where many a dark pile of ruins told of their disastrous visit on the preceding autumn. They kept the highroad to Tlascala, and, at not many leagues' distance from that capital, fell in with Father Olmedo and his companions on their return from the camp of Narvaez, to which, it will be remembered, they had been sent as envoys. The ecclesiastic bore a letter from that commander, in which he summoned Cortés and his followers to submit to his authority as captain-general of the country, menacing them with condign punishment in case of refusal or delay. Olmedo gave many curious particulars of the state of the enemy's camp. Narvaez he described as puffed up by authority, and negligent of precautions against a foe whom he held in contempt. He was surrounded by a number of pompous, conceited officers, who ministered to his vanity, and whose braggart tones the good father, who had an eye for the ridiculous, imitated, to the no small diversion of Cortés and the soldiers. Many of the troops, he said, showed no great partiality for their commander, and were strongly disinclined to a rupture with their countrymen; a state of feeling much promoted by the accounts they had received of Cortés, by his own arguments and promises, and by the liberal distribution of the gold with which he had been provided. In addition to these matters, Cortés gathered much important intelligence respecting the position of the enemy's force and his general plan of operations.

At Tlascala the Spaniards were received with a frank and friendly hospitality. It is not said whether any of the Tlascalan allies had accompanied them from Mexico. If they did, they went no farther than their native city. Cortés requested a reinforcement of six hundred fresh troops to attend him on his present expedition. It was readily granted; but, before the army had proceeded many miles on its route, the Indian

---

1 So says Oviedo,—and with truth: "Si aquel capitan Juan Velasquez de Leon no estubiera mal con su pariente Diego Velasquez, é se pasara con los 150 Hombres, que havia llevado á Guaçacalco, á la parte de Pánfilo de Narvaez su cuñado, acabado oviera Cortés su oficio." Hist. de las Ind., MS., lib. 33, cap. 12.

auxiliaries fell off, one after another, and returned to their city. They had no personal feeling of animosity to gratify in the present instance, as in a war against Mexico. It may be, too, that, although intrepid in a contest with the bravest of the Indian races, they had had too fatal experience of the prowess of the white men to care to measure swords with them again. At any rate, they deserted in such numbers that Cortés dismissed the remainder at once, saying, good-humouredly, " He had rather part with them then than in the hour of trial."

The troops soon entered on that wild district in the neighbourhood of Perote, strewed with the wreck of volcanic matter, which forms so singular a contrast to the general character of beauty with which the scenery is stamped. It was not long before their eyes were gladdened by the approach of Sandoval and about sixty soldiers from the garrison of Vera Cruz, including several deserters from the enemy. It was a most important reinforcement, not more on account of the numbers of the men than of the character of the commander, in every respect one of the ablest captains in the service. He had been compelled to fetch a circuit in order to avoid falling in with the enemy, and had forced his way through thick forests and wild mountain-passes, till he had fortunately, without accident, reached the appointed place of rendezvous and stationed himself once more under the banner of his chieftain.[1]

At the same place, also, Cortés was met by Tobillos, a Spaniard whom he had sent to procure the lances from Chinantla. They were perfectly well made, after the pattern which had been given,—double-headed spears, tipped with copper, and of great length. Tobillos drilled the men in the exercise of this weapon, the formidable uses of which, especially against horse, had been fully demonstrated, towards the close of the last century, by the Swiss battalions, in their encounters with the Burgundian chivalry, the best in Europe.[2]

Cortés now took a review of his army,—if so paltry a force may be called an army,—and found their numbers were two hundred and sixty-six, only five of whom were mounted. A few muskets and crossbows were sprinkled among them. In defensive armour they were sadly deficient. They were for the most part cased in the quilted doublet of the country, thickly stuffed with cotton, the *escaupil*, recommended by its superior lightness, but which, though competent to turn the arrow of the Indian, was ineffectual against a musket-ball. Most of this cotton mail was exceedingly out of repair, giving evidence, in its unsightly gaps, of much rude service and hard blows. Few, in this emergency, but would have given almost any price—the best of the gold chains which they wore in tawdry

[1] Rel. Seg. de Cortés, ap. Lorenzana, pp. 123, 124. —Bernal Diaz, Hist. de la Conquista, cap. 115-117. —Oviedo, Hist. de las Ind., MS., lib. 33, cap. 12.
[2] But, although irresistible against cavalry, the long pike of the German proved no match for the short sword and buckler of the Spaniard, in the great battle of Ravenna, fought a few years before this, 1512. Machiavelli makes some excellent reflections on the comparative merit of these arms. Arte della Guerra, lib. 2, ap. Opere, tom. iv. p. 67.

display over their poor habiliments—for a steel morion or cuirass, to take the place of their own hacked and battered armour.[1]

Under this coarse covering, however, they bore hearts stout and courageous as ever beat in human bosoms. For they were the heroes, still invincible, of many a hard-fought field, where the odds had been incalculably against them. They had large experience of the country and of the natives, and knew well the character of their own commander, under whose eye they had been trained till every movement was in obedience to him. The whole body seemed to constitute but a single individual, in respect of unity of design and of action. Thus its real effective force was incredibly augmented; and, what was no less important, the humblest soldier felt it to be so.

The troops now resumed their march across the table-land, until reaching the eastern slope, their labours were lightened, as they descended towards the broad plains of the *tierra caliente*, spread out like a boundless ocean of verdure below them. At some fifteen leagues' distance from Cempoalla, where Narvaez, as has been noticed, had established his quarters, they were met by another embassy from that commander. It consisted of the priest, Guevara, Andres de Duero, and two or three others. Duero, the fast friend of Cortés, had been the person most instrumental, originally, in obtaining him his commission from Velasquez. They now greeted each other with a warm embrace, and it was not till after much preliminary conversation on private matters that the secretary disclosed the object of his visit.

He bore a letter from Narvaez, couched in terms somewhat different from the preceding. That officer required, indeed, the acknowledgment of his paramount authority in the land, but offered his vessels to transport all, who desired it, from the country, together with their treasures and effects, without molestation or inquiry. The more liberal tenor of these terms was, doubtless, to be ascribed to the influence of Duero. The secretary strongly urged Cortés to comply with them, as the most favourable that could be obtained, and as the only alternative affording him a chance of safety in his desperate condition. "For, however valiant your men may be, how can they expect," he asked, "to face a force so much superior in numbers and equipment as that of their antagonist?" But Cortés had set his fortunes on the cast, and he was not the man to shrink from it. "If Narvaez bears a royal commission," he returned, "I will readily submit to him. But he has produced none. He is a deputy of my rival, Velasquez. For myself, I am a servant of the king; I have conquered the country for him; and for him I and my brave followers will defend it, be assured, to the last drop of our blood. If we fall, it will be glory enough to have perished in the discharge of our duty."[2]

---

1 Bernal Diaz, Hist. de la Conquista, cap. 118.— "Tambien quiero dezir la gran necessidad que teniamos de armas, que por vn peto, ó capacete, ó casco, ó babera de hierro, dieramos aquella noche quãto nos pidiera por ello, y todo quãto auiamos ganado." Cap. 122.

2 "Yo les respondí, que no via provision de Vuestra Alteza, por donde le debiesse entregar la Tierra; é

His friend might have been somewhat puzzled to comprehend how the authority of Cortés rested on a different ground from that of Narvaez; and if they both held of the same superior, the governor of Cuba, why that dignitary should not be empowered to supersede his own officer, in case of dissatisfaction, and appoint a substitute.[1] But Cortés here reaped the full benefit of that legal fiction, if it may be so termed, by which his commission, resigned to the self-constituted municipality of Vera Cruz, was again derived through that body from the crown. The device, indeed, was too palpable to impose on any but those who chose to be blinded. Most of the army were of this number. To them it seemed to give additional confidence, in the same manner as a strip of painted canvas, when substituted, as it has sometimes been, for a real parapet of stone, has been found not merely to impose on the enemy, but to give a sort of artificial courage to the defenders concealed behind it.[2]

Duero had arranged with his friend in Cuba, when he took command of the expedition, that he himself was to have a liberal share of the profits. It is said that Cortés confirmed this arrangement at the present juncture, and made it clearly for the other's interest that he should prevail in the struggle with Narvaez. This was an important point, considering the position of the secretary.[3] From this authentic source the general derived much information respecting the designs of Narvaez, which had escaped the knowledge of Olmedo. On the departure of the envoys, Cortés intrusted them with a letter for his rival, a counterpart of that which he had received from him. This show of negotiation intimated a desire on his part to postpone, if not avoid, hostilities, which might the better put Narvaez off his guard. In the letter he summoned that commander and his followers to present themselves before him without delay, and to acknowledge his authority as the representative of his sovereign. He should otherwise be compelled to proceed against them as rebels to the crown![4] With this missive, the vaunting tone of which was intended quite as much for his own troops as the enemy, Cortés dismissed the envoys. They returned to disseminate among their comrades their

que si alguna trahia, que la presentasse ante mí, y ante el Cabildo de la Vera Cruz, segun órden, y costumbre de España, y que yo estaba presto de la obedecer, y cumplir; y que hasta tanto, por ningun interese, ni partido haria lo que él decia; ántes yo, y los que conmigo estaban, moririamos en defensa de la Tierra, pues la habiamos ganado, y tenido por Vuestra Magestad pacífica, y segura, y por no ser Traydores y desleales á nuestro Rey. . . . Considerando, que morir en servicio de mi Rey, y por defender, y amparar sus Tierras, y no las dejar usurpar, á mí, y á los de mi Compañía se nos seguia farta gloria." Rel. Seg. de Cortés, ap. Lorenzana, pp. 125-127.

[1] Such are the natural reflections of Oviedo, speculating on the matter some years later. "É tambien que me parece donaire, ó no bastante la escusa que Cortés da para fundar é justificar su negocio, que es decir, que el Narvaez presentase las provisiones que llevaba de S. M. Como si el dicho Cortés oviera ido á aquella tierra por mandado de S M. ó con nuas, ni tanta autoridad como llebaba

Narvaez; pues que es claro é notorio, que el Adelantado Diego Velasquez, que embió á Cortés, era parte, segun derecho, para le embiar á remover, y el Cortés obligado á le obedecer. No quiero decir mas en esto por no ser odioso á ninguna de las partes." Hist. de las Ind., MS., lib. 33, cap. 12.

[2] More than one example of this *ruse* is mentioned by Mariana in Spanish history, though the precise passages have escaped my memory.

[3] Bernal Diaz, Hist. de la Conquista, cap. 119.

[4] "É assimismo mandaba, y mandé por el dicho Mandamiento á todas las Personas, que con el dicho Narvaez estaban, que no tubiessen, ni obedeciessen al dicho Narvaez por tal Capitan, ni Justicia; ántes, dentro de cierto término, que en el dicho Mandamiento señalé, pareciessen ante mí, para que yo les dijesse, lo que debian hacer en servicio de Vuestra Alteza: con protestacion, que lo contrario haciendo, procederia contra ellos, como contra Traydores, y aleves, y malos Vasallos, que se rebelaban contra su Rey, y quieren usurpar sus Tierras, y Señoríos." Rel. Seg. de Cortés, ap. Lorenzana, p. 127.

admiration of the general, and of his unbounded liberality, of which he took care they should experience full measure, and they dilated on the riches of his adherents, who, over their wretched attire, displayed, with ostentatious profusion, jewels, ornaments of gold, collars, and massive chains winding several times round their necks and bodies, the rich spoil of the treasury of Montezuma.

The army now took its way across the level plains of the *tierra caliente*, on which Nature has exhausted all the wonders of creation; it was covered more thickly then than at the present day with noble forests, where the towering cottonwood-tree, the growth of ages, stood side by side with the light bamboo or banana, the product of a season, each in its way attesting the marvellous fecundity of the soil, while innumerable creeping flowers, muffling up the giant branches of the trees, waved in bright festoons above their heads, loading the air with odours. But the senses of the Spaniards were not open to the delicious influences of nature. Their minds were occupied by one idea.

Coming upon an open reach of meadow, of some extent, they were at length stopped by a river, or rather stream, called *Rio de Canoas*, "the River of Canoes," of no great volume ordinarily, but swollen at this time by excessive rains. It had rained hard that day, although at intervals the sun had broken forth with intolerable fervour, affording a good specimen of those alternations of heat and moisture which give such activity to vegetation in the tropics, where the process of forcing seems to be always going on.

The river was about a league distant from the camp of Narvaez. Before seeking out a practicable ford by which to cross it, Cortés allowed his men to recruit their exhausted strength by stretching themselves on the ground. The shades of evening had gathered round; and the rising moon, wading through dark masses of cloud, shone with a doubtful and interrupted light. It was evident that the storm had not yet spent its fury.[1] Cortés did not regret this. He had made up his mind to an assault that very night, and in the darkness and uproar of the tempest his movements would be most effectually concealed.

Before disclosing his design, he addressed his men in one of those stirring, soldierly harangues to which he had recourse in emergencies of great moment, as if to sound the depths of their hearts, and, where any faltered, to reanimate them with his own heroic spirit. He briefly recapitulated the great events of the campaign, the dangers they had surmounted, the victories they had achieved over the most appalling odds, the glorious spoil they had won. But of this they were now to be defrauded; not by men holding a legal warrant from the crown, but by adventurers, with no better title than that of superior force. They had established a claim on the gratitude of their country and their sovereign. This claim was now

---

[1] " Y aun llouia de rato en rato, y entonces salia la Luna, que quãdo allí llegámos hazia muy escuro, y llouia, y tambien la escuridad ayudó." Hist. de la Conquista, cap. 122.

to be dishonoured, their very services were converted into crimes, and their names branded with infamy as those of traitors. But the time had at last come for vengeance. God would not desert the soldier of the Cross. Those whom he had carried victorious through greater dangers would not be left to fail now. And, if they should fail, better to die like brave men on the field of battle, than, with fame and fortune cast away, to perish ignominiously like slaves on the gibbet. This last point he urged home upon his hearers; well knowing there was not one among them so dull as not to be touched by it.

They responded with hearty acclamations, and Velasquez de Leon, and de Lugo, in the name of the rest, assured their commander, if they failed, it should be his fault, not theirs. They would follow wherever he led. The general was fully satisfied with the temper of his soldiers, as he felt that his difficulty lay not in awakening their enthusiasm, but in giving it a right direction. One thing is remarkable. He made no allusion to the defection which he knew existed in the enemy's camp. He would have his soldiers, in this last pinch, rely on nothing but themselves.

He announced his purpose to attack the enemy that very night, when he should be buried in slumber, and the friendly darkness might throw a veil over their own movements and conceal the poverty of their numbers. To this the troops, jaded though they were by incessant marching, and half famished, joyfully assented. In their situation, suspense was the worst of evils. He next distributed the commands among his captains. To Gonzalo de Sandoval he assigned the important office of taking Narvaez. He was commanded, as *alguacil mayor*, to seize the person of that officer as a rebel to his sovereign, and, if he made resistance, to kill him on the spot.[1] He was provided with sixty picked men to aid him in this difficult task, supported by several of the ablest captains, among whom were two of the Alvarados, de Avila, and Ordaz. The largest division of the force was placed under Cristóval de Olid, or, according to some authorities, of Pizarro, one of that family so renowned in the subsequent conquest of Peru. He was to get possession of the artillery, and to cover the assault of Sandoval by keeping those of the enemy at bay who would interfere with it. Cortés reserved only a body of twenty men for himself, to act on any point that occasion might require. The watchword was *Espíritu Santo*, it being the evening of Whitsunday. Having made these arrangements, he prepared to cross the river.[2]

During the interval thus occupied by Cortés, Narvaez had remained at Cempoalla, passing his days in idle and frivolous amusement. From this he was at length roused, after the return of Duero, by the remonstrances

---

[1] The Attorney of Narvaez, in his complaint before the crown, expatiates on the diabolical enormity of these instructions. "El dho Fernando Corttés como traidor aleboso, sin apercibir al dho mi partte, con un diabólico pensamto é infernal osadía, en contemtto é menosprecio de V. M. ó de sus provisiones R.ˢ, no mirando ni asattando la lealtad qᵉ debia á V. M., el dho Corttés dió un

Mandamienitto al dho Gonzalo de Sandobal para que prendiese al dho Pánfilo de Narvaez, é si se defendiese qᵉ lo mattase." Demanda de Zavallos en nombre de Narvaez, MS.

[2] Oviedo, Hist. de las Ind., MS., lib. 33, cap. 12, 47.—Bernal Diaz, Hist. de la Conquista, cap. 122. — Herrera, Hist. general, dec. 2, lib. 10, cap. 1.

of the old cacique of the city. "Why are you so heedless?" exclaimed the latter; "do you think Malinche is so? Depend on it, he knows your situation exactly, and when you least dream of it, he will be upon you." [1]

Alarmed at these suggestions and those of his friends, Narvaez at length put himself at the head of his troops, and, on the very day on which Cortés arrived at the River of Canoes, sallied out to meet him. But, when he had reached this barrier, Narvaez saw no sign of an enemy. The rain, which fell in torrents, soon drenched the soldiers to the skin. Made somewhat effeminate by their long and luxurious residence at Cempoalla, they murmured at their uncomfortable situation. "Of what use was it to remain there fighting with the elements? There was no sign of an enemy, and little reason to apprehend his approach in such tempestuous weather. It would be wiser to return to Cempoalla, and in the morning they should be all fresh for action, should Cortés make his appearance."

Narvaez took counsel of these advisers, or rather of his own inclinations. Before retracing his steps, he provided against surprise by stationing a couple of sentinels at no great distance from the river, to give notice of the approach of Cortés. He also detached a body of forty horse in another direction, by which he thought it not improbable the enemy might advance on Cempoalla. Having taken these precautions, he fell back again before night on his own quarters.

He there occupied the principal *teocalli.* It consisted of a stone building on the usual pyramidal basis; and the ascent was by a flight of steep steps on one of the faces of the pyramid. In the edifice or sanctuary above he stationed himself with a strong party of arquebusiers and cross-bowmen. Two other *teocallis* in the same area were garrisoned by large detachments of infantry. His artillery, consisting of seventeen or eighteen small guns, he posted in the area below, and protected it by the remainder of his cavalry. When he had thus distributed his forces, he returned to his own quarters, and soon after to repose, with as much indifference as if his rival had been on the other side of the Atlantic, instead of a neighbouring stream.

That stream was now converted by the deluge of waters into a furious torrent. It was with difficulty that a practicable ford could be found. The slippery stones, rolling beneath the feet, gave way at every step. The difficulty of the passage was much increased by the darkness and driving tempest. Still, with their long pikes, the Spaniards contrived to make good their footing,—at least, all but two, who were swept down by the fury of the current. When they had reached the opposite side, they had new impediments to encounter, in traversing a road, never good, now made doubly difficult by the deep mire, and the tangled brushwood with which it was overrun.

---

[1] "Que hazeis, que estais mui descuidado? pensais que Malinche, y los Teules que trae cōsigo, que son assí como vosotros? Pues yo os digo, que quādo no os cataredes, será aquí, y os matará." Bernal Diaz, Hist. de la Conquista, cap. 121.

Here they met with a cross, which had been raised by them on their former march into the interior. They hailed it as a good omen; and Cortés, kneeling before the blessed sign, confessed his sins, and declared his great object to be the triumph of the holy Catholic faith. The army followed his example, and, having made a general confession, received absolution from Father Olmedo, who invoked the blessing of Heaven on the warriors who had consecrated their swords to the glory of the Cross. Then rising up and embracing one another, as companions in the good cause, they found themselves wonderfully invigorated and refreshed. The incident is curious, and well illustrates the character of the time,—in which war, religion, and rapine were so intimately blended together. Adjoining the road was a little coppice; and Cortés, and the few who had horses, dismounting, fastened the animals to the trees, where they might find some shelter from the storm. They deposited there, too, their baggage, and such superfluous articles as would encumber their movements. The general then gave them a few last words of advice. "Everything," said he, "depends on obedience. Let no man, from desire of distinguishing himself, break his ranks. On silence, despatch, and, above all, obedience to your officers, the success of our enterprise depends."

Silently and stealthily they held on their way, without beat of drum or sound of trumpet, when they suddenly came on the two sentinels who had been stationed by Narvaez to give notice of their approach. This had been so noiseless that the vedettes were both of them surprised on their post, and one only, with difficulty, effected his escape. The other was brought before Cortés. Every effort was made to draw from him some account of the present position of Narvaez. But the man remained obstinately silent; and, though threatened with the gibbet, and having a noose actually drawn round his neck, his Spartan heroism was not to be vanquished. Fortunately, no change had taken place in the arrangements of Narvaez since the intelligence previously derived from Duero.

The other sentinel, who had escaped, carried the news of the enemy's approach to the camp. But his report was not credited by the lazy soldiers whose slumbers he had disturbed. "He had been deceived by his fears," they said, "and mistaken the noise of the storm and the waving of the bushes for the enemy. Cortés and his men were far enough on the other side of the river, which they would be slow to cross in such a night." Narvaez himself shared in the same blind infatuation, and the discredited sentinel slunk abashed to his own quarters, vainly menacing them with the consequences of their incredulity.[1]

Cortés, not doubting that the sentinel's report must alarm the enemy's camp, quickened his pace. As he drew near, he discerned a light in one of the lofty towers of the city. "It is the quarters of Narvaez," he

---

[1] Rel. Seg. de Cortés, ap. Lorenzana, p. 128.—Oviedo, Hist. de las Ind., MS., lib. 33, cap. 47.—Herrera, Hist. general, dec. 2, lib. 10, cap. 2, 3.

exclaimed to Sandoval, "and that light must be your beacon." On entering the suburbs, the Spaniards were surprised to find no one stirring, and no symptom of alarm. Not a sound was to be heard except the measured tread of their own footsteps, half drowned in the howling of the tempest. Still they could not move so stealthily as altogether to elude notice, as they defiled through the streets of this populous city. The tidings were quickly conveyed to the enemy's quarters, where in an instant all was bustle and confusion. The trumpets sounded to arms. The dragoons sprang to their steeds, the artillerymen to their guns. Narvaez hastily buckled on his armour, called his men around him, and summoned those in the neighbouring *teocallis* to join him in the area. He gave his orders with coolness; for, however wanting in prudence, he was not deficient in presence of mind, or courage.

All this was the work of a few minutes. But in those minutes the Spaniards had reached the avenue leading to the camp. Cortés ordered his men to keep close to the walls of the buildings, that the cannon-shot might pass between the two files.[1] No sooner had they presented themselves before the enclosure, than the artillery of Narvaez opened a general fire. Fortunately, the pieces were pointed so high that most of the balls passed over their heads, and three men only were struck down. They did not give the enemy time to reload. Cortés shouting the watchword of the night, "Espíritu Santo! Espíritu Santo! Upon them!" in a moment Olid and his division rushed on the artillerymen, whom they pierced or knocked down with their pikes, and got possession of their guns. Another division engaged the cavalry, and made a diversion in favour of Sandoval, who with his gallant little band sprang up the great stairway of the temple. They were received with a shower of missiles, —arrows and musket-balls, which, in the hurried aim, and the darkness of the night, did little mischief. The next minute the assailants were on the platform, engaged hand to hand with their foes. Narvaez fought bravely in the midst, encouraging his followers. His standard-bearer fell by his side, run through the body. He himself received several wounds; for his short sword was no match for the long pikes of the assailants. At length he received a blow from a spear, which struck out his left eye. "Santa María!" exclaimed the unhappy man, "I am slain!" The cry was instantly taken up by the followers of Cortés, who shouted "Victory!"

Disabled, and half mad with agony from his wound, Narvaez was withdrawn by his men into the sanctuary. The assailants endeavoured to force an entrance, but it was stoutly defended. At length a soldier, getting possession of a torch or firebrand, flung it on the thatched roof, and in a few moments the combustible materials of which it was composed were in a

---

[1] "Ya que se acercaban al Aposento de Narvaez, Cortés, que andaba reconociendo, i ordenando á todas partes, dixo á la Tropa de Sandoval : Señores, arrimaos á las dos aceras de la Calle, para que las balas del Artillería pasen por medio, sin hacer daño." Herrera, Hist. general, dec. 2, lib. 10, cap. 3.

blaze. Those within were driven out by the suffocating heat and smoke. A soldier named Farfan grappled with the wounded commander, and easily brought him to the ground; when he was speedily dragged down the steps, and secured with fetters. His followers, seeing the fate of their chief, made no further resistance.[1]

During this time, Cortés and the troops of Olid had been engaged with the cavalry, and had discomfited them, after some ineffectual attempts on the part of the latter to break through the dense array of pikes, by which several of their number were unhorsed and some of them slain. The general then prepared to assault the other *teocallis*, first summoning the garrisons to surrender. As they refused, he brought up the heavy guns to bear on them, thus turning the artillery against its own masters. He accompanied this menacing movement with offers of the most liberal import ; an amnesty for the past, and a full participation in all the advantages of the Conquest. One of the garrisons was under the command of Salvatierra, the same officer who talked of cutting off the ears of Cortés. From the moment he had learned the fate of his own general, the hero was seized with a violent fit of illness which disabled him from further action. The garrison waited only for one discharge of the ordnance, when they accepted the terms of capitulation. Cortés, it is said, received, on this occasion, support from an unexpected auxiliary. The air was filled with the *cocuyos*,—a species of large beetle which emits an intense phosphoric light from its body, strong enough to enable one to read by it. These wandering fires, seen in the darkness of the night, were converted, by the excited imaginations of the besieged, into an army with matchlocks ! Such is the report of an eyewitness.[2] But the facility with which the enemy surrendered may quite as probably be referred to the cowardice of the commander, and the disaffection of the soldiers, not unwilling to come under the banners of Cortés.

The body of cavalry, posted, it will be remembered, by Narvaez, on one of the roads to Cempoalla, to intercept his rival, having learned what had been passing, were not long in tendering their submission. Each of the soldiers in the conquered army was required, in token of his obedience, to deposit his arms in the hands of the alguacils, and to take the oaths to Cortés as Chief Justice and Captain-General of the colony.

The number of the slain is variously reported. It seems probable that not more than twelve perished on the side of the vanquished, and of the victors half that number. The small amount may be explained by the short duration of the action, and the random aim of the missiles in the darkness. The number of the wounded was much more considerable.[3]

---

[1] Demanda de Zavallos en nombre de Narvaez, MS.—Oviedo, Hist. de las Ind., MS., lib. 33, cap. 47;

[2] "Como hazia tan escuro auia muchos cocayos (ansí los llaman en Cuba) que relumbrauan de noche, é los de Narvaez creyéron que erā muchas de las escopetas." Bernal Diaz, Hist. de la Conquista, cap. 122.

[3] Narvaez, or rather his attorney, swells the amount of slain on his own side much higher. But it was his cue to magnify the mischief sustained by his employer. The collation of this account with

The field was now completely won. A few brief hours had sufficed to change the condition of Cortés from that of a wandering outlaw at the head of a handful of needy adventurers, a rebel with a price upon his head, to that of an independent chief, with a force at his disposal strong enough not only to secure his present conquests, but to open a career for still loftier ambition. While the air rang with the acclamations of the soldiery, the victorious general, assuming a deportment corresponding with his change of fortune, took his seat in a chair of state, and, with a rich, embroidered mantle thrown over his shoulders, received, one by one, the officers and soldiers, as they came to tender their congratulations. The privates were graciously permitted to kiss his hand. The officers he noticed with words of compliment or courtesy; and when Duero, Bermudez, the treasurer, and some others of the vanquished party, his old friends, presented themselves, he cordially embraced them.[1]

Narvaez, Salvatierra, and two or three of the other hostile leaders were led before him in chains. It was a moment of deep humiliation for the former commander, in which the anguish of the body, however keen, must have been forgotten in that of the spirit. "You have great reason, Señor Cortés," said the discomfited warrior, "to thank Fortune for having given you the day so easily, and put me in your power." "I have much to be thankful for," replied the general; "but for my victory over you, I esteem it as one of the least of my achievements since my coming into the country!"[2] He then ordered the wounds of the prisoners to be cared for, and sent them under a strong guard to Vera Cruz.

Notwithstanding the proud humility of his reply, Cortés could scarcely have failed to regard his victory over Narvaez as one of the most brilliant achievements in his career. With a few scores of followers, badly clothed, worse fed, wasted by forced marches, under every personal disadvantage, deficient in weapons and military stores, he had attacked in their own quarters, routed, and captured the entire force of the enemy, thrice his superior in numbers, well provided with cavalry and artillery, admirably equipped, and complete in all the munitions of war! The amount of troops engaged on either side was, indeed, inconsiderable. But the proportions are not affected by this; and the relative strength of the parties made a result so decisive one of the most remarkable events in the annals of war.

---

those of Cortés and his followers affords the best means of approximation to the truth. " É allí le mattáron quince hombres qᵉ muriéron de las feridas qᵉ les diéron é les quemáron seis hombres del dho Incendio qᵉ despues pareciéron las cabezas de ellos quemadas, é pusiéron á sacomano todo quantto ttenian los que benian con el dho mi partte como si fueran Moros y al dho mi partte robáron é saque-áron todos sus vienes, oro, é Platta é Joyas." Demanda de Zavallos en nombre de Narvaez, MS.

[1] " Entre ellos venia Andres de Duero, y Agustin Bermudez, y muchos amigos de nuestro Capitã, y assí como veniã, ivan á besar las manos á Cortés, q̃ estaua sentado en vna silla de caderas, con vna ropa larga de color como narãjada, cõ sus armas debaxo, acõpañado de nosotros. Pues ver la gracia con que les hablaua, y abraçaua, y las palabras de tãtos cumplimiẽtos que les dezia, era cosa de ver que alegre estaua : y tenia mucha razon de verse en aquel pũto tan señor, y pujãte : y assí como le besauã la mano, se fuéró cada vno á su posada." Bernal Diaz, Hist. de la Conquista, cap. 122.

[2] Ibid., loc. cit.—"Dixose que como Narvaez vido á Cortés estando así preso le dixo : Señor Cortés, tened en mucho la ventura que habeis tenido, é lo mucho que habeis hecho en tener mi persona, ó en tomar mi persona. É que Cortés le respondió, é dixo : Lo menos que yo he hecho en esta tierra donde estais, es haberos prendido : é luego le hizo poner á buen recaudo é le tubo mucho tiempo preso." Oviedo, Hist. de las Ind., MS., lib. 33, cap. 47.

It is true there were some contingencies on which the fortunes of the day depended, that could not be said to be entirely within his control. Something was the work of chance. If Velasquez de Leon, for example, had proved false, the expedition must have failed.[1] If the weather, on the night of the attack, had been fair, the enemy would have had certain notice of his approach, and been prepared for it. But these are the chances that enter more or less into every enterprise. He is the skilful general who knows how to turn them to account; to win the smiles of Fortune, and make even the elements fight on his side.

If Velasquez de Leon was, as it proved, the very officer whom the general should have trusted with the command, it was his sagacity which originally discerned this and selected him for it. It was his address that converted this dangerous foe into a friend, and one so fast that in the hour of need he chose rather to attach himself to his desperate fortunes than to those of the governor of Cuba, powerful as the latter was, and his near kinsman. It was the same address which gained Cortés such an ascendency over his soldiers and knit them to him so closely that in the darkest moment not a man offered to desert him.[2] If the success of the assault may be ascribed mainly to the dark and stormy weather which covered it, it was owing to him that he was in a condition to avail himself of this. The shortest possible time intervened between the conception of his plan and its execution. In a very few days he descended by extraordinary marches from the capital to the sea-coast. He came like a torrent from the mountains, pouring on the enemy's camp, and sweeping everything away, before a barrier could be raised to arrest it. This celerity of movement, the result of a clear head and determined will, has entered into the strategy of the greatest captains, and forms a prominent feature in their most brilliant military exploits. It was undoubtedly in the present instance a great cause of success.

But it would be taking a limited view of the subject to consider the battle which decided the fate of Narvaez as wholly fought at Cempoalla. It was begun in Mexico. With that singular power which he exercised over all who came near him, Cortés converted the very emissaries of Narvaez into his own friends and agents. The reports of Guevara and his companions, the intrigues of Father Olmedo, and the general's gold, were

---

[1] Oviedo says that military men discussed whether Velasquez de Leon should have obeyed the commands of Cortés rather than those of his kinsman, the governor of Cuba. They decided in favour of the former, on the ground of his holding his commission immediately from him. "Visto he platicar sobre esto á caballeros é personas militares sobre si este Juan Velasquez de Leon hizo lo que debia, en acudir ó no á Diego Velasquez, ó al Pánfilo en su nombre; É combienen los veteranos milites, é á mi parecer determinan bien la question, en que si Juan Velasquez tubo conducta de capitan para que con aquella Gente que él le dió ó toviese en aquella tierra como capitan particular le acudiese á él ó á quien le mandase. Juan Velasquez faltó á lo que era obligado en no pasar á Pánfilo de Narvaez siendo requerido de Diego Velasquez, mas si le hizo capitan Hernando Cortés, é le dió él la Gente, á él havia de acudir, como acudió, excepto si viera carta, á mandamiento expreso del Rey en contrario." Hist. de las Ind., MS., lib. 33, cap. 12.

[2] This ascendency the thoughtful Oviedo refers to his dazzling and liberal manners, so strongly contrasted with those of the governor of Cuba. "En lo demas valerosa persona ha seido, é para mucho; y este deseo de mandar juntamente con que fué mui bien partido é gratificador de los que le viniéron, fué mucha causa juntamente con ser mal quisto Diego Velasquez, para que Cortés se saliese con lo que emprendió, é se quedase en el oficio, é governacion." Hist. de las Ind., MS., lib. 33, cap. 12.

all busiiy at work to shake the loyalty of the soldiers, and the battle was half won before a blow had been struck. It was fought quite as much with gold as with steel. Cortés understood this so well that he made it his great object to seize the person of Narvaez. In such an event, he had full confidence that indifference to their own cause and partiality to himself would speedily bring the rest of the army under his banner. He was not deceived. Narvaez said truly enough, therefore, some years after this event, that "he had been beaten by his own troops, not by those of his rival; that his followers had been bribed to betray him."[1] This affords the only explanation of their brief and ineffectual resistance.

CHAPTER VIII.

DISCONTENT OF THE TROOPS.—INSURRECTION IN THE CAPITAL.—RETURN OF CORTÉS.—GENERAL SIGNS OF HOSTILITY.—MASSACRE BY ALVARADO. —RISING OF THE AZTECS.

(1520.)

THE tempest, that had raged so wildly during the night, passed away with the morning, which rose bright and unclouded on the field of battle. As the light advanced, it revealed more strikingly the disparity of the two forces so lately opposed to each other. Those of Narvaez could not conceal their chagrin; and murmurs of displeasure became audible, as they contrasted their own superior numbers and perfect appointments with the wayworn visages and rude attire of their handful of enemies! It was with some satisfaction, therefore, that the general beheld his dusky allies from Chinantla, two thousand in number, arrive upon the field. They were a fine, athletic set of men; and, as they advanced in a sort of promiscuous order, so to speak, with their gay banners of feather-work, and their long lances tipped with *itztli* and copper glistening in the morning sun, they had something of an air of military discipline. They came too late for the action, indeed, but Cortés was not sorry to exhibit to his new followers the extent of his resources in the country. As he had now no occasion for his Indian allies, after a courteous reception and a liberal recompense he dismissed them to their homes.[2]

---

[1] It was in a conversation with Oviedo himself, at Toledo, in 1525, in which Narvaez descanted with much bitterness, as was natural, on his rival's conduct. The gossip, which has never appeared in print, may have some interest for the Spanish reader. "Que el año de 1525, estando Cesar en la cibdad de Toledo, ví allí al dicho Narvaez, é publicamente decia, que Cortés era vr. traidor: É que dándole S. M. licencia se lo haria conocer de su persona á la suya, é que era hombre sin verdad, é otras muchas é feas palabras llamándole alevoso é tirano, é ingrato á su Señor, é á quien le havia embiado á la Nueva España, que era el Adelantado Diego Velasquez á su propia costa, é se le havia alzado con la tierra, é con la Gente é Hacienda, é otras muchas cosas que mal sonaban. Y en la manera de su prision la contaba mui al reves de lo que está dicho. Lo que yo noto de esto es, que con todo lo que oí á Narvaez, (como yo se lo dixe) no puedo hallarle desculpa para su descuido, porque ninguna necesidad tenia de andar con Cortés en pláticas, sino estar en vela mejor que la que hizo. É á esto decia él que le havian vendido aquellos de quien se fiaba, que Cortés le havia sobornado." Oviedo, Hist. de las Ind., MS., lib. 33, cap. 12.

[2] Herrera, Hist. general, dec. 2, lib. 10, cap. 6.— Oviedo, Hist. de las Ind., MS., lib. 33, cap. 47.— Bernal Diaz, Hist. de la Conquista, cap. 123.

He then used his utmost endeavours to allay the discontent of the troops. He addressed them in his most soft and insinuating tones, and was by no means frugal of his promises.[1] He suited the action to the word. There were few of them but had lost their accoutrements or their baggage, or horses taken and appropriated by the victors. This last article was in great request among the latter, and many a soldier, weary with the long marches hitherto made on foot, had provided himself, as he imagined, with a much more comfortable as well as creditable conveyance for the rest of the campaign. The general now commanded everything to be restored.[2] "They were embarked in the same cause," he said, "and should share with one another equally." He went still further, and distributed among the soldiers of Narvaez a quantity of gold and other precious commodities gathered from the neighbouring tribes or found in his rival's quarters.[3]

These proceedings, however politic in reference to his new followers, gave great disgust to his old. "Our commander," they cried, "has forsaken his friends for his foes. We stood by him in his hour of distress, and are rewarded with blows and wounds, while the spoil goes to our enemies!" The indignant soldiery commissioned the priest Olmedo and Alonso de Avila to lay their complaints before Cortés. The ambassadors stated them without reserve, comparing their commander's conduct to the ungrateful proceeding of Alexander, who, when he gained a victory, usually gave away more to his enemies than to the troops who enabled him to beat them. Cortés was greatly perplexed. Victorious or defeated, his path seemed equally beset with difficulties.

He endeavoured to soothe their irritation by pleading the necessity of the case. "Our new comrades," he said, "are formidable from their numbers, so much so that we are even now much more in their power than they are in ours. Our only security is to make them not merely confederates, but friends. On any cause of disgust, we shall have the whole battle to fight over again, and, if they are united, under a much greater disadvantage than before. I have considered your interests," he added, "as much as my own. All that I have is yours. But why should there be any ground for discontent, when the whole country, with its riches, is before us? And our augmented strength must henceforth secure the undisturbed control of it."

But Cortés did not rely wholly on argument for the restoration of tranquillity. He knew this to be incompatible with inaction, and he made arrangements to divide his forces at once and to employ them on distant

---

[1] Diaz, who had often listened to it, thus notices his eloquence: "Comenzó vn parlamento por tan lindo estilo, y plática, tãbiẽ dichas cierto otras palabras mas sabrosas, y llenas de ofertas, q̃ yo aqui no sabré escriuir." Hist. de la Conquista, cap. 122.

[2] Captain Diaz had secured for his share of the spoil of the Philistines, as he tells us, a very good horse with all his accoutrements, a brace of swords,

three daggers, and a buckler,—a very beautiful outfit for the campaign. The general's orders were, naturally enough, not at all to his taste. Ibid., cap. 124.

[3] Narvaez alleges that Cortés plundered him of property to the value of 100,000 castellanos of gold! (Demanda de Zavallos en nombre de Narvaez, MS.) If so, the pillage of the leader may have supplied the means of liberality to the privates.

services. He selected a detachment of two hundred men, under Diego de Ordaz, whom he ordered to form the settlement before meditated on the Coatzacualco. A like number was sent with Velasquez de Leon, to secure the province of Panuco, some three degrees to the north, on the Mexican Gulf. Twenty in each detachment were drafted from his own veterans.

Two hundred men he despatched to Vera Cruz, with orders to have the rigging, iron, and everything portable on board of the fleet of Narvaez, brought on shore, and the vessels completely dismantled. He appointed a person named Cavallero superintendent of the marine, with instructions that if any ships hereafter should enter the port they should be dismantled in like manner, and their officers imprisoned on shore.[1]

But, while he was thus occupied with new schemes of discovery and conquest, he received such astounding intelligence from Mexico as compelled him to concentrate all his faculties and his forces on that one point. The city was in a state of insurrection. No sooner had the struggle with his rival been decided, than Cortés despatched a courier with the tidings to the capital. In less than a fortnight the messenger returned with a letter from Alvarado, conveying the alarming information that the Mexicans were in arms and had vigorously assaulted the Spaniards in their own quarters. The enemy, he added, had burned the brigantines, by which Cortés had secured the means of retreat in case of the destruction of the bridges. They had attempted to force the defences, and had succeeded in partially undermining them, and they had overwhelmed the garrison with a tempest of missiles, which had killed several and wounded a great number. The letter concluded with beseeching the commander to hasten to the relief of his men, if he would save them or keep his hold on the capital.

These tidings were a heavy blow to the general,—the heavier, it seemed, coming as they did in the hour of triumph, when he had thought to have all his enemies at his feet. There was no room for hesitation. To lose his footing in the capital, the noblest city in the Western World, would be to lose the country itself, which looked up to it as its head.[2] He opened the matter fully to his soldiers, calling on all who would save their countrymen to follow him. All declared their readiness to go; showing an alacrity, says Diaz, which some would have been slow to manifest had they foreseen the future.

Cortés now made preparations for instant departure. He countermanded the orders previously given to Velasquez and Ordaz, and directed them to join him with their forces at Tlascala. He called

[1] Demanda de Zavallos en nombre de Narvaez, MS —Bernal Diaz, Hist. de la Conquista, cap. 124. —Oviedo, Hist. de las Ind., MS., lib. 33, cap. 47. —Rel. Seg. de Cortés, ap. Lorenzana, p. 130.— Camargo, Hist. de Tlascala, MS.—The visit of Narvaez left melancholy traces among the natives, that made it long remembered. A negro in his suite brought with him the smallpox. The disease spread rapidly in that quarter of the country, and great numbers of the Indian population soon fell victims to it. Herrera, Hist. general, dec. 2, lib. 10, cap. 6.

[2] " Se perdia la mejor, y mas Noble Ciudad de todo lo nuevamente descubierto del Mundo ; y ella perdida, se perdia todo lo que estaba ganado, por ser la Cabeza de todo, y á quien todos obedecian." Rel. Seg. de Cortés, ap. Lorenzana, p. 131.

Fac-Simile of the Signature of Cortes.

*The above signature (*Fernando Cortes*) together with the* ☩ *rubrica* ☩ *or flourish which forms an indispensable appendage to a Spanish name, was the Conqueror's signature before he was made* Marquess of The Valley of Oaxaca. *It is not easy to meet with it, as after that time he always subscribed himself by his TITLE.*

the troops from Vera Cruz, leaving only a hundred men in garrison there, under command of one Rodrigo Rangre ; for he could not spare the services of Sandoval at this crisis. He left his sick and wounded at Cempoalla, under charge of a small detachment, directing that they should follow as soon as they were in marching order. Having completed these arrangements, he set out from Cempoalla, well supplied with provisions by its hospitable cacique, who attended him some leagues on his way. The Totonac chief seems to have had an amiable facility of accommodating himself to the powers that were in the ascendant.

Nothing worthy of notice occurred during the first part of the march. The troops everywhere met with a friendly reception from the peasantry, who readily supplied their wants. For some time before reaching Tlascala, the route lay through a country thinly settled ; and the army experienced considerable suffering from want of food, and still more from that of water. Their distress increased to an alarming degree, as, in the hurry of their forced march, they travelled with the meridian sun beating fiercely on their heads. Several faltered by the way, and, throwing themselves down by the roadside, seemed incapable of further effort, and almost indifferent to life.

In this extremity, Cortés sent forward a small detachment of horse to procure provisions in Tlascala, and speedily followed in person. On arriving, he found abundant supplies already prepared by the hospitable natives. They were sent back to the troops ; the stragglers were collected one by one ; refreshments were administered ; and the army, restored in strength and spirits, entered the republican capital.

Here they gathered little additional news respecting the events in Mexico, which a popular rumour attributed to the secret encouragement and machinations of Montezuma. Cortés was commodiously lodged in the quarters of Maxixca, one of the four chiefs of the republic. They readily furnished him with two thousand troops. There was no want of heartiness, when the war was with their ancient enemy the Aztec.[1]

The Spanish commander, on reviewing his forces after the junction with his two captains, found that they amounted to about a thousand foot, and one hundred horse, besides the Tlascalan levies.[2] In the infantry were nearly a hundred arquebusiers, with as many crossbowmen ; and the part of the army brought over by Narvaez was admirably equipped. It was inferior, however, to his own veterans in what is better than any outward appointments,—military training, and familiarity with the peculiar service in which they were engaged.

Leaving these friendly quarters, the Spaniards took a more northerly

[1] Rel. Seg. de Cortés, ap. Lorenzana, p. 131.— Oviedo, Hist. de las Ind., MS., lib. 33, cap. 13, 14. —Bernal Diaz, Hist. de la Conquista, cap. 124, 125. Peter Martyr, De Orbe Novo, dec. 5, cap. 5.— Camargo, Hist. de Tlascala, MS.

[2] Gomara, Crónica, cap. 103.—Herrera, Hist. general, dec. 2, lib. 10, cap. 7.—Bernal Diaz raises the amount to 1300 foot and 96 horse. (Hist. de la Conquista, cap. 125.) Cortés diminishes it to less than half that number. (Rel. Seg., ubi supra.) The estimate cited in the text from the two preceding authorities corresponds nearly enough with that already given from official documents of the forces of Cortés and Narvaez before the junction.

route, as more direct than that by which they had before penetrated into the Valley. It was the road to Tezcuco. It still compelled them to climb the same bold range of the Cordilleras, which attains its greatest elevation in the two mighty *volcans* at whose base they had before travelled. The sides of the sierra were clothed with dark forests of pine, cypress, and cedar,[1] through which glimpses now and then opened into fathomless dells and valleys, whose depths, far down in the sultry climate of the tropics, were lost in a glowing wilderness of vegetation. From the crest of the mountain range the eye travelled over the broad expanse of country, which they had lately crossed, far away to the green plains of Cholula. Towards the west, they looked down on the Mexican Valley, from a point of view wholly different from that which they had before occupied, but still offering the same beautiful spectacle, with its lakes trembling in the light, its gay cities and villas floating on their bosom, its burnished *teocallis* touched with fire, its cultivated slopes and dark hills of porphyry stretching away in dim perspective to the verge of the horizon. At their feet lay the city of Tezcuco, which, modestly retiring behind her deep groves of cypress, formed a contrast to her more ambitious rival on the other side of the lake, who seemed to glory in the unveiled splendours of her charms as Mistress of the Valley.

As they descended into the populous plains, their reception by the natives was very different from that which they had experienced on the preceding visit. There were no groups of curious peasantry to be seen gazing at them as they passed, and offering their simple hospitality. The supplies they asked were not refused, but granted with an ungracious air, that showed the blessing of the giver did not accompany them. This air of reserve became still more marked as the army entered the suburbs of the ancient capital of the Acolhuans. No one came forth to greet them, and the population seemed to have dwindled away,—so many of them were withdrawn to the neighbouring scene of hostilities at Mexico.[2] Their cold reception was a sensible mortification to the veterans of Cortés, who, judging from the past, had boasted to their new comrades of the sensation their presence would excite among the natives. The cacique of the place, who, as it may be remembered, had been created through the influence of Cortés, was himself absent. The general drew an ill omen from all these circumstances, which even raised an uncomfortable apprehension in his mind respecting the fate of the garrison in Mexico.[3]

---

[1] "Las sierras altas de Tetzcuco á que le mostrasen desde la mas alta cumbre de aquellas montañas y sierras de Tetzcuco, que son las sierras de Tlallocan altisimas y humbrosas, en las cuales he estado y visto, y puedo decir que son bastante para descubrir el un emisferio y otro, porque son los mayores puertos y mas altos de esta Nueva España, de árboles y montes de grandísima altura, de cedras, cipreses y pinares." Camargo, Hist. de Tlascala, MS.

[2] The historian partly explains the reason: "En la misma Ciudad de Tezcuco habia algunos apasionados de los deudos y amigos de los que matáron Pedro de Alvarado y sus compañeros en México." Ixtlilxochitl, Hist. Chich., MS., cap. 88.

[3] "En todo el camino nunca me salió á recibir ninguna Persona de el dicho Mutezuma, como ántes lo solian facer; y toda la Tierra estaba alborotada, y casi despoblada : de que concebí mala sospecha, creyendo que los Españoles que en la dicha Ciudad habian quedado, eran muertos." Rel. Seg. de Cortés, ap. Lorenzana, p. 132.

But his doubts were soon dispelled by the arrival of a messenger in a canoe from that city, whence he had escaped through the remissness of the enemy, or, perhaps, with their connivance. He brought despatches from Alvarado, informing his commander that the Mexicans had for the last fortnight desisted from active hostilities and converted their operations into a blockade. The garrison had suffered greatly, but Alvarado expressed his conviction that the siege would be raised, and tranquillity restored, on the approach of his countrymen. Montezuma sent a messenger, also, to the same effect. At the same time, he exculpated himself from any part in the late hostilities, which he said had been conducted not only without his privity, but contrary to his inclination and efforts.

The Spanish general, having halted long enough to refresh his wearied troops, took up his march along the southern margin of the lake, which led him over the same causeway by which he had before entered the capital. It was the day consecrated to St. John the Baptist, the 24th of June 1520. But how different was the scene from that presented on his former entrance![1] No crowds now lined the roads, no boats swarmed on the lake, filled with admiring spectators. A single pirogue might now and then be seen in the distance, like a spy stealthily watching their movements, and darting away the moment it had attracted notice. A deathlike stillness brooded over the scene,—a stillness that spoke louder to the heart than the acclamations of multitudes.

Cortés rode on moodily at the head of his battalions, finding abundant food for meditation, doubtless, in this change of circumstances. As if to dispel these gloomy reflections, he ordered his trumpets to sound, and their clear, shrill notes, borne across the waters, told the inhabitants of the beleaguered fortress that their friends were at hand. They were answered by a joyous peal of artillery, which seemed to give a momentary exhilaration to the troops, as they quickened their pace, traversed the great drawbridges, and once more found themselves within the walls of the imperial city.

The appearance of things here was not such as to allay their apprehensions. In some places they beheld the smaller bridges removed, intimating too plainly, now that their brigantines were destroyed, how easy it would be to cut off their retreat.[2] The town seemed even more deserted than Tezcuco. Its once busy and crowded population had mysteriously vanished. And, as the Spaniards defiled through the empty streets, the tramp of their horses' feet upon the pavement was answered by dull and melancholy echoes that fell heavily on their hearts. With saddened feelings they reached the great gates of the palace of Axayacatl. The gates were thrown open, and Cortés and his veterans, rushing in, were

---

[1] "Y como asomó á la vista de la Ciudad de México, parecióle que estaba toda yerma, y que no parecia persona por todos los caminos, ni casas, ni plazas, ni nadie le salió á recibir, ni de los suyos, ni de los enemigos; y fué esto señal de indignacion y enemistad por lo que habia pasado." Sahagun, Hist. de Nueva-España, MS., lib. 12, cap. 19.

[2] "Pontes ligneos qui tractim lapideos intersecant, sublatos, ac vias aggeribus munitas reperit." Peter Martyr, De Orbe Novo, dec. 5, cap. 5.

cordially embraced by their companions in arms, while both parties soon forgot the present in the interesting recapitulation of the past.[1]

The first inquiries of the general were respecting the origin of the tumult. The accounts were various. Some imputed it to the desire of the Mexicans to release their sovereign from confinement ; others to the design of cutting off the garrison while crippled by the absence of Cortés and their country-men. All agreed, however, in tracing the immediate cause to the violence of Alvarado. It was common for the Aztecs to celebrate an annual festival in May, in honour of their patron war-god. It was called the " incensing of Huitzilopochtli," and was commemorated by sacrifice, religious songs, and dances, in which most of the nobles engaged, for it was one of the great festivals which displayed the pomp of the Aztec ritual. As it was held in the court of the *teocalli*, in the immediate neighbourhood of the Spanish quarters, and as a part of the temple itself was reserved for a Christian chapel, the caciques asked permission of Alvarado to perform their rites there. They requested also, it is said, to be allowed the presence of Montezuma. This latter petition Alvarado declined, in obedience to the injunctions of Cortés ; but acquiesced in the former, on condition that the Aztecs should celebrate no human sacrifices, and should come without weapons.

They assembled accordingly on the day appointed, to the number of six hundred, at the smallest computation.[2] They were dressed in their most magnificent gala costumes, with their graceful mantles of feather-work sprinkled with precious stones, and their necks, arms, and legs ornamented with collars and bracelets of gold. They had that love of gaudy splendour which belongs to semi-civilized nations, and on these occasions displayed all the pomp and profusion of their barbaric wardrobes.

Alvarado and his soldiers attended as spectators, some of them taking their station at the gates as if by chance, and others mingling in the crowd. They were all armed,—a circumstance which, as it was usual, excited no attention. The Aztecs were soon engrossed by the exciting movement of the dance, accompanied by their religious chant and wild, discordant minstrelsy. While thus occupied, Alvarado and his men, at a concerted signal, rushed with drawn swords on their victims. Unprotected by armour or weapons of any kind, they were hewn down without resistance by their assailants, who in their bloody work, says a contemporary, showed no touch of pity or compunction.[3] Some fled to

---

1 Probanza á pedimento de Juan de Lexalde, MS. —Rel. Seg. de Cortés, ap. Lorenzana, p. 133.— " Esto causó gran admiracion en todos los que venian, pero no dejáron de marchar, hasta entrar donde estaban los Españoles acorralados. Venian todos muy casados y muy fatigados y con mucho deseo de llegar á donde estaban sus hermanos ; los de dentro cuando los vieron, recibiéron singular consolacion y esfuerzo y recibiéronlos con la artil-leria que tenian, saludándolos, y dándolos el para-bien de su venida." Sahagun, Hist. de Nueva-España, MS., lib. 12. cap. 22.

2 " F. así los Ind.os, todos Señores, mas de 600

desnudos é con muchas joyas de oro é hermosos penachos, é muchas piedras preciosas, é como mas aderezados é gentiles hombres se pudiéron é supiéron aderezar, é sin arma alguna defensiva ni ofensiva bailaban é cantaban é hacian su areito é fiesta segun su costumbre." (Oviedo, Hist. de las Ind., MS., lib. 33, cap. 54.) Some writers carry the number as high as eight hundred or even one thousand. Las Casas, with a more modest exaggeration than usual, swells it only to two thousand. Brevissima Relatione, p. 48.

3 " Sin duelo ni piedad Christiana los acuchilló, i mató." Gomara, Crónica, cap. 104.

the gates, but were caught on the long pikes of the soldiers. Others, who attempted to scale the *coatepantli*, or Wall of Serpents, as it was called, which surrounded the area, shared the like fate, or were cut to pieces, or shot by the ruthless soldiery. The pavement, says a writer of the age, ran with streams of blood, like water in a heavy shower.[1] Not an Aztec, of all that gay company, was left alive! It was repeating the dreadful scene of Cholula with the disgraceful addition that the Spaniards, not content with slaughtering their victims, rifled them of the precious ornaments on their persons! On this sad day fell the flower of the Aztec nobility. Not a family of note but had mourning and desolation brought within its walls.[2] And many a doleful ballad, rehearsing the tragic incidents of the story, and adapted to the plaintive national airs, continued to be chanted by the natives long after the subjugation of the country.[3]

Various explanations have been given of this atrocious deed. But few historians have been content to admit that of Alvarado himself. According to this, intelligence had been obtained through his spies—some of them Mexicans—of an intended rising of the Indians. The celebration of this festival was fixed on as the period for its execution, when the caciques would be met together and would easily rouse the people to support them. Alvarado, advised of all this, had forbidden them to wear arms at their meeting. While affecting to comply, they had secreted their weapons in the neighbouring arsenals, whence they could readily withdraw them. But his own blow, by anticipating theirs, defeated the design, and, as he confidently hoped, would deter the Aztecs from a similar attempt in future.[4]

Such is the account of the matter given by Alvarado. But, if true, why did he not verify his assertion by exposing the arms thus secreted? Why did he not vindicate his conduct in the eyes of the Mexicans generally, by publicly avowing the treason of the nobles, as was done by Cortés at Cholula? The whole looks much like an apology devised after the commission of the deed, to cover up its atrocity.

---

[1] "Fué tan grande el derramamiento de Sangre, que corrian arroyos de ella por el Patio, como agua cuando mucho llueve." Sahagun, Hist. de Nueva-España, MS., lib. 12, cap. 20.

[2] [In the process instituted against Alvarado this massacre forms one of the most important charges. He is there accused of having killed four hundred of the principal nobles and a great number of the common people, of whom more than three thousand, it is stated, were assembled to celebrate the festival in honour of their war-god. "Ynbio al patyo donde todos baylaban y syn cabsa ni razon alguna dieron sobrellos y mataron todos los mas de los señores que estavan presos con el dicho Motenzuma y mataron cuatro cientos señores e prencipales que con el estavan e mataron mucho numero de yndios que estavan baylando en mas cantydad de tres mill personas." (Procesos de Residencia, instruidos contra Pedro de Alvarado y Nuño de Guzman, p. 53.) The public are under great obligations to the licentiate Don Ignacio Rayon for bringing into light this important document, which for more than three centuries had lain hid in the General Archives of Mexico. We have hardly less reason to thank him for placing the manuscript in the hands of so competent a scholar as Don José Fernando Ramirez, to enrich it with the stores of his critical erudition. The publication of the process did not take place till some years after that of my own history of the Conquest of Mexico. But, as it contains a minute specification of the various charges against Alvarado, and his own defence, it furnishes me with the means of correcting any errors into which I have fallen in reference to that commander, while it corroborates, I may add, the general tenor of the statements I have derived from contemporary chroniclers.]

[3] "Y de aquí á que se acabe el mundo, ó ellos del todo se acaben, no dexarán de lamentar, y cantar en sus areytos, y bayles, como en romances, que acá dezimos, aquella calamidad, y perdida de la sucession de toda su nobleza, de que se preciauan de tantos años atras." Las Casas, Brevíssima Relatione, p. 49.

[4] See Alvarado's reply to queries of Cortés, as reported by Diaz (Hist. de la Conquista, cap. 125), with some additional particulars in Torquemada (Monarch. Ind., lib. 4, cap. 66), Solis (Conquista, lib. 4, cap. 12), and Herrera (Hist. general, dec. 2, lib. 10, cap. 8), who all seem content to endorse Alvarado's version of the matter. I find no other authority, of any weight, in the same charitable vein.

Some contemporaries assign a very different motive for the massacre, which, according to them, originated in the cupidity of the Conquerors, as shown by their plundering the bodies of their victims.[1] Bernal Diaz, who, though not present, had conversed familiarly with those who were, vindicates them from the charge of this unworthy motive. According to him, Alvarado struck the blow in order to intimidate the Aztecs from any insurrectionary movement.[2] But whether he had reason to apprehend such, or even affected to do so before the massacre, the old chronicler does not inform us.

On reflection, it seems scarcely possible that so foul a deed, and one involving so much hazard to the Spaniards themselves, should have been perpetrated from the mere desire of getting possession of the baubles worn on the persons of the natives. It is more likely this was an after-thought, suggested to the rapacious soldiery by the display of the spoil before them. It is not improbable that Alvarado may have gathered rumours of a conspiracy among the nobles,—rumours, perhaps, derived through the Tlascalans, their inveterate foes, and for that reason very little deserving of credit.[3] He proposed to defeat it by imitating the example of his commander at Cholula. But he omitted to imitate his leader in taking precautions against the subsequent rising of the populace. And he grievously miscalculated when he confounded the bold and warlike Aztec with the effeminate Cholulan.[4]

No sooner was the butchery accomplished, than the tidings spread like

---

[1] Oviedo mentions a conversation which he had some years after this tragedy with a noble Spaniard, Don Thoan Cano, who came over in the train of Narvaez and was present at all the subsequent operations of the army. He married a daughter of Montezuma, and settled in Mexico after the Conquest. Oviedo describes him as a man of sense and integrity. In answer to the historian's queries respecting the cause of the rising, he said that Alvarado had wantonly perpetrated the massacre from pure avarice; and the Aztecs, enraged at such unprovoked and unmerited cruelty, rose, as they well might, to avenge it. (Hist. de las Ind., MS., lib. 33, cap. 54.) See the original dialogue in Appendix, Part 2, No. 11.

[2] "Verdaderamente dió en ellos por metelles temor." Hist. de la Conquista, cap. 125.

[3] Such, indeed, is the statement of Ixtlilxochitl, derived, as he says, from the native Tezcucan annalists. According to them, the Tlascalans, urged by their hatred of the Aztecs and their thirst for plunder, persuaded Alvarado, nothing loth, that the nobles meditated a rising on the occasion of these festivities. The testimony is important, and I give it in the author's words: "Fué que ciertos Tlascaltecas (segun las Historias de Tescuco que son las que Io sigo y la carta que otras veces he referido) por embidia lo uno acordándose que en semejante fiesta los Mexicanos solian sacrificar gran suma de cautivos de los de la Nacion Tlascalteca, y lo otro que era !a mejor ocasion que ellos podian tener para poder hinchir las manos de despojos y hartar su codicia, y vengarse de sus Enemigos (porque hasta entonces no habian tenido lugar, ni Cortés se les diera, ni admitiera sus dichos, porque siempre hacia las cosas con mucho acuerdo) fuéron con esta invencion al capitan Pedro de Albarado, que estaba en lugar de Cortés, el qual no fué menester mucho para darles crédito porque tan buenos

filos, y pensamientos tenia como ellos, y mas viendo que allí en aquella fiesta habian acudido todos los Señores y Cabezas del Imperio y que muertos no tenian mucho trabajo en sojuzgarles." Hist. Chich., MS., cap. 88.

[4] [Alvarado intimates, in the defence of his conduct which forms part of the process, one source of the rumours respecting the rising of the Aztecs, by saying that the existence of such a scheme was matter of public notoriety among the Tlascalans. He adds that he obtained more precise intelligence from two or three Indians, one a Tezcucan, another a slave whom he had rescued from the sacrifice to which he had been doomed by the Aztecs; that these latter, under cover of the festivities, had planned an insurrection against the Spaniards, in which he and his countrymen were all to be exterminated. At the same time they determined to tear down the image of the Virgin which had been raised in the temple, and in its place to substitute that of their war-god, Huitzilopochtli. Montezuma was accused of being privy to this conspiracy. Thus instructed, Alvarado, as he asserts, got his men in readiness to resist the enemy, who, after a short encounter, was repulsed with slaughter, while one Spaniard was slain, and he himself, with several others, severely wounded (Proceso, pp. 66, 67). But although a long array of witnesses, most of them probably his ancient friends and comrades, are introduced to endorse his statement, one who reflects on the submissive spirit hitherto shown, not only by Montezuma, but his subjects, in their dealings with the Spaniards, and contrasts it with the fierce and unscrupulous temper displayed by Alvarado, will have little doubt on whose head the guilt of the massacre must rest; and as little seems to have been felt by most of the writers of the time who have spoken of the affair.]

wildfire through the capital. Men could scarcely credit their senses. All they had hitherto suffered, the desecration of their temples, the imprisonment of their sovereign, the insults heaped on his person, all were forgotten in this one act.[1] Every feeling of long-smothered hostility and rancour now burst forth in the cry for vengeance. Every former sentiment of superstitious dread was merged in that of inextinguishable hatred. It required no effort of the priests—though this was not wanting—to fan these passions into a blaze. The city rose in arms to a man; and on the following dawn, almost before the Spaniards could secure themselves in their defences, they were assaulted with desperate fury. Some of the assailants attempted to scale the walls; others succeeded in partially undermining and setting fire to the works. Whether they would have succeeded in carrying the place by storm is doubtful. But, at the prayers of the garrison, Montezuma himself interfered, and, mounting the battlements, addressed the populace, whose fury he endeavoured to mitigate by urging considerations for his own safety. They respected their monarch so far as to desist from further attempts to storm the fortress, but changed their operations into a regular blockade. They threw up works around the palace to prevent the egress of the Spaniards. They suspended the *tianguez*, or market, to preclude the possibility of their enemy's obtaining supplies; and they then quietly sat down, with feelings of sullen desperation, waiting for the hour when famine should throw their victims into their hands.

The condition of the besieged, meanwhile, was sufficiently distressing. Their magazines of provisions, it is true, were not exhausted; but they suffered greatly from want of water, which, within the enclosure, was exceedingly brackish, for the soil was saturated with the salt of the surrounding element. In this extremity, they discovered, it is said, a spring of fresh water in the area. Such springs were known in some other parts of the city; but, discovered first under these circumstances, it was accounted as nothing less than a miracle. Still they suffered much from their past encounters. Seven Spaniards, and many Tlascalans, had fallen, and there was scarcely one of either nation who had not received several wounds. In this situation, far from their own countrymen, without expectation of succour from abroad, they seemed to have no alternative before them but a lingering death by famine, or one more dreadful on the altar of sacrifice. From this gloomy state they were relieved by the coming of their comrades.[2]

Cortés calmly listened to the explanation made by Alvarado. But,

---

[1] Martyr well recapitulates these grievances, showing that they seemed such in the eyes of the Spaniards themselves,--of those, at least, whose judgment was not warped by a share in the transactions. "Emori statuerunt malle, quam diutius ferre tales hospites qui regem suum sub tutoris vitæ specie detineant, civitatem occupent, antiquos hostes Tascaltecanos et alios præterea in contumeliam ante illorum oculos ipsorum impensa conseruent; . . . qui demum simulachra deorum confregerint, et ritus veteres ac ceremonias antiquas illis abstulerint." De Orbe Novo, dec. 5, cap. 5.

[2] Camargo, Hist. de Tlascala, MS. — Oviedo, Hist. de las Ind., MS., lib. 33, cap. 13, 47.— Gomara, Crónica, cap. 105.

before it was ended, the conviction must have forced itself on his mind that he had made a wrong selection for this important post. Yet the mistake was natural. Alvarado was a cavalier of high family, gallant and chivalrous, and his warm personal friend. He had talents for action, was possessed of firmness and intrepidity, while his frank and dazzling manners made the *Tonatiuh* an especial favourite with the Mexicans. But underneath this showy exterior the future conqueror of Guatemala concealed a heart rash, rapacious, and cruel. He was altogether destitute of that moderation which, in the delicate position he occupied, was a quality of more worth than all the rest.

When Alvarado had concluded his answers to the several interrogatories of Cortés, the brow of the latter darkened, as he said to his lieutenant, "You have done badly. You have been false to your trust. Your conduct has been that of a madman!" And, turning abruptly on his heel, he left him in undisguised displeasure.

Yet this was not a time to break with one so popular, and, in many respects, so important to him, as this captain, much less to inflict on him the punishment he merited. The Spaniards were like mariners labouring in a heavy tempest, whose bark nothing but the dexterity of the pilot and the hearty co-operation of the crew can save from foundering. Dissensions at such a moment must be fatal. Cortés, it is true, felt strong in his present resources. He now found himself at the head of a force which could scarcely amount to less than twelve hundred and fifty Spaniards, and eight thousand native warriors, principally Tlascalans.[1] But, though relying on this to overawe resistance, the very augmentation of numbers increased the difficulty of subsistence. Discontented with himself, disgusted with his officer, and embarrassed by the disastrous consequences in which Alvarado's intemperance had involved him, he became irritable, and indulged in a petulance by no means common; for, though a man of lively passions by nature, he held them habitually under control.[2]

On the day that Cortés arrived, Montezuma had left his own quarters to welcome him. But the Spanish commander, distrusting, as it would seem, however unreasonably, his good faith, received him so coldly that the Indian monarch withdrew, displeased and dejected, to his apartment. As the Mexican populace made no show of submission, and brought no supplies to the army, the general's ill-humour with the emperor continued. When, therefore, Montezuma sent some of the nobles to ask an interview with Cortés, the latter, turning to his own officers, haughtily exclaimed, "What have I to do with this dog of a king who suffers us to starve before his eyes?"

---

[1] He left in garrison, on his departure from Mexico, 140 Spaniards and about 6500 Tlascalans, including a few Cempoallan warriors. Supposing five hundred of these—a liberal allowance—to have perished in battle and otherwise, it would still leave a number which, with the reinforcement now brought, would raise the amount to that stated in the text.

[2] "Seeing how all went contrary to his expectations and that we still received no supplies, he grew extremely sad, and showed himself in his bearing towards the Spaniards fretful and haughty." Bernal Diaz, Hist. de la Conquista, cap. 126.

His captains, among whom were Olid, De Avila, and Velasquez de Leon, endeavoured to mitigate his anger, reminding him, in respectful terms, that had it not been for the emperor the garrison might even now have been overwhelmed by the enemy. This remonstrance only chafed him the more. " Did not the dog," he asked, repeating the opprobrious epithet, " betray us in his communications with Narvaez ? And does he not now suffer his markets to be closed, and leave us to die of famine ? " Then, turning fiercely to the Mexicans, he said, " Go tell your master and his people to open the markets, or we will do it for them, at their cost ! " The chiefs, who had gathered the import of his previous taunt on their sovereign, from his tone and gesture, or perhaps from some comprehension of his language, left his presence swelling with resentment, and, in communicating his message, took care it should lose none of its effect.[1]

Shortly after, Cortés, at the suggestion, it is said, of Montezuma, released his brother Cuitlahua, lord of Iztapalapan, who, it will be remembered, had been seized on suspicion of co-operating with the chief of Tezcuco in his meditated revolt. It was thought he might be of service in allaying the present tumult and bringing the populace to a better state of feeling. But he returned no more to the fortress.[2] He was a bold, ambitious prince, and the injuries he had received from the Spaniards rankled deep in his bosom. He was presumptive heir to the crown, which, by the Aztec laws of succession, descended much more frequently in a collateral than in a direct line. The people welcomed him as the representative of their sovereign, and chose him to supply the place of Montezuma during his captivity. Cuitlahua willingly accepted the post of honour and of danger. He was an experienced warrior, and exerted himself to reorganize the disorderly levies and to arrange a more efficient plan of operations. The effect was soon visible.

Cortés meanwhile had so little doubt of his ability to overawe the insurgents, that he wrote to that effect to the garrison of Villa Rica by the same despatches in which he informed them of his safe arrival in the capital. But scarcely had his messenger been gone half an hour, when he returned breathless with terror and covered with wounds. " The city," he said, " was all in arms ! The drawbridges were raised, and the enemy would soon be upon them ! " He spoke truth. It was not long before a hoarse, sullen sound became audible, like that of the roaring of distant waters. It grew louder and louder ; till, from the parapet surrounding the enclosure, the great avenues which led to it might be seen dark with the masses of warriors, who came rolling on in a confused tide towards the fortress. At the same time, the terraces and *azoteas* or flat roofs, in the neighbourhood, were thronged with combatants brandishing their missiles, who seemed to have risen up as if by magic ![3] It was a spectacle to

---

[1] The scene is reported by Diaz, who was present. (Hist. de la Conquista, cap. 126.) See, also, the Chronicle of Gomara, the chaplain of Cortés. (Cap. 106.) It is further confirmed by Don Thoan Cano, an eyewitness, in his conversation with Oviedo. See Appendix, Part 2, No. 11.

[2] Herrera, Hist. general, dec. 2, lib. 10, cap. 8.
[3] " El qual Mensajero bolvió dende á media hora todo descalabrado, y herido, dando voces, que todos los Indios de la Ciudad venian de Guerra y que tenian todas las Puentes alzadas ; é junto tras él da sobre nosotros tanta multitud de Gente por

appal the stoutest. But the dark storm to which it was the prelude, and which gathered deeper and deeper round the Spaniards during the remainder of their residence in the capital, must form the subject of a separate Book.

———————————

Gonzalo Fernandez de Oviedo y Valdés was born in 1478. He belonged to an ancient family of the Asturias. Every family, indeed, claims to be ancient in this last retreat of the intrepid Goths. He was early introduced at court, and was appointed page to Prince Juan, the only son of Ferdinand and Isabella, on whom their hopes, and those of the nation, deservedly rested. Oviedo accompanied the camp in the latter campaigns of the Moorish war, and was present at the memorable siege of Granada. On the untimely death of his royal master, in 1496, he passed over to Italy and entered the service of King Frederick of Naples. At the death of that prince he returned to his own country, and in the beginning of the sixteenth century we find him again established in Castile, where he occupied the place of keeper of the crown jewels. In 1513 he was named by Ferdinand the Catholic *veedor*, or inspector, of the gold founderies in the American colonies. Oviedo, accordingly, transported himself to the New World, where he soon took a commission under Pedrarias, governor of Darien, and shared in the disastrous fortunes of that colony. He obtained some valuable privileges from the Crown, built a fortress on Tierra Firme, and entered into traffic with the natives. In this we may presume he was prosperous, since we find him at length established with a wife and family at Hispaniola, or Fernandina, as it was then called. Although he continued to make his principal residence in the New World, he made occasional visits to Spain, and in 1526 published at Madrid his *Sumario*. It is dedicated to the Emperor Charles the Fifth, and contains an account of the West Indies, their geography, climate, the races who inhabited them, together with their animals and vegetable productions. The subject was of great interest to the inquisitive minds of Europe, and one of which they had previously gleaned but scanty information. In 1535, in a subsequent visit to Spain, Oviedo gave to the world the first volume of his great work, which he had been many years in compiling,—the *Historia de las Indias occidentales*. In the same year he was appointed by Charles the Fifth alcayde of the fortress of Hispaniola. He continued in the island the ten following years, actively engaged in the prosecution of his historical researches, and then returned for the last time to his native land. The veteran scholar was well received at court, and obtained the honourable appointment of Chronicler of the Indies. He occupied this post until the period of his death, which took place at Valladolid in 1557, in the seventy-ninth year of his age, at the very time when he was employed in preparing the residue of his history for the press.

Considering the intimate footing on which Oviedo lived with the eminent persons of his time, it is singular that so little is preserved of his personal history and his character. Nic. Antonio speaks of him as a "man of large experience, courteous in his manners, and of great probity." His long and active life is a sufficient voucher for his experience, and one will hardly doubt his good breeding when we know the high society in which he moved. He left a large mass of manuscripts, embracing a vast range both of civil and natural history. By far the most important is his *Historia general de las Indias*. It is divided into three parts, containing fifty books. The first part, consisting of nineteen books, is the one already noticed as having been published during his lifetime. It gives in a more extended form the details of geographical and natural history embodied in his *Sumario*, with a narrative, moreover, of the discoveries and conquests of the Islands. A translation of this portion of the work was made by the learned Ramusio, with whom Oviedo was in correspondence, and is published in the third volume of his inestimable

———————————

todas partes que ni las calles ni Azoteas se parecian con Gente ; la qual venia con los mayores alaridos, y grita mas espantable, que en el Mundo se puede pensar." Rel. Seg. de Cortés, ap. Lorenzana, p. 134.— Oviedo, Hist. de las Ind., MS., lib. 33, cap. 13.

collection. The two remaining parts relate to the conquests of Mexico, of Peru, and other countries of South America. It is that portion of the work consulted for these pages. The manuscript was deposited, at his death, in the *Casa de la Contratacion*, at Seville. It afterwards came into the possession of the Dominican monastery of Monserrat. In process of time, mutilated copies found their way into several private collections; when, in 1775, Don Francisco Cerda y Rico, an officer in the Indian department, ascertained the place in which the original was preserved, and, prompted by his literary zeal, obtained an order from the government for its publication. Under his supervision the work was put in order for the press, and Oviedo's biographer, Alvarez y Baena, assures us that a complete edition of it, prepared with the greatest care, would soon be given to the world. (Hijos de Madrid (Madrid, 1790), tom. ii. pp. 354-361.) It still remains in manuscript.

No country has been more fruitful in the field of historical composition than Spain. Her ballads are chronicles done into verse. The chronicles themselves date from the twelfth and thirteenth centuries. Every city, every small town, every great family, and many a petty one, has its chronicler. These were often mere monkish chroniclers, who in the seclusion of the convent found leisure for literary occupation. Or, not unfrequently, they were men who had taken part in the affairs they described, more expert with the sword than with the pen. The compositions of this latter class have a general character of that indifference to fine writing which shows a mind intent on the facts with which it is occupied, much more than on forms of expression. The monkish chroniclers, on the other hand, often make a pedantic display of obsolete erudition, which contrasts rather whimsically with the homely texture of the narrative. The chronicles of both the one and the other class of writers may frequently claim the merit of picturesque and animated detail, showing that the subject was one of living interest, and that the writer's heart was in his subject.

Many of the characteristic blemishes of which I have been speaking may be charged on Oviedo. His style is cast in no classic mould. His thoughts find themselves a vent in tedious, interminable sentences, that may fill the reader with despair; and the thread of the narrative is broken by impertinent episodes that lead to nothing. His scholarship was said to be somewhat scanty. One will hardly be led to doubt it, from the tawdry display of Latin quotations with which he garnishes his pages, like a poor gallant who would make the most of his little store of finery. He affected to take the elder Pliny as his model, as appears from the preface to his *Sumario*. But his own work fell far short of the model of erudition and eloquence which that great writer of natural history has bequeathed to us.

Yet, with his obvious defects, Oviedo showed an enlightened curiosity, and a shrewd spirit of observation, which place him far above the ordinary range of chroniclers. He may even be said to display a philosophic tone in his reflections, though his philosophy must be regarded as cold and unscrupulous wherever the rights of the aborigines are in question. He was indefatigable in amassing materials for his narratives, and for this purpose maintained a correspondence with the most eminent men of his time who had taken part in the transactions which he commemorates. He even condescended to collect information from more humble sources, from popular tradition and the reports of the common soldiers. Hence his work often presents a medley of inconsistent and contradictory details, which perplex the judgment, making it exceedingly difficult, at this distance of time, to disentangle the truth. It was perhaps for this reason that Las Casas complimented the author by declaring that "his works were a wholesale fabrication, as full of lies as of pages!" Yet another explanation of this severe judgment may be found in the different characters of the two men. Oviedo shared in the worldly feelings common to the Spanish Conquerors, and, while he was ever ready to magnify the exploits of his countrymen, held lightly the claims and the sufferings of the unfortunate aborigines. He was incapable of appreciating the generous philanthropy of Las Casas, or of rising to his lofty views, which he doubtless derided as those of a benevolent, it might be, but visionary, fanatic. Las Casas, on the other hand, whose voice had been constantly uplifted against the abuses of the Conquerors, was filled with abhorrence at the sentiments avowed by Oviedo, and it was natural that his aversion to the principles should be extended to the person who professed them. Probably no two men could have been found less competent to form a right estimate of each other.

Oviedo showed the same activity in gathering materials for natural history as he had done for the illustration of civil. He collected the different plants of the Islands in his garden, and domesticated many of the animals, or kept them in confinement under his eye, where he could study their peculiar habits. By this course, if he did not himself rival Pliny and Hernandez in science, he was, at least, enabled to furnish the man of science with facts of the highest interest and importance.

Besides these historical writings, Oviedo left a work in six volumes, called by the whimsical title of *Quincuagenas*. It consists of imaginary dialogues between the most eminent Spaniards of the time, in respect to their personal history, their families, and genealogy. It is a work of inestimable value to the historian of the times of Ferdinand and Isabella, and of Charles the Fifth. But it has attracted little attention in Spain, where it still remains in manuscript. A complete copy of Oviedo's History of the Indies is in the archives of the Royal Academy of History in Madrid, and it is understood that this body has now an edition prepared for the press. Such parts as are literally transcribed from preceding narratives, like the Letters of Cortés, which Oviedo transferred without scruple entire and unmutilated into his own pages, though enlivened, it is true, by occasional criticism of his own, might as well be omitted. But the remainder of the great work affords a mass of multifarious information which would make an important contribution to the colonial history of Spain.

An authority of frequent reference in these pages is Diego Muñoz Camargo. He was a noble Tlascalan *mestee*, and lived in the latter half of the sixteenth century. He was educated in the Christian faith, and early instructed in Castilian, in which tongue he composed his *Historia de Tlascala*. In this work he introduces the reader to the different members of the great Nahuatlac family who came successively up the Mexican plateau. Born and bred among the aborigines of the country, when the practices of the pagan age had not wholly become obsolete. Camargo was in a position perfectly to comprehend the condition of the ancient inhabitants; and his work supplies much curious and authentic information respecting the social and religious institutions of the land at the time of the Conquest. His patriotism warms as he recounts the old hostilities of his countrymen with the Aztecs; and it is singular to observe how the detestation of the rival nations survived their common subjection under the Castilian yoke.

Camargo embraces in his narrative an account of this great event, and of the subsequent settlement of the country. As one of the Indian family, we might expect to see his chronicle reflect the prejudices, or, at least, partialities, of the Indian. But the Christian convert yielded up his sympathies as freely to the Conquerors as to his own countrymen. The desire to magnify the exploits of the latter, and at the same time to do full justice to the prowess of the white men, produces occasionally a most whimsical contrast in his pages, giving the story a strong air of inconsistency. In point of literary execution the work has little merit; as great, however, as could be expected from a native Indian, indebted for his knowledge of the tongue to such imperfect instruction as he could obtain from the missionaries. Yet in style of composition it may compare not unfavourably with the writings of some of the missionaries themselves.

The original manuscript was long preserved in the convent of *San Felipe Neri* in Mexico, where Torquemada, as appears from occasional references, had access to it. It has escaped the attention of other historians, but was embraced by Muñoz in his magnificent collection, and deposited in the archives of the Royal Academy of History at Madrid; from which source the copy in my possession was obtained. It bears the title of *Pedazo de Historia verdadera*, and is without the author's name, and without division into books or chapters.

BOOK V.

EXPULSION FROM MEXICO.

———

CHAPTER I.

DESPERATE ASSAULT ON THE QUARTERS.—FURY OF THE MEXICANS.—
SALLY OF THE SPANIARDS.—MONTEZUMA ADDRESSES THE PEOPLE.—
DANGEROUSLY WOUNDED.

(1520.)

THE palace of Axayacatl, in which the Spaniards were quartered, was,
as the reader may remember, a vast, irregular pile of stone buildings,
having but one floor, except in the centre, where another story was added,
consisting of a suite of apartments which rose like turrets on the main
building of the edifice. A vast area stretched around, encompassed by
a stone wall of no great height. This was supported by towers or
bulwarks at certain intervals, which gave it some degree of strength, not,
indeed, as compared with European fortifications, but sufficient to resist
the rude battering enginery of the Indians. The parapet had been
pierced here and there with embrasures for the artillery, which consisted
of thirteen guns; and smaller apertures were made in other parts for the
convenience of the arquebusiers. The Spanish forces found accommodations within the great building; but the numerous body of Tlascalan
auxiliaries could have had no other shelter than what was afforded by
barracks or sheds hastily constructed for the purpose in the spacious
courtyard. Most of them, probably, bivouacked under the open sky, in
a climate milder than that to which they were accustomed among the
rude hills of their native land. Thus crowded into a small and compact
compass, the whole army could be assembled at a moment's notice; and,
as the Spanish commander was careful to enforce the strictest discipline
and vigilance, it was scarcely possible that he could be taken by surprise.
No sooner, therefore, did the trumpet call to arms, as the approach of
the enemy was announced, than every soldier was at his post, the cavalry
mounted, the artillerymen at their guns, and the archers and arquebusiers
stationed so as to give the assailants a warm reception.

On they came, with the companies, or irregular masses, into which the multitude was divided, rushing forward each in its own dense column, with many a gay banner displayed, and many a bright gleam of light reflected from helmet, arrow, and spear-head, as they were tossed about in their disorderly array. As they drew near the enclosure, the Aztecs set up a hideous yell, or rather that shrill whistle used in fight by the nations of Anahuac, which rose far above the sound of shell and atabal and their other rude instruments of warlike melody. They followed this by a tempest of missiles,—stones, darts, and arrows,—which fell thick as rain on the besieged, while volleys of the same kind descended from the crowded terraces in the neighbourhood.[1]

The Spaniards waited until the foremost column had arrived within the best distance for giving effect to their fire, when a general discharge of artillery and arquebuses swept the ranks of the assailants and mowed them down by hundreds.[2] The Mexicans were familiar with the report of these formidable engines as they had been harmlessly discharged on some holiday festival; but never till now had they witnessed their murderous power. They stood aghast for a moment, as with bewildered looks they staggered under the fury of the fire;[3] but, soon rallying, the bold barbarians uttered a piercing cry, and rushed forward over the prostrate bodies of their comrades. A second and a third volley checked their career, and threw them into disorder, but still they pressed on, letting off clouds of arrows; while their comrades on the roofs of the houses took more deliberate aim at the combatants in the courtyard. The Mexicans were particularly expert in the use of the sling;[4] and the stones which they hurled from their elevated positions on the heads of their enemies did even greater execution than the arrows. They glanced, indeed, from the mail-covered bodies of the cavaliers, and from those who were sheltered under the cotton panoply, or *escaupil*. But some of the soldiers, especially the veterans of Cortés, and many of their Indian allies, had but slight defences, and suffered greatly under this stony tempest.

The Aztecs, meanwhile, had advanced close under the walls of the intrenchment, their ranks broken and disordered and their limbs mangled by the unintermitting fire of the Christians. But they still pressed on,

---

[1] " Eran tantas las Piedras, que nos echaban con Hondas dentro en la Fortaleza, que no parecia sino que el Cielo las llovia; é las Flechas, y Tiraderas eran tantas, que todas las paredes y Patios estaban llenos, que casi no podiamos andar con ellas." (Rel. Seg. de Cortés, ap. Lorenzana, p. 134.) No wonder that they should have found some difficulty in wading through the arrows, if Herrera's account be correct, that *forty cartloads* of them were gathered up and burnt by the besieged every day ! Hist. general, dec. 2, lib. 10, cap. 9.

[2] " Luego sin tardanza se juntáron los Mexicanos, en gran copia, puestos á punto de Guerra, que no parecia, sino que habian salido debajo de tierra todos juntos, y comenzáron luego á dar grita y pelear, y los Españoles les comenzáron á responder de dentro con toda la artillería que de nuebo habian traido, y con toda la gente que de nuevo habia venido, y los Españoles hiciéron gran destrozo en los Indios, con la artillería, arcabuzes, y ballestas y todo el otro artificio de pelear." (Sahagun, Hist. de Nueva-España, MS., lib. 12, cap. 22.) The good father waxes eloquent in his description of the battle-scene.

[3] The enemy presented so easy a mark, says Gomara, that the gunners loaded and fired with hardly the trouble of pointing their pieces. "Tan recio, que los artilleros sin asestar jugaban con los tiros." Crónica, cap. 106.

[4] " Hondas, que eran la mas fuerte arma de pelea que los Mejicanos tenian." Camargo, Hist. de Tlascala, MS.

under the very muzzles of the guns. They endeavoured to scale the parapet, which, from its moderate height, was in itself a work of no great difficulty. But the moment they showed their heads above the rampart they were shot down by the unerring marksmen within, or stretched on the ground by a blow of a Tlascalan *maquahuitl.* Nothing daunted, others soon appeared to take the place of the fallen, and strove by raising themselves on the writhing bodies of their dying comrades, or by fixing their spears in the crevices of the wall, to surmount the barrier. But the attempt proved equally vain.

Defeated here, they tried to effect a breach in the parapet by battering it with heavy pieces of timber. The works were not constructed on those scientific principles by which one part is made to overlook and protect another. The besiegers, therefore, might operate at their pleasure, with but little molestation from the garrison within, whose guns could not be brought into a position to bear on them, and who could mount no part of their own works for their defence without exposing their persons to the missiles of the whole besieging army. The parapet, however, proved too strong for the efforts of the assailants. In their despair, they endeavoured to set the Christian quarters on fire, shooting burning arrows into them, and climbing up so as to dart their firebrands through the embrasures. The principal edifice was of stone. But the temporary defences of the Indian allies, and other parts of the exterior works, were of wood. Several of these took fire, and the flame spread rapidly among the light, combustible materials. This was a disaster for which the besieged where wholly unprepared. They had little water, scarcely enough for their own consumption. They endeavoured to extinguish the flames by heaping on earth. But in vain. Fortunately, the great building was of materials which defied the destroying element. But the fire raged in some of the outworks, connected with the parapet, with a fury which could only be checked by throwing down a part of the wall itself, thus laying open a formidable breach. This, by the general's order, was speedily protected by a battery of heavy guns, and a file of arquebusiers, who kept up an incessant volley through the opening on the assailants.[1]

The fight now raged with fury on both sides. The walls around the palace belched forth an unintermitting sheet of flame and smoke. The groans of the wounded and dying were lost in the fiercer battle-cries of the combatants, the roar of the artillery, the sharper rattle of the musketry, and the hissing sound of Indian missiles. It was the conflict of the European with the American ; of civilized man with the barbarian ; of the science of the one with the rude weapons and warfare of the other. And as the ancient walls of Tenochtitlan shook under the thunders of the

---

[1] " En la Fortaleza daban tan recio combate, que por muchas partes nos pusiéron fuego, y por la una se quemó mucha parte de ella, sin la poder remediar, hasta que la atajámos, cortando las paredes, y derrocando un pedazo que mató el fuego. É si no fuera por la mucha Guarda, que allí puse de Escopeteros, y Ballesteros, y otros tiros de pólvora, nos entraran á escala vista, sin los poder resistir." Rel. Seg. de Cortés, ap. Lorenzana, p. 134.

artillery, it announced that the white man, the destroyer, had set his foot within her precincts.[1]

Night at length came, and drew her friendly mantle over the contest. The Aztec seldom fought by night. It brought little repose, however, to the Spaniards, in hourly expectation of an assault; and they found abundant occupation in restoring the breaches in their defences and in repairing their battered armour. The beleaguering host lay on their arms through the night, giving token of their presence, now and then, by sending a stone or shaft over the battlements, or by a solitary cry of defiance from some warrior more determined than the rest, till all other sounds were lost in the vague, indistinct murmurs which float upon the air in the neighbourhood of a vast assembly.

The ferocity shown by the Mexicans seems to have been a thing for which Cortés was wholly unprepared. His past experience, his uninterrupted career of victory with a much feebler force at his command, had led him to underrate the military efficiency, as well as the valour, of the Indians. The apparent facility with which the Mexicans had acquiesced in the outrages on their sovereign and themselves had led him to hold their courage, in particular, too lightly. He could not believe the present assault to be anything more than a temporary ebullition of the populace, which would soon waste itself by its own fury. And he proposed, on the following day, to sally out and inflict such chastisement on his foes as should bring them to their senses and show who was master in the capital.

With early dawn, the Spaniards were up and under arms; but not before their enemies had given evidence of their hostility by the random missiles which from time to time were sent into the enclosure. As the grey light of morning advanced, it showed the besieging army, far from being diminished in numbers, filling up the great square and neighbouring avenues in more dense array than on the preceding evening. Instead of a confused, disorderly rabble, it had the appearance of something like a regular force, with its battalions distributed under their respective banners, the devices of which showed a contribution from the principal cities and districts in the Valley. High above the rest was conspicuous the ancient standard of Mexico, with its well-known cognizance, an eagle pouncing on an ocelot, emblazoned on a rich mantle of feather-work. Here and there priests might be seen mingling in the ranks of the besiegers, and, with frantic gestures, animating them to avenge their insulted deities.

The greater part of the enemy had little clothing save the *maxtlatl*, or sash round the loins. They were variously armed, with long spears tipped with copper or flint, or sometimes merely pointed and hardened in the fire. Some were provided with slings, and others with darts, having two or three points, with long strings attached to them, by which, when dis-

[1] Rel. Seg. de Cortés, ap. Lorenzana, ubi supra. —Gomara, Crónica, cap. 106.—Oviedo, Hist. de las Ind., MS., lib. 33, cap. 13. — Sahagun, Hist. de Nueva-España, MS., lib. 12, cap. 22.—Gonzalo de las Casas, Defensa, MS., Parte 1, cap. 26.—Bernal Diaz, Hist. de la Conquista, cap. 126.

charged, they could be torn away again from the body of the wounded. This was a formidable weapon, much dreaded by the Spaniards. Those of a higher order wielded the terrible *maquahuitl*, with its sharp and brittle blades of obsidian. Amidst the motley bands of warriors were seen many whose showy dress and air of authority intimated persons of high military consequence. Their breasts were protected by plates of metal, over which was thrown the gay surcoat of feather-work. They wore casques resembling in their form the head of some wild and ferocious animal, crested with bristly hair, or overshadowed by tall and graceful plumes of many a brilliant colour. Some few were decorated with the red fillet bound round the hair, having tufts of cotton attached to it, which denoted by their number that of the victories they had won, and their own pre-eminent rank among the warriors of the nation. The motley assembly plainly showed that priest, warrior, and citizen had all united to swell the tumult.

Before the sun had shot his beams into the Castilian quarters, the enemy were in motion, evidently preparing to renew the assault of the preceding day. The Spanish commander determined to anticipate them by a vigorous sortie, for which he had already made the necessary dispositions. A general discharge of ordnance and musketry sent death far and wide into the enemy's ranks, and, before they had time to recover from their confusion, the gates were thrown open, and Cortés, sallying out at the head of his cavalry, supported by a large body of infantry and several thousand Tlascalans, rode at full gallop against them. Taken thus by surprise, it was scarcely possible to offer much resistance. Those who did were trampled down under the horses' feet, cut to pieces with the broadswords, or pierced with the lances of the riders. The infantry followed up the blow, and the rout for the moment was general.

But the Aztecs fled only to take refuge behind a barricade, or strong work of timber and earth, which had been thrown across the great street through which they were pursued. Rallying on the other side, they made a gallant stand, and poured in turn a volley of their light weapons on the Spaniards, who, saluted with a storm of missiles at the same time from the terraces of the houses, were checked in their career and thrown into some disorder.[1]

Cortés, thus impeded, ordered up a few pieces of heavy ordnance, which soon swept away the barricades and cleared a passage for the army. But it had lost the momentum acquired in its rapid advance. The enemy had time to rally and to meet the Spaniards on more equal terms. They were attacked in flank, too, as they advanced, by fresh battalions, who swarmed in from the adjoining streets and lanes. The canals were alive with boats filled with warriors, who with their formidable darts searched every crevice or weak place in the armour of proof, and made havoc on the unprotected bodies of the Tlascalans. By repeated and vigorous

---

[1] Carta del Exército, MS.

charges, the Spaniards succeeded in driving the Indians before them; though many, with a desperation which showed they loved vengeance better than life, sought to embarrass the movements of their horses by clinging to their legs, or, more successfully, strove to pull the riders from their saddles. And woe to the unfortunate cavalier who was thus dismounted,—to be despatched by the brutal *maquahuitl*, or to be dragged on board a canoe to the bloody altar of sacrifice!

But the greatest annoyance which the Spaniards endured was from the missiles from the *azoteas*, consisting often of large stones, hurled with a force that would tumble the stoutest rider from his saddle. Galled in the extreme by these discharges, against which even their shields afforded no adequate protection, Cortés ordered fire to be set to the buildings. This was no very difficult matter, since, although chiefly of stone, they were filled with mats, canework, and other combustible materials, which were soon in a blaze. But the buildings stood separated from one another by canals and drawbridges, so that the flames did not easily communicate to the neighbouring edifices. Hence the labour of the Spaniards was incalculably increased, and their progress in the work of destruction—fortunately for the city—was comparatively slow.[1] They did not relax their efforts, however, till several hundred houses had been consumed, and the miseries of a conflagration, in which the wretched inmates perished equally with the defenders, were added to the other horrors of the scene.

The day was now far spent. The Spaniards had been everywhere victorious. But the enemy, though driven back on every point, still kept the field. When broken by the furious charges of the cavalry, he soon rallied behind the temporary defences, which, at different intervals, had been thrown across the streets, and, facing about, renewed the fight with undiminished courage, till the sweeping away of the barriers by the cannon of the assailants left a free passage for the movements of their horse. Thus the action was a succession of rallying and retreating, in which both parties suffered much, although the loss inflicted on the Indians was probably tenfold greater than that of the Spaniards. But the Aztecs could better afford the loss of a hundred lives than their antagonists that of one. And, while the Spaniards showed an array broken and obviously thinned in numbers, the Mexican army, swelled by the tributary levies which flowed in upon it from the neighbouring streets, exhibited, with all its losses, no sign of diminution. At length, sated with carnage, and exhausted by toil and hunger, the Spanish commander drew off his men, and sounded a retreat.[2]

---

[1] "Están todas en el agua, y de casa á casa vna puente leuadiza, passalla á nado, era cosa muy peligrosa; porque desde las açuteas tirauan tanta piedra, y cantos, que era cosa perdida ponernos en ello. Y demas desto, en alguna: casas que les poniamos fuego, tardaua vna casa en se quemar vn dia entero, y no se podia pegar fuego de vna casa á otra; lo vno, por estar apartadas la vna de otra el agua en medio; y lo otro, por ser de açuteas." Bernal Diaz, Hist. de la Conquista, cap. 126.

[2] "The Mexicans fought with such ferocity," says Diaz, "that, if we had had the assistance on that day of ten thousand Hectors, and as many Orlandos, we should have made no impression on them.

On his way back to his quarters, he beheld his friend the secretary Duero, in a street adjoining, unhorsed, and hotly engaged with a body of Mexicans, against whom he was desperately defending himself with his poniard. Cortés, roused at the sight, shouted his war-cry, and, dashing into the midst of the enemy, scattered them like chaff by the fury of his onset ; then, recovering his friend's horse, he enabled him to remount, and the two cavaliers, striking their spurs into their steeds, burst through their opponents and joined the main body of the army.[1] Such displays of generous gallantry were not uncommon in these engagements, which called forth more feats of personal adventure than battles with antagonists better skilled in the science of war. The chivalrous bearing of the general was emulated in full measure by Sandoval, De Leon, Olid, Alvarado, Ordaz, and his other brave companions, who won such glory under the eye of their leader as prepared the way for the independent commands which afterwards placed provinces and kingdoms at their disposal.

The undaunted Aztecs hung on the rear of their retreating foes, annoying them at every step by fresh flights of stones and arrows ; and, when the Spaniards had re-entered their fortress, the Indian host encamped around it, showing the same dogged resolution as on the preceding evening. Though true to their ancient habits of inaction during the night, they broke the stillness of the hour by insulting cries and menaces, which reached the ears of the besieged. "The gods have delivered you, at last, into our hands," they said ; "Huitzilopochtli has long cried for his victims. The stone of sacrifice is ready. The knives are sharpened. The wild beasts in the palace are roaring for their offal. And the cages," they added, taunting the Tlascalans with their leanness, "are waiting for the false sons of Anahuac, who are to be fattened for the festival!" These dismal menaces, which sounded fearfully in the ears of the besieged, who understood too well their import, were mingled with piteous lamentations for their sovereign, whom they called on the Spaniards to deliver up to them.

Cortés suffered much from a severe wound which he had received in the hand in the late action. But the anguish of his mind must have been still greater as he brooded over the dark prospect before him. He had mistaken the character of the Mexicans. Their long and patient endurance had been a violence to their natural temper, which, as their whole history proves, was arrogant and ferocious beyond that of most of the races of Anahuac. The restraint which, in deference to their monarch more than to their own fears, they had so long put on their natures, being once removed, their passions burst forth with accumulated violence.

There were several of our troops," he adds, "who had served in the Italian wars, but neither there nor in the battles with the Turk had they ever seen anything like the desperation shown by these Indians." Hist. de la Conquista, cap. 126. See, also, for the last pages, Rel. Seg. de Cortés, ap. Lorenzana, p.

135,—Ixtlilxochitl, Relaciones, MS.,—Probanza á pedimento de Juan de Lexalde, MS.,—Oviedo, Hist. de las Ind., MS., lib. 33, cap. 13,—Gomara, Crónica, cap. 196.
[1] Herrera, Hist. general, dec. 2, lib. 10, cap. 9.— Torquemada, Monarch. Ind., lib. 4, cap. 69.

The Spaniards had encountered in the Tlascalan an open enemy, who had no grievance to complain of, no wrong to redress. He fought under the vague apprehension only of some coming evil to his country. But the Aztec, hitherto the proud lord of the land, was goaded by insult and injury, till he had reached that pitch of self-devotion which made life cheap in comparison with revenge. Armed thus with the energy of despair, the savage is almost a match for the civilized man; and a whole nation, moved to its depths by a common feeling, which swallows up all selfish considerations of personal interest and safety, becomes, whatever be its resources, like the earthquake and the tornado, the most formidable among the agencies of nature.

Considerations of this kind may have passed through the mind of Cortés, as he reflected on his own impotence to restrain the fury of the Mexicans, and resolved, in despite of his late supercilious treatment of Montezuma, to employ his authority to allay the tumult,—an authority so successfully exerted in behalf of Alvarado at an earlier stage of the insurrection. He was the more confirmed in his purpose on the following morning, when the assailants, redoubling their efforts, succeeded in scaling the works in one quarter and effecting an entrance into the enclosure. It is true, they were met with so resolute a spirit that not a man of those who entered was left alive. But, in the impetuosity of the assault, it seemed, for a few moments, as if the place was to be carried by storm.[1]

Cortés now sent to the Aztec emperor to request his interposition with his subjects in behalf of the Spaniards. But Montezuma was not in the humour to comply. He had remained moodily in his quarters ever since the general's return. Disgusted with the treatment he had received, he had still further cause for mortification in finding himself the ally of those who were the open enemies of his nation. From his apartment he had beheld the tragical scenes in his capital, and seen another, the presumptive heir to his throne, taking the place which he should have occupied at the head of his warriors and fighting the battles of his country.[2] Distressed by his position, indignant at those who had placed him in it, he coldly answered, "What have I to do with Malinche? I do not wish to hear from him. I desire only to die. To what a state has my willingness to serve him reduced me!"[3] When urged still further to comply by Olid and Father Olmedo, he added, "It is of no use. They will neither believe me, nor the false words and promises of Malinche. You will never leave these walls alive." On being assured, however, that the Spaniards would willingly depart if a way were opened to them by their enemies, he

[1] Bernal Diaz, Hist. de la Conquista, cap. 126.—Oviedo, Hist. de las Ind., MS., lib. 33, cap. 13.—Gomara, Crónica, cap. 107.

[2] Cortés sent Marina to ascertain from Montezuma the name of the gallant chief, who could be easily seen from the walls animating and directing his countrymen. The emperor informed him that it was his brother Cuitlahua, the presumptive heir to his crown, and the same chief whom the Spanish commander had released a few days previous. Herrera, Hist. general, dec. 2, lib. 10, cap. 10.

[3] "¿Que quiere de mí ya Malinche, que yo no deseo viuir ni oille? pues en tal estado por su causa mi ventura me ha traido." Bernal Diaz, Hist. de la Conquista, cap. 126.

at length—moved, probably, more by the desire to spare the blood of his subjects than of the Christians—consented to expostulate with his people.[1]

In order to give the greater effect to his presence, he put on his imperial robes. The *tilmatli*, his mantle of white and blue, flowed over his shoulders, held together by its rich clasp of the green *chalchivitl*. The same precious gem, with emeralds of uncommon size, set in gold, profusely ornamented other parts of his dress. His feet were shod with the golden sandals, and his brows covered by the *copilli*, or Mexican diadem, resembling in form the pontifical tiara. Thus attired, and surrounded by a guard of Spaniards and several Aztec nobles, and preceded by the golden wand, the symbol of sovereignty, the Indian monarch ascended the central turret of the palace. His presence was instantly recognized by the people, and, as the royal retinue advanced along the battlements, a change, as if by magic, came over the scene. The clang of instruments, the fierce cries of the assailants, were hushed, and a deathlike stillness pervaded the whole assembly, so fiercely agitated, but a few moments before, by the wild tumult of war! Many prostrated themselves on the ground; others bent the knee; and all turned with eager expectation towards the monarch whom they had been taught to reverence with slavish awe, and from whose countenance they had been wont to turn away as from the intolerable splendours of divinity. Montezuma saw his advantage; and, while he stood thus confronted with his awestruck people, he seemed to recover all his former authority and confidence, as he felt himself to be still a king. With a calm voice, easily heard over the silent assembly, he is said by the Castilian writers to have thus addressed them:—

"Why do I see my people here in arms against the palace of my fathers? Is it that you think your sovereign a prisoner, and wish to release him? If so, you have acted rightly. But you are mistaken. I am no prisoner. The strangers are my guests. I remain with them only from choice, and can leave them when I list. Have you come to drive them from the city? That is unnecessary. They will depart of their own accord, if you will open a way for them. Return to your homes, then. Lay down your arms. Show your obedience to me, who have a right to it. The white men shall go back to their own land; and all shall be well again within the walls of Tenochtitlan."

As Montezuma announced himself the friend of the detested strangers, a murmur ran through the multitude; a murmur of contempt for the pusillanimous prince who could show himself so insensible to the insults and injuries for which the nation was in arms. The swollen tide of their passions swept away all the barriers of ancient reverence, and, taking a new direction, descended on the head of the unfortunate monarch, so far degenerated from his warlike ancestors. "Base Aztec," they exclaimed,

---

[1] Bernal Diaz, Hist. de la Conquista, ubi supra.—Ixtlilxochitl, Hist. Chich., MS., cap. 88.

" woman, coward ! the white men have made you a woman,—fit only to weave and spin ! " These bitter taunts were soon followed by still more hostile demonstrations. A chief, it is said, of high rank, bent a bow or brandished a javelin with an air of defiance against the emperor,[1] when, in an instant, a cloud of stones and arrows descended on the spot where the royal train was gathered. The Spaniards appointed to protect his person had been thrown off their guard by the respectful deportment of the people during their lord's address. They now hastily interposed their bucklers. But it was too late. Montezuma was wounded by three of the missiles, one of which, a stone, fell with such violence on his head, near the temple, as brought him senseless to the ground. The Mexicans, shocked at their own sacrilegious act, experienced a sudden revulsion of feeling, and, setting up a dismal cry, dispersed, panic-struck, in different directions. Not one of the multitudinous array remained in the great square before the palace !

The unhappy prince, meanwhile, was borne by his attendants to his apartments below. On recovering from the insensibility caused by the blow, the wretchedness of his condition broke upon him. He had tasted the last bitterness of degradation. He had been reviled, rejected, by his people. The meanest of the rabble had raised their hands against him. He had nothing more to live for. It was in vain that Cortés and his officers endeavoured to soothe the anguish of his spirit and fill him with better thoughts. He spoke not a word in answer. His wound, though dangerous, might still, with skilful treatment, not prove mortal. But Montezuma refused all the remedies prescribed for it. He tore off the bandages as often as they were applied, maintaining, all the while, the most determined silence. He sat with eyes dejected, brooding over his fallen fortunes, over the image of ancient majesty and present humiliation. He had survived his honour. But a spark of his ancient spirit seemed to kindle in his bosom, as it was clear he did not mean to survive his disgrace. From this painful scene the Spanish general and his followers were soon called away by the new dangers which menaced the garrison.[2]

---

[1] Acosta reports a tradition that Guatemozin, Montezuma's nephew, who himself afterwards succeeded to the throne, was the man that shot the first arrow. Lib. 7, cap. 26.

[2] I have reported this tragical event, and the circumstances attending it, as they are given, in more or less detail, but substantially in the same way, by the most accredited writers of that and the following age,—several of them eyewitnesses. (See Bernal Diaz, Hist. de la Conquista, cap. 126.—Oviedo, Hist. de las Ind., MS., lib. 33, cap. 47.—Rel. Seg. de Cortés, ap. Lorenzana, p. 136.—Camargo, Hist. de Tlascala, MS.—Ixtlilxochitl, Hist. Chich., MS., cap. 88.—Herrera, Hist. general, dec. 2, lib. 10, cap. 10.—Torquemada, Monarch. Ind., lib. 4, cap. 70.—Acosta, ubi supra.—Martyr, De Orbe Novo, dec. 5, cap. 5.) It is also confirmed by Cortés in the instrument granting to Montezuma's favourite daughter certain estates by way of dowry. (See Appendix, Part 2, No. 12.) Don Thoan Cano, indeed, who married this princess, assured Oviedo that the Mexicans respected the person of the monarch so long as they saw him, and were not aware, when they discharged their missiles, tnat he was

present, being hid from sight by the shields of the Spaniards. (See Appendix, Part 2, No. 11.) This improbable statement is repeated by the chaplain Gomara. (Crónica, cap. 107.) It is rejected by Oviedo, however, who says that Alvarado, himself present at the scene, in a conversation with him afterwards, explicitly confirmed the narrative given in the text. (Hist. de las Ind., MS., lib. 33, cap. 47.) The Mexicans gave a very different account of the transaction. According to them, Montezuma, together with the lords of Tezcuco and Tlatelolco, then detained as prisoners in the fortress by the Spaniards, were all strangled by means of the *garrote*, and their dead bodies thrown over the walls to their countrymen. I quote the original of Father Sahagun, who gathered the story from the Aztecs themselves :—

" De esta manera se determináron los Españoles á morir ó vencer varonilmente ; y así habláron á todos los amigos Indios, y todos ellos estuviéron firmes en esta determinacion : y lo primero que hiciéron fué que diéron garrote á todos los Señores que tenian presos, y los echáron muertos fuera del fuerte : y antes que esto hiciesen les dijéron muchas

CHAPTER II.

STORMING OF THE GREAT TEMPLE.—SPIRIT OF THE AZTECS.—DISTRESSES OF THE GARRISON. — SHARP COMBATS IN THE CITY. — DEATH OF MONTEZUMA.

(1520.)

OPPOSITE to the Spanish quarters, at only a few rods' distance, stood the great *teocalli* of Huitzilopochtli. This pyramidal mound, with the sanctuaries that crowned it, rising altogether to the height of near a hundred and fifty feet, afforded an elevated position that completely commanded the palace of Axayacatl, occupied by the Christians. A body of five or six hundred Mexicans, many of them nobles and warriors of the highest rank, had got possession of the *teocalli*, whence they discharged such a tempest of arrows on the garrison that no one could leave his defences for a moment without imminent danger ; while the Mexicans, under shelter of the sanctuaries, were entirely covered from the fire of the besieged. It was obviously necessary to dislodge the enemy, if the Spaniards would remain longer in their quarters.

Cortés assigned this service to his chamberlain, Escobar, giving him a hundred men for the purpose, with orders to storm the *teocalli* and set fire to the sanctuaries. But that officer was thrice repulsed in the attempt, and, after the most desperate efforts, was obliged to return with considerable loss and without accomplishing his object.

Cortés, who saw the immediate necessity of carrying the place, determined to lead the storming party himself. He was then suffering much from the wound in his left hand, which had disabled it for the present. He made the arm serviceable, however, by fastening his buckler to it,[1] and, thus crippled, sallied out at the head of three hundred chosen cavaliers and several thousand of his auxiliaries.

In the courtyard of the temple he found a numerous body of Indians prepared to dispute his passage. He briskly charged them ; but the flat

---

cosas, y les hiciéron saber su determinacion, y que de ellos habia de comenzar esta obra, y luego todos los demas habian de ser muertos á sus manos, dijéronles, no es posible que vuestros ídolos os libren de nuestras manos. Y desque les hubiéron dado Garrote, y viéron que estaban muertos, mandáronlos .char por las azoteas, fuera de la casa, en un lugar que se llama Tortuga de Piedra, porque allí estaba una piedra labrada á manera de Tortuga. Y desque supiéron y viéron los de á fuera, que aquellos Señores tan principales habian sido muertos por las manos de los Españoles, luego tomáron los cuerpos, y les hiciéron sus exequias, al modo de su Idolatría, y quemáron sus cuerpos, y tomáron sus cenizas, y las pusiéron en lugares apropiadas á sus dignidades y valor." Hist. de Nueva - España, MS., lib. 12, cap. 23.

It is hardly necessary to comment on the absurdity of this monstrous imputation, which, however, has found favour with some later writers. Independently of all other considerations, the Spaniards would have been slow to compass the Indian monarch's death, since, as the Tezcucan Ixtlilxochitl truly observes, it was the most fatal blow which could befall them, by dissolving the last tie which held them to the Mexicans. Hist. Chich., MS., ubi supra.

[1] " Salí fuera de la Fortaleza, aunque manco de la mano izquierda de una herida que el primer dia me habian dado : y liada la rodela en el brazo fuý á la Torre con algunos Españoles, que me siguiéron." Rel. Seg. de Cortés, ap. Lorenzana, p. 138.

smooth stones of the pavement were so slippery that the horses lost their footing and many of them fell. Hastily dismounting, they sent back the animals to their quarters, and, renewing the assault, the Spaniards succeeded without much difficulty in dispersing the Indian warriors and opening a free passage for themselves to the *teocalli*. This building, as the reader may remember, was a huge pyramidal structure, about three hundred feet square at the base. A flight of stone steps on the outside, at one of the angles of the mound, led to a platform, or terraced walk, which passed round the building until it reached a similar flight of stairs directly over the preceding, that conducted to another landing as before. As there were five bodies or divisions of the *teocalli*, it became necessary to pass round its whole extent four times, or nearly a mile, in order to reach the summit, which, it may be recollected, was an open area, crowned only by the two sanctuaries dedicated to the Aztec deities.[1]

Cortés, having cleared a way for the assault, sprang up the lower stairway, followed by Alvarado, Sandoval, Ordaz, and the other gallant cavaliers of his little band, leaving a file of arquebusiers and a strong corps of Indian allies to hold the enemy in check at the foot of the monument. On the first landing, as well as on the several galleries above, and on the summit, the Aztec warriors were drawn up to dispute his passage. From their elevated position they showered down volleys of lighter missiles, together with heavy stones, beams, and burning rafters, which, thundering along the stairway, overturned the ascending Spaniards and carried desolation through their ranks. The more fortunate, eluding or springing over these obstacles, succeeded in gaining the first terrace; where, throwing themselves on their enemies, they compelled them, after a short resistance, to fall back. The assailants pressed on, effectually supported by a brisk fire of the musketeers from below, which so much galled the Mexicans in their exposed situation that they were glad to take shelter on the broad summit of the *teocalli*.

Cortés and his comrades were close upon their rear, and the two parties soon found themselves face to face on this aerial battle-field, engaged in mortal combat in presence of the whole city, as well as of the troops in the courtyard, who paused, as if by mutual consent, from their own hostilities, gazing in silent expectation on the issue of those above. The area, though somewhat smaller than the base of the *teocalli*, was large enough to afford a fair field of fight for a thousand combatants. It was paved with broad, flat stones. No impediment occurred over its surface, except the huge sacrificial block, and the temples of stone which rose to the height of forty feet, at the farther extremity of the arena. One of these had been consecrated to the Cross. The other was still occupied by the Mexican war-god. The Christian and the Aztec contended for their religions under the very

---

[1] See *ante*, pp. 298, 299.—I have ventured to repeat the description of the temple here, as it is important that the reader, who may perhaps not turn to the preceding pages, should have a distinct image of it in his own mind before beginning the account of the combat.

shadow of their respective shrines; while the Indian priests, running to and fro, with their hair wildly streaming over their sable mantles, seemed hovering in mid-air, like so many demons of darkness urging on the work of slaughter !

The parties closed with the desperate fury of men who had no hope but in victory. Quarter was neither asked nor given; and to fly was impossible. The edge of the area was unprotected by parapet or battlement. The least slip would be fatal; and the combatants, as they struggled in mortal agony, were sometimes seen to roll over the sheer sides of the precipice together.[1] Cortés himself is said to have had a narrow escape from this dreadful fate. Two warriors, of strong, muscular frames, seized on him, and were dragging him violently towards the brink of the pyramid. Aware of their intention, he struggled with all his force, and, before they could accomplish their purpose, succeeded in tearing himself from their grasp and hurling one of them over the walls with his own arm ! The story is not improbable in itself, for Cortés was a man of uncommon agility and strength. It has been often repeated; but not by contemporary history.[2]

The battle lasted with unintermitting fury for three hours. The number of the enemy was double that of the Christians; and it seemed as if it were a contest which must be determined by numbers and brute force, rather than by superior science. But it was not so. The invulnerable armour of the Spaniard, his sword of matchless temper, and his skill in the use of it, gave him advantages which far outweighed the odds of physical strength and numbers. After doing all that the courage of despair could enable men to do, resistance grew fainter and fainter on the side of the Aztecs. One after another they had fallen. Two or three priests only survived, to be led away in triumph by the victors. Every other combatant was stretched a corpse on the bloody arena, or had been hurled from the giddy heights. Yet the loss of the Spaniards was not inconsiderable. It amounted to forty-five of their best men; and nearly all the remainder were more or less injured in the desperate conflict.[3]

---

[1] Many of the Aztecs, according to Sahagun, seeing the fate of such of their comrades as fell into the hands of the Spaniards on the narrow terraces below, voluntarily threw themselves headlong from the lofty summit, and were dashed in pieces on the pavement. "Y los de arriba viendo á los de abajo muertos, y á los de arriba que los iban matando los que habian subido, comenzáron á arrojarse del cu abajo, desde lo alto, los cuales todos morian despeñados, quebrados brazos y piernas, y hechos pedazos, porque el cu era muy alto; y otros los mesmos Españoles los arrojaban de lo alto del cu, y así todos cuantos allá habian subido de los Mexicanos, muriéron mala muerte." Sahagun, Hist. de Neuva-España, MS., lib. 12, cap. 22.

[2] Among others, see Herrera, Hist. general, dec. 2, lib. 10, cap. 9,—Torquemada, Monarch. Ind., lib. 4, cap. 69,—and Solís, very circumstantially, as usual, Conquista, lib. 4, cap. 16.—The first of these authors had access to some contemporary sources, the chronicle of the old soldier, Ojeda, for example,

not now to be met with. It is strange that so valiant an exploit should not have been communicated by Cortés himself, who cannot be accused of diffidence in such matters.

[3] Captain Diaz, a little loth sometimes, is emphatic in his encomiums on the valour shown by his commander on this occasion. "Here Cortés showed himself a very man, such as he always was. Oh what a fighting, what a strenuous battle, did we have ! It was a memorable thing to see us flowing with blood and full of wounds, and more than forty soldiers slain." (Hist. de la Conquista, cap. 126.) The pens of the old chroniclers keep pace with their swords in the display of this brilliant exploit:—"colla penna e colla spada," equally fortunate. See Rel. Seg. de Cortés, ap. Lorenzana, p. 138.—Gomara, Crónica, cap. 106.—Sahagun, Hist. de Nueva-España, MS., lib. 12, cap. 22.—Herrera, Hist. general, dec. 2, lib. 10, cap. 9.—Oviedo, Hist. de las Ind., MS., lib. 33, cap. 13.—Torquemada, Monarch. Ind., lib. 4, cap. 69.

The victorious cavaliers now rushed towards the sanctuaries. The lower story was of stone ; the two upper were of wood. Penetrating into their recesses, they had the mortification to find the image of the Virgin and the Cross removed.[1] But in the other edifice they still beheld the grim figure of Huitzilopochtli, with his censer of smoking hearts, and the walls of his oratory reeking with gore,—not improbably of their own countrymen ! With shouts of triumph the Christians tore the uncouth monster from his niche, and tumbled him, in the presence of the horror-struck Aztecs, down the steps of the *teocalli*,[2] they then set fire to the accursed building. The flames speedily ran up the slender towers, sending forth an ominous light over city, lake, and valley, to the remotest hut among the mountains. It was the funeral pyre of paganism, and proclaimed the fall of that sanguinary religion which had so long hung like a dark cloud over the fair regions of Anahuac ![3]

Having accomplished this good work, the Spaniards descended the winding slopes of the *teocalli* with more free and buoyant step, as if conscious that the blessing of Heaven now rested on their arms. They passed through the dusky files of Indian warriors in the courtyard, too much dismayed by the appalling scenes they had witnessed to offer resistance, and reached their own quarters in safety. That very night they followed up the blow by a sortie on the sleeping town, and burned three hundred houses, the horrors of conflagration being made still more impressive by occurring at the hour when the Aztecs, from their own system of warfare, were least prepared for them.[4]

Hoping to find the temper of the natives somewhat subdued by these reverses, Cortés now determined, with his usual policy, to make them a vantage-ground for proposing terms of accommodation. He accordingly invited the enemy to a parley, and, as the principal chiefs, attended by their followers, assembled in the great square, he mounted the turret before occupied by Montezuma, and made signs that he would address them. Marina, as usual, took her place by his side, as his interpreter.

[1] Archbishop Lorenzana is of opinion that this image of the Virgin is the same now seen in the church of *Nuestra Señora de los Remedios!* (Rel. Seg. de Cortés, ap. Lorenzana, p. 138, nota.) In what way the Virgin survived the sack of the city and was brought to light again, he does not inform us. But the more difficult to explain, the more undoubted the miracle.

[2] [Sir Arthur Helps speaks, rather oddly, of Cortés having set fire to this image. Neither Cortés himself nor Bernal Diaz mentions any such attempt to burn what is described as a "huge block of basalt, covered with sculptured figures." It is now in the museum at Mexico, having lain undiscovered in the great square, close to the site of the *teocalli*, till the end of the last century. "For some years after that it was kept buried, lest the sight of one of their old deities might be too exciting for the Indians, who had certainly not forgotten it, and secretly ornamented it with flowers as long as it remained above ground." Tylor, Anahuac, p. 223. —ED.]

[3] No achievement in the war struck more awe into the Mexicans than this storming of the great

temple, in which the white men seemed to bid defiance equally to the powers of God and man. Hieroglyphical paintings minutely commemorating it were to be frequently found among the natives after the Conquest. The sensitive Captain Diaz intimates that those which he saw made full as much account of the wounds and losses of the Christians as the facts would warrant. (Hist. de la Conquista, ubi supra.) It was the only way in which the conquered could take their revenge.

[4] "Sequenti nocte, nostri erumpentes in vna viarum arci vicina, domos combussère tercentum : in altera plerasque e quibus arci molestia fiebat. Ita nunc trucidando, nunc diruendo, et interdum vulnera recipiendo, in pontibus et in viis, diebus noctibusque multis laboratum est utrinque. (Martyr, De Orbe Novo, dec. 5, cap. 6.) In the number of actions and their general result, namely, the victories, barren victories, of the Christians, all writers are agreed. But as to time, place, circumstance, or order, no two hold together. How shall the historian of the present day make a harmonious tissue out of these motley and many-coloured threads?

The multitude gazed with earnest curiosity on the Indian girl, whose influence with the Spaniards was well known, and whose connection with the general, in particular, had led the Aztecs to designate him by her Mexican name of Malinche.[1] Cortés, speaking through the soft, musical tones of his mistress, told his audience they must now be convinced that they had nothing further to hope from opposition to the Spaniards. They had seen their gods trampled in the dust, their altars broken, their dwellings burned, their warriors falling on all sides. "All this," continued he, "you have brought on yourselves by your rebellion. Yet, for the affection the sovereign whom you have so unworthily treated still bears you, I would willingly stay my hand, if you will lay down your arms and return once more to your obedience. But, if you do not," he concluded, "I will make your city a heap of ruins, and leave not a soul alive to mourn over it!"

But the Spanish commander did not yet comprehend the character of the Aztecs, if he thought to intimidate them by menaces. Calm in their exterior, and slow to move, they were the more difficult to pacify when roused; and now that they had been stirred to their inmost depths, it was no human voice that could still the tempest. It may be, however, that Cortés did not so much misconceive the character of the people. He may have felt that an authoritative tone was the only one he could assume with any chance of effect in his present position, in which milder and more conciliatory language would, by intimating a consciousness of inferiority, have too certainly defeated its own object.

It was true, they answered, he had destroyed their temples, broken in pieces their gods, massacred their countrymen. Many more, doubtless, were yet to fall under their terrible swords. But they were content so long as for every thousand Mexicans they could shed the blood of a single white man![2] "Look out," they continued, "on our terraces and streets; see them still thronged with warriors, as far as your eyes can reach. Our numbers are scarcely diminished by our losses. Yours, on the contrary, are lessening every hour. You are perishing from hunger and sickness. Your provisions and water are failing. You must soon fall into our hands. *The bridges are broken down, and you cannot escape!*[3] There will be too few of you left to glut the vengeance of our gods!" As they concluded, they sent a volley of arrows over the battlements, which compelled the Spaniards to descend and take refuge in their defences.

The fierce and indomitable spirit of the Aztecs filled the besieged with dismay. All, then, that they had done and suffered, their battles by day,

---

[1] It is the name by which she is still celebrated in the popular minstrelsy of Mexico. Was the famous Tlascalan mountain, *sierra de Malinche,*—anciently "Mattalcueye,"—named in compliment to the Indian damsel? At all events, it was an honour well merited from her adopted countrymen.

[2] According to Cortés, they boasted, in somewhat loftier strain, they could spare twenty-five thousand for one: "á morir veinte y cinco mil de ellos, y uno de los nuestros." Rel. Seg. de Cortés, ap. Lorenzana, p. 139.

[3] "Que todas las calzadas de las entradas de la ciudad eran deshechas, como de hecho passaba." Ibid., loc. cit.—Oviedo, Hist. de las Ind., MS., lib. 33, cap. 13.

their vigils by night, the perils they had braved, even the victories they had won, were of no avail. It was too evident that they had no longer the spring of ancient superstition to work upon in the breasts of the natives, who, like some wild beast that has burst the bonds of his keeper, seemed now to swell and exult in the full consciousness of their strength. The annunciation respecting the bridges fell like a knell on the ears of the Christians. All that they had heard was too true ; and they gazed on one another with looks of anxiety and dismay.

The same consequences followed which sometimes take place among the crew of a shipwrecked vessel. Subordination was lost in the dreadful sense of danger. A spirit of mutiny broke out, especially among the recent levies drawn from the army of Narvaez. They had come into the country from no motive of ambition, but attracted simply by the glowing reports of its opulence, and they had fondly hoped to return in a few months with their pockets well lined with the gold of the Aztec monarch. But how different had been their lot! From the first hour of their landing, they had experienced only trouble and disaster, privations of every description, sufferings unexampled, and they now beheld in perspective a fate yet more appalling. Bitterly did they lament the hour when they left the sunny fields of Cuba for these cannibal regions ; and heartily did they curse their own folly in listening to the call of Velasquez, and still more in embarking under the banner of Cortés ![1]

They now demanded, with noisy vehemence, to be led instantly from the city, and refused to serve longer in defence of a place where they were cooped up like sheep in the shambles, waiting only to be dragged to slaughter. In all this they were rebuked by the more orderly, soldier-like conduct of the veterans of Cortés. These latter had shared with their general the day of his prosperity, and they were not disposed to desert him in the tempest. It was, indeed, obvious, on a little reflection, that the only chance of safety, in the existing crisis, rested on subordination and union, and that even this chance must be greatly diminished under any other leader than their present one.

Thus pressed by enemies without and by factions within, that leader was found, as usual, true to himself. Circumstances so appalling as would have paralyzed a common mind only stimulated his to higher action and drew forth all its resources. He combined, what is most rare, singular coolness and constancy of purpose with a spirit of enterprise that might well be called romantic. His presence of mind did not now desert him. He calmly surveyed his condition and weighed the difficulties which surrounded him, before coming to a decision. Independently of the hazard of a retreat in the face of a watchful and desperate foe, it was a deep mortification to

---

[1] "Pues tambien quiero dezir las maldiciones que los de Narvaez echauan á Cortés, y las palabras que dezian, que renegauan dél, y de la tierra, y aun de Diego Velasquez, que acá les embió, que bien   pacíficos estauan en sus casas en la Isla de Cuba, y estavan embelesados, y sin sentido." Bernal Diaz, Hist. de la Conquista, ubi supra.

surrender up the city where he had so long lorded it as a master; to abandon the rich treasures which he had secured to himself and his followers; to forego the very means by which he had hoped to propitiate the favour of his sovereign and secure an amnesty for his irregular proceedings. This, he well knew, must, after all, be dependent on success. To fly now was to acknowledge himself further removed from the conquest than ever. What a close was this to a career so auspiciously begun! What a contrast to his magnificent vaunts! What a triumph would it afford to his enemies! The governor of Cuba would be amply revenged.

But, if such humiliating reflections crowded on his mind, the alternative of remaining, in his present crippled condition, seemed yet more desperate.[1] With his men daily diminishing in strength and numbers, their provisions reduced so low that a small daily ration of bread was all the sustenance afforded to the soldier under his extraordinary fatigues,[2] with the breaches every day widening in his feeble fortifications, with his ammunition, in fine, nearly expended, it would be impossible to maintain the place much longer—and none but men of iron constitutions and tempers, like the Spaniards, could have held it so long—against the enemy. The chief embarrassment was as to the time and manner in which it would be expedient to evacuate the city. The best route seemed to be that of Tlacopan (Tacuba). For the causeway, the most dangerous part of the road, was but two miles long in that direction, and would, therefore, place the fugitives, much sooner than either of the other great avenues, on terra firma. Before his final departure, however, Cortés proposed to make another sally, in order to reconnoitre the ground, and, at the same time, divert the enemy's attention from his real purpose by a show of active operations.

For some days his workmen had been employed in constructing a military machine of his own invention. It was called a *manta*, and was contrived somewhat on the principle of the mantelets used in the wars of the Middle Ages. It was, however, more complicated, consisting of a tower made of light beams and planks, having two chambers, one over the other. These were to be filled with musketeers, and the sides were provided with loopholes, through which a fire could be kept up on the enemy. The great advantage proposed by this contrivance was to afford a defence to the troops against the missiles hurled from the terraces. These machines, three of which were made, rested on rollers, and were provided with strong ropes, by which they were to be dragged along the streets by the Tlascalan auxiliaries.[3]

---

[1] Notwithstanding this, in the petition or letter from Vera Cruz, addressed by the army to the Emperor Charles V., after the Conquest, the importunity of the soldiers is expressly stated as the principal motive that finally induced their general to abandon the city. Carta del Exército, MS.

[2] "The scarcity was such that the ration of the Indians was a small cake, and that of the Spaniards fifty grains of maize." Herrera, Hist. general, dec. 2, lib. 10, cap. 9.

[3] Rel. Seg. de Cortés, ap. Lorenzana, p. 135.—Gomara, Crónica, cap. 106.—Dr. Bird, in his picturesque romance of "Calavar," has made good use of these *mantas*, better, indeed, than can be permitted to the historian. He claims the privilege of the romancer; though it must be owned he does not

The Mexicans gazed with astonishment on this warlike machinery, and, as the rolling fortresses advanced, belching forth fire and smoke from their entrails, the enemy, incapable of making an impression on those within, fell back in dismay. By bringing the *mantas* under the walls of the houses, the Spaniards were enabled to fire with effect on the mischievous tenants of the *azoteas*, and, when this did not silence them, by letting a ladder, or light drawbridge, fall on the roof from the top of the *manta*, they opened a passage to the terrace, and closed with the combatants hand to hand. They could not, however, thus approach the higher buildings, from which the Indian warriors threw down such heavy masses of stone and timber as dislodged the planks that covered the machines, or, thundering against their sides, shook the frail edifices to their foundations, threatening all within with indiscriminate ruin. Indeed, the success of the experiment was doubtful, when the intervention of a canal put a stop to their further progress.

The Spaniards now found the assertion of their enemies too well confirmed. The bridge which traversed the opening had been demolished; and, although the canals which intersected the city were, in general, of no great width or depth, the removal of the bridges not only impeded the movements of the general's clumsy machines, but effectually disconcerted those of his cavalry. Resolving to abandon the *mantas*, he gave orders to fill up the chasm with stone, timber, and other rubbish drawn from the ruined buildings, and to make a new passage-way for the army. While this labour was going on, the Aztec slingers and archers on the other side of the opening kept up a galling discharge on the Christians, the more defenceless from the nature of their occupation. When the work was completed, and a safe passage secured, the Spanish cavaliers rode briskly against the enemy, who, unable to resist the shock of the steel-clad column, fell back with precipitation to where another canal afforded a similar strong position for defence.[1]

There were no less than seven of these canals intersecting the great street of Tlacopan,[2] and at every one the same scene was renewed, the Mexicans making a gallant stand and inflicting some loss, at each, on their persevering antagonists. These operations consumed two days, when, after incredible toil, the Spanish general had the satisfaction to find the line of communication completely re-established through the whole length of the avenue, and the principal bridges placed under strong detachments

abuse this privilege, for he has studied with great care the costume, manners, and military usages of the natives. He has done for them what Cooper has done for the wild tribes of the North,—touched their rude features with the bright colouring of a poetic fancy. He has been equally fortunate in his delineation of the picturesque scenery of the land. If he has been less so in attempting to revive the antique dialogue of the Spanish cavalier, we must not be surprised. Nothing is more difficult than the skilful execution of a modern antique. It requires all the genius and learning of Scott to execute

it so that the connoisseur shall not detect the counterfeit.

[1] Carta del Exército, MS.—Rel. Seg. de Cortés, ap. Lorenzana, p. 140.—Gomara, Crónica, cap. 109.

[2] Clavigero is mistaken in calling this the street of Iztapalapan! (Stor. del Messico, tom. iii. p. 120.) It was not the street by which the Spaniards entered, but by which they finally left the city, and is correctly indicated by Lorenzana as that of Tlacopan,—or, rather, Tacuba, into which the Spaniards corrupted the name. See p. 282.

of infantry. At this juncture, when he had driven the foe before him to the farthest extremity of the street, where it touches on the causeway, he was informed that the Mexicans, disheartened by their reverses, desired to open a parley with him respecting the terms of an accommodation, and that their chiefs awaited his return for that purpose at the fortress. Overjoyed at the intelligence, he instantly rode back, attended by Alvarado, Sandoval, and about sixty of the cavaliers, to his quarters.

The Mexicans proposed that he should release the two priests captured in the temple, who might be the bearers of his terms and serve as agents for conducting the negotiation. They were accordingly sent with the requisite instructions to their countrymen. But they did not return. The whole was an artifice of the enemy, anxious to procure the liberation of their religious leaders, one of whom was their *teoteuctli*, or high-priest, whose presence was indispensable in the probable event of a new coronation.

Cortés, meanwhile, relying on the prospects of a speedy arrangement, was hastily taking some refreshment with his officers, after the fatigues of the day, when he received the alarming tidings that the enemy were in arms again, with more fury than ever; that they had overpowered the detachments posted under Alvarado at three of the bridges, and were busily occupied in demolishing them. Stung with shame at the facility with which he had been duped by his wily foe, or rather by his own sanguine hopes, Cortés threw himself into the saddle, and, followed by his brave companions, galloped back at full speed to the scene of action. The Mexicans recoiled before the impetuous charge of the Spaniards. The bridges were again restored; and Cortés and his chivalry rode down the whole extent of the great street, driving the enemy, like frightened deer, at the points of their lances. But, before he could return on his steps, he had the mortification to find that the indefatigable foe, gathering from the adjoining lanes and streets, had again closed on his infantry, who, worn down by fatigue, were unable to maintain their position at one of the principal bridges. New swarms of warriors now poured in on all sides, overwhelming the little band of Christian cavaliers with a storm of stones, darts, and arrows, which rattled like hail on their armour and on that of their well-barbed horses. Most of the missiles, indeed, glanced harmless from the good panoplies of steel, or thick quilted cotton, but, now and then, one better aimed penetrated the joints of the harness and stretched the rider on the ground.

The confusion became greater around the broken bridge. Some of the horsemen were thrown into the canal, and their steeds floundered wildly about without a rider. Cortés himself, at this crisis, did more than any other to cover the retreat of his followers. While the bridge was repairing, he plunged boldly into the midst of the barbarians, striking down an enemy at every vault of his charger, cheering on his own men, and spreading terror through the ranks of his opponents by the well-known sound of his battle-cry. Never did he display greater hardihood, or more freely expose his person, emulating, says an old chronicler, the feats ot the Roman Cocles.[1] In this way he stayed the tide of assailants till the last man had crossed the bridge, when, some of the planks having given way, he was compelled to leap a chasm of full six feet in width, amidst a cloud of missiles, before he could place himself in safety.[2] A report ran through the army that the general was slain. It soon spread through the city, to the great joy of the Mexicans, and reached the fortress, where the besieged were thrown into no less consternation. But, happily for them, it was false. He, indeed, received two severe contusions on the knee, but in other respects remained uninjured. At no time, however, had he been in such extreme danger; and his escape, and that of his companions, were esteemed little less than a miracle. More than one grave historian refers the preservation of the Spaniards to the watchful care of their patron Apostle, St. James, who, in these desperate conflicts, was beheld careering on his milk-white steed at the head of the Christian squadrons, with his sword flashing lightning, while a lady robed in white —supposed to be the Virgin—was distinctly seen by his side, throwing dust in the eyes of the infidel! The fact is attested both by Spaniards and Mexicans, — by the latter after their conversion to Christianity. Surely, never was there a time when the interposition of their tutelar saint was more strongly demanded.[3]

The coming of night dispersed the Indian battalions, which, vanishing like birds of ill omen from the field, left the well-contested pass in possession of the Spaniards. They returned, however, with none of the joyous feelings of conquerors to their citadel, but with slow step and dispirited, with weapons hacked, armour battered, and fainting under the loss of blood, fasting, and fatigue. In this condition they had yet to learn the tidings of a fresh misfortune in the death of Montezuma.[4]

---

[1] It is Oviedo who finds a parallel for his hero in the Roman warrior; the same, to quote the spirit-stirring legend of Macaulay,

"Who kept the bridge so well
In the brave days of old."

"Mui digno es Cortés que se compare este fecho suyo desta jornada al de Oracio Cocles, que se tocó de suso, porque con su esfuerzo é lanza sola dió tanto lugar, que los caballos pudieran pasar, é hizo desembarazar la puente é pasó, á pesar de los Enemigos, aunque con harto trabajo." Hist. de las Ind., MS., lib. 33, cap. 13.

[2] It was a fair leap, for a knight and horse in armour. But the general's own assertion to the emperor (Rel. Seg., ap. Lorenzana, p. 142) is fully confirmed by Oviedo, who tells us he had it from several who were present : "Y segun lo que yo he entendido de algunos que presentes se halláron, demas de la resistencia de aquellos havia de la vna parte á la otra casi vn estado de saltar con el caballo sin le faltar muchas pedradas de diversas partes, é manos, é por ir él, é su caballo bien armados no los hiriéron ; pero no dexó de quedar atormentado de los golpes que le diéron." Hist. de las Ind., MS., ubi supra.

[3] Truly, "dignus vindice nodus"! The intervention of the celestial chivalry on these occasions is testified in the most unqualified manner by many

respectable authorities. It is edifying to observe the combat going on in Oviedo's mind between the dictates of strong sense and superior learning, and those of the superstition of the age. It was an unequal combat, with odds sorely against the former, in the sixteenth century. I quote the passage, as characteristic of the times. "Afirman que se vido el Apóstol Santiago á caballo peleandc sobre vn caballo blanco en favor de los Christianos ; é decian los Indios que el caballo con los pies y manos é con la boca mataba muchos dellos, de forma, que en poco discurso de tiempo no pareció Indio, é reposáron los Christianos lo restante de aquel dia. Ya sé que los incrédulos ó poco devotos dirán, que mi ocupacion en esto destos miraglos, pues no los vi, es superflua, ó perder tiempo novelando, y yo hablo, que esto é mas se puede creer ; pues que los gentiles é sin fé, é Idólatras escriben, que ovo grandes misterios é miraglos en sus tiempos, é aquellos sabemos que eran causados é fechos por el Diablo, pues mas fácil cosa es á Dios é á la inmaculata Vírgen Nuestra Señora é al glorioso Apóstol Santiago, é á los santos é amigos de Jesu Christo hacer esos miraglos, que de suso estan dichos, é otros maiores." Hist. de las Ind., MS., lib. 33, cap. 47.

[4] "Multi restiterunt lapidibus et iaculis confossi, fuit et Cortesius grauiter percussus, pauci evaserunt incolumes, et hi adeò languidi, vt neque lacertos

The Indian monarch had rapidly declined, since he had received his injury, sinking, however, quite as much under the anguish of a wounded spirit as under disease. He continued in the same moody state of insensibility as that already described; holding little communication with those around him, deaf to consolation, obstinately rejecting all medical remedies as well as nourishment. Perceiving his end approach, some of the cavaliers present in the fortress, whom the kindness of his manners had personally attached to him, were anxious to save the soul of the dying prince from the sad doom of those who perish in the darkness of unbelief. They accordingly waited on him, with Father Olmedo at their head, and in the most earnest manner implored him to open his eyes to the error of his creed, and consent to be baptized. But Montezuma—whatever may have been suggested to the contrary—seems never to have faltered in his hereditary faith, or to have contemplated becoming an apostate; for surely he merits that name in its most odious application, who, whether Christian or pagan, renounces his religion without conviction of its false-hood.[1] Indeed, it was a too implicit reliance on its oracles which had led him to give such easy confidence to the Spaniards. His intercourse with them had, doubtless, not sharpened his desire to embrace their communion; and the calamities of his country he might consider as sent by his gods to punish him for his hospitality to those who had desecrated and destroyed their shrines.[2]

When Father Olmedo, therefore, kneeling at his side, with the uplifted crucifix, affectionately besought him to embrace the sign of man's redemption, he coldly repulsed the priest, exclaiming, "I have but a few moments to live, and will not at this hour desert the faith of my fathers."[3] One thing, however, seemed to press heavily on Montezuma's mind. This was

---

erigere quirent. Postquam vero se in arcem receperunt, non commodè satis conditas dapes, quibus reficerentur, inuenerunt, nec fortè asperi maiicii panis bucellas, aut aquam potabilem, de vino aut carnibus sublata erat cura." (Martyr, De Orbe Novo, dec. 5, cap. 6.) See also, for the hard fighting described in the last pages, Oviedo, Hist. de las Ind., MS., lib. 33, cap. 13,—Rel. Seg. de Cortés, ap. Lorenzana, pp. 140–142,—Carta del Exército, MS.,—Gonzalo de las Casas, Defensa, MS., Parte 1, cap. 26,—Herrera, Hist. general, dec. 2, lib. 10, cap. 9, 10,—Gomara, Crónica, cap. 107.

[1] The sentiment is expressed with singular energy in the verses of Voltaire :—

" Mais rénoncer aux dieux que l'on croît dans son
cœur,
C'est le crime d'un lâche, et non pas une erreur ;
C'est trahir à la fois, sous un masque hypocrite,
Et le dieu qu'on préfère, et le dieu que l'on quitte :
C'est mentir au Ciel même, à l'univers, à soi."
ALZIRE, acte 5, sc. 5.

[2] Camargo, the Tlascalan convert, says he was told by several of the Conquerors that Montezuma was baptized at his own desire in his last moments, and that Cortés and Alvarado stood sponsors on the occasion. " Muchos afirman de los conquistadores que yo conocí, que en el artículo de la muerte, pidió agua de batismo é que fué batizado y murió Cristiano, aunque en esto hay grandes dudas y diferentes paresceres ; mas como digo que de

personas fidedignas conquistadores de los primeros desta tierra de quien fuimos informados, supímos que murió batizado y Cristiano, é que fuéron sus padrinos del batismo Fernando Cortés y Don Pedro de Alvarado." (Hist. de Tlascala, MS.) According to Gomara, the Mexican monarch desired to be baptized before the arrival of Narvaez. The ceremony was deferred till Easter, that it might be performed with greater effect. But in the hurry and bustle of the subsequent scenes it was forgotten, and he died without the stain of infidelity having been washed away from him. (Crónica, cap. 107.) Torquemada, not often a Pyrrhonist where the honour of the faith is concerned, rejects these tales as irreconcilable with the subsequent silence of Cortés himself, as well as of Alvarado, who would have been loud to proclaim an event so long in vain desired by them. (Monarch. Ind., lib. 4, cap. 70.) The criticism of the father is strongly supported by the fact that neither of the preceding accounts is corroborated by writers of any weight, while they are contradicted by several, by popular tradition, and, it may be added, by one another.

[3] " Respondió, Que por la media .hora que le quedaba de vida, no se quería apartar de la religion de sus Padres." (Herrera, Hist. general, dec. 2, lib. 10, cap. 10.) " Ya he dicho," says Diaz, " la tristeza que todos nosotros huvímos por ello, y aun al Frayle de la Merced, que siempre estaua con él, y no le pudo atraer á que se bolviesse Christiano." Hist. de la Conquista, cap. 127

the fate of his children, especially of three daughters, whom he had by his two wives; for there were certain rites of marriage which distinguished the lawful wife from the concubine. Calling Cortés to his bedside, he earnestly commended these children to his care, as " the most precious jewels that he could leave him." He besought the general to interest his master, the emperor, in their behalf, and to see that they should not be left destitute, but be allowed some portion of their rightful inheritance. "Your lord will do this," he concluded, " if it were only for the friendly offices I have rendered the Spaniards, and for the love I have shown them, —though it has brought me to this condition ! But for this I bear them no ill-will." [1] Such, according to Cortés himself, were the words of the dying monarch. Not long after, on the 30th of June 1520,[2] he expired in the arms of some of his own nobles, who still remained faithful in their attendance on his person. "Thus," exclaims a native historian, one of his enemies, a Tlascalan, "thus died the unfortunate Montezuma, who had swayed the sceptre with such consummate policy and wisdom, and who was held in greater reverence and awe than any other prince of his lineage, or any, indeed, that ever sat on the throne in this Western World. With him may be said to have terminated the royal line of the Aztecs, and the glory to have passed away from the empire, which under him had reached the zenith of its prosperity." [3] "The tidings of his death," says the old Castilian chronicler, Diaz, " were received with real grief by every cavalier and soldier in the army who had had access to his person ; for we all loved him as a father,—and no wonder, seeing how good he was." [4] This simple but emphatic testimony to his desert, at such a time, is in itself the best refutation of the suspicions occasionally entertained of his fidelity to the Christians.[5]

---

[1] *Aunque no le pesaba dello;* literally, "although he did not repent of it." But this would be rather too much for human nature to assert ; and it is probable the language of the Indian prince underwent some little change as it was sifted through the interpretation of Marina. The Spanish reader will find the original conversation, as reported by Cortés himself, in the remarkable document in the Appendix, Part 2, No. 12. The general adds that he faithfully complied with Montezuma's request, receiving his daughters, after the Conquest, into his own family, where, *agreeably to their royal father's desire, they were baptized,* and instructed in the doctrines and usages of the Christian faith. They were afterwards married to Castilian hidalgos, and handsome dowries were assigned them by the government. See p. 396, note 4.

[2] I adopt Clavigero's chronology, which cannot be far from truth. (Stor. del Messico, tom. iii. p. 131.) And yet there are reasons for supposing he must have died at least a day sooner.

[3] " De suerte que le tiráron una pedrada con una honda y le diéron en la cabeza, de que vino á morir el desdichado Rey, habiendo gobernado este nuevo Mundo con la mayor prudencia y gobierno que se puede imaginar, siendo el mas tenido y reverenciado y adorado Señor que en el mundo ha habido, y en su linaje, como es cosa pública y notoria en toda la maquina deste Nuevo Mundo, donde con la muerte de tan gran Señor se acabáron los Reyes Culhuaques Mejicanos, y todo su poder y mando,

estando en la mayor felicidad de su monarquía ; y ansí no hay de que fiar en las cosas desta vida sino en solo Dios." Hist. de Tlascala, MS.

[4] "Y Cortés lloró por él, y todos nuestros Capitanes, y soldados : é hombres huvo entre nosotros de los que le conociamos, y tratauamos que tan llorado fué, como si fuera nuestro padre, y no nos hemos de maravillar dello, viendo que tan bueno era." Hist. de la Conquista, cap. 126.

[5] " He loved the Christians," says Herrera, "as well as could be judged from appearances." (Hist. general, dec. 2, lib. 10, cap. 10.) "They say," remarks the general's chaplain, "that Montezuma, though often urged to it, never consented to the death of a Spaniard, nor to the injury of Cortés, whom he loved exceedingly. But there are those who dispute this." (Gomara, Crónica, cap. 107.) Don Thoan Cano assured Oviedo that during all the troubles of the Spaniards with the Mexicans, both in the absence of Cortés and after his return, the emperor did his best to supply the camp with provisions. (See Appendix, Part 2, No. 11.) And, finally, Cortés himself, in an instrument already referred to, dated six years after Montezuma's death, bears emphatic testimony to the goodwill he had shown the Spaniards, and particularly acquits him of any share in the late rising, which, says the Conqueror, "I had trusted to suppress through his assistance." See Appendix, Part 2, No. 12.—The Spanish historians, in general,—notwithstanding an occasional intimation of a doubt as

It is not easy to depict the portrait of Montezuma in its true colours, since it has been exhibited to us under two aspects, of the most opposite and contradictory character. In the accounts gathered of him by the Spaniards on coming into the country, he was uniformly represented as bold and warlike, unscrupulous as to the means of gratifying his ambition, hollow and perfidious, the terror of his foes, with a haughty bearing which made him feared even by his own people. They found him, on the contrary, not merely affable and gracious, but disposed to waive all the advantages of his own position, and to place them on a footing with himself; making their wishes his law; gentle even to effeminacy in his deportment, and constant in his friendship while his whole nation was in arms against them. Yet these traits, so contradictory, were truly enough drawn. They are to be explained by the extraordinary circumstances of his position.

When Montezuma ascended the throne, he was scarcely twenty-three years of age. Young, and ambitious of extending his empire, he was continually engaged in war, and is said to have been present himself in nine pitched battles.[1] He was greatly renowned for his martial prowess, for he belonged to the *Quachictin*, the highest military order of his nation, and one into which but few even of its sovereigns had been admitted.[2] In later life, he preferred intrigue to violence, as more consonant to his character and priestly education. In this he was as great an adept as any prince of his time, and, by arts not very honourable to himself, succeeded in filching away much of the territory of his royal kinsman of Tezcuco. Severe in the administration of justice, he made important reforms in the arrangement of the tribunals. He introduced other innovations in the royal household, creating new offices, introducing a lavish magnificence and forms of courtly etiquette unknown to his ruder predecessors. He was, in short, most attentive to all that concerned the exterior and pomp of royalty.[3] Stately and decorous, he was careful of his own dignity, and might be said to be as great an "actor of majesty" among the barbarian potentates of the New World as Louis the Fourteenth was among the polished princes of Europe.

He was deeply tinctured, moreover, with that spirit of bigotry which threw such a shade over the latter days of the French monarch. He received the Spaniards as the beings predicted by his oracles. The anxious

to his good faith towards their countrymen,—make honourable mention of the many excellent qualities of the Indian prince. Solís, however, the most eminent of all, dismisses the account of his death with the remark that "his last hours were spent in breathing vengeance and maledictions against his people; until he surrendered up to Satan—with whom he had frequent communication in his lifetime—the eternal possession of his soul!" (Conquista de México, lib. 4, cap. 15.) Fortunately, the historiographer of the Indians could know as little of Montezuma's fate in the next world as he appears to have known of it in this. Was it bigotry, or a desire to set his own hero's character in a

brighter light, which led him thus unworthily to darken that of his Indian rival?

[1] "Dicen que venció nueve Batallas, i otros nueve Campos, en desafío vno á vno." Gomara, Crónica, cap. 107.

[2] One other only of his predecessors, Tizoc, is shown by the Aztec paintings to have belonged to this knightly order, according to Clavigero. Stor. del Messico, tom. ii. p. 140.

[3] "Era mas cauteloso, y ardidoso, que valeroso. En las Armas, y modo de su govierno, fué muy justiciero; en las cosas tocantes á ser estimado y tenido en su Dignidad y Majestad Real de condicion muy severo, aunque cuerdo y gracioso." Ixtlilxochitl, Hist. Chich., MS., cap. 88.

dread with which he had evaded their proffered visit was founded on the same feelings which led him so blindly to resign himself to them on their approach. He felt himself rebuked by their superior genius. He at once conceded all that they demanded,—his treasures, his power, even his person. For their sake, he forsook his wonted occupations, his pleasures, his most familiar habits. He might be said to forego his nature, and, as his subjects asserted, to change his sex and become a woman. If we cannot refuse our contempt for the pusillanimity of the Aztec monarch, it should be mitigated by the consideration that his pusillanimity sprung from his superstition, and that superstition in the savage is the substitute for religious principle in the civilized man.

It is not easy to contemplate the fate of Montezuma without feelings of the strongest compassion ;—to see him thus borne along the tide of events beyond his power to avert or control ; to see him, like some stately tree, the pride of his own Indian forests, towering aloft in the pomp and majesty of its branches, by its very eminence a mark for the thunderbolt, the first victim of the tempest which was to sweep over its native hills ! When the wise king of Tezcuco addressed his royal relative at his coronation, he exclaimed, " Happy the empire which is now in the meridian of its prosperity, for the sceptre is given to one whom the Almighty has in his keeping ; and the nations shall hold him in reverence ! "[1] Alas ! the subject of this auspicious invocation lived to see his empire melt away like the winter's wreath ; to see a strange race drop, as it were, from the clouds on his land ; to find himself a prisoner in the palace of his fathers, the companion of those who were the enemies of his gods and his people ; to be insulted, reviled, trodden in the dust, by the meanest of his subjects, by those who, a few months previous, had trembled at his glance ; drawing his last breath in the halls of the stranger,—a lonely outcast in the heart of his own capital ! He was the sad victim of destiny,—a destiny as dark and irresistible in its march as that which broods over the mythic legends of antiquity ![2]

Montezuma, at the time of his death, was about forty-one years old, of which he reigned eighteen. His person and manners have been already described. He left a numerous progeny by his various wives, most of whom, having lost their consideration after the Conquest, fell into obscurity, as they mingled with the mass of the Indian population.[3] Two of them, however, a son and a daughter, who embraced Christianity, became the founders of noble houses in Spain.[4] The government, willing

---

[1] The whole address is given by Torquemada, Monarch. Ind., lib. 4, cap. 68.

[2] " Τέχνη δ' ἀνάγκης ἀσθενεστέρα μακρῷ.
Τίς οὖν ἀνάγκης ἐστὶν οἰακοστρόφος ;
Μοῖραι τρίμορφοι, μνήμονές τ' Ἐρινύες.
Τούτων ἄρ' Ζεύς ἐστιν ἀσθενέστερος ;
Οὔκουν ἂν ἐκφύγοι γε τὴν πεπρωμένην."
ÆSCHYL., Prometh., v. 522-526.

[3] Señor de Calderon, the late Spanish minister at Mexico, informs me that he has more than once passed by an Indian dwelling where the Indians in his suite made a reverence, saying it was occupied by a descendant of Montezuma.

[4] This son, baptized by the name of Pedro, was descended from one of the royal concubines. Montezuma had two lawful wives. By the first of these, named Teçalco, he had a son, who perished in the flight from Mexico ; and a daughter named

to show its gratitude for the large extent of empire derived from their ancestor, conferred on them ample estates and important hereditary honours ; and the counts of Montezuma and Tula, intermarrying with the best blood of Castile, intimated by their names and titles their illustrious descent from the royal dynasty of Mexico.[1]

Montezuma's death was a misfortune to the Spaniards. While he lived, they had a precious pledge in their hands, which, in extremity, they might possibly have turned to account. Now the last link was snapped which connected them with the natives of the country. But, independently of interested feelings, Cortés and his officers were much affected by his death, from personal considerations, and, when they gazed on the cold remains of the ill-starred monarch, they may have felt a natural compunction, as they contrasted his late flourishing condition with that to which his friendship for them had reduced him.

The Spanish commander showed all respect for his memory. His body, arrayed in its royal robes, was laid decently on a bier, and borne on the shoulders of his nobles to his subjects in the city. What honours, if any, indeed, were paid to his remains, is uncertain. A sound of wailing, distinctly heard in the western quarters of the capital, was interpreted by the Spaniards into the moans of a funeral procession, as it bore the body to be laid among those of his ancestors, under the princely shades of Chapoltepec.[2] Others state that it was removed to a burial-place in the city named Copalco, and there burned with the usual solemnities and signs of lamentation by his chiefs, but not without some unworthy insults from the Mexican populace.[3] Whatever be the fact, the people, occupied

---

Tecuichpo, who embraced Christianity and received the name of Isabella. She was married, when very young, to her cousin Guatemozin, and lived long enough after his death to give her hand to four Castilians, all of honourable family. From two of these, Don Thoan Cano and Don Juan Andrada, descended the illustrious families of the Cano and Andrada Montezuma. From the last came the counts of Miravalle noticed by Humboldt (Essai politique, tom. ii. p. 73, note). See Alaman, Disertaciones históricas, tom. ii. p. 325.—Montezuma, by his second wife, the princess Acatlan, left two daughters, named, after their conversion, Maria and Leonor. The former died without issue. Doña Leonor married a Spanish cavalier, Cristóval de Valderrama, from whom descended the family of the Sotelos de Montezuma.—The royal genealogy is minutely exhibited in a Memorial setting forth the claims of Montezuma's grandsons to certain property in right of their respective mothers. The document, which is without date, is among the MSS. of Muñoz.

[1] It is interesting to know that a descendant of the Aztec emperor, Don José Sarmiento Valladares, count of Montezuma, ruled as viceroy, from 1697 to 1701, over the dominions of his barbaric ancestors. (Humboldt, Essai politique, tom. ii. p. 93, note.)* Solís speaks of this noble house, grandees of Spain, who intermingled their blood with that of the Guzmans and the Mendozas. Clavigero has traced their descent from the emperor's son Iohualicahua, or Don Pedro Montezuma (as he was called after his baptism), down to the close of the eighteenth century. (See Solís, Conquista, lib. 4, cap. 15.— Clavigero, Stor. del Messico, tom. i. p. 302, tom. iii. p. 132.) The title of count was bestowed on the head of the family by Philip the Second, in 1556. In 1765, under Charles the Third, the count of Montezuma was made a grandee of Spain, and he was in receipt of a yearly pension of 40,000 *pesos.* (Alaman, Disertaciones históricas, tom. i. p. 159.) The last of the line, of whom I have been able to obtain any intelligence, died not long since in this country. He was very wealthy, having large estates in Spain,—but was not, as it appears, very wise. When seventy years old or more, he passed over to Mexico, in the vain hope that the nation, in deference to his descent, might place him on the throne of his Indian ancestors, so recently occupied by the presumptuous Iturbide. But the modern Mexicans, with all their detestation of the old Spaniards, showed no respect for the royal blood of the Aztecs. The unfortunate nobleman retired to New Orleans, where he soon after put an end to his existence by blowing out his brains,—not for ambition, however, if report be true, but disappointed love !

[2] Gomara, Crónica, cap. 107.—Herrera, Hist. general, dec. 2, lib. 10, cap. 10.

[3] Torquemada, Monarch. Ind., lib. 4, cap. 7.

* [Señor Alaman, in a note on this passage, says it was not the viceroy, but his wife, Doña María Gerónima Montezuma, who was a descendant of the Aztec emperor. She was third countess of Montezuma in her own right, her husband's title being duke of Atlixco.—Ed]

with the stirring scenes in which they were engaged, were probably not long mindful of the monarch who had taken no share in their late patriotic movements. Nor is it strange that the very memory of his sepulchre should be effaced in the terrible catastrophe which afterwards overwhelmed the capital and swept away every landmark from its surface.

CHAPTER III.

COUNCIL OF WAR.—SPANIARDS EVACUATE THE CITY.—NOCHE TRISTE, OR "THE MELANCHOLY NIGHT."—TERRIBLE SLAUGHTER.—HALT FOR THE NIGHT.—AMOUNT OF LOSSES.

(1520.)

THERE was no longer any question as to the expediency of evacuating the capital. The only doubt was as to the time of doing so, and the route. The Spanish commander called a council of officers to deliberate on these matters. It was his purpose to retreat on Tlascala, and in that capital to decide, according to circumstances, on his future operations. After some discussion, they agreed on the causeway of Tlacopan as the avenue by which to leave the city. It would, indeed, take them back by a circuitous route, considerably longer than either of those by which they had approached the capital. But, for that reason, it would be less likely to be guarded, at least suspected; and the causeway itself, being shorter than either of the other entrances, would sooner place the army in comparative security on the mainland.

There was some difference of opinion in respect to the hour of departure. The daytime, it was argued by some, would be preferable, since it would enable them to see the nature and extent of their danger and to provide against it. Darkness would be much more likely to embarrass their own movements than those of the enemy, who were familiar with the ground. A thousand impediments would occur in the night, which might prevent their acting in concert, or obeying, or even ascertaining the orders of the commander. But, on the other hand, it was urged that the night presented many obvious advantages in dealing with a foe who rarely carried his hostilities beyond the day. The late active operations of the Spaniards had thrown the Mexicans off their guard, and it was improbable they would anticipate so speedy a departure of their enemies. With celerity and caution they might succeed, therefore, in making their escape from the town, possibly over the causeway, before their retreat should be discovered; and, could they once get beyond that pass of peril, they felt little apprehension for the rest.

These views were fortified, it is said, by the counsels of a soldier named Botello, who professed the mysterious science of judicial astrology. He had gained credit with the army by some predictions which had been verified by the events; those lucky hits which make chance pass for calculation with the credulous multitude.[1] This man recommended to his countrymen by all means to evacuate the place in the night, as the hour most propitious to them, although he should perish in it. The event proved the astrologer better acquainted with his own horoscope than with that of others.[2]

It is possible Botello's predictions had some weight in determining the opinion of Cortés. Superstition was the feature of the age, and the Spanish general, as we have seen, had a full measure of its bigotry. Seasons of gloom, moreover, dispose the mind to a ready acquiescence in the marvellous. It is, however, quite as probable that he made use of the astrologer's opinion, finding it coincided with his own, to influence that of his men and inspire them with higher confidence. At all events, it was decided to abandon the city that very night.

The general's first care was to provide for the safe transportation of the treasure. Many of the common soldiers had converted their share of the prize, as we have seen, into gold chains, collars, or other ornaments, which they easily carried about their persons. But the royal fifth, together with that of Cortés himself, and much of the rich booty of the principal cavaliers, had been converted into bars and wedges of solid gold, and deposited in one of the strong apartments of the palace. Cortés delivered the share belonging to the crown to the royal officers, assigning them one of the strongest horses, and a guard of Castilian soldiers, to transport it.[3] Still, much of the treasure, belonging both to the crown and to individuals, was necessarily abandoned, from the want of adequate means of conveyance. The metal lay scattered in shining heaps along the floor, exciting the cupidity of the soldiers. " Take what you will of it," said Cortés to his men. " Better you should have it, than these Mexican hounds.[4] But be careful not to overload yourselves. He travels safest in the dark night who travels lightest." His own more wary followers took heed to his counsel, helping themselves to a few articles of least bulk, though, it

---

[1] Oviedo, Hist. de las Ind., MS., lib. 33, cap. 47.—The astrologer predicted that Cortés would be reduced to the greatest extremity of distress, and afterwards come to great honour and fortune. (Bernal Diaz, Hist. de la Conquista, cap. 128.) He showed himself as cunning in his art as the West Indian sibyl who foretold the destiny of the unfortunate Josephine.

[2] " Pues al astrólogo Botello, no le aprouechó su astrología, que tambien allí murió." Bernal Diaz, ubi supra.

[3] The disposition of the treasure has been stated with some discrepancy, though all agree as to its ultimate fate. The general himself did not escape the imputation of negligence, and even peculation, most unfounded, from his enemies. The account in the text is substantiated by the evidence, under oath, of the most respectable names in the expedition, as given in the instrument already more than once referred to. " Hizo sacar el oro é joyas de sus Altezas é le dió é entregó á los otros oficiales Alcaldes é Regidores, é les dixo á la rason que así se lo entregó, que todos viesen el mejor modo é manera que habia para lo poder salvar, que él allí estaba para por su parte hacer lo que fuese posible é poner su persona á qualquier trance é riesgo que sobre lo salvar le viniese. . . . El qual les dió para ello una muy buena yegua, é quatro ó cinco Españoles de mucha confianza, á quien se encargó la dha yegua cargado con el otro oro." Probanza á pedimento de Juan de Lexalde.

[4] " Desde aquí se lo doi, como se ha de quedar aquí perdido entre estos perros." Bernal Diaz, Hist. de la Conquista, cap. 128.—Oviedo, Hist. de las Ind., MS., lib. 33, cap. 47.

might be, of greatest value.[1]   But the troops of Narvaez, pining for riches of which they had heard so much and hitherto seen so little, showed no such discretion.   To them it seemed as if the very mines of Mexico were turned up before them, and, rushing on the treacherous spoil, they greedily loaded themselves with as much of it, not merely as they could accommodate about their persons, but as they could stow away in wallets, boxes, or any other means of conveyance at their disposal.[2]

Cortés next arranged the order of march.   The van, composed of two hundred Spanish foot, he placed under the command of the valiant Gonzalo de Sandoval, supported by Diego de Ordaz, Francisco de Lujo, and about twenty other cavaliers.   The rear-guard, constituting the strength of the infantry, was intrusted to Pedro de Alvarado and Velasquez de Leon.   The general himself took charge of the "battle," or centre, in which went the baggage, some of the heavy guns, most of which, however, remained in the rear, the treasure, and the prisoners.   These consisted of a son and two daughters of Montezuma, Cacama, the deposed lord of Tezcuco, and several other nobles, whom Cortés retained as important pledges in his future negotiations with the enemy.   The Tlascalans were distributed pretty equally among the three divisions; and Cortés had under his immediate command a hundred picked soldiers, his own veterans most attached to his service, who, with Cristóval de Olid, Francisco de Morla, Alonso de Avila, and two or three other cavaliers, formed a select corps, to act wherever occasion might require.

The general had already superintended the construction of a portable bridge to be laid over the open canals in the causeway.   This was given in charge to an officer named Magarino, with forty soldiers under his orders, all pledged to defend the passage to the last extremity.   The bridge was to be taken up when the entire army had crossed one of the breaches, and transported to the next.   There were three of these openings in the causeway, and most fortunate would it have been for the expedition if the foresight of the commander had provided the same number of bridges.   But the labour would have been great, and time was short.[3]

At midnight the troops were under arms, in readiness for the march. Mass was performed by Father Olmedo, who invoked the protection of the Almighty through the awful perils of the night.   The gates were thrown open, and on the first of July 1520 the Spaniards for the last time sallied forth from the walls of the ancient fortress, the scene of so much suffering and such indomitable courage.[4]

---

[1] Captain Diaz tells us that he contented himself with four *chalchivitl*,—the green stone so much prized by the natives,—which he cunningly picked out of the royal coffers before Cortés' majordomo had time to secure them.   The prize proved of great service, by supplying him the means of obtaining food and medicine when in great extremity, afterwards, from the people of the country.   Hist. de la Conquista, cap. 128.

[2] Oviedo, Hist. de las Ind., MS., ubi supra.

[3] Gomara, Crónica, cap. 109.— Rel. Seg. de Cortés, ap. Lorenzana, p. 143.—Oviedo, Hist. de las Ind., MS., lib. 33, cap. 13, 47.

[4] There is some difficulty in adjusting the precise date of their departure, as, indeed, of most events in the Conquest; attention to chronology being deemed somewhat superfluous by the old chroniclers. Ixtlilxochitl, Gomara, and others fix the date at July 10th.   But this is wholly contrary to the letter of Cortés, which states that the army reached

The night was cloudy, and a drizzling rain, which fell without inter-mission, added to the obscurity. The great square before the palace was deserted, as, indeed, it had been since the fall of Montezuma. Steadily, and as noiselessly as possible, the Spaniards held their way along the great street of Tlacopan, which so lately had resounded with the tumult of battle. All was now hushed in silence; and they were only reminded of the past by the occasional presence of some solitary corpse, or a dark heap of the slain, which too plainly told where the strife had been hottest. As they passed along the lanes and alleys which opened into the great street, or looked down the canals, whose polished surface gleamed with a sort of ebon lustre through the obscurity of night, they easily fancied that they discerned the shadowy forms of their foe lurking in ambush and ready to spring on them. But it was only fancy; and the city slept undisturbed even by the prolonged echoes of the tramp of the horses and the hoarse rumbling of the artillery and baggage-trains. At length, a lighter space beyond the dusky line of buildings showed the van of the army that it was emerging on the open causeway. They might well have congratulated themselves on having thus escaped the dangers of an assault in the city itself, and that a brief time would place them in comparative safety on the opposite shore. But the Mexicans were not all asleep.

As the Spaniards drew near the spot where the street opened on the causeway, and were preparing to lay the portable bridge across the uncovered breach, which now met their eyes, several Indian sentinels, who had been stationed at this, as at the other approaches to the city, took the alarm, and fled, rousing their countrymen by their cries. The priests, keeping their night-watch on the summit of the *teocallis*, instantly caught the tidings and sounded their shells, while the huge drum in the desolate temple of the war-god sent forth those solemn tones, which, heard only in seasons of calamity, vibrated through every corner of the capital. The Spaniards saw that no time was to be lost. The bridge was brought forward and fitted with all possible expedition. Sandoval was the first to try its strength, and, riding across, was followed by his little body of chivalry, his infantry, and Tlascalan allies, who formed the first division of the army. Then came Cortés and his squadrons, with the baggage, ammunition-waggons, and a part of the artillery. But before they had time to defile across the narrow passage, a gathering sound was heard, like that of a mighty forest agitated by the winds. It grew louder and louder, while on the dark waters of the lake was heard a plashing noise, as of many oars. Then came a few stones and arrows striking at random among the hurrying troops. They fell every moment faster and more furious, till they thickened into a terrible tempest, while the very heavens

---

Tlascala on the eighth of July, not the tenth, as Clavigero misquotes him (Stor. del Messico, tom. iii. pp. 135, 136, nota); and from the general's accurate account of their progress each day, it appears that they left the capital on the last night of June, or rather the morning of July 1st. It was the night, he also adds, following the affair of the bridges in the city. Comp. Rel. Seg., ap. Loren-zana, pp. 142–149.

were rent with the yells and war-cries of myriads of combatants, who seemed all at once to be swarming over land and lake!

The Spaniards pushed steadily on through this arrowy sleet, though the barbarians, dashing their canoes against the sides of the causeway, clambered up and broke in upon their ranks. But the Christians, anxious only to make their escape, declined all combat except for self-preservation. The cavaliers, spurring forward their steeds, shook off their assailants and rode over their prostrate bodies, while the men on foot with their good swords or the butts of their pieces drove them headlong again down the sides of the dike.

But the advance of several thousand men, marching, probably, on a front of not more than fifteen or twenty abreast, necessarily required much time, and the leading files had already reached the second breach in the causeway before those in the rear had entirely traversed the first.[1] Here they halted, as they had no means of effecting a passage, smarting all the while under unintermitting volleys from the enemy, who were clustered thick on the waters around this second opening. Sorely distressed, the van-guard sent repeated messages to the rear to demand the portable bridge. At length the last of the army had crossed, and Magarino and his sturdy followers endeavoured to raise the ponderous framework. But it stuck fast in the sides of the dike. In vain they strained every nerve. The weight of so many men and horses, and above all of the heavy artillery, had wedged the timbers so firmly in the stones and earth that it was beyond their power to dislodge them. Still they laboured amidst a torrent of missiles, until, many of them slain, and all wounded, they were obliged to abandon the attempt.

The tidings soon spread from man to man, and no sooner was their dreadful import comprehended than a cry of despair arose, which for a moment drowned all the noise of conflict. All means of retreat were cut off. Scarcely hope was left. The only hope was in such desperate exertions as each could make for himself. Order and subordination were at an end. Intense danger produced intense selfishness. Each thought only of his own life. Pressing forward, he trampled down the weak and the wounded, heedless whether it were friend or foe. The leading files, urged on by the rear, were crowded on the brink of the gulf. Sandoval, Ordaz, and the other cavaliers dashed into the water. Some succeeded in swimming their horses across. Others failed, and some who reached the opposite bank, being overturned in the ascent, rolled headlong with their steeds into the lake. The infantry followed pellmell, heaped promiscuously on one another, frequently pierced by the shafts or struck down by the war-clubs of the Aztecs; while many an unfortunate victim

---

[1] [This second breach, says Ramirez, "the scene of the rout and slaughter of the Spaniards, was in front of *San Hipolito*, where a chapel was built, to commemorate the event, and dedicated to the *Martyrs*,—though assuredly none of those who had fallen there had any claim to the crown of martyrdom." Notas y Esclarecimientos, p. 104.]

was dragged half stunned on board their canoes, to be reserved for a protracted but more dreadful death.[1]

The carnage raged fearfully along the length of the causeway. Its shadowy bulk presented a mark of sufficient distinctness for the enemy's missiles, which often prostrated their own countrymen in the blind fury of the tempest. Those nearest the dike, running their canoes alongside with a force that shattered them to pieces, leaped on the land, and grappled with the Christians, until both came rolling down the side of the causeway together. But the Aztec fell among his friends, while his antagonist was borne away in triumph to the sacrifice. The struggle was long and deadly. The Mexicans were recognized by their white cotton tunics, which showed faint through the darkness. Above the combatants rose a wild and discordant clamour, in which horrid shouts of vengeance were mingled with groans of agony, with invocations of the saints and the blessed Virgin, and with the screams of women;[2] for there were several women, both natives and Spaniards, who had accompanied the Christian camp. Among these, one named María de Estrada is particularly noticed for the courage she displayed, battling with broadsword and target like the stanchest of the warriors.[3]

The opening in the causeway, meanwhile, was filled up with the wreck of matter which had been forced into it, ammunition-waggons, heavy guns, bales of rich stuffs scattered over the waters, chests of solid ingots, and bodies of men and horses, till over this dismal ruin a passage was gradually formed, by which those in the rear were enabled to clamber to the other side.[4] Cortés, it is said, found a place that was fordable, where, halting, with the water up to his saddle-girths, he endeavoured to check the confusion, and lead his followers by a safer path to the opposite bank. But his voice was lost in the wild uproar, and finally, hurrying on with the tide, he pressed forwards with a few trusty cavaliers, who remained near his person, to the van; but not before he had seen his favourite page, Juan de Salazar, struck down, a corpse, by his side. Here he found Sandoval and his companions, halting before the third and last breach, endeavouring to cheer on their followers to surmount it. But their resolution faltered. It was wide and deep; though the passage was not so closely beset by the

---

[1] Rel. Seg. de Cortés, ap. Lorenzana, p. 143.— Camargo, Hist. de Tlascala, MS.—Bernal Diaz, Hist. de la Conquista, cap. 128.—Oviedo, Hist. de las Ind., MS., lib. 33, cap. 13, 47.—Sahagun, Hist. de Nueva-España, MS., lib. 12, cap. 24.—Martyr, De Orbe Novo, dec. 5, cap. 6.—Herrera, Hist. general, dec. 2, lib. 10, cap. 4.—Probanza en la Villa Segura, MS.

[2] "Pues la grita, y lloros, y lástimas q̃ deziã demãdando socorro: Ayudadme, q̃ me ahogo, otros: Socorredme, q̃ me matã, otros demãdando ayuda á N. Señora Santa María, y á Señor Santiago." Bernal Diaz, Hist. de la Conquista, cap. 128.

[3] "In this combat María de Estrada, oblivious of her sex, showed herself most valorous, and armed with sword and shield did marvellous deeds, rushing into the midst of the enemy with a courage and spirit equal to that of the bravest of men. . . . This lady became the wife of Pedro Sanchez Farfan, and the village of Tetela was granted to them *en encomienda.*" Torquemada, Monarch. Ind., lib. 4, cap. 72.

[4] Camargo, Hist. de Tlascala, MS.—Bernal Diaz, Hist. de la Conquista, cap. 128.—"Por la gran priesa que daban de ambas partes de el camino, comenzáron á caer en aquel foso, y cayéron juntos, que de Españoles, que de Indios y de caballos, y de cargas, el foso se hinchó hasta arriba, cayendo los unos sobre los otros, y los otros sobre los otros, de manera que todos los del bagage quedáron allí ahogados, y los de la retaguardia pasáron sobre los muertos." Sahagun, Hist. de Nueva-España, MS., lib. 12, cap. 24.

enemy as the preceding ones. The cavaliers again set the example by plunging into the water. Horse and foot followed as they could, some swimming, others with dying grasp clinging to the manes and tails of the struggling animals. Those fared best, as the general had predicted, who travelled lightest ; and many were the unfortunate wretches who, weighed down by the fatal gold which they loved so well, were buried with it in the salt floods of the lake.[1] Cortés, with his gallant comrades, Olid, Morla, Sandoval, and some few others, still kept in the advance, leading his broken remnant off the fatal causeway. The din of battle lessened in the distance ; when the rumour reached them that the rear-guard would be wholly overwhelmed without speedy relief. It seemed almost an act of desperation ; but the generous hearts of the Spanish cavaliers did not stop to calculate danger when the cry for succour reached them. Turning their horses' bridles, they galloped back to the theatre of action, worked their way through the press, swam the canal, and placed themselves in the thick of the *mêlée* on the opposite bank.[2]

The first grey of the morning was now coming over the waters. It showed the hideous confusion of the scene which had been shrouded in the obscurity of night. The dark masses of combatants, stretching along the dike, were seen struggling for mastery, until the very causeway on which they stood appeared to tremble, and reel to and fro, as if shaken by an earthquake ; while the bosom of the lake, as far as the eye could reach, was darkened by canoes crowded with warriors, whose spears and bludgeons, armed with blades of " volcanic glass," gleamed in the morning light.

The cavaliers found Alvarado unhorsed, and defending himself with a poor handful of followers against an overwhelming tide of the enemy. His good steed, which had borne him through many a hard fight, had fallen under him.[3] He was himself wounded in several places, and was striving in vain to rally his scattered column, which was driven to the verge of the canal by the fury of the enemy, then in possession of the whole rear of the causeway, where they were reinforced every hour by fresh combatants from the city. The artillery in the earlier part of the engagement had not been idle, and its iron shower, sweeping along the dike, had mowed down the assailants by hundreds. But nothing could resist their impetuosity. The front ranks, pushed on by those behind, were at length forced up to the pieces, and, pouring over them like a torrent, overthrew men and guns in one general ruin. The resolute charge of the Spanish cavaliers, who had now arrived, created a temporary check, and gave time for their country-

1 " É los que habian ido con Narvaez arrojáronse en la sala, é cargáronse de aquel oro é plata quanto pudiéron : pero los menos lo gozáron, porque la carga no los dexaba pelear, é los Indios los tomaban vivos cargados ; é á otros llevaban arrastrando, é á otros mataban allí ; É así no se salvaron sino los desocupados é que iban en la delantera." Oviedo, Hist. de las Ind., MS., lib. 33, cap. 47

2 Herrera, Hist. general, dec. 2, lib. 10, cap. 11. —Oviedo, Hist. de las Ind., MS., lib. 33, cap. 13. —Bernal Diaz, Hist. de la Conquista, cap. 128.

3 " Luego encontráron con Pedro de Alvarado bien herido con vna lança en la mano á pie, que la yegua alaçana ya se la auian muerto." Bernal Diaz, Hist. de la Conquista, cap. 128.

men to make a feeble rally. But they were speedily borne down by the returning flood. Cortés and his companions were compelled to plunge again into the lake,—though all did not escape. Alvarado stood on the brink for a moment, hesitating what to do. Unhorsed as he was, to throw himself into the water, in the face of the hostile canoes that now swarmed around the opening, afforded but a desperate chance of safety. He had but a second for thought. He was a man of powerful frame, and despair gave him unnatural energy. Setting his long lance firmly on the wreck which strewed the bottom of the lake, he sprung forward with all his might, and cleared the wide gap at a leap! Aztecs and Tlascalans gazed in stupid amazement, exclaiming, as they beheld the incredible feat, "This is truly the *Tonatiuh*,—the child of the Sun!"[1] The breadth of the opening is not given. But it was so great that the valorous captain Diaz, who well remembered the place, says the leap was impossible to any man.[2] Other contemporaries, however, do not discredit the story.[3] It was, beyond doubt, matter of popular belief at the time; it is to this day familiarly known to every inhabitant of the capital; and the name of the *Salto de Alvarado*, "Alvarado's Leap," given to the spot, still commemorates an exploit which rivalled those of the demi-gods of Grecian fable.[4]

Cortés and his companions now rode forward to the front, where the troops, in a loose, disorderly manner, were marching off the fatal causeway. A few only of the enemy hung on their rear, or annoyed them by occasional flights of arrows from the lake. The attention of the Aztecs was

---

[1] "Y los amigos vista tan gran hazaña quedáron maravillados, y al instante que esto viéron se arrojáron por el suelo postrados por tierra en señal de hecho tan heroico, espantable y raro, que ellos no habian visto hacer á ningun hombre, y ansí adoráron al Sol, comiendo puñados de tierra, arrancando yervas del campo, diciendo á grandes voces, verdaderamente que este hombre es *hijo del Sol*." (Camargo, Hist. de Tlascala, MS.) This writer consulted the process instituted by Alvarado's heirs, in which they set forth the merits of their ancestor, as attested by the most valorous captains of the Tlascalan nation, present at the Conquest. It *may be* that the famous leap was among these "merits" of which the historian speaks. M. de Humboldt, citing Camargo, so considers it. (Essai politique, tom. ii. p. 75.) This would do more than anything else to establish the fact. But Camargo's language does not seem to me necessarily to warrant the inference.

[2] "Se llama aora la puente del salto de Alvarado: y platicauamos muchos soldados sobre ello, y no hallavamos razon, ni soltura de vn hombre que tal saltasse." Hist. de la Conquista, cap. 128.

[3] Gomara, Crónica, cap. 109.—Camargo, Hist. de Tlascala, ubi supra.—Oviedo, Hist. de las Ind., MS., lib. 33, cap. 47.—Which last author, however, frankly says that many who had seen the place declared that it seemed to them impossible. "Fué tan estremado de grande el salto, que á muchos hombres que han visto aquello, he oido decir que parece cosa imposible haberlo podido saltar ninguno hombre humano. En fin él lo saltó é ganó por ello la vida, é perdiéronla muchos que atras quedaban."

[4] The spot is pointed out to every traveller. It is where a ditch, of no great width, is traversed by a small bridge not far from the western extremity of the Alameda. A house, lately erected there, may

somewhat interfere with the meditations of the antiquary. (Alaman, Disertaciones históricas, tom. i. p. 202.) As the place received its name in Alvarado's time, the story could scarcely have been discountenanced by him. But, since the length of the leap, strange to say, is nowhere given, the reader can have no means of passing his own judgment on its probability. [Unfortunately for the lovers of the marvellous, another version is now given of the account of Alvarado's escape, which deprives him of the glory claimed for him by this astounding feat. In the process against him, which was not brought to light till several years after the present work was published, one of the charges was that he fled from the field, leaving his soldiers to their fate, and escaping by means of a beam which had survived the demolition of the bridge and still stretched across the chasm from one side to the other. The chief, in his reply, said that, far from deserting his men, they deserted him, and that he did not fly till he was wounded and his horse killed under him, when he escaped across the breach, was taken up behind a mounted cavalier on the other side, and carried out of the fray. That he should not have alluded to the account given of the manner of his escape, so much less glorious than that usually claimed for him, may lead us to infer that it was too true to be disputed. Such is the judgment of Señor Ramirez, who, in his account of the affair, tells us that, far from being an object of admiration, Alvarado's escape was, in his own time, deemed rather worthy of punishment, as an act of desertion which cost the lives of many brave follower whom he left behind him. (See the Proceso de Alvarado, pp. 53, 68, with the caustic remarks of Ramirez, pp. xiv., 288, et seq.) It is natural that a descendant of the conquered race should hold in peculiar detestation the most cruel persecutor of the Aztecs.]

diverted by the rich spoil that strewed the battle-ground; fortunately for the Spaniards, who, had their enemy pursued with the same ferocity with which he had fought, would, in their crippled condition, have been cut off, probably, to a man. But little molested, therefore, they were allowed to defile through the adjacent village, or suburbs, it might be called, of Popotla.[1]

The Spanish commander there dismounted from his jaded steed, and, sitting down on the steps of an Indian temple, gazed mournfully on the broken files as they passed before him. What a spectacle did they present! The cavalry, most of them dismounted, were mingled with the infantry, who dragged their feeble limbs along with difficulty; their shattered mail and tattered garments dripping with the salt ooze, showing through their rents many a bruise and ghastly wound; their bright arms soiled, their proud crests and banners gone, the baggage, artillery, all, in short, that constitutes the pride and panoply of glorious war, for ever lost. Cortés, as he looked wistfully on their thin and disordered ranks, sought in vain for many a familiar face, and missed more than one dear companion who had stood side by side with him through all the perils of the Conquest. Though accustomed to control his emotions, or, at least, to conceal them, the sight was too much for him. He covered his face with his hands, and the tears, which trickled down, revealed too plainly the anguish of his soul.[2]

He found some consolation, however, in the sight of several of the cavaliers on whom he most relied. Alvarado, Sandoval, Olid, Ordaz, Avila, were yet safe. He had the inexpressible satisfaction, also, of learning the safety of the Indian interpreter, Marina, so dear to him, and so important to the army. She had been committed, with a daughter of a Tlascalan chief, to several of that nation. She was fortunately placed in the van, and her faithful escort had carried her securely through all the dangers of the night. Aguilar, the other interpreter, had also escaped. And it was with no less satisfaction that Cortés learned the safety of the shipbuilder, Martin Lopez.[3] The general's solicitude for the fate of this man, so indispensable, as he proved, to the success of his subsequent operations, showed that, amidst all his affliction, his indomitable spirit was looking forward to the hour of vengeance.

Meanwhile, the advancing column had reached the neighbouring city of Tlacopan (Tacuba), once the capital of an independent principality. There it halted in the great street, as if bewildered and altogether uncertain what course to take; like a herd of panic-struck deer, who, flying from the hunters, with the cry of hound and horn still ringing in their ears, look wildly around for some glen or copse in which to plunge for concealment.

---

[1] "Fué Dios servido de que los Mejicanos se ocupasen en recojer, los despojos de los muertos, y las riquezas de oro y piedras que llevaba el bagage, y de sacar los muertos de aquel acequia, y á los caballos y otros bestias. Y por esto no siguiéron el alcanze, y los Españoles pudiéron ir poco á poco por su camino sin tener mucha molestia de enemigos." Sahagun, Hist. de Nueva-España, MS., lib. 12, cap. 25.

[2] Oviedo, Hist. de las Ind., MS., lib. 33, cap. 47.—Ixtlilxochitl, Hist. Chich., MS., cap. 89.— Gomara, Crónica, cap. 109.

[3] Herrera, Hist. general. dec. 2, lib. 10, cap. 12.

Cortés, who had hastily mounted and rode on to the front again, saw the danger of remaining in a populous place, where the inhabitants might sorely annoy the troops from the *azoteas*, with little risk to themselves. Pushing forward, therefore, he soon led them into the country. There he endeavoured to re-form his disorganized battalions and bring them to something like order.[1]

Hard by, at no great distance on the left, rose an eminence, looking towards a chain of mountains which fences in the Valley on the west. It was called the Hill of Otoncalpolco, and sometimes the Hill of Montezuma [2] It was crowned with an Indian *teocalli*, with its large outworks of stone covering an ample space, and by its strong position, which commanded the neighbouring plain, promised a good place of refuge for the exhausted troops. But the men, disheartened and stupefied by their late reverses, seemed for the moment incapable of further exertion ; and the place was held by a body of armed Indians. Cortés saw the necessity of dislodging them if he would save the remains of his army from entire destruction. The event showed he still held a control over their wills stronger than circumstances themselves. Cheering them on, and supported by his gallant cavaliers, he succeeded in infusing into the most sluggish something of his own intrepid temper, and led them up the ascent in face of the enemy. But the latter made slight resistance, and, after a few feeble volleys of missiles which did little injury, left the ground to the assailants.

It was covered by a building of considerable size, and furnished ample accommodations for the diminished numbers of the Spaniards. They found there some provisions ; and more, it is said, were brought to them, in the course of the day, from some friendly Otomi villages in the neighbourhood. There was, also, a quantity of fuel in the courts, destined to the uses of the temple. With this they made fires to dry their drenched garments, and busily employed themselves in dressing one another's wounds, stiff and extremely painful from exposure and long exertion. Thus refreshed, the weary soldiers threw themselves down on the floor and courts of the temple, and soon found the temporary oblivion which Nature seldom denies even in the greatest extremity of suffering.[3]

There was one eye in that assembly, however, which we may well believe did not so speedily close. For what agitating thoughts must have crowded on the mind of their commander, as he beheld his poor remnant of followers thus huddled together in this miserable bivouac ! And this was all that survived of the brilliant array with which but a few weeks since he had entered the capital of Mexico ! Where now were his dreams of

---

[1] " Tacuba," says that interesting traveller, Latrobe, " lies near the foot of the hills, and is at the present day chiefly noted for the large and noble church which was erected there by Cortés. And hard by you trace the lines of a Spanish encampment. I do not hazard the opinion, but it might appear by the coincidence, that this was the very position chosen by Cortés for his intrenchment, after the retreat just mentioned, and before he commenced his painful route towards Otumba." (Rambler in Mexico, Letter 5.) It is evident, from our text, that Cortés could have thrown up no intrenchment here, at least on his retreat from the capital.

[2] Lorenzana, Viage, p. xiii.

[3] Sahagun, Hist. de Nueva-España, MS., lib. 12, cap. 24.—Bernal Diaz, Hist. de la Conquista, cap. 128.—Camargo, Hist. de Tlascala, MS.—Ixtlilxochitl, Hist. Chich., MS., cap. 89.

conquest and empire? And what was he but a luckless adventurer, at whom the finger of scorn would be uplifted as a madman? Whichever way he turned, the horizon was almost equally gloomy, with scarcely one light spot to cheer him. He had still a weary journey before him, through perilous and unknown paths, with guides of whose fidelity he could not be assured. And how could he rely on his reception at Tlascala, the place of his destination,—the land of his ancient enemies, where, formerly as a foe, and now as a friend, he had brought desolation to every family within its borders?

Yet these agitating and gloomy reflections, which might have crushed a common mind, had no power over that of Cortés; or, rather, they only served to renew his energies and quicken his perceptions, as the war of the elements purifies and gives elasticity to the atmosphere. He looked with an unblenching eye on his past reverses; but, confident in his own resources, he saw a light through the gloom which others could not. Even in the shattered relics which lay around him, resembling in their haggard aspect and wild attire a horde of famished outlaws, he discerned the materials out of which to reconstruct his ruined fortunes. In the very hour of discomfiture and general despondency, there is no doubt that his heroic spirit was meditating the plan of operations which he afterwards pursued with such dauntless constancy.

The loss sustained by the Spaniards on this fatal night, like every other event in the history of the Conquest, is reported with the greatest discrepancy. If we believe Cortés' own letter, it did not exceed one hundred and fifty Spaniards and two thousand Indians. But the general's bulletins, while they do full justice to the difficulties to be overcome and the importance of the results, are less scrupulous in stating the extent either of his means or of his losses. Thoan Cano, one of the cavaliers present, estimates the slain at eleven hundred and seventy Spaniards and eight thousand allies. But this is a greater number than we have allowed for the whole army. Perhaps we may come nearest the truth by taking the computation of Gomara, who was the chaplain of Cortés, and who had free access, doubtless, not only to the general's papers, but to other authentic sources of information. According to him, the number of Christians killed and missing was four hundred and fifty, and that of natives four thousand. This, with the loss sustained in the conflicts of the previous week, may have reduced the former to something more than a third, and the latter to a fourth, or perhaps fifth, of the original force with which they entered the capital.[1] The brunt of the action fell on the rear-guard, few of whom

---

[1] The table below may give the reader some idea of the discrepancies in numerical estimates even among eyewitnesses, and writers who, having access to the actors, are nearly of equal authority:—

	Killed and Missing.	
	Spaniards.	Indians.
Cortés, ap. Lorenzana, p. 145,	150	2000
Cano, ap. Oviedo, lib. 33, cap. 54,	1170	8000
Probanza, etc.,	200	2000
	Killed and Missing.	
	Spaniards.	Indians.
Oviedo, Hist. de las Ind., lib. 33, cap. 13,	150	2000
Camargo,	450	4000
Gomara, cap. 109,	450	4000
Ixtlilxochitl, Hist. Chich., cap. 88,	450	4000
Sahagun, lib. 12, cap. 24,	300	2000
Herrera, dec. 2, lib. 10, cap. 12,	150	4000

escaped. It was formed chiefly of the soldiers of Narvaez, who fell the victims, in some measure, of their cupidity.[1] Forty-six of the cavalry were cut off, which with previous losses reduced the number in this branch of the service to twenty-three, and some of these in very poor condition. The greater part of the treasure, the baggage, the general's papers, including his accounts, and a minute diary of transactions since leaving Cuba,—which, to posterity at least, would have been of more worth than the gold,—had been swallowed up by the waters.[2] The ammunition, the beautiful little train of artillery with which Cortés had entered the city, were all gone. Not a musket even remained, the men having thrown them away, eager to disencumber themselves of all that might retard their escape on that disastrous night. Nothing, in short, of their military apparatus was left, but their swords, their crippled cavalry, and a few damaged crossbows, to assert the superiority of the European over the barbarian.

The prisoners, including, as already noticed, the children of Montezuma and the cacique of Tezcuco, all perished by the hands of their ignorant countrymen, it is said, in the indiscriminate fury of the assault. There were, also, some persons of consideration among the Spaniards whose names were inscribed on the same bloody roll of slaughter. Such was Francisco de Morla, who fell by the side of Cortés on returning with him to the rescue. But the greatest loss was that of Juan Velasquez de Leon, who, with Alvarado, had command of the rear. It was the post of danger on that night, and he fell, bravely defending it, at an early part of the retreat. He was an excellent officer, possessed of many knightly qualities, though somewhat haughty in his bearing, being one of the best-connected cavaliers in the army. The near relation of the governor of Cuba, he looked coldly, at first, on the pretensions of Cortés; but, whether from a conviction that the latter had been wronged, or from personal preference, he afterwards attached himself zealously to his leader's interests. The general requited this with a generous confidence, assigning him, as we have seen, a separate and independent command, where misconduct, or even a mistake, would have been fatal to the expedition. Velasquez proved himself worthy of the trust; and there was no cavalier in the army, with the exception, perhaps, of Sandoval and Alvarado, whose loss would have

---

Bernal Diaz does not take the trouble to agree with himself. After stating that the rear, on which the loss fell heaviest, consisted of 120 men, he adds, in the same paragraph, that 150 of these were slain, which number swells to 200 in a few lines further! Falstaff's men in buckram! See Hist. de la Conquista, cap. 128.—Cano's estimate embraces, it is true, those—but their number was comparatively small—who perished subsequently on the march. The same authority states that 270 of the garrison, ignorant of the proposed departure of their country-men, were perfidiously left in the palace of Axayacatl, where they subsequently all sacrificed by the Aztecs! (See Appendix, Part 2, No. 11.) The improbability of this monstrous story, by which the army with all its equipage could leave the citadel without the know-

ledge of so many of their comrades,—and this be permitted, too, at a juncture which made every man's co-operation so important,—is too obvious to require refutation. Herrera records, what is much more probable, that Cortés gave particular orders to the captain, Ojeda, to see that none of the sleeping or wounded should, in the hurry of the moment, be overlooked in their quarters. Hist. general, dec. 2, lib. 10, cap. 11.

[1] "Pues de los de Narvaez, todos los mas en las puentes quedáron, cargados de oro." Bernal Diaz, Hist. de la Conquista, cap. 128.

[2] According to Diaz, part of the gold intrusted to the *Tlascalan* convoy was preserved. (Hist. de la Conquista, cap. 136.) From the document already cited,—Probanza de Villa Segura, MS.,—it appears that it was a Castilian guard who had charge of it.

been so deeply deplored by the commander. Such were the disastrous
results of this terrible passage of the causeway; more disastrous than those
occasioned by any other reverse which has stained the Spanish arms in
the New World; and which have branded the night on which it happened,
in the national annals, with the name of the *noche triste,* "the sad or
melancholy night." [1]

CHAPTER IV.

RETREAT OF THE SPANIARDS.—DISTRESSES OF THE ARMY.—PYRAMIDS OF
TEOTIHUACAN.—GREAT BATTLE OF OTUMBA.

(1520.)

THE Mexicans, during the day which followed the retreat of the Spaniards,
remained, for the most part, quiet in their own capital, where they found
occupation in cleansing the streets and causeways from the dead, which
lay festering in heaps that might have bred a pestilence. They may have
been employed, also, in paying the last honours to such of their warriors
as had fallen, solemnizing the funeral rites by the sacrifice of their wretched
prisoners, who, as they contemplated their own destiny, may well have
envied the fate of their companions who left their bones on the battle-field.
It was most fortunate for the Spaniards, in their extremity, that they had
this breathing-time allowed them by the enemy. But Cortés knew that he
could not calculate on its continuance, and, feeling how important it was
to get the start of his vigilant foe, he ordered his troops to be in readiness
to resume their march by midnight. Fires were left burning, the better to
deceive the enemy; and at the appointed hour the little army, without
sound of drum or trumpet, but with renewed spirits, sallied forth from the
gates of the *teocalli,* within whose hospitable walls they had found such
seasonable succour. The place is now indicated by a Christian church,
dedicated to the Virgin, under the title of *Nuestra Señora de los Remedios,*
whose miraculous image—the very same, *it is said,* brought over by the
followers of Cortés [2]—still extends her beneficent sway over the neighbouring capital; and the traveller who pauses within the precincts of the consecrated fane may feel that he is standing on the spot made memorable
by the refuge it afforded to the Conquerors in the hour of their deepest
despondency. [3]

---

[1] Gomara, Crónica, cap. 109.—Oviedo, Hist. de
las Ind., MS., lib. 33, cap. 13.—Probanza en la
Villa Segura, MS.—Bernal Diaz, Hist. de la Conquista, cap. 128.

[2] Lorenzana, Viage, p. xiii.

[3] The last instance, I believe, of the direct interposition of the Virgin in behalf of the metropolis
was in 1833, when she was brought into the city to

avert the cholera. She refused to pass the night in
town, however, but was found the next morning in
her own sanctuary at Los Remedios, showing, by
the mud with which she was plentifully bespattered,
that she must have performed the distance—several
leagues—through the miry ways on foot! See
Latrobe, Rambler in Mexico, Letter 5.

It was arranged that the sick and wounded should occupy the centre, transported on litters, or on the backs of the *tamanes*, while those who were strong enough to keep their seats should mount behind the cavalry. The able-bodied soldiers were ordered to the front and rear, while others protected the flanks, thus affording all the security possible to the invalids.

The retreating army held on its way unmolested under cover of the darkness. But, as morning dawned, they beheld parties of the natives moving over the heights, or hanging at a distance, like a cloud of locusts, on their rear. They did not belong to the capital, but were gathered from the neighbouring country, where the tidings of their rout had already penetrated. The charm which had hitherto covered the white men was gone. The dread *Teules* were no longer invincible.[1]

The Spaniards, under the conduct of their Tlascalan guides, took a circuitous route to the north, passing through Quauhtitlan, and round lake Tzompanco (Zumpango), thus lengthening their march, but keeping at a distance from the capital. From the eminences, as they passed along, the Indians rolled down heavy stones, mingled with volleys of darts and arrows, on the heads of the soldiers. Some were even bold enough to descend into the plain and assault the extremities of the column. But they were soon beaten off by the horse, and compelled to take refuge among the hills, where the ground was too rough for the rider to follow. Indeed, the Spaniards did not care to do so, their object being rather to fly than to fight.

In this way they slowly advanced, halting at intervals to drive off their assailants when they became too importunate, and greatly distressed by their missiles and their desultory attacks. At night, the troops usually found shelter in some town or hamlet, whence the inhabitants, in anticipation of their approach, had been careful to carry off all the provisions. The Spaniards were soon reduced to the greatest straits for subsistence. Their principal food was the wild cherry, which grew in the woods or by the roadside. Fortunate were they if they found a few ears of corn unplucked. More frequently nothing was left but the stalks; and with them, and the like unwholesome fare, they were fain to supply the cravings of appetite. When a horse happened to be killed, it furnished an extraordinary banquet; and Cortés himself records the fact of his having made one of a party who thus sumptuously regaled themselves, devouring the animal even to his hide.[2]

---

[1] The epithet by which, according to Diaz, the Castilians were constantly addressed by the natives, and which—whether correctly or not—he interprets into *gods* or *divine beings*. (See Hist. de la Conquista, cap. 48, et alibi.) One of the stanzas of Ercilla intimates the existence of a similar delusion among the South American Indians,—and a similar cure of it :—

"Por dioses, como dixe, eran tenidos
de los Indios los nuestros ; pero oliéron
que de muger y hombre eran nacidos,
y todas sus flaquezas entendiéron :

viéndolos á miserias sometidos,
el error ignorante conociéron,
ardiendo en viva rabia avergonzados
por verse de mortales conquistados."

LA ARAUCANA, Parte 1, Canto 2.

[2] Rel. Seg. de Cortés, ap. Lorenzana, p. 147.— Hunger furnished them a sauce, says Oviedo, which made their horse-flesh as relishing as the far-famed sausages of Naples, the delicate kid of Avila, or the savoury veal of Saragossa ! "Con la carne del caballo tubiéron buen pasto, é se consoláron ó mitigáron en parte su hambre, é se lo comiéron sin

The wretched soldiers, faint with famine and fatigue, were sometimes seen to drop down lifeless on the road. Others loitered behind, unable to keep up with the march, and fell into the hands of the enemy, who followed in the track of the army like a flock of famished vultures, eager to pounce on the dying and the dead. Others, again, who strayed too far, in their eagerness to procure sustenance, shared the same fate. The number of these, at length, and the consciousness of the cruel lot for which they were reserved, compelled Cortés to introduce stricter discipline, and to enforce it by sterner punishments than he had hitherto done,—though too often ineffectually, such was the indifference to danger, under the overwhelming pressure of present calamity.

In their prolonged distresses, the soldiers ceased to set a value on those very things for which they had once been content to hazard life itself. More than one who had brought his golden treasure safe through the perils of the *noche triste* now abandoned it as an intolerable burden : and the rude Indian peasant gleaned up, with wondering delight, the bright fragments of the spoils of the capital.[1]

Through these weary days Cortés displayed his usual serenity and fortitude. He was ever in the post of danger, freely exposing himself in encounters with the enemy ; in one of which he received a severe wound in the head that afterwards gave him much trouble.[2] He fared no better than the humblest soldier, and strove, by his own cheerful countenance and counsels, to fortify the courage of those who faltered, assuring them that their sufferings would soon be ended by their arrival in the hospitable "land of bread."[3] His faithful officers co-operated with him in these efforts ; and the common file, indeed, especially his own veterans, must be allowed, for the most part, to have shown a full measure of the constancy and power of endurance so characteristic of their nation,—justifying the honest boast of an old chronicler, "that there was no people so capable of supporting hunger as the Spaniards, and none of them who were ever more severely tried than the soldiers of Cortés."[4] A similar fortitude was shown by the Tlascalans, trained in a rough school that made them familiar with hardship and privations. Although they sometimes threw themselves on the ground, in the extremity of famine, imploring their gods not to abandon them, they did their duty as warriors, and, far from manifesting coldness towards the Spaniards as

---

dexar cuero, ni otra cosa dél sino los huesos, é las viñas, y el pelo ; é aun las tripas no les pareció de menos buen gusto que las sobreasados de Nápoles, ó los gentiles cabritos de Abila, ó las sabrosas Terneras de Zaragosa, segun la estrema necesidad que llevaban ; por que despues que de la gran cibdad de Temixtitan havian salido, ninguna otra cosa comiéron sino mahiz tostado, é cocido, é yervas del campo, y desto no tanto quanto quisieran ó ovieran menester." Hist. de las Ind., MS., lib. 33, cap. 13.
[1] Herrera mentions one soldier who had succeeded in carrying off his gold to the value of 3000

castellanos across the causeway, and afterwards flung it away by the advice of Cortés. "The devil take your gold," said the commander bluntly to him, "if it is to cost you your life." Hist. general, dec. 2, lib. 10, cap. 11.
[2] Gomara, Crónica, cap. 110.
[3] The meaning of the word *Tlascala*, and so called from the abundance of maize raised in the country. Boturini, Idea, p. 78.
[4] "Empero la Nacion nuestra Española sufre mas hambre que otra ninguna, i estos de Cortés mas que todos." Gomara, Crónica, cap. 110.

the cause of their distresses, seemed only the more firmly knit to them by the sense of a common suffering.

On the seventh morning, the army had reached the mountain rampart which overlooks the plains of Otompan, or Otumba, as commonly called, from the Indian city—now a village—situated in them. The distance from the capital is hardly nine leagues. But the Spaniards had travelled more than thrice that distance, in their circuitous march round the lakes. This had been performed so slowly that it consumed a week, two nights of which had been passed in the same quarters, from the absolute necessity of rest. It was not, therefore, till the seventh of July that they reached the heights commanding the plains which stretched far away towards the territory of Tlascala, in full view of the venerable pyramids of Teotihuacan, two of the most remarkable monuments of the antique American civilization now existing north of the Isthmus. During all the preceding day they had seen parties of the enemy hovering like dark clouds above the highlands, brandishing their weapons, and calling out, in vindictive tones, "Hasten on! You will soon find yourselves where you cannot escape!" words of mysterious import, which they were made fully to comprehend on the following morning.[1]

The monuments of San Juan Teotihuacan are, with the exception of the temple of Cholula, the most ancient remains, probably, on the Mexican soil. They were found by the Aztecs, according to their traditions, on their entrance into the country, when Teotihuacan, *the habitation of the gods*, now a paltry village, was a flourishing city, the rival of Tula, the great Toltec capital.[2] The two principal pyramids were dedicated to *Tonatiuh*, the Sun, *Meztli*, the Moon. The former, which is considerably the larger, is found by recent measurements to be six hundred and eighty-two feet long at the base, and one hundred and eighty feet high, dimensions not inferior to those of some of the kindred monuments of Egypt.[3] They were divided into four stories, of which three are now discernible, while the vestiges of the intermediate gradations are nearly effaced. In fact, time has dealt so roughly with them, and the materials have been so much displaced by the treacherous vegetation of the tropics, muffling up with its flowery mantle the ruin which it causes, that it is not easy to discern at once the pyramidal form of the structures.[4] The huge masses bear such resemblance to the North American mounds that some have fancied them

---

[1] For the foregoing pages, see Camargo, Hist. de Tlascala, MS.,—Bernal Diaz, Hist. de la Conquista, cap. 128,—Oviedo, Hist. de las Ind., MS., lib. 33, cap. 13,—Gomara, Crónica, ubi supra,—Ixtlilxochitl, Hist. Chich., MS., cap. 89,—Martyr, De Orbe Novo, dec. 5, cap. 6,—Rel. Seg. de Cortés, ap. Lorenzana, pp. 147, 148,—Sahagun, Hist. de Nueva-España, MS., lib. 12, cap. 25, 26.

[2] "Su nombre, que quiere decir *habitacion de los Dioses*, y que ya por estos tiempos era ciudad tan famosa, que no solo competia, pero excedia con muchas ventajas á la corte de Tollan." Veytia, Hist. antig., tom. i. cap. 27.

[3] The pyramid of Mycerinos is 280 feet only at the base, and 162 feet in height. The great pyramid of Cheops is 728 feet at the base, and 448 feet high. See Denon, Egypt Illustrated (London, 1825), p. 9.

[4] "It requires a particular position," says Mr. Tudor, "united with some little faith, to discover the pyramidal form at all." (Tour in North America, vol. ii. p. 277.) Yet Mr. Bullock says, "The general figure of the square is as perfect as the great pyramid of Egypt." (Six Months in Mexico, vol. ii. chap. 26.) Eyewitnesses both! The historian must often content himself with repeating, in the words of the old French lay,—

"*Si com je l'ai trové escrite,*
Vos conterai la vérité.*"

to be only natural eminences shaped by the hand of man into a regular form, and ornamented with the temples and terraces the wreck of which still covers their slopes. But others, seeing no example of a similar eleva-tion in the wide plain in which they stand, infer, with more probability, that they are wholly of an artificial construction.[1]

The interior is composed of clay mixed with pebbles, incrusted on the surface with the light porous stone, *tetzontli*, so abundant in the neighbour-ing quarries. Over this was a thick coating of stucco, resembling, in its reddish colour, that found in the ruins of Palenque. According to tradi-tion, the pyramids are hollow; but hitherto the attempt to discover the cavity in that dedicated to the Sun has been unsuccessful. In the smaller mound an aperture has been found on the southern side, at two-thirds of the elevation. It is formed by a narrow gallery, which, after penetrating to the distance of several yards, terminates in two pits or wells. The largest of these is about fifteen feet deep,[2] and the sides are faced with unbaked bricks; but to what purpose it was devoted, nothing is left to show. It may have been to hold the ashes of some powerful chief, like the solitary apartment discovered in the great Egyptian pyramid. That these monu-ments were dedicated to religious uses, there is no doubt; and it would be only conformable to the practice of antiquity in the Eastern continent that they should have served for tombs as well as temples.[3]

Distinct traces of the latter destination are said to be visible on the summit of the smaller pyramid, consisting of the remains of stone walls showing a building of considerable size and strength.[4] There are no remains on the top of the pyramid of the Sun. But the traveller who will take the trouble to ascend its bald summit will be amply compensated by the glorious view it will open to him;—towards the south-east, the hills of Tlascala, surrounded by their green plantations and cultivated corn-fields, in the midst of which stands the little village, once the proud capital of the republic. Somewhat farther to the south, the eye passes across the beautiful plains lying around the city of Puebla de los Angeles, founded by the old Spaniards, and still rivalling, in the splendour of its churches, the most brilliant capitals of Europe; and far in the west he may behold the Valley of Mexico, spread out like a map, with its diminished lakes, its princely capital rising in still greater glory from its ruins, and its rugged hills gathering darkly around it, as in the days of Montezuma.

The summit of this larger mound is said to have been crowned by a temple, in which was a colossal statue of its presiding deity, the Sun, made of one entire block of stone, and facing the east. Its breast was protected

---

[1] This is M. de Humboldt's opinion. (See his Essai politique, tom. ii. pp. 66–70.) He has also discussed these interesting monuments in his Vues des Cordillères, p. 25, et seq.

[2] Latrobe gives the description of this cavity, into which he and his fellow-travellers penetrated. Rambler in Mexico, Letter 7.

[3] "Et tot templa deûm Romæ, quot in urbe sepulcra

Heroum numerare licet: quos fabula manes Nobilitat, noster populus veneratus adorat."
PRUDENTIUS, Contra Sym., lib. 1.

[4] The dimensions are given by Bullock (Six Months in Mexico, vol. ii. chap. 26), who has some-times seen what has eluded the optics of other travellers.

by a plate of burnished gold and silver, on which the first rays of the rising luminary rested.[1] An antiquary, in the early part of the last century, speaks of having seen some fragments of the statue. It was still standing, according to report, on the invasion of the Spaniards, and was demolished by the indefatigable Bishop Zumárraga, whose hand fell more heavily than that of Time itself on the Aztec monuments.[2]

Around the principal pyramids are a great number of smaller ones, rarely exceeding thirty feet in height, which, according to tradition, were dedicated to the stars and served as sepulchres for the great men of the nation. They are arranged symmetrically in avenues terminating at the sides of the great pyramids, which face the cardinal points. The plain on which they stand was called *Micoatl*, or "Path of the Dead." The labourer, as he turns up the ground, still finds there numerous arrow-heads, and blades of obsidian, attesting the warlike character of its primitive population.[3]

What thoughts must crowd on the mind of the traveller as he wanders amidst these memorials of the past; as he treads over the ashes of the generations who reared these colossal fabrics, which take us from the present into the very depths of time! But who were their builders? Was it the shadowy Olmecs, whose history, like that of the ancient Titans, is lost in the mists of fable? or, as commonly reported, the peaceful and industrious Toltecs, of whom all that we can glean rests on traditions hardly more secure? What has become of the races who built them? Did they remain on the soil, and mingle and become incorporated with the fierce Aztecs who succeeded them? Or did they pass on to the South, and find a wider field for the expansion of their civilization, as shown by the higher character of the architectural remains in the distant regions of Central America and Yucatan? It is all a mystery,—over which time has thrown an impenetrable veil, that no mortal hand may raise. A nation has passed away,—powerful, populous, and well advanced in refinement, as attested by their monuments,—but it has perished without a name. It has died and made no sign!

Such speculations, however, do not seem to have disturbed the minds of the Conquerors, who have not left a single line respecting these time-honoured structures, though they passed in full view of them,—perhaps under their very shadows. In the sufferings of the present they had little leisure to bestow on the past. Indeed, the new and perilous position in which at this very spot they found themselves must naturally have excluded every other thought from their bosoms but that of self-preservation.

As the army was climbing the mountain steeps which shut in the Valley

---

[1] Such is the account given by the cavalier Boturini. Idea, pp. 42, 43.

[2] Both Ixtlilxochitl and Boturini, who visited these monuments, one early in the seventeenth, the other in the first part of the eighteenth century, testify to their having seen the remains of this statue. They had entirely disappeared by 1757, when Veytia examined the pyramid. Hist. antig., tom. i. cap. 26.

[3] "Agricola, incurvo terram molitus aratro, Exesa inveniet scabra rubigine pila," etc.
GEORG., lib. i.

of Otompan, the vedettes came in with the intelligence that a powerful body was encamped on the other side, apparently awaiting their approach. The intelligence was soon confirmed by their own eyes, as they turned the crest of the sierra, and saw spread out, below, a mighty host, filling up the whole depth of the valley, and giving to it the appearance, from the white cotton mail of the warriors, of being covered with snow.[1] It consisted of levies from the surrounding country, and especially the populous territory of Tezcuco, drawn together at the instance of Cuitlahua, Montezuma's successor, and now concentrated on this point to dispute the passage of the Spaniards. Every chief of note had taken the field with his whole array gathered under his standard, proudly displaying all the pomp and rude splendour of his military equipment. As far as the eye could reach, were to be seen shields and waving banners, fantastic helmets, forests of shining spears, the bright feather-mail of the chief, and the coarse cotton panoply of his follower, all mingled together in wild confusion and tossing to and fro like the billows of a troubled ocean.[2] It was a sight to fill the stoutest heart among the Christians with dismay, heightened by the previous expectation of soon reaching the friendly land which was to terminate their wearisome pilgrimage. Even Cortés, as he contrasted the tremendous array before him with his own diminished squadrons, wasted by disease and enfeebled by hunger and fatigue, could not escape the conviction that his last hour had arrived.[3]

But his was not the heart to despond; and he gathered strength from the very extremity of his situation. He had no room for hesitation; for there was no alternative left to him. To escape was impossible. He could not retreat on the capital, from which he had been expelled. He must advance,—cut through the enemy, or perish. He hastily made his dispositions for the fight. He gave his force as broad a front as possible, protecting it on each flank by his little body of horse, now reduced to twenty. Fortunately, he had not allowed the invalids, for the last two days, to mount behind the riders, from a desire to spare the horses, so that these were now in tolerable condition; and, indeed, the whole army had been refreshed by halting, as we have seen, two nights and a day in the same place, a delay, however, which had allowed the enemy time to assemble in such force to dispute its progress.

Cortés instructed his cavaliers not to part with their lances, and to direct them at the face. The infantry were to thrust, not strike, with their swords; passing them at once through the bodies of their enemies. They were, above all, to aim at the leaders, as the general well knew how much depends on the life of the commander in the wars of barbarians, whose want of

---

[1] "Y como iban vestidos de blanco, parecia el campo nevado." Herrera, Hist. general, dec. 2, lib. 10, cap. 13.
[2] "Vistosa confusion," says Solís, "de armas y penachos, en que tenian su hermosura los horrores." (Conquista, lib. 4, cap. 20.) His painting shows the hand of a great artist,—which he certainly was. But he should not have put firearms into the hands of his countrymen on this occasion.
[3] "Y cierto creimos ser aquel el último de nuestros dias." Rel. Seg. de Cortés, ap. Lorenzana, p. 148.

subordination makes them impatient of any control but that to which they are accustomed.

He then addressed to his troops a few words of encouragement, as customary with him on the eve of an engagement. He reminded them of the victories they had won with odds nearly as discouraging as the present; thus establishing the superiority of science and discipline over numbers. Numbers, indeed, were of no account, where the arm of the Almighty was on their side. And he bade them have full confidence that He who had carried them safely through so many perils would not now abandon them and his own good cause to perish by the hand of the infidel. His address was brief, for he read in their looks that settled resolve which rendered words unnecessary. The circumstances of their position spoke more forcibly to the heart of every soldier than any eloquence could have done, filling it with that feeling of desperation which makes the weak arm strong and turns the coward into a hero. After they had earnestly commended themselves, therefore, to the protection of God, the Virgin, and St. James, Cortés led his battalions straight against the enemy.[1]

It was a solemn moment, that in which the devoted little band, with steadfast countenances and their usual intrepid step, descended on the plain to be swallowed up, as it were, in the vast ocean of their enemies. The latter rushed on with impetuosity to meet them, making the mountains ring to their discordant yells and battle-cries, and sending forth volleys of stones and arrows which for a moment shut out the light of day. But, when the leading files of the two armies closed, the superiority of the Christians was felt, as their antagonists, falling back before the charges of cavalry, were thrown into confusion by their own numbers who pressed on them from behind. The Spanish infantry followed up the blow, and a wide lane was opened in the ranks of the enemy, who, receding on all sides, seemed willing to allow a free passage for their opponents. But it was to return on them with accumulated force, as rallying they poured upon the Christians, enveloping the little army on all sides, which, with its bristling array of long swords and javelins, stood firm,—in the words of a contemporary,—like an islet against which the breakers, roaring and surging, spend their fury in vain.[2] The struggle was desperate of man against man. The Tlascalan seemed to renew his strength, as he fought almost in view of his own native hills; as did the Spaniard, with the horrible doom of the captive before his eyes. Well did the cavaliers do their duty on that day; charging in little bodies of four or five abreast, deep into the enemy's ranks, riding over the broken files, and by this temporary advantage giving

---

[1] Camargo, Hist. de Tlascala, MS.—Oviedo, Hist. de las Ind., MS., lib. 33, cap. 14.—Bernal Diaz, Hist. de la Conquista, cap. 128.—Sahagun, Hist. de Nueva-España, MS., lib. 12, cap. 27.—Cortés might have addressed his troops, as Napoleon did his in the famous battle with the Mamelukes: "From yonder pyramids forty centuries look down upon you." But the situation of the Spaniards was altogether too serious for theatrical display.

[2] It is Sahagun's simile: "Estaban los Españoles como una Isleta en el mar, combatida de las olas por todas partes." (Hist. de Nueva-España, MS., lib. 12, cap. 27.) The venerable missionary gathered the particulars of the action, as he informs us, from several who were present in it.

2 D

strength and courage to the infantry. Not a lance was there which did not reek with the blood of the infidel. Among the rest, the young captain Sandoval is particularly commemorated for his daring prowess. Managing his fiery steed with easy horsemanship, he darted, when least expected, into the thickest of the *mêlée*, overturning the stanchest warriors, and rejoicing in danger as if it were his natural element.[1]

But these gallant displays of heroism served only to ingulf the Spaniards deeper and deeper in the mass of the enemy, with scarcely any more chance of cutting their way through his dense and interminable battalions than of hewing a passage with their swords through the mountains. Many of the Tlascalans and some of the Spaniards had fallen, and not one but had been wounded. Cortés himself had received a second cut on the head, and his horse was so much injured that he was compelled to dismount, and take one from the baggage train, a strong-boned animal, who carried him well through the turmoil of the day.[2] The contest had now lasted several hours. The sun rode high in the heavens, and shed an intolerable fervour over the plain. The Christians, weakened by previous sufferings, and faint with loss of blood, began to relax in their desperate exertions. Their enemies, constantly supported by fresh relays from the rear, were still in good heart, and, quick to perceive their advantage, pressed with redoubled force on the Spaniards. The horse fell back, crowded on the foot ; and the latter, in vain seeking a passage amidst the dusky throngs of the enemy, who now closed up the rear, were thrown into some disorder. The tide of battle was setting rapidly against the Christians. The fate of the day would soon be decided ; and all that now remained for them seemed to be to sell their lives as dearly as possible.

At this critical moment, Cortés, whose restless eye had been roving round the field in quest of any object that might offer him the means of arresting the coming ruin, rising in his stirrups, descried at a distance, in the midst of the throng, the chief who from his dress and militaiy cortége he knew must be the commander of the barbarian forces. He was covered with a rich surcoat of feather-work; and a panache of beautiful plumes, gorgeously set in gold and precious stones, floated above his head. Rising above this, and attached to his back, between the shoulders, was a short staff bearing a golden net for a banner,—the singular, but customary, symbol of authority for an Aztec commander. The cacique, whose name was Cihuaca, was borne on a litter, and a body of young warriors, whose gay and ornamented dresses showed them to be the

---

[1] The epic bard Ercilla's spirited portrait of the young warrior Tucapél may be applied without violence to Sandoval, as described by the Castilian chroniclers :—

    " Cubierto Tucapél de fina malla
      saltó como un ligero y suelto pardo
      en medio de la timida canalla,
      haciendo plaza el bárbaro gallardo :

      con silvos grita en desigual batalla :
      con piedra, palo, flecha, lanza y dardo
      le persigue la gente de manera
      como si fuera toro, ó brava fiera."
            LA ARAUCANA, Parte 1, canto 8.

[2] Herrera, Hist. general, dec. 2, lib. 10, cap. 13. —" Este caballo harriero," says Camargo, " le sirvió en la conquista de Méjico, y en la última guerra que se dió se le matáron." Hist. de Tlascala, MS.

flower of the Indian nobles, stood round as a guard of his person and the sacred emblem.

The eagle eye of Cortés no sooner fell on this personage than it lighted up with triumph. Turning quickly round to the cavaliers at his side, among whom were Sandoval, Olid, Alvarado, and Avila, he pointed out the chief, exclaiming, "There is our mark! Follow and support me!" Then, crying his war-cry, and striking his iron heel into his weary steed, he plunged headlong into the thickest of the press. His enemies fell back, taken by surprise and daunted by the ferocity of the attack. Those who did not were pierced through with his lance or borne down by the weight of his charger. The cavaliers followed close in the rear. On they swept with the fury of a thunderbolt, cleaving the solid ranks asunder, strewing their path with the dying and the dead, and bounding over every obstacle in their way. In a few minutes they were in the presence of the Indian commander, and Cortés, overturning his supporters, sprang forward with the strength of a lion, and, striking him through with his lance, hurled him to the ground. A young cavalier, Juan de Salamanca, who had kept close by his general's side, quickly dismounted and despatched the fallen chief. Then, tearing away his banner, he presented it to Cortés, as a trophy to which he had the best claim.[1] It was all the work of a moment. The guard, overpowered by the suddenness of the onset, made little resistance, but, flying, communicated their own panic to their comrades. The tidings of the loss soon spread over the field. The Indians, filled with consternation, now thought only of escape. In their blind terror, their numbers augmented their confusion. They trampled on one another, fancying it was the enemy in their rear.[2]

The Spaniards and Tlascalans were not slow to avail themselves of the marvellous change in their affairs. Their fatigue, their wounds, hunger, thirst, all were forgotten in the eagerness for vengeance; and they followed up the flying foe, dealing death at every stroke, and taking ample retribution for all they had suffered in the bloody marshes of Mexico.[3] Long did they pursue, till, the enemy having abandoned the field, they returned, sated with slaughter, to glean the booty which he had left. It was great, for the ground was covered with the bodies of chiefs, at whom the Spaniards, in obedience to the general's instructions, had particularly aimed; and their dresses displayed all the barbaric pomp of ornament in

---

[1] The brave cavalier was afterwards permitted by the emperor Charles V. to assume this trophy on his own escutcheon, in commemoration of his exploit. Bernal Diaz, Hist. de la Conquista, cap. 128.

[2] The historians all concur in celebrating this glorious achievement of Cortés; who, concludes Gomara, "by his single arm saved the whole army from destruction." See Crónica, cap. 110.—Also Sahagun, Hist. de Nueva-España, MS., lib. 12, cap. 27.—Camargo, Hist. de Tlascala, MS.—Bernal Diaz, Hist. de la Conquista, cap. 128.—Oviedo, Hist. de las Ind., MS., lib. 33, cap. 47.—Herrera, Hist. general, dec. 2, lib. 10, cap. 13.—Ixtlilxochitl, Hist. Chich., MS., cap. 89.—The brief and extremely modest notice of the affair in the general's own letter forms a beautiful contrast to the style of panegyric by others: "In this arduous contest we consumed a great part of the day, until it pleased God that a person was slain in their ranks of such consequence that his death put an end to the battle." Rel. Seg., ap. Lorenzana, p. 148.

[3] "Pues á nosotros," says the doughty Captain Diaz, "no nos dolian las heridas, ni teniamos hambre, ni sed, sino que parecia que no auiamos auido, ni passado ningun mal trabajo. Seguimos la vitoria matando, é hiriendo. Pues nuestros amigos los de Tlascala estavan hechos vnos leones, y con sus espadas, y montantes, y otras armas que allí apañárun, hazianlo muy biē y esforçadamente.' Hist. de la Conquista. loc. cit.

which the Indian warrior delighted.[1] When his men had thus indemnified themselves, in some degree, for their late reverses, Cortés called them again under their banners ; and, after offering up a grateful acknowledgment to the Lord of Hosts for their miraculous preservation,[2] they renewed their march across the now deserted valley. The sun was declining in the heavens, but, before the shades of evening had gathered around, they reached an Indian temple on an eminence, which afforded a strong and commodious position for the night.

Such was the famous battle of Otompan,—or Otumba, as commonly called, from the Spanish corruption of the name. It was fought on the eighth of July 1520. The whole amount of the Indian force is reckoned by Castilian writers at two hundred thousand ! that of the slain at twenty thousand ! Those who admit the first part of the estimate will find no difficulty in receiving the last.[3] It is about as difficult to form an accurate calculation of the numbers of a disorderly savage multitude as of the pebbles on the beach or the scattered leaves in autumn. Yet it was, undoubtedly, one of the most remarkable victories ever achieved in the New World. And this, not merely on account of the disparity of the forces, but of their unequal condition. For the Indians were in all their strength, while the Christians were wasted by disease, famine, and long-protracted sufferings; without cannon or firearms, and deficient in the military apparatus which had so often struck terror into their barbarian foe,—deficient even in the terrors of a victorious name. But they had discipline on their side, desperate resolve, and implicit confidence in their commander. That they should have triumphed against such odds furnishes an inference of the same kind as that established by the victories of the European over the semi-civilized hordes of Asia.

Yet even here all must not be referred to superior discipline and tactics. For the battle would certainly have been lost had it not been for the fortunate death of the Indian general. And, although the selection of the victim may be called the result of calculation, yet it was by the most precarious chance that he was thrown in the way of the Spaniards. It is, indeed, one among many examples of the influence of fortune in determining the fate of military operations. The star of Cortés was in the ascendant. Had it been otherwise, not a Spaniard would have survived that day to tell the bloody tale of the battle of Otumba.

---

[1] Bernal Diaz, Hist. de la Conquista, ubi supra.

[2] The belligerent apostle St. James, riding, as usual, his milk-white courser, came to the rescue on this occasion ; an event commemorated by the dedication of a hermitage to him in the neighbourhood. (Camargo, Hist. de Tlascala.) Diaz, a sceptic on former occasions, admits his indubitable appearance on this. (Hist. de la Conquista, ubi supra.) According to the Tezcucan chronicler, he was supported by the Virgin and St. Peter. (Hist. Chich., MS.,

cap. 89.) Voltaire sensibly remarks, "Ceux qui ont fait les relations de ces étranges événemens les ont voulu relever par des miracles, qui ne servent en effet qu'à les rabaisser. Le vrai miracle fut la conduite de Cortés." Voltaire, Essai sur les Mœurs, chap. 147.

[3] See Oviedo, Hist. de las Ind., MS., lib. 33, cap. 47.—Herrera, Hist. general, dec. 2, lib. 10, cap. 13. —Gomara, Crónica, cap. 110.

CHAPTER V.

ARRIVAL IN TLASCALA.—FRIENDLY RECEPTION.—DISCONTENTS OF THE
ARMY.—JEALOUSY OF THE TLASCALANS.—EMBASSY FROM MEXICO.

(1520.)

On the following morning the army broke up its encampment at an early
hour. The enemy does not seem to have made an attempt to rally.
Clouds of skirmishers, however, were seen during the morning, keeping
at a respectful distance, though occasionally venturing near enough to
salute the Spaniards with a volley of missiles.

On a rising ground they discovered a fountain, a blessing not too
often met with in these arid regions, and gratefully commemorated by the
Christians for the refreshment it afforded by its cool and abundant waters.[1]
A little farther on they descried the rude works which served as the
bulwark and boundary of the Tlascalan territory. At the sight, the allies
sent up a joyous shout of congratulation, in which the Spaniards heartily
joined, as they felt they were soon to be on friendly and hospitable
ground.

But these feelings were speedily followed by others of a different
nature; and, as they drew nearer the territory, their minds were disturbed
with the most painful apprehensions as to their reception by the people
among whom they were bringing desolation and mourning, and who
might so easily, if ill disposed, take advantage of their present crippled
condition. "Thoughts like these," says Cortés, "weighed as heavily
on my spirit as any which I ever experienced in going to battle with the
Aztecs."[2] Still he put, as usual, a good face on the matter, and encouraged his men to confide in their allies, whose past conduct had afforded
every ground for trusting to their fidelity in future. He cautioned them,
however, as their own strength was so much impaired, to be most careful
to give no umbrage or ground for jealousy to their high-spirited allies.
"Be but on your guard," continued the intrepid general, "and we have
still stout hearts and strong hands to carry us through the midst of
them!"[3] With these anxious surmises, bidding adieu to the Aztec

---

[1] Is it not the same fountain of which Toribio
makes honourable mention in his topographical
account of the country? "Nace en Tlaxcala una
fuente grande á la parte del Norte, cinco leguas de
la principal ciudad; nace en un pueblo que se llama
Azumba, que en su lengua quiere decir *cabeza*, y así
es, porque esta fuente es cabeza y principio del
mayor rio de los que entran en la mar del Sur, el
cual entra en la mar por Zacatula." Hist. de los
Indios, MS., Parte 3, cap. 16.

[2] "El qual pensamiento, y sospecha nos puso en

tanta afliccion, quanta trahiamos viniendo peleando
con los de Culúa." Rel. Seg. de Cortés, ap. Lorenzana, p. 149.

[3] "Y mas dixo, que tenia esperança en Dios que
los hallariamos buenos, y leales; é que si otra cosa
fuesse, lo que Dios no permita, que nos han de
tornar á andar los puños con coraçones fuertes, y
braços vigorosos, y que para esso fuessemos muy
apercibidos." Bernal Diaz, Hist. de la Conquista,
cap. 128.

domain, the Christian army crossed the frontier, and once more trod the soil of the Republic.

The first place at which they halted was the town of Huejotlipan, a place of about twelve or fifteen thousand inhabitants.[1] They were kindly greeted by the people, who came out to receive them, inviting the troops to their habitations, and administering all the relief of their simple hospitality. Yet this was not so disinterested, according to some of the Spaniards, as to prevent their expecting in requital a share of the plunder taken in the late action.[2] Here the weary forces remained two or three days, when, the news of their arrival having reached the capital, not more than four or five leagues distant, the old chief Maxixca, their efficient friend on their former visit, and Xicotencatl, the young warrior who, it will be remembered, had commanded the troops of his nation in their bloody encounters with the Spaniards, came with a numerous concourse of the citizens to welcome the fugitives to Tlascala. Maxixca, cordially embracing the Spanish commander, testified the deepest sympathy for his misfortunes. That the white men could so long have withstood the confederated power of the Aztecs was proof enough of their marvellous prowess. "We have made common cause together," said the lord of Tlascala, "and we have common injuries to avenge; and, come weal or come woe, be assured we will prove true and loyal friends and stand by you to the death." [3]

This cordial assurance and sympathy, from one who exercised a control over the public councils beyond any other ruler, effectually dispelled the doubts that lingered in the mind of Cortés. He readily accepted his invitation to continue his march at once to the capital, where he would find so much better accommodations for his army than in a small town on the frontier. The sick and wounded, placed in hammocks, were borne on the shoulders of the friendly natives; and, as the troops drew near the city, the inhabitants came flocking out in crowds to meet them, rending the air with joyous acclamations and wild bursts of their rude Indian minstrelsy. Amidst the general jubilee, however, were heard sounds of wailing and sad lament, as some unhappy relative or friend, looking earnestly into the diminished files of their countrymen, sought in vain for some dear and familiar countenance, and, as they turned disappointed away, gave utterance to their sorrow in tones that touched the heart of every soldier in the army. With these mingled accompaniments of joy and woe, —the motley web of human life,—the wayworn columns of Cortés at length re-entered the republican capital.[4]

---

[1] Called Gualipan by Cortés. (Rel. Seg., ap. Lorenzana, p. 149.) An Aztec would have found it hard to trace the route of his enemies by their itineraries.

[2] Ibid., ubi supra.—Thoan Cano, however, one of the army, denies this, and asserts that the natives received them like their children, and would take no recompense. (See Appendix, Part 2, No. 11.)

[3] " Y que tubiesse por cierto, que me serian muy

ciertos, y verdaderos Amigos, hasta la muerte." Ibid., p. 150.

[4] Camargo, Hist. de Tlascala, MS.—Bernal Diaz, Hist. de la Conquista, ubi supra.—" Sobreviniéron las mugeres Tlascaltecas, y todas puestas de luto, y llorando á donde estaban los Españoles, las unas preguntaban por sus maridos, las otras por sus hijos y hermanos, las otras por sus parientes que habian ido con los Españoles, y quedaban todos allá

The general and his suite were lodged in the rude but spacious palace of Maxixca. The rest of the army took up their quarters in the district over which the Tlascalan lord presided. Here they continued several weeks, until, by the attentions of the hospitable citizens, and such medical treatment as their humble science could supply, the wounds of the soldiers were healed, and they recovered from the debility to which they had been reduced by their long and unparalleled sufferings. Cortés was one of those who suffered severely. He lost the use of two of the fingers of his left hand.[1] He had received, besides, two injuries on the head; one of which was so much exasperated by his subsequent fatigues and excitement of mind that it assumed an alarming appearance. A part of the bone was obliged to be removed.[2] A fever ensued, and for several days the hero who had braved danger and death in their most terrible forms lay stretched on his bed, as helpless as an infant. His excellent constitution, however, got the better of disease, and he was at length once more enabled to resume his customary activity. The Spaniards, with politic generosity, requited the hospitality of their hosts by sharing with them the spoils of their recent victory, and Cortés especially rejoiced the heart of Maxixca by presenting him with the military trophy which he had won from the Indian commander.[3]

But while the Spaniards were thus recruiting their health and spirits under the friendly treatment of their allies, and recovering the confidence and tranquillity of mind which had sunk under their hard reverses, they received tidings, from time to time, which showed that their late disaster had not been confined to the Mexican capital. On his descent from Mexico to encounter Narvaez, Cortés had brought with him a quantity of gold, which he left for safe keeping at Tlascala. To this was added a considerable sum collected by the unfortunate Velasquez de Leon in his expedition to the coast, as well as contributions from other sources. From the unquiet state of the capital, the general thought it best, on his return there, still to leave the treasure under the care of a number of invalid soldiers, who, when in marching condition, were to rejoin him in Mexico. A party from Vera Cruz, consisting of five horsemen and forty foot, had since arrived at Tlascala, and, taking charge of the invalids and treasure, undertook to escort them to the capital. He now learned that they had been intercepted on the route and all cut off, with the entire loss of the treasure. Twelve other soldiers, marching in the same direction,

---

muertos : no es menos, sino que de esto llanto causó gran sentimiento en el corazon del Capitan, y de todos los Españoles, y él procuró lo mejor que pudo consolarles por medio de sus Intérpretes." Sahagun, Hist. de Nueva-España, MS., lib. 12, cap. 28.

[1] "Yo assimismo quedé manco de dos dedos de la mano izquierda "—is Cortés' own expression in his letter to the emperor. (Rel. Seg., ap. Lorenzana, p. 152.) Don Thoan Cano, however, whose sympathies—from his Indian alliance, perhaps—seem to have been quite as much with the Aztecs as with his own countrymen, assured Oviedo, who was lamenting the general's loss, that he might spare his regrets, since Cortés had as many fingers on his hand at that hour as when he came from Castile. (See Appendix, Part 2, No. 11.) May not the word *manco*, in his letter, be rendered by "maimed"?

[2] "Hiriéron á Cortés con Honda tan mal, que se le pasmó la Cabeça, ó porque no le curáron bien, sacándole Cascos, ó por el demasiado trabajo que pasó." Gomara, Crónica, cap. 110.

[3] Herrera, Hist. general, dec. 2, lib. 10, cap. 13.—Bernal Diaz, Hist. de la Conquista, ubi supra.

had been massacred in the neighbouring province of Tepeaca; and accounts continually arrived of some unfortunate Castilian, who, presuming on the respect hitherto shown to his countrymen, and ignorant of the disasters in the capital, had fallen a victim to the fury of the enemy.[1]

These dismal tidings filled the mind of Cortés with gloomy apprehensions for the fate of the settlement at Villa Rica,—the last stay of their hopes. He despatched a trusty messenger, at once, to that place, and had the inexpressible satisfaction to receive a letter in return from the commander of the garrison, acquainting him with the safety of the colony and its friendly relations with the neighbouring Totonacs. It was the best guarantee of the fidelity of the latter, that they had offended the Mexicans too deeply to be forgiven.

While the affairs of Cortés wore so gloomy an aspect without, he had to experience an annoyance scarcely less serious from the discontents of his followers. Many of them had fancied that their late appalling reverses would put an end to the expedition, or, at least, postpone all thoughts of resuming it for the present. But they knew little of Cortés who reasoned thus. Even while tossing on his bed of sickness, he was ripening in his mind fresh schemes for retrieving his honour, and for recovering the empire which had been lost more by another's rashness than his own. This was apparent, as he became convalescent, from the new regulations he made respecting the army, as well as from the orders sent to Vera Cruz for fresh reinforcements.

The knowledge of all this occasioned much disquietude to the disaffected soldiers. They were, for the most part, the ancient followers of Narvaez, on whom, as we have seen, the brunt of the war had fallen the heaviest. Many of them possessed property in the Islands, and had embarked on this expedition chiefly from the desire of increasing it. But they had gathered neither gold nor glory in Mexico. Their present service filled them only with disgust; and the few, comparatively, who had been so fortunate as to survive, languished to return to their rich mines and pleasant farms in Cuba, bitterly cursing the day when they had left them.

Finding their complaints little heeded by the general, they prepared a written remonstrance, in which they made their demand more formally. They represented the rashness of persisting in the enterprise in his present impoverished state, without arms or ammunition, almost without men; and this, too, against a powerful enemy, who had been more than a match for him with all the strength of his late resources. It was madness to think of it. The attempt would bring them all to the sacrifice-block. Their only course was to continue their march to Vera Cruz. Every hour of delay

---

[1] Rel. Seg. de Cortés, ap. Lorenzana, p. 150.—Oviedo, Hist. de las Ind., MS., lib. 33, cap. 15.—Herrera gives the following inscription, cut on the bark of a tree by some of these unfortunate Spaniards: "By this road passed Juan Juste and his wretched companions, who were so much pinched by hunger that they were obliged to give a solid bar of gold, weighing eight hundred ducats, for a few cakes of maize bread." Hist. general, dec. 2, lib. 10, cap. 13.

might be fatal. The garrison in that place might be overwhelmed from want of strength to defend itself; and thus their last hope would be annihilated. But, once there, they might wait in comparative security for such reinforcements as would join them from abroad ; while in case of failure they could the more easily make their escape. They concluded with insisting on being permitted to return at once to the port of Villa Rica. This petition, or rather remonstrance, was signed by all the disaffected soldiers, and, after being formally attested by the royal notary, was presented to Cortés.[1]

It was a trying circumstance for him. What touched him most nearly was to find the name of his friend the secretary Duero, to whose good offices he had chiefly owed his command, at the head of the paper. He was not, however, to be shaken from his purpose for a moment ; and, while all outward resources seemed to be fading away, and his own friends faltered, or failed him, he was still true to himself. He knew that to retreat to Vera Cruz would be to abandon the enterprise. Once there, his army would soon find a pretext and a way for breaking up and returning to the Islands. All his ambitious schemes would be blasted. The great prize, already once in his grasp, would then be lost for ever. He would be a ruined man.

In his celebrated letter to Charles the Fifth, he says that, in reflecting on his position, he felt the truth of the old adage, "that fortune favours the brave. The Spaniards were the followers of the Cross ; and, trusting in the infinite goodness and mercy of God, he could not believe that He would suffer them and his own good cause thus to perish among the heathen.[2] He was resolved, therefore, not to descend to the coast, but at all hazards to retrace his steps and beard the enemy again in his capital."

It was in the same resolute tone that he answered his discontented followers.[3] He urged every argument which could touch their pride or honour as cavaliers. He appealed to that ancient Castilian valour which had never been known to falter before an enemy ; besought them not to discredit the great deeds which had made their name ring throughout Europe ; not to leave the emprise half achieved, for others more daring and adventurous to finish. How could they with any honour, he asked, desert their allies whom they had involved in the war, and leave them unprotected to the vengeance of the Aztecs ? To retreat but a single step towards Villa Rica would be to proclaim their own weakness. It would dishearten their friends and give confidence to their foes. He implored

---

[1] One is reminded of the similar remonstrance made by Alexander's soldiers to him on reaching the Hystaspis,—but attended with more success; as, indeed, was reasonable. For Alexander continued to advance from the ambition of indefinite conquest, while Cortés was only bent on carrying out his original enterprise. What was madness in the one was heroism in the other.

[2] "Acordándome, que siempre á los osados ayuda la fortuna, y que eramos Christianos y confiando en la grandíssima Bondad, y Misericordia de Dios, que no permitiria, que del todo pereciessemos, y se perdiesse tanta, y tan noble Tierra." Rel. Seg., ap. Lorenzana, p. 152.

[3] This reply, exclaims Oviedo, showed a man of unconquerable spirit and high destinies : "Paréceme que la respuesta que á esto les dió Hernando Cortés, é lo que hizo en ello, fué vna cosa de ánimo invencible, é de varon de mucha suerte é valor." Hist. de las Ind., MS., lib. 33, cap. 15.

them to resume the confidence in him which they had ever showed, and to reflect that, if they had recently met with reverses, he had up to that point accomplished all, and more than all, that he had promised. It would be easy now to retrieve their losses, if they would have patience and abide in this friendly land until the reinforcements, which would be ready to come in at his call, should enable them to act on the offensive. If, however, there were any so insensible to the motives which touch a brave man's heart, as to prefer ease at home to the glory of this great achievement, he would not stand in their way. Let them go, in God's name. Let them leave their general in his extremity. He should feel stronger in the service of a few brave spirits than if surrounded by a host of the false or the faint-hearted.[1]

The disaffected party, as already noticed, was chiefly drawn from the troops of Narvaez. When the general's own veterans heard this appeal,[2] their blood warmed with indignation at the thoughts of abandoning him or the cause at such a crisis. They pledged themselves to stand by him to the last; and the malcontents, silenced, if not convinced, by this generous expression of sentiment from their comrades, consented to postpone their departure for the present, under the assurance that no obstacle would be thrown in their way when a more favourable season should present itself.[3]

Scarcely was this difficulty adjusted, when Cortés was menaced with one more serious, in the jealousy springing up between his soldiers and their Indian allies. Notwithstanding the demonstrations of regard by Maxixca and his immediate followers, there were others of the nation who looked with an evil eye on their guests, for the calamities in which they had involved them; and they tauntingly asked if, in addition to this, they were now to be burdened by the presence and maintenance of the strangers. These sallies of discontent were not so secret as altogether to escape the ears of the Spaniards, in whom they occasioned no little disquietude. They proceeded for the most part, it is true, from persons of little consideration, since the four great chiefs of the republic appear to have been steadily secured to the interests of Cortés. But they derived some importance from the countenance of the warlike Xicotencatl, in whose bosom still lingered the embers of that implacable hostility which he had displayed so courageously on the field of battle; and sparkles of this fiery temper occasionally gleamed forth in the intimate inter-

---

[1] "É no me hable ninguno en otra cosa; y él que desta opinion no estuviere váyase en buen hora, que mas holgaré de quedar con los pocos y osados, que en compañía de muchos, ni de ninguno cobarde, ni desacordado de su propia honra." Hist. de las Ind., MS., loc. cit.

[2] Oviedo has expanded the harangue of Cortés into several pages, in the course of which the orator quotes Xenophon, and borrows largely from the old Jewish history, a style of eloquence savouring much more of the closet than the camp. Cortés was no pedant, and his soldiers were no scholars.

[3] For the account of this turbulent transaction, see Bernal Diaz, Hist. de la Conquista, cap. 129,—Rel. Seg. de Cortés, ap. Lorenzana, p. 152,—Oviedo, Hist. de las Ind., MS., lib. 33, cap. 15,—Gomara, Crónica, cap. 112, 113,—Herrera, Hist. general, dec. 2, lib. 10, cap. 14.—Diaz is exceedingly wroth with the chaplain Gomara for not discriminating between the old soldiers and the levies of Narvaez, whom he involves equally in the sin of rebellion. The captain's own version seems a fair one, and I have followed it, therefore, in the text.

course into which he was now reluctantly brought with his ancient opponents.

Cortés, who saw with alarm the growing feeling of estrangement which must sap the very foundations on which he was to rest the lever for future operations, employed every argument which suggested itself, to restore the confidence of his own men. He reminded them of the good services they had uniformly received from the great body of the nation. They had a sufficient pledge of the future constancy of the Tlascalans in their long-cherished hatred of the Aztecs, which the recent disasters they had suffered from the same quarter could serve only to sharpen. And he urged, with much force, that if any evil designs had been meditated by them against the Spaniards the Tlascalans would, doubtless, have taken advantage of their late disabled condition, and not waited till they had recovered their strength and means of resistance.[1]

While Cortés was thus endeavouring, with somewhat doubtful success, to stifle his own apprehensions, as well as those in the bosoms of his followers, an event occurred which happily brought the affair to an issue, and permanently settled the relations in which the two parties were to stand to each other. This will make it necessary to notice some events which had occurred in Mexico since the expulsion of the Spaniards.

On Montezuma's death, his brother, Cuitlahua, lord of Iztapalapan, conformably to the usage regulating the descent of the Aztec crown, was chosen to succeed him. He was an active prince, of large experience in military affairs, and, by the strength of his character, was well fitted to sustain the tottering fortunes of the monarchy. He appears, moreover, to have been a man of liberal, and what may be called enlightened, taste, to judge from the beautiful gardens which he had filled with rare exotics and which so much attracted the admiration of the Spaniards in his city of Iztapalapan. Unlike his predecessor, he held the white men in detestation, and had, probably, the satisfaction of celebrating his own coronation by the sacrifice of many of them. From the moment of his release from the Spanish quarters, where he had been detained by Cortés, he entered into the patriotic movements of his people. It was he who conducted the assaults both in the streets of the city and on the " Melancholy Night ; " and it was at his instigation that the powerful force had been assembled to dispute the passage of the Spaniards in the Vale of Otumba.[2]

Since the evacuation of the capital, he had been busily occupied in repairing the mischief it had received,—restoring the buildings and the bridges and putting it in the best posture of defence. He had endeavoured to improve the discipline and arms of his troops. He introduced

[1] Oviedo, Hist. de las Ind., MS., lib. 33, cap. 15. —Herrera, Hist. general, dec. 2, lib. 10, cap. 14. —Sahagun, Hist. de Nueva-España, MS., lib. 12, cap. 29.
[2] Oviedo, Hist. de las Ind., MS., lib. 33, cap. 47. —Rel. Seg. de Cortés, ap. Lorenzana, p. 166.— Sahagun, Hist. de Nueva-España, MS., lib. 12,

cap. 27, 29.—Or, rather, it was "at the instigation of the great Devil, the captain of all the devils, called Satan, who regulated everything in New Spain by his freewill and pleasure, before the coming of the Spaniards," according to Father Sahagun, who begins his chapter with this eloquent exordium.

the long spear among them, and, by attaching the sword-blades taken from the Christians to long poles, contrived a weapon that should be formidable against the cavalry He summoned his vassals, far and near, to hold themselves in readiness to march to the relief of the capital, if necessary, and, the better to secure their goodwill, relieved them from some of the burdens usually laid on them. But he was now to experience the insta-bility of a government which rested not on love, but on fear. The vassals in the neighbourhood of the Valley remained true to their allegiance; but others held themselves aloof, uncertain what course to adopt; while others, again, in the more distant provinces, refused obedience altogether, con-sidering this a favourable moment for throwing off the yoke which had so long galled them.[1]

In this emergency, the government sent a deputation to its ancient enemies the Tlascalans. It consisted of six Aztec nobles, bearing a present of cotton cloth, salt, and other articles rarely seen, of late years, in the republic. The lords of the state, astonished at this unprecedented act of condescension in their ancient foe, called the council or senate of the great chiefs together, to give the envoys audience.

Before this body the Aztecs stated the purpose of their mission. They invited the Tlascalans to bury all past grievances in oblivion, and to enter into a treaty with them. All the nations of Anahuac should make common cause in defence of their country against the white men. The Tlascalans would bring down on their own heads the wrath of the gods, if they longer harboured the strangers who had violated and destroyed their temples. If they counted on the support and friendship of their guests, let them take warning from the fate of Mexico, which had received them kindly within its walls, and which, in return, they had filled with blood and ashes. They conjured them, by their reverence for their common religion, not to suffer the white men, disabled as they now were, to escape from their hands, but to sacrifice them at once to the gods, whose temples they had profaned. In that event, they proffered them their alliance, and the renewal of that friendly traffic which would restore to the republic the possession of the comforts and luxuries of which it had been so long deprived.

The proposals of the ambassadors produced different effects on their audience. Xicotencatl was for embracing them at once. Far better was it, he said, to unite with their kindred, with those who held their own language, their faith and usages, than to throw themselves into the arms of the fierce strangers, who, however they might talk of religion, wor-shipped no god but gold. This opinion was followed by that of the younger warriors, who readily caught the fire of his enthusiasm. But the elder chiefs, especially his blind old father, one of the four rulers of the state, who seem to have been all heartily in the interests of the Spaniards, and one of them, Maxixca, their stanch friend, strongly expressed their

---

[1] Ixtlilxochitl, Hist. Chich., MS., cap. 88.— | cap. 29.—Herrera, Hist. general, dec. 2, lib. 10, Sahagun, Hist. de Nueva-España, MS., lib. 12, | cap. 19.

aversion to the proposed alliance with the Aztecs. They were always the same, said the latter,—fair in speech, and false in heart. They now proffered friendship to the Tlascalans. But it was fear which drove them to it, and, when that fear was removed, they would return to their old hostility. Who was it, but these insidious foes, that had so long deprived the country of the very necessaries of life, of which they were now so lavish in their offers? Was it not owing to the white men that the nation at length possessed them? Yet they were called on to sacrifice the white men to the gods!—the warriors who, after fighting the battles of the Tlascalans, now threw themselves on their hospitality. But the gods abhorred perfidy. And were not their guests the very beings whose coming had been so long predicted by the oracles? "Let us avail ourselves of it," he concluded, "and unite and make common cause with them, until we have humbled our haughty enemy."

This discourse provoked a sharp rejoinder from Xicotencatl, till the passion of the elder chieftain got the better of his patience, and substituting force for argument, he thrust his younger antagonist, with some violence, from the council-chamber. A proceeding so contrary to the usual decorum of Indian debate astonished the assembly. But, far from bringing censure on its author, it effectually silenced opposition. Even the hot-headed followers of Xicotencatl shrunk from supporting a leader who had incurred such a mark of contemptuous displeasure from the ruler whom they most venerated. His own father openly condemned him; and the patriotic young warrior, gifted with a truer foresight into futurity than his countrymen, was left without support in the council, as he had formerly been on the field of battle. The proffered alliance of the Mexicans was unanimously rejected; and the envoys, fearing that even the sacred character with which they were invested might not protect them from violence, made their escape secretly from the capital.[1]

The result of the conference was of the last importance to the Spaniards, who, in their present crippled condition, especially if taken unawares, would have been, probably, at the mercy of the Tlascalans. At all events, the union of these latter with the Aztecs would have settled the fate of the expedition; since, in the poverty of his own resources, it was only by adroitly playing off one part of the Indian population against the other that Cortés could ultimately hope for success.

---

[1] The proceedings in the Tlascalan senate are reported in more or less detail, but substantially alike, by Camargo, Hist. de Tlascala, MS.,—Sahagun, Hist. de Nueva-España, MS., lib. 12, cap. 29,—Herrera, Hist. general, dec. 2, lib. 12, cap. 14.—See, also, Bernal Diaz, Hist. de la Conquista, cap. 129,—Gomara, Crónica, cap. 111.

CHAPTER VI.

WAR WITH THE SURROUNDING TRIBES.—SUCCESSES OF THE SPANIARDS.—
DEATH OF MAXIXCA.—ARRIVAL OF REINFORCEMENTS.—RETURN IN
TRIUMPH TO TLASCALA.

(1520.)

THE Spanish commander, reassured by the result of the deliberations in
the Tlascalan senate, now resolved on active operations, as the best means
of dissipating the spirit of faction and discontent inevitably fostered by a
life of idleness.   He proposed to exercise his troops, at first, against some
of the neighbouring tribes who had laid violent hands on such of the
Spaniards as, confiding in their friendly spirit, had passed through their
territories.   Among these were the Tepeacans, a people often engaged in
hostility with the Tlascalans, and who, as mentioned in the preceding
chapter, had lately massacred twelve Spaniards in their march to the
capital.   An expedition against them would receive the ready support of
his allies, and would assert the dignity of the Spanish name, much dimmed
in the estimation of the natives by the late disasters.

The Tepeacans were a powerful tribe of the same primitive stock as the
Aztecs, to whom they acknowledged allegiance.   They had transferred
this to the Spaniards, on their first march into the country, intimidated
by the bloody defeats of their Tlascalan neighbours.   But, since the
troubles in the capital, they had again submitted to the Aztec sceptre.
Their capital, now a petty village, was a flourishing city at the time of the
Conquest, situated in the fruitful plains that stretch far away towards the
base of Orizaba.[1]   The province contained, moreover, several towns of
considerable size, filled with a bold and warlike population.

As these Indians had once acknowledged the authority of Castile,
Cortés and his officers regarded their present conduct in the light of
rebellion, and, in a council of war, it was decided that those engaged in
the late massacre had fairly incurred the doom of slavery.[2]   Before
proceeding against them, however, the general sent a summons requiring
their submission, and offering full pardon for the past, but, in case
of refusal, menacing them with the severest retribution.   To this the
Indians, now in arms, returned a contemptuous answer, challenging the
Spaniards to meet them in fight, as they were in want of victims for their
sacrifices.

Cortés, without further delay, put himself at the head of his small

---

[1] The Indian name of the capital,—the same as
that of the province,—*Tepejacac*, was corrupted by
the Spaniards into *Tepeaca*.   It must be admitted
to have gained by the corruption.

[2] "Y como aquello vió Cortés, comunicólo con
todos nuestros Capitanes, y soldados: y fué
acordado, que se hiziesse vn auto por ante
Escriuano, que diesse fe de todo lo passado, y
que se diessen por esclauos." Bernal Diaz, Hist.
de la Conquista, cap. 130.

corps of Spaniards and a large reinforcement of Tlascalan warriors. They were led by the younger Xicotencatl, who now appeared willing to bury his recent animosity, and desirous to take a lesson in war under the chief who had so often foiled him in the field.[1]

The Tepeacans received their enemy on their borders. A bloody battle followed, in which the Spanish horse were somewhat embarrassed by the tall maize that covered part of the plain. They were successful in the end, and the Tepeacans, after holding their ground like good warriors, were at length routed with great slaughter. A second engagement, which took place a few days after, was followed by like decisive results; and the victorious Spaniards with their allies, marching straightway on the city of Tepeaca, entered it in triumph.[2] No further resistance was attempted by the enemy, and the whole province, to avoid further calamities, eagerly tendered its submission. Cortés, however, inflicted the meditated chastisement on the places implicated in the massacre. The inhabitants were branded with a hot iron as slaves, and, after the royal fifth had been reserved, were distributed between his own men and the allies.[3] The Spaniards were familiar with the system of *repartimientos* established in the Islands; but this was the first example of slavery in New Spain.[4] It was justified, in the opinion of the general and his military casuists, by the aggravated offences of the party. The sentence, however, was not countenanced by the crown,[5] which, as the colonial legislation abundantly shows, was ever at issue with the craving and mercenary spirit of the colonist.

Satisfied with this display of his vengeance, Cortés now established his headquarters at Tepeaca, which, situated in a cultivated country, afforded easy means for maintaining an army, while its position on the Mexican frontier made it a good *point d'appui* for future operations.

The Aztec government, since it had learned the issue of its negotiations at Tlascala, had been diligent in fortifying its frontier in that quarter. The garrisons usually maintained there were strengthened, and large bodies of men were marched in the same direction, with orders to occupy the strong positions on the borders. The conduct of these troops was in their usual style of arrogance and extortion, and greatly disgusted the inhabitants of the country.

---

[1] The chroniclers estimate his army at 50,000 warriors; one-half, according to Toribio, of the disposable military force of the republic. "De la cual (Tlascala), como ya tengo dicho, solian salir cien mil hombres de pelea." Hist. de los Indios, MS., Parte 3, cap. 16.

[2] "That night," says the credulous Herrera, speaking of the carouse that followed one of their victories, "the Indian allies had a grand supper of legs and arms; for, besides an incredible number of roasts on wooden spits, they had fifty thousand pots of stewed human flesh"! (Hist. general, dec. 2, lib. 10, cap. 15.) Such a banquet would not have smelt savoury in the nostrils of Cortés.

[3] "Y allí hiziéron hazer el hierro con que se auian de herrar los que se tomauan por esclauos,

que era una G., que quiere decir *guerra*." Bernal Diaz, Hist. de la Conquista, cap. 130.

[4] [It may have been the first instance of natives being reduced to slavery by the Spaniards, but female slaves at least had been given to them on several previous occasions by the Mexican chiefs. The present case has also no connection with the system of *repartimientos*, by which, after the conquest was effected, the soil and its inhabitants were divided among the new possessors. In the case of the Tepeacans, no attempt was made to enslave the adult males, whose services were not needed, and who would have brought only embarrassment to their captors. See Bernal Diaz, Hist. de la Conquista, cap. 135.—ED.]

[5] Solís, Conquista, lib. 5, cap. 3.

Among the places thus garrisoned by the Aztecs was Quauhquechollan,[1] a city containing thirty thousand inhabitants, according to the historians, and lying to the south-west twelve leagues or more from the Spanish quarters. It stood at the extremity of a deep valley, resting against a bold range of hills, or rather mountains, and flanked by two rivers with exceedingly high and precipitous banks. The only avenue by which the town could be easily approached was protected by a stone wall more than twenty feet high and of great thickness.[2] Into this place, thus strongly defended by art as well as by nature, the Aztec emperor had thrown a garrison of several thousand warriors, while a much more formidable force occupied the heights commanding the city.

The cacique of this strong post, impatient of the Mexican yoke, sent to Cortés, inviting him to march to his relief, and promising a co-operation of the citizens in an assault on the Aztec quarters. The general eagerly embraced the proposal, and detached Cristóval de Olid, with two hundred Spaniards and a strong body of Tlascalans, to support the friendly cacique.[3] On the way, Olid was joined by many volunteers from the Indian city and from the neighbouring capital of Cholula, all equally pressing their services. The number and eagerness of these auxiliaries excited suspicions in the bosom of the cavalier. They were strengthened by the surmises of the soldiers of Narvaez, whose imaginations were still haunted, it seems, by the horrors of the *noche triste*, and who saw in the friendly alacrity of their new allies evidence of an insidious understanding with the Aztecs. Olid, catching this distrust, made a countermarch on Cholula, where he seized the suspected chiefs, who had been most forward in offering their services, and sent them under a strong guard to Cortés.

The general, after a careful examination, was satisfied of the integrity of the suspected parties. He, expressing his deep regret at the treatment they had received, made them such amends as he could by liberal presents, and, as he now saw the impropriety of committing an affair of such importance to other hands, put himself at the head of his remaining force and effected a junction with his officer in Cholula.

He had arranged with the cacique of the city against which he was marching, that on the appearance of the Spaniards the inhabitants should rise on the garrison. Everything succeeded as he had planned. No sooner had the Christian battalions defiled on the plain before the town, than the inhabitants attacked the garrison with the utmost fury. The latter, abandoning the outer defences of the place, retreated to their own quarters in the principal *teocalli*, where they maintained a hard struggle

---

[1] Called by the Spaniards *Huacachula*, and spelt with every conceivable diversity by the old writers, who may be excused for stumbling over such a confusion of consonants.

[2] "Y toda la Ciudad está cercada de muy fuerte Muro de cal y canto, tan alto, como quatro estados por de fuera de la Ciudad : ó por de dentro está casi igual con el suelo. Y por toda la Muralla va su petril, tan alto, como medio estado, para pelear, tiene quatro entradas, tan anchas, como uno puede entrar á Caballo." Rel. Seg., p. 162.

[3] This cavalier's name is usually spelt Olid by the chroniclers. In a copy of his own signature I find it written Oli.

with their adversaries. In the heat of it, Cortés, at the head of his little body of horse, rode into the place, and directed the assault in person. The Aztecs made a fierce defence. But, fresh troops constantly arriving to support the assailants, the works were stormed, and every one of the garrison was put to the sword.[1]

The Mexican forces, meanwhile, stationed on the neighbouring eminences, had marched down to the support of their countrymen in the town, and formed in order of battle in the suburbs, where they were encountered by the Tlascalan levies. "They mustered," says Cortés, speaking of the enemy, "at least thirty thousand men; and it was a brave sight for the eye to look on,—such a beautiful array of warriors glistening with gold and jewels and variegated feather-work."[2] The action was well contested between the two Indian armies. The suburbs were set on fire, and, in the midst of the flames, Cortés and his squadrons, rushing on the enemy, at length broke their array, and compelled them to fall back in disorder into the narrow gorge of the mountain, from which they had lately descended. The pass was rough and precipitous. Spaniards and Tlascalans followed close in the rear, and the light troops, scaling the high wall of the valley, poured down on the enemy's flanks. The heat was intense, and both parties were so much exhausted by their efforts that it was with difficulty, says the chronicler, that the one could pursue, or the other fly.[3] They were not too weary, however, to slay. The Mexicans were routed with terrible slaughter. They found no pity from their Indian foes, who had a long account of injuries to settle with them. Some few sought refuge by flying higher up into the fastnesses of the sierra. They were followed by their indefatigable enemy, until, on the bald summit of the ridge, they reached the Mexican encampment. It covered a wide tract of ground. Various utensils, ornamented dresses, and articles of luxury, were scattered round, and the number of slaves in attendance showed the barbaric pomp with which the nobles of Mexico went to their campaigns.[4] It was a rich booty for the victors, who spread over the deserted camp, and loaded themselves with the spoil, until the gathering darkness warned them to descend.[5]

---

[1] "I should have been very glad to have taken some alive," says Cortés, "who could have informed me of what was going on in the great city, and who had been lord there since the death of Montezuma. But I succeeded in saving only one; and he was more dead than alive." Rel. Seg. de Cortés, ap. Lorenzana, p. 159.

[2] "Y á ver que cosa era aquella, los quales eran mas de treinta mil Hombres, y la mas lúcida Gente, que hemos visto, porque trahian muchas Joyas de Oro, y Plata, y Plumajes." Ibid., p. 160.

[3] "Alcanzando muchos por una Cuesta arriba muy agra; y tal, que quando acabámos de encumbrar la Sierra, ni los Enemigos, ni nosotros podiamos ir atras, ni adelante : é assi caiéron muchos de ellos muertos, y ahogados de la calor, sin herida ninguna." Ibid., p. 160.

[4] "Porque demas de la Gente de Guerra, tenian mucho aparato de Servidores, y fornecimiento para su Real." Ibid., p. 160.

[5] The story of the capture of this strong post is told very differently by Captain Diaz. According to him, Olid, when he had fallen back on Cholula, in consequence of the refusal of his men to advance, under the strong suspicion which they entertained of some foul practice from their allies, received such a stinging rebuke from Cortés that he compelled his troops to resume their march, and, attacking the enemy "with the fury of a tiger," totally routed them. (Hist. de la Conquista, cap. 132.) But this version of the affair is not endorsed, so far as I am aware, by any contemporary. Cortés is so compendious in his report that it is often necessary to supply the omissions with the details of other writers. But where he is positive in his statements,—unless there be some reason to suspect a bias,—his practice of writing on the spot, and the peculiar facilities for information afforded by his position, make him decidedly the best authority.

Cortés followed up the blow by assaulting the strong town of Itzocan, held also by a Mexican garrison, and situated in the depths of a green valley watered by artificial canals and smiling in all the rich abundance of this fruitful region of the plateau.[1] The place, though stoutly defended, was stormed and carried ; the Aztecs were driven across a river which ran below the town, and, although the light bridges that traversed it were broken down in the flight, whether by design or accident, the Spaniards, fording and swimming the stream as they could, found their way to the opposite bank, following up the chase with the eagerness of bloodhounds. Here, too, the booty was great ; and the Indian auxiliaries flocked by thousands to the banners of the chief who so surely led them on to victory and plunder.[2]

Soon afterwards, Cortés returned to his headquarters at Tepeaca. Thence he detached his officers on expeditions which were usually successful. Sandoval, in particular, marched against a large body of the enemy lying between the camp and Vera Cruz, defeated them in two decisive battles, and thus restored the communications with the port.

The result of these operations was the reduction of that populous and cultivated territory which lies between the great *volcan*, on the west, and the mighty skirts of Orizaba, on the east. Many places, also, in the neighbouring province of Mixtecapan acknowledged the authority of the Spaniards, and others from the remote region of Oaxaca sent to claim their protection. The conduct of Cortés towards his allies had gained him great credit for disinterestedness and equity. The Indian cities in the adjacent territory appealed to him, as their umpire, in their differences with one another, and cases of disputed succession in their governments were referred to his arbitration. By his discreet and moderate policy he insensibly acquired an ascendency over their counsels which had been denied to the ferocious Aztec. His authority extended wider and wider every day; and a new empire grew up in the very heart of the land, forming a counterpoise to the colossal power which had so long overshadowed it.[3]

Cortés now felt himself strong enough to put in execution the plans for recovering the capital, over which he had been brooding ever since the hour of his expulsion. He had greatly undervalued the resources of

---

[1] Cortés, with an eye less sensible to the picturesque than his great predecessor in the track of discovery, Columbus, was full as quick in detecting the capabilities of the soil. "Tiene un Valle redondo muy fertil de Frutas, y Algodon, que en ninguna parte de los Puertos arriba se hace por la gran frialdad ; y allí es Tierra caliente, y caúsalo, que está muy abrigada de Sierras ; todo este Valle se riega por muy buenas Azequias, que tienen muy bien sacadas, y concertadas." Rel. Seg. de Cortés, ap. Lorenzana, pp. 164, 165.

[2] So numerous, according to Cortés, that they covered hill and dale, as far as the eye could reach, mustering more than a hundred and twenty thousand strong ! (Ibid., p. 162.) When the Conquerors attempt anything like a precise numeration, it will be as safe to substitute "a multitude," "a great force," etc., trusting the amount to the reader's own imagination.

[3] For the hostilities with the Indian tribes, noticed in the preceding pages, see, in addition to the Letter of Cortés, so often cited, Oviedo, Hist. de las Ind., MS., lib. 33, cap. 15,—Herrera, Hist. general, dec. 2, lib. 10, cap. 15, 16,—Ixtlilxochitl, Hist. Chich., MS., cap. 90,—Bernal Diaz, Hist. de la Conquista, cap. 130, 132, 134,—Gomara, Crónica, cap. 114–117,—P. Martyr, De Orbe Novo, dec. 5, cap. 6,—Camargo, Hist. de Tlascala. MS.

the Aztec monarchy. He was now aware, from bitter experience, that, to vanquish it, his own forces, and all he could hope to muster, would be incompetent, without a very extensive support from the Indians themselves. A large army would, moreover, require large supplies for its maintenance, and these could not be regularly obtained, during a protracted siege, without the friendly co-operation of the natives. On such support he might now safely calculate from Tlascala and the other Indian territories, whose warriors were so eager to serve under his banners. His past acquaintance with them had instructed him in their national character and system of war; while the natives who had fought under his command, if they had caught little of the Spanish tactics, had learned to act in concert with the white men and to obey him implicitly as their commander. This was a considerable improvement in such wild and disorderly levies, and greatly augmented the strength derived from numbers.

Experience showed that in a future conflict with the capital it would not do to trust to the causeways, but that, to succeed, he must command the lake. He proposed, therefore, to build a number of vessels like those constructed under his orders in Montezuma's time and afterwards destroyed by the inhabitants. For this he had still the services of the same experienced shipbuilder, Martin Lopez, who, as we have seen, had fortunately escaped the slaughter of the " Melancholy Night." Cortés now sent this man to Tlascala, with orders to build thirteen brigantines, which might be taken to pieces and carried on the shoulders of the Indians to be launched on the waters of Lake Tezcuco. The sails, rigging, and ironwork were to be brought from Vera Cruz, where they had been stored since their removal from the dismantled ships. It was a bold conception, that of constructing a fleet to be transported across forest and mountain before it was launched on its destined waters ! But it suited the daring genius of Cortés, who, with the co-operation of his stanch Tlascalan confederates, did not doubt his ability to carry it into execution.

It was with no little regret that the general learned at this time the death of his good friend Maxixca, the old lord of Tlascala, who had stood by him so steadily in the hour of adversity. He had fallen a victim to that terrible epidemic, the smallpox, which was now sweeping over the land like fire over the prairies, smiting down prince and peasant, and adding another to the long train of woes that followed the march of the white men. It was imported into the country, it is said, by a negro slave in the fleet of Narvaez.[1] It first broke out in Cempoalla. The poor natives, ignorant of the best mode of treating the loathsome disorder, sought relief in their usual practice of bathing in cold water, which greatly aggravated their trouble. From Cempoalla it spread rapidly over the

---

[1] "La primera fué de viruela, y comenzó de esta manera. Siendo Capitan y Governador Hernando Cortés al tiempo que el Capitan Pánfilo de Narvaez desembarcó en esta tierra, en uno de sus navíos vino un negro herido de viruelas, la cual enfermedad nunca en esta tierra se habia visto, y esta sazon estaba esta nueva España en estremo muy llena de gente." Toribio, Hist. de los Indios, MS., Parte 1, cap. 1.

neighbouring country, and, penetrating through Tlascala, reached the Aztec capital, where Montezuma's successor, Cuitlahua, fell one of its first victims. Thence it swept down towards the borders of the Pacific, leaving its path strewn with the dead bodies of the natives, who, in the strong language of a contemporary, perished in heaps like cattle stricken with the murrain.[1] It does not seem to have been fatal to the Spaniards, many of whom, probably, had already had the disorder, and who were, at all events, acquainted with the proper method of treating it.

The death of Maxixca was deeply regretted by the troops, who lost in him a true and most efficient ally. With his last breath he commended them to his son and successor, as the great beings whose coming into the country had been so long predicted by the oracles.[2] He expressed a desire to die in the profession of the Christian faith. Cortés no sooner learned his condition than he despatched Father Olmedo to Tlascala. The friar found that Maxixca had already caused a crucifix to be placed before his sick couch, as the object of his adoration. After explaining, as intelligibly as he could, the truths of revelation, he baptized the dying chieftain; and the Spaniards had the satisfaction to believe that the soul of their benefactor was exempted from the doom of eternal perdition that hung over the unfortunate Indian who perished in his unbelief.[3]

Their late brilliant successes seem to have reconciled most of the disaffected soldiers to the prosecution of the war. There were still a few among them, the secretary Duero, Bermudez the treasurer, and others high in office, or wealthy hidalgos, who looked with disgust on another campaign, and now loudly reiterated their demand of a free passage to Cuba. To this Cortés, satisfied with the support on which he could safely count, made no further objection. Having once given his consent, he did all in his power to facilitate their departure and provide for their comfort. He ordered the best ship at Vera Cruz to be placed at their disposal, to be well supplied with provisions and everything necessary for the voyage, and sent Alvarado to the coast to superintend the embarkation. He took the most courteous leave of them, with assurances of his own unalterable regard. But, as the event proved, those who could part from him at this crisis had little sympathy with his fortunes; and we find Duero not long afterwards in Spain, supporting the claims of Velasquez before the emperor, in opposition to those of his former friend and commander.

The loss of these few men was amply compensated by the arrival of others, whom Fortune—to use no higher term—most unexpectedly threw in his way. The first of these came in a small vessel sent from Cuba by

---

[1] "Morian como chinches á montones." (Toribio, Hist. de los Indios, ubi supra.) "So great was the number of those who died of this disease that there was no possibility of burying them, and in Mexico the dead were thrown into the canals, then filled with water, until the air was poisoned with the stench of putrid bodies." Sahagun, Hist. de Nueva-España, lib. 8, cap. 1.

[2] Bernal Diaz, Hist. de la Conquista, cap. 136.

[3] Hist. de la Conquista, ubi supra.—Herrera, Hist. general, dec. 2, lib. 10, cap. 19.—Sahagun, Hist. de Nueva-España, MS., lib. 12, cap 30

the governor, Velasquez, with stores for the colony at Vera Cruz. He was not aware of the late transactions in the country, and of the discomfiture of his officer. In the vessel came despatches, it is said, from Fonseca, bishop of Burgos, instructing Narvaez to send Cortés, if he had not already done so, for trial to Spain.[1] The alcalde of Vera Cruz, agreeably to the general's instructions, allowed the captain of the bark to land, who had no doubt that the country was in the hands of Narvaez. He was undeceived by being seized, together with his men, so soon as they had set foot on shore. The vessel was then secured; and the commander and his crew, finding out their error, were persuaded without much difficulty to join their countrymen in Tlascala.

A second vessel, sent soon after by Velasquez, shared the same fate, and those on board consented, also, to take their chance in the expedition under Cortés.

About the same time, Garay, the governor of Jamaica, fitted out three ships with an armed force to plant a colony on the Panuco, a river which pours into the Gulf a few degrees north of Villa Rica. Garay persisted in establishing this settlement, in contempt of the claims of Cortés, who had already entered into a friendly communication with the inhabitants of that region. But the crews experienced such a rough reception from the natives on landing, and lost so many men, that they were glad to take to their vessels again. One of these foundered in a storm. The others put into the port of Vera Cruz to restore the men, much weakened by hunger and disease. Here they were kindly received, their wants supplied, their wounds healed; when they were induced, by the liberal promises of Cortés, to abandon the disastrous service of their employer and enlist under his own prosperous banner. The reinforcements obtained from these sources amounted to full a hundred and fifty men, well provided with arms and ammunition, together with twenty horses. By this strange concurrence of circumstances, Cortés saw himself in possession of the supplies he most needed; that, too, from the hands of his enemies, whose costly preparations were thus turned to the benefit of the very man whom they were designed to ruin.

His good fortune did not stop here. A ship from the Canaries touched at Cuba, freighted with arms and military stores for the adventurers in the New World. Their commander heard there of the recent discoveries in Mexico, and, thinking it would afford a favourable market for him, directed his course to Vera Cruz. He was not mistaken. The alcalde, by the general's orders, purchased both ship and cargo; and the crews, catching the spirit of adventure, followed their countrymen into the interior. There seemed to be a magic in the name of Cortés, which drew all who came within hearing of it under his standard.[2]

---

[1] Bernal Diaz, Hist. de la Conquista, cap. 131.
[2] Bernal Diaz, Hist. de la Conquista, cap. 131, 133, 136.—Herrera, Hist. general, ubi supra.—Rel.

Seg. de Cortés, ap. Lorenzana, pp. 154, 167.—Oviedo, Historia de las Indias, MS., lib. 33. cap. 16.

Having now completed the arrangements for settling his new conquests, there seemed to be no further reason for postponing his departure to Tlascala. He was first solicited by the citizens of Tepeaca to leave a garrison with them, to protect them from the vengeance of the Aztecs. Cortés acceded to the request, and, considering the central position of the town favourable for maintaining his conquests, resolved to plant a colony there. For this object he selected sixty of his soldiers, most of whom were disabled by wounds or infirmity. He appointed the alcaldes, regidores, and other functionaries of a civic magistracy. The place he called *Segura de la Frontera*, or Security of the Frontier.[1] It received valuable privileges as a city, a few years later, from the emperor Charles the Fifth,[2] and rose to some consideration in the age of the Conquest. But its consequence soon after declined. Even its Castilian name, with the same caprice which has decided the fate of more than one name in our own country, was gradually supplanted by its ancient one, and the little village of Tepeaca is all that now commemorates the once flourishing Indian capital, and the second Spanish colony in Mexico.

While at Segura, Cortés wrote that celebrated letter to the emperor— the second in the series—so often cited in the preceding pages. It takes up the narrative with the departure from Vera Cruz, and exhibits in a brief and comprehensive form the occurrences up to the time at which we are now arrived. In the concluding page, the general, after noticing the embarrassments under which he labours, says, in his usual manly spirit, that he holds danger and fatigue light in comparison with the attainment of his object, and that he is confident a short time will restore the Spaniards to their former position and repair all their losses.[3]

He notices the resemblance of Mexico, in many of its features and productions, to the mother country, and requests that it may henceforth be called "New Spain of the Ocean Sea."[4] He finally requests that a commission may be sent out, at once, to investigate his conduct and to verify the accuracy of his statements.

This letter, which was printed at Seville the year after its reception, has been since reprinted, and translated, more than once.[5] It excited a great sensation at the court, and among the friends of science generally. The previous discoveries in the New World had disappointed the expectations which had been formed after the solution of the grand problem of its existence. They had brought to light only rude tribes, which, however

---

1 Rel. Seg. de Cortés, ap. Lorenzana, p. 156.

2 Clavigero, Stor. del Messico, tom. iii. p. 153.

3 "É creo, como ya á Vuestra Magestad he dicho, que en muy breve tomará al estado, en que antes yo la tenia, é se restaurarán las pérdidas pasadas." Rel. Seg., ap. Lorenzana, p. 167.

4 "Me pareció, que el mas conveniente nombre para esta dicha Tierra, era llamarse *la Nueva España del Mar Océano:* y assí en nombre de Vuestra Magestad se le puso aqueste nombre; humildemente suplico á Vuestra Alteza lo tenga por bien, y mande, que se nombre assi." (Ibid., p. 169.) The

name of "New Spain," without other addition, had been before given by Grijalva to Yucatan. *Ante*, Book 2, Chapter 1.

5 It was dated, "De la Villa Segura de la Frontera de esta Nueva-España, á treinta de Octubre de mil quinientos veinte años." But, in consequence of the loss of the ship intended to bear it, the letter was not sent till the spring of the following year; leaving the nation still in ignorance of the fate of the gallant adventurers in Mexico, and the magnitude of their discoveries.

gentle and inoffensive in their manners, were still in the primitive stages of barbarism. Here was an authentic account of a vast nation, potent and populous, exhibiting an elaborate social polity, well advanced in the arts of civilization, occupying a soil that teemed with mineral treasures and with a boundless variety of vegetable products, stores of wealth, both natural and artificial, that seemed, for the first time, to realize the golden dreams in which the great discoverer of the New World had so fondly, and in his own day so fallaciously, indulged. Well might the scholar of that age exult in the revelation of these wonders, which so many had long, but in vain, desired to see.[1]

With this letter went another to the emperor, signed, as it would seem, by nearly every officer and soldier in the camp. It expatiated on the obstacles thrown in the way of the expedition by Velasquez and Narvaez, and the great prejudice this had caused to the royal interests. It then set forth the services of Cortés, and besought the emperor to confirm him in his authority, and not to allow any interference with one who, from his personal character, his intimate knowledge of the land and its people, and the attachment of his soldiers, was the man best qualified in all the world to achieve the conquest of the country.[2]

It added not a little to the perplexities of Cortés that he was still in entire ignorance of the light in which his conduct was regarded in Spain. He had not even heard whether his despatches, sent the year preceding from Vera Cruz, had been received. Mexico was as far removed from all intercourse with the civilized world as if it had been placed at the antipodes. Few vessels had entered, and none had been allowed to leave, its ports. The governor of Cuba, an island distant but a few days' sail, was yet ignorant, as we have seen, of the fate of his armament. On the arrival of every new vessel or fleet on these shores, Cortés might well doubt whether it brought aid to his undertaking, or a royal commission to supersede him. His sanguine spirit relied on the former; though the latter was much the more probable, considering the intimacy of his enemy, the governor, with Bishop Fonseca, a man jealous of his authority, and one who, from his station at the head of the Indian department, held a predominant control over the affairs of the New World. It was the policy of Cortés, therefore, to lose no time; to push forward his preparations, lest another should be permitted to snatch the laurel now almost within his grasp. Could he but reduce the Aztec capital, he felt that he should be safe, and that, in whatever light his irregular proceedings might now be

---

[1] The state of feeling occasioned by these discoveries may be seen in the correspondence of Peter Martyr, then residing at the court of Castile. See, in particular, his epistle, dated March 1521, to his noble pupil, the Marquis de Mondejar, in which he dwells with unbounded satisfaction on all the rich stores of science which the expedition of Cortés had thrown open to the world. Opus Epistolarum, ep. 771.

[2] This memorial is in that part of my collection made by the former President of the Spanish Academy, Vargas Ponçe. It is signed by four hundred and forty-four names; and it is remarkable that this roll, which includes every other familiar name in the army, should not contain that of Bernal Diaz del Castillo. It can only be accounted for by his illness; as he tells us he was confined to his bed by a fever about this time. Hist. de la Conquista, cap. 134.

viewed, his services in that event would far more than counterbalance them in the eyes both of the crown and of the country.

The general wrote, also, to the Royal Audience at St. Domingo, in order to interest them in his cause. He sent four vessels to the same island, to obtain a further supply of arms and ammunition; and, the better to stimulate the cupidity of adventurers and allure them to the expedition, he added specimens of the beautiful fabrics of the country, and of its precious metals.[1] The funds for procuring these important supplies were, probably, derived from the plunder gathered in the late battles, and the gold which, as already remarked, had been saved from the general wreck by the Castilian convoy.

It was the middle of December when Cortés, having completed all his arrangements, set out on his return to Tlascala, ten or twelve leagues distant. He marched in the van of the army, and took the way of Cholula. How different was his condition from that in which he had left the republican capital not five months before! His march was a triumphal procession, displaying the various banners and military ensigns taken from the enemy, long files of captives, and all the rich spoils of conquest gleaned from many a hard-fought field. As the army passed through the towns and villages, the inhabitants poured out to greet them, and, as they drew near to Tlascala, the whole population, men, women, and children, came forth, celebrating their return with songs, dancing, and music. Arches decorated with flowers were thrown across the streets through which they passed, and a Tlascalan orator addressed the general, on his entrance into the city, in a lofty panegyric on his late achievements, proclaiming him the "avenger of the nation." Amidst this pomp and triumphal show, Cortés and his principal officers were seen clad in deep mourning in honour of their friend Maxixca. And this tribute of respect to the memory of their venerated ruler touched the Tlascalans more sensibly than all the proud display of military trophies.[2]

The general's first act was to confirm the son of his deceased friend in the succession, which had been contested by an illegitimate brother. The youth was but twelve years of age; and Cortés prevailed on him without difficulty to follow his father's example and receive baptism. He afterwards knighted him with his own hand; the first instance, probably, of the order of chivalry being conferred on an American Indian.[3] The elder Xicotencatl was also persuaded to embrace Christianity; and the example of their rulers had its obvious effect in preparing the minds of the people for the reception of the truth. Cortés, whether

---

[1] Rel. Terc. de Cortés, ap. Lorenzana, p. 179.—Herrera, Hist. general, dec. 2, lib. 10, cap. 18.—Alonso de Avila went as the bearer of despatches to St. Domingo. Bernal Diaz, who is not averse, now and then, to a fling at his commander, says that Cortés was willing to get rid of this gallant cavalier, because he was too independent and plain-spoken. Hist. de la Conquista, cap. 136.

[2] Bernal Diaz, Hist. de la Conquista, cap. 136.—Herrera, Hist. general, dec. 2, lib. 10, cap. 19.
[3] Ibid., ubi supra.—"Híçolo," says Herrera, "i armóle caballero, al vso de Castilla; i porque lo fuese de Jesu-Christo, le hiço bautiçar, se llamó D. Lorenço Maxiscatzin."

from the suggestions of Olmedo, or from the engrossing nature of his own affairs, did not press the work of conversion further at this time, but wisely left the good seed, already sown, to ripen in secret, till time should bring forth the harvest.

The Spanish commander, during his short stay in Tlascala, urged forward the preparations for the campaign. He endeavoured to drill the Tlascalans and to give them some idea of European discipline and tactics. He caused new arms to be made, and the old ones to be put in order. Powder was manufactured with the aid of sulphur obtained by some adventurous cavaliers from the smoking throat of Popocatepetl.[1] The construction of the brigantines went forward prosperously under the direction of Lopez, with the aid of the Tlascalans.[2] Timber was cut in the forests, and pitch, an article unknown to the Indians, was obtained from the pines on the neighbouring Sierra de Malinche. The rigging and other appurtenances were transported by the Indian *tamanes* from Villa Rica; and by Christmas the work was so far advanced that it was no longer necessary for Cortés to delay the march to Mexico.

CHAPTER VII.

GUATEMOZIN, EMPEROR OF THE AZTECS.—PREPARATIONS FOR THE MARCH. —MILITARY CODE.—SPANIARDS CROSS THE SIERRA.—ENTER TEZCUCO. —PRINCE IXTLILXOCHITL.

(1520.)

WHILE the events related in the preceding chapter were passing, an important change had taken place in the Aztec monarchy. Montezuma's brother and successor, Cuitlahua, had suddenly died of the smallpox, after a brief reign of four months,—brief, but glorious, for it had witnessed the overthrow of the Spaniards and their expulsion from Mexico.[3] On the death of their warlike chief, the electors were convened, as usual, to supply the vacant throne. It was an office of great responsibility in the dark hour of their fortunes. The *teoteuctli*, or high-priest, invoked the

---

[1] For an account of the manner in which this article was procured by Montaño and his doughty companion, see *ante*, p. 253.

[2] "Ansi se hicieron trece bergantines en el barrio de Atempa, junto á una hermita que se llama San Buenaventura, los quales hizo y otro Martin Lopez uno de los primeros conquistadores, y le ayudó Neguez Gomez." Hist. de Tlascala, MS.

[3] Solís dismisses this prince with the remark "that he reigned but a few days; long enough, however, for his indolence and apathy to efface the memory of his name among the people." (Conquista, lib. 4, cap. 16.) Whence the historiographer of the Indies borrowed the colouring for this portrait I cannot conjecture; certainly not from the ancient authorities, which uniformly delineate the character and conduct of the Aztec sovereign in the light represented in the text. Cortés, who ought to know, describes him "as held to be very wise and valiant." Rel. Seg., ap. Lorenzana, p. 166.—See, also, Sahagun, Hist. de Nueva-España, MS., lib. 12, cap. 29,—Herrera, Hist. general, dec. 2, lib. 10, cap. 19,—Ixtlilxochitl, Hist. Chich., MS., cap. 88, —Oviedo, Hist. de las Ind., MS., lib. 33, cap. 16.— Gomara, Crónica, cap. 118.

blessing of the supreme God on their deliberations. His prayer is still extant. It was the last one ever made on a similar occasion in Anahuac, and a few extracts from it may interest the reader, as a specimen of Aztec eloquence :—

"O Lord! thou knowest that the days of our sovereign are at an end, for thou hast placed him beneath thy feet. He abides in the place of his retreat; he has trodden the path which we are all to tread; he has gone to the house whither we are all to follow,—the house of eternal darkness, where no light cometh. He is gathered to his rest, and no one henceforth shall disquiet him. . . . All these were the princes, his predecessors, who sat on the imperial throne, directing the affairs of thy kingdom ; for thou art the universal lord and emperor, by whose will and movement the whole world is directed; thou needest not the counsel of another. They laid down the intolerable burden of government, and left it to him, their successor. Yet he sojourned but a few days in his kingdom,—but a few days had we enjoyed his presence, when thou summonedst him away to follow those who had ruled over the land before him. And great cause has he for thankfulness, that thou hast relieved him from so grievous a load, and placed him in tranquillity and rest. . . . Who now shall order matters for the good of the people and the realm? Who shall appoint the judges to administer justice to thy people? Who now shall bid the drum and the flute to sound, and gather together the veteran soldiers and the men mighty in battle? Our Lord and our Defence! wilt thou, in thy wisdom, elect one who shall be worthy to sit on the throne of thy kingdom; one who shall bear the grievous burden of government; who shall comfort and cherish thy poor people, even as the mother cherisheth her offspring? . . . O Lord most merciful! pour forth thy light and thy splendour over this thine empire! . . . Order it so that thou shalt be served in all, and through all." [1]

The choice fell on Quauhtemotzin, or Guatemozin, as euphoniously

---

[1] The reader of Spanish will see that in the version in the text I have condensed the original, which abounds in the tautology and repetitions characteristic of the compositions of a rude people. "Señor nuestro! ya V. M. sabe como es muerto nuestro N. : ya lo habeis puesto debajo de vuestros pies : ya está en su recogimiento, y es ido por el camino que todos hemos de ir y á la casa donde hemos de morar, casa de perpetuas tinieblas, donde ni hay ventana, ni luz alguna : ya está en el reposo donde nadie le desasosegará. . . . Todos estos señores y reyes rigiéron, gobernáron, y gozáron del señorío y dignidad real, y del trono y sitial del imperio, los cuales ordenáron y concertáron las cosas de vuestro reino, que sois el universal señor y emperador, por cuyo albedrio y motivo se rige todo el universo, y que no teneis necesidad de consejo de ningun otro. Ya estos dichos dejáron la carga intolerable del gobierno que tragéron sobre sus hombros, y lo dejáron á su succesor N., el cual por algunos dias tuvo en pie su señorío y reino, y ahora ya se ha ido en pos de ellos al otro mundo, porque vos le mandásteis que fuese y le llamásteis, y por haberle descargado de tan gran carga, y quitado de tan gran trabajo, y haberle puesto en paz y en reposo, está muy obligado á daros gracias. Algunos pocos dias le lográmos, y ahora para siempre se ausentó de nosotros para nunca mas volver al mundo. . . . ¿Quien ordenará y dispondrá las cosas necesarias al bien del pueblo, señorío y reino? ¿Quien elegirá á los jueces particulares, que tengan carga de la gente baja por los barrios? ¿Quien mandará tocar el atambor y pífano para juntar gente para la guerra? ¿Y quien reunirá y acaudillará á los soldados viejos, y hombres diestros en la pelea? Señor nuestro y amparador nuestro! tenga por bien V. M. de elegir, y señalar alguna persona suficiente para que tenga vuestro trono, y lleve á cuestas la carga pesada del régimen de la república, regocige y regale á los populares, bien asi como la madre regala á su hijo, poniéndole en su regazo. . . . O señor nuestro humanísimo! dad lumbre y resplandor de vuestra mano á esto reino ! . . . Hágase como V. M. fuere servido en todo, y por todo." Sahagun, Hist. de Nueva-España, lib 6. cap. 5.

corrupted by the Spaniards.[1] He was nephew to the two last monarchs, and married his cousin, the beautiful princess Tecuichpo, Montezuma's daughter. "He was not more than twenty-five years old, and elegant in his person for an Indian," says one who had seen him often ; "valiant, and so terrible that his followers trembled in his presence."[2] He did not shrink from the perilous post that was offered to him ; and, as he saw the tempest gathering darkly around, he prepared to meet it like a man. Though young, he had ample experience in military matters, and had distinguished himself above all others in the bloody conflicts of the capital. He bore a sort of religious hatred to the Spaniards, like that which Hannibal is said to have sworn, and which he certainly cherished, against his Roman foes.

By means of his spies, Guatemozin made himself acquainted with the movements of the Spaniards and their design to besiege the capital. He prepared for it by sending away the useless part of the population, while he called in his potent vassals from the neighbourhood. He continued the plans of his predecessor for strengthening the defences of the city, reviewed his troops, and stimulated them by prizes to excel in their exercises. He made harangues to his soldiers to rouse them to a spirit of desperate resistance. He encouraged his vassals throughout the empire to attack the white men wherever they were to be met with, setting a price on their heads, as well as on the persons of all who should be brought alive to him in Mexico.[3] And it was no uncommon thing for the Spaniards to find hanging up in the temples of the conquered places the arms and accoutrements of their unfortunate countrymen who had been seized and sent to the capital for sacrifice.[4] Such was the young monarch who was now called to the tottering throne of the Aztecs ; worthy, by his bold and magnanimous nature, to sway the sceptre of his country in the most flourishing period of her renown, and now, in her distress, devoting himself in the true spirit of a patriot prince to uphold her falling fortunes or bravely perish with them.[5]

We must now return to the Spaniards in Tlascala, where we left them preparing to resume their march on Mexico. Their commander had the satisfaction to see his troops tolerably complete in their appointments ; varying, indeed, according to the condition of the different reinforcements which had arrived from time to time, but, on the whole, superior to those

---

[1] The Spaniards appear to have changed the *Qua*, beginning Aztec names, into *Gua*, in the same manner as, in the mother country, they changed the *Wad* at the beginning of Arabic names into *Guad*. (See Condé, El Nubiense, Descripcion de España, notas, passim.) The Aztec *tzin* was added to the names of sovereigns and great lords, as a mark of reverence. Thus, Cuitlahua was called Cuitlahuatzin. This termination, usually dropped by the Spaniards, has been retained from accident, or perhaps for the sake of euphony, in Guatemozin's name.

[2] "Mancebo de hasta veynte y cinco años, bien gentil hombre para ser Indio, y muy esforçado, y se hizo temer de tal manera, que todos los suyos temblauan dél; y estaua casado con vna hija de Montecuma, bien hermosa muger para ser India." Bernal Diaz, Hist. de la Conquista, cap. 130.

[3] Herrera, Hist. general, dec. 2, lib. 10, cap. 19.

[4] Bernal Diaz, Hist. de la Conquista, cap. 134.

[5] One may call to mind the beautiful invocation which Racine has put into the mouth of Joad :—

"Venez, cher rejeton d'une vaillante race, Remplir vos défenseurs d'une nouvelle audace ; Venez du diadème à leurs yeux vous couvrir, Et périssez du moins en roi, s'il faut périr."

ATHALIE, acte 4, scène 5.

of the army with which he had first invaded the country. His whole force fell little short of six hundred men; forty of whom were cavalry, together with eighty arquebusiers and crossbowmen. The rest were armed with sword and target, and with the copper-headed pike of Chinantla. He had nine cannon of a moderate calibre, and was indifferently supplied with powder.[1]

As his forces were drawn up in order of march, Cortés rode through the ranks, exhorting his soldiers, as usual with him on these occasions, to be true to themselves and the enterprise in which they were embarked. He told them they were to march against *rebels*, who had once acknowledged allegiance to the Spanish sovereign;[2] against barbarians, the enemies of their religion. They were to fight the battles of the Cross and of the crown; to fight their own battles, to wipe away the stain from their arms, to avenge their injuries, and the loss of the dear companions who had been butchered on the field or on the accursed altar of sacrifice. Never was there a war which offered higher incentives to the Christian cavalier; a war which opened to him riches and renown in this life, and an imperishable glory in that to come.[3]

Thus did the politic chief touch all the secret springs of devotion, honour, and ambition in the bosoms of his martial audience, waking the mettle of the most sluggish before leading him on the perilous emprise. They answered with acclamations that they were ready to die in defence of the Faith, and would either conquer, or leave their bones with those of their countrymen in the waters of the Tezcuco.

The army of the allies next passed in review before the general. It is variously estimated by writers from a hundred and ten to a hundred and fifty thousand soldiers! The palpable exaggeration, no less than the discrepancy, shows that little reliance can be placed on any estimate. It is certain, however, that it was a multitudinous array, consisting not only of the flower of the Tlascalan warriors, but of those of Cholula, Tepeaca, and the neighbouring territories, which had submitted to the Castilian crown.[4]

They were armed, after the Indian fashion, with bows and arrows, the glassy *maquahuitl*, and the long pike, which formidable weapon Cortés, as we have seen, had introduced among his own troops. They were divided into battalions, each having its own banner, displaying the appropriate arms or emblem of its company. The four great chiefs of the nation marched in the van; three of them venerable for their years, and showing, in the insignia which decorated their persons, the evidence

---

[1] Rel. Tercera de Cortés, ap. Lorenzana, p. 183. —Most, if not all, of the authorities—a thing worthy of note—concur in this estimate of the Spanish forces.

[2] "Y como sin causa ninguna todos los Naturales de Colúa, que son los de la gran Ciudad de Temixtitan, y los de todas las otras Provincias á ellas sujetas, no solamente se habian *rebelado* contra Vuestra Magestad." Ibid., ubi supra.

[3] Rel. Tercera de Cortés, ap. Lorenzana, p. 184. —"Porque demas del premio, que les davia en el cielo, se les seguirian en esto mundo grandíssima honra, riquezas inestimables." Ixtlilxochitl, Hist. Chichimeca, MS., cap. 91.

[4] "Cosa muy de ver," says Father Sahagun, without hazarding any precise number, "en la cantidad y en los aparejos que llevaban." Hist. de Nueva-España, lib. 12, cap. 30, MS.

of many a glorious feat in arms. The panache of many-coloured plumes floated from their casques, set in emeralds or other precious stones. Their *escaupil,* or stuffed doublet of cotton, was covered with the graceful surcoat of feather-work, and their feet were protected by sandals embossed with gold. Four young pages followed, bearing their weapons, and four others supported as many standards, on which were emblazoned the armorial bearings of the four great divisions of the republic.[1] The Tlascalans, though frugal in the extreme, and rude in their way of life, were as ambitious of display in their military attire as any of the races on the plateau. As they defiled before Cortés, they saluted him by waving their banners and by a flourish of their wild music, which the general acknowledged by courteously raising his cap as they passed.[2] The Tlascalan warriors, and especially the younger Xicotencatl, their commander, affected to imitate their European masters, not merely in their tactics, but in minuter matters of military etiquette.

Cortés, with the aid of Marina, made a brief address to his Indian allies. He reminded them that he was going to fight their battles against their ancient enemies. He called on them to support him in a manner worthy of their renowned republic. To those who remained at home, he committed the charge of aiding in the completion of the brigantines, on which the success of the expedition so much depended; and he requested that none would follow his banner who were not prepared to remain till the final reduction of the capital.[3] This address was answered by shouts, or rather yells, of defiance, showing the exultation felt by his Indian confederates at the prospect of at last avenging their manifold wrongs and humbling their haughty enemy.

Before setting out on the expedition, Cortés published a code of ordinances, as he terms them, or regulations for the army, too remarkable to be passed over in silence. The preamble sets forth that in all institutions, whether divine or human,—if the latter have any worth,—order is the great law. The ancient chronicles inform us that the greatest captains in past times owed their successes quite as much to the wisdom of their ordinances as to their own valour and virtue. The situation of the Spaniards eminently demanded such a code; a mere handful of men as they were, in the midst of countless enemies, most cunning in the management of their weapons and in the art of war. The instrument then reminds the army that the conversion of the heathen is the work most acceptable in the eye of the Almighty, and one that will be sure to receive his support. It calls on every soldier to regard this as the prime object of the expedition, *without which the war would be manifestly unjust, and every acquisition made by it, a robbery.*[4]

---

1 Herrera, Hist. general, dec. 2, lib. 10, cap. 20.
2 Ibid., ubi supra.
3 Ibid., loc. cit.
4 "Que su principal motivo é intencion sea apartar y desarraigar de las dichas idolatrías á todos los naturales destas partes y reducillos ó á lo menos desear su salvacion y que sean reducidos al conocimiento de Dios y de su Santa Fe católica: porque si con otra intencion se hiciese la dicha guerra seria injusta y todo lo que en ella se oviese Onoloxio é obligado á restitucion." Ordenanzas militares, MS

The general solemnly protests that the principal motive which operates in his own bosom is the desire to wean the natives from their gloomy idolatry and to impart to them the knowledge of a purer faith ; and next, to recover for his master, the emperor, the dominions which of right belong to him.[1]

The ordinances then prohibit all blasphemy against God or the saints ; a vice much more frequent among Catholic than Protestant nations, arising, perhaps, less from difference of religion than of physical tempera- ment,—for the warm sun of the South, under which Catholicism prevails, stimulates the sensibilities to the more violent expression of passion.[2]

Another law is directed against gaming, to which the Spaniards, in all ages, have been peculiarly addicted. Cortés, making allowance for the strong national propensity, authorizes it under certain limitations, but prohibits the use of dice altogether.[3] Then follow other laws against brawls and private combats, against personal taunts and the irritating sarcasms of rival companies ; rules for the more perfect discipline of the troops, whether in camp or the field. Among others is one prohibiting any captain, under pain of death, from charging the enemy without orders ; a practice noticed as most pernicious and of too frequent occur- rence,—showing the impetuous spirit and want of true military subordina- tion in the bold cavaliers who followed the standard of Cortés.

The last ordinance prohibits any man, officer or private, from securing to his own use any of the booty taken from the enemy, whether it be gold, silver, precious stones, feather-work, stuffs, slaves, or other commodity, however or wherever obtained, in the city or in the field, and requires him to bring it forthwith to the presence of the general, or the officer appointed to receive it. The violation of this law was punished with death and confiscation of property. So severe an edict may be thought to prove that, however much the *Conquistador* may have been influenced by spiritual considerations, he was by no means insensible to those of a temporal character.[4]

These provisions were not suffered to remain a dead letter. The

---

[1] "É desde ahora protesto en nombre de S. M. que mi principal intencion é motivo es facer esta guerra é las otras que ficiese por traer y reducir á los dichos naturales al dicho conocimiento de nu- estra Santa Fe é creencia ; y despues por los sozjugar é supeditar debajo del yugo é dominio imperial é real de su Sacra Magestad, á quien juridicamente el Señorío de todas estas partes." Ordenanzas militares, MS.

[2] "Ce n'est qu'en Espagne et en Italie," says the penetrating historian of the Italian Republics, "qu'on rencontre cette habitude vicieuse, absolument inconnue aux peuples protestants, et qu'il ne faut point confondre avec les grossiers juremens que le peuple en tout pays mêle à ses discours. Dans tous les accès de colère des peuples du Midi, ils s'atta- quent aux objets de leur culte, ils les menacent, et ils accablent de paroles outrageantes la Divinité elle-même, le Rédempteur ou ses saints." Sismondi, Républiques Italiennes, cap. 126.

[3] Lucio Marineo, who witnessed all the dire effects of this national propensity at the Castilian

court, where he was residing at this time, breaks out into the following animated apostrophe against it : "The gambler is he who wishes and conspires the death of his parents, he who swears falsely by God and by the life of his king and lord, he who kills his own soul and casts it into hell. What will not the gambler do, when he is not ashamed to lose his money, his time, his sleep, his reputation, his honour, and even life itself ? So that, considering how great a number of men are incessantly engaged in play, the opinion seems to me well founded of those who say that *hell is filled with gamblers.*" Cosas memorables de España (ed. Sevilla, 1539), fol. 165.

[4] These regulations are reported with much uni- formity by Herrera, Solís, Clavigero, and others, but with such palpable inaccuracy that it is clear they never could have seen the original instrument. The copy in my possession was taken from the Muñoz collection. As the document, though curious and highly interesting, has never been published, I have given it entire in the Appendix, Part 2, No. 13.

Spanish commander, soon after their proclamation, made an example of two of his own slaves, whom he hanged for plundering the natives. A similar sentence was passed on a soldier for the like offence, though he allowed him to be cut down before the sentence was entirely executed. Cortés knew well the character of his followers; rough and turbulent spirits, who required to be ruled with an iron hand. Yet he was not eager to assert his authority on light occasions. The intimacy into which they were thrown by their peculiar situation, perils, and sufferings, in which all equally shared, and a common interest in the adventure, induced a familiarity between men and officers, most unfavourable to military discipline. The general's own manners, frank and liberal, seemed to invite this freedom, which, on ordinary occasions, he made no attempt to repress; perhaps finding it too difficult, or at least impolitic, since it afforded a safety-valve for the spirits of a licentious soldiery, that, if violently coerced, might have burst forth into open mutiny. But the limits of his forbearance were clearly defined; and any attempt to overstep them, or to violate the established regulations of the camp, brought a sure and speedy punishment on the offender. By thus tempering severity with indulgence, masking an iron will under the open bearing of a soldier, Cortés established a control over his band of bold and reckless adventurers, such as a pedantic martinet, scrupulous in enforcing the minutiæ of military etiquette, could never have obtained.

The ordinances, dated on the twenty-second of December, were proclaimed to the assembled army on the twenty-sixth. Two days afterwards, the troops were on their march, and Cortés, at the head of his battalions, with colours flying and music playing, issued forth from the gates of the republican capital, which had so generously received him in his distress, and which now, for the second time, supplied him with the means for consummating his great enterprise. The population of the city, men, women, and children, hung on the rear of the army, taking a last leave of their countrymen, and imploring the gods to crown their arms with victory.

Notwithstanding the great force mustered by the Indian confederates, the Spanish general allowed but a small part of them now to attend him. He proposed to establish his headquarters at some place on the Tezcucan lake, whence he could annoy the Aztec capital by reducing the surrounding country, cutting off the supplies, and thus placing the city in a state of blockade.[1]

The direct assault on Mexico itself he intended to postpone until the arrival of the brigantines should enable him to make it with the greatest advantage. Meanwhile, he had no desire to encumber himself with a superfluous multitude, whom it would be difficult to feed; and he preferred

---

[1] Herrera, Hist. general, dec. 2, lib. 10, cap. 20.—Bernal Diaz, Hist. de la Conquista, cap. 127. The former historian states the number of Indian allies who followed Cortés, at eighty thousand; the latter at ten thousand! *¿Quien sabe?*

to leave them at Tlascala, whence they might convey the vessels, when completed, to the camp, and aid him in his future operations.

Three routes presented themselves to Cortés by which he might penetrate into the Valley. He chose the most difficult, traversing the bold sierra which divides the eastern plateau from the western, and so rough and precipitous as to be scarcely practicable for the march of an army. He wisely judged that he should be less likely to experience annoyance from the enemy in this direction, as they might naturally confide in the difficulties of the ground for their protection.

The first day, the troops advanced five or six leagues, Cortés riding in the van, at the head of his little body of cavalry. They halted at the village of Tetzmellocan, at the base of the mountain chain which traverses the country, touching, at its southern limit, the mighty Iztaccihuatl, or "White Woman,"—white with the snows of ages.[1] At this village they met with a friendly reception, and on the following morning began the ascent of the sierra.

The path was steep and exceedingly rough. Thick matted bushes covered its surface, and the winter torrents had broken it into deep stony channels, hardly practicable for the passage of artillery, while the straggling branches of the trees, flung horizontally across the road, made it equally difficult for cavalry. The cold, as they rose higher, became intense. It was keenly felt by the Spaniards, accustomed of late to a warm, or at least temperate, climate ; though the extreme toil with which they forced their way upward furnished the best means of resisting the weather. The only vegetation to be seen in these higher regions was the pine, dark forests of which clothed the sides of the mountains, till even these dwindled into a thin and stunted growth. It was night before the wayworn soldiers reached the bald crest of the sierra, where they lost no time in kindling their fires ; and, huddling round their bivouacs, they warmed their frozen limbs and prepared their evening repast.

With the earliest dawn, the troops were again in motion. Mass was said, and they began their descent, more difficult and painful than their ascent on the day preceding ; for, in addition to the natural obstacles of the road, they found it strewn with huge pieces of timber and trees, obviously felled for the purpose by the natives. Cortés ordered up a body of light troops to clear away the impediments, and the army again resumed its march, but with the apprehension that the enemy had prepared an ambuscade, to surprise them when they should be entangled in the pass. They moved cautiously forward, straining their vision to pierce the thick gloom of the forest, where the wily foe might be lurking. But they saw no living thing, except only the wild inhabitants of the woods, and flocks

---

[1] This mountain, which, with its neighbour Popocatepetl, forms the great barrier—the *Herculis columnæ*—of the Mexican Valley, has been fancifully likened, from its long dorsal swell, to the back of a dromedary. (Tudor's Tour in North America, Let. 22.) It rises far above the limits of perpetual snow in the tropics, and its huge crest and sides, enveloped in its silver drapery, form one of the most striking objects in the magnificent *coup-d'œil* presented to the inhabitants of the capital.

of the *zopilote*, the voracious vulture of the country, which, in anticipation of a bloody banquet, hung, like a troop of evil spirits, on the march of the army.

As they descended, the Spaniards felt a sensible and most welcome change in the temperature. The character of the vegetation changed with it, and the funereal pine, their only companion of late, gave way to the sturdy oak, to the sycamore, and, lower down, to the graceful pepper-tree mingling its red berry with the dark foliage of the forest; while, in still lower depths, the gaudy-coloured creepers might be seen flinging their gay blossoms over the branches and telling of a softer and more luxurious climate.

At length the army emerged on an open level, where the eye, unobstructed by intervening wood or hill-top, could range, far and wide, over the Valley of Mexico. There it lay bathed in the golden sunshine, stretched out, as it were, in slumber, in the arms of the giant hills which clustered, like a phalanx of guardian genii, around it. The magnificent vision, new to many of the spectators, filled them with rapture. Even the veterans of Cortés could not withhold their admiration, though this was soon followed by a bitter feeling, as they recalled the sufferings which had befallen them within these beautiful but treacherous precincts. It made us feel, says the lion-hearted Conqueror, in his Letters, that " we had no choice but victory or death; and, our minds once resolved, we moved forward with as light a step as if we had been going on an errand of certain pleasure." [1]

As the Spaniards advanced, they beheld the neighbouring hill-tops blazing with beacon-fires, showing that the country was already alarmed and mustering to oppose them. The general called on his men to be mindful of their high reputation; to move in order, closing up their ranks, and to obey implicitly the commands of their officers.[2] At every turn among the hills, they expected to meet the forces of the enemy drawn up to dispute their passage. And, as they were allowed to pass the defiles unmolested, and drew near to the open plains, they were prepared to see them occupied by a formidable host, who would compel them to fight over again the battle of Otumba. But, although clouds of dusky warriors were seen, from time to time, hovering on the highlands, as if watching their progress, they experienced no interruption till they reached a *barranca*, or deep ravine, through which flowed a little river, crossed by a bridge partly demolished. On the opposite side a considerable body of Indians was stationed, as if to dispute the passage; but, whether distrusting their own numbers, or intimidated by the steady advance of the Spaniards,

---

[1] "Y prometímos todos de nunca de ella salir, sin Victoria, ó dejar allí las vidas. Y con esta determinacion ibamos todos tan alegres, como si fueramos á cosa de mucho placer." Rel. Terc., ap. Lorenzana, p. 188.

[2] "Y yo torné á rogar, y encomendar mucho á los Españoles, que hiciessen, como siempre habian hecho, y como se esperaba de sus Personas; y que nadie no se desmandasse, y que fuessen con mucho concierto, y órden por su Camino." Ibid., ubi supra.

2 F

they offered them no annoyance, and were quickly dispersed by a few resolute charges of cavalry. The army then proceeded, without molestation, to a small town, called Coatepec, where they halted for the night. Before retiring to his own quarters, Cortés made the rounds of the camp, with a few trusty followers, to see that all was safe.[1] He seemed to have an eye that never slumbered, and a frame incapable of fatigue. It was the indomitable spirit within, which sustained him.[2]

Yet he may well have been kept awake through the watches of the night, by anxiety and doubt. He was now but three leagues from Tezcuco, the far-famed capital of the Acolhuans. He proposed to establish his headquarters, if possible, at this place. Its numerous dwellings would afford ample accommodations for his army. An easy communication with Tlascala, by a different route from that which he had traversed, would furnish him with the means of readily obtaining supplies from that friendly country, and for the safe transportation of the brigantines, when finished, to be launched on the waters of the Tezcuco. But he had good reason to distrust the reception he should meet with in the capital; for an important revolution had taken place there since the expulsion of the Spaniards from Mexico, of which it will be necessary to give some account.

The reader will remember that the cacique of that place, named Cacama, was deposed by Cortés, during his first residence in the Aztec metropolis, in consequence of a projected revolt against the Spaniards, and that the crown had been placed on the head of a younger brother, Cuicuitzca. The deposed prince was among the prisoners carried away by Cortés, and perished with the others in the terrible passage of the causeway, on the *noche triste*. His brother, afraid, probably, after the flight of the Spaniards, of continuing with his own vassals, whose sympathies were altogether with the Aztecs, accompanied his friends in their retreat, and was so fortunate as to reach Tlascala in safety.

Meanwhile, a second son of Nezahualpilli, named Coanaco, claimed the crown, on his elder brother's death, as his own rightful inheritance. As he heartily joined his countrymen and the Aztecs in their detestation of the white men, his claims were sanctioned by the Mexican emperor. Soon after his accession, the new lord of Tezcuco had an opportunity of showing his loyalty to his imperial patron in an effectual manner.

A body of forty-five Spaniards, ignorant of the disasters in Mexico, were transporting thither a large quantity of gold, at the very time their countrymen were on the retreat to Tlascala. As they passed through the

---

[1] "É como la Gente de pie venia algo cansada, y se hacia tarde, dormímos en una Poblacion, que se dice Coatepeque. . . . É yo con diez de Caballo comenzé la Vela, y Ronda de la prima, y hice, que toda la Gente estubiesse muy apercibida." Rel. Terc., ap. Lorenzana, pp. 188, 189.

[2] For the preceding pages, giving the account of the march, besides the Letter of Cortés, so often

quoted, see Gomara, Crónica, cap. 121,—Oviedo, Hist. de las Ind., MS., lib. 33, cap. 18,—Bernal Diaz, Hist. de la Conquista, cap. 137,—Camargo, Hist. de Tlascala, MS.,—Herrera, Hist. general, dec. 2, lib. 10, cap. 20,—Ixtlilxochitl, Relacion de la Venida de los Españoles y Principio de la Ley Evangélica (México, 1829), p. 9.

Tezcucan territory, they were attacked by Coanaco's orders, most of them massacred on the spot, and the rest sent for sacrifice to Mexico. The arms and accoutrements of these unfortunate men were hung up as trophies in the temples, and their skins, stripped from their dead bodies, were suspended over the bloody shrines, as the most acceptable offering to the offended deities.[1]

Some months after this event, the exiled prince, Cuicuitzca, wearied with his residence in Tlascala, and pining for his former royal state, made his way back secretly to Tezcuco, hoping, it would seem, to raise a party there in his favour. But, if such were his expectations, they were sadly disappointed; for no sooner had he set foot in the capital than he was betrayed to his brother, who, by the advice of Guatemozin, put him to death, as a traitor to his country.[2] Such was the posture of affairs in Tezcuco when Cortés, for the second time, approached its gates; and well might he doubt, not merely the nature of his reception there, but whether he would be permitted to enter it at all, without force of arms.

These apprehensions were dispelled the following morning, when, before the troops were well under arms, an embassy was announced from the lord of Tezcuco. It consisted of several nobles, some of whom were known to the companions of Cortés. They bore a golden flag in token of amity, and a present of no great value to Cortés. They brought also a message from the cacique, imploring the general to spare his territories, inviting him to take up his quarters in his capital, and promising on his arrival to become the vassal of the Spanish sovereign.

Cortés dissembled the satisfaction with which he listened to these overtures, and sternly demanded of the envoys an account of the Spaniards who had been massacred, insisting, at the same time, on the immediate restitution of the plunder. But the Indian nobles excused themselves by throwing the whole blame upon the Aztec emperor, by whose orders the deed had been perpetrated, and who now had possession of the treasure. They urged Cortés not to enter the city that day, but to pass the night in the suburbs, that their master might have time to prepare suitable accommodations for him. The Spanish commander, however, gave no heed to this suggestion, but pushed forward his march, and at noon, on the thirty-first of December 1520, entered, at the head of his legions, the venerable walls of Tezcuco, "the place of rest," as not inaptly denominated.[3]

He was struck, as when he before visited this populous city, with the solitude and silence which reigned throughout its streets. He was conducted to the palace of Nezahualpilli, which was assigned as his quarters. It was an irregular pile of low buildings, covering a wide extent of ground,

---

[1] See *ante*, p. 423.—The skins of those immolated on the sacrificial stone were a common offering in the Indian temples, and the mad priests celebrated many of their festivals by publicly dancing with their own persons enveloped in these disgusting spoils of their victims. See Sahagun, Hist. de Nueva-España, passim.

[2] Rel. Terc. de Cortés, ap. Lorenzana, p. 187.—Oviedo, Hist. de las Ind., MS., lib. 33, cap. 19.

[3] Tezcuco, a Chichimec name, according to Ixtlilxochitl, signifying "place of detention or rest," because the various tribes from the North halted there on their entrance into Anahuac. Hist. Chich., MS., cap. 10.

like the royal residence occupied by the troops in Mexico. It was spacious enough to furnish accommodations not only for all the Spaniards, says Cortés, but for twice their number.[1] He gave orders, on his arrival, that all regard should be paid to the persons and property of the citizens, and forbade any Spaniard to leave his quarters, under pain of death.

His commands were not effectual to suppress some excesses of his Indian allies, if the report of the Tezcucan chronicler be correct, who states that the Tlascalans burnt down one of the royal palaces soon after their arrival. It was the depository of the national archives; and the conflagration, however it may have occurred, may well be deplored by the antiquary, who might have found in its hieroglyphic records some clue to the migrations of the mysterious races which first settled on the highlands of Anahuac.[2]

Alarmed at the apparent desertion of the place, as well as by the fact that none of its principal inhabitants came to welcome him, Cortés ordered some soldiers to ascend the neighbouring *teocalli* and survey the city. They soon returned with the report that the inhabitants were leaving it in great numbers, with their families and effects, some in canoes upon the lake, others on foot towards the mountains. The general now comprehended the import of the cacique's suggestion that the Spaniards should pass the night in the suburbs,—in order to secure time for evacuating the city. He feared that the chief himself might have fled. He lost no time in detaching troops to secure the principal avenues, where they were to turn back the fugitives, and arrest the cacique, if he were among the number. But it was too late. Coanaco was already far on his way across the lake to Mexico.

Cortés now determined to turn this event to his own account, by placing another ruler on the throne, who should be more subservient to his interests. He called a meeting of the few principal persons still remaining in the city, and, by their advice and ostensible election, advanced a brother of the late sovereign to the dignity, which they declared vacant. This prince, who consented to be baptized, was a willing instrument in the hands of the Spaniards. He survived but a few months,[3] and was succeeded by another member of the royal house, named Ixtlilxochitl, who, indeed, as general of his armies, may be said to have held the reins of government in his hands during his brother's

---

[1] "La qual es tan grande, que aunque fueramos doblados los Españoles, nos pudieramos aposentar bien á placer en ella." Rel. Terc., ap. Lorenzana, p. 191.

[2] "De tal manera que se quemáron todos los Archivos Reales de toda la Nueva España, que fué una de las mayores pérdidas que tuvo esta tierra, porque con esto toda la memoria de sus antiguayas y otras cosas que eran como Escrituras y recuerdos pereciéron desde este tiempo. La obra de las Casas era la mejor y la mas artificiosa que hubo en esta tierra." Ixtlilxochitl, Hist. Chich., MS., cap. 91.

[3] The historian Ixtlilxochitl pays the following high tribute to the character of his royal kinsman, whose name was Tecocol. Strange that this name is not to be found—with the exception of Sahagun's work—in any contemporary record! "Fué el primero que lo fué en Tezcoco, con harta pena de los Españoles, porque fué nobilísimo y los quiso mucho. Fué D. Fernando Tecocoltzin muy gentil hombre, alto de cuerpo y muy blanco, tanto cuanto podia ser cualquier Español por muy blanco que fuese, y que mostraba su persona y término descender, y ser del linage que era. Supo la lengua Castellana, y así casi las mas noches despues de haber cenado, trataban él y Cortés de todo lo que se debia hacer acerca de las guerras." Ixtlilxochitl, Venida de los Españoles. pp. 12, 13.

lifetime. As this person was intimately associated with the Spaniards in their subsequent operations, to the success of which he essentially contributed, it is proper to give some account of his early history, which, in truth, is as much enveloped in the marvellous as that of any fabulous hero of antiquity.[1]

He was son, by a second queen, of the great Nezahualpilli. Some alarming prodigies at his birth, and the gloomy aspect of the planets, led the astrologers who cast his horoscope to advise the king, his father, to take away the infant's life, since, if he lived to grow up, he was destined to unite with the enemies of his country and overturn its institutions and religion. But the old monarch replied, says the chronicler, that "the time had arrived when the sons of Quetzalcoatl were to come from the East to take possession of the land; and, if the Almighty had selected his child to co-operate with them in the work, His will be done."[2]

As the boy advanced in years, he exhibited a marvellous precocity not merely of talent, but of mischievous activity, which afforded an alarming prognostic for the future. When about twelve years old, he formed a little corps of followers of about his own age, or somewhat older, with whom he practised the military exercises of his nation, conducting mimic fights and occasionally assaulting the peaceful burghers and throwing the whole city as well as palace into uproar and confusion. Some of his father's ancient counsellors, connecting this conduct with the predictions at his birth, saw in it such alarming symptoms that they repeated the advice of the astrologers to take away the prince's life, if the monarch would not see his kingdom one day given up to anarchy. This unpleasant advice was reported to the juvenile offender, who was so much exasperated by it that he put himself at the head of a party of his young desperadoes, and, entering the houses of the offending counsellors, dragged them forth and administered to them the *garrote*,—the mode in which capital punishment was inflicted in Tezcuco.

He was seized and brought before his father. When questioned as to his extraordinary conduct, he coolly replied "that he had done no more than he had a right to do. The guilty ministers had deserved their fate, by endeavouring to alienate his father's affections from him, for no other reason than his too great fondness for the profession of arms,—

---

[1] The accession of Tecocol, as, indeed, his existence, passes unnoticed by some historians, and by others is mentioned in so equivocal a manner—his Indian name being omitted—that it is very doubtful if any other is intended than his younger brother Ixtlilxochitl. The Tezcucan chronicler bearing this last melodious name * has alone given the particulars of his history. I have followed him, as, from his personal connections, having had access to the best sources of information; though, it must be confessed, he is far too ready to take things on trust, to be always the best authority.

[2] "Él respondió, que era por demas ir contra lo determinado por el Dios Criador de todas las cosas, pues no sin misterio y secreto juicio suyo le daba tal Hijo al tiempo y quando se acercaban las profecías de sus Antepasados, que haviase venir nuevas Gentes á poseer la Tierra, como eran los Hijos de Quetzalcoatl que aguardaban su venida de la parte oriental." Ixtlilxochitl, Hist. Chich., MS., cap. 69.

* [This name — "which," says Mr. Tylor, "sticks in the throats of readers of Prescott"— signifies "vanilla-face," being compounded of *ixtli*, face, and *tlilxochitl*, vanilla, the latter being itself a compound of *tlilli*, black, and *xochitl*, flower.—Buschmann, Ueber die Aztekischen Ortsnamen, S. 681.—ED.]

the most honourable profession in the state, and the one most worthy of a prince. If they had suffered death, it was no more than they had intended for him." The wise Nezahualpilli, says the chronicler, found much force in these reasons; and, as he saw nothing low and sordid in the action, but rather the ebullition of a daring spirit, which in after-life might lead to great things, he contented himself with bestowing a grave admonition on the juvenile culprit.[1] Whether this admonition had any salutary effect on his subsequent demeanour, we are not informed. It is said, however, that as he grew older he took an active part in the wars of his country, and, when no more than seventeen, had won for himself the insignia of a valiant and victorious captain.[2]

On his father's death, he disputed the succession with his elder brother, Cacama. The country was menaced with a civil war, when the affair was compromised by his brother's ceding to him that portion of his territories which lay among the mountains. On the arrival of the Spaniards, the young chieftain—for he was scarcely twenty years of age—made, as we have seen, many friendly demonstrations towards them, induced, no doubt, by his hatred of Montezuma, who had supported the pretensions of Cacama.[3] It was not, however, till his advancement to the lordship of Tezcuco that he showed the full extent of his good-will. From that hour he became the fast friend of the Christians, supporting them with his personal authority and the whole strength of his military array and resources, which, although much shorn of their ancient splendour since the days of his father, were still considerable, and made him a most valuable ally. His important services have been gratefully commemorated by the Castilian historians; and history should certainly not defraud him of his just meed of glory,—the melancholy glory of having contributed more than any other chieftain of Anahuac to rivet the chains of the white man round the necks of his countrymen.

The two pillars on which the story of the Conquest mainly rests are the Chronicles of Gomara and of Bernal Diaz, two individuals having as little resemblance to each other as the courtly and cultivated churchman has to the unlettered soldier.

The first of these, Francisco Lopez de Gomara, was a native of Seville. On the return of Cortés to Spain after the Conquest, Gomara became his chaplain, and on his patron's death continued in the service of his son, the second Marquis of the Valley. It was then that he wrote his Chronicle; and the circumstances under which it was produced might lead one to conjecture that the narrative would not be conducted on the strict

---

[1] "Con que el Rey no supo con que ocacion poderle castigar, porque lo pareciéron sus razones tan vivas y fundadas que su parte no habia hecho cosa indebida ni vileza para poder ser castigado, mas tan solo una ferocidad de ánimo; pronóstico de lo mucho que habia de venir á saber por las Armas, y así el Rey dijo, que se fuese á la mano." Ixtlilxochitl. Hist. Chich., MS., cap. 69.

[2] Ibid., ubi supra.—Among other anecdotes recorded of the young prince's early development

is one of his having, when only three years old, pitched his nurse into a well, as she was drawing water, to punish her for certain improprieties of conduct of which he had been witness. But I spare the reader the recital of these astonishing proofs of precocity, as it is very probable his appetite for the marvellous may not keep pace with that of the chronicler of Tezcuco.

[3] Ante, p. 147.

principles of historic impartiality. Nor would such a conjecture be without foundation. The history of the Conquest is necessarily that of the great man who achieved it. But Gomara has thrown his hero's character into so bold relief that it has entirely overshadowed that of his brave companions in arms ; and, while he has tenderly drawn the veil over the infirmities of his favourite, he is ever studious to display his exploits in the full blaze of panegyric. His situation may in some degree excuse his partiality. But it did not vindicate him in the eyes of the honest Las Casas, who seldom concludes a chapter of his own narrative of the Conquest without administering a wholesome castigation to Gomara. He even goes so far as to tax the chaplain with "downright falsehood," assuring us "that he had neither eyes nor ears but for what his patron chose to dictate to him." That this is not literally true is evident from the fact that the narrative was not written till several years after the death of Cortés. Indeed, Gomara derived his information from the highest sources ; not merely from his patron's family, but also from the most distinguished actors in the great drama, with whom his position in society placed him in intimate communication.

The materials thus obtained he arranged with a symmetry little understood by the chroniclers of the time. Instead of their rambling incoherencies, his style displays an elegant brevity ; it is as clear as it is concise. If the facts are somewhat too thickly crowded on the reader, and occupy the mind too busily for reflection, they at least all tend to a determinate point, and the story, instead of dragging its slow length along till our patience and interest are exhausted, steadily maintains its onward march. In short, the execution of the work is not only superior to that of most contemporary narratives, but, to a certain extent, may aspire to the rank of a classical composition.

Owing to these circumstances, Gomara's History soon obtained general circulation and celebrity ; and, while many a letter of Cortés, and the more elaborate compositions of Oviedo and Las Casas, were suffered to slumber in manuscript, Gomara's writings were printed and reprinted in his own day, and translated into various languages of Europe. The first edition of the *Crónica de la Nueva-España* appeared at Medina, in 1553 ; it was republished at Antwerp the following year. It has since been incorporated in Barcia's collection, and lastly, in 1826, made its appearance on this side of the water from the Mexican press. The circumstances attending this last edition are curious. The Mexican government appropriated a small sum to defray the expense of translating what was supposed to be an original chronicle of Chimalpain, an Indian writer who lived at the close of the sixteenth century. The care of the translation was committed to the laborious Bustamante. But this scholar had not proceeded far in his labour when he ascertained that the supposed original was itself an Aztec translation of Gomara's Chronicle. He persevered, however, in his editorial labours, until he had given to the public an American edition of Gomara. It is a fact more remarkable that the editor in his different compilations constantly refers to this same work as the Chronicle of Chimalpain.

The other authority to which I have adverted is Bernal Diaz del Castillo, a native of Medina del Campo in Old Castile. He was born of a poor and humble family, and in 1514 came over to seek his fortunes in the New World. He embarked as a common soldier under Cordova in the first expedition to Yucatan. He accompanied Grijalva in the following year to the same quarter, and finally enlisted under the banner of Cortés. He followed this victorious chief in his first march up the great plateau ; descended with him to make the assault on Narvaez ; shared the disasters of the *noche triste ;* and was present at the seige and surrender of the capital. In short, there was scarcely an event or an action of importance in the whole war in which he did not bear a part. He was engaged in a hundred and nineteen different battles and rencountres, in several of which he was wounded, and in more than one narrowly escaped falling into the enemy's hands. In all these Bernal Diaz displayed the old Castilian valour, and a loyalty which made him proof against the mutinous spirit that too often disturbed the harmony of the camp. On every occasion he was found true to his commander and to the cause in which he was embarked. And his fidelity is attested not only by his own report, but by the emphatic commendations of his general ; who selected him on this account for offices of trust and responsibility, which furnished the future chronicler with access to the best means of information in respect to the Conquest.

On the settlement of the country, Bernal Diaz received his share of the *repartimientos* of land and labourers. But the arrangement was not to his satisfaction ; and he loudly murmurs at the selfishness of his commander, too much engrossed by the care for his own emoluments to think of his followers. The division of spoil is usually an unthankful office. Diaz had been too long used to a life of adventure to be content with one of torpid security. He took part in several expeditions conducted by the captains of Cortés, and he accompanied that chief in his terrible passage through the forests of Honduras. At length, in 1568, we find the veteran established as regidor of the city of Guatemala, peacefully employed in recounting the valorous achievements of his youth. It was then nearly half a century after the Conquest. He had survived his general and nearly all his ancient companions in arms. Five only remained of that gallant band who had accompanied Cortés on his expedition from Cuba ; and those five, to borrow the words of the old chronicler, were "poor, aged, and infirm, with children and grandchildren looking to them for support, but with scarcely the means of affording it,—ending their days, as they had begun them, in toil and trouble." Such was the fate of the Conquerors of golden Mexico.

The motives which induced Bernal Diaz to take up his pen at so late a period of life were to vindicate for himself and his comrades that share of renown in the Conquest which fairly belonged to them. Of this they had been deprived, as he conceived, by the exaggerated reputation of their general ; owing, no doubt, in part, to the influence of Gomara's writings. It was not, however, till he had advanced beyond the threshold of his own work that Diaz met with that of the chaplain. The contrast presented by his own homely diction to the clear and polished style of his predecessor filled him with so much disgust that he threw down his pen in despair. But, when he had read further, and saw the gross inaccuracies and what he deemed disregard of truth in his rival, he resumed his labours, determined to exhibit to the world a narrative which should at least have the merit of fidelity. Such was the origin of the *Historia verdadera de la Conquista de la Nueva-España.*

The chronicler may be allowed to have succeeded in his object. In reading his pages, we feel that, whatever are the errors into which he has fallen, from oblivion of ancient transactions, or from unconscious vanity,—of which he had full measure,—or from credulity, or any other cause, there is nowhere a wilful perversion of truth. Had he attempted it, indeed, his very simplicity would have betrayed him. Even in relation to Cortés, while he endeavours to adjust the true balance between his pretensions and those of his followers, and while he freely exposes his cunning or cupidity, and sometimes his cruelty, he does ample justice to his great and heroic qualities. With all his defects, it is clear that he considers his own chief as superior to any other of ancient or modern times. In the heat of remonstrance, he is ever ready to testify his loyalty and personal attachment. When calumnies assail his commander, or he experiences unmerited slight or indignity, the loyal chronicler is prompt to step forward and shield him. In short, it is evident that, however much he may at times censure Cortés, he will allow no one else to do it.

Bernal Diaz, the untutored child of nature, is a most true and literal copyist of nature. He transfers the scenes of real life by a sort of *daguerreotype* process, if I may so say, to his pages. He is among chroniclers what De Foe is among novelists. He introduces us into the heart of the camp, we huddle round the bivouac with the soldiers, loiter with them on their wearisome marches, listen to their stories, their murmurs of discontent, their plans of conquest, their hopes, their triumphs, their disappointments. All the picturesque scenes and romantic incidents of the campaign are reflected in his page as in a mirror. The lapse of fifty years has had no power over the spirit of the veteran. The fire of youth glows in every line of his rude history ; and, as he calls up the scenes of the past, the remembrance of the brave companions who are gone gives, it may be, a warmer colouring to the picture than if it had been made at an earlier period. Time, and reflection, and the apprehensions for the future, which might steal over the evening of life, have no power over the settled opinions of his earlier days. He has no misgivings as to the right of conquest, or as to the justice of the severities inflicted on the natives. He is still the soldier of the Cross; and those who fell by his side in the fight were martyrs for the faith. "Where are now my companions?" he asks; "they have fallen in battle or been devoured by the cannibal, or been thrown to fatten the wild beasts in their cages! they whose remains should rather have been gathered under monuments emblazoned with their achievements, which deserve to be commemorated in letters of gold; for they died in the service of God and of his Majesty, and to give light to those who sat in darkness,—*and also to acquire that wealth which most men covet.*" The last motive—thus tardily and incidentally expressed—may be thought by some to furnish a better key than either of the preceding to the conduct of the Conquerors. It is, at all events, a specimen of that *naïveté* which gives an irresistible charm to the old chronicler, and which, in spite of himself, unlocks his bosom, as it were, and lays it open to the eye of the reader.

It may seem extraordinary that, after so long an interval, the incidents of his campaign should have been so freshly remembered. But we must consider that they were of the most strange and romantic character, well fitted to make an impression on a young and susceptible imagination. They had probably been rehearsed by the veteran again and again to his family and friends, until every passage of the war was as familiar to his mind as the "tale of Troy" to the Greek rhapsodist, or the interminable adventures of Sir Lancelot or Sir Gawain to the Norman minstrel. The throwing of his narrative into the form of chronicle was but repeating it once more.

The literary merits of the work are of a very humble order; as might be expected from the condition of the writer. He has not even the art to conceal his own vulgar vanity, which breaks out with a truly comic ostentation in every page of the narrative. And yet we should have charity for this, when we find that it is attended with no disposition to depreciate the merits of others, and that its display may be referred in part to the singular simplicity of the man. He honestly confesses his infirmity, though, indeed, to excuse it. "When my chronicle was finished," he says, "I submitted it to two licentiates, who were desirous of reading the story, and for whom I felt all the respect which an ignorant man naturally feels for a scholar. I besought them, at the same time, to make no change or correction in the manuscript, as all there was set down in good faith. When they had read the work, they much commended me for my wonderful memory. The language, they said, was good old Castilian, without any of the flourishes and finicalities so much affected by our fine writers. But they remarked that it would have been as well if I had not praised myself and my comrades so liberally, but had left that to others. To this I answered that it was common for neighbours and kindred to speak kindly of one another; and, if we did not speak well of ourselves, who would? Who else witnessed our exploits and our battles,—unless, indeed, the clouds in the sky, and the birds that were flying over our heads?"

Notwithstanding the liberal encomiums passed by the licentiates on our author's style, it is of a very homely texture, abounding in colloquial barbarisms, and seasoned occasionally by the piquant sallies of the camp. It has the merit, however, of clearly conveying the writer's thoughts, and is well suited to their simple character. His narrative is put together with even less skill than is usual among his craft, and abounds in digressions and repetitions, such as vulgar gossips are apt to use in telling their stories. But it is superfluous to criticise a work by the rules of art which was written manifestly in total ignorance of those rules, and which, however we may criticise it, will be read and re-read by the scholar and the schoolboy, while the compositions of more classic chroniclers sleep undisturbed on their shelves.

In what, then, lies the charm of the work? In that spirit of truth which pervades it;

which shows us situations as they were, and sentiments as they really existed in the heart of the writer. It is this which imparts a living interest to his story, and which is more frequently found in the productions of the untutored penman solely intent upon facts, than in those of the ripe and fastidious scholar occupied with the mode of expressing them.

It was by a mere chance that this inimitable chronicle was rescued from the oblivion into which so many works of higher pretensions have fallen in the Peninsula. For more than sixty years after its composition the manuscript lay concealed in the obscurity of a private library, when it was put into the hands of Father Alonso Remon, Chronicler-General of the Order of Mercy. He had the sagacity to discover, under its rude exterior, its high value in illustrating the history of the Conquest. He obtained a license for the publication of the work, and under his auspices it appeared at Madrid in 1632,— the edition used in the preparation of this work.

BOOK VI.

SIEGE AND SURRENDER OF MEXICO.

—o—

CHAPTER I.

ARRANGEMENTS AT TEZCUCO.—SACK OF IZTAPALAPAN.—ADVANTAGES OF THE SPANIARDS.—WISE POLICY OF CORTÉS.—TRANSPORTATION OF THE BRIGANTINES.

(1521.)

The city of Tezcuco was the best position, probably, which Cortés could have chosen for the headquarters of the army. It supplied all the accommodations for lodging a numerous body of troops, and all the facilities for subsistence, incident to a large and populous town.[1] It furnished, moreover, a multitude of artisans and labourers for the uses of the army. Its territories, bordering on the Tlascalan, afforded a ready means of intercourse with the country of his allies; while its vicinity to Mexico enabled the general, without much difficulty, to ascertain the movements in that capital. Its central situation, in short, opened facilities for communication with all parts of the Valley, and made it an excellent *point d'appui* for his future operations.

The first care of Cortés was to strengthen himself in the palace assigned to him, and to place his quarters in a state of defence which might secure them against surprise not only from the Mexicans, but from the Tezcucans themselves. Since the election of their new ruler, a large part of the population had returned to their homes, assured of protection in person and property. But the Spanish general, notwithstanding their show of submission, very much distrusted its sincerity; for he knew that many of them were united too intimately with the Aztecs, by marriage and other social relations, not to have their sympathies engaged in their behalf.[2]

---

[1] "Así mismo hizo juntar todos los bastimentos que fuéron necesarios para sustentar el Exército y Guarniciones de Gente que andaban en favor de Cortés, y así hizo traer á la Ciudad de Tezcuco el Maiz que habia en las Troxes y Graneros de las Provincias sugetas al Reyno de Tezcuco." Ixtlilxochitl, Hist. Chich., MS., cap. 91.

[2] "No era de espantar que tuviese este recelo, porque sus Enemigos, y los de esta Ciudad eran todos Deudos y Parientes mas cercanos, mas despues el tiempo lo desengañó, y vido la gran lealtad de Ixtlilxochitl, y de todos." Ixtlilxochitl, Hist. Chich., MS., cap. 92.

The young monarch, however, seemed wholly in his interests; and, to secure him more effectually, Cortés placed several Spaniards near his person, whose ostensible province it was to instruct him in their language and religion, but who were in reality to watch over his conduct and prevent his correspondence with those who might be unfriendly to the Spanish interests.[1]

Tezcuco stood about half a league from the lake. It would be necessary to open a communication with it, so that the brigantines, when put together in the capital, might be launched upon its waters. It was proposed, therefore, to dig a canal, reaching from the gardens of Nezahual-coyotl, as they were called, from the old monarch who planned them, to the edge of the basin. A little stream, or rivulet, which flowed in that direction, was to be deepened sufficiently for the purpose; and eight thousand Indian labourers were forthwith employed on this great work, under the direction of the young Ixtlilxochitl.[2]

Meanwhile, Cortés received messages from several places in the neighbourhood, intimating their desire to become the vassals of his sovereign and to be taken under his protection. The Spanish commander required, in return, that they should deliver up every Mexican who should set foot in their territories. Some noble Aztecs, who had been sent on a mission to these towns, were consequently delivered into his hands. He availed himself of it to employ them as bearers of a message to their master the emperor. In it he deprecated the necessity of the present hostilities. Those who had most injured him, he said, were no longer among the living. He was willing to forget the past, and invited the Mexicans, by a timely submission, to save their capital from the horrors of a siege.[3] Cortés had no expectation of producing any immediate result by this appeal. But he thought it might lie in the minds of the Mexicans, and that, if there was a party among them disposed to treat with him, it might afford them encouragement, as showing his own willingness to co-operate with their views. At this time, however, there was no division of opinion in the capital. The whole population seemed animated by a spirit of resistance, as one man.

In a former page I have mentioned that it was the plan of Cortés, on entering the Valley, to commence operations by reducing the subordinate cities before striking at the capital itself, which, like some goodly tree whose roots had been severed one after another, would be thus left without support against the fury of the tempest. The first point of attack which he selected was the ancient city of Iztapalapan; a place containing fifty thousand inhabitants, according to his own account, and situated about six leagues distant, on the narrow tongue of land which divides the

[1] Bernal Diaz, Hist. de la Conquista, cap. 137.
[2] Ibid., ubi supra.—Ixtlilxochitl, Hist. Chich., MS., cap. 91.
[3] "Los principales, que habian sido en hacerme la Guerra pasada, eran ya muertos; y que lo pasado fuesse pasado, y que no quisiessen dar causa á que destruyesse sus Tierras, y Ciudades, porque me pesaba mucho de ello." Rel. Terc. de Cortés, ap. Lorenzana, p. 193.

waters of the great salt lake from those of the fresh. It was the private domain of the last sovereign of Mexico ; where, as the reader may remember, he entertained the white men the night before their entrance into the capital, and astonished them by the display of his princely gardens. To this monarch they owed no goodwill, for he had conducted the operations on the *noche triste.* He was, indeed, no more ; but the people of his city entered heartily into his hatred of the strangers, and were now the most loyal vassals of the Mexican crown.

In a week after his arrival at his new quarters, Cortés, leaving the command of the garrison to Sandoval, marched against this Indian city, at the head of two hundred Spanish foot, eighteen horse, and between three and four thousand Tlascalans. Their route lay along the eastern border of the lake, gemmed with many a bright town and hamlet, or, unlike its condition at the present day, darkened with overhanging groves of cypress and cedar, and occasionally opening a broad expanse to their view, with the Queen of the Valley rising gloriously from the waters, as if proudly conscious of her supremacy over the fair cities around her. Farther on, the eye ranged along the dark line of causeway connecting Mexico with the mainland, and suggesting many a bitter recollection to the Spaniards.

They quickened their step, and had advanced within two leagues of their point of destination, when they were encountered by a strong Aztec force drawn up to dispute their progress. Cortés instantly gave them battle. The barbarians showed their usual courage, but, after some hard fighting, were compelled to give way before the steady valour of the Spanish infantry, backed by the desperate fury of the Tlascalans, whom the sight of an Aztec seemed to inflame almost to madness. The enemy retreated in disorder, closely followed by the Spaniards. When they had arrived within half a league of Iztapalapan, they observed a number of canoes filled with Indians, who appeared to be labouring on the mole which hemmed in the waters of the salt lake. Swept along in the tide of pursuit, they gave little heed to it, but, following up the chase, entered pellmell with the fugitives into the city.

The houses stood some of them on dry ground, some on piles in the water. The former were deserted by the inhabitants, most of whom had escaped in canoes across the lake, leaving, in their haste, their effects behind them. The Tlascalans poured at once into the vacant dwellings and loaded themselves with booty ; while the enemy, making the best of their way through this part of the town, sought shelter in the buildings erected over the water, or among the reeds which sprung from its shallow bottom. In the houses were many of the citizens also, who still lingered with their wives and children, unable to find the means of transporting themselves from the scene of danger.

Cortés, supported by his own men, and by such of the allies as could be brought to obey his orders, attacked the enemy in this last place of their retreat. Both parties fought up to their girdles in the water. A desperate struggle ensued; as the Aztec fought with the fury of a tiger driven to bay by the huntsmen. It was all in vain. The enemy was overpowered in every quarter. The citizen shared the fate of the soldier, and a pitiless massacre succeeded, without regard to sex or age. Cortés endeavoured to stop it. But it would have been as easy to call away the starving wolf from the carcass he was devouring, as the Tlascalan who had once tasted the blood of an enemy. More than six thousand, including women and children, according to the Conqueror's own statement, perished in the conflict.[1]

Darkness meanwhile had set in; but it was dispelled in some measure by the light of the burning houses, which the troops had set on fire in different parts of the town. Their insulated position, it is true, prevented the flames from spreading from one building to another, but the solitary masses threw a strong and lurid glare over their own neighbourhood, which gave additional horror to the scene. As resistance was now at an end, the soldiers abandoned themselves to pillage, and soon stripped the dwellings of every portable article of any value.

While engaged in this work of devastation, a murmuring sound was heard as of the hoarse rippling of waters, and a cry soon arose among the Indians that the dikes were broken! Cortés now comprehended the business of the men whom he had seen in the canoes at work on the mole which fenced in the great basin of Lake Tezcuco.[2] It had been pierced by the desperate Indians, who thus laid the country under an inundation, by suffering the waters of the salt lake to spread themselves over the lower level, through the opening. Greatly alarmed, the general called his men together, and made all haste to evacuate the city. Had they remained three hours longer, he says, not a soul could have escaped.[3] They came staggering under the weight of booty, wading with difficulty through the water, which was fast gaining upon them. For some distance their path was illumined by the glare of the burning buildings. But, as the light faded away in the distance, they wandered with uncertain steps, sometimes up to their knees, at others up to their waists, in the water, through which they floundered on with the greatest difficulty. As they reached the opening in the dike, the stream became deeper, and flowed out with such a current that the men were unable to maintain their footing. The Spaniards, breasting the flood, forced their way through; but many of the Indians, unable to swim, were borne down by the waters. All the plunder was lost. The powder was spoiled; the arms and clothes of the

---

[1] "Muriéron de ellos mas de seis mil ánimas, entre Hombres, y Mugeres, y Niños; porque los Indios nuestros Amigos, vista la Victoria, que Dios nos daba, no entendian en otra cosa, sino en matar á diestro y á siniestro." Rel. Terc. de Cortés, ap. Lorenzana, p. 195.

[2] "Estándolas quemando, pareció que Nuestro Señor me inspiró, y trujo á la memoria la Calzada,

ó Presa, que habia visto rota en el Camino, y representóseme el gran daño, que era." Ibid., loc. cit.

[3] "Y certifico á Vuestra Magestad, que si aquella noche no pasaramos el Agua, ó aguardaramos tres horas mas, que ninguno de nosotros escapara, porque quedabamos cercados de Agua, sin tener paso por parte ninguna." Ibid., ubi supra.

soldiers were saturated with the brine, and the cold night-wind, as it blew over them, benumbed their weary limbs till they could scarcely drag them along. At dawn they beheld the lake swarming with canoes, full of Indians, who had anticipated their disaster, and who now saluted them with showers of stones, arrows, and other deadly missiles. Bodies of light troops, hovering in the distance, disquieted the flanks of the army in like manner. The Spaniards had no desire to close with the enemy. They only wished to regain their comfortable quarters in Tezcuco, where they arrived on the same day, more disconsolate and fatigued than after many a long march and hard-fought battle.[1]

The close of the expedition, so different from its brilliant commencement, greatly disappointed Cortés. His numerical loss had, indeed, not been great ; but this affair convinced him how much he had to apprehend from the resolution of a people who, with a spirit worthy of the ancient Hollanders, were prepared to bury their country under water rather than to submit. Still, the enemy had little cause for congratulation ; since, independently of the number of slain, they had seen one of their most flourishing cities sacked, and in part, at least, laid in ruins,—one of those, too, which in its public works displayed the nearest approach to civilization. Such are the triumphs of war !

The expedition of Cortés, notwithstanding the disasters which checkered it, was favourable to the Spanish cause. The fate of Iztapalapan struck a terror throughout the Valley. The consequences were soon apparent in the deputations sent by the different places eager to offer their submission. Its influence was visible, indeed, beyond the mountains. Among others, the people of Otumba, the town near which the Spaniards had gained their famous victory, sent to tender their allegiance and to request the protection of the powerful strangers. They excused themselves, as usual, for the part they had taken in the late hostilities, by throwing the blame on the Aztecs.

But the place of most importance which thus claimed their protection was Chalco, situated on the eastern extremity of the lake of that name. It was an ancient city, peopled by a kindred tribe of the Aztecs, and once their formidable rival. The Mexican emperor, distrusting their loyalty, had placed a garrison within their walls to hold them in check. The rulers of the city now sent a message secretly to Cortés, proposing to put themselves under his protection, if he would enable them to expel the garrison.

The Spanish commander did not hesitate, but instantly detached a considerable force under Sandoval for this object. On the march, his rear-guard, composed of Tlascalans, was roughly handled by some light

---

[1] The general's own Letter to the emperor is so full and precise that it is the very best authority for this event. The story is told also by Bernal Diaz, Hist. de la Conquista, cap. 138,—Oviedo. Hist. de las Ind., MS., lib. 33, cap. 18,—Ixtlilxochitl, Hist. Chich., MS., cap. 92,—Herrera, Hist. general, dec. 3, lib. 1, cap. 2, et auct. aliis.

troops of the Mexicans.   But he took his revenge in a pitched battle which took place with the main body of the enemy at no great distance from Chalco.   They were drawn up on a level ground, covered with green crops of maize and maguey.   The field is traversed by the road which at this day leads from the last-mentioned city to Tezcuco.[1] Sandoval, charging the enemy at the head of his cavalry, threw them into disorder.   But they quickly rallied, formed again, and renewed the battle with greater spirit than ever.   In a second attempt he was more fortunate ; and, breaking through their lines by a desperate onset, the brave cavalier succeeded, after a warm but ineffectual struggle on their part, in completely routing and driving them from the field.   The conquering army continued its march to Chalco, which the Mexican garrison had already evacuated, and was received in triumph by the assembled citizens, who seemed eager to testify their gratitude for their deliverance from the Aztec yoke.   After taking such measures as he could for the permanent security of the place, Sandoval returned to Tezcuco, accompanied by the two young lords of the city, sons of the late cacique.

They were courteously received by Cortés ; and they informed him that their father had died, full of years, a short time before.   With his last breath he had expressed his regret that he should not have lived to see Malinche.   He believed that the white men were the beings predicted by the oracles as one day to come from the East and take possession of the land ;[2] and he enjoined it on his children, should the strangers return to the Valley, to render them their homage and allegiance.   The young caciques expressed their readiness to do so ; but, as this must bring on them the vengeance of the Aztecs, they implored the general to furnish a sufficient force for their protection.[3]

Cortés received a similar application from various other towns, which were disposed, could they do so with safety, to throw off the Mexican yoke.   But he was in no situation to comply with their request.   He now felt more sensibly than ever the incompetency of his means to his undertaking.   " I assure your Majesty," he writes in his letter to the emperor, " the greatest uneasiness which I feel, after all my labours and fatigues, is from my inability to succour and support our Indian friends, your Majesty's loyal vassals."[4] Far from having a force competent to this, he had scarcely enough for his own protection.   His vigilant enemy had an eye on all his movements, and, should he cripple his strength by sending away too many detachments or by employing them at too great a distance, would be prompt to take advantage of it.   His only expeditions, hitherto,

---

[1] Lorenzana, p. 199, nota.

[2] " Porque ciertamente sus antepassados les auian dicho, que auian de señorear aquellas tierras hombres que vernian con barbas de hazia donde sale el Sol, y que por las cosas que han visto, eramos nosotros." Bernal Diaz, Hist. de la Conquista, cap. 139.

[3] Ibid., ubi supra.—Rel. Terc. de Cortés, ap.

Lorenzana, p. 200.—Gomara, Crónica, cap. 122.— Venida de los Españoles, p. 15.

[4] " Y certifico á Vuestra Magestad, allende de nuestro trabajo y necesidad, la mayor fatiga, que tenia, era no poder ayudar, y socorrer á los Indios nuestros Amigos, que por ser Vassallos de Vuestra Magestad, eran molestados y trabajados de los de Culúa." Rel. Terc., ap. Lorenzana, p. 204.

had been in the neighbourhood, where the troops, after striking some sudden and decisive blow, might speedily regain their quarters. The utmost watchfulness was maintained there, and the Spaniards lived in as constant preparation for an assault as if their camp was pitched under the walls of Mexico.

On two occasions the general had sallied forth and engaged the enemy in the environs of Tezcuco. At one time a thousand canoes, filled with Aztecs, crossed the lake to gather in a large crop of Indian corn, nearly ripe, on its borders. Cortés thought it important to secure this for himself. He accordingly marched out and gave battle to the enemy, drove them from the field, and swept away the rich harvest to the granaries of Tezcuco. Another time a strong body of Mexicans had established themselves in some neighbouring towns friendly to their interests. Cortés, again sallying, dislodged them from their quarters, beat them in several skirmishes, and reduced the places to obedience. But these enterprises demanded all his resources, and left him nothing to spare for his allies. In this exigency, his fruitful genius suggested an expedient for supplying the deficiency of his means.

Some of the friendly cities without the Valley, observing the numerous beacon-fires on the mountains, inferred that the Mexicans were mustering in great strength, and that the Spaniards must be hard pressed in their new quarters. They sent messengers to Tezcuco, expressing their apprehension, and offering reinforcements, which the general, when he set out on his march, had declined. He returned many thanks for the proffered aid; but, while he declined it for himself, as unnecessary, he indicated in what manner their services might be effectual for the defence of Chalco and the other places which had invoked his protection. But his Indian allies were in deadly feud with these places, whose inhabitants had too often fought under the Aztec banner not to have been engaged in repeated wars with the people beyond the mountains.

Cortés set himself earnestly to reconcile these differences. He told the hostile parties that they should be willing to forget their mutual wrongs, since they had entered into new relations. They were now vassals of the same sovereign, engaged in a common enterprise against the formidable foe who had so long trodden them in the dust. Singly they could do little, but united they might protect each other's weakness and hold their enemy at bay till the Spaniards could come to their assistance. These arguments finally prevailed; and the politic general had the satisfaction to see the high-spirited and hostile tribes forego their long-cherished rivalry, and, resigning the pleasures of revenge, so dear to the barbarian, embrace one another as friends and champions in a common cause. To this wise policy the Spanish commander owed quite as much of his subsequent successes as to his arms.[1]

---

1 Rel. Terc. de Cortés, ap. Lorenzana, pp. 2c4, 205.—Oviedo, Hist. de las Ind., MS., lib. 33, cap. 19.

Thus the foundations of the Mexican empire were hourly loosening, as the great vassals around the capital, on whom it most relied, fell off one after another from their allegiance. The Aztecs, properly so called, formed but a small part of the population of the Valley. This was principally composed of cognate tribes, members of the same great family of the Nahuatlacs who had come upon the plateau at nearly the same time. They were mutual rivals, and were reduced one after another by the more warlike Mexican, who held them in subjection, often by open force, always by fear. Fear was the great principle of cohesion which bound together the discordant members of the monarchy; and this was now fast dissolving before the influence of a power more mighty than that of the Aztec. This, it is true, was not the first time that the conquered races had attempted to recover their independence. But all such attempts had failed for want of concert. It was reserved for the commanding genius of Cortés to extinguish their old hereditary feuds, and, combining their scattered energies, to animate them with a common principle of action.[1]

Encouraged by this state of things, the Spanish general thought it a favourable moment to press his negotiations with the capital. He availed himself of the presence of some noble Mexicans, taken in the late action with Sandoval, to send another message to their master. It was in substance a repetition of the first, with a renewed assurance that, if the city would return to its allegiance to the Spanish crown, the authority of Guatemozin should be confirmed and the persons and property of his subjects be respected. To this communication no reply was made. The young Indian emperor had a spirit as dauntless as that of Cortés himself. On his head descended the full effects of that vicious system of government bequeathed to him by his ancestors. But, as he saw his empire crumbling beneath him, he sought to uphold it by his own energy and resources. He anticipated the defection of some vassals by establishing garrisons within their walls. Others he conciliated by exempting them from tributes or greatly lightening their burdens, or by advancing them to posts of honour and authority in the state. He showed, at the same time, his implacable animosity towards the Christians by commanding that every one taken within his dominions should be straightway sent to the capital, where he was sacrificed, with all the barbarous ceremonies prescribed by the Aztec ritual.[2]

---

[1] Oviedo, in his admiration of his hero, breaks out into the following panegyric on his policy, prudence, and military science, which, as he truly predicts, must make his name immortal. It is a fair specimen of the manner of the sagacious old chronicler. "Sin dubda alguna la habilidad y esfuerzo, é prudencia de Hernando Cortés mui dignas son que entre los cavalleros, é gente militar en nuestros tiempos se tengan en mucha estimacion, y en los venideros nunca se desacuerden. Por causa suya me acuerdo muchas veces de aquellas cosas que se escriven del capitan Viriato nuestro Español y Estremeño; y por Hernando Cortés me ocurren al sentido las muchas fatigas de aquel espejo de caballería Julio César dictador, como parece por sus comentarios, é por Suetonio é Plutarco é otros autores que en conformidad escriviéron los grandes hechos suyos. Pero los de Hernando Cortés en un Mundo nuevo, é tan apartadas provincias de Europa, é con tantos trabajos é necesidades é pocas fuerzas, é con gente tan innumerable, é tan bárbara é bellicosa, é apacentada en carne humana, é aun habida por excelente é sabroso manjar entre sus adversarios; é faltándole á él ó á sus mílites el pan é vino é los otros mantenimientos todos de España, y en tan diferenciadas regiones é aires é tan desviado é léjos de socorro é de su príncipe, cosas son de admiracion." Hist. de las Ind., MS., lib. 33, cap. 20.

[2] Among other chiefs, to whom Guatemozin applied for assistance in the perilous state of his affairs.

While these occurrences were passing, Cortés received the welcome intelligence that the brigantines were completed and waiting to be transported to Tezcuco. He detached a body for the service, consisting of two hundred Spanish foot and fifteen horse, which he placed under the command of Sandoval. This cavalier had been rising daily in the estimation both of the general and of the army. Though one of the youngest officers in the service, he possessed a cool head and a ripe judgment, which fitted him for the most delicate and difficult undertakings. There were others, indeed, as Alvarado and Olid, for example, whose intrepidity made them equally competent to achieve a brilliant *coup-de-main*. But the courage of Alvarado was too often carried to temerity or perverted by passion; while Olid, dark and doubtful in his character, was not entirely to be trusted. Sandoval was a native of Medellin, the birthplace of Cortés himself. He was warmly attached to his commander, and had on all occasions proved himself worthy of his confidence. He was a man of few words, showing his worth rather by what he did than what he said. His honest, soldier-like deportment made him a favourite with the troops, and had its influence even on his enemies. He unfortunately died in the flower of his age. But he discovered talents and military skill which, had he lived to later life, would undoubtedly have placed his name on the roll with those of the greatest captains of his nation.

Sandoval's route was to lead him by Zoltepec, a small city where the massacre of the forty-five Spaniards, already noticed, had been perpetrated. The cavalier received orders to find out the guilty parties, if possible, and to punish them for their share in the transaction.

When the Spaniards arrived at the spot, they found that the inhabitants, who had previous notice of their approach, had all fled. In the deserted temples they discovered abundant traces of the fate of their countrymen; for, besides their arms and clothing, and the hides of their horses, the heads of several soldiers, prepared in such a way that they could be well preserved, were found suspended as trophies of the victory. In a neighbouring building, traced with charcoal on the walls, they found the

---

was Tangapan, lord of Michoacán, an independent and powerful state in the West, which had never been subdued by the Mexican army. The accounts which the Aztec emperor gave him, through his ambassadors, of the white men, were so alarming, according to Ixtlilxochitl, who tells the story, that the king's sister voluntarily starved herself to death, from her apprehensions of the coming of the terrible strangers. Her body was deposited, as usual, in the vaults reserved for the royal household, until preparations could be made for its being burnt. On the fourth day, the attendants who had charge of it were astounded by seeing the corpse exhibit signs of returning life. The restored princess, recovering her speech, requested her brother's presence. On his coming, she implored him not to think of hurting a hair of the heads of the mysterious visitors. She had been permitted, she said, to see the fate of the departed in the next world. The souls of all her ancestors she had beheld tossing about in unquenchable fire; while those who embraced the faith of the strangers were in glory. As a proof of the truth of her assertion, she added that her brother would see, on a great festival near at hand, a young warrior, armed with a torch brighter than the sun, in one hand, and a flaming sword, like that worn by the white men, in the other, passing from east to west over the city. Whether the monarch waited for the vision, or ever beheld it, is not told us by the historian. But, relying perhaps on the miracle of her resurrection as quite a sufficient voucher, he disbanded a very powerful force which he had assembled on the plains of Avalos for the support of his brother of Mexico. This narrative, with abundance of supernumerary incidents, not necessary to repeat, was commemorated in the Michoacán picture-records, and reported to the historian of Tezcuco by the grandson of Tangapan. (See Ixtlilxochitl, Hist. Chich., MS., cap. 91.) Whoever reported to him, it is not difficult to trace the same pious fingers in it which made so many wholesome legends for the good of the Church on the Old Continent, and which now found, in the credulity of the New, a rich harvest for the same godly work.

following inscription in Castilian: "In this place the unfortunate Juan Juste, with many others of his company, was imprisoned."[1] This hidalgo was one of the followers of Narvaez, and had come with him into the country in quest of gold, but had found, instead, an obscure and inglorious death. The eyes of the soldiers were suffused with tears as they gazed on the gloomy record, and their bosoms swelled with indignation as they thought of the horrible fate of the captives. Fortunately, the inhabitants were not then before them. Some few, who subsequently fell into their hands, were branded as slaves. But the greater part of the population, who threw themselves, in the most abject manner, on the mercy of the Conquerors, imputing the blame of the affair to the Aztecs, the Spanish commander spared, from pity, or contempt.[2]

He now resumed his march on Tlascala; but scarcely had he crossed the borders of the republic, when he descried the flaunting banners of the convoy which transported the brigantines, as it was threading its way through the defiles of the mountains. Great was his satisfaction at the spectacle, for he had feared a detention of some days at Tlascala before the preparations for the march could be completed.

There were thirteen vessels in all, of different sizes. They had been constructed under the direction of the experienced shipbuilder, Martin Lopez, aided by three or four Spanish carpenters and the friendly natives, some of whom showed no mean degree of imitative skill. The brigantines, when completed, had been fairly tried on the waters of the Zahuapan. They were then taken to pieces, and, as Lopez was impatient of delay, the several parts, the timbers, anchors, ironwork, sails, and cordage, were placed on the shoulders of the *tamanes*, and, under a numerous military escort, were thus far advanced on the way to Tezcuco.[3] Sandoval dismissed a part of the Indian convoy as superfluous.

Twenty thousand warriors he retained, dividing them into two equal bodies for the protection of the *tamanes* in the centre.[4] His own little body of Spaniards he distributed in like manner. The Tlascalans in the van marched under the command of a chief who gloried in the name of Chichemecatl. For some reason Sandoval afterwards changed the order of march, and placed this division in the rear,—an arrangement which gave great umbrage to the doughty warrior that led it, who asserted his right to the front, the place which he and his ancestors had always occupied, as the post of danger. He was somewhat appeased by Sandoval's assurance that it was for that very reason he had been transferred

---

[1] "Aqui estuvo preso el sin ventura de Juã Iuste cõ otros muchos que traia en mi compañia." Bernal Diaz, Hist. de la Conquista, cap. 140.

[2] Ibid., ubi supra.—Oviedo, Hist. de las Ind., MS., lib. 33, cap. 19.—Rel. Terc. de Cortés, ap. Lorenzana, p. 206.

[3] "Y despues de hechos por orden de Cortés, y probados en el rio que llaman de Tlaxcalla Zahuapan, que se atajó para probarlos los bergantines, y los tornáron á desbaratar por llevarlos á cuestas

sobre hombros de los de Tlaxcalla á la ciudad de Tetzcuco, donde se echáron en la laguna, y se armáron de artillería y municion." Camargo, Hist. de Tlascala, MS.

[4] Rel. Terc. de Cortés, ap. Lorenzana, p. 207.—Bernal Diaz says sixteen thousand. (Hist. de la Conquista, ubi supra.) There is a wonderful agreement between the several Castilian writers as to the number of forces, the order of march, and the events that occurred on it.

to the rear, the quarter most likely to be assailed by the enemy. But even then he was greatly dissatisfied on finding that the Spanish commander was to march by his side, grudging, it would seem, that any other should share the laurel with himself.

Slowly and painfully, encumbered with their heavy burden, the troops worked their way over steep eminences and rough mountain-passes, presenting, one might suppose, in their long line of march, many a vulnerable point to an enemy. But, although small parties of warriors were seen hovering at times on their flanks and rear, they kept at a respectful distance, not caring to encounter so formidable a foe. On the fourth day the warlike caravan arrived in safety before Tezcuco.

Their approach was beheld with joy by Cortés and the soldiers, who hailed it as the signal of a speedy termination of the war. The general, attended by his officers, all dressed in their richest attire, came out to welcome the convoy. It extended over a space of two leagues; and so slow was its progress that six hours elapsed before the closing files had entered the city.[1] The Tlascalan chiefs displayed all their wonted bravery of apparel, and the whole array, composed of the flower of their warriors, made a brilliant appearance. They marched by the sound of atabal and cornet, and, as they traversed the streets of the capital amidst the acclamations of the soldiery, they made the city ring with the shouts of " Castile and Tlascala, long live our sovereign, the emperor ! " [2]

" It was a marvellous thing," exclaims the Conqueror, in his Letters, " that few have seen, or even heard of,—this transportation of thirteen vessels of war on the shoulders of men for nearly twenty leagues across the mountains ! " [3] It was, indeed, a stupendous achievement, and not easily matched in ancient or modern story; one which only a genius like that of Cortés could have devised, or a daring spirit like his have so successfully executed. Little did he foresee, when he ordered the destruction of the fleet which first brought him to the country, and with his usual forecast commanded the preservation of the ironwork and rigging,—little did he foresee the important uses for which they were to be reserved; so important, that on their preservation may be said to have depended the successful issue of his great enterprise.[4]

---

[1] "Estendíase tanto la Gente, que dende que los primeros comenzáron á entrar, hasta que los postreros hobiéron acabado, se pasáron mas de seis horas; sin quebrar el hilo de la Gente." Rel. Terc. de Cortés, ap. Lorenzana, p. 208.

[2] "Dando vozes y silvos y diziendo : Viua, viua el Emperador, nuestro Señor, y Castilla, Castilla, y Tlascala, Tlascala." (Bernal Diaz, Hist. de la Conquista, cap. 140.) For the particulars of Sandoval's expedition, see, also, Oviedo, Hist. de las Ind., MS., lib. 33, cap. 19,—Gomara, Crónica, cap. 124,—Torquemada, Monarch. Ind., lib. 4, cap. 84, —Ixtlilxochitl, Hist. Chich., MS., cap. 92,—Herrera, Hist. general, dec. 3, lib. 1, cap. 2.

[3] "Que era cosa maravillosa de ver, y assí me parece que es de oir, llevar trece Fustas diez y ocho leguas por Tierra." (Rel. Terc. de Cortés, ap. Lorenzana, p. 207.) " En rem Romano populo,"

exclaims Martyr, " quando illustrius res illorum vigebant, non facilem ! " De Orbe Novo, dec. 5, cap. 8.

[4] Two memorable examples of a similar transportation of vessels across the land are recorded, the one in ancient, the other in modern history ; and both, singularly enough, at the same place, Tarentum, in Italy. The first occurred at the siege of that city by Hannibal (see Polybius, lib. 8) ; the latter some seventeen centuries later, by the Great Captain, Gonsalvo de Cordova. But the distance they were transported was inconsiderable. A more analogous example is that of Balboa, the bold discoverer of the Pacific. He made arrangements to have four brigantines transported a distance of twenty-two leagues across the Isthmus of Darien, a stupendous labour, and not entirely successful, as only two reached their point of destination. (See Herrera,

He greeted his Indian allies with the greatest cordiality, testifying his sense of their services by those honours and attentions which he knew would be most grateful to their ambitious spirits. "We come," exclaimed the hardy warriors, "to fight under your banner; to avenge our common quarrel, or to fall by your side;" and, with their usual impatience, they urged him to lead them at once against the enemy. "Wait," replied the general, bluntly, "till you are rested, and you shall have your hands full."[1]

CHAPTER II.

CORTÉS RECONNOITRES THE CAPITAL.—OCCUPIES TACUBA.—SKIRMISHES WITH THE ENEMY.—EXPEDITION OF SANDOVAL.—ARRIVAL OF REIN-FORCEMENTS.

(1521.)

In the course of three or four days, the Spanish general furnished the Tlascalans with the opportunity so much coveted, and allowed their boiling spirits to effervesce in active operations. He had for some time meditated an expedition to reconnoitre the capital and its environs, and to chastise, on the way, certain places which had sent him insulting messages of defiance and which were particularly active in their hostilities. He disclosed his design to a few only of his principal officers, from his distrust of the Tezcucans, whom he suspected to be in correspondence with the enemy.

Early in the spring, he left Tezcuco, at the head of three hundred and fifty Spaniards and the whole strength of his allies. He took with him Alvarado and Olid, and intrusted the charge of the garrison to Sandoval. Cortés had had practical acquaintance with the incompetence of the first of these cavaliers for so delicate a post, during his short but disastrous rule in Mexico.

But all his precautions had not availed to shroud his designs from the vigilant foe, whose eye was on all his movements; who seemed even to divine his thoughts and to be prepared to thwart their execution. He had advanced but a few leagues, when he was met by a considerable body of Mexicans, drawn up to dispute his progress. A sharp skirmish took place, in which the enemy were driven from the ground, and the way was left open to the Christians. They held a circuitous route to the north, and their first point of attack was the insular town of Xaltocan,

---

Hist. general, dec. 2, lib. 2, cap. 11.) This took place in 1516, in the neighbourhood, as it were, of Cortés, and may have suggested to his enterprising spirit the first idea of his own more successful, as well as more extensive, undertaking.

[1] "Y ellos me dijéron, que trahian deseo de se ver con los de Culúa, y que viesse lo que mandaba, que ellos, y aquella Gente venian con deseos, y voluntad de se vengar, ó morir con nosotros; y yo les dí las gracias, y les dije, que reposassen, y que presto les daria las manos llenas." Rel. Terc. de Cortés, ap. Lorenzana, p. 208.

situated on the northern extremity of the lake of that name, now called San Christóbal. The town was entirely surrounded by water, and communicated with the mainland by means of causeways, in the same manner as the Mexican capital. Cortés, riding at the head of his cavalry, advanced along the dike till he was brought to a stand by finding a wide opening in it, through which the waters poured, so as to be altogether impracticable, not only for horse, but for infantry. The lake was covered with canoes filled with Aztec warriors, who, anticipating the movement of the Spaniards, had come to the aid of the city. They now began a furious discharge of stones and arrows on the assailants, while they were themselves tolerably well protected from the musketry of their enemy by the light bulwarks with which, for that purpose, they had fortified their canoes.

The severe volleys of the Mexicans did some injury to the Spaniards and their allies, and began to throw them into disorder, crowded as they were on the narrow causeway, without the means of advancing, when Cortés ordered a retreat. This was followed by renewed tempests of missiles, accompanied by taunts and fierce yells of defiance. The battle-cry of the Aztec, like the war-whoop of the North American Indian, was an appalling note, according to the Conqueror's own acknowledgment, in the ears of the Spaniards.[1] At this juncture, the general fortunately obtained information from a deserter, one of the Mexican allies, of a ford, by which the army might traverse the shallow lake and penetrate into the place. He instantly despatched the greater part of the infantry on the service, posting himself with the remainder and with the horse at the entrance of the passage, to cover the attack and prevent any interruption in the rear.

The soldiers, under the direction of the Indian guide, forded the lake without much difficulty, though in some places the water came above their girdles. During the passage, they were annoyed by the enemy's missiles ; but when they had gained the dry level they took ample revenge, and speedily put all who resisted to the sword. The greater part, together with the townsmen, made their escape in the boats. The place was now abandoned to pillage. The troops found in it many women, who had been left to their fate ; and these, together with a considerable quantity of cotton stuffs, gold, and articles of food, fell into the hands of the victors, who, setting fire to the deserted city, returned in triumph to their comrades.[2]

Continuing his circuitous route, Cortés presented himself successively before three other places, each of which had been deserted by the inhabitants in anticipation of his arrival.[3] The principal of these, Azca-

1 "De lejos comenzáron á gritar, como lo suelen hacer en la Guerra, que cierto es cosa espantosa oillos." Rel. Terc., ap. Lorenzana, p. 209.

2 Ibid., loc. cit.—Bernal Diaz, Hist. de la Conquista, cap. 141.—Oviedo, Hist de las Ind., MS., lib. 33, cap. 20.—Ixtlilxochitl, Venida de los Españoles, pp. 13, 14.—Idem, Hist. Chich., MS., cap. 92.—Gomara, Crónica, cap. 125.

3 These towns rejoiced in the melodious names of Tenajocoan, Quauhtitlan, and Azcapozalco. I have

constantly endeavoured to spare the reader, in the text, any unnecessary accumulation of Mexican names, which, as he is aware by this time, have not even brevity to recommend them. [Alaman, with some justice, remarks that these names appear unmelodious to an English writer who does not know how to pronounce them, for the same reason as English names would appear unmelodious to a Mexican. Conquista de Méjico (trad. de Vega), tom. ii. p. 115.]

pozalco, had once been the capital of an independent state.   It was now
the great slave-market of the Aztecs, where their unfortunate captives
were brought and disposed of at public sale.   It was also the quarter
occupied by the jewellers, and the place whence the Spaniards obtained
the goldsmiths who melted down the rich treasures received from Montezuma.   But they found there only a small supply of the precious metals,
or, indeed, of anything else of value, as the people had been careful to
remove their effects.   They spared the buildings, however, in consideration of their having met with no resistance.

During the nights, the troops bivouacked in the open fields, maintaining
the strictest watch, for the country was all in arms, and beacons were
flaming on every hill-top, while dark masses of the enemy were occasionally descried in the distance.   The Spaniards were now traversing the
most opulent region of Anahuac.   Cities and villages were scattered over
hill and valley, with cultivated environs blooming around them, all giving
token of a dense and industrious population.   In the centre of this
brilliant circumference stood the Indian metropolis, with its gorgeous tiara
of pyramids and temples, attracting the eye of the soldier from every other
object, as he wound round the borders of the lake.   Every inch of ground
which the army trod was familiar to them,—familiar as the scenes of
childhood, though with very different associations, for it had been written
on their memories in characters of blood.   On the right rose the Hill of
Montezuma,[1] crowned by the *teocalli* under the roof of which the shattered
relics of the army had been gathered on the day following the flight from
the capital.   In front lay the city of Tacuba, through whose inhospitable
streets they had hurried in fear and consternation; and away to the east
of it stretched the melancholy causeway.

It was the general's purpose to march at once on Tacuba and establish
his quarters in that ancient capital for the present.   He found a strong
force encamped under its walls, prepared to dispute his entrance.   Without waiting for their advance, he rode at full gallop against them with his
little body of horse.   The arquebuses and crossbows opened a lively volley
on their extended wings, and the infantry, armed with their swords and
copper-headed lances and supported by the Indian battalions, followed up
the attack of the horse with an alacrity which soon put the enemy to flight.
The Spaniards usually opened the combat with a charge of cavalry.   But,
had the science of the Aztecs been equal to their courage, they might
with their long spears have turned the scale of battle, sometimes at least,
in their own favour; for it was with the same formidable weapon that the
Swiss mountaineers, but a few years before this period of our history,
broke and completely foiled the famous *ordonnance* of Charles the Bold,
the best-appointed cavalry of their day.   But the barbarians were ignorant
of the value of this weapon when opposed to cavalry.   And, indeed, the

---

[1] [The Hill of Los Remedios.   Conquista de Méjico (trad. de Vega), tom. ii. p. 116.]

appalling apparition of the war-horse and his rider still held a mysterious power over their imaginations, which contributed, perhaps, quite as much as the effective force of the cavalry itself, to their discomfiture. Cortés led his troops without further opposition into the suburbs of Tacuba, the ancient Tlacopan, where he established himself for the night.

On the following morning he found the indefatigable Aztecs again under arms, and, on the open ground before the city, prepared to give him battle. He marched out against them, and, after an action hotly contested, though of no long duration, again routed them. They fled towards the town, but were driven through the streets at the point of the lance, and were compelled, together with the inhabitants, to evacuate the place. The city was then delivered over to pillage ; and the Indian allies, not content with plundering the houses of everything portable within them, set them on fire, and in a short time a quarter of the town—the poorer dwellings, probably, built of light, combustible materials—was in flames. Cortés and his troops did all in their power to stop the conflagration, but the Tlascalans were a fierce race, not easily guided at any time, and when their passions were once kindled it was impossible even for the general himself to control them. They were a terrible auxiliary, and, from their insubordination, as terrible sometimes to friend as to foe.[1]

Cortés proposed to remain in his present quarters for some days, during which time he established his own residence in the ancient palace of the lords of Tlacopan. It was a long range of low buildings, like most of the royal residences in the country, and offered good accommodations for the Spanish forces. During his halt here, there was not a day on which the army was not engaged in one or more rencontres with the enemy. They terminated almost uniformly in favour of the Spaniards, though with more or less injury to them and to their allies. One encounter, indeed, had nearly been attended with more fatal consequences.

The Spanish general, in the heat of pursuit, had allowed himself to be decoyed upon the great causeway,—the same which had once been so fatal to his army. He followed the flying foe until he had gained the farther side of the nearest bridge, which had been repaired since the disastrous action of the *noche triste*. When thus far advanced, the Aztecs, with the rapidity of lightning, turned on him, and he beheld a large reinforcement in their rear, all fresh on the field, prepared to support their countrymen. At the same time, swarms of boats, unobserved in the eagerness of the chase, seemed to start up as if by magic, covering the waters around. The Spaniards were now exposed to a perfect hailstorm of missiles, both from the causeway and the lake; but they stood unmoved

1 They burned this place, according to Cortés, in retaliation of the injuries inflicted by the inhabitants on their countrymen in the retreat : " Y en amaneciendo los Indios nuestros Amigos comenzáron á saquear, y quemar toda la Ciudad, salvo el Aposento donde estabamos, y pusiéron tanta diligencia, que aun de él se quemó un Quarto ; y esto se hizo, porque quando salímos la otra vez desbaratados de Temixtitan, pasando por esta Ciudad, los Naturales de ella juntamente con los de Temixtitan nos hiciéron muy cruel Guerra, y nos matáron muchos Españoles." Rel. Terc., ap. Lorenzana, p. 210.

amidst the tempest, when Cortés, too late perceiving his error, gave orders for the retreat. Slowly, and with admirable coolness, his men receded, step by step, offering a resolute front to the enemy.[1] The Mexicans came on with their usual vociferation, making the shores echo to their war-cries, and striking at the Spaniards with their long pikes, and with poles, to which the swords taken from the Christians had been fastened. A cavalier, named Volante, bearing the standard of Cortés, was felled by one of their weapons, and, tumbling into the lake, was picked up by the Mexican boats. He was a man of a muscular frame, and, as the enemy were dragging him off, he succeeded in extricating himself from their grasp, and, clenching his colours in his hand, with a desperate effort sprang back upon the causeway. At length, after some hard fighting, in which many of the Spaniards were wounded and many of their allies slain, the troops regained the land, where Cortés, with a full heart, returned thanks to Heaven for what he might well regard as a providential deliverance.[2] It was a salutary lesson; though he should scarcely have needed one, so soon after the affair of Iztapalapan, to warn him of the wily tactics of his enemy.

It had been one of Cortés' principal objects in this expedition to obtain an interview, if possible, with the Aztec emperor, or with some of the great lords at his court, and to try if some means for an accommodation could not be found, by which he might avoid the appeal to arms. An occasion for such a parley presented itself when his forces were one day confronted with those of the enemy, with a broken bridge interposed between them. Cortés, riding in advance of his people, intimated by signs his peaceful intent, and that he wished to confer with the Aztecs. They respected the signal, and, with the aid of his interpreter, he requested that if there were any great chief among them he would come forward and hold a parley with him. The Mexicans replied, in derision, they were all chiefs, and bade him speak openly whatever he had to tell them. As the general returned no answer, they asked why he did not make another visit to the capital, and tauntingly added, "Perhaps Malinche does not expect to find there another Montezuma, as obedient to his commands as the former."[3] Some of them complimented the Tlascalans with the epithet of *women*, who, they said, would never have ventured so near the capital but for the protection of the white men.

The animosity of the two nations was not confined to these harmless though bitter jests, but showed itself in regular cartels of defiance, which daily passed between the principal chieftains. These were followed by combats, in which one or more champions fought on a side, to vindicate

---

[1] "Luego mandó, que todos se retraxessen; y con el mejor concierto que pudo, y no bueltas las espaldas, sino los rostros á los contrarios, pie contra pie, como quien haze represas." Bernal Diaz, Hist. de la Conquista, cap. 141

[2] "Desta manera se escapó Cortés aquella vez del poder de México, y quando se vió en tierra firme, dió muchas gracias á Dios." Ibid., ubi supra.

[3] "Pensais, que hay agora otro Muteczuma, para que haga todo, lo que quisieredes?" Rel. Terc. de Cortés, ap. Lorenzana, p. 211.

the honour of their respective countries. A fair field of fight was given to the warriors, who conducted these combats *à l'outrance* with the punctilio ot a European tourney; displaying a valour worthy of the two boldest of the races of Anahuac, and a skill in the management of their weapons, which drew forth the admiration of the Spaniards.[1]

Cortés had now been six days in Tacuba. There was nothing further to detain him, as he had accomplished the chief objects of his expedition. He had humbled several of the places which had been most active in their hostility; and he had revived the credit of the Castilian arms, which had been much tarnished by their former reverses in this quarter of the Valley. He had also made himself acquainted with the condition of the capital, which he found in a better posture of defence than he had imagined. All the ravages of the preceding year seemed to be repaired, and there was no evidence, even to his experienced eye, that the wasting hand of war had so lately swept over the land. The Aztec troops, which swarmed through the Valley, seemed to be well appointed, and showed an invincible spirit, as if prepared to resist to the last. It is true, they had been beaten in every encounter. In the open field they were no match for the Spaniards, whose cavalry they could never comprehend, and whose firearms easily penetrated the cotton mail which formed the stoutest defence of the Indian warrior. But, entangled in the long streets and narrow lanes of the metropolis, where every house was a citadel, the Spaniards, as experience had shown, would lose much of their superiority. With the Mexican emperor, confident in the strength of his preparations, the general saw there was no probability of effecting an accommodation. He saw, too, the necessity of the most careful preparations on his own part—indeed, that he must strain his resources to the utmost—before he could safely venture to rouse the lion in his lair.

The Spaniards returned by the same route by which they had come. Their retreat was interpreted into a flight by the natives, who hung on the rear of the army, uttering vainglorious vaunts, and saluting the troops with showers of arrows, which did some mischief. Cortés resorted to one ot their own stratagems to rid himself of this annoyance. He divided his cavalry into two or three small parties, and concealed them among some thick shrubbery which fringed both sides of the road. The rest of the army continued its march. The Mexicans followed, unsuspicious of the ambuscade, when the horse, suddenly darting from their place of concealment, threw the enemy's flanks into confusion, and the retreating columns of infantry, facing about suddenly, commenced a brisk attack, which completed their consternation. It was a broad and level plain, over which the panic-struck Mexicans made the best ot their way, without attempting resistance; while the cavalry, riding them down and piercing the fugitives with their lances, followed up the chase for several miles, in what Cortés

---

1 "Y peleaban los unos con los otros muy hermosamente." Rel. Terc. de Cortés, ubi supra.—Oviedo, Hist. de las Ind., MS., lib. 33, cap. 20.

calls a truly beautiful style.[1] The army experienced no further annoyance from the enemy.

On their arrival at Tezcuco they were greeted with joy by their comrades, who had received no tidings of them during the fortnight which had elapsed since their departure. The Tlascalans, immediately on their return, requested the general's permission to carry back to their own country the valuable booty which they had gathered in their foray,—a request which, however unpalatable, he could not refuse.[2]

The troops had not been in quarters more than two or three days, when an embassy arrived from Chalco, again soliciting the protection of the Spaniards against the Mexicans, who menaced them from several points in their neighbourhood. But the soldiers were so much exhausted by unintermitted vigils, forced marches, battles, and wounds, that Cortés wished to give them a breathing-time to recruit, before engaging in a new expedition. He answered the application of the Chalcans by sending his missives to the allied cities, calling on them to march to the assistance of their confederate. It is not to be supposed that they could comprehend the import of his despatches. But the paper, with its mysterious characters, served for a warrant to the officer who bore it, as the interpreter of the general's commands.

But, although these were implicitly obeyed, the Chalcans felt the danger so pressing that they soon repeated their petition for the Spaniards to come in person to their relief. Cortés no longer hesitated; for he was well aware of the importance of Chalco, not merely on its own account, but from its position, which commanded one of the great avenues to Tlascala, and to Vera Cruz, the intercourse with which should run no risk of interruption. Without further loss of time, therefore, he detached a body of three hundred Spanish foot and twenty horse, under the command of Sandoval, for the protection of the city.

That active officer soon presented himself before Chalco, and, strengthened by the reinforcement of its own troops and those of the confederate towns, directed his first operations against Huaxtepec, a place of some importance, lying five leagues or more to the south among the mountains. It was held by a strong Mexican force, watching their opportunity to make a descent upon Chalco. The Spaniards found the enemy drawn up at a distance from the town, prepared to receive them. The ground was broken and tangled with bushes, unfavourable to the cavalry, which, in consequence, soon fell into disorder; and Sandoval, finding himself embarrassed by their movements, ordered them, after sustaining some loss, from the field. In their place he brought up his musketeers and crossbow-

---

[1] "Y comenzámos á lanzear en ellos, y duró el alcanze cerca de dos leguas todas llanas, como la palma, que fué muy hermosa cosa." Rel. Terc., ap. Lorenzana, p. 212.

[2] For the particulars of this expedition of Cortés, see, besides his own Commentaries so often quoted, Oviedo, Hist. de las Ind., MS., lib. 33, cap. 20,—Torquemada, Monarch. Ind., lib. 4, cap. 85,—Gomara, Crónica, cap. 125,—Ixtlilxochitl, Venida de los Españoles, pp. 13, 14,—Bernal Diaz, Hist. de la Conquista, cap. 141.

men, who poured a rapid fire into the thick columns of the Indians. The rest of the infantry, with sword and pike, charged the flanks of the enemy, who, bewildered by the shock, after sustaining considerable slaughter, fell back in an irregular manner, leaving the field of battle to the Spaniards.

The victors proposed to bivouac there for the night. But while engaged in preparations for their evening meal, they were aroused by the cry of "To arms, to arms! the enemy is upon us!" In an instant the trooper was in his saddle, the soldier grasped his musket or his good Toledo, and the action was renewed with greater fury than before. The Mexicans had received a reinforcement from the city. But their second attempt was not more fortunate than their first; and the victorious Spaniards, driving their antagonists before them, entered and took possession of the town itself, which had already been evacuated by the inhabitants.[1]

Sandoval took up his quarters in the dwelling of the lord of the place, surrounded by gardens which rivalled those of Iztapalapan in magnificence and surpassed them in extent. They are said to have been two leagues in circumference, having pleasure-houses, and numerous tanks stocked with various kinds of fish; and they were embellished with trees, shrubs, and plants, native and exotic, some selected for their beauty and fragrance, others for their medicinal properties. They were scientifically arranged; and the whole establishment displayed a degree of horticultural taste and knowledge of which it would not have been easy to find a counterpart, at that day, in the more civilized communities of Europe.[2] Such is the testimony not only of the rude Conquerors, but of men of science, who visited these beautiful repositories in the day of their glory.[3]

After halting two days to refresh his forces in this agreeable spot, Sandoval marched on Jacapichtla, about twelve miles to the eastward. It was a town, or rather fortress, perched on a rocky eminence almost inaccessible from its steepness. It was garrisoned by a Mexican force, who rolled down on the assailants, as they attempted to scale the heights, huge fragments of rock, which, thundering over the sides of the precipice, carried ruin and desolation in their path. The Indian confederates fell back in dismay from the attempt. But Sandoval, indignant that any achievement should be too difficult for a Spaniard, commanded his cavaliers to dismount, and, declaring that he "would carry the place or die in the attempt," led on his men with the cheering cry of "St. Jago."[4] With

---

[1] Rel. Terc. de Cortés, ap. Lorenzana, pp. 214, 215.—Gomara, Crónica, cap. 146.—Bernal Diaz, Hist. de la Conquista, cap. 142.—Oviedo, Hist. de las Ind., MS., lib. 33, cap. 21.

[2] "Which gardens," says Cortés, who afterwards passed a day there, "are the largest, freshest, and most beautiful that were ever seen. They have a circuit of two leagues, and through the middle flows a very pleasant stream of water. At distances of two bowshots are buildings surrounded by grounds planted with fruit-trees of various kinds, with many shrubs and odorous flowers. Truly the whole place is wonderful for its pleasantness and its extent." (Rel. Terc., ap. Lorenzana, pp. 221, 222.) Bernal

Diaz is not less emphatic in his admiration. Hist. de la Conquista, cap. 142.

[3] The distinguished naturalist Hernandez has frequent occasion to notice this garden, which furnished him with many specimens for his great work. It had the good fortune to be preserved after the Conquest, when particular attention was given to its medicinal plants, for the use of a great hospital established in the neighbourhood. See Clavigero, Stor. del Messico, tom. ii. p. 153.

[4] "É como esto vió el dicho Alguacil Mayor, y los Españoles, determináron de morir, ó subilles por fuerza á lo alto del Pueblo, y con el apellido de *Señor Santiago,* comenzáron á subir." Rel. Terc.,

renewed courage, they now followed their gallant leader up the ascent, under a storm of lighter missiles, mingled with huge masses of stone, which, breaking into splinters, overturned the assailants and made fearful havoc in their ranks.   Sandoval, who had been wounded on the preceding day, received a severe contusion on the head, while more than one of his brave comrades were struck down by his side.   Still they clambered up, sustaining themselves by the bushes or projecting pieces of rock, and seemed to force themselves onward as much by the energy of their wills as by the strength of their bodies.

After incredible toil, they stood on the summit, face to face with the astonished garrison.   For a moment they paused to recover breath, then sprang furiously on their foes.   The struggle was short, but desperate. Most of the Aztecs were put to the sword.   Some were thrown headlong over the battlements, and others, letting themselves down the precipice, were killed on the borders of a little stream that wound round its base, the waters of which were so polluted with blood that the victors were unable to slake their thirst with them for a full hour ! [1]

Sandoval, having now accomplished the object of his expedition, by reducing the strongholds which had so long held the Chalcans in awe, returned in triumph to Tezcuco.   Meanwhile, the Aztec emperor, whose vigilant eye had been attentive to all that had passed, thought that the absence of so many of its warriors afforded a favourable opportunity for recovering Chalco.   He sent a fleet of boats, for this purpose, across the lake, with a numerous force under the command of some of his most valiant chiefs. [2]   Fortunately the absent Chalcans reached their city before the arrival of the enemy ; but, though supported by their Indian allies, they were so much alarmed by the magnitude of the hostile array that they sent again to the Spaniards, invoking their aid.

The messengers arrived at the same time with Sandoval and his army. Cortés was much puzzled by the contradictory accounts. He suspected some negligence in his lieutenant, and, displeased with his precipitate return in this unsettled state of the affair, ordered him back at once, with such of his forces as were in fighting condition.   Sandoval felt deeply injured by this proceeding, but he made no attempt at exculpation, and, obeying his commander in silence, put himself at the head of his troops and made a rapid countermarch on the Indian city. [3]

Before he reached it, a battle had been fought between the Mexicans and the confederates, in which the latter, who had acquired unwonted confidence from their recent successes, were victorious.   A number of

ap. Lorenzana, p. 214.—Oviedo, Hist. de las Ind., MS., lib. 33, cap. 21.

[1] So says the *Conquistador*. (Rel. Terc., ap. Lorenzana, p. 215.) Diaz, who will allow no one to hyperbolize but himself, says, "For as long as one might take to say an Ave Maria !" (Hist. de la Conquista, cap. 142.) Neither was present.

[2] The gallant Captain Diaz, who affects a sobriety in his own estimates, which often leads him to dis-

parage those of the chaplain Gomara, says that the force consisted of 20,000 warriors in 2000 canoes. Hist. de la Conquista, loc. cit.

[3] "El Cortés no le quiso escuchar á Sandoual de enojo, creyendo que por su culpa, ó descuido, recibiá mala obra nuestros amigos los de Chalco ; y luego sin mas dilacion, ni le oyr, le mandó bolver" Ibid., ubi supra.

Aztec nobles fell into their hands in the engagement, whom they delivered to Sandoval to be carried off as prisoners to Tezcuco. On his arrival there, the cavalier, wounded by the unworthy treatment he had received, retired to his own quarters without presenting himself before his chief.

During his absence, the inquiries of Cortés had satisfied him of his own precipitate conduct, and of the great injustice he had done his lieutenant. There was no man in the army on whose services he set so high a value, as the responsible situations in which he had placed him plainly showed; and there was none for whom he seems to have entertained a greater personal regard. On Sandoval's return, therefore, Cortés instantly sent to request his attendance ; when, with a soldier's frankness, he made such an explanation as soothed the irritated spirit of the cavalier,—a matter of no great difficulty, as the latter had too generous a nature, and too earnest a devotion to his commander and the cause in which they were embarked, to harbour a petty feeling of resentment in his bosom.[1]

During the occurrence of these events the work was going forward actively on the canal, and the brigantines were within a fortnight of their completion. The greatest vigilance was required, in the mean time, to prevent their destruction by the enemy, who had already made three ineffectual attempts to burn them on the stocks. The precautions which Cortés thought it necessary to take against the Tezcucans themselves added not a little to his embarrassment.

At this time he received embassies from different Indian states, some of them on the remote shores of the Mexican Gulf, tendering their allegiance and soliciting his protection. For this he was partly indebted to the good offices of Ixtlilxochitl, who, in consequence of his brother's death, was now advanced to the sovereignty of Tezcuco. This important position greatly increased his consideration and authority through the country, of which he freely availed himself to bring the natives under the dominion of the Spaniards.[2]

The general received also at this time the welcome intelligence of the arrival of three vessels at Villa Rica, with two hundred men on board, well provided with arms and ammunition, and with seventy or eighty horses. It was a most seasonable reinforcement. From what quarter it came is uncertain; most probably from Hispaniola. Cortés, it may be remembered, had sent for supplies to that place; and the authorities of the island, who had general jurisdiction over the affairs of the colonies, had shown themselves, on more than one occasion, well inclined towards him, probably considering him, under all circumstances, as better fitted than any other man to achieve the conquest of the country.[3]

---

[1] Besides the authorities already quoted for Sandoval's expedition, see Gomara, Crónica, cap. 126,—Ixtlilxochitl, Hist. Chich., MS., cap. 92,—Torquemada, Monarch. Ind., lib. 4, cap. 86.

[2] "Ixtlilxochitl procuraba siempre traer á la devocion y amistad de los Cristianos no tan solamente á los de el Reyno de Tezcuco sino aun los de

las Provincias remotas, rogándoles que todos se procurasen dar de paz al Capitan Cortés, y que aunque de las guerras pasadas algunos tuviesen culpa, era tan afable y deseaba tanto la paz que luego al punto los reciviria en su amistad." Ixtlilxochitl, Hist. Chich., MS., cap. 92.

[3] Cortés speaks of these vessels as coming at the

The new recruits soon found their way to Tezcuco; as the communications with the port were now open and unobstructed. Among them were several cavaliers of consideration, one of whom, Julian de Alderete, the royal treasurer, came over to superintend the interests of the crown.

There was also in the number a Dominican friar, who brought a quantity of pontifical bulls, offering indulgences to those engaged in war against the infidel. The soldiers were not slow to fortify themselves with the good graces of the Church; and the worthy father, after driving a prosperous traffic with his spiritual wares, had the satisfaction to return home, at the end of a few months, well freighted, in exchange, with the more substantial treasures of the Indies.[1]

CHAPTER III.

SECOND RECONNOITRING EXPEDITION. — ENGAGEMENTS ON THE SIERRA. —CAPTURE OF CUERNAVACA. — BATTLES AT XOCHIMILCO. — NARROW ESCAPE OF CORTÉS.—HE ENTERS TACUBA.

(1521.)

NOTWITHSTANDING the relief which had been afforded to the people of Chalco, it was so ineffectual that envoys from that city again arrived at Tezcuco, bearing a hieroglyphical chart, on which were depicted several strong places in their neighbourhood, garrisoned by the Aztecs, from which they expected annoyance. Cortés determined, this time, to take the affair into his own hands, and to scour the country so effectually as to place Chalco, if possible, in a state of security. He did not confine himself to this object, but proposed, before his return, to pass quite round the great lakes, and reconnoitre the country to the south of them, in the same manner as he had before done to the west. In the course of his march he would direct his arms against some of the strong places from which the Mexicans might expect support in the siege. Two or three weeks must elapse before the completion of the brigantines; and, if no other good resulted from the expedition, it would give active occupation to his troops, whose turbulent spirits might fester into discontent in the monotonous existence of a camp.

He selected for the expedition thirty horse and three hundred Spanish

same time, but does not intimate from what quarter. (Rel. Terc., ap. Lorenzana, p. 216.) Bernal Diaz, who notices only one, says it came from Castile. (Hist. de la Conquista, cap. 143.) But the old soldier wrote long after the events he commemorates, and may have confused the true order of things. It seems hardly probable that so important a reinforcement should have arrived from Castile, considering that Cortés had yet received none of the royal patronage, or even sanction, which would stimulate adventurers in the mother country to enlist under his standard.

[1] Bernal Diaz, Hist. de la Conquista, cap 143.— Oviedo, Hist. de las Ind., MS., lib. 33, cap. 21.— Herrera, Hist. general, dec. 3, lib. 1, cap. 6.

infantry, with a considerable body of Tlascalan and Tezcucan warriors. The remaining garrison he left in charge of the trusty Sandoval, who, with the friendly lord of the capital, would watch over the construction of the brigantines and protect them from the assaults of the Aztecs.

On the fifth of April he began his march, and on the following day arrived at Chalco, where he was met by a number of the confederate chiefs. With the aid of his faithful interpreters, Doña Marina and Aguilar, he explained to them the objects of his present expedition, stated his purpose soon to enforce the blockade of Mexico, and required their co-operation with the whole strength of their levies. To this they readily assented ; and he soon received a sufficient proof of their friendly disposition in the forces which joined him on the march, amounting, according to one of the army, to more than had ever before followed his banner.[1]

Taking a southerly direction, the troops, after leaving Chalco, struck into the recesses of the wild sierra, which, with its bristling peaks, serves as a formidable palisade to fence round the beautiful Valley ; while within its rugged arms it shuts up many a green and fruitful pasture of its own. As the Spaniards passed through its deep gorges, they occasionally wound round the base of some huge cliff or rocky eminence, on which the inhabitants had built their towns, in the same manner as was done by the people of Europe in the feudal ages ; a position which, however favourable to the picturesque, intimates a sense of insecurity as the cause of it, which may reconcile us to the absence of this striking appendage of the land-scape in our own more fortunate country.

The occupants of these airy pinnacles took advantage of their situation to shower down stones and arrows on the troops as they defiled through the narrow passes of the sierra. Though greatly annoyed by their incessant hostilities, Cortés held on his way, till, winding round the base of a castellated cliff occupied by a strong garrison of Indians, he was so severely pressed that he felt to pass on without chastising the aggressors would imply a want of strength which must disparage him in the eyes of his allies. Halting in the valley, therefore, he detached a small body of light troops to scale the heights, while he remained with the main body of the army below, to guard against surprise from the enemy.

The lower region of the rocky eminence was so steep that the soldiers found it no easy matter to ascend, scrambling, as well as they could, with hand and knee. But, as they came into the more exposed view of the garrison, the latter rolled down huge masses of rock, which, bounding along the declivity and breaking into fragments, crushed the foremost assailants and mangled their limbs in a frightful manner. Still they strove to work their way upward, now taking advantage of some gulley worn by the winter torrent, now sheltering themselves behind a projecting

---

[1] "Viniéron tantos, que en todas las entradas que yo auia ido, despues que en la Nueua España entré, nunca vi tanta gente de guerra de nuestros amigos, como aora fuéron en nuestra compañía." Bernal Diaz, Hist. de la Conquista, cap. 144.

cliff, or some straggling tree anchored among the crevices of the mountain. It was all in vain. For no sooner did they emerge again into open view than the rocky avalanche thundered on their heads with a fury against which steel helm and cuirass were as little defence as gossamer. All the party were more or less wounded. Eight of the number were killed on the spot,—a loss the little band could ill afford,—and the gallant ensign, Corral, who led the advance, saw the banner in his hand torn into shreds.[1] Cortés, at length, convinced of the impracticability of the attempt, at least without a more severe loss than he was disposed to incur, commanded a retreat. It was high time; for a large body of the enemy were on full march across the valley to attack him.

He did not wait for their approach, but, gathering his broken files together, headed his cavalry and spurred boldly against them. On the level plain the Spaniards were on their own ground. The Indians, unable to sustain the furious onset, broke, and fell back before it. The flight soon became a rout, and the fiery cavaliers, dashing over them at full gallop, or running them through with their lances, took some revenge for their late discomfiture. The pursuit continued for some miles, till the nimble foe made their escape into the rugged fastnesses of the sierra, where the Spaniards did not care to follow. The weather was sultry, and, as the country was nearly destitute of water, the men and horses suffered extremely. Before evening they reached a spot overshadowed by a grove of wild mulberry-trees, in which some scanty springs afforded a miserable supply to the army.

Near the place rose another rocky summit of the sierra, garrisoned by a stronger force than the one which they had encountered in the former part of the day; and at no great distance stood a second fortress at a still greater height, though considerably smaller than its neighbour. This was also tenanted by a body of warriors, who, as well as those of the adjoining cliff, soon made active demonstration of their hostility by pouring down missiles on the troops below. Cortés, anxious to retrieve the disgrace of the morning, ordered an assault on the larger and, as it seemed, more practicable eminence. But, though two attempts were made with great resolution, they were repulsed with loss to the assailants. The rocky sides of the hill had been artificially cut and smoothed, so as greatly to increase the natural difficulties of the ascent. The shades of evening now closed around; and Cortés drew off his men to the mulberry-grove, where he took up his bivouac for the night, deeply chagrined at having been twice foiled by the enemy on the same day.

During the night, the Indian force which occupied the adjoining height passed over to their brethren, to aid them in the encounter which they foresaw would be renewed on the following morning. No sooner did the Spanish general, at the break of day, become aware of this manœuvre,

---

1 "Todos descalabrados. v corriendo sangre, y las vanderas rotas, y ocho muertos." Bernal Diaz, Hist. de la Conquista, ubi supra

than, with his usual quickness, he took advantage of it. He detached a body of musketeers and crossbowmen to occupy the deserted eminence, purposing, as soon as this was done, to lead the assault in person against the other. It was not long before the Castilian banner was seen streaming from the rocky pinnacle, when the general instantly led up his men to the attack. And, while the garrison were meeting them resolutely on that quarter, the detachment on the neighbouring heights poured into the place a well-directed fire, which so much distressed the enemy that in a very short time they signified their willingness to capitulate.[1]

On entering the place, the Spaniards found that a plain of some extent ran along the crest of the sierra, and that it was tenanted not only by men, but by women and their families, with their effects. No violence was offered by the victors to the property or persons of the vanquished; and the knowledge of this lenity induced the Indian garrison, who had made so stout a resistance on the morning of the preceding day, to tender their submission.[2]

After a halt of two days in this sequestered region, the army resumed its march in a south-westerly direction on Huaxtepec, the same city which had surrendered to Sandoval. Here they were kindly received by the cacique, and entertained in his magnificent gardens, which Cortés and his officers, who had not before seen them, compared with the best in Castile.[3] Still threading the wild mountain mazes, the army passed through Jauhtepec and several other places, which were abandoned at their approach. As the inhabitants, however, hung in armed bodies on their flanks and rear, doing them occasionally some mischief, the Spaniards took their revenge by burning the deserted towns.

Thus holding on their fiery track, they descended the bold slope of the Cordilleras, which on the south are far more precipitous than on the Atlantic side. Indeed, a single day's journey is sufficient to place the traveller on a level several thousand feet lower than that occupied by him in the morning; thus conveying him, in a few hours, through the climates of many degrees of latitude. The route of the army led them across many an acre covered with lava and blackened scoriæ, attesting the volcanic character of the region; though this was frequently relieved by patches of verdure, and even tracts of prodigal fertility, as if Nature were desirous to compensate by these extraordinary efforts for the curse of barrenness which elsewhere had fallen on the land. On the ninth day of

[1] For the assault on the rocks,—the topography of which it is impossible to verify from the narratives of the Conquerors,—see Bernal Diaz, Hist. de la Conquista, cap. 144,—Rel. Terc. de Cortés, ap. Lorenzana, pp. 218–221,—Gomara, Crónica, cap. 127,—Ixtlilxochitl, Venida de los Españoles, pp. 16, 17,—Oviedo, Hist. de las Ind., MS., lib. 33, cap. 21.

[2] Cortés, according to Bernal Diaz, ordered the troops who took possession of the second fortress "not to meddle with a grain of maize belonging to the besieged." Diaz, giving this a very liberal interpretation, proceeded forthwith to load his Indian *tamanes* with everything but maize, as fair booty. He was interrupted in his labours, however, by the captain of the detachment, who gave a more narrow construction to his general's orders, much to the dissatisfaction of the latter, if we may trust the doughty chronicler. Hist. de la Conquista, ubi supra.

[3] "Adonde estaua la huerta que he dicho, que es la mejor que auia visto en toda mi vida, y ansí lo torno á dezir, que Cortés, y el Tesorero Alderete, desque entonces la viéron, y passeáron algo de ella, se admiráron, y dixéron, que mejor cosa de huerta no auian visto en Castilla." Ibid., cap. 144.

their march the troops arrived before the strong city of Quauhnahuac, or Cuernavaca, as since called by the Spaniards.[1] It was the ancient capital of the Tlahuicas, and the most considerable place for wealth and population in this part of the country. It was tributary to the Aztecs, and a garrison of this nation was quartered within its walls. The town was singularly situated, on a projecting piece of land, encompassed by *barrancas*, or formidable ravines, except on one side, which opened on a rich and well-cultivated country. For, though the place stood at an elevation of between five and six thousand feet above the level of the sea, it had a southern exposure so sheltered by the mountain barrier on the north that its climate was as soft and genial as that of a much lower region.

The Spaniards, on arriving before this city, the limit of their southerly progress, found themselves separated from it by one of the vast barrancas before noticed, which resembled one of those frightful rents not unfrequent in the Mexican Andes, the result, no doubt, of some terrible convulsion in earlier ages. The rocky sides of the ravine sank perpendicularly down, so bare as scarcely to exhibit even a vestige of the cactus, or of the other hardy plants with which Nature in these fruitful regions so gracefully covers up her deformities. The bottom of the chasm, however, showed a striking contrast to this, being literally choked up with a rich and spontaneous vegetation ; for the huge walls of rock which shut in these barrancas, while they screen them from the cold winds of the Cordilleras, reflect the rays of a vertical sun, so as to produce an almost suffocating heat in the enclosure, stimulating the soil to the rank fertility of the *tierra caliente*. Under the action of this forcing apparatus,—so to speak,—the inhabitants of the towns on their margin above may with ease obtain the vegetable products which are to be found on the sultry level of the lowlands.[2]

At the bottom of the ravine was seen a little stream, which, oozing from the stony bowels of the sierra, tumbled along its narrow channel and contributed by its perpetual moisture to the exuberant fertility of the valley. This rivulet, which at certain seasons of the year was swollen to a torrent, was traversed at some distance below the town, where the sloping sides of the barranca afforded a more practicable passage, by two rude bridges, both of which had been broken in anticipation of the coming of the Spaniards. The latter had now arrived on the brink of the chasm which intervened between them and the city. It was, as has been remarked, of no great width, and the army drawn up on its borders was directly exposed to the archery of the garrison, on whom its own fire made little impression, protected as they were by their defences.

---

[1] This barbarous Indian name is tortured into all possible variations by the old chroniclers. The town soon received from the Spaniards the name which it now bears, of Cuernavaca, and by which it is indicated on modern maps. " Prevalse poi quello di *Cuernabaca*, col quale è presentemente conosciuta dagli Spagnuoli." Clavigero, Stor. del Messico, tom. iii. p. 185, nota.

[2] [" The whole of this description," remarks Alaman, " agrees perfectly with the present aspect of Cuernavaca and the *barrancas* surrounding it."—ED.]

The general, annoyed by his position, sent a detachment to seek a passage lower down, by which the troops might be landed on the other side. But, although the banks of the ravine became less formidable as they descended, they found no means of crossing the river, till a path unexpectedly presented itself, on which, probably, no one before had ever been daring enough to venture.

From the cliffs on the opposite side of the barranca, two huge trees shot up to an enormous height, and, inclining towards each other, interlaced their boughs so as to form a sort of natural bridge. Across this avenue, in mid-air, a Tlascalan conceived it would not be difficult to pass to the opposite bank. The bold mountaineer succeeded in the attempt, and was soon followed by several others of his countrymen, trained to feats of agility and strength among their native hills. The Spaniards imitated their example. It was a perilous effort for an armed man to make his way over this aerial causeway, swayed to and fro by the wind, where the brain might become giddy, and where a single false movement of hand or foot would plunge him in the abyss below. Three of the soldiers lost their hold and fell. The rest, consisting of some twenty or thirty Spaniards and a considerable number of Tlascalans, alighted in safety on the other bank.[1] There hastily forming, they marched with all speed on the city. The enemy, engaged in their contest with the Castilians on the opposite brink of the ravine, were taken by surprise,—which, indeed, could scarcely have been exceeded if they had seen their foe drop from the clouds on the field of battle.

They made a brave resistance, however, when fortunately the Spaniards succeeded in repairing one of the dilapidated bridges in such a manner as to enable both cavalry and foot to cross the river, though with much delay. The horse, under Olid and Andrés de Tápia, instantly rode up to the succour of their countrymen. They were soon followed by Cortés at the head of the remaining battalions, and the enemy, driven from one point to another, were compelled to evacuate the city and to take refuge among the mountains. The buildings in one quarter of the town were speedily wrapt in flames. The place was abandoned to pillage, and, as it was one of the most opulent marts in the country, it amply compensated the victors for the toil and danger they had encountered. The trembling caciques, returning soon after to the city, appeared before Cortés, and, deprecating his resentment by charging the blame, as usual, on the Mexicans, threw themselves on his mercy. Satisfied with their submission, he allowed no further violence to the inhabitants.[2]

---

[1] The stout-hearted Diaz was one of those who performed this dangerous feat, though his head swam so, as he tells us, that he scarcely knew how he got on. " Porque de mí digo, que verdaderamēte quando passaua, q̃ lo ví mui peligroso, é malo de passar, y se me desvanecia la cabeça, y todavía passé yo, y otros veinte, ó treinta soldados, y muchos Tlascaltecas." Hist. de la Conquista, ubi supra.

[2] For the preceding account of the capture of Cuernavaca, see Bernal Diaz, ubi supra,—Oviedo, Hist. de las Ind., MS., lib. 33, cap. 21,—Ixtlilxochitl, Hist. Chich., MS., cap. 93,—Herrera, Hist. general, dec. 3, lib. 1, cap. 8,—Torquemada, Monarch. Ind., lib. 4, cap. 87,—Rel. Terc. de Cortés, ap. Lorenzana, pp. 223, 224.

Having thus accomplished the great object of his expedition across the mountains, the Spanish commander turned his face northwards, to recross the formidable barrier which divided him from the Valley. The ascent, steep and laborious, was rendered still more difficult by fragments of rock and loose stones, which encumbered the passes. The mountain sides and summits were shaggy with thick forests of pine and stunted oak, which threw a melancholy gloom over the region, still further heightened at the present day by its being a favourite haunt of banditti.

The weather was sultry, and, as the stony soil was nearly destitute of water, the troops suffered severely from thirst. Several of them, indeed, fainted on the road, and a few of the Indian allies perished from exhaustion.[1] The line of march must have taken the army across the eastern shoulder of the mountain called the *Cruz del Marques*, or Cross of the Marquess, from a huge stone cross erected there to indicate the boundary of the territories granted by the Crown to Cortés, as Marquis of the Valley. Much, indeed, of the route lately traversed by the troops lay across the princely domain subsequently assigned to the Conqueror.[2]

The Spaniards were greeted from these heights with a different view from any which they had before had of the Mexican Valley, made more attractive in their eyes, doubtless, by contrast with the savage scenery in which they had lately been involved. It was its most pleasant and populous quarter; for nowhere did its cities and villages cluster together in such numbers as round the lake of sweet water. From whatever quarter seen, however, the enchanting region presented the same aspect of natural beauty and cultivation, with its flourishing villas, and its fair lake in the centre, whose dark and polished surface glistened like a mirror, deep set in the huge framework of porphyry in which nature had enclosed it.

The point of attack selected by the general was Xochimilco, or "the field of flowers," as its name implies, from the floating gardens which rode at anchor, as it were, on the neighbouring waters.[3] It was one of the most potent and wealthy cities in the Valley, and a stanch vassal of the Aztec crown. It stood, like the capital itself, partly in the water, and was approached in that quarter by causeways of no great length. The town was composed of houses like those of most other places of like magnitude in the country, mostly of cottages or huts made of clay and the light bamboo, mingled with aspiring *teocallis*, and edifices of stone, belonging to the more opulent classes.

As the Spaniards advanced, they were met by skirmishing parties of the enemy, who, after dismissing a light volley of arrows, rapidly retreated

---

[1] "Una Tierra de Pinales, despoblada, y sin ninguna agua, la qual y un Puerto pasámos con grandíssimo trabajo, y sin beber : tanto, que muchos de los Indios que iban con nosotros pereciéron de sed." Rel. Terc. de Cortés, ap. Lorenzana, p. 224.

[2] The city of Cuernavaca was comprehended in the patrimony of the dukes of Monteleone, descend-

ants and heirs of the *Conquistador*.—The Spaniards, in their line of march towards the north, did not deviate far, probably, from the great road which now leads from Mexico to Acapulco, still exhibiting in this upper portion of it the same characteristic features as at the period of the Conquest.

[3] Clavigero, Stor. del Messico, tom. iii. p. 187, nota.

before them. As they took the direction of Xochimilco, Cortés inferred that they were prepared to resist him in considerable force. It exceeded his expectations.

On traversing the principal causeway, he found it occupied at the farther extremity by a numerous body of warriors, who, stationed on the opposite side of a bridge, which had been broken, were prepared to dispute his passage. They had constructed a temporary barrier of palisades, which screened them from the fire of the musketry. But the water in its neighbourhood was very shallow, and the cavaliers and infantry, plunging into it, soon made their way, swimming or wading, as they could, in face of a storm of missiles, to the landing near the town. Here they closed with the enemy, and hand to hand, after a sharp struggle, drove them back on the city; a few, however, taking the direction of the open country, were followed up by the cavalry. The great mass, hotly pursued by the infantry, were driven through street and lane, without much further resistance. Cortés, with a few followers, disengaging himself from the tumult, remained near the entrance of the city. He had not been there long when he was assailed by a fresh body of Indians, who suddenly poured into the place from a neighbouring dike. The general, with his usual fearlessness, threw himself into the midst, in hopes to check their advance. But his own followers were too few to support him, and he was overwhelmed by the crowd of combatants. His horse lost his footing and fell; and Cortés, who received a severe blow on the head before he could rise, was seized and dragged off in triumph by the Indians. At this critical moment, a Tlascalan, who perceived the general's extremity, sprang, like one of the wild ocelots of his own forests, into the midst of the assailants, and endeavoured to tear him from their grasp. Two of the general's servants also speedily came to the rescue, and Cortés, with their aid and that of the brave Tlascalan, succeeded in regaining his feet and shaking off his enemies. To vault into the saddle and brandish his good lance was but the work of a moment. Others of his men quickly came up, and the clash of arms reaching the ears of the Spaniards, who had gone in pursuit, they returned, and, after a desperate conflict, forced the enemy from the city. Their retreat, however, was intercepted by the cavalry, returning from the country, and, thus hemmed in between the opposite columns, they were cut to pieces, or saved themselves only by plunging into the lake.[1]

This was the greatest personal danger which Cortés had yet encountered. His life was in the power of the barbarians, and, had it not been for their eagerness to take him prisoner, he must undoubtedly have lost it. To the same cause may be frequently attributed the preservation of

[1] Rel. Terc. de Cortés, ap. Lorenzana, p. 226.— Herrera, Hist. general, dec. 3, lib. 1, cap. 8.— Oviedo, Hist. de las Ind., MS., lib. 33, cap. 21.— This is the general's own account of the matter. Diaz, however, says that he was indebted for his rescue to a Castilian, named Olea, supported by some Tlascalans, and that his preserver received three severe wounds himself on the occasion. (Hist. de la Conquista, cap. 145.) This was an affair, however, in which Cortés ought to be better informed than any one else, and one, moreover, not likely to slip his memory. The old soldier has probably confounded it with another and similar adventure of his commander.

the Spaniards in these engagements. The next day he sought, it is said, for the Tlascalan who came so boldly to his rescue, and, as he could learn nothing of him, he gave the credit of his preservation to his patron, St. Peter.[1] He may well be excused for presuming the interposition of his good Genius to shield him from the awful doom of the captive,—a doom not likely to be mitigated in his case. That heart must have been a bold one, indeed, which, from any motive, could voluntarily encounter such a peril! Yet his followers did as much, and that, too, for a much inferior reward.

The period which we are reviewing was still the age of chivalry,— that stirring and adventurous age, of which we can form little conception in the present day of sober, practical reality. The Spaniard, with his nice point of honour, high romance, and proud, vainglorious vaunt, was the true representative of that age. The Europeans generally had not yet learned to accommodate themselves to a life of literary toil, or to the drudgery of trade or the patient tillage of the soil. They left these to the hooded inmate of the cloister, the humble burgher, and the miserable serf. Arms was the only profession worthy of gentle blood,—the only career which the high-mettled cavalier could tread with honour. The New World, with its strange and mysterious perils, afforded a noble theatre for the exercise of his calling ; and the Spaniard entered on it with all the enthusiasm of a paladin of romance.

Other nations entered on it also, but with different motives. The French sent forth their missionaries to take up their dwelling among the heathen, who, in the good work of winning souls to Paradise, were content to wear—nay, sometimes seemed to court—the crown of martyrdom. The Dutch, too, had their mission, but it was one of worldly lucre, and they found a recompense for toil and suffering in their gainful traffic with the natives. While our own Puritan fathers, with the true Anglo-Saxon spirit, left their pleasant homes across the waters, and pitched their tents in the howling wilderness, that they might enjoy the sweets of civil and religious freedom. But the Spaniard came over to the New World in the true spirit of a knight-errant, courting adventure however perilous, wooing danger, as it would seem, for its own sake. With sword and lance, he was ever ready to do battle for the Faith ; and, as he raised his old war-cry of " St. Jago," he fancied himself fighting under the banner of the military apostle, and felt his single arm a match for more than a hundred infidels ! It was the expiring age of chivalry ; and Spain, romantic Spain, was the land where its light lingered longest above the horizon.

It was not yet dusk when Cortés and his followers re-entered the city ; and the general's first act was to ascend a neighbouring *teocalli* and reconnoitre the surrounding country. He there beheld a sight which

---

[1] " Otro Dia buscó Cortés al Indio, que le ocorrió, i muerto, ni vivo no pareció ; i Cortés, por la devocion de San Pedro, juzgo que él le avia aiudado." Herrera, Hist. general, dec. 3, lib. 1, cap. 8.

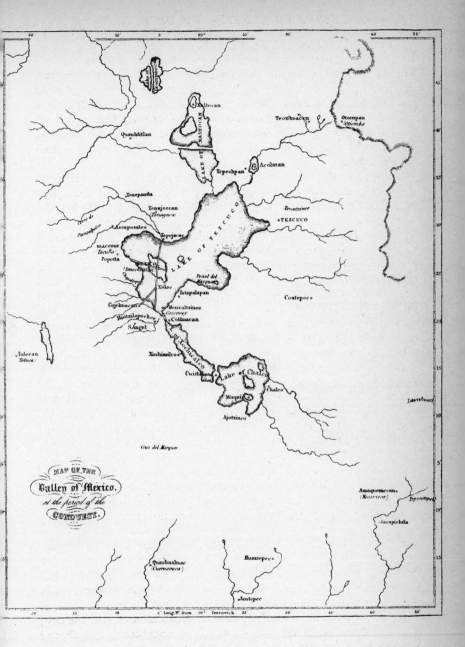

MAP OF THE
Valley of Mexico,
at the period of the
CONQUEST.

might have troubled a bolder spirit than his. The surface of the salt lake was darkened with canoes, and the causeway, for many a mile, with Indian squadrons, apparently on their march towards the Christian camp. In fact, no sooner had Guatemozin been apprised of the arrival of the white men at Xochimilco than he mustered his levies in great force to relieve the city. They were now on their march, and, as the capital was but four leagues distant, would arrive soon after nightfall.[1]

Cortés made active preparations for the defence of his quarters. He stationed a corps of pikemen along the landing where the Aztecs would be likely to disembark. He doubled the sentinels, and, with his principal officers, made the rounds repeatedly in the course of the night. In addition to other causes for watchfulness, the bolts of the crossbowmen were nearly exhausted, and the archers were busily employed in preparing and adjusting shafts to the copper heads, of which great store had been provided for the army. There was little sleep in the camp that night.[2]

It passed away, however, without molestation from the enemy. Though not stormy, it was exceedingly dark. But, although the Spaniards on duty could see nothing they distinctly heard the sound of many oars in the water, at no great distance from the shore. Yet those on board the canoes made no attempt to land, distrusting, or advised, it may be, of the preparations made for their reception. With early dawn they were under arms, and, without waiting for the movement of the Spaniards, poured into the city and attacked them in their own quarters.

The Spaniards, who were gathered in the area round one of the *teocallis*, were taken at disadvantage in the town, where the narrow lanes and streets, many of them covered with a smooth and slippery cement, offered obvious impediments to the manœuvres of cavalry. But Cortés hastily formed his musketeers and crossbowmen, and poured such a lively, well-directed fire into the enemy's ranks as threw him into disorder and compelled him to recoil. The infantry, with their long pikes, followed up the blow ; and the horse, charging at full speed as the retreating Aztecs emerged from the city, drove them several miles along the mainland.

At some distance, however, they were met by a strong reinforcement of their countrymen, and, rallying, the tide of battle turned, and the cavaliers, swept along by it, gave the rein to their steeds and rode back at full gallop towards the town. They had not proceeded very far, when they came upon the main body of the army, advancing rapidly to their support. Thus strengthened, they once more returned to the charge, and the rival hosts met together in full career, with the shock of an earthquake. For a time, victory seemed to hang in the balance, as the mighty press

---

[1] "Por el Agua á una muy grande flota de Canoas, que creo, que pasaban de dos mil ; y en ellas venian mas de doce mil Hombres de Guerra ; é por la Tierra llegó tanta multitud de Gente, que todos los Campos cubrian." Rel. Terc. de Cortés, ap. Lorenzana, p. 227.

[2] "Y acordóse que huviesse mui buena vela en todo nuestro Real, repartida á los puertos, é azequias por donde auian de venir á desembarcar, y los de acauallo mui á punto toda la noche ensillados y enfrenados, aguardando en la calçada, y tierra firme, y todos los Capitanes, y Cortés con ellos, haziendo vela y ronda toda la noche." Bernal Diaz, Hist. de la Conquista, cap. 145.

reeled to and fro under the opposite impulse, and a confused shout rose up towards heaven, in which the war-whoop of the savage was mingled with the battle-cry of the Christian,—a still stranger sound on these sequestered shores. But, in the end, Castilian valour, or rather Castilian arms and discipline, proved triumphant. The enemy faltered, gave way, and, recoiling step by step, the retreat soon terminated in a rout, and the Spaniards, following up the flying foe, drove them from the field with such dreadful slaughter that they made no further attempt to renew the battle.

The victors were now undisputed masters of the city. It was a wealthy place, well stored with Indian fabrics, cotton, gold, feather-work, and other articles of luxury and use, affording a rich booty to the soldiers. While engaged in the work of plunder, a party of the enemy, landing from their canoes, fell on some of the stragglers, laden with merchandise, and made four of them prisoners. It created a greater sensation among the troops than if ten times that number had fallen on the field. Indeed, it was rare that a Spaniard allowed himself to be taken alive. In the present instance the unfortunate men were taken by surprise. They were hurried to the capital, and soon after sacrificed ; when their arms and legs were cut off, by the command of the ferocious young chief of the Aztecs, and sent round to the different cities, with the assurance that this should be the fate of the enemies of Mexico ![1]

From the prisoners taken in the late engagement, Cortés learned that the forces already sent by Guatemozin formed but a small part of his levies; that his policy was to send detachment after detachment, until the Spaniards, however victorious they might come off from the contest with each individually, would, in the end, succumb from mere exhaustion, and thus be vanquished, as it were, by their own victories.

The soldiers having now sacked the city, Cortés did not care to await further assaults from the enemy in his present quarters. On the fourth morning after his arrival, he mustered his forces on a neighbouring plain. They came, many of them reeling under the weight of their plunder. The general saw this with uneasiness. They were to march, he said, through a populous country, all in arms to dispute their passage. To secure their safety, they should move as light and unencumbered as possible. The sight of so much spoil would sharpen the appetite of their enemies, and draw them on, like a flock of famished eagles after their prey. But his eloquence was lost on his men, who plainly told him they had a right to the fruit of their victories, and that what they had won with their swords they knew well enough how to defend with them.

Seeing them thus bent on their purpose, the general did not care to balk

---

[1] Diaz, who had an easy faith, states, as a fact, that the limbs of the unfortunate men were cut off *before* their sacrifice : "Manda cortar pies y braços á los tristes nuestros compañeros, y las embia por muchos pueblos nuestros amigos de los q̃ nos auian venido de paz, y les embia á dezir, que antes que bolvamos á Tezcuco, piensa no quedará ninguno de nosotros á vida, y con los coraçones y sangre hizo sacrificio á sus ídolos." (Hist. de la Conquista, cap. 145.)—This is not very probable. The Aztecs did not, like our North American Indians, torture their enemies from mere cruelty, but in conformity to the prescribed regulations of their itual. The captive was a religious victim.

their inclinations. He ordered the baggage to the centre, and placed a few of the cavalry over it ; dividing the remainder between the front and rear, in which latter post, as that most exposed to attack, he also stationed his arquebusiers and crossbowmen. Thus prepared, he resumed his march, but first set fire to the combustible buildings of Xochimilco, in retaliation for the resistance he had met there.[1] The light of the burning city streamed high into the air, sending its ominous glare far and wide across the waters, and telling the inhabitants on their margin that the fatal strangers so long predicted by their oracles had descended like a consuming flame upon their borders.[2]

Small bodies of the enemy were seen occasionally at a distance, but they did not venture to attack the army on its march, which, before noon, brought them to Cojohuacan, a large town about two leagues distant from Xochimilco. One could scarcely travel that distance in this populous quarter of the Valley without meeting with a place of considerable size, oftentimes the capital of what had formerly been an independent state. The inhabitants, members of different tribes, and speaking dialects somewhat different, belonged to the same great family of nations, who had come from the real or imaginary region of Aztlan, in the far North-west. Gathered round the shores of their Alpine sea, these petty communities continued, after their incorporation with the Aztec monarchy, to maintain a spirit of rivalry in their intercourse with one another, which—as with the cities on the Mediterranean in the feudal ages—quickened their mental energies, and raised the Mexican Valley higher in the scale of civilization than most other quarters of Anahuac.

The town at which the army had now arrived was deserted by its inhabitants ; and Cortés halted two days there to restore his troops and give the needful attention to the wounded.[3] He made use of the time to reconnoitre the neighbouring ground, and, taking with him a strong detachment, descended on the causeway which led from Cojohuacan to the great avenue of Iztapalapan.[4] At the point of intersection, called

[1] "Y al cabo dejándola toda quemada y asolada nos partímos ; y cierto era mucho para ver, porque tenia muchas Casas, y Torres de sus Idolos de cal y canto." Rel. Terc. de Cortés, ap. Lorenzana, p. 228.

[2] For other particulars of the actions at Xochimilco, see Oviedo, Hist. de las Ind., MS., lib. 23, cap. 21,—Herrera, Hist. general, dec. 3, lib. 1, cap. 8, 11,—Ixtlilxochitl, Venida de los Españoles, p. 18, —Torquemada, Monarch. Ind., lib. 4, cap. 87, 88, —Bernal Diaz, Hist. de la Conquista, cap. 145.— The Conqueror's own account of these engagements has not his usual perspicuity, perhaps from its brevity. A more than ordinary confusion, indeed, prevails in the different reports of them, even those proceeding from contemporaries, making it extremely difficult to collect a probable narrative from authorities not only contradicting one another, but themselves. It is rare, at any time, that two accounts of a battle coincide in all respects ; the range of observation for each individual is necessarily so limited and different, and it is so difficult to make a cool observation at all, in the hurry and heat of conflict. Any one who has conversed with the sur-

vivors will readily comprehend this, and be apt to conclude that, wherever he may look for truth, it will hardly be on the battle-ground.

[3] This place, recommended by the exceeding beauty of its situation, became, after the Conquest, a favourite residence of Cortés, who founded a nunnery in it, and commanded in his will that his bones should be removed thither from any part of the world in which he might die : "Que mis huesos —los lleven á la mi Villa de Coyoacan, y allí les den tierra en el Monesterio de Monjas, que mando hacer y edificar en la dicha mi Villa." Testamento de Hernan Cortés, MS.

[4] This, says Archbishop Lorenzana, was the modern *calzada de la Piedad.* (Rel. Terc. de Cortés, p. 229, nota.) But it is not easy to reconcile this with the elaborate chart which M. de Humboldt has given of the Valley. A short arm, which reached from this city in the days of the Aztecs, touched obliquely the great southern avenue by which the Spaniards first entered the capital. As the waters which once entirely surrounded Mexico have shrunk into their narrow basin, the face of the country has undergone a great change, and, though the founda-

Xoloc, he found a strong barrier, or fortification, behind which a Mexican force was intrenched. Their archery did some mischief to the Spaniards as they came within bowshot. But the latter, marching intrepidly forward in face of the arrowy shower, stormed the works, and, after an obstinate struggle, drove the enemy from their position.[1] Cortés then advanced some way on the great causeway of Iztapalapan; but he beheld the farther extremity darkened by a numerous array of warriors, and, as he did not care to engage in unnecessary hostilities, especially as his ammunition was nearly exhausted, he fell back and retreated to his own quarters.

The following day, the army continued its march, taking the road to Tacuba, but a few miles distant. On the way it experienced much annoyance from straggling parties of the enemy, who, furious at the sight of the booty which the invaders were bearing away, made repeated attacks on their flanks and rear. Cortés retaliated, as on the former expedition, by one of their own stratagems, but with less success than before; for, pursuing the retreating enemy too hotly, he fell with his cavalry into an ambuscade which they had prepared for him in their turn. He was not yet a match for their wily tactics. The Spanish cavaliers were enveloped in a moment by their subtle foe, and separated from the rest of the army. But, spurring on their good steeds, and charging in a solid column together, they succeeded in breaking through the Indian array, and in making their escape, except two individuals, who fell into the enemy's hands. They were the general's own servants, who had followed him faithfully through the whole campaign, and he was deeply affected by their loss,—rendered the more distressing by the consideration of the dismal fate that awaited them. When the little band rejoined the army, which had halted, in some anxiety at their absence, under the walls of Tacuba, the soldiers were astonished at the dejected mien of their commander, which too visibly betrayed his emotion.[2]

The sun was still high in the heavens when they entered the ancient capital of the Tepanecs. The first care of Cortés was to ascend the principal *teocalli* and survey the surrounding country. It was an admirable point of view, commanding the capital, which lay but little more than a league distant, and its immediate environs. Cortés was accompanied by Alderete, the treasurer, and some other cavaliers, who had lately joined his banner. The spectacle was still new to them; and, as they gazed on the stately city, with its broad lake covered with boats and barges hurrying to and fro, some laden with merchandise, or fruits and vegetables, for the

---

tions of the principal causeways are still maintained, it is not always easy to discern vestiges of the ancient avenues.*

1 "We came to a wall which they had built across the causeway, and the foot-soldiers began to attack it; and though it was very thick and stoutly defended, and ten Spaniards were wounded, at length

they gained it, killing many of the enemy, although the musketeers were without powder and the bowmen without arrows." Rel. Terc., ubi supra.

2 "Y estando en esto viene Cortés, con el qual nos alegrámos, puesto que él venia muy triste y como lloroso." Bernal Diaz, Hist. de la Conquista, cap. 145.

* ["La calzada de Iztapalapan," says Alaman, who has made a minute study of the topography, "es la de San Antonio Abad, que conduce á San Augustin de las Cuevas ó Tlalpam."—Ed.]

markets of Tenochtitlan, others crowded with warriors, they could not withhold their admiration at the life and activity of the scene, declaring that nothing but the hand of Providence could have led their countrymen safe through the heart of this powerful empire.[1]

In the midst of the admiring circle, the brow of Cortés alone was observed to be overcast, and a sigh, which now and then stole audibly from his bosom, showed the gloomy working of his thoughts.[2] "Take comfort," said one of the cavaliers, approaching his commander, and wishing to console him, in his rough way, for his recent loss; "you must not lay these things so much to heart; it is, after all, but the fortune of war." The general's answer showed the nature of his meditations. "You are my witness," said he, "how often I have endeavoured to persuade yonder capital peacefully to submit. It fills me with grief when I think of the toil and the dangers my brave followers have yet to encounter before we can call it ours. But the time is come when we must put our hands to the work."[3]

There can be no doubt that Cortés, with every other man in his army, felt he was engaged on a holy crusade, and that, independently of personal considerations, he could not serve Heaven better than by planting the Cross on the blood-stained towers of the heathen metropolis. But it was natural that he should feel some compunction as he gazed on the goodly scene, and thought of the coming tempest, and how soon the opening blossoms of civilization which there met his eye must wither under the rude breath of War. It was a striking spectacle, that of the great Conqueror thus brooding in silence over the desolation he was about to bring on the land! It seems to have made a deep impression on his soldiers, little accustomed to such proofs of his sensibility; and it forms the burden of some of those *romances*, or national ballads, with which the Castilian minstrel, in the olden time, delighted to commemorate the favourite heroes of his country, and which, coming mid-way between oral tradition and chronicle, have been found as imperishable a record as chronicle itself.[4]

Tacuba was the point which Cortés had reached on his former expedition round the northern side of the Valley. He had now, therefore, made

---

1 "Pues quando viéron la gran ciudad de México, y la laguna, y tanta multitud de canoas, que vnas ivan cargadas con bastimentos, y otras ivan á pescar, y otras valdías, mucho mas se espantáron, porque no las auian visto, hasta en aquella saçon : y dixéron, que nuestra venida en esta Nueua España, que no eran cosas de hombres humanos, sino que la gran misericordia de Dios era quiē nos sostenia." Bernal Diaz, Hist. de la Conquista, cap. 145.

2 "En este instante suspiró Cortés cō vna muy grā tristeza, mui mayor q̃ la q̃ de antes traia." Ibid., loc. cit.

3 "Y Cortés le dixo, que ya veia quantas vezes auia embiado á México á rogalles con la paz, y que la tristeza no la tenia por sola vna cosa, sino en pensar en los grandes trabajos en que nos auiamos de ver, hasta tornar á señorear ; y que con la ayuda de Dios presto lo porniamos por la obra." Ibid., ubi supra.

4 Diaz gives the opening *redondillas* of the *romance*, which I have not been able to find in any of the printed collections :—

"En Tacuba está Cortés,
cō su esquadron esforçado,
triste estaua, y muy penoso,
triste, y con gran cuidado,
la vna mano en la mexilla,
y la otra en el costado," etc.

It may be thus done into pretty literal doggerel :—

In Tacuba stood Cortés,
With many a care opprest,
Thoughts of the past came o'er him,
And he bowed his haughty crest.
One hand upon his cheek he laid,
The other on his breast,
While his valiant squadrons round him, etc.

the entire circuit of the great lake; had reconnoitred the several approaches to the capital, and inspected with his own eyes the dispositions made on the opposite quarters for its defence.   He had no occasion to prolong his stay in Tacuba, the vicinity of which to Mexico must soon bring on him its whole warlike population.

Early on the following morning he resumed his march, taking the route pursued in the former expedition north of the small lakes.   He met with less annoyance from the enemy than on the preceding days ; a circumstance owing in some degree, perhaps, to the state of the weather, which was exceedingly tempestuous.   The soldiers, with their garments heavy with moisture, ploughed their way with difficulty through miry roads flooded by the torrents.   On one occasion, as their military chronicler informs us, the officers neglected to go the rounds of the camp at night, and the sentinels to mount guard, trusting to the violence of the storm for their protection.   Yet the fate of Narvaez might have taught them not to put their faith in the elements.

At Acolman, in the Acolhuan territory, they were met by Sandoval, with the friendly cacique of Tezcuco, and several cavaliers, among whom were some recently arrived from the Islands.   They cordially greeted their countrymen, and communicated the tidings that the canal was completed, and that the brigantines, rigged and equipped, were ready to be launched on the bosom of the lake.   There seemed to be no reason, therefore, for longer postponing operations against Mexico.—With this welcome intelligence, Cortés and his victorious legions made their entry for the last time into the Acolhuan capital, having consumed just three weeks in completing the circuit of the Valley.

CHAPTER IV.

CONSPIRACY IN THE ARMY.—BRIGANTINES LAUNCHED.—MUSTER OF FORCES. —EXECUTION OF XICOTENCATL.—MARCH OF THE ARMY.—BEGINNING OF THE SIEGE.

(1521.)

AT the very time when Cortés was occupied with reconnoitring the Valley, preparatory to his siege of the capital, a busy faction in Castile was labouring to subvert his authority and defeat his plans of conquest altogether.   The fame of his brilliant exploits had spread not only through the Isles, but to Spain and many parts of Europe, where a general admiration was felt for the invincible energy of the man who with his single arm, as it were, could so long maintain a contest with the powerful Indian empire.   The absence of the Spanish monarch from his dominions, and the troubles of the country, can alone explain the supine indifference shown by the government to the prosecution of this great enterprise. To the same causes it may be ascribed that no action was had in regard to the suits of Velasquez and Narvaez, backed as they were by so potent an advocate as Bishop Fonseca, president of the Council of the Indies. The reins of government had fallen into the hands of Adrian of Utrecht, Charles's preceptor, and afterwards Pope,—a man of learning, and not without sagacity, but slow and timid in his policy, and altogether incapable of that decisive action which suited the bold genius of his predecessor, Cardinal Ximenes.

In the spring of 1521, however, a number of ordinances passed the Council of the Indies, which threatened an important innovation in the affairs of New Spain. It was decreed that the Royal Audience of His- paniola should abandon the proceedings already instituted against Narvaez for his treatment of the commissioner Ayllon; that that unfortunate commander should be released from his confinement at Vera Cruz; and that an arbitrator should be sent to Mexico with authority to investigate the affairs and conduct of Cortés and to render ample justice to the governor of Cuba. There were not wanting persons at court who looked with dissatisfaction on these proceedings, as an unworthy requital of the services of Cortés, and who thought the present moment, at any rate, not the most suitable for taking measures which might discourage the general and perhaps render him desperate. But the arrogant temper of the bishop of Burgos overruled all objections; and the ordinances, having been approved by the Regency, were signed by that body, April 11, 1521. A person named Tápia, one of the functionaries of the Audience at St. Domingo, was selected as the new commissioner to be despatched to Vera Cruz. Fortunately, circumstances occurred which postponed the execu- tion of the design for the present, and permitted Cortés to go forward unmolested in his career of conquest.[1]

But while thus allowed to remain, for the present at least, in possession of authority, he was assailed by a danger nearer home, which menaced not only his authority, but his life. This was a conspiracy in the army, of a more dark and dangerous character than any hitherto formed there. It was set on foot by a common soldier, named Antonio Villafaña, a native of Old Castile, of whom nothing is known but his share in this transaction. He was one of the troop of Narvaez,—that leaven of dis- affection, which had remained with the army, swelling with discontent on every light occasion, and ready at all times to rise into mutiny. They had voluntarily continued in the service after the secession of their comrades at Tlascala; but it was from the same mercenary hopes with which they had originally embarked in the expedition, — and in these they were destined still to be disappointed. They had little of the true spirit of adventure which distinguished the old companions of Cortés; and they

1 Herrera, Hist. general, dec. 3, lib. 1, cap. 15.—Relacion de Alonso de Verzara, Escrivano Público de Vera Cruz, MS., dec. 21.

found the barren laurels of victory but a sorry recompense for all their toils and sufferings.

With these men were joined others, who had causes of personal disgust with the general; and others, again, who looked with distrust on the result of the war. The gloomy fate of their countrymen who had fallen into the enemy's hands filled them with dismay. They felt themselves the victims of a chimerical spirit in their leader, who, with such inadequate means, was urging to extremity so ferocious and formidable a foe; and they shrank with something like apprehension from thus pursuing the enemy into his own haunts, where he would gather tenfold energy from despair.

These men would have willingly abandoned the enterprise and returned to Cuba; but how could they do it? Cortés had control over the whole route from the city to the sea-coast; and not a vessel could leave its ports without his warrant. Even if he were put out of the way, there were others, his principal officers, ready to step into his place and avenge the death of their commander. It was necessary to embrace these, also, in the scheme of destruction; and it was proposed, therefore, together with Cortés to assassinate Sandoval, Olid, Alvarado, and two or three others most devoted to his interests. The conspirators would then raise the cry of liberty, and doubted not that they should be joined by the greater part of the army, or enough, at least, to enable them to work their own pleasure. They proposed to offer the command, on Cortés' death, to Francisco Verdugo, a brother-in-law of Velasquez. He was an honourable cavalier, and not privy to their design. But they had little doubt that he would acquiesce in the command thus in a manner forced upon him, and this would secure them the protection of the governor of Cuba, who, indeed, from his own hatred of Cortés, would be disposed to look with a lenient eye on their proceedings.

The conspirators even went so far as to appoint the subordinate officers, an *alguacil mayor* in place of Sandoval, a quartermaster-general to succeed Olid, and some others.[1] The time fixed for the execution of the plot was soon after the return of Cortés from his expedition. A parcel, pretended to have come by a fresh arrival from Castile, was to be presented to him while at table, and, when he was engaged in breaking open the letters, the conspirators were to fall on him and his officers and despatch them with their poniards. Such was the iniquitous scheme devised for the destruction of Cortés and the expedition. But a conspiracy, to be successful, especially when numbers are concerned, should allow but little time to elapse between its conception and its execution.

On the day previous to that appointed for the perpetration of the deed, one of the party, feeling a natural compunction at the commission of the crime, went to the general's quarters and solicited a private interview with

---

1. "Haziā Alguazil mayor é Alférez, y Alcaldes, y Regidores, y Contador, y Tesorero, y Ueedor, y otras cosas deste arte, y aun repartido entre ellos nuestros bienes, y cauallos." Bernal Diaz, Hist. de la Conquista, cap. 146.

him. He threw himself at his commander's feet, and revealed all the particulars relating to the conspiracy, adding that in Villafaña's possession a paper would be found, containing the names of his accomplices. Cortés, thunderstruck at the disclosure, lost not a moment in profiting by it. He sent for Alvarado, Sandoval, and one or two other officers marked out by the conspirator, and, after communicating the affair to them, went at once with them to Villafaña's quarters, attended by four alguacils.

They found him in conference with three or four friends, who were instantly taken from the apartment and placed in custody. Villafaña, confounded at this sudden apparition of his commander, had barely time to snatch a paper, containing the signatures of the confederates, from his bosom, and attempt to swallow it. But Cortés arrested his arm, and seized the paper. As he glanced his eye rapidly over the fatal list, he was much moved at finding there the names of more than one who had some claim to consideration in the army. He tore the scroll in pieces, and ordered Villafaña to be taken into custody. He was immediately tried by a military court hastily got together, at which the general himself presided. There seems to have been no doubt of the man's guilt. He was condemned to death, and, after allowing him time for confession and absolution, the sentence was executed by hanging him from the window of his own quarters.[1]

Those ignorant of the affair were astonished at the spectacle; and the remaining conspirators were filled with consternation when they saw that their plot was detected, and anticipated a similar fate for themselves. But they were mistaken. Cortés pursued the matter no further. A little reflection convinced him that to do so would involve him in the most disagreeable, and even dangerous, perplexities. And, however much the parties implicated in so foul a deed might deserve death, he could ill afford the loss even of the guilty, with his present limited numbers. He resolved, therefore, to content himself with the punishment of the ringleader.

He called his troops together, and briefly explained to them the nature of the crime for which Villafaña had suffered. He had made no confession, he said, and the guilty secret had perished with him. He then expressed his sorrow that any should have been found in their ranks capable of so base an act, and stated his own unconsciousness of having wronged any individual among them; but, if he had done so, he invited them frankly to declare it, as he was most anxious to afford them all the redress in his power.[2] But there was no one of his audience, whatever might be his grievances, who cared to enter his complaint at such a moment; least of all were the conspirators willing to do so, for they were too happy at having, as they fancied, escaped detection, to stand forward now in the ranks of the malcontents. The affair passed off, therefore, without further consequences.

1 Bernal Diaz, Hist. de la Conquista, cap. 146.—Oviedo, Hist. de las Ind., MS., lib. 33, cap. 48.—Herrera, Hist. general, dec. 3, lib. 1, cap. 1.　　　2 Herrera, Hist. general, ubi supra.

The conduct of Cortés in this delicate conjuncture shows great coolness, and knowledge of human nature. Had he suffered his detection, or even his suspicion, of the guilty parties to take air, it would have placed him in hostile relations with them for the rest of his life. It was a disclosure of this kind, in the early part of Louis the Eleventh's reign, to which many of the troubles of his later years were attributed.[1] The mask once torn away, there is no longer occasion to consult even appearances. The door seems to be closed against reform. The alienation, which might have been changed by circumstances or conciliated by kindness, settles into a deep and deadly rancour. And Cortés would have been surrounded by enemies in his own camp more implacable than those in the camp of the Aztecs.

As it was, the guilty soldiers had suffered too serious apprehensions to place their lives hastily in a similar jeopardy. They strove, on the contrary, by demonstrations of loyalty, and the assiduous discharge of their duties, to turn away suspicion from themselves. Cortés, on his part, was careful to preserve his natural demeanour, equally removed from distrust and—what was perhaps more difficult—that studied courtesy which intimates, quite as plainly, suspicion of the party who is the object of it. To do this required no little address. Yet he did not forget the past. He had, it is true, destroyed the scroll containing the list of the conspirators. But the man that has once learned the names of those who have conspired against his life has no need of a written record to keep them fresh in his memory. Cortés kept his eye on all their movements, and took care to place them in no situation, afterwards, where they could do him injury.[2]

This attempt on the life of their commander excited a strong sensation in the army, with whom his many dazzling qualities and brilliant military talents had made him a general favourite. They were anxious to testify their reprobation of so foul a deed, coming from their own body, and they felt the necessity of taking some effectual measures for watching over the safety of one with whom their own destinies, as well as the fate of the enterprise, were so intimately connected. It was arranged, therefore, that he should be provided with a guard of soldiers, who were placed under the direction of a trusty cavalier named Antonio de Quiñones. They constituted the general's body-guard during the rest of the campaign, watching over him day and night, and protecting him from domestic treason no less than from the sword of the enemy.

As was stated at the close of the last chapter, the Spaniards, on their return to quarters, found the construction of the brigantines completed,

---

[1] So says M. de Barante in his picturesque *rifacimento* of the ancient chronicles: "Les procès du connétable et de monsieur de Némours, bien d'autres révélations, avaient fait éclater leur mauvais vouloir, ou du moins leur peu de fidélité pour le roi; ils ne pouvaient donc douter qu'il désirât ou complotât leur ruine." Histoire des Ducs de Bourgogne (Paris, 1838), tom. xi. p. 169.

[2] "Y desde allí adelante, aunque mostraua gran voluntad á las personas que eran en la cõjuraciõ, siempre se rezelaua dellos." Bernal Diaz, Hist. de la Conquista, cap. 146.

and that they were fully rigged, equipped, and ready for service. The canal, also, after having occupied eight thousand men for nearly two months, was finished.

It was a work of great labour; for it extended half a league in length, was twelve feet wide, and as many deep. The sides were strengthened by palisades of wood, or solid masonry. At intervals, dams and locks were constructed, and part of the opening was through the hard rock. By this avenue the brigantines might now be safely introduced on the lake.[1]

Cortés was resolved that so auspicious an event should be celebrated with due solemnity. On the 28th of April, the troops were drawn up under arms, and the whole population of Tezcuco assembled to witness the ceremony. Mass was performed, and every man in the army, together with the general, confessed and received the sacrament. Prayers were offered up by Father Olmedo, and a benediction invoked on the little navy, the first—worthy of the name—ever launched on American waters.[2] The signal was given by the firing of a cannon, when the vessels, dropping down the canal, one after another, reached the lake in good order; and, as they emerged on its ample bosom, with music sounding, and the royal ensign of Castile proudly floating from their masts, a shout of admiration arose from the countless multitudes of spectators, which mingled with the roar of artillery and musketry from the vessels and the shore![3] It was a novel spectacle to the simple natives; and they gazed with wonder on the gallant ships, which, fluttering like sea-birds on their snowy pinions, bounded lightly over the waters, as if rejoicing in their element. It touched the stern hearts of the Conquerors with a glow of rapture, and, as they felt that Heaven had blessed their undertaking, they broke forth, by general accord, into the noble anthem of the *Te Deum*. But there was no one of that vast multitude for whom the sight had deeper interest than their commander. For he looked on it as the work, in a manner, of his own hands; and his bosom swelled with exultation, as he felt he was now possessed of a power strong enough to command the lake, and to shake the haughty towers of Tenochtitlan.[4]

The general's next step was to muster his forces in the great square of the capital. He found they amounted to eighty-seven horse, and eight

---

[1] Ixtlilxochitl, Venida de los Españoles, p. 19.—Rel. Terc. de Cortés, ap. Lorenzana, p. 234.—"Obra grandíssima," exclaims the Conqueror, "y mucho para ver."—"Fuéron en guarde de estos bergantines," adds Camargo, "mas de diez mil hombres de guerra con los maestros dellas, hasta que los armáron y echáron en el agua y laguna de Méjico, que fué obra de mucho efecto para tomarse Méjico." Hist. de Tlascala, MS.

[2] The brigantines were still to be seen, preserved, as precious memorials, long after the conquest, in the dockyards of Mexico. Toribio, Hist. de los Indios, MS., Parte 1, cap. 1.

[3] "Dada la señal, soltó la Presa, fuéron saliendo los Vergantines, sin tocar vno á otro, i apartándose por la Laguna, desplegáron las Vanderas, tocó la Música, dispararón su Artillería, respondió la del Exército, así de Castellanos, como de Indios." Herrera, Hist. general, dec. 3, lib. 1, cap. 6.

[4] Ibid., ubi supra.—Rel. Terc. de Cortés, ap. Lorenzana, p. 234.—Ixtlilxochitl, Venida de los Españoles, p. 19.—Oviedo, Hist. de las Ind., MS., lib. 33, cap. 48.—The last-mentioned chronicler indulges in no slight swell of exultation at this achievement of his hero, which in his opinion throws into shade the boasted exploits of the great Sesostris. "Otras muchas é notables cosas, cuenta este actor que he dicho de aqueste Rey Sesori, en que no me quiero detener, ni las tengo en tanto como esta tranchea, ó canja que es dicho, y los Vergantines de que tratamos, los quales diéron ocasion á que se oviesen mayores Thesoros é Provincias, é Reynos, que no tuvo Sesori, para la corona Real de Castilla por la industria de Hernando Cortés." Ibid., lib. 33, cap. 22.

hundred and eighteen foot, of which one hundred and eighteen were arquebusiers and crossbowmen. He had three large field-pieces of iron, and fifteen lighter guns or falconets of brass.[1] The heavier cannon had been transported from Vera Cruz to Tezcuco, a little while before, by the faithful Tlascalans. He was well supplied with shot and balls, with about ten hundred-weight of powder, and fifty thousand copper-headed arrows, made after a pattern furnished by him to the natives.[2] The number and appointments of the army much exceeded what they had been at any time since the flight from Mexico, and showed the good effects of the late arrivals from the Islands. Indeed, taking the fleet into the account, Cortés had never before been in so good a condition for carrying on his operations. Three hundred of the men were sent to man the vessels, thirteen, or rather twelve, in number, one of the smallest having been found, on trial, too dull a sailer to be of service. Half of the crews were required to navigate the ships. There was some difficulty in finding hands for this, as the men were averse to the employment. Cortés selected those who came from Palos, Moguer, and other maritime towns, and, notwithstanding their frequent claims of exemption, as hidalgos, from this menial occupation, he pressed them into the service.[3] Each vessel mounted a piece of heavy ordnance, and was placed under an officer of respectability, to whom Cortés gave a general code of instructions for the government of the little navy, of which he proposed to take the command in person.

He had already sent to his Indian confederates, announcing his purpose of immediately laying siege to Mexico, and called on them to furnish their promised levies within the space of ten days at furthest. The Tlascalans he ordered to join him in Tezcuco; the others were to assemble at Chalco, a more convenient place of rendezvous for the operations in the southern quarter of the Valley. The Tlascalans arrived within the time prescribed, led by the younger Xicotencatl, supported by Chichemecatl, the same doughty warrior who had convoyed the brigantines to Tezcuco. They came fifty thousand strong, according to Cortés,[4] making a brilliant show with their military finery, and marching proudly forward under the great national banner, emblazoned with a spread eagle, the arms of the republic.[5] With as blithe and manly a step as if they

[1] Rel. Terc. de Cortés, ap. Lorenzana, p. 234.

[2] Bernal Diaz, Hist. de la Conquista, cap. 147.

[3] Ibid., ubi supra.—*Hidalguía*, besides its legal privileges, brought with it some fanciful ones to its possessor; if, indeed, it be considered a privilege to have excluded him from many a humble, but honest calling, by which the poor man might have gained his bread. (For an amusing account of these, see Doblado's Letters from Spain, let. 2.) In no country has the *poor gentleman* afforded so rich a theme for the satirist, as the writings of Le Sage, Cervantes, and Lope de Vega abundantly show.

[4] "Y los Capitanes de Tascaltecal con toda su gente, muy lúcida, y bien armada, . . . y segun la cuenta, que los Capitanes nos diéron, pasaban de

cinquenta mil Hombres de Guerra." (Rel. Terc. de Cortés, ap. Lorenzana, p. 236.) "I toda la Gente," adds Herrera, "tardó tres Dias en entrar, segun en sus Memoriales dice Alonso de Ojeda, ni con ser Tezcuco tan gran Ciudad, cabian en ella." Hist. general, dec. 3, lib. 1, cap. 13.

[5] "Y sus váderas tēdidas, y el aue blāca q̃ tienen por armas, q̃ parece águila, con sus alas tendidas." (Bernal Diaz, Hist. de la Conquista, cap. 149.) A spread eagle of gold, Clavigero considers as the arms of the republic. (Clavigero, Stor. del Messico, tom. ii. p. 145.) But, as Bernal Diaz speaks of it as "white," it may have been the white heron, which belonged to the house of Xicotencatl.

were going to the battle-ground, they defiled through the gates of the capital, making its walls ring with the friendly shouts of "Castile and Tlascala."

The observations which Cortés had made in his late tour of reconnoissance had determined him to begin the siege by distributing his forces into three separate camps, which he proposed to establish at the extremities of the principal causeways. By this arrangement the troops would be enabled to move in concert on the capital, and be in the best position to intercept its supplies from the surrounding country. The first of these points was Tacuba, commanding the fatal causeway of the *noche triste.* This was assigned to Pedro de Alvarado, with a force consisting, according to Cortés' own statement, of thirty horse, one hundred and sixty-eight Spanish infantry, and five-and-twenty thousand Tlascalans. Cristóval de Olid had command of the second army, of much the same magnitude, which was to take up its position at Cojohuacan, the city, it will be remembered, overlooking the short causeway connected with that of Iztapalapan. Gonzalo de Sandoval had charge of the third division, of equal strength with each of the two preceding, but which was to draw its Indian levies from the forces assembled at Chalco. This officer was to march on Iztapalapan and complete the destruction of that city, begun by Cortés soon after his entrance into the Valley. It was too formidable a post to remain in the rear of the army. The general intended to support the attack with his brigantines, after which the subsequent movements of Sandoval would be determined by circumstances.[1]

Having announced his intended dispositions to his officers, the Spanish commander called his troops together, and made one of those brief and stirring harangues with which he was wont on great occasions to kindle the hearts of his soldiery. "I have taken the last step," he said; "I have brought you to the goal for which you have so long panted. A few days will place you before the gates of Mexico,—the capital from which you were driven with so much ignominy. But we now go forward under the smiles of Providence. Does any one doubt it? Let him but compare our present condition with that in which we found ourselves not twelve months since, when, broken and dispirited, we sought shelter within the walls of Tlascala; nay, with that in which we were but a few months since, when we took up our quarters in Tezcuco.[2] Since that time our strength has been nearly doubled. We are fighting the battles of the Faith, fighting for our honour, for riches, for revenge. I have brought you face to face with your foe. It is for you to do the rest."[3]

---

[1] The precise amount of each division, as given by Cortés, was,—in that of Alvarado, 30 horse, 168 Castilian infantry, and 25,000 Tlascalans; in that of Olid, 33 horse, 178 infantry, 20,000 Tlascalans; and in Sandoval's, 24 horse, 167 infantry, 30,000 Indians. (Rel. Terc., ap. Lorenzana, p. 236.) Diaz reduces the number of native troops to one-third. Hist. de la Conquista, cap. 150.

[2] "Que se alegrassen, y esforzassen mucho, pues que veian, que nuestro Señor nos encaminaba para haber victoria de nuestros Enemigos: porque bien sabian, que quando habiamos entrado en Tesaico, no habiamos trahido mas de quarenta de Caballo, y que Dios nos habia socorrido mejor, que lo habiamos pensado." Rel. Terc. de Cortés, ap. Lorenzana, p. 235.

[3] Oviedo expands what he nevertheless calls the "brebe é substancial oracion" of Cortés into treble

The address of the bold chief was answered by the thundering acclamations of his followers, who declared that every man would do his duty under such a leader; and they only asked to be led against the enemy.[1] Cortés then caused the regulations for the army, published at Tlascala, to be read again to the troops, with the assurance that they should be enforced to the letter.

It was arranged that the Indian forces should precede the Spanish by a day's march, and should halt for their confederates on the borders of the Tezcucan territory. A circumstance occurred soon after their departure which gave bad augury for the future. A quarrel had arisen in the camp at Tezcuco between a Spanish soldier and a Tlascalan chief, in which the latter was badly hurt. He was sent back to Tlascala, and the matter was hushed up, that it might not reach the ears of the general, who, it was known, would not pass it over lightly. Xicotencatl was a near relative of the injured party, and on the first day's halt he took the opportunity to leave the army, with a number of his followers, and set off for Tlascala. Other causes are assigned for his desertion.[2] It is certain that from the first he had looked on the expedition with an evil eye, and had predicted that no good would come of it. He came into it with reluctance, as, indeed, he detested the Spaniards in his heart.

His partner in the command instantly sent information of the affair to the Spanish general, still encamped at Tezcuco. Cortés, who saw at once the mischievous consequences of this defection at such a time, detached a party of Tlascalan and Tezcucan Indians after the fugitive, with instructions to prevail on him, if possible, to return to his duty. They overtook him on the road, and remonstrated with him on his conduct, contrasting it with that of his countrymen generally, and of his own father in particular, the steady friend of the white men. "So much the worse," replied the chieftain: "if they had taken my counsel, they would never have become the dupes of the perfidious strangers."[3] Finding their remonstrances received only with anger or contemptuous taunts, the emissaries returned without accomplishing their object.

Cortés did not hesitate on the course he was to pursue. "Xicotencatl," he said, "had always been the enemy of the Spaniards, first in the field, and since in the council-chamber; openly, or in secret, still the same,— their implacable enemy. There was no use in parleying with the false-hearted Indian." He instantly despatched a small body of horse with an

---

the length of it as found in the general's own pages; in which he is imitated by most of the other chroniclers. Hist. de las Ind., MS., lib. 33, cap. 22.

[1] "Y con estas últimas palabras cesó; y todos respondiéron sin discrepancia, é á una voce dicentes; Sirvanse Dios y el Emperador nuestro Señor de tan buen capitan, y de nosotros, que asi lo harémos todos como quien somos, y como se debe esperar de buenos Españoles, y con tanta voluntad, y deseo, dicho que parecia que cada hora les era perder vn año de tiempo por estar ya á las manos con los Enemigos." Oviedo, Hist. de las Ind., MS., ubi supra.

[2] According to Diaz, the desire to possess himself of the lands of his comrade Chichemecatl, who remained with the army (Hist. de la Conquista, cap. 150); according to Herrera, it was an amour that carried him home. (Hist. general, dec. 3, lib. 1, cap. 17.) Both and all agree on the chief's aversion to the Spaniards and to the war.

[3] "Y la respuesta que le embió á dezir fué, que si el viejo de su padre, y Masse Escaci le huvieran creido, que no se huvieran señoreado tanto dellos, que les haze hazer todo lo que quiere: *y por no gastar mas palabras, dixo, que no queria venir.*" Bernal Diaz, Hist. de la Conquista, cap. 150.

alguacil to arrest the chief wherever he might be found, even though it were in the streets of Tlascala, and to bring him back to Tezcuco. At the same time, he sent information of Xicotencatl's proceedings to the Tlascalan senate, adding that desertion among the Spaniards was punished with death.

The emissaries of Cortés punctually fulfilled his orders. They arrested the fugitive chief,—whether in Tlascala or in its neighbourhood is uncertain,—and brought him a prisoner to Tezcuco, where a high gallows, erected in the great square, was prepared for his reception. He was instantly led to the place of execution; his sentence and the cause for which he suffered were publicly proclaimed, and the unfortunate cacique expiated his offence by the vile death of a malefactor. His ample property, consisting of lands, slaves, and some gold, was all confiscated to the Castilian crown.[1]

Thus perished Xicotencatl, in the flower of his age,—as dauntless a warrior as ever led an Indian army to battle. He was the first chief who successfully resisted the arms of the invaders; and, had the natives of Anahuac, generally, been animated with a spirit like his, Cortés would probably never have set foot in the capital of Montezuma. He was gifted with a clearer insight into the future than his countrymen; for he saw that the European was an enemy far more to be dreaded than the Aztec. Yet, when he consented to fight under the banner of the white men, he had no right to desert it, and he incurred the penalty prescribed by the code of savage as well as of civilized nations. It is said, indeed, that the Tlascalan senate aided in apprehending him, having previously answered Cortés that his crime was punishable with death by their own laws.[2] It was a bold act, however, thus to execute him in the midst of his people. For he was a powerful chief, heir to one of the four seigniories of the republic. His chivalrous qualities made him popular, especially with the younger part of his countrymen; and his garments were torn into shreds at his death and distributed as sacred relics among them. Still, no resistance was offered to the execution of the sentence, and no commotion followed it. He was the only Tlascalan who ever swerved from his loyalty to the Spaniards.

According to the plan of operations settled by Cortés, Sandoval, with his division, was to take a southern direction, while Alvarado and Olid would make the northern circuit of the lakes. These two cavaliers, after getting possession of Tacuba, were to advance to Chapoltepec and

---

[1] So says Herrera, who had in his possession the memorial of Ojeda, one of the Spaniards employed to apprehend the chieftain. (Hist. general, dec. 3, lib. 1, cap. 17, and Torquemada, Monarch. Ind., lib. 4, cap. 90.) Bernal Diaz, on the other hand, says that the Tlascalan chief was taken and executed on the road. (Hist. de la Conquista, cap. 150.) But the latter chronicler was probably absent at the time with Alvarado's division, in which he served. Solís, however, prefers his testimony, on the ground that Cortés would not have hazarded the execution of Xicotencatl before the eyes of his own troops.

(Conquista, lib. 5, cap. 19.) But the Tlascalans were already well on their way towards Tacuba. A very few only could have remained in Tezcuco, which was occupied by the citizens and the Castilian army,—neither of them very likely to interfere in the prisoner's behalf. His execution there would be an easier matter than in the territory of Tlascala, which he had probably reached before his apprehension.

[2] Herrera, Hist. general, dec. 3, lib. 1, cap. 17.—Torquemada, Monarch. Ind., lib. 4, cap. 90.

demolish the great aqueduct there, which supplied Mexico with water. On the tenth of May they commenced their march; but at Acolman, where they halted for the night, a dispute arose between the soldiers of the two divisions, respecting their quarters. From words they came to blows, and a defiance was even exchanged between the leaders, who entered into the angry feelings of their followers.[1] Intelligence of this was soon communicated to Cortés, who sent at once to the fiery chiefs, imploring them, by their regard for him and the common cause, to lay aside their differences, which must end in their own ruin and that of the expedition. His remonstrance prevailed, at least, so far as to establish a show of reconciliation between the parties. But Olid was not a man to forget, or easily to forgive; and Alvarado, though frank and liberal, had an impatient temper much more easily excited than appeased. They were never afterwards friends.[2]

The Spaniards met with no opposition on their march. The principal towns were all abandoned by the inhabitants, who had gone to strengthen the garrison of Mexico, or taken refuge with their families among the mountains. Tacuba was in like manner deserted, and the troops once more established themselves in their old quarters in the lordly city of the Tepanecs.[3]

Their first undertaking was to cut off the pipes that conducted the water from the royal streams of Chapoltepec to feed the numerous tanks and fountains which sparkled in the courtyards of the capital. The aqueduct, partly constructed of brickwork and partly of stone and mortar, was raised on a strong though narrow dike, which transported it across an arm of the lake; and the whole work was one of the most pleasing monuments of Mexican civilization. The Indians, well aware of its importance, had stationed a large body of troops for its protection. A battle followed, in which both sides suffered considerably, but the Spaniards were victorious. A part of the aqueduct was demolished, and during the siege no water found its way again to the capital through this channel.

On the following day the combined forces descended on the fatal causeway, to make themselves masters, if possible, of the nearest bridge. They found the dike covered with a swarm of warriors, as numerous as on the night of their disaster, while the surface of the lake was dark with the multitude of canoes. The intrepid Christians strove to advance under a perfect hurricane of missiles from the water and the land, but they made

[1] "Y sobre ello ya auiamos echado mano á las armas los de nuestra Capitania contra los de Christóual de Oli, y aun los Capitanes desafiados." Bernal Diaz, Hist. de la Conquista, cap. 150.

[2] Bernal Diaz, Hist. de la Conquista, cap. 150.—Rel. Terc. de Cortés, ap. Lorenzana, p. 237.—Gomara, Crónica, cap. 130.—Oviedo, Hist. de las Ind., MS., lib. 33, cap. 22.

[3] The Tepanec capital, shorn of its ancient splendours, is now only interesting from its historic associations. "These plains of Tacuba." says the spirited author of "Life in Mexico," "once the theatre of fierce and bloody conflicts, and where, dur ng the siege of Mexico, Alvarado 'of the leap' fixed his camp, now present a very tranquil scene. Tacuba itself is now a small village of mud huts, with some fine old trees, a few very old ruined houses, a ruined church, and some traces of a building, which —— assured us had been the palace of their last monarch; whilst others declare it to have been the site of the Spanish encampment." Vol. i. let. 13.

slow progress. Barricades thrown across the causeway embarrassed the cavalry and rendered it nearly useless. The sides of the Indian boats were fortified with bulwarks, which shielded the crews from the arquebuses and crossbows ; and, when the warriors on the dike were hard pushed by the pikemen, they threw themselves fearlessly into the water, as if it were their native element, and, reappearing along the sides of the dike, shot off their arrows and javelins with fatal execution. After a long and obstinate struggle, the Christians were compelled to fall back on their own quarters with disgrace, and—including the allies—with nearly as much damage as they had inflicted on the enemy. Olid, disgusted with the result of the engagement, inveighed against his companion as having involved them in it by his wanton temerity, and drew off his forces the next morning to his own station at Cojohuacan.

The camps, separated by only two leagues, maintained an easy communication with each other. They found abundant employment in foraging the neighbouring country for provisions, and in repelling the active sallies of the enemy ; on whom they took their revenge by cutting off his supplies. But their own position was precarious, and they looked with impatience for the arrival of the brigantines under Cortés. It was in the latter part of May that Olid took up his quarters at Cojohuacan ; and from that time may be dated the commencement of the siege of Mexico.[1]

CHAPTER V.

INDIAN FLOTILLA DEFEATED.— OCCUPATION OF THE CAUSEWAYS.— DESPERATE ASSAULTS.—FIRING OF THE PALACES.—SPIRIT OF THE BESIEGED.—BARRACKS FOR THE TROOPS.

(1521.)

No sooner had Cortés received intelligence that his two officers had established themselves in their respective posts, than he ordered Sandoval to march on Iztapalapan. The cavalier's route led him through a country for the most part friendly ; and at Chalco his little body of Spaniards was swelled by the formidable muster of Indian levies who awaited there his approach. After this junction, he continued his march without opposition till he arrived before the hostile city, under whose walls he found a

---

[1] Rel. Terc. de Cortés, ap. Lorenzana, pp. 237–239.—Ixtlilxochitl, Hist. Chich., MS., cap. 94.—Oviedo, Hist. de las Ind., MS., lib. 33, cap. 22.—Bernal Diaz, Hist. de la Conquista, cap. 50.—Gomara, Crónica, cap. 130.—Clavigero settles this date at the day of Corpus Christi, May 30th. (Clavigero, Stor. del Messico, tom. iii. p. 196.) But the Spaniards left Tezcuco May 10th, according to Cortés ; and three weeks could not have intervened between their departure and their occupation of Cojohuacan. Clavigero disposes of this difficulty, it is true, by dating the beginning of their march on the 20th instead of the 10th of May : following the chronology of Herrera, instead of that of Cortés. Surely the general is the better authority of the two.

large force drawn up to receive him. A battle followed, and the natives, after maintaining their ground sturdily for some time, were compelled to give way, and to seek refuge either on the water, or in that part of the town which hung over it. The remainder was speedily occupied by the Spaniards.

Meanwhile, Cortés had set sail with his flotilla, intending to support his lieutenant's attack by water. On drawing near the southern shore of the lake, he passed under the shadow of an insulated peak, since named from him the "Rock of the Marquis." It was held by a body of Indians, who saluted the fleet, as it passed, with showers of stones and arrows. Cortés, resolving to punish their audacity, and to clear the lake of his troublesome enemy, instantly landed with a hundred and fifty of his followers. He placed himself at their head, scaled the steep ascent, in the face of a driving storm of missiles, and, reaching the summit, put the garrison to the sword. There was a number of women and children, also, gathered in the place, whom he spared.[1]

On the top of the eminence was a blazing beacon, serving to notify to the inhabitants of the capital when the Spanish fleet weighed anchor. Before Cortés had regained his brigantine, the canoes and *piraguas* of the enemy had left the harbours of Mexico, and were seen darkening the lake for many a rood. There were several hundred of them, all crowded with warriors, and advancing rapidly by means of their oars over the calm bosom of the waters.[2]

Cortés, who regarded his fleet, to use his own language, as "the key of the war," felt the importance of striking a decisive blow in the first encounter with the enemy.[3] It was with chagrin, therefore, that he found his sails rendered useless by the want of wind. He calmly awaited the approach of the Indian squadron, which, however, lay on their oars at something more than musket-shot distance, as if hesitating to encounter these leviathans of their waters. At this moment, a light air from land rippled the surface of the lake ; it gradually freshened into a breeze, and Cortes, taking advantage of the friendly succour, which he may be excused, under all the circumstances, for regarding as especially sent him by Heaven, extended his line of battle, and bore down, under full press of canvas, on the enemy.[4]

The latter no sooner encountered the bows of their formidable opponents than they were overturned and sent to the bottom by the shock, or so much damaged that they speedily filled and sank. The water was

---

[1] "It was a beautiful victory," exclaims the Conqueror. "É entrámoslos de tal manera, que ninguno de ellos se escapó, excepto las Mugeres, y Niños ; y en este combate me hiriéron veinte y cinco Españoles, pero fué muy hermosa Victoria." Rel. Terc. ap. Lorenzana, p. 241.

[2] About five hundred boats, according to the general's own estimate (Ibid., loc. cit.) ; but more than four thousand, according to Bernal Diaz (Hist. de la Conquista, cap. 150) : who, however, was not present.

[3] "Y como yo deseaba mucho, que el primer reencuentro, que con ellos obiessemos, fuesse de mucha victoria ; y se hiciesse de manera, que ellos cobrassen mucho temor de los bergantines, porque la llave de toda la Guerra estaba en ellos." Rel. Terc., ap. Lorenzana, pp. 241, 242.

[4] "Plugo á nuestro Señor, que estándonos mirando los unos á los otros, vino un viento de la Tierra muy favorable para embestir con ellos." Ibid., p. 242.

covered with the wreck of broken canoes, and with the bodies of men struggling for life in the waves and vainly imploring their companions to take them on board their overcrowded vessels. The Spanish fleet, as it dashed through the mob of boats, sent off its volleys to the right and left with a terrible effect, completing the discomfiture of the Atecs. The latter made no attempt at resistance, scarcely venturing a single flight of arrows, but strove with all their strength to regain the port from which they had so lately issued. They were no match in the chase, any more than in the fight, for their terrible antagonist, who, borne on the wings of the wind, careered to and fro at his pleasure, dealing death widely around him, and making the shores ring with the thunders of his ordnance. A few only of the Indian flotilla succeeded in recovering the port, and, gliding up the canals, found a shelter in the bosom of the city, where the heavier burden of the brigantines made it impossible for them to follow. This victory, more complete than even the sanguine temper of Cortés had prognosticated, proved the superiority of the Spaniards, and left them, henceforth, undisputed masters of the Aztec sea.[1]

It was nearly dusk when the squadron, coasting along the great southern causeway, anchored off the point of junction, called Xoloc, where the branch from Cojohuacan meets the principal dike. The avenue widened at this point, so as to afford room for two towers, or turreted temples, built of stone, and surrounded by walls of the same material, which presented altogether a position of some strength, and, at the present moment, was garrisoned by a body of Aztecs. They were not numerous, and Cortés, landing with his soldiers, succeeded without much difficulty in dislodging the enemy and in getting possession of the works.

It seems to have been originally the general's design to take up his own quarters with Olid at Cojohuacan. But, if so, he now changed his purpose, and wisely fixed on this spot as the best position for his encampment. It was but half a league distant from the capital, and, while it commanded its great southern avenue, had a direct communication with the garrison at Cojohuacan, through which he might receive supplies from the surrounding country. Here, then, he determined to establish his headquarters. He at once caused his heavy iron cannon to be transferred from the brigantines to the causeway, and sent orders to Olid to join him with half his force, while Sandoval was instructed to abandon his present quarters and advance to Cojohuacan, whence he was to detach fifty picked men of his infantry to the camp of Cortés. Having made these arrange-

[1] Rel. Terc., ap. Lorenzana, loc. cit.—Oviedo, Hist. de las Ind., MS., lib. 33, cap. 48.—Sahagun, Hist. de Nueva-España, MS., lib. 12, cap. 32.—I may be excused for again quoting a few verses from a beautiful description in "Madoc," and one as pertinent as it is beautiful:—

"Their thousand boats, and the ten thousand oars,
From whose broad bowls the waters fall and flash,
And twice ten thousand feathered helms, and shields,
Glittering with gold and scarlet plumery.
Onward they come with song and swelling horn;
. . . . . On the other side
Advance the *British* barks; the freshening breeze
Fills the broad sail; around the rushing keel
The waters sing, while proudly they sail on,
Lords of the water."
MADOC, Part 2, canto 25.

ments, the general busily occupied himself with strengthening the works at Xoloc and putting them in the best posture of defence.

During the first five or six days after their encampment the Spaniards experienced much annoyance from the enemy, who too late endeavoured to prevent their taking up a position so near the capital, and which, had they known much of the science of war, they would have taken better care themselves to secure.   Contrary to their usual practice, the Indians made their attacks by night as well as by day.   The water swarmed with canoes, which hovered at a distance in terror of the brigantines, but still approached near enough, especially under cover of the darkness, to send showers of arrows into the Christian camp, that fell so thick as to hide the surface of the ground and impede the movements of the soldiers.   Others ran along the western side of the causeway, unprotected as it was by the Spanish fleet, and plied their archery with such galling effect that the Spaniards were forced to make a temporary breach in the dike, wide enough to admit two of their own smaller vessels, which, passing through, soon obtained as entire command of the interior basin as they before had of the outer.   Still, the bold barbarians, advancing along the causeway, marched up within bowshot of the Christian ramparts, sending forth such yells and discordant battle-cries that it seemed, in the words of Cortés, " as if heaven and earth were coming together."   But they were severely punished for their temerity, as the batteries, which commanded the approaches to the camp, opened a desolating fire, that scattered the assailants and drove them back in confusion to their own quarters.[1]

The two principal avenues to Mexico, those on the south and the west, were now occupied by the Christians.   There still remained a third, the great dike of Tepejacac, on the north, which, indeed, taking up the principal street, that passed in a direct line through the heart of the city, might be regarded as a continuation of the dike of Iztapalapan.   By this northern route a means of escape was still left open to the besieged, and they availed themselves of it, at present, to maintain their communications with the country and to supply themselves with provisions.   Alvarado, who observed this from his station at Tacuba, advised his commander of it, and the latter instructed Sandoval to take up his position on the causeway. That officer, though suffering at the time from a severe wound received from a lance in one of the late skirmishes, hastened to obey, and thus, by shutting up its only communication with the surrounding country, completed the blockade of the capital.[2]

But Cortés was not content to wait patiently the effects of a dilatory blockade, which might exhaust the patience of his allies and his

[1] " Y era tanta la multitud," says Cortés, "que por el Agua, y por la Tierra no viamos sino Gente, y daban tantas gritas, y alaridos, que parecia que se hundia el Mundo." Rel. Terc., p. 245.—Oviedo, Hist. de las Ind., MS., lib. 33, cap. 23.—Ixtlilxochitl, Hist. Chich., MS., cap. 95.—Sahagun, Historia de Nueva-España, MS., lib. 12, cap. 32.

[2] Rel. Terc. de Cortés, ap. Lorenzana, pp. 246, 247.—Bernal Diaz, Hist. de la Conquista, cap. 150. —Herrera, Hist. de las Ind., dec. 3, lib. 1, cap. 17. —Defensa, MS., cap. 28.

own resources. He determined to support it by such active assaults on the city as should still further distress the besieged and hasten the hour of surrender. For this purpose he ordered a simultaneous attack, by the two commanders at the other stations, on the quarters nearest their encampments.

On the day appointed, his forces were under arms with the dawn. Mass, as usual, was performed; and the Indian confederates, as they listened with grave attention to the stately and imposing service, regarded with undisguised admiration the devotional reverence shown by the Christians, whom, in their simplicity, they looked upon as little less than divinities themselves.[1] The Spanish infantry marched in the van, led on by Cortés, attended by a number of cavaliers, dismounted like himself. They had not moved far upon the causeway, when they were brought to a stand by one of the open breaches, that had formerly been traversed by a bridge. On the farther side a solid rampart of stone and lime had been erected, and behind this a strong body of Aztecs were posted, who discharged on the Spaniards, as they advanced, a thick volley of arrows. The latter vainly endeavoured to dislodge them with their firearms and crossbows; they were too well secured behind their defences.

Cortés then ordered two of the brigantines, which had kept along, one on each side of the causeway, in order to co-operate with the army, to station themselves so as to enfilade the position occupied by the enemy. Thus placed between two well-directed fires, the Indians were compelled to recede. The soldiers on board the vessels, springing to land, bounded like deer up the sides of the dike. They were soon followed by their countrymen under Cortés, who, throwing themselves into the water, swam the undefended chasm and joined in pursuit of the enemy. The Mexicans fell back, however, in something like order, till they reached another opening in the dike, like the former, dismantled of its bridge, and fortified in the same manner by a bulwark of stone, behind which the retreating Aztecs, swimming across the chasm, and reinforced by fresh bodies of their countrymen, again took shelter.

They made good their post, till, again assailed by the cannonade from the brigantines, they were compelled to give way. In this manner breach after breach was carried; and at every fresh instance of success a shout went up from the crews of the vessels, which, answered by the long files of the Spaniards and their confederates on the causeway, made the Valley echo to its borders.

Cortés had now reached the end of the great avenue, where it entered the suburbs. There he halted to give time for the rear-guard to come up with him. It was detained by the labour of filling up the breaches in

<hr/>

[1] " Así como fué de dia se dixo vna misa de Espíritu Santo, que todos los Christianos oyéron con mucha devocion; é aun los Indios, como simples, é no entendientes de tan alto misterio, con admiracion estaban atentos notando el silencio de los cathólicos y el acatamiento que al altar, y al sacerdote los Christianos toviéron hasta recevir la benedicion." Oviedo, Hist. de las Ind., MS., lib. 33, cap. 24.

such a manner as to make a practicable passage for the artillery and horse and to secure one for the rest of the army on its retreat. This important duty was intrusted to the allies, who executed it by tearing down the ramparts on the margins and throwing them into the chasms, and, when this was not sufficient,—for the water was deep around the southern causeway,—by dislodging the great stones and rubbish from the dike itself, which was broad enough to admit of it, and adding them to the pile, until it was raised above the level of the water.

The street on which the Spaniards now entered was the great avenue that intersected the town from north to south, and the same by which they had first visited the capital.[1] It was broad and perfectly straight, and, in the distance, dark masses of warriors might be seen gathering to the support of their countrymen, who were prepared to dispute the further progress of the Spaniards. The sides were lined with buildings, the terraced roofs of which were also crowded with combatants, who, as the army advanced, poured down a pitiless storm of missiles on their heads, which glanced harmless, indeed, from the coat of mail, but too often found their way through the more common *escaupil* of the soldier, already gaping with many a ghastly rent. Cortés, to rid himself of this annoyance for the future, ordered his Indian pioneers to level the principal buildings as they advanced; in which work of demolition, no less than in the repair of the breaches, they proved of inestimable service.[2]

The Spaniards, meanwhile, were steadily, but slowly, advancing, as the enemy recoiled before the rolling fire of musketry, though turning, at intervals, to discharge their javelins and arrows against their pursuers. In this way they kept along the great street until their course was interrupted by a wide ditch or canal, once traversed by a bridge, of which only a few planks now remained. These were broken by the Indians the moment they had crossed, and a formidable array of spears was instantly seen bristling over the summit of a solid rampart of stone, which protected the opposite side of the canal. Cortés was no longer supported by his brigantines, which the shallowness of the canals prevented from penetrating into the suburbs. He brought forward his arquebusiers, who, protected by the targets of their comrades, opened a fire on the enemy. But the balls fell harmless from the bulwarks of stone; while the assailants presented but too easy a mark to their opponents.

The general then caused the heavy guns to be brought up, and opened a lively cannonade, which soon cleared a breach in the works, through which the musketeers and crossbowmen poured in their volleys thick as

[1] [This street, which is now called the Calle del Rastro, and traverses the whole city from north to south, leading from the Calle del Relox to the causeway of Guadalupe or Tepeyacac, was known at the period immediately following the Conquest as the Calle de Iztapalapa, which name was given to it through its whole extent. In the time of the ancient Mexicans its course was intercepted by the great temple, the principal door of which fronted upon it. After this edifice had been demolished, the street was opened from one end to the other. Conquista de Méjico, (trad. de Vega), tom. ii. p. 157.]

[2] Sahagun, Hist. de Nueva-España, MS., lib. 12, cap. 32.—Ixtlilxochitl, Hist. Chich., MS., cap. 95.—Oviedo, Hist. de las Ind., MS., lib. 33, cap. 23.—Rel. Terc. de Cortés, ap. Lorenzana, pp. 247, 248.

hail. The Indians now gave way in disorder, after having held their antagonists at bay for two hours.[1] The latter, jumping into the shallow water, scaled the opposite bank without further resistance, and drove the enemy along the street towards the square, where the sacred pyramid reared its colossal bulk high over the other edifices of the city.

It was a spot too familiar to the Spaniards. On one side stood the palace of Axayacatl, their old quarters, the scene to many of them of so much suffering.[2] Opposite was the pile of low, irregular buildings once the residence of the unfortunate Montezuma;[3] while a third side of the square was flanked by the *Coatepantli*, or Wall of Serpents, which encompassed the great *teocalli* with its little city of holy edifices.[4] The Spaniards halted at the entrance of the square, as if oppressed, and for the moment overpowered, by the bitter recollections that crowded on their minds. But their intrepid leader, impatient at their hesitation, loudly called on them to advance before the Aztecs had time to rally; and, grasping his target in one hand, and waving his sword high above his head with the other, he cried his war-cry of "St. Jago," and led them at once against the enemy.[5]

The Mexicans, intimidated by the presence of their detested foe, who, in spite of all their efforts, had again forced his way into the heart of their city, made no further resistance, but retreated, or rather fled, for refuge into the sacred enclosure of the *teocalli*, where the numerous buildings scattered over its ample area afforded many good points of defence. A few priests, clad in their usual wild and blood-stained vestments, were to be seen lingering on the terraces which wound round the stately sides of the pyramid, chanting hymns in honour of their god, and encouraging the warriors below to battle bravely for his altars.[6]

The Spaniards poured through the open gates into the area, and a small party rushed up the winding corridors to its summit. No vestige now remained there of the Cross, or of any other symbol of the pure faith to which it had been dedicated. A new effigy of the Aztec war-god had taken the place of the one demolished by the Christians, and raised its

[1] Rel. Terc. de Cortés, ubi supra.—Ixtlilxochitl, Hist. Chich., MS., cap. 95.—Here terminates the work last cited of the Tezcucan chronicler; who has accompanied us from the earliest period of our narrative down to this point in the final siege of the capital. Whether the concluding pages of the manuscript have been lost, or whether he was interrupted by death, it is impossible to say. But the deficiency is supplied by a brief sketch of the principal events of the siege, which he has left in another of his writings. He had, undoubtedly, uncommon sources of information in his knowledge of the Indian languages and picture-writing, and in the oral testimony which he was at pains to collect from the actors in the scenes he describes. All these advantages are too often counterbalanced by a singular incapacity for discriminating—I will not say, between historic truth and falsehood (for what is truth?)—but between the probable, or rather the possible, and the impossible. One of the generation of primitive converts to the Romish faith, he lived in a state of twilight civilization, when, if miracles

were not easily wrought, it was at least easy to believe them.

[2] [In the street of Santa Teresa. Conquista de Méjico (trad. de Vega), tom. ii. p. 158.]

[3] [Which forms now what is called "El Empedradillo." Ibid.]

[4] [This wall, adorned with serpents, and crowned with the heads, strung together on stakes, of the human victims sacrificed in the temple, formed the front of the Plaza on the south side, extending from the corner of the Calle de Plateros east, towards the chains that enclose the cemetery of the cathedral. Ibid.]

[5] "I con todo eso no se determinaban los Christianos de entrar en la Plaça; por lo qual diciendo Hernando Cortés, que no era tiempo de mostrar cansancio, ni cobardia, con vna Rodela en la mano, apellidando Santiago, arremetió el primero." Herrera, Hist. general, dec. 3, lib. 1, cap. 18.

[6] Sahagun, Hist. de Nueva-España, MS., lib. 12, cap. 32.

fantastic and hideous form in the same niche which had been occupied by its predecessor. The Spaniards soon tore away its golden mask and the rich jewels with which it was bedizened, and, hurling the struggling priests down the sides of the pyramid, made the best of their way to their comrades in the area. It was full time.[1]

The Aztecs, indignant at the sacrilegious outrage perpetrated before their eyes, and gathering courage from the inspiration of the place, under the very presence of their deities, raised a yell of horror and vindictive fury, as, throwing themselves into something like order, they sprang, by a common impulse, on the Spaniards. The latter, who had halted near the entrance, though taken by surprise, made an effort to maintain their position at the gateway. But in vain; for the headlong rush of the assailants drove them at once into the square, where they were attacked by other bodies of Indians, pouring in from the neighbouring streets. Broken, and losing their presence of mind, the troops made no attempt to rally, but, crossing the square, and abandoning the cannon, planted there, to the enemy, they hurried down the great street of Iztapalapan. Here they were soon mingled with the allies, who choked up the way, and who, catching the panic of the Spaniards, increased the confusion, while the eyes of the fugitives, blinded by the missiles that rained on them from the *azoteas*, were scarcely capable of distinguishing friend from foe. In vain Cortés endeavoured to stay the torrent, and to restore order. His voice was drowned in the wild uproar, as he was swept away, like drift-wood, by the fury of the current.

All seemed to be lost ;—when suddenly sounds were heard in an adjoining street, like the distant tramp of horses galloping rapidly over the pavement. They drew nearer and nearer, and a body of cavalry soon emerged on the great square. Though but a handful in number, they plunged boldly into the thick of the enemy. We have often had occasion to notice the superstitious dread entertained by the Indians of the horse and his rider. And, although the long residence of the cavalry in the capital had familiarized the natives in some measure with their presence, so long a time had now elapsed since they had beheld them that all their former mysterious terrors revived in full force ; and, when thus suddenly assailed in flank by the formidable apparition, they were seized with a panic and fell into confusion. It soon spread to the leading files, and Cortés, perceiving his advantage, turned with the rapidity of lightning, and, at this time supported by his followers, succeeded in driving the enemy with some loss back into the enclosure.

It was now the hour of vespers, and, as night must soon overtake them,

[1] Ixtlilxochitl, in his Thirteenth Relacion, embracing among other things a brief notice of the capture of Mexico, of which an edition has been given to the world by the industrious Bustamante, bestows the credit of this exploit on Cortés himself. "En la capilla mayor donde estaba Huitzilopoxctli, que llegáron Cortés é Ixtlilxuchitl á un tiempo, y ambos embistiéron con el ídolo. *Cortés cogió la máscara de oro que tenia puesta este ídolo* con ciertas piedras preciosas que estaban engastadas en ella." Venida de los Españoles, p. 29.

ne made no further attempt to pursue his advantage. Ordering the trumpets, therefore, to sound a retreat, he drew off his forces in good order, taking with him the artillery which had been abandoned in the square. The allies first went off the ground, followed by the Spanish infantry, while the rear was protected by the horse, thus reversing the order of march on their entrance. The Aztecs hung on the closing files, and, though driven back by frequent charges of the cavalry, still followed in the distance, shooting off their ineffectual missiles, and filling the air with wild cries and howlings, like a herd of ravenous wolves disappointed of their prey. It was late before the army reached its quarters at Xoloc.[1]

Cortés had been well supported by Alvarado and Sandoval in this assault on the city; though neither of these commanders had penetrated the suburbs, deterred, perhaps, by the difficulties of the passage, which in Alvarado's case were greater than those presented to Cortés, from the greater number of breaches with which the dike in his quarter was intersected. Something was owing, too, to the want of brigantines, until Cortés supplied the deficiency by detaching half of his little navy to the support of his officers. Without their co-operation, however, the general himself could not have advanced so far, nor, perhaps, have succeeded at all in setting foot within the city. The success of this assault spread consternation not only among the Mexicans, but their vassals, as they saw that the formidable preparations for defence were to avail little against the white man, who had so soon, in spite of them, forced his way into the very heart of the capital. Several of the neighbouring places, in consequence, now showed a willingness to shake off their allegiance, and claimed the protection of tne Spaniards. Among these were the territory of Xochimilco, so roughly treated by the invaders, and some tribes of Otomies, a rude but valiant people, who dwelt on the western confines of the Valley.[2] Their support was valuable, not so much from the additional reinforcements which it brought, as from the greater security it gave to the army, whose outposts were perpetually menaced by these warlike barbarians.[3]

The most important aid which the Spaniards received at this time was from Tezcuco, whose prince, Ixtlilxochitl, gathered the whole strength of his levies, to the number of fifty thousand, if we are to credit Cortés, and led them in person to the Christian camp. By the general's orders, they were distributed among the three divisions of the besiegers.[4]

[1] "Los de Caballo revolvian sobre ellos, que siempre alanceaban, ó mataban algunos; é como la Calle era muy larga, hubo lugar de hacerse esto quatro, ó cinco veces. É aunque los Enemigos vian que recibian daño, venian los Perros tan rabiosos, que en ninguna manera los podiamos detener, ni que nos dejassen de seguir." Rel. Terc. de Cortés, ap. Lorenzana, p. 250.—Herrera, Hist. general, dec. 3, lib. 1, cap. 18.—Sahagun, Hist. de Nueva-España, MS., lib. 12, cap. 32.—Oviedo, Hist. de las Ind., MS., lib. 33, cap. 23.

[2] The great mass of the Otomies were an untamed race, who roamed over the broad tracts of the plateau, far away to the north. But many of them, who found their way into the Valley, became blended with the Tezcucan, and even with the Tlascalan nation, making some of the best soldiers in their armies.

[3] [The Otomies inhabited all the country of Tula on the west, where their language is well preserved. Conquista de Méjico (trad. de Vega), tom. ii. p. 161.]

[4] "Istrisuchil [Ixtlilxochitl], que es de edad de veinte y tres, ó veinte y quatro años, muy esforzado, amado, y temido de todos." (Rel. Terc. de Cortés, ap. Lorenzana, p. 251.) The greatest obscurity

Thus strengthened, Cortés prepared to make another attack upon the capital, and that before it should have time to recover from the former. Orders were given to his lieutenants on the other causeways to march at the same time, and co-operate with him, as before, in the assault. It was conducted in precisely the same manner as on the previous entry, the infantry taking the van, and the allies and cavalry following. But, to the great dismay of the Spaniards, they found two-thirds of the breaches restored to their former state, and the stones and other materials, with which they had been stopped, removed by the indefatigable enemy. They were again obliged to bring up the cannon, the brigantines ran alongside, and the enemy was dislodged, and driven from post to post, in the same manner as on the preceding attack. In short, the whole work was to be done over again. It was not till an hour after noon, that the army had won a footing in the suburbs.

Here their progress was not so difficult as before ; for the buildings, from the terraces of which they had experienced the most annoyance, had been swept away. Still, it was only step by step that they forced a passage in face of the Mexican militia, who disputed their advance with the same spirit as before. Cortés, who would willingly have spared the inhabitants, if he could have brought them to terms, saw them with regret, as he says, thus desperately bent on a war of extermination. He conceived that there would be no way more likely to affect their minds than by destroying at once some of the principal edifices, which they were accustomed to venerate as the pride and ornament of the city.[1]

Marching into the great square, he selected, as the first to be destroyed, the old palace of Axayacatl, his former barracks. The ample range of low buildings was, it is true, constructed of stone ; but the interior, as well as the outworks, the turrets, and roofs, was of wood. The Spaniards, whose associations with the pile were of so gloomy a character, sprang to the work of destruction with a satisfaction like that which the French mob may have felt in the demolition of the Bastile. Torches and firebrands were thrown about in all directions ; the lower parts of the building were speedily on fire, which, running along the inflammable hangings and wood-work of the interior, rapidly spread to the second floor. There the element took freer range, and, before it was visible from without, sent up from every aperture and crevice a dense column of vapour, that hung like a funeral pall over the city. This was dissipated by a bright sheet of flame, which enveloped all the upper regions of the vast pile, till, the supporters giving

---

prevails among historians in respect to this prince, whom they seem to have confounded very often with his brother and predecessor on the throne of Tezcuco. It is rare that either of them is mentioned by any other than his baptismal name of Hernando ; and, if Herrera is correct in the assertion that this name was assumed by both, it may explain in some degree the confusion. (Hist. general, dec. 3, lib. 1, cap. 18.) I have conformed in the main to the old Tezcucan chronicler, who gathered his account of his kinsman, as he tells us, from the records of his

nation, and from the oral testimony of the contemporaries of the prince himself. Venida de los Españoles, pp. 30, 31.

[1] " Daban ocasion, y nos forzaban á que totalmente les destruyessemos. É de esta postrera tenia mas sentimiento, y me pesaba en el alma, y pensaba que forma ternia para los atemorizar, de manera, que viniessen en conocimiento de su yerro, y de el daño, que podian recibir de nosotros, y no hacia sino quemalles, y derrocalles las Torres de sus Idolos, y sus Casas." Rel. Terc. de Cortés, ap. Lorenzana, p. 254.

way, the wide range of turreted chambers fell, amidst clouds of dust and ashes, with an appalling crash, that for a moment stayed the Spaniards in the work of devastation.[1]

It was but for a moment. On the other side of the square, adjoining Montezuma's residence, were several buildings, as the reader is aware, appropriated to animals. One of these was now marked for destruction,—the House of Birds, filled with specimens of all the painted varieties which swarmed over the wide forests of Mexico. It was an airy and elegant building, after the Indian fashion, and, viewed in connection with its object, was undoubtedly a remarkable proof of refinement and intellectual taste in a barbarous monarch. Its light, combustible materials, of wood and bamboo, formed a striking contrast to the heavy stone edifices around it, and made it obviously convenient for the present purpose of the invaders. The torches were applied, and the fanciful structure was soon wrapped in flames, that sent their baleful splendours far and wide over city and lake. Its feathered inhabitants either perished in the fire, or those of stronger wing, bursting the burning lattice-work of the aviary, soared high into the air, and, fluttering for a while over the devoted city, fled with loud screams to their native forests beyond the mountains.

The Aztecs gazed with inexpressible horror on this destruction of the venerable abode of their monarchs and of the monuments of their luxury and splendour. Their rage was exasperated almost to madness as they beheld their hated foes the Tlascalans busy in the work of desolation, and aided by the Tezcucans, their own allies, and not unfrequently their kinsmen. They vented their fury in bitter execrations, especially on the young prince Ixtlilxochitl, who, marching side by side with Cortés, took his full share in the dangers of the day. The warriors from the house-tops poured the most opprobrious epithets on him as he passed, denouncing him as a false-hearted traitor ; false to his country and his blood,—reproaches not altogether unmerited, as his kinsman, who chronicles the circumstance, candidly confesses.[2] He gave little heed to their taunts, however, holding on his way with the dogged resolution of one true to the cause in which he was embarked ; and, when he entered the great square, he grappled with the leader of the Aztec forces, wrenched a lance from his grasp, won by the latter from the Christians, and dealt him a blow with his mace, or *maquahuitl*, which brought him lifeless to the ground.[3]

The Spanish commander, having accomplished the work of destruction, sounded a retreat, sending on the Indian allies, who blocked up the way before him. The Mexicans, maddened by their losses, in wild transports of fury hung close on his rear, and, though driven back by the cavalry, still

[1] [The ruins of this building were brought to light in the process of laying the foundations of the houses recently constructed on the southern side of the street of Santa Teresa, adjoining the convent of the Conception. Conquista de Méjico (trad. de Vega), tom. ii. p. 162.]

[2] "Y desde las azoteas deshonrarle llamándole de

traidor contra su patria y deudos, y otras razones pesadas, que á la verdad *á ellos les sobraba la razon ;* mas Ixtlilxuchitl callaba y peleaba, que mas estimaba la amistad y salud de los Cristianos que todo esto." Venida de los Españoles, p. 32.

[3] Ibid., p. 29.

returned, throwing themselves desperately under the horses, striving to tear the riders from their saddles, and content to throw away their own lives for one blow at their enemy. Fortunately, the greater part of their militia was engaged with the assailants on the opposite quarters of the city, but, thus crippled, they pushed the Spaniards under Cortés so vigorously that few reached the camp that night without bearing on their bodies some token of the desperate conflict.[1]

On the following day, and, indeed, on several days following, the general repeated his assaults with as little care for repose as if he and his men had been made of iron. On one occasion he advanced some way down the street of Tacuba, in which he carried three of the bridges, desirous, if possible, to open a communication with Alvarado, posted on the contiguous causeway. But the Spaniards in that quarter had not penetrated beyond the suburbs, still impeded by the severe character of the ground, and wanting, it may be, somewhat of that fiery impetuosity which the soldier feels who fights under the eye of his chief.

In each of these assaults the breaches were found more or less restored to their original state by the pertinacious Mexicans, and the materials, which had been deposited in them with so much labour, again removed. It may seem strange that Cortés did not take measures to guard against the repetition of an act which caused so much delay and embarrassment to his operations. He notices this in his Letter to the Emperor, in which he says that to do so would have required either that he should have established his quarters in the city itself, which would have surrounded him with enemies and cut off his communications with the country, or that he should have posted a sufficient guard of Spaniards—for the natives were out of the question—to protect the breaches by night, a duty altogether beyond the strength of men engaged in so arduous service through the day.[2]

Yet this was the course adopted by Alvarado; who stationed at night a guard of forty soldiers for the defence of the opening nearest to the enemy. This was relieved by a similar detachment, in a few hours, and this again by a third, the two former still lying on their post; so that on an alarm a body of one hundred and twenty soldiers was ready on the spot to repel an attack. Sometimes, indeed, the whole division took up their bivouac in the neighbourhood of the breach, resting on their arms, and ready for instant action.[3]

But a life of such incessant toil and vigilance was almost too severe even for the stubborn constitutions of the Spaniards. "Through the long

---

[1] For the preceding pages relating to this second assault, see Rel. Terc. de Cortés, ap. Lorenzana, pp. 254-256,—Sahagun, Hist. de Nueva-España, MS., lib. 12, cap. 33,—Oviedo, Hist. de las Ind., MS., lib. 33, cap. 24,—Defensa, MS., cap. 28.

[2] Rel. Terc., ap. Lorenzana, p. 219.

[3] Bernal Diaz, Hist. de la Conquista, cap. 151.—According to Herrera, Alvarado and Sandoval did

not conceal their disapprobation of the course pursued by their commander in respect to the breaches : "I Alvarado, i Sandoval, por su parte, tambien lo hiciéron mui bien, culpando á Hernando Cortés por estas retiradas, queriendo muchos que se quedara en lo ganado, por no bolver tantas veces á ello." Hist. general, dec. 3, lib. i, cap. 19.

night," exclaims Diaz, who served in Alvarado's division, "we kept our dreary watch; neither wind, nor wet, nor cold availing anything. There we stood, smarting as we were from the wounds we had received in the fight of the preceding day." [1] It was the rainy season, which continues in that country from July to September; [2] and the surface of the causeways, flooded by the storms, and broken up by the constant movement of such large bodies of men, was converted into a marsh, or rather quagmire, which added inconceivably to the distresses of the army.

The troops under Cortés were scarcely in a better situation. But few of them could find shelter in the rude towers that garnished the works of Xoloc. The greater part were compelled to bivouac in the open air, exposed to all the inclemency of the weather. Every man, unless his wounds prevented it, was required by the camp regulations to sleep on his arms; and they were often roused from their hasty slumbers by the midnight call to battle. For Guatemozin, contrary to the usual practice of his countrymen, frequently selected the hours of darkness to aim a blow at the enemy. "In short," exclaims the veteran soldier above quoted, "so unintermitting were our engagements, by day and by night, during the three months in which we lay before the capital, that to recount them all would but exhaust the reader's patience, and make him fancy he was perusing the incredible feats of a knight-errant of romance." [3]

The Aztec emperor conducted his operations on a systematic plan, which showed some approach to military science. He not unfrequently made simultaneous attacks on the three several divisions of the Spaniards established on the causeways, and on the garrisons at their extremities. To accomplish this, he enforced the service not merely of his own militia of the capital, but of the great towns in the neighbourhood, who all moved in concert, at the well-known signal of the beacon-fire, or of the huge drum struck by the priests on the summit of the temple. One of these general attacks, it was observed, whether from accident or design, took place on the eve of St. John the Baptist, the anniversary of the day on which the Spaniards made their second entry into the Mexican capital. [4]

Notwithstanding the severe drain on his forces by this incessant warfare, the young monarch contrived to relieve them in some degree by different detachments, which took the place of one another. This was apparent from the different uniforms and military badges of the Indian battalions that successively came and disappeared from the field. At night a strict guard was maintained in the Aztec quarters, a thing not common with the

1 "Porque còmo era de noche, no aguardauan mucho, y desta manera que he dichò velauamos, que ni porque llouiesse, ni vientos, ni frios, y aunque estauamos metidos en medio de grandes lodos, y heridos, allí auiamos de estar." Hist. de la Conquista, cap. 154.

2 [That is to say, the more violent part of the rainy season, which lasts, in fact, from May or June to October. Conquista de Méjico (trad. de Vega). tom. ii. p. 165.]

3 "Porque nouenta y tres dias estuuimos sobre esta tan fuerte ciudad, cada dia é de noche teniamos guerras, y combates; é no lo pongo aqui por capítulos lo que cada dia haziamos, porque me parece que seria gran proligidad, é seria cosa para nunca acabar, y pareceria a los libros de Amadis, é de otros corros de caualleros." Hist. de la Conquista, ubi supra.

4 Bernal Diaz, Hist. de la Conquista, ubi supra. —Sahagun, Hist. de Nueva-España, MS., lib. 12 cap. 33.

nations of the plateau.   The outposts of the hostile armies were stationed within sight of each other.   That of the Mexicans was usually placed in the neighbourhood of some wide breach, and its position was marked by a large fire in front.   The hours for relieving guard were intimated by the shrill Aztec whistle, while bodies of men might be seen moving behind the flame, which threw a still ruddier glow over the cinnamon-coloured skins of the warriors.

While thus active on land, Guatemozin was not idle on the water. He was too wise, indeed, to cope with the Spanish navy again in open battle ; but he resorted to stratagem, so much more congenial to Indian warfare.   He placed a large number of canoes in ambuscade among the tall reeds which fringed the southern shores of the lake, and caused piles, at the same time, to be driven into the neighbouring shallows.   Several *piraguas,* or boats of a larger size, then issued forth, and rowed near the spot where the Spanish brigantines were moored.   Two of the smallest vessels, supposing the Indian barks were conveying provisions to the besieged, instantly stood after them, as had been foreseen.   The Aztec boats fled for shelter to the reedy thicket where their companions lay in ambush.   The Spaniards, following, were soon entangled among the palisades under the water.   They were instantly surrounded by the whole swarm of Indian canoes, most of the men were wounded, several, including the two commanders, slain, and one of the brigantines fell—a useless prize—into the hands of the victors.   Among the slain was Pedro Barba, captain of the crossbowmen, a gallant officer, who had highly distinguished himself in the Conquest.   This disaster occasioned much mortification to Cortés.   It was a salutary lesson, that stood him in good stead during the remainder of the war.[1]

Thus the contest was waged by land and by water,—on the causeway, the city, and the lake.   Whatever else might fail, the capital of the Aztec empire was true to itself, and, mindful of its ancient renown, opposed a bold front to its enemies in every direction.   As in a body whose extremities have been struck with death, life still rallied in the heart, and seemed to beat there, for the time, with even a more vigorous pulsation than ever.

It may appear extraordinary that Guatemozin should have been able to provide for the maintenance of the crowded population now gathered in the metropolis, especially as the avenues were all in the possession of the besieging army.[2]   But, independently of the preparations made with this view before the siege, and of the loathsome sustenance daily furnished by the victims for sacrifice, supplies were constantly obtained from the surrounding country across the lake.   This was so conducted, for a time, as in a great

---

[1] Bernal Diaz, Hist. de la Conquista, cap. 151.— Sahagun, Hist. de Nueva-España, MS., lib. 12, cap. 34.

[2] I recollect meeting with no estimate of their numbers ; nor, in the loose arithmetic of the Con- querors, would it be worth much.   They must, however, have been very great, to enable them to meet the assailants so promptly and efficiently on every point.

measure to escape observation; and even when the brigantines were commanded to cruise day and night, and sweep the waters of the boats employed in this service, many still contrived, under cover of the darkness, to elude the vigilance of the cruisers, and brought their cargoes into port. It was not till the great towns in the neighbourhood cast off their allegiance that the supply began to fail, from the failure of its sources. This defection was more frequent, as the inhabitants became convinced that the government, incompetent to its own defence, must be still more so to theirs; and the Aztec metropolis saw its great vassals fall off one after another, as the tree over which decay is stealing parts with its leaves at the first blast of the tempest.[1]

The cities which now claimed the Spanish general's protection supplied the camp with an incredible number of warriors; a number which, if we admit Cortes' own estimate, one hundred and fifty thousand,[2] could have only served to embarrass his operations on the long extended causeways. Yet it is true that the Valley, teeming with towns and villages, swarmed with a population—and one, too, in which every man was a warrior—greatly exceeding that of the present day. These levies were distributed among the three garrisons at the terminations of the causeways; and many found active employment in foraging the country for provisions, and yet more in carrying on hostilities against the places still unfriendly to the Spaniards.

Cortés found further occupation for them in the construction of barracks for his troops, who suffered greatly from exposure to the incessant rains of the season, which were observed to fall more heavily by night than by day. Quantities of stone and timber were obtained from the buildings that had been demolished in the city. They were transported in the brigantines to the causeway, and from these materials a row of huts or barracks was constructed, extending on either side of the works of Xoloc. It may give some idea of the great breadth of the causeway at this place, one of the deepest parts of the lake, to add that, although the barracks were erected in parallel lines on the opposite sides of it, there still remained space enough for the army to defile between.[3]

By this arrangement, ample accommodations were furnished for the Spanish troops and their Indian attendants, amounting in all to about two thousand. The great body of the allies, with a small detachment of horse and infantry, were quartered at the neighbouring post of Cojohuacan, which served to protect the rear of the encampment and to maintain its communications with the country. A similar disposition of forces took place in the other divisions of the army, under Alvarado and Sandoval, though

[1] Defensa, MS., cap. 28.—Sahagun, Hist. de Nueva-España, MS., lib. 12, cap. 34.—The principal cities were Mexicaltzinco, Cuitlahuac, Iztapalapan, Mizquiz, Huitzilopochco, Colhuacan.

[2] "Y como aquel dia llevabamos mas de ciento y cincuenta mil Hombres de Guerra." Rel. Terc., ap. Lorenzana, p. 280.

[3] "Y vea Vuestra Magestad," says Cortés to the emperor, "que tan ancha puede ser la Calzada, que va por lo mas hondo de la Laguna, que de la una parte, y de la otra iban estas Casas, y quedaba en medio hecha Calle, que muy á placer á pie, y á caballo ibamos, y veniamos por ella." Rel. Terc., ap. Lorenzana, p. 260.

the accommodations provided for the shelter of the troops on their causeways were not so substantial as those for the division of Cortés.

The Spanish camp was supplied with provisions from the friendly towns
in the neighbourhood, and especially from Tezcuco.[1] They consisted of
fish, the fruits of the country, particularly a sort of fig borne by the *tuna*
(*Cactus opuntia*), and a species of cherry, or something much resembling
it, which grew abundantly at this season. But their principal food was the
tortillas, cakes of Indian meal, still common in Mexico, for which bake-
houses were established, under the care of the natives, in the garrison towns
commanding the causeways.[2] The allies, as appears too probable, reinforced their frugal fare with an occasional banquet on human flesh, for
which the battle-field unhappily afforded them too much facility, and
which, however shocking to the feelings of Cortés, he did not consider
himself in a situation, at that moment, to prevent.[3]

Thus the tempest, which had been so long mustering, broke at length,
in all its fury, on the Aztec capital. Its unhappy inmates beheld the hostile
regions encompassing them about, with their glittering files stretching as
far as the eye could reach. They saw themselves deserted by their allies
and vassals in their utmost need; the fierce stranger penetrating into their
secret places, violating their temples, plundering their palaces, wasting the
fair city by day, firing its suburbs by night, and intrenching himself in
solid edifices under their walls, as if determined never to withdraw his
foot while one stone remained upon another. All this they saw; yet their
spirits were unbroken; and, though famine and pestilence were beginning
to creep over them, they still showed the same determined front to their
enemies. Cortés, who would gladly have spared the town and its inhabitants, beheld this resolution with astonishment. He intimated more than
once, by means of the prisoners whom he released, his willingness to grant
them fair terms of capitulation. Day after day he fully expected his
proffers would be accepted. But day after day he was disappointed.[4]

---

[1] The greatest difficulty under which the troops
laboured, according to Diaz, was that of obtaining
the requisite medicaments for their wounds. But
this was in a great degree obviated by a Catalan
soldier, who by virtue of his prayers and incanta-
tions wrought wonderful cures both on the Spaniards
and their allies. The latter, as the more ignorant,
flocked in crowds to the tent of this military Æscu-
lapius, whose success was doubtless in a direct ratio
to the faith of his patients. Hist. de la Conquista,
ubi supra.

[2] Diaz mourns over this unsavoury diet. (Hist.
de la Conquista, loc. cit.) Yet the Indian fig is an
agreeable, nutritious fruit; and the *tortilla*, made of
maize flour, with a slight infusion of lime, though
not precisely a *morceau friand*, might pass for very
tolerable camp fare. According to the lively author
of "Life in Mexico," it is made now precisely as it
was in the days of the Aztecs. If so, a cooking
receipt is almost the only thing that has not changed
in this country of revolutions.

[3] "Quo strages," says Martyr, "erat crudelior,
eo magis copiose ac opipare coenabant Guazuzingui
& Tascaltecani, cæterique prouinciales auxiliarii,
qui soliti sunt hostes in proelio cadentes intra suos

ventres sepelire; nec vetare ausus fuisset Cortesius."
(De Orbe Novo, dec. 5, cap. 8.) "Y los otros les
mostraban los de su Ciudad hechos pedazos, diciéndoles, que los habian de cenar aquella noche, y
almorzar otro dia, como de hecho lo hacian." (Rel.
Terc. de Cortés, ap. Lorenzana, p. 256.) Yet one
may well be startled by the assertion of Oviedo,
that the carnivorous monsters fished up the bloated
bodies of those drowned in the lake to swell their
repast! "Ni podian ver los ojos de los Christianos,
é Cathólicos, mas espantable é aborrecida cosa, que
ver en el Real de los Amigos confederados el continuo
exercicio de comer carne asada, ó cocida de los
Indios enemigos, é aun de los que mataban en las
canoas, ó se ahogaban, é despues el agua los echaba
en la superficie de la laguna, ó en la costa, no los
dexaban de pescar, é aposentar en sus vientres."
Hist. de las Ind., MS., lib. 33, cap. 24.

[4] "I confidently expected both on that and the
preceding day that they would come with proposals
of peace, as I had myself, whether victorious or
otherwise, constantly made overtures to that end.
But on their part we never perceived a sign of such
intention." Rel. Terc. de Cortés, ap. Lorenzana
p. 261.

He had yet to learn how tenacious was the memory of the Aztecs, and that, whatever might be the horrors of their present situation, and their fears for the future, they were all forgotten in their hatred of the white man.

CHAPTER VI.

GENERAL ASSAULT ON THE CITY.—DEFEAT OF THE SPANIARDS.—THEIR DISASTROUS CONDITION.—SACRIFICE OF THE CAPTIVES.—DEFECTION OF THE ALLIES.—CONSTANCY OF THE TROOPS.

(1521.)

FAMINE was now gradually working its way into the heart of the beleaguered city. It seemed certain that, with this strict blockade, the crowded population must in the end be driven to capitulate, though no arm should be raised against them. But it required time; and the Spaniards, though constant and enduring by nature, began to be impatient of hardships scarcely inferior to those experienced by the besieged. In some respects their condition was even worse, exposed as they were to the cold, drenching rains, which fell with little intermission, rendering their situation dreary and disastrous in the extreme.

In this state of things, there were many who would willingly have shortened their sufferings and taken the chance of carrying the place by a *coup de main.* Others thought it would be best to get possession of the great market of Tlatelolco, which, from its situation in the north-western part of the city, might afford the means of communication with the camps of both Alvarado and Sandoval. This place, encompassed by spacious porticoes, would furnish accommodations for a numerous host; and, once established in the capital, the Spaniards would be in a position to follow up the blow with far more effect than at a distance.

These arguments were pressed by several of the officers, particularly by Alderete, the royal treasurer, a person of much consideration, not only from his rank, but from the capacity and zeal he had shown in the service. In deference to their wishes, Cortés summoned a council of war, and laid the matter before it. The treasurer's views were espoused by most of the high-mettled cavaliers, who looked with eagerness to any change of their present forlorn and wearisome life; and Cortés, thinking it, probably, more prudent to adopt the less expedient course than to enforce a cold and reluctant obedience to his own opinion, suffered himself to be overruled.[1]

---

[1] Such is the account explicitly given by Cortes to the emperor. (Rel. Terc., ap. Lorenzana, p. 264.) Bernal Diaz, on the contrary, speaks of the assault as first conceived by the general himself. (Hist. de la Conquista, cap. 151.) Yet Diaz had not the best means of knowing; and Cortés would hardly have sent home a palpable misstatement that could have been so easily exposed.

A day was fixed for the assault, which was to be made simultaneously by the two divisions under Alvarado and the commander-in-chief. Sandoval was instructed to draw off the greater part of his forces from the northern causeway and to unite himself with Alvarado, while seventy picked soldiers were to be detached to the support of Cortés.

On the appointed morning, the two armies, after the usual celebration of mass, advanced along their respective causeways against the city.[1] They were supported, in addition to the brigantines, by a numerous fleet of Indian boats, which were to force a passage up the canals, and by a countless multitude of allies, whose very numbers served in the end to embarrass their operations. After clearing the suburbs, three avenues presented themselves, which all terminated in the square of Tlatelolco. The principal one, being of much greater width than the other two, might rather be called a causeway than a street, since it was flanked by deep canals on either side. Cortés divided his force into three bodies. One of them he placed under Alderete, with orders to occupy the principal street. A second he gave in charge to Andrés de Tápia and Jorge de Alvarado; the former a cavalier of courage and capacity, the latter a younger brother of Don Pedro, and possessed of the intrepid spirit which belonged to that chivalrous family. These were to penetrate by one of the parallel streets, while the general himself, at the head of the third division, was to occupy the other. A small body of cavalry, with two or three field-pieces, was stationed as a reserve in front of the great street of Tacuba, which was designated as the rallying-point for the different divisions.[2]

Cortés gave the most positive instructions to his captains not to advance a step without securing the means of retreat by carefully filling up the ditches and the openings in the causeway. The neglect of this precaution by Alvarado, in an assault which he had made on the city but a few days before, had been attended with such serious consequences to his army that Cortés rode over, himself, to his officer's quarters, for the purpose of publicly reprimanding him for his disobedience of orders. On his arrival at the camp, however, he found that his offending captain had conducted the affair with so much gallantry, that the intended reprimand—though well deserved—subsided into a mild rebuke.[3]

The arrangements being completed, the three divisions marched at once up the several streets. Cortés, dismounting, took the van of his own

---

[1] This punctual performance of mass by the army, in storm and in sunshine, by day and by night, among friends and enemies, draws forth a warm eulogium from the archiepiscopal editor of Cortés: "En el Campo, en una Calzada, entre Enemigos, trabajando dia, y noche, nunca se omitia la Missa, páraque toda la obra se atribuyesse á Dios, y mas en unos Meses, en que incomodan las Aguas de el Cielo; y encima del Agua las Habitaciones, ó malas Tiendas." Lorenzana, p. 266, nota.

[2] In the treasurer's division, according to the general's Letter, there were 70 Spanish foot, 7 or 8 horse, and 15,000 or 20,000 Indians; in Tápia's, 80 foot, and 10,000 allies; and in his own, 8 horse, 100 infantry, and "an infinite number of allies." (Ibid., ubi supra.) The looseness of the language shows that a few thousands more or less were of no great moment in the estimate of the Indian forces.

[3] "Otro dia de mañana acordé de ir á su Real para le reprehender lo pasado. . . . Y visto, no les impute tanta culpa, como antes parecia tener, y platicado cerca de lo que habia de hacer, yo me bolví á nuestro Real aquel dia." Rel. Terc. de Cortés, ap. Lorenzana, pp. 263, 264.

squadron, at the head of his infantry. The Mexicans fell back as he advanced, making less resistance than usual. The Spaniards pushed on, carrying one barricade after another, and carefully filling up the gaps with rubbish, so as to secure themselves a footing. The canoes supported the attack, by moving along the canals and grappling with those of the enemy; while numbers of the nimble-footed Tlascalans, scaling the terraces, passed on from one house to another, where they were connected, hurling the defenders into the streets below. The enemy, taken apparently by surprise, seemed incapable of withstanding for a moment the fury of the assault; and the victorious Christians, cheered on by the shouts of triumph which arose from their companions in the adjoining streets, were only the more eager to be first at the destined goal.

Indeed, the facility of his success led the general to suspect that he might be advancing too fast; that it might be a device of the enemy to draw them into the heart of the city and then surround or attack them in the rear. He had some misgivings, moreover, lest his too ardent officers, in the heat of the chase, should, notwithstanding his commands, have overlooked the necessary precaution of filling up the breaches. He accordingly brought his squadron to a halt, prepared to baffle any insidious movement of his adversary. Meanwhile he received more than one message from Alderete, informing him that he had nearly gained the market. This only increased the general's apprehension that, in the rapidity of his advance, he might have neglected to secure the ground. He determined to trust no eyes but his own, and, taking a small body of troops, proceeded at once to reconnoitre the route followed by the treasurer.

He had not proceeded far along the great street, or causeway, when his progress was arrested by an opening ten or twelve paces wide, and filled with water at least two fathoms deep, by which a communication was formed between the canals on the opposite sides. A feeble attempt had been made to stop the gap with the rubbish of the causeway, but in too careless a manner to be of the least service; and a few straggling stones and pieces of timber only showed that the work had been abandoned almost as soon as begun.[1] To add to his consternation, the general observed that the sides of the causeway in this neighbourhood had been pared off, and, as was evident, very recently. He saw in all this the artifice of the cunning enemy, and had little doubt that his hot-headed officer had rushed into a snare deliberately laid for him. Deeply alarmed, he set about repairing the mischief as fast as possible, by ordering his men to fill up the yawning chasm.

But they had scarcely begun their labours, when the hoarse echoes of

---

[1] " Y hallé, que habian pasado una quebrada de la Calle, que era de diez, ó doce pasos de ancho ; y el Agua, que por ella pasaba, era de hondura de mas de dos estados, y al tiempo que la pasáron habian echado en ella madera, y cañas de carrizo, y como pasaban pocos á pocos, y con tiento, no se habia hundido la madera y cañas." Rel. Terc. de Cortés, ap. Lorenzana, p. 268.—See also Oviedo, Hist. de las Ind., MS., ib. 33, cap. 48.

conflict in the distance were succeeded by a hideous sound of mingled yells and war-whoops, that seemed to rend the very heavens. This was followed by a rushing noise, as of the tread of thronging multitudes, showing that the tide of battle was turned back from its former course, and was rolling on towards the spot where Cortés and his little band of cavaliers were planted.

His conjecture proved too true. Alderete had followed the retreating Aztecs with an eagerness which increased with every step of his advance. He had carried the barricades which had defended the breach, without much difficulty, and, as he swept on, gave orders that the opening should be stopped. But the blood of the high-spirited cavaliers was warmed by the chase, and no one cared to be detained by the ignoble occupation of filling up the ditches, while he could gather laurels so easily in the fight; and they all pressed on, exhorting and cheering one another with the assurance of being the first to reach the square of Tlatelolco. In this way they suffered themselves to be decoyed into the heart of the city; when suddenly the horn of Guatemozin—the sacred symbol, heard only in seasons of extraordinary peril—sent forth a long and piercing note from the summit of a neighbouring *teocalli*. In an instant, the flying Aztecs, as if maddened by the blast, wheeled about, and turned on their pursuers. At the same time, countless swarms of warriors from the adjoining streets and lanes poured in upon the flanks of the assailants, filling the air with the fierce, unearthly cries which had reached the ears of Cortés, and drowning, for a moment, the wild dissonance which reigned in the other quarters of the capital.[1]

The army, taken by surprise, and shaken by the fury of the assault, was thrown into the utmost disorder. Friends and foes, white men and Indians, were mingled together in one promiscuous mass. Spears, swords, and war-clubs were brandished together in the air. Blows fell at random. In their eagerness to escape, they trod down one another. Blinded by the missiles which now rained on them from the *azoteas*, they staggered on, scarcely knowing in what direction, or fell, struck down by hands which they could not see. On they came, like a rushing torrent sweeping along some steep declivity, and rolling in one confused tide towards the open breach, on the farther side of which stood Cortés and his companions horror-struck at the sight of the approaching ruin. The foremost files soon plunged into the gulf, treading one another under the flood, some striving ineffectually to swim, others, with more success, to clamber over the heaps of their suffocated comrades. Many, as they attempted to scale the opposite sides of the slippery dike, fell into the water, or were

[1] Gomara, Crónica, cap. 138.—Ixtlilxochitl, Venida de los Españoles, p. 37.—Oviedo, Hist. de las Ind., MS., lib. 33, cap. 26.—Guatemozin's horn rang in the ears of Bernal Diaz for many a day after the battle. "Guatemuz, y manda tocar su corneta, q. era vna señal q. quando a uella se tocasse, era q. avian de pelear sus Capitanes de maner. q. hiziessen presa, ó morir sobre ello; y retumbaua el sonido, q. se metia en los oidos, y de q. lo oyéro aquellos sus esquadrones, y Capitanes : saber yo aqui dezir aora, con q. rabia, y esfuerço se metian entre nosotros á nos echar mano, es cosa de espanto." Hist. de la Conquista, cap. 152.

hurried off by the warriors in the canoes, who added to the horrors of the rout by the fresh storm of darts and javelins which they poured on the fugitives.

Cortés, meanwhile, with his brave followers, kept his station undaunted on the other side of the breach. " I had made up my mind," he says, " to die, rather than desert my poor followers in their extremity ! " [1] With outstretched hands he endeavoured to rescue as many as he could from the watery grave, and from the more appalling fate of captivity. He as vainly tried to restore something like presence of mind and order among the distracted fugitives. His person was too well known to the Aztecs, and his position now made him a conspicuous mark for their weapons. Darts, stones, and arrows fell around him thick as hail, but glanced harmless from his steel helmet and armour of proof. At length a cry of " Malinche," " Malinche," arose among the enemy ; and six of their number, strong and athletic warriors, rushing on him at once, made a violent effort to drag him on board their boat. In the struggle he received a severe wound in the leg, which for the time disabled it. There seemed to be no hope for him ; when a faithful follower, Cristóval de Olea, perceiving his general's extremity, threw himself on the Aztecs, and with a blow cut off the arm of one savage, and then plunged his sword in the body of another. He was quickly supported by a comrade named Lerma, and by a Tlascalan chief, who, fighting over the prostrate body of Cortés, despatched three more of the assailants ; though the heroic Olea paid dearly for his self-devotion, as he fell mortally wounded by the side of his general. [2]

The report soon spread among the soldiers that their commander was taken ; and Quiñones, the captain of his guard, with several others, pouring in to the rescue, succeeded in disentangling Cortés from the grasp of his enemies, who were struggling with him in the water, and, raising him in their arms, placed him again on the causeway. One of his pages, meanwhile, had advanced some way through the press, leading a horse for his master to mount. But the youth received a wound in the throat from

---

[1] " É como el negocio fué tan de súpito, y ví que mataban la Gente, determiné de me quedar allí, y morir peleando." Rel. Terc., ap. Lorenzana, p. 268.

[2] Ixtlilxochitl, who would fain make his royal kinsman a sort of residuary legatee for all unappropriated, or even doubtful, acts of heroism, puts in a sturdy claim for him on this occasion. A painting, he says, on one of the gates of a monastery of Tlatelolco, long recorded the fact that it was the Tezcucan chief who saved the life of Cortés. (Venida de los Españoles, p. 38.) But Camargo gives the full credit of it to Olea, on the testimony of " a famous Tlascalan warrior," present in the action, who reported it to him. (Hist. de Tlascala, MS.) The same is stoutly maintained by Bernal Diaz, the townsman of Olea, to whose memory he pays a hearty tribute, as one of the best men and bravest soldiers in the army. (Hist. de la Conquista, cap. 152, 204.) Saavedra, the poetic chronicler,—something more of chronicler than poet,—who came on the stage before all that had borne arms in the Conquest had

left it, gives the laurel also to Olea, whose fate he commemorates in verses that at least aspire to historic fidelity :—

" Túvole con las manos abraçado,
Y Francisco de Olea el valeroso,
Vn valiente Español, y su criado,
Le tiró vn tajo brauo y riguroso :
Las dos manos á cercen le ha cortado,
Y él le libró del trance trabajoso.
Huuo muy gran rumor, porque dezian,
Que ya en prision amarga le tenian.

" Llegáron otros Indios arriscados,
Y á Olea matáron en vn punto,
Cercáron á Cortés por todos lados,
Y al miserable cuerpo ya difunto :
Y viendo sus sentidos recobrados,
Fuso mano á la espada y daga junto.
Antonio de Quiñones llegó luego,
Capitan de la guarda ardiendo en fuego."

EL PEREGRINO INDIANO, Canto 20.

a javelin, which prevented him from effecting his object. Another of his attendants was more successful. It was Guzman, his chamberlain; but, as he held the bridle while Cortés was assisted into the saddle, he was snatched away by the Aztecs, and, with the swiftness of thought, hurried off by their canoes. The general still lingered, unwilling to leave the spot while his presence could be of the least service. But the faithful Quiñones, taking his horse by the bridle, turned his head from the breach, exclaiming, at the same time, that " his master's life was too important to the army to be thrown away there." [1]

Yet it was no easy matter to force a passage through the press. The surface of the causeway, cut up by the feet of men and horses, was knee-deep in mud, and in some parts was so much broken that the water from the canals flowed over it. The crowded mass, in their efforts to extricate themselves from their perilous position, staggered to and fro like a drunken man. Those on the flanks were often forced by the lateral pressure of their comrades down the slippery sides of the dike, where they were picked up by the canoes of the enemy, whose shouts of triumph proclaimed the savage joy with which they gathered in every new victim for the sacrifice Two cavaliers, riding by the general's side, lost their footing, and rolled down the declivity into the water. One was taken and his horse killed. The other was happy enough to escape. The valiant ensign, Corral, had a similar piece of good fortune. He slipped into the canal, and the enemy felt sure of their prize, when he again succeeded in recovering the causeway, with the tattered banner of Castile still flying above his head. The barbarians set up a cry of disappointed rage as they lost possession of a trophy to which the people of Anahuac attached, as we have seen, the highest importance, hardly inferior in their eyes to the capture of the commander-in-chief himself. [2]

Cortés at length succeeded in regaining the firm ground, and reaching the open place before the great street of Tacuba. Here, under a sharp fire of the artillery, he rallied his broken squadrons, and, charging at the head of the little body of horse, which, not having been brought into action, were still fresh, he beat off the enemy. He then commanded the retreat of the two other divisions. The scattered forces again united; and the general, sending forward his Indian confederates, took the rear with a chosen body of cavalry to cover the retreat of the army, which was effected with but little additional loss. [3]

Andrés de Tápia was despatched to the western causeway to acquaint

---

1 " É aquel Capitan que estaba con el General, que se decia Antonio de Quiñones, dixole : Vamos, Señor, de aqui, y salvemos vuestra Persona, pues que ya esto está de manera, que es morir desesperado atender ; é sin vos, ninguno de nosotros puede escapar, que no es esfuerzo, sino poquedad, porfiar aqui otra cosa." Oviedo, Hist. de las Ind., MS., lib. 33, cap. 26.

2 It may have been the same banner which is noticed by Mr. Bullock as treasured up in the Hospital of Jesus, " where," says he, " we beheld

the identical embroidered standard under which the great captain wrested this immense empire from the unfortunate Montezuma." Six Months in Mexico, vol. i. chap. 10.

3 For this disastrous affair, besides the Letter of Cortés, and the Chronicle of Diaz, so often quoted, see Sahagun, Hist. de Nueva-España, MS., lib. 12, cap. 33,—Camargo, Hist. de Tlascala, MS.,—Gomara, Crónica, cap. 138,—Torquemada, Monarch. Ind., lib. 4, cap. 94,—Oviedo, Hist. de las Ind., MS., lib. 33, cap. 26, 48.

Alvarado and Sandoval with the failure of the enterprise. Meanwhile the two captains had penetrated far into the city. Cheered by the triumphant shouts of their countrymen in the adjacent streets, they had pushed on with extraordinary vigour, that they might not be outstripped in the race of glory. They had almost reached the market-place, which lay nearer to their quarters than to the general's, when they heard the blast from the dread horn of Guatemozin,[1] followed by the overpowering yell of the barbarians, which had so startled the ears of Cortés; till at length the sounds of the receding conflict died away in the distance. The two captains now understood that the day must have gone hard with their countrymen. They soon had further proof of it, when the victorious Aztecs, returning from the pursuit of Cortés, joined their forces to those engaged with Sandoval and Alvarado, and fell on them with redoubled fury. At the same time they rolled on the ground two or three of the bloody heads of the Spaniards, shouting the name of "Malinche." The captains, struck with horror at the spectacle,—though they gave little credit to the words of the enemy,—instantly ordered a retreat. Indeed, it was not in their power to maintain their ground against the furious assaults of the besieged, who poured on them, swarm after swarm, with a desperation of which, says one who was there, "although it seems as if it were now present to my eyes, I can give but a faint idea to the reader. God alone could have brought us off safe from the perils of that day."[2] The fierce barbarians followed up the Spaniards to their very intrenchments. But here they were met, first by the cross-fire of the brigantines, which, dashing through the palisades planted to obstruct their movements, completely enfiladed the causeway, and next by that of the small battery erected in front of the camp, which, under the management of a skilful engineer, named Medrano, swept the whole length of the defile. Thus galled in front and on flank, the shattered columns of the Aztecs were compelled to give way and take shelter under the defences of the city.

The greatest anxiety now prevailed in the camp regarding the fate of Cortés; for Tápia had been detained on the road by scattered parties of the enemy, whom Guatemozin had stationed there to interrupt the communication between the camps. He arrived at length, however, though bleeding from several wounds. His intelligence, while it reassured the Spaniards as to the general's personal safety, was not calculated to allay their uneasiness in other respects.

Sandoval, in particular, was desirous to acquaint himself with the actual state of things and the further intentions of Cortés. Suffering as he was

---

1 "El resonido de la corneta de Guatemuz."—
Astolfo's magic horn was not more terrible:—

  "Dico che 'l corno è di sì orribil suono,
  Ch' ovunque s' oda, fa fuggir la gente.
  Non può trovarsi al mondo un cor sì buono,
  Che possa non fuggir come lo sente.
  Rumor di vento e di tremuoto, e 'l tuono,
  A par del suon di questo, era niente."
      ORLANDO FURIOSO, Canto 15, st. 15.

2 "Por q. yo no lo sé aquí escriuir q. aora q. me pongo á pensar en ello, es como si visiblemente lo viesse, mas bueluo á dezir, y ansí es verdad, q. si Dios no nos diera esfuerço, segun estauamos todos heridos: él nos saluo, q. de otra manera no nos podiamos llegar á nuestros ranchos." Bernal Diaz, Hist. de la Conquista, cap. 152.

from three wounds, which he had received in that day's fight, he resolved to visit in person the quarters of the commander-in-chief. It was mid-day —for the busy scenes of the morning had occupied but a few hours—when Sandoval remounted the good steed on whose strength and speed he knew he could rely. It was a noble animal, well known throughout the army, and worthy of its gallant rider, whom it had carried safe through all the long marches and bloody battles of the Conquest.[1]   On the way he fell in with Guatemozin's scouts, who gave him chase, and showered around him volleys of missiles, which, fortunately, found no vulnerable point in his own harness or that of his well-barbed charger.

On arriving at the camp, he found the troops there much worn and dispirited by the disaster of the morning. They had good reason to be so. Besides the killed, and a long file of wounded, sixty-two Spaniards, with a multitude of allies, had fallen alive into the hands of the enemy,— an enemy who was never known to spare a captive. The loss of two field-pieces and seven horses crowned their own disgrace and the triumph of the Aztecs. This loss, so insignificant in European warfare, was a great one here, where both horses and artillery, the most powerful arms of war against the barbarians, were not to be procured without the greatest cost and difficulty.[2]

Cortés, it was observed, had borne himself throughout this trying day with his usual intrepidity and coolness. The only time he was seen to falter was when the Mexicans threw down before him the heads of several Spaniards, shouting, at the same time, "Sandoval," "Tonatiuh," the well-known epithet of Alvarado. At the sight of the gory trophies he grew deadly pale; but, in a moment recovering his usual confidence, he endeavoured to cheer up the drooping spirits of his followers. It was with a cheerful countenance that he now received his lieutenant; but a shade of sadness was visible through this outward composure, showing how the catastrophe of the *puente cuidada*, "the sorrowful bridge," as he mournfully called it, lay heavy at his heart.

To the cavalier's anxious inquiries as to the cause of the disaster, he replied, "It is for my sins that it has befallen me, son Sandoval;" for such was the affectionate epithet with which Cortés often addressed his best-beloved and trusty officer. He then explained to him the immediate cause, in the negligence of the treasurer. Further conversation followed, in which the general declared his purpose to forego active hostilities for a few days. "You must take my place," he continued, "for I am too much crippled at present to discharge my duties. You must watch over

---

[1] This renowned steed, who might rival the Babieca of the Cid, was named Motilla, and, when one would pass unqualified praise on a horse, he would say, "He is as good as Motilla." So says that prince of chroniclers, Diaz, who takes care that neither beast nor man shall be defrauded of his fair guerdon in these campaigns against the infidel. He was of a chestnut colour, it seems, with a star in his forehead, and, luckily for his credit, with only one foot white. See Historia de la Conquista, cap. 152, 205.

[2] The cavaliers might be excused for not wantonly venturing their horses, if, as Diaz asserts, they could only be replaced at an expense of eight hundred or a thousand dollars apiece: "Porque costaua en aquella sazon vn cauallo ochocientos pesos, y aun algunos costauan á mas de mil." Hist. de la Conquista, cap. 151. See, also, *ante*, p. 124, note 3.

the safety of the camps. Give especial heed to Alvarado's. He is a gallant soldier, I know it well; but I doubt the Mexican hounds may, some hour, take him at disadvantage."[1] These few words showed the general's own estimation of his two lieutenants; both equally brave and chivalrous, but the one uniting with these qualities the circumspection so essential to success in perilous enterprises, in which the other was signally deficient. The future conqueror of Guatemala had to gather wisdom, as usual, from the bitter fruits of his own errors. It was under the training of Cortés that he learned to be a soldier. The general, having concluded his instructions, affectionately embraced his lieutenant, and dismissed him to his quarters.

It was late in the afternoon when he reached them; but the sun was still lingering above the western hills, and poured his beams wide over the Valley, lighting up the old towers and temples of Tenochtitlan with a mellow radiance, that little harmonized with the dark scenes of strife in which the city had so lately been involved. The tranquillity of the hour, however, was on a sudden broken by the strange sounds of the great drum in the temple of the war-god,—sounds which recalled the *noche triste*, with all its terrible images, to the minds of the Spaniards, for that was the only occasion on which they had ever heard them.[2] They intimated some solemn act of religion within the unhallowed precincts of the *teocalli;* and the soldiers, startled by the mournful vibrations, which might be heard for leagues across the Valley, turned their eyes to the quarter whence they proceeded. They there beheld a long procession winding up the huge sides of the pyramid; for the camp of Alvarado was pitched scarcely a mile from the city, and objects are distinctly visible at a great distance in the transparent atmosphere of the table-land.

As the long file of priests and warriors reached the flat summit of the *teocalli*, the Spaniards saw the figures of several men stripped to their waists, some of whom, by the whiteness of their skins, they recognized as their own countrymen. They were the victims for sacrifice. Their heads were gaudily decorated with coronals of plumes, and they carried fans in their hands. They were urged along by blows, and compelled to take part in the dances in honour of the Aztec war-god. The unfortunate captives, then stripped of their sad finery, were stretched, one after another, on the great stone of sacrifice. On its convex surface their breasts were heaved up conveniently for the diabolical purpose of the priestly executioner, who cut asunder the ribs by a strong blow with his sharp razor of *itztli*, and, thrusting his hand into the wound, tore away the heart, which, hot and reeking, was deposited on the golden censer

1 "Mira pues veis que yo no puedo ir á todas partes, á vos os encomiendo estos trabajos, pues veis q̃ estoy herido y coxo; ruego os pongais cobro en estos tres reales; bien sé q̃ Pedro de Alvarado, y sus Capitanes, y soldados aurán batallado, y hecho como caualleros, mas temo el gran poder destos perros no les ayan desbaratado." Bernal Diaz, Hist. de la Conquista, cap. 152.

2 "Vn atambor de muy triste sonido, enfin como instrumento de demonios, y retumbaua tanto, que se oia dos, ó tres leguas." Bernal Diaz, Hist. de la Conquista, loc. cit.

before the idol. The body of the slaughtered victim was then hurled down the steep stairs of the pyramid, which, it may be remembered, were placed at the same angle of the pile, one flight below another; and the mutilated remains were gathered up by the savages beneath, who soon prepared with them the cannibal repast which completed the work of abomination![1]

We may imagine with what sensations the stupefied Spaniards must have gazed on this horrid spectacle, so near that they could almost recognize the persons of their unfortunate friends, see the struggles and writhing of their bodies, hear—or fancy that they heard—their screams of agony! yet so far removed that they could render them no assistance. Their limbs trembled beneath them, as they thought what might one day be their own fate; and the bravest among them, who had hitherto gone to battle as careless and light-hearted as to the banquet or the ball-room, were unable, from this time forward, to encounter their ferocious enemy without a sickening feeling, much akin to fear, coming over them.[2]

Such was not the effect produced by this spectacle on the Mexican forces, gathered at the end of the causeway. Like vultures maddened by the smell of distant carrion, they set up a piercing cry, and, as they shouted that "such should be the fate of all their enemies," swept along in one fierce torrent over the dike. But the Spaniards were not to be taken by surprise; and, before the barbarian horde had come within their lines, they opened such a deadly fire from their battery of heavy guns, supported by the musketry and crossbows, that the assailants were compelled to fall back slowly, but fearfully mangled, to their former position.

The five following days passed away in a state of inaction, except, indeed, so far as was necessary to repel the sorties made from time to time by the militia of the capital. The Mexicans, elated with their success, meanwhile, abandoned themselves to jubilee; singing, dancing, and feasting on the mangled relics of their wretched victims. Guatemozin sent several heads of the Spaniards, as well as of the horses, round the country, calling on his old vassals to forsake the banners of the white men, unless they would share the doom of the enemies of Mexico. The priests now cheered the young monarch and the people with the declaration that the

---

[1] Bernal Diaz, Hist. de la Conquista, ubi supra.—Oviedo, Hist. de las Ind., MS., lib. 33, cap. 48.—"Sacándoles los corazones, sobre una piedra que era como un pilar cortado, tan grueso como un hombre y algo mas, y tan alto como medio estadio; allí á cada uno echado de espaldas sobre aquella piedra, que se llama Techcatl, uno le tiraba por un brazo, y otro por el otro, y tambien por las piernas otros dos, y venia uno de aquellos Sátrapas, con un pedernal, como un hierro de lanza enhastado, en un palo de dos palmos de largo, le daba un golpe con ambas manos en el pecho; y sacando aquel pedernal, por la misma llaga metia la mano, y arrancábale el corazon, y luego fregaba con él la boca del Ídolo; y echaba á rodar el cuerpo por las gradas abajo, que serian como cinquenta ó sesenta gradas, por allí abajo iba quebrando las piernas y los brazos, y dando cabezasos con la cabeza, *hasta que llegaba abajo aun vivo.*" Sahagun, Hist. de Nueva-España, MS., lib. 12, cap. 35.

[2] At least, such is the honest confession of Captain Diaz, as stout-hearted a soldier as any in the army. He consoles himself, however, with the reflection that the tremor of his limbs intimated rather an excess of courage than a want of it, since it arose from a lively sense of the great dangers into which his daring spirit was about to hurry him! The passage in the original affords a good specimen of the inimitable *naïveté* of the old chronicler: "Digan agora todos aquellos caualleros, que desto del militar entienden, y se han hallado en trances peligrosos de muerte, á que fin echarán mi temor, si es á mucha flaqueza de animo, ó á mucho esfuerço, porque como he dicho, sentia yo en mi pensamiento, que auia de poner por mi persona, batallando en parte que por fuerça auia de temer la muerte mas que otras vezes, y por esto me temblaua el coraçon, y temia la muerte." Hist. de la Conquista, cap. 156.

dread Huitzilopochtli, their offended deity, appeased by the sacrifices offered up on his altars, would again take the Aztecs under his protection, and deliver their enemies, before the expiration of eight days, into their hands.[1]

This comfortable prediction, confidently believed by the Mexicans, was thundered in the ears of the besieging army in tones of exultation and defiance. However it may have been contemned by the Spaniards, it had a very different effect on their allies. The latter had begun to be disgusted with a service so full of peril and suffering and already protracted far beyond the usual term of Indian hostilities. They had less confidence than before in the Spaniards. Experience had shown that they were neither invincible nor immortal, and their recent reverses made them even distrust the ability of the Christians to reduce the Aztec metropolis. They recalled to mind the ominous words of Xicotencatl, that "so sacrilegious a war could come to no good for the people of Anahuac." They felt that their arm was raised against the gods of their country. The prediction of the oracle fell heavy on their hearts. They had little doubt of its fulfilment, and were only eager to turn away the bolt from their own heads by a timely secession from the cause.

They took advantage, therefore, of the friendly cover of night to steal away from their quarters. Company after company deserted in this manner, taking the direction of their respective homes. Those belonging to the great towns of the Valley, whose allegiance was the most recent, were the first to cast it off. Their example was followed by the older confederates, the militia of Cholula, Tepeaca, Tezcuco, and even the faithful Tlascala. There were, it is true, some exceptions to these, and among them Ixtlilxochitl, the young lord of Tezcuco, and Chichemecatl, the valiant Tlascalan chieftain, who, with a few of their immediate followers, still remained true to the banner under which they had enlisted. But their number was insignificant. The Spaniards beheld with dismay the mighty array, on which they relied for support, thus silently melting away before the breath of superstition. Cortés alone maintained a cheerful countenance. He treated the prediction with contempt, as an invention of the priests, and sent his messengers after the retreating squadrons, beseeching them to postpone their departure, or at least to halt on the road, till the time, which would soon elapse, should show the falsehood of the prophecy.

The affairs of the Spaniards at this crisis must be confessed to have worn a gloomy aspect. Deserted by their allies, with their ammunition nearly exhausted, cut off from the customary supplies from the neighbourhood, harassed by unintermitting vigils and fatigues, smarting under wounds of which every man in the army had his share, with an unfriendly country in

1 Herrera, Hist. general, dec. 3, lib. 2, cap. 20.—Ixtlilxochitl, Venida de los Españoles, pp. 41, 42.—" Y ros dezian, que de ai á ocho dias no auia de quedar ninguno de nosotros á vida, poique assi se lo auian prometido la noche antes sus Dioses " Fernal Diaz, Hist. de la Conquista, cap. 153.

their rear and a mortal foe in front, they might well be excused for faltering in their enterprise.   They found abundant occupation by day in foraging the country, and in maintaining their position on the causeways against the enemy, now made doubly daring by success and by the promises of their priests ; while at night their slumbers were disturbed by the beat of the melancholy drum, the sounds of which, booming far over the waters, tolled the knell of their murdered comrades.   Night after night fresh victims were led up to the great altar of sacrifice ; and, while the city blazed with the illumination of a thousand bonfires on the terraced roofs of the dwellings and in the areas of the temples, the dismal pageant, showing through the fiery glare like the work of the ministers of hell, was distinctly visible from the camp below.   One of the last of the sufferers was Guzman, the unfortunate chamberlain of Cortés, who lingered in captivity eighteen days before he met his doom.[1]

Yet in this hour of trial the Spaniards did not falter.   Had they faltered, they might have learned a lesson of fortitude from some of their own wives, who continued with them in the camp, and who displayed a heroism on this occasion, of which history has preserved several examples. One of these, protected by her husband's armour, would frequently mount guard in his place when he was wearied.   Another, hastily putting on a soldier's *escaupil* and seizing a sword and lance, was seen, on one occasion, to rally their retreating countrymen and lead them back against the enemy.   Cortés would have persuaded these Amazonian dames to remain at Tlascala ; but they proudly replied, "It was the duty of Castilian wives not to abandon their husbands in danger, but to share it with them,—and die with them, if necessary."   And well did they do their duty.[2]

Amidst all the distresses and multiplied embarrassments of their situation, the Spaniards still remained true to their purpose.   They relaxed in no degree the severity of the blockade.   Their camps still occupied the only avenues to the city ; and their batteries, sweeping the long defiles at every fresh assault of the Aztecs, mowed down hundreds of the assailants.   Their brigantines still rode on the waters, cutting off the communication with the shore.   It is true, indeed, the loss of the auxiliary canoes left a passage open for the occasional introduction of supplies to the capital.[3]   But the whole amount of these supplies was small ; and its

---

[1] Sahagun, Hist. de Nueva-España, MS., lib. 12, cap. 36.—Ixtlilxochitl, Venida de los Españoles, pp. 41, 42.—The Castilian scholar will see that I have not drawn on my imagination for the picture of these horrors : "Digamos aora lo que los Mexicanos hazian de noche en sus grandes, y altos Cues ; y es, q̃ tañian su maldito atambor, que dixe otra vez que era el de mas maldito sonido, y mas triste q̃ se podia inuẽtar, y sonaua muy lexos ; y tañian otros peores instrumentos. En fin, cosas diabólicas, y teniã grandes lumbres, y dauã grãdissimos gritos, y siluos, y en aquel instãte estauan sacrificando de nuestros cõpañeros, de los q̃ tomárõ á Cortés, que supímos q̃ sacrificáron diez dias arreo, hasta que los acabáron, y el postrero dexárõ á

Christoual de Guzman, q̃ viuo lo tuuiéron diez y ocho dias, segun dixérõ tres Capitanes Mexicanos q̃ prẽdímos.   Bernal Diaz, Hist. de la Conquista, cap. 153.

[2] "Que no era bien, que Mugeres Castellanas dexasen á sus Maridos, iendo á la Guerra, i que adonde ellos muriesen, moririan ellas." (Herrera, Hist. general, dec. 3, lib. 1, cap. 22.)   The historian has embalmed the names of several of these heroines in his pages, who are, doubtless, well entitled to share the honours of the Conquest : Beatriz de Palacios, María de Estrada, Juana Martin, Isabel Rodriguez, and Beatriz Bermudez.

[3] Ibid., ubi supra.

crowded population, while exulting in their temporary advantage and the delusive assurances of their priests, were beginning to sink under the withering grasp of an enemy within, more terrible than the one which lay before their gates.

CHAPTER VII.

SUCCESSES OF THE SPANIARDS.—FRUITLESS OFFERS TO GUATEMOZIN.—BUILDINGS RAZED TO THE GROUND.—TERRIBLE FAMINE.—THE TROOPS GAIN THE MARKET-PLACE.—BATTERING-ENGINE.

(1521.)

THUS passed away the eight days prescribed by the oracle; and the sun which rose upon the ninth beheld the fair city still beset on every side by the inexorable foe. It was a great mistake of the Aztec priests—one not uncommon with false prophets, anxious to produce a startling impression on their followers—to assign so short a term for the fulfilment of their prediction.[1]

The Tezcucan and Tlascalan chiefs now sent to acquaint their troops with the failure of the prophecy, and to recall them to the Christian camp. The Tlascalans, who had halted on the way, returned, ashamed of their credulity, and with ancient feelings of animosity heightened by the artifice of which they had been the dupes. Their example was followed by many of the other confederates, with the levity natural to a people whose convictions are the result not of reason, but of superstition. In a short time the Spanish general found himself at the head of an auxiliary force which, if not so numerous as before, was more than adequate to all his purposes. He received them with politic benignity; and, while he reminded them that they had been guilty of a great crime in thus abandoning their commander, he was willing to overlook it in consideration of their past services. They must be aware that these services were not necessary to the Spaniards, who had carried on the siege with the same vigour during their absence as when they were present. But he was unwilling that those who had shared the dangers of the war with him should not also partake its triumphs, and be present at the fall of their enemy, which he promised, with a confidence better founded than that of the priests in their prediction, should not be long delayed.

Yet the menaces and machinations of Guatemozin were still not

---

[1] And yet the priests were not so much to blame, if, as Solis assures us, "the Devil went about very industriously in those days, insinuating into the ears of his flock what he could not into their hearts." *Conquista,* lib. 5, cap. 22.

without effect in the distant provinces. Before the full return of the confederates, Cortés received an embassy from Cuernavaca, ten or twelve leagues distant, and another from some friendly towns of the Otomies, still farther off, imploring his protection against their formidable neighbours, who menaced them with hostilities as allies of the Spaniards. As the latter were then situated, they were in a condition to receive succour much more than to give it.[1] Most of the officers were, accordingly, opposed to granting a request compliance with which must still further impair their diminished strength. But Cortés knew the importance, above all, of not betraying his own inability to grant it. "The greater our weakness," he said, "the greater need have we to cover it under a show of strength."[2]

He immediately detached Tápia with a body of about a hundred men in one direction, and Sandoval with a somewhat larger force in the other, with orders that their absence should not in any event be prolonged beyond ten days.[3] The two captains executed their commissions promptly and effectually. They each met and defeated his adversary in a pitched battle, laid waste the hostile territories, and returned within the time prescribed. They were soon followed by ambassadors from the conquered places, soliciting the alliance of the Spaniards; and the affair terminated by an accession of new confederates, and, what was more important, a conviction in the old that the Spaniards were both willing and competent to protect them.

Fortune, who seldom dispenses her frowns or her favours single-handed, further showed her goodwill to the Spaniards, at this time, by sending a vessel into Vera Cruz laden with ammunition and military stores. It was part of the fleet destined for the Florida coast by the romantic old knight, Ponce de Leon. The cargo was immediately taken by the authorities of the port, and forwarded, without delay, to the camp, where it arrived most seasonably, as the want of powder, in particular, had begun to be seriously felt.[4] With strength thus renovated, Cortés determined to resume active operations, but on a plan widely differing from that pursued before.

In the former deliberations on the subject, two courses, as we have seen, presented themselves to the general. One was to intrench himself in the heart of the capital and from this point carry on hostilities; the other was the mode of proceeding hitherto followed. Both were open to serious objections, which he hoped would be obviated by the one now

---

[1] "Y teniamos necesidad antes de ser socorridos, que de dar socorro." Rel. Terc. de Cortés, ap. Lorenzana, p. 272.

[2] "God knows," says the general, "the peril in which we all stood; pero como nos convenia mostrar mas esfuerzo y ánimo, que nunca, y morir peleando, disimulabamos nuestro flaqueza assí con los Amigos como con los Enemigos." Rel. Terc. de Cortés, ap. Lorenzana, p. 275.

[3] Tápia's force consisted of 10 horse and 80 foot; the chief alguacil, as Sandoval was styled, had 18 horse and 100 infantry. Ibid., loc. cit.—Also Oviedo, Hist. de las Ind., MS., lib. 33, cap. 26.

[4] "Pólvora y Ballestas, de que teniamos muy estrema necesidad." (Rel. Terc. de Cortés, ap. Lorenzana, p. 278.) It was probably the expedition in which Ponce de Leon lost his life; an expedition to the very land which the chivalrous cavalier had himself first visited in quest of the Fountain of Health. The story is pleasantly told by Irving, as the reader may remember, in his "Companions of Columbus."

adopted. This was to advance no step without securing the entire safety of the army, not only on its immediate retreat, but in its future inroads. Every breach in the causeway, every canal in the streets, was to be filled up in so solid a manner that the work should not be again disturbed. The materials for this were to be furnished by the buildings, every one of which, as the army advanced, whether public or private, hut, temple, or palace, was to be demolished! Not a building in their path was to be spared. They were all indiscriminately to be levelled, until, in the Conqueror's own language, "the water should be converted into dry land," and a smooth and open ground be afforded for the manœuvres of the cavalry and artillery! [1]

Cortés came to this terrible determination with great difficulty. He sincerely desired to spare the city, "the most beautiful thing in the world," [2] as he enthusiastically styles it, and which would have formed the most glorious trophy of his conquest. But in a place where every house was a fortress and every street was cut up by canals so embarrassing to his movements, experience proved it was vain to think of doing so and becoming master of it. There was as little hope of a peaceful accommodation with the Aztecs, who, so far from being broken by all they had hitherto endured, and the long perspective of future woes, showed a spirit as haughty and implacable as ever. [3]

The general's intentions were learned by the Indian allies with unbounded satisfaction; and they answered his call for aid by thousands of pioneers, armed with their *coas*, or hoes of the country, all testifying the greatest alacrity in helping on the work of destruction. [4] In a short time the breaches in the great causeways were filled up so effectually that they were never again molested. Cortés himself set the example by carrying stones and timber with his own hands. [5] The buildings in the suburbs were then thoroughly levelled, the canals were filled up with the rubbish, and a wide space around the city was thrown open to the manœuvres of the cavalry, who swept over it free and unresisted. The Mexicans did not look with indifference on these preparations to lay waste their town and leave them bare and unprotected against the enemy. They made incessant efforts to impede the labours of the besiegers; but the latter, under cover of their guns, which kept up an unintermitting fire, still advanced in the work of desolation. [6]

---

1 The calm and simple manner in which the *Conquistador*, as usual, states this in his *Commentaries*, has something appalling in it from its very simplicity : "Acordé de tomar un medio para nuestra seguridad, y para poder mas estrechar á los Enemigos ; y fué, que como fuessemos ganando por las Calles de la Ciudad, que fuessen derrocando todas las Casas de ellas, del un lado, y del otro ; por manera, que no fuessemos un paso adelante, sin lo dejar todo asolado, y lo que era Agua, hacerlo Tierra-firme, aunque hobiesse toda la dilacion, que se pudiesse seguir." Rel. Terc., ap. Lorenzana, p. 279.
2 "Porque era la mas hermosa cosa del Mundo." Ibid., p. 278.

3 "Mas antes en el pelear, y en todos sus ardides, los hallabamos con mas ánimo, que nunca." Ibid., p. 279.
4 Yet we shall hardly credit the Tezcucan historian's assertion that a hundred thousand Indians flocked to the camp for this purpose ! "Viniesen todos los labradores con sus coas para este efecta con toda brevedad : . . . llegáron *mas de cien mil de ellos*." Ixtlilxochitl, Venida de los Españoles, p. 42.
5 Bernal Diaz, Hist. de la Conquista, cap. 153.
6 Sahagun, who gathered the story from the actors, and from the aspect of the scene before the devastation had been wholly repaired, writes with the animation of an eyewitness : "La guerra por

The gleam of fortune which had so lately broken out on the Mexicans again disappeared; and the dark mist, after having been raised for a moment, settled on the doomed capital more heavily than before. Famine, with all her hideous train of woes, was making rapid strides among its accumulated population. The stores provided for the siege were exhausted. The casual supply of human victims, or that obtained by some straggling pirogue from the neighbouring shores, was too inconsiderable to be widely felt.[1] Some forced a scanty sustenance from a mucilaginous substance gathered in small quantities on the surface of the lake and canals.[2] Others appeased the cravings of appetite by devouring rats, lizards, and the like loathsome reptiles, which had not yet deserted the starving city. Its days seemed to be already numbered. But the page of history has many an example to show that there are no limits to the endurance of which humanity is capable, when animated by hatred and despair.

With the sword thus suspended over it, the Spanish commander, desirous to make one more effort to save the capital, persuaded three Aztec nobles, taken in one of the late actions, to bear a message from him to Guatemozin; though they undertook it with reluctance, for fear of the consequences to themselves. Cortés told the emperor that all had now been done that brave men could do in defence of their country. There remained no hope, no chance of escape, for the Mexicans. Their provisions were exhausted; their communications were cut off; their vassals had deserted them; even their gods had betrayed them. They stood alone, with the nations of Anahuac banded against them. There was no hope but in immediate surrender. He besought the young monarch to take compassion on his brave subjects, who were daily perishing before his eyes; and on the fair city, whose stately buildings were fast crumbling into ruins. "Return to the allegiance," he concludes, "which you once proffered to the sovereign of Castile. The past shall be forgotten. The persons and property, in short, all the rights, of the Aztecs shall be respected. You shall be confirmed in your authority, and Spain will once more take your city under her protection."[3]

The eye of the young monarch kindled, and his dark cheek flushed with sudden anger, as he listened to proposals so humiliating. But, though his bosom glowed with the fiery temper of the Indian, he had

---

agua y por tierra fué tan porfiada y tan sangrienta, que era espanto de verla, y no hay posibilidad, para decir las particularidades que pasaban; eran tan espesas las saetas, y dardos, y piedras, y palos, que se arrojavan los unos á los otros, que quitavan la claridad del sol; era tan grande la voceria, y grita, de hombres y mugeres, y niños que voceaban y lloraban, que era cosa de grima; era tan grande la polvareda, y ruido, en derrocar y quemar casas, y robar lo que en ellas habia, y cautivar niños y mugeres, *que parecia un juicio.*" Hist. de Nueva-España, MS., lib. 12, cap. 38.

[1] The flesh of the Christians failed to afford them even the customary nourishment, since the Mexicans said it was intolerably bitter; a miracle considered by Captain Diaz as expressly wrought for this occasion. Hist. de la Conquista, cap. 153.
[2] Ibid., ubi supra.—When dried in the sun, this slimy deposit had a flavour not unlike that of cheese, and formed part of the food of the poorer classes at all times, according to Clavigero. Stor. del Messico, tom. ii. p. 222.*
[3] Bernal Diaz, Hist. de la Conquista, cap. 154.

* [This was the *ahuahutle* before described. See *ante*, p. 284, note 3.—Ed.]

the qualities of a "gentle cavalier," says one of his enemies, who knew him well.[1] He did no harm to the envoys; but, after the heat of the moment had passed off, he gave the matter a calm consideration, and called a council of his wise men and warriors to deliberate upon it. Some were for accepting the proposals, as offering the only chance of preservation. But the priests took a different view of the matter. They knew that the ruin of their own order must follow the triumph of Christianity. "Peace was good," they said, "but not with the white men." They reminded Guatemozin of the fate of his uncle Montezuma, and the requital he had met with for all his hospitality; of the seizure and imprisonment of Cacama, the cacique of Tezcuco; of the massacre of the nobles by Alvarado; of the insatiable avarice of the invaders, which had stripped the country of its treasures; of their profanation of the temples; of the injuries and insults which they had heaped without measure on the people and their religion. "Better," they said, "to trust in the promises of their own gods, who had so long watched over the nation. Better, if need be, give up our lives at once for our country, than drag them out in slavery and suffering among the false strangers."[2]

The eloquence of the priests, artfully touching the various wrongs of his people, roused the hot blood of Guatemozin. "Since it is so," he abruptly exclaimed, "let us think only of supplying the wants of the people. Let no man, henceforth, who values his life, talk of surrender. We can at least die like warriors."[3]

The Spaniards waited two days for the answer to their embassy. At length it came, in a general sortie of the Mexicans, who, pouring through every gate of the capital, like a river that has burst its banks, swept on, wave upon wave, to the very intrenchments of the besiegers, threatening to overwhelm them by their numbers. Fortunately, the position of the latter on the dikes secured their flanks, and the narrowness of the defile gave their small battery of guns all the advantages of a larger one. The fire of artillery and musketry blazed without intermission along the several causeways, belching forth volumes of sulphurous smoke, that, rolling heavily over the waters, settled dark around the Indian city and hid it from the surrounding country. The brigantines thundered, at the same time, on the flanks of the columns, which, after some ineffectual efforts to maintain themselves, rolled back in wild confusion, till their impotent fury died away in sullen murmurs within the capital.

Cortés now steadily pursued the plan he had laid down for the devastation of the city. Day after day the several armies entered by their

---

[1] "Mas como el Guatemuz era mancebo, *y muy gentil-hombre* y de buena disposicion." Bernal Diaz, Hist. de la Conquista, ubi supra.
[2] "Mira primero lo que nuestros Dioses te han prometido, toma buen consejo sobre ello y no te fies de Malinche, ni de sus palabras, que mas vale que todos muramos en esta ciudad peleando, que no vernos en poder de quiē nos harán esclauos, y nos atormentarán." Ibid., cap. 154.

[3] "Y entonces el Guatemuz medio enojado les dixo: Pues assi quereis que sea, guardad mucho el maiz, y bastimentos que tenemos, y muramos todos peleando: y desde aqui adelante ninguno sea osado á me demandar pazes, si no yo le mataré: y alli todos prometiéron de pelear noches, y dias, y morir en la defensa de su ciudad." Bernal Diaz, Hist. de la Conquista, ubi supra.

respective quarters, Sandoval probably directing his operations against the north-eastern district. The buildings, made of the porous *tetzontli*, though generally low, were so massy and extensive, and the canals were so numerous, that their progress was necessarily slow. They, however, gathered fresh accessions of strength every day from the numbers who flocked to the camp from the surrounding country, and who joined in the work of destruction with a hearty goodwill which showed their eagerness to break the detested yoke of the Aztecs. The latter raged with impotent anger as they beheld their lordly edifices, their temples, all they had been accustomed to venerate, thus ruthlessly swept away; their canals, constructed with so much labour and what to them seemed science, filled up with rubbish; their flourishing city, in short, turned into a desert, over which the insulting foe now rode triumphant. They heaped many a taunt on the Indian allies. "Go on," they said bitterly: "the more you destroy, the more you will have to build up again hereafter. If we conquer, you shall build for us; and if your white friends conquer, they will make you do as much for them."[1] The event justified the prediction.

In their rage they rushed blindly on the corps which covered the Indian pioneers. But they were as often driven back by the impetuous charge of the cavalry, or received on the long pikes of Chinantla, which did good service to the besiegers in their operations. At the close of day, however, when the Spaniards drew off their forces, taking care to send the multitudinous host of confederates first from the ground, the Mexicans usually rallied for a more formidable attack. Then they poured out from every lane and byway, like so many mountain streams, sweeping over the broad level cleared by the enemy, and falling impetuously on their flanks and rear. At such times they inflicted considerable loss in their turn, till an ambush, which Cortés laid for them among the buildings adjoining the great temple, did them so much mischief that they were compelled to act with more reserve.

At times the war displayed something of a chivalrous character, in the personal rencontres of the combatants. Challenges passed between them, and especially between the native warriors. These combats were usually conducted on the *azoteas*, whose broad and level surface afforded a good field of fight. On one occasion, a Mexican of powerful frame, brandishing a sword and buckler which he had won from the Christians, defied his enemies to meet him in single fight. A young page of Cortés', named Nuñez, obtained his master's permission to accept the vaunting challenge of the Aztec, and, springing on the *azotea*, succeeded, after a hard struggle, in discomfiting his antagonist, who fought at a disadvantage with

---

[1] "Los de la Ciudad como veian tanto estrago, por esforzarse, decian á nuestros Amigos, que no ficiessen sino quemar, y destruir, que ellos se las harian tornar á hacer de nuevo, porque si ellos eran vencedores, ya ellos sabian, que habia de ser assi, y si no que las habian de hacer para nosotros." Rel. Terc. de Cortés, ap. Lorenzana, p. 286.

weapons in which he was unpractised, and, running him through the body, brought off his spoils in triumph and laid them at the general's feet.[1]

The division of Cortés had now worked its way as far north as the great street of Tacuba, which opened a communication with Alvarado's camp, and near which stood the palace of Guatemozin. It was a spacious stone pile, that might well be called a fortress. Though deserted by its royal master, it was held by a strong body of Aztecs, who made a temporary defence, but of little avail against the battering enginery of the besiegers. It was soon set on fire, and its crumbling walls were levelled in the dust, like those other stately edifices of the capital, the boast and admiration of the Aztecs, and some of the fairest fruits of their civilization. "It was a sad thing to witness their destruction," exclaims Cortés; "but it was part of our plan of operations, and we had no alternative." [2]

These operations had consumed several weeks, so that it was now drawing towards the latter part of July. During this time the blockade had been maintained with the utmost rigour, and the wretched inhabitants were suffering all the extremities of famine. Some few stragglers were taken, from time to time, in the neighbourhood of the Christian camp, whither they had wandered in search of food. They were kindly treated, by command of Cortés, who was in hopes to induce others to follow their example, and thus to afford a means of conciliating the inhabitants, which might open the way to their submission. But few were found willing to leave the shelter of the capital, and they preferred to take their chance with their suffering countrymen rather than trust themselves to the mercies of the besiegers.

From these few stragglers, however, the Spaniards heard a dismal tale of woe respecting the crowded population in the interior of the city. All the ordinary means of sustenance had long since failed, and they now supported life as they could, by means of such roots as they could dig from the earth, by gnawing the bark of trees, by feeding on the grass,— on anything, in short, however loathsome, that could allay the craving of appetite. Their only drink was the brackish water of the soil saturated with the salt lake.[3] Under this unwholesome diet, and the diseases engendered by it, the population was gradually wasting away. Men sickened and died every day, in all the excruciating torments produced by hunger, and the wan and emaciated survivors seemed only to be waiting for their time.

The Spaniards had visible confirmation of all this as they penetrated

[1] Rel. Terc. de Cortés, ap. Lorenzana, pp. 282-284.—Herrera, Hist. general, dec. 3, lib. 1, cap. 22, lib. 2, cap. 2.—Gomara, Crónica, cap. 140.—Oviedo, Hist. de las Ind., MS., lib. 33, cap. 28.—Ixtlilxochitl, Venida de los Españoles, p. 43.

[2] "No se entendió sino en quemar, y hallanar Casas, que era lástima cierto de lo ver ; pero como no nos convenia hacer otra cosa, eramos forzado seguir aquella órden." Rel. Terc. de Cortés, p. 286.

[3] "No tenian agua dulce para beber, ni para de ninguna manera de comer ; bebian del agua salada y hedionda, comian ratones y lagartijas, y cortezas de árboles, y otras cosas no comestibles ; y de esta causa enfermáron muchos, y muriéron muchos." Sahagun, Hist. de Nueva-España, MS., lib. 12, cap. 39.—Also Rel. Terc. de Cortés, ap. Lorenzana, p. 289.

deeper into the city and approached the district of Tlatelolco, now occupied by the besieged. They found the ground turned up in quest of roots
and weeds, the trees stripped of their green stems, their foliage, and their
bark. Troops of famished Indians flitted in the distance, gliding like ghosts
among the scenes of their former residence. Dead bodies lay unburied
in the streets and courtyards, or filled up the canals. It was a sure sign
of the extremity of the Aztecs; for they held the burial of the dead as
a solemn and imperative duty. In the early part of the siege they had
religiously attended to it. In its latter stages they were still careful to
withdraw the dead from the public eye, by bringing their remains within
the houses. But the number of these, and their own sufferings, had now
so fearfully increased that they had grown indifferent to this, and they
suffered their friends and their kinsmen to lie and moulder on the spot
where they drew their last breath ! [1]

As the invaders entered the dwellings, a more appalling spectacle
presented itself;—the floors covered with the prostrate forms of the
miserable inmates, some in the agonies of death, others festering in their
corruption; men, women, and children inhaling the poisonous atmosphere,
and mingled promiscuously together; mothers with their infants in their
arms perishing of hunger before their eyes, while they were unable to
afford them the nourishment of nature; men crippled by their wounds,
with their bodies frightfully mangled, vainly attempting to crawl away, as
the enemy entered. Yet even in this state they scorned to ask for mercy,
and glared on the invaders with the sullen ferocity of the wounded tiger
that the huntsmen have tracked to his forest cave. The Spanish commander issued strict orders that mercy should be shown to these poor and
disabled victims. But the Indian allies made no distinction. An Aztec,
under whatever circumstances, was an enemy; and, with hideous shouts
of triumph, they pulled down the burning buildings on their heads,
consuming the living and the dead in one common funeral pile !

Yet the sufferings of the Aztecs, terrible as they were, did not incline
them to submission. There were many, indeed, who, from greater strength
of constitution, or from the more favourable circumstances in which they
were placed, still showed all their wonted energy of body and mind, and
maintained the same undaunted and resolute demeanour as before. They
fiercely rejected all the overtures of Cortés, declaring they would rather
die than surrender, and adding, with a bitter tone of exultation, that the
invaders would be at least disappointed in their expectations of treasure,
for it was buried where they could never find it ! [2]

---

[1] " Y es verdad y juro amen, que toda la laguna,
y casas, y barbacoas estauan llenas de cuerpos, y
cabeças de hombres muertos, que yo no sé de que
manera lo escriua." (Bernal Diaz, Hist. de la Conquista, cap. 156.) Clavigero considers that it was a
scheme of the Mexicans to leave the dead unburied,
in order that the stench might annoy and drive off
the Spaniards. (Stor. del Messico, tom. iii. p. 231,
nota.) But this policy would have operated much

more to the detriment of the besieged than of the
besiegers, whose presence in the capital was but
transitory. It is much more natural to refer it to
the same cause which has led to a similar conduct
under similar circumstances elsewhere, whether
occasioned by pestilence or famine.
[2] Gonzalo de las Casas, Defensa, MS., cap. 28.—
Martyr, De Orbe Novo, dec. 5, cap. 8.—Ixtlilxochitl, Venida de los Españoles, p. 45.—Rel. Terc.

The women, it is said, shared in this desperate—it should rather be called heroic—spirit. They were indefatigable in nursing the sick and dressing their wounds ; they aided the warriors in battle, by supplying them with the Indian ammunition of stones and arrows, prepared their slings, strung their bows, and displayed, in short, all the constancy and courage shown by the noble maidens of Saragossa in our day, and by those of Carthage in the days of antiquity.[1]

Cortés had now entered one of the great avenues leading to the market-place of Tlatelolco, the quarter towards which the movements of Alvarado were also directed. A single canal only lay in his way ; but this was of great width and stoutly defended by the Mexican archery. At this crisis, the army one evening, while in their intrenchments on the causeway, were surprised by an uncommon light that arose from the huge *teocalli* in that part of the city which, being at the north, was the most distant from their own position. This temple, dedicated to the dread war-god, was inferior only to the pyramid in the great square ; and on it the Spaniards had more than once seen their unhappy countrymen led to slaughter. They now supposed that the enemy were employed in some of their diabolical ceremonies,—when the flame, mounting higher and higher, showed that the sanctuaries themselves were on fire. A shout of exultation at the sight broke forth from the assembled soldiers, as they assured one another that their countrymen under Alvarado had got possession of the building.

It was indeed true. That gallant officer, whose position on the western causeway placed him near the district of Tlatelolco, had obeyed his commander's instructions to the letter, razing every building to the ground in his progress, and filling up the ditches with their ruins. He at length found himself before the great *teocalli* in the neighbourhood of the market. He ordered a company, under a cavalier named Gutierre de Badajoz, to storm the place, which was defended by a body of warriors, mingled with priests, still more wild and ferocious than the soldiery. The garrison, rushing down the winding terraces, fell on the assailants with such fury as compelled them to retreat in confusion and with some loss. Alvarado ordered another detachment to their support. This last was engaged, at the moment, with a body of Aztecs, who hung on its rear as it wound up the galleries of the *teocalli.* Thus hemmed in between two enemies, above and below, the position of the Spaniards was critical. With sword and buckler, they plunged desperately on the ascending Mexicans, and drove them into the courtyard below, where Alvarado plied them with such lively volleys of musketry as soon threw them into disorder and compelled

---

de Cortés, ap. Lorenzana, p. 289.—Oviedo, Hist. de las Ind., MS., lib. 33, cap. 29.

[1] " Muchas cosas acaeciéron en este cerco, que entre otras generaciones estobieran discantadas é tenidas en mucho, en especial de las Mugeres de Temixtitan, de quien ninguna mencion se ha fecho.

Y soy certificado, que fué cosa maravillosa y para espantar, ver la prontitud y constancia que tobiéron en servir á sus maridos, y en curar los heridos, é en el labrar de las piedras para los que tiraban con hondas, é en otros oficios para mas que mugeres." Oviedo, Hist. de las Ind., MS., lib. 33, cap. 48.

them to abandon the ground. Being thus rid of annoyance in the rear, the Spaniards returned to the charge. They drove the enemy up the heights of the pyramid, and, reaching the broad summit, a fierce encounter followed in mid-air,—such an encounter as takes place where death is the certain consequence of defeat. It ended, as usual, in the discomfiture of the Aztecs, who were either slaughtered on the spot still wet with the blood of their own victims, or pitched headlong down the sides of the pyramid.

The area was covered with the various symbols of the barbarous worship of the country, and with two lofty sanctuaries, before whose grinning idols were displayed the heads of several Christian captives who had been immolated on their altars. Although overgrown by their long, matted hair and bushy beards, the Spaniards could recognize in the livid countenances, their comrades who had fallen into the hands of the enemy. Tears fell from their eyes as they gazed on the melancholy spectacle and thought of the hideous death which their countrymen had suffered. They removed the sad relics with decent care, and after the Conquest deposited them in consecrated ground, on a spot since covered by the Church of the Martyrs.[1]

They completed their work by firing the sanctuaries, that the place might be no more polluted by these abominable rites. The flame crept slowly up the lofty pinnacles, in which stone was mingled with wood, till at length, bursting into one bright blaze, it shot up its spiral volume to such a height that it was seen from the most distant quarters of the Valley. It was this which had been hailed by the soldiery of Cortés, and it served as the beacon-light to both friend and foe, intimating the progress of the Christian arms.

The commander-in-chief and his division, animated by the spectacle, made, in their entrance on the following day, more determined efforts to place themselves alongside of their companions under Alvarado. The broad canal, above noticed as the only impediment now lying in his way, was to be traversed ; and on the farther side the emaciated figures of the Aztec warriors were gathered in numbers to dispute the passage, like the gloomy shades that wander—as ancient poets tell us—on the banks of the infernal river. They poured down, however, a storm of missiles, which were no shades, on the heads of the Indian labourers while occupied with filling up the wide gap with the ruins of the surrounding buildings. Still they toiled on in defiance of the arrowy shower, fresh numbers taking the place of those who fell. And when at length the work was completed, the cavalry rode over the rough plain at full charge against the enemy, followed by the deep array of spearmen, who bore down all opposition with their invincible phalanx.

The Spaniards now found themselves on the same ground with Alvarado's

---

[1] Oviedo, Hist. de las Ind., MS., lib. 33, cap. 29.—Bernal Diaz, Hist. de la Conquista, cap. 155.-Rel. Terc. de Cortés, ap. Lorenzana, pp. 287–289.

division. Soon afterwards, that chief, attended by several of his staff, rode into their lines, and cordially embraced his countrymen and companions in arms, for the first time since the beginning of the siege. They were now in the neighbourhood of the market. Cortés, taking with him a few of his cavaliers, galloped into it. It was a vast enclosure, as the reader has already seen, covering many an acre.[1] Its dimensions were suited to the immense multitudes who gathered there from all parts of the Valley in the flourishing days of the Aztec monarchy. It was surrounded by porticoes and pavilions for the accommodation of the artisans and traders who there displayed their various fabrics and articles of merchandise. The flat roofs of the piazzas were now covered with crowds of men and women, who gazed in silent dismay on the steel-clad horsemen, that profaned these precincts with their presence for the first time since their expulsion from the capital. The multitude, composed for the most part, probably, of unarmed citizens, seemed taken by surprise; at least they made no show of resistance; and the general, after leisurely viewing the ground, was permitted to ride back unmolested to the army.

On arriving there, he ascended the *teocalli*, from which the standard of Castile, supplanting the memorials of Aztec superstition, was now triumphantly floating. The Conqueror, as he strode among the smoking embers on the summit, calmly surveyed the scene of desolation below. The palaces, the temples, the busy marts of industry and trade, the glittering canals, covered with their rich freights from the surrounding country, the royal pomp of groves and gardens, all the splendours of the imperial city, the capital of the Western World, for ever gone,—and in their place a barren wilderness! How different the spectacle which the year before had met his eye, as it wandered over the same scenes from the heights of the neighbouring *teocalli*, with Montezuma at his side! Seven-eighths of the city were laid in ruins, with the occasional exception, perhaps, of some colossal temple which it would have required too much time to demolish.[2] The remaining eighth, comprehending the district of Tlatelolco, was all that now remained to the Aztecs, whose population— still large after all its losses—was crowded into a compass that would hardly have afforded accommodations for a third of their numbers. It was the quarter lying between the great northern and western causeways, and is recognized in the modern capital as the *Barrio de San Jago* and its vicinity. It was the favourite residence of the Indians after the Conquest,[3] though

[1] *Ante*, p. 294.—The *tianguez* still continued cf great dimensions, though with faded magnificence, after the Conquest, when it is thus noticed by Father Sahagun: "Entráron en la plaza ó Tianguez de esta Tlaltilulco (lugar muy espacioso mucho mas de lo que ahora es), el cual se podia llamar emporio de toda esta nueva España: al cual venian á tratar gentes de toda esta nueva España, y aun de los Reinos á ella contiguos, y donde se vendian y compraban todas cuantas cosas hay en toda esta tierra, y en los Reinos de Quahtimalla y Xalisco (cosa cierto mucho de ver), y lo ví

por muchos años morando en esta Casa del Señor Santiago aunque ya no era tanto como antes de la Conquista." Hist. de Nueva-España, MS., lib. 12, cap. 37.

[2] "É yo miré dende aquella Torre, lo que teniamos ganado de la Ciudad, que sin duda de ocho partes teniamos ganado las siete." Rel. Terc. de Cortés, ap. Lorenzana, p. 289.

[3] Toribio, Hist. de los Ind., MS., Parte 3, cap. 7.—The remains of the ancient foundations may still be discerned in this quarter, while in every other *etiam periêre ruinæ!*

at the present day thinly covered with humble dwellings, forming the straggling suburbs, as it were, of the metropolis. Yet it still affords some faint vestiges of what it was in its prouder days; and the curious antiquary, and occasionally the labourer, as he turns up the soil, encounters a glittering fragment of obsidian, or the mouldering head of a lance or arrow, or some other warlike relic, attesting that on this spot the retreating Aztecs made their last stand for the independence of their country.[1]

On the day following, Cortés, at the head of his battalions, made a second entry into the great *tianguez*. But this time the Mexicans were better prepared for his coming. They were assembled in considerable force in the spacious square. A sharp encounter followed; but it was short. Their strength was not equal to their spirit, and they melted away before the rolling fire of musketry, and left the Spaniards masters of the enclosure.

The first act was to set fire to some temples, of no great size, within the market-place, or more probably on its borders. As the flames ascended, the Aztecs, horror-struck, broke forth into piteous lamentations at the destruction of the deities on whom they relied for protection.[2]

The general's next step was at the suggestion of a soldier named Sotelo, a man who had served under the Great Captain in the Italian wars, where he professed to have gathered knowledge of the science of engineering, as it was then practised. He offered his services to construct a sort of catapult, a machine for discharging stones of great size, which might take the place of the regular battering-train in demolishing the buildings. As the ammunition, notwithstanding the liberal supplies which from time to time had found their way into the camp, now began to fail, Cortés eagerly acceded to a proposal so well suited to his exigences. Timber and stone were furnished, and a number of hands were employed, under the direction of the self-styled engineer, in constructing the ponderous apparatus, which was erected on a solid platform of masonry, thirty paces square and seven or eight feet high, that covered the centre of the market-place. This was a work of the Aztec princes, and was used as a scaffolding on which mountebanks and jugglers might exhibit their marvellous feats for the amusement of the populace, who took great delight in these performances.[3]

The erection of the machine consumed several days, during which hostilities were suspended, while the artisans were protected from interruption by a strong corps of infantry. At length the work was completed; and

[1] Bustamante, the Mexican editor of Sahagun, mentions that he has now in his possession several of these military spoils. "Toda la llanura del Santuario de nuestra Señora de los Ángeles y de Santiago Tlaltilolco se ve sembrada de fragmentos de lanzas cortantes, de macanas, y flechas de piedra obsidiana, de que usaban los Mexicanos ó sea Chinapos, y yo he recogido no pocos que conservo en mi poder." Hist. de Nueva-España, lib. 12, nota 21.

[2] "Y como comenzó á arder, levantóse una llama tan alta que parecia llegar al cielo, al espectáculo de esta quema, todos los hombres y mugeres que se habian acogido á las tiendas que cercaban todo el Tianguez comenzáron á llorar á voz en grito, que fué cosa de espanto oirlos ; porque quemado aquel delubro satánico luego entendiéron que habian de ser del todo destruidos y robados." Sahagun, Hist. de Nueva-España, MS., lib. 12, cap. 37.

[3] Vestiges of the work are still visible, according to M. de Humboldt, within the limits of the porch of the chapel of St. Jago. Essai politique, tom. ii. p. 44.

the besieged, who with silent awe had beheld from the neighbouring *azoteas* the progress of the mysterious engine which was to lay the remainder of their capital in ruins, now looked with terror for its operation. A stone of huge size was deposited on the timber. The machinery was set in motion; and the rocky fragment was discharged with a tremendous force from the catapult. But, instead of taking the direction of the Aztec buildings, it rose high and perpendicularly into the air, and, descending whence it sprung, broke the ill-omened machine into splinters! It was a total failure. The Aztecs were released from their apprehensions, and the soldiery made many a merry jest on the catastrophe, somewhat at the expense of their commander, who testified no little vexation at the disappointment, and still more at his own credulity.[1]

CHAPTER VIII.

DREADFUL SUFFERINGS OF THE BESIEGED. — SPIRIT OF GUATEMOZIN.— MURDEROUS ASSAULTS. — CAPTURE OF GUATEMOZIN. — EVACUATION OF THE CITY.—TERMINATION OF THE SIEGE.—REFLECTIONS.

(1521.)

THERE was no occasion to resort to artificial means to precipitate the ruin of the Aztecs. It was accelerated every hour by causes more potent than those arising from mere human agency. There they were,—pent up in their close and suffocating quarters, nobles, commoners, and slaves, men, women, and children, some in houses, more frequently in hovels,—for this part of the city was not the best,—others in the open air in canoes, or in the streets, shivering in the cold rains of night, and scorched by the burning heat of day.[2] An old chronicler mentions the fact of two women of rank remaining three days and nights up to their necks in the water among the reeds, with only a handful of maize for their support.[3] The ordinary means of sustaining life were long since gone. They wandered about in search of anything, however unwholesome or revolting, that might mitigate the fierce gnawings of hunger. Some hunted for insects and worms on the borders of the lake, or gathered the salt weeds and moss from its bottom, while at times they might be seen casting a wistful look at the green hills beyond, which many of them had left to share the fate of their brethren in the capital.

[1] Bernal Diaz, Hist. de la Conquista, cap. 155.— Rel. Terc. de Cortés, ap. Lorenzana, p. 290.— Sahagun, Hist. de Nueva-España, MS., lib. 12, cap. 37.

[2] "Estaban los tristes Mejicanos, hombres y mugeres, niños y niñas, viejos y viejas, heridos y enfermos, en un lugar bien estrecho, y bien apre-

tados los unos con los otros, y con grandísima falta de bastimentos, y al calor del Sol, y al frio de la noche, y cada hora esperando la muerte." Sahagun, Hist. de Nueva-España, MS., lib. 12, cap. 39.

[3] Torquemada had the anecdote from a nephew of one of the Indian matrons, then a very old man himself. Monarch. Ind., lib. 4, cap. 102.

To their credit, it is said by the Spanish writers that they were not driven, in their extremity, to violate the laws of nature by feeding on one another.[1] But, unhappily, this is contradicted by the Indian authorities, who state that many a mother, in her agony, devoured the offspring which she had no longer the means of supporting. This is recorded of more than one siege in history; and it is the more probable here, where the sensibilities must have been blunted by familiarity with the brutal practices of the national superstition.[2]

But all was not sufficient, and hundreds of famished wretches died every day from extremity of suffering. Some dragged themselves into the houses, and drew their last breath alone and in silence. Others sank down in the public streets. Wherever they died, there they were left. There was no one to bury or to remove them. Familiarity with the spectacle made men indifferent to it. They looked on in dumb despair, waiting for their own turn. There was no complaint, no lamentation, but deep, unutterable woe.

If in other quarters of the town the corpses might be seen scattered over the streets, here they were gathered in heaps. "They lay so thick," says Bernal Diaz, "that one could not tread except among the bodies."[3] "A man could not set his foot down," says Cortés, yet more strongly, "unless on the corpse of an Indian."[4] They were piled one upon another, the living mingled with the dead. They stretched themselves on the bodies of their friends, and lay down to sleep there. Death was everywhere. The city was a vast charnel-house, in which all was hastening to decay and decomposition. A poisonous steam arose from the mass of putrefaction, under the action of alternate rain and heat, which so tainted the whole atmosphere that the Spaniards, including the general himself, in their brief visits to the quarter, were made ill by it, and it bred a pestilence that swept off even greater numbers than the famine.[5]

Men's minds were unsettled by these strange and accumulated horrors. They resorted to all the superstitious rites prescribed by their religion, to stay the pestilence. They called on their priests to invoke the gods in their behalf. But the oracles were dumb, or gave only gloomy responses. Their deities had deserted them, and in their place they saw signs of celestial wrath, telling of still greater woes in reserve. Many, after the siege, declared that, among other prodigies, they beheld a stream of light,

[1] Torquemada, Monarch. Ind., ubi supra.— Bernal Diaz, Hist. de la Conquista, cap. 156.

[2] "De los niños, no quedó nadie, que las mismas madres y padres los comian (que era gran lástima de ver, y mayormente de sufrir)." (Sahagun, Hist. de Nueva-España, MS., lib. 12, cap. 39.) The historian derived his accounts from the Mexicans themselves, soon after the event.—One is reminded of the terrible denunciations of Moses: "The tender and delicate woman among you, which would not adventure to set the sole of her foot upon the ground for delicateness and tenderness, her eye shall be evil toward . . . her children which she shall bear; for she shall eat them, for want of all things, secretly, in the siege and straitness wherewith thine enemy shall distress thee in thy gates." Deuteronomy, chap. 28, vs. 56, 57.

[3] "No podiamos andar sino entre cuerpos, y cabeças de Indios muertos." Hist. de la Conquista, cap. 156.

[4] "No tenian donde estar sino sobre los cuerpos muertos de los suyos." Rel. Terc., ap. Lorenzana, p. 291.

[5] Bernal Diaz, Hist. de la Conquista, ubi supra. —Herrera, Hist. general, dec. 3, lib. 2, cap. 8.— Sahagun, Hist. de Nueva-España, MS., lib. 12, cap. 41.—Gonzalo de las Casas, Defensa, MS., cap. 28.

of a blood-red colour, coming from the north in the direction of Tepejacac, with a rushing noise like that of a whirlwind, which swept round the district of Tlatelolco, darting out sparkles and flakes of fire, till it shot far into the centre of the lake! [1] In the disordered state of their nerves, a mysterious fear took possession of their senses. Prodigies were of familiar occurrence, and the most familiar phenomena of nature were converted into prodigies. [2] Stunned by their calamities, reason was bewildered, and they became the sport of the wildest and most superstitious fancies.

In the midst of these awful scenes, the young emperor of the Aztecs remained, according to all accounts, calm and courageous. With his fair capital laid in ruins before his eyes, his nobles and faithful subjects dying around him, his territory rent away, foot by foot, till scarce enough remained for him to stand on, he rejected every invitation to capitulate, and showed the same indomitable spirit as at the commencement of the siege. When Cortés, in the hope that the extremities of the besieged would incline them to listen to an accommodation, persuaded a noble prisoner to bear to Guatemozin his proposals to that effect, the fierce young monarch, according to the general, ordered him at once to be sacrificed. [3] It is a Spaniard, we must remember, who tells the story.

Cortés, who had suspended hostilities for several days, in the vain hope that the distresses of the Mexicans would bend them to submission, now determined to drive them to it by a general assault. Cooped up as they were within a narrow quarter of the city, their position favoured such an attempt. He commanded Alvarado to hold himself in readiness, and directed Sandoval—who, besides the causeway, had charge of the fleet, which lay off the Tlatelolcan district—to support the attack by a cannonade on the houses near the water. He then led his forces into the city, or rather across the horrid waste that now encircled it.

On entering the Indian precincts, he was met by several of the chiefs, who, stretching forth their emaciated arms, exclaimed, " You are the children of the Sun. But the Sun is swift in his course. Why are you, then, so tardy? Why do you delay so long to put an end to our miseries? Rather kill us at once, that we may go to our god Huitzilopochtli, who waits for us in heaven to give us rest from our sufferings! " [4]

Cortés was moved by their piteous appeal, and answered that he desired not their death, but their submission. " Why does your master refuse to treat with me," he said, " when a single hour will suffice for me to crush

---

[1] " Un torbellino de fuego como sangre embuelto en brasas y en centellas, que partia de hacia Tepeacac (que es donde está ahora Santa María de Guadalupe) y fué haciendo gran ruido, hacia donde estaban acorralados los Mejicanos y Tlaltilulcanos; y dió una vuelta para enrededor de ellos, y no dicen si los empeció algo, sino que habiendo dado aquella vuelta, se entró por la laguna adelante; y allí desapareció." Sahagun, Hist. de Nueva-España, MS., lib. 12, cap. 40.

[2] " Inclinatis ad credendum animis," says the philosophic Roman historian, " loco ominum etiam fortuita." Tacitus, Hist., lib. 2, sec. 1.

[3] " Y como lo lleváron delante de Guatimucin su Señor, y él le comenzó á hablar sobre la Paz, dizque luego lo mandó matar y sacrificar." Rel. Terc., ap. Lorenzana, p. 293.

[4] " Que pues ellos me tenian por Hijo del Sol, y el Sol en tanta brevedad como era en un dia y una noche daba vuelta á todo el Mundo, que porque yo assí brevemente no los acababa de matar, y los quitaba de penar tanto, porque ya ellos tenian deseos de morir, y irse al Cielo para su Ochilobus [Huitzilopochtli], que los estaba esperando para descansar." Ibid., p. 292.

him and all his people ? " He then urged them to request Guatemozin to confer with him, with the assurance that he might do it in safety, as his person should not be molested.

The nobles, after some persuasion, undertook the mission; and it was received by the young monarch in a manner which showed—if the anecdote before related of him be true—that misfortune had at length asserted some power over his haughty spirit. He consented to the interview, though not to have it take place on that day, but the following, in the great square of Tlatelolco. Cortés, well satisfied, immediately withdrew from the city and resumed his position on the causeway.

The next morning he presented himself at the place appointed, having previously stationed Alvarado there with a strong corps of infantry, to guard against treachery. The stone platform in the centre of the square was covered with mats and carpets, and a banquet was prepared to refresh the famished monarch and his nobles. Having made these arrangements, he awaited the hour of the interview.

But Guatemozin, instead of appearing himself, sent his nobles, the same who had brought to him the general's invitation, and who now excused their master's absence on the plea of illness. Cortés, though disappointed, gave a courteous reception to the envoys, considering that it might still afford the means of opening a communication with the emperor. He persuaded them, without much entreaty, to partake of the good cheer spread before them, which they did with a voracity that told how severe had been their abstinence. He then dismissed them with a seasonable supply of provisions for their master, pressing him to consent to an interview, without which it was impossible their differences could be adjusted.

The Indian envoys returned in a short time, bearing with them a present of fine cotton fabrics, of no great value, from Guatemozin, who still declined to meet the Spanish general. Cortés, though deeply chagrined, was unwilling to give up the point. "He will surely come," he said to the envoys, "when he sees that I suffer you to go and come unharmed, you who have been my steady enemies, no less than himself, throughout the war. He has nothing to fear from me." [1] He again parted with them, promising to receive their answer the following day.

On the next morning the Aztec chiefs, entering the Christian quarters, announced to Cortés that Guatemozin would confer with him at noon in the market-place. The general was punctual at the hour; but without success. Neither monarch nor ministers appeared there. It was plain that the Indian prince did not care to trust the promises of his enemy. A thought of Montezuma may have passed across his mind. After he had waited three hours, the general's patience was exhausted, and, as he

1 " Y. yo les torné á repetir, que no sabia la causa, porque él se recelaba venir ante mí, pues veia que á ellos, que yo sabia q̃ habian sido los causadores principales de la Guerra, y que la habian sustentado, les hacia buen tratamiento, que los dejaba ir, y venir seguramente, sin recibir enojo alguno ; que les rogaba, que le tornassen á hablar, y mirassen mucho en esto de su venida, pues á él le convenia, y yo lo hacia por su provecho." Rel. Terc., ap. Lorenzana, pp. 294. 295.

learned that the Mexicans were busy in preparations for defence, he made immediate dispositions for the assault.[1]

The confederates had been left without the walls; for he did not care to bring them within sight of the quarry before he was ready to slip the leash. He now ordered them to join him, and, supported by Alvarado's division, marched at once into the enemy's quarters. He found them prepared to receive him. Their most able-bodied warriors were thrown into the van, covering their feeble and crippled comrades. Women were seen occasionally mingling in the ranks, and, as well as children, thronged the *azoteas*, where, with famine-stricken visages and haggard eyes, they scowled defiance and hatred on their invaders.

As the Spaniards advanced, the Mexicans set up a fierce war-cry, and sent off clouds of arrows with their accustomed spirit, while the women and boys rained down darts and stones from their elevated position on the terraces. But the missiles were sent by hands too feeble to do much damage; and, when the squadrons closed, the loss of strength became still more sensible in the Aztecs. Their blows fell feebly and with doubtful aim, though some, it is true, of stronger constitution, or gathering strength from despair, maintained to the last a desperate fight.

The arquebusiers now poured in a deadly fire. The brigantines replied by successive volleys, in the opposite quarter. The besieged, hemmed in, like deer surrounded by the huntsmen, were brought down on every side. The carnage was horrible. The ground was heaped up with slain, until the maddened combatants were obliged to climb over the human mounds to get at one another. The miry soil was saturated with blood, which ran off like water and dyed the canals themselves with crimson.[2] All was uproar and terrible confusion. The hideous yells of the barbarians, the oaths and execrations of the Spaniards, the cries of the wounded, the shrieks of women and children, the heavy blows of the Conquerors, the death-struggle of their victims, the rapid, reverberating echoes of musketry, the hissing of innumerable missiles, the crash and crackling of blazing buildings, crushing hundreds in their ruins, the blinding volumes of dust and sulphurous smoke shrouding all in their gloomy canopy, made a scene appalling even to the soldiers of Cortés, steeled as they were by many a rough passage of war, and by long familiarity with blood and violence. "The piteous cries of the women and children, in particular," says the general, "were enough to break one's heart."[3] He commanded that they should be spared, and that

---

[1] The testimony is most emphatic and unequivocal to these repeated efforts on the part of Cortés to bring the Aztecs peaceably to terms. Besides his own Letter to the emperor, see Bernal Diaz, cap. 155,—Herrera, Hist. general, lib. 2, cap. 6, 7,—Torquemada, Monarch. Ind., lib. 4, cap. 100,—Ixtlilxochitl, Venida de los Españoles, pp. 44-48,—Oviedo, Hist. de las Ind., MS., lib. 33, cap. 29, 30.

[2] "Corrian Arroios de Sangre por las Calles,

como pueden correr de Agua, quando llueve, y con ímpetu, y fuerça." Torquemada, Monarch. Ind., lib. 4, cap. 103.

[3] "Era tanta la grita, y lloro de los Niños, y Mugeres, que no habia Persona, á quien no quebrantasse el corazon." (Rel. Terc., ap. Lorenzana, p. 296.) They were a rash and stiff-necked race, exclaims his reverend editor, the archbishop, with a charitable commentary! "*Gens duræ cervicis gens absque consilio.*" Nota.

all who asked it should receive quarter. He particularly urged this on the confederates, and placed Spaniards among them to restrain their violence.[1] But he had set an engine in motion too terrible to be controlled. It were as easy to curb the hurricane in its fury, as the passions of an infuriated horde of savages. "Never did I see so pitiless a race," he exclaims, "or anything wearing the form of man so destitute of humanity."[2] They made no distinction of sex or age, and in this hour of vengeance seemed to be requiting the hoarded wrongs of a century. At length, sated with slaughter, the Spanish commander sounded a retreat. It was full time, if, according to his own statement,—we may hope it is an exaggeration,—forty thousand souls had perished![3] Yet their fate was to be envied, in comparison with that of those who survived.

Through the long night which followed, no movement was perceptible in the Aztec quarter. No light was seen there, no sound was heard, save the low moaning of some wounded or dying wretch, writhing in his agony. All was dark and silent,—the darkness of the grave. The last blow seemed to have completely stunned them. They had parted with hope, and sat in sullen despair, like men waiting in silence the stroke of the executioner. Yet, for all this, they showed no disposition to submit. Every new injury had sunk deeper into their souls, and filled them with a deeper hatred of their enemy. Fortune, friends, kindred, home,—all were gone. They were content to throw away life itself, now that they had nothing more to live for.

Far different was the scene in the Christian camp, where, elated with their recent successes, all was alive with bustle and preparation for the morrow. Bonfires were seen blazing along the causeways, lights gleamed from tents and barracks, and the sounds of music and merriment, borne over the waters, proclaimed the joy of the soldiers at the prospect of so soon terminating their wearisome campaign.

On the following morning the Spanish commander again mustered his forces, having decided to follow up the blow of the preceding day before the enemy should have time to rally, and at once put an end to the war. He had arranged with Alvarado, on the evening previous, to occupy the market-place of Tlatelolco; and the discharge of an arquebuse was to be the signal for a simultaneous assault. Sandoval was to hold the northern causeway, and, with the fleet, to watch the movements of the Indian emperor, and to intercept the flight to the mainland, which Cortés knew he meditated. To allow him to effect this would be to leave a formidable enemy in his own neighbourhood, who might at any time

---

[1] "Como la gente de la Cibdad se salia á los nuestros, habia el general proveido, que por todas las calles estubiesen Españoles para estorvar á los amigos, que no matasen aquellos tristes, que eran sin número. É tambien dixo á todos los amigos capitanes, que no consintiesen á su gente que matasen á ninguno de los que salian." Oviedo, Hist. de las Ind., MS., lib. 33, cap. 50.

[2] "La qual crueldad nunca en Generacion tan recia se vió, ni tan fuera de toda órden de naturaleza, como en los Naturales de estas partes." Rel. Terc. de Cortés, ap. Lorenzana, p. 296.

[3] Rel. Terc. de Cortés, ap. Lorenzana, ubi supra.—Ixtlilxochitl says, 50,000 were slain and taken in this dreadful onslaught. Venida de los Españoles, p. 48.

kindle the flame of insurrection throughout the country. He ordered Sandoval, however, to do no harm to the royal person, and not to fire on the enemy at all, except in self-defence.[1]

It was the memorable thirteenth of August 1521, the day of St. Hippolytus, — from this circumstance selected as the patron saint of modern Mexico, — that Cortés led his warlike array for the last time across the black and blasted environs which lay around the Indian capital. On entering the Aztec precincts, he paused, willing to afford its wretched inmates one more chance of escape before striking the fatal blow. He obtained an interview with some of the principal chiefs, and expostulated with them on the conduct of their prince. "He surely will not," said the general, "see you all perish, when he can so easily save you." He then urged them to prevail on Guatemozin to hold a conference with him, repeating the assurances of his personal safety.

The messengers went on their mission, and soon returned with the *cihuacoatl* at their head, a magistrate of high authority among the Mexicans. He said, with a melancholy air, in which his own disappointment was visible, that "Guatemozin was ready to die where he was, but would hold no interview with the Spanish commander;" adding, in a tone of resignation, "it is for you to work your pleasure." "Go, then," replied the stern Conqueror, "and prepare your countrymen for death. Their hour is come."[2]

He still postponed the assault for several hours. But the impatience of his troops at this delay was heightened by the rumour that Guatemozin and his nobles were preparing to escape with their effects in the *piraguas* and canoes which were moored on the margin of the lake. Convinced of the fruitlessness and impolicy of further procrastination, Cortés made his final dispositions for the attack, and took his own station on an *azotea* which commanded the theatre of operations.

When the assailants came into the presence of the enemy, they found them huddled together in the utmost confusion, all ages and sexes, in masses so dense that they nearly forced one another over the brink of the causeways into the water below. Some had climbed on the terraces, others feebly supported themselves against the walls of the buildings. Their squalid and tattered garments gave a wildness to their appearance which still further heightened the ferocity of their expression, as they glared on their enemy with eyes in which hate was mingled with despair. When the Spaniards had approached within bowshot, the Aztecs let off a flight of impotent missiles, showing to the last the resolute spirit, though

---

1 "Adonde estauan retraidos el Guatemuz con toda la flor de sus Capitanes, y personas mas nobles que en Mexico auia, y le mandó que no matasse ni hiriesse á ningunos Indios, saluo si no le diessen guerra, é que aunque se la diessen, que solamente se defendiesse." Bernal Diaz, Hist. de la Conquista, cap. 156.

2 "Y al fin me dijo, que en ninguna manera el Señor vernia ante mí; y antes queria por allá morir, y que á él pesaba mucho de esto, que hiciesse yo lo que quisiesse; y como ví en esto su determinacion, yo le dije; que se bolviesse á los suyos, y que él, y ellos se aparejassen, porque los queria combatir, y acabar de matar, y assi se fué." Rel. Terc. de Cortés, ap. Lorenzana, p. 298.

they had lost the strength, of their better days. The fatal signal was then given by the discharge of an arquebuse,—speedily followed by peals of heavy ordnance, the rattle of firearms, and the hellish shouts of the confederates as they sprang upon their victims. It is unnecessary to stain the page with a repetition of the horrors of the preceding day. Some of the wretched Aztecs threw themselves into the water and were picked up by the canoes. Others sank and were suffocated in the canals. The number of these became so great that a bridge was made of their dead bodies, over which the assailants could climb to the opposite banks. Others again, especially the women, begged for mercy, which, as the chroniclers assure us, was everywhere granted by the Spaniards, and, contrary to the instructions and entreaties of Cortés, everywhere refused by the confederates.[1]

While this work of butchery was going on, numbers were observed pushing off in the barks that lined the shore, and making the best of their way across the lake. They were constantly intercepted by the brigantines, which broke through the flimsy array of boats, sending off their volleys to the right and left, as the crews of the latter hotly assailed them. The battle raged as fiercely on the lake as on the land. Many of the Indian vessels were shattered and overturned. Some few, however, under cover of the smoke, which rolled darkly over the waters, succeeded in clearing themselves of the turmoil, and were fast nearing the opposite shore.

Sandoval had particularly charged his captains to keep an eye on the movements of any vessel in which it was at all probable that Guatemozin might be concealed. At this crisis, three or four of the largest *piraguas* were seen skimming over the water and making their way rapidly across the lake. A captain, named Garci Holguin, who had command of one of the best sailers in the fleet, instantly gave them chase. The wind was favourable, and every moment he gained on the fugitives, who pulled their oars with a vigour that despair alone could have given. But it was in vain; and, after a short race, Holguin, coming alongside of one of the *piraguas*, which, whether from its appearance or from information he had received, he conjectured might bear the Indian emperor, ordered his men to level their crossbows at the boat. But, before they could discharge them, a cry arose from those in it that their lord was on board. At the same moment a young warrior, armed with buckler and *maquahuitl*, rose up, as if to beat off the assailants. But, as the Spanish captain ordered his men not to shoot, he dropped his weapons, and exclaimed, " I am Guatemozin. Lead me to Malinche ; I am his prisoner ; but let no harm come to my wife and my followers." [2]

1 Oviedo, Hist. de las Ind., MS., lib. 33, cap. 30.—Ixtlilxochitl, Venida de los Españoles, p. 48.—Herrera, Hist. general, dec. 3, lib. 2, cap. 7.—Rel. Terc. de Cortés, ap. Lorenzana, pp. 297, 298.—Gomara, Crónica, cap. 142.

2 Ixtlilxochitl, Venida de los Españoles, p. 49.—" No me tiren, que yo soy el Rey de México, y desta tierra, y lo que te ruego es, que no me llegues á mi muger, ni á mis hijos ; ni á ninguna muger, ni á ninguna cosa de lo que aquí traygo, sino que me tomes á mi, y me lleues á Malinche." (Bernal Diaz, Hist. de la Conquista, cap. 156.) M. de Humboldt has taken much pains to identify the place of Guatemozin's capture,—now become dry land,—which he

Holguin assured him that his wishes should be respected, and assisted him to get on board the brigantine, followed by his wife and attendants. These were twenty in number, consisting of Coanaco, the deposed lord of Tezcuco, the lord of Tlacopan, and several other caciques and dignitaries, whose rank, probably, had secured them some exemption from the general calamities of the siege. When the captives were seated on the deck of his vessel, Holguin requested the Aztec prince to put an end to the combat by commanding his people in the other canoes to surrender. But, with a dejected air, he replied, "It is not necessary. They will fight no longer, when they see that their prince is taken." He spoke truth. The news of Guatemozin's capture spread rapidly through the fleet, and on shore, where the Mexicans were still engaged in conflict with their enemies. It ceased, however, at once. They made no further resistance; and those on the water quickly followed the brigantines, which conveyed their captive monarch to land. It seemed as if the fight had been maintained thus long the better to divert the enemy's attention and cover their master's retreat.[1]

Meanwhile, Sandoval, on receiving tidings of the capture, brought his own brigantine alongside of Holguin's and demanded the royal prisoner to be surrendered to him. But the captain claimed him as his prize. A dispute arose between the parties, each anxious to have the glory of the deed, and perhaps the privilege of commemorating it on his escutcheon. The controversy continued so long that it reached the ears of Cortés, who, in his station on the *azotea*, had learned with no little satisfaction the capture of his enemy. He instantly sent orders to his wrangling officers to bring Guatemozin before him, that he might adjust the difference between them.[2] He charged them, at the same time, to treat their prisoner with respect. He then made preparations for the interview, caused the terrace to be carpeted with crimson cloth and matting, and a table to be spread with provisions, of which the unhappy Aztecs stood so much in need.[3] His lovely Indian mistress, Doña Marina, was present to act as interpreter. She had stood by his side through all the troubled scenes of the Conquest, and she was there now to witness its triumphant termination.

considers to have been somewhere between the Garita de Peralvillo, the square of Santiago, Tlatelolco, and the bridge of Amaxac. Essai politique, tom. ii. p. 76.*

[1] For the preceding account of the capture of Guatemozin, told with little discrepancy, though with more or less minuteness, by the different writers, see Bernal Diaz, Hist. de la Conquista, ubi supra,—Rel. Terc. de Cortés, p. 299,—Gonzalo de las Casas, Defensa, MS.,—Oviedo, Hist. de las Ind., MS., lib. 33, cap. 30.—Torquemada, Monarch. Ind., lib. 4, cap. 101.

[2] The general, according to Diaz, rebuked his officers for their ill-timed contention, reminding them of the direful effects of a similar quarrel between Marius and Sylla respecting Jugurtha.

(Hist. de la Conquista, cap. 156.) This piece of pedantry savours much more of the old chronicler than his commander. The result of the whole—not an uncommon one in such cases—was that the emperor granted to neither of the parties, but to Cortés, the exclusive right of commemorating the capture of Guatemozin on his escutcheon. He was permitted to bear three crowns of gold on a sable field, one above the other two, in token of his victory over the three lords of Mexico, Montezuma, his brother Cuitlahua, and Guatemozin. A copy of the instrument containing the grant of the arms of Cortés may be found in the "Disertaciones históricas" of Alaman, tom. ii. apénd. 2.

[3] Sahagun, Hist. de Nueva-España, lib. 12, cap. 40, MS.

* [According to an old tradition, it was on the Puente del Cabildo, which is within the limits designated by Humboldt. Alaman, Conquista de Méjico (trad. de Vega), tom. ii. p. 209, note.—Ed.]

Guatemozin, on landing, was escorted by a company of infantry to the presence of the Spanish commander. He mounted the *azotea* with a calm and steady step, and was easily to be distinguished from his attendant nobles, though his full, dark eye was no longer lighted up with its accustomed fire, and his features wore an expression of passive resignation, that told little of the fierce and fiery spirit that burned within. His head was large, his limbs well proportioned, his complexion fairer than that of his bronze-coloured nation, and his whole deportment singularly mild and engaging.[1]

Cortés came forward with a dignified and studied courtesy to receive him. The Aztec monarch probably knew the person of his conqueror,[2] for he first broke silence by saying, "I have done all that I could to defend myself and my people. I am now reduced to this state. You will deal with me, Malinche, as you list." Then, laying his hand on the hilt of a poniard stuck in the general's belt, he added, with vehemence, "Better despatch me with this, and rid me of life at once."[3] Cortés was filled with admiration at the proud bearing of the young barbarian, showing in his reverses a spirit worthy of an ancient Roman. "Fear not," he replied: "you shall be treated with all honour. You have defended your capital like a brave warrior. A Spaniard knows how to respect valour even in an enemy."[4] He then inquired of him where he had left the princess his wife; and, being informed that she still remained under protection of a Spanish guard on board the brigantine, the general sent to have her escorted to his presence.

She was the youngest daughter of Montezuma, and was hardly yet on the verge of womanhood. On the accession of her cousin Guatemozin to the throne, she had been wedded to him as his lawful wife.[5] She is celebrated by her contemporaries for her personal charms; and the beautiful princess Tecuichpo is still commemorated by the Spaniards, since from her by a subsequent marriage are descended some of the illustrious families of their own nation.[6] She was kindly received by Cortés, who showed her the respectful attentions suited to her rank. Her birth, no doubt, gave her an additional interest in his eyes, and he may have felt some touch of compunction as he gazed on the daughter of the unfor-

---

[1] For the portrait of Guatemozin I again borrow the faithful pencil of Diaz, who knew him—at least his person—well: "Guatemuz era de muy gentil disposicion, assí de cuerpo, como de fayciones, y la cata algo larga, y alegre, y los ojos mas parecian que quando miraua, que eran con grauedad, y halagüeños, y no auia falta en ellos, y era de edad de veinte y tres, ó veinte y quatro años, y el color tiraua mas á blanco, que al color, y matiz de essotros Indios morenos." Hist. de la Conquista, cap. 156.

[2] [It was unnecessary to qualify the statement, as they had often seen each other at the court of Montezuma. Alaman, Conquista de Méjico (trad. de Vega), tom. ii. p. 211, note.—ED.]

[3] "Llegóse á mi, y díjome en su lengua: que ya él habia hecho todo, lo que de su parte era obligado para defenderse á si, y á los suyos, hasta venir en aquel estado; que ahora fíciesse de él lo que yo quisiese; y puso la mano en un puñal, que yo tenia,

diciéndome, que le diesse de puñaladas, y le matasse." (Rel. Terc. de Cortés, ap. Lorenzana, p. 300.) This remarkable account by the Conqueror himself is confirmed by Diaz, who does not appear to have seen this letter of his commander. Hist. de la Conquista, cap. 156.

[4] Ibid., cap. 156.—Also Oviedo, Hist. de las Ind., MS., lib. 33, cap. 48,—and Martyr (De Orbe Novo, dec. 5, cap. 8), who, by the epithet of *magnanimo regi*, testifies the admiration which Guatemozin's lofty spirit excited in the court of Castile.

[5] The ceremony of marriage, which distinguished the "lawful wife" from the concubine, is described by Don Thoan Cano, in his conversation with Oviedo. According to this, it appears that the only legitimate offspring which Montezuma left at his death was a son and a daughter, this same princess.—See Appendix, Part 2, No. 11.

[6] For a further account of Montezuma's daughter, see Book VII., chapter iii. of this History.

tunate Montezuma. He invited his royal captives to partake of the refreshments which their exhausted condition rendered so necessary. Meanwhile the Spanish commander made his dispositions for the night, ordering Sandoval to escort the prisoners to Cojohuacan, whither he proposed himself immediately to follow. The other captains, Olid and Alvarado, were to draw off their forces to their respective quarters. It was impossible for them to continue in the capital, where the poisonous effluvia from the unburied carcasses loaded the air with infection. A small guard only was stationed to keep order in the wasted suburbs. It was the hour of vespers when Guatemozin surrendered,[1] and the siege might be considered as then concluded. The evening set in dark, and the rain began to fall before the several parties had evacuated the city.[2]

During the night, a tremendous tempest, such as the Spaniards had rarely witnessed, and such as is known only within the tropics, burst over the Mexican Valley. The thunder, reverberating from the rocky amphitheatre of hills, bellowed over the waste of waters, and shook the *teocallis* and crazy tenements of Tenochtitlan—the few that yet survived—to their foundations. The lightning seemed to cleave asunder the vault of heaven, as its vivid flashes wrapped the whole scene in a ghastly glare, for a moment, to be again swallowed up in darkness. The war of elements was in unison with the fortunes of the ruined city. It seemed as if the deities of Anahuac, scared from their ancient abodes, were borne along shrieking and howling in the blast, as they abandoned the fallen capital to its fate![3]

On the day following the surrender, Guatemozin requested the Spanish commander to allow the Mexicans to leave the city and to pass unmolested into the open country. To this Cortés readily assented, as, indeed, without it he could take no steps for purifying the capital. He gave his orders, accordingly, for the evacuation of the place, commanding that no one, Spaniard or confederate, should offer violence to the Aztecs or in any

[1] The event is annually commemorated—or rather was, under the colonial government—by a solemn procession round the walls of the city. It took place on the 13th of August, the anniversary of the surrender, and consisted of the principal cavaliers and citizens on horseback, headed by the viceroy, and displaying the venerable standard of the Conqueror.*

[2] Toribio, Hist. de los Ind., MS., Parte 3, cap. 7.—Sahagun, Hist. de Nueva-España, MS., lib. 12, cap. 42.—Bernal Diaz, Hist. de la Conquista, cap. 156.—" The lord of Mexico having surrendered," says Cortés, in his letter to the emperor, " the war, by the blessing of Heaven, was brought to an end, on Wednesday, the 13th day of August 1521. So that from the day when we first sat down before the city, which was the 30th of May, until its final occupation, seventy-five days elapsed." (Rel. Terc., ap. Lorenzana, p. 300.) It is not easy to tell what event occurred on May 30th to designate the beginning of the siege. Clavigero considers it the occu-

pation of Cojohuacan by Olid. (Stor. del Messico, tom. iii. p. 196.) But I know not on what authority. Neither Bernal Diaz, nor Herrera, nor Cortés, so fixes the date. Indeed, Clavigero says that Alvarado and Olid left Tezcuco May 20th, while Cortés says May 10th. Perhaps Cortés dates from the time when Sandoval established himself on the northern causeway, and when the complete investment of the capital began. Bernal Diaz, more than once, speaks of the siege as lasting three months, computing, probably, from the time when his own division, under Alvarado, took up its position at Tacuba.

[3] It did not, apparently, disturb the slumbers of the troops, who had been so much deafened by the incessant noises of the siege that, now these had ceased, "we felt," says Diaz, in his homely way, " like men suddenly escaped from a belfry, where we had been shut up for months with a chime of bells ringing in our ears!" Hist. de la Conquista, ubi supra.

* [It was the royal standard, not that of Cortés, which was carried on this occasion. The celebration was suppressed by a decree of the córtes of Cadiz in 1812. Alaman, Conquista de Méjico (trad. de Vega), tom. ii. p. 212, note.—ED.]

way obstruct their departure. The whole number of these is variously estimated at from thirty to seventy thousand, besides women and children, who had survived the sword, pestilence, and famine.[1] It is certain they were three days in defiling along the several causeways,—a mournful train ;[2] husbands and wives, parents and children, the sick and the wounded, leaning on one another for support, as they feebly tottered along, squalid, and but half covered with rags, that disclosed at every step hideous gashes, some recently received, others festering from long neglect, and carrying with them an atmosphere of contagion. Their wasted forms and famine-stricken faces told the whole history of the siege ; and, as the straggling files gained the opposite shore, they were observed to pause from time to time, as if to take one more look at the spot so lately crowned by the imperial city, once their pleasant home, and endeared to them by many a glorious recollection.

On the departure of the inhabitants, measures were immediately taken to purify the place, by means of numerous fires kept burning day and night, especially in the infected quarter of Tlatelolco, and by collecting the heaps of dead, which lay mouldering in the streets, and consigning them to the earth. Of the whole number who perished in the course of the siege it is impossible to form any probable computation. The accounts range widely, from one hundred and twenty thousand, the lowest estimate, to two hundred and forty thousand.[3] The number of the Spaniards who fell was comparatively small, but that of the allies must have been large, if the historian of Tezcuco is correct in asserting that thirty thousand perished of his own countrymen alone.[4] That the number of those destroyed within the city was immense cannot be doubted, when we consider that, besides its own redundant population, it was thronged with that of the neighbouring towns, who, distrusting their strength to resist the enemy, sought protection within its walls.

The booty found there—that is, the treasures of gold and jewels, the only booty of much value in the eyes of the Spaniards—fell far below their expectations. It did not exceed, according to the general's state-

---

[1] Herrera (Hist. general, dec. 3, lib. 2, cap. 7) and Torquemada (Monarch. Ind., lib. 4, cap. 101) estimate them at 30,000. Ixtlilxochitl says that 60,000 fighting men laid down their arms (Venida de los Españoles, p. 49) ; and Oviedo swells the amount still higher, to 70,000. (Hist. de las Ind., MS., lib. 33, cap. 48.)—After the losses of the siege, these numbers are startling.

[2] "Digo que en tres dias con sus noches iban todas tres calçadas llenas de Indios, é Indias, y muchachos, llenas de bote en bote, que nunca dexauan de salir, y tan flacos, y suzios, é amarillos, é hediondos, que era lástima de los ver." Bernal Diaz, Hist. de la Conquista, cap. 156.

[3] Cortés estimates the losses of the enemy in the three several assaults at 67,000, which with 50,000 whom he reckons to have perished from famine and disease, would give 117,000. (Rel. Terc., ap. Lorenzana, p. 298, et alibi.) But this is exclusive of those who fell previously to the commencement of the vigorous plan of operations for demolishing the city. Ixtlilxochitl, who seldom allows any one to beat him in figures, puts the dead, in round numbers, at 240,000, comprehending the flower of the Aztec nobility. (Venida de los Españoles, p. 51.) Bernal Diaz observes, more generally, "I have read the story of the destruction of Jerusalem, but I doubt if there was as great mortality there as in this siege ; for there was assembled in the city an immense number of Indian warriors from all the provinces and towns subject to Mexico, the most of whom perished." (Hist. de la Conquista, cap. 156.) "I have conversed," says Oviedo, "with many hidalgos and other persons, and have heard them say that the number of the dead was incalculable,—greater than that at Jerusalem, as described by Josephus." (Hist. de las Ind., MS., lib. 30, cap. 30.) As the estimate of the Jewish historian amounts to 1,100,000 (Antiquities of the Jews, Eng. trans., book vii. chap. xvii.), the comparison may stagger the most accommodating faith. It will be safer to dispense with arithmetic where the data are too loose and slippery to afford a foothold for getting at truth.

[4] Ixtlilxochitl, Venida de los Españoles, p. 51.

ment, a hundred and thirty thousand *castellanos* of gold, including the sovereign's share, which, indeed, taking into account many articles of curious and costly workmanship, voluntarily relinquished by the army, greatly exceeded his legitimate fifth.[1] Yet the Aztecs must have been in possession of a much larger treasure, if it were only the wreck of that recovered from the Spaniards on the night of the memorable flight from Mexico. Some of the spoil may have been sent away from the capital, some spent in preparations for defence, and more of it buried in the earth, or sunk in the water of the lake. Their menaces were not without a meaning. They had, at least, the satisfaction of disappointing the avarice of their enemies.

Cortés had no further occasion for the presence of his Indian allies. He assembled the chiefs of the different squadrons, thanked them for their services, noticed their valour in flattering terms, and, after distributing presents among them, with the assurance that his master the emperor would recompense their fidelity yet more largely, dismissed them to their own homes. They carried off a liberal share of the spoils of which they had plundered the dwellings,—not of a kind to excite the cupidity of the Spaniards,—and returned in triumph, short-sighted triumph! at the success of their expedition and the downfall of the Aztec dynasty.

Great, also, was the satisfaction of the Spaniards at this brilliant termination of their long and laborious campaign. They were, indeed, disappointed at the small amount of treasure found in the conquered city. But the soldier is usually too much absorbed in the present to give much heed to the future; and, though their discontent showed itself afterwards in a more clamorous form, they now thought only of their triumph, and abandoned themselves to jubilee. Cortés celebrated the event by a banquet, as sumptuous as circumstances would permit, to which all the cavaliers and officers were invited. Loud and long was their revelry, which was carried to such an excess as provoked the animadversion of Father Olmedo, who intimated that this was not the fitting way to testify their sense of the favours shown them by the Almighty. Cortés admitted the justice of the rebuke, but craved some indulgence for a soldier's license in the hour of victory. The following day was appointed for the commemoration of their successes in a more suitable manner.

A procession of the whole army was then formed, with Father Olmedo at its head. The soiled and tattered banners of Castile, which had waved over many a field of battle, now threw their shadows on the peaceful array of the soldiery, as they slowly moved along, rehearsing the litany and displaying the image of the Virgin and the blessed symbol of man's redemption. The reverend father pronounced a discourse, in which he briefly reminded the troops of their great cause for thankfulness to Provi-

---

[1] Rel. Terc., ap. Lorenzana, p. 301.—Oviedo goes into some further particulars respecting the amount of the treasure, and especially of the imperial fifth, to which I shall have occasion to advert hereafter Hist. de las Ind., MS., lib. 33, cap. 31.

dence for conducting them safe through their long and perilous pilgrimage; and, dwelling on the responsibility incurred by their present position, he besought them not to abuse the rights of conquest, but to treat the unfortunate Indians with humanity. The sacrament was then administered to the commander-in-chief and the principal cavaliers, and the services concluded with a solemn thanksgiving to the God of battles, who had enabled them to carry the banner of the Cross triumphant over this barbaric empire.[1]

Thus, after a siege of nearly three months' duration, unmatched in history for the constancy and courage of the besieged, seldom surpassed for the severity of its sufferings, fell the renowned capital of the Aztecs. Unmatched, it may be truly said, for constancy and courage, when we recollect that the door of capitulation on the most honourable terms was left open to them throughout the whole blockade, and that, sternly rejecting every proposal of their enemy, they, to a man, preferred to die rather than surrender. More than three centuries had elapsed since the Aztecs, a poor and wandering tribe from the far North-west, had come on the plateau. There they built their miserable collection of huts on the spot—as tradition tells us—prescribed by the oracle. Their conquests, at first confined to their immediate neighbourhood, gradually covered the Valley, then, crossing the mountains, swept over the broad extent of the table-land, descended its precipitous sides, and rolled onwards to the Mexican Gulf and the distant confines of Central America. Their wretched capital, meanwhile, keeping pace with the enlargement of territory, had grown into a flourishing city, filled with buildings, monuments of art, and a numerous population, that gave it the first rank among the capitals of the Western World. At this crisis came over another race from the remote East, strangers like themselves, whose coming had also been predicted by the oracle, and, appearing on the plateau, assailed them in the very zenith of their prosperity, and blotted them out from the map of nations for ever! The whole story has the air of fable rather than of history! a legend of romance, —a tale of the genii!

Yet we cannot regret the fall of an empire which did so little to promote the happiness of its subjects or the real interests of humanity. Notwithstanding the lustre thrown over its latter days by the glorious defence of its capital, by the mild munificence of Montezuma, by the dauntless heroism of Guatemozin, the Aztecs were emphatically a fierce and brutal race, little calculated, in their best aspects, to excite our sympathy and regard. Their civilization, such as it was, was not their own, but reflected, perhaps imperfectly, from a race whom they had succeeded in the land. It was in respect to the Aztecs, a generous graft on a vicious stock, and could have brought no fruit to perfection. They ruled over their wide domains

[1] Herrera, Hist. general, dec. 3, lib. 2, cap. 8.— Bernal Diaz, Hist. de la Conquista, cap. 156.— Sahagun, Hist. de Nueva-España, MS., lib. 12, cap. 42.—Oviedo, Hist. de las Ind., MS., lib. 33, cap. 30.—Ixtlilxochitl, Venida de los Españoles, pp. 51, 52.

with a sword, instead of a sceptre. They did nothing to ameliorate the condition or in any way promote the progress of their vassals. Their vassals were serfs, used only to minister to their pleasure, held in awe by armed garrisons, ground to the dust by imposts in peace, by military conscriptions in war. They did not, like the Romans, whom they resembled in the nature of their conquests, extend the rights of citizenship to the conquered. They did not amalgamate them into one great nation, with common rights and interests. They held them as aliens,—even those who in the Valley were gathered round the very walls of the capital. The Aztec metropolis, the heart of the monarchy, had not a sympathy, not a pulsation, in common with the rest of the body politic. It was a stranger in its own land.

The Aztecs not only did not advance the condition of their vassals, but, morally speaking, they did much to degrade it. How can a nation where human sacrifices prevail, and especially when combined with cannibalism, further the march of civilization? How can the interests of humanity be consulted where man is levelled to the rank of the brutes that perish? The influence of the Aztecs introduced their gloomy superstition into lands before unacquainted with it, or where, at least, it was not established in any great strength. The example of the capital was contagious. As the latter increased in opulence, the religious celebrations were conducted with still more terrible magnificence; in the same manner as the gladiatorial shows of the Romans increased in pomp with the increasing splendour of the capital. Men became familiar with scenes of horror and the most loathsome abominations. Women and children — the whole nation — became familiar with and assisted at them. The heart was hardened, the manners were made ferocious, the feeble light of civilization, transmitted from a milder race, was growing fainter and fainter, as thousands and thousands of miserable victims, throughout the empire, were yearly fattened in its cages, sacrificed on its altars, dressed and served at its banquets! The whole land was converted into vast human shambles! The empire of the Aztecs did not fall before its time.

Whether these unparalleled outrages furnish a sufficient plea to the Spaniards for their invasion, whether, with the Protestant, we are content to find a warrant for it in the natural rights and demands of civilization, or, with the Roman Catholic, in the good pleasure of the Pope,—on the one or other of which grounds the conquests by most Christian nations in the East and the West have been defended, — it is unnecessary to discuss, as it has already been considered in a former chapter. It is more material to inquire whether, assuming the right, the conquest of Mexico was conducted with a proper regard to the claims of humanity. And here we must admit that, with all allowance for the ferocity of the age and the laxity of its principles, there are passages which every Spaniard who cherishes the fame of his countrymen would be glad to see expunged from their history; passages not to be vindicated on the score of self-defence, or of necessity of any kind, and which must for ever leave a dark spot on the annals of the Conquest. And yet, taken as a whole, the invasion, up to the capture of the capital, was conducted on principles less revolting to humanity than most, perhaps than any, of the other conquests of the Castilian crown in the New World.

It may seem slight praise to say that the followers of Cortés used no blood-hounds to hunt down their wretched victims, as in some other parts of the Continent, nor exterminated a peaceful and submissive population in mere wantonness of cruelty, as in the Islands. Yet it is something that they were not so far infected by the spirit of the age, and that their swords were rarely stained with blood unless it was indispensable to the success of their enterprise. Even in the last siege of the capital, the sufferings of the Aztecs, terrible as they were, do not imply any unusual cruelty in the victors ; they were not greater than those inflicted on their own countrymen at home, in many a memorable instance, by the most polished nations, not merely of ancient times, but of our own. They were the inevitable consequences which follow from war when, instead of being confined to its legitimate field, it is brought home to the hearthstone, to the peaceful community of the city,—its burghers untrained to arms, its women and children yet more defenceless. In the present instance, indeed, the sufferings of the besieged were in a great degree to be charged on themselves,—on their patriotic but desperate self-devotion. It was not the desire, as certainly it was not the interest, of the Spaniards to destroy the capital or its inhabitants. When any of these fell into their hands, they were kindly entertained, their wants supplied, and every means taken to infuse into them a spirit of conciliation ; and this, too, it should be remembered, in despite of the dreadful doom to which they consigned their Christian captives. The gates of a fair capitulation were kept open, though unavailingly, to the last hour.

The right of conquest necessarily implies that of using whatever force may be necessary for overcoming resistance to the assertion of that right. For the Spaniards to have done otherwise than they did would have been to abandon the siege, and, with it, the conquest of the country. To have suffered the inhabitants, with their high-spirited monarch, to escape, would but have prolonged the miseries of war by transferring it to another and more inaccessible quarter. They literally, so far as the success of the expedition was concerned, had no choice. If our imagination is struck with the amount of suffering in this and in similar scenes of the Conquest, it should be borne in mind that it was a natural result of the great masses of men engaged in the conflict. The amount of suffering does not of itself show the amount of cruelty which caused it ; and it is but justice to the Conquerors of Mexico to say that the very brilliancy and importance of their exploits have given a melancholy celebrity to their misdeeds, and thrown them into somewhat bolder relief than strictly belongs to them. It is proper that thus much should be stated, not to excuse their excesses, but that we may be enabled to make a more impartial estimate of their conduct as compared with that of other nations under similar circumstances, and that we may not visit them with peculiar obloquy for evils which necessarily flow from the condition of war.[1] I have not drawn a veil over these evils; for the historian should not shrink from depicting in their true colours the atrocities of a condition over which success is apt to throw a false halo of glory, but which, bursting asunder the strong bonds of human fellowship, purchases its triumphs by arming the hand of man against his brother, makes a savage of the civilized, and kindles the fires of hell in the bosom of the savage.

Whatever may be thought of the Conquest in a moral view, regarded as a military achievement it must fill us with astonishment. That a handful of adventurers, indifferently armed and equipped, should have landed on the shores of a powerful empire inhabited by a fierce and war-like race, and, in defiance of the reiterated prohibitions of its sovereign, have forced their way into the interior;—that they should have done this without knowledge of the language or of the land, without chart or compass to guide them, without any idea of the difficulties they were to encounter, totally uncertain whether the next step might bring them on a hostile nation or on a desert, feeling their way along in the dark, as it were;—that, though nearly overwhelmed in their first encounter with the inhabitants, they should have still pressed on to the capital of the empire, and, having reached it, thrown themselves unhesitatingly into the midst of their enemies;—that, so far from being daunted by the extraordinary spectacle there exhibited of power and civilization, they should have been but the more confirmed in their original design;—that they should have seized the monarch, have executed his ministers before the eyes of his subjects, and, when driven forth with ruin from the gates, have gathered their scattered wreck together, and, after a system of operations pursued with consummate policy and daring, have succeeded in overturning the capital and establishing their sway over the country;—that all this should have been so effected by a mere handful of indigent adventurers, is a fact little short of the miraculous,—too startling for the probabilities demanded by fiction, and without a parallel in the pages of history.

Yet this must not be understood too literally; for it would be unjust to the Aztecs themselves, at least to their military prowess, to regard the Conquest as directly achieved by the Spaniards alone. This would indeed

---

[1] By none has this obloquy been poured with such unsparing hand on the heads of the old Conquerors as by their own descendants, the modern Mexicans. Ixtlilxochitl's editor, Bustamante, concludes an animated invective against the invaders with recommending that a monument should be raised on the spot—now dry land—where Guatemozin was taken, which, as the proposed inscription itself intimates, should "devote to eternal execration the detested memory of these banditti!" (Venida de los Españoles, p. 52, nota.) One would suppose that the pure Aztec blood, uncontaminated by a drop of Castilian, flowed in the veins of the indignant editor and his compatriots, or at least that their sympathies for the conquered race would make them anxious to reinstate them in their ancient rights. Notwithstanding these bursts of generous indignation, however, which plentifully season the writings of the Mexicans of our day, we do not find that the Revolution, or any of its numerous brood of *pronunciamientos*, has resulted in restoring to them an acre of their ancient territory.

be to arm the latter with the charmed shield of Ruggiero, and the magic lance of Astolfo, overturning its hundreds at a touch. The Indian empire was in a manner conquered by Indians. The first terrible encounter of the Spaniards with the Tlascalans, which had nearly proved their ruin, did in fact insure their success. It secured to them a strong native support on which to retreat in the hour of trouble, and round which they could rally the kindred races of the land for one great and overwhelming assault. The Aztec monarchy fell by the hands of its own subjects, under the direction of European sagacity and science. Had it been united, it might have bidden defiance to the invaders. As it was, the capital was dissevered from the rest of the country, and the bolt, which might have passed off comparatively harmless had the empire been cemented by a common principle of loyalty and patriotism, now found its way into every crack and crevice of the ill-compacted fabric and buried it in its own ruins. Its fate may serve as a striking proof that a government which does not rest on the sympathies of its subjects cannot long abide ; that human institutions, when not connected with human prosperity and progress, must fall,—if not before the increasing light of civilization, by the hand of violence ; by violence from within, if not from without. And who shall lament their fall ?

With the events of this Book terminates the history, by Solís, of the *Conquista de Méjico ;* a history, in many points of view, the most remarkable in the Castilian language. Don Antonio de Solís was born of a respectable family, in October 1610, at Alcalá de Henares, the nursery of science, and the name of which is associated in Spain with the brightest ornaments of both Church and State. Solís, while very young, exhibited the sparks of future genius, especially in the vivacity of his imagination and a sensibility to the beautiful. He showed a decided turn for dramatic composition, and produced a comedy, at the age of seventeen, which would have reflected credit on a riper age. He afterwards devoted himself with assiduity to the study of ethics, the fruits of which are visible in the moral reflections which give a didactic character to the lightest of his compositions.

At the usual age he entered the University of Salamanca, and went through the regular course of the canon and civil law. But the imaginative spirit of Solís took much more delight in the soft revels of the Muses than in the severe discipline of the schools ; and he produced a number of pieces for the theatre, much esteemed for the richness of the diction and for the ingenious and delicate texture of the intrigue. His taste for dramatic composition was, no doubt, nourished by his intimacy with the great Calderon, for whose dramas he prepared several *loas,* or prologues. The amiable manners and brilliant acquisitions of Solís recommended him to the favour of the Conde de Oropesa, Viceroy of Navarre, who made him his secretary. The letters written by him while in the service of this nobleman, and afterwards, have some of them been given to the public, and are much commended for the suavity and elegance of expression characteristic of all the writings of their author.

The increasing reputation of Solís attracted the notice of the Court, and in 1661 he was made secretary of the queen dowager,—an office which he had declined under Philip the Fourth,—and he was also preferred to the still more important post of Historiographer of the Indies, an appointment which stimulated his ambition to a bold career, different from anything he had yet attempted. Five years after this event, at the age of fifty-six, he made a most important change in his way of life, by embracing the religious profession, and was admitted to priest's orders in 1666. From this time he discontinued his addresses to the comic Muse, and, if we may credit his biographers, even refused, from conscientious scruples, to engage in the composition of the religious dramas, styled *autos sacramentales*, although the field was now opened to him by the death of the poet Calderon. But such tenderness of conscience it seems difficult to reconcile with the publication of his various comedies, which took place in 1681. It is certain, however, that he devoted himself zealously to his new profession, and to the historical studies in which his office of chronicler had engaged him. At length the fruits of these studies were given to the world in his *Conquista de Méjico*, which appeared at Madrid in 1684. He designed, it is said, to continue the work to the times after the Conquest. But, if so, he was unfortunately prevented by his death, which occurred about two years after the publication of his history, on the 13th of April 1686. He died at the age of seventy-six, much regarded for his virtues and admired for his genius, but in that poverty with which genius and virtue are too often requited.

The miscellaneous poems of Solís were collected and published a few years after his death, in one volume quarto; which has since been reprinted. But his great work, that on which his fame is permanently to rest, is his *Conquista de Méjico*. Notwithstanding the field of history had been occupied by so many eminent Spanish scholars, there was still a new career open to Solís. His predecessors, with all their merits, had shown a strange ignorance of the principles of art. They had regarded historical writing not as a work of art, but as a science. They had approached it on that side only, and thus divorced it from its legitimate connection with *belles-lettres*. They had thought only of the useful, and nothing of the beautiful; had addressed themselves to the business of instruction, not to that of giving pleasure; to the man of letters, studious to hive up knowledge, not to the man of leisure, who turns to books as a solace or a recreation. Such writers are never in the hands of the many,—not even of the cultivated many. They are condemned to the closet of the student, painfully toiling after truth, and little mindful of the coarse covering under which she may be wrapped. Some of the most distinguished of the national historiographers, as, for example, Herrera and Zurita, two of the greatest names in Castile and Aragon, fall under this censure. They display acuteness, strength of argument, judicious criticism, wonderful patience and industry in accumulating details for their varied and voluminous compilations; but in all the graces of composition—in elegance of style, skilful arrangement of the story, and selection of incidents—they are lamentably deficient. With all their high merits, intellectually considered, they are so defective on the score of art that they can neither be popular, nor reverenced as the great classics of the nation. Solís saw that the field was unappropriated by his predecessors, and had the address to avail himself of it. Instead of spreading himself over a vast range, where he must expend his efforts on cold and barren generalities, he fixed his attention on one great theme,—one that, by its picturesque accompaniments, the romantic incidents of the story, the adventurous character of the actors and their exploits, was associated with many a proud and patriotic feeling in the bosom of the Spaniard,—one, in fine, that, by the brilliant contrast it afforded of European civilization to the barbaric splendours of an Indian dynasty, was remarkably suited to the kindling imagination of the poet. It was accordingly under its poetic aspect that the eye of Solís surveyed it. He distributed the whole subject with admirable skill, keeping down the subordinate parts, bringing the most important into high relief, and by a careful study of its proportions giving an admirable symmetry to the whole. Instead of bewildering the attention by a variety of objects, he presented to it one great and predominant idea, which shed its light, if I may so say, over his whole work. Instead of the numerous episodes, leading, like so many blind galleries, to nothing, he took the student along a great road, conducting straight towards the mark. At every step which we take in the narrative, we feel ourselves on the advance. The story never falters or stands still. That admirable *liaison* of the parts is maintained, by which one part is held to another, and each preceding event prepares the way for that which is to follow. Even those occasional interruptions, th‿ great stumbling-block of the historian, which cannot be avoided, in consequence of the important bearing which the events that cause them have on the story, are managed with such address that, if the interest is suspended, it is never snapped. Such halting-places, indeed, are so contrived as to afford a repose not unwelcome after the stirring scenes in which the reader has been long involved; as the traveller, exhausted by the fatigues of his journey, finds refreshment at places which in their own character have little to recommend them.

The work, thus conducted, affords the interest of a grand spectacle,—of some well-ordered drama, in which scene succeeds to scene, act to act, each unfolding and preparing the mind for the one that is to follow, until the whole is consummated by the grand and decisive *dénouement*. With this *dénouement*, the fall of Mexico, Solís has closed his history, preferring to leave the full impression unbroken on the reader's mind rather than to weaken it by prolonging the narrative to the Conqueror's death. In this he certainly consulted effect.

Solís used the same care in regard to style that he showed in the arrangement of his story. It is elaborated with the nicest art, and displays that varied beauty and brilliancy which remind us of those finely variegated woods which, under a high polish, display all the rich tints that lie beneath the surface. Yet this style finds little favour with foreign critics, who are apt to condemn it as tumid, artificial, and verbose. But let the foreign critic beware how he meddles with style, that impalpable essence which surrounds thought as with an atmosphere, giving to it its life and peculiar tone of colour, differing in different nations, like the atmospheres which envelop the different planets of our system, and which require to be comprehended that we may interpret the character of the objects seen through their medium. None but a native can pronounce with any confidence upon style, affected as it is by so many casual and local associations that determine its propriety and its elegance. In the judgment of eminent Spanish critics, the style of Solís claims the merits of perspicuity, copiousness, and classic elegance. Even the foreigner will not be insensible to its power of conveying a living picture to the eye. Words are the colours of the writer, and Solís uses them with the skill of a consummate artist; now displaying the dark tumult of battle, and now refreshing the mind by scenes of quiet magnificence or of soft luxury and repose.

Solís formed himself to some extent on the historical models of antiquity. He introduced set speeches into the mouths of his personages, speeches of his own composing. The practice may claim high authority among moderns as well as ancients, especially among the great Italian historians. It has its advantages, in enabling the writer to convey in a dramatic form the sentiments of the actors, and thus to maintain the charm of historic illusion by never introducing the person of the historian. It has also another advantage, that of exhibiting the author's own sentiments under cover of his hero's,—a more effective mode than if they were introduced as his own. But to one trained in the school of the great English historians the practice has something in it unsatisfactory and displeasing. There is something like deception in it. The reader is unable to determine what are the sentiments of the characters and what those of the author. History assumes the air of romance, and the bewildered student wanders about in an uncertain light, doubtful whether he is treading on fact or fiction.

It is open to another objection, when, as it frequently does, it violates the propriety of costume. Nothing is more difficult than to preserve the keeping of the piece when the new is thus laid on the old,—the imitation of the antique on the antique itself. The declamations of Solís are much prized as specimens of eloquence. But they are too often misplaced; and the rude characters in whose mouths they are inserted are as little in keeping with them as were the Roman heroes with the fashionable wig and sword with which they strutted on the French stage in Louis the Fourteenth's time.

As to the value of the researches made by Solís in the compilation of his work it is not easy to speak, for the page is supported by none of the notes and references which enable us to track the modern author to the quarry whence he has drawn his materials. It was not the usage of the age. The people of that day, and, indeed, of preceding times, were content to take the author's word for his facts. They did not require to know why he affirmed this thing or doubted that ; whether he built his story on the authority of a friend or of a foe, of a writer of good report or of evil report. In short, they did not demand a reason for their faith. They were content to take it on trust. This was very comfortable to the historian. It saved him a world of trouble in the process, and it prevented the detection of error, or, at least, of negligence. It prevented it with all who did not carefully go over the same ground with himself. They who have occasion to do this with Solís will probably rise from the examination with no very favourable idea of the extent of his researches ; they will find that, though his situation gave him access to the most valuable repositories in the kingdom, he rarely ascends to original documents, but contents himself with the most obvious and accessible ; that he rarely discriminates between the contemporary testimony and that of later date ; in a word, that in all that constitutes the *scientific* value of history he falls far below his learned predecessor Herrera —rapid as was the composition of this last.

Another objection that may be made to Solís is his bigotry, or rather his fanaticism. This defect, so repugnant to the philosophic spirit which should preside over the labours of the historian, he possessed, it is true, in common with many of his countrymen. But in him it was carried to an uncommon height ; and it was peculiarly unfortunate, since his subject, being the contest between the Christian and the Infidel, naturally drew forth the full display of this failing. Instead of regarding the benighted heathen with the usual measure of aversion in which they were held in the Peninsula after the subjugation of Granada, he considered them as part of the grand confederacy of Satan, not merely breathing the spirit and acting under the invisible influence of the Prince of Darkness, but holding personal communication with him. He seems to have regarded them, in short, as his regular and organized militia. In this view, every act of the unfortunate enemy was a crime. Even good acts were misrepresented, or referred to evil motives ; for how could goodness originate with the Spirit of Evil ? No better evidence of the results of this way of thinking need be given than that afforded by the ill-favoured and unauthorized portrait which the historian has left us of Montezuma,—even in his dying hours. The war of the Conquest was, in short, in the historian's eye, a conflict between light and darkness, between the good principle and the evil principle, between the soldiers of Satan and the chivalry of the Cross. It was a Holy War, in which the sanctity of the cause covered up the sins of the Conquerors, and every one—the meanest soldier who fell in it—might aspire to the crown of martyrdom. With sympathies thus preoccupied, what room was there for that impartial criticism which is the life of history ?

The historian's overweening partiality to the Conquerors is still further heightened by those feelings of patriotism—a bastard patriotism—which, identifying the writer's own glory with that of his countrymen, makes him blind to their errors. This partiality is especially shown in regard to Cortés, the hero of the piece. The lights and shadows of the picture are all disposed with reference to this principal character. The good is ostentatiously paraded before us, and the bad is winked out of sight. Solís does not stop here, but, by the artful gloss which makes the worse appear the better cause, he calls on us to admire his hero sometimes for his very transgressions. No one, not even Gomara himself, is such a wholesale encomiast of the great Conqueror ; and, when his views are contradicted by the statements of honest Diaz, Solís is sure to find a motive for the discrepancy in some sinister purpose of the veteran. He knows more of Cortés, of his actions and his motives, than his companion in arms or his admiring chaplain.

In this way Solís has presented a beautiful image of his hero,—but it is a hero of romance ; a character without a blemish. An eminent Castilian critic has commended him for "having conducted his history with so much art that it has become a panegyric." This may be true ; but, if history be panegyric, panegyric is not history.

Yet, with all these defects,—the existence of which no candid critic will be disposed to deny,—the History of Solís has found such favour with his own countrymen that it has been printed and reprinted, with all the refinements of editorial luxury. It has been translated into the principal languages of Europe ; and such is the charm of its composition, and its exquisite finish as a work of art, that it will doubtless be as imperishable as the language in which it is written, or the memory of the events which it records.

At this place also we are to take leave of Father Sahagun, who has accompanied us through our narrative. As his information was collected from the traditions of the natives, the contemporaries of the Conquest, it has been of considerable importance in corroborating or contradicting the statements of the Conquerors. Yet its value in this respect is much impaired by the wild and random character of many of the Aztec traditions,—so absurd, indeed, as to carry their own refutation with them. Where the passions are enlisted, what is too absurd to find credit ?

The Twelfth Book—as it would appear from his Preface, the Ninth Book originally—of his *Historia de la Nueva-España* is devoted to the account of the Conquest. In 1585, thirty years after the first draft, he rewrote this part of his great work, moved to it, as he tells us. " by the desire to correct the defects of the first account, in which some things had found their way that had better been omitted, and other things omitted which were well deserving of record." [1] It might be supposed that the obloquy which the missionary had brought on his head by his honest recital of the Aztec traditions would have made him more circumspect in this *rifacimento* of his former narrative. But I have not found it so, or that there has been any effort to mitigate the statements that bore hardest on his countrymen. As this manuscript copy must have been that which the author himself deemed the most correct, since it is his last revision, and as it is more copious than the printed narrative, I have been usually guided by it.

Señor Bustamante is mistaken in supposing that the edition of this Twelfth Book which he published in Mexico in 1829 is from the *reformed* copy of Sahagun. The manuscript cited in these pages is undoubtedly a transcript of that copy. For in the Preface to it, as we have seen, the author himself declares it. In the intrinsic value of the two drafts there is, after all, but little difference.

---

[1] " En el libro nono, donde se trata esta Conquista, se hiciéron ciertos defectos ; y fué, que algunas cosas se pusiéron en la narracion de este Conquista que fuéron mal puestas ; y otras se calláron, que fuéron mal calladas. Por esta causa, este año de mil quinientos ochenta y cinco, enmende este Libro." MS.

BOOK VII.

(CONCLUSION.)

SUBSEQUENT CAREER OF CORTÉS.

——o——

CHAPTER I.

TORTURE OF GUATEMOZIN.—SUBMISSION OF THE COUNTRY.—REBUILDING
OF THE CAPITAL.—MISSION TO CASTILE.—COMPLAINTS AGAINST CORTÉS.
—HE IS CONFIRMED IN HIS AUTHORITY.

(1521–1522.)

THE history of the Conquest of Mexico terminates with the surrender of
the capital. But the history of the Conquest is so intimately blended with
that of the extraordinary man who achieved it, that there would seem to
be an incompleteness in the narrative if it were not continued to the close
of his personal career. This part of the subject has been very imperfectly
treated by preceding writers. I shall therefore avail myself of the authentic
materials in my possession to give a brief sketch of the brilliant but
checkered fortunes which marked the subsequent career of Cortés.

The first ebullition of triumph was succeeded in the army by very
different feelings, as they beheld the scanty spoil gleaned from the conquered city, and as they brooded over the inadequate compensation they
were to receive for all their toils and sufferings. Some of the soldiers
of Narvaez, with feelings of bitter disappointment, absolutely declined to
accept their shares. Some murmured audibly against the general, and
others against Guatemozin, who, they said, could reveal, if he chose, the
place where the treasures were secreted. The white walls of the barracks
were covered with epigrams and pasquinades levelled at Cortés, whom they
accused of taking "one-fifth of the booty as commander-in-chief, and
another fifth as king." As Guatemozin refused to make any revelation in
respect to the treasure, or rather declared there was none to make, the
soldiers loudly insisted on his being put to the torture. But for this act
of violence, so contrary to the promise of protection recently made to the

Indian prince, Cortés was not prepared; and he resisted the demand, until the men, instigated, it is said, by the royal treasurer, Alderete, accused the general of a secret understanding with Guatemozin, and of a design to defraud the Spanish sovereigns and themselves. These unmerited taunts stung Cortés to the quick, and in an evil hour he delivered the Aztec prince into the hands of his enemies, to work their pleasure on him.

But the hero who had braved death in its most awful forms was not to be intimidated by bodily suffering. When his companion, the cacique of Tacuba, who was put to the torture with him, testified his anguish by his groans, Guatemozin coldly rebuked him by exclaiming, "And do you think I, then, am taking my pleasure in my bath?"[1] At length Cortés, ashamed of the base part he was led to play, rescued the Aztec prince from his tormentors before it was too late,—not, however, before it was too late for his own honour, which has suffered an indelible stain from this treatment of his royal prisoner.

All that could be wrung from Guatemozin by the extremity of his sufferings was the confession that much gold had been thrown into the water. But, although the best divers were employed, under the eye of Cortés himself, to search the oozy bed of the lake, only a few articles of inconsiderable value were drawn from it. They had better fortune in searching a pond in Guatemozin's gardens, where a sun, as it is called, probably one of the Aztec calendar wheels, made of pure gold, of great size and thickness, was discovered. The cacique of Tacuba had confessed that a quantity of treasure was buried in the ground at one of his own villas. But when the Spaniards carried him to the spot he alleged that "his only motive for saying so was the hope of dying on the road!" The soldiers, disappointed in their expectations, now, with the usual caprice of an unlicensed mob, changed their tone, and openly accused their commander of cruelty to his captive. The charge was well deserved, —but not from them.[2]

The tidings of the fall of Mexico were borne on the wings of the wind over the plateau, and down the broad sides of the Cordilleras. Many envoys made their appearance from the remote Indian tribes, anxious to learn the truth of the astounding intelligence and to gaze with their own eyes on the ruins of the detested city. Among these were ambassadors from the kingdom of Michoacán, a powerful and independent state, inhabited by one of the kindred Nahuatlac races, and lying between the Mexican Valley and the Pacific. The embassy was soon followed by the king of the country in person, who came in great state to the Castilian quarters. Cortés received him with equal parade, astonished him by the brilliant evolutions of his cavalry and by the thunders of his ordnance, and

---

[1] "¿Estoi yo en algun deleite, ó baño?" (Gomara, Crónica, cap. 145.) The literal version is not so poetical as "the bed of flowers," into which this exclamation of Guatemozin is usually rendered.

[2] The most particular account of this disgraceful transaction is given by Bernal Diaz, one of those selected to accompany the lord of Tacuba to his villa. (Hist. de la Conquista, cap. 157.) He notices the affair with becoming indignation, but excuses Cortés from a voluntary part in it.

escorted him in one of the brigantines round the fallen city, whose pile of smouldering palaces and temples was all that now remained of the once dread capital of Anahuac. The Indian monarch gazed with silent awe on the scene of desolation, and eagerly craved the protection of the invincible beings who had caused it.[1] His example was followed by ambassadors from the remote regions which had never yet had intercourse with the Spaniards. Cortés, who saw the boundaries of his empire thus rapidly enlarging, availed himself of the favourable dispositions of the natives to ascertain the products and resources of their several countries.

Two small detachments were sent into the friendly state of Michoacán, through which country they penetrated to the borders of the grea⁺ Southern ocean. No European had as yet descended on its shores so faɪ north of the equator. The Spaniards eagerly advanced into its waters, erected a cross on the sandy margin, and took possession of it, with all the usual formalities, in the name of their Catholic Majesties. On their return, they visited some of the rich districts towards the north, since celebrated for their mineral treasures, and brought back samples of gold and Californian pearls, with an account of their discovery of the ocean. The imagination of Cortés was kindled, and his soul swelled with exultation, at the splendid prospects which their discoveries unfolded. " Most of all," he writes to the emperor, " do I exult in the tidings brought me of the Great Ocean. For in it, as cosmographers, and those learned men who know most about the Indies, inform us, are scattered the rich isles teeming with gold and spices and precious stones."[2] He at once sought a favourable spot for a colony on the shores of the Pacific, and made arrangements for the construction of four vessels to explore the mysteries of these unknown seas. This was the beginning of his noble enterprises for discovery in the Gulf of California.

Although the greater part of Anahuac, overawed by the successes of the Spaniards, had tendered their allegiance, there were some, especially on the southern slopes of the Cordilleras, who showed a less submissive disposition. Cortés instantly sent out strong detachments under Sandoval and Alvarado to reduce the enemy and establish colonies in the conquered provinces. The highly coloured reports which Alvarado, who had a quick scent for gold, gave of the mineral wealth of Oaxaca, no doubt operated with Cortés in determining him to select this region for his own particular domain.

The commander-in-chief, with his little band of Spaniards, now daily recruited by reinforcements from the Islands, still occupied the quarters of

---

[1] Rel. Terc. de Cortés, ap. Lorenzana, p. 308.—The simple statement of the Conqueror contrasts strongly with the pompous narrative of Herrera (Hist. general, dec. 3, lib. 3, cap. 3), and with that of Father Cavo, who may have drawn a little on his own imagination. " Cortés en una canoa ricamente entapizada, llevó á el Rey Vehichilze, y á los nobles de Michoacan á México. Este es uno de los palacios de Moctheuzoma (les decia); allí está el gran templo de Huitzilopuctli; estas ruinas son del grande edificio de Quauhtemoc, aquellos de la gran plaza del mercado. Conmovido Vehichilze de este espectáculo se le saltáron las lágrimas." Los tres Siglos de México (México, 1836), tom. i. p. 13.

[2] " Que todos los que tienen alguna ciencia, y experiencia en la Navegacion de las Indias, han tenido por muy cierto, que descubriendo por estas Partes la Mar del Sur, se habian de hallar muchas Islas ricas de Oro, y Perlas, y Piedras preciosas, y Especeria, y se habian de descubrir y hallar otros muchos secretos y cosas admirables." Rel. Terc. de Cortés, ap. Lorenzana, pp. 302, 303.

Cojohuacan, which they had taken up at the termination of the siege. Cortés did not immediately decide in what quarter of the Valley to establish the new capital which was to take the place of the ancient Tenochtitlan. The situation of the latter, surrounded by water and exposed to occasional inundations, had some obvious disadvantages. But there was no doubt that in some part of the elevated and central plateau of the Valley the new metropolis should be built, to which both European and Indian might look up as to the head of the colonial empire of Spain. At length he decided on retaining the site of the ancient city, moved to it, as he says, " by its past renown, and the memory "—not an enviable one, surely—" in which it was held among the nations ; " and he made preparations for the reconstruction of the capital on a scale of magnificence which should, in his own language, " raise her to the rank of Queen of the surrounding provinces, in the same manner as she had been of yore."[1]

The labour was to be performed by the Indian population, drawn from all quarters of the Valley, and including the Mexicans themselves, great numbers of whom still lingered in the neighbourhood of their ancient residence. At first they showed reluctance, and even symptoms of hostility, when called to this work of humiliation by their conquerors. But Cortés had the address to secure some of the principal chiefs in his interests, and under their authority and direction the labour of their countrymen was conducted. The deep groves of the Valley and the forests of the neighbouring hills supplied cedar, cypress, and other durable woods for the interior of the buildings, and the quarries of *tetzontli* and the ruins of the ancient edifices furnished abundance of stone. As there were no beasts of draught employed by the Aztecs, an immense number of hands was necessarily required for the work. All within the immediate control of Cortés were pressed into the service. The spot so recently deserted now swarmed with multitudes of Indians of various tribes, and with Europeans, the latter directing, while the others laboured. The prophecy of the Aztecs was accomplished.[2] And the work of reconstruction went forward with a rapidity like that shown by an Asiatic despot, who concentrates the population of an empire on the erection of a favourite capital.[3]

Yet the condition of Cortés, notwithstanding the success of his arms, suggested many causes for anxiety. He had not received a word of encouragement from home, — not a word, indeed, of encouragement or censure. In what light his irregular course was regarded by the government or the nation was still matter of painful uncertainty. He now

---

[1] " Y crea Vuestra Magestad, que cada dia se irá ennobleciendo en tal manera, que como antes fué Principal, y Señora de todas estas Provincias, que lo será tambien de aquí adelante." Rel. Terc. de Cortés, ap. Lorenzana, p. 307.

[2] *Ante*, p. 538.

[3] Herrera, Hist. general, dec. 3, lib. 4, cap. 8.— Oviedo, Hist. de las Ind., MS., lib. 33, cap. 32.— Camargo, Hist. de Tlascala, MS.—Gomara, Crónica, cap. 162.—" En la cual (la edificacion de la ciudad)

los primeros años andaba mas gente que en la edificacion del templo de Jerusalem, porque era tanta la gente que andaba en las obras, que apénas podia hombre romper por algunas calles y calzadas, aunque son muy anchas." (Toribio, Hist. de los Indios, MS., Parte 1, cap. 1.) Ixtlilxochitl supplies any blank which the imagination might leave, by filling it up with 400,000, as the number of natives employed in this work by Cortés ! Venida de los Españoles, p. 60.

prepared another Letter to the emperor, the Third in the published series, written in the same simple and energetic style which has entitled his Commentaries, as they may be called, to a comparison with those of Cæsar. It was dated at Cojohuacan, May 15th, 1522, and in it he recapitulated the events of the final siege of the capital, and his subsequent operations, accompanied by many sagacious reflections, as usual, on the character and resources of the country. With this letter he proposed to send the royal fifth of the spoils of Mexico, and a rich collection of fabrics, especially of gold and jewellery wrought into many rare and fanciful forms. One of the jewels was an emerald, cut in a pyramidal shape, of so extraordinary a size that the base was as broad as the palm of the hand! [1] The collection was still further augmented by specimens of many of the natural products, as well as of animals peculiar to the country. [2]

The army wrote a letter to accompany that of Cortés, in which they expatiated on his manifold services and besought the emperor to ratify his proceedings and confirm him in his present authority. The important mission was intrusted to two of the general's confidential officers, Quiñones and Avila. It proved to be unfortunate. The agents touched at the Azores, where Quiñones lost his life in a brawl. Avila, resuming his voyage, was captured by a French privateer, and the rich spoils of the Aztecs went into the treasury of his Most Christian Majesty. Francis the First gazed with pardonable envy on the treasures which his Imperial rival drew from his colonial domains; and he intimated his discontent by peevishly expressing a desire "to see the clause in Adam's testament which entitled his brothers of Castile and Portugal to divide the New World between them." Avila found means, through a private hand, of

---

[1] "Sirviéron al Emperador con muchas piedras, i entre ellas con una esmeralda fina, como la palma, pero quadrada, i que se remataba en punta como pirámide." (Gomara, Crónica, cap. 146.) Martyr confirms the account of this wonderful emerald, which, he says, "was reported to the king and council to be nearly as broad as the palm of the hand, and which those who had seen it thought could not be procured for any sum." De Orbe Novo, dec. 8, cap. 4.*

[2] [Cortés availed himself of the same opportunity by which the royal fifth was despatched, to send costly or curious presents to numerous individuals and churches in Spain. For this fact I am indebted to the kindness of Mr. George Sumner, who, when in Spain, made a visit to the Archives of Simancas, from which he has furnished me with some interesting particulars for the period on which I am engaged. In a file endorsed *Papeles de Cortés* he met with a

list, without date, but evidently belonging to the year 1522, of the gold, plumage, and ornaments sent by Cortés to the different persons and institutions in Spain. "The policy of Cortés and his clear-sightedness," Mr. Sumner justly remarks, "are well shown by this. Not a church, not a shrine of any fame, throughout Spain, has been forgotten. To Santa María del Antigua in Sevilla, a rich offering of gold and of plumage; to Santa Maria del Pilar in Zaragoza, the same: another again to San Jago de Compostella; and one to the Cartuja of Seville, in which the bones of Columbus were then lying. There are plumages and gold for every place of importance. Then the bishops and men of power are not forgotten; for to them also are rich presents sent. In a time when there were no gazettes to trumpet one's fame, what surer way to notoriety than this? What surer way, in Spain, for gaining that security which Cortés so much needed?"]

---

* [Alaman, however, denies that this stone was an emerald, or that any true emeralds were found by the Conquerors in Mexico, notwithstanding the frequent mention of them in contemporary relations. "There are no emeralds," he says, "in our republic; and the stones mistaken for them at the time of the Conquest were jade or serpentine." As an evidence of the ignorance on this subject common in Europe at a former period, he cites the famous instance of the *Sacro Catino* at Genoa, regarded for ages as an emerald of priceless value, but now proved to be an imitation. (Disertaciones históricas, tom. i. p. 161.) It is certain that no emeralds are now found in any part of North America. Yet the Conquerors would seem to have been more discriminating than Señor Alaman represents them. They distinguished the *chalchivitl*, supposed to have been jade, from the emerald, and rejected as valueless other green stones prized by the natives. The case of the *Sacro Catino* does not apply, since it is not pretended that the Mexicans possessed the art of imitating precious stones by means of paste. The fact, therefore, that the emeralds sent and taken to Europe by Cortés were there recognized as genuine affords a presumptive proof in their favour, which has been generally accepted as sufficient by modern writers on the subject.—ED.]

transmitting his letters, the most important part of his charge, to Spain, where they reached the court in safety.[1]

While these events were passing, affairs in Spain had been taking an unfavourable turn for Cortés. It may seem strange that the brilliant exploits of the Conqueror of Mexico should have attracted so little notice from the government at home. But the country was at that time distracted by the dismal feuds of the *comunidades.* The sovereign was in Germany, too much engrossed by the cares of the empire to allow leisure for those of his own kingdom. The reins of government were in the hands of Adrian, Charles's preceptor; a man whose ascetic and studious habits better qualified him to preside over a college of monks than to fill, as he successively did, the most important posts in Christendom, — first as Regent of Castile, afterwards as Head of the Church. Yet the slow and hesitating Adrian could not have so long passed over in silence the important services of Cortés, but for the hostile interference of Velasquez, the governor of Cuba, sustained by Fonseca, bishop of Burgos, the chief person in the Spanish colonial department. This prelate, from his elevated station, possessed paramount authority in all matters relating to the Indies, and he had exerted it from the first, as we have already seen, in a manner most prejudicial to the interests of Cortés. He had now the address to obtain a warrant from the regent, which was designed to ruin the Conqueror at the very moment when his great enterprise had been crowned with success. The instrument, after recapitulating the offences of Cortés in regard to Velasquez, appoints a commissioner with full power to visit the country, to institute an inquiry into the general's conduct, to suspend him from his functions, and even to seize his person and sequestrate his property, until the pleasure of the Castilian court could be known. The warrant was signed by Adrian, at Burgos, on the 11th of April 1521, and countersigned by Fonseca.[2]

The individual selected for the delicate task of apprehending Cortés and bringing him to trial on the theatre of his own discoveries and in the heart of his own camp was named Cristóval de Tápia, *veedor,* or inspector, of the gold foundries in St. Domingo. He was a feeble, vacillating man, as little competent to cope with Cortés in civil matters as Narvaez had shown himself to be in military.

The commissioner, clothed in his brief authority, landed, in December, at Villa Rica. But he was coldly received by the magistrates of the city. His credentials were disputed, on the ground of some technical informality. It was objected, moreover, that his commission was founded on obvious misrepresentations to the government ; and, notwithstanding a

---

1 Peter Martyr, De Orbe Novo, dec. 8, cap. 4.— Bernal Diaz, Hist. de la Conquista, cap. 169.

2 The instrument also conferred similar powers in respect to an inquiry into Narvaez's treatment of the licentiate Ayllon. The whole document is cited in a deposition drawn up by the notary, Alonso de Vergara, setting forth the proceedings of Tápia and the municipality of Villa Rica, dated at Cempoalla, December 24, 1521. The MS. forms part of the collection of Don Vargas Ponçe, in the archives of the Academy of History at Madrid.

most courteous and complimentary epistle which he received from Cortés, congratulating him, as an old friend, on his arrival, the *veedor* soon found that he was neither to be permitted to penetrate far into the country nor to exercise any control there. He loved money; and, as Cortés knew the weak side of his "old friend," he proposed to purchase his horses, slaves, and equipage, at a tempting price. The dreams of disappointed ambition were gradually succeeded by those of avarice; and the discomfited commissioner consented to re-embark for Cuba, well freighted with gold, if not with glory, and provided with fresh matter of accusation against the high-handed measures of Cortés.[1]

Thus left in undisputed possession of authority, the Spanish commander went forward with vigour in his plans for the settlement of his conquests. The Panuchese, a fierce people on the borders of the Panuco, on the Atlantic coast, had taken up arms against the Spaniards. Cortés marched at the head of a considerable force into their country, defeated them in two pitched battles, and, after a severe campaign, reduced the warlike tribe to subjection.

A subsequent insurrection was punished with greater severity. They rose on the Spaniards, massacred five hundred of their oppressors, and menaced with destruction the neighbouring settlement of San Estevan. Cortés ordered Sandoval to chastise the insurgents; and that officer, after a campaign of incredible hardship, completely routed the barbarians, captured four hundred of their chiefs, and, after the affected formalities of a trial, sentenced every man of them to the stake or the gibbet. "By which means," says Cortés, "God be praised! the safety of the Spaniards was secured, and the province once more restored to tranquillity and peace."[2] He had omitted to mention in his letter his ungenerous treatment of Guatemozin. But the undisguised and *naïve* manner, so to speak, in which he details these circumstances to the emperor, shows that he attached no discredit to the deed. It was the just recompense of *rebellion;* a word that has been made the apology for more atrocities than any other word,—save *religion.*

During this interval the great question in respect to Cortés and the colony had been brought to a decisive issue. The general must have succumbed under the insidious and implacable attacks of his enemies, but for the sturdy opposition of a few powerful friends zealously devoted to his interests. Among them may be mentioned his own father, Don Martin Cortés, a discreet and efficient person,[3] and the duke de Bejar, a powerful nobleman, who from an early period had warmly espoused

1 Relacion de Vergara, MS.—Rel. Terc. de Cortés, ap. Lorenzana, pp. 309-314.—Bernal Diaz, Hist. de la Conquista, cap. 158.—The *regidores* of Mexico and other places remonstrated against Cortés' leaving the Valley to meet Tápia, on the ground that his presence was necessary to overawe the natives. (MS., Coyoacan, Dec. 12, 1521.) The general acquiesced in the force of a remonstrance which it is not improbable was made at his own suggestion.

2 "Como ya (loado nuestro Señor) estaba toda la Provincia muy pacifica, y segura." Rel. Quarta de Cortés, ap. Lorenzana, p. 367.

3 The Muñoz collection of MSS. contains a power of attorney given by Cortés to his father, authorizing him to manage all negotiations with the emperor and with private persons, to conduct all lawsuits on his behalf, to pay over and receive money, etc.

the cause of Cortés.   By their representations the timid regent was at
length convinced that the measures of Fonseca were prejudicial to the
interests of the crown, and an order was issued interdicting him from
further interference in any matters in which Cortés was concerned.

While the exasperated prelate was chafing under this affront, both the
commissioners Tápia and Narvaez arrived in Castile.   The latter had
been ordered to Cojohuacan after the surrender of the capital, where his
cringing demeanour formed a striking contrast to the swaggering port
which he had assumed on first entering the country.   When brought into
the presence of Cortés, he knelt down, and would have kissed his hand,
but the latter raised him from the ground, and, during his residence in
his quarters, treated him with every mark of respect.   The general soon
afterwards permitted his unfortunate rival to return to Spain, where he
proved, as might have been anticipated, a most bitter and implacable
enemy.[1]

These two personages, reinforced by the discontented prelate, brought
forward their several charges against Cortés with all the acrimony which
mortified vanity and the thirst of vengeance could inspire.   Adrian was
no longer in Spain, having been called to the chair of St. Peter; but
Charles the Fifth, after his long absence, had returned to his dominions,
in July 1522.   The royal ear was instantly assailed with accusations of
Cortés on the one hand and his vindication on the other, till the young
monarch, perplexed, and unable to decide on the merits of the question,
referred the whole subject to the decision of a board selected for the
purpose.   It was drawn partly from the members of his privy council,
and partly from the Indian department, with the Grand Chancellor of
Naples as its president, and constituted altogether a tribunal of the
highest respectability for integrity and wisdom.[2]

By this learned body a patient and temperate hearing was given to the
parties.   The enemies of Cortés accused him of having seized and finally
destroyed the fleet intrusted to him by Velasquez and fitted out at the
governor's expense; of having afterwards usurped powers in contempt of
the royal prerogative; of the unjustifiable treatment of Narvaez and Tápia,
when they had been lawfully commissioned to supersede him; of cruelty
to the natives, and especially to Guatemozin; of embezzling the royal
treasures, and remitting but a small part of its dues to the crown; of
squandering the revenues of the conquered countries in useless and
wasteful schemes, and particularly in rebuilding the capital on a plan of
unprecedented extravagance; of pursuing, in short, a system of violence
and extortion, without respect to the public interest or any other end than
his own selfish aggrandizement.

---

[1] Bernal Diaz, Hist. de la Conquista, cap. 158.
[2] Sayas, Annales de Aragon (Zaragoza, 1666),
cap. 63, 78.—It is a sufficient voucher for the respectability of this court that we find in it the name of

Dr. Galindez de Carbajal, an eminent Castilian
jurist, grown grey in the service of Ferdinand and
Isabella, whose confidence he enjoyed to the highest
degree.

In answer to these grave charges, the friends of Cortés adduced evidence to show that he had defrayed with his own funds two-thirds of the cost of the expedition. The powers of Velasquez extended only to traffic, not to establish a colony. Yet the interest of the crown required the latter. The army had therefore necessarily assumed this power to themselves; but, having done so, they had sent intelligence of their proceedings to the emperor and solicited his confirmation of them. The rupture with Narvaez was that commander's own fault; since Cortés would have met him amicably, had not the violent measures of his rival, threatening the ruin of the expedition, compelled him to an opposite course. The treatment of Tápia was vindicated on the grounds alleged to that officer by the municipality at Cempoalla. The violence to Guatemozin was laid at the door of Alderete, the royal treasurer, who had instigated the soldiers to demand it. The remittances to the crown, it was clearly proved, so far from falling short of the legitimate fifth, had considerably exceeded it. If the general had expended the revenues of the country on costly enterprises and public works, it was for the interest of the country that he did so, and he had incurred a heavy debt by straining his own credit to the utmost for the same great objects. Neither did they deny that, in the same spirit, he was now rebuilding Mexico on a scale suited to the metropolis of a vast and opulent empire.

They enlarged on the opposition he had experienced throughout his whole career from the governor of Cuba, and still more from the bishop of Burgos, which latter functionary, instead of affording him the aid to have been expected, had discouraged recruits, stopped his supplies, sequestered such property as from time to time he had sent to Spain, and falsely represented his remittances to the crown as coming from the governor of Cuba. In short, such and so numerous were the obstacles thrown in his path that Cortés had been heard to say " he had found it more difficult to contend against his own countrymen than against the Aztecs." They concluded with expatiating on the brilliant results of his expedition, and asked if the council were prepared to dishonour the man who, in the face of such obstacles and with scarcely other resources than what he found in himself, had won an empire for Castile such as was possessed by no European potentate![1]

This last appeal was irresistible. However irregular had been the manner of proceeding, no one could deny the grandeur of the results. There was not a Spaniard that could be insensible to such services, or that would not have cried out " Shame!" at an ungenerous requital of them. There were three Flemings in the council; but there seems to have been no difference of opinion in the body. It was decided that neither Velasquez nor Fonseca should interfere further in the concerns of New Spain. The difficulties of the former with Cortés were regarded in

[1] Sayas, Annales de Aragon, cap. 78.—Herrera, Hist. general, dec. 3, lib. 4, cap. 3.—Probanza en la Villa Segura, MS.—Declaraciones de Puertocarrero y de Montejo, MS.

the nature of a private suit ; and, as such, redress must be sought by the regular course of law. The acts of Cortés were confirmed in their fuli extent. He was constituted Governor, Captain-General, and Chief Justice of New Spain, with power to appoint to all offices, civil and military, and to order any person to leave the country whose residence there he might deem prejudicial to the interests of the crown. This judgment of the council was ratified by Charles the Fifth, and the commission investing Cortés with these ample powers was signed by the emperor at Valladolid, October 15th, 1522. A liberal salary was provided, to enable the governor of New Spain to maintain his office with suitable dignity. The favour of his sovereign was rendered still more welcome by a letter of the same date, written by him to the general, in which, after expatiating on the services of Cortés, he declares it to be his intention to make him such a requital as they well deserve.[1] The principal officers were recompensed with honours and substantial emoluments ; and the troops, together with some privileges grateful to the vanity of the soldier, received the promise of liberal grants of land. The emperor still further complimented them by a letter written to the army with his own hand, in which he acknowledged its services in the fullest manner.[2]

From this hour the influence of Fonseca in the Indian department was at an end. He did not long survive his chagrin, as he died in the following year. No man was in a situation to do more for the prosperity of his country than the bishop of Burgos. For more than thirty years, ever since the first dawn of discovery under Columbus, he had held supreme control over colonial affairs ; and it lay with him, therefore, in an especial degree, to give ardour to enterprise, and to foster the youthful fortunes of the colonies. But he lay like a blight upon them. He looked with an evil eye on the most illustrious of the Spanish discoverers, and sought only to throw impediments in their career. Such had been his conduct towards Columbus, and such to Cortés. By a wise and generous policy, he might have placed his name among the great lights of his age. As it was, he only served to bring these into greater lustre by contrast with his own dark and malignant nature. His career shows the overweening ascendency which the ecclesiastical profession possessed in Castile in the sixteenth century ; when it could raise a man to so important a station, for which he was totally unfit, and keep him there after he had proved himself to be so.[3]

The messengers who bore the commission of Cortés to Mexico touched

---

[1] ["E porque soy certificado de lo mucho que vos en ese descubrimiento é conquista y en tornar á ganar la dicha ciudad é provincias habeis fecho é trabajado, de que me he *enido é tengo por muy servido, é tengo la voluntad que es razon para vos favorecer y hacer la merced que vuestros servicios y trabajos merecen."—The whole letter is inserted by Alaman in his Disertaciones históricas, tom. i. apénd. 2, p. 144, et seq.]

[2] Nombramiento de Governador y Capitan General y Justicia Mayor de Nueva-España, MS.

—Also Bernal Diaz, Hist. de la Conquista, cap. 168.

[3] The character of Fonseca has been traced by the same hand which has traced that of Columbus. (Irving's Life and Voyages of Columbus, Appendix, No. 32.) Side by side they will go down to posterity in the beautiful page of the historian, though the characters of the two individuals have been inscribed with pens as different from each other as the golden and iron pen which Paolo Giovio tells us he employed in his compositions.

on their way at Cuba, where the tidings were proclaimed by sound of trumpet. It was a deathblow to the hopes of Velasquez. Exasperated by the failure of his schemes, impoverished by the expense of expeditions of which others had reaped the fruits, he had still looked forward to eventual redress, and cherished the sweet hope of vengeance, — long delayed. That hope was now gone. There was slight chance of redress, he well knew, in the tedious and thorny litigation of the Castilian courts. Ruined in fortune, dishonoured before the nation, the haughty spirit of the governor was humbled in the dust. He would take no comfort, but fell into a sullen melancholy, and in a few months died—if report be true —of a broken heart.[1]

The portrait usually given of Velasquez is not favourable. Yet Las Casas speaks kindly of him, and, when his prejudices are not involved, there can be no better authority. But Las Casas knew him when, in his earlier days, the missionary first landed in Cuba. The governor treated him with courtesy, and even confidence ; and it was natural that the condescension of a man of high family and station should have made its impression on the feelings of the poor ecclesiastic. In most accounts he is depicted as a haughty, irascible person, jealous of authority and covetous of wealth. He quarrelled with Grijalva, Cortés' predecessor, apparently, without cause. With as little reason, he broke with Cortés before he left the port. He proposed objects to himself in their nature incompatible. He proposed that others should fight his battles, and that he should win the laurels; that others should make discoveries, and that he should reap the fruits of them. None but a weak mind would have conformed to his conditions, and a weak mind could not have effected his objects. His appointment of Cortés put him in a false position for the rest of his life. His efforts to retrieve his position only made things worse. The appointment of Cortés to the command was scarcely a greater error than the subsequent appointment of Narvaez and of Tápia. The life of Velasquez was a series of errors.

Narvaez had no better fate than his friend the governor of Cuba. In the hope of retrieving his fortunes, he continued to pursue his adventurous career, and embarked in an expedition to Honduras. It was his last ; and Las Casas, who had little love for the Conquerors, and who had watched the acts of cruelty perpetrated by Narvaez, concludes the notice of his death with the assurance that the " devil took possession of his soul."

The announcement of the emperor's commission confirming Cortés in the supreme authority of New Spain was received there with general acclamation. The army rejoiced in having at last secured not merely an amnesty for their irregular proceedings, but a distinct acknowledgment of their services. The nomination of Cortés to the supreme command put

---

[1] Bernal Diaz, Hist. de la Conquista, cap. 158.

his mind at ease as to the past, and opened to him a noble theatre for future enterprise. The soldiers congratulated themselves on the broad powers conferred on their commander, and, as they reckoned up their scars and their services, indulged in golden dreams and the most vague and visionary expectations. It is not strange that their expectations should have been disappointed.

CHAPTER II.

MODERN MEXICO.—SETTLEMENT OF THE COUNTRY.—CONDITION OF THE NATIVES.—CHRISTIAN MISSIONARIES.—CULTIVATION OF THE SOIL.— VOYAGES AND EXPEDITIONS.

(1522–1524.)

IN less than four years from the destruction of Mexico, a new city had risen on its ruins, which, if inferior to the ancient capital in extent, surpassed it in magnificence and strength. It occupied so exactly the same site as its predecessor, that the *plaza mayor*, or great square, was the same spot which had been covered by the huge *teocalli* and the palace of Montezuma; while the principal streets took their departure as before from this central point, and, passing through the whole length of the city, terminated at the principal causeways. Great alterations, however, took place in the fashion of the architecture. The streets were widened, many of the canals were filled up, and the edifices were constructed on a plan better accommodated to European taste and the wants of a European population.

On the site of the temple of the Aztec war-god rose the stately cathedral dedicated to St. Francis;[1] and, as if to complete the triumphs of the Cross, the foundations were laid with the broken images of the Aztec gods.[2] In a corner of the square, on the ground once covered by the House of Birds, stood a Franciscan convent, a magnificent pile, erected a few years after the Conquest by a lay brother, Pedro de Gante, a natural son, it is said, of Charles the Fifth.[3] In an opposite quarter of the same square Cortés caused his own palace to be constructed. It was built of hewn stone, and seven thousand cedar beams are said to have been used for the interior.[4] The government afterwards appropriated it to the residence of the viceroys; and the Conqueror's descendants, the dukes of Monteleone, were allowed to erect a new mansion in another part of the *plaza*, on the spot which, by an ominous coincidence, had been covered by the palace of Montezuma.[5]

---

[1] [According to Señor Alaman, the cathedral, instead of being dedicated to Saint Francis, was consecrated to the Assumption of the Virgin. Conquista de Méjico (trad. de Vega), tom. ii. p. 254.]
[2] Herrera, Hist. general, dec. 3, lib. 4, cap. 8.

[3] Clavigero, Stor. del Messico, tom. i. p. 271.—Humboldt, Essai politique, tom. ii. p. 58.
[4] Herrera, Hist. general, ubi supra.
[5] Humboldt, Essai politique, tom. ii. p. 72.

The houses occupied by the Spaniards were of stone, combining with elegance a solid strength which made them capable of defence like so many fortresses.[1] The Indian buildings were for the most part of an inferior quality. They were scattered over the ancient district of Tlatelolco, where the nation had made its last stand for freedom. This quarter was also provided with a spacious cathedral;[2] and thirty inferior churches attested the care of the Spaniards for the spiritual welfare of the natives.[3] It was in watching over his Indian flock, and in the care of the hospitals with which the new capital was speedily endowed, that the good Father Olmedo, when oppressed by growing infirmities, spent the evening of his days.[4]

To give greater security to the Spaniards, Cortés caused a strong fortress to be erected in a place since known as the *Matadero*.[5] It was provided with a dockyard, and the brigantines which had served in the siege of Mexico were long preserved there as memorials of the Conquest. When the fortress was completed, the general, owing to the evil offices of Fonseca, found himself in want of artillery and ammunition for its defence. He supplied the former deficiency by causing cannon to be cast in his own foundries, made of the copper which was common in the country, and tin which he obtained with more difficulty from the mines of Tasco. By this means, and a contribution which he received from the shipping, he contrived to mount his walls with seventy pieces of ordnance. Stone balls, much used in that age, could easily be made; but for the manufacture of his powder, although there was nitre in abundance, he was obliged to seek the sulphur by a perilous expedition into the bowels of the great *volcan*.[6] Such were the resources displayed by Cortés, enabling him to supply every deficiency, and to triumph over every obstacle which the malice of his enemies had thrown in his path.

The general's next care was to provide a population for the capital. He invited the Spaniards thither by grants of lands and houses, while the Indians, with politic liberality, were permitted to live under their own chiefs as before, and to enjoy various immunities. With this encouragement, the Spanish quarter of the city in the neighbourhood of the great square could boast in a few years two thousand families; while the Indian district of Tlatelolco included no less than thirty thousand.[7] The various trades and occupations were resumed; the canals were again covered with barges; two vast markets in the respective quarters of the capital displayed all the different products and manufactures of the surrounding country; and the city swarmed with a busy, industrious population, in which the white man

1 Rel. d'un gentil' huomo, ap. Ramusio, tom. iii. fol. 309.

2 [Alaman asserts that there was no cathedral in Tlatelolco, but a Franciscan convent, dedicated to St. James, which still exists. Conquista de Méjico (trad. de Vega), tom. ii. p. 255.]

3 Rel. d'un gentil' huomo, ap. Ramusio, ubi supra.

4 Bernal Diaz, Hist. de la Conquista, cap. 177.

5 Rel. Quarta de Cortés, ap. Lorenzana, p. 376 nota.

6 For an account of this singular enterprise, see *ante*, p. 253.

7 Cortés, reckoning only the Indian population, says *treinta mil vecinos*. (Rel. Quarta, ap. Lorenzana, p. 375.) Gomara, speaking of Mexico some years later, estimates the number of Spanish householders as in the text. Crónica, cap. 162.

and the Indian, the conqueror and the conquered, mingled together promiscuously in peaceful and picturesque confusion. Not twenty years had elapsed since the Conquest, when a missionary who visited it had the confidence, or the credulity, to assert that "Europe could not boast a single city so fair and opulent as Mexico." [1]

The metropolis of our day would seem to stand in a different situation from that reared by the Conquerors ; for the waters no longer flow through its streets, nor wash the ample circumference of its walls. These waters have retreated within the diminished basin of Tezcuco ; and the causeways, which anciently traversed the depths of the lake, are not now to be distinguished from the other avenues to the capital. But the city, embellished, it is true, by the labours of successive viceroys, is substantially the same as in the days of the Conquerors ; and the massive grandeur of the few buildings that remain of the primitive period, and the general magnificence and symmetry of its plan, attest the far-sighted policy of its founder, which looked beyond the present to the wants of coming generations.

The attention of Cortés was not confined to the capital. He was careful to establish settlements in every part of the country which afforded a favourable position for them. He founded Zacatula on the shores of the miscalled Pacific, Coliman in the territory of Michoacán, San Estevan on the Atlantic coast, probably not far from the site of Tampico, Medellin (so called after his own birthplace) in the neighbourhood of the modern Vera Cruz, and a port near the river Antigua, from which it derived its name. It was designed to take the place of Villa Rica, which, as experience had shown, from its exposed situation, afforded no protection to shipping against the winds that sweep over the Mexican Gulf. Antigua, sheltered within the recesses of a bay, presented a more advantageous position. Cortés established there a board of trade, connected the settlement by a highway with the capital, and fondly predicted that his new city would become the great emporium of the country. [2] But in this he was mistaken. From some cause, not very obvious, the port of entry was removed, at the close of the sixteenth century, to the modern Vera Cruz, which, without any superiority, probably, of topographical position, or even of salubrity of climate, has remained ever since the great commercial capital of New Spain.

Cortés stimulated the settlement of his several colonies by liberal grants of land and municipal privileges. The great difficulty was to induce women to reside in the country ; and without them he felt that the colonies, like a tree without roots, must soon perish. By a singular provision, he

---

[1] Toribio, Hist. de los Indios, MS., Parte 3, cap. 7.—Yet this is scarcely stronger language than that of the Anonymous Conqueror : "Cosi ben ordinato et di si belle piazze et strade, quanto d' altre città che siano al mondo." Rel. d'un gentil' huomo, ap. Ramusio, tom. iii. fol. 309.

[2] "Y tengo por cierto, que aquel Pueblo ha de ser, despues de esta Ciudad, el mejor que obiere en esta Nueva España." (Rel. Quarta, ap. Lorenzana, p. 382.) The archbishop confounds this town with the modern Vera Cruz. But the general's description of the port refutes this supposition, and confirms our confidence in Clavigero's statement that the present city was founded by the Conde de Monterey, at the time mentioned in the text. See *ante*, p. 167, note.

required every settler, if a married man, to bring over his wife within eighteen months, on pain of forfeiting his estate. If he were too poor to do this himself, the government would assist him. Another law imposed the same penalty on all bachelors who did not provide themselves with wives within the same period. The general seems to have considered celibacy as too great a luxury for a young country.[1]

His own wife, Doña Catalina Xuarez, was among those who came over from the Islands to New Spain. According to Bernal Diaz, her coming gave him no particular satisfaction.[2] It is possible; since his marriage with her seems to have been entered into with reluctance, and her lowly condition and connections stood somewhat in the way of his future advancement. Yet they lived happily together for several years, according to the testimony of Las Casas;[3] and, whatever he may have felt, he had the generosity, or the prudence, not to betray his feelings to the world. On landing, Doña Catalina was escorted by Sandoval to the capital, where she was kindly received by her husband, and all the respect paid to her to which she was entitled by her elevated rank. But the climate of the table-land was not suited to her constitution, and she died in three months after her arrival.[4] An event so auspicious to his worldly prospects did

---

[1] Ordenanzas municipales, Tenochtitlan, Marzo, 1524, MS.*—The Ordinances made by Cortés for the government of the country during his viceroyalty are still preserved in Mexico; and the copy in my possession was transmitted to me from that capital. They give ample evidence of the wise and penetrating spirit which embraced every object worthy of the attention of an enlightened ruler; and I will quote, in the original, the singular provisions mentioned in the text:—

"Item. Por que mas se manifieste la voluntad que los pobladores de estas partes tienen de residir y permanecer en ellas, mando que todas las personas que tuvieren Indios, que fueren casados en Castilla ó en otras partes, que traigan sus mugeres dentro de un año y medio primero siguientes de como estas ordenanzas fueren pregonadas, so pena de perder los Indios, y todo lo con ellos adquirido é grangeado; y por que muchas personas podrian poner por achaque aunque tuviesen aparejo de decir que no tienen dineros para enviar por ellas, por hende las tales personas que tuvieran esta necesidad parescan ante el R⁰. P⁰. Fray Juan de Tecto y ante Alonso de Estrada, tesorero de su Magestad, á les informar de su necesidad, para que ellos la comuniquen á mí, y su necesidad se remedie; y si algunas personas hay que casados y no tienen sus mugeres en esta tierra, y quisieran traerlas, sepan que trayéndolas serán ayudadas así mismo para las traer, dando fianzas.

"Item. Por quanto en esta tierra hay muchas personas que tienen Indios de encomienda y no son casados, por hende por que conviene así para *la salud de sus conciencias de los tales* por estar en buen estado, como por la poblacion é noblecimiento de sus tierras, mando que las tales personas se casen, traigan y tengan sus mugeres en esta tierra dentro de un año y medio, despues que fueren pregonadas estas dichas Ordenanzas, é que no haciendo lo por el mismo caso sean privados y pierdan los tales Indios que así tienen."

[2] Bernal Diaz, Hist. de la Conquista, cap. 160.

[3] *Ante*, p. 112.

[4] Of asthma, according to Bernal Diaz (Hist. de la Conquista, cap. 160); but her death seems to have been too sudden to be attributed to that disease. I shall return to the subject hereafter.

---

* [The exact date is given at the close of the document—"fecha en esta dicha ciudad [de Temixtitan] á veinte dias del mes de marzo de mil y quinientos é veinte y cuatro años." Sir Arthur Helps says a copy sent by Cortés to the emperor in October of the same year "has been lost, but the orders manifestly related to this subject of *encomiendas*." The original seems also to have disappeared. But an ancient copy of these, as well as of subsequent ordinances and instructions of a similar nature, is preserved in the archives of the duke of Terranova y Monteleone in the Hospital of Jesus at Mexico, and the whole series was published, so far back as 1844, by Señor Alaman, in his Disertaciones históricas, tom. i. pp. 105-143. The contents, therefore, are not a matter of inference. They do not relate chiefly or directly to the *encomiendas*, that system having been already established and become, in the language of Alaman, "the basis of the whole organization of the country." The "Ordenanzas," while they incidentally modify the system, consist for the most part of regulations suggested by the general condition and circumstances of a new colony. They make provision for the military equipment and inspection of the settlers, with a view to their readiness for service; for their permanent residence in the country, which is made a condition of their holding *repartimientos;* for the conversion of the natives, their protection against robbery and oppression, and the education of the children of their chiefs; for the cultivation of imported plants and grain, and the raising of cattle, sheep, and swine; for facilitating traffic by the establishment of markets, adjustment of prices, etc.; and for the organization of the municipalities, prescribing their powers and forms of administration. Some of these provisions are still in force, while others, though obsolete, indicate the origin of certain existing customs. Taken together, they contain, in the opinion of Alaman, the foundation of all the later institutions of the country,—"el fundamento de todas nuestras instituciones."—ED.]

not fail, as we shall see hereafter, to provoke the tongue of scandal to the most malicious, but, it is scarcely necessary to say, unfounded, inferences.

In the distribution of the soil among the Conquerors, Cortés adopted the vicious system of *repartimientos*, universally practised among his countrymen. In a letter to the emperor, he states that the superior capacity of the Indians in New Spain had made him regard it as a grievous thing to condemn them to servitude, as had been done in the Islands. But, on further trial, he had found the Spaniards so much harassed and impoverished that they could not hope to maintain themselves in the land without enforcing the services of the natives, and for this reason he had at length waived his own scruples in compliance with their repeated remonstrances.[1] This was the wretched pretext used on the like occasions by his countrymen to cover up this flagrant act of injustice. The crown, however, in its instructions to the general, disavowed the act and annulled the *repartimientos*.[2] It was all in vain. The necessities, or rather the cupidity, of the colonists, easily evaded the royal ordinances.[3] The colonial legislation of Spain shows, in the repetition of enactments against slavery, the perpetual struggle that subsisted between the crown and the colonists, and the impotence of the former to enforce measures

---

[1] Rel. Terc., ap. Lorenzana, pp. 319, 320.

[2] Herrera, Hist. general, dec. 3, lib. 5, cap. 1.

[3] [This remark would imply that the instructions were published and some attempts at least made to enforce them. That such was not the case we learn from a remarkable private letter of Cortés to the emperor, sent with the " Relacion Quarta," and bearing the same date,—October 15, 1524. Referring first to an order that the Spanish settlers should be allowed to have free intercourse with the Indian population as a means of promoting conversion, he declines to comply with it, on the ground that the effects would be most pernicious. The natives, he says, would be subjected to violence, robbery, and vexations of all kinds. Even with the present rigorous rule forbidding any Spaniard to leave his settlement and go among the Indians without a special license, the evils resulting from this intercourse were so great that if he and his officers should attend solely to their suppression they would be unable to effect it, the territory being so vast. If all the Spaniards now in the country or on their way to it were friars engaged in the work of conversion, entire freedom of intercourse would no doubt be profitable. But, the reverse being the case, such also would be the effect. Most of the Spaniards who came were men of base condition and manners, addicted to every sort of vice and sin ; and if free intercourse were allowed, the natives would be converted to evil rather than to good, and, seeing the difference between what was preached and what was practised, would make a jest of what was taught them by the priests, thinking it was meant merely to bring them into servitude. The injuries done them would lead to rebellion ; they would profit by their acquired knowledge to arm themselves better, and being so many and the Spaniards so few, the latter would be cut off singly, as had already happened in many cases, and the greatest work of conversion since the time of the apostles would come to a stop.

Turning then to the emperor's prohibition of the *repartimientos*, as a thing which his conscience would not suffer, the theologians having declared that since God had made the Indians free their liberty ought not to be taken away, Cortés states that he has not only not complied with this order, but he has kept it secret except from the officials, whom he has forbidden to make it public. His reasons for thus acting are as follows : 1st. The Spaniards are unable to live except by the labour of the Indians, and if deprived of this they would be obliged to leave the country. 2d. His system of *repartimientos* is such that by it the Indians are in fact taken out of captivity, their condition under their former masters having been one of intolerable servitude, in which they were not only deprived of all but the barest means of subsistence, but they and their children were sacrificed to the idols in numbers horrible to hear of, it being a certified fact that in the great temple of Mexico alone, at a single festival, one of many that were held annually, eight thousand persons had been sacrificed ; all this, with innumerable other wrongs, had now ceased ; and the surest punishment which could be inflicted on the Indians was the threat to send them back to their former masters. 3d. Enumerating the various provisions he has made for obviating the evils of the system as practised in the Islands, where, during a residence of twenty years, he had ample knowledge of its workings, he asserts that, in the mode in which it has been established and regulated by him, it will lead not to the diminution but to the preservation and increase of the natives, besides securing a provision for the settlers and large revenues to the crown, and he contends that the *repartimientos*, instead of being abrogated, should be made hereditary, so that the possessors might have a stronger interest in the proper cultivation of the soil, instead of seeking to extract from it the most that was possible in a given time.

The letter, which concludes by noticing and rejecting some minor points in the emperor's instructions, has been recently discovered, and is perhaps the ablest document that has come down to us with the signature of Cortés. It has been published by Señor Icazbalceta, in his Col. de Doc. para la Hist. de México, tom. i.—Ed.]

repugnant to the interests, at all events to the avarice, of the latter. New Spain furnishes no exception to the general fact.

The Tlascalans, in gratitude for their signal services, were exempted, at the recommendation of Cortés, from the doom of slavery. It should be added that the general, in granting the *repartimientos*, made many humane regulations for limiting the power of the master, and for securing as many privileges to the natives as were compatible with any degree of compulsory service.[1] These limitations, it is true, were too often disregarded; and in the mining districts, in particular, the situation of the poor Indian was often deplorable. Yet the Indian population, clustering together in their own villages and living under their own magistrates, have continued to prove by their numbers, fallen as these have below their primitive amount, how far superior was their condition to that in most other parts of the vast colonial empire of Spain.[2] This condition has been gradually ameliorated, under the influence of higher moral views and larger ideas of government, until the servile descendants of the ancient lords of the soil have been permitted, in republican Mexico, to rise— nominally, at least—to a level with the children of their conquerors.

Whatever disregard he may have shown to the political rights of the natives, Cortés manifested a commendable solicitude for their spiritual welfare. He requested the emperor to send out holy men to the country; not bishops and pampered prelates, who too often squandered the substance of the Church in riotous living, but godly persons, members of religious fraternities, whose lives might be a fitting commentary on their teaching. Thus only, he adds,—and the remark is worthy of note,—can they exercise any influence over the natives, who have been accustomed to see the least departure from morals in their own priesthood punished with the utmost rigour of the law.[3] In obedience to these suggestions, twelve Franciscan friars embarked for New Spain, which they reached early in 1524. They were men of unblemished purity of life, nourished with the learning of the cloister, and, like many others whom the Romish Church has sent forth on such apostolic missions, counted all personal sacrifices as little in the sacred cause to which they were devoted.[4]

---

[1] Herrera, Hist. general, dec. 4, lib. 6, cap. 5.— Ordenanzas, MS.—The ordinances prescribe the service of the Indians, the hours they may be employed, their food, compensation, and the like. They require the *encomendero* to provide them with suitable means of religious instruction and places of worship. But what avail good laws, which in their very nature imply the toleration of a great abuse?

[2] The whole population of New Spain in 1810 is estimated by Don Fernando Navarro y Noriega at about 6,000,000; of whom more than half were pure Indians. The author had the best means for arriving at a correct result. See Humboldt, Essai politique, tom. i. pp. 318, 319, note.

[3] Rel. Quarta, ap. Lorenzana, pp. 391–394.—The petition of the Conquerors was acceded to by the government, which further prohibited "attorneys and men learned in the law from setting foot in the country, on the ground that experience had shown they would be sure by their evil practices to disturb

the peace of the community." (Herrera, Hist. general, dec. 3, lib. 5, cap. 2.) These enactments are but an indifferent tribute to the character of the two professions in Castile.

[4] Toribio, Hist. de los Indios, MS., Parte 1, cap. 1.—Camargo, Hist. de Tlascala, MS. [My views of the character of the Spanish missionaries find favour with Señor Alaman, who warmly eulogizes the spirit of self-sacrifice and the untiring zeal which they showed in propagating the gospel among the natives : "El Sr. Prescott hace de los misioneros el justo aprecio que sus virtudes merecieron, y sus elogios son tanto mas recomendables, cuanto que sus opiniones religiosas parece deberian hacerle contrario á ellos. En efecto, solo la iglesia católica ha producido misioneros inflamados de un verdadero celo religioso, que los ha hecho sacrificar su vida por la propagacion de la religion y en beneficio de la humanidad." Conquista de Méjico (trad. de Vega), tom. ii. p. 255. Mr. Gallatin, also, in his "Notes

The presence of the reverend fathers in the country was greeted with general rejoicing. The inhabitants of the towns through which they passed cam. out in a body to welcome them; processions were formed of the natives bearing wax tapers in their hands, and the bells of the churches rang out a joyous peal in honour of their arrival. Houses of refreshment were provided for them along their route to the capital; and when they entered it they were met by a brilliant cavalcade of the principal cavaliers and citizens, with Cortés at their head. The general, dismounting, and bending one knee to the ground, kissed the robes of Father Martin of Valencia, the principal of the fraternity. The natives, filled with amazement at the viceroy's humiliation before men whose naked feet and tattered garments gave them the aspect of mendicants, henceforth regarded them as beings of a superior nature. The Indian chronicler of Tlascala does not conceal his admiration of this edifying condescension of Cortés, which he pronounces " one of the most heroical acts of his life ! " [1]

The missionaries lost no time in the good work of conversion. They began their preaching through interpreters, until they had acquired a competent knowledge of the language themselves. They opened schools and founded colleges, in which the native youth were instructed in profane as well as Christian learning.[2] The ardour of the Indian neophyte emulated that of his teacher. In a few years every vestige of the primitive *teocallis* was effaced from the land. The uncouth idols of the country, and, unhappily, the hieroglyphical manuscripts, shared the same fate. Yet the missionary and the convert did much to repair these losses by their copious accounts of the Aztec institutions, collected from the most authentic sources.[3]

---

on the Semi-civilized Nations of America," pays a hearty tribute to the labours of the Roman Catholic missionaries in the New World : "The Dominican monks, though inquisitors and relentless persecutors in Spain, became in America the protectors of the Indians. . . . The praise must be extended to all the Catholic priests, whether Franciscans or Jesuits, monks or curates. All, from the beginning, were, have ever been, and continue to be, the protectors and the friends of the Indian race." Transactions of the American Ethnological Society, i. 213.]

[1] "Cuyo hecho del rotísimo y humilde recebimiento fué uno de los heroicos hechos que este Capitan hizo, porque fué documento para que con mayor fervor los naturales desta tierra viniesen á la conversion de nuestra fee." (Camargo, Hist. de Tlascala, MS.—See also Bernal Diaz, Hist. de la Conquista, cap. 171.) Archbishop Lorenzana falls nothing short of the Tlascalan historian in his admiration of the religious zeal of the great *Conquistador*, which, he assures us, entirely overwhelming him, as savouring so much more of the apostolic missionary than of the soldier !" Lorenzana, p. 393, nota.

[2] [A singular tribute to the thoroughness of the instruction thus given, and the facility with which it was imbibed, is rendered in a long complaint on the subject addressed to the emperor by Gerónimo Lopez, under date of October 20, 1541. The writer, a person evidently commissioned to send home reports on the condition of the country, denounces

the system of education instituted by the Franciscan monks as diabolically pernicious,—"muy dañoso como el diablo." He considers that the Indians should at the most be taught to repeat the Pater Noster and Ave Maria, the Creed and the Commandments, without any expositions, or any distinction of the persons of the Trinity and their attributes, above all without learning to read and write. Instead of this, they are taught not only these pernicious branches of knowledge but punctuation, music,—nay, even grammar ! Their natural ability is so great, and the devil is so largely interested in the matter, that they have acquired a skill in forming different kinds of letters which is marvellous, and a great number of them are thus enabled to carry on a correspondence and learn what is going on in the country from one sea to the other. There are boys among them who speak as elegant Latin as Tullius. They have translated and read the whole of the Scriptures,—the same thing that has ruined so many in Spain and given birth to a thousand heresies. A secular ecclesiastic told him that, having visited one of the colleges, he found there two hundred students, who stunned him with questions about religion, till the place seemed to him hell, and its inmates disciples of Satan.—Icazbalceta, Col. de Doc. para la Hist. de México, tom. ii.—ED.]

[3] Toribio, Hist. de los Indios, MS., Parte 3, cap. 1.—Father Sahagun, who has done better service in this way than any other of his order, describes

The business of conversion went on prosperously among the several tribes of the great Nahuatlac family. In about twenty years from the first advent of the missionaries, one of their body could make the pious vaunt that nine millions of converts—a number probably exceeding the population of the country—had been admitted within the Christian fold![1] The Aztec worship was remarkable for its burdensome ceremonial, and prepared its votaries for the pomp and splendours of the Romish ritual. It was not difficult to pass from the fasts and festivals of the one religion to the fasts and festivals of the other; to transfer their homage from the fantastic idols of their own creation to the beautiful forms in sculpture and in painting which decorated the Christian cathedral. It is true, they could have comprehended little of the dogmas of their new faith, and little, it may be, of its vital spirit. But, if the philosopher may smile at the reflection that conversion, under these circumstances, was one of form rather than of substance, the philanthropist will console himself by considering how much the cause of humanity and good morals must have gained by the substitution of these unsullied rites for the brutal abominations of the Aztecs.

The Conquerors settled in such parts of the country as best suited their inclinations. Many occupied the south-eastern slopes of the Cordilleras towards the rich valley of Oaxaca. Many more spread themselves over the broad surface of the table-land, which, from its elevated position, reminded them of the plateau of their own Castiles. Here, too, they were in the range of those inexhaustible mines which have since poured their silver deluge over Europe. The mineral resources of the land were not, indeed, fully explored or comprehended till at a much later period; but some few, as the mines of Zacatecas, Guanaxuato, and Tasco,—the last of which was also known in Montezuma's time,—had begun to be wrought within a generation after the Conquest.[2]

But the best wealth of the first settlers was in the vegetable products of the soil, whether indigenous, or introduced from abroad by the wise economy of Cortés. He had earnestly recommended the crown to require all vessels coming to the country to bring over a certain quantity of seeds and plants.[3] He made it a condition of the grants of land on the plateau, that the proprietor of every estate should plant a specified number of vines in it.[4] He further stipulated that no one should get a clear title to his

---

with simple brevity the rapid process of demolition. "We took the children of the caciques," he says, "into our schools, where we taught them to read and write, and to chant. The children of the poorer natives were brought together in the courtyard, and instructed there in the Christian faith. After our teaching, one or two brethren took the pupils to some neighbouring *teocalli*, and, by working at it for a few days, they levelled it to the ground. In this way they demolished, in a short time, all the Aztec temples, great and small, *so that not a vestige of them remained.*" (Hist. de Nueva-España, tom. iii. p. 77.) This passage helps to explain why so few architectural relics of the Indian era still survive in Mexico.

[1] "De manera que á mi juicio y verdaderamente serán bautizados en este tiempo que digo, que serán quince años, mas de nueve millones de ánimas de Indios." Toribio, Hist. de los Indios, MS., Parte 2, cap. 3.

[2] Clavigero, Stor. del Messico, tom. i. p. 43.—Humboldt, Essai politique, tom. iii. pp. 115, 145.—Esposicion de Don Lúcas Alaman (México, 1828), p. 59.

[3] "Páraque cada Navío traiga cierta cantidad de Plantas, y que no pueda salir sin ellas, porque será mucha causa para la Poblacion, y perpetuacion de ella." Rel. Quarta de Cortés, ap. Lorenzana, p. 397.

[4] "Item, que cualquier vecino que tubiere Indios

estate until he had occupied it eight years.[1] He knew that permanent residence could alone create that interest in the soil which would lead to its efficient culture, and that the opposite system had caused the impoverishment of the best plantations in the Islands. His various regulations, some of them not a little distasteful to the colonists, augmented the agricultural resources of the country by the addition of the most important European grains and other vegetables, for which the diversified climate of New Spain was admirably adapted. The sugar-cane was transplanted from the neighbouring islands to the lower level of the country, and, together with indigo, cotton, and cochineal, formed a more desirable staple for the colony than its precious metals. Under the sun of the tropics, the peach, the almond, the orange, the vine, and the olive, before unknown there, flourished in the gardens of the table-land, at an elevation twice as great as that at which the clouds are suspended in summer above our heads. The importation of a European fruit or vegetable was hailed by the simple colonists with delight. The first produce of the exotic was celebrated by a festival, and the guests greeted each other, as on the appearance of an old familiar friend, who called up the remembrance of the past and the tender associations of their native land.[2]

While thus occupied with the internal economy of the country, Cortés was still bent on his great schemes of discovery and conquest. In the preceding chapter we have seen him fitting out a little fleet at Zacatula to explore the shores of the Pacific. It was burnt in the dockyard when nearly completed. This was a serious calamity, as most of the materials were to be transported across the country from Villa Rica. Cortés, however, with his usual promptness, took measures to repair the loss. He writes to the emperor that another squadron will soon be got ready at the same port, and, "he doubts not, will put his Majesty in possession of more lands and kingdoms than the nation has ever heard of"![3] This magnificent vaunt shows the common sentiment of the Spaniards at that time, who looked on the Pacific as the famed Indian Ocean, studded with golden islands and teeming with the rich treasures of the East.

A principal object of this squadron was the discovery of a strait which should connect the Atlantic with the Pacific. Another squadron, consisting of five vessels, was fitted out in the Gulf of Mexico, to take the direction of Florida, with the same view of detecting a strait. For Cortés trusted —we at this day may smile at the illusion—that one might be found in

---

de repartimiento sea obligado á poner en ellos en cada un año con cada cien Indios de los que tuvieren de repartimiento mil sarmientos aunque sean de la planta de su tierra, escogiendo la mejor que pudiesse hallar." Ordenanzas municipales, año de 1524, MS.

[1] Ordenanzas municipales, año de 1524, MS.

[2] ["No general interest would attach to the private undertakings of Cortés, if the sole object of them had been the aggrandizement of his own fortune. But they were, in fact, the germs of what are now the most important branches of the national wealth; and they prove the grandeur of those views which in the times of the Conquest gave an impulse to whatever promised to contribute to the prosperity of the country." Alaman, Disertaciones históricas, tom. ii. p. 63.]

[3] "Tengo de ser causa, que Vuestra Cesarea Magestad sea en estas partes Señor de mas Reynos, y Señorios que los que hasta hoy en nuestra Nacion se tiene noticia." Rel. Quarta de Cortés, ap. Lorenzana, p. 374.

that direction which should conduct the navigator to those waters which had been traversed by the keels of Magellan ! [1]

The discovery of a strait was the great object to which nautical enter-prise in that day was directed, as it had been ever since the time of Columbus. It was in the sixteenth century what the discovery of the North-west passage has been in our own age,—the *ignis fatuus* of navigators. The vast extent of the American continent had been ascertained by the voyages of Cabot in the North, and of Magellan very recently in the South. The proximity, in certain quarters, of the two great oceans that washed its eastern and western shores had been settled by the discoveries both of Balboa and of Cortés. European scholars could not believe that Nature had worked on a plan so repugnant, apparently, to the interests of humanity, as to interpose, through the whole length of the great continent, such a barrier to communication between the adjacent waters. The cor-respondence of men of science,[2] the instructions of the Court, the letters of Cortés, like those of Columbus, touch frequently on this favourite topic. "Your Majesty may be assured," he writes, "that, as I know how much you have at heart the discovery of *this great secret of a strait*, I shall post-pone all interests and projects of my own, some of them of the highest moment, for the fulfilment of this great object." [3]

It was partly with the same view that the general caused a considerable armament to be equipped and placed under the command of Cristóval de Olid, the brave officer who, as the reader will remember, had charge of one of the great divisions of the besieging army. He was to steer for Honduras and plant a colony on its northern coast. A detachment of Olid's squadron was afterwards to cruise along its southern shore towards Darien in search of the mysterious strait. The country was reported to be full of gold ; so full that "the fishermen used gold weights for their nets." The life of the Spanish discoverers was one long day-dream. Illusion after illusion chased one another like the bubbles which the child throws off from his pipe, as bright, as beautiful, and as empty. They lived in a world of enchantment.[4]

Together with these maritime expeditions, Cortés fitted out a powerful expedition by land. It was intrusted to Alvarado, who, with a large force of Spaniards and Indians, was to descend the southern slant of the Cordilleras and penetrate into the countries that lay beyond the rich valley of Oaxaca. The campaigns of this bold and rapacious chief terminated in the important conquest of Guatemala. The general required his captains to send him minute accounts of the countries which they

---

[1] " Much as I esteem Hernando Cortés," exclaims Oviedo, "for the greatest captain and most practised in military matters of any we have known, I think such an opinion shows he was no great cosmo-grapher." (Hist. de las Ind., MS., lib. 33, cap. 41.) Oviedo had lived to see its fallacy.

[2] Martyr, Opus Epist., ep. 811

[3] Rel. Quarta, ap. Lorenzana, p. 385.

[4] The illusion at home was kept up, in some measure, by the dazzling display of gold and jewels remitted from time to time, wrought into fanciful and often fantastic forms. One of the articles sent home by Cortés was a piece of ordnance, made of gold and silver, of very fine workmanship, the metal of which alone cost 25,000 *pesos de oro*. Oviedo, who saw it in the palace, speaks with admiration of this magnificent toy. Hist. de las Ind., MS., lib. 33, cap. 41.

visited, the productions of the soil, and their general resources. The result was several valuable and interesting communications.[1] In his instructions for the conduct of these expeditions, he enjoined a considerate treatment of the natives, and inculcated a policy which may be called humane, as far as humanity is compatible with a system of subjugation.[2] Unfortunately the character of his officers too often rendered these instructions unavailing.

In the prosecution of his great enterprises, Cortés, within three short years after the Conquest, had reduced under the dominion of Castile an extent of country more than four hundred leagues in length, as he affirms, on the Atlantic coast, and more than five hundred on the Pacific, and, with the exception of a few interior provinces of no great importance, had brought them to a condition of entire tranquillity.[3] In accomplishing this, he had freely expended the revenues of the crown, drawn from tributes similar to those which had been anciently paid by the natives to their own sovereigns ; and he had, moreover, incurred a large debt on his own account, for which he demanded remuneration from the government. The celebrity of his name, and the dazzling reports of the conquered countries, drew crowds of adventurers to New Spain, who furnished the general with recruits for his various enterprises.

Whoever would form a just estimate of this remarkable man must not confine himself to the history of the Conquest. His military career, indeed, places him on a level with the greatest captains of his age. But the period subsequent to the Conquest affords different, and in some respects nobler, points of view for the study of his character. For we then see him devising a system of government for the motley and antagonist races, so to speak, now first brought under a common dominion ; repairing the mischiefs of war ; and employing his efforts to detect the latent resources of the country and to stimulate it to its highest power of production. The narrative may seem tame, after the recital of exploits as bold and adventurous as those of a paladin of romance. But it is only by the perusal of this narrative that we can form an adequate conception of the acute and comprehensive genius of Cortés.

---

[1] Among these may be particularly mentioned the Letters of Alvarado and Diego de Godoy, transcribed by Oviedo in his Hist. de las Ind., MS. (lib. 33, cap. 42–44), and translated by Ramusio for his rich collection, Viaggi, tom. iii.

[2] See, among others, his orders to his kinsman, Francisco Cortés,—"Instruccion civil y militar por la Expedicion de la Costa de Colima." The paper is dated in 1524, and forms part of the Muñoz collection of MSS.

[3] Rel. Quarta, ap. Lorenzana, p. 371.—"Well may we wonder," exclaims his archiepiscopal editor, "that Cortés and his soldiers could have overrun and subdued, in so short a time, countries, many of them so rough and difficult of access that even at the present day we can hardly penetrate them !" Ibid., nota.

CHAPTER III.

DEFECTION OF OLID.—DREADFUL MARCH TO HONDURAS.—EXECUTION OF GUATEMOZIN.—DOÑA MARINA.—ARRIVAL AT HONDURAS.

(1524–1526.)

IN the last chapter we have seen that Cristóval de Olid was sent by Cortés to plant a colony in Honduras. The expedition was attended with consequences which had not been foreseen. Made giddy by the possession of power, Olid, when he had reached his place of destination, determined to assert an independent jurisdiction for himself. His distance from Mexico, he flattered himself, might enable him to do so with impunity. He misunderstood the character of Cortés, when he supposed that any distance would be great enough to shield a rebel from his vengeance.

It was long before the general received tidings of Olid's defection. But no sooner was he satisfied of this than he despatched to Honduras a trusty captain and kinsman, Francisco de las Casas, with directions to arrest his disobedient officer. Las Casas was wrecked on the coast, and fell into Olid's hands, but eventually succeeded in raising an insurrection in the settlement, seized the person of Olid, and beheaded that unhappy delinquent in the market-place of Naco.[1]

Of these proceedings, Cortés learned only what related to the shipwreck of his lieutenant. He saw all the mischievous consequences that must arise from Olid's example, especially if his defection were to go unpunished. He determined to take the affair into his own hands, and to lead an expedition in person to Honduras. He would thus, moreover, be enabled to ascertain from personal inspection the resources of the country, which were reputed great on the score of mineral wealth, and would perhaps detect the point of communication between the great oceans, which had so long eluded the efforts of the Spanish discoverers. He was still further urged to this step by the uncomfortable position in which he had found himself of late in the capital. Several functionaries had recently been sent from the mother country for the ostensible purpose of administering the colonial revenues. But they served as spies on the general's conduct, caused him many petty annoyances, and sent back to court the most malicious reports of his purposes and proceedings. Cortés, in short, now that he was made Governor-General of the country, had less real power than when he held no legal commission at all.

The Spanish force which he took with him did not probably exceed a hundred horse and forty or perhaps fifty foot; to which were added about

---

[1] Carta, Quinta de Cortés, MS.

three thousand Indian auxiliaries.[1]   Among them were Guatemozin and the cacique of Tacuba, with a few others of highest rank, whose consideration with their countrymen would make them an obvious nucleus round which disaffection might gather.   The general's personal retinue consisted of several pages, young men of good family, and among them Montejo, the future conqueror of Yucatan ; a butler and steward ; several musicians, dancers, jugglers, and buffoons, showing, it might seem, more of the effeminacy of an Oriental satrap than the hardy valour of a Spanish cavalier.[2]   Yet the imputation of effeminacy is sufficiently disproved by the terrible march which he accomplished.

Towards the end of October 1524, Cortés began his march.   As he descended the sides of the Cordilleras, he was met by many of his old companions in arms, who greeted their commander with a hearty welcome, and some of them left their estates to join the expedition.[3]   He halted in the province of Coatzacualco (Huazacualco) until he could receive intelligence respecting his route from the natives of Tabasco.   They furnished him with a map, exhibiting the principal places whither the Indian traders who wandered over these wild regions were in the habit of resorting.   With the aid of this map, a compass, and such guides as from time to time he could pick up on his journey, he proposed to traverse that broad and level tract which forms the base of Yucatan and spreads from the Coatzacualco River to the head of the Gulf of Honduras.   " I shall give your Majesty," he begins his celebrated Letter to the emperor, describing this expedition, " an account, as usual, of the most remarkable events of my journey, every one of which might form the subject of a separate narration."   Cortés did not exaggerate.[4]

The beginning of the march lay across a low and marshy level, intersected by numerous little streams, which form the head-waters of the Rio de Tabasco, and of the other rivers that discharge themselves, to the

---

[1] Carta de Albornos, MS., Mexico, Dec. 15, 1525. —Carta Quinta de Cortés, MS.—The authorities do not precisely agree as to the numbers, which were changing, probably, with every step of their march across the table-land.

[2] Bernal Diaz, Hist. de la Conquista, cap. 175.

[3] Among these was Captain Diaz, who, however, left the pleasant farm, which he occupied in the province of Coatzacualco, with a very ill grace, to accompany the expedition.   "But Cortés commanded it, and we dared not say no," says the veteran.   Ibid., cap. 174.

[4] This celebrated Letter, which has never been published, is usually designated as the *Carta Quinta*, or " Fifth Letter," of Cortés.   It is nearly as long as the longest of the printed letters of the Conqueror, is written in the same clear, simple, business-like manner, and is as full of interest as any of the preceding.   It gives a minute account of the expedition to Honduras, together with events that occurred in the year following.   It bears no date, but was probably written in that year from Mexico.   The original manuscript is in the Imperial Library at Vienna, which, as the German sceptre was swayed at that time by the same hand which held the Castilian, contains many documents of value for the illustration of Spanish history.*

* [It is scarcely credible that a long and important document in an official form should have borne no date, and we may therefore suspect that the manuscript at Vienna, if unmutilated, is *not* the original.   A copy in the Royal Library at Madrid, purporting to have been made " from the original " by Alonso Diaz, terminates as follows : " De la cibdad de Temixtitan, desta Nueva España á *tres del mes de setiembre del nascimiento de nuestro Señor é Salvador Jesu-Cristo de* 1526."   This date is confirmed by a passage in a letter which will be found cited in the notes to the next chapter with the date of Sept. 11, but of which there are in fact two originals, the duplicate being dated Sept. 3.   It gives a summary, for the emperor's own perusal, of the matters narrated at length, in the *Carta Quinta*, which it thus describes : " Asi mesmo *envio agora* á V. M. *con lo presente* una relacion bien larga y particular de todo lo que me subcedió en el camino que hice á las Hibueras, y al cabo della hago saber á V. M. muy por extenso lo que ha pasado y se ha hecho en esta Nueva España despues que yo parté de la isla de Cuba para ella."   See Col. de Doc. inéd. para la Historia de España, tom. i.—ED.]

north, into the Mexican Gulf. The smaller streams they forded, or
passed in canoes, suffering their horses to swim across as they held them
by the bridle. Rivers of more formidable size they crossed on floating
bridges. It gives one some idea of the difficulties they had to encounter
in this way, when it is stated that the Spaniards were obliged to construct
no less than fifty of these bridges in a distance of less than a hundred
miles![1] One of them was more than nine hundred paces in length.
Their troubles were much augmented by the difficulty of obtaining
subsistence, as the natives frequently set fire to the villages on their
approach, leaving to the wayworn adventurers only a pile of smoking
ruins.

It would be useless to encumber the page with the names of Indian
towns which lay in the route of the army, but which may be now obsolete,
and, at all events, have never found their way into a map of the country.[2]
The first considerable place which they reached was Iztapan, pleasantly
situated in the midst of a fruitful region, on the banks of one of the
tributaries of the Rio de Tabasco. Such was the extremity to which the
Spaniards had already, in the course of a few weeks, been reduced by
hunger and fatigue, that the sight of a village in these dreary solitudes was
welcomed by his followers, says Cortés, "with a shout of joy that was
echoed back from all the surrounding woods." The army was now at no
great distance from the ancient city of Palenque, the subject of so much
speculation in our time. The village of *Las Tres Cruzes*, indeed, situated
between twenty and thirty miles from Palenque, is said still to commemorate the passage of the Conquerors by the existence of three crosses which
they left there. Yet no allusion is made to the ancient capital. Was it
then the abode of a populous and flourishing community, such as once
occupied it, to judge from the extent and magnificence of its remains?
Or was it, even then, a heap of mouldering ruins, buried in a wilderness
of vegetation, and thus hidden from the knowledge of the surrounding
country? If the former, the silence of Cortés is not easy to be explained.

On quitting Iztapan, the Spaniards struck across a country having the
same character of a low and marshy soil, checkered by occasional patches
of cultivation, and covered with forests of cedar and Brazil wood, which
seemed absolutely interminable. The overhanging foliage threw so deep
a shade that, as Cortés says, the soldiers could not see where to set their
feet.[3] To add to their perplexity, their guides deserted them ; and, when

---

[1] " Es tierra mui baja y de muchas sienegas, tanto
que en tiempo de invierno no se puede andar, ni se
sirve sino en canoas, y con pasarla yo en tiempo de
seca, desde la entrada hasta la salida de ella, que
puede aver veinti leguas, se hiziéron mas de cinquenta puentes, que sin se hazer, fuera imposible
pasar." Carta Quinta de Cortés, MS.
[2] I have examined some of the most ancient maps
of the country, by Spanish, French, and Dutch cosmographers, in order to determine the route of
Cortés. An inestimable collection of these maps,
made by the learned German Ebeling, is to be

found in the library of Harvard University. I can
detect on them only four or five of the places indicated by the general. They are the places mentioned in the text, and, though few, may serve to
show the general direction of the march of the
army.
[3] " Donde se ponian los pies en el suelo açia
arriba la claridad del cielo no se veia, tanta era la
espesura y alteza de los árboles, que aunque se
subian en algunos, no podian descubrir un tiro de
piedra." Carta Quinta de Cortés, MS.

they climbed to the summits of the tallest trees, they could see only the same cheerless, interminable line of waving woods. The compass and the map furnished the only clue to extricate them from this gloomy labyrinth; and Cortés and his officers, among whom was the constant Sandoval, spreading out their chart on the ground, anxiously studied the probable direction of their route. Their scanty supplies meanwhile had entirely failed them, and they appeased the cravings of appetite by such roots as they dug out of the earth, or by the nuts and berries that grew wild in the woods. Numbers fell sick, and many of the Indians sank by the way, and died of absolute starvation.

When at length the troops emerged from these dismal forests, their path was crossed by a river of great depth, and far wider than any which they had hitherto traversed. The soldiers, disheartened, broke out into murmurs against their leader, who was plunging them deeper and deeper in a boundless wilderness, where they must lay their bones. It was in vain that Cortés encouraged them to construct a floating bridge, which might take them to the opposite bank of the river. It seemed a work of appalling magnitude, to which their wasted strength was unequal. He was more successful in his appeal to the Indian auxiliaries, till his own men, put to shame by the ready obedience of the latter, engaged in the work with a hearty goodwill, which enabled them, although ready to drop from fatigue, to accomplish it at the end of four days. It was, indeed, the only expedient by which they could hope to extricate themselves from their perilous situation. The bridge consisted of one thousand pieces of timber, each of the thickness of a man's body and full sixty feet long.[1] When we consider that the timber was all standing in the forest at the commencement of the labour, it must be admitted to have been an achievement worthy of the Spaniards. The well-compacted beams presented a solid structure which nothing, says Cortés, but fire could destroy. It excited the admiration of the natives, who came from a great distance to see it; and "the bridge of Cortés" remained for many a year the enduring monument of that commander's energy and perseverance.

The arrival of the army on the opposite bank of the river involved them in new difficulties. The ground was so soft and saturated with water that the horses floundered up to their girths, and, sometimes plunging into quagmires, were nearly buried in the mud. It was with the greatest difficulty that they could be extricated by covering the wet soil with the foliage and the boughs of trees, when a stream of water, which forced its way through the heart of the morass, furnished the jaded animals with the means of effecting their escape by swimming.[2] As the Spaniards emerged

---

[1] "Porque lleva mas que mil bigas, que la menor es casi tan gorda como un cuerpo de un hombre, y de nueve y diez brazas en largo." Carta Quinta de Cortés, MS.

[2] "Pasada toda la gente y cavallos de la otra parte del alcon dímos luego en una gran çienega, que durava bien tres tiros de ballesta, la cosa mas espantosa que jamas las gentes viéron, donde todos los cavallos desençillados se sumiéron hasta las orejas sin parecerse otra cosa, y querer forçeiar á salir, sumianse mas, de manera que allí perdimos toda la esperanza de poder escapar cavallos ningunos, pero todavía comenzámos á trabajar y componerles haçes de yerba y ramas grandes de bajo,

from these slimy depths, they came on a broad and rising ground, which, by its cultivated fields teeming with maize, *agi*, or pepper of the country, and the *yuca* plant, intimated their approach to the capital of the fruitful province of Aculan. It was in the beginning of Lent, 1525, a period memorable for an event of which I shall give the particulars from the narrative of Cortés.

The general at this place was informed, by one of the Indian converts in his train, that a conspiracy had been set on foot by Guatemozin, with the cacique of Tacuba, and some other of the principal Indian nobles, to massacre the Spaniards. They would seize the moment when the army should be entangled in the passage of some defile, or some frightful morass like that from which it had just escaped, where, taken at disadvantage, it could be easily overpowered by the superior number of the Mexicans. After the slaughter of the troops, the Indians would continue their march to Honduras and cut off the Spanish settlements there. Their success would lead to a rising in the capital, and, indeed, throughout the land, until every Spaniard should be exterminated, and the vessels in the ports be seized, and secured from carrying the tidings across the waters.

No sooner had Cortés learned the particulars of this formidable plot than he arrested Guatemozin and the principal Aztec lords in his train. The latter admitted the fact of the conspiracy, but alleged that it had been planned by Guatemozin and that they had refused to come into it. Guatemozin and the chief of Tacuba neither admitted nor denied the truth of the accusation, but maintained a dogged silence. Such is the statement of Cortés.[1] Bernal Diaz, however, who was present in the expedition, assures us that both Guatemozin and the cacique of Tacuba declared their innocence. They had indeed, they said, talked more than once together of the sufferings they were then enduring, and had said that death was preferable to seeing so many of their poor followers dying daily around them. They admitted, also, that a project for rising on the Spaniards had been discussed by some of the Aztecs; but Guatemozin had discouraged it from the first, and no scheme of the kind could have been put into execution without his knowledge and consent.[2] These protestations did not avail the unfortunate princes; and Cortés, having satisfied, or affected to satisfy, himself of their guilt, ordered them to immediate execution.

When brought to the fatal tree, Guatemozin displayed the intrepid spirit worthy of his better days. "I knew what it was," said he, "to trust to your false promises, Malinche; I knew that you had destined me to this fate, since I did not fall by my own hand when you entered my city of

sobre que se sostuviesen y no se sumiesen, remediávanse algo, y andando trabajando y yendo y viniendo de la una parte á la otra, abrióse por medio de un calejon de agua y cieno, que los cavallos comenzáron algo á nadar, y con esto plugo á nuestro Señor que saliéron todos sin peligro ninguno." Carta Quinta de Cortés, MS.

[1] Carta Quinta de Cortés, MS.
[2] Hist. de la Conquista, cap. 177.

Tenochtitlan. Why do you slay me so unjustly? God will demand it of you!"[1] The cacique of Tacuba, protesting his innocence, declared that he desired no better lot than to die by the side of his lord. The unfortunate princes, with one or more inferior nobles (for the number is uncertain), were then executed by being hung from the huge branches of a *ceiba*-tree which overshadowed the road.[2]

Such was the sad end of Guatemozin, the last emperor of the Aztecs, if we might not rather call him "the last of the Aztecs;" since from this time, broken in spirit and without a head, the remnant of the nation resigned itself, almost without a struggle, to the stern yoke of its oppressors. Among all the names of barbarian princes, there are few entitled to a higher place on the roll of fame than that of Guatemozin. He was young, and his public career was not long; but it was glorious. He was called to the throne in the convulsed and expiring hours of the monarchy, when the banded nations of Anahuac and the fierce European were thundering at the gates of the capital. It was a post of tremendous responsibility; but Guatemozin's conduct fully justified the choice of him to fill it. No one can refuse his admiration to the intrepid spirit which could prolong a defence of his city while one stone was left upon another; and our sympathies, for the time, are inevitably thrown more into the scale of the rude chieftain, thus battling for his country's freedom, than into that of his civilized and successful antagonist.[3]

In reviewing the circumstances of Guatemozin's death, one cannot attach much weight to the charge of conspiracy brought against him. That the Indians, brooding over their wrongs and present sufferings, should have sometimes talked of revenge, would not be surprising. But that any chimerical scheme of an insurrection, like that above mentioned, should have been set on foot, or even sanctioned by Guatemozin, is altogether improbable. That prince's explanation of the affair, as given by Diaz, is, to say the least, quite as deserving of credit as the accusation of the Indian informer.[4] The defect of testimony and the distance of time make it difficult for us, at the present day, to decide the question. We have a surer criterion of the truth in the opinion of those who were eyewitnesses of the transaction. It is given in the words of the old

---

[1] Bernal Diaz, Hist. de la Conquista, ubi supra.

[2] According to Diaz, both Guatemozin and the prince of Tacuba had embraced the religion of their conquerors, and were confessed by a Franciscan friar before their execution. We are further assured by the same authority that "they were, *for Indians*, very good Christians, and believed well and truly." (Ibid., loc. cit.) One is reminded of the last hours of Caupolican, converted to Christianity by the same men who tied him to the stake. See the scene, painted in the frightful colouring of a master-hand, in the Araucana, Canto 34.

[3] Guatemozin's beautiful wife, the princess Tecuichpo, the daughter of Montezuma, lived long enough after his death to give her hand to four Castilians, all of noble descent. (See *ante*, p. 396, note 4.) She is described as having been as well

instructed in the Catholic faith as any woman in Castile, as most gracious and winning in her deportment, and as having contributed greatly, by her example, and the deference with which she inspired the Aztecs, to the tranquillity of the conquered country. This pleasing portrait, it may be well enough to mention, is by the hand of her husband, Don Thoan Cano. See Appendix, Part 2, No. 11.

[4] The Indian chroniclers regard the pretended conspiracy of Guatemozin as an invention of Cortés. The informer himself, when afterwards put to the torture by the cacique of Tezcuco, declared that he had made no revelation of this nature to the Spanish commander. Ixtlilxochitl vouches for the truth of this story. (Venida de los Españoles, pp. 83–93.) But who will vouch for Ixtlilxochitl?

chronicler so often quoted. "The execution of Guatemozin," says Diaz, "was most unjust, and was thought wrong by all of us." [1]

The most probable explanation of the affair seems to be that Guatemozin was a troublesome and, indeed, formidable captive. Thus much is intimated by Cortés himself, in his Letter to the emperor. [2] The fallen sovereign of Mexico, by the ascendency of his character, as well as by his previous station, maintained an influence over his countrymen which would have enabled him with a breath, as it were, to rouse their smothered, not extinguished, animosity into rebellion. The Spaniards, during the first years after the Conquest, lived in constant apprehension of a rising of the Aztecs. This is evident from numerous passages in the writings of the time. It was under the same apprehension that Cortés consented to embarrass himself with his royal captive on this dreary expedition. And in such distrust did he hold him that, even while in Mexico, he neither rode abroad, nor walked to any great distance, according to Gomara, without being attended by Guatemozin. [3]

Parties standing in such relations to each other could have been the objects only of mutual distrust and aversion. The forlorn condition of the Spaniards on the present march, which exposed them in a peculiar degree to any sudden assault from their wily Indian vassals, increased the suspicions of Cortés. Thus predisposed to think ill of Guatemozin, the general lent a ready ear to the first accusation against him. Charges were converted into proofs, and condemnation followed close upon the charges. By a single blow he proposed to rid himself and the state for ever of a dangerous enemy,—the more dangerous, that he was an enemy in disguise. Had he but consulted his own honour and his good name, Guatemozin's head was the last on which he should have suffered an injury to fall. " He should have cherished him," to borrow the homely simile of his encomiast, Gomara, "like gold in a napkin, as the best trophy of his victories." [4]

Whatever may have been the real motives of his conduct in this affair, it seems to have left the mind of Cortés but ill at ease. For a long time he was moody and irritable, and found it difficult to sleep at night. On one occasion, as he was pacing an upper chamber of a *teocalli* in which he was quartered, he missed his footing in the dark, and was precipitated from a height of some twelve feet to the ground, which occasioned him a severe contusion on the head,—a thing too palpable to be concealed, though he endeavoured, says the gossiping Diaz, to hide the knowledge of it, as well as he could, from the soldiers. [5]

It was not long after the sad scene of Guatemozin's execution that the

---

1 "Y fué esta muerte que les diéron muy injustamente dada, y pareció mal á todos los que ibamos aquella jornada." Hist. de la Conquista, cap. 177.

2 "Guatemozin, Señor que fué de esta Ciudad de Temixtitan, á quien yo despues que la gané he tenido siempre preso, teniéndole por hombre bullicioso, y le llevé conmigo." Carta Quinta, MS.

3 "Y le hacian aquella mesma reverencia, i ceremonias, que á Moteçuma, i creo que por eso le llevaba siempre consigo por la Ciudad á Caballo si cavalgaba, i sino á pie como él iba." Crónica, cap. 170.

4 "I Cortés debiera guardarlo vivo, como Oro en paño, que era el triumpho, i gloria de sus Victorias." Crónica, cap. 170.

5 Hist. de la Conquista, ubi supra.

wearied troops entered the head town of the great province of Aculan; a thriving community of traders, who carried on a profitable traffic with the farthest quarters of Central America. Cortés notices in general terms the excellence and beauty of the buildings, and the hospitable reception which he experienced from the inhabitants.

After renewing their strength in these comfortable quarters, the Spaniards left the capital of Aculan, the name of which is to be found on no map, and held on their toilsome way in the direction of what is now called the Lake of Peten. It was then the property of an emigrant tribe of the hardy Maya family, and their capital stood on an island in the lake, "with its houses and lofty *teocallis* glistening in the sun," says Bernal Diaz, "so that it might be seen for the distance of two leagues." [1] These edifices, built by one of the races of Yucatan, displayed, doubtless, the same peculiarities of construction as the remains still to be seen in that remarkable peninsula. But, whatever may have been their architectural merits, they are disposed of in a brief sentence by the Conquerors.

The inhabitants of the island showed a friendly spirit, and a docility unlike the warlike temper of their countrymen of Yucatan. They willingly listened to the Spanish missionaries who accompanied the expedition, as they expounded the Christian doctrines through the intervention of Marina. The Indian interpreter was present throughout this long march, the last in which she remained at the side of Cortés. As this, too, is the last occasion on which she will appear in these pages, I will mention, before parting with her, an interesting circumstance that occurred when the army was traversing the province of Coatzacualco. This, it may be remembered, was the native country of Marina, where her infamous mother sold her, when a child, to some foreign traders, in order to secure her inheritance to a younger brother. Cortés halted for some days at this place, to hold a conference with the surrounding caciques on matters of government and religion. Among those summoned to this meeting was Marina's mother, who came, attended by her son. No sooner did they make their appearance than all were struck with the great resemblance of the cacique to her daughter. The two parties recognized each other, though they had not met since their separation. The mother, greatly terrified, fancied that she had been decoyed into a snare in order to punish her inhuman conduct. But Marina instantly ran up to her, and endeavoured to allay her fears, assuring her that she should receive no harm, and, addressing the bystanders, said "that she was sure her mother knew not what she did when she sold her to the traders, and that she forgave her." Then, tenderly embracing her unnatural parent, she gave her such jewels and other little ornaments as she wore about her own person, to win back, as it would seem, her lost affection. Marina added that "she felt much happier than before, now

----

1 Hist. de la Conquista, cap. 178.

that she had been instructed in the Christian faith and given up the bloody worship of the Aztecs."[1]

In the course of the expedition to Honduras, Cortés gave Marina away to a Castilian knight, Don Juan Xaramillo,[2] to whom she was wedded as his lawful wife. She had estates assigned to her in her native province, where she probably passed the remainder of her days.[3] From this time the name of Marina disappears from the page of history. But it has been always held in grateful remembrance by the Spaniards, for the important aid which she gave them in effecting the Conquest, and by the natives, for the kindness and sympathy which she showed them in their misfortunes. Many an Indian ballad commemorates the gentle virtues of Malinche,—her Aztec epithet. Even now her spirit, if report be true, watches over the capital which she helped to win; and the peasant is occasionally startled by the apparition of an Indian princess, dimly seen through the evening shadows, as it flits among the groves and grottos of the royal Hill of Chapoltepec.[4]

By the Conqueror, Marina left one son, Don Martin Cortés. He rose to high consideration, and was made a *comendador* of the order of St. Jago. He was subsequently suspected of treasonable designs against the government; and neither his parents' extraordinary services, nor his own deserts, could protect him from a cruel persecution; and in 1568 the son of Hernando Cortés was shamefully subjected to the torture in the very capital which his father had acquired for the Castilian crown!

The inhabitants of the isles of Peten—to return from our digression —listened attentively to the preaching of the Franciscan friars, and consented to the instant demolition of their idols, and the erection of the Cross upon their ruins.[5] A singular circumstance showed the value of these hurried conversions. Cortés, on his departure, left among this friendly people one of his horses, which had been disabled by an injury in the foot. The Indians felt a reverence for the animal, as in some way connected with the mysterious power of the white men. When their visitors had gone, they offered flowers to the horse, and, as it is said, prepared for him many savoury messes of poultry, such as they would have

---

[1] Diaz, who was present, attests the truth of this account by the most solemn adjuration : " Y todo esto que digo, se lo oi muy certificadamente y se lo juro, amen." Hist. de la Conquista, cap. 37.

[2] [Alaman, from an examination of the municipal archives of Mexico, finds that Juan de Jaramillo was commander of one of the brigantines in the siege of Mexico. He subsequently filled the office of royal standard-bearer of the city, and was several times chosen to represent it in the assemblies of the cities of New Spain. Conquista de Méjico (trad. de Vega), tom. ii. p. 269.]

[3] [The Spanish government showed its sense of the services of Marina by the grant of several estates both in the town and country. The house in which she usually resided in Mexico was in the street of Medinas, as it is now called, which then bore the name of her husband, Jaramillo. She had a pleasure-house at Chapultepec, and in Cuyoacan a garden that had belonged to Montezuma. She lived in the enjoyment of wealth and much consideration from her countrymen ; and, as we see mention made of her grandchild during her lifetime, we may presume she reached a good old age. Conquista de Méjico (trad. de Vega), tom. ii. p. 269.— Alaman, Disertaciones históricas, tom. ii. p. 293.]

[4] Life in Mexico, let. 8.—The fair author does not pretend to have been favoured with a sight of the apparition.

[5] Villagutierre says that the Iztacs, by which name the inhabitants of these islands were called, did not destroy their idols while the Spaniards remained there. (Historia de la Conquista de la Provincia de el Itza (Madrid, 1701), pp. 49, 50.) The historian is wrong, since Cortés expressly asserts that the images were broken and burnt in his presence. Carta Quinta, MS.

administered to their own sick. Under this extraordinary diet the poor animal pined away and died. The affrighted Indians raised his effigy in stone, and, placing it in one of their *teocallis,* did homage to it, as to a deity. In 1618, when two Franciscan friars came to preach the gospel in these regions, then scarcely better known to the Spaniards than before the time of Cortés, one of the most remarkable objects which they found was this statue of a horse, receiving the homage of the Indian worshippers, as the god of thunder and lightning![1]

It would be wearisome to recount all the perils and hardships endured by the Spaniards in the remainder of their journey. It would be repeating only the incidents of the preceding narrative, the same obstacles in their path, the same extremities of famine and fatigue,—hardships more wearing on the spirits than encounters with an enemy, which, if more hazardous, are also more exciting. It is easier to contend with man than with Nature. Yet I must not omit to mention the passage of the *Sierra de los Pedernales,* "the Mountain of Flints," which, though only twenty-four miles in extent, consumed no less than twelve days in crossing it! The sharp stones cut the horses' feet to pieces, while many were lost down the precipices and ravines; so that when they had reached the opposite side sixty-eight of these valuable animals had perished, and the remainder were, for the most part, in an unserviceable condition![2]

The rainy season had now set in, and torrents of water, falling day and night, drenched the adventurers to the skin, and added greatly to their distresses. The rivers, swollen beyond their usual volume, poured along with a terrible impetuosity that defied the construction of bridges; and it was with the greatest difficulty that, by laying trunks of trees from one huge rock to another, with which these streams were studded, they effected a perilous passage to the opposite banks.[3]

At length the shattered train drew near the Golfo Dolce, at the head of the Bay of Honduras. Their route could not have been far from the site of Copan, the celebrated city whose architectural ruins have furnished such noble illustrations for the pencil of Catherwood. But the Spaniards passed on in silence. Nor, indeed, can we wonder that at this stage of the enterprise they should have passed on without heeding the vicinity of a city in the wilderness, though it were as glorious as the capital of Zenobia; for they were arrived almost within view of the Spanish settlements, the object of their long and wearisome pilgrimage.

The place which they were now approaching was Naco, or San Gil de Buena Vista, a Spanish settlement on the Golfo Dolce. Cortés advanced

---

[1] The fact is recorded by Villagutierre, Conquista de el Itza, pp. 100-102, and Cojullado, Hist. de Yucathan, lib. i, cap. 16.

[2] "Y querer dezir la aspereza y fragosidad de este Puerto y sierras, ni quien lo dixese lo sabria significar, ni quien lo oyese podria entender, sino que sepa V. M. que en ocho leguas que duró hasta este puerto estuvimos en las andar doze dias, digo los postreros en llegar al cabo de él, en que muriéron sesenta y ocho cavallos despeñados y desxaretados, y todos los demas viniéron heridos y tan lastimados que no pensámos aprovecharnos de ninguno." Carta Quinta de Cortés, MS.

[3] "If any unhappy wretch had become giddy in this transit," says Cortés, "he must inevitably have been precipitated into the gulf and perished. There were upwards of twenty of these frightful passes." Carta Quinta, MS.

cautiously, prepared to fall on the town by surprise. He had held on his way with the undeviating step of the North American Indian, who, traversing morass and mountain and the most intricate forests, guided by the instinct of revenge, presses straight towards the mark, and, when he has reached it, springs at once on his unsuspecting victim. Before Cortés made his assault, his scouts fortunately fell in with some of the inhabitants of the place, from whom they received tidings of the death of Olid, and of the re-establishment of his own authority. Cortés, therefore, entered the place like a friend, and was cordially welcomed by his countrymen, greatly astonished, says Diaz, "by the presence among them of the general so renowned throughout these countries."[1]

The colony was at this time sorely suffering from famine; and to such extremity was it soon reduced that the troops would probably have found a grave in the very spot to which they had looked forward as the goal of their labours, but for the seasonable arrival of a vessel with supplies from Cuba. With a perseverance which nothing could daunt, Cortés made an examination of the surrounding country, and occupied a month more in exploring dismal swamps, steaming with unwholesome exhalations, and infected with bilious fevers, and with swarms of venomous insects which left peace neither by day nor night. At length he embarked with a part of his forces on board of two brigantines, and, after touching at one or two ports in the bay, anchored off Truxillo, the principal Spanish settlement on that coast. The surf was too high for him easily to effect a landing; but the inhabitants, overjoyed at his arrival, rushed into the shallow water and eagerly bore back the general in their arms to the shore.[2]

After he had restored the strength and spirits of his men, the indefatigable commander prepared for a new expedition, the object of which was to explore and to reduce the extensive province of Nicaragua. One may well feel astonished at the adventurous spirit of the man who, unsubdued by the terrible sufferings of his recent march, should so soon be prepared for another enterprise equally appalling. It is difficult, in this age of sober sense, to conceive the character of a Castilian cavalier of the sixteenth century, a true counterpart of which it would not have been easy to find in any other nation, even at that time,—or anywhere, indeed, save in those tales of chivalry, which, however wild and extravagant they may seem, were much more true to character than to situation. The mere excitement of exploring the strange and the unknown was a sufficient compensation to the Spanish adventurer for all his toils and trials. It seems to have been ordered by Providence that such a race of men should exist contemporaneously with the discovery of the New World, that those regions should be brought to light which were beset with dangers and difficulties

---

[1] "Espantáronse en gran manera, y como supiéron que era Cortés q̃ tan nombrado era en todas estas partes de las Indias, y en Castilla, no sabiã que se hazer de placer." Hist. de la Conquista, cap. 179.

[2] Bernal Diaz, Hist. de la Conquista, cap. 179, et seq.—Herrera, Hist. general, dec. 3, lib. 8, cap. 3, 4.—Carta Quinta de Cortés, MS.

so appalling as might have tended to overawe and to discourage the ordinary spirit of adventure. Yet Cortés, though filled with this spirit, proposed nobler ends to himself than those of the mere vulgar adventurer. In the expedition to Nicaragua he designed, as he had done in that to Honduras, to ascertain the resources of the country in general, and, above all, the existence of any means of communication between the great oceans on its borders. If none such existed, it would at least establish this fact, the knowledge of which, to borrow his own language, was scarcely less important.

The general proposed to himself the further object of enlarging the colonial empire of Castile. The conquest of Mexico was but the commencement of a series of conquests. To the warrior who had achieved this, nothing seemed impracticable; and scarcely would anything have been so, had he been properly sustained. It is no great stretch of imagination to see the Conqueror of Mexico advancing along the provinces of the vast Isthmus,—Nicaragua, Costa Rica, and Darien,—until he had planted his victorious banner on the shores of the Gulf of Panamá; and, while it was there fanned by the breezes from the golden South, the land of the Incas, to see him gathering such intelligence of this land as would stimulate him to carry his arms still farther, and to anticipate, it might be, the splendid career of Pizarro!

But from these dreams of ambition Cortés was suddenly aroused by such tidings as convinced him that his absence from Mexico was already too far prolonged, and that he must return without delay, if he would save the capital or the country.

CHAPTER IV.

DISTURBANCES IN MEXICO.—RETURN OF CORTÉS.—DISTRUST OF THE COURT. —CORTÉS RETURNS TO SPAIN.—DEATH OF SANDOVAL.—BRILLIANT RECEPTION OF CORTÉS.—HONOURS CONFERRED ON HIM.

(1526–1530.)

THE intelligence alluded to in the preceding chapter was conveyed in a letter to Cortés from the licentiate Zuazo, one of the functionaries to whom the general had committed the administration of the country during his absence. It contained full particulars of the tumultuous proceedings in the capital. No sooner had Cortés quitted it, than dissensions broke out among the different members of the provisional government. The misrule increased as his absence was prolonged. At length tidings were received that Cortés with his whole army had perished in the morasses of Chiapa. The members of the government showed no reluctance to credit this story. They now openly paraded their own authority; proclaimed the general's death; caused funeral ceremonies to be performed in his honour; took possession of his property wherever they could meet with it, piously devoting a small part of the proceeds to purchasing masses for his soul, while the remainder was appropriated to pay off what was called his debt to the state. They seized, in like manner, the property of other individuals engaged in the expedition. From these outrages they proceeded to others against the Spanish residents in the city, until the Franciscan missionaries left the capital in disgust, while the Indian population were so sorely oppressed that great apprehensions were entertained of a general rising. Zuazo, who communicated these tidings, implored Cortés to quicken his return. He was a temperate man, and the opposition which he had made to the tyrannical measures of his comrades had been rewarded with exile.[1]

The general, greatly alarmed by this account, saw that no alternative was .eft but to abandon all further schemes of conquest, and to return at once, f he would secure the preservation of the empire which he had won. He accordingly made the necessary arrangements for settling the administration of the colonies at Honduras, and embarked with a small number of followers for Mexico.

He had not been long at sea when he encountered such a terrible tempest as seriously damaged his vessel and compelled him to return to port and refit. A second attempt proved equally unsuccessful; and Cortés, feeling that his good star had deserted him, saw in this repeated disaster an intimation from Heaven that he was not to return.[2] He contented himself, therefore, with sending a trusty messenger to advise his friends of his personal safety in Honduras. He then instituted processions and public prayers to ascertain the will of Heaven and to deprecate its anger. His health now showed the effects of his recent sufferings, and declined under a wasting fever. His spirits sank with it, and he fell into a state of gloomy despondency. Bernal Diaz, speaking of him at this time, says that nothing could be more wan and emaciated than his person, and that so strongly was he possessed with the idea of his approaching end that he procured a Franciscan habit,—for it was common to be laid out in the habit of some one or other of the monastic orders,—in which to be carried to the grave.[3]

From this deplorable apathy Cortés was roused by fresh advices urging his presence in Mexico, and by the judicious efforts of his good friend Sandoval, who had lately returned, himself, from an excursion into the interior. By his persuasion, the general again consented to try his fortunes on the seas. He embarked on board of a brigantine, with a few followers, and bade adieu to the disastrous shores of Honduras, April 25,

---

[1] Carta Quinta de Cortés, MS.—Bernal Diaz, Hist. de la Conquista, cap. 185.—Relacion del Tesorero Strada, MS., México, 1526.

[2] Carta Quinta de Cortés, MS.
[3] Hist. de la Conquista, cap. 184, et seq.—Carta Quinta de Cortés, MS.

1526. He had nearly made the coast of New Spain, when a heavy gale threw him off his course and drove him to the island of Cuba. After staying there some time to recruit his exhausted strength, he again put to sea, on the 16th of May, and in eight days landed near San Juan de Ulua, whence he proceeded about five leagues on foot to Medellin.

Cortés was so much changed by disease that his person was not easily recognized. But no sooner was it known that the general had returned than crowds of people, white men and natives, thronged from all the neighbouring country to welcome him. The tidings spread far and wide on the wings of the wind, and his progress to the capital was a triumphal procession. The inhabitants came from the distance of eighty leagues to have a sight of him; and they congratulated one another on the presence of the only man who could rescue the country from its state of anarchy. It was a resurrection of the dead,—so industriously had the reports of his death been circulated, and so generally believed.[1]

At all the great towns where he halted he was sumptuously entertained. Triumphal arches were thrown across the road, and the streets were strewed with flowers as he passed. After a night's repose at Tezcuco, he made his entrance in great state into the capital. The municipality came out to welcome him, and a brilliant cavalcade of armed citizens formed his escort; while the lake was covered with barges of the Indians, all fancifully decorated with their gala dresses, as on the day of his first arrival among them. The streets echoed to music, and dancing, and sounds of jubilee, as the procession held on its way to the great convent of St. Francis, where thanksgivings were offered up for the safe return of the general, who then proceeded to take up his quarters once more in his own princely residence.[2] It was in June 1526 when Cortés re-entered Mexico; nearly two years had elapsed since he had left it, on his difficult march to Honduras, — a march which led to no important results, but which consumed nearly as much time, and was attended with sufferings quite as severe, as the Conquest of Mexico itself.[3]

Cortés did not abuse his present advantage. He, indeed, instituted proceedings against his enemies; but he followed them up so languidly as to incur the imputation of weakness. It is the only instance in which he has been accused of weakness; and, since it was shown in redressing his own injuries, it may be thought to reflect no discredit on his character.[4]

---

[1] Carta Quinta de Cortés, MS.—Bernal Diaz, Hist. de la Conquista, cap. 189, 190.—Carta de Cortés al Emperador, MS., México, Sept. 11, 1526.

[2] Carta de Ocaña, MS., Agosto 31, 1526.—Carta Quinta de Cortés, MS.

[3] "What Cortés suffered," says Dr. Robertson, "on this march,—a distance, according to Gomara, of 3000 miles" (the distance must be greatly exaggerated),—"from famine, from the hostility of the natives, from the climate, and from hardships of every species, has nothing in history parallel to it, but what occurs in the adventures of the other discoverers and conquerors of the New World. Cortés was employed in this dreadful service above two years; and, though it was not distinguished by any

splendid event, he exhibited, during the course of it, greater personal courage, more fortitude of mind, more perseverance and patience, than in any other period or scene in his life." (Hist. of America, note 96.) The historian's remarks are just; as the passages which I have borrowed from the extraordinary record of the Conqueror may show. Those who are desirous of seeing something of the narrative told in his own way will find a few pages of it translated in the Appendix, Part 2, No. 14.

[4] "Y esto yo lo oí dezir á los del Real Consejo de Indias, estando presente el señor Obispo Fray Bartolomé de las Casas, que se descuidó mucho Cortés en ello, y se lo tuviéron á floxedad." Bernal Diaz, Hist. de la Conquista, cap. 190.

He was not permitted long to enjoy the sweets of triumph. In the month of July he received advices of the arrival of a *juez de residencia* on the coast, sent by the court of Madrid to supersede him temporarily in the government. The crown of Castile, as its colonial empire extended, became less and less capable of watching over its administration. It was therefore obliged to place vast powers in the hands of its viceroys ; and, as suspicion naturally accompanies weakness, it was ever prompt to listen to accusations against these powerful vassals. In such cases the government adopted the expedient of sending out a commissioner, or *juez de residencia*, with authority to investigate the conduct of the accused, to suspend him in the meanwhile from his office, and, after a judicial examination, to reinstate him in it or to remove him altogether, according to the issue of the trial. The enemies of Cortés had been for a long time busy in undermining his influence at court, and in infusing suspicions of his loyalty in the bosom of the emperor. Since his elevation to the government of the country they had redoubled their mischievous activity, and they assailed his character with the foulest imputations. They charged him with appropriating to his own use the gold which belonged to the crown, and especially with secreting the treasures of Montezuma. He was said to have made false reports of the provinces he had conquered, that he might defraud the exchequer of its lawful revenues. He had distributed the principal offices among his own creatures, and had acquired an unbounded influence, not only over the Spaniards, but the natives, who were all ready to do his bidding. He had expended large sums in fortifying both the capital and his own palace ; and it was evident, from the magnitude of his schemes and his preparations, that he designed to shake off his allegiance and to establish an independent sovereignty in New Spain.[1]

The government, greatly alarmed by these formidable charges, the probability of which they could not estimate, appointed a commissioner with full powers to investigate the matter. The person selected for this delicate office was Luis Ponce de Leon, a man of high family, young for such a post, but of a mature judgment and distinguished for his moderation and equity. The nomination of such a minister gave assurance that the crown meant to do justly by Cortés.

The emperor wrote at the same time with his own hand to the general, advising him of this step, and assuring him that it was taken, not from distrust of his integrity, but to afford him the opportunity of placing that integrity in a clear light before the world.[2]

Ponce de Leon reached Mexico in July 1526. He was received with all respect by Cortés and the municipality of the capital; and the two parties interchanged those courtesies with each other which gave augury that the

---

[1] Memorial de Luis Cardenas, MS.—Carta de Diego de Ocaña, MS.—Herrera, Hist. general, dec. 3, lib. 8, cap. 14, 15.

[2] Carta del Emperador, MS., Toledo, Nov. 4, 1525.

future proceedings would be conducted in a spirit of harmony. Unfortunately, this fair beginning was blasted by the death of the commissioner in a few weeks after his arrival, a circumstance which did not fail to afford another item in the loathsome mass of accusation heaped upon Cortés. The commissioner fell the victim of a malignant fever, which carried off a number of those who had come over in the vessel with him.[1]

On his deathbed, Ponce de Leon delegated his authority to an infirm old man, who survived but a few months,[2] and transmitted the reins of government to a person named Estrada, or Strada, the royal treasurer, one of the officers sent from Spain to take charge of the finances, and who was personally hostile to Cortés. The Spanish residents would have

---

[1] Bernal Diaz, Hist. de la Conquista, cap. 192.— Carta de Cortés al Emperador, MS., México, Set. 11, 1526.

[2] [This person, the licentiate Marcos de Aguilar, showed, during his short tenure of office, much greater zeal and activity than would be inferred from the slight mention of him by historians. Prescott has omitted to state that a principal point in the instructions given to Ponce de Leon related to the question of the *repartimientos* and other methods of treating the Indians, in regard to which he was to obtain the opinions of the authorities and other principal persons and of the Dominican and Franciscan friars. Sir Arthur Helps, who notices this fact, adds that it "led to no result," the instructions on this subject to Ponce de Leon being on his death "forgotten or laid aside." But a series of documents published by Señor Icazbalceta (Col. de Doc. para la Hist. de México, tom. ii.) shows, on the contrary, that they were promptly and fully carried out by Aguilar, who considered this to be the principal business of the commission, and one, as he wrote to the emperor, requiring despatch, since the very existence of the native population depended on immediate action. He accordingly consulted all the officials, Cortés himself included, the other chief residents of the city, such as Alvarado and Sandoval, and the members of the two religious orders, obtaining written opinions, individual as well as collective, which he transmitted with his own report to the emperor. The great majority of the persons consulted, including all the monks, while differing on some matters of detail, concurred in urging the necessity of the *repartimientos* and in recommending that they should be made hereditary.

The same result followed an inquiry instituted in 1532 and the following years. Among the opinions delivered on that occasion is one deserving of particular notice, both for the manner in which it is enforced and the character of the writer, — Fray Domingo de Batanzos, whose career has been agreeably sketched, though his views on the present matter have been misapprehended, by Sir Arthur Helps. The three objects to be kept in view, he begins by remarking, are the good treatment and preservation of the natives, the establishment and security of the Spanish settlers, and the augmentation of the royal revenues. The proper means to be adopted are also threefold: the *repartimientos* extended and perpetuated, the abandonment of the idea of reserving certain *pueblos* to be held by the crown and managed by its officers, and the appointment of good governors, since the best measures are of no avail if not ably administered. The objections to the crown's reserving any *pueblos* for itself are, that the officers will be employed solely in collecting the tribute, the Indians will receive no protection or religious instruction, and the cultivation of the soil will be always degenerating, since no one will have an interest in maintaining or improving its condition. The *repartimientos*, on the contrary, by giving the holders a direct interest in the better cultivation of the soil and the increase of the people, will insure both these results; and though under this system the royal revenues may be diminished for a time, they will in the end be greatly augmented through the general improvement of the country. The great misfortune has been that the authorities at home pursue a policy which directly contravenes their own intentions: wishing to benefit, they destroy; wishing to enrich, they impoverish; wishing to save the Indians, they exterminate them. There is needed a man with the mind and resolution of Charlemagne or Cæsar, to adopt a plan and carry it out. Instead of this, the course pursued is that of endless changes and experiments, like a perpetual litigation. It is a sure sign that God intends destruction when men are unable to find a remedy. In the present case well-meaning and holy men have sought one in vain. In his opinion, which he knows will be unheeded, the system which has in it the least evil and the most good is that of hereditary *repartimientos*, which should be established once for all. In a later letter he says, "The person least deceived about the affairs of this country is I, who know its fate as if I saw it with my eyes and touched it with my hands." He predicts the extermination of the Indians within fifty years. He has always believed and asserted that they would perish, and the laws and measures founded on any other supposition have all been bad. The wonderful thing is, he remarks, with an apparent allusion to Las Casas, that the men of greatest sanctity and zeal for good are those who have done the most harm. (Icazbalceta, Col. de Doc. para la Hist. de México, tom. ii.) That the prediction of Batanzos has been falsified by the event may be attributed to a variety of causes: the vastness of the country and the comparative density of the native population; the social and industrial habits of the latter, so different from those of more northern tribes; the decline of the Spanish power and of that spirit of conquest which, by keeping up a constant stream of emigration and ardour of enterprise, might have led to a conflict of races; and the sedulous protection afforded to the Indians by the government and the church. Their welfare was the object of constant investigation and a long series of enactments. Slavery was in their case entirely abolished. The *repartimientos* were made hereditary, but the rights and power of the *encomenderos* were carefully restricted, and the personal services at first exacted were ultimately commuted for a fixed tribute. Living together in communities which resembled so many small republics, governed by their own laws and chiefs, guided and protected by the priests, exempt from military service and all the burdens imposed by the state on the rest of the population, the Indians constituted, down to the period of Independence, a separate and privileged class, despised, it is true, but not oppressed, by the superior race.—Ed.]

persuaded Cortés to assert for himself at least an equal share of the authority, to which they considered Estrada as having no sufficient title. But the general, with singular moderation, declined a competition in this matter, and determined to abide a more decided expression of his sovereign's will. To his mortification, the nomination of Estrada was confirmed; and this dignitary soon contrived to inflict on his rival all those annoyances by which a little mind in possession of unexpected power endeavours to assert superiority over a great one. The recommendations of Cortés were disregarded, his friends mortified and insulted, his attendants outraged by injuries. One of the domestics of his friend Sandoval, for some slight offence, was sentenced to lose his hand; and when the general remonstrated against these acts of violence he was peremptorily commanded to leave the city! The Spaniards, indignant at this outrage, would have taken up arms in his defence; but Cortés would allow no resistance, and, simply remarking "that it was well that those who at the price of their blood had won the capital should not be allowed a footing in it," withdrew to his favourite villa of Cojohuacan, a few miles distant, to await there the result of these strange proceedings.[1]

The suspicions of the court of Madrid, meanwhile, fanned by the breath of calumny, had reached the most preposterous height. One might have supposed that it fancied the general was organizing a revolt throughout the colonies and meditated nothing less than an invasion of the mother country. Intelligence having been received that a vessel might speedily be expected from New Spain, orders were sent to the different ports of the kingdom, and even to Portugal, to sequestrate the cargo, under the expectation that it contained remittances to the general's family which belonged to the crown; while his letters, affording the most luminous account of all his proceedings and discoveries, were forbidden to be printed. Fortunately, however, three letters, constituting the most important part of the Conqueror's correspondence, had been given to the public, some years previous, by the indefatigable press of Seville.

The court, moreover, made aware of the incompetency of the treasurer, Estrada, to the present delicate conjuncture, now intrusted the whole affair of the inquiry to a commission dignified with the title of the Royal Audience of New Spain. This body was clothed with full powers to examine into the charges against Cortés, with instructions to send him back, as a preliminary measure, to Castile,—peacefully if they could, but forcibly if necessary. Still afraid that its belligerent vassal might defy the authority of this tribunal, the government resorted to artifice to effect his return. The president of the Indian Council was commanded to write to him, urging his presence in Spain to vindicate himself from the charges of his enemies, and offering his personal co-operation in his defence. The emperor further wrote a letter to the Audience, containing his commands

---

[1] Bernal Diaz, Hist. de la Conquista, cap. 194.—Carta de Cortés al Emperador, MS., Set. 11, 1526.

for Cortés to return, as the government wished to consult him on matters relating to the Indies, and to bestow on him a recompense suited to his high deserts. This letter was intended to be shown to Cortés.[1]

But it was superfluous to put in motion all this complicated machinery to effect a measure on which Cortés was himself resolved. Proudly conscious of his own unswerving loyalty, and of the benefits he had rendered to his country, he was deeply sensible to this unworthy requital of them, especially on the very theatre of his achievements. He determined to abide no longer where he was exposed to such indignities, but to proceed at once to Spain, present himself before his sovereign, boldly assert his innocence, and claim redress for his wrongs and a just reward for his services. In the close of his letter to the emperor, detailing the painful expedition to Honduras, after enlarging on the magnificent schemes he had entertained of discovery in the South Sea, and vindicating himself from the charge of a too lavish expenditure, he concludes with the lofty yet touching declaration "that he trusts his Majesty will in time acknowledge his deserts; but, if that unhappily shall not be, the world at least will be assured of his loyalty, and he himself shall have the conviction of having done his duty; and no better inheritance than this shall he ask for his children."[2]

No sooner was the intention of Cortés made known, than it excited a general sensation through the country. Even Estrada relented; he felt that he had gone too far, and that it was not his policy to drive his noble enemy to take refuge in his own land. Negotiations were opened, and an attempt at a reconciliation was made, through the bishop of Tlascala. Cortés received these overtures in a courteous spirit, but his resolution was unshaken. Having made the necessary arrangements, therefore, in Mexico, he left the Valley, and proceeded at once to the coast. Had he entertained the criminal ambition imputed to him by his enemies, he might have been sorely tempted by the repeated offers of support which were made to him, whether in good or in bad faith, on the journey, if he would but reassume the government and assert his independence of Castile. But these disloyal advances he rejected with the scorn they merited.[3]

On his arrival at Villa Rica he received the painful tidings of the death of his father, Don Martin Cortés, whom he had hoped so soon to embrace after his long and eventful absence. Having celebrated his obsequies with every mark of filial respect, he made preparations for his speedy departure. Two of the best vessels in the port were got ready and provided with everything requisite for a long voyage. He was attended by

---

[1] Herrera, Hist. general, dec. 4, lib. 2, cap. 1; and lib. 3, cap. 8.

[2] "Todas estas entradas están ahora para partir casi á una, plega á Dios de los guiar como él se sirva, que yo aunque V. M. mas me mande desfavoreçer no tengo de dejar de servir, que no es posible que por tiempo V. M. no conosca mis servicios, y ya que esto no sea, yo me satisfago con hazer lo que debo, y con saber que á todo el mundo tengo satisfecho, y les son notorios mis servicios y lealdad, con que los hago, y no quiero otro mayorazgo sino este." Carta Quinta, MS.

[3] Bernal Diaz, Hist. de la Conquista, cap. 194.— Carta de Ocaña, MS., Agosto 31, 1526.

his friend the faithful Sandoval, by Tápia, and some other cavaliers most attached to his person. He also took with him several Aztec and Tlascalan chiefs, and among them a son of Montezuma, and another of Maxixca, the friendly old Tlascalan lord, both of whom were desirous to accompany the general to Castile. He carried home a large collection of plants and minerals, as specimens of the natural resources of the country; several wild animals, and birds of gaudy plumage; various fabrics of delicate workmanship, especially the gorgeous feather-work; and a number of jugglers, dancers, and buffoons, who greatly astonished the Europeans by the marvellous facility of their performances, and were thought a suitable present for his Holiness the Pope.[1] Lastly, Cortés displayed his magnificence in a rich treasure of jewels, among which were emeralds of extraordinary size and lustre, gold to the amount of two hundred thousand *pesos de oro*, and fifteen hundred marks of silver. "In fine," says Herrera, "he came in all the state of a great lord." [2]

After a brief and prosperous voyage, Cortés came in sight once more of his native shores, and, crossing the bar of Saltes, entered the little port of Palos in May 1528,—the same spot where Columbus had landed five-and-thirty years before, on his return from the discovery of the Western World. Cortés was not greeted with the enthusiasm and public rejoicings which welcomed the great navigator; and, indeed, the inhabitants were not prepared for his arrival. From Palos he soon proceeded to the convent of La Rabida, the same place, also, within the hospitable walls of which Columbus had found a shelter. An interesting circumstance is mentioned by historians, connected with his short stay at Palos. Francisco Pizarro, the Conqueror of Peru, had arrived there, having come to Spain to solicit aid for his great enterprise.[3] He was then in the commencement of his brilliant career, as Cortés might be said to be at the close of his. He was an old acquaintance, and a kinsman, as is affirmed, of the general, whose mother was a Pizarro.[4] The meeting of these two extraordinary men, the Conquerors of the North and of the South in the New World, as they set foot, after their eventful absence, on the shores of their native land, and that, too, on the spot consecrated by the presence of Columbus, has something in it striking to the imagination. It has accordingly attracted the attention of one of the most illustrious of living poets, who, in a brief and beautiful sketch, has depicted the scene in the genuine colouring of the age.[5]

While reposing from the fatigues of his voyage, at La Rabida, an event occurred which afflicted Cortés deeply and which threw a dark cloud

---

[1] The Pope, who was of the joyous Medici family, Clement VII., and the cardinals, were greatly delighted with the feats of the Indian jugglers, according to Diaz; and his Holiness, who, it may be added, received at the same time from Cortés a substantial donative of gold and jewels, publicly testified, by prayers and solemn processions, his great sense of the services rendered to Christianity by the Conquerors of Mexico, and generously requited them by bulls granting plenary absolution from their sins. Hist. de la Conquista, cap. 195.

[2] "Y en fin venia como gran Señor." Hist. gen., dec. 4, lib. 3, cap. 8.

[3] Herrera, Hist. general, dec. 4, lib. 4, cap. 1.—Cavo, Los tres Siglos de México, tom. i. p. 78.

[4] Pizarro y Orellana, Varones ilustres, p. 121.

[5] See the conclusion of Rogers's Voyage of Columbus.

over his return. This was the death of Gonzalo de Sandoval, his trusty friend, and so long the companion of his fortunes. He was taken ill in a wretched inn at Palos, soon after landing; and his malady gained ground so rapidly that it was evident his constitution, impaired, probably, by the extraordinary fatigues he had of late years undergone, would be unable to resist it. Cortés was instantly sent for, and arrived in time to administer the last consolations of friendship to the dying cavalier. Sandoval met his approaching end with composure, and, having given the attention which the short interval allowed to the settlement of both his temporal and spiritual concerns, he breathed his last in the arms of his commander.

Sandoval died at the premature age of thirty-one.[1] He was in many respects the most eminent of the great captains formed under the eye of Cortés. He was of good family, and a native of Medellin, also the birth-place of the general, for whom he had the warmest personal regard. Cortés soon discerned his uncommon qualities, and proved it by uniformly selecting the young officer for the most difficult commissions. His conduct on these occasions fully justified the preference. He was a decided favourite with the soldiers; for, though strict in enforcing discipline, he was careful of their comforts and little mindful of his own. He had nothing of the avarice so common in the Castilian cavalier, and seemed to have no other ambition than that of faithfully discharging the duties of his profession. He was a plain man, affecting neither the showy manners nor the bravery in costume which distinguished Alvarado, the Aztec *Tonatiuh.* The expression of his countenance was open and manly; his chestnut hair curled close to his head; his frame was strong and sinewy. He had a lisp in his utterance, which made his voice somewhat indistinct. Indeed, he was no speaker; but, if slow of speech, he was prompt and energetic in action. He had precisely the qualities which fitted him for the perilous enterprise in which he had embarked. He had accomplished his task; and, after having escaped death, which lay waiting for him in every step of his path, had come home, as it would seem, to his native land, only to meet it there.

His obsequies were performed with all solemnity by the Franciscan friars of La Rabida, and his remains were followed to their final resting-place by the comrades who had so often stood by his side in battle. They were laid in the cemetery of the convent, which, shrouded in its forest of pines, stood, and may yet stand, on the bold eminence that overlooks the waste of waters so lately traversed by the adventurous soldier.[2]

It was not long after this melancholy event that Cortés and his suite began their journey into the interior. The general stayed a few days at the castle of the duke of Medina Sidonia, the most powerful of the

---

[1] Bernal Diaz says that Sandoval was twenty-two years old when he first came to New Spain, in 1519. —Hist. de la Conquista, cap. 205.

[2] Bernal Diaz, Hist. de la Conquista, cap. 195.

Andalusian lords, who hospitably entertained him, and, at his departure, presented him with several noble Arabian horses. Cortés first directed his steps towards Guadalupe, where he passed nine days, offering up prayers and causing masses to be performed at Our Lady's shrine for the soul of his departed friend.

Before his departure from La Rabida, he had written to the court, informing it of his arrival in the country. Great was the sensation caused there by the intelligence; the greater, that the late reports of his treasonable practices had made it wholly unexpected. His arrival produced an immediate change of feeling. All cause of jealousy was now removed; and, as the clouds which had so long settled over the royal mind were dispelled, the emperor seemed only anxious to show his sense of the distinguished services of his so dreaded vassal. Orders were sent to different places on the route to provide him with suitable accommodations, and preparations were made to give him a brilliant reception in the capital.

Meanwhile, Cortés had formed the acquaintance at Guadalupe of several persons of distinction, and among them of the family of the *comendador* of Leon, a nobleman of the highest consideration at court. The general's conversation, enriched with the stores of a life of adventure, and his manners, in which the authority of habitual command was tempered by the frank and careless freedom of the soldier, made a most favourable impression on his new friends; and their letters to the court, where he was yet unknown, heightened the interest already felt in this remarkable man. The tidings of his arrival had by this time spread far and wide throughout the country; and, as he resumed his journey, the roads presented a spectacle such as had not been seen since the return of Columbus. Cortés did not usually affect an ostentation of dress, though he loved to display the pomp of a great lord in the number and magnificence of his retainers. His train was now swelled by the Indian chieftains, who by the splendours of their barbaric finery gave additional brilliancy, as well as novelty, to the pageant. But his own person was the object of general curiosity. The houses and the streets of the great towns and villages were thronged with spectators, eager to look on the hero who with his single arm, as it were, had won an empire for Castile, and who, to borrow the language of an old historian, "came in the pomp and glory, not so much of a great vassal, as of an independent monarch." [1]

As he approached Toledo, then the rival of Madrid, the press of the multitude increased, till he was met by the duke de Bejar, the count de Aguilar, and others of his steady friends, who, at the head of a large body of the principal nobility and cavaliers of the city, came out to receive him, and attended him to the quarters prepared for his residence. It was a

---

[1] "Vino de las Indias despues de la conquista de Mexico, con tanto acompañamiento y magestad, que mas parecia de Príncipe, ó señor poderosíssimo, que de Capitan y vasallo de algun Rey ó Emperador." Lanuza, Historias ecclesiásticas y seculares de Aragon (Zaragoza, 1622), lib. 3, cap. 14.

2 Q

proud moment for Cortés; and distrusting, as he well might, his reception by his countrymen, it afforded him a greater satisfaction than the brilliant entrance which, a few years previous, he had made into the capital of Mexico.

The following day he was admitted to an audience by the emperor, and Cortés, gracefully kneeling to kiss the hand of his sovereign, presented to him a memorial which succinctly recounted his services and the requital he had received for them. The emperor graciously raised him, and put many questions to him respecting the countries he had conquered. Charles was pleased with the general's answers, and his intelligent mind took great satisfaction in inspecting the curious specimens of Indian ingenuity which his vassal had brought with him from New Spain. In subsequent conversations the emperor repeatedly consulted Cortés on the best mode of administering the government of the colonies, and by his advice introduced some important regulations, especially for ameliorating the condition of the natives and for encouraging domestic industry.

The monarch took frequent opportunity to show the confidence which he now reposed in Cortés. On all public occasions he appeared with him by his side; and once, when the general lay ill of a fever, Charles paid him a visit in person, and remained some time in the apartment of the invalid. This was an extraordinary mark of condescension in the haughty court of Castile; and it is dwelt upon with becoming emphasis by the historians of the time, who seem to regard it as an ample compensation for all the sufferings and services of Cortés.[1]

The latter had now fairly triumphed over opposition. The courtiers, with that ready instinct which belongs to the tribe, imitated the example of their master; and even envy was silent, amidst the general homage that was paid to the man who had so lately been a mark for the most envenomed calumny. Cortés, without a title, without a name but what he had created for himself, was at once, as it were, raised to a level with the proudest nobles in the land.

He was so still more effectually by the substantial honours which were accorded to him by his sovereign in the course of the following year. By an instrument dated July 6th, 1529, the emperor raised him to the dignity of the Marquis of the Valley of Oaxaca;[2] and the title of "marquis," when used without the name of the individual, has been always appropriated in the colonies, in an especial manner, to Cortés, as the title of "admiral" was to Columbus.[3]

Two other instruments, dated in the same month of July, assigned to Cortés a vast tract of land in the rich province of Oaxaca, together with

[1] Gomara, Crónica, cap. 183.—Herrera, Hist. general, dec. 4, lib. 4, cap. 1.—Bernal Diaz, Hist. de la Conquista, cap. 195.

[2] Titulo de Marques, MS., Barcelona, 6 de Julio, 1529.

[3] Humboldt, Essai politique, tom. ii. p. 30, note. —According to Lanuza, he was offered by the emperor the Order of St. Jago, but declined it, because no *encomienda* was attached to it. (Hist. de Aragon, tom. i. lib. 3, cap. 14.) But Caro de Torres, in his History of the Military Orders of Castile, enumerates Cortés among the members of the Compostellan fraternity. Hist. de las Ordenes militares (Madrid, 1629), fol. 103, et seq.

large estates in the city of Mexico, and other places in the Valley.[1] The princely domain thus granted comprehended more than twenty large towns and villages, and twenty-three thousand vassals. The language in which the gift was made greatly enhanced its value. The preamble of the instrument, after enlarging on the "good services rendered by Cortés in the Conquest, and the great benefits resulting therefrom, both in respect to the increase of the Castilian empire and the advancement of the Holy Catholic Faith," acknowledges "the sufferings he had undergone in accomplishing this glorious work, and the fidelity and obedience with which, as a good and trusty vassal, he had ever served the crown."[2] It declares, in conclusion, that it grants this recompense of his deserts because it is "the duty of princes to honour and reward those who serve them well and loyally, in order that the memory of their great deeds should be perpetuated, and others be incited by their example to the performance of the like illustrious exploits." The unequivocal testimony thus borne by his sovereign to his unwavering loyalty was most gratifying to Cortés,—how gratifying, every generous soul who has been the subject of suspicion undeserved will readily estimate. The language of the general in aftertime shows how deeply he was touched by it.[3]

Yet there was one degree in the scale, above which the royal gratitude would not rise. Neither the solicitations of Cortés, nor those of the duke de Bejar and his other powerful friends, could prevail on the emperor to reinstate him in the government of Mexico. The country, reduced to tranquillity, had no longer need of his commanding genius to control it; and Charles did not care to place again his formidable vassal in a situation which might revive the dormant spark of jealousy and distrust. It was the policy of the crown to employ one class of its subjects to effect its conquests, and another class to rule over them. For the latter it selected men in whom the fire of ambition was tempered by a cooler judgment naturally, or by the sober influence of age. Even Columbus, notwithstanding the terms of his original "capitulation" with the crown, had not been permitted to preside over the colonies; and still less likely would it be to concede this power to one possessed of the aspiring temper of Cortés.

But, although the emperor refused to commit the civil government of the colony into his hands, he reinstated him in his military command. By a royal ordinance, dated also in July, 1529, the Marquis of the Valley

---

[1] Merced de Tierras inmediatas á Mexico, MS., Barcelona, 23 de Julio, 1529.—Merced de los Vasallos, MS., Barcelona, 6 de Julio, 1529.

[2] "É nos habemos recibido y tenemos de vos por bien servido en ello, y acatando los grandes provechos que de vuestros servicios han redundado, ansi para el servicio de Nuestro Señor y aumento de su santa fé católica, y en las dichas tierras que estaban sin conocimiento ni fé se han plantado, como el acrecentamiento que dello ha redundado á nuestra corona real destos reynos, y los trabajos que en ello habeis pasado, y la fidelidad y obediencia con que siempre nos habeis servido como bueno é fiel servidor y vasallo nuestro, de que somos ciertos y confiados." Merced de los Vasallos, MS.

[3] "The benignant reception which I experienced, on my return, from your Majesty," says Cortés, "your kind expressions and generous treatment, make me not only forget all my toils and sufferings, but even cause me regret that I have not been called to endure more in your service." (Carta de Cortés al Lic. Nuñez, MS., 1535.) This memorial, addressed to his agent in Castile, was designed for the emperor.

was named Captain-General of New Spain and of the coasts of the South Sea. He was empowered to make discoveries in the Southern Ocean, with the right to rule over such lands as he should colonize,[1] and by a subsequent grant he was to become proprietor of one-twelfth of all his discoveries.[2] The government had no design to relinquish the services of so able a commander. But it warily endeavoured to withdraw him from the scene of his former triumphs, and to throw open a new career of ambition, that might stimulate him still further to enlarge the dominions of the crown.

Thus gilded by the sunshine of royal favour, "rivalling," to borrow the homely comparision of an old chronicler, "Alexander in the fame of his exploits, and Crassus in that of his riches,"[3] with brilliant manners, and a person which, although it showed the effects of hard service, had not yet lost all the attractions of youth, Cortés might now be regarded as offering an enviable alliance for the best houses in Castile. It was not long before he paid his addresses, which were favourably received, to a member of that noble house which had so steadily supported him in the dark hour of his fortunes. The lady's name was Doña Juana de Zuñiga, daughter of the second count de Aguilar, and niece of the duke de Bejar.[4] She was much younger than himself, beautiful, and, as events showed, not without spirit. One of his presents to his youthful bride excited the admiration and envy of the fairer part of the court. This was five emeralds, of wonderful size and brilliancy. These jewels had been cut by the Aztecs into the shapes of flowers, fishes, and into other fanciful forms, with an exquisite style of workmanship which enhanced their original value.[5] They were, not improbably, part of the treasure of the unfortunate Montezuma, and, being easily portable, may have escaped the general wreck of the *noche triste.* The queen of Charles the Fifth, it is said,—it may be the idle gossip of a court,—had intimated a willingness to become proprietor of some of these magnificent baubles ; and the preference which Cortés gave to his fair bride caused some feelings of estrangement in the royal bosom, which had an unfavourable influence on the future fortunes of the Marquis.

Late in the summer of 1529, Charles the Fifth left his Spanish dominions

---

[1] Título de Capitan General de la Nueva-España y Costa del Sur, MS., Barcelona, 6 de Julio, 1529.

[2] Asiento y Capitulacion que hizo con el Emperador Don H. Cortés, MS., Madrid, 27 de Oct., 1529.

[3] "Que, segun se dezia, excedia en las hazañas á Alexandro Magno, y en las riquezas á Crasso." (Lanuza, Hist. de Aragon. lib. 3, cap. 14.) The rents of the marquis of the Valley, according to L. Marineo Siculo, who lived at the court at this time, were about 60,000 ducats a year. Cosas memorables de España (Alcalá de Henares, 1539), fol. 24.

[4] Doña Juana was of the house of Arellano, and of the royal lineage of Navarre. Her father was not a very wealthy noble. L. Marineo Siculo, Cosas memorables, fol. 24, 25.

[5] One of these precious stones was as valuable as Shylock's turquoise. Some Genoese merchants in

Seville offered Cortés, according to Gomara, 40,000 ducats for it. The same author gives a more particular account of the jewels, which may interest some readers. It shows the ingenuity of the artist, who, without steel, could so nicely cut so hard a material. One emerald was in the form of a rose ; the second, in that of a horn ; a third, like a fish, with eyes of gold ; the fourth was like a little bell with a fine pearl for the tongue, and on the rim was this inscription, in Spanish : *Blessed is he who created thee.* The fifth, which was the most valuable, was a small cup with a foot of gold, and with four little chains, of the same metal, attached to large pearl as a button. The edge of the cup was of gold, on which was engraven this Latin sentence : *Inter natos mulierum non surrexit major.* Gomara, Crónica, cap. 184.

for Italy. Cortés accompanied him on his way, probably to the place of embarkation ; and in the capital of Aragon we find him, according to the national historian, exciting the same general interest and admiration among the people as he had done in Castile. On his return, there seemed no occasion for him to protract his stay longer in the country. He was weary of the life of idle luxury which he had been leading for the last year, and which was so foreign to his active habits and the stirring scenes to which he had been accustomed. He determined, therefore, to return to Mexico, where his extensive property required his presence, and where a new field was now opened to him for honourable enterprise.

CHAPTER V.

CORTÉS REVISITS MEXICO.—RETIRES TO HIS ESTATES.—HIS VOYAGES OF DISCOVERY.—FINAL RETURN TO CASTILE.—COLD RECEPTION.—DEATH OF CORTÉS.—HIS CHARACTER.

(1530-1547.)

EARLY in the spring of 1530, Cortés embarked for New Spain. He was accompanied by the marchioness, his wife, together with his aged mother, who had the good fortune to live to see her son's elevation, and by a magnificent retinue of pages and attendants, such as belonged to the household of a powerful noble. How different from the forlorn condition in which, twenty-six years before, he had been cast loose, as a wild adventurer, to seek his bread upon the waters !

The first point of his destination was Hispaniola, where he was to remain until he received tiding of the organization of the new government that was to take charge of Mexico.[1] In the preceding chapter it was stated that the administration of the country had been intrusted to a body called the Royal Audience ; one of whose first duties it was to investigate the charges brought against Cortés. Nuñez de Guzman, his avowed enemy, was placed at the head of this board ; and the investigation was conducted with all the rancour of personal hostility. A remarkable document still exists called the *Pesquisa Secreta*, or "Secret Inquiry," which contains a record of the proceedings against Cortés. It was prepared by the secretary of the Audience, and signed by the several members. The document is very long, embracing nearly a hundred folio pages. The name and the testimony of every witness are given, and the whole forms a mass of loathsome details, such as might better suit a prosecution in a petty municipal court than that of a great officer of the crown.

---

[1] Carta de Cortés al Emperador, MS., Tezcuco, 10 de Oct., 1530.

The charges are eight in number; involving, among other crimes, that of a deliberate design to cast off his allegiance to the crown; that of the murder of two of the commissioners who had been sent out to supersede him; of the murder of his own wife, Catalina Xuarez;[1] of extortion, and of licentious practices,—of offences, in short, which, from their private nature, would seem to have little to do with his conduct as a public man. The testimony is vague and often contradictory; the witnesses are for the most part obscure individuals, and the few persons of consideration among them appear to have been taken from the ranks of his decided enemies. When it is considered that the inquiry was conducted in the absence of Cortés, before a court the members of which were personally unfriendly to him, and that he was furnished with no specification of the charges, and had no opportunity, consequently, of disproving them, it is impossible, at this distance of time, to attach any importance to this paper as a legal document. When it is added that no action was taken on it by the government to whom it was sent, we may be disposed to regard it simply as a monument of the malice of his enemies. It has been drawn by the curious antiquary from the obscurity to which it had been so long consigned in the Indian archives at Seville; but it can be of no further use to the historian than to show that a great name in the sixteenth century exposed its possessor to calumnies as malignant as it has at any time since.[2]

The high-handed measures of the Audience, and the oppressive conduct of Guzman, especially towards the Indians, excited general indignation in the colony and led to serious apprehensions of an insurrection. It became necessary to supersede an administration so reckless and unprincipled. But Cortés was detained two months at the island, by the slow movements of the Castilian court, before tidings reached him of the

---

[1] Doña Catalina's death happened so opportunely for the rising fortunes of Cortés, that this charge of murder by her husband has found more credit with the vulgar than the other accusations brought against him. Cortés, from whatever reason, perhaps from the conviction that the charge was too monstrous to obtain credit, never condescended to vindicate his innocence. But, in addition to the arguments mentioned in the text for discrediting the accusation generally, we should consider that this particular charge attracted so little attention in Castile, where he had abundance of enemies, that he found no difficulty, on his return there, seven years afterwards, in forming an alliance with one of the noblest houses in the kingdom; that no writer of that day (except Bernal Diaz, who treats it as a base calumny), not even Las Casas, the stern accuser of the Conquerors, intimates a suspicion of his guilt; and that, lastly, no allusion whatever is made to it in the suit instituted, some years after her death, by the relatives of Doña Catalina, for the recovery of property from Cortés, pretended to have been derived through her marriage with him,—a suit conducted with acrimony and protracted for several years. I have not seen the documents connected with this suit, which are still preserved in the archives of the house of Cortés, but the fact has been communicated to me by a distinguished Mexican who has carefully examined them, and I cannot

but regard it as of itself conclusive that the family at least of Doña Catalina did not attach credit to the accusation. Yet so much credit has been given to this in Mexico, where the memory of the old Spaniards is not held in especial favour at the present day, that it has formed the subject of an elaborate discussion in the public periodicals of that city.

[2] This remarkable paper, forming part of the valuable collection of Don Vargas Ponçe, is without date. It was doubtless prepared in 1529, during the visit of Cortés to Castile. The following Title is prefixed to it:

"Pesquisa secreta.

"Relacion de los cargos que resultan de la pesquisa secreta contra Don Hernando Cortés, de los quales no se le dió copia ni traslado á la parte del dicho Don Hernando, así por ser los dichos cargos de la calidad que son, como por estar la persona del dicho Don Hernando ausente como está. Los quales yo Gregorio de Saldaña, escribano de S. M. y escribano de la dicha Residencia, saqué de la dicha pesquisa secreta por mandado de los Señores, Presidente y Oidores de la Audiencia y Chancillería Real que por mandado de S. M. en esta Nueva España reside. Los quales dichos Señores, Presidente y Oidores, envian á S. M. para que los mande ver, y vestos mande proveer lo que á su servicio convenga." MS.

appointment of a new Audience for the government of the country. The person selected to preside over it was the bishop of St Domingo, a prelate whose acknowledged wisdom and virtue gave favourable augury for the conduct of his administration. After this, Cortés resumed his voyage, and landed at Villa Rica on the 15th of July, 1530.

After remaining for a time in the neighbourhood, where he received some petty annoyances from the Audience, he proceeded to Tlascala, and publicly proclaimed his powers as Captain-General of New Spain and the South Sea. An edict issued by the empress during her husband's absence had interdicted Cortés from approaching within ten leagues of the Mexican capital while the present authorities were there.[1] The empress was afraid of a collision between the parties. Cortés, however, took up his residence on the opposite side of the lake, at Tezcuco.

No sooner was his arrival there known in the metropolis than multitudes both of Spaniards and natives crossed the lake to pay their respects to their old commander, to offer him their services, and to complain of their manifold grievances. It seemed as if the whole population of the capital was pouring into the neighbouring city, where the Marquis maintained the state of an independent potentate. The members of the Audience, indignant at the mortifying contrast which their own diminished court presented, imposed heavy penalties on such of the natives as should be found in Tezcuco, and, affecting to consider themselves in danger, made preparations for the defence of the city. But these belligerent movements were terminated by the arrival of the new Audience; though Guzman had the address to maintain his hold on a northern province, where he earned a reputation for cruelty and extortion unrivalled even in the annals of the New World.

Everything seemed now to assure a tranquil residence to Cortés. The new magistrates treated him with marked respect, and took his advice on the most important measures of government. Unhappily, this state of things did not long continue; and a misunderstanding arose between the parties, in respect to the enumeration of the vassals assigned by the crown to Cortés, which the marquis thought was made on principles prejudicial to his interests and repugnant to the intentions of the grant.[2] He was still further displeased by finding that the Audience were intrusted, by their commission, with a concurrent jurisdiction with himself in military affairs.[3] This led occasionally to an interference, which the proud spirit of Cortés, so long accustomed to independent rule, could ill brook. After submitting to it for a time, he left the capital in disgust, no more to return there, and took up his residence in his city of Cuernavaca. It was the place won by his own sword from the Aztecs previous to the

---

[1] MS., Tordelaguna, 22 de Marzo, 1530.
[2] The principal grievance alleged was that slaves, many of them held temporarily by their masters, according to the old Aztec usage, were comprehended in the census. The complaint forms part of a catalogue of grievances embodied by Cortés in a memorial to the emperor. It is a clear and business-like paper. Carta de Cortés á Nuñez, MS.
[3] Ibid., MS.

siege of Mexico. It stood on the southern slope of the Cordilleras, and overlooked a wide expanse of country, the fairest and most flourishing portion of his own domain.[1] He had erected a stately palace on the spot, and henceforth made this city his favourite residence.[2] It was well situated for superintending his vast estates, and he now devoted himself to bringing them into proper cultivation. He introduced the sugar-cane from Cuba, and it grew luxuriantly in the rich soil of the neighbouring lowlands. He imported large numbers of merino sheep and other cattle, which found abundant pastures in the country around Tehuantepec. His lands were thickly sprinkled with groves of mulberry-trees, which furnished nourishment for the silk-worm. He encouraged the cultivation of hemp and flax, and, by his judicious and enterprising husbandry, showed the capacity of the soil for the culture of valuable products before unknown in the land; and he turned these products to the best account, by the erection of sugar-mills, and other works for the manufacture of the raw material. He thus laid the foundation of an opulence for his family, as substantial, if not as speedy, as that derived from the mines. Yet this latter source of wealth was not neglected by him, and he drew gold from the region of Tehuantepec, and silver from that of Zacatecas. The amount derived from these mines was not so abundant as at a later day. But the expense of working them, on the other hand, was much less in the earlier stages of the operation, when the metal lay so much nearer the surface.[3]

But this tranquil way of life did not long content his restless and adventurous spirit; and it sought a vent by availing itself of his new charter of discovery to explore the mysteries of the great Southern Ocean. In 1527, two years before his return to Spain, he had sent a little squadron to the Moluccas. The expedition was attended with some important consequences; but as they do not relate to Cortés, an account of it will find a more suitable place in the maritime annals of Spain, where it has been given by the able hand which has done so much for the country in this department.[4]

Cortés was preparing to send another squadron of four vessels in the same direction, when his plans were interrupted by his visit to Spain; and

---

1 ["Dominando una vista muy extensa sobre el valle hácia el Sur, lo que al Norte y Oriente se termina con la magestuosa cordillera que separa el valle de Cuernavaca del de Méjico." Alaman, Disertaciones históricas, tom. ii. p. 35.]

2 The palace has crumbled into ruins, and the spot is now only remarkable for its natural beauty and its historic associations. "It was the capital," says Madame de Calderon, "of the Tlahuica nation, and, after the Conquest, Cortés built here a splendid palace, a church, and a convent for Franciscans, believing that he had laid the foundation of a great city. . . . It is, however, a place of little importance, though so favoured by nature; and the Conqueror's palace is a half-ruined barrack, though a most picturesque object, standing on a hill, behind which starts up the great white volcano." Life in Mexico, vol. ii. let. 31. [The beautiful church

of San Francisco, now the parish church, was constructed by Cortés, and enriched with jewels and sacred vessels by his wife, manifesting, says Alaman, the good taste and the piety of *the marquis* and *the marchioness,*—as, in consequence of their being the first and at that time the only persons who bore the title in Mexico, they were styled and always subscribed themselves. Disertaciones históricas, tom. ii. p. 35.]

3 These particulars respecting the agricultural economy of Cortés I have derived in part from a very able argument, prepared, in January, 1828, for the Mexican Chamber of Deputies, by Don Lúcas Alaman, in defence of the territorial rights possessed at this day by the Conqueror's descendant, the duke of Monteleone.]

4 Navarrete, Coleccion de los Viages y Descubrimientos (Madrid, 1837), tom. v., Viages al Maluco;

his unfinished little navy, owing to the malice of the Royal Audience, who drew off the hands employed in building it, went to pieces on the stocks. Two other squadrons were now fitted out by Cortés in the years 1532 and 1533, and sent on a voyage of discovery to the Northwest.[1] They were unfortunate, though in the latter expedition the Californian peninsula was reached, and a landing effected on its southern extremity at Santa Cruz, probably the modern port of La Paz. One of the vessels, thrown on the coast of New Galicia, was seized by Guzman, the old enemy of Cortés, who ruled over that territory ; the crew were plundered, and the ship was detained as a lawful prize. Cortés, indignant at the outrage, demanded justice from the Royal Audience; and as that body was too feeble to enforce its own decrees in his favour, he took redress into his own hands.[2]

He made a rapid but difficult march on Chiametla, the scene of Guzman's spoliation ; and as the latter did not care to face his incensed antagonist, Cortés recovered his vessel, though not the cargo. He was then joined by the little squadron which he had fitted out from his own port of Tehuantepec,—a port which in the sixteenth century promised to hold the place since occupied by that of Acapulco.[3] The vessels were provided with everything requisite for planting a colony in the newly-discovered region, and transported four hundred Spaniards and *three hundred negro slaves*, which Cortés had assembled for that purpose. With this intention he crossed the Gulf, the Adriatic—to which an old writer compares it—of the Western World.

Our limits will not allow us to go into the details of this disastrous expedition, which was attended with no important results either to its projector or to science. It may suffice to say that, in the prosecution of it, Cortés and his followers were driven to the last extremity by famine ; that he again crossed the Gulf, was tossed about by terrible tempests, without a pilot to guide him, was thrown upon the rocks, where his shattered vessel nearly went to pieces, and, after a succession of dangers and disasters as formidable as any which he had ever encountered on land, succeeded, by means of his indomitable energy, in bringing his crazy bark safe into the same port of Santa Cruz from which he had started.

While these occurrences were passing, the new Royal Audience, after a faithful discharge of its commission, had been superseded by the arrival of a viceroy, the first ever sent to New Spain. Cortés, though invested with similar powers, had the title only of Governor. This was the commencement of the system, afterwards pursued by the crown, of intrusting the colonial administration to some individual whose high rank and personal consideration might make him the fitting representative of majesty. The jealousy of the court did not allow the subject clothed

---

[1] Instruccion que dió el Marques del Valle á Juan de Avellaneda, etc., MS.

[2] Provision sobre los Descubrimientos del Sur, MS., Setiembre, 1534

[3] The river Huasacualco furnished great facilities for transporting across the isthmus, from Vera Cruz, materials to build vessels on the Pacific. Humboldt, Essai politique, tom. iv. p. 50.

with such ample authority to remain long enough in the same station to form dangerous schemes of ambition, but at the expiration of a few years he was usually recalled, or transferred to some other province of the vast colonial empire. The person now sent to Mexico was Don Antonio de Mendoza, a man of moderation and practical good sense, and one of that illustrious family who in the preceding reign furnished so many distinguished ornaments to the Church, to the camp, and to letters.

The long absence of Cortés had caused the deepest anxiety in the mind of his wife, the marchioness of the Valley. She wrote to the viceroy immediately on his arrival, beseeching him to ascertain, if possible, the fate of her husband, and, if he could be found, to urge his return. The viceroy, in consequence, despatched two ships in search of Cortés, but whether they reached him before his departure from Santa Cruz is doubtful. It is certain that he returned safe, after his long absence, to Acapulco, and was soon followed by the survivors of his wretched colony.

Undismayed by these repeated reverses, Cortés, still bent on some discovery worthy of his reputation, fitted out three more vessels, and placed them under the command of an officer named Ulloa. This expedition, which took its departure in July, 1539, was attended with more important results. Ulloa penetrated to the head of the Gulf, then, returning and winding round the coast of the peninsula, doubled its southern point, and ascended as high as the twenty-eighth or twenty-ninth degree of north latitude on its western borders. After this, sending home one of the squadron, the bold navigator held on his course to the north, but was never more heard of.[1]

Thus ended the maritime enterprises of Cortés, sufficiently disastrous in a pecuniary view, since they cost him three hundred thousand *castellanos* of gold, without the return of a ducat.[2] He was even obliged to borrow money, and to pawn his wife's jewels, to procure funds for the last enterprise;[3] thus incurring a debt which, increased by the great charges of his princely establishment, hung about him during the remainder of his life. But, though disastrous in an economical view, his generous efforts added important contributions to science. In the course of these expeditions, and those undertaken by Cortés previous to his visit to Spain,

---

[1] Instruccion del Marques del Valle, MS.—The most particular and authentic account of Ulloa's cruise will be found in Ramusio. (Tom. iii. pp. 340–354.) It is by one of the officers of the squadron. My limits will not allow me to give the details of the voyages made by Cortés, which, although not without interest, were attended with no permanent consequences.* A good summary of his expeditions in the Gulf has been given by Navarrete in the Introduction to his

Relacion del Viage hecho por las Goletas Sutil y Mexicana (Madrid, 1802), pp. vi.-xxvi. ; and the English reader will find a brief account of them in Greenhow's valuable Memoir on the Northwest Coast of North America (Washington, 1840), pp. 22–27.

[2] Memorial al Rey del Marques del Valle, MS., 25 de Junio, 1540.

[3] Provision sobre los Descubrimientos del Sur, MS.

* [The restless and determined spirit with which Cortés pursued his mainly ineffectual projects of discovery is exemplified by a letter to the Council of the Indies, September 20, 1538, begging that body to assist his agents in procuring pilots for him. He has at present, he says, nine vessels, very good and well equipped, and is only waiting for pilots, having tried in vain to obtain some from Panamá and Leon. Though he has not yet secured the fruits he had expected from his expeditions, he trusts in God that they will be henceforth attended with better fortune. Col. de Doc. inéd. relativos al Descubrimiento, Conquista y Colonizacion de las Posesiones españolas en América y Oceanía, tom. iii.—Ed.]

the Pacific had been coasted from the Bay of Panamá to the Rio Colorado. The great peninsula of California had been circumnavigated as far as to the isle of Cedros, or Cerros, into which the name has since been corrupted. This vast tract, which had been supposed to be an archipelago of islands, was now discovered to be a part of the continent ; and its general outline, as appears from the maps of the time, was nearly as well understood as at the present day.[1] Lastly, the navigator had explored the recesses of the Californian Gulf, or *Sea of Cortés*, as, in honour of the great discoverer, it is with more propriety named by the Spaniards ; and he had ascertained that, instead of the outlet before supposed to exist towards the north, this unknown ocean was locked up within the arms of the mighty continent. These were results that might have made the glory and satisfied the ambition of a common man ; but they are lost in the brilliant renown of the former achievements of Cortés.

Notwithstanding the embarrassments of the Marquis of the Valley, he still made new efforts to enlarge the limits of discovery, and prepared to fit out another squadron of five vessels, which he proposed to place under the command of a natural son, Don Luis. But the viceroy Mendoza, whose imagination had been inflamed by the reports of an itinerant monk respecting an *El Dorado* in the north, claimed the right of discovery in that direction. Cortés protested against this, as an unwarrantable inter-ference with his own powers. Other subjects of collision arose between them ; till the marquis, disgusted with this perpetual check on his authority and his enterprises, applied for redress to Castile.[2] He finally determined to go there to support his claims in person, and to obtain, if possible, remuneration for the heavy charges he had incurred by his maritime expeditions, as well as for the spoliation of his property by the Royal Audience during his absence from the country ; and, lastly, to procure an assignment of his vassals on principles more conformable to the original intentions of the grant. With these objects in view, he bade adieu to his family, and taking with him his eldest son and heir, Don Martin, then only eight years of age, he embarked at Mexico in 1540, and, after a favourable voyage, again set foot on the shores of his native land.

The emperor was absent from the country. But Cortés was honourably received in the capital, where ample accommodations were provided for him and his retinue. When he attended the Royal Council of the Indies to urge his suit, he was distinguished by uncommon marks of respect. The president went to the door of the hall to receive him, and a seat was pro-vided for him among the members of the Council.[3] But all evaporated in this barren show of courtesy. Justice, proverbially slow in Spain, did

---

[1] See the map prepared by the pilot Domingo del Castillo, in 1541, ap. Lorenzana, p. 328.

[2] In the collection of Vargas Ponçe is a petition of Cortés, setting forth his grievances, and demand-ing an investigation of the viceroy's conduct. It is without date. Peticion contra Don Antonio de Mendoza Virrey, pediendo residencia contra él, MS.

[3] Bernal Diaz, Hist. de la Conquista, cap. 200.

not mend her gait for Cortés; and at the expiration of a year he found himself no nearer the attainment of his object than on the first week after his arrival in the capital.

In the following year, 1541, we find the marquis of the Valley embarked as a volunteer in the memorable expedition against Algiers. Charles the Fifth, on his return to his dominions, laid siege to that stronghold of the Mediterranean corsairs. Cortés accompanied the forces destined to meet the emperor, and embarked on board the vessel of the Admiral of Castile. But a furious tempest scattered the navy, and the admiral's ship was driven a wreck upon the coast. Cortés and his son escaped by swimming, but the former, in the confusion of the scene, lost the inestimable set of jewels noticed in the preceding chapter; "a loss," says an old writer, "that made the expedition fall more heavily on the marquis of the Valley than on any other man in the kingdom, except the emperor." [2]

It is not necessary to recount the particulars of this disastrous siege, in which Moslem valour, aided by the elements, set at defiance the combined forces of the Christians. A council of war was called, and it was decided to abandon the enterprise and return to Castile. This determination was indignantly received by Cortés, who offered, with the support of the army, to reduce the place himself; and he only expressed the regret that he had not a handful of those gallant veterans by his side who had served him in the Conquest of Mexico. But his offers were derided, as those of a romantic enthusiast. He had not been invited to take part in the discussions of the council of war. It was a marked indignity; but the courtiers, weary of the service, were too much bent on an immediate return to Spain, to hazard the opposition of a man who, when he had once planted his foot, was never known to raise it again till he had accomplished his object. [2]

On arriving in Castile, Cortés lost no time in laying his suit before the emperor. His applications were received by the monarch with civility,— a cold civility, which carried no conviction of its sincerity. His position was materially changed since his former visit to the country. More than ten years had elapsed, and he was now too well advanced in years to give promise of serviceable enterprise in future. Indeed, his undertakings of late had been singularly unfortunate. Even his former successes suffered the disparagement natural to a man of declining fortunes. They were already eclipsed by the magnificent achievements in Peru, which had poured a golden tide into the country, that formed a striking contrast to the streams of wealth that as yet had flowed in but scantily from the silver-mines of Mexico. Cortés had to learn that the gratitude of a court has reference to the future much more than to the past. He stood in the position of an importunate suitor whose claims, however just, are too large

[1] Gomara, Crónica, cap. 237.
[2] Sandoval, Hist. de Cárlos V., lib. 12, cap. 25.—   Ferreras (trad. d'Hermilly), Hist. d'Espagne, tom. ix. p. 231.

to be readily allowed. He found, like Columbus, that it was possible to deserve too greatly.[1]

In the month of February, 1544, he addressed a letter to the emperor,—it was the last he ever wrote him,—soliciting his attention to his suit. He begins by proudly alluding to his past services to the crown. " He had hoped that the toils of youth would have secured him repose in his old age. For forty years he had passed his life with little sleep, bad food, and with his arms constantly by his side. He had freely exposed his person to peril, and spent his substance in exploring distant and unknown regions, that he might spread abroad the name of his sovereign and bring under his sceptre many great and powerful nations. All this he had done, not only without assistance from home, but in the face of obstacles thrown in his way by rivals and by enemies who thirsted like leeches for his blood. He was now old, infirm, and embarrassed with debt. Better had it been for him not to have known the liberal intentions of the emperor, as intimated by his grants; since he should then have devoted himself to the care of his estates, and not have been compelled, as he now was, to contend with the officers of the crown, against whom it was more difficult to defend himself than to win the land from the enemy." He concludes with beseeching his sovereign to " order the Council of the Indies, with the other tribunals which had cognizance of his suits, to come to a decision; since he was too old to wander about like a vagrant, but ought rather, during the brief remainder of his life, to stay at home and settle his account with Heaven, occupied with the concerns of his soul, rather than with his substance." [2]

This appeal to his sovereign, which has something in it touching from a man of the haughty spirit of Cortés, had not the effect to quicken the determination of his suit. He still lingered at the court from week to week, and from month to month, beguiled by the deceitful hopes of the litigant, tasting all that bitterness of the soul which arises from hope deferred. After three years more, passed in this unprofitable and humiliating occupation, he resolved to leave his ungrateful country and return to Mexico.

He had proceeded as far as Seville, accompanied by his son, when he fell ill of an indigestion, caused, probably, by irritation and trouble of mind. This terminated in dysentery, and his strength sank so rapidly under the disease that it was apparent his mortal career was drawing towards its close. He prepared for it by making the necessary arrangements for the settlement of his affairs. He had made his will some time before; and he now executed it. It is a very long document, and in some respects a remarkable one.

---

[1] Voltaire tells us that, one day, Cortés, unable to obtain an audience of the emperor, pushed through the press surrounding the royal carriage, and mounted the steps; and when Charles inquired "who that man was," he replied, " One who has given you more kingdoms than you had towns before." (Essai sur les Mœurs, chap. 147.) For this most improbable anecdote I have found no authority whatever. It served, however, very well to point a moral,—the main thing with the philosopher of Ferney.

[2] The Letter, dated February 3, 1544, Valladolid, may be found entire, in the original, in Appendix, Part 2, No. 15.

The bulk of his property was entailed to his son, Don Martin, then fifteen years of age. In the testament he fixes his majority at twenty-five; but at twenty his guardians were to allow him his full income, to maintain the state becoming his rank. In a paper accompanying the will, Cortés specified the names of the agents to whom he had committed the management of his vast estates scattered over many different provinces; and he requests his executors to confirm the nomination, as these agents have been selected by him from a knowledge of their peculiar qualifications. Nothing can better show the thorough supervision which, in the midst of pressing public concerns, he had given to the details of his widely-extended property.

He makes a liberal provision for his other children, and a generous allowance to several old domestics and retainers in his household. By another clause he gives away considerable sums in charity, and he applies the revenues of his estates in the city of Mexico to establish and permanently endow three public institutions,—a hospital in the capital, which was to be dedicated to Our Lady of the Conception, a college in Cojohuacan for the education of missionaries to preach the gospel among the natives, and a convent, in the same place, for nuns. To the chapel of this convent situated in his favourite town, he orders that his own body shall be transported for burial, in whatever quarter of the world he may happen to die.

After declaring that he has taken all possible care to ascertain the amount of the tributes formerly paid by his Indian vassals to their native sovereigns, he enjoins on his heir that, in case those which they have hitherto paid shall be found to exceed the right valuation, he shall restore them a full equivalent. In another clause he expresses a doubt whether it is right to exact personal service from the natives, and commands that a strict inquiry shall be made into the nature and value of such services as he had received, and that in all cases a fair compensation shall be allowed for them. Lastly, he makes this remarkable declaration : " It has long been a question whether one can conscientiously hold property in Indian slaves. Since this point has not yet been determined, I enjoin it on my son Martin and his heirs that they spare no pains to come to an exact knowledge of the truth ; as a matter which deeply concerns the conscience of each of them, no less than mine." [1]

Such scruples of conscience, not to have been expected in Cortés, were still less likely to be met with in the Spaniards of a later generation. The state of opinion in respect to the great question of slavery, in the sixteenth century, at the commencement of the system, bears some resemblance to

---

[1] " Item. Porque acerca de los esclavos naturales de la dicha Nueva España, así de guerra como de rescate, ha habido y hay muchas dudas y opiniones sobre si se han podido tener con buena conciencia ó no, y hasta ahora no está determinado : Mando que todo aquello que generalmente se averiguare, que en este caso se debe hacer para descargo de las conciencias en lo que toca á estos esclavos de la dicha Nueva España, que se haya y cumpla en todos los que yo tengo, é encargo y mando á D. Martin mi hijo subcesor, y á los que despues del subcedieren en mi Estado, que para averiguar esto hagan todas las diligencias que combengan al descargo de mi conciencia y suyas." Testamento de Hernan Cortés, MS.

that which exists in our time, when we may hope it is approaching its conclusion. Las Casas and the Dominicans of the former age, the abolitionists of their day, thundered out their uncompromising invectives against the system on the broad ground of natural equity and the rights of man. The great mass of proprietors troubled their heads little about the question of right, but were satisfied with the expediency of the institution. Others, more considerate and conscientious, while they admitted the evil, found an argument for its toleration in the plea of necessity, regarding the constitution of the white man as unequal, in a sultry climate, to the labour of cultivating the soil.[1] In one important respect the condition of slavery in the sixteenth century differed materially from its condition in the nineteenth. In the former, the seeds of the evil, but lately sown, might have been, with comparatively little difficulty, eradicated. But in our time they have struck their roots deep into the social system, and cannot be rudely handled without shaking the very foundations of the political fabric. It is easy to conceive that a man who admits all the wretchedness of the institution and its wrong to humanity may nevertheless hesitate to adopt a remedy until he is satisfied that the remedy itself is not worse than the disease. That such a remedy will come with time, who can doubt, that has confidence in the ultimate prevalence of the right and the progressive civilization of his species?

Cortés names as his executors, and as guardians of his children, the duke of Medina Sidonia, the marquis of Astorga, and the count of Aguilar. For his executors in Mexico, he appoints his wife, the marchioness, the archbishop of Toledo, and two other prelates. The will was executed at Seville, October 11th, 1547.[2]

Finding himself much incommoded, as he grew weaker, by the presence of visitors to which he was necessarily exposed at Seville, he withdrew to the neighbouring village of Castilleja de la Cuesta, attended by his son, who watched over his dying parent with filial solicitude.[3] Cortés seems to have contemplated his approaching end with a composure not always to be found in those who have faced death with indifference on the field of battle. At length, having devoutly confessed his sins and received the sacrament, he expired on the 2d of December, 1547, in the sixty-third year of his age.[4]

The inhabitants of the neighbouring country were desirous to show

---

[1] This is the argument controverted by Las Casas in his elaborate Memorial, addressed to the government in 1542, on the best method of arresting the destruction of the aborigines.

[2] This interesting document is in the Royal Archives of Seville; and a copy of it forms part of the valuable collection of Don Vargas Ponçe.

[3] [My friend Mr. Picard has furnished me with the copy of an inscription which may be seen, or could a few years since, on the house in which Cortés expired. "Here died, on the second of September, 1544, victim of sorrow and misfortune, the renowned Hernan Cortés, the glory of our country and the conqueror of the Mexican empire." It is strange that the author of the inscription should have made a blunder of more than three years in the date of the hero's death.]

[4] Zuñiga, Annales de Sevilla, p. 504.—Gomara, Crónica, cap. 237.—In his last letter to the emperor, dated in February, 1544, he speaks of himself as being "sixty years of age." But he probably did not mean to be exact to a year. Gomara's statement that he was born in the year 1485 (Crónica, cap. 1), is confirmed by Diaz, who tells us that Cortés used to say that when he first came over to Mexico, in 1519, he was thirty-four years old. (Hist. de la Conquista, cap. 205.) This would coincide with the age mentioned in the text.

every mark of respect to the memory of Cortés. His funeral obsequies were celebrated with due solemnity by a long train of Andalusian nobles and of the citizens of Seville, and his body was transported to the chapel of the monastery of San Isidro, in that city, where it was laid in the family vault of the duke Medina Sidonia.[1] In the year 1562, it was removed, by order of his son, Don Martin, to New Spain, not, as directed by his will, to Cojohuacan,[2] but to the monastery of St. Francis, in Tezcuco, where it was laid by the side of a daughter, and of his mother, Doña Catalina Pizarro. In 1629 the remains of Cortés were again removed; and on the death of Don Pedro, fourth marquis of the Valley, it was decided by the authorities of Mexico to transfer them to the church of St. Francis, in that capital. The ceremonial was conducted with the pomp suited to the occasion. A military and religious procession was formed, with the archbishop of Mexico at its head. He was accompanied by the great dignitaries of church and state, the various associations with their respective banners, the several religious fraternities, and the members of the Audience. The coffin, containing the relics of Cortés, was covered with black velvet, and supported by the judges of the royal tribunals. On either side of it was a man in complete armour, bearing, on the right, a standard of pure white, with the arms of Castile embroidered in gold, and, on the left, a banner of black velvet, emblazoned in like manner with the armorial ensigns of the house of Cortés. Behind the corpse came the viceroy and a numerous escort of Spanish cavaliers, and the rear was closed by a battalion of infantry, armed with pikes and arquebuses, and with their banners trailing on the ground. With this funeral pomp, by the sound of mournful music, and the slow beat of the muffled drum, the procession moved forward, with measured pace, till it reached the capital, when the gates were thrown open to receive the mortal remains of the hero who, a century before, had performed there such prodigies of valour.

Yet his bones were not permitted to rest here undisturbed; and in 1794 they were removed to the Hospital of Jesus of Nazareth. It was a more fitting place, since it was the same institution which, under the name of " Our Lady of the Conception," had been founded and endowed by Cortés, and which, with a fate not too frequent in similar charities, has been administered to this day on the noble principles of its foundation. The mouldering relics of the warrior, now deposited in a crystal coffin secured by bars and plates of silver, were laid in the chapel, and over them was raised a simple monument, displaying the arms of the family, and surmounted by a bust of the Conqueror, executed in bronze by Tolsa, a sculptor worthy of the best period of the arts.[3]

---

[1] Noticia del Archivero de la Santa Eclesia de Sevilla, MS.

[2] [This may be accounted for by the fact that his intention to found a convent at Cuyoacan, as the place is now called, had, according to Alaman, never been carried out.—Ed.]

[3] The full particulars of the ceremony described in the text may be found in Appendix, Part 2, No. 16, translated into English from a copy of the original document, existing in the Archives of the Hospital of Jesus, in Mexico.

Unfortunately for Mexico, the tale does not stop here. In 1823, the patriot mob of the capital, in their zeal to commemorate the era of the national independence, and their detestation of the "old Spaniards," prepared to break open the tomb which held the ashes of Cortés, and to scatter them to the winds! The authorities declined to interfere on the occasion; but the friends of the family, as is commonly reported, entered the vault by night, and, secretly removing the relics, prevented the commission of a sacrilege which must have left a stain, not easy to be effaced, on the scutcheon of the fair city of Mexico.[1] Humboldt, forty years ago, remarked that "we may traverse Spanish America from Buenos Ayres to Monterey, and in no quarter shall we meet with a national monument which the public gratitude has raised to Christopher Columbus or Hernando Cortés."[2] It was reserved for our own age to conceive the design of violating the repose of the dead and insulting their remains! Yet the men who meditated this outrage were not the descendants of Montezuma, avenging the wrongs of their fathers and vindicating their own rightful inheritance. They were the descendants of the old Conquerors, and their countrymen, depending on the right of conquest for their ultimate title to the soil.[3]

Cortés had no children by his first marriage. By his second he left four; a son, Don Martin,—the heir of his honours, and of persecutions even more severe than those of his father,[4]—and three daughters, who formed splendid alliances. He left, also, five natural children, whom he particularly mentions in his testament and honourably provides for. Two of these, Don Martin, the son of Marina, and Don Luis Cortés, attained considerable distinction, and were created *comendadores* of the Order of St. Jago.[5]

The male line of the marquises of the Valley became extinct in the third generation. The title and estates descended to a female, and by her marriage were united with those of the house of Terranova, descendants of the "Great Captain," Gonsalvo de Cordova.[6] By a subsequent mar-

---

[1] [The bust of Cortés and the arms of gilt bronze were secretly removed from his monument, and sent to his descendant, the duke of Monteleone, at Palermo. The remains of the Conqueror were soon after sent in the same direction, according to Doctor Mora, cited by Alaman, who does not contradict it: "Aun se habrian profanado las cenizas del héroe, sin la precaucion de personas despreocupadas, que deseando evitar el deshonor de su patria por tan reprensible é irreflexivo procedimiento, lograron ocultarlas de pronto y despues las remitieron á Italia á su familia." Disertaciones históricas, tom. ii. p. 61.]

[2] Essai politique, tom. ii. p. 60.

[3] [They entertained, says Alaman, the rather extravagant idea that, as descendants of the conquering nation, they were the heirs of the rights of the conquered, and bound to avenge their wrongs. Conquista de Méjico (trad. de Vega), tom. ii. p. 309.]

[4] Don Martin Cortés, second marquis of the Valley, was accused, like his father, of an attempt to establish an independent sovereignty in New Spain. His natural brothers, Don Martin and Don

Luis, were involved in the same accusation with himself, and the former—as I have elsewhere remarked—was in consequence subjected to the torture. Several others of his friends, on charge of abetting his treasonable designs, suffered death. The marquis was obliged to remove with his family to Spain, where the investigation was conducted; and his large estates in Mexico were sequestered until the termination of the process, a period of seven years, from 1567 to 1574, when he was declared innocent. But his property suffered irreparable injury, under the wretched administration of the royal officers, during the term of sequestration.

[5] [The illegitimate children were Don Martin Cortés, Don Luis Cortés, Doña Catalina Pizarro (daughter of Doña Leonor Pizarro), also two other daughters, Leonor and María, born of two Indian women of noble birth. Alaman, Disertaciones históricas, tom. ii. p. 48.]

[6] [Señor Alaman, in reference to this passage, says, "It is a mistake to suppose that the heirs of Cortés and Gonsalvo de Cordova were ever united by marriage. The fact appears to be that the title of duke of Terranova was held by the descendants

---

riage they were carried into the family of the duke of Monteleone, a Neapolitan noble. The present proprietor of these princely honours and of vast domains, both in the Old and the New World, dwells in Sicily, and boasts a descent—such as few princes can boast—from two of the most illustrious commanders of the sixteenth century, the "Great Captain," and the Conqueror of Mexico.

The personal history of Cortés has been so minutely detailed in the preceding narrative that it will be only necessary to touch on the more prominent features of his character. Indeed, the history of the Conquest, as I have already had occasion to remark, is necessarily that of Cortés, who is, if I may so say, not merely the soul, but the body, of the enterprise, present everywhere in person, in the thick of the fight or in the building of the works, with his sword or with his musket, sometimes leading his soldiers, and sometimes directing his little navy. The negotiations, intrigues, correspondence, are all conducted by him ; and, like Cæsar, he wrote his own Commentaries in the heat of the stirring scenes which form the subject of them. His character is marked with the most opposite traits, embracing qualities apparently the most incompatible. He was avaricious, yet liberal ; bold to desperation, yet cautious and calculating in his plans ; magnanimous, yet very cunning ; courteous and affable in his deportment, yet inexorably stern ; lax in his notions of morality, yet (not uncommon) a sad bigot. The great feature in his character was constancy of purpose ; a constancy not to be daunted by danger, nor baffled by disappointment, nor wearied out by impediments and delays.

He was a knight-errant, in the literal sense of the word. Of all the band of adventurous cavaliers whom Spain, in the sixteenth century, sent forth on the career of discovery and conquest, there was none more deeply filled with the spirit of romantic enterprise than Hernando Cortés. Dangers and difficulties, instead of deterring, seemed to have a charm in his eyes. They were necessary to rouse him to a full consciousness of his powers. He grappled with them at the outset, and, if I may so express myself, seemed to prefer to take his enterprises by the most difficult side. He conceived, at the first moment of his landing in Mexico, the design of its conquest. When he saw the strength of its civilization, he was not turned from his purpose. When he was assailed by the superior force of Narvaez, he still persisted in it ; and when he was driven in ruin from the capital, he still cherished his original idea. How successfully he carried it into execution, we have seen. After the few years of repose which succeeded the Conquest, his adventurous spirit impelled him to that dreary march across the marshes of Chiapa, and, after another interval, to seek his fortunes on the stormy Californian Gulf. When he found that no other

---

of both ; but the Terranova assigned to the Great Captain was in Calabria, while the place from which the descendants of Cortés took the title was in Sicily. Conquista de Méjico (trad. de Vega), tom. ii. p. 308.]

continent remained for him to conquer, he made serious proposals to the emperor to equip a fleet at his own expense, with which he would sail to the Moluccas and subdue the Spice Islands for the crown of Castile ! [1]

This spirit of knight-errantry might lead us to undervalue his talents as a general and to regard him merely in the light of a lucky adventurer. But this would be doing him injustice ; for Cortés was certainly a great general if that man be one who performs great achievements with the resources which his own genius has created. There is probably no instance in history where so vast an enterprise has been achieved by means apparently so inadequate. He may be truly said to have effected the Conquest by his own resources. If he was indebted for his success to the co-operation of the Indian tribes, it was the force of his genius that obtained command of such materials. He arrested the arm that was lifted to smite him, and made it do battle in his behalf. He beat the Tlascalans, and made them his stanch allies. He beat the soldiers of Narvaez, and doubled his effective force by it. When his own men deserted him, he did not desert himself. He drew them back by degrees, and compelled them to act by his will, till they were all as one man. He brought together the most miscellaneous collection of mercenaries who ever fought under one standard : adventurers from Cuba and the Isles, craving for gold ; hidalgos, who came from the old country to win laurels ; broken-down cavaliers, who hoped to mend their fortunes in the New World ; vagabonds flying from justice ; the grasping followers of Narvaez, and his own reckless veterans,—men with hardly a common tie, and burning with the spirit of jealousy and faction ; wild tribes of the natives from all parts of the country, who had been sworn enemies from their cradles, and who had met only to cut one another's throats and to procure victims for sacrifice ; men, in short, differing in race, in language, and in interests, with scarcely anything in common among them. Yet this motley congregation was assembled in one camp, compelled to bend to the will of one man, to consort together in harmony, to breathe, as it were, one spirit, and to move on a common principle of action ! It is in this wonderful power over the discordant masses thus gathered under his banner that we recognize the genius of the great commander, no less than in the skill of his military operations.

His power over the minds of his soldiers was a natural result of their confidence in his abilities. But it is also to be attributed to his popular manners,—that happy union of authority and companionship which fitted him for the command of a band of roving adventurers. It would not have done for him to fence himself round with the stately reserve of a

---

[1] "Yo me ofresco á descubrir por aquí toda la espeçería, y otras Islas si huviere cerca de Moluco, ó Melaca, y la China, y aun de dar tal órden que V. M. no aiga la espeçeria por via de rescate, como la ha el Rey de Portugal, sino que la tenga por cosa propria, y los naturales de aquellas Islas le reconos- can y sirvan como á su Rey y señor natural, porque yo me ofresco con el dicho additamento de embiar á ellas tal armada, *ó ir yo con mi persona por manera que la sojusge y pueble.*" Carta Quinta de Cortés, MS.

commander of regular forces. He was embarked with his men in a common adventure, and nearly on terms of equality, since he held his commission by no legal warrant. But, while he indulged this freedom and familiarity with his soldiers, he never allowed it to interfere with their strict obedience nor to impair the severity of discipline. When he had risen to higher consideration, although he affected more state, he still admitted his veterans to the same intimacy. "He preferred," says Diaz, "to be called 'Cortés' by us, to being called by any title; and with good reason," continues the enthusiastic old cavalier, "for the name of Cortés is as famous in our day as was that of Cæsar among the Romans, or of Hannibal among the Carthaginians." [1] He showed the same kind regard towards his ancient comrades in the very last act of his life. For he appropriated a sum by his will for the celebration of two thousand masses for the souls of those who had fought with him in the campaigns of Mexico. [2]

His character has been unconsciously traced by the hand of a master:

> "And oft *the chieftain* deigned to aid
> And mingle in the mirth they made ;
> For, though with men of high degree
> The proudest of the proud was he,
> Yet, trained in camps, he knew the art
> To win the soldiers' hardy heart.
> They love a captain to obey,
> Boisterious as March, yet fresh as May ;
> With open hand, and brow as free,
> Lover of wine and minstrelsy ;
> Ever the first to scale a tower,
> As venturous in a lady's bower;—
> Such buxom chief shall lead his host
> From India's fires to Zembla's frost."

Cortés, without much violence, might have sat for this portrait of Marmion.

Cortés was not a vulgar conqueror. He did not conquer from the mere ambition of conquest. If he destroyed the ancient capital of the Aztecs, it was to build up a more magnificent capital on its ruins. If he desolated the land and broke up its existing institutions, he employed the short period of his administration in digesting schemes for introducing there a more improved culture and a higher civilization. In all his

---

[1] The comparison to Hannibal is better founded than the old soldier probably imagined. Livy's description of the Carthaginian warrior has a marvellous application to Cortés,—better, perhaps, than that of the imaginary personage quoted a few lines below in the text. "Plurimum audaciæ ad pericula capessenda, plurimum consilii inter ipsa pericula erat : nullo labore aut corpus fatigari, aut animus vinci poterat. Caloris ac frigoris patientia par : cibi potionisque desiderio naturali, non voluptate, modus finitus : vigiliarum somnique nec die, nec nocte discriminata tempora. Id, quod gerendis rebus superesset, quieti datum ; ea neque molli strato, neque silentio arcessita. Multi sæpe militari sagulo opertum, humi jacentem, inter custodias stationesque militum, conspexerunt. Vestitus nihil inter æquales excellens ; arma atque equi conspiciebantur. Equitum peditumque idem longe primus erat ; princeps in prœlium ibat ; ultimus conserto prœlio excedebat." (Hist., lib. xxi. sec. 5.) The reader who reflects on the fate of Guatemozin may possibly think that the extract should have embraced the "perfidia plus quám Punica," in the succeeding sentence.

[2] Testamento de Hernan Cortés, MS.

expeditions he was careful to study the resources of the country, its social organization, and its physical capacities. He enjoined it on his captains to attend particularly to these objects. If he was greedy of gold, like most of the Spanish cavaliers in the New World, it was not to hoard it, nor merely to lavish it in the support of a princely establishment, but to secure funds for prosecuting his glorious discoveries. Witness his costly expeditions to the Gulf of California. His enterprises were not undertaken solely for mercenary objects; as is shown by the various expeditions he set on foot for the discovery of a communication between the Atlantic and the Pacific. In his schemes of ambition he showed a respect for the interests of science, to be referred partly to the natural superiority of his mind, but partly, no doubt, to the influence of early education. It is, indeed, hardly possible that a person of his wayward and mercurial temper should have improved his advantages at the University; but he brought away from it a tincture of scholarship seldom found among the cavaliers of the period, and which had its influence in enlarging his own conceptions. His celebrated Letters are written with a simple elegance that, as I have already had occasion to remark, have caused them to be compared to the military narrative of Cæsar. It will not be easy to find in the chronicles of the period a more concise yet comprehensive statement, not only of the events of his campaigns, but of the circumstances most worthy of notice in the character of the conquered countries.

Cortés was not cruel; at least, not cruel as compared with most of those who followed his iron trade. The path of the conqueror is necessarily marked with blood. He was not too scrupulous, indeed, in the execution of his plans. He swept away the obstacles which lay in his track; and his fame is darkened by the commission of more than one act which his boldest apologists will find it hard to vindicate. But he was not wantonly cruel. He allowed no outrage on his unresisting foes. This may seem small praise; but it is an exception to the usual conduct of his countrymen in their conquests, and it is something to be in advance of one's time. He was severe, it may be added, in enforcing obedience to his orders for protecting their persons and their property. With his licentious crew, it was, sometimes, not without a hazard that he was so. After the Conquest, he sanctioned the system of *repartimientos;* but so did Columbus. He endeavoured to regulate it by the most humane laws, and continued to suggest many important changes for ameliorating the condition of the natives. The best commentary on his conduct in this respect is the deference that was shown him by the Indians, and the confidence with which they appealed to him for protection in all their subsequent distresses.

In private life he seems to have had the power of attaching to himself warmly those who were near his person. The influence of this attachment is shown in every page of Bernal Diaz, though his work was written to vindicate the claims of the soldiers in opposition to those of the general. He seems to have led a happy life with his first wife, in their humble retirement in Cuba, and regarded the second, to judge from the expressions in his testament, with confidence and love. Yet he cannot be acquitted from the charge of those licentious gallantries which entered too generally into the character of the military adventurer of that day. He would seem also, by the frequent suits in which he was involved, to have been of an irritable and contentious spirit. But much allowance must be made for the irritability of a man who had been too long accustomed to independent sway, patiently to endure the checks and control of the petty spirits who were incapable of comprehending the noble character of his enterprises. " He thought," says an eminent writer, "to silence his enemies by the brilliancy of the new career on which he had entered. He did not reflect that these enemies had been raised by the very grandeur and rapidity of his success."[1] He was rewarded for his efforts by the misinterpretation of his motives ; by the calumnious charges of squandering the public revenues and of aspiring to independent sovereignty. But, although we may admit the foundation of many of the grievances alleged by Cortés, yet, when we consider the querulous tone of his correspondence and the frequency of his litigation, we may feel a natural suspicion that his proud spirit was too sensitive to petty slights and too jealous of imaginary wrongs.

One trait more remains to be noticed in the character of this remarkable man ; that is, his bigotry, the failing of the age,—for surely it should be termed only a failing.[2] When we see the hand, red with the blood of the wretched native, raised to invoke the blessing of Heaven on the cause which it maintains, we experience something like a sensation of disgust at the act, and a doubt of its sincerity. But this is unjust. We should throw ourselves back (it cannot be too often repeated) into the age,—the age of the Crusades. For every Spanish cavalier, however sordid and selfish might be his private motives, felt himself to be the soldier of the Cross. Many of them would have died in defence of it. Whoever has read the correspondence of Cortés, or, still more, has attended to the circumstances of his career, will hardly doubt that he would have been among the first to lay down his life for the Faith. He more than once perilled life, and fortune, and the success of his whole enterprise, by the premature and most impolitic manner in which he would have forced conversion on the natives.[3] To the more rational spirit of the present day, enlightened by a purer Christianity, it may seem difficult to reconcile gross deviations from morals with such devotion to

---

[1] Humboldt, Essai politique, tom. ii. p. 267.

[2] An extraordinary anecdote is related by Cavo of this bigotry (shall we call it policy?) of Cortés. "In Mexico," says the historian, "it is commonly reported that after the Conquest he commanded that on Sundays and holidays all should attend, under pain of a certain number of stripes, to the expounding of the Scriptures. The general was himself guilty of an omission on one occasion, and, after having listened to the admonition of the priest, submitted, with edifying humility, to be chastised by him, to the unspeakable amazement of the Indians." Hist. de los tres Siglos, tom. i. p. 151.

[3] " Al Rey infinitas tierras,
 Y á Dios infinitas almas,"

says Lope de Vega, commemorating in this couplet the double glory of Cortés. It is the light in which the Conquest was viewed by every devout Spaniard of the sixteenth century.

the cause of religion. But the religion taught in that day was one of form and elaborate ceremony. In the punctilious attention to discipline, the spirit of Christianity was permitted to evaporate. The mind, occupied with forms, thinks little of substance. In a worship that is addressed too exclusively to the senses, it is often the case that morality becomes divorced from religion, and the measure of righteousness is determined by the creed rather than by the conduct.

In the earlier part of the History I have given a description of the person of Cortés.[1] It may be well to close this review of his character by the account of his manners and personal habits left us by Bernal Diaz, the old chronicler, who has accompanied us through the whole course of our narrative, and who may now fitly furnish the conclusion of it. No man knew his commander better; and, if the avowed object of his work might naturally lead to a disparagement of Cortés, this is more than counterbalanced by the warmth of his personal attachment, and by that *esprit de corps* which leads him to take a pride in the renown of his general.

" In his whole appearance and presence," says Diaz, " in his discourse, his table, his dress, in everything, in short, he had the air of a great lord. His clothes were in the fashion of the time; he set little value on silk, damask, or velvet, but dressed plainly and exceedingly neat;[2] nor did he wear massy chains of gold, but simply a fine one, of exquisite workmanship, from which was suspended a jewel having the figure of our Lady the Virgin and her precious Son, with a Latin motto cut upon it. On his finger he wore a splendid diamond ring; and from his cap, which, according to the fashion of that day, was of velvet, hung a medal the device of which I do not remember. He was magnificently attended, as became a man of his rank, with chamberlains and major-domos and many pages; and the service of his table was splendid, with a quantity of both gold and silver plate. At noon he dined heartily, drinking about a pint of wine mixed with water. He supped well, though he was not dainty in regard to his food, caring little for the delicacies of the table, unless, indeed, on such occasions as made attention to these matters of some consequence.[3]

" He was acquainted with Latin, and, as I have understood, was made Bachelor of Laws; and when he conversed with learned men who addressed him in Latin, he answered them in the same language. He was also something of a poet; his conversation was agreeable, and he had a pleasant elocution. In his attendance on the services of the Church he was most punctual, devout in his manner, and charitable to the poor.[4]

" When he swore, he used to say, ' On my conscience; ' and when he

---

[1] *Ante*, p. 122.
[2] So Gomara : "He dressed neatly rather than richly, and was always scrupulously clean." Crónica, cap. 236.
[3] " Fué mui gran comedor, i templado en el beber,

teniendo abundancia. Sufria mucho la hambre con necesidad." Ibid., ubi supra.
[4] He dispensed a thousand ducats every year in his ordinary charities, according to Gomara. "Grandísimo limosnero; daba cada un año mil ducados de limosna ordinaria." Crónica, cap. 238.

was vexed with any one, 'Evil betide you.' With his men he was very patient ; and they were sometimes impertinent and even insolent. When very angry, the veins in his throat and forehead would swell, but he uttered no reproaches against either officer or soldier.

" He was fond of cards and dice, and, when he played, was always in good humour, indulging freely in jests and repartees. He was affable with his followers, especially with those who came over with him from Cuba. In his campaigns he paid strict attention to discipline, frequently going the rounds himself during the night, and seeing that the sentinels did their duty. He entered the quarters of his soldiers without ceremony, and chided those whom he found without their arms and accoutrements, saying, ' It was a bad sheep that could not carry its own wool.' On the expedition to Honduras he acquired the habit of sleeping after his meals, feeling unwell if he omitted it ; and, however sultry or stormy the weather. he caused a carpet or his cloak to be thrown under a tree, and slept soundly for some time. He was frank and exceedingly liberal in his disposition, until the last few years of his life, when he was accused of parsimony. But we should consider that his funds were employed on great and costly enterprises, and that none of these, after the Conquest, neither his expedition to Honduras nor his voyages to California, were crowned with success. It was perhaps intended that he should receive his recompense in a better world ; and I fully believe it ; for he was a good cavalier, most true in his devotions to the Virgin, to the Apostle St. Peter, and to all the other Saints." [1]

Such is the portrait, which has been left to us by the faithful hand most competent to trace it, of Hernando Cortés, the Conqueror of Mexico.

---

[1] Hist. de la Conquista, cap. 203.

APPENDIX.

——o——

PART I.

ORIGIN OF THE MEXICAN CIVILIZATION.

PRELIMINARY NOTICE.

—o—

THE following Essay was originally designed to close the Introductory Book, to which it properly belongs. It was written three years since, at the same time with that part of the work. I know of no work of importance, having reference to the general subject of discussion, which has appeared since that period, except Mr. Bradford's valuable treatise on *American Antiquities*. But in respect to that part of the discussion which treats of American Architecture a most important contribution has been made by Mr. Stephens's two works, containing the account of his visits to Central America and Yucatan, and especially by the last of these publications. Indeed, the ground, before so imperfectly known, has now been so diligently explored that we have all the light, which we can reasonably expect, to aid us in making up our opinion in regard to the mysterious monuments of Yucatan. It only remains that the exquisite illustrations of Mr. Catherwood should be published on a larger scale, like the great works on the subject in France and England, in order to exhibit to the eye a more adequate representation of these magnificent ruins than can be given in the limited compass of an octavo page.

But, notwithstanding the importance of Mr. Stephens's researches, I have not availed myself of them to make any additions to the original draft of this Essay, nor have I rested my conclusions in any instance on his authority. These conclusions had been formed from a careful study of the narratives of Dupaix and Waldeck, together with that of their splendid illustrations of the remains of Palenque and Uxmal, two of the principal places explored by Mr. Stephens; and the additional facts collected by him from the vast field which he has surveyed, so far from shaking my previous deductions, have only served to confirm them. The only object of my own speculations on these remains was to ascertain their probable origin, or rather to see what light, if any, they could throw on the origin of Aztec Civilization. The reader, on comparing my reflections with those of Mr. Stephens in the closing chapters of his two works, will see that I have arrived at inferences, as to the origin and probable antiquity of these structures, precisely the same as his. Conclusions formed under such different circumstances serve to corroborate each other; and, although the reader will find here some things which would have been different had I been guided by the light now thrown on the path, yet I prefer not to disturb the foundations on which the argument stands, nor to impair its value—if it has any—as a distinct and independent testimony.

APPENDIX.

PART I.

—*o*—

ORIGIN OF THE MEXICAN CIVILIZATION.—ANALOGIES WITH THE OLD WORLD.

WHEN the Europeans first touched the shores of America, it was as if they had alighted on another planet,—everything there was so different from what they had before seen. They were introduced to new varieties of plants, and to unknown races of animals; while man, the lord of all, was equally strange, in complexion, language, and institutions.[1] It was what they emphatically styled it,—a New World. Taught by their faith to derive all created beings from one source, they felt a natural perplexity as to the manner in which these distant and insulated regions could have obtained their inhabitants. The same curiosity was felt by their countrymen at home, and the European scholars bewildered their brains with speculations on the best way of solving this interesting problem.

In accounting for the presence of animals there, some imagined that the two hemispheres might once have been joined in the extreme north, so as to have afforded an easy communication.[2] Others, embarrassed by the difficulty of transporting inhabitants of the tropics across the Arctic regions, revived the old story of Plato's Atlantis, that huge island, now submerged, which might have stretched from the shores of Africa to the eastern borders of the new continent;[3] while they saw vestiges of a similar con-

---

[1] The names of many animals in the New World, indeed, have been frequently borrowed from the Old; but the species are very different. "When the Spaniards landed in America," says an eminent naturalist, "they did not find a single animal they were acquainted with; not one of the quadrupeds of Europe, Asia, or Africa." Lawrence, Lectures on Physiology, Zoology, and the Natural History of Man (London, 1819), p. 250.

[2] Acosta, lib. 1, cap. 16.

[3] [The existence at some former period of such an island, or rather continent, seems to be regarded by geologists as a well-attested fact. But few would admit that its subsidence can have taken place through any sudden convulsion or within the period of human existence. Such, however, is the theory maintained by M. Brasseur de Bourbourg, who dates the event "six or seven thousand years ago,"

and believes that the traditions of it have been faithfully preserved. This is the great cataclysm with which all mythology begins. It may be traced through the myths of Greece, Egypt, India, and America, all being identical and having a common origin. It is the subject of the *Teo-Amoxtli*, of which several of the Mexican manuscripts, the Borgian and Dresden Codices in particular, are the hieroglyphical transcriptions, and of which "the actual letter," "in the Nahuatlac language," is found in a manuscript in Boturini's Collection. This manuscript is "in appearance" a history of the Toltecs and of the kings of Colhuacan and Mexico; but "under the ciphers of a fastidious chronology, under the recital more or less animated of the Toltec history, are concealed the profoundest mysteries concerning the geological origin of the world in its existing form and the cradle of the

vulsion of nature in the green islands sprinkled over the Pacific, once the mountain summits of a vast continent, now buried beneath the waters.[4] Some, distrusting the existence of revolutions of which no record was preserved, supposed that animals might have found their way across the ocean by various means; the birds of stronger wing by flight over the narrowest spaces; while the tamer kinds of quadrupeds might easily have been transported by men in boats, and even the more ferocious, as tigers, bears, and the like, have been brought over, in the same manner, when young, "for amusement and the pleasure of the chase!"[5] Others, again, maintained the equally probable opinion that angels, who had, doubtless, taken charge of them in the Ark, had also superintended their distribution afterwards over the different parts of the globe.[6] Such were the extremities to which even thinking minds were reduced, in their eagerness to reconcile the literal interpretation of Scripture with the phenomena of nature ! The philosophy of a later day conceives that it is no departure from this sacred authority to follow the suggestions of science, by referring the new tribes of animals to a creation, since the Deluge, in those places for which they were clearly intended by constitution and habits.[7]

Man would not seem to present the same embarrassments, in the discussion, as the inferior orders. He is fitted by nature for every climate, the burning sun of the tropics and the icy atmosphere of the North. He wanders indifferently over the sands of the desert, the waste of polar snows, and the pathless ocean. Neither mountains nor seas intimidate him, and, by the aid of mechanical contrivances, he accomplishes journeys which birds of boldest wing would perish in attempting. Without ascending to the high northern latitudes, where the continents of Asia and America approach within fifty miles of each other, it would be easy for the inhabitant of Eastern Tartary or Japan to steer his canoe from islet to islet, quite across to the American shore, without ever being on the ocean more than two days at a time.[8] The communication is somewhat

---

religions of antiquity." The Toltecs are " telluric powers, agents of the subterranean fire;" they are identical with the Cabiri, who reappear as the Cyclops, having "hollowed an eye in their forehead; that is to say, raised themselves with masses of earth above the surface and filled the craters of the volcanoes with fire." " The Chichimecs and the Aztecs are also symbolical names, borrowed from the forces of nature." Tollan, " the marshy or reedy place," was "the low fertile region" now covered by the Gulf of Mexico. Quetzalcoatl is ' merely the personification of the land swallowed up by the ocean." Tlapallan, Aztlan, and other names are similarly explained. Osiris, Pan, Hercules, and Bacchus have their respective parts assigned to them; for "not only all the sources of ancient mythology, but even the most mysterious details, even the obscurest enigmas, with which that mythology is enveloped, are to be sought in the two mediterraneans hollowed out by the cataclysm, and in the islands, great and small, which separate them from the ocean." (Quatre Lettres sur le Mexique.) There can be no refutation of such a theory, or of the assumptions on which it rests; but it may be proper to remark that this author has not succeeded in deciphering a single hieroglyphical character, and has published no translation of the real or supposed *Teo-Amoxtli*,—a point on which some misapprehension seems to exist.—ED.]

[4] Count Carli shows much ingenuity and learning in support of the famous Egyptian tradition, recorded by Plato in his "Timæus,"—of the good faith of which the Italian philosopher nothing doubts. Lettres Améric., tom. ii. let. 36–39.

[5] Garcia, Orígen de los Indios, de el nuevo Mundo (Madrid, 1729), cap. 4.

[6] Torquemada, Monarch. Ind., lib. 1, cap. 8.

[7] Prichard, Researches into the Physical History of Mankind (London, 1826), vol. i. p. 81, et seq.— He may find an orthodox authority of respectable antiquity, for a similar hypothesis, in St. Augustine, who plainly intimates his belief that, "as by God's command, at the time of the creation, the earth brought forth the living creature after his kind, so a similar process must have taken place after the Deluge, in islands too remote to be reached by animals from the continent." De Civitate Dei, ap Opera (Parisiis, 1. 36), tom. v. p. 987.

[8] Beechey, Voyage to the Pacific and Beering's Strait (London, 1831), Part 2, Appendix.—Hum-

more difficult on the Atlantic side. But even there, Iceland was occupied by colonies of Europeans many hundred years before the discovery by Columbus; and the transit from Iceland to America is comparatively easy.[9] Independently of these channels, others were opened in the Southern hemisphere, by means of the numerous islands in the Pacific. The population of America is not nearly so difficult a problem as that of these little spots. But experience shows how practicable the communication may have been, even with such sequestered places.[10] The savage has been picked up in his canoe, after drifting hundreds of leagues on the open ocean, and sustaining life, for months, by the rain from heaven, and such fish as he could catch.[11] The instances are not very rare; and it would be strange if these wandering barks should not sometimes have been intercepted by the great continent which stretches across the globe, in unbroken continuity, almost from pole to pole. No doubt, history could reveal to us more than one example of men who, thus driven upon the American shores, have mingled their blood with that of the primitive races who occupied them.

The real difficulty is not, as with the animals, to explain how man could have reached America, but from what quarter he actually has reached it. In surveying the whole extent of the New World, it was found to contain two great families, one in the lowest stage of civilization, composed of hunters, and another nearly as far advanced in refinement as the semi-civilized empires of Asia. The more polished races were probably unacquainted with the existence of each other on the different continents of America, and had as little intercourse with the barbarian tribes by whom they were surrounded. Yet they had some things in common both with these last and with one another, which remarkably distinguished them from the inhabitants of the Old World. They had a common complexion and physical organization,—at least, bearing a more uniform character than is found among the nations of any other quarter of the globe. They had some usages and institutions in common, and spoke languages of similar construction, curiously distinguished from those in the Eastern hemisphere.

Whence did the refinement of these more polished races come? Was

---

boldt, Examen critique de l'Histoire de la Géographie du Nouveau-Continent (Paris, 1837), tom. ii. p. 58.

[9] Whatever scepticism may have been entertained as to the visit of the Northmen, in the eleventh century, to the coasts of the great continent, it is probably set at rest in the minds of most scholars since the publication of the original documents by the Royal Society at Copenhagen. (See, in particular, Antiquitates Americanæ (Hafniæ, 1837), pp. 79-200.) How far south they penetrated is not so easily settled.

[10] The most remarkable example, probably, of a direct intercourse between remote points is furnished us by Captain Cook, who found the inhabitants of New Zealand not only with the same religion, but speaking the same language, as the people of Otaheite, distant more than 2000 miles. The comparison of the two vocabularies establishes the fact. Cook's Voyages (Dublin, 1784), vol. i. book 1, chap. 8.

[11] The eloquent Lyell closes an enumeration of some extraordinary and well-attested instances of this kind with remarking, "Were the whole of mankind now cut off, with the exception of one family, inhabiting the old or new continent, or Australia, or even some coral islet of the Pacific, we should expect their descendants, though they should never become more enlightened than the South Sea Islanders or the Esquimaux, to spread, in the course of ages, over the whole earth, diffused partly by the tendency of population to increase beyond the means of subsistence in a limited district, and partly by the accidental drifting of canoes by tides and currents to distant shores." Principles of Geology (London, 1832), vol. ii. p. 121.

it only a higher development of the same Indian character which we see, in the more northern latitudes, defying every attempt at permanent civilization? Was it engrafted on a race of higher order in the scale originally, but self-instructed, working its way upward by its own powers? Was it, in short, an indigenous civilization? or was it borrowed in some degree from the nations in the Eastern World? If indigenous, how are we to explain the singular coincidence with the East in institutions and opinions? If Oriental, how shall we account for the great dissimilarity in language, and for the ignorance of some of the most simple and useful arts, which, once known, it would seem scarcely possible should have been forgotten? This is the riddle of the Sphinx, which no Œdipus has yet had the ingenuity to solve. It is, however, a question of deep interest to every curious and intelligent observer of his species. And it has accordingly occupied the thoughts of men, from the first discovery of the country to the present time; when the extraordinary monuments brought to light in Central America have given a new impulse to inquiry, by suggesting the probability—the possibility, rather—that surer evidences than any hitherto known might be afforded for establishing the fact of a positive communication with the other hemisphere.

It is not my intention to add many pages to the volumes already written on this inexhaustible topic. The subject—as remarked by a writer of a philosophical mind himself, and who has done more than any other for the solution of the mystery—is of too speculative a nature for history, almost for philosophy.[12] But this work would be incomplete without affording the reader the means of judging for himself as to the true sources of the peculiar civilization already described, by exhibiting to him the alleged points of resemblance with the ancient continent. In doing this, I shall confine myself to my proper subject, the Mexicans, or to what, in some way or other, may have a bearing on this subject; proposing to state only real points of resemblance, as they are supported by evidence, and stripped, as far as possible, of the illusions with which they have been invested by the pious credulity of one party, and the visionary system-building of another.

An obvious analogy is found in *cosmogonal traditions* and *religious usages*. The reader has already been made acquainted with the Aztec system of four great cycles, at the end of each of which the world was destroyed, to be again regenerated.[13] The belief in these periodical convulsions of nature, through the agency of some one or other of the elements, was familiar to many countries in the Eastern hemisphere; and, though varying in detail, the general resemblance of outline furnishes an argument in favour of a common origin.[14]

---

[12] "La question générale de la première origine des habitans d'un continent est au-delà des limites prescrites à l'histoire; peut-être même n'est-elle pas une question philosophique." Humboldt, Essai politique, tom. i. p. 349.

[13] *Ante*, p. 30.

[14] The fanciful division of time into four or five cyles or ages was found among the Hindoos (Asiatic Researches, vol. ii. mem. 7), the Thibetians (Humboldt, Vues des Cordillères, p. 210), the Persians

No tradition has been more widely spread among nations than that of a Deluge. Independently of tradition, indeed, it would seem to be naturally suggested by the interior structure of the earth, and by the elevated places on which marine substances are found to be deposited. It was the received notion, under some form or other, of the most civilized people in the Old World, and of the barbarians of the New.[15] The Aztecs combined with some particular circumstances of a more arbitrary character, resembling the accounts of the East. They believe that two persons survived the Deluge,—a man, named Coxcox, and his wife. Their heads are represented in ancient paintings, together with a boat floating on the waters, at the foot of a mountain. A dove is also depicted, with a hieroglyphical emblem of languages in his mouth, which he is distributing to the children of Coxcox, who were born dumb.[16] The neighbouring people of Michoacán, inhabiting the same high plains of the Andes, had a still further tradition, that the boat in which Tezpi, their Noah, escaped, was filled with various kinds of animals and birds. After some time, a vulture was sent out from it, but remained feeding on the dead bodies of the giants, which had been left on the earth, as the waters subsided. The little humming-bird, *huitzitzilin*, was then sent forth, and returned with a twig in its mouth. The coincidence of both these accounts with the Hebrew and Chaldean narratives is obvious. It were to be wished that the authority for the Michoacán version were more satisfactory.[17]

On the way between Vera Cruz and the capital, not far from the modern city of Puebla, stands the venerable relic—with which the reader has become familiar in the course of the narrative—called the temple of Cholula. It is, as he will remember, a pyramidal mound, built, or rather cased, with unburnt brick, rising to the height of nearly one hundred and eighty feet. The popular tradition of the natives is that it was erected by

---

(Bailly, Traité de l'Astronomie (Paris, 1787), tom. i. discours préliminaire), the Greeks (Hesiod, Ἔργα καὶ Ἡμέραι, v. 108, et seq.), and other people, doubtless. The five ages in the Grecian cosmogony had reference to moral rather than physical phenomena,—a proof of higher civilization.

[15] The Chaldean and Hebrew accounts of the Deluge are nearly the same. The parallel is pursued in Palfrey's ingenious Lectures on the Jewish Scriptures and Antiquities (Boston, 1840), vol. ii. lect. 21, 22. Among the pagan writers, none approach so near to the Scripture narrative as Lucian, who, in his account of the Greek traditions, speaks of the Ark, and the pairs of different kinds of animals. De Deâ Syriâ, sec. 12.) The same thing is found in the Bhagawatn Purana, a Hindoo poem of great antiquity. (Asiatic Researches, vol. ii. mem. 7.) The simple tradition of a universal inundation was preserved among most of the aborigines, probably, of the Western World. See McCulloh, Researches, p. 147.

[16] This tradition of the Aztecs is recorded in an ancient hieroglyphical map, first published in Gemelli Carreri's Giro del Mondo. (See tom. vi. p. 38, ed. Napoli, 1700.) Its authenticity, as well as the integrity of Carreri himsel', on which some suspicions have been thrown (See Robertson's America (London, 1796), vol. iii. note 26), has been

successfully vindicated by Boturini, Clavigero, and Humboldt, all of whom trode in the steps of the Italian traveller. (Boturini, Idea, p. 54.—Humboldt, Vues des Cordillères, pp. 223, 224.—Clavigero, Stor. del Messico, tom. i. p. 24.) The map is a copy from one in the curious collection of Siguenza. It has all the character of a genuine Aztec picture, with the appearance of being retouched, especially in the costumes, by some later artist. The painting of the four ages, in the Vatican Codex, No. 3730, represents, also, the two figures in the boat, escaping the great cataclysm. Antiq. of Mexico, vol. i. Pl. 7.

[17] I have met with no other voucher for this remarkable tradition than Clavigero (Stor. del Messico, dissert. 1), a good, though certainly not the best, authority, when he gives us no reason for our faith. Humboldt, however, does not distrust the tradition. (See Vues des Cordillères, p. 226.) He is not so sceptical as Vater ; who, in allusion to the stories of the Flood, remarks, "I have purposely omitted noticing the resemblance of religious notions, for I do not see how it is possible to separate from such views every influence of Christian ideas, if it be only from an imperceptible confusion in the mind of the narrator." Mithridates, oder allgemeine Sprachenkunde (Berlin, 1812), Theil iii. Abtheil. 3, p. 82, note.

a family of giants, who had escaped the great inundation and designed to raise the building to the clouds; but the gods, offended with their presumption, sent fires from heaven on the pyramid, and compelled them to abandon the attempt.[18]   The partial coincidence of this legend with the Hebrew account of the Tower of Babel, received also by other nations of the East, cannot be denied.[19]   But one who has not examined the subject will scarcely credit what bold hypotheses have been reared on this slender basis.

Another point of coincidence is found in the goddess Cioacoatl, " our lady and mother;" " the first goddess who brought forth;" " who bequeathed the sufferings of childbirth to women, as the tribute of death;" "by whom sin came into the world."   Such was the remarkable language applied by the Aztecs to this venerated deity.   She was usually represented with a serpent near her; and her name signified the "serpent-woman."   In all this we see much to remind us of the mother of the human family, the Eve of the Hebrew and Syrian nations.[20]

But none of the deities of the country suggested such astonishing analogies with Scripture as Quetzalcoatl, with whom the reader has already been made acquainted.[21]   He was the white man, wearing a long beard, who came from the East, and who, after presiding over the golden age of Anahuac, disappeared as mysteriously as he had come, on the great Atlantic Ocean.   As he promised to return at some future day, his reappearance was looked for with confidence by each succeeding generation. There is little in these circumstances to remind one of Christianity.   But the curious antiquaries of Mexico found out that to this god were to be referred the institution of ecclesiastical communities, reminding one of the monastic societies of the Old World; that of the rites of confession and

---

[18] This story, so irreconcilable with the vulgar Aztec tradition, which admits only two survivors of the Deluge, was still lingering among the natives of the place on M. de Humboldt's visit there. (Vues des Cordillères, pp. 31, 32.) It agrees with that given by the interpreter of the Vatican Codex (Antiq. of Mexico, vol. vi. p. 192, et seq.); a writer —probably a monk of the sixteenth century—in whom ignorance and dogmatism contend for mastery.   See a precious specimen of both in his account of the Aztec chronology, in the very pages above referred to.

[19] A tradition, very similar to the Hebrew one, existed among the Chaldeans and the Hindoos. (Asiatic researches, vol. iii. mem. 16.) The natives of Chiapa, also, according to the bishop Nuñez de la Vega, had a story, cited as genuine by Humboldt (Vues des Cordillères, p. 148), which not only agrees with the Scripture account of the manner in which Babel was built, but with that of the subsequent dispersion and confusion of tongues.   A very marvellous coincidence!   But who shall vouch for the authenticity of the tradition?   The bishop flourished towards the close of the seventeenth century.   He drew his information from hieroglyphical maps, and an Indian MS., which Boturini in vain endeavoured to recover.   In exploring these, he borrowed the aid of the natives, who, as Boturini informs us, frequently led the good man into errors and absurdities; of which he gives several specimens. (Idea,

p. 116, et seq.)—Boturini himself has fallen into an error equally great, in regard to a map of this same Cholulan pyramid, which Clavigero shows, far from being a genuine antique, was the forgery of a later day. (Stor. del Messico, tom. i. p. 130, nota.) It is impossible to get a firm footing in the quicksands of tradition.   The further we are removed from the Conquest, the more difficult it becomes to decide what belongs to the primitive Aztec and what to the Christian convert.

[20] Sahagun, Hist. de Nueva-España, lib. 1, cap. 6; lib. 6, cap. 28, 33.—Torquemada, not content with the honest record of his predecessor, whose MS. lay before him, tells us that the Mexican Eve had two sons, Cain and Abel. (Monarch. Ind., lib. 6, cap. 31.)   The ancient interpreters of the Vatican and Tellerian Codices add the further tradition of her bringing sin and sorrow into the world by plucking the forbidden *rose* (Antiq. of Mexico, vol. vi., explan. of Pl. 7, 20); and Veytia remembers to have seen a Toltec or Aztec map representing a garden with a single tree in it, round which was coiled the serpent with a human face! (Hist. antig., lib. 1, cap. 1.)   After this we may be prepared for Lord Kingsborough's deliberate conviction that the "Aztecs had a clear knowledge of the Old Testament, and, most probably, of the New, though somewhat corrupted by time and hieroglyphics"! Antiq. of Mexico, vol. vi. p. 409.

[21] *Ante*, p. 29.

penance; and the knowledge even of the great doctrines of the Trinity and the Incarnation![22] One party, with pious industry, accumulated proofs to establish his identity with the Apostle St. Thomas;[23] while another, with less scrupulous faith, saw, in his anticipated advent to regenerate the nation, the type, dimly veiled, of the Messiah![24]

Yet we should have charity for the missionaries who first landed in this world of wonders, where, while man and nature wore so strange an aspect, they were astonished by occasional glimpses of rites and ceremonies which reminded them of a purer faith. In their amazement, they did not reflect whether these things were not the natural expression of the religious feeling common to all nations who have reached even a moderate civilization. They did not inquire whether the same things were not practised by other idolatrous people. They could not suppress their wonder, as they beheld the Cross, the sacred emblem of their own faith, raised as an object of worship in the temples of Anahuac. They met with it in various places; and the image of a cross may be seen at this day, sculptured in bas-relief, on the walls of one of the buildings of Palenque, while a figure bearing some resemblance to that of a child is held up to it, as if in adoration.[25]

Their surprise was heightened when they witnessed a religious rite which reminded them of the Christian communion. On these occasions an image of the tutelary deity of the Aztecs was made of the flour of maize, mixed with blood, and, after consecration by the priests, was distributed among the people, who, as they ate it, "showed signs of humiliation and sorrow, declaring it was the flesh of the deity!"[26] How could the Roman Catholic fail to recognize the awful ceremony of the Eucharist?

With the same feelings they witnessed another ceremony, that of the Aztec baptism; in which, after a solemn invocation, the head and lips of the infant were touched with water, and a name was given to it; while the goddess Cioacoatl, who presided over childbirth, was implored "that the

---

[22] Veytia, Hist. antig., lib. 1, cap. 15.

[23] Ibid., lib. 1, cap. 19.—A sorry argument, even for a casuist. See, also, the elaborate dissertation of Dr. Mier (apud Sahagun, lib. 3, Suplem.), which settles the question entirely to the satisfaction of his reporter, Bustamante.

[24] See, among others, Lord Kingsborough's reading of the Borgian Codex, and the interpreters of the Vatican (Antiq. of Mexico, vol. vi., explan. of Pl. 3, 10, 41), equally well skilled with his lordship —and Sir Hudibras—in unravelling mysteries.

" Whose primitive tradition reaches
     As far as Adam's first green breeches."

[25] Antiquités Mexicaines, exped. 3, Pl. 36.—The figures are surrounded by hieroglyphics of most arbitrary character, perhaps phonetic. (See, also, Herrera, Hist. general, dec. 2, lib. 3, cap. 1.— Gomara, Crónica de la Nueva-España, cap. 15, ap. Barcia, tom. ii.) Mr. Stephens considers that the celebrated "Cozumel Cross," preserved at Merida, which claims the credit of being the same originally worshipped by the natives of Cozumel, is, after all, nothing but a cross that was erected by the Spaniards

in one of their own temples in that island after the Conquest. This fact he regards as "completely invalidating the strongest proof offered at this day that the Cross was recognized by the Indians as a symbol of worship." (Travels in Yucatan, vol. ii. chap. 20.) But, admitting the truth of this statement, that the Cozumel Cross is only a Christian relic, which the ingenious traveller has made extremely probable, his inference is by no means admissible. Nothing could be more natural than that the friars in Merida should endeavour to give celebrity to their convent by making it the possessor of so remarkable a monument as the very relic which proved, in their eyes, that Christianity had been preached at some earlier date among the natives. But the real proof of the existence of the Cross, as an object of worship, in the New World, does not rest on such spurious monuments as these, but on the unequivocal testimony of the Spanish discoverers themselves.

[26] "Lo recibian con gran reverencia, humiliacion, y lágrimas, diciendo que comian la carne de su Dios." Veytia, Hist. antig., lib. 1, cap. 18.—Also, Acosta, lib. 5, cap. 24.

sin which was given to us before the beginning of the world might not visit the child, but that, cleansed by these waters, it might live and be born anew ! " [27]

It is true, these several rites were attended with many peculiarities, very unlike those in any Christian church. But the fathers fastened their eyes exclusively on the points of resemblance. They were not aware that the Cross was a symbol of worship, of the highest antiquity, in Egypt and Syria,[28] and that rites resembling those of communion [29] and baptism were practised by pagan nations on whom the light of Christianity had never shone.[30] In their amazement, they not only magnified what they saw, but were perpetually cheated by the illusions of their own heated imaginations. In this they were admirably assisted by their Mexican converts, proud to establish—and half believing it themselves—a correspondence between their own faith and that of their conquerors.[31]

The ingenuity of the chronicler was taxed to find out analogies between the Aztec and Scripture histories, both old and new. The migration from Aztlan to Anahuac was typical of the Jewish exodus.[32] The places where the Mexicans halted on the march were identified with those in the journey of the Israelites ; [33] and the name of Mexico itself was found to be

---

[27] *Ante,* p. 31. — Sahagun, Hist. de Nueva-España, lib. 6, cap. 37.—That the reader may see for himself how like, yet how unlike, the Aztec rite was to the Christian, I give the translation of Sahagun's account at length : " When everything necessary for the baptism had been made ready, all the relations of the child were assembled, and the midwife, who was the person that performed the rite of baptism, was summoned. At early dawn, they met together in the courtyard of the house. When the sun had risen, the midwife, taking the child in her arms, called for a little earthen vessel of water, while those about her placed the ornaments which had been prepared for the baptism in the midst of the court. To perform the rite of baptism, she placed herself with her face towards the west, and immediately began to go through certain ceremonies. . . . After this she sprinkled water on the head of the infant, saying, ' O my child ! take and receive the water of the Lord of the world, which is our life, and is given for the increasing and renewing of our body. It is to wash and to purify. I pray that these heavenly drops may enter into your body, and dwell there ; that they may destroy and remove from you all the evil and sin which was given to you before the beginning of the world ; since all of us are under its power, being all the children of Chalchivitlycue ' [the goddess of water]. She then washed the body of the child with water, and spoke in this manner : ' Whencesoever thou comest, thou that art hurtful to this child, leave him and depart from him, for he now liveth anew, and is born anew ; now is he purified and cleansed afresh, and our mother Chalchivitlycue again bringeth him into the world.' Having thus prayed, the midwife took the child in both hands, and, lifting him towards heaven, said, ' O Lord, thou seest here thy creature, whom thou hast sent into this world, this place of sorrow, suffering, and penitence. Grant him, O Lord, thy gifts, and thine inspiration, for thou art the great God, and with thee is the great goddess.' Torches of pine were kept burning during the performance of these ceremonies. When these things were ended, they gave the child the name of some one of his ancestors in the hope that he might shed a new

lustre over it. The name was given by the same midwife, or priestess who baptized him."

[28] Among Egyptian symbols we meet with several specimens of the Cross. One, according to Justus Lipsius, signified "life to come." See his treatise, De Cruce (Lutetiæ Parisiorum, 1598), lib. 3, cap. 8.) We find another in Champollion's catalogue, which he interprets "support or saviour." Précis, tom. ii., Tableau gén., Nos. 277, 348.) Some curious examples of the reverence paid to this sign by the ancients have been collected by McCulloh (Researches, p. 330, et seq.), and by Humboldt in his late work, Géographie du Nouveau-Continent, tom. ii. p. 354, et seq.

[29] " Ante, Deos homini quod conciliare valaret
Far erat,"
says Ovid. (Fastorum, lib. 1, v. 337.) Count Carli has pointed out a similar use of consecrated bread, and wine or water, in the Greek and Egyptian mysteries. Lettres Améric., tom. i. let. 27.) See, also, McCulloh, Researches, p. 240, et seq.

[30] Water for purification and other religious rites is frequently noticed by the classical writers. Thus Euripides :

" Ἁγνοῖς καθαρμοῖς πρῶτά νιν νίψαι θέλω.
Θάλασσα κλύζει πάντα τἀνθρώπων κακά."
Iphig. in Taur., vv. 1192, 1194.

The notes on this place, in the admirable Variorum edition of Glasgow, 1821, contain references to several passages of similar import in different authors.

[31] The difficulty of obtaining anything like a faithful report from the natives is the subject of complaint from more than one writer, and explains the great care taken by Sahagun to compare their narratives with each other. See Hist. de Nueva-España, Prólogo,— Ixtlilxochitl, Hist. Chich., MS., Pról.,—Boturini, Idea, p. 116.

[32] The parallel was so closely pressed by Torquemada that he was compelled to suppress the chapter containing it, on the publication of his book. See the Proemio to the edition of 1723, sec. 2.

[33] "The devil," says Herrera, " chose to imitate,

nearly identical with the Hebrew name for the Messiah.[34] The Mexican hieroglyphics afforded a boundless field for the display of this critical acuteness. The most remarkable passages in the Old and New Testaments were read in their mysterious characters; and the eye of faith could trace there the whole story of the Passion, the Saviour suspended from the cross, and the Virgin Mary with her attendant angels![35]

The Jewish and Christian schemes were strangely mingled together, and the brains of the good fathers were still further bewildered by the mixture of heathenish abominations which were so closely intertwined with the most orthodox observances. In their perplexity, they looked on the whole as the delusion of the devil, who counterfeited the rites of Christianity and the traditions of the chosen people, that he might allure his wretched victims to their own destruction.[36]

But, although it is not necessary to resort to this startling supposition, nor even to call up an apostle from the dead, or any later missionary, to explain the coincidences with Christianity, yet these coincidences must be allowed to furnish an argument in favour of some primitive communication with that great brotherhood of nations on the old continent, among whom similar ideas have been so widely diffused. The probability of such a communication, especially with Eastern Asia, is much strengthened by the resemblance of sacerdotal institutions, and of some religious rites, as those of marriage,[37] and the burial of the dead;[38] by the practice of human sacrifices, and even of cannibalism, traces of which are discernible in the Mongol races;[39] and, lastly, by a conformity of social usages and manners, so striking that the description of Montezuma's court may well pass for that of the Grand Khan's, as depicted by Maundeville and Marco Polo.[40] It would occupy too much room to go into details in this matter, without which, however, the strength of the argument cannot be felt, nor

---

[34] in everything, the departure of the Israelites from Egypt, and their subsequent wanderings." (Hist. general, dec. 3, lib. 3, cap. 10. But all that has been done by monkish annalist and missionary to establish the parallel with the children of Israel falls far short of Lord Kingsborough's learned labours, spread over nearly two hundred folio pages. (See Antiq. of Mexico, tom. vi. pp. 282-410.) *Quantum inane!*

[34] The word מׁשׁיח, from which is derived *Christ,* "the anointed," is still more nearly—not "precisely," as Lord Kingsborough states (Antiq. of Mexico, vol. vi. p. 186)—identical with that of Mexi, or Mesi, the chief who was said to have led the Aztecs on the plains of Anahuac.

[35] Interp. of Cod. Tel.-Rem. et Vat., Antiq. of Mexico, vol. vi.—Sahagun, Hist. de Nueva-España, lib. 3, Suplem.—Veytia, Hist. antig., lib. 1, cap. 16.

[36] This opinion finds favour with the best Spanish and Mexican writers, from the Conquest downwards. Solís sees nothing improbable in the fact that "the malignant influence, so frequently noticed in sacred history, should be found equally in profane." Hist. de la Conquista, lib. 2, cap. 4.

[37] The bridal ceremony of the Hindoos, in particular, contains curious points of analogy with the Mexican. (See Asiatic Researches, vol. vii. mem. 9.) The institution of a numerous priesthood, with the practices of confession and penance, was familiar to the Tartar people. (Maundeville, Voiage, chap. 23.) And monastic establishments were found in Thibet and Japan from the earliest ages. Humboldt, Vues des Cordillères, p. 179.

[38] "Doubtless," says the ingenious Carli, "the fashion of burning the corpse, collecting the ashes in a vase, burying them under pyramidal mounds, with the immolation of wives and servants at the funeral, all remind one of the customs of Egypt and Hindostan." Lettres Améric., tom. ii. let. 10.

[39] Marco Polo notices a civilized people in Southeastern China, and another in Japan, who drank the blood and ate the flesh of their captives, esteeming it the most savoury food in the world,—"la più saporita et migliore, che si possa truovar al mondo." (Viaggi, lib. 2, cap. 75; lib. 3, 13, 14.) The Mongols, according to Sir John Maundeville, regarded the ears "sowced in vynegre" as a particular dainty. Voiage, chap. 23.

[40] Marco Polo, Viaggi, lib. 2, cap. 10.—Maundeville, Voiage, cap. 20, et alibi.—See, also, a striking parallel between the Eastern Asiatics and Americans, in the Supplement to Ranking's "Historical Researches;" a work embodying many curious details of Oriental history and manners in support of a whimsical theory.

fully established. It has been done by others ; and an occasional coincidence has been adverted to in the preceding chapters.

It is true, we should be very slow to infer identity, or even correspondence, between nations, from a partial resemblance of habits and institutions. Where this relates to manners, and is founded on caprice, it is not more conclusive than when it flows from the spontaneous suggestions of nature, common to all. The resemblance, in the one case, may be referred to accident ; in the other, to the constitution of man. But there are certain arbitrary peculiarities, which, when found in different nations, reasonably suggest the idea of some previous communication between them. Who can doubt the existence of an affinity, or, at least, intercourse, between tribes who had the same strange habit of burying the dead in a sitting posture, as was practised to some extent by most, if not all, of the aborigines, from Canada to Patagonia ? [41] The habit of burning the dead, familiar to both Mongols and Aztecs, is in itself but slender proof of a common origin. The body must be disposed of in some way ; and this, perhaps, is as natural as any other. But when to this is added the circumstance of collecting the ashes in a vase and depositing the single article of a precious stone along with them, the coincidence is remarkable.[42] Such minute coincidences are not unfrequent ; while the accumulation of those of a more general character, though individually of little account, greatly strengthens the probability of a communication with the East.

A proof of a higher kind is found in the analogies of *science.* We have seen the peculiar chronological system of the Aztecs ; their method of distributing the years into cycles, and of reckoning by means of periodical series, instead of numbers. A similar process was used by the various Asiatic nations of the Mongol family from India to Japan. Their cycles, indeed, consisted of sixty, instead of fifty-two, years ; and for the terms of their periodical series they employed the names of the elements and the signs of the zodiac, of which latter the Mexicans, probably, had no knowledge. But the principle was precisely the same.[43]

A correspondence quite as extraordinary is found between the hieroglyphics used by the Aztecs for the signs of the days, and those zodiacal signs which the Eastern Asiatics employed as one of the terms of their series. The symbols in the Mongolian calendar are borrowed from animals. Four of the twelve are the same as the Aztec. Three others are as nearly the same as the different species of animals in the two hemispheres

[41] Morton, Crania Americana (Philadelphia, 1839), pp. 224-246.—The industrious author establishes this singular fact by examples drawn from a great number of nations in North and South America.
[42] Gomara, Cronica de la Nueva-España, cap. 202, ap. Barcia, tom. ii.—Clavigero, Stor. del Messico, tom. i. pp. 94, 95.—McCulloh (Researches, p. 198), who cites the Asiatic Researches.—Dr. McCulloh, in his single volume, has probably brought together a larger mass of materials for the illustration of the aboriginal history of the continent than any other writer in the language. In the selection of his facts he has shown much sagacity, as well as industry ; and, if the formal and somewhat repulsive character of the style has been unfavourable to a popular interest, the work must always have an interest for those who are engaged in the study of the Indian antiquities. His fanciful speculations on the subject of Mexican mythology may amuse those whom they fail to convince.
[43] *Ante*, p. 53, et seq.

would allow. The remaining five refer to no creature then found in Anahuac.[44] The resemblance went as far as it could.[45] The similarity of these conventional symbols among the several nations of the East can hardly fail to carry conviction of a common origin for the system, as regards them. Why should not a similar conclusion be applied to the Aztec calendar, which, although relating to days instead of years, was, like the Asiatic, equally appropriated to chronological uses and to those of divination?[46]

I shall pass over the further resemblance to the Persians, shown in the adjustment of time by a similar system of intercalation;[47] and to the Egyptians, in the celebration of the remarkable festival of the winter solstice;[48] since, although sufficiently curious, the coincidences might be accidental, and add little to the weight of evidence offered by an agreement in combinations of so complex and artificial a character as those before stated.

Amid these intellectual analogies, one would expect to meet with that of *language*, the vehicle of intellectual communication, which usually exhibits traces of its origin even when the science and literature that are embodied in it have widely diverged. No inquiry, however, has led to less satisfactory results. The languages spread over the Western continent far exceed in number those found in any equal population in the Eastern.[49] They exhibit the remarkable anomaly of differing as widely in etymology as they agree in organization; and, on the other hand, while they bear some slight affinity to the languages of the Old World in the former particular,

---

[44] This will be better shown by enumerating the zodiacal signs, used as the *names of the years* by the Eastern Asiatics. Among the Mongols, these were—1, mouse; 2, ox; 3, leopard; 4, hare; 5, crocodile; 6, serpent; 7, horse; 8, sheep; 9, monkey; 10, hen; 11, dog; 12, hog. The Mantchou Tartars, Japanese, and Thibetians have nearly the same terms, substituting, however, for No. 3, tiger; 5, dragon; 8, goat. In the Mexican signs for the names of the days we also meet with *hare, serpent, monkey, dog*. Instead of the "leopard," "crocodile," and "hen,"—neither of which animals was known in Mexico at the time of the Conquest, —we find the *ocelotl*, the *lizard*, and the *eagle*.— The lunar calendar of the Hindoos exhibits a correspondence equally extraordinary. Seven of the terms agree with those of the Aztecs, namely, *serpent, cane, razor, path of the sun, dog's tail, house*. (Humboldt, Vues des Cordillères, p. 152.) These terms, it will be observed, are still more arbitrarily selected, not being confined to animals; as, indeed, the hieroglyphics of the Aztec calendar were derived indifferently from them, and other objects, like the signs of our zodiac. These scientific analogies are set in the strongest light by M. de Humboldt, and occupy a large and, to the philosophical inquirer, the most interesting portion of his great work. (Vues des Cordillères, pp. 125-194.) He has not embraced in his tables, however, the Mongol calendar, which affords even a closer approximation to the Mexican than that of the other Tartar races. Comp. Ranking, Researches, pp. 370, 371, note.

[45] There is some inaccuracy in Humboldt's definition of the *ocelotl* as "the tiger," "the jaguar." (Ibid., p. 159.) It is smaller than the jaguar, though quite as ferocious, and is as graceful and beautiful as the leopard, which it more nearly resembles. It is a native of New Spain, where the tiger is not known. (See Buffon, Histoire naturelle (Paris, An VIII), tom. ii., *vox Ocelotl*.) The adoption of this latter name, therefore, in the Aztec calendar, leads to an inference somewhat exaggerated.

[46] Both the Tartars and the Aztecs indicated the year by its sign; as the "year of the hare" or "rabbit," etc. The Asiatic signs, likewise, far from being limited to the years and months, presided also over days, and even hours. (Humboldt, Vues des Cordillères, p. 165.) The Mexicans had also astrological symbols appropriated to the hours. Gama, Descripcion, Parte 2, p. 117.

[47] *Ante*, p. 53, note. 7.

[48] Achilles Tatius notices a custom of the Egyptians,—who, as the sun descended towards Capricorn, put on mourning, but, as the days lengthened, their fears subsided, they robed themselves in white, and, crowned with flowers, gave themselves up to jubilee, like the Aztecs. This account, transcribed by Carli's French translator, and by M. de Humboldt, is more fully criticised by M. Jomard in the Vues des Cordillères, p. 309, et seq.

[49] Jefferson (Notes on Virginia (London, 1787), p. 164), confirmed by Humboldt (Essai politique, tom. i. p. 353). Mr. Gallatin comes to a different conclusion. (Transactions of American Antiquarian Society (Cambridge, 1836), vol. ii. p. 161.) The great number of American dialects and languages is well explained by the unsocial nature of a hunter's life, requiring the country to be parcelled out into small and separate territories for the means of subsistence.

they have no resemblance to them whatever in the latter.[50] The Mexican was spoken for an extent of three hundred leagues. But within the boundaries of New Spain more than twenty languages were found; not simply dialects, but, in many instances, radically different.[51] All this these idioms, however, with one exception, conformed to that peculiar synthetic structure by which every Indian dialect appears to have been fashioned, from the land of the Esquimaux to Terra del Fuego;[52] a system which, bringing the greatest number of ideas within the smallest possible compass, condenses whole sentences into a single word,[53] displaying a curious mechanism, in which some discern the hand of the philosopher, and others only the spontaneous efforts of the savage.[54]

The etymological affinities detected with the ancient continent are not very numerous, and they are drawn indiscriminately from all the tribes scattered over America. On the whole, more analogies have been found with the idioms of Asia than of any other quarter. But their amount is too inconsiderable to balance the opposite conclusion inferred by a total dissimilarity of structure.[55] A remarkable exception is found in the Othomi or Otomi language, which covers a wider territory than any other but the Mexican in New Spain,[56] and which, both in its monosyllabic composition, so different from those around it, and in its vocabulary, shows a very singular affinity to the Chinese.[57] the existence of this insulated idiom in the heart of this vast continent offers a curious theme for speculation, entirely beyond the province of history.

The American languages, so numerous and widely diversified, present an immense field of inquiry, which, notwithstanding the labours of several distinguished philologists, remains yet to be explored. It is only after a

---

[50] Philologists have, indeed, detected two curious exceptions, in the Congo and primitive Basque; from which, however, the Indian languages differ in many essential points. See Du Ponceau's Report, ap. Transactions of the Lit. and Hist. Committee of the Am. Phil. Society, vol. i.

[51] Vater (Mithridates, Theil iii. Abtheil. 3, p. 70), who fixes on the Rio Gila and the Isthmus of Darien as the boundaries within which traces of the Mexican language were to be discerned. Clavigero estimates the number of dialects at thirty-five. I have used the more guarded statement of M. de Humboldt, who adds that fourteen of these languages have been digested into dictionaries and grammars. Essai politique, tom. i. p. 352.

[52] No one has done so much towards establishing this important fact as that estimable scholar, Mr. Du Ponceau. And the frankness with which he has admitted the exception that disturbed his favourite hypothesis shows that he is far more wedded to science than to system. See an interesting account of it, in his prize essay before the Institute, Mémoire sur le Système grammaticale des Langues de quelques Nations Indiennes de l'Amérique. (Paris, 1838.)

[53] The Mexican language, in particular, is most flexible; admitting of combinations so easily that the most simple ideas are often buried under a load of accessories. The forms of expression, though picturesque, were thus made exceedingly cumbrous. A "priest," for example, was called *notiazomahuisteopixcatatzin*, meaning "venerable minister of

God, that I love as my father." A still more comprehensive word is *amatlacuilolitquitcatlaxtlahuitli*, signifying "the reward given to a messenger who bears a hieroglyphical map conveying intelligence."

[54] See, in particular, for the latter view of the subject, the arguments of Mr. Gallatin, in his acute and masterly disquisition on the Indian tribes; a disquisition that throws more light on the intricate topics of which it treats than whole volumes that have preceded it. Transactions of the American Antiquarian Society, vol. ii., Introd., sec. 6.

[55] This comparative anatomy of the languages of the two hemispheres, begun by Barton (Origin of the Tribes and Nations of America (Philadelphia, 1797)), has been extended by Vater (Mithridates, Theil iii. Abtheil. 1, p. 348, et seq.). A selection of the most striking analogies may be found, also, in Malte Brun, book 75, table.

[56] *Othomi*, from *otho* "stationary," and *mi*, "nothing." (Najera, Dissert., *ut infra*.) The etymology intimates the condition of this rude nation of warriors, who, imperfectly reduced by the Aztec arms, roamed over the high lands north of the Valley of Mexico.

[57] See Najera's Dissertatio De Lingua Othomitorum, ap. Transactions of the American Philosophical Society, vol. v. New Series.—The author, a learned Mexican, has given a most satisfactory analysis of this remarkable language, which stands alone among the idioms of the New World, as the Basque—the solitary wreck, perhaps, of a primitive age—exists among those of the Old.

wide comparison of examples that conclusions founded on analogy can be trusted. The difficulty of making such comparisons increases with time, from the facility which the peculiar structure of the Indian languages affords for new combinations ; while the insensible influence of contact with civilized man, in producing these, must lead to a still further distrust of our conclusions.

The theory of an Asiatic origin for Aztec civilization derives stronger confirmation from the light of *tradition*, which, shining steadily from the far Northwest, pierces through the dark shadows that history and mythology have alike thrown around the traditions of the country. Traditions of a Western or Northwestern origin were found among the more barbarous tribes,[58] and by the Mexicans were preserved both orally and in their hieroglyphical maps, where the different stages of their migration are carefully noted. But who, at this day, shall read them ?[59] They are admitted to agree, however, in representing the populous North as the prolific hive of the American races.[60] In this quarter were placed their Aztlan and their Huehuetlapallan,—the bright abodes of their ancestors, whose warlike exploits rivalled those which the Teutonic nations have recorded of Odin and the mythic heroes of Scandinavia. From this quarter the Toltecs, the Chichimecs, and the kindred races of the Nahuatlacs came successively up the great plateau of the Andes, spreading over its hills and valleys, down to the Gulf of Mexico.[61]

Antiquaries have industriously sought to detect some still surviving traces of these migrations. In the northwestern districts of New Spain, at the distance of a thousand miles from the capital, dialects have been discovered showing intimate affinity with the Mexicans.[62] Along the Rio Gila, remains of populous towns are to be seen, quite worthy of the Aztecs in their style of architecture.[63] The country north of the great Rio

---

[58] Barton, p. 92.—Heckewelder, chap. 1, ap. Transactions of the Hist. and Lit. Committee of the Am. Phil. Soc., vol. i.—The various traditions have been assembled by M. Warden, in the Antiquités Mexicaines, part 2, p. 185, et seq.

[59] The recent work of Mr. Delafield (Inquiry into the Origin of the Antiquities of America (Cincinnati, 1839)) has an engraving of one of these maps, said to have been obtained by Mr. Bullock from Boturini's collection. Two such are specified on page 10 of that antiquary's Catalogue. This map has all the appearance of a genuine Aztec painting of the rudest character. We may recognize, indeed, the symbols of some dates and places, with others denoting the aspect of the country, whether fertile or barren, a state of war or peace, etc. But it is altogether too vague, and we know too little of the allusions, to gather any knowledge from it of the course of the Aztec migration.—Gemelli Carreri's celebrated chart contains the names of many places on the route, interpreted, perhaps, by Siguenza himself, to whom it belonged (Giro del Mondo, tom. vi. p. 56); and Clavigero has endeavoured to ascertain the various localities with some precision. (Stor. del Messico, tom. i. p. 160, et seq.) But, as they are all within the boundaries of New Spain, and, indeed, south of the Rio Gila, they throw little light, of course, on the vexed question of the primitive abodes of the Aztecs.

[60] This may be fairly gathered from the agreement of the *traditionary* interpretations of the maps of the various people of Anahuac, according to Veytia ; who, however, admits that it is "next to impossible," with the lights of the present day, to determine the precise route taken by the Mexicans. (Hist. antig., tom. i. cap. 2.) Lorenzana is not so modest. "Los Mexicanos por tradicion viniéron por el norte," says he, "y se saben ciertamente sus mansiones." (Hist. de Nueva-España, p. 81, nota.) There are some antiquaries who see best in the dark.

[61] Ixtlilxochitl, Hist. Chich., MS., cap. 2, et seq. —Idem, Relaciones, MS.—Veytia, Hist. antig., ubi supra.—Torquemada, Monarch. Ind., tom. i. lib. 1.

[62] In the province of Sonora, especially along the Californian Gulf. The Cora language, above all, of which a regular grammar has been published, and which is spoken in New Biscay, about 30° north, so much resembles the Mexican that Vater refers them both to a common stock. Mithridates, Theil iii. Abtheil. 3, p. 143.

[63] On the southern bank of this river are ruins of large dimensions, described by the missionary Pedro Font on his visit there in 1775. (Antiq. of Mexico, vol. vi. p. 538.)—At a place of the same name, Casas Grandes, about 33° north, and, like the former, a supposed station of the Aztecs, still more extensive remains are to be found ; large enough, indeed,

Colorado has been imperfectly explored; but in the higher latitudes, in the neighbourhood of Nootka, tribes still exist whose dialects, both in the termination and general sound of the words, bear considerable resemblance to the Mexican.[64] Such are the vestiges, few, indeed, and feeble, that still exist to attest the truth of traditions which themselves have remained steady and consistent through the lapse of centuries and the migrations of successive races.

The conclusions suggested by the intellectual and moral analogies with Eastern Asia derive considerable support from those of a *physical nature.* The aborigines of the Western World were distinguished by certain peculiarities of organization, which have led physiologists to regard them as a separate race. These peculiarities are shown in their reddish complexion, approaching a cinnamon colour; their straight, black, and exceedingly glossy hair; their beard thin, and usually eradicated;[65] their nigh cheek-bones, eyes obliquely directed towards the temples, prominent noses, and narrow foreheads falling backwards with a greater inclination than those of any other race except the African.[66] From this general standard, however, there are deviations, in the same manner, if not to the same extent, as in other quarters of the globe, though these deviations do not seem to be influenced by the same laws of local position.[67] Anatomists, also, have discerned in crania disinterred from the mounds, and in those of the inhabitants of the high plains of the Cordilleras, an obvious difference from those of the more barbarous tribes. This is seen especially in the ampler forehead, intimating a decided intellectual superiority.[68] These characteristics are found to bear a close resemblance to those of the Mongolian family, and especially to the people of Eastern Tartary;[69] so that, notwithstanding certain differences recognized by

---

according to a late traveller, Lieut. Hardy, for a population of 20,000 or 30,000 souls. The country for leagues is covered with these remains, as well as with utensils of earthenware, obsidian, and other relics. A drawing which the author has given of a painted jar or vase may remind one of the Etruscan. "There were, also, good specimens of earthen images in the Egyptian style," he observes, "which are, *to me at least, so perfectly uninteresting* that I was at no pains to procure any of them." (Travels in the Interior of Mexico (London, 1829), pp. 464-466.) The lieutenant was neither a Boturini nor a Belzoni.

[64] Vater has examined the languages of three of these nations, between 50° and 60° north, and collated their vocabularies with the Mexican, showing the probability of a common origin of many of the words in each. Mithridates, Theil iii. Abtheil. 3, p. 212.

[65] The Mexicans are noticed by M. de Humboldt as distinguished from the other aborigines whom he had seen, by the quantity both of beard and moustaches. (Essai politique, tom. i. p. 361.) The modern Mexican, however, broken in spirit and fortunes, bears as little resemblance, probably, in physical as in moral characteristics to his ancestors, the fierce and independent Aztecs.

[66] Prichard, Physical History, vol. i. pp. 167-169, 182, et seq.—Morton, Crania Americana, pp. 66.—

McCulloh, Researches, p. 18.—Lawrence Lectures, pp. 317, 565.

[67] Thus we find, amidst the generally prevalent copper or cinnamon tint, nearly all gradations of colour, from the European white, to a black, almost African; while the complexion capriciously varies among different tribes in the neighbourhood of each other. See examples in Humboldt (Essai politique, tom. i. pp. 358, 359), also Prichard (Physical History, vol. ii. pp. 452, 522, et alibi), a writer whose various research and dispassionate judgment have made his work a text-book in this department of science.

[68] Such is the conclusion of Dr. Warren, whose excellent collection has afforded him ample means for study and comparison. (See his remarks before the British Association for the Advancement of Science, ap. London Athenæum, Oct. 1837.) In the specimens collected by Dr. Morton, however, the barbarous tribes would seem to have a somewhat larger facial angle, and a greater quantity of brain, than the semi-civilized. Crania Americana, p. 259.

[69] "On ne peut se refuser d'admettre que l'espèce humaine n'offre pas de races plus voisines que le sont celles des Américains, des Mongols, des Mantchoux, et des Malais." Humboldt, Essai politique, tom. i. p. 367.—Also, Prichard, Physical History, vol. i. pp. 184-186; vol. ii. pp. 365-367.—Lawrence, Lectures, p. 365.

physiologists, the skulls of the two races could not be readily distinguished from one another by a common observer. No inference can be surely drawn, however, without a wide range of comparison. That hitherto made has been chiefly founded on specimens from the barbarous tribes.[70] Perhaps a closer comparison with the more civilized may supply still stronger evidence of affinity.[71]

In seeking for analogies with the Old World, we should not pass by in silence the *architectural remains* of the country, which, indeed, from their resemblance to the pyramidal structures of the East, have suggested to more than one antiquary the idea of a common origin.[72] The Spanish invaders, it is true, assailed the Indian buildings, especially those of a religious character, with all the fury of fanaticism. The same spirit survived in the generations which succeeded. The war has never ceased against the monuments of the country; and the few that fanaticism has spared have been nearly all demolished to serve the purposes of utility. Of all the stately edifices, so much extolled by the Spaniards who first visited the country, there are scarcely more vestiges at the present day than are to be found in some of those regions of Europe and Asia which once swarmed with populous cities, the great marts of luxury and commerce.[73] Yet some of these remains, like the temple of Xochicalco,[74] the palaces of

---

[70] Dr. Morton's splendid work on American crania has gone far to supply the requisite information. Out of about one hundred and fifty specimens of skulls, of which he has ascertained the dimensions with admirable precision, one-third belong to the semi-civilized races; and of them thirteen are Mexican. The number of these last is too small to found any general conclusions upon, considering the great diversity found in individuals of the same nation, not to say kindred.—Blumenbach's observations on American skulls were chiefly made, according to Prichard (Physical History, vol. i. pp. 183, 184), from specimens of the Carib tribes, as unfavourable, perhaps, as any on the continent.

[71] Yet these specimens are not so easy to be obtained. With uncommon advantages for procuring these myself in Mexico, I have not succeeded in obtaining any specimens of the genuine Aztec skull. The difficulty of this may be readily comprehended by any one who considers the length of time that has elapsed since the Conquest, and that the burial-places of the ancient Mexicans have continued to be used by their descendants. Dr. Morton more than once refers to his specimens as those of the "genuine Toltec skull, from cemeteries in Mexico older than the Conquest." (Crania Americana, pp. 152, 155, 231, et alibi.) But how does he know that the heads are Toltec? That nation is reported to have left the country about the middle of the eleventh century, nearly eight hundred years ago,—according to Ixtlilxochitl, indeed, a century earlier; and it seems much more probable that the specimens now found in these burial-places should belong to some of the races who have since occupied the country, than to one so far removed. The presumption is manifestly too feeble to authorize any positive inference.

[72] The tower of Belus, with its retreating stories, described by Herodotus (Clio, sec. 181), has been selected as the model of the *teocalli*; which leads Vater somewhat shrewdly to remark that it is strange no evidence of this should appear in the erection of similar structures by the Aztecs in the whole course of their journey to Anahuac. (Mithridates, Theil

iii. Abtheil. 3, pp. 74, 75.) The learned Niebuhr finds the elements of the Mexican temple in the mythic tomb of Porsenna. (Roman History, Eng. trans. (London, 1827), vol. i. p. 88.) The resemblance to the accumulated pyramids composing this monument is not very obvious. Comp. Pliny (Hist. Nat., lib. 36, sec. 19). Indeed, the antiquarian may be thought to encroach on the poet's province when he finds in Etruscan *fable*—"cum omnia excedat fabulositas," as Pliny characterizes this—the origin of Aztec science.

[73] See the powerful description of Lucan, Pharsalia, lib. 9, v. 966.—The Latin bard has been surpassed by the Italian, in the beautiful stanza beginning *Giace l' alta Cartago* (Gierusalemme Liberata, c. 15, s. 20), which may be said to have been expanded by Lord Byron into a canto,—the fourth of Childe Harold.

[74] The most remarkable remains on the proper Mexican soil are the temple or fortress of Xochicalco, not many miles from the capital. It stands on a rocky eminence, nearly a league in circumference, cut into terraces faced with stone. The building on the summit is seventy-five feet long and sixty-six broad. It is of hewn granite, put together without cement, but with great exactness. It was constructed in the usual pyramidal, terraced form, rising by a succession of stories, each smaller than that below it. The number of these is now uncertain; the lower one alone remaining entire. This is sufficient, however, to show the nice style of execution, from the sharp, salient cornices, and the hieroglyphical emblems with which it is covered, all cut in the hard stone. As the detached blocks found among the ruins are sculptured with bas-reliefs in like manner, it is probable that the whole building was covered with them. It seems probable, also, as the same pattern extends over different stones, that the work was executed after the walls were raised.—In the hill beneath, subterraneous galleries, six feet wide and high, have been cut to the length of one hundred and eighty feet, where they terminate in two halls, the vaulted ceilings of which connect by a sort of tunnel with the buildings

Tezcotzinco,[75] the colossal calendar stone in the capital, are of sufficient magnitude, and wrought with sufficient skill, to attest mechanical powers in the Aztecs not unworthy to be compared with those of the ancient Egyptians.

But, if the remains on the Mexican soil are so scanty, they multiply as we descend the south-eastern slope of the Cordilleras, traverse the rich Valley of Oaxaca, and penetrate the forests of Chiapa and Yucatan. In the midst of these lonely regions we meet with the ruins, recently discovered, of several ancient cities, Mitla, Palenque, and Itzalana or Uxmal,[76] which argue a higher civilization than anything yet found on the American continent; and, although it was not the Mexicans who built these cities, yet, as they are probably the work of cognate races, the present inquiry would be incomplete without some attempt to ascertain what light they can throw on the origin of the Indian, and consequently of the Aztec, civilization.[77]

Few works of art have been found in the neighbourhood of any of the ruins. Some of them, consisting of earthen or marble vases, fragments of statues, and the like, are fantastic, and even hideous; others show much grace and beauty of design, and are apparently well executed.[78] It may seem extraordinary that no iron in the buildings themselves, nor iron tools, should have been discovered, considering that the materials used are chiefly granite, very hard, and carefully hewn and polished. Red copper chisels and axes have been picked up in the midst of large blocks of granite imperfectly cut, with fragments of pillars and architraves, in the quarries near Mitla.[79] Tools of a similar kind have been discovered, also, in the quarries near Thebes; and the difficulty, nay, impossibility, of cutting such masses from the living rock with any tools which we possess, except iron, has confirmed an ingenious writer in the supposition that this metal must have been employed by the Egyptians, but that its tendency to decomposition, especially in a nitrous soil, has prevented

---

above. These subterraneous works are also lined with hewn stone. The size of the blocks, and the hard quality of the granite of which they consist, have made the buildings of Xochicalco a choice quarry for the proprietors of a neighbouring sugar-refinery, who have appropriated the upper stories of the temple to this ignoble purpose! The Barberini at least built palaces, beautiful themselves, as works of art, with the plunder of the Coliseum. See the full description of this remarkable building, both by Dupaix and Alzate. (Antiquités Mexicaines, tom. i. Exp. 1, pp. 15–20; tom. iii. Exp. 1, Pl. 33.) A recent investigation has been made by order of the Mexican government, the report of which differs, in some of its details, from the preceding. Revista Mexicana, tom. i. mem. 5.

[75] *Ante*, p. 87.

[76] It is impossible to look at Waldeck's finished drawings of buildings, where Time seems scarcely to have set his mark on the nicely chiselled stone, and the clear tints are hardly defaced by a weather-stain, without regarding the artist's work as a *restoration*; a picture true, it may be, of those buildings in the day of their glory, but not of their decay.—Cogolludo, who saw them in the middle of the

seventeenth century, speaks of them with admiration, as works of "accomplished architects," of whom history has preserved no tradition. Historia de Yucatan (Madrid, 1688), lib. 4, cap. 2.

[77] In the original text is a description of some of these ruins, especially of those of Mitla and Palenque. It would have had novelty at the time in which it was written, since the only accounts of these buildings were in the colossal publications of Lord Kingsborough, and in the Antiquités Mexicaines, not very accessible to most readers. But it is unnecessary to repeat descriptions now familiar to every one, and so much better executed than they can be by me in the spirited pages of Stephens.

[78] See, in particular, two terra-cotta busts with helmets, found in Oaxaca, which might well pass for Greek, both in the style of the heads and the casques that cover them. Antiquités Mexicaines, tom. iii. Exp. 2, Pl. 36.

[79] Dupaix speaks of these tools as made of pure copper. But doubtless there was some alloy mixed with it, as was practised by the Aztecs and Egyptians; otherwise their edges must have been easily turned by the hard substances on which they were employed.

any specimens of it from being preserved.[80]   Yet iron has been found, after the lapse of some thousands of years, in the remains of antiquity ; and it is certain that the Mexicans, down to the time of the Conquest, used only copper instruments, with an alloy of tin, and a silicious powder, to cut the hardest stones, some of them of enormous dimensions.[81]   This fact, with the additional circumstances that only similar tools have been found in Central America, strengthens the conclusion that iron was neither known there nor in ancient Egypt.

But what are the nations of the Old Continent whose style of architecture bears most resemblance to that of the remarkable monuments of Chiapa and Yucatan?   The points of resemblance will probably be found neither numerous nor decisive.   There is, indeed, some analogy both to the Egyptian and Asiatic style of architecture in the pyramidal, terrace-formed bases on which the buildings repose, resembling also the Toltec and Mexican *teocalli*.   A similar care, also, is observed in the people of both hemispheres to adjust the position of their buildings by the cardinal points.   The walls in both are covered with figures and hieroglyphics, which, on the American as on the Egyptian, may be designed, perhaps, to record the laws and historical annals of the nation.   These figures, as well as the buildings themselves, are found to have been stained with various dyes, principally vermilion ;[82] a favourite colour with the Egyptians also, who painted their colossal statues and temples of granite.[83]   Notwithstanding these points of similarity, the Palenque architecture has little to remind us of the Egyptian or of the Oriental.   It is, indeed, more conformable, in the perpendicular elevation of the walls, the moderate size of the stones, and the general arrangement of the parts, to the European.   It must be admitted, however, to have a character of originality peculiar to itself.

More positive proofs of communication with the East might be looked for in their sculpture and in the conventional forms of their hieroglyphics. But the sculptures on the Palenque buildings are in relief, unlike the Egyptian, which are usually in *intaglio*.   The Egyptians were not very successful in their representations of the human figure, which are on the same invariable model, always in profile, from the greater facility of execution this presents over the front view ; the full eye is placed on the side of the head, while the countenance is similar in all, and perfectly destitute of expression.[84]   The Palenque artists were equally awkward in

---

[80] Wilkinson, Ancient Egyptians, vol. iii. pp. 246–254.

[81] *Ante*, p. 67.

[82] Waldeck, Atlas pittoresque, p. 73.—The fortress of Xochiaalco was also coloured with a red paint (Antiquités Mexicaines, tom. i. p. 20) ; and a cement of the same colour covered the Toltec pyramid at Teotihuacan, according to Mr. Bullock, Six Months in Mexico, vol, ii. p. 143.

[83] Description de l'Égypte, Antiq., tom. ii. cap. 9, sec. 4.—The huge image of the Sphinx was originally coloured red. (Clarke's Travels, vol. v. p. 202.)   Indeed, many of the edifices, as well as statues, of ancient Greece, also, still exhibit traces of having been painted.

[84] The various causes of the stationary condition of art in Egypt, for so many ages, are clearly exposed by the duke di Serradifalco, in his *Antichità della Sicilia* (Palermo, 1834, tom. ii. pp. 33, 34) ; a work in which the author, while illustrating the antiquities of a little island, has thrown a flood of light on the arts and literary culture of ancient Greece.

representing the various attitudes of the body, which they delineated also in profile. But the parts are executed with much correctness, and sometimes gracefully; the costume is rich and various; and the ornamented head-dress, typical, perhaps, like the Aztec, of the name and condition of the person represented, conforms in its magnificence to the Oriental taste. The countenance is various, and often expressive. The contour of the head is, indeed, most extraordinary, describing almost a semicircle from the forehead to the tip of the nose, and contracted towards the crown, whether from the artificial pressure practised by many of the aborigines, or from some preposterous notion of ideal beauty.[85] But, while superior in the execution of the details, the Palenque artist was far inferior to the Egyptian in the number and variety of the objects displayed by him, which on the Theban temples comprehend animals as well as men, and almost every conceivable object of use or elegant art.

The hieroglyphics are too few on the American buildings to authorize any decisive inference. On comparing them, however, with those of the Dresden Codex, probably from this same quarter of the country,[86] with those on the monument of Xochicalco, and with the ruder picture-writing of the Aztecs, it is not easy to discern anything which indicates a common system. Still less obvious is the resemblance to the Egyptian characters, whose refined and delicate abbreviations approach almost to the simplicity of an alphabet. Yet the Palenque writing shows an advanced stage of the art, and, though somewhat clumsy, intimates, by the conventional and arbitrary forms of the hieroglyphics, that it was symbolical, and perhaps phonetic, in its character.[87] That its mysterious import will ever be deciphered is scarcely to be expected. The language of the race who employed it, the race itself, is unknown. And it is not likely that another Rosetta stone will be found, with its trilingual inscription, to supply the means of comparison, and to guide the American Champollion in the path of discovery.

It is impossible to contemplate these mysterious monuments of a lost civilization without a strong feeling of curiosity as to who were their architects and what is their probable age. The data on which to rest our conjectures of their age are not very substantial; although some find in them a warrant for an antiquity of thousands of years, coeval with the architecture of Egypt and Hindostan.[88] But the interpretation of hiero-

---

[85] "The ideal is not always the beautiful," as Winckelmann truly says, referring to the Egyptian figures. (Histoire de l'Art chez les Anciens, liv. 4, chap. 2, trad. Fr.) It is not impossible, however, that the portraits mentioned in the text may be copies from life. Some of the rude tribes of America distorted their infants' heads into forms quite as fantastic; and Garcilaso de la Vega speaks of a nation discovered by the Spaniards in Florida, with a formation apparently not unlike the Palenque: "*Tienen cabezas increiblemente largas, y ahusadas para arriba*, que las ponen así con artificio, atándoselas desde el punto, que nascen las criaturas, hasta que son de nueve ó diez años." La Florida (Madrid, 1723), p. 190.

[86] For a notice of this remarkable codex, see *ante*, p. 50. There is, indeed, a resemblance, in the use of straight lines and dots, between the Palenque writing and the Dresden MS. Possibly these dots denoted years, like the rounds in the Mexican system.

[87] The hieroglyphics are arranged in perpendicular lines. The heads are uniformly turned towards the right, as in the Dresden MS.

[88] "Les ruines," says the enthusiastic chevalier Le Noir, "sans nom, à qui l'on a donné celui de

glyphics, and the apparent duration of trees, are vague and unsatisfactory.[89] And how far can we derive an argument from the discoloration and dilapidated condition of the ruins, when we find so many structures of the Middle Ages dark and mouldering with decay, while the marbles of the Acropolis and the grey stone of Pæstum still shine in their primitive splendour ?

There are, however, undoubted proofs of considerable age to be found there. Trees have shot up in the midst of the buildings, which measure, it is said, more than nine feet in diameter.[90] A still more striking fact is the accumulation of vegetable mould in one of the courts, to the depth of nine feet above the pavement.[91] This in our latitude would be decisive of a very great antiquity. But in the rich soil of Yucatan, and under the ardent sun of the tropics, vegetation bursts forth with irrepressible exuberance, and generations of plants succeed each other without intermission, leaving an accumulation of deposits that would have perished under a northern winter. Another evidence of their age is afforded by the circumstance that in one of the courts of Uxmal the granite pavement, on which the figures of tortoises were raised in relief, is worn nearly smooth by the feet of the crowds who have passed over it ;[92] a curious fact, suggesting inferences both in regard to the age and population of the place. Lastly, we have authority for carrying back the date of many of these ruins to a certain period, since they were found in a deserted, and probably dilapidated, state by the first Spaniards who entered the country. Their notices, indeed, are brief and casual, for the old Conquerors had little respect for works of art ;[93] and it is fortunate for

---

Palenque, peuvent remonter comme les plus anciennes ruines du monde à trois mille ans. Ceci n'est point mon opinion seule ; c'est celle de *tous* les voyageurs qui ont vu les ruines dont il s'agit, de *tous* les archéologues qui en ont examiné les dessins ou lu les descriptions, enfin des historiens qui ont fait des recherches, et qui n'ont rien trouvé dans les annales du monde qui fasse soupçonner l'époque de la fondation de tels monuments, dont l'origine se perd dans la nuit des temps." (Antiquités Mexicaines, tom. ii., Examen, p. 73.) Colonel Galindo, fired with the contemplation of the American ruins, pronounces this country the true cradle of civilization, whence it passed over to China, and latterly to Europe, which, whatever "its foolish vanity" may pretend, has but just started in the march of improvement ! See his Letter on Copan, ap. Trans. of Am. Ant. Soc., vol. ii.

[89] From these sources of information, and especially from the number of the concentric rings in some old trees and the incrustation of stalactites found on the ruins of Palenque, M. Waldeck computes their age at between two and three thousand years. (Voyage en Yucatan, p. 78.) The criterion, as far as the trees are concerned, cannot be relied on in an advanced stage of their growth ; and as to the stalactite formations, they are obviously affected by too many casual circumstances, to afford the basis of an accurate calculation.

[90] Waldeck, Voyage en Yucatan, ubi supra.

[91] Antiquités Mexicaines, Examen, p. 76.—Hardly deep enough, however, to justify Captain Dupaix's surmise of the antediluvian existence of these buildings ; especially considering that the accumulation was in the sheltered position of an interior court.

[92] Waldeck, Voyage en Yucatan, p. 97.

[93] The chaplain of Grijalva speaks with admiration of the "lofty towers of stone and lime, some of them very ancient," found in Yucatan. (Itinerario, MS. (1518).) Bernal Diaz, with similar expressions of wonder, refers the curious antique relics found there to the Jews. (Hist. de la Conquista, cap. 2, 6.) Alvarado, in a letter to Cortés, expatiates on the "maravillosos et grandes edificios" to be seen in Guatemala. (Oviedo, Hist. de las Ind., MS., lib. 33, cap. 42.) According to Cogolludo, the Spaniards, who could get no tradition of their origin, referred them to the Phœnicians or Carthaginians. (Hist. de Yucatan, lib. 4, cap. 2.) He cites the following emphatic notice of these remains from Las Casas : "Ciertamente la tierra de Yucathan d.. á entender cosas mui especiales, y de mayor antiguedad, por las grandes, admirables, y excessivas maneras de edificios, y letreros de ciertos caracteres, que en otra ninguna parte se hallan." (Loc. cit.) Even the inquisitive Martyr has collected no particulars respecting them, merely noticing the buildings of this region with general expressions of admiration. (De Insulis nuper Inventis, pp. 334-340.) What is quite as surprising is the silence of Cortés, who traversed the country forming the base of Yucatan, in his famous expedition to Honduras, of which he has given many details we would gladly have exchanged for a word respecting these interesting memorials. Carta Quinta de Cortés, MS.—I must add that some remarks in the above paragraph in the text would have been omitted, had I enjoyed the benefit of Mr. Stephens's researches when it was originally written. This is especially the case with the reflections on the probable condition of these

these structures that they had ceased to be the living temples of the gods, since no merit of architecture, probably, would have availed to save them from the general doom of the monuments of Mexico.

If we find it so difficult to settle the age of these buildings, what can we hope to know of their architects? Little can be gleaned from the rude people by whom they are surrounded. The old Tezcucan chronicler so often quoted by me, the best authority for the traditions of his country, reports that the Toltecs, on the breaking up of their empire,—which he places, earlier than most authorities, in the middle of the tenth century,— migrating from Anahuac, spread themselves over Guatemala, Tehuantepec, Campeachy, and the coasts and neighbouring isles on both sides of the Isthmus.[94] This assertion, important, considering its source, is confirmed by the fact that several of the nations in that quarter adopted systems of astronomy and chronology, as well as sacerdotal institutions, very similar to the Aztec,[95] which, as we have seen, were also probably derived from the Toltecs, their more polished predecessors in the land.

If so recent a date for the construction of the American buildings be thought incompatible with this oblivion of their origin, it should be remembered how treacherous a thing is tradition, and how easily the links of the chain are severed. The builders of the pyramids had been forgotten before the time of the earliest Greek historians.[96] The antiquary still disputes whether the frightful inclination of that architectural miracle, the tower of Pisa, standing as it does in the heart of a populous city, was the work of accident or design. And we have seen how soon the Tezcucans, dwelling amidst the ruins of their royal palaces, built just before the Conquest, had forgotten their history, while the more inquisitive traveller refers their construction to some remote period before the Aztecs.[97]

The reader has now seen the principal points of coincidence insisted on between the civilization of ancient Mexico and the Eastern hemisphere. In presenting them to him, I have endeavoured to confine myself to such as rest on sure historic grounds, and not so much to offer my own opinion as to enable him to form one for himself. There are some material embarrassments in the way to this, however, which must not be passed over in silence. These consist, not in explaining the fact that, while the mythic system and the science of the Aztecs afford some striking points of analogy with the Asiatic, they should differ in so many more; for the same phenomenon is found among the nations of the Old World, who seem

structures at the time of the Conquest ; when some of them would appear to have been still used for their original purposes.

94 "Asimismo los Tultecas que escapáron se fuéron por las costas del Mar del Sur y Norte, como son Huatimala, Tecuantepec, Cuauhzacualco, Campechy, Tecolotlan, y los de las Islas y Costas de una mar y otra, que despues se viniéron á multiplicar." Ixtlilxochitl, Relaciones, MS., No. 5.

95 Herrera, Hist. general, dec. 4, lib. 10, cap. 1–4.—Cogolludo, Hist. de Yucatan, lib. 4, cap. 5. —Pet. Martyr, De Insulis, ubi supra.—M. Wal-

deck comes to just the opposite inference, namely, that the inhabitants of Yucatan were the true sources of the Toltec and Aztec civilization. (Voyage en Yucatan, p. 72.) "Doubt must be our lot in everything," exclaims the honest Captain Dupaix,—"*the true faith always excepted.*" Antiquités Mexicaines, tom. i. p. 21.

96 "Inter omnes eos non constat a quibus factæ sint, justissimo casu, obliteratis tantæ vanitatis auctoribus." Pliny, Hist. Nat., lib. 36, cap. 17.

97 *Ante*, p. 88.

to have borrowed from one another those ideas, only, best suited to their peculiar genius and institutions. Nor does the difficulty lie in accounting for the great dissimilarity of the American languages to those in the other hemisphere; for the difference with these is not greater than what exists among themselves; and no one will contend for a separate origin for each of the aboriginal tribes.[98] But it is scarcely possible to reconcile the knowledge of -Oriental science with the total ignorance of some of the most serviceable and familiar arts, as the use of milk and iron, for example; arts so simple, yet so important to domestic comfort, that when once acquired they could hardly be lost.

The Aztecs had no useful domesticated animals. And we have seen that they employed bronze, as a substitute for iron, for all mechanical purposes. The bison, or wild cow of America, however, which ranges in countless herds over the magnificent prairies of the west, yields milk like the tame animal of the same species in Asia and Europe; [99] and iron was scattered in large masses over the surface of the table-land. Yet there have been people considerably civilized in Eastern Asia who were almost equally strangers to the use of milk.[100] The buffalo range was not so much on the western coast as on the eastern slopes of the Rocky Mountains; [101] and the migratory Aztec might well doubt whether the wild, uncouth monsters whom he occasionally saw bounding with such fury over the distant plains were capable of domestication, like the meek animals which he had left grazing in the green pastures of Asia. Iron, too, though met with on the surface of the ground, was more tenacious, and harder to work, than copper, which he also found in much greater quantities on his route. It is possible, moreover, that his migration may have been previous to the time when iron was used by his nation; for we have seen more than one people in the Old World employing bronze and copper, with entire ignorance, apparently, of any more serviceable metal.[102]—

---

[98] At least, this is true of the etymology of these languages, and as such, was adduced by Mr. Edward Everett, in his Lectures on the Aboriginal Civilization of America, forming part of a course delivered some years since by that acute and highly accomplished scholar.

[99] The mixed breed, from the buffalo and European stock, was known formerly in the northwestern counties of Virginia, says Mr. Gallatin (Synopsis, sec. 5); who is, however, mistaken in asserting that "the bison is not known to have ever been domesticated by the Indians." (Ubi supra.) Gomara speaks of a nation, dwelling about 40° north latitude, on the northwestern borders of New Spain, whose chief wealth was in droves of these cattle (buyes con una giba sobre la cruz, "oxen with a hump on the shoulders,") from which they got their clothing, food, and drink; which last, however, appears to have been only the blood of the animal. Historia de las Indias, cap. 214, ap. Barcia, tom. ii.

[100] The people of parts of China, for example, and, above all, of Cochin China, who never milk their cows, according to Macartney, cited by Humboldt, Essai politique, tom. iii. p. 58, note. See, also, p. 118.

[101] The native regions of the buffalo were the vast prairies of the Missouri, and they wandered over the long reach of country east of the Rocky Mountains, from 55° north, to the headwaters of the streams between the Mississippi and the Rio del Norte. The Columbia plains, says Gallatin, were as naked of game as of trees. (Synopsis, sec. 5.) That the bison was sometimes found also on the other side of the mountains, is plain from Gomara's statement. (Hist. de las Ind., loc. cit.) See, also, Laet, who traces their southern wanderings to the river Vaquimi (?), in the province of Cinaloa, on the Californian Gulf. Novus Orbis (Lugd. Bat., 1633), p. 286.

[102] Ante, p. 67.
Thus Lucretius:

" Et prior æris erat, quam ferri cognitus usus,
Quo facilis magis est natura, et copia major.
Ære solum terræ tractabant, æreque belli
Miscebant fluctus."

De Rerum Natura, lib. 5.

According to Carli, the Chinese were acquainted with iron 3000 years before Christ. (Lettres Améric., tom. ii. p. 63.) Sir J. G. Wilkinson, in an elaborate inquiry into its first appearance among the people of Europe and Western Asia, finds no traces of it earlier than the sixteenth century before the Christian era. (Ancient Egyptians, vol. iii. pp. 241-246.)

Such is the explanation, unsatisfactory, indeed, but the best that suggests itself, of this curious anomaly.

The consideration of these and similar difficulties has led some writers to regard the antique American civilization as purely indigenous. Whichever way we turn, the subject is full of embarrassment. It is easy, indeed, by fastening the attention on one portion of it, to come to a conclusion. In this way, while some feel little hesitation in pronouncing the American civilization original, others, no less certainly, discern in it a Hebrew, or an Egyptian, or a Chinese, or a Tartar origin, as their eyes are attracted by the light of analogy too exclusively to this or the other quarter. The number of contradictory lights, of itself, perplexes the judgment, and prevents us from arriving at a precise and positive inference. Indeed, the affectation of this, in so doubtful a matter, argues a most unphilosophical mind. Yet where there is most doubt there is often the most dogmatism.

The reader of the preceding pages may perhaps acquiesce in the general conclusions—not startling by their novelty—

First, that the coincidences are sufficiently strong to authorize a belief that the civilization of Anahuac was in some degree influenced by that of Eastern Asia.

And, secondly, that the discrepancies are such as to carry back the communication to a very remote period ; so remote that this foreign influence has been too feeble to interfere materially with the growth of what may be regarded in its essential features as a peculiar and indigenous civilization.

The origin of the most useful arts is lost in darkness. Their very utility is one cause of this, from the rapidity with which they are diffused among distant nations. Another cause is, that in the first ages of the discovery men are more occupied with availing themselves of it than with recording its history ; until time turns history into fiction. Instances are familiar to every schoolboy.

APPENDIX.

PART II.

——o——

ORIGINAL DOCUMENTS.

No. I.—See p. 72, *note* 3.

ADVICE OF AN AZTEC MOTHER TO HER DAUGHTER; TRANS-
LATED FROM SAHAGUN'S "HISTORIA DE NUEVA-ESPAÑA,"
LIB. VI. CAP. XIX.

[I have thought it best to have this translation made in the most literal
manner, that the reader may have a correct idea of the strange mixture of
simplicity, approaching to childishness, and moral sublimity, which belongs to the original. It is the product of the twilight of civilization.]

My beloved daughter, very dear little dove, you have already heard and
attended to the words which your father has told you. They are precious
words, and such as are rarely spoken or listened to, and which have proceeded
from the bowels and heart in which they were treasured up ; and your beloved
father well knows that you are his daughter, begotten of him, are his blood,
and his flesh ; and God our Lord knows that it is so. Although you are a
woman, and are *the image of your father*, what more can I say to you than
has already been said ? What more can you hear than what you have heard
from your lord and father ? who has fully told you what it is becoming for you
to do and to avoid ; nor is there anything remaining, which concerns you, that
he has not touched upon. Nevertheless, that I may do towards you my whole
duty, I will say to you some few words.—The first thing that I earnestly charge
upon you is, that you observe and do not forget what your father has now told
you, since it is all very precious ; and persons of his condition rarely publish
such things ; for they are the words which belong to the noble and wise,—valuable as rich jewels. See, then, that you take them and lay them up in your
heart, and write them in your bowels. If God gives you life, with these same
words will you teach your sons and daughters, if God shall give you them.—
The second thing that I desire to say to you is, that I love you much, that you
are my dear daughter. Remember that nine months I bore you in my womb,
that you were born and brought up in my arms. I placed you in your cradle,
and in my lap, and with my milk I nursed you. This I tell you, in order that
you may know that I and your father are the source of your being ; it is we

2 T

who now instruct you. See that you receive our words, and treasure them in your breast.—Take care that your garments are such as are decent and proper ; and observe that you do not adorn yourself with much finery, since this is a mark of vanity and of folly. As little becoming is it, that your dress should be very mean, dirty, or ragged ; since rags are a mark of the low, and of those who are held in contempt. Let your clothes be becoming and neat, that you may neither appear fantastic nor mean. When you speak, do not hurry your words from uneasiness, but speak deliberately and calmly. Do not raise your voice very high, nor speak very low, but in a moderate tone. Neither mince, when you speak, nor when you salute, nor speak through your nose ; but let your words be proper, of a good sound, and your voice gentle. Do not be nice in the choice of your words. In walking, my daughter, see that you behave becomingly, neither going with haste, nor too slowly ; since it is an evidence of being puffed up, to walk too slowly, and walking hastily causes a vicious habit of restlessness and instability. Therefore neither walk very fast, nor very slow ; yet, when it shall be necessary to go with haste, do so,—in this use your discretion. And when you may be obliged to jump over a pool of water, do it with decency, that you may neither appear clumsy nor light. When you are in the street, do not carry your head much inclined, or your body bent ; nor as little go with your head very much raised ; since it is a mark of ill breeding ; walk erect, and with your head slightly inclined. Do not have your mouth covered, or your face, from shame, nor go looking like a near-sighted person, nor, on your way, make fantastic movements with your feet. Walk through the street quietly, and with propriety. Another thing that you must attend to, my daughter, is, that when you are in the street you do not go looking hither and thither, nor turning your head to look at this and that ; walk neither looking at the skies nor on the ground. Do not look upon those whom you meet with the eyes of an offended person, nor have the appearance of being uneasy, but of one who looks upon all with a serene countenance ; doing this, you will give no one occasion of being offended with you. Show a becoming countenance ; that you may neither appear morose, nor, on the other hand, too complaisant. See, my daughter, that you give yourself no concern about the words you may hear, in going through the street, nor pay any regard to them, let those who come and go say what they will. Take care that you neither answer nor speak, but act as ·if you neither heard nor understood them ; since, doing in this manner, no one will be able to say with truth that you have said anything amiss. See, likewise, my daughter, that you never paint your face, or stain it or your lips with colours, in order to appear well ; since this is a mark of vile and unchaste women. Paints and colouring are things which bad women use,—the immodest, who have lost all shame and even sense, who are like fools and drunkards, and are called *rameras* [prostitutes]. But, that your husband may not dislike you, adorn yourself, wash yourself, and cleanse your clothes ; and let this be done with moderation ; since if every day you wash yourself and your clothes it will be said of you that you are over-nice,—too delicate ; they will call you *tapepetzon tinemaxoch.*— My daughter, this is the course you are to take ; since in this manner the ancestors from whom you spring brought us up. Those noble and venerable dames, your grandmothers, told us not so many things as I have told you,— they said but few words, and spoke thus : " Listen, my daughters ; in this world it is necessary to live with much prudence and circumspection. Hear this allegory, which I shall now tell you, and preserve it, and take from it a warning and example for living aright. Here, in this world, we travel by a very narrow, steep, and dangerous road, which is as a lofty mountain ridge, on whose top passes a narrow path ; on either side is a great gulf without bottom ; and if you deviate from the path you will fall into it. There is need, therefore, of much discretion in pursuing the road. ' My tenderly loved daughter, my little dove, keep this illustration in your heart, and see that you do not forget it,—it will be to you as a lamp and a beacon so long as you shall live in this world. Only one thing remains to be said, and I have done. If God shall give you life, if you shall continue some years upon the earth, see that you guard yourself carefully, that no stain come upon you ; should you forfeit your chastity, and afterwards be asked in marriage, and should marry any one, you will never be fortunate, nor have true love,—he will always remember that you were not a virgin, and this will be the cause of great affliction and distress ; you will never be at peace, for your husband will always be suspicious of you. O my dearly beloved daughter, if you shall live upon the earth, see that not more than one man approaches you ; and observe what I now shall tell you, as a strict command. When it shall please God that you receive a husband, and you are placed under his authority, be free from arrogance, see that you do not neglect him, nor allow your heart to be in opposition to him. Be not disrespectful to him. Beware that in no time or place you commit the treason against him called adultery. See that you give no favour to another ; since this, my dear and much-loved daughter, is to fall into a pit without bottom, from which there will be no escape. According to the custom of the world, if it shall be known, for this crime they will kill you, they will throw you into the street, for an example to all the people, where your head will be crushed and dragged upon the ground. Of these says a proverb, " You will be stoned and dragged upon the earth, and others will take warning at your death. " From this will arise a stain and dishonour upon our ancestors, the nobles and senators from whom we are descended. You will tarnish their illustrious fame, and their glory, by the filthiness and impurity of your sin. You will, likewise, lose your reputation, your nobility, and honour of birth ; your name will be forgotten and abhorred. Of you will it be said that you were buried in the dust of your sins. And remember, my daughter, that, though no man shall see you, nor your husband ever know what happens, *God, who is in every place, sees you,* will be angry with you, and will also excite the indignation of the people against you, and will be avenged upon you as he shall see fit. By his command, you shall either be maimed, or struck blind, or your body will wither, or you will come to extreme poverty, for daring to injure your husband. Or perhaps he will give you to death, and put you under his feet, sending you to the place of torment. Our Lord is compassionate ; but, if you commit treason against your husband, God, who is in every place, shall take vengeance on your sin, and will permit you to have neither contentment, nor repose, nor a peaceful life ; and he will excite your husband to be always unkind towards you, and always to speak to you with anger. My dear daughter, whom I tenderly love, see that you live in the world in peace, tranquillity, and contentment, all the days that you shall live. See that you disgrace not yourself, that you stain not your honour, nor pollute the lustre and fame of your ancestors. See that you honour me and your father, and reflect glory on us by your good life. May God prosper you, my first-born, and may you come to God, who is in every place.

No. II.—See p. 83.

A CASTILIAN AND AN ENGLISH TRANSLATION OF A POEM ON THE MUTABILITY OF LIFE, BY NEZAHUALCOYOTL, LORD OF TEZCUCO.

[This poem was fortunately rescued from the fate of too many of the Indian MSS., by the chevalier Boturini, and formed part of his valuable *Muséo*. It was subsequently incorporated in the extensive collection of documents made by Father Manuel de la Vega, in Mexico, 1792. This magnificent collection was made in obedience to an enlightened order of the Spanish government, "that all such MSS. as could be found in New Spain, fitted to illustrate the antiquities, geography, civil, ecclesiastical, and natural history of America, should be copied and transmitted to Madrid." This order was obeyed, and the result was a collection of thirty-two volumes in folio, which, amidst much that is trivial and of little worth, contains also a mass of original materials, of inestimable value to the historian of Mexico and of the various races who occupied the country of New Spain.]

Un rato cantar quiero,
pues la ocasion y el tiempo se ofrece ;
ser admitido espero,
si intento lo merece ;
y comienzo mi canto,
aunque fuera mejor llamarle llanto.

Y tú, querido Amigo,
goza la amenidad de aquestas flores,
alégrate conmigo ;
desechemos de pena los temores,
que el gusto trae medida,
por ser al fin con fin la mala vida.

Io tocaré cantando
el músico instrumento sonoroso,
tú de flores gozando
danza, y festeja á Dios que es Poderoso ;
gocemos de esta gloria,
porque la humana vida es transitoria.

De Ocblehacan pusíste
en esta noble Corte, y siendo tuyo,
tus sillas, y quisiste
vestirlas ; donde arguyo,
que con grandeza tanta
el Imperio se aumenta y se levanta.

Oyoyotzin prudente,
famoso Rey y singular Monarca,
goza del bien presente.

que lo presente lo florido abarca;
porque vendrá algun dia
que busques este gusto y alegría.

  Entonces tu Fortuna
te ha de quitar el Cetro de la mano,
ha de menguar tu Luna
no te verás tan fuerte y tan ufano;
entonces tus criados
de todo bien serán desamparados.

  Y en tan triste suceso
los nobles descendientes de tu nido,
de Príncipes el peso,
los que de nobles Padres han nacido,
faltando tú Cabeza,
gustarán la amargura de pobreza.

  Y traerán á la memoria
quien fuíste en pompa de todos envidiada
tus triunfos y victoria;
y con la gloria y Magestad pasada
cotejando pesares,
de lágrimas harán crecidas Mares.

  Y estos tus descendientes,
que te sirven de pluma y de corona
de tí viéndose ausentes,
de Culhuacan estrañarán la cuna,
y tenidos por tales
con sus desdichas crecerán sus males.

  Y de esta grandeza rara,
digna de mil coronas y blasones,
será la fama avara;
solo se acordarán en las naciones,
lo bien que governáron,
las tres Cabezas que el imperio honráron.

  En México famosa
Moctezumá, valor de pecho Indiano;
á Culhuacan dichosa
de Neçahualcoyotl rigió la mano;
Acatlapan la fuerte
Totoquilhuastli le salió por suerte.

  Y ningun olvido temo
de lo bien que tu reyno dispusíste,
estando en el supremo
lugar, que de la mano recibíste
de aquel Señor del Mundo,
factor de aquestas cosas sin segundo.

  Y goza pues muy gustoso,
O Neçahualcoyotl, lo que agora tienes
con flores de este hermoso
jardin corona tus ilustres sienes;
oye mi canto, y lira
que á darte gustos y placeres tira.

Y los gustos de esta vida,
sus riquezas, y mandos son prestados
son sustancia fingida,
con apariencias solo matizados ;
y es tan gran verdad esta,
que á una pregunta me has de dar respuesta.
        ¿ Y que es de Cihuapan,
y Quantzintecomtzin el valiente,
y Conahuatzin ;
que es de toda esa gente ?
sus voces ; ¡ agora acaso !
ya están en la otra vida, este es el caso.
        ¡ Ojala los, que agora
juntos los tiene del amor el hilo,
que amistad atesora,
vieramos de la muerte el duro filo !
porque no hay bien seguro,
que siempre trae mudanza á lo futuro.

Now would I sing, since time and place
        Are mine,—and oh ! with thee
May this my song obtain the grace
        My purpose claims for me.
I wake these notes on song intent,
But call it rather a lament.
Do thou, beloved, now delight
In these my flowers, pure and bright,
        Rejoicing with thy friend ;
Now let us banish pain and fear,
For, if our joys are measured here,
        Life's sadness hath its end.

And I will strike, to aid my voice,
        The deep, sonorous chord ;
Thou, dancing, in these flowers rejoice,
        And feast Earth's mighty Lord ;
Seize we the glories of to-day,
For mortal life fleets fast away.—
In Ocblehacan, all thine own,
Thy hand hath placed the noble throne
        Which thou hast richly dressed ;
From whence I argue that thy sway
Shall be augmented day by day,
        In rising greatness blessed.

Wise Oyoyotzin ! prudent king !
        Unrivalled Prince, and great !
Enjoy the fragrant flowers that spring
        Around thy kingly state :

A day will come which shall destroy
Thy present bliss,—thy present joy,—
When fate the sceptre of command
Shall wrench from out thy royal hand,—
   Thy moon diminished rise ;
And, as thy pride and strength are quenched,
From thy adherents shall be wrenched
   All that they love or prize.

When sorrow shall my truth attest,
   And this thy throne decline,—
The birds of thy ancestral nest,
   The princes of thy line,—
The mighty of thy race,—shall see
The bitter ills of poverty ;—
And then shall memory recall
Thy envied greatness, and on all
   Thy brilliant triumphs dwell ;
And as they think on bygone years,
Compared with present shame, their tears
   Shall to an ocean swell.

And those who, though a royal band,
   Serve thee for crown, or plume,
Remote from Culhuacan's land
   Shall find the exile's doom.
Deprived of thee,—their rank forgot,—
Misfortune shall o'erwhelm their lot.
Then fame shall grudgingly withhold
Her meed to greatness, which of old
   Blazons and crowns displayed ;
The people will retain alone
Remembrance of that *triple throne*
   Which this our land obeyed.

Brave Moctezuma's Indian land
   Was Mexico the great,
And Nezahualcoyotl's hand
   Blessed Culhuacan's state,
Whilst Totoquil his portion drew
In Acatlapan, strong and true ;
But no oblivion can I fear,
Of good by thee accomplished here,
   Whilst high upon thy throne ;
That station, which, to match thy worth,
Was given by the Lord of Earth,
   Maker of good alone.

Then, Nezahualcoyotl,—now,
   In what thou *hast*, delight ;
And wreathe around thy royal brow
   Life's garden blossoms bright ;

List to my lyre and my lay,
Which aim to please thee, and obey.
The pleasures which our lives present—
Earth's sceptres, and its wealth—are lent,
    Are shadows fleeting by ;
Appearance colours all our bliss ;
A truth so great, that now to this
    One question, make reply.

What has become of Cihuapan,
    Quantzintecomtzin brave,
And Conahuatzin, mighty man ;
    Where are they ?   In the grave !
Their names remain, but they are fled,
For ever numbered with the dead.
Would that those now in friendship bound,
We whom Love's thread encircles round,
    Death's cruel edge might see !
Since good on earth is insecure,
And all things must a change endure
    In dark futurity !

No. III.—See p. 84.

DESCRIPTION OF THE RESIDENCE OF NEZAHUALCOYOTL AT TEZCOTZINCO, EXTRACTED FROM IXTLILXOCHITL'S "HISTORIA CHICHIMECA," MS., Cap. XLII.

De los jardines el mas ameno y de curiosidades fué el Bosque de Tezcotzinco ; porque demas de la cerca tan grande que tenia, para subir á la cumbre de él, y andarlo todo, tenia sus gradas, parte de ellas de argamasa, parte labrada en la misma peña ; y el agua que se trahia para las Fuentes, Pilas, y Baños, y los caños que se repartian para el riego de las Flores y arboledas de este Bosque, para poderla traer desde su Nacimiento, fué menester hacer fuertes y altíssimas murallas de argamasa desde unas sierras á otras, de increible grandeza ; sobre la qual hizo una Fargea hasta venir á dar á la mas alta del Bosque, y á las espaldas de la cumbre de él En el primer Estanque de Agua estaba una Peña esculpida en ella en circunferencia los años desde que havia nacido el Rey Nezahualcoiotzin hasta la edad de aquel tiempo ; y por la parte de afuera los años en fin de cada uno de ellos, así mismo esculpidas las cosas mas memorables que hizo ; y por dentro de la rueda esculpidas sus Armas, que eran una casa, que estaba ardiendo, en llamas y desaciéndose ; otra que estaba muy ennoblecida de edificios : y en medio de las dos un pie de venado, atada en él una piedra preciosa, y salian del pie unos penachos de plumas preciosas, y así mismo una cierva, y en ella un Brazo asido de un Arco con unas Flechas, y como un Hombre armado con su Morrion y oregeras, coselete, y dos tigres á los Lados, de cuias bocas salian agua y fuego, y por orla, doce cabezas de Reyes y Señores, y otras cosas que el primer Arzobispo de México,

Don Fray Juan de Zumarraga, mandó hacer pedazos, entendiendo ser algunos Ídolos ; y todo lo referido era la etimología de sus Armas. Y de allí se partia esta agua en dos partes, que la una iba cercando y rodeando el Bosque por la parte del Norte, y la otra por la parte del Sur. En la cumbre de este Bosque estaban edificadas unas casas á manera de torre, y por remate y Chapitel estaba hecha de cantería una como á manera de Mazeta, y dentra de ella salian unos Penachos y plumeros, que era la etimología del nombre del Bosque ; y luego mas abajo, hecho de una Peña, un Leon de mas de dos brazas de largo con sus alas y plumas : estaba hechado y mirando á la parte del Oriente, en cuia boca asomaba un rostro, que era el mismo retrato del Rey, el qual Leon estaba de ordinario debajo de un palio hecho de oro y plumería. Un poquito mas abajo estaban tres Albercas de agua, y en la de en medio estaban en sus Bordos tres Damas esculpidas y labradas en la misma Peña, que significaban la gran Laguna y las Ramas las cabezas del Imperio ; y por un lado (que era hacia la parte del Norte) otra Alberca, y en una Peña esculpido el nombre y Escudo de Armas de la Ciudad de Tolan, que fué cabecera de los Tultecas ; y por el lado izquierdo, que caia hacia la parte del Sur, estaba la otra Alberca, y en la peña esculpido el Escudo de Armas y nombre de la Ciudad de Tenaiocan, que fué la cabecera del Imperio de los Chichimecas ; y de esta Alberca salia un caño de Agua, que saltando sobre unas peñas salpicaba el Agua, que iba á caer á un Jardin de todas flores olorosas de Tierra caliente, que parecia que llovia con la precipitacion y golpe que daba el agua sobre la peña. Tras este jardin se seguian los Baños hechos y labrados de peña viva, que con dividirse en dos Baños eran de una pieza ; y por aquí se bajaba por una peña grandísima de unas gradas hechas de la misma peña, tan bien gravadas y lizas, que parecian Espejos ; y por el pretil de estas gradas estaba esculpido el dia, mes, y año, y hora, en que se le dió aviso al Rey Nezahualcoiotzin de la muerte de un Señor de Huexotzinco, á quien quisó y amó notablemente, y le cojió esta nueva quando se estaban haciendo estas gradas. Luego consecutivamente estaba el Alcazar y Palacio que el Rey tenia en el Bosque, en los quales havia, entre otras muchas salas, aposentos, y retretes, una muy grandísima, y delante de ella un Patio, en la qual recivia á los Reyes de México y Tlacopan, y á otros Grandes Señores, quando se iban á holgar con él, y en el Patio se hacian las Damas, y algunas representaciones de gusto y entretenimiento. Estaban estos alcazares con tan admirable y maravillosa hechura, y con tanta diversidad de piedras, que no parecian ser hechos de industria humana. El Aposento donde el Rey dormia era redondo ; todo lo demas de este Bosque, como dicho tengo, estaba plantado de diversidad de Árboles, y flores odoríferas, y en ellos diversidad de Aves, sin las que el Rey tenia en jaulas, traidas de diversas partes, que hacian una armonia, y canto, que no se oian las Gentes. Fuera de las florestas, que las dividia, una Pared entraba la Montaña, en que havia muchos venados, conejos, y liebres, que si de cada cosa muy particular se describiese, y de los demas Bosques de este Reyno, era menester hacer Historia muy particular.

No. IV.—See p. 96, *note* 1.

TRANSLATION FROM IXTLILXOCHITL'S "HISTORIA CHICHIMECA," MS., Cap. LXIV.

OF THE EXTRAORDINARY SEVERITY WITH WHICH THE KING NEZAHUALPILLI PUN-
ISHED THE MEXICAN QUEEN FOR HER ADULTERY AND TREASON.

When Axaiacatzin, king of Mexico, and other lords, sent their daughters to king Nezahualpilli, for him to choose one to be his queen and lawful wife, whose son might succeed to the inheritance, she who had highest claims among them, from nobility of birth and rank, was Chachiuhnenetzin, daughter of the Mexican king. But being at that time very young, she was brought up by the monarch in a separate palace, with great pomp and numerous attendants, as became the daughter of so great a king. The number of servants attached to her household exceeded two thousand. Young as she was, she was yet exceedingly artful and vicious ; so that, finding herself alone, and seeing that her people feared her on account of her rank and import-ance, she began to give way to the unlimited indulgence of her lust. When-ever she saw a young man who pleased her fancy, she gave secret orders to have him brought to her, and, having satisfied her desires, caused him to be put to death. She then ordered a statue or effigy of his person to be made, and, adorning it with rich clothing, gold, and jewellery, had it placed in the apartment in which she lived. The number of statues of those whom she thus put to death was so great as almost to fill the apartment. When the king came to visit her, and inquired respecting these statues, she answered that they were her gods ; and he, knowing how strict the Mexicans were in the worship of their false deities, believed her. But, as no iniquity can be long committed with entire secrecy, she was finally found out in this manner. Three of the young men, for some reason or other, she had left alive. Their names were Chicuhcoatl, Huitzilimitzin, and Maxtla, one of whom was lord of Tesoyucan, and one of the grandees of the kingdom ; and the other two nobles of high rank. It happened that one day the king recognized on one of these a very precious jewel, which he had given to the queen ; and although he had no fear of treason on her part, it gave him some uneasiness. Pro-ceeding to visit her that night, her attendants told him that she was asleep, supposing that the king would then return, as he had done at other times. But the affair of the jewel made him insist on entering the chamber in which she slept ; and, going to awake her, he found only a statue in the bed, adorned with her hair, and closely resembling her. This being seen by the king, and also that the attendants around were in much trepidation and alarm, he called his guards, and, assembling all the people of the house, made a general search for the queen, who was shortly found at an entertainment with the three young lords, who were likewise arrested with her. The king referred the case to the judges of his court, in order that they might make an inquiry into the matter and examine the parties implicated. These discovered many individuals, servants of the queen, who had in some way or other been acces-sory to her crimes, workmen who had been engaged in making and adorning the statues, others who had aided in introducing the young men into the palace, and others again who had put them to death and concealed their bodies. The case having been sufficiently investigated, he despatched ambassadors to the kings of Mexico and Tlacopan, giving them information of the event, and signifying the day on which the punishment of the queen and her accomplices was to take place ; and he likewise sent through the empire to summon all the lords to bring their wives and their daughters, however young they might be, to be witnesses of a punishment which he designed for a great example.   He also made a truce with all the enemies of the empire, in order that they might come freely to see it.   The time being arrived, so great was the concourse of people gathered on the occasion, that, large as was the city of Tezcuco, they could scarcely all find room in it.   The execution took place publicly, in sight of the whole city.   The queen was put to the *garrote* [a method of strangling by means of a rope twisted round a stick]. as well as her three gallants ; and, from their being persons of high birth, their bodies were burned, together with the effigies before mentioned.   The other parties who had been accessory to the crime, who were more than two thousand persons, were also put to the *garrote*, and buried in a pit made for the purpose in a ravine near a temple of the Idol of Adulterers.   All applauded so severe and exemplary a punishment, except the Mexican lords, the relations of the queen, who were much incensed at so public an example, and, although for the present they concealed their resentment, meditated future revenge.   It was not without cause that the king experienced this disgrace in his household, since he was thus punished for the unworthy means made use of by his father to obtain his mother as a wife.

<hr />

No. V.—See p. 118.

INSTRUCTIONS GIVEN BY VELASQUEZ, GOVERNOR OF CUBA, TO CORTES ON HIS TAKING COMMAND OF THE EXPEDITION ; DATED AT FERNANDINA, OCTOBER 23, 1518.

[The instrument forms part of the Muñoz collection.]

Por quanto yo Diego Velasquez, Alcalde, capitan general, é repartidor de los caciques é yndios de esta isla Fernandina por sus Altezas, &c., embié los dias pasados, en nombre é servicio de sus Altezas, aver é bojar la ysla de Yucatan Sᵗᵃ María de los remedios, que neuvamente habia descubierto, é á descobrir lo demas que Dios Nʳᵒ Sᵒʳ fuese servido, y en nombre de sus Altezas tomar la posesion de todo, una armada con la gente necesaria, en que fué é nombre por capitan della á Juan de Grijalva, vezino de la villa de la Trinidad desta ysla, el qual me embió una caravela de las que llevava, porque le facia mucha agua, é en ella cierta gente, que los Indios en la dicha Sᵗᵃ María de los remedios le habian herido, é otros adolecido, y con la razon de todo lo que le habia ocurrido hasta otras yslas é tierras que de nuebo descubrió ; que là una es una ysla que se dice Cozumel, é le puso por nombre Sᵗᵃ Cruz ; y la otra es una tierra grande, que parte della se llama Ulua, que puso por nombre Sᵗᵃ María de las Niebes ; desde donde me embió la dicha caravela é gente, é me escribió como iba siguiendo su demanda principalmente á saber si aquella tierra era Isla, ó tierra firme ; é ha muchos dias que de razon habia de haber sabido nueva dél, de que se presume, pues tal nueva dél fasta oy no se sabe, que debe de tener ó estar en alguna ó estrema necesidad de socorro : é así mesmo porque una caravela, que yo embié al dicho Juan de Grijalva desdel puerto desta cibdad de Santiago, para que con él é la armada que lleva se juntase en el puerto de S^n Cristóbal de la Havana, porque muy mas proveido de todo é como al servicio de sus Altezas convenia fuesen, quando llegó donde pensó fallarle, el d^ho Juan de Grijalva se habia fecho á la bela é hera ido con toda la dicha armada, puesto que dejó abiso del viage que la d^ha carabela habia de llebar ; é como la d^ha carabela, en que iban ochenta, ó noventa hombres, no falló la d^ha armada, tomó el dicho aviso, y fué en seguimiento del d^ho Juan de Grijalva ; y segun paresze é se ha sabido por informacion de las personas feridas é dolientes, que el d^ho Juan de Grijalva me embió, no se habia juntado con él, ni della habia habido ninguna nueba, ni los d^hos dolientes ni feridos la supiéron á la buelta, puesto que viniéron mucha parte del biage costa á costa de la ysla de Sta M^a de los remedios por donde habian ydo ; de que se presume que con tiempo forzoso podria de caer acia tierra firme, ó llegar á alguna parte donde los dichos ochenta ó noventa ombres españoles corran detrimento por el nabío, ó por ser pocos, ó por andar perdidos en busca del d^ho Juan de Grijalva, puesto que iban muy bien pertrechados de todo lo necesario : ademas de esto porque despues que con el d^ho Juan de Grijalva embié la dicha armada he sido informado de muy cierto por un yndio de los de la d^ha ysla de Yucatan Sta María de los remedios, como en poder de ciertos Caciques principales della están seis cristianos cautibos, y los tienen por esclabos, é se sirben dellos en sus haciendas, que los tomáron muchos dias ha de una carabela que con tiempo por allí diz que aportó perdida, que se cree que alguno dellos deve ser Nicuesa capitan, que el católico Rey D^n Fernando de gloriosa memoria mandó ir á tierra firme, é redimirlos seria grandísimo servicio de Dios N^ro S^or é de sus Altezas : por todo lo qual pareciéndome que al servicio de Dios N^ro S^nr é de sus Altezas convenia inhiar así en seguimiento é socorro de la d^ha armada quel d^ho Juan de Grijalva llebó, y busca de la carabela que tras él en su seguimiento fué como á redimir si posible fuese los d^hos cristianos que en poder de los d^hos Indios están cautivos ; acorde, habiendo muchas veces pensado, é pesado, é platicadolo con personas cuerdas, de embiar como embié otra armada tal, é tambien bastecida é aparejada ansí de nabíos é mantenimientos como de gente é todo lo demas para semejante negocio necesario ; que si por caso á la gente de la otra primera armada, ó de la d^ha carabela que fué en su seguimiento hallase en alguna parte cerca de infieles, sea bastante para los socorrer ó descercar ; é si ansí no los hallare, por sí sola pueda seguramente andar é calar en su busca todas aquellas yslas tierras, é saber el secreto dellas, y faser todo lo demas que al servicio é de Dios N^ro S^or cumpla é al de sus Altezas combenga : é para ello he acordado de la encomendar á vos Fernando Cortés, é os imbiar por capitan della, por la esperiencia que de vos tengo del tiempo que ha que en esta ysla en mi compañia habeis servido á sus Altezas, confiando que soys persona cuerda, y que con toda pendencia é zelo de su real servicio daréis buena razon é quenta de todo lo que por mí en nombre de sus Altezas os fuere mandado acerca de la dicha negociacion, y la guiaréis ó encaminaréis como mas al servicio de Dios N^ro S^or é de sus Altezas combenga ; y porque mejor guiada la negociacion de todo vaya, lo que habeis de fazer, y mirar, é con mucha vigilancia y deligencia ynquirir é saber, es lo siguiente.

1. Hágase el servicio de Dios en todo, y quien saltaré castiga con rigor.

2. Castigaréis en particular la fornicacion.

3. Proibiréis dados y naipes, ocasion de discordias y otros excesos.

4. Ya salido la armada del p^{to} desta ciud^d de Santiago en los otros, dotaréis desta esta cuidado no se haga agravio á Españoles ni Indios.

5. Tomados los bastimentos necesarios en d^{hos} puertos, partiréis á v^{ro} destino, haciendo antes alarde de gente ó armas.

6. No consentiréis vaya ningun Indio ni India.

7. Salido al mar y metidas las barcas, en la de v^{ro} navío visitaréis los otros, y reconoceréis otra vez la gente con las copias [las listas] de cada uno.

8. Apercibiréis á los capitanes y Maestres de los otros navíos que jamas se aparten de v^{ra} conserva, y haréis quanto convenga para llegar todos juntos á la ysla de Cozumel Santa Cruz, donde será vuestra derecha derrota.

9. Si por algun caso llegaren antes que vos, les mandaréis que nadie sea osado á tratar mal á los Indios, ni les diga la causa porque vais, ni les demande ó interrogue por los cristianos captivos en la Isla de Sta María de los remedios : digan solo que vos hablaréis en llegando.

10. Llegado á d^{ha} ysla de Sta Cruz veréis y sondearéis los puertos, entradas, y aguadas, así della como de Sta María de los remedios, y la punta de Sta María de las Nieves, para dar cumplida relacion de todo.

11. Diréis á los Indios de Cozumel, Sta Cruz, y demas partes, que vais por mandado del Rey á visitarles ; hablaréis de su poder y conquistas, individuando las hechas en estas Islas y Tierra firme, de sus mercedes á quantos le sirven ; que ellos se vengan á su obediencia y den muestras dello, regalándole, como los otros han hecho, con oro, perlas, &c., para que eche de ver su buena voluntad y les favorezca y defienda : que yo les aseguro de todo en su nombre, que me pesó mucho de la batalla que con ellos ovo Francisco Hernandez, y os embió para darles á entender como Su Alteza quiere que sean bien tratados, &c,

12. Tomaréis entera informacion de las cruces que diz se hallan en d^{ha} Isla Sta Cruz adoradas por los Indios, del orígen y causas de semejante costumbre.

13. En general sabréis quanto concierne á la religion de la tierra.

14. Y cuidad mucho de doctrinarlos en la verdadera fee, pues esta es la causa principal porque sus Altezas permiten estos descubrimientos.

15. Inquirid de la armada de Juan de Grijalva, y de la caravela que llevó en su seguimiento Cristóv. de Olid.

16. Caso de juntaros con la armada, búsquese la caravela, y concertad donde podréis juntaros otra vez todos.

17. Lo mismo haréis si 1° se halla la caravela.

18. Iréis por la costa de la Isla de Yucatan Sta María de los remedios, do están seis cristianos en poder de unos caciques á quienes dice conocer Melchor Indio de allí, que con vos llevais. Tratadlo con mucho amor, para que os le tenga y sirva fielmente. No sea que os suceda algun daño, por que los Indios de aquella tierra son de ordinario en caso de guerra so mañosos.

19. Donde quiera, trataréis muy bien á los Indios.

20. Quantos rescates hicieredes meteréis en arca de tres llaves de que tendréis vos una, las otras el Veedor y el Tesorero que nombraredes.

21. Quando se necesite hacer agua, ó leña, &c., embiaréis personas cuerdas al mando dél de mayor confianza, que ni causen escándalo ni se pongan en peligro.

22. Si adentro la tierra viereis alguna poblacion de Indios que ofrecieren amistad, podréis ir á ella con la gente mas pacífica y bien armada, mirando mucho en que ningun agravio se les haga en sus bienes y mugeres.

23. En tal caso dejaréis á mui buen recabdo los navíos ; estaréis mui sobre aviso que no os engañen ni se entrometan muchos Indios entre los Españoles, &c.

24. Avisdo que placiendo á Dios N. S. ayais los X^{nos} que en la d^{ha} Isla de Sta M^a de los remedios están captivos, y buscado que por ella ayais la d^{ha} armada é la d^{ha} caravela, seguiréis vuestro viage á la punta llana ques el principio de la tierra grande que agora nuevamente el d^{ho} J. de Grijalva descubrió, y correréis en su busca por la costa della adelante buscando todos los rios é puertos della fasta llegar á la baia de S. Juan, y Sta M^a de los Nieves, que es desde donde el d^{ho} J. de Grijalva me embió los heridos é dolientes, é me escrivió lo que hasta allí le habia occurrido ; é si allí hallaredes, juntaros é ir con el J. ; porque entre los Españoles que llevais ó allá están no haya diferencias, . . . cada uno tenga cargo de la gente que consigo lleva, . . . y entramos mui conformes, consultaréis lo que mas convenga conforme á esta instruccion, y á la que Grijalva llevó de sus Paternidades y mias : en tal caso los rescates todos se harán en presencia de Francisco de Peñalosa, veedor nombrado por sus Paternidades.

25. Inquiriréis las cosas de las tierras á do llegareis, así morales como físicas, si hai perlas, especiería, oro, &c., part^{te} en Sta M^a de las Nieves, de donde Grijalva me embió ciertos granos de oro por fundir é fundidos.

26. Quando salteis en tierra sea ante v^{ro} S^{no} y muchos testigos, y tomaréis posesion della con las solemnidades usadas : inquirid la calidad de las gentes : porque diz que hay gentes de orejas grandes y anchas, y otras que tienen las caras como perros, . . . á que parte están las Amazonas, que dicen estos Indios que con vos llevais, que están cerca de allí.

27. Las demas cosas dejo á v^{ra} prudencia, confiando de vos que en todo tomeis el cuidadoso cuidado de hacer lo que mas cumpla al servicio de Dios y de SS. AA.

28. En todos los puertos de esta ysla do hallareis Españoles que quieran ir con vos, no lleveis á quien tuviere deudas, si antes no las paga ó da fianzas suficientes.

29. Luego en llegando á Sta M^a de las Nieves, me embiaréis en el navío que menos falta hiciere, quanto hubieredes rescatado y hallado de oro, perlas, especiería, animales, aves, &c., con relacion de lo hecho y lo que pensais hacer, p^a que yo lo mande y diga al Rey.

30. Conoceréis conforme á derecho de las causas civiles y criminales que ocurran, como Capitan desta armada con todos los poderes, &c. &c. F^{ha} en esta cibdad de Santiago puerto desta isla Fernandina, á 23 Oct., 1518.

No. VI.—See p. 129, *note* 1.

EXTRACT FROM LAS CASAS' "HISTORIA GENERAL DE LAS INDIAS," MS., LIB. III. CAP. CXVI.

[Few Spanish scholars have had access to the writings of Las Casas ; and I have made this short extract from the original, as a specimen of the rambling but vigorous style of a work the celebrity of which has been much enhanced by the jealous reserve with which it has been withheld from publication.]

Esto es uno de los herrores y disparates que muchos han tenido y echo en estas partes ; porque simprimero por mucho tiempo aver-á los yndios y á qual-quiera nacion ydolatria dotrinado es gran desvario quitarles los ýdolos ; lo qual nunca se hace por voluntad sino contra de los ydólatras ; porque ninguno puede dexar por su voluntad é de buena gana aquello que tiene de muchos años por Dios y en la leche mamado y autorizado por sus mayores, sin que primero tenga entendido que aquello que les dan ó en que les comutan su Dios, sea verdadero Dios. Mirad que doctrina les podian dar en dos ó en tres ó en quatro ó en diez dias, que allí estuviéron, y que mas estuvieran, del ver-dadero Dios, y tampoco les supieran dar para desarraygalles la opinion erro-nea de sus dioses, que en yéndose, que se fuéron, no tornáron á ydolatrar. Primero se han de rraer de los corazones los ydolos, conviene á saber el con-cepto y estima que tienen de ser aquellos Dios los ydólatras por diuturna y deligente é continua dotrina, ý pintalles en ellos el concepto y verdad del ver-dadero Dios, y despues ellos mismos viendo su engaño y error an de derrocar é destruir, con sus mismas manos y de toda su voluntad, los ýdolos que vener-aban por Dios é por dioses. Yasí lo enseña San Agustin en el sermon, *De puero centurionis, de verbis Domini.* Pero no fué aqueste el postrero disparate que en estas yndias cerca desta materia se a hecho poner cruces, ynduciendo á los yndios á la rreverencia dellas. Si ay tiempo para ello con sinificacion alguna del fruto que pueden sacar dello, si se lo pueden dar á entender para hacerse y bien hacerse, pero no aviendo tiempo ni lengua ni sazon, cosa super-flua é ynútil parece. Porque pueden pensar los yndios que les dan algun ýdolo de aquella figura que tienen por Dios los christianos, y así lo arán ydólatra adorando por Dios aquel palo. La mas cierta é conveniente regla é dotrina que por estas tierras y otras de ynfieles semejantes á estos los christianos deben dar é tener, quando van de pasada como estos yvan, é quando tambien quisieren morar entre ellas, es dalles muy buen exem-plo de hobras virtuosas y christianas, para que, como dice nuestro Redemptor, viéndolas alaben y den gloria al Dios é padre de los cristianos, é por ellas juzguen que quien tales cultores tiene no puede ser sino bueno é verdadero Dios.

No. VII.—See p. 156.

DEPOSITION OF ALONSO HERNANDEZ DE PUERTO-CARRERO, MS.

[Puerto-Carrero and Montejo were the two officers sent home by Cortés from Villa Rica with despatches to the government. The emissaries were examined under oath before the venerable Dr. Carbajal, one of the Council of the Indies, in regard to the proceedings of Velasquez and Cortés ; and the following is the deposition of Puerto-Carrero. He was a man of good family, superior in this respect to most of those embarked in the expedition. The original is in the Archives of Simancas.]

En la cibdad de la Coruña, á 30 dias del mes de Abril, de 1520 años, se tomó el d^{ho} é depusicion de Alonso Hernandez Puerto-Carrero por mí, Joan de Samano, del qual haviendo jurado en forma so cargo del juramento dijo lo sig^{te}.

Primeramente dijo, que en ell armada que hizo Fran^{co} Hernandez de Cordova é Caycedo é su compañero él no fué en ella; de la qual armada fué el d^{ho} Fran^{co} Hernandez de Cordova por Capitan General é principal armador; é que ha oido decir como estos descubrieron la Isla que se llama de Yucatan.

Item : dijo que en ell armada de que fué Capⁿ General Joan de Grijalva este testigo no fué; pero que vido un Capⁿ, que se dice Pedro de Alvarado, que embió Juan de Grijalva en una caravela con cierto oro é joyas á Diego Velasquez; é que oyó decir, que des que Diego Velasquez vido que traian tan poco oro, é el Capitan Joan de Grijalva se queria luego bolver é no hacer mas rescate, acordó de hablar á Hernandez Cortés para que hiciesen esta armada, por que al presente en Santiago no havia persona que mejor aparejo tuviese, i que mas bien quisto en la isla fuese, por que al presente tenia tres navíos; fuéle preguntado, como savia lo susod^{ho}; respondió, que porque lo avia oido decir á muchas personas de la isla.

Dice mas que se pregonó en el pueblo don este testigo vivia, que todas las personas que quisiesen ir en ell armada, de todo lo que se oviese ó rescátase habria la una tercera parte, é las otras dos partes eran para los armadores i navíos.

Fuéle preguntado, quien hizo dar el d^{ho} pregun, é en cuyo nombre se hacia, é quien se decia entonces que hacia la d^{ha} armada; respondió, que oyó decir, que Hernando Cortés havia escripto una carta á un Alc^e de aquel pueblo para que hiciese á pregonarlo; é que oyó decir, que Diego Velasquez habló con Hern^{do} Cortés para que juntam^{te} con él hiciesen la d^{ha} armada, por que al presente no habia otra persona que mejor aparejo en la dicha isla para ello tuviese, porque al presente tenia tres navíos, é era bien quisto en la isla; é que oyó decir, que si él no fuera por Capitan, que no fuera la tercera parte de la gente que con él fué; é que no sabe el concierto que entre sí tienen, mas de que oyó decir, que amvos hacian aquella armada, é que ponia Hern^{do} Cortés mas de las dos partes della, é que la otra parte cree este testigo que la puso Diego Velasquez, porque lo oyó decir, e despues que fué en la d^{ha} armada vido ciertos navíos que puso Hern^{do} Cortés, en lo que gastaba con la gente, que le pareció que ponia las dos partes ó mas, é que de diez navíos que fuéron en ell armada los tres puso Diego Velasquez, é los siete Cortés suyos é de sus amigos.

Dijo que le dijéron muchas personas que ivan en ell armada como Hern^{do} Cortés hizo pregonar, que todos los que quisiesen ir en su compañía, si toviesen nescésida de dineros así para comprar vestidos como provisiones ó armas para ellos, que fuesen á él, é que él les socoreria é les daria lo que hoviesen menester, é que á todos los que á él acodian que lo dava, é que esto sabe, porque muchas personas á quien el socorria con dineros que le dijéron; é que estando en la villa de la Trenidad, vió que él é sus amigos davan á toda la gente que allí estaba todo lo que havian menester; é así mesmo estando en la villa de Sant Cristobal en la Havana, vió hacer lo mismo, é comprar muchos puercos é pan, que podian ser tres ó cuatro meses.

Fuéle preguntado, á quien tenian por principal armador desta armada, é quien era público que la hacia; dijo que lo que oyó decir é vido, que Hern^{do} Cortés gastava las dos partes, é que los d^{hos} Diego Velasquez é Hern^{do} Cortés la hiciéron como d^{ho} tiene, é que no sabe mas en esto de este artículo.

Fuéle preguntado, si sabia quel d^{ho} Diego Valesquez fuese el principal por respecto de ser Governador por su Al. en las tierras é islas que por su industria se descobriesen ; que no lo sabe, por que no le eran entonces llegados Gonzalo de Guzman é Narvaez.

Fuéle preguntado, si sabe el d^{ho} Diego Velasquez sea lugar teniente de Governador é capitan de la isla de Cuba; dijo que ha oido decir, ques teniente de Almirante.

Fuéle preguntado, si sabia dellasi^{to} é capitulac^{n} que el dicho Diego Velasquez tomó con los Frailes Gerónimos en nombre de S. M., é de la instruccion que ellos para el descubrimiento le diéron ; dijo que oyó decir, que les havia f^{ho} relacion que havia descovierto una t^{rra} que era mui rica, é les embió á pedir le diesen lic^{a} para vojallá é para rescatar en ella, é los Padres Gerónimos que la diéron, é que esto sabe por que lo oyó decir : fuéle preguntado, si vió este asiento ó poderes algunos de los d^{hos} Padres ó la d^{ha} instruccion ; dijo que bien los puede haver visto, mas lo que en ellos iva, no se acuerda mas que lo arriva d^{ho}.

Fuéle preguntado, si vió ó oyó decir, que los dichos poderes é capitulac^{n} de los d^{hos} Padres Gerónimos fuese nombrado Diego Velasquez ó el d^{ho} Cortés ; dijo que en los poderes que los P^{es} Gerónimos embiáron á Diego Velasquez que á él seria, é no há Hernando Cortés, por que el d^{ho} Diego Velasquez lo embió á pedir.

Fuéle preguntado, como é porque causa obedecia á Hern^{do} Cortés por Cap^{n} General de aquella armada ; dijo que porque Diego Velasquez le dió su poder en nombre de su Al. para ir hacer aquel rescate ; é que lo sabe, porque vió el poder é lo oyó decir á todos ellos.

Fuéle preguntado, que fué la causa por que no usáron con el d^{ho} Hern^{do} Cortés de los poderes que llevaba del d^{ho} Diego Velasquez ; dijo que esta armada iva en achaque de buscar á Juan de Grijalva ; que oyó decir, que no tenia poder Diego Velasquez de los P^{res} Gerónimos para hacer esta armada ; é con este achaque que arriva dice hiciéron esta armada, é que él usó del poder que Diego Velasquez le dió, é allí rescató.

Fuéle preguntado, qué fué la causa porque, quando quisiéron poblar, le nombráron ellos por Capitan General é justicia mayor de nuevo ; dijo que Hernando Cortés, desque havia rescatado é vido que tenia pocos vastim^{tos}, que no havia mas de para bolver tasadamente á la isla de Cuba, dijo que se queria bolver ; é entonces toda la gente se juntaron é le requiriéron que poblase, pues los Yndios les tenian buena voluntad é mostravan que holgaban con ellos, é la t^{rra} era tan aparejada para ello, é S. M. seria dello mui servido ; é respondió, que él no traia poder para poblar, que él responderia ; é respondió, que pues era servicio de S. M. poblar, otejaba que poblasen ; é hiciéron Alc^{s} é Rexidores, é se juntáron en su cabildo, é le proveyéron de Xusticia mayor é Capitan General en nombre de S. M.

Fuéle preguntado, que se hiciéron los navios que llebáron ; dijo que desque pobláron venian los maestres de los navíos, á decir al capitan que todos los navíos se ivan á fondo, que no los podian tener encima dell agua ; i el d^{ho} Capitan mandó á ciertos maestres é pilotos que entrasen en los navíos é viesen los que estavan para poder navegar, é ver si se podiesen remediar ; é los d^{hos} maestres é pilotos digéron, que no havia mas de tres navíos que pudiesen navegar é remediarse, é que havia de ser con mucha costa ; é que los demas que no havia medio ninguno en ellos, é que alguno dellos se undió en la mar, estando echada el ancla ; é que con los demas que no estavan para poder navegar é remediarse, los dejáron ir al traves ; é que esta es la verdad, é firmólo de su nombre

2 U

Dijo que se acuerda que oyó decir, que Hernando Cortés havia gastado en esta armada cinco mill ducados ó castellanos ; é que Diego Velasquez oyó decir, que havia gastado mill é setecientos, poco mas ó menos ; é que esto que gastó fué en vinos é aceites é vinagre é ropas de vestir, las que les vendió un factor que ellá está de Diego Velasquez, en que les vendia el arroba de vino á cuatro castellanos que salia al respecto por una pipa cient. castellanos, el arroba del aceite á seis castellanos, é alomesmo la arrova del vinagre, é las camisas á dos pesos, y el par de los alpargates á castellano, é un mazo de cuentas de valoría á dos castellanos costándole á él á dos reales, é á este respecto fuéron todas las otras cosas ; é que esto que gastó Diego Velasquez lo sabe, porque lo vido vender, é este testigo se le vendió hasta parte dello.—Alonso Hernandez Portocarrero declaró ante mí, Johan de Samano.

No. VIII.—See p. 158.

EXTRACT FROM THE "CARTA DE VERA CRUZ," MS.

[The following extract from this celebrated letter of the Municipality of La Villa Rica de la Vera Cruz to the Emperor gives a succinct view of the foundation of the first colony in Mexico, and of the appointment of Cortés by that body as Chief Justice and Captain-General. The original is preserved in the Imperial Library at Vienna.]

Despues de se aver despedido de nosotros el dicho Caçique, y buelto á su casa, en mucha conformidad, como en esta armada venimos, personas nobles, cavalleros, hijos dalgo, zelosos del servicio de n^{ro} Señor y de V^{ras} Reales Altezas, y deseosos de ensalzar su Corona Real, de acrecentar sus Señoríos, y de aumentar sus rentas, nos juntámos y platicámos con el dicho capitan Fernando Cortés, diciendo que esta tierra era buena, y que segun la muestra de oro que aquel Caçique avia traido, se creia que debia de ser mui rica, y que segun las muestras que el dicho Caçique avia dado, era de creer que él y todos sus Indios nos tenian muy buena voluntad ; por tanto que nos pareçia que nos convenia al servicio de V^{ras} Magestades, y que en tal tierra se hiziese lo que Diego Velasquez avia mandado hacer al dicho Capitan Fernando Cortés, que era rescatar todo el oro que pudiese, y rescatado bolverse con todo ello á la Isla Fernandina, para gozar solamente de ello el dicho Diego Velasquez y el dicho Capitan ; y que lo mejor que á todos nos parecia era, que en nombre de V^{ras} Reales Altezas se poblase y fundase allí un pueblo en que huviese justicia, para que en esta tierra tuviesen Señorío, como en sus Reinos y Señoríos lo tienen ; porque siendo esta tierra poblada de Españoles, de mas de acreçentar los Reinos y Señoríos de V^{ras} Magestades, y sus rentas, nos podrian hacer mercedes á nosotros y á los pobladores que de mas allá viniesen adelante ; y acordado esto, nos juntámos todos en concordes de un ánimo y voluntad, y hizímos un requerimiento al dicho capitan, en el qual diximos, que pues él veia quanto al servicio de Dios n^{ro} Señor y al de V^{ras} Magestades convenia, que esta tierra estuviese poblada, dándole las causas de que arriba á V^{ras} Altezas se ha hecho relaçion, que le requerímos que luego cesase de hacer rescates de la manera que los venia á hacer, porque seria destruir la

tierra en mucha manera, y V^{ras} Magestades serian en ellos muy desservidos ;
y que ansí mismo le pedímos y requerímos que luego nombrase para
aquélla villa, que se avia por nosotros de hacer y fundar, Alcaldes y Regidores,
en nombre de V^{ras} Reales Altezas, con ciertas protestaciones, en forma que
contra él protestámos si ansí no lo hiziesen ; y hecho este requerimiento al
dicho Capitan, dixo que daria su respuesta el dia siguiente ; y viendo pues el
dicho Capitan como convenia al servicio de V^{ras} Reales Altezas lo que le
pediamos, luego otro dia nos respondió diciendo, que su voluntad estava mas
inclinada al servicio de V^{ras} Magestades que á otra cosa alguna, y que no
mirando al interese que á él se le siguiese, si prosiguiera en el rescate que
traia propuesto de rehacer los grandes gastos que de su hacienda avia hecho
en aquella armada juntamente con el dicho Diego Velasquez, antes poniéndolo
todo le placia y era contento de hacer lo que por nosotros le era pedido, pues
que tanto convenia al servicio de V^{ras} Reales Altezas ; y luego comenzó con
gran diligencia á poblar y á fundar una villa la qual puso por nombre la rica
Villa de Vera Cruz, y nombrónos á los que lá delantes subscribímos, por
Alcaldes y Regidores de la dicha Villa, y en nombre de V^{ras} Reales Altezas
recibió de nosotros el juramento y solenidad que en tal caso se acostumbra
y suele hacer ; despues de lo qual otro dia siguiente entrámos en nuestro
cabildo y ajuntamiento, y estando así juntos embiamos á llamar al dicho
Capitan Fernando Cortés, y le pedímos en nombre de V^{ras} Reales Altezas
que nos mostrase los poderes y instrucciones que el dicho Diego Velasquez le
avia dado para venir á estas partes, el qual embió luego por ellos y nos los
mostró ; y vistos y leidos por nosotros, bien examinados segun lo que pudímos
mejor entender, hallámos á nuestro parecer que por los dichos poderes y
instrucciones no tenia mas poder el dicho capitan Fernando Cortés, y que por
aver ya espirado no podia usar de justicia ni de Capitan de allí adelante ;
pareciéndonos pues, mui Excellentíssimos Príncipes ! que para la pacificacion
y concordia de entre nosotros, y para nos gobernar bien, convenia poner una
persona para su Real servicio, que estuviese en nombre de V^{ras} Magestades en
la dicha villa y en estas partes por justicia mayor y capitan y cabeza, á quien
todos acatasemos hasta hacer relacion de ello á V^{ras} Reales Altezas para que
en ello proveyesen lo que mas servidos fuesen, y visto que á ninguna persona
se podria dar mejor el dicho cargo que al dicho Fernando Cortés, porque
demas de ser persona tal qual para ello conviene, tiene muy gran zelo y
deseo del servicio de V^{ras} Magestades, y ansí mismo por la mucha experiencia
que de estas partes y Islas tiene, de causa de los quales ha siempre dado
buena cuenta, y por haver gastado todo quanto tenia por venir como vino
con esta armada en servicio de V^{ras} Magestades, y por aver tenido en
poco, como hemos hecho relacion, todo lo que podia ganar y interese que
se le podia seguir si rescatara como traia concertado, y le proveimos en
nombre de V^{ras} Reales Altezas de justicia y Alcalde mayor, del qual recibímos
el juramento que en tal caso se requiere, y hecho como convenia al Real
servicio de V^{ra} Magestad, lo recibímos en su Real nombre en n^{ro} ajuntamiento
y cabildo por Justicia mayor y capitan de V^{ras} Reales armas, y ansí está y
estará hasta tanto que V^{ras} Magestades provean lo que mas á su servicio
convenga : hemos querido hacer de todo esto relaçion á V^{ras} Reales Altezas,
porque sepan lo que acá se ha hecho, y el estado y manera en que quedamos.

No. IX.—See p. 197.

EXTRACT FROM CAMARGO'S "HISTORIA DE TLASCALA" MS.

[This passage from the Indian chronicler relates to the ceremony of inauguration of a Tecuhtle, or merchant-knight, in Tlascala. One might fancy himself reading the pages of Ste.-Palaye, or any other historian of European chivalry.]

Esta ceremonia de armarse caballeros los naturales de México y Tlaxcalla y otras provincias de la Laguna Mejicana es cosa muy notoria ; y así no nos detendrémos en ella, mas de pasar secuntamente. Es de saber, que cualquier Señor, ó hijos de Señores, que por sus personas habian ganado alguna cosa en la guerra, ó que hubiesen hecho ó emprendido cosas señaladas y aventajadas, como tubiese indicios de mucho valor, y que fuese de buen consejo y aviso en la república, le armaban caballero ; que como fuesen tan ricos que por sus riquezas se enoblecian y hacian negocios de hijos y dalgo y caballero, los armaban caballeros por dos, diferentemente que los caballeros, de linea recta, porque los llamaban Tepilhuan : Al Mercader que era armado caballero, y á los finos que por descendencia lo eran, llamaban Tecuhtles. Estos Tecuhtles se armaban caballeros con muchas ceremonias. Ante todas cosas, estaban encerrados 40 ó 60 dias en un templo de sus Ídolos, y ayunaban todo este tiempo, y no trataban con gente mas que con aquellos que les servian, y al cabo de los cuales eran llevados al templo mayor, y allí se les daban grandes doctrinas de la vida que habian de tener y guardar ; y antes de todas estas cosas les daban grandes bejamenes con muchas palabras afrentosas y satíricas, y les daban de puñadas con grandes reprensiones, y aun en su propio rostro, segun atras dejámos tratado, y les horadaban las narices y labios y orejas ; y la sangre que de ellos salia la ofrecian á sus Ídolos. Allí les daban publicamente sus arcos y flechas y macanas y todo género de armas usadas en su arte militar. Del templo era llevado por las calles y plazas acostumbradas con gran pompa y regocijo y solemnidad : poníanles en las orejas orejeras de oro, y bezotes de lo mismo, llevando adelante muchos truhanes y chocarreros que decian grandes donaires, con que hacian reir las gentes ; pero como vamos tratando, se ponian en las narices piedras ricas, oradábanles las orejas y narices y bezos, no con yerros ni cosa de oro ni plata, sino con guesos de Tigres y leones y águilas agudos. Este armado caballero hacia muy solemnes fiestas y costosas, y daban muy grandes presentes á los antiguos Señores caballeros así de ropas como de esclavos, oro y piedras preciosas y plumerías ricas, y divisas, escudos, rodelas y arcos y flechas, á manera de propinas cuando se doctoran nuestros letrados. Andan de casa en casa de estos Tecuhtles dándoles estos presentes y dadivas, y lo propio hacen con estos armados caballeros despues que lo eran, y se tenia cuenta con todos ellos. Y era república ; y así no se armaban muchos caballeros hidalgos pobres, por su poca posibilidad, sino eran aquellos que por sus nobles y loables hechos lo habian merecido, que en tal caso los caciques cabeceros y los mas supremos Señores Reyes, pues tenian meromixto imperio con sus tierras, y orca y cuchillo para ejecutar los casos de justicia, como en efecto era así. Finalmente.

que los que oradaban las orejas, bezos, y narices de estos, que así se armaban caballeros, eran caballeros ancianos y muy antiguos, los cuales estaban dedicados para esto; y así como para en los casos de justicia y consejos de guerra. Servian estos caballeros veteranos en la república, los cuales eran temidos, obedecidos, y reverenciados en muy gran veneracion y estima. Y como atras dejámos dicho, que al cabo de los 40 ó 60 dies de ayuno de los caballeros nobles los sacaban de allí para llevarlos al templo mayor donde tenian sus simulacros ; no les oradaban entonces las orejas, narices, ni labios, que son los labios de la parte de abajo, sino que cuando se ponian en el ayuno, entonces ; y ante todas cosas les hacian estos bestiales espectáculos ; y en todo el tiempo de ayuno estaba en cura, para que el dia de la mayor ceremonia fuese sano de las heridas, que pudiesen ponerle las orejeras y bezotes sin ningun detrimento ni dolor ; y en todo este tiempo no se lavaban, antes estaban todo tiznados y embiajados de negro, y con muestras de gran humildad para conseguir y alcanzar tan gran merced y premio, velando las armas todo el tiempo del ayuno segun sus ordenanzas, constitutiones, y usos y costumbres entre ellos tan celebrados. Tambien usaban tener las puertas donde estaban ayunando cerradas con ramos de laurel, cuyo árbol entre los naturales era muy estimado.

No. X.—See p. 289.

EXTRACT FROM OVIEDO'S " HISTORIA DE LAS INDIAS," MS. LIB. XXXIII. CAP. LXVI.

[This chapter, which has furnished me with many particulars for the narrative, contains a minute account of Montezuma's household and way of life, gathered by the writer, as he tells us, from the testimony of different individuals of credit, who had the best means of information. It affords a good specimen of the historian's manner, and may have interest to the Castilian scholar, since the original has never been published, and, to judge from appearances, is not likely to be so.]

Quando este gran Príncipe Montezuma comia, estaba en una gran sala encalada é mui pintada de pinturas diversas ; allí tenia enanos é chocarreros que le decian gracias é donaires, é otros que jugaban con vn palo puesto sobre los pies grande, é le traian é meneaban con tanta facilidad é ligereza, que parecia cosa imposible ; é otros hacian otros juegos é cosas de mucho para se admirar los hombres. Á la puerta de la sala estaba vn patio mui grande, en que habia cien aposentos de 25 ó 30 pies de largo, cada uno sobre sí, en torno de dicho patío, é allí estaban los Señores principales aposentados como guardas del palacio ordinarias, y estos tales aposentos se llaman galpones, los quales á la contina ocupan mas de 600 hombres, que jamas se quitaban de allí, é cada vno de aquellos tenian mas de 30 servidores, de manera que á lo menos nunca faltaban 3000 hombres de guerra en esta guarda cotediana del palacio. Quando queria comer aquel príncipe grande, daban le agua á manos sus Mugeres, é salian allí hasta 20 dellas las mas queridas é mas hermosas é estaban en pie en tanto que él comia ; É traíale vn Mayordomo ó Maestresala 3000 platos ó mas de diversos manjares de gallinas, codornices, palomas, tórtolas, é otras aves, é algunos platos de muchachos tiernos guisados á su modo, é todo mui lleno de axi, é el comia de lo que las mugeres le trahian ó queria. Despues que habia acabado de comer se tornaba á labar las manos, é las Mugeres se iban á su aposento dellas, donde eran mui bien servidas ; É luego ante el señor allegábanse á sus burlas é gracias aquellos chocarreros é donosos, é mandaba les dar de comer sentados á vn cabo de la sala ; é todo lo restante de la comida mandaba dar á la otra gente que se ha dicho que estaban en aquel gran patio ; y luego venian 3000 Xicalos i cantaros ó ánforas de brevage, é despues que el señor habia comido ó bebido, é labádose las manos, íbanse las Mugeres, é acabadas de salir de la sala, entraban los negociantes de muchas partes, así de la misma cibdad como de sus señoríos ; é los que le habian de hablar incábanse de rodillas quatro varas de medir ó mas, apartados dél é descalzos, é sin manta de algodon que algo valiese ; é sin mirarle á la cara decian su razonamiento ; é él proveia lo que le parecia ; é aquellos se levantaban é tornaban atras retraiéndose sin volver las espaldas vn buen tiro de piedra, como lo acostumbraban hacer los Moros de Granada delante de sus señores é príncipes. Allí habia muchos jugadores de diversos juegos, en especial con vnos fesoles á manera de habas, é apuntadas como dados, que es cosa de ver ; é juegan cuanto tienen los que son Tahures entrellos. Ivan los Españoles á ver á Montezuma, é mandábales dar duchos, que son vnos banquillos ó escabelos, en que se sentasen, mui lindamente labrados, é de gentil madera, é decíanles que querian, que lo pidiesen é dárselo han. Su persona era de pocas carnes, pero de buena gracia é afabil, é tenia cinco ó seis pelos en la barba tan luengos como un geme. Si le parecia buena alguna ropa que el Español tubiese, pedíasela, é si se la dada liberalmente sin le pedir nada por ella, luego se la cobria é la miraba mui particularmente, é con placer la loaba ; mas si le pedian precio por ella hacíalo dar luego, é tomaba la ropa é tornábasela á dar á los christianos sin se la cobrir, é como descontento de la mala crianza dél que pedia el precio, decia : Para mí no ha de haber precio alguno, porque yo soy señor, é no me han de pedir nada deso ; que yo lo daré sin que me den alguna cosa ; que es mui gran afrenta poner precio de ninguna cosa á los que son señores, ni ser ellos Mercaderes. Con esto concuerdan las palabras que de Scipion Africano, que de sí decian aquella contienda de prestancia, que escrive Luciano, entre los tres capitanes mas excelentes de los antiguos, que son Alexandro Magno, é Anibal, é Scipion : Desde que nascí, ni vendí ni compré cosa ninguna. Así que decia Montezuma quando así le pedian prescio : Otro dia no te pediré cosa alguna, porque me has hecho mercader ; vete con Dios á tu casa, é lo que obieses menester pídelo, é dársete ha : É no tornes aca, que no soy amigo desos tratos, ni de los que en ellos entienden, para mas de dexárselos vsar con otros hombres en mi Señorío. Tenia Montezuma mas de 3000 señores que le eran subgetos, é aquellos tenian muchos vasallos cada uno dellos ; É cada qual tenia casa principal en Temixtitan, é habia de residir en ella ciertos meses del año ; É quando se habian de ir á su tierra con licencia de Montezuma, habia de quedar en la casa su hijo ó hermano hasta quel señor della tornase. Esto hacia Montezuma por tener su tierra segura, é que ninguno se le alzase sin ser sentido. Tenia vna seña, que trahian sus Almoxarifes é Mensageros quando recogian los tributos, é él que erraba lo mataban á él é á quantos dél venian. Dábanle sus vasallos en tributo ordinario de tres hijos uno, é él que no tenia hijos habia de dar vn Indio ó India para sacrificar á sus Dioses, é sino lo daban, habian de sacrificarle á él : Dábanle tres hanegas de mahiz vna, é de todo lo que grangeaban, ó comian, ó bebian ; En fin, de todo se le daba el tercio ; É él que desto faltaba pagaba con la cabeza. En cada pueblo tenian Mayordomo con sus libros del número de la gente é de todo lo demas asentado por tales figuras é caracteres quellos se entendian sin discrepancia, como entre nosotros con nuestras letras se entenderia vna cuenta mui bien ordenada. É aquellos particulares Mayordomos daban quenta á aquellos que residian en Temixtitan, é tenian sus alholíes é magazenes é depósitos donde se recogian los tributos, é oficiales para ello, é ponian en cárceles los que á su tiempo no pagaban, é dábanles término para la paga, é aquel pasado é no pagado, justiciaban al tal deudor, ó le hacian esclavo.

. . . .

Dexemos esta materia, é volvamos á este gran Príncipe Montezuma, el qual en vna gran sala de 150 pies de largo, é de 50 de ancho, de grandes vigas é postes de madera que lo sostenian, encima de la qual, era todo vn terrado é azutea, é tenia dentro desta sala muchos géneros de aves, é de animales. Havia 50 águilas caudales en jaolas, tigres, lobos, culebras, tan gruesas como la pierna, de mucho espanto, é en sus jaolas así mismo, é allí se les llevaba la sangre de los hombres é mugeres é niños que sacrificaban, é cebaban con ella aquellas bestias ; é habia vn suelo hecho de la mesma sangre humana en toda la dicha sala, é si se metia vn palo ó vara temblaba el suelo. En entrando por la sala, el hedor era mucho é aborrecible é asqueroso ; las culebras daban grandes é horribles silvos, é los gemidos é tonos de los otros animales allí presos era una melodía infernal, é para poner espanto ; tenian 500 gallinas de racion cada dia para la sustentacion desos animales. En medio de aquella sala habia vna capilla á manera de vn horno grande, é por encima chapada de las minas de oro é plata é piedras de muchas maneras, como ágatas é cornesinas, nides, topacios, planas desmeraldas, é de otras suertes, muchas é mui bien engastadas. Allí entraba Montezuma é se retrahia á hablar con el Dieblo, al qual nombraban Atezcatepoca, que aquella gente tienen por Dios de la guerra, y él les daba á entender, que era Señor y criador de todo, y que en su mano era el vencer ; é los Indios en sus arreitos y cantares é hablas le dan gracias y lo invocan en sus necesidades. En aquel patio é sala habia continuamente 5000 hombres pintados de cierto betun ó tinta, los quales no llegan á mugeres é son castos ; llámanlos papas, é aquestos son religiosos.

. . . .

Tenia Montezuma vna casa mui grande en que estaban sus Mugeres, que eran mas de 4000 hijas de señores, que se las daban para ser sus Mugeres, é él lo mandaba hacer así ; é las tenia mui guardadas y servidas ; y algunas veces él daba algunas dellas á quien queria favorecer y honrar de sus principales : Ellos las recibian como vn don grandísimo. Habia en su casa muchos jardines é 100 vaños, ó mas, como los que vsan los Moros, que siempre estaban calientes, en que se bañaban aquellas sus Mugeres, las quales tenian sus guardas, é otras mugeres como Prioras que las governaban : É á estas mayores, que eran ancianas, acataban como á Madres, y ellas las trataban como á hijas. Tuvo su padre de Montezuma 150 hijos é hijas, de los quales los mas mató Montezuma, y las hermanas casó muchas dellas con quien le pareció ; y él tubo 50 hijos y hijas, ó mas ; y acaeció algunas veces tener 50 mugeres preñadas, y las mas dellas mataban las criaturas en el cuerpo, porque así dicen que se lo mandaba el Diablo, que hablaba con ellas y decíales que se sacrificasen ellas las orejas y las lenguas y sus naturas, é se sacasen mucha sangre é se la ofreciesen, é así lo hacian en efeto. Parecia la casa de Montezuma vna cibdad mui poblada. Tenia sus porteros en cada puerta. Tenia

20 puertas de servicio ; entraban muchas calles de agua á ellas, por las quales entraban é salian las canoas con mahiz, é otros bastimentos, é leña. Entraba en esta casa vn caño de agua dulce, que venia de dos leguas de allí, por encima de vna calzada de piedra, que venia de vna fuente, que se dice cha-pictepeque, que nace en vn peñon, que está en la Laguna salada, de mui excelente agua.

No. XI.—See p. 594, *et alibi.*

DIALOGUE OF OVIEDO WITH DON THOAN CANO, AP. "HISTORIA DE LAS INDIAS," MS., LIB. XXXIII. CAP. LIV.

[The most remarkable, in some respects, of Oviedo's compositions is his *Quincuagenas,* a collection of imaginary dialogues with the most eminent persons of his time, frequently founded, no doubt, on the personal communications which he had held with them. In his "History of the Indies" he has also introduced a dialogue which he tells us he actually had with Don Thoan Cano, a Castilian hidalgo, who married Guatemozin's widow, the lovely daughter of Montezuma. He came into the country originally with Narvaez ; and as he was a man of intelligence, according to Oviedo, and his peculiar position both before and after the Conquest opened to him the best sources of information, his testimony is of the highest value. As such I have made frequent use of it in the preceding pages, and I now transcribe it entire, in the original, as an important document for the history of the Conquest.]

DIÁLOGO DEL ALCAYDE DE LA FORTALEZA DE LA CIBDAD É PUERTO DE SANTO DOMINGO DE LA ISLA ESPAÑOLA, AUTOR Y CHRONISTA DESTAS HISTORIAS, DE LA VNA PARTE, É DE LA OTRA, VN CABALLERO VECINO DE LA GRAND CIBDAD DE MÉXICO, LLAMADO THOAN CANO.

ALC. Señor, ayer supe que Vm. vive en la grand cibdad de México, y que os llamais Thoan Cano ; y porque yo tube amistad con vn caballero llamado Diego Cano, que fué criado del sereníssimo Príncipe Don Thoan, mi señor, de gloriosa memoria, deseo saber si es vivo, é donde sois señor natural, é como quedástes avecindado en estas partes, é rescibiré merced, que no rescibais pesadumbre de mis preguntas ; porque tengo necesidad de saber algunas cosas de la Nueva España, y es razon, que para mi satisfaccion yo procure entender lo que deseo de tales personas é hábito que merezcan crédito ; y ansí, Señor, recibiré mucha merced de la vuestra en lo que digo.

THOAN CANO. Señor Alcayde, yo soy él que gano mucho en conoceros ; y tiempo ha que deseaba ver vuestra persona, porque os soi aficionado, y querria que mui de veras me tubiesedes por tan amigo é servidor como yo os lo seré. É satisfaciendo á lo que Vm. quiere saber de mí, digo, que Diego Cano, Escribano de Cámara del Príncipe Don Thoan, y camarero de la Tapicería de su Alteza, fué mi tio, é ha poco tiempo que murió en la cibdad de Caceres, donde vivia é yo soy natural : Y quanto á lo demas, yo, Señor, pasé desde la Isla de Cuba á la Nueva España con el capitan Pámphilo de

Narvaez, é aunque mozo é de poco edad, yo me hallé cerca dél quando fué preso por Hernando Cortés é sus mañas ; é en ese trance le quebráron vn ojo, peleando él como mui valiente hombre ; pero como no le acudió su gente, é con él se halláron mui pocos, quedó preso é herido, é se hizo Cortés señor del campo, é truxo á su devocion la gente que con Pámphilo habia ido, é en rencuentros é en batallas de manos en México ; y todo lo que ha sucedido despues yo me he hallado en ello.   Mandais que diga como quedé avecindado en estas partes, y que no reciba pesadumbre de vuestras preguntas ; satisfaciendo á mi asiento, digo, Señor, que yo me casé con una Señora hija legítima de Montezuma, llamada doña Isabel, tal persona, que aunque se hobiera criado en nuestra España, no estobiera mas enseñada é bien dotrinada é Católica, é de tal conversacion é arte, que os satisfaria su manera é buena gracia ; y no es poco útil é provechosa al sosiego é contentamientos de los naturales de la tierra ; porque, como es Señora en todas sus cosas é amiga de los christianos, por su respecto é exemplo mas quietud é reposo se imprime en los ánimos de los Mexicanos.   En lo demas que se me preguntare, é de que yo tenga memoria, yo, Señor, diré lo que supiere conforme á la verdad.

ALC. Io acepto la merced que en eso recibiré ; y quiero comenzar á decir lo que me ocurre, porque me acuerdo, que fuí informado que su padre de Montezuma tubo 150 hijos é hijas, ó mas, é que le acaeció tener 50 mugeres preñadas ; É ansí escrebí esto, é otras cosas á este propósito en el capítulo 46 ; lo qual si así fué, queria saber, ¿como podeis vos tener por legítima hija de Montezuma á la S^{ra} Doña Isabel vuestra Muger, é que forma tenia vuestro suegro para que se conociesen los hijos bastardos entre los legítimos ó espurios, é quales eran mugeres legítimas é concubinas ?

CAN. Fué costumbre vsada y guardada entre los Mexicanos, que las mugeres legítimas que tomaban, era de la manera que agora se dirá.   Concertados el hombre é muger que habian de contraer matrimonio, para le efectuar se juntaban los parientes de ambas partes é hacian vn areito despues que habian comido ó cenado ; é al tiempo que los Novios se habian de acostar é dormir en vno, tomaban la halda delantera de la camisa de la Novia é atábanla á la manta de algodon que tenia cubierto el Novio.   É así ligados tomábanlos de las manos los principales parientes de ambos, é metian los en una cámara, donde los dejaban solos é oscuros por tres dias contiguos sin que de allí saliesen él ni ella, ni allá entraba mas de vna India á los proveer de comer é lo que habian menester ; en el qual tiempo deste encerramiento siempre habia bailes ó areitos, que ellos llaman mitote ; é en fin de los tres dias no hai mas fiesta. É los que sin esta cerimonia se casan no son habidos por matrimonios, ni los hijos que proceden por legítimos, ni heredan.   Ansí como murió Montezuma, quedáronle solamente por hijos legítimos mi Muger é vn hermano suio, é muchachos ambos ; á causa de lo qual fué elegido por Señor vn hermano de Montezuma, que se decia Cuitcavaci, Señor de Iztapalapa, el qual vivió despues de su eleccion solos 60 dias, y murió de viruelas ; á causa de lo qual vn sobrino de Montezuma, que era Papa ó sacerdote maior entre los Indios, que se llamaba Guatimuci, mató al primo hijo legítimo de Montezuma, que se decia Asupacaci, hermano de padre é madre de doña Isabel, é hizose señor, é fué mui valeroso.   Este fué él que perdió á Mexico, é fué preso, é despues injustamente muerto con otros principales Señores é Indios ; pues como Cortés é los christianos fuéron enseñoreados de México, ningun hijo quedó legítimo sino bastardos de Montezuma, ecepto mi Muger, que quedaba viuda, porque Guatimuci señor de México, su primo, por fixar mejor su estado, siendo ella mui muchacha, la tubo por muger con la cerimonia ya dicha del atar la camisa con la manta ; é no obiéron hijos, ni tiempo para procreallos ; é ella se convirtió á nuestra santa fee católica, é casóse con vn hombre de bien de los conquistadores primeros, que se llamaba Pedro Gallego, é ovo vn hijo en ella, que se llama Thoan Gallego Montezuma ; é murió el dicho Pedro Gallego, é yo casé con la dicha doña Isabel, en la qual me ha dado Dios tres hijos é dos hijas, que se llaman Pedro Cano, Gonzalo Cano de Saavedra, Thoan Cano, doña Isabel, é doña Catalina.

ALC. Señor Thoan Cano, suplícoos que me digais porque mató Hernando Cortés á Guatimuci : ¿revelóse despues, ó que hizo para que muriese ?

CAN. Habeis de saber, que así á Guatimuci, como al Rey de Tacuba, que se decia Tetepanquezal, é al Señor de Tezcuco, el capitan Hernando Cortés les hizo dar muchos tormentos é crudos, quemándoles los pies, é untándoles las plantas con aceite, é poniéndoselas cerca de las brasas, é en otras diversas maneras, porque les diesen sus tesoros ; é teniéndolos en contiguas fatigas, supo como el capitan Cristóval de Olit se le habia alzado en puerto de Caballos é Honduras, la qual provincia los Indios llaman Guaimuras, é determinó de ir á buscar é castigar el dicho Christóval de Olit, é partió de México por tierra con mucha gente de Españoles, é de los naturales de la tierra : é llevóse consigo aquellos tres principales ya dichos, y despues los ahorcó en el camino ; é ansí enviudó doña Isabel, é despues ella se casó de la manera que he dicho con Pedro Gallego, é despues conmigo.

ALC. Pues en cierta informacion, que se envió al Emperador Nuestro Señor, dice Hernando Cortés, que habia sucedido Guatimuci en el Señorío de México tras Montezuma, porque en las puentes murió el hijo é heredero de Montezuma, é que otros dos hijos que quedáron vivos, el vno era loco ó mentecapto, é el otro paralítico, é inaviles por sus enfermedades : É yo lo he escripto así en el capítulo 16, pensando quello seria así.

CAN. Pues escriba Vm. lo que mandare, y el Marques Hernando Cortés lo que quisiere, que yo digo en Dios y en mi conciencia la verdad, y esto es mui notorio.

ALC. Señor Thoan Cano, dígame Vm. ¿de que procedió el alzamiento de los Indios de México en tanto que Hernando Cortés salió de aquella cibdad é fué á buscar á Pámphilo de Narvaez, é dexó preso á Montezuma en poder de Pedro de Alvarado ? Porque he oido sobre esto muchas cosas, é mui diferentes las vnas de las otras ; é yo querria escrebir verdad, así Dios salve mi ánima.

CAN. Señor Alcayde, eso que preguntais es vn paso en que pocos de los que hai en la tierra sabrán dar razon, aunque ello fué mui notorio, é mui manifiesta la sinrazon que á los Indios se les hizo, y de allí tomáron tanto odio con los Christianos que no fiáron mas dellos, y se siguiéron quantos males ovo despues, é la rebelion de México, y pienso desta manera : Esos Mexicanos tenian entre las otras sus idolatrías ciertas fiestas del año en que se juntaban á sus ritos é cerimonias ; y llegado el tiempo de vna de aquellas, estaba Alvarado en guarda de Montezuma, é Cortés era ido donde habeis dicho, é muchos Indios principales juntáronse é pidiéron licencia al capitan Alvarado, para ir á celebrar sus fiestas en los patios de sus mezquitas ó qq. maiores junto al aposento de los españoles, porque no pensasan que aquel aiuntamiento se hacia á otro fin ; É el dicho Capitan les dió la licencia. É así los Indios, todos Señores, mas de 600, desnudos, é con muchas joyas de oro, é hermosos penachos, é muchas piedras preciosas, é como mas aderezados é gentiles hombres se pudiéron é supiéron aderezar, é sin arma alguna defensiva ni ofensiva, bailaban é cantaban é hacian su areito é fiesta segund su costumbre ; é al mejor tiempo que ellos estaban embebecidos en su regocijo, movido de cobdicia el Alvarado hizo poner en cinco puertas del patio cada 15 hombres, é en él entró con la gente restante de los Españoles, é comenzáron á acuchillar é matar los Indios sin perdonar á vno ni á ninguno, hasta que á todos los acabáron en poco espacio de hora. I esta fué la causa porque los de México, viendo muertos é robados aquellos sobre seguro, é sin haber merecido que tal crueldad en ellos hobiese fecho, se alzáron é hiciéron la guerra al dicho Alvarado, é á los christianos que con él estaban en guarda de Montezuma, é con mucha razon que tenian para ello.

ALC. ¿ Montezuma, como murió ? porque diversamente lo he entendido, y ansí lo he yo escripto diferenciadamente.

CAN. Montezuma murió de vna pedrada que los de fuera tiráron, lo qual no se hiciera, si delante dél no se pusiera vn rodelero, porque como le vieran ninguno tirara ; y ansí por le cubrir con la rodela, é no creer que allí estaba Montezuma, le diéron vna pedrada de que murió. Pero quiero que sepais, Señor Alcayde, que desde la primera revelion de los Indios hasta que el Marques volvió á la cibdad despues de preso Narvaez, non obstante la pelea ordinaria que con los christianos tenian, siempre Montezuma les hacia dar de comer ; é despues que el Marques tornó se le hizo grand recebimiento, é le diéron á todos los Españoles mucha comida. Mas habeis de saber, que el capitan Alvarado, como le acusaba la conciencia, é no arrepentido de su culpa, mas queriéndole dar color, é por aplacar el ánimo de Montezuma, dixo á Hernando Cortés, que fingiese que le queria prender é castigar, porque Montezuma le rogase por él, é que se fuesen muertos por muertos ; lo qual Hernando Cortés no quiso hacer, antes mui enojado dixo, que eran vnos perros, é que no habia necesidad de aquel cumplimiento ; é envió á vn principal á que hiciesen el Franquez ó Mercado ; el qual principal enojado de ver la ira de Cortés y la poca estimacion que hacia de los Indios vivos, y lo poco que se le daba de los muertos, desdeñado el principal é determinado en la venganza fué el primero que renovó la guerra contra los Españoles dentro de vna hora.

ALC. Siempre oí decir que es buena la templanza, é sancta la piedad, é abominable la soberbia. Dicen que fué grandísimo el tesoro que Hernando Cortés repartió entre sus mílites todos, quando determinó de dexar la cibdad é irse fuera della por consejo de vn Botello, que se preciaba de pronosticar lo que estaba por venir.

CAN. Bien sé quien era ese, y en verdad que él fué de parecer que Cortés y los Christianos se saliesen ; y al tiempo del efectuarlo no lo hizo saber á todos, antes no lo supiéron, sino los que con él se halláron á esa plática ; é los demas que estaban en sus aposentos é cuarteles se quedáron, que eran 270 hombres ; los quales se defendiéron ciertos dias peleando hasta que de hambre se diéron á los Indios, é guardáronles la palabra de la manera que Alvarado la guardó á los que es dicho ; é así los 270 Christianos, é los que dellos no habian sido muertos peleando todos, quando se rindiéron, fuéron cruelmente sacrificados : pero habeis, Señor, de saber, que desa liberalidad que Hernando Cortés vsó, como decis, entre sus mílites, los que mas parte alcanzáron della, é mas se cargáron de oro é joyás, mas presto los matáron ; porque por salvar el albarda murió el Asno que mas pesado la tomó ; é los que no la quisiéron, sino sus espaldas é armas, pasáron con menos ocupacion, haciéndose el camino con el espada.

ALC. Grand lástima fué perderse tanto Thesoro y 154 Españoles, é 45 yeguas, é mas de 2000 Indios, é entrellos al Hijo é Hijas de Montezuma, é á todos los otros Señores que trahian presos. Io así lo tengo escripto en el capítulo 14 de esta Historia.

CAN. Señor Alcayde, en verdad quien tal os dixo, ó no lo vidó, ni supo ó uiso callar la verdad. Io os certifico, que fuéron los Españoles muertos en eso, con los que como dixe de suso que quedáron en la cibdad y en los que se perdiéron en el camino siguiendo á Cortés, y continuándose nuestra fuga, mas de 1170; é así pareció por alarde; é de los Indios nuestros amigos de Tascaltecle, que decis 2000, sin dubda fuéran mas de 8000.

ALC. Maravíllome como despues que Cortés se acogió, é los que escapáron á la tierra de Tascaltecle, como no acabáron á él é á los christianos dexando allá muertos á los amigos; y aun así diz, que no les daban de comer sino por rescate los de Guaulip, que es ya término de Tascaltecle, é el rescate no le querian sino era oro.

CAN. Tenedlo, Señor, por falso todo eso; porque en casa de sus Padres no pudiéron hallar mas buen acogimiento los Christianos, é todo quanto quisiéron, é aun sin pedirlo, se les dió gracioso é de mui buena voluntad.

ALC. Para mucho ha sido el Marques é digno es de quanto tiene, é de mucho mas. É tengo lástima de ver lisiado vn cavallero tan valeroso é manco de dos dedos de la mano izquierda, como lo escrebí é saqué de su relacion, é puse en el capítulo 15. Pero las cosas de la guerra ansí son, é los honores, é la palma de la victoria no se adquieren durmiendo.

CAN. Sin dubda, Señor, Cortés ha sido venturoso é sagaz capitan, é los principales suelen hacer mercedes á quien los sirve, y es bien las hagan á todos los que en su servicio real trabajan; pero algunos he visto yo que trabajan é sirven é nunca medran, é otros que no hacen tanto como aquellos son gratificados é aprovechados; pera ansí fuesen todos remunerados como el Marques lo ha sido en lo de sus dedos de lo que la habeis lástima. Tubo Dios poco que hacer en sanarlo; y salid, Señor, de ese cuidado, que así como los sacó de Castilla, quando pasó la primera vez á estas partes, así se los tiene agora en España; porque nunca fué manco dellos, ni le faltan; y ansí, ni hubo menester cirujano ni milagro para guarecer de ese trabajo.

ALC. Señor Thoan Cano, ¿ es verdad aquella crueldad que dicen que el Marques vsó con Chulula, que es vna Cibdad por donde pasó la primera vez que fué á México?

CAN. Mui grand verdad es, pero eso yo no lo ví, porque aun no era yo ido á la tierra; pero supe lo despues de muchos que los viéron é se halláron en esa cruel hazaña.

ALC. ¿ Como oístes decir que pasó?

CAN. Lo que oí por cosa mui notoria es, que en aquella cibdad pidió Hernando Cortés 3000 Indios para que llevasen el fardage, é se los diéron, é los hizo todos poner á cuchillo sin que escapase ninguno.

ALC. Razon tiene el Emperador Nuestro Señor de mandar quitar los Indios á todos los Christianos.

CAN. Hágase lo que S. M. mandare é fuese servido, que eso es lo que es mejor; pero yono querria que padeciesen justos por pecadores: ¿ quien hace crueldades paguelas, mas él que no comete delicto porque le han de castigar? Esto es materia para mas espacio; y yo me tengo de envarcar esta noche, é es ya quasi hora del Ave María. Mirad, Señor Alcayde, si hay en México en que pueda yo emplearme en vuestro servicio, que yo lo haré con entera voluntad é obra. Y en lo que toca á la libertad de los Indios, sin dubda á vnos se les habia de rogar con ellos á que los tuviesen é governasen, é los industrasen en las cosas de nuestra sancta fee Católica, é á otros se debian quitar : Pero pues aquí está el Obispo de Chiapa, Fr. Bartolomé de las Casas, que ha sido el movedor é inventor destas mudanzas, é va cargado de frailes mancebos de su órden, con él podeis, Señor Alcayde, desenvolver esta materia de Indios. É yo no me quiero mas entremeter ni hablar en ella, aunque sabria decir mi parte.

ALC. Sin duda, Señor Thoan Cano, Vmd. habla como prudente, y estas cosas deben ser así ordenadas de Dios, y es de pensar, que este reverendo Obispo de Cibdad Real en la provincia de Chiapa, como celoso del servicio de Dios é de S. M., se ha movido á estas peregrinaciones en que anda, y plega á Dios que el y sus Frailes acierten á servirles ; pero él no está tan bien con migo como pensais, antes se ha quexado de mí por lo que escrebí cerca de aquellos Labradores é nuevos cavalleros que quiso hacer, y con sendas cruces, que querian parecer á las de Calatrava, seiendo labradores é de otras mezclas é género de gente baja, quando fué á Cubagua é á Cumaná, é lo dixo al Señor Obispo de S. Joan, don Rodrigo de Bastidas, para que me lo dixese, y ansí me lo dixo ; y lo que yo respondí á su quexa no lo hice por satisfacer al Obispo de San Joan, é su sancta intencion ; fué que le supliqué que le dixese, que en verdad yo no tube cuenta ni respecto, quando aquello escreví, á le hacer pesar ni placer, sino á decir lo que pasó ; y que viese vn Libro, que es la primera parte destas Historias de Indias, que se imprimió el año de 1535, y allí estaba lo que escrebí ; é que holgaba porque estabamos en parte que todo lo que dixe y lo que dexé de decir se provaria facilmente ; y que supiese que aquel Libro estaba ya en Lengua Toscana y Francesa é Alemana é Latina é Griega é Turca é Aráviga, aunque yo le escreví en Castellana ; y que pues él continuaba nuevas empresas, y yo no habia de cesar de escrebir las materias de Indias en tanto que S. S. M. M. desto fuesen servidos, que yo tengo esperanza en Dios que le dexara mejor acertar en lo porvenir que en lo pasado, y ansí adelante le pareceria mejor mi pluma. Y como el Señor Obispo de San Joan es tan noble é le consta la verdad, y quan sin pasion yo escribo, el Obispo de Chiapa quedó satisfecho, aun yo no ando por satisfacer á su paladar ni otro, sino por cumplir con lo que debo, hablando con vos, Señor, lo cierto ; y por tanto quanto á la carga de los muchos Frailes me parece en verdad que estas tierras manan, ó que llueven Frailes, pero pues son sin canas todos y de 30 años abajo, plega á Dios que todos acierten á servirle. Ya los ví entrar en esta Cibdad de dos en dos hasta 30 dellos, con sendos bordones, é sus sayas é escapularios é sombreros é sin capas, é el Obispo detras dellos. É no parecia vna devota farsa, é agora la comienzan no sabemos en que parará ; el tiempo lo dirá, y esto haga Nuestra Señor al propósito de su sancto servicio. Pero pues van hacia aquellos nuevos vulcanes, decidme, Señor, ¿ que cosa son, si los habeis visto, y que cosa es otro que teneis allá en la Nueva España, que se dice Guaxocingo ?

CAN. El Vulcan de Chalco ó Guaxocingo todo es vna cosa, é alumbraba de noche 3 ó 4 leguas ó mas, é de dia salia continuo humo é á veces llamas de fuego, lo qual está en vn escollo de la sierra nevada, en la qual nunca falta perpetua nieve, é está á 9 leguas de México ; pero este fuego é humo que he dicho turó hasta 7 años, poco mas ó menos, despues que Hernando Cortés pasó á aquellas partes, é ya no sale fuego alguno de allí ; pero ha quedado mucho azufre é mui bueno, que se ha sacado para hacer pólvora, é hai quanto quisiéron sacar dello : pero en Guatimala hai dos volcanes é montes fogosos, é echan piedras mui grandísimas fuera de sí quemadas, é lanzan aquellas bocas mucho humo, é es cosa de mui horrible aspecto. en especial como le viéron quando murió la pecadora de doña Beatriz de la

Cueva, Muger del Adelantado Don Pedro de Alvarado. Plega á nuestro Señor de quedar con Vmd., Señor Alcaide, é dadme licencia que atiende la Barca para irme á la Nao.

ALC. Señor Thoan Cano, el Espíritu Sancto vaya con Vm., y os dé tan próspero viage é navegacion, que en pocos dias y en salvamento llegueis á Vuestra Casa, y halleis á la S^ra doña Isabel y los hijos é hijas con la salud que Vmd. y ellos os deseais.

No. XII.—See p. 394.

GRANT OF CORTÉS TO DOÑA ISABEL MONTEZUMA, DAUGHTER OF THE EMPEROR MONTEZUMA ; DATED AT MEXICO, June 27, 1526.

[Montezuma, on his deathbed, commended, as we have seen in the History, three favourite daughters to the protection of Cortés. After their father's death they were baptized, and after the Conquest were married to Spaniards of honourable family, and from them have descended several noble houses in Spain. Cortés granted, by way of dowry, to the eldest, Doña Isabel, the city of Tacuba and several other places, embracing an extensive and very populous district. I have given here the instrument containing this grant, which has a singular degree of interest, from the notices it contains of Montezuma's last moments, and the strong testimony it bears to his unswerving friendship for the Spaniards. Some allowance must be made by the reader for the obvious endeavour of Cortés to exhibit Montezuma's conduct in so favourable a light to the Castilian government as might authorize the extensive grant to his daughter.

The instrument in the Muñoz collection was taken from an ancient copy in the library of Don Rafael Floranes of Valladolid.]

PRIVILEGIO DE DOÑA ISABEL MONTEZUMA, HIJA DEL GRAN MOTEZUMA, ÚLTIMO REY INDIO DEL GRAN REYNO Y CIBDAD DE MÉXICO, QUE BAUTIZADA Y SIENDO CHRISTIANA CASÓ CON ALONSO GRADO, NATURAL DE LA VILLA DE ALCANTARA, HIDALGO, Y CRIADO DE SU MAGESTAD, QUE HABIA SERVIDO Y SERVIA EN MUCHOS OFFICIOS EN AQUEL REYNO.

OTORGADO POR DON HERNANDO CORTÉS, CONQUISTADOR DEL DICHO REYNO, EN NOMBRE DE SU MAGESTAD, COMO SU CAPITAN GENERAL Y GOVERNADOR DE LA NUEVA ESPAÑA.

Por quanto al tiempo que yo, Don Hernando Cortés, capitan general é Governador desta nueva España é sus provincias por S. Mag^d, pasé á estas partes con ciertos Navíos é gente para las pacificar é poblar y traher las gentes della al dominio y servidumbre de la Corona Imperial de S. M. como al presente está, y despues de á ellos benido tuve noticia de un gran Señor, que en esta gran cibdad de Tenextitan residió, y hera Señor della, y de todas las demas provincias y tierras á ella comarcanas, que se llamaba Moteçuma, al qual hize saber mi venida, y como le supo por los Mensageros que le envié para que me obedeciese en nombre de S. M. y se ofreciese por su vasallo : Tuvo por bien la dicha mi venida, é por mejor mostrar su buen celo y voluntad de servir á S. M., y obedecer lo que por mí en su Real nombre le fuese mandado, me mostró mucho amor, é mandó, que per todas las partes que pasasen los Españoles hasta llegar á esta Cibdad se nos hiciese mui buen acogimiento, y se nos diese todo lo que hubiesemos menester, como siempre se hizo, y mui mejor despues que á esta cibdad llegámos, donde fuímos mui

bien recevidos, yo y todos los que en mi compañía benímos ; y aun mostró
haberle pesado mucho de algunos recuentros y batallas que en el camino se
me ofreciéron antes de la llegada á esta dicha cibdad, queriéndose él desculpar
dello ; y que de lo demas dicho para efetuar y mostrar mejor su buen deseo,
huvo por bien el dicho Moteçuma de estar debajo de la obediencia de S. M.,
y en mi poder á manera de preso asta que yo hiciese relacion á S. M., y del
estado y cosas destas partes, y de la voluntad del dicho Moteçuma ; y que
estando en esta paz y sosiego, y teniendo yo pacificada esta dicha tierra
docientas leguas y mas hacia una parte y otra con el sello y seguridad del dicho
señor Moteçuma, por la voluntad y amor que siempre mostró al servicio de
S. M., y complacerme á mí en su real nombre, hasta mas de un año, que se
ofreció la venida de Pánfilo de Narvaez, que los alborotó y escandalizó con
sus dañadas palabras y temores que les puso ; por cuyo respeto se levantó
contra el dicho señor Moteçuma un hermano suyo, llamado Auit Lavaci, Señor
de Iztapalapa, y con mucha gente que traxo assí hizo mui cruda guerra al
dicho Moteçuma y a mí y á los Españoles que en mi compañía estavan,
poniéndonos mui recio cerco en los aposentos y casas donde estavamos ; y
para quel dicho su hermano y los principales que con él venian cesasen la
dicha guerra y alzasen el cerco, se puso de una ventana el dicho Moteçuma,
y estándoles mandando y amonestando que no lo hiciesen, y que fuesen
vasallos de S. M. y obedeciesen los mandamientos que yo en su real nombre le
mandaba, le tiráron con muchas hondas, y le diéron con una piedra en la cabeza,
que le hiciéron mui gran herida ; y temiendo de morir della, me hizo ciertos
razonamientos, trayéndome á la memoria que por el entrañable amor que
tenia al servicio de S. M. y á mí en su Real nombre y á todos los Españoles,
padecia tantas heridas y afrentas, lo qual dava por bien empleado ; y que si
él de aquella herida fallecia, que me rogava y encargaba muy afetuosamente,
que aviendo respeto á lo mucho que me queria y deseava complacer, tuviese
por bien de tomar á cargo tres hijas suyas que tenia, y que las hiciese bautizar
y mostrar nuestra doctrina, porque conocia que era muibuena ; á las quales,
despues que yo gané esta dicha cibdad, hize luego bautizar, y poner por
nombres á la una que es la mayor, su legítima heredera, Doña Isabel, y á las
otras dos, Doña María y Doña Marina ; y estando en finamiento de la dicha
herida me tornó á llamar y rogar mui ahincadamente, que si él muriese, que
quirase por aquellas hijas, que eran las mejores joyas que él me daba, y que
partiese con ellas de lo que tenia, por que no quedasen perdidas, especialmente
á la mayor, que esta queria él mucho ; y que si por ventura Dios le escapaba
de aquella enfermedad, y le daba Victoria en aquel cerco, que él mostraria
mas largamente el deseo que tenia de servir á S. M. y pagarme con obras la
voluntad y amor que me tenia ; y que demas desto yo hiciese relacion á su
Magestad de como me dexaba estas sus hijas, y le suplicase en su nombre se
sirviese de mandarme que yo mirase por ellas y las tuviese so mi amparo y
administracion, pues él hera tan servidor y vasallo de S. M. y siempre tuvo
mui buena voluntad á los Españoles, como yo havia visto y via, y por el
amor que les tenia le havian dado el pago que tenia, aunque no le pesaba dello.
Y aun en su lengua me dixo, y entre estos razonamientos que encargaba la conciencia sobre ello.—Por ende acatando los mucho servicios que el dicho Señor
Moteçuma hizo á S. M. en las buenas obras que siempre en su vida me hizo,
y buenos tratamientos de los Españoles que en mi compañía yo tena en su real
nombre, y la voluntad que me mostró en su real servicio ; y que sin duda él no
fué parte en el levantamiento desta dicha cibdad, sino el dicho su hermano ; antes
se esperaba, como yo tenia por cierto, que su vida fuera mucha ayuda para que la

tierra estuviera siempre mui pacífica, y vinieran los naturales della en verdadero conocimiento, y se sirviera S. M. con mucha suma de pesos de oro y joyas y otras cosas, y por causa de la venida del dicho Narvaez y de la guerra que el dicho su hermano Auit Lavaci levantó, se perdiéron ; y considerando así mismo que Dios nuestro señor y S. M. son mui servidos que en estas partes planté nuestra santíssima Religion, como de cada dia la en crecimiento : Y que las dichas hijas de Moteçuma y los demas Señores y principales y otras personas de los naturales desta Nueva España se les dé y muestre toda la mas y mejor Dotrina que fuere posible, para quitarlos de las idolatrías en que hasta aquí han estado, y traerlos al verdadero conocimiento de nuestra sancta fee cathólica, especialmente los hijos de los mas principales, como lo era este Señor Moteçuma, y que en esto se descargava la conciencia de S. M. y la mia ; en su real nombre tuve por bien de azetar su ruego, y tener en mi casa á las dichas tres sus hijas, y hacer, como he hecho, que se les haga todo el mejor tratamiento y acogimiento que ha podido, haciéndoles administrar y enseñar los mandamientos de nuestra santa fe cathólica y las otras buenas costumbres de Christianos, para que con mejor voluntad y amor sirvan á Dios nuestro Señor y conozcan y los Artículos della, y que los demas naturales tomen exemplo. Me pareció que segun la calidad de la persona de la dicha Doña Isabel, que es la mayor y legítima heredera del dicho Señor Moteçuma, y que mas encargada me dejó, y que su edad requeria tener compañía, le he dado por marido y esposo á una persona de honra, Hijo-Dalgo, y que ha servido á S. M. en mi compañía dende el principio que á estas partes pasó, teniendo por mí y en nombre de S. M. cargos y oficios mui honrosos, así de Contador y mi lugartheniente de Capitan Governador como de otras muchas, y dado dellas mui buena cuenta, y al presente está á su administracion el cargo y oficio de visitador general de todos los Indios desta dicha Nueva España, el qual se dice y nombra Alonso Grado, natural de la villa de Alcantara. Con la qual dicha Doña Isabel le prometo y doi en dote y arras á la dicha Doña Isabel y sus descendientes, en nombre de S. M., como su Governador y Capitan General destas partes, y porque de derecho le pertenece de su patrimonio y legítima, el Señorío y naturales del Pueblo de Tacuba, que tiene ciento é veinte casas ; y Yeteve, que es estancia que tiene quarenta casas ; y Izqui Luca, otra estancia, que tiene otras ciento y veinte casas ; y Chimalpan, otra estancia, que tiene quarenta casas ; y Chapulma Loyan, que tiene otras quarenta casas ; y Escapucaltango, que tiene veinte casas ; é Xiloango, que tiene quarenta casas ; y otra estancia que se dice Ocoiacaque, y otra que se dice Castepeque, y otra que se dice Talanco, y otra estancia que se dice Goatrizco, y otra estancia que se dice Duotepeque, y otra que se dice Tacala, que podrá haver en todo mil y docientas y quarenta casas ; las quales dichas estancias y pueblos son subjetos al pueblo de Tacuba y al Señor della. Lo qual, como dicho es, doy en nombre de S. M. en dote y arras á la dicha Doña Isabel para que lo haya y tenga y goce por juro de heredad, para agora y para siempre jamas, con título de Señora de dicho Pueblo y de lo demas aquí contenido. Lo qual le doy en nombre de S. M. por descargar su Real conciencia y la mia en su nombre.—Por esta digo; que no le será quitado ni removido por cosa alguna, en ningun tiempo, ni por alguna manera ; y para mas saneamiento prometo y doy mi fe en nombre de S. M., que si se lo escriviese, le haré relacion de todo, para que S. M. se sirva de confirmar esta Merced de la dicha Doña Isabel y á los dichos sus herederos y subcesores del dicho Pueblo de Tacuba y lo demas aquí contenido, y de otras estancias á él subjetas, que están en poder de algunos Españoles, para que S. M. asimismo se sirva de-

mandárselas dar y confirmar juntamente con las que al presente le doy ; que por estar, como dicho es, en poder de Españoles, no se las dí hasta ver si S. M. es dello servido ; y doy por ninguna y de ningun valor y efeto qualquier cédula de encomienda y depósito que del dicho pueblo de Tacuba y de las otras estancias aquí contenidas y declaradas yo aya dado á qualquiera persona; por quanto yo en nombre de S. M. las revoco y lo restituyo y doi á la dicha Doña Isabel, para que lo tenga como cosa suya propia y que de derecho le pertenece. Y mando á todas y qualesquier personas, vecinos y moradores desta dicha Nueva España, estantes y habitantes en ella, que hayan y tengan á la dicha Doña Isabel por Señora del dicho pueblo de Tacuba con las dichas estancias, y que no le impidan ni estorven cosa alguna della, so pena de quinientos pesos de oro para la cámara y fino de S. Mag^d.—Fecho á veinte y siete dias del mes de Junio de mil y quinientos y veinte y seis años.—Don Hernando de Cortés.—Por mandado del Governador mi señor.—Alonso Baliente.

No. XIII.—See p. 447.

MILITARY CODE ; DATED AT TLASCALA, DEC. 22, 1520.

[These Regulations, proclaimed by Cortés at Tlascala on the eve of the final march against Mexico, show the careful discipline established in his camp, and, to some extent, the nature of his military policy. The Code forms part of the collection of Muñoz.]

ORDENANZAS MILITARES.

Este dia á voz de pregonero publicó sus Ordenanzas, cuyo proemio es este.

Porque por muchas escrituras y corónicas auténticas nos es notorio é manifiesto quanto los antiguos que siguiéron el exercicio de la guerra procuráron é travaxáron de introducir tales y tan buenas costumbres y ordenaciones, con las cuales y con su propia virtud y fortaleza pudiesen alcanzar y conseguir victoria y próspero fin en las conquistas y guerras, que hobiesen de hacer é seguir ; é por el contrario vemos haber sucedido grandes infortunios, desastres, é muertes á los que no siguiéron la buena costumbre y órden que en la guerra se debe tener ; e les haber sucedido semejantes casos con poca pujanza de los enemigos, segun parece claro por muchos exemplos antiguos é modernos, que aquí se podrian espresar ; é porque la órden es tan loable, que no tan solamente en las cosas humanas mas aun en las divinas se ama y sigue, y sin ella ninguna cosa puede haber cumplido efecto, como que ello sea un principio, medio, y fin para el buen reximiento de todas las cosas : Por ende yo, H. C., Capitan general é Justicia mayor en esta Nueva España del mar occéano por el mui alto, mui poderoso, é mui católico D. Cárlo nuestro Señor, electo Rey de Romanos, futuro Emperador semper Augusto, Rey de España é de otros muchos grandes reynos é Señoríos, considerando todo lo suso dicho, y que si los pasados falláron ser necesario hacer Ordenanzas é costumbres por donde se rigiesen é gobernasen aquellos que hubiesen de seguir y exercer el uso de la guerra, á los Españoles que en mi compañía agora están é estubiesen é á mí nos es mucho mas necesario é conveniente seguir y observar toda la mejor costumbre y órden que nos sea posible, así por lo que toca al servicio de Dios nuestro Señor y de la sacra Católica Magestad, como por tener por enemigos y contrarios á la mas belicosa y astuta gente en la guerra é de mas géneros de armas que ninguna otra generacion, especialmente por ser tanta que no tiene número, é nosotros tan pocos y tan apartados y destituidos de todo humano socorro ; viendo ser mui necesario y cumplidero al servicio de su Cesarea Magestad é utilidad nuestra, Mandé hacer é hicemas Ordenanzas que de yuso serán contenidas é irán firmadas de mi nombre é del infrascrito en la manera siguiente.

PRIMERAMENTE, por quanto por la experiencia que habemos visto é cada dia vemos quanta solicitud y vigilancia los naturales de estas partes tienen en la cultura y veneracion de sus ídolos, de que á Dios nuestro Señor se hace gran deservicio, y el demonio por la ceguedad y engaño en que los trae es de ellos muy venerado ; y en los apartar de tanto

2 X

error é idolatría y en los reducir al conocimiento de nuestra Santa Fe católica nuestro Señor será muy servido, y demas de adquirir gloria para nuestras ánimas con ser causa que de aquí adelante no se pierdan ni condenen tantos, acá en lo temporal seria Dios siempre en nuestra ayuda y socorro : por ende, con toda la justicia que puedo y debo, exhorto y ruego á todos los Españoles que en mi compañia fuesen á esta guerra que al presente vamos, y á todas las otras guerras y conquistas que en nombre de S. M. por mi mandado hubiesen de ir, que su principal motivo é intencion sea apartar y desarraigar de las dichas idolatrías á todos los naturales destas partes, y reducillos, ó á lo menos desear su salvacion, y que sean reducidos al conocimiento de Dios y de su Santa Fe católica ; porque si con otra intencion se hiciese la dicha guerra, seria injusta, y todo lo que en ella se oviese Onoloxio é obligado á restitucion, é S. M. no ternia razon de mandar gratificar á los que en ellas sirviesen. É sobre ello encargo la conciencia á los dichos Españoles, é desde ahora protesto en nombre de S. M. que mi principal intencion é motivo en facer esta guerra é las otras que ficiese por traer y reducir á los dichos naturales al dicho conocimiento de nuestra Santa Fe é creencia ; y despues por los sozjugar é supeditar debajo del yugo é dominio imperial é real de su Sacra Magestad, á quien juridicamente el Señorío de todas estas partes.

Yt. En por quanto de los reniegos é blasfemias Dios nuestro Señor es mucho deservido, y es la mayor ofensa que á su Santísimo nombre se puede hacer, y por eso permite en las gentes recios y duros castigos ; y no basta que seamos tan malos que por los inmensos beneficios que de cada dia dél recibimos no le demos gracias, mas decimos mal é blasfemamos de su santo nombre ; y por evitar tan aborrecible uso y pecado, mando que ninguna persona, de qualquiera condicion que sea, no sea osado decir, No creo en Dios, ni Pese, ni Reniego, ni Del cielo, ni No ha poder en Dios ; y que lo mismo se entienda de Nuestra Señora y de todos los otros Santos : sopena que demas de ser executadas las penas establecidas por las leyes del reyno contra los blasfemos, la persona que en lo susodicho incurriese pague 15 castellanos de oro, la tercera parte para la primera Cofradía de Nuestra Señora que en estas partes se hiciese, y la otra tercera parte para el ñeco de S. M., y la otra tercera parte para el juez que lo sentenciase.

Yt. Porque de los juegos muchas y las muchas veces resultan reniegos y blasfemias, é nacen otros inconvenientes, é es justo que del todo se prohiban y defiendan ; por ende mando que de aquí adelante ninguna persona sea osada de jugar á naypes ni á otros juegos vedados dineros ni preseas ni otra cosa alguna ; sopena de perdimiento de todo lo que jugase é de 20 pesos de oro, la mitad de todo ello para la Cámara, y la otra mitad para el juez que lo sentenciase. Pero por quanto en las guerras es bien que tenga la gente algun exercicio, y se acostumbra y permítese que jueguen por que se eviten otros mayores inconvenientes ; permítese que en el aposento donde estubiese se jueguen naypes é otros juegos moderadamente, con tanto que no sea á los dados, porque allí es curarse han de no de decir mal, é á lo menos si lo dixesen serán castigados.

Yt. Que ninguno sea osado de echar mano á la espada ó puñal ó otra arma alguna para ofender á ningun Español ; sopena que él que lo contrario hiciere, si fuese hidalgo, pague 100 pesos de oro, la mitad para el fisco de S. M., y la otra mitad para los gastos de la Xusticia ; y al que no fuese hidalgo se le han de dar 100 azotes publicamente.

Yt. Por quanto acaese que algunos Españoles por no valar é hacer otras cosas se dexan de aputar en las copias de los Capitanes que tienen gente : por ende mando que todos se alisten en las Capitanías que yo tengo hechas é hiciese, excepto los que yo señalaré que queden fuera dellas, con apercibimiento que dende agora se les face, que él que ansí no lo hiciese, no se le dará parte ni partes algunas.

Otrosí, por quanto algunas veces suele acaecer, que en burlas é por pasar tiempo algunas personas que están en una capitanía burlan é porfian de algunos de las otras Capitanías, y los unos dicen de los otros, y los otros de los otros, de que se suelen recrecer quistiones é escándalos ; por ende mando que de aquí adelante ninguno sea osado de burlar ni decir mal de ninguna Capitanía ni la perjudicar ; sopena de 20 pesos de oro, la mitad para la Cámara, y la otra mitad para los gastos de Xusticia.

Otrosí, que ninguno de los dichos Españoles no se aposente ni pose en ninguna parte, exepto en el lugar é parte donde estubiese aposentada su capitan ; supena de 12 pesos de oro, aplicados en la forma contenida en el capítulo antecedente.

Yt. Que ningun capitan se aposente en ninguna poblacion ó villa ó ciudad, sino en el pueblo que le fuese señalado por el Maestro de Campo, sopena de 10 pesos de oro, aplicados en la forma suso dicha.

Yt. Por quanto cada Capitan tenga mejor acaudillada su gente, mando que cada uno de los dichos Capitanes tenga sus cuadrillas de 20 en 20 Españoles, y con cada una quadrilla un quadrillero ó cabo de escuadra, que sea persona hábil y de quien se deba confiar ; so la dicha pena.

Otrosí, que cada uno de los dichos quadrilleros ó cabos desquadra ronden sobre las velas todos los quartos que les cupiese de velar, so la dicha pena ; é que la vela que hallasen durmiendo, ó ausente del lugar donde debiese velar, pague cuatro Castellanos, aplicados en la forma suso dicha, y demas que esté atado medio dia.

Otrosí, que los dichos quadrilleros tengan cuidado de avisar y avisen á las velas que hubiesen de poner, que puesto que recaudo en el Real no desamparen ni dexen los portillos ó calles ó pasos donde les fuese mandado velar y se vayan de allí á otra parte por ninguna necesidad que digan que les constriñó hasta que sean mandado ; sopena de 50 castellanos, aplicados en la forma suso dicha al que fuese hijo dalgo ; y sino lo fuese, que le sean dados 100 azotes publicamente.

Otrosí, que cada Capitan que por mí fuese nombrado tenga y traiga consigo su tambor é bandera para que rija y acaudille mejor la gente que tenga á su cargo ; sopena de 10 pesos de oro, aplicados en la forma suso dicha.

Otrosí, que cada Español que oyese tocar el atambor de su compañía sea obligado á salir e salga á acompañar su bandera con todas sus armas en forma y á punto de guerra ; sopena de 20 castellanos, aplicados en la forma arriba declarada.

Otrosí, que todas las veces que yo mandase mover le Real para alguna parte cada Capitan sea obligado de llevar por el camino toda su gente junta y apartada de las otras Capitanías, sinque se entrometa en ella ningun Español de otra Capitanía ninguna ; y para ello constriñan é apremien á los que asi llevasen debaxo de su bandera segun uso de guerra ; sopena de 10 pesos de oro, aplicados en la forma suso declarada.

Yt. Por quanto acaece que antes ó al tiempo de romper en los enemigos algunos Españoles se meten entre el fardage, demas de ser pusilanimidad, es cosa fea el mal exemplo para los Indios nuestros amigos que nos acompañan en la guerra : por ende mando que ningun Español se entremeta ni vaya con el fardage, salvo aquellos que para ello fuesen dados é señalados : sopena de 20 pesos de oro, aplicados segun que de suso contiene.

Otrosí, por quanto acaece algunas veces que algunos Españoles fuera de órden y sin les ser mandado arremeten ó rompen en algun esquadron de los enemigos, é por se desmandar ansí se desbaratan y salen fuera de ordenanza, de que suele recrecerse peligro á los mas : por ende mando que ningun Capitan se desmande á romper por los enemigos sin que primeramente por mí le sea mandado ; sopena de muerte. En otra persona se desmanda, si fuese hijodalgo, pena de 100 pesos, aplicados en la forma suso dicha ; y si no fuese hidalgo, le sean dados 100 azotes publicamente.

Yt. Por quanto podria ser que al tiempo que entran á tomar por fuerza alguna poblacion ó villa ó ciudad á los enemigos, antes de ser del todo echados fuera, con codicia de robar, algun Español se entrase en alguna casa de los Enemigos, de que se podria seguir daño : por ende mando que ningun Español ni Españoles entren á robar ni á otra cosa alguna en las tales casas de los enemigos, hasta ser del todo echados fuera, y haber conseguido el fin de la victoria ; sopena de 20 pesos de oro, aplicados en la manera que dicha es.

Yt. Si por escusar y evitar los hurtos encubiertos y fraudes que se hacen en las cosas habidas en la guerra ó fuera de ella, así por lo que toca al quinto que dellas pertenece á su católica Magestad, como porque han de ser repartidas conforme á lo que cada una sirve é merece : por ende mando que todo el oro, plata, perlas, piedras, plumage, ropa, esclavos, y otras cosas qualesquier que se adquieran, hubiesen, ó tomasen en qualquier manera, ansí en las dichas poblaciones, villas, ó ciudades, como en el campo, que la persona ó personas á cuyo poder viniese ó la hallasen ó tomasen, en qualquier forma que sea, lo traigan luego incontinente é manifiesten ante mí ó ante otra persona que fuese sin lo meter ni llevar á su posada ni á otra parte alguna ; sopena de muerte é perdimiento de todos sus bienes para la Cámara é fisco de S. M.

É por quanto lo suso dicho é cada una cosa é parte dello se guarde é cumpla segun é de la manera que aquí de suso se contiene, y de ninguna cosa de lo aquí contenida pretendan ignorancia, mando que sea apregonado publicamente, para que venga á noticia de todos : Que fuéron hechas las dichas Ordenanzas en la ciudad y provincia de Taxclateque selado 22 dias del mes de Diciembre, año del nascimiento de nuestro Salvador Jesu Christo de 1520 años.

Pregonáronse las dichas Ordenanzas desuso contenidas en la ciudad é provincia de Taxclatecle, miércoles dia de San Estéban, que fuesen 26 dias del mes de Diciembre, año del nacimiento de nuestro Salvador Jesu Christo de 1520 años ; estando presente el magnífico Señor Fernando Cortés, capitan general é Justicia mayor de esta Nueva España del mar Océano por el Emperador nuestro Señor, por ante mí, Juan de Rivera, escribano é Notario público en todos los Reinos é Señoríos de España por las Autoridades apostólica y Real. Lo qual pregonó en vcz alta Anton Garcia pregonero, en el Alarde que la gente de á caballo é de á pie que su merced mandó facer é se fizo el dicho dia. Á lo qual fuéron testigos que estaban presentes, Gonzalo de Sandoval, Alguacil mayor, é Alonso de Prado, contador, é Rodrigo Alvarez Chico, veedor por S. M., é otras muchas personas.—Fecho ut supra.—Juan de Rivera.

No. XIV.—See p. 602.

TRANSLATION OF PASSAGES IN THE HONDURAS LETTER OF CORTÉS.

[I have noticed this celebrated Letter, the *Carta Quinta* of Cortés, so particularly in the body of the work, that little remains to be said about it here. I have had these passages translated to show the reader the circumstantial and highly graphic manner of the general's narrative. The latter half of the Letter is occupied with the events which occurred in Mexico in the absence of Cortés and after his return. It may be considered, therefore, as part of the regular series of his historical correspondence, the publication of which was begun by Archbishop Lorenzana. Should another edition of the Letters of Cortés be given to the world, this one ought undoubtedly to find a place in it.]

A lake of great width and proportionate depth was the difficulty which we had to encounter. In vain did we turn to the right and to the left ; the lake was equally wide in every direction. My guides told me that it was useless to look for a ford in the vicinity, as they were certain the nearest one was towards the mountains, to reach which would necessarily be a journey of five or six days. I was extremely puzzled what measure to adopt. To return was certain death ; as, besides being at a loss for provisions, the roads, in consequence of the rains which had prevailed, were absolutely impassable. Our situation was now perilous in the extreme ; on every side was room for despair, and not a single ray of hope illumined our path. My followers had become sick of their continual labour, and had as yet reaped no benefit from their toils. It was therefore useless for me to look to them for advice in our present truly critical position. Besides the primitive band and the horses, there were upwards of three thousand five hundred Indians who followed in our train. There was one solitary canoe lying on the beach, in which, doubtless, those whom I had sent in advance had crossed. At the entrance of the lake, and on the other side, were deep marshes, which rendered our passage of the lake considerably more doubtful. One of my companions entered into the canoe, and found the depth of the lake to be five-and-twenty feet, and, with some lances tied together, I ascertained that the mud and slime were twelve feet more, making in all a depth of nearly forty feet. In this juncture, I resolved that a floating bridge should be made, and for this purpose requested that the Indians would lend their assistance in felling the wood, whilst I and my followers would employ ourselves in preparing the bridge. The undertaking seemed to be of such magnitude that scarcely any one entertained an idea of its being completed before our provisions were all exhausted. The Indians, however, set to work with the most commendable zeal. Not so with the Spaniards, who already began to comment upon the labours they had undergone, and the little prospect which appeared of their termination. They proceeded to communicate their thoughts one to another, and the spirit of disaffection had now attained such a height that some had the hardihood to express their disapprobation of my proceedings to my very face. Touched to the quick with this show of desertion when I had least expected it, I said to them that I needed not their assistance ; and, turning towards the Indians who accompanied me, exposed to them the necessity we lay under of using the most strenuous exertions to reach the other side, for if this point were not effected we should all perish from hunger. I then pointed in the opposite direction, in which the province of Acalan lay, and cheered their spirits with the prospect of there obtaining provisions in abundance, without taking into consideration the ample supply which would be afforded us by the caravels. I also promised them, in the name of your Majesty, that they should be recompensed to the fullest extent of their wishes, and that not a person who contributed his assistance should go unrewarded. My little oration had the best possible effect with the Indians, who promised, to a man, that their exertions should only terminate with their lives. The Spaniards, ashamed of their previous conduct, surrounded me, and requested that I would pardon their late act ; alleging, in extenuation of their offence, the miserable position in which they were placed, obliged to support themselves with the unsavoury roots which the earth supplied, and which were scarcely sufficient to keep them alive. They immediately proceeded to work, and though frequently ready to fall from fatigue, never made another complaint. After four days' incessant labour the bridge was completed, and both horse and man passed without the slightest accident. The bridge was constructed in so solid a manner that it would be impossible to destroy it otherwise than by fire. More than one thousand beams were united for its completion, and every one of them was thicker than a man's body, and sixty feet long.

. . . .

At two leagues' distance from this place the mountains commenced. From no words of mine, nor of a more gifted man, can your Majesty form an adequate idea of the asperity and unevenness of the place which we were now ascending. He alone who has experienced the hardships of the route, and who himself has been an eye-witness, can be fully sensible of its difficulty. It will be sufficient for me to say, in order that your Majesty may have some notion of the labour which we had to undergo, that we were twelve days before we got entirely free of it,—a distance altogether of eight leagues ! Sixty-eight horses died on the passage, the greater part having fallen down the precipices which abounded on every side ; and the few that escaped seemed so overcome that we thought not a single one would ever afterwards proved serviceable. More than three months elapsed before they recovered from the effects of the journey. It never ceased to rain, day or night, from the time we entered the mountain until we left it ; and the rock was of such a nature that the water passed away without collecting in any place in sufficient quantity to allow us to drink. Thus, in addition to the other hardships which we had to encounter, was that most pressing of all, thirst. Some of the horses suffered considerably from the want of this truly necessary article, and but for the culinary and other vessels which we had with us, and which served to receive some of the rain, neither man nor horse could possibly have escaped. A nephew of mine had a fall upon a piece of sharp rock, and fractured his leg in three or four places ; thus was our labour increased, as the men had to carry him by turns. We had now but a league to journey before we could arrive at Tenas, the place which I mentioned as belonging to the chief of Tayco ; but here a formidable obstacle presented itself, in a very wide and very large river, which was swollen by the continued rains. After searching for some time, one of the most surprising fords ever heard of was discovered. Some huge jutting cliffs arrest the progress of the river, in consequence of which it extends for a considerable space around. Between these cliffs are narrow channels, through which the water rushes with an impetuosity which baffles description. From one of these rocks to another we threw large trunks of trees, which had been felled with much labour. Ropes of bass-weed were affixed to these trunks ; and thus, though at imminent risk of our lives, we crossed the river· If anybody had become giddy in the transit, he must unavoidably have perished. Of these passes there were upwards of twenty, and we took two whole days to get clear by this extraordinary way.

. . . .

It were indeed an arduous task for me to describe to your Majesty the joy which pervaded every countenance when this truly inspiring account was received. To be near the termination of a journey so beset with hardships and labour as ours had been, was an event that could not but be hailed with rapture. Our last four days' march subjected us to innumerable trials ; as, besides being without any certainty of our proceeding in the right direction, we were ever in the heart of mountains abounding with precipices on every side. Many horses dropped on the way ; and a cousin of mine, Juan Davilos by name, fell down a precipice and broke an arm. Had it not been for the suit of armour which he wore, he would have been infallibly dashed to pieces. As it was, besides having his arm broken, he was dreadfully lacerated. His horse, upon which he was mounted, having no protection, was so wounded by the fall that we were obliged to leave him behind. With much difficulty we succeeded in extricating my cousin from his perilous situation. It would be an endless task to relate to your Majesty the many sufferings which we endured, amongst which the chief was from hunger ; for, although we had some swine which we had brought from Mexico, upwards of eight days had elapsed without our having tasted bread. The fruit of the palm-tree boiled with hog's flesh, and without any salt, which we had exhausted some time previous, formed our only sustenance. They were alike destitute of provisions at the place at which we had now arrived, where they lived in constant dread of an attack from the adjoining Spanish settlement. They needed not to fear such an event, as, from the situation in which I found the Spaniards, they were incapable of doing the slightest mischief. So elated were we all with our neighbourhood to Nico that all our past troubles were soon forgotten, as are the dangers of the sea by the weather-beaten sailor, who on his arrival in port thinks no more of the perils he has encountered. We still suffered greatly from hunger, for even the unsavoury roots were procured with the greatest difficulty ; and, after we had been occupied many hours in collecting them, they were devoured with the greatest eagerness, in the shortest space of time imaginable.

No. XV.—See p. 621.

LAST LETTER OF CORTÉS TO THE EMPEROR.

[I give this letter of Cortés entire, *Ultima y sentidísima Carta*, his "Last and most touching Letter," as it is styled by Vargas Ponçe, who has embraced it in his important collection from the archives of Seville.[1] It may be called touching, when we consider the tone of it, as compared with the former correspondence of its author, and the gloomy circumstances under which it was written. Yet we are not to take the complaints contained in it of his poverty too literally; since at his death, but three years after, he left immense estates. But these estates were so much embarrassed by his expensive and disastrous expeditions in the South Sea that his income during the rest of his life seems to have been scarcely sufficient to meet his ordinary expenditure. The last days of Cortés, wasted in ineffectual attempts to obtain redress from the court whom he had so signally served, remind us of the similar fate of Columbus. The history of both may teach us that the most brilliant career too often leads only to sorrow and disappointment, as the clouds gather round the sun at his setting.]

Pensé que haber trabajado en la juventud me aprovechara para que en la vejez tubiera descanso, y así ha quarenta años que me he ocupado en no dormir, mal comer, y á las veces ni bien ni mal, traer las armas á cuestas, poner la persona en peligro, gastar mi hacienda y edad, todo en servicio de Dios, trayendo obejas en su corral muy remotas de nuestro hemisferio, ignotas, y no escriptas en nuestras Escrituras, y acrecentando y dilatando el nombre y patrimonio de mi Rey, ganándole y trayéndole á su yugo y Real cetro muchos y muy grandes reynos y señoríos de muchas bárvaras naciones y gentes, ganados por mi propia persona y espensas, sin ser ayudado de cosa alguna, hantes muy estorvado por muchos émulos y invidiosos, que como sanguijuelas han reventado de artos de mi sangre. De la parte que á Dios cupo de mis trabajos y vigilias asaz estoy pagado, porque seyendo la obra suya, quiso tomarme por medio, y que las gentes me atribuyesen alguna parte, aunque quien conociere de mí lo que yo, beré claro que no sin causa la divina providencia quiso que una hobra tan grande se acavase por el mas flaco é inútil medio que se pudo hallar, porque á solo dios fuese el atributo. De lo que á mi rey quedó, la remuneracion siempre estuve satisfecho, que ceteris paribus no fuera menor por ser en tiempo de V. M., que nunca estos reynos de España, donde yo soy natural y á quien cupo este beneficio, fuéron poseydos de tan grande y Católico príncipe, magnánimo y poderoso Rey; y así V. M., la primera vez que vesé las manos y entregué los frutos de mis servicios, mostró reconocimiento dellos y comenzó á mostrar voluntad de me hacer gratificacion, honrrando mi persona con palabras y hobras, que pareciéndome á mí que no se equiparaban á mis méritos, V. M. sabe que rehusé yo de recibir. V. M. me dijo y mandó que las aceptase, porque pareciese que me comenzaba á hacer alguna merced, y que no las reciviese por pago de mis servicios; porque V. M. se queria haber con migo, como se han los que se muestran á tirar la ballesta, que los primeros tiros dan fuera del terrero, y enmendando dan en él y en el blanco y fiel; que la merced que V. M. me hacia hera dar fuera del terrero, y que iria enmendando hasta dar en el fiel de lo que yo merecia; y pues que no se me quitava nada de lo que tenia, ni se me habia de quitar, que reciviese lo que me dava; y ansí vesé las manos á V. M. por ello, y enbolviendo las espaldas quitóseme lo que tenia todo, y no se me cumplió la merced que V. M. me hizo. Y demas destas palabras que V. M. me dijo, y obras que me prometió, que, pues tiene tan buena memoria, no se le habrán olvidado, por cartas de V. M. firmadas de su real nombre tengo otras muy mayores. Y pues mis servicios hechos hasta allí son beneméritos de las obras y promesas que V. M. me hizo, y despues acá no lo han desmerecido; antes nunca he cesado de servir y acrecentar el Patrimonio de estos reynos, con mil estorvos, que si no obiera tenido no fuera menos lo acrecentado, despues que la merced se me hizo, que lo hecho porque la merecí, no sé porque no se me cumple la promesa de las merecedes ofrecidas, y se me quitan las hechas. Y si quisieren decir

[1] [It has since been printed in the Col. de Doc. inéd. para la Hist. de España, tom. i., affording an opportunity for correcting the almost innumerable errors which disfigure the transcription of Vargas Ponçe, and render it scarcely intelligible.— Ed.]

que no se me quitan, pues poseo algo ; cierto es que nada é inútil son una mesma cosa, y lo que tengo es tan sin fruto, que me fuera arto mejor no tenerlo, porque obiera entendido en mis grangerías, y no gastado el fruto de ellas por defenderme del fiscal de V. M., que a sido y es mas dificultoso que ganar la tierra de los enemigos ; así que mi trabajo aprovechó para mi contentamiento de haber hecho el dever, y no para conseguir el efecto dél, pues no solo no se me siguió reposo á la vejez, mas trabajo hasta la muerte ; y pluguiese á Dios que no passase adelante, sino que con la corporal se acabase, y no se estendiese á la perpetua, porque quien tanto trabajo tiene en defender el cuerpo no puede dejar de ofender al ánima. Suplico á V. M. no permita que á tan notorios servicios haya tan poco miramiento, y pues es de creer que no es á culpa de V. M. que las gentes lo sepan ; porque como esta obra que Dios hizo por mi medio es tan grande y maravillosa, y se ha estendido la fama de ella por todos los reynos de V. M. y de los otros reyes cristianos y aun por algunos infieles, en estos donde hay noticia del pleito de entre el fiscal y mí, no se trata de cosa mas ; y unos atribuyen la culpa al fiscal, otros á culpas mias ; y estas no las hallan tan grandes, que si bastasen para por ellas negárseme el premio, no bastasen tambien para quitarme la vida, honrra, y hacienda ; y que pues esto no se hace que no deve ser mia la culpa. Á V. M. ninguna se atribuye ; porque si V. M. quisiese quitarme lo que me dió, poder tiene para ejecutarlo, pues al que quiere y puede nada hay imposible ; decir que se vuscan formas para colorar la obra, y que no se sienta el intento, no caven ni pueden caber en los reyes unjidos por Dios tales medios, porque para con él no hay color que no sea transparente, para con el mundo no hay para que colorarlo, por que así lo quiero, así lo mando, es el descargo de lo que los reyes hacen. Yo supliqué á V. M. en Madrid fuese servido de aclarar la boluntad que tubo de hacerme merced en pago de mis servicios, y le traje á la memoria algunos de ellos ; díjome V. M. que mandaria á los del su consejo que me despachasen ; pensé que se les dejava mandado lo que abian de hacer, porque V. M. me dijo que no queria que trajese pleyto con el fiscal : cuando quise saberlo, dijéronme que me defendiese de la demanda del fiscal, porque havia de ir por tela de justicia, y por ella se habia de sentenciar ; sentílo por grave, y escrebí á V. M. á Barcelona, suplicándole que pues era servido de entrar en juicio de su siervo, lo fuese en que obiese Juezes sin sospecha y V. M. mandase que con los del Consejo de las Indias se juntasen algunos de los otros, pues todos son criados de V. M., y que juntos lo determinasen ; no fué V. M. servido, que no puedo alcanzar la causa, pues quantos mas lo viesen mejor alcanzarian lo que se devia hacer. Véome viejo y pobre y empeñado en este reyno en mas de veinte mil ducados, sin mas de ciento otros, que he gastado de los que traje é me han enviado, que algunos de ellos debo tambien que los an tomado prestados para enviarme, y todos corren cambios ; y en cinco años poco menos que ha que salí de mi casa, no es mucho lo que he gastado, pues nunca ha salido de la Corte, con tres hijos que traygo en ella, con letrados, procuradores, y solicitadores ; que todo fuera mejor empleado que V. M. se sirviera de ello y de lo que yo mas hoviera adquirido en este tiempo ; ha ayudado tambien la ida de Argel. Pareceme que al cojer del fruto de mis trabajos no devia hecharlo en basijas rotas, y dejarlo en juicio de pocos, sino tornar á suplicar á V. M. sea servido que todos quantos jueces V. M. tiene en sus Consejos conozcan de esta causa, y conforme á justicia la sentenciase.—Yo he sentido del obispo de Cuenca que desea que obiese para esto otros jueces demas de los que hay ; porque él y el licenciado Salmeron, nuebo Oidor en este Consejo de Indias, son los que me despejáron sin hoyrme de hecho, siendo jueces en la nueva España, como lo tengo provado, y con quien yo traigo pleito sobre el dicho despojo, y les pido cantidad de dineros de los intereses y rentas de lo que me despojáron ; y está claro que no han de sentenciar contra sí. No les he querido recusar en este caso, porque siempre crey que V. M. fuera servido que no llegara á estos términos ; y no seyendo V. M. servido que hayan mas jueces que determinen esta causa, serme ha forzado recusar al Obispo de Cuenca y á Salmeron, y pesar mehía en el ánima porque no podrá ser sin alguna dilacion ; que para mí no puede ser cosa mas dañosa, porque he sesenta años, y anda en cinco que salí de mi casa, y no tengo mas de un hijo Varon que me suceda ; y aunque tengo la muger moza para poder tener mas, mi hedad no sufre esperar mucho ; y si no tubiera otro, y dios dispusiera de este sin dejar sucesion, ¿ que me habria aprovechado lo adquirido ? pues subcediendo hijas se pierde la memoria. Otra y otra vez torno á suplicar á V. M. sea servido que con los Jueces del Consejo de Indias se junten otros jueces de estos otros Consejos ; pues todos son criados de V. M., y les fia la governacion de sus reynos y su real conciencia, no es inconveniente fiarles que determinen sobre una escriptura de merced, que V. M. hizo á un su vasallo de una partecica de un gran todo con que le sirvió á V. M., sin costar trabajo ni peligro en su real persona, ni ciudado de espíritu de proveer como se hiciese, ni costa de dineros para pagar la gente que lo hizo, y que tan limpia y lealmente sirvió, no solo en la tierra que ganó, pero con mucha cantidad de oro y plata y piedra de los despojos que en ella ubo ; y que V. M. mande á los jueces que fuere servido que entiendan en ello, que en un cierto tiempo, que V. M. les señale, lo determinen y sentencien sin que haya esta dilacion ; y esta será para mí muy gran merced ; porque á dilatarse, dejarlo hé perder y volvermehé á mi casa : porque no tengo ya edad para andar por mesones, sino para recogerme á aclarar mi cuenta con Dios, pues la tengo larga, y poca vida para dar los descargos, y será mejor dejar perder la acienda que el ánima. Sacra Magestad : Dios Nuestro Señor guarde la muy Real persona de V. M. con el acrecentamiento de Reynos y estados que V. M. desea. De Valladolid, á tres de Febrero de quinientos quarenta y quatro años. De V. C. M. muy humilde siervo y vasallo, que sus muy reales pies y manos besa.—El Marques de Valle.

Cuvierta á la S. C. C. M., El Emperador y Rey de las Españas.

Tiene este decreto :—Á su Mag. del Marques del Valle, 3 de Febrero de 44 :—*Nay que responder :* parece letra de Covos.

Original. Archivo de Indias.

No. XVI.—See p. 624.

FUNERAL OBSEQUIES OF CORTÉS.

[The original of this document is in the Hospital of Jesus at Mexico ; and the following literal translation was made from a copy sent to me from that capital.]

THE INTERMENT OF THE MARQUIS OF THE VALLEY OF OAJACA, HERNAN CORTÉS, AND OF HIS DESCENDANT, DON PEDRO CORTÉS, WHICH TOOK PLACE IN THE CITY OF MEXICO, FEB. 24, 1629.

The remains of Don Hernan Cortés (the first Marquis of the Valley of Oajaca), which lay in the monastery of St. Francis for more than fifty years since they had been brought from Castilleja de la Cuesta, were carried in funeral procession. It also happened that Don Pedro Cortés, Marquis of the Valley, died at the court of Mexico, Jan. 30, 1629. The Lord Archbishop of Mexico, D. Francisco Manso de Zuñiga, and his Excellency the Viceroy, Marquis of Serralbo, agreed that the two funerals should be conducted together, paying the greatest honour to the ashes of Hernando Cortés. The place of interment was the church of St. Francis in Mexico. The procession set forth from the palace of the Marquis of the Valley. In the advance were carried the banners of the various associations ; then followed the different orders of the religious fraternities, all the tribunals of Mexico, and the members of the Audience. Next came the Archbishop and the Chapter of the cathedral. Then was borne along the corpse of the Marquis Don Pedro Cortés in an open coffin, succeeded by the remains of Don Hernando Cortés in a coffin covered with black velvet. A banner of pure white, with a crucifix, an image of the Virgin and of St. John the Evangelist, embroidered in gold, was carried on one side. On the other were the armorial bearings of the King of Spain, also worked in gold. This standard was on the right hand of the body. On the left hand was carried another banner, of black velvet, with the arms of the Marquis of the Valley embroidered upon it in gold. The standard-bearers were armed. Next came the teachers of divinity, the mourners, and a horse with sable trappings, the whole procession being conducted with the greatest order. The members of the University followed. Behind them came the Viceroy with a large escort of cavaliers ; then four armed captains with their plumes, and with pikes on their shoulders. These were succeeded by four companies of soldiers with their arquebuses, and some with lances. Behind them banners were trailed upon the ground, and muffled drums were struck at intervals. The coffin enclosing the remains of the Conqueror was borne by the Royal Judges, while the knights of the order of Santiago supported the body of the Marquis Don Pedro Cortés. The crowd was immense, and there were six stations where the coffins were exposed to view, and at each of these the responses were chanted by the members of the religious fraternities.

The bones of Cortés were secretly removed from the church of St. Francis, with the permission of his Excellency the Archbishop, on the 2d of July, 1794, at eight o'clock in the evening, in the carriage of the Governor, the Marques de Sierra Nevada, and were placed in a vault, made for this purpose, in the church of Jesus of Nazareth. The bones were deposited in a wooden coffin enclosed in one of lead, being the same in which they came from Castilleja de la Cuesta, near Seville. This was placed in another of crystal, with its cross-bars and plates of silver ; and the remains were shrouded in a winding-sheet of cambric embroidered with gold, with a fringe of black lace four inches deep.

INDEX.

**PHOENIX
PRESS**

GENERAL EDITORS:
SIMON SCHAMA AND ANTONIA FRASER

*Phoenix Press publishes and re-publishes hundreds of the very best new
and out of print books about the past. For a free colour catalogue listing
more than 500 titles please*

telephone: +44 (0) 1903 828 503
fax: +44 (0) 1903 828 802
e-mail: mailorder@lbsltd.co.uk
or visit our website at www.phoenixpress.co.uk

The following books might be of interest to you:

History of the Conquest of Peru

W. H. PRESCOTT

'The most brilliant passages in the history of Spanish adventure in
the New World are undoubtedly afforded by the conquests of
Mexico and Peru' wrote William Hickling Prescott in 1847 when
History of the Conquest of Peru was first published. Since then
Prescott's two books *History of the Conquest of Mexico* and *History of
the Conquest of Peru* have become revered classics.

Paperback
UK: £14.99   752pp   1 84212 594 X
USA: $21.95
CAN: $33.95

Prince of Princes

The Life of Potemkin

SIMON SEBAG MONTEFIORE

'A headlong gallop of a read' said Antony Beevor about this massive
new biography of Catherine the Great's lover and co-ruler;
conqueror of the Ukraine and Crimea. Exhaustively researched
and beautifully written. 'Magnificent' *Independent*, 'Superb', *Daily
Telegraph*, 'Splendidly written' *Sunday Telegraph*, 'This well
researched and highly ambitious biography has succeeded
triumphantly in re-creating the life of an extraordinary man'

Antony Beevor, *Sunday Times*. Shortlisted for the Duff Cooper
Memorial Prize and the Samuel Johnson Prize.

Paperback
UK: £9.99   656pp·+ 24pp col. b/w   1 84212 438 2

Dr Johnson's London
LIZA PICARD

The first paperback edition of this celebrated account of London
from 1740–1770. With erudition and wit, Liza Picard extracts
nuggets from all sorts of contemporary records to expose the substance of everyday life in the biggest city in Europe – houses and
coffee-houses, climbing boys and gardens, medicine, toothpaste
and gin, sex, food, manners, etiquette, crime and punishment; the
practical realities of everyday life in the mid 18th century.

Paperback
UK: £9.99   384pp + 32pp col. b/w   1 84212 437 4

Empire
The British Imperial Experience From 1765 to the Present
DENIS JUDD

'Wonderfully ambitious . . . a pungent and attractive survey of the
British Empire from 1765 to the present.' *London Review of Books*,
'An indispensable one-volume source.' John Keegan

Paperback
UK: £14.99   544pp + 24pp b/w + Maps   1 84212 498 6
USA: $21.95
CAN: $31.95

The Rise of the Greeks
MICHAEL GRANT

The irrepressible Michael Grant takes the reader on an intriguing
detective trail to understand the world of the early Greeks. With
fluency and scholarship he shows how the extraordinary epoch
between 1000 and 495BC was one of the most creative in history.

Paperback
UK: £12.99   416pp + 16pp b/w + Maps   1 84212 265 7
USA: $19.95
CAN: $29.95

The Classical Greeks

MICHAEL GRANT

The Golden Age of ancient Greek city-state civilization lasted from 480 to 336 BC, the period between the first wars against Persia and Carthage and the accession of Alexander the Great. Never has there been such a multiplication of talents and genius within so limited a period and Michael Grant captures this astonishing civilization at the height of its powers.

Paperback
UK: £12.99   352pp + 16pp b/w   1 84212 447 1
USA: $19.95
CAN: $29.95

The Fall of the Roman Empire

MICHAEL GRANT

The fall of the western Roman empire was one of the most significant transformations throughout the whole of human history. Michael Grant explores the past with clarity and depth.

Paperback
UK: £12.99   256pp   1 85799 975 4

The Muslim Discovery of Europe

BERNARD LEWIS

A lively exploration of the sources and nature of Muslim knowledge of the West. 'No one writes about Muslim history with greater authority, or intelligence, or literary charm than Professor Bernard Lewis.' Hugh Trevor-Roper, *Sunday Times*

Paperback
UK: £14.99   352pp + 28pp b/w   1 84212 195 2

The Age of Arthur

JOHN MORRIS

A history of the British Isles from 350 to 650, 'the starting point of future British history'. 'From the resources of a mind vastly learned in the documents of the Arthurian age, John Morris has created more than the most devoted of Arthurian enthusiasts could have hoped for . . . Winston Churchill would have loved this book.' *TLS*

Paperback
UK: £14.99   684pp + Maps   1 84212 477 3
USA: $21.95
CAN: $31.95

Londinium

JOHN MORRIS

The authoritative account of earliest London from pre-Roman Britain to the Age of Arthur, examining subjects as diverse as food, religion, politics and sport.

Paperback
UK: £14.99   400pp + 8pp b/w   0 75380 660 6

The Birth of the Modern
World Society 1815–1830

PAUL JOHNSON

An examination of how the matrix of the modern world was formed. 'A work of this kind stands or falls . . . on the richness of its material, the scope of its coverage, the intelligence of its arguments, and on all these counts this book not merely stands, but towers above any other history of the period.' *Sunday Telegraph*

Paperback
UK: £11.99   1120pp   1 85799 366 7

Collision of Empires
Britain in Three World Wars 1793–1945

A. D. HARVEY

'Delightfully opinionated, well-documented insights into the three wars which constituted the rise, stagger and fall of the British Empire.' Andrew Roberts, *The Times*

Paperback
UK: £14.99   800pp   1 85799 125 7

History of the Dutch-Speaking Peoples 1555–1648

PIETER GEYL

An unforgettable portrait of Dutch life during the sixteenth and seventeenth centuries, this new paperback edition combines the two volumes *The Revolt of the Netherlands 1555–1609* and *The*

Netherlands in the Seventeenth Century 1609–1648 of Pieter Geyl's magnificent History.

Paperback
UK: £16.99   640pp + Maps   1 84212 225 8
USA: $24.95
CAN: $36.95

The European Powers 1900–1945
MARTIN GILBERT

Martin Gilbert analyses the dramatic changes that altered the face of Europe from the strong and prosperous European Empires of 1900 to a new order reeling from the effect of two wasteful wars with influence transferred to the United States and the Soviet Union.

Paperback
UK: £12.99   316pp + 16pp b/w + Maps   1 84212 216 9
USA: $19.95
CAN: $29.95

The Discoverers
A History of Man's Search to Know the World and Himself
DANIEL J. BOORSTIN

This Pulitzer Prize-winning saga of human discovery, the first in the trilogy, is the story of countless Columbuses. 'A new and fascinating approach to history . . . rich in unknowns and surprises' Barbara Tuchman. 'A ravishing book . . . [with] a verve, an audacity and a grasp of every sort of knowledge that is outrageous and wonderful . . . I can't think of any other living writer who could have attempted, let alone accomplished it.' Alistair Cooke, 'An adventure story . . . great fun to read.' *New York Times*

Paperback
UK: £16.99   768pp   1 84212 227 4

The Creators
A History of Heroes of the Imagination
DANIEL J. BOORSTIN

A panoramic yet minutely detailed history of the arts from Homer and Giotto to Picasso and Virginia Woolf encompassing 3,000 years of academic and intellectual invention. 'He combines lively opinion and a distinguished historian's erudition, with a first-class journalist's clarity and eye for the revealing anecdote . . . Irresistible.' *USA Today*

Paperback
UK: £16.99   832pp   1 84212 229 0

The Seekers
The Story of Man's Continuing Quest to Understand his World
DANIEL J. BOORSTIN

The final volume in the trilogy looks at the great men in history who sought meaning and purpose in our existence from Moses, Plato and Socrates through to Marx, Toynbee, Carlyle and Einstein. 'This completion of the trilogy on humanity's quest for understanding confirms Boorstin's rank as one of the giants of 20th century American scholarship.' George F. Will

Paperback
UK: £12.99   320pp   1 84212 228 2

Barbarossa
The Russian–German Conflict 1941–1945
ALAN CLARK

The classic account of the war on the Eastern Front, written by the eminent military historian, diarist and politician Alan Clark.

Paperback
UK: £14.99   544pp + 16pp b/w   1 84212 434 x

Second World War
MARTIN GILBERT

A new edition of the first total, global history of the Second World War, by the foremost historian of the twentieth century. 'Gilbert's epic is a remarkable achievement.' *Daily Express*

Paperback
UK: £18.99   864pp + 130 b/w photos + 102 maps   1 84212 262 8

The Klemperer Diaries, Volumes I & II

1933–1945

VICTOR KLEMPERER

A single paperback edition of the two volumes *I Shall Bear Witness* and *To the Bitter End* of Victor Klemperer's diaries of his experiences as a Jew in Nazi Germany. 'Klemperer's diary deserves to rank alongside that of Anne Frank', *Sunday Times*, 'Few English readers will fail to be moved as I was – ultimately to the point of tears.' Niall Ferguson, *Sunday Telegraph*

UK: £16.99   1070pp   1 84212 022 0